PSYCHOLOGICAL PROCESSES THAT AFFECT CRITICAL THINKING

Psychological research has helped to clarify how people think critically–and why, often, they do not. Here are a few of the topics relevant to critical thinking that are discussed in this book, and the chapters in which they appear.

BARRIERS TO CRITICAL THINKING

Pseudoscientific thinking (chapters 1 and 2)

Conformity (chapter 8)

Diffusion of responsibility (chapter 8)

Entrapment (chapter 8)

Groupthink (chapter 8)

Coercive persuasion (chapter 8)

Prejudice and ethnocentrism (chapter 8)

Stereotypes (chapter 8)

Self-serving bias (chapter 8)

Mindlessness (chapter 9)

Cognitive biases (e.g., confirmation and hindsight biases) (chapter 9)

Cognitive dissonance (chapter 9)

Mental sets (chapter 9)

Nonreflective judgment (chapter 9)

Fallibility of memory (chapter 10)

Emotional reasoning (chapter 11)

Defense mechanisms (chapter 13)

Vulnerability to the "Barnum Effect" (chapter 13)

Cognitive distortions in mood disorders (chapters 11, 16)

FACTORS ENHANCING CRITICAL THINKING

Scientific methods and reasoning (chapter 2)

Conditions promoting independent action and nonconformity (chapter 8)

Conditions promoting individuation and mindfulness (chapter 8)

Inductive, deductive, and dialectical reasoning (chapter 9)

Reflective judgment (chapter 9)

Creative problem solving (chapter 9)

Algorithms, heuristics (chapter 9)

Intelligence (chapter 9)

Metacognition (chapter 9)

Improving memory (chapter 10)

Reducing negative emotions (chapter 11)

Cognitive development (chapter 14)

Wisdom derived from life experiences (chapter 14)

Role of appraisals and rethinking in coping with stress and illness (chapter 15)

Attributions that affect feelings and behavior (chapters 8, 11, 12)

Cognitive therapy (chapter 17)

PSYCHOLOGY

PSYCHOLOGY

Sixth Edition

CAROLE WADE
Dominican College of San Rafael

CAROL TAVRIS

Prentice Hall
Upper Saddle River, NJ 07458

Library of Congress Cataloging-in-Publication

VP/Editorial Director: Laura Pearson
Executive Editor: Bill Webber
Editor in Chief of Development: Susanna Lesan
Development Editor: Lisa Pinto
Editorial Assistant: Abigail Ruth
AVP/Director of Production and Manufacturing: Barbara Kittle
Managing Editor: Mary Rottino
Project Manager: Maureen Richardson
Manufacturing Manager: Nick Sklitsis
Prepress and Manufacturing Buyer: Tricia Kenny
Creative Design Director: Leslie Osher
Art Director and Designer: Ximena Tamvakopoulos
Design Assistance: Kathryn Foot
Director, Image Resource Center: Melinda Reo
Manager, Rights and Permissions: Kay Dellosa
Image Specialist: Beth Boyd
Permission Coordinator: Nancy Seise
Photo Research: Julie Tesser, Karen Pugliano
Line Art Coordinator: Guy Ruggiero
Electronic Art Creation: Titan Digital Limited, Mirella Signoretto
Copy Editor: Shari Dorantes Hatch
Proofreader: Rainbow Graphics

Photo and text credits appear on pages C-1–C-5 which constitute a
continuation of the copyright page.

This book was set in 10/12.5 Sabon by TSI Graphics, Effingham and was printed and bound
by Von Hoffman Press. The cover was printed by The Lehigh Press, Inc.

© 2000 by Prentice-Hall, Inc.
Upper Saddle River, NJ 07458

(Previous editions of this book were published by Addison Wesley Longman, Inc.
and HarperCollins Publishers, Inc.)

Printed in the United States of America
10 9 8 7 6 5 4 3 2

ISBN 0-321-04931-4

Prentice-Hall International (UK) Limited, *London*
Prentice-Hall of Australia Pty. Limited, *Sydney*
Prentice-Hall Canada Inc., *Toronto*
Prentice-Hall Hispanoamericana, S.A., *Mexico*
Prentice-Hall of India Private Limited, *New Delhi*
Prentice-Hall of Japan, Inc., *Tokyo*
Pearson Education Asia Pte. Ltd., *Singapore*
Editora Prentice-Hall do Brasil. Ltda., *Rio de Janiero*

CONTENTS AT A GLANCE

CONTENTS

5 BODY RHYTHMS AND MENTAL STATES   139

6 SENSATION AND PERCEPTION   179

PART THREE / THE ENVIRONMENT AND BEHAVIOR

7 LEARNING AND CONDITIONING   225

10 MEMORY   347

11 EMOTION 391

12 MOTIVATION 421

PART FIVE / THE DEVELOPING PERSON

13 THEORIES OF PERSONALITY 457

14 DEVELOPMENT OVER THE LIFE SPAN   497

PART SIX / HEALTH AND DISORDER

TO THE INSTRUCTOR

When we began work on the first edition of this textbook in the mid-1980s, we had five goals, some of which then were considered quite daring: (1) to make critical thinking integral to the introductory psychology course; (2) to represent psychology as the study of *all* human beings by mainstreaming research on culture and gender; (3) to foster active learning, so that students would become involved with the material and see how it applies to their personal and social lives; (4) to keep "ahead of the curve" with research as psychology moves in new directions; and (5) to acknowledge forthrightly the many controversies in the field.

THINKING ABOUT CRITICAL AND CREATIVE THINKING

Our first ambition, unique to textbooks at the time, was to get students to reflect on what they were learning—to show them what it is like to think like a psychologist. Psychology is not just a body of knowledge; it is also a way of approaching and analyzing the world. From the beginning, therefore, our approach has been based on **critical thinking**: the understanding that knowledge is advanced when people resist leaping to conclusions on the basis of personal experience alone (so tempting in psychological matters), when they apply rigorous standards of evidence, and when they listen to competing views. Because many students equate the word "critical" with "negative" (as in "He was critical of her dress"), we later added an emphasis on the creative, forward-moving aspects of critical thinking—the importance of generating alternative explanations of events, asking questions, and using one's imagination.

In a textbook, true critical thinking cannot be reduced to a set of rhetorical questions or to a formula for analyzing studies; it is a process that must be woven seamlessly into the narrative. The primary way we "do" critical and creative thinking, therefore, is by modeling it in our evaluations of research and popular ideas. In this book, for example, we encourage critical thinking about concepts that many students approach uncritically, such as astrology, "premenstrual syndrome," and the "instinctive" nature of sexuality. And we also apply it to some ideas that many psychologists have accepted unquestioningly, such as the decisive importance of childhood to later life, Maslow's motivational hierarchy, and the disease model of

THINKING **CRITICALLY** AND CREATIVELY ABOUT PSYCHOLOGICAL ISSUES

ASK QUESTIONS, BE WILLING TO WONDER
A Chinese man standing alone against awesome military might inspired millions during the 1989 rebellion in Tiananmen Square. Why do some people have the courage to risk their lives for their beliefs? Why do so many others go along with the crowd or mindlessly obey authority? Social psychologists probe these questions in depth, as we will see in Chapter 8.

DEFINE YOUR TERMS
People refer to intelligence all the time, but what is it exactly? Does the musical genius of a world-class violinist like Anne-Sophie Mutter count as intelligence? Is intelligence captured by an IQ score, or does it also include wisdom and practical "smarts"? We will consider some answers in Chapter 9.

EXAMINE THE EVIDENCE
When demonstrating "levitation" and other supposedly magical phenomena, illusionists such as André Kole exploit people's tendency to trust the evidence of their own eyes even when such evidence is misleading, as discussed in Chapter 6.

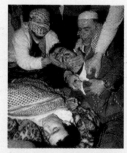

ANALYZE ASSUMPTIONS AND BIASES
Many North Americans assume that men are by nature less emotionally expressive than women. But this Palestinian man, grieving over his dead son, does not fit Western stereotypes of male emotionality. Cultural rules have a powerful influence on how men and women express their feelings, as we will see in Chapter 11.

addiction. By probing beneath assumptions and presenting the most recent evidence, we hope to convey the excitement and open-ended nature of psychological research and inquiry.

The first chapter starts right off with an extended discussion of what critical thinking is and what it isn't, and why critical thought is particularly relevant to the study of psychology. This discussion introduces **eight guidelines to critical thinking**, guidelines that we draw on throughout the text as we evaluate research and popular ideas. (These guidelines are also listed and described briefly, with examples, on the inside front cover of this book.)

Many, though by no means all, of these critical discussions in the text are signaled by the *critical-thinking lightbulb symbol* shown in the margin, along with marginal "signposts" containing provocative questions that alert students to the issues. We have explicitly identified the relevant guidelines in each signpost so that students can see more easily how the guidelines are actually applied. The questions in the signposts are *not*, in themselves, illustrations of critical thinking; rather, they serve as pointers to critical analyses in the text and invite the reader into the discussion.

THINKING CRITICALLY

AVOID EMOTIONAL REASONING

Many people get upset at the idea that their earliest experiences are lost to memory and angrily insist that memories from the first two years must be true. How can research help us think clearly about this issue?

MAINSTREAMING CULTURE AND GENDER

At the time of our first edition, some considered our goal of incorporating research on gender, ethnicity, and culture into introductory psychology to be quite radical—either a sop to political correctness or a fluffy and superficial fad. Today, the issue is no longer whether to include these topics, but how best to do it. From the beginning, our own answer has been to include studies of gender and culture in the main body of the text, wherever they are relevant to the larger discussion, rather than relegating these studies to separate chapters or boxed features. Thus, research on sex differences in the brain is critically evaluated in the brain chapter; cultural and gender influences on emotion are discussed in the emotion chapter; and cultural influences on childrearing practices and children's attachment styles are described in the development chapter.

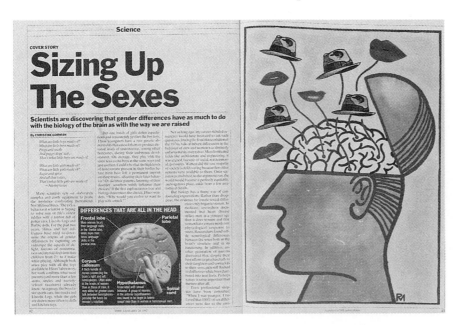

Our Approach to Gender. You will find many gender differences covered in this book—in pain, sexual attitudes and motives, sexual coercion, body satisfaction, depression, eating disorders, antisocial personality disorder, children's play preferences, and ways of expressing love, intimacy, and emotion, to mention just a few. (Other topics are listed in the index.) In these discussions, we have tried to go beyond mere description of differences, by examining competing explanations for them: biological and evolutionary influences, social roles, gender socialization, gender schemas, and the power of current situations and experiences in shaping people's choices and lives.

"Mainstreaming gender," however, does not mean focusing exclusively on differences.

Many gender differences, though reliable, are trivial in terms of real-life importance. And gender *similarities*, though they are often overlooked, are every bit as important and interesting as the eternal search for differences. We therefore include findings on similarities, too—for example, that men and women do not, overall, differ in moral reasoning (Chapter 14), obedience to authority (Chapter 8), experiences with having had unwanted sex (Chapter 12), or mood swings in the course of an average month (Chapter 5).

Our Approach to Culture. Research on cultural and cross-cultural psychology is as important in our culturally diverse world, we believe, as is research on genetics or the brain. Culture is not merely a superficial gloss on human behavior; it has a profound influence on all aspects of life. However, the scientific study of human diversity is not synonymous with the popular movement called multiculturalism. The study of culture, in our view, should increase students' understanding of what culture means, and how and why ethnic and national groups differ.

Thus we raise empirical findings about culture and ethnicity as topics warrant, throughout the book—for example, in our discussions of addiction, anxiety symptoms, differing cultural norms (e.g., for cleanliness, risk, and conversational distance), emotional expression, group differences in IQ scores and academic achievement, motivational conflicts, personality, psychotherapy, rules about time, attitudes toward weight and the ideal body, and the effectiveness of medication. (Again, we refer you to the index for a complete listing of topics.) In addition, Chapter 8 (Behavior in Social and Cultural Context) highlights the sociocultural perspective in psychology and includes extended discussions of ethnocentrism, prejudice, and cross-cultural relations. And Chapter 13 (Theories of Personality) includes a discussion of the personality "traits" that cultures may reward or discourage (see Table 13.1).

Instructors whose classes consist of students from diverse ethnic backgrounds may want, at the outset, to confront some sensitive issues evoked by the study of culture and cultural differences. One such issue is ethnocentrism. We have found that many students cannot read about group differences without assuming that one group (usually theirs) is being "trashed" for its typical way of doing things. They reason emotionally about cultural differences—as many people do!—and it is often difficult for them to separate a *research finding* from its *emotional connotations*. We encourage instructors to raise this issue in class if possible, to avoid student misunderstandings or unspoken resentments.

Another sensitive issue, reflecting the tension between minority groups' self-identities and accommodation to the mainstream culture, is the touchy question of group labels. "Eskimo" and "Sioux" were labels given to these groups by the dominant culture; their own preferred names are Inuit and Lakota, respectively. The label *Hispanic* is used by the United States government to include all Spanish-speaking groups, but many "Hispanics" prefer national-origin labels such as Cuban or Cuban-American, Chicano or Chicana, Latino or Latina. Likewise, Koreans, Japanese,

TABLE 13.1	Some Average Differences Between Individualist and Collectivist Cultures	
Members of individualist cultures	**Members of collectivist cultures**
Define the self as autonomous, independent of groups	Define the self as an interdependent part of groups
Give priority to individual, personal goals	Give priority to the needs and goals of the in-group
Value independence, leadership, achievement, "self-fulfillment"	Value group harmony, duty, obligation, security
Give more weight to an individual's attitudes and preferences than to group norms as explanations of behavior	Give more weight to group norms than to individual attitudes as explanations of behavior
Attend to the benefits and costs of relationships; if costs exceed advantages, a person is likely to drop a relationship	Attend to the needs of group members; if a relationship is beneficial to the group but costly to the individual, the individual is likely to stay in the relationship

Chinese, and Vietnamese are all Asian, but many individuals in these groups resent being lumped into a single category. Some African-Americans feel no kinship to Africa and prefer the term "black." And no one knows what to call "whites." European- or Anglo-American doesn't do it, as most white North Americans do not identify with any European nation and many are not from England or other European countries; "Caucasian" is out of favor as a race label, as "Negro" is. (In this book, we have used the admittedly vague term "white" simply because of general consensus on what that term refers to.) Finally, growing numbers of people of multi-ethnic backgrounds are irritated by society's efforts to squeeze them into only one category; they consider themselves "both" and sometimes "all of the above." Again, we recommend that instructors raise the question of ethnic labels at the outset, showing how these terms change in response to changing social conditions and are associated with ethnic self-identity.

APPLICATIONS AND ACTIVE LEARNING: GETTING INVOLVED

Throughout this book, we have kept in mind one of the soundest findings about learning: that it requires the active encoding of material. You can't just sit there and expect it to happen. Several pedagogical features in particular encourage students to become actively involved in what they are reading.

What's Ahead, which is new to this edition, consists of a brief set of questions introducing each major section within a chapter. These questions are not merely rhetorical; they are intended to be provocative and intriguing enough to arouse students' curiosity about the material to follow: Why do some people get depressed even though they "have it all"? How are your beliefs about love affected by your income? Which part of the anatomy do psychologists think is the "sexiest sex organ"? What is the difference between ordinary techniques of persuasion and the coercive techniques used by cults?

Looking Back, at the end of each chapter, lists all of the *What's Ahead* questions along with page numbers to show where the material for each question was covered. Students can check their retention and can easily review if they have trouble answering a question. This feature gives students a sense of how much they are learning about matters of personal and social importance, and helps them appreciate that psychology offers more than "common sense." Some instructors may want to turn some of the Looking Back questions into essay or short-answer test items or written assignments.

Get Involved exercises in each chapter make active learning entertaining. Some consist of quick demonstrations (e.g., clasping your hands together to find out if you are genetically a "right thumb over left" person or the reverse). Some are simple mini-studies (e.g., observing seating patterns in the school cafeteria). Some help students relate course

---

WHAT'S AHEAD

- Why does a note played on a flute sound different from the same note on an oboe?
- If you habitually listen to loud music through headphones, what kind of hearing impairment are you risking?
- To locate the source of a sound, why does it sometimes help to turn or tilt your head?

LOOKING BACK

- What kind of code in the nervous system helps explain why a pinprick and a kiss feel different? (p. 182)
- Why does your dog hear a "silent" doggie whistle when you can't? (p. 182)
- What kind of bias can influence whether you think you hear the phone ringing when you're in the shower? (p. 184)
- What happens when people are deprived of all external sensory stimulation? (p. 186)
- How does the eye differ from a camera? (p. 190)
- Why can we describe a color as bluish green but not as reddish green? (p. 193)
- If you were blind in one eye, why might you misjudge the distance of a painting on the wall but not of buildings a

- Why does a note played on a flute sound different from the same note on an oboe? (p. 201)
- If you habitually listen to loud music through headphones, what kind of hearing impairment are you risking? (p. 202)
- To locate the source of a sound, why does it sometimes help to turn or tilt your head? (p. 204)
- Why do saccharin and caffeine taste bitter to some people but not to others? (p. 205)
- Why do you have trouble tasting your food when you have a cold? (p. 206)
- Why do people often continue to "feel" limbs that have been amputated? (p. 209)
- Do babies see the world the way adults do? (p. 212)

GET → INVOLVED

THUMBS UP!

Ask the members of your family, one person at a time, to clasp their hands together. Include aunts and uncles, grandparents—as many of your biological relatives as possible. Which thumb does each person put on top?

About half of all people fold the left thumb over the right, and about half fold the right thumb over the left, and these responses tend to run in families. Do your own relatives show one tendency over the other? (If your family is an adoptive one, of course, there is less chance of finding a trend.) Try the same exercise with someone else's family; do you get the same results? Even for behavior as simple as thumb folding, the details of how genes exert their effect remain uncertain (Jones, 1994).

material to their own lives (e.g., if they drink, listing their own motives for doing so). Instructors may want to assign some of these exercises to the entire class and then discuss the results and what they might mean.

Conceptual graphics, most of them new to this edition, help students visualize material in order to understand and retain it better. By using these graphics, students can see at a glance, for example, the various types of attachment, distinctions between different types of memories, the difference between positive and negative reinforcement, and the elements of successful therapy. We have tried to keep these visual summaries simple, straightforward, and appealing.

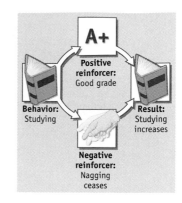

Review tables, which are new to this edition, summarize and contrast theories and approaches discussed in the text—for example, methods used in brain research, theories of dreaming, theories of personality, and approaches to psychotherapy. This feature helps students extract main points, organize what they have learned, and study for exams.

Quick Quizzes are periodic self-tests that encourage students to check their progress, and to go back and review if necessary. These quizzes do more than just test for memorization of definitions; they tell students whether they comprehend the issues. Mindful of the common tendency to skip quizzes or to peek at the answers, we have used various formats and have included engaging examples in order to motivate students to test themselves.

Many of the quizzes also include critical–thinking items, identified by the critical-thinking symbol. These items invite the student to reflect on the implications of findings and consider how psychological principles might illuminate real-life issues. For example: What kinds of questions should a critical thinker ask about a new drug for depression? How might a hypothetical study of testosterone and hostility be improved? How should a critical consumer evaluate someone's claim that health is entirely a matter of "mind over matter"? Although we offer some answers to these questions, students may have valid, well-reasoned answers that differ from our own.

Other pedagogical features designed to help students study and learn better include a **running glossary** that defines boldfaced technical terms on the pages where they occur for handy reference and study; a **cumulative glossary** at the back of the book; a list of **key terms** at the end of each chapter that includes page numbers so that students can find the sections where the terms are covered; **chapter outlines;** and **chapter summaries** in numbered paragraph form to help students review major concepts.

Taking Psychology with You, a feature that concludes each chapter, illustrates the practical implications of psychological research for individuals, groups, institutions, and society. This feature tackles topics of personal interest and relevance, such as living with pain (Chapter 6), improving study habits (Chapter 7), getting along with people from other cultures (Chapter 8), becoming more creative (Chapter 9), managing anger (Chapter 11), boosting motivation (Chapter 12), and choosing a therapist (Chapter 17).

REVIEW 1.2

FIVE MAJOR PSYCHOLOGICAL PERSPECTIVES

	Perspective	Major Topics of Study	Sample Finding on Violence
	Biological	The nervous system, hormones, brain chemistry, heredity, evolutionary influences	Brain damage caused by birth complications or child abuse might incline some people toward violence.
	Learning	Environment and experience	
	Behavioral	Environmental determinants of observable behavior	Violence increases when it pays off.
	Social cognitive	Environmental influences, observation and imitation, beliefs and values	Violent role models can influence some children to behave aggressively.
	Cognitive	Thinking, memory, language, problem solving, perceptions	Violent people are often quick to perceive provocation and insult.
	Sociocultural	Social and cultural contexts	
	Social psychology	Social rules and roles, groups, relationships	People are often more aggressive in a crowd than they would be on their own.
	Cultural psychology	Cultural norms, values, and expectations	Cultures based on herding rather than agriculture tend to train boys to be aggressive.
	Psychodynamic	Unconscious thoughts, desires, and conflicts	A man who murders prostitutes may have unconscious conflicts about his mother and about sexuality.

QUICK QUIZ

Is all this information about eating making you hungry for knowledge?

1. *True or false:* Emotional problems explain why fat people are heavy.

2. Falling and rising levels of leptin help the brain regulate _____ and metabolism in order to maintain a person's genetically influenced _____.

3. Rising rates of obesity can best be explained by (a) genetic changes over the past few decades, (b) a lack of will power, (c) an abundance of high-fat food and sedentary lifestyles, (d) the increase in eating disorders.

4. Bill, who is thin, reads in the newspaper that genes set the range of body weight and shape. "Oh, good," he exclaims, "now I can eat all the junk food I want; I was born to be skinny." What's wrong with Bill's conclusion?

Answers:

1. False 2. appetite, set point 3. c 4. Bill is right to recognize that there may be limits to how heavy he can become. But he may also be oversimplifying and jumping to conclusions. Even people who have a set point for leanness will gain some weight on fatty foods and excess calories, especially if they don't exercise; also, rich junk food is unhealthy for reasons that have nothing to do with overweight.

FOOD FOR THOUGHT: DIET AND NEUROTRANSMITTERS

Vitamin improves sex! Mineral boosts brainpower! Chocolate chases the blues! Claims such as these have long given nutritional theories of behavior a bad reputation. In the late 1960s, when Nobel laureate Linus Pauling proposed that some mental disorders be treated with massive doses of vitamins, few researchers listened. Mainstream medical authorities classified Pauling's vitamin therapy with such infamous cure-alls as snake oil and leeches.

Today, most mental-health professionals remain skeptical of nutritional cures for mental illness. But the underlying premise of nutritional treatments, that diet affects the brain and therefore behavior, is getting a second look. Claims that sugar or common food additives lead to undesirable behavior in otherwise normal people remain doubtful, but in some cases of disturbance, diet may make a difference. In one double-blind study, researchers asked depressed patients to abstain from refined sugar and caffeine. Over a three-month period, these patients showed significantly more improvement in their symptoms

The final "Taking Psychology with You" in the book is an **Epilogue**, a unique effort to show students that the vast number of seemingly disparate studies and points of view they have just read about are related. The Epilogue contains a typical problem that everyone can be expected to encounter: conflicts in a close relationship. We show how topics discussed in previous chapters can be applied to understanding and coping with such conflicts. Many instructors have told us that they find the Epilogue a useful tool for helping students integrate the diverse approaches of contemporary psychology. Asking students to come up with research findings that might apply to other problems also makes for a good term-paper assignment.

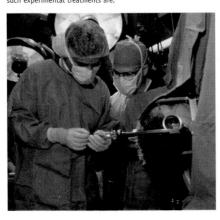

In 1998, in the operation shown here, surgeons attempted for the first time to treat a stroke victim by injecting specially prepared precursor cells into her brain. Scientists will soon learn how effective such experimental treatments are.

REFLECTING NEW DIRECTIONS AND RESEARCH IN THE FIELD

Psychology is an expanding, constantly evolving enterprise. New areas of interest emerge, and suddenly research on a topic that was previously overlooked explodes into prominence. Accordingly, this edition includes prominent coverage of three rapidly growing fields: evolutionary psychology (Chapter 3), behavioral genetics (Chapters 3 and 13), and cultural psychology (throughout the book). We have also added up-to-date research in every chapter, including some astonishing findings on neuronal growth throughout life (Chapters 4 and 14), the limits of parental influence on children's personality and behavior (Chapters 13 and 14), and the continuing mysteries of pain (Chapter 6), memory (Chapter 10), and dreaming (Chapter 5).

FACING THE CONTROVERSIES

Psychology has always been full of lively, sometimes angry, debates, and we feel that students should not be sheltered from them. They are what make psychology so interesting! Sociobiologists and feminist psychologists often differ strongly in their analyses of gender relations (Chapters 3 and 12). Psychodynamic clinicians and experimental psychologists differ strongly in their assumptions about memory, child development, and trauma; these differences have heated repercussions for, among other things, "recovered memory" therapy and the questioning of children as eyewitnesses (Chapter 10). The "scientist-practitioner" gap between researchers and psychodynamic psychotherapists is continuing to widen (Chapters 13 and 17). Developmental psychologists are hotly debating the extent and limits of parental influence on children (Chapter 14). And psychologists continue to argue among themselves about the genetic and cultural origins of addiction, in a debate that has profound importance for reducing and treating drug abuse (Chapters 5 and 16). In this book we candidly address these and other controversies, try to show why they are occurring, and suggest the kinds of questions that might lead to useful answers in each case.

A NOTE TO USERS OF PREVIOUS EDITIONS

In response to suggestions from users of earlier editions of *Psychology,* we have made a special effort to reduce the "density" of the narrative, by reducing the level of detail in many discussions, resisting the temptation to digress, and keeping the focus on main points. Expert reviewers, of course, tend to want students to appreciate all the complexities of their particular area of research. However, while acknowledging areas of debate and trying to make sure that the research we cite is absolutely current, we have worked hard to keep the student's focus on the fundamental points and conclusions. In addition, we have reorganized some sections to make them clearer and easier to study and teach.

A detailed explanation of all deletions, additions, and changes in the sixth edition is available to adopters of the fifth edition, so that no one will have to guess why we made particular changes. We hope this support will make the transition from one edition to the next as painless for instructors as possible. You can obtain this description from your Prentice Hall representative or by writing to: Marketing Manager, Psychology, Prentice Hall Publishers, One Lake Street, Saddle River, New Jersey 07458.

SUPPLEMENTS PACKAGE

Psychology, Sixth Edition, is supported by a complete teaching and learning package.

For the Instructor

Instructor's Resource Manual. We believe that you will find a wealth of helpful information and teaching resources in the *Instructor's Resource Manual,* developed by Barbara Brown of Georgia Perimeter College. Professor Brown brings a number of innovative ideas to the IRM, which includes learning objectives, chapter outlines, lecture supplements, classroom demonstrations, and critical-thinking exercises, mini-experiments, self-test exercises and suggestions for additional readings, and an extensive guide to audiovisual materials.

Test Banks I and II. Scott Johnson of John Wood Community College and Steve Charlton of Kwantlen College designed these excellent test banks. Each contains over 2500 multiple-choice, true-false, short-answer, and essay questions that test factual, applied, and conceptual knowledge. Items are referenced by learning objectives, cognitive type, topic, and skill.

Prentice Hall Test Manager. *Psychology, Sixth Edition,* is now accompanied by the best-selling test-generating software on the market. The software runs on IBM (Windows), Macintosh and Apple IIE. It contains the following modules:

- GRADE: Gradebook
- GUIDE: Tutoring system
- PAINT: Creates graphical artwork and illustrations
- On-Line Network Testing

Tests are created through the custom-test software, administered through the On-line Testing module, and then transferred to the gradebook for evaluation.

Prentice Hall Transparencies for Introductory Psychology, Series V.
You can add visual impact to the study of psychology with Prentice Hall's collection of four-color transparencies. Designed in a large-type format for lecture settings, many of these quality illustrations are not found in the text and offer a wealth of additional resources to enhance lectures and reinforce student learning.

Powerpoint Slides and Electronic Text Art. A set of Powerpoint Slides and nearly all of the line art found in the text is available on a CD-ROM and can also be downloaded from the Faculty Section of the Psychology Interactive Center.

Teaching Psychology, 2/E by Fred W. Whitford, Montana State University, is an excellent guide for new instructors or teaching assistants who want to learn to manage the myriad tasks required to teach effectively from the start.

ABC News/Prentice Hall Video Library. Prentice Hall has assembled a collection of feature segments from award-winning news programs. The following libraries are currently available to qualified adopters:

■ ABC News Videos for Introductory Psychology Series III consists of segments from such programs as Nightline, 20/20, Prime Time Live, and The Health Show. A summary and questions, designed to stimulate critical thinking for each segment, are included in the Instructor's Resource Manual.

■ The Alliance Series: The Annenberg/CPB Collection. The Alliance Series is the most extensive collection of professionally produced videos available with any introductory psychology textbook. Selections include videos in the following Annenberg series: The Brain, the Brain Teaching Modules, Discovering Psychology, The Mind, and The Mind Teaching Modules. Available to qualified adopters. Please contact your local Prentice Hall representative for more information.

On-Line Course Management. For instructors interested in distance learning, Prentice Hall and Pearson Education offer a fully customizable, on-line course with World Wide Web links, on-line testing, and many other course management tools. See your local Prentice Hall representative or visit Prentice Hall's special Demonstration Central website at http://www.prenhall.com/demo for more information.

For the Instructor and the Student

Multimedia, Internet, and World Wide Web Materials: The Psychology Interactive Center. Prentice Hall and Peregrine Publishers have melded two acclaimed interactive learning resources: Prentice Hall's Companion Website with Peregrine's The Psychology Place. Available at http://www.prenhall.com/wade, the Companion Website portion of this new center was developed by Professor Kenneth Carter of the Oxford College of Emory University. It provides materials to help students review chapter content and test their knowledge of what they have read. It also provides exciting World Wide Web destinations where students can find related information that expands on material found in their text. Chat rooms and Message Boards allow students to share their ideas about psychology with students from their own classroom or from colleges across the country.

The Psychology Interactive Center provides a jumping-off point for students to explore the more than 200 articles, demonstrations, frequently asked questions, and interactive exercises from The Psychology Place, which has been customized for the sixth edition of *Psychology* to provide extra information for motivated students.

Both the Instructor's Resource Manual and the new Media Users Guide inform instructors and students on how to get the most out of this unique resource.

For the Student

Practice Test and Review Manual. Prepared by Professor Tina Stern of Georgia Perimeter College, this manual has been extensively updated to reflect the new coverage in the Sixth Edition. It includes learning objectives, chapter outlines, critical-thinking questions on important concepts in the text, practice tests with suggested answers, key-term reviews, and a "How to Study" section.

"Psychobabble and Biobunk" by Carol Tavris. This expanded and updated collection of opinion essays, written for the *Los Angeles Times* and the *New York Times* by Carol Tavris, applies psychological research to current issues in the news. These essays may be used to encourage debate in the classroom or as a basis for student papers. Using them as models, students can write or present their own points of view on a topic, drawing on evidence from the textbook, lectures, or independent research to support their conclusions.

Media User's Guide. The Media User's Guide is provided to students at no charge with the purchase of a new text. Students who use this guide should have no trouble taking advantage of everything the web has to offer for their introductory psychology experience. The guide includes:

■ Written explanations and navigational instructions for using the Psychology Interactive Center (see above description under Multimedia, Internet, and the World Wide Web).

■ Summaries of the content of every article, demonstration and exercise found in The Psychology Place.

■ A hands-on Internet Tutorial that features web sites related to psychology.

The New York Times Supplement. The core subject matter provided in the text is supplemented by a collection of timely articles from one of the world's most distinguished newspapers, the *New York Times.* Also included are discussion and critical thinking questions that relate psychological perspectives and topics in the text to issues in the articles.

SUPPLEMENTAL TEXTS AVAILABLE FOR PACKAGING WITH THE SIXTH EDITION

Several Prentice Hall textbooks are available, at reduced prices, for packaging with *Psychology, Sixth Edition,* to enhance your students' experience:

The Psychology Major: Careers and Strategies for Success by Eric Landrum (Boise State University), Stephen Davis (Emporia State University), and Terri Landrum (Boise State University). This 160-page paperback provides valuable information on career options available to psychology majors, tips for improving academic performance, and a guide to the APA style of research reporting.

Forty Studies that Changed Psychology, Third Edition by Roger Hock (Mendocino College). Presenting the seminal research studies that have shaped modern psychological study, this brief supplement provides an overview of the environment that gave rise to each study, its experimental design, its findings, and its impact on current thinking in the discipline.

How to Think Like a Psychologist by Donald McBurney (University of Pittsburgh). This unique supplementary text uses a question-answer format to explore some of the most common questions students ask about psychology.

Experiencing Psychology by Gary Brannigan (State University of New York at Plattesburgh). This hands-on activity book contains 39 active-learning experiences corresponding to major topics in psychology to provide students with hands-on experience in "doing" psychology.

ACKNOWLEDGMENTS

Like any other cooperative effort, writing a textbook requires a support team. We are indebted to the following reviewers and consultants, who made many valuable suggestions during the development of this and previous editions of *Psychology*. (Please note that affiliations of some individuals may have changed since they reviewed our book.)

Benton E. Allen, *Mt. San Antonio College*
Susan M. Andersen, *University of California, Santa Barbara*
Lynn R. Anderson, *Wayne State University*
Emir Andrews, *Memorial University of Newfoundland*
Richard Anglin, *Oklahoma City Community College*
Alan Auerbach, *Wilfrid Laurier University*
Lynn Haller Augsbach, *Morehead State University*
Harold Babb, *Binghamton University*
Brian C. Babbitt, *Missouri Southern State College*
MaryAnn Baenninger, *Trenton State College*
Patricia Barker, *Schenectady County Community College*
Ronald K. Barrett, *Loyola Marymount University*
Allan Basbaum, *University of California, San Francisco*
Carol Batt, *Sacred Heart University*
William M. Baum, *University of New Hampshire*
Gordon Bear, *Ramapo College of New Jersey*
Peter A. Beckett, *Youngstown State University*
Bill E. Beckwith, *University of North Dakota*
Helen Bee, *Madison, Wisconsin*
David F. Berger, *SUNY at Cortland*
Michael Bergmire, *Jefferson College*
Philip J. Bersh, *Temple University*
Randolph Blake, *Vanderbilt University*
Richard Bowen, *Loyola University of Chicago*
Laura L. Bowman, *Kent State University*
Edward N. Brady, *Belleville Area College*
Ann Brandt-Williams, *Glendale Community College*
John R. Braun, *University of Bridgeport*
Sharon S. Brehm, *SUNY at Binghamton*
Sylvester Briggs, *Kent State University*
Gwen Briscoe, *College of Mt. St. Joseph*
Barbara L. Brown, *Georgia Perimeter College*
Robert C. Brown, Jr., *Georgia State University*
Linda L. Brunton, *Columbia State Community College*
Stephen R. Buchanan, *University of South Carolina, Union*
Peter R. Burzvnski, *Vincennes University*
Frank Calabrese, *Community College of Philadelphia*
Jean Caplan, *Concordia University*
Bernardo J. Carducci, *Indiana University Southeast*
Sally S. Carr, *Lakeland Community College*
Michael Catchpole, *North Island College*
Paul Chance, *Seaford, DE*
Herbert H. Clark, *Stanford University*
Job B. Clément, *Daytona Beach Community College*

Samuel Clement, *Marianopolis College*
Eva Conrad, *San Bernardino Valley College*
Richard L. Cook, *University of Colorado*
Robert Cormack, *New Mexico Institute of Mining and Technology*
Wendi Cross, *Ohio University*
Gaylen Davidson-Podgorny, *Santa Rosa Junior College*
Robert M. Davis, *Purdue University School of Science, IUPUI*
Michael William Decker, *University of California, Irvine*
Geri Anne Dino, *Frostburg State University*
Susan H. Evans, *University of Southern California*
Fred Fahringer, *Southwest Texas State University*
Ronald Finke, *SUNY at Stony Brook*
Deborah Finkel, *Indiana University Southeast*
John H. Flowers, *University of Nebraska-Lincoln*
William F. Ford, *Bucks County Community College*
Donald G. Forgays, *University of Vermont*
Sheila Francis, *Creighton University*
Charles A. Fuller, *University of California, Davis*
Grace Galliano, *Kennesaw State College*
Mary Gauvain, *Oregon State University*
Ron Gerrard, *SUNY at Oswego*
David Gersh, *Houston Community College*
Jessica B. Gillooly, *Glendale Community College*
Margaret Gittis, *Youngstown State University*
Carlos Goldberg, *Indiana University-Purdue University at Indianapolis*
Carol Grams, *Orange Coast College*
Patricia Greenfield, *University of California, Los Angeles*
Richard A. Griggs, *University of Florida*
Sarmi Gulgoz, *Auburn University*
Jimmy G. Hale, *McLennan Community College*
Pryor Hale, *Piedmont Virginia Community College*
Len Hamilton, *Rutgers University*
George Hampton, *University of Houston*
Algea Harrison, *Oakland University*
Neil Helgeson, *The University of Texas at San Antonio*
John E. Hesson, *Metropolitan State College*
Robert Higgins, *Oakland Community College*
John P. Hostetler, *Albion College*
Kenneth I. Howard, *Northwestern University*
John Hunsley, *University of Ottawa*
William G. Iacono, *University of Minnesota*
David E. Irwin, *University of Illinois*

James Johnson, *University of North Carolina at Wilmington*

Robert D. Johnson, *Arkansas State University*

Timothy P. Johnston, *University of North Carolina at Greensboro*

Susan Joslyn, *University of Washington*

Chadwick Karr, *Portland State University*

Yoshito Kawahara, *San Diego Mesa College*

Michael C. Kennedy, *Allegheny University*

Geoffrey Keppel, *University of California, Berkeley*

Harold O. Kiess, *Framingham State College*

Gary King, *Rose State College*

Jack Kirschenbaum, *Fullerton College*

Donald Kline, *University of Calgary*

Stephen M. Kosslyn, *Harvard University*

Janet E. Keubli, *St. Louis University*

Michael J. Lambert, *Brigham Young University*

George S. Larimer, *West Liberty State College*

Herbert Leff, *University of Vermont*

Patricia Lefler, *Lexington Community College*

S. David Leonard, *University of Georgia*

Robert Levy, *Indiana State University*

Lewis Lieberman, *Columbus College*

R. Martin Lobdell, *Pierce College*

Walter J. Lonner, *Western Washington University*

Nina Lott, *National University*

Bonnie Lustigman, *Montclair State College*

Debra Moehle McCallum, *University of Alabama at Birmingham*

D. F. McCoy, *University of Kentucky*

C. Sue McCullough, *Texas Woman's University*

Elizabeth McDonel, *University of Alabama*

Susanne Wicks McKenzie, *Dawson College*

Mark B. McKinley, *Lorain County Community College*

Ronald K. McLaughlin, *Juniata College*

Frances K. McSweeney, *Washington State University*

James E. Maddux, *George Mason University*

Marc Marschark, *University of North Carolina at Greensboro*

Monique Martin, *Champlain Regional College*

Maty Jo Meadow, *Mankato State University*

Linda Mealey, *College of St. Benedict*

Ronald Melzack, *McGill University*

Dorothy Mercer, *Eastern Kentucky University*

Laura J. Metallo, *Five Towns College*

Denis Mitchell, *University of Southern California*

Timothy H. Monk, *University of Pittsburgh Medical Center*

Maribel Montgomery, *Linn-Benton Community College*

Douglas G. Mook, *University of Virginia*

T. Mark Morey, *SUNY College at Oswego*

Joel Morgovsky, *Brookdale Community College (NJ)*

Micah Mukabi, *Essex County College (NJ)*

Sarah Murray, *Kwantlen University College, Vancouver, BC*

James S. Nairne, *University of Texas at Arlington*

Michael Nash, *University of Tennessee-Knoxville*

Douglas Navarick, *California State University, Fullerton*

Robert A. Neimever, *Memphis State University*

Todd Nelson, *California State University, Stanislaus*

Nora Newcombe, *Temple University*

Linda Noble, *Kennesaw State College*

Keith Oatley, *Ontario Institute for Studies in Education, Toronto*

Peter Oliver, *University of Hartford*

Patricia Owen-Smith, *Oxford College*

Elizabeth Weiss Ozorak, *Allegheny College*

David Page, *Nazareth College*

M. Carr Payne, Jr., *Georgia Institute of Technology*

Dan G. Perkins, *Richland College*

Gregory Pezzetti, *Rancho Santiago Community College*

Wayne Poniewaz, *University of Arkansas, Monticello*

Debra Poole, *Central Michigan University*

Paula M. Popovich, *Ohio University*

Lyman Porter, *University of California, Irvine*

Robert Prochnow, *St. Cloud State University*

Janet Proctor, *Purdue University*

Eric Ravussin, *Obesity Research & Clinical Investigation, Lilly Research Laboratories*

Reginald L. Razzi, *Upsala College*

Sheena Rogers, *University of Wisconsin-Madison*

Jayne Rose, *Augustana State College*

Gary Ross-Reynolds, *Nicholls State University*

Peter J. Rowe, *College of Charleston*

Gerald Rubin, *Central Virginia Community College*

Joe Rubinstein, *Purdue University*

Karen P. Saenz, *Houston Community College, Southeast*

Nancy Sauerman, *Kirkwood Community College*

H. R. Schiffman, *Rutgers University*

Lael Schooler, *Indiana University*

David A. Schroeder, *University of Arkansas*

Marvin Schwartz, *University of Cincinnati*

Shelley Schwartz, *Vanier College*

Joyce Segreto, *Youngstown State University*

Kimron Shapiro, *University of Calgary*

Phillip R. Shaver, *University of California, Davis*

Susan A. Shodahl, *San Bernardino Valley College*

Dale Simmons, *Oregon State University*

Art Skibbe, *Appalachian State University*

William P. Smotherman, *SUNY at Binghamton*

Samuel Snyder, *North Carolina State University*

Barbara A. Spellman, *University of Texas at Austin*

Larry R. Squire, *University of California, San Diego*

Granville L. Sydnor, *San Jacinto College North*

Tina Stern, *Georgia Perimeter College*

A. Stirling, *John Abbott College*

Milton E. Strauss, *Johns Hopkins University*

Judith Sugar, *Colorado State University*

Shelley E. Taylor, *University of California, Los Angeles*
Dennis C. Turk, *University of Washington*
Barbara Turpin, *Southwest Missouri State University*
Ronald J. Venhorst, *Kean College of New Jersey*
Wayne A. Viney, *Colorado State University*
Benjamin Wallace, *Cleveland State University*
Phyllis Walrad, *Macomb Community College*
Charles R. Walsmith, *Bellevue Community College*
Phillip Wann, *Missouri Western State College*

Thomas J. Weatherly, *DeKalb College-Central Campus*
Mary Wellman, *Rhode Island University*
Gary L. Wells, *University of Alberta*
Warner Wilson, *Wright State University*
Loren Wingblade, *Jackson Community College*
Judith K. Winters, *DeKalb College*
Rita S. Wolpert, *Caldwell College*
James M. Wood, *University of Texas at El Paso*
Phyllis Zee, *Northwestern University Medical School*

We are grateful to the many talented and hardworking people who were involved in planning and producing this edition of *Psychology*. We thank Psychology Editor Rebecca Pascal and Developmental Director Lisa Pinto for their many insightful editorial suggestions in launching this revision; and editorial assistant Abigail Ruth for so accurately and efficiently coordinating the book's many elements through its early stages. We are also grateful to Donna DeBenedictis and Rubina Yeh for their excellent contributions to the early stages of production and design.

We are beholden to the editorial and production team at Prentice Hall for handling the transition of this book into their capable hands with such professionalism, energy, and good humor. Our special thanks go to Executive Editor Bill Webber, Senior Project Manager Maureen Richardson, Managing Editor Mary Rottino, and Editor in Chief of Development Susanna Lesan, for all the long hours they put in, the wonderful suggestions they made, and their unflagging commitment to the quality of the book. We also thank Senior Marketing Manager Sharon Cosgrove for her innovative and enthusiastic contributions to the launching of this edition.

The art team who gave *Psychology, Sixth Edition,* its clear and inviting new look have all been a delight to work with: Art Director Ximena Tamvakopolous, who created the fresh, elegant, and readable design; Shanti Marlar, who suggested the many delightful conceptual ideas for rendering graphics and tables; Rose Turner at Titan Digital Limited, the artist who executed Shanti's ideas so brilliantly; and Mirella Signoretto, who made necessary corrections to the line art. Photo researcher Julie Tesser did a superb job of selecting photographs and cartoons. And our special kudos to Connie Blacker and her formatting team at TSI Graphics, who did the layouts with unsurpassed care and attention to quality.

Finally, our thanks and affection to Jennifer Bass, daughter of the late Saul Bass, for permission to use the stunning cover image created by her father, who had designed the award-winning covers of our first four editions.

Most of all, we thank Howard Williams and Ronan O'Casey, who from the first edition to this one have bolstered us with their love, humor, and good cheer, not to mention an endless supply of freshly brewed coffee.

We have enjoyed writing this book, and we hope you will enjoy reading and using it. Your questions, comments, and reactions on earlier editions helped us make many improvements. Please let us hear from you.

Carole Wade

Carol Tavris

TO THE STUDENT

If you are reading this introduction, you are starting your introductory psychology course on the right foot. It is always a good idea to get a general picture of what you are about to read before charging forward.

Our goal in writing this book is to guide you to think critically and imaginatively about psychological issues, and to help you apply what you learn to your own life and the world around you. We ourselves have never gotten over our initial excitement about psychology, and we have done everything we can think of to make the field as absorbing for you as it is for us. However, what you bring to this book is as important as what we have written—we can pitch ideas to you, but you have to step up to the plate to connect with them. This text will remain only a collection of pages with ink on them unless you choose to read actively.

GETTING INVOLVED

To encourage you to read and study actively, we have included some special features.

In the first chapter, we will introduce you to the basic guidelines of **critical and creative thinking**—the principles we hope will help you learn the difference between unsupported claims or "psychobabble" and good, scientific reasoning. The identifying symbol for critical thinking is a lightbulb, like the one in the margin. Throughout the book, some (but not all) of our **critical-thinking discussions** are signaled in the text by a "signpost" in the margin that includes this lightbulb and one of the critical-thinking guidelines. We will be telling you about many lively and passionate debates in psychology—over gender differences, psychotherapy, memory, multiple personality disorder, and many other topics—and we hope our coverage of these debates will increase your involvement with the ongoing discoveries of psychology.

Before each major section in a chapter, a feature called **What's Ahead** lists some preview questions designed to stir your curiosity and give you an overview of what the section will cover. For example: Why does paying children for good grades sometimes backfire? Do people remember better when they're hypnotized? Do men and women differ in the ability to love? When you finish the chapter, you will encounter these questions again, under the heading **Looking Back**. Use this list as a self-test; if you can't answer a question, you can go to the page indicated after the question and review the material.

Each chapter also contains several **Get Involved** exercises, entertaining little experiments or explorations you can do that relate to what you are reading about. In Chapter 3, for instance, you can find out immediately whether you are genetically disposed to cross your right thumb over your left or vice versa when you clasp your hands together; and in Chapter 11 you can find out how your own thoughts affect your emotions. Some of these exercises take only a minute; others are "mini-studies" that you can do by observing or interviewing others.

Every chapter contains several **Quick Quizzes** that permit you to test your understanding and retention of what you have just read and give you practice in applying the material to examples. Do not let the word "quiz" give you a sinking feeling. These quizzes are for your practical use and, we hope, for your enjoyment. When you have trouble with a question, do not go on; pause right then and there, review what you have read, and then try again.

Some of the Quick Quizzes contain a *critical-thinking item*, denoted by the lightbulb symbol. The answers we give for these items are only suggestions; feel free to come up with different ones. Quick Quizzes containing critical-thinking questions are not really so quick, because they ask you to reflect on what you have read and to apply the guidelines to critical thinking that are introduced in Chapter 1. But if you take the time to respond thoughtfully to them, we think you will learn more and become a more sophisticated user of psychology.

At the end of each chapter, a feature called **Taking Psychology with You** draws on research to suggest ways you can apply what you have learned to everyday problems and concerns, such as how to boost your motivation, improve your memory, and get a better night's sleep, as well as more urgent ones, such as how to live with chronic pain or help a friend who seems suicidal. The very last "Taking Psychology with You," at the end of the book, is an **Epilogue** that shows how you might integrate and use the findings and theories you have read about to solve problems in your own relationships.

HOW TO STUDY

In our years of teaching, we have found that certain study strategies can vastly improve learning, and so we offer the following suggestions. (Reading Chapter 7, on learning, and Chapter 10, on memory, will also be helpful!)

Before you even start the book, we suggest you read the Table of Contents to get an overall view of the book's organization and coverage. Likewise, before starting a chapter, read the chapter title and outline to get an idea of what is in store. Browse through the chapter, looking at the pictures and reading the headings.

Do not try to read the text the same way you might read a novel, taking in large chunks at a sitting. To get the most from your studying, we recommend that you read only a part of each chapter at a time.

Instead of simply reading silently, nodding along saying "hmmmmm" to yourself, try to restate what you have read in your own words at the end of each major section. Some people find it helpful to write down main points on a piece of paper or on index cards. Others prefer to recite main points aloud to someone else—or even to a patient pet. Do not count on getting by with just one reading of a chapter. Most people need to go through the material at least twice, and then revisit the main points several times before an exam. Special tables called **Reviews** will help you summarize, integrate, and compare psychological theories and approaches discussed in the chapter.

When you have finished a chapter, read the **Summary**. (Some students find it useful to write down their own summary first, then compare it with the book's.) Use the list of **key terms** at the end of each chapter as a checklist. Try to define and discuss each term to see how well you understand and remember it. If you need to check your recall, the page number that follows each term refers you to the term's first mention in the chapter. Finally, go over the **Looking Back** questions to be sure you can answer them.

Important new terms in this textbook are printed in **boldface** and are defined in the margin of the page on which they appear, or on the facing page. The **marginal glossary** permits you to find all key terms and concepts easily, and will help you when you study for exams. A complete glossary appears at the end of the book.

The **Study Guide** for this book, available at your bookstore, is an excellent resource. It contains review material, exercises, and practice tests to help you understand and apply the concepts in the book.

If you are assigned a term project or a report, you may need to track down some references we provide or do further reading. Throughout the book, all studies and theories include *citations* in parentheses, like this: (Aardvark and Zebra, 2000). A citation tells you who the authors of a book, article, or paper are and when the work was published. The full reference can then be looked up in the alphabetical **bibliography** at the end of the book. At the back of the book you will also find an **name index** and a **subject index.** The name index lists the name of every author cited and the pages where the person's work is discussed. If you remember the name of a psychologist but not where he or she was mentioned, look for the person in the name index. The subject index lists all the major topics mentioned in the book. If you want to review material on, say, depression, you can look up "depression" in the subject index and find each place it is mentioned.

We have done our utmost to convey our own enthusiasm about psychology, but in the end, it is your efforts as much as ours that will determine whether you find psychology to be exciting or boring, and whether the field will matter in your own life. We welcome your ideas and reactions so that we will know what works for you and what doesn't. In the meantime, welcome to psychology!

Carole Wade

Carol Tavris

ABOUT THE AUTHORS

Carole Wade earned her Ph.D. in cognitive psychology at Stanford University. She began her academic career at the University of New Mexico; was professor of psychology for ten years at San Diego Mesa College; then taught at College of Marin; and is now at Dominican College of San Rafael. She is coauthor, with Carol Tavris, of *Invitation to Psychology; Psychology in Perspective; Critical and Creative Thinking: The Case of Love and War;* and *The Longest War: Sex Differences in Perspective.* Dr. Wade has a long-standing interest in making psychology accessible to students and the general public through public lectures, workshops, general interest articles, and the electronic media. For many years she has focused her efforts on the teaching and promotion of critical-thinking skills and the enhancement of undergraduate education in psychology. She chaired the APA Board of Educational Affairs's Task Force on Diversity Issues at the Precollege and Undergraduate Levels of Education in Psychology; is a past chair of the APA's Public Information Committee; and served on the APA's Committee on Undergraduate Education and the Steering Committee for the APA's National Conference on Enhancing the Quality of Undergraduate Education. Dr. Wade is a Fellow of the American Psychological Association and is a charter member of the American Psychological Society. When she isn't teaching or writing, she can be found riding the trails of northern California on her horse, Condé.

Carol Tavris earned her Ph.D. in the interdisciplinary program in social psychology at the University of Michigan, and ever since has sought to bring research from the many fields of psychology to the public. She is author of *The Mismeasure of Woman,* which won the Distinguished Media Contribution Award from the American Association from Applied and Preventive Psychology, and the Heritage Publications Award from Division 35 of the APA. Dr. Tavris is also the author of *Anger: The Misunderstood Emotion* and coauthor with Carole Wade of *Invitation to Psychology; Psychology in Perspective; Critical and Creative Thinking: The case of love and war;* and *The Longest War: Sex Differences in Perspective.* She has written on psychological topics for many different magazines, journals, edited books, and newspapers, notably the *Los Angeles Times* and the *New York Times.* She has given keynote addresses and workshops on, among other topics, critical thinking, pseudoscience in psychology, anger, gender, and psychology and the media. She has taught in the psychology department at UCLA and at the Human Relations Center of the New School for Social Research in New York. Dr. Tavris is a Fellow of the American Psychological Association and a charter Fellow of the American Psychological Society; and, for fun, a Fellow of the Committee for the Scientific Investigation of Claims of the Paranormal. When she is not writing or lecturing, she can be found walking the trails of the Hollywood Hills with her border collie, Sophie.

PSYCHOLOGY

1

THE SCIENCE OF PSYCHOLOGY

The purpose of psychology is to give us a completely

different idea of the things we know best.

PHILOSOPHER PAUL VALÉRY

W

HAT IS PSYCHOLOGY? If you were to wander through the psychology section of your local bookstore (perhaps called "self-help" or "personal growth"), you would find books offering the following answers:

- Psychology is all about finding happiness. It will teach you that *You Can Be Happy No Matter What*, presumably if you also read *I Don't Have to Make Everything All Better*. And if you are feeling that nothing will ever get better, you might be cheered up by *The Joy of Stress* and *The Joy of Failure*.
- Psychology will make you rich and successful if you read *Baby Steps to Success* or *Giant Steps* or *How to Succeed in Life*. You can learn *How to Make the Impossible Possible* and also how to *Get What You Deserve*.
- Psychology will help you fall in love, stay in love, or get over love. *Love Is the Answer*, but only if you are *Learning to Love Yourself* first and don't develop *Obsessive Love*. You can learn *How to Make Anyone Fall in Love with You* as long as you *Don't Say Yes When You Want to Say No*. Once you're in love, of course, you will need *The Art of Intimacy* and *The Art of Staying Together*.
- Psychology is full of contradictory advice. It provides *Toughness Training for Life* and will show you how to say *Good-bye to Guilt* but will also teach you *How to Turn the Other Cheek and Still Survive in Today's World*. You can develop your inner child, *The Animal in You*, or maybe even *Grow Up!*

The psychology that you are about to study, however, bears little relation to the popular psychology ("pop psych") found in many self-help books. It is more complex, more informative, and, we think, far more helpful because it is based on scientific research and empirical evidence—evidence gathered by careful observation, experimentation, and measurement.

The psychology you will be studying also addresses a far broader range of issues than does popular psychology. When people think of psychology, they often think of mental and emotional disorders, abnormal acts, personal problems, and psychotherapy. But psychologists do not confine their attention to mental and emotional problems. They take as their subject the entire spectrum of brave and cowardly, intelligent and foolish, beautiful and brutish things that people do. Their aim is to examine and explain how human beings (and other animals, too) learn, remember, solve problems, perceive, feel, and get along (or fail to get along) with others. They are therefore as likely to study commonplace experiences as exceptional ones—rearing children, gossiping, remembering a shopping list, daydreaming, making love, and making a living.

Most psychologists today would agree that *psychology is the scientific study of behavior and mental processes and how they are affected by an organism's physical*

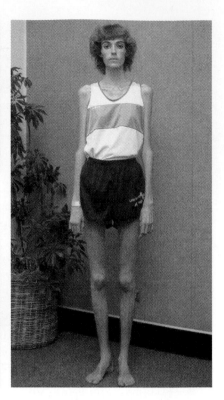

Psychologists use scientific methods to study many puzzles of human behavior. Why do people dress in funny outfits? Why do some people pursue their goals in the face of daunting disabilities, whereas others give up? Why do people develop eating disorders, in some cases literally starving themselves to death? And why do some people obliterate their own identities in the service of cults, like members of Japan's Aum Shinrikyo ("Supreme Truth"), shown here wearing masks of their leader's face?

state, mental state, and external environment. This definition, however, is a little like defining a car as a vehicle for transporting people from one place to another, without explaining how a car differs from a train or a bus, how a Ford differs from a Ferrari, or how a catalytic converter works. To get a clear picture of what psychology is, you are going to need to know more about its methods, its findings, and its ways of interpreting information. We will begin by looking more closely at what psychology is *not*.

WHAT'S AHEAD

● **How does "psychobabble" differ from serious psychology?**
● **How accurate are psychology's nonscientific competitors, such as astrologers and psychics?**

PSYCHOLOGY, PSEUDOSCIENCE, AND POPULAR OPINION

empirical Relying on or derived from observation, experimentation, or measurement.

psychology The scientific study of behavior and mental processes and how they are affected by an organism's physical state, mental state, and external environment; the term is often represented by Ψ, the Greek letter psi (usually pronounced "sy").

In recent years, the public's appetite for psychological information has created a huge market for what R. D. Rosen (1977) called "psychobabble": pseudoscience and quackery covered by a veneer of psychological language. The examples that Rosen analyzed in the 1970s included group encounters designed to transform a person's rotten life in one weekend; "primal scream therapy," in which people are supposed to link their current unhappiness to the trauma of being born (this therapy still exists); and "Theta," a "rebirthing" therapy whose leader asserted that "no one dies if they don't want to"—certainly the ultimate belief in mind over matter!

GET → INVOLVED

HOW WISE IS POPULAR WISDOM?

How reliable a guide to experience are "popular opinion" and "common sense"? For each of the following popular sayings, see whether you can think of another one that contradicts it. (You'll find some possible answers listed at the end of this chapter.)

■ Birds of a feather flock together.
■ Haste makes waste.
■ Actions speak louder than words.
■ It's not whether you win or lose, it's how you play the game.
■ You can't teach an old dog new tricks.

The particular programs and groups based on psychobabble have changed their names and leaders since Rosen wrote, but the common elements remain. ~~All promise simple, quick fixes for emotional problems and needs~~. All rely on vaguely psychological and scientific-sounding language, such as "getting in touch with your real self," "reprogramming your brain," and "identifying your unconscious talents." Some forms of psychobabble play on the modern consumer's love of technology. Thus all sorts of electrical gizmos have been marketed with the promise that they will get both halves of your brain working at their peak (Chance, 1989): the Graham Potentializer, the Tranquilite, the Floatarium, the Transcutaneous Electro-Neural Stimulator, the Brain SuperCharger, and the Whole Brain Wave Form Synchro-Energizer. (We are not making these up.)

The promise of a simple answer to meet an obvious and universal human need—coated with what Rosen called "a light dusting of psychology"—is the sign of psychobabble. Because so many pop-psych ideas have filtered into public consciousness,

Nonscientific and pseudoscientific approaches to psychological problems promise easy answers and quick solutions. For example, fortune tellers—who never seem to go out of style—claim they can analyze your personality and foresee your future from the lines on your palm. And the marriage of old-fashioned pseudoscience and modern technology has produced gizmos like the "Synchro-Energizer," which supposedly alters consciousness, boosts intelligence, aids digestion, and enhances sexual functioning, all by simply bombarding you with lights and sounds of different frequencies and intensities.

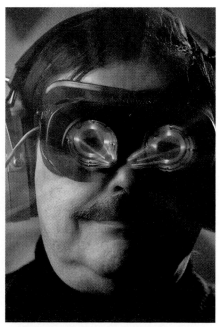

the media, education, and even the law, we all need to distinguish between psycho-babble and serious psychology, and between unsupported *popular opinion* and findings based on *research evidence*. Are unhappy memories "repressed" and then accurately recalled years later, as if they had been tape recorded? Do most women suffer from emotional symptoms of "PMS"? Do policies of abstinence from alcohol reduce rates of alcoholism? As you will learn in this book, all of these common beliefs and many others are contradicted by the evidence.

Beliefs about psychological topics are not trivial; they can affect our lives. For example, a woman wrote to the *Los Angeles Times*, "As a child of alcoholic parents, I realized many years ago that I would not make a good mother since I did not have a proper role model. In the case of inheriting bad genes, I would not want to make a child of mine go through the nights of yelling and beatings that I experienced." This writer had uncritically accepted the popular notions that all children of alcoholics become alcoholic; that all children who are abused become abusive parents themselves; and that "bad genes" determine behavior. As you will see in this book, all of these assumptions have been disproved by empirical evidence.

I see you being less gullible in the future.

The study of psychology can make this prediction come true.

Psychology has many nonscientific competitors: palm reading, graphology, fortune-telling, numerology, and the most popular, astrology. Like psychologists, promoters of these competing systems try to explain people's problems and predict their behavior. If you are having romantic problems, for example, an astrologer may advise you to choose an Aries instead of an Aquarius as your next love, and a "past-lives channeler" may say it's because you were jilted in a former life. But whenever they are put to the test, the claims of psychics, astrologers, and the like turn out to be so vague that they are meaningless—or they are just plain wrong (Dean, 1987; Rowe, 1993).

For example, psychics predicted that 1997 was going to be the year that Mick Jagger became a member of the British Parliament, Congress suspended the baseball season after a brawl left dozens of people dead, Hillary Clinton got pregnant again, and Rush Limbaugh became a liberal Democrat after having a little talk with Barbra Streisand (Emery, 1998). Obviously, they were mistaken! Likewise, no psychic predicted the impeachment trial of President Clinton in 1999. Nor has any psychic ever predicted anything that was truly a horrible shock, such as the bombing of the federal building in Oklahoma that left 168 people dead. Nor has any psychic ever found a missing child, identified a serial killer, or helped police solve any other crime solely by using "psychic powers"—in spite of frequent reports in the mass media that psychics do this all the time (Rowe, 1993; Shermer, 1997).

Perhaps the ultimate difference between psychobabble and scientific psychology is that psychobabble *confirms* our existing beliefs and prejudices (which is why it is so appealing), whereas psychology often *challenges* them. You do not have to be a psychologist to know that people don't always take kindly to having their beliefs challenged. You rarely hear someone say, cheerfully, "Oh, thank you for explaining to me why my lifelong philosophy of child rearing is wrong! I'm so grateful for your facts!" The person is more likely to say, "Oh, buzz off, and take your stupid ideas with you." (In Chapter 9 you will learn why this is so.)

However, although psychologists often challenge prevailing beliefs, they also seek to extend and deepen our understanding of generally accepted facts. After all, everyone knows that an apple will fall to the ground if it drops from a tree, but it took Isaac Newton to discover the laws of gravity and to explain why the apple falls and why it travels at a particular speed. Psychologists, like scientists in other fields, strive not only to discover new phenomena, but also to deepen our understanding of an already familiar world.

WHAT'S AHEAD

- Are "critical thinkers" always critical?
- Are all opinions created equal?
- What guidelines can help you evaluate psychological claims?

THINKING CRITICALLY AND CREATIVELY ABOUT PSYCHOLOGY

In this book, you will gain practice in distinguishing scientific psychology from pseudoscience by thinking critically. Critical thinking is the ability and willingness to assess claims and make objective judgments on the basis of well-supported reasons and evidence, rather than emotion and anecdote. Critical thinkers are able to look for flaws in arguments and to resist claims that have no support. Critical thinking, however, is not merely negative thinking. It includes the ability to be creative and constructive—the ability to come up with various possible explanations for events, think of implications of research findings, and apply new knowledge to social and personal problems.

Most people know that you have to exercise the body to keep it in shape, but they may not realize that clear thinking also requires effort and practice. Unlike breathing, it is not automatic. All around us we can see examples of flabby thinking. Sometimes people justify their mental laziness by proudly telling you they are "open-minded." "It's good to be open-minded," philosopher Jacob Needleman once replied, "but not so open that your brains fall out."

One prevalent misreading of what it means to be open-minded is the idea that all opinions are created equal and that everybody's beliefs are as good as everybody else's. On matters of personal preference, that is true; if you prefer the look of a Ford Escort to the look of a Honda Civic, no one can argue with you. But if you say, "The Ford is a better car than a Honda," you have uttered more than mere opinion. Now you have to support your belief with evidence of the car's reliability, track record, and safety (Ruggiero, 1997). And if you say, "Fords are the best in the world and Hondas do not exist; they are a conspiracy of the Japanese government," you forfeit the right to have your opinion taken seriously. Your opinion, if it ignores reality, is *not* equal to any other.

As we will see in Chapter 9, many people do not use critical-thinking skills until they are in their mid-20s, or until they have had many years of higher education (King & Kitchener, 1994). Yet even young children have the basic capacity to think critically, although they may not get much credit for it. We know one fourth-grader, who, when told that ancient Greece was the "cradle of democracy," replied, "But what about women and slaves, who couldn't vote and had no rights? Was Greece a democracy for them?" That's critical thinking!

Many educators, philosophers, and psychologists believe that contemporary education shortchanges students by not encouraging them to think critically and creatively. Too often, say these critics, teachers and students view the mind as a bin for storing "the right answers" or a sponge for "soaking up knowledge." The mind is neither a bin nor a sponge. Remembering, thinking, and understanding require judgment, choice, and the weighing of evidence. Many high school and college graduates have learned to memorize the "right" answers but cannot formulate a rational argument or see through misleading advertisements that play on their emotions. They may not know how to assess a political proposal or candidate, decide whether or when to have children, or come up with constructive solutions to their problems.

critical thinking The ability and willingness to assess claims and to make judgments on the basis of well-supported reasons and evidence, rather than emotion or anecdote.

Many spend huge amounts of money on medical remedies that lack any evidence of effectiveness and that can even be life-threatening (Halpern, 1998).

Critical thinking is not only indispensable in ordinary life, but also fundamental to all science. And it is particularly relevant in psychology. For one thing, the field itself includes the study of reasoning, problem solving, creativity, curiosity, and other aspects of critical thought. It also includes the study of *barriers* to clear thinking, such as the human propensity for rationalization, self-deception, and misperception. Most important, the field of psychology generates many competing findings on hot topics of personal and social relevance, such as addiction, memory, sexual orientation, and the role of genetics in behavior; people need to know how to think critically in order to evaluate these findings and their possible implications.

Critical thinking requires logical skills, but other skills are also important (Ennis, 1985; Halpern, 1995; Levy, 1997; Paul, 1984; Ruggiero, 1997). Here are eight essential critical-thinking guidelines that are emphasized throughout this book.

Ask Questions; Be Willing to Wonder. What is the one kind of question that most exasperates parents of young children? "Why is the sky blue, Mommy?" "Why doesn't the plane fall?" "Why don't pigs have wings?" Unfortunately, as children grow up, they tend to stop asking "why" questions like these. (Why do you think this is?)

"The trigger mechanism for creative thinking is the disposition to be curious, to wonder, to inquire," observed Vincent Ruggiero (1988). "Asking 'What's wrong here?' and/or 'Why is this the way it is, and how did it come to be that way?' leads to the identification of problems and challenges." Psychologist Bob Perloff (1992) once reflected on a few questions he would like to have answered: "Why are moths attracted to wool but indifferent to cotton?" he wondered. "Why is a rainbow arched? I used to feel foolish, even dumb, because I didn't know why or how the sun shines until I learned very recently that the astrophysicists themselves are in a quandary about this."

We hope that you will not approach psychology as "received wisdom" but will ask many questions about the theories and findings presented in this book. Be on the lookout, too, for questions about human behavior that have not yet been asked. If you do that, you will be not only learning psychology, but also learning to think the way psychologists do.

Define Your Terms. Once you have raised a general question, the next step is to frame it in clear and concrete terms. "What makes people happy?" is a fine question for midnight reveries, but it will not lead to answers until you have defined what you mean by "happy." Do you mean being in a state of euphoria most of the time? Do you mean feeling pleasantly content with life? Do you mean the absence of serious problems or pain?

Poorly defined terms can produce misleading or incomplete answers to psychological questions. For example, have you ever wondered whether animals use language? The answer depends on how you define "language." If you mean "a system of communication," then birds do it, bees do it, and even plants do it. But if you define language as "a system of communication that combines sounds or gestures into an infinite number of structured utterances that convey meaning" (which is the way linguists define it), then as far as anyone can tell, only people use language. And if, instead of a "yes-no"-type question, you ask, "Which aspects of language might some animals be able to acquire in special settings?" you will discover similarities between humans and other primates that you might never have imagined, as we will see in Chapter 9.

💡 *Examine the Evidence.* Have you ever heard someone in the heat of argument exclaim, "I just know it's true, no matter what you say" or "That's my opinion; nothing's going to change it"? Have you ever made such statements yourself? Accepting a conclusion without evidence, or expecting others to do so, is a sure sign of lazy thinking. A critical thinker asks, "What evidence supports or refutes this argument and its opposition? How reliable is the evidence?" If checking the reliability of the evidence directly is not possible, the person considers whether it came from a reliable source.

Some pop-psych ideas have been widely accepted on the basis of poor evidence or even no evidence at all. For example, many people think it is healthy to ventilate their anger at the first person, pet, or piece of furniture that gets in their way. Actually, studies across many fields suggest that sometimes expressing anger is beneficial, but more often it is not. Often it makes the angry person angrier, makes the target of the anger become angry in return, lowers everybody's self-esteem, and fosters hostility and aggression (Tavris, 1989). Yet the belief that expressing anger is always healthy persists, despite the evidence to the contrary. Perhaps you can think of some reasons why this might be so.

💡 *Analyze Assumptions and Biases.* Assumptions are beliefs that are taken for granted. Critical thinkers try to identify the unspoken assumptions on which claims and arguments may rest. The assumption might be "All Democrats (or Republicans) are idiots," or "You have a need for the product we are selling," or "People have free will and are therefore entirely responsible for any crimes they commit" (or, conversely, "People's behavior is a result of their biology or upbringing, so they aren't responsible for anything they do"). Everyone, of course, carries around a headful of assumptions about how the world works; we could not function otherwise. But if we do not make our own and other people's assumptions explicit, our ability to judge an argument's merits may be impaired.

When an assumption or belief keeps us from considering the evidence fairly, or causes us to ignore the evidence completely, it becomes a *bias.* Sometimes we are unaware that we have a bias until someone challenges our belief and we get defensive and angry. For example, most of us, psychologists included, believe that parents are the most important influence in shaping a child's personality. Could anything be more obvious? Isn't that what parenting books, therapists, and magazine articles have been telling us for years? In 1998, in her book *The Nurture Assumption*, Judith Rich Harris dared to question that assumption. Genes and peers, she argued, are more important influences on a child's personality than how parents raise their children. Because this idea challenged a widespread bias, it immediately provoked a storm of disbelief, outrage, and scorn. Some critics focused on Harris's lack of credentials instead of her facts or her logic (she does not have a Ph.D.), and some attacked the book without even bothering to read it. That is the nature of a bias: It causes us to put on intellectual blinders. (You may be wondering whether Harris is right about parents and peers. In Chapter 14 we will look more closely at her argument—in as unbiased a manner as possible.)

💡 *Avoid Emotional Reasoning: "If I Feel This Way, It Must Be True."*
Emotion has a place in critical thinking. Passionate commitment to a view can motivate a person to think boldly, defend an unpopular idea, and seek evidence for a creative new theory. But when "gut feelings" replace clear thinking, the results can be dangerous. "Persecutions and wars and lynchings," observed Edward de Bono (1985), "are all a result of gut feeling."

Because our feelings feel so *right*, so natural, we may not realize that people who hold an opposing viewpoint feel just as strongly as we do. But they usually do, which means that emotional conviction alone cannot settle arguments. You probably hold strong feelings about many topics, such as drugs, the causes of crime, racism, the origins of intelligence, gender differences, homosexuality, and other issues of concern to psychologists. As you read this book, you may find yourself quarreling with findings that you dislike. Disagreement is fine; it means that you are reading actively. All we ask is that you think about why you are disagreeing: Is it because the evidence is unpersuasive or because the results make you feel anxious or annoyed?

Don't Oversimplify. A critical thinker looks beyond the obvious, resists easy generalizations, and rejects either/or thinking. For example, is it better to feel you have control over everything that happens to you, or to accept with tranquility whatever life serves up? Either position oversimplifies. As we will see in Chapter 15, a sense of control has many important benefits, but sometimes it is best to "go with the flow."

One common form of oversimplification is *argument by anecdote*—generalizing from a personal experience or a few examples to everyone. One crime committed by a paroled ex-convict means that parole should be abolished; one friend who hates her school means that everybody who goes there hates it. Anecdotes are often the source of

THINKING CRITICALLY AND CREATIVELY ABOUT PSYCHOLOGICAL ISSUES

ASK QUESTIONS, BE WILLING TO WONDER

A Chinese man standing alone against awesome military might inspired millions during the 1989 rebellion in Tiananmen Square. Why do some people have the courage to risk their lives for their beliefs? Why do so many others go along with the crowd or mindlessly obey authority? Social psychologists probe these questions in depth, as we will see in Chapter 8.

DEFINE YOUR TERMS

People refer to intelligence all the time, but what is it exactly? Does the musical genius of a world-class violinist like Anne-Sophie Mutter count as intelligence? Is intelligence captured by an IQ score, or does it also include wisdom and practical "smarts"? We will consider some answers in Chapter 9.

stereotyping as well? One dishonest welfare mother means they are all dishonest; one encounter with an unconventional Californian means they are all flaky. Critical thinkers want more evidence than one or two stories before drawing such sweeping conclusions.

Consider Other Interpretations. Critical thinkers generate as many interpretations of the evidence as possible before settling on the most likely one. For example, suppose a news magazine reports that chronically depressed people are more likely than nondepressed people to develop cancer. Before concluding that depression causes cancer, you would need to consider some other possibilities. Perhaps depressed people are more likely to smoke and drink too much, and it is those unhealthful habits that increase their cancer risk. Perhaps, in studies of depression and cancer, early undetected cancers were responsible for the feelings of depression felt by the patients. Alternative explanations such as these must be ruled out by further investigation before we can conclude that depression is a direct cause of cancer.

Once several explanations of a phenomenon have been generated, a critical thinker chooses the one that accounts for the most evidence and makes the fewest unverified assumptions. For example, suppose that a fortune-teller reads your palm and predicts that soon you will fall in love on a blind date, travel to Zanzibar, and have twins. One of two things must be true (Steiner, 1989):

EXAMINE THE EVIDENCE

When demonstrating "levitation" and other supposedly magical phenomena, illusionists such as André Kole exploit people's tendency to trust the evidence of their own eyes even when such evidence is misleading, as discussed in Chapter 6.

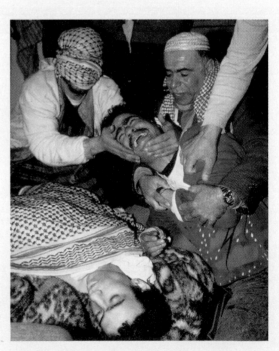

ANALYZE ASSUMPTIONS AND BIASES

Many North Americans assume that men are by nature less emotionally expressive than women. But this Palestinian man, grieving over his dead son, does not fit Western stereotypes of male emotionality. Cultural rules have a powerful influence on how men and women express their feelings, as we will see in Chapter 11.

- The fortune-teller can actually sort out the infinite number of interactions among people, animals, events, objects, and circumstances that could affect your life and can know for sure the outcome. Moreover, this fortune-teller is able to alter all the known laws of physics and defy the hundreds of studies showing that no one, under proper procedures for validating psychic predictions, has been able to predict the future for any given individual.

OR

- The fortune-teller is faking it.

A critical thinker would prefer the second alternative because it requires fewer assumptions and has the most supporting evidence.

Tolerate Uncertainty. Ultimately, learning to think critically teaches us one of the hardest lessons of life: how to live with uncertainty. Sometimes there is little or no evidence to examine. Sometimes the evidence permits only tentative conclusions. Sometimes the evidence seems strong enough to permit conclusions . . . until, exasperatingly, new evidence throws our beliefs into disarray. Critical thinkers are willing to accept this state of uncertainty. They are not afraid to say, "I don't know" or "I'm not sure" or, the hardest, "I was wrong." This admission is not an evasion but a spur to further creative inquiry.

AVOID EMOTIONAL REASONING

Passionate feelings about controversial issues can keep us from considering other viewpoints. The resolution of differences requires that we move beyond emotional reasoning and instead weigh point and counterpoint, as discussed in Chapter 9.

DON'T OVERSIMPLIFY

Is the left side of the brain entirely analytic, rational, and sensible and the right side always intuitive, emotional, and spontaneous? The two hemispheres of the brain do have some specialized talents, but it is easy to exaggerate the differences, as we will see in Chapter 4.

The desire for certainty often makes people uncomfortable when experts cannot give them "the" answer to a question. Patients may demand of their doctors, "What do you mean you don't know what's wrong with me? Find out and fix it!" Students may demand of their professors, "What do you mean it's a controversial issue? Just tell me the answer!" Critical thinkers know that the more important the question, the less likely it is to have a single simple answer.

The need to accept a certain amount of uncertainty does not mean that we must live without beliefs and convictions. That would be impossible, in any case: We all need values and principles to guide our actions. As Vincent Ruggiero (1988) wrote, "It is not the embracing of an idea that causes problems—it is the refusal to relax that embrace when good sense dictates doing so. It is enough to form convictions with care and carry them lightly, being willing to reconsider them whenever new evidence calls them into question."

Of course, critical thinking cannot provide answers to all of life's quandaries. Some questions, such as whether there is a God and what the nature of God might be, are ultimately matters of faith. Moreover, critical thinking is a process, not a once-and-for-all accomplishment. No one ever becomes a perfect critical thinker, entirely unaffected by emotional reasoning and wishful thinking. We are all less open-minded than we think; it is always easier to poke holes in another person's argument than to critically examine our own position. As philosopher Richard W. Paul (1984) observed, critical thinking is really "fair-mindedness brought into the heart of everyday life."

CONSIDER OTHER INTERPRETATIONS

The Rastafarian church regards marijuana as a "wisdom weed." Will these young Jamaican members react to the drug in the same way as someone who buys it on the street and smokes it alone or at a party? Although people commonly attribute the effects of psychoactive substances solely to the drugs, an alternative explanation emphasizes the impact of setting, motives, and cultural practices, as we will see in Chapters 5 and 16.

TOLERATE UNCERTAINTY

Many questions have no current answers. For example, several theories have been offered to explain sexual orientation, but no single explanation can account for the many variations of homosexuality or of heterosexuality, as we will see in Chapter 12.

REVIEW 1.1

GUIDELINES TO THINKING CRITICALLY ABOUT PSYCHOLOGICAL ISSUES

	Guideline	Example
	Ask questions; be willing to wonder	"Can I recall events from my childhood accurately?"
	Define your terms	"By 'childhood' I mean ages 3 to 12; by 'events' I mean things that happened to me personally, like a trip to the zoo or a stay in the hospital; by 'accurately' I mean the event basically happened the way I think it did."
	Examine the evidence	"I *feel* I recall my fifth birthday party perfectly, but studies show that people often reconstruct past events inaccurately."
	Analyze assumptions and biases	"I've always assumed that memory is like a tape recorder —perfectly accurate for every moment of my life— but maybe this is just a bias, because it's so reassuring."
	Avoid emotional reasoning	"I really *want* to believe this memory is true, but that doesn't mean it *is*."
	Don't oversimplify	"Some of my childhood memories could be accurate, others mistaken, and some partly right and partly wrong."
	Consider other interpretations	"Some 'memories' could be based on what my parents told me later, not on my own recall."
	Tolerate uncertainty	"I may never know for sure whether some of my childhood memories are real or accurate."

Note: You will be reading a lot more about the reliability of memory in Chapter 10.

As you read this book, keep in mind the eight guidelines we have described, which are summarized for you in Review 1.1. You will have many opportunities to apply them to psychological theories and to the personal and social issues that affect us all. From time to time, questions in the margin, accompanied by a lightbulb symbol (like the ones next to our descriptions of the critical-thinking guidelines) will draw your attention to a discussion where one of the guidelines is especially relevant. In Quick Quizzes, the lightbulb symbol will identify questions that ask you to apply the guidelines yourself. Keep in mind, however, that critical thinking is important throughout every chapter, not just where the lightbulb appears.

QUICK QUIZ

Amelia and Harold are arguing about the death penalty. "Look, I just feel strongly that it's barbaric, ineffective, and wrong," says Harold. "You're nuts," says Amelia, "I believe in an eye for an eye, and besides, I'm absolutely sure it's a deterrent to further crime." Which lapses of critical thinking might Amelia and Harold be committing?

Answers:

Here are some problems in their style of argument; feel free to think of others. (1) They are reasoning emotionally ("I feel strongly about this, so I'm right and you're wrong"). (2) They have not examined evidence that supports or contradicts their arguments. What do studies show about the link between the death penalty and crime? Is the death penalty applied fairly to rich and poor, men and women, black and white? (3) They have not examined the assumptions and biases they bring to the discussion. (4) They may not be clearly defining the problem they are arguing about. What is the goal of the death penalty, for example? Is it to deter criminals, to satisfy the public desire for revenge, or to keep criminals from being paroled and returned to the streets?

WHAT'S AHEAD

- **What is the lesson of phrenology for modern psychology?**
- **How old is the science of psychology?**
- **Was Sigmund Freud the official founder of psychology?**

PSYCHOLOGY'S PAST: FROM THE ARMCHAIR TO THE LABORATORY

Now that you know what psychology is and what it isn't, and why studying it requires critical thinking, let us see how psychology developed into a modern science. Until the nineteenth century, psychology was not a formal discipline. Of course, most of the great thinkers of history, from Aristotle to Zoroaster, raised questions that today would be called psychological. They wanted to know how people take in information through their senses, use information to solve problems, and become motivated to act in brave or villainous ways. They wondered about the elusive nature of emotion, and whether it controls us or is something we can control. Like today's psychologists, they wanted to *describe, predict, understand,* and *modify* behavior in order to add to human knowledge and increase human happiness. But unlike modern psychologists, scholars of the past did not rely heavily on empirical evidence. Often, their observations were based simply on anecdotes or descriptions of individual cases.

This does not mean that the forerunners of modern psychology were always wrong. On the contrary, they often had insights and made observations that were verified by later work. Hippocrates (c. 460 B.C.–c. 377 B.C.), the Greek physician known as the founder of modern medicine, observed patients with head injuries and inferred that the brain must be the ultimate source of "our pleasures, joys, laughter, and jests as well as our sorrows, pains, griefs, and tears." And so it is. In the first century A.D., the Stoic philosophers observed that people do not become angry or sad or anxious because of actual events, but because of their explanations of those events. And so they do. In the seventeenth century, the French philosopher René Descartes (1596–1650) promoted scientific thinking by searching for physical explanations of behavior. Later in the same century, the English philosopher John Locke (1643–1704) argued that the mind works by associating ideas arising from experience, a notion that continues to influence many psychologists today.

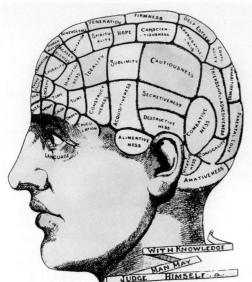

Phrenology, a nineteenth-century pseudoscientific fad, linked bumps on the skull with character traits. On this phrenological "map," notice the tiny space allocated to self-esteem and the large one devoted to cautiousness!

But without empirical methods, the forerunners of psychology also committed some terrible blunders. A good example of how prescientific psychology could lead down a blind alley comes from the early 1800s, when the theory of *phrenology* (Greek for "study of the mind") became wildly popular. Inspired by the writings and lectures of Austrian physician Joseph Gall (1758–1828), phrenologists argued that different brain areas accounted for specific character and personality traits, such as "stinginess" and "religiosity," and that such traits could be "read" from bumps on the skull. Thieves, for example, supposedly had large bumps above the ears. When phrenologists examined people with "stealing bumps" who were *not* thieves, they explained away this counterevidence by saying that other bumps on the skull represented positive traits that must be holding the person's thieving impulses in check.

In the United States, all sorts of people eagerly sought the services of phrenologists. Parents used them to make decisions about child rearing and to decide whether their children could benefit from music lessons; schools used them to decide which teachers to hire; young people used them when deciding on a career or a mate; and businesses used them to find out which employees were likely to be loyal and honest (Benjamin, 1998). For communities that were too small to afford their own phrenologist, there were even circuit-riding phrenologists who traveled around the country giving readings. Some phrenologists offered classes or self-study programs for people who wanted to overcome their deficiencies—the forerunners of today's many self-improvement programs and seminars. Enthusiasm for phrenology did not disappear until well into the twentieth century, even though phrenology was a classic pseudoscience—utter nonsense.

The Birth of Modern Psychology

At the same time that phrenologists were having a heyday, several pioneering researchers in Europe and America were starting to study psychological issues using scientific methods. Indeed, psychology has many forefathers—and several foremothers, too, although their accomplishments were often unacknowledged or were attributed to others (Scarborough & Furumoto, 1987). But credit for the establishment of psychology as a science usually goes to Wilhelm Wundt [VIL-helm Voont], who formally founded the first psychological laboratory in 1879, in Leipzig, Germany. Wundt (1832–1920), who was trained in medicine and philosophy, wrote many volumes on psychology, physiology, natural history, ethics, and logic. But he is especially revered by psychologists because he was the first person to announce (in 1873) that he intended to make psychology a science and because his laboratory was the first to have its results published in a scholarly journal. Although it started out as just a few rooms in an old building, the Leipzig laboratory soon became the place to go for anyone who wanted to become a psychologist. Many of America's first psychologists got their training there.

Researchers in Wundt's laboratory did not study the entire gamut of topics that today's psychologists do. Most concentrated on sensation, perception, reaction times, imagery, and attention, and they avoided learning, personality, and abnormal behavior. One of Wundt's favorite research methods was *trained introspection*, in which specially trained people carefully observed, analyzed, and described their own sensations, mental images, and emotional reactions. This was not as easy as it sounds. Wundt's introspectors had to make 10,000 practice observations before they were allowed to participate in an actual study. Once trained, they might take as long as 20 minutes to report their inner experiences during a 1.5-second experiment.

Wilhelm Wundt (1832–1920), on the right, with co-workers.

GET ➔ INVOLVED

LOOKING INWARD

How reliable is introspection as a method for arriving at generalizations about human experience? Find out for yourself by asking some friends what they experience mentally when they think of a chair. Tell them to be specific about color, shape, size, style, orientation, and so on. Which aspects of the experience do they agree on, and which do they report differently?

Although Wundt hoped that his methods would produce reliable, verifiable results, most psychologists eventually rejected trained introspection as too subjective. But Wundt still gets the credit for initiating the movement to make psychology a science.

Three Early Psychologies

During the early decades of psychology's existence as a formal discipline, three schools of psychological thought became popular. One soon faded, another disappeared as a separate school but continued to influence the field, and the third remains alive today, despite passionate debate about whether it belongs in scientific psychology at all.

Structuralism. In America, Wundt's ideas were popularized in somewhat modified form by one of his students, E. B. Titchener (1867–1927), who gave Wundt's approach the name structuralism. Like Wundt, structuralists hoped to analyze sensations, images, and feelings into basic elements, much as a chemist might analyze water into hydrogen and oxygen atoms. For example, a person might be asked to listen to a metronome clicking and to report exactly what he or she heard. Most people said they perceived a pattern (such as, CLICK click click CLICK click click), even though the clicks of a metronome are actually all the same. Or a person might be asked to break down all the different components of taste when biting into an orange (sweet, tart, wet, etc.).

Despite an intensive program of research, however, structuralism soon went the way of the dinosaur. After you have discovered the building blocks of a particular sensation or image and how they link up, then what? Years after structuralism's demise, Wolfgang Köhler (1959) recalled how he and his colleagues had responded to it as students: "What had disturbed us was . . . the implication that human life, apparently so colorful and so intensely dynamic, is actually a frightful bore."

The structuralists' reliance on introspection also got them into trouble. Despite their training, introspectors often produced conflicting reports. For example, when asked what image came to mind when they heard the word *triangle*, most respondents said they imagined a visual image of a form with three sides and three corners, but one person might report a flashing red form with equal angles, whereas another reported a revolving colorless form with one angle larger than the other two. Some people even claimed they could think about a triangle without forming any visual image at all (Boring, 1953). It was hard, therefore, to know what mental attributes of a triangle were basic.

structuralism An early psychological approach that emphasized the analysis of immediate experience into basic elements.

William James (1842–1910)

Sigmund Freud (1856–1939)

functionalism An early psychological approach that emphasized the function or purpose of behavior and consciousness.

psychoanalysis A theory of personality and a method of psychotherapy, originally formulated by Sigmund Freud, that emphasizes unconscious motives and conflicts.

Functionalism. Another early approach to scientific psychology, called functionalism, emphasized the function or purpose of behavior, as opposed to its analysis and description. One of functionalism's leaders was William James (1842–1910), an American philosopher, physician, and psychologist who argued that searching for building blocks of experience, as Wundt and Titchener tried to do, was a waste of time. The brain and the mind are constantly changing, he noted. Permanent ideas—of triangles or anything else—do not appear periodically before the "footlights of consciousness." Attempting to grasp the nature of the mind through introspection, wrote James (1890/1950), is "like seizing a spinning top to catch its motion, or trying to turn up the gas quickly enough to see how the darkness looks."

Where the structuralists asked *what* happens when an organism does something, the functionalists asked *how* and *why.* They were inspired in part by the evolutionary theories of British naturalist Charles Darwin (1809–1882). Darwin had argued that a biologist's job is not merely to describe, say, the brilliant plumage of a peacock or the drab markings of a lizard, but also to figure out how these attributes enhance survival. Do they help the animal attract a mate or hide from its enemies? Similarly, the functionalists wanted to know how specific behaviors and mental processes help a person or animal adapt to the environment, so they looked for underlying causes and practical consequences of these behaviors and processes. Unlike the structuralists, they felt free to pick and choose among many methods, and they broadened the field of psychology to include the study of children, animals, religious experiences, and what James called the "stream of consciousness"—a term still used because it so beautifully describes the way thoughts flow like a river, tumbling over each other in waves, sometimes placid, sometimes turbulent.

As a school of psychology, functionalism, like structuralism, was short-lived. It lacked the kind of precise theory or program of research that wins recruits, and it endorsed the study of consciousness just as that concept was about to fall out of favor. Yet the functionalists' emphasis on the causes and consequences of behavior was to set the course of psychological science.

Psychoanalysis. Psychology also has roots in Vienna, Austria, where it first developed as a method of psychotherapy. While researchers in Europe and America were working in their laboratories, struggling to make psychology more scientific, Sigmund Freud (1856–1939), an obscure neurologist, was in his office, listening to his patients' reports of depression, nervousness, and obsessive habits. Freud became convinced that many of his patients' symptoms had mental, not bodily, causes. Their distress, he concluded, was due to conflicts and emotional traumas that had occurred in early childhood and that were too threatening to be remembered consciously.

Freud argued that conscious awareness is merely the tip of a mental iceberg. Beneath the visible tip, he said, lies the unconscious part of the mind, containing unrevealed wishes, passions, guilty secrets, unspeakable yearnings, and conflicts between desire and duty. We are not aware of our unconscious urges and thoughts as we go blithely about our daily business, yet they make themselves known—in dreams, slips of the tongue, apparent accidents, and even jokes. Freud (1905a) wrote, "No mortal can keep a secret. If the lips are silent, he chatters with his fingertips; betrayal oozes out of him at every pore."

Freud's proposals were not an overnight sensation; his first book, *The Interpretation of Dreams* (1900), managed to sell only 600 copies in the eight years following publication. Eventually, however, his ideas evolved into a broad theory of personality and a method of psychotherapy, both of which became known as psychoanalysis. Freudian concepts had a profound influence on the philosophy, literature, and art of the twentieth century, and his name is now as much a household word as Einstein's.

From these early beginnings in philosophy, natural science, and medicine, psychology has grown into a complex field consisting of different specialties and perspectives. Today, psychology is like a large, sprawling family; the members of this family share common great-grandparents, but some of the cousins have formed alliances, some are quarreling, and a few are barely speaking to one another.

QUICK QUIZ

A. Make sure psychology's past is still present in your memory by choosing the correct response from each pair of terms in parentheses.

1. Psychology has been a science for a little over (2,000/100) years.
2. The forerunners of modern psychology depended heavily on (casual observation/empirical methods).
3. Credit for founding modern psychology is generally given to (William James/Wilhelm Wundt).
4. Early psychologists who emphasized how behavior helps an organism adapt to its environment were known as (structuralists/functionalists).

B. The psychological treatment of emotional problems has its origins in Freud's theory of _____.

Answers:

A. 1. 100 2. casual observation 3. Wilhelm Wundt 4. functionalists B. psychoanalysis

WHAT'S AHEAD

- **What are the five major perspectives in psychology?**
- **Why is psychoanalysis the "thumb on the hand of psychology"?**
- **How have humanism and feminism influenced psychology?**

PSYCHOLOGY'S PRESENT: BEHAVIOR, BODY, MIND, AND CULTURE

If you had a noisy, rude, surly neighbor, and you asked a group of psychologists to explain why this guy was such a miserable person, they might give you different answers. Depending on their theoretical perspective, they might cite your neighbor's biological makeup, his belligerent attitude toward the world, the way he was brought up (or not brought up!), the environment that encourages his nasty temper, or the influence of his unconscious motives. Modern psychologists tend to examine human behavior through several lenses.

The Major Psychological Perspectives

The five lenses that predominate in psychology today are the *biological, learning, cognitive, sociocultural,* and *psychodynamic* perspectives. These approaches reflect different questions about human behavior, different assumptions about how the mind works, and, most important, different kinds of explanations of why people do what they do.

1 *The* biological perspective *focuses on how bodily events affect behavior, feelings, and thoughts.* Electrical impulses shoot along the intricate pathways of the nervous system. Hormones course through the bloodstream, telling internal organs to slow down or speed up. Chemical substances flow across the tiny gaps that separate one microscopic brain cell from another. Biological psychologists want to know how these physical events interact with events in the external environment to produce perceptions, memories, and behavior.

Researchers in this perspective study how biology affects learning and performance, perceptions of reality, the experience of emotion, and vulnerability to emotional disorder. They study how the mind and body interact in illness and health. They investigate the contributions of genes and other biological factors in the development of traits and abilities. And in a popular new specialty, *evolutionary psychology*, researchers have been studying how our species' evolutionary past may help explain some of our present behaviors and psychological traits. The message of the biological approach is that we cannot really know ourselves if we do not know our bodies.

2 *The* learning perspective *is concerned with how the environment and experience affect a person's (or an animal's) actions.* Within this perspective, *behaviorists* focus on the environmental conditions—the rewards and punishers—that maintain or discourage specific behaviors. Behaviorists do not invoke the mind or mental states to explain behavior: They stick to what they can observe and measure directly—acts and events taking place in the environment. *Social-cognitive learning theorists*, on the other hand, combine elements of behaviorism with research on thoughts, values, expectations, and intentions. They believe that people learn not only by adapting their behavior to the environment, but also by imitating others and by thinking about the events happening around them.

The learning perspective has many practical applications. Behavioral programs have helped people get rid of unwanted habits and acquire better ones; social-cognitive learning techniques have helped people boost their motivation and become more self-confident. Historically, the behaviorists' insistence on precision and objectivity has done much to advance psychology as a science, and learning research in general has given psychology some of its most reliable findings.

3 *The* cognitive perspective *emphasizes what goes on in people's heads*—how people reason, remember, understand language, solve problems, explain experiences, and form beliefs. (The word *cognitive* comes from the Latin for "to know.") One of this perspective's most important contributions has been to show how people's thoughts and explanations affect their actions, feelings, and choices. Cognitive researchers do not rely on the structuralists' method of introspection; instead, they have developed clever ways to infer mental processes from observable behavior. With these methods, they have been able to study phenomena that were once only the stuff of speculation, such as sleeping, dreaming, and hypnosis. They are designing computer programs that model how humans perform complex tasks; discovering what goes on in the mind of an infant; and identifying types of intelligence not measured by conventional IQ tests. The cognitive approach is one of the strongest forces in psychology today, and it has inspired an explosion of research on the intricate workings of the mind.

4 *The* sociocultural perspective *focuses on social and cultural forces outside the individual.* These forces shape every aspect of behavior, from how (and whether!) we kiss to what and where we eat. Most of us underestimate the impact of other people, group affiliations, and cultural rules on our actions. We are like fish that are unaware they live in water, so obvious is water in their lives. Sociocultural psychologists study the water—the social and cultural environment that people "swim" in every day.

---

biological perspective A psychological approach that emphasizes bodily events and changes associated with actions, feelings, and thoughts.

learning perspective A psychological approach that emphasizes how the environment and experience affect a person's or animal's actions; it includes *behaviorism* and *social-cognitive learning theories.*

cognitive perspective A psychological approach that emphasizes mental processes in perception, memory, language, problem solving, and other areas of behavior.

sociocultural perspective A psychological approach that emphasizes social and cultural influences on behavior.

Within this perspective, social psychologists focus on social rules and roles, how groups affect attitudes and behavior, why people obey authority, and how each of us is affected by other people—spouses, lovers, friends, bosses, parents, and strangers. Cultural psychologists examine how cultural rules and values—both explicit and unspoken—affect people's development, behavior, and feelings. For example, they might study how culture influences people's willingness to help a stranger in distress, or how it influences what people do when they are angry. Because human beings are social animals who are profoundly affected by their different cultural worlds, the sociocultural perspective has made psychology a more representative and rigorous discipline.

5 *The* psychodynamic perspective *deals with unconscious dynamics within the individual, such as inner forces, conflicts, or instinctual energy.* It has its origins in Freud's theory of psychoanalysis, but many other psychodynamic theories also exist. Psychodynamic psychologists try to dig below the surface of a person's behavior to get to its unconscious roots; they think of themselves as archeologists of the mind.

Psychodynamic psychology is the thumb on the hand of psychology—connected to the other fingers, but also set apart from them because it differs radically in its language, methods, and standards of acceptable evidence. Although some psychological scientists are doing empirical studies of psychodynamic concepts, many others believe that psychodynamic approaches belong in philosophy or literature rather than in academic psychology. Outside of empirical psychology, however, many psychotherapists, novelists, and laypeople are attracted to the psychodynamic emphasis on unconscious forces and on such grand psychological issues as relations between the sexes, the power of sexuality, and the universal fear of death. Later in this book, we will candidly discuss the many controversies surrounding psychodynamic ideas.

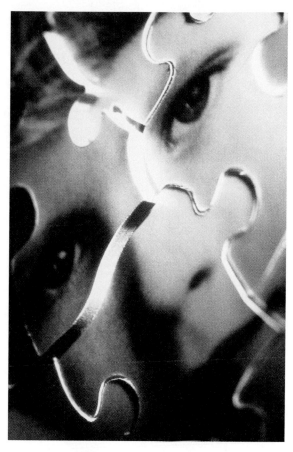

What makes us who we are? Psychologists approach questions about human behavior from five major perspectives: biological, learning, cognitive, sociocultural, and psychodynamic.

Review 1.2 on page 20 presents a summary of these five perspectives and shows you how they might be applied to a concrete issue, the problem of violence.

Two Influential Movements in Psychology

Throughout psychology's history, various movements and intellectual trends have emerged that do not fit neatly into any of the major perspectives. In the 1960s, for example, humanist psychologists rejected the psychoanalytic emphasis on unconscious conflict as too pessimistic a view of human nature, and they rejected the behavioral approach as too mechanistic and "mindless" a view of human nature. Humanists argued that psychoanalysts were limiting themselves to just a partial view of human nature—one that dealt with unconscious conflicts and emotional problems but overlooked human resilience and the capacity for joy. Likewise, said the humanists, the behaviorists' emphasis on observable acts ignored what really matters to most people—their uniquely human hopes and aspirations. Human behavior, in the humanists' view, is not completely determined by either unconscious dynamics or the environment. People are capable of free will and therefore have the ability to make more of themselves than either psychoanalysts or behaviorists would predict. The goal of humanist psychology was to help people express themselves creatively and achieve their full potential.

Although humanism is no longer a dominant movement in psychology, it has had considerable influence both inside and outside the field. Many psychologists across all perspectives embrace some humanist ideas, although most regard humanism

psychodynamic perspective A psychological approach that emphasizes unconscious dynamics within the individual, such as inner forces, conflicts, or the movement of instinctual energy.

humanist psychology A psychological approach that emphasizes personal growth and the achievement of human potential, rather than the scientific understanding and assessment of behavior.

FIVE MAJOR PSYCHOLOGICAL PERSPECTIVES

Perspective	Major Topics of Study	Sample Finding on Violence
Biological	The nervous system, hormones, brain chemistry, heredity, evolutionary influences	Brain damage caused by birth complications or child abuse might incline some people toward violence.
Learning	Environment and experience	
Behavioral	Environmental determinants of observable behavior	Violence increases when it pays off.
Social cognitive	Environmental influences, observation and imitation, beliefs and values	Violent role models can influence some children to behave aggressively.
Cognitive	Thinking, memory, language, problem solving, perceptions	Violent people are often quick to perceive provocation and insult.
Sociocultural	Social and cultural contexts	
Social psychology	Social rules and roles, groups, relationships	People are often more aggressive in a crowd than they would be on their own.
Cultural psychology	Cultural norms, values, and expectations	Cultures based on herding rather than agriculture tend to train boys to be aggressive.
Psychodynamic	Unconscious thoughts, desires, and conflicts	A man who murders prostitutes may have unconscious conflicts about his mother and about sexuality.

as a philosophy of life rather than a systematic approach to psychology. Further, many topics raised by the humanists, such as creativity, joy, humor, and courage, have been studied by scientific psychologists in other perspectives. But humanism has had its greatest influence in psychotherapy and in the human-potential and self-help movements.

Another important movement, which emerged in the 1970s, was **feminist psychology**. As women began to enter psychology in greater numbers, they documented evidence of a pervasive bias in the research methods used and in the very

feminist psychology A psychological approach that analyzes the influence of social inequities on gender relations and on the behavior of the two sexes.

questions that researchers had been asking (Bem, 1993; Crawford & Marecek, 1989; Hare-Mustin & Marecek, 1990). They noted that many studies used only men as subjects—and usually only young, white, middle-class men, at that—and they showed why it was often inappropriate to generalize to everyone else from such a narrow research base.

Today, women and men who call themselves feminist psychologists may identify with any of the five major perspectives, or they may draw on research from several approaches in analyzing gender relations and the behavior of the sexes. Feminist psychologists have spurred the growth of research on topics that were long ignored in psychology, including menstruation, menopause, motherhood, the dynamics of power and sexuality in close relationships, definitions of masculinity and femininity, gender roles, and sexist attitudes (Fisher & Good, 1988; Frieze & McHugh, 1998; Spence & Hahn, 1997). They have also critically examined the male bias in psychotherapy, starting with Freud's own case studies (Hare-Mustin, 1991). And they have analyzed the social consequences of psychological findings, showing how research has often been used to justify the lower status of women and other disadvantaged groups.

Critics, both outside and within this movement, worry that some feminists are replacing a male bias in research with a female bias—for example, by doing studies of women only and then drawing conclusions about gender differences, or by replacing the "women are inferior to men" stereotype with a "women are superior to men" stereotype (Yoder & Kahn, 1993). They also note that the political goal of gender equality sometimes leads feminist psychologists to embrace conclusions that lack solid empirical support (Mednick, 1989; Peplau & Conrad, 1989; Stimpson, 1996).

Feminist psychologists, however, remind us that research and psychotherapy are social processes, affected by all the attitudes and values that people bring to any enterprise. To improve psychology and make it more socially useful, they say, we must become aware of our biases and attempt to correct them. This argument has inspired other efforts to eliminate bias in studies of cultural groups, gay men and lesbians, old people, disabled people, and the poor.

QUICK QUIZ

Anxiety is a common problem. To test your understanding of the five major perspectives in psychology, match each possible explanation of anxiety on the left with a perspective on the right.

1. Anxious people often think about the future in distorted ways.

2. Anxiety is due to forbidden, unconscious desires.

3. Anxiety symptoms often bring hidden rewards, such as being excused from exams.

4. Excessive anxiety can be caused by a chemical imbalance.

5. A national emphasis on competition and success promotes anxiety about failure.

a. behavioral

b. psychodynamic

c. sociocultural

d. biological

e. cognitive

Answers:

1.e 2.b 3.a 4.d 5.c

WHAT'S AHEAD

● If someone tells you that he or she is a psychologist, why can't you assume that the person is a therapist?

● If you decided to call yourself a "psychotherapist," would you be breaking the law?

● What's the difference between a clinical psychologist and a psychiatrist?

WHAT PSYCHOLOGISTS DO

Now you know the main viewpoints that guide psychologists in their work. But what do psychologists actually do with their time between breakfast and dinner?

To most people, the word *psychologist* conjures up an image of a therapist listening intently while a client, perhaps stretched out on a couch, pours forth his or her troubles. Many psychologists do in fact fit this image (though chairs are more common than couches these days). Many others, however, do not. The professional activities of psychologists generally fall into three categories: (1) teaching and doing research in colleges and universities; (2) providing health or mental health services, often referred to as *psychological practice*; and (3) conducting research or applying its findings in nonacademic settings such as business, sports, government, law, the military, and private research institutes (see Review 1.3). Some psychologists move flexibly across these areas. A researcher might also provide counseling services in a mental-health setting, such as a clinic or a hospital; a university professor might teach, do research, and serve as a professional consultant in legal cases or to government policymakers.

REVIEW 1.3

WHAT IS A PSYCHOLOGIST?

Many psychologists are psychotherapists, but others do research, teach, work in business, or consult.

Academic/Research Psychologists	Clinical Psychologists	Psychologists in Industry, Law, or Other Settings
Specialize in areas of pure or applied research, such as:	*May work in any of these settings, or in some combination:*	*Do research or serve as consultants to institutions on, for example:*
Human development	Private practice	Sports
Psychometrics (testing)	Mental-health clinics or services	Consumer issues
Health	Hospitals	Advertising
Education	Research laboratories	Organizational problems
Industrial/organizational psychology	Colleges and universities	Environmental issues
Physiological psychology		Public policy
Sensation and perception		Survey research and opinion polls

Psychological Research

Most psychologists who do research have doctoral degrees (Ph.D.s or Ed.D.s, doctorates in education). Some, seeking knowledge for its own sake, work in basic psychology, doing "pure" research. Others, concerned with the practical uses of knowledge, work in applied psychology. A psychologist doing basic research might ask, "How do children, adolescents, and adults differ in their approach to moral issues such as honesty?" An applied psychologist might ask, "How can knowledge about moral development be used to prevent teenage violence?" A psychologist in basic science might ask, "Can a chimpanzee or a gorilla learn to use sign language?" An applied psychologist might ask, "Can techniques used to teach language to a chimpanzee be used to help mentally impaired or disturbed children who do not speak?"

Applied psychologists have made important contributions in areas as diverse as education, health, marketing, management, consumer behavior, industrial design, worker productivity, and urban planning. Although basic psychology can sometimes lead to useful discoveries by accident, such accidents cannot be depended on. On the other hand, insisting that psychological research always be relevant is like trying to grow flowers by concentrating only on the blossoms and ignoring the roots (Walker, 1970). Basic research is root research. Without it, there would be little scientific knowledge to apply.

Psychologists' findings, both basic and applied, fill this book, so you can get a good idea of *what* psychologists study and teach by scanning the Table of Contents on pages vii to xvi. Here are a few of the major nonclinical specialties in psychology:

■ *Experimental psychologists* conduct laboratory studies of learning, motivation, emotion, sensation and perception, physiology, and cognition. Do not be misled by the term *experimental*, though; other researchers also do experiments.

■ *Educational psychologists* study psychological principles that explain learning and search for ways to improve educational systems. Their interests range from the application of findings on memory and thinking to the use of rewards to encourage achievement.

■ *Developmental psychologists* study how people change and grow over time— physically, mentally, and socially. In the past, their focus was mainly on childhood, but many now study adolescence, young adulthood, the middle years, or old age.

■ *Industrial/organizational psychologists* study behavior in the workplace. They are concerned with group decision making, employee morale, work motivation, productivity, job stress, personnel selection, marketing strategies, equipment design, and many other issues.

■ *Psychometric psychologists* design and evaluate tests of mental abilities, aptitudes, interests, and personality. Nearly all of us have had firsthand experience with one or more of these tests in school, at work, or in the military.

Psychological Practice

Psychological practitioners, whose goal is to understand and improve physical and mental health, work in mental hospitals, general hospitals, clinics, schools, counseling centers, and private practice. Since the 1970s, the proportion of psychologists who are practitioners has greatly increased; today, practitioners account for over two-thirds of new psychology doctorates and members of the American Psychological Association (APA), psychology's largest professional organization (APA Research Office, 1998; Shapiro & Wiggins, 1994).

basic psychology The study of psychological issues in order to seek knowledge for its own sake rather than for its practical application.

applied psychology The study of psychological issues that have direct practical significance and the application of psychological findings.

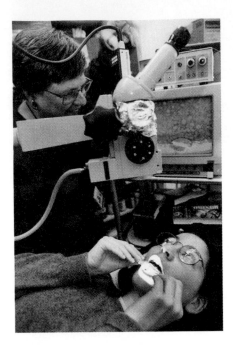

Some psychologists are researchers, others are practitioners, and some are both. On the left, researcher Linda Bartoshuk uses technology to study how the anatomy of the tongue influences the way we experience different tastes. On the right, a clinical psychologist helps a couple in therapy.

Some practitioners are *counseling psychologists*, who generally help people deal with problems of everyday life, such as test anxiety, family conflicts, or low job motivation. Others are *school psychologists*, who work with parents, teachers, and students to enhance students' performance and resolve emotional difficulties. The majority, however, are *clinical psychologists*, who diagnose, treat, and study mental or emotional problems. Clinical psychologists are trained to do psychotherapy with highly disturbed people, as well as with those who are simply troubled or unhappy or who want to learn to handle their problems better.

To practice psychology, you need a license, and in almost all states, a clinical psychology license requires a doctorate. Most clinical psychologists have a Ph.D., some have an Ed.D., and a smaller but growing number have a Psy.D. (doctorate in psychology, pronounced "sy-dee"). Clinical psychologists typically do four or five years of graduate work in psychology, plus at least a year's internship under the direction of a practicing psychologist. Clinical programs leading to a Ph.D. or Ed.D. are usually designed to prepare a person both as a scientist and as a clinical practitioner; they require completion of a dissertation, a major scholarly project (usually involving research) that contributes to knowledge in the field. Programs leading to a Psy.D. focus on professional practice and do not usually require a research dissertation, although they typically require the student to complete a study, literature review, or other scholarly project.

People often confuse *clinical psychologist* with three other terms: *psychotherapist, psychoanalyst,* and *psychiatrist.* But these terms mean different things:

- A *psychotherapist* is simply anyone who does any kind of psychotherapy. The term is not legally regulated; in fact, in most states, anyone can say that he or she is a "therapist" of one sort or another without having any training at all.

- A *psychoanalyst* is a person who practices one particular form of therapy, psychoanalysis. To call yourself a psychoanalyst, you must get specialized training at a psychoanalytic institute and undergo extensive psychoanalysis yourself. Until recently, admission to a psychoanalytic institute required an M.D. or a Ph.D., but increasingly this requirement is being waived; for example, clinical social workers with master's degrees are often now admitted.

■ A *psychiatrist* is a medical doctor (M.D.) who has done a residency in psychiatry, the medical specialty concerned with mental disorders, maladjustment, and abnormal behavior. During the residency period, a psychiatrist learns to diagnose and treat mental disorders under the supervision of more experienced physicians. Some psychiatrists (like some clinical psychologists) do research on mental problems, such as depression or schizophrenia, rather than work with patients.

Psychiatrists and clinical psychologists do similar work, but psychiatrists, because of their medical training, tend to focus on possible biological causes of mental disorders and to treat these problems with medication. They can write prescriptions, whereas clinical psychologists cannot (or at least not yet; in many states, psychologists are pressing for prescription-writing privileges). Psychiatrists, however, are often untrained in current psychological theories and methods.

As if all these credentials and labels were not confusing enough, many other people work in related mental-health fields, including social workers, school counselors, and marriage, family, and child counselors. These professionals ordinarily treat general problems in adjustment rather than severe mental disturbance, although their work may bring them into contact with people who have serious problems—violent delinquents, sex offenders, individuals involved in domestic and child abuse. Licensing requirements vary from state to state but usually include a master's degree in psychology or social work and one or two years of supervised experience. (For a summary of the types of psychotherapists and the training they receive, see Review 1.4.)

Many research psychologists are worried about the recent increase in the number of psychotherapists who are unschooled in research methods, who know little about empirical findings, and who use unvalidated therapy techniques (Dawes, 1994; Poole et al., 1995). Some practitioners, too, are concerned about the lack of uniform standards in professional education (Fox, 1994). In 1987, such concerns contributed to the formation of the American Psychological Society, an organization

REVIEW 1.4

TYPES OF PSYCHOTHERAPISTS

Psychotherapist	A person who does psychotherapy: may have anything from no degree to an advanced professional degree; the term is unregulated
Clinical psychologist	Has a Ph.D., an Ed.D., or a Psy.D.
Psychoanalyst	Has specific training in psychoanalysis after an advanced degree (usually, but not always, an M.D. or a Ph.D.)
Psychiatrist	A medical doctor (M.D.) with a specialty in psychiatry
Licensed social worker (LSW); school psychologist; marriage, family, and child counselor (MFCC)	Licensing requirements vary; generally has at least an M.A. in psychology or social work

devoted to the needs and interests of psychology as a science. Many practitioners, on the other hand, argue that psychotherapy is an art, and that therefore research findings are largely irrelevant to the work they do with clients. In Chapter 17, we will return to the important issue of the widening gap in training and attitudes between scientists and some therapists.

Partly because of these tensions, and partly because the media and the public persist in equating "psychologist" with "psychotherapist," some psychological scientists think it is time to use other labels to describe what they do and to yield the word *psychologist* to its popular meaning. Research psychologists, they say, should call themselves "cognitive scientists," "behavioral scientists," "neuroscientists," and so forth, depending on their area of study. This change in language is already underway. At present, however, the word *psychologist* still embraces all the cousins in psychology's sprawling family.

Psychology in the Community

Since World War II, psychology has expanded rapidly in terms of scholars, publications, and specialties. The American Psychological Association now has 50 divisions. Some represent major fields such as developmental psychology or physiological psychology. Others represent specific research or professional interests, such as the psychology of women, the psychology of men, ethnic minority issues, sports, the arts, environmental concerns, gay and lesbian issues, peace, psychology and the law, and health.

As psychology has grown, psychologists have found ways to contribute to their communities in about as many fields as you can think of. They consult with companies to improve worker satisfaction and productivity. They establish programs to improve race relations and reduce ethnic tensions. They advise commissions on how pollution and noise affect mental health. They do rehabilitation training for people who are physically or mentally disabled. They educate judges and juries about the reliability of eyewitness testimony. They assist the police in emergencies involving hostages or disturbed persons. They conduct public-opinion surveys. They run suicide-prevention hot lines. They advise zoos on the care and training of animals. They help coaches improve the athletic performance of their teams. And on and on.

Is it any wonder that people are a little fuzzy about what a psychologist is?

Psychologists work in all sorts of settings, from classrooms to courtrooms. On the left, sports psychologist Sean McCain helps an Olympic athlete relax and rehearse mentally what he would do physically during an actual athletic event. On the right, Louis Herman studies a dolphin's ability to understand an artificial language consisting of hand signals. In response to the gestural sequence "person" and "over," the dolphin will leap over the person in the pool.

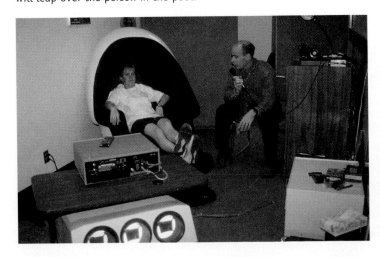

QUICK QUIZ

Can you match the specialties on the left with their defining credentials and approaches on the right?

1. psychotherapist
2. psychiatrist
3. clinical psychologist
4. research psychologist
5. psychoanalyst

a. Trained in an approach started by Freud
b. Has Ph.D., Psy.D., or Ed.D. and does research on, or psychotherapy for, mental-health problems
c. May have any credential or none
d. Has advanced degree (usually a Ph.D. or Ed.D.) and does applied or basic research
e. Has M.D.; tends to take a medical approach to emotional problems

Answers:

1.c 2.e 3.b 4.d 5.a

THE MOSAIC OF PSYCHOLOGY

The differences we have described among the psychological perspectives are very real, and they have produced many passionate arguments. These differences are compounded by the fact that psychologists earn their livelihoods in many ways and are often trying to achieve different goals: knowledge for its own sake, practical knowledge, the application of knowledge in real-life settings, the ability to help people in distress. Not all psychologists, however, feel they must swear allegiance to one approach or another. Many, perhaps most, are *eclectic*, applying in their research or practice what they believe to be the best features of diverse schools of thought.

Today, the field of psychology is like a giant mosaic made up of many fragments, yielding a rich, multi-colored psychological portrait. Psychologists may argue about which part of the portrait is most important, but most psychological scientists and scientist-clinicians agree on basic guidelines about what is and what is not acceptable in their discipline. Most believe in the importance of gathering empirical evidence instead of relying on hunches. Nearly all reject supernatural explanations of events—evil spirits, psychic forces, miracles, and so forth. And one thing will always unite psychologists: a fascination with the unending mysteries of human behavior and the human mind.

If you have ever wondered what makes people tick; if you love a mystery and want to know not only who did it but also why they did it; if you are willing to reconsider what you think you think . . . then you are in the right course. We invite you now to step into the world of psychology, the discipline that dares to explore the most complex topic on earth: *you*.

© 1990 Creators Syndicate, Inc.

2-2

TAKING PSYCHOLOGY WITH YOU

WHAT PSYCHOLOGY CAN DO FOR YOU—AND WHAT IT CAN'T

If you intend to become a research psychologist or a mental-health professional, you have an obvious reason for taking a course in psychology. But psychology can contribute to your life in many ways, whether you plan to work in the field or not. Here are a few things psychology can do for you:

■ *Make you a better-informed person.* One purpose of education is to acquaint people with their cultural heritage and with humanity's achievements in literature, philosophy, the arts, and science. Because psychology plays a large role in contemporary society, being a well-informed person requires knowing something about psychological methods and findings.

■ *Satisfy your curiosity about human nature.* When the ancient Greek philosopher Socrates admonished his students to "know thyself," he was only telling them to do what they wanted to do anyway. Psychology—

along with the other social sciences, literature, history, and philosophy—can help you better understand yourself and others.

■ *Help you increase your control over your life.* Throughout this book we will be suggesting ways in which you can apply the findings of psychology to your own life. Psychology cannot solve all your problems, but it does offer techniques for handling your emotions, improving your memory, and eliminating unwanted habits. It can also foster an attitude of objectivity that is useful for analyzing your behavior and your relationships with others.

■ *Help you on the job.* Many people who get a bachelor's degree in psychology go on to study other fields (see Figure 1.1). A background in psychology is useful for getting a job in a helping profession—for example, as a welfare caseworker or a rehabilitation counselor. Anyone who works

as a nurse, doctor, religious counselor, police officer, or teacher can also put psychology to work on the job. So can waiters, flight attendants, bank tellers, salespeople, receptionists, and others whose jobs involve customer service. Finally, psychology can be useful to those whose jobs require them to predict people's behavior—for example, labor negotiators, politicians, advertising copywriters, managers, product designers, buyers, market researchers, magicians. . . .

■ *Give you insights into political and social issues.* Crime, drug abuse, discrimination, and war are not only social issues but also psychological ones. Psychological knowledge alone cannot solve the complex political, social, and ethical problems that plague every society, but it can help you make informed judgments about them. For example, if you know how social and cultural practices affect rates of drug use and abuse, this knowledge may affect your views about the war on drugs.

There are also things that psychology *cannot* do for you. Some people follow individual psychologists the way others follow religious leaders and gurus, hoping for spiritual or philosophical enlightenment. But a philosophy of life requires more than psychological knowledge; it requires reflection and a willingness to learn

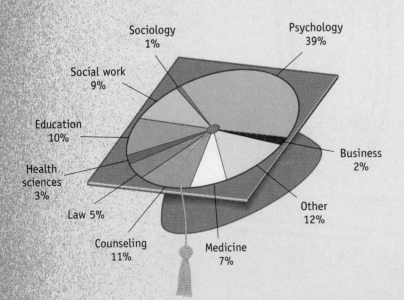

Sociology 1%

Psychology 39%

Social work 9%

Education 10%

Health sciences 3%

Law 5%

Counseling 11%

Medicine 7%

Business 2%

Other 12%

FIGURE 1.1

WHAT UNDERGRADUATE PSYCHOLOGY MAJORS GO ON TO STUDY IN GRADUATE SCHOOL

This chart, from a 1995 APA survey, shows graduate fields of study reported by students who had earlier received a bachelor's degree in psychology.

from life's experiences. Some people think that psychological explanations of behavior will relieve them of responsibility for their faults and misdeeds. But knowing that your short temper is a result, in part, of your unhappy childhood does not give you a green light to yell at your family.

Many people look to psychology for simple answers to complex questions ("Medication will one day cure all mental illnesses"; "With the right environment, any child can become a Mozart"). But as we have repeatedly emphasized, serious psychology, unlike pop psychology, does not offer simple answers or one-note explanations. Instead it offers research findings from many perspectives, which the critical thinker will try to evaluate and integrate. (In the epilogue to this book, we suggest how such an integration might apply to problems in love.)

Many years ago, George Miller, in a presidential address to the American Psychological Association (1969), called on his colleagues to "give psychology away" and to pass out psychological facts "to all who need and can use them." Ever since, critics have complained that psychologists don't know enough to "give it away." We disagree. Human behavior is complicated, but psychologists have made enormous progress in unraveling the secrets of the human brain, mind, and heart. At the end of each chapter, starting with the next one, the "Taking Psychology with You" feature will suggest ways to apply psychological findings to your own life—at school, on the job, and in your relationships.

SUMMARY

PSYCHOLOGY, PSEUDOSCIENCE, AND POPULAR OPINION

1. *Psychology* is the study of behavior and mental processes and of how they are affected by an organism's external and internal environment. In its methods and its reliance on *empirical evidence,* it differs from pseudoscience and "psychobabble."

2. Psychologists have many pseudoscientific competitors, such as astrologers and psychics. But when put to the test, the claims and predictions of these competitors have only chance-level accuracy. Psychobabble is appealing because it confirms our beliefs and prejudices; in contrast, psychology often challenges them, although it also seeks to extend our understanding of familiar facts.

THINKING CRITICALLY AND CREATIVELY ABOUT PSYCHOLOGY

3. One benefit of studying psychology is the development of *critical thinking* skills and attitudes. These skills and attitudes can help people evaluate competing findings on psychological issues that are personally and socially important.

4. The critical thinker asks questions, defines problems clearly and accurately, examines the evidence, analyzes assumptions and biases, avoids emotional reasoning, avoids oversimplification, considers alternative interpretations, and tolerates uncertainty. Critical thinking is an evolving process rather than a once-and-for-all accomplishment.

PSYCHOLOGY'S PAST: FROM THE ARMCHAIR TO THE LABORATORY

5. Psychology's forerunners made some valid observations and had useful insights, but until the late 1800s, psychology was not a science. A lack of empirical evidence often led to serious errors in the description and explanation of behavior.

6. The official founder of scientific psychology was Wilhelm Wundt, who formally established the first psychological laboratory, in Leipzig, Germany, and whose work led to *structuralism,* the first of many approaches to the field. Structuralism emphasized the analysis of immediate experience into basic elements. It was soon abandoned because of its reliance on *introspection.*

7. Another early approach, *functionalism,* which was inspired in part by the evolutionary theories of Charles Darwin, emphasized the purpose of behavior. One of its leading proponents was William James. Functionalism, too, did not last long as a distinct school of psychology, but it greatly affected the course of psychological science.

8. Psychology as a method of psychotherapy has roots in Freud's theory of *psychoanalysis,* which emphasizes unconscious causes of mental and emotional problems.

PSYCHOLOGY'S PRESENT: BEHAVIOR, BODY, MIND, AND CULTURE

9. Five points of view predominate today in psychology. The *biological perspective* emphasizes bodily events associated with actions, thoughts, and feelings. The *learning perspective* emphasizes the study of observable behavior and rejects mentalistic explanations (*behaviorism*) or combines elements of behaviorism with the study of thoughts, values, and intentions (*social-cognitive learning theory*). The *cognitive perspective* emphasizes mental processes in perception, problem solving, belief formation, and other human activities. The *sociocultural perspective* explores how the social context and cultural rules affect an individual's beliefs and behavior. The *psychodynamic perspective*, which originated with Freud's theory of psychoanalysis, emphasizes unconscious motives, conflicts, and desires.

10. Not all approaches to psychology fit neatly into one of the five major perspectives. For example, two important social movements, *humanist psychology* and *feminist psychology*, have influenced the questions researchers ask, the methods they use, and their awareness of biases in the field.

WHAT PSYCHOLOGISTS DO

11. Psychologists do research and teach in colleges and universities; provide mental-health services (*psycho-logical practice*); and conduct research and apply findings in a wide variety of nonacademic settings. *Applied psychologists* are concerned with the practical uses of psychological knowledge. *Basic psychologists* are concerned with knowledge for its own sake. Among the many psychological specialties are experimental, educational, developmental, industrial/organizational, psychometric, counseling, school, and clinical psychology.

12. *Psychotherapist* is an unregulated word for anyone who does therapy, including persons who have no credentials or training at all. Licensed therapists differ according to their training and approach: *Clinical psychologists* have a Ph.D., an Ed.D., or a Psy.D.; *psychiatrists* have an M.D.; *psychoanalysts* are trained in psychoanalytic institutes; and social workers, school counselors, and marriage, family, and child counselors may have a variety of postgraduate degrees.

THE MOSAIC OF PSYCHOLOGY

13. Many, if not most, psychologists are eclectic, drawing on more than one school of psychology. Although psychologists differ in their perspectives and goals, psychological scientists and scientist-practitioners generally agree on which methods of study are acceptable, and all psychologists are united by their fascination with the mysteries of behavior.

KEY TERMS

Use this list to check your understanding of terms and people in this chapter. If you have trouble with a term, you can find it on the page listed here.

empirical 1
psychology 1
"psychobabble" 2
critical thinking 5
Wilhelm Wundt 14
trained introspection 14
structuralism 15
functionalism 16
William James 16
Charles Darwin 16
Sigmund Freud 16
psychoanalysis 16

biological perspective 18
evolutionary psychology 18
behaviorists 18
social-cognitive learning theorists 18
cognitive perspective 18
sociocultural perspective 18
social psychologists 19
cultural psychologists 19
psychodynamic perspective 19
humanist psychology 19
feminist psychology 20
psychological practice 22

basic psychology 23
applied psychology 23
experimental psychologist 23
educational psychologist 23
developmental psychologist 23
industrial/organizational psychologist 23
psychometric psychologist 23
counseling psychologist 24
school psychologist 24
clinical psychologist 24
psychotherapist 24
psychiatrist 25

LOOKING BACK

Now that you have read this chapter, see whether you can answer the "What's Ahead" questions that preceded each major section. By using these questions to "look back," you can find out how much you have learned—and what you may need to review.

- How does "psychobabble" differ from serious psychology? (pp. 3–4)

- How accurate are psychology's nonscientific competitors, such as astrologers and psychics? (p. 4)

- Are "critical thinkers" always critical? (p. 5)

- Are all opinions created equal? (p. 5)

- What guidelines can help you evaluate psychological claims? (pp. 6–11)

- What is the lesson of phrenology for modern psychology? (p. 14)

- How old is the science of psychology? (p. 14)

- Was Sigmund Freud the official founder of psychology? (p. 14)

- What are the five major perspectives in psychology? (pp. 17–19)

- Why is psychoanalysis the "thumb on the hand of psychology"? (p. 19)

- How have humanism and feminism influenced psychology? (pp. 19–21)

- If someone tells you that he or she is a psychologist, why can't you assume that the person is a therapist? (p. 22)

- If you decided to call yourself a "psychotherapist," would you be breaking the law? (p. 24)

- What's the difference between a clinical psychologist and a psychiatrist? (p. 25)

Possible answers for the Get Involved exercise on p. 3: "Opposites attract"; "He who hesitates is lost"; "The pen is mightier than the sword"; "Winning isn't everything, it's the only thing" (often attributed to Vince Lombardi); "You're never too old to learn."

2 HOW PSYCHOLOGISTS DO RESEARCH

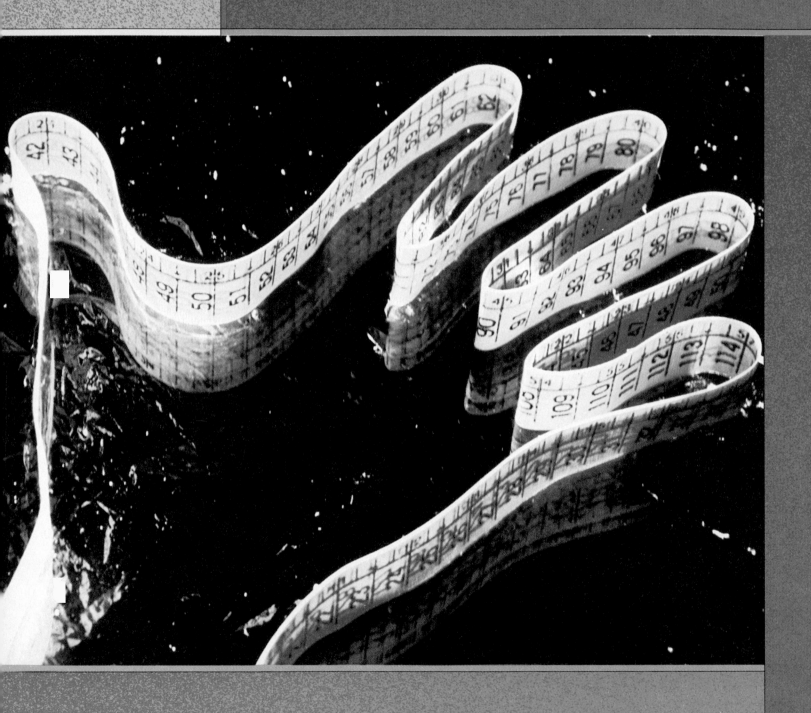

The negative cautions of science

are never popular.

ANTHROPOLOGIST MARGARET MEAD

Suppose that you are the parent of a 9-year-old boy who has been diagnosed as autistic. Your child lives in a silent world of his own, cut off from normal social interaction. He does not speak, and he rarely looks you in the eyes. Sometimes he spends hours just rocking back and forth, and occasionally, in frustration, he does self-destructive things, like poking pencils in his ears. He has never been able to function in a public classroom.

You are ecstatic, then, when you hear about a new technique, called "facilitated communication," that promises to release your child from his mental prison. According to proponents of this technique, when autistic or mentally impaired children are placed in front of a keyboard and an adult "facilitator" gently places a hand over the child's hand or forearm, amazing things happen. Children who have never used words are suddenly able to peck out complete sentences, answer questions, and divulge their thoughts. One child reportedly typed, "I amn not a utistivc on thje typ" (I am not autistic on the typewriter). Some children, through their facilitators, have supposedly even mastered high-school-level subjects, or have written poetry of astonishing beauty. The fee is steep, but it certainly seems worth it.

Or is it?

The situation we have described is not hypothetical; thousands of hopeful parents have been drawn to the promise of facilitated communication. Psychological scientists, however, have been more cautious. Before accepting claims and testimonials about any program or therapy, they put those claims and testimonials to the test. In the case of facilitated communication, they have done experiments involving hundreds of autistic children and their facilitators (Eberlin et al., 1993; Jacobson, Mulick, & Schwartz, 1995; Mulick, 1994). Their techniques have been simple: They show the child a picture to identify but show the facilitator a different picture, or no picture at all; or they keep the facilitator from hearing the questions being put to the child. Under these conditions, the child types out only what the facilitator sees or hears—not what the child does.

This research shows that what happens in facilitated communication is exactly what happens when a medium guides a person's hand over a Ouija board to help the person receive "messages" from a "spirit": The person doing the "facilitating" is unconsciously nudging the other person's hand in the desired direction (Burgess et al., 1998; Spitz, 1997). Facilitated communication, on closer inspection, turns out to be *facilitator* communication. This finding is vitally important, because if parents waste their time and money on a treatment that doesn't work, they may never get genuine help for their children, and they will suffer when their false hopes are finally shattered by reality.

  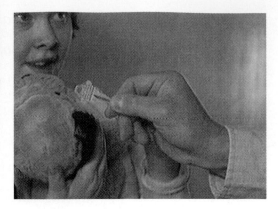

WHY SCIENTIFIC METHODS MATTER

Using "facilitated communication (FC)" (see text), Betsy Wheaton, a child with autism, appeared to type that she had been sexually abused by her entire family; she was promptly removed from her home. But when researcher Howard Shane tested her by showing pictures of objects separately to her and then to her facilitator, Betsy could type only what the facilitator saw. For example, if Betsy saw a cup but the facilitator saw a hat (left), Betsy typed "hat" (center). And when Shane gave Betsy a key out of sight of the facilitator (right), she could not type what it was; only when the facilitator also saw the key could Betsy "produce" the answer. Because of these results, the facilitator stopped using FC and persuaded Betsy's school to do the same, and Betsy was reunited with her family.

You can see why research methods matter so much to psychologists. Some students would rather not study research methods; "let's just cut straight to the findings," they say. But these methods are the tools that allow psychologists to separate truth from unfounded belief, to sort out conflicting views, and to correct false ideas that may cause people harm. We hope that when you hear and read about psychological issues, you will consider not only what the findings say, but also how the information was obtained and how the results were interpreted, using information in this chapter.

> ### WHAT'S AHEAD
>
> - Where do psychological scientists get their hypotheses?
> - In what way are scientists risk-takers?
> - Why is secrecy a big "no-no" in science?

WHAT MAKES PSYCHOLOGICAL RESEARCH SCIENTIFIC?

When we refer to psychologists as scientists, we do not mean that they work with complicated gadgets and machines or wear white lab coats (although some do). The scientific enterprise has more to do with attitudes and procedures than with apparatus and apparel. Here are a few key characteristics of the ideal scientist.

1 *Precision.* Scientists sometimes launch an investigation because they have a hunch about some behavior, based on previous findings or casual observations. Often, however, they start out with a general **theory**, an organized system of assumptions and principles that purports to explain certain phenomena and how they are related. A scientific theory is not just someone's personal opinion, as people imply when they say "It's only a theory." Theories that come to be accepted by the scientific community are those that account for many empirical findings.

From a hunch or theory, the psychological scientist derives a **hypothesis**, a statement that attempts to describe or explain a given behavior. Initially, this statement may be quite general, as in, say, "Misery loves company." But before any research can be done, the hypothesis must be made more precise. For example, "Misery loves company" might be rephrased as "People who are anxious about a threatening situation tend to seek out others facing the same threat."

A hypothesis, in turn, leads to predictions about what will happen in a particular situation. In a prediction, terms such as *anxiety* or *threatening situation* are given

---

theory An organized system of assumptions and principles that purports to explain a specified set of phenomena and their interrelationships.

hypothesis A statement that attempts to predict or to account for a set of phenomena; scientific hypotheses specify relationships among events or variables and are empirically tested.

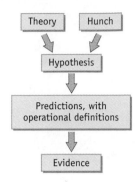

operational definitions, which specify how the phenomena in question are to be observed and measured. "Anxiety" might be defined operationally as a score on an anxiety questionnaire; "threatening situation" might be defined as the threat of an electric shock. The prediction might be, "If you raise people's anxiety scores by telling them they are going to receive electric shocks, and then give them the choice of waiting alone or with others in the same situation, they will be more likely to choose to wait with others than they would be if they were not anxious." The prediction can then be tested, using systematic methods.

2 *Skepticism.* Scientists do not accept ideas on faith or authority; their motto is "Show me!" Some of the greatest scientific advances have been made by those who dared to doubt what everyone else assumed to be true: that the sun revolves around the earth, that illness can be cured by applying leeches to the skin, that madness is a sign of demonic possession. In the world of the researcher, skepticism means treating conclusions, both new and old, with caution. Caution, however, must be balanced by an openness to new ideas and evidence. Otherwise, the scientist may wind up as shortsighted as the famous physicist Lord Kelvin, who at the end of the nineteenth century reputedly declared with great confidence that radio had no future, x-rays were a hoax, and "heavier-than-air flying machines" were impossible.

3 *Reliance on empirical evidence.* Unlike plays and poems, scientific theories and hypotheses are not judged by how pleasing or entertaining they are. An idea may initially generate excitement because it is plausible or imaginative, but eventually it must be backed by empirical evidence if it is to be taken seriously. A collection of anecdotes or an appeal to authority will not do. Nor will the "intuitive" appeal of the idea, or its popularity. As Nobel Prize–winning scientist Peter Medawar (1979) wrote, "The intensity of the conviction that a hypothesis is true has no bearing on whether it is true or not."

4 *Willingness to make "risky predictions."* A related principle is that a scientist must state an idea in such a way that it can be *refuted*, or disproved by counterevidence. This principle, known as the **principle of falsifiability**, does not mean that the idea *will be* disproved, only that it *could be* if contrary evidence were to be discovered. Another way of saying this is that a scientist must risk disconfirmation by predicting not only what will happen, but also what will not happen. In the "misery loves company" study, the hypothesis would be refuted if most anxious people went off alone to sulk and worry, or if anxiety had no effect on their behavior (see Figure 2.1 on page 36). A willingness to make "risky" predictions forces the scientist to take negative evidence seriously. Any researcher who refuses to go out on a limb and risk disconfirmation is not a true scientist; and any theory that purports to explain everything that could conceivably happen is unscientific.

Nonscientists violate the principle of falsifiability all the time. For example, some police officers and therapists believe that murderous satanic cults are widespread, even though research psychologists, the FBI, and police investigators have been unable to substantiate this claim (Goodman et al., 1995; Hicks, 1991). Believers say they are not surprised by the lack of evidence because satanic cults cover up their activities by eating bodies or burying them. The FBI's failure to find the evidence is "proof," they say, that the FBI is part of a conspiracy to support the satanists. To believers, then, the lack of evidence of satanic cults is actually a sign of the cults' success. But think about that claim. If a lack of evidence can count as evidence, then what could possibly count as counterevidence?

5 *Openness.* Scientists must be willing to tell others where they got their ideas, how they tested them, and what the results were. They must do this clearly and in detail so that other scientists can repeat, or *replicate*, their studies and verify—or challenge—the findings. Secrecy is a big "no-no" in science.

operational definition A precise definition of a term in a hypothesis, which specifies the operations for observing and measuring the process or phenomenon being defined.

principle of falsifiability The principle that a scientific theory must make predictions that are specific enough to expose the theory to the possibility of disconfirmation; that is, the theory must predict not only what will happen, but also what will not happen.

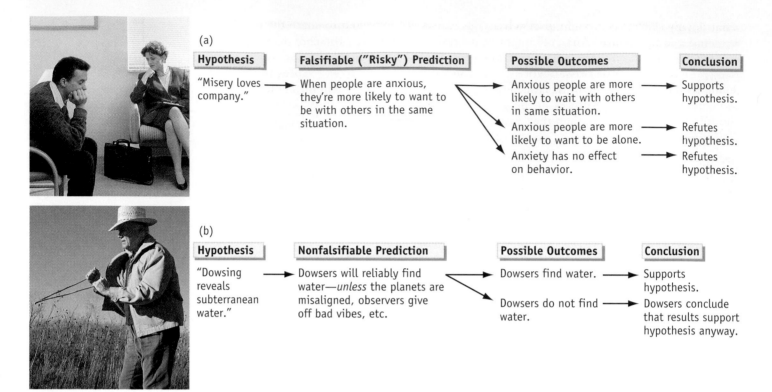

FIGURE 2.1

THE PRINCIPLE OF FALSIFIABILITY

The scientific method requires researchers to expose their ideas to the possibility of counterevidence, as in row (a). In contrast, people claiming psychic powers, such as dowsers (who say they can find underground water with a "dowsing rod" that bends when water is present), typically interpret *all* possible outcomes as support for their assertions, as in row (b). By doing so, they make their claims untestable.

Sometimes replication shows that an apparently fabulous phenomenon was just a fluke. A famous example occurred many years ago, when a team of researchers trained flatworms to cringe in response to a flashing light, then killed the worms, ground them into a mash, and fed the mash to a second set of worms. This cannibalistic diet, the researchers reported, sped up acquisition of the cringe response in the second group of worms (McConnell, 1962). As you can imagine, this finding caused tremendous excitement. If worms could learn faster by ingesting the "memory molecules" of their fellow worms, what might this mean for human memory? Students joked about grinding up professors; professors joked about doing brain transplants in students. But alas, other researchers were never able to replicate the results.

If you think about it, you will see that these principles of good science correspond to some of the critical-thinking guidelines described in Chapter 1. Formulating a prediction with operational definitions corresponds to "define your terms." Openness to new ideas encourages scientists to "consider other interpretations." The principle of falsifiability forces scientists to "analyze assumptions and biases" in a fair-minded fashion. And until their results have been replicated and verified, scientists must "tolerate uncertainty."

Do psychologists and other scientists always live up to the lofty standards expected of them? Of course not. Being human, they may put too much trust in their personal experiences. They may permit ambition to interfere with openness. They may fail to put their theories fully to the test: It is always easier to be skeptical about someone else's ideas than about your own.

Commitment to one's theories is not in itself a bad thing. Passion is the fuel of progress. It motivates researchers to think boldly, defend unpopular ideas, and do the exhaustive testing that is often required to support an idea. But passion can also cloud perceptions and in some sad cases has even led to deception and fraud.

That is why science is a communal activity. ~~Scientists are expected to share their evidence and procedures with others.~~ They are expected to submit their results to professional journals, which send the findings to experts in the field for comment before publishing them. Through this process, called *peer review*, scientists demonstrate that their position is well supported. Peer review precedes any announcements to the public through press releases or popular books. The research community—in our case, the psychological community—acts as a jury, scrutinizing and sifting the evidence, approving some viewpoints and relegating others to the scientific scrap heap.

This public process is not perfect, but it does give science a built-in system of checks and balances. Individuals are not necessarily objective, honest, or even rational, but science forces them to justify their claims.

QUICK QUIZ

Test your understanding of science by identifying which of its rules was violated in each of the following cases.

1. For years, writer Norman Cousins told how he had cured himself of a rare, life-threatening disease through a combination of humor and vitamins. In a best-selling book about his experience, he recommended the same approach to others.

2. Benjamin Rush, an 18th-century physician, believed that illnesses accompanied by fever should be treated by bloodletting. Although many patients whom he treated in this manner died, Rush did not lose faith in his approach. He attributed each recovery to his treatment and each death to the severity of the disease (Stanovich, 1996).

Answers:

1. Cousins offered only a personal account and did not gather empirical evidence from controlled studies or consider cases of sick people who were not helped by humor and vitamins. 2. Rush violated the principle of falsifiability: He interpreted a patient's survival as support for his treatment and explained a death by saying that the person had been too ill for the treatment to work. Thus, there was no possible counterevidence that could refute the theory (which, by the way, was dead wrong—the "treatment" was actually as dangerous as the disease).

WHAT'S AHEAD

- When are psychological case studies informative, and when are they useless?
- Why do psychologists often observe people's behavior in laboratories instead of in everyday situations?
- Why should you be skeptical about psychological tests you find in magazines and newspapers?
- What's the difference between a psychological survey and a poll of listeners by a radio DJ?

DESCRIPTIVE STUDIES: ESTABLISHING THE FACTS

Psychologists gather evidence to support their hypotheses by ~~using different methods, depending on the kinds of questions they want to answer.~~ These methods are not mutually exclusive. Just as a detective may use a magnifying glass *and* a fingerprint duster *and* interviews of suspects to figure out "who done it," psychological sleuths often draw on different techniques at different stages of an ongoing investigation. As you read about these methods, we suggest that you list their advantages

This picture, drawn by Genie, a young girl who endured years of isolation and mistreatment, shows one of her favorite pastimes: listening to researcher Susan Curtiss play the piano. Genie's drawings were used along with other case material to study her mental and social development.

and disadvantages in order to remember them better. When you finish this and the next two sections, you can check your list against the one in the Review table on page 53.

We will begin with descriptive methods, which allow psychologists to describe and predict behavior but not necessarily to choose one explanation over competing ones.

Case Studies

A case study (or *case history*) is a detailed description of a particular individual based on careful observation or on formal psychological testing. It may include information about the person's childhood, dreams, fantasies, experiences, relationships, and hopes—anything that will provide insight into the person's behavior. Case studies are most commonly used by clinicians, but sometimes academic researchers use them as well, especially when they are just beginning to study a topic or when practical or ethical considerations prevent them from gathering information in other ways.

For example, suppose you want to know whether the first few years of life are critical for acquiring a first language. Can children who have missed out on hearing speech (or, in the case of deaf children, seeing signs) catch up later? Obviously, psychologists cannot answer this question by isolating children and seeing what happens! So instead, they have studied unusual cases of language deprivation.

One such case involved a 13-year-old girl who had been cruelly locked up in a small room since the age of 1½. During the day her parents usually kept her strapped in a potty seat. At night, they confined her to a straitjacket-like sleeping bag. Her mother, a battered wife, barely cared for the child. The little girl might have been able to hear some speech through the walls of her room, but the family had no television or radio, and no one spoke a word to her. If she made the slightest sound, her severely disturbed father beat her with a large piece of wood.

When Genie, as researchers later called her, was finally rescued, she did not know how to chew or stand erect, and she was not toilet trained. She slobbered uncontrollably, masturbated in public, and spat on anything that was handy, including herself and other people. Her only sounds were high-pitched whimpers. Yet she was alert and curious. Placed in a rehabilitation center and then a foster home, she developed physically and learned some rules of social conduct. Gradually, she began to understand short sentences. She was able to use words to convey her needs, to describe her moods, and—like other human beings—to lie. Even after many years, however, Genie's grammar and pronunciation remained abnormal. She never learned to use pronouns correctly, ask questions, produce proper negative sentences, or use the little word endings that communicate tense, number, and possession (Curtiss, 1977, 1982; Rymer, 1993). This sad case, along with similar ones, suggests that a critical period exists for language development, with the likelihood of fully mastering a first language declining steadily after early childhood and falling off drastically at puberty (Pinker, 1994; Tartter, 1986).

Case studies illustrate psychological principles in a way that abstract generalizations and cold statistics never can, and they produce a more detailed picture of an individual than other methods do. However, the case-study method also has many drawbacks. First, vital information is often missing, so the case may be hard to interpret. For example, no one knows what Genie's language development was like before she was locked up, or whether she was born with mental deficits that might have interfered with her language development even if she had had a normal childhood. Second, many case studies depend on people's memories of the past, and such memories may be both selective and inaccurate. Third, and most important, this method has limited usefulness for deriving general principles of behavior, because

---

descriptive methods Methods that yield descriptions of behavior but not necessarily causal explanations.

case study A detailed description of a particular individual being studied or treated.

the person who is the focus of the study may be *unrepresentative* of the group that a researcher is interested in.

For all these reasons, case studies are usually only sources, rather than tests, of hypotheses. When people draw conclusions solely on the basis of case studies, the results can be disastrous. For example, for many years, physicians believed that autism in children was caused by rejecting, cold, "refrigerator" mothers. This belief was based on the writings of the eminent psychoanalyst Bruno Bettelheim (1967), who drew his conclusions from three published cases of autistic children whose mothers had psychological problems, and from a few other unpublished cases. When proper studies were finally done, using objective testing procedures and a larger, representative group of autistic children and their parents, scientists learned that parents of autistic children are as psychologically healthy as any other parents. Today, we know that autism stems from a neurological problem rather than from any psychological problems of the mothers. But because so many people accepted Bettelheim's claims, thousands of women blamed themselves for their children's disorder and suffered needless guilt and remorse.

Observational Studies

In **observational studies**, the researcher observes, measures, and records behavior, taking care not to be intrusive or to interfere with the people (or animals) being observed. Unlike case studies, observational studies usually involve many participants ("subjects"). Often, an observational study is the first step in a program of research; it is helpful to have a good description of behavior before you try to explain it.

The primary purpose of *naturalistic observation* is to find out how people or animals act in their normal social environments. Ethologists such as Jane Goodall and the late Dian Fossey used this method to study apes and other animals in the wild. Psychologists use naturalistic observation wherever people happen to be—at home, on playgrounds or streets, in schoolrooms, or in offices. In one study, a social psychologist and his students ventured into a common human habitat: bars. They wanted to know whether people in bars drink more when they are in groups than when they are alone. They visited all 32 pubs in a midsized city, ordered beers, and recorded on napkins and pieces of newspaper how much the other patrons imbibed. They found that drinkers in groups consumed more than individuals who were alone. Those in groups did not drink any faster; they just lingered in the bar longer (Sommer, 1977).

observational study A study in which the researcher carefully and systematically observes and records behavior without interfering with the behavior; it may involve either naturalistic or laboratory observation.

GET ➜ INVOLVED

A STUDY OF "PERSONAL SPACE"

Try a little naturalistic observation of your own. Go to a public place where people voluntarily seat themselves near others, such as a movie theater or a cafeteria with large tables. If you choose a setting where many people enter at once, you might recruit some friends to help you; you can divide the area into sections and give each observer one section to observe. As individuals and groups sit down, note how many seats they leave between themselves and the next person. On the average, how far do people tend to sit from strangers? Once you have your results, see how many possible explanations you can come up with.

The man asking for a handout is in reality a psychologist doing observational research to find out how people react to panhandlers. A tape recorder hidden beneath his shirt records their responses.

Note that the students who did this study did not rely on their impressions or memories of how much people drank. In observational studies, researchers count, rate, or measure behavior in a systematic way. These procedures help to minimize the tendency of observers to notice only what they expect or want to see. Careful record keeping ensures accuracy and allows different observers to cross-check their observations for consistency. Observers must also take pains to avoid being obvious about what they are doing and to disguise their intentions so they can see people as they really are. If the researchers who studied drinking habits had marched in with video cameras and announced that they were psychology students, the bar patrons might not have behaved naturally.

Sometimes psychologists prefer to make observations in a laboratory setting. In *laboratory observation*, psychologists have more control. They can use sophisticated equipment, determine how many people will be observed at once, maintain a clear line of vision while observing, remain hidden behind a one-way mirror, and so forth. Suppose that you wanted to know how infants of different ages respond when left with a stranger. Visiting private homes might be slow and inconvenient, and you would have to worry about interruptions. A more efficient approach might be to have parents and their infants come to your laboratory, observe them playing together for a while through a one-way window, then have a stranger enter the room and, a few minutes later, have the parent leave. You could record signs of distress, interactions with the stranger, and other behavior. If you did this, you would find that very young infants carry on cheerfully with whatever they are doing when the parent leaves. However, by the age of about 8 months, many children will burst into tears or show other signs of what child psychologists call "separation anxiety" (Ainsworth, 1979).

One shortcoming of laboratory observation is that the presence of researchers and special equipment may cause subjects to behave differently than they would in their usual surroundings. And observational studies, like other descriptive studies, are more useful for describing behavior than for explaining it. For example, the barroom results we described do not necessarily mean that being in a group makes

SLUMBERING FOR SCIENCE

By sleeping in the laboratory instead of the natural environment of their own homes, volunteers can provide researchers with valuable information about brain and muscle activity during sleep.

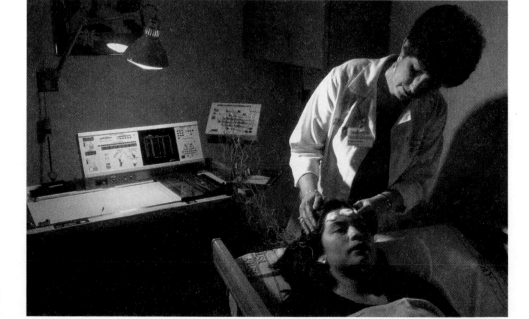

people drink a lot. People may join a group because they are already interested in drinking and find it more comfortable to hang around the bar if they are with others. Similarly, if we observe infants protesting whenever a parent leaves the room, we cannot be sure *why* they are protesting. Is it because they have become attached to their parents and want them nearby? Is it because they learned from experience that crying brings an adult with a cookie and a cuddle? Observational studies alone cannot answer such questions.

Tests

Psychological tests, sometimes called *assessment instruments*, are procedures used for measuring and evaluating personality traits, emotional states, aptitudes, interests, abilities, and values. Hundreds of psychological tests are used in industry, education, the military, and the helping professions. Typically, these tests require people to answer a series of written or oral questions. The answers may then be totaled to yield a single numerical score, or a set of scores. *Objective tests*, also called "inventories," measure beliefs, feelings, or behaviors of which an individual is aware; *projective tests* are designed to tap unconscious feelings or motives (see Chapter 13).

At one time or another, most people have taken a psychological test, such as an intelligence test, an achievement test, or a vocational-aptitude test. These measures help clarify differences among people, as well as differences in the reactions of the same person on different occasions or at different stages of life. Tests may be used to promote self-understanding, to evaluate psychological treatments, or, in scientific research, to draw generalizations about human behavior. Well-constructed psychological tests are a great improvement over simple self-evaluation, because many people have a distorted view of their own abilities and traits.

One test of a good test is whether it is standardized—that is, whether uniform procedures exist for giving and scoring the test. It would hardly be fair to give some people detailed instructions and plenty of time and others only vague instructions and limited time. Those who administer the test must know exactly how to explain the tasks involved, how much time to allow, and what materials to use. Scoring is usually done by referring to norms, established standards of performance. The usual procedure for developing norms is to give the test to a large group of people who resemble those for whom the test is intended. Norms determine which scores can be considered high, low, or average.

Test construction presents many challenges. For one thing, the test must be reliable—that is, it must produce the same results from one time and place to the next. A vocational-interest test is not reliable if it tells Tom that he would make a wonderful engineer but a poor journalist, but then gives different results when Tom retakes the test a week later. Psychologists can measure *test–retest reliability* by giving the test twice to the same group of people, then comparing the two sets of scores statistically. If the test is reliable, individuals' scores will be similar from one session to another. This method has a drawback, however: People tend to do better the second time they take a test, after they have become familiar with the strategies required and the actual test items used. A solution is to compute *alternate-forms reliability* by giving different versions of the same test to the same group on two separate occasions. The items on the two forms are similar in format but are not identical in content. With this method, performance cannot improve because of familiarity with the items, although people may still do somewhat better the second time around because they have learned the procedures expected of them.

psychological tests Procedures used to measure and evaluate personality traits, emotional states, aptitudes, interests, abilities, and values.

standardize In test construction, to develop uniform procedures for giving and scoring a test.

norms In test construction, established standards of performance.

reliability In test construction, the consistency of scores derived from a test, from one time and place to another.

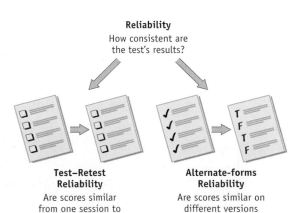

Reliability
How consistent are the test's results?

Test–Retest Reliability
Are scores similar from one session to another?

Alternate-forms Reliability
Are scores similar on different versions of the test?

validity The ability of a test to measure what it was designed to measure.

To be useful, a test must also be ~~valid~~; that is, ~~it must measure what it sets out to measure~~. A creativity test is not valid if what it actually measures is verbal sophistication. If the items broadly represent the trait in question, the test is said to have *content validity*. If you were measuring employees' job satisfaction, and your test tapped a broad array of relevant beliefs and behaviors (e.g., "Do you feel you have reached a dead end at work?" "Are you bored with your assignments?"), it would have content validity. If the test asked only how workers felt about their salary level, it would lack content validity and would be of little use; after all, highly paid people are not always satisfied with their jobs, and people who earn low wages are not always dissatisfied.

Most tests are also judged on ~~*criterion validity*~~, ~~the ability to predict other, independent measures, or criteria, of the trait in question~~. The criterion for a scholastic aptitude test might be college grades; the criterion for a test of shyness might be behavior in social situations. To find out whether your job-satisfaction test had criterion validity, you might return a year later to see whether it correctly predicted absenteeism, resignations, or requests for job transfers.

Unfortunately, teachers, parents, and employers do not always stop to question a test's validity, especially when the results are summarized in a single precise-sounding number, such as an IQ score of 115 or a job applicant's ranking of 5. But among psychologists and educators, controversy exists about the validity of even some widely used tests. For example, "integrity tests," which probe for such traits as hostility to authority, conscientiousness, and "wayward impulses," are given to millions of job applicants each year in an effort to predict dishonesty and drug use in the workplace. Such tests may be more reliable and valid than interviews, but many people who fail them are not actually dishonest, nor will they become bad employees (Camera & Schneider, 1994; Sackett, 1994; Saxe, 1994).

The Scholastic Assessment Test (SAT) and the Graduate Record Exam (GRE) have also come under fire. Undergraduates can do pretty well on the SAT's reading-comprehension section even without reading the passages (although not as well as when they do read them) (Katz & Lautenschlager, 1994). This finding suggests that the items measure general knowledge and test-taking skills, as well as reading comprehension. As for the GRE, it is somewhat useful for predicting first-year grades in graduate psychology programs, but it is *not* good at predicting second-year grades, professors' ratings of students, or the quality of students' dissertations (Sternberg & Williams, 1997). (See why you should know about test validity?)

Criticisms and reevaluations of psychological tests keep psychological assessment honest and scientifically rigorous. In contrast, the "pop-psych" tests frequently found in magazines and newspapers usually have not been evaluated for either validity or reliability. These questionnaires have inviting headlines, such as "Are You Self-destructive?" or "The Seven Types of Lover," but they are merely lists of questions that someone thought sounded good. Similarly, pseudoscientific methods of assessing personality and ability, such as handwriting analysis, lack the reliability and validity that scientists demand (see Chapter 13).

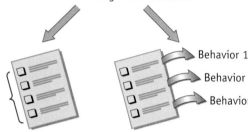

Validity
Does the test measure
what it was designed to measure?

Content Validity
Do items broadly
represent the
trait in question?

Criterion Validity
Do the test results
predict other measures
of the trait?

Behavior 1
Behavior 2
Behavior 3

Many people attach a *lot* of importance to their test scores!

HERE LIES
FREDERICK
JONES

VERBAL — MATH
680   720

R. Chw

Surveys

Psychological tests usually generate information about people indirectly. In contrast, surveys are questionnaires and interviews that gather information about people by asking them *directly* about their experiences or attitudes. Most of us are familiar with national opinion surveys, such as the Gallup and Roper polls. Surveys have been done on many topics, including consumer preferences, sexual behavior, political opinions, child rearing practices, use of the internet, and just about any attitude you can think of.

Social scientists like them because they produce bushels of data—but they are not easy to do well. The biggest hurdle is getting a representative sample, a group of subjects that accurately represents the larger population that the researcher wishes to describe. Suppose you wanted to know about drug use among college sophomores. Questioning every college sophomore in the country would be impractical; instead, you would need to recruit a sample. You would use special selection procedures to ensure that this sample contained the same proportion of women, men, blacks, whites, poor people, rich people, Catholics, Jews, and so on as in the general population of college sophomores. If you questioned students only from your own school, city, or state, the results might not apply to the entire country.

Most people do not realize that a sample's size is less critical than its representativeness. A small but representative sample may yield extremely accurate results; and a survey or poll that fails to use proper sampling methods may yield questionable results, no matter how large the sample was. When a TV show asks viewers to call in to vote on a controversial question or a magazine invites its readers to tell about their sexual habits, they will not get scientifically valid results that apply to the population in general—even if thousands of people respond. Why? As a group, people who watch MTV or read *Cosmo* are likely to hold different opinions than people who watch the Discovery Channel or read *Scientific American*.

Popular polls and surveys also suffer from a volunteer bias: People who feel strongly enough to volunteer their opinions may differ from those who remain silent. When you read about a survey (or any other kind of study), always ask who participated. A biased, nonrepresentative sample does not necessarily mean that a survey is worthless or uninteresting, but it does mean that the results may not hold for other groups.

Another problem with surveys is that people sometimes lie—especially when the survey is about a touchy topic ("What? Me do that disgusting/dishonest/fattening thing? Never!"). The likelihood of lying is reduced when respondents are guaranteed anonymity. Also, there are ways to check for lying—for example, by asking a question several times with different wording. But not all surveys use these techniques, and even when people are trying to be truthful, they may misinterpret the survey questions or misremember the past.

Finally, when you hear about the results of a survey or opinion poll, check to see how the questions were phrased. Political pollsters often design questions to produce the results they want. A Republican might ask people whether they support "increasing the amount spent on Medicare at a slower rate" whereas a Democrat might ask whether people favor "cuts in the projected growth of Medicare." The two phrases mean exactly the same thing, but respondents are likely to react more negatively when the word "cuts" is used (Kolbert, 1995).

As you can see, although surveys can be extremely informative, they must be conducted and interpreted carefully.

Every time I think I'm part of a normal relationship...

— Someone publishes a new survey.

THINKING CRITICALLY

ANALYZE ASSUMPTIONS AND BIASES

A magazine has just published a survey of its female readers, called "The Sex Life of the American Wife." It reports that "Eighty-seven percent of all wives like to make love in rubber boots." Is the assumption that the sample represents all married American women justified? What would be a more accurate title for the survey?

surveys Questionnaires and interviews that ask people directly about their experiences, attitudes, or opinions.

representative sample A group of subjects, selected from a population for study, which matches that population on important characteristics such as age and sex.

volunteer bias A shortcoming of findings derived from a sample of volunteers instead of a representative sample; the volunteers may differ from those who did not volunteer.

QUICK QUIZ

A. Which descriptive method would be most appropriate for studying each of the following topics? (All of them, by the way, have been investigated by psychologists.)

1. Ways in which the games of boys differ from those of girls.

2. Changes in attitudes toward nuclear disarmament after a television movie about nuclear holocaust.

3. The math skills of children in the United States versus Japan.

4. Physiological changes that occur when people watch violent movies.

5. The development of a male infant who was reared as a female after his penis was accidentally burned off during a routine surgery.

a. case study
b. naturalistic observation
c. laboratory observation
d. survey
e. test

B. Professor Flummox gives her new test of aptitude for studying psychology to her psychology students at the start of the year. At the end of the year, she finds that those who did well on the test averaged only a C in the course. The test lacks _____.

C. Over a period of 55 years, a British woman sniffed large amounts of cocaine, which she obtained legally under British regulations for the treatment of addicts. Yet, she appeared to show no negative effects, other than drug dependence (Brown & Middlefell, 1989). What does this case tell us about the dangers or safety of cocaine?

Answers:

A. 1. b 2. d 3. e 4. c 5. a   B. validity (more specifically, criterion validity)   C. Not much. Snorting cocaine may be relatively harmless for some people, such as this woman, but extremely harmful for others. Also, the cocaine she received may have been less potent than cocaine purchased on the street. Critical thinking requires that we resist generalizing from a single case.

WHAT'S ·AHEAD

- If two things are "negatively" correlated, like grades and TV watching, what is the relationship between them?

- If depression and illness are correlated, does that mean depression causes illness?

CORRELATIONAL STUDIES: LOOKING FOR RELATIONSHIPS

correlational study A descriptive study that looks for a consistent relationship between two phenomena.

correlation A measure of how strongly two variables are related to one another.

variables Characteristics of behavior or experience that can be measured or described by a numeric scale; variables are manipulated and assessed in scientific studies.

In descriptive research, psychologists often want to know whether two or more phenomena are related and, if so, how strongly. For example, is there a relationship between the number of hours students spend watching television and students' grade-point averages? To find out, psychologists do correlational studies.

The word correlation is often used as a synonym for relationship. Technically, however, a correlation is a numerical measure of the *strength* of the relationship between two things. The "things" may be events, scores, or anything else that can be recorded and tallied. In psychological studies, such things are called variables because they can vary in quantifiable ways. Height, weight, age, income, IQ scores, number of items recalled on a memory test, number of smiles in a given time period—anything that can be measured, rated, or scored can serve as a variable.

Correlations always occur between *sets* of observations. In psychological research, these sets of observations usually come from many individuals or are used to compare groups of people. For example, in research on the origins of intelligence, psychologists look for a correlation between the IQ scores of parents and those of their children. To do this, the researchers must gather scores from a set of parents and from the children of these parents. You cannot compute a correlation if you know the IQs of only one particular parent–child pair. To say that a relationship exists, you need more than one pair of values to compare.

A *positive correlation* means that high values of one variable are associated with high values of the other, and that low values of one variable are associated with low values of the other.

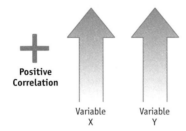

Positive Correlation

Variable X   Variable Y

Height and weight are positively correlated, for example; so are IQ scores and school grades. Rarely is a correlation perfect, however. Some tall people weigh less than some short ones; some people with average IQs are superstars in the classroom and some with high IQs get poor grades. Figure 2.2a on page 46, shows a positive correlation between men's educational level and their annual income. Each dot represents a man; you can find each man's educational level by drawing a horizontal line from his dot to the vertical axis. You can find his income by drawing a vertical line from his dot to the horizontal axis.

A *negative correlation* means that *high* values of one variable are associated with *low* values of the other.

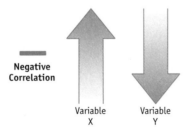

Negative Correlation

Variable X   Variable Y

Figure 2.2b shows a negative correlation between average income and the incidence of dental disease for groups of 100 families. Each dot represents one group. In general, as you can see, the higher the income, the fewer the dental problems. In the automobile business, the older the car, the lower the price, except for antiques and models favored by collectors. As for human beings, in general, the older adults are, the fewer miles they can run, the fewer crimes they are likely to commit, and the fewer hairs they have on their heads. And remember that correlation between hours spent watching TV and grade-point averages? It's a negative one: Lots of hours in front of the television are associated with lower grades (Potter, 1987; Ridley-Johnson, Cooper, & Chance, 1983). See whether you can think of other variables that are negatively correlated. Remember, though: A negative correlation means that a relationship exists—the more of one thing, the less of another. If there is no relationship between two variables, we say that they are *uncorrelated*. Adult shoe size and IQ scores are uncorrelated.

positive correlation An association between increases in one variable and increases in another.

negative correlation An association between increases in one variable and decreases in another.

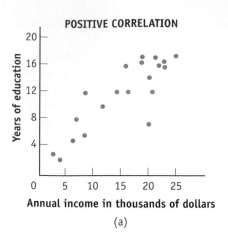

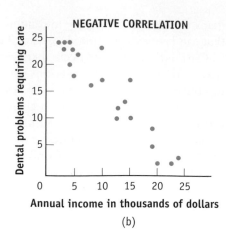

**FIGURE 2.2
CORRELATIONS**

Graph (a) shows a positive correlation; in general, the more education people have, the higher their income. Graph (b) shows a negative correlation; in general, the higher people's income, the fewer dental problems they have. (From Wright, 1976.)

The statistic used to express a correlation is called the coefficient of correlation. This number conveys both the size of the correlation and its direction. A perfect positive correlation has a coefficient of +1.00, and a perfect negative correlation has a coefficient of −1.00. If you weighed ten people and listed them from lightest to heaviest, then measured their heights and listed them from shortest to tallest, and the names on the two lists were in exactly the same order, the correlation between weight and height would be +1.00. If the correlation between two variables is +.80, it means that they are strongly (though not perfectly) related. If the correlation is −.80, the relationship is just as strong, but it is negative. When there is no association between two variables, the coefficient is zero or close to zero.

Correlational findings are common in psychology and are often reported in the news. But beware; correlations can be misleading. The important thing to remember is that *a correlation does not show causation*. It is easy to assume that if variable A predicts variable B, A must be causing B—that is, making B happen—but it's not necessarily so. The number of storks nesting in some European villages is reportedly correlated (positively) with the number of human births in those villages. Therefore, knowing when the storks nest allows you to predict when more births than usual will occur. But that doesn't mean that storks bring babies or that babies attract storks! Human births seem to be somewhat more frequent at certain times of the year (you might want to speculate on the reasons), and the peaks just happen to coincide with the storks' nesting periods.

The coincidental nature of the correlation between nesting storks and human births may seem obvious, but in other cases, unwarranted conclusions about causation are more tempting. For example, television watching is positively correlated with children's aggressiveness. Therefore, many people assume that watching television (A), with its violent programs, causes aggressiveness (B):

coefficient of correlation A measure of correlation that ranges in value from −1.00 to +1.00.

But it is also possible that being highly aggressive (B) causes children to watch more television (A):

And there is yet another possibility: Growing up in a violent household (C) could cause children both to be aggressive (B) and to watch television (A):

Actually, there is evidence for all three of these relationships (APA Commission on Violence and Youth, 1993; Eron, 1982, 1995).

Similarly, the negative correlation between TV watching and grades might exist because heavy TV watchers have less time to study, because they have some personality trait that attracts them to TV and makes them dislike studying, because they use TV as an escape when their grades are low . . . you get the idea. The moral of the story: When two variables are associated, one variable may or may not be causing the other.

QUICK QUIZ

A. Are you clear about correlations? Find out by indicating whether each of the following findings is a positive correlation or a negative correlation.

1. The higher a child's score on an intelligence test, the less likely her parents are to have spanked her.

2. The higher a male monkey's level of the hormone testosterone, the more aggressive he is likely to be.

3. The older people are, the less frequently they tend to have sexual intercourse.

4. The hotter the weather, the more crimes against persons (such as muggings) tend to occur.

B. Now see whether you can generate two or three alternative explanations for each of the preceding findings.

Answers:

A. 1. negative correlation   2. positive correlation   3. negative correlation   4. positive correlation   B. 1. Spanking may impair a child's intellectual growth; brighter children may require less physical discipline from their parents; brighter mothers may tend to have brighter children, or may be able to think of alternative methods of discipline.   2. The hormone may cause aggressiveness, or acting aggressively may stimulate hormone production.   3. Older people may have less interest in sex than younger people, have less energy or more physical ailments, or simply have more trouble finding sexual partners.   4. Hot temperatures may make people edgy and cause them to commit crimes; potential victims may be more plentiful in warm weather because more people go outside; criminals may find it more comfortable to be out committing their crimes in warm weather than in cold. (Our explanations are not the only ones possible.)

WHAT'S AHEAD

● Why do psychologists rely so heavily on experiments?
● What, exactly, do control groups control for?
● In a double-blind experiment, who is "blind," and what aren't they supposed to "see"?

EXPERIMENTS: HUNTING FOR CAUSES

Researchers gain plenty of illuminating information from descriptive studies, but when they want to actually track down the causes of behavior, they rely heavily on the experimental method. An experiment allows the researcher to *control* the situation being studied. Instead of being a passive recorder of what is going on, the researcher actively does something to affect people's behavior and then observes what happens. These procedures allow the experimenter to draw conclusions about cause and effect—about what causes what.

Experimental Variables

Suppose you are a psychologist and you come across reports suggesting that cigarette smoking improves reaction time on simple tasks. You have a hunch that nicotine has the opposite effect, however, when the task is as complex and demanding as driving a car. You know that on average, smokers have more car accidents than nonsmokers. But you realize that this relationship does not prove that smoking *causes* accidents. Smokers may simply be greater risk-takers than nonsmokers, whether the risk is lung cancer or trying to beat a red light. Or perhaps the distraction of lighting up accounts for the increased accident risk, rather than smoking itself. So you decide to do an experiment to test your hypothesis.

In a laboratory, you ask smokers to "drive" using a computerized driving simulator equipped with a stick shift and a gas pedal. The object, you tell them, is to maximize distance by driving as fast as possible on a winding road while avoiding rear-end collisions. At your request, some of the subjects smoke a cigarette immediately before climbing into the driver's seat. Others do not. You are interested in comparing how many collisions the two groups have. The basic design of this experiment is illustrated in Figure 2.3, which you may want to refer to as you read the next few pages.

The aspect of an experimental situation manipulated or varied by the researcher is known as the independent variable. The reaction of the subjects—the behavior that the researcher tries to predict—is the dependent variable. Every experiment has at least one independent and one dependent variable. In our example, the independent variable is nicotine use: one cigarette versus none. The dependent variable is the number of rear-end collisions.

Ideally, everything in the experimental situation *except* the independent variable is held constant—that is, kept the same for all participants. You would not have some people use a stick shift and others an automatic, unless shift type were an independent variable. Similarly, you would not have some people go through the experiment alone and others perform in front of an audience. Holding everything but the independent variable constant ensures that whatever happens is due to the researcher's manipulation and nothing else. It allows you to rule out other interpretations.

Understandably, students often have trouble keeping independent and dependent variables straight. You might think of it this way: The dependent variable—the outcome of the study—*depends* on the independent variable. When psychologists set up an experiment, they think, "If I do X, the subjects in my study will do Y."

experiment A controlled test of a hypothesis in which the researcher manipulates one variable to discover its effect on another.

independent variable A variable that an experimenter manipulates.

dependent variable A variable that an experimenter predicts will be affected by manipulations of the independent variable.

The "X" represents manipulation of the independent variable; the "Y" represents the dependent variable:

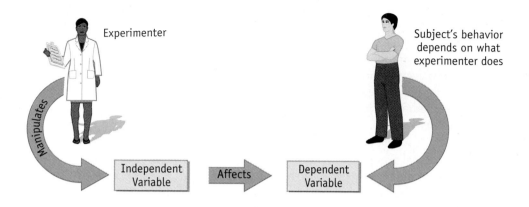

Most variables may be either independent or dependent, depending on what the experimenter wishes to find out. If you want to know whether eating chocolate makes people nervous, then the amount of chocolate eaten is the independent variable. If you want to know whether feeling nervous makes people eat chocolate, then the amount of chocolate eaten is the dependent variable.

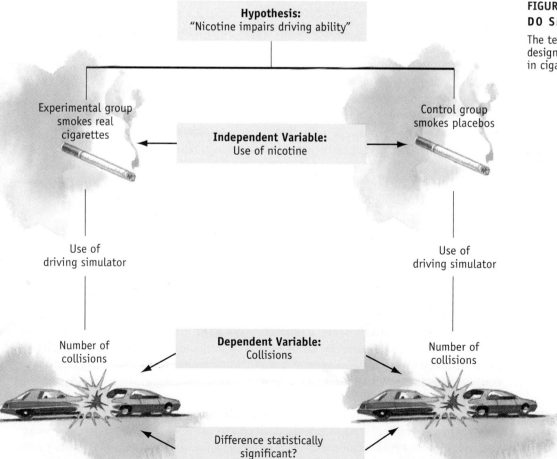

FIGURE 2.3

DO SMOKING AND DRIVING MIX?

The text describes this experimental design to test the hypothesis that nicotine in cigarettes impairs driving skills.

Experimental and Control Conditions

Experiments usually require both an experimental condition and a comparison, or control condition. In the control condition, subjects are treated exactly as they are in the experimental condition, except that they are not exposed to the same treatment, or manipulation of the independent variable. Without a control condition, you cannot be sure that the behavior you are interested in would not have occurred anyway, even without your manipulation.

In our nicotine experiment, the people who smoke before driving make up the experimental group, and those who refrain from smoking make up the control group. We want these two groups to be roughly the same in terms of average driving skill. It would not do to start out with a bunch of reckless roadrunners in the experimental group and a bunch of tired tortoises in the control group. We probably also want the two groups to be similar in age, education, smoking history, and other characteristics so that none of these variables will affect our results. One way to accomplish this is to use random assignment of people to one group or another—for example, by randomly assigning them numbers and putting those with even numbers in one group and those with odd numbers in another. If we have enough participants, individual characteristics that could possibly affect the results are likely to be roughly balanced in the two groups, so we can forget about them.

Sometimes, researchers use several experimental or control groups. For example, in our nicotine study, we might want to examine the effects of different levels of nicotine by having people smoke one, two, or three cigarettes before "driving," and then comparing each of these experimental groups to each other and to a control group of nonsmokers as well. For now, however, let's focus just on experimental subjects who smoked one cigarette.

We now have two groups. We also have a problem. In order to smoke, the experimental subjects must light up and inhale. These acts might set off certain expectations—of feeling relaxed, nervous, confident, or whatever. These expectations, in turn, might affect driving performance. It would be better to have the control group do everything the experimental group does except use nicotine.

Therefore, we will change the experimental design a bit. Instead of having the control subjects refrain from smoking, we will give them a placebo, a fake treatment. Placebos, which are critical when testing new drugs, often take the form of pills or injections containing no active ingredients. In our study, we will use phony cigarettes that taste and smell like the real thing but contain no nicotine. Our control subjects will not know their cigarettes are fake and will have no way of distinguishing them from real ones. Now if they have substantially fewer collisions than the experimental group, we will feel safe in concluding that nicotine increases the probability of an auto accident.

Experimenter Effects

Because expectations can influence the results of a study, subjects should not know whether they are in an experimental or a control group. When this is so (as it usually is), the experiment is said to be a single-blind study. But subjects are not the only ones who bring expectations to the laboratory; so do researchers. And researchers' expectations and hopes for a particular result may cause them to inadvertently influence the participants' responses through facial expressions, posture, tone of voice, or some other cue.

Many years ago, Robert Rosenthal (1966) demonstrated how powerful such experimenter effects can be. He had students teach rats to run a maze. Half the students were told that their rats had been bred to be "maze bright," and half were told that their rats had been bred to be "maze dull." In reality, there were no genetic differences between the two groups of rats, yet the supposedly brainy rats actually did learn the maze more

control condition In an experiment, a comparison condition in which subjects are not exposed to the same treatment as in the experimental condition.

random assignment A procedure for assigning people to experimental and control groups in which each individual has the same probability as any other of being assigned to a given group.

placebo An inactive substance or fake treatment used as a control in an experiment or given by a medical practitioner to a patient.

single-blind study An experiment in which subjects do not know whether they are in an experimental or a control group.

experimenter effects Unintended changes in subjects' behavior due to cues inadvertently given by the experimenter.

GET →INVOLVED

THE POWER OF A SMILE

Prove to yourself how easy it is for experimenters to affect the behavior of a study's partici-pants by giving off nonverbal cues. As you walk around campus, quickly glance at individuals approaching you and either smile or maintain a neutral expression. Try to keep the duration of your glance the same whether you smile or not. You might record the results on a piece of paper as you collect them instead of relying on your memory. Chances are that people you smile at will smile back, whereas those you approach with a neutral expression will do the same. What does this tell you about the importance of doing double-blind studies?

quickly, apparently because of the way the students treated them. If an experimenter's expectations can affect a rodent's behavior, reasoned Rosenthal, surely they can affect a human being's. He went on to demonstrate this point in many other studies (Rosenthal, 1994). Even the most subtle cue from an experimenter, like a friendly smile, can affect people's responses in a study.

One solution to the problem of experimenter effects is to do a **double-blind study.** In such a study, the person running the experiment does not know which subjects are in which groups until the data have been gathered. Double-blind procedures are standard in drug research. Different doses of a drug are coded in some way, and the person administering the drug is kept in the dark about the code's meaning until af-ter the experiment is completed. To run our nicotine study in a double-blind fashion, we would keep the person dispensing the cigarettes from knowing which ones were real and which were placebos.

	Experimenter	Subject
Single-blind Study Experimenter knows who is in which group; subjects do not.		

	Experimenter	Subject
Double-blind Study Neither experimenter nor subjects know who is in which group.		

Advantages and Limitations of Experiments

Because experiments allow conclusions about cause and effect, and because they per-mit researchers to distinguish real effects from placebo effects, they have long been the method of choice in psychology.

However, like all methods, the experiment has its limitations. Just as in other kinds of studies, the participants are not always representative of the larger population. Most volunteers in academic experiments are college students, who differ in many ways from people who are not in school. Moreover, in an experiment, the researcher determines what questions are asked and what behaviors are recorded, and the participants try to do as they are told. In their desire to cooperate with the experimenter or present them-selves in a positive light, participants may act in ways that they ordinarily would not (Kihlstrom, 1995).

double-blind study An experiment in which neither the subjects nor the individuals running the study know which subjects are in the control group and which are in the experimental group until after the results are tallied.

field research Descriptive or experimental research conducted in a natural setting outside the laboratory.

Thus, research psychologists confront a dilemma: The more control they exercise over the situation, the more unlike real life it may be. For this reason, many psychologists are calling for more **field research,** the careful study of behavior in natural contexts such as schools and the workplace, using both descriptive and experimental methods.

As we have seen, every research method has its strengths and weaknesses. Now that we have come to the end of our discussion of these methods, how did you do on your list of their advantages and disadvantages? You can find out by comparing your list with the one in Review 2.1.

QUICK QUIZ

A. Name the independent and dependent variables in studies designed to answer the following questions:

1. Whether sleeping after learning a poem improves memory for the poem.
2. Whether the presence of other people affects a person's willingness to help someone in distress
3. Whether people get agitated from listening to heavy-metal music

 B. On a talk show, Dr. Blitznik announces a fabulous new program: Chocolate Immersion Therapy. "People who spend one day a week doing nothing but eating chocolate are soon cured of eating disorders, depression, and poor study habits," claims Dr. Blitznik. What should you find out about C.I.T. before signing up?

Answers:

1. Opportunity to sleep after learning is the independent variable; memory for the poem is the dependent variable. 2. The presence of other people is the independent variable; willingness to help others is the dependent variable. 3. Exposure to heavy-metal music is the independent variable; agitation is the dependent variable. B. Some questions to ask: Is there research showing that people who go through C.I.T. did better than those in a control group who did not have the therapy, or who had a different therapy—say, Broccoli Immersion Therapy? If so, how many people were studied? How were they selected, and how were they assigned to the therapy and no-therapy groups? Did the person running the experiment know who was getting C.I.T. and who was not? How long did the "cures" last? Has the research been peer reviewed? Has it been replicated?

WHAT'S AHEAD

● **In psychological studies, why are averages sometimes misleading?**
● **How can psychologists tell whether a finding is impressive or trivial?**
● **Why are some findings significant statistically but unimportant in practical terms?**

EVALUATING THE FINDINGS

If you are a psychologist who has just done an observational study, a survey, or an experiment, your work has only just begun. Once you have some results in hand, you must do three things: (1) describe them, (2) assess how reliable and meaningful they are, and (3) figure out how to explain them.

Descriptive Statistics: Finding Out What's So

Let's say that 30 people in the nicotine experiment smoked real cigarettes, and 30 smoked placebos. We have recorded the number of collisions for each person on the driving simulator. Now we have 60 numbers. What can we do with them?

REVIEW 2.1

RESEARCH METHODS IN PSYCHOLOGY: THEIR ADVANTAGES AND DISADVANTAGES

Method	Advantages	Disadvantages
Case study	Good source of hypotheses. Provides in-depth information on individuals. Unusual cases can shed light on situations or problems that are unethical or impractical to study in other ways.	Vital information may be missing, making the case hard to interpret. The person's memories may be selective or inaccurate. Individual may not be representative or typical.
Naturalistic observation	Allows description of behavior as it occurs in the natural environment. Often useful in first stages of a research program.	Allows researcher little or no control of the situation. Observations may be biased. Does not allow firm conclusions about cause and effect.
Laboratory observation	Allows more control than naturalistic observation. Allows use of sophisticated equipment.	Allows researcher only limited control of the situation. Observations may be biased. Does not allow firm conclusions about cause and effect. Behavior in the laboratory may differ from behavior in the natural environment.
Test	Yields information on personality traits, emotional states, aptitudes, abilities.	Difficult to construct tests that are valid and reliable.
Survey	Provides a large amount of information on large numbers of people.	If sample is nonrepresentative or biased, it may be impossible to generalize from the results. Responses may be inaccurate or untrue.
Correlational study	Shows whether two or more variables are related. Allows general predictions.	Does not permit identification of cause and effect.
Experiment	Allows researcher to control the situation. Permits researcher to identify cause and effect, and distinguish placebo effects from real effects.	Situation is artificial, and results may not generalize well to the real world. Sometimes difficult to avoid experimenter effects.

Averages can be misleading if you don't know the extent to which events deviated from the statistical mean and how they were distributed.

FIGURE 2.4

SAME MEAN, DIFFERENT MEANING

In both distributions of scores, the mean is 5, but in (a) the scores are clustered around the mean, whereas in (b) they are widely dispersed, so the standard deviations for the distributions will be quite different. In which distribution is the mean more "typical" of all scores?

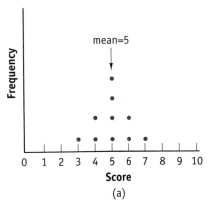

(a)

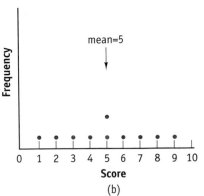

(b)

The first step is to summarize the data. The world does not want to hear how many collisions each person had. It wants to know what happened in the nicotine group as a whole, compared to what happened in the control group. To provide this information, we need numbers that sum up our data. Such numbers, known as descriptive statistics, are often depicted in graphs and charts.

A good way to summarize the data is to compute group averages. The most commonly used type of average is the arithmetic mean. The mean is calculated by adding up all the individual scores and dividing the result by the number of scores. We can compute a mean for the nicotine group by adding up the 30 collision scores and dividing the sum by 30. Then we can do the same for the control group. Now our 60 numbers have been boiled down to 2. Let's assume that the nicotine group had an average of 10 collisions, whereas the control group's average was only 7.

We must be careful, however, about how we interpret these averages. It is possible that no one in our nicotine group actually had 10 collisions. Perhaps half the people in the group were motoring maniacs and had 15 collisions, whereas the others were more cautious and had only 5. Perhaps almost all the subjects had 9, 10, or 11 collisions. Perhaps the number of accidents ranged from 0 to 15. The mean does not tell us about such variability in the subjects' responses. For that, we need other descriptive statistics. These statistics—the most common one is called a *standard deviation*—tell us how clustered or spread out the individual scores are around the mean (see Figure 2.4). The more spread out the scores are, the less "typical" the mean is. Unfortunately, when research is reported in the media, you usually hear only about the mean. (To learn how to calculate the standard deviation, as well as other descriptive statistics, see the Statistical Appendix at the end of this book.)

Inferential Statistics: Asking "So What?"

At this point in our nicotine study, we have one group with an average of 10 collisions and another with an average of 7. Should we break out the champagne? Try to get on TV? Call our mothers?

Better hold off. Perhaps if one group had an average of 15 collisions and the other an average of 1, we could get excited. But rarely does a psychological study hit you between the eyes with a sensationally clear result. In most cases, it is possible that the difference between the two groups was due simply to chance. Despite all our precautions, perhaps the people in the nicotine group just happened to be a little more accident-prone, and their behavior had nothing to do with the nicotine.

To find out how impressive the data are, psychologists use inferential statistics. These statistics do not merely describe or summarize the data. They permit a researcher to draw *inferences* (conclusions based on evidence) about how meaningful the findings are. Like descriptive statistics, inferential statistics involve the application of mathematical formulas to the data. (Again, see the Statistical Appendix for details.)

The most commonly used inferential statistics are ~~significance tests~~ that ~~tell re-searchers how likely a result was to have occurred by chance~~. In our nicotine study, a significance test will tell us how likely it is that the difference between the nicotine group and the placebo group occurred by chance. It is impossible to rule out chance entirely, but ~~if the likelihood that a result occurred by chance is extremely low, we can say that the result is~~ *statistically significant*. This means that the probability that the difference is "real" is overwhelming—not certain, mind you, but overwhelming.

By convention, psychologists consider a result to be significant if it would be expected to occur by chance 5 or fewer times in 100 repetitions of the study. Another way of saying this is that the result is significant at the .05—"point oh five"—level. If the difference could be expected to occur by chance in 6 out of 100 studies, we would have to say that the results failed to support the hypothesis—that the difference we obtained might well have occurred merely by chance. You can see that psychologists refuse to be impressed by just any old result.

Statistically significant results allow psychologists to make general predictions about human behavior. These predictions are usually stated as probabilities ("On average, we can expect 60 percent of all students to do X, Y, or Z"). However, they usually do not tell us with any certainty what a particular individual will do in a particular situation. Probabilistic results are typical not only in psychology but in all of the sciences. Medical research, for example, can tell us that the odds are high that someone who smokes will get lung cancer, but because many variables interact to produce any particular case of cancer, research cannot tell us for sure whether Aunt Bessie, a two-pack-a-day smoker, will come down with the disease.

By the way, a nicotine study similar to our hypothetical example has actually been done, using somewhat more complicated procedures (Spilich, June, & Renner, 1992). Participants who lit up before driving got a little farther on the simulated road, but they also had significantly more rear-end collisions on average (10.7) than did temporarily abstaining smokers (5.2) or nonsmokers (3.1). After hearing about this research, the head of Federal Express banned smoking on the job among all of the company's 12,000 drivers (George Spilich, personal communication).

Interpreting the Findings

The last step in any study is to figure out what the findings mean. Trying to understand behavior from uninterpreted findings is like trying to become fluent in Swedish by reading a Swedish–English dictionary. Just as you need the grammar of Swedish to tell you how the words fit together, the psychologist needs hypotheses and theories to explain how the facts that emerge from research fit together.

Choosing the Best Explanation. Sometimes it is hard to choose between competing explanations. Does nicotine disrupt driving by impairing coordination, by increasing a driver's vulnerability to distraction, by interfering with the processing of information, by distorting the perception of danger—or by some combination of these factors? In interpreting any study, we must not go too far beyond the facts; several explanations may fit those facts equally well, which means that more research will be needed to determine the best one. Rarely does one study prove anything, in psychology or any other field.

Sometimes the best interpretation of a finding does not emerge until a hypothesis has been tested in different ways. Although the methods we have described tend to be appropriate for different questions (see Review 2.2), sometimes one method can be used to confirm, disconfirm, or extend the results obtained with another. If the findings of studies using various methods converge, there is greater reason to

descriptive statistics Statistical procedures that organize and summarize a body of data.

arithmetic mean An average that is calculated by adding up a set of quantities and dividing the sum by the total number of quantities in the set.

inferential statistics Statistical procedures that allow researchers to draw inferences about how statistically meaningful a study's results are.

significance tests Statistical tests that show how likely it is that a study's results occurred merely by chance.

REVIEW 2.2

PSYCHOLOGICAL RESEARCH METHODS CONTRASTED

Psychologists may use different methods to answer different questions about a topic. To illustrate, this table shows some ways in which the methods described in this chapter can be used to study different questions about aggression. The methods listed are not mutually exclusive. That is, sometimes two or more methods can be used to investigate the same question. As discussed in the text, findings based on one method may extend, support, or disconfirm findings based on another.

Method	Purpose	Example
Case study	To understand the development of aggressive behavior in a particular individual; to formulate research hypotheses about the origins of aggressiveness	Developmental history of a serial killer
Naturalistic observation	To describe the nature of aggressive acts in early childhood	Observation, tallying, and description of hitting, kicking, etc., during free-play periods in a preschool
Laboratory observation	To find out whether aggressiveness in pairs of same-sex and different-sex children differs in frequency or intensity	Observation through a one-way window of same-sex and different-sex pairs of preschoolers; pairs must negotiate who gets to play with an attractive toy that has been promised to each child
Test	To compare the personality traits of aggressive and nonaggressive persons	Administration of personality tests to violent and nonviolent prisoners
Survey	To find out how common domestic violence is in the general population	Questionnaire asking anonymous respondents (in a sample representative of the population) about the occurrence of slapping, hitting, etc. in their homes
Correlational study	To examine the relationship between aggressiveness and television viewing	Administration to college students of a paper-and-pencil test of aggressiveness and a questionnaire on number of hours spent watching TV weekly; computation of correlation coefficient
Experiment	To find out whether high air temperatures elicit aggressive behavior	Arrangement for individuals to "shock" a "learner" (actually a confederate of the experimenter) while seated in a room heated to either 72°F or 85°F

be confident about them. If they conflict, researchers must modify their hypotheses or do more research.

Here is an example. When psychologists compare the mental-test scores of young people and old people, they usually find that younger people outscore older ones. This type of research, in which groups are compared at a given time, is called cross-sectional.

CROSS-SECTIONAL STUDY

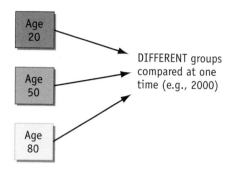

But longitudinal studies can also be used to investigate mental abilities across the life span. In a longitudinal study, the same people are followed over a period of time and are reassessed at regular intervals.

LONGITUDINAL STUDY
SAME group compared at different times

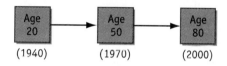

In contrast to cross-sectional studies, longitudinal studies find that as people age, they often perform as well as they ever did on many mental tests. A general decline in ability does not usually occur until people reach their 70s or 80s (Salthouse, 1998; Schaie, 1993). Why do results from the two types of studies conflict? Apparently, cross-sectional studies measure generational differences; younger generations may outperform older ones because they are better educated, had better nutrition as children, or are more familiar with the tests used. Without longitudinal studies, we might falsely conclude that mental ability inevitably declines with age.

Judging the Result's Importance. Sometimes psychologists agree on the reliability and meaning of a finding, but not on its ultimate relevance for theory or practice. Statistical significance alone does not provide the answer. A result may be statistically significant at the "point oh five level" yet be small and of little consequence in everyday life, because the independent variable did not explain most of the variation in the subjects' behavior. On the other hand, a result may not quite reach statistical significance yet be worth following up (Falk & Greenbaum, 1995; Hunter, 1997). Because of these problems, many psychologists now prefer other statistical procedures that reveal how powerful the independent variable really is—how much of the variation in the data the independent variable accounts for.

One popular statistical technique, called meta-analysis, combines and analyzes data from many studies, instead of assessing each study's results separately. Meta-analysis

cross-sectional study A study in which subjects of different ages are compared at a given time.

longitudinal study A study in which subjects are followed and periodically reassessed over time.

meta-analysis A procedure for combining and analyzing data from many studies; it determines how much of the variance in scores across all studies can be explained by a particular variable.

tells the researcher how much of the variation in scores across *all* the studies examined can be explained by a particular variable. For example, a meta-analysis of nearly 50 years of research found that gender accounts for a great deal of the variance in performance on certain spatial–visual tasks, with males doing better on the average (Voyer, Voyer, & Bryden, 1995). But other meta-analyses have shown that gender accounts for only 1 to 5 percent of the variance on tests of verbal and math ability (Feingold, 1988; Hyde, Fennema, & Lamon, 1990; Hyde & Linn, 1988). Although gender differences on these tests are reliable, they are small, and scores for males and females greatly overlap.

Meta-analysis is not a perfect technique: If you throw flawed studies into the pot along with the good ones, you might get a tasteless stew. However, it has been a useful way to find overall patterns in topics that have generated dozens and even hundreds of studies.

QUICK QUIZ

A. Check your understanding of the descriptive–inferential distinction by placing a check in the appropriate column for each phrase:

	Descriptive statistics	Inferential statistics
1. Summarize the data	_____	_____
2. Give likelihood of data occurring by chance	_____	_____
3. Include the mean	_____	_____
4. Give measure of statistical significance	_____	_____
5. Tell you whether to call your mother about your results	_____	_____

B. If a researcher studies the same group over many years, the study is said to be _____.

C. On the Internet, you read a posting about a "Fantastic Psychological Breakthrough!!!" Why should you be cautious about this announcement?

Answers:

A. 1. descriptive 2. inferential 3. descriptive 4. inferential 5. inferential B. longitudinal C. Scientific progress, in psychology or any field, usually proceeds gradually, not all at once. (And besides, anyone can post anything on the Internet, so you will want to ask, "What's the source of this information?")

WHAT'S AHEAD

- Why do psychologists often lie to their subjects?
- Why do psychologists study nonhuman animals?

KEEPING THE ENTERPRISE ETHICAL

Rigorous research methods are the very heart of science, so it is not surprising that psychologists spend considerable time discussing and debating their procedures for collecting and evaluating data. They are also concerned about the ethics of their activities. In most colleges and universities, an ethics committee must approve all studies and be sure they conform to federal regulations. In addition, the American Psychological Association (APA) has a code of ethics that all members must follow.

The Ethics of Studying Human Beings

The APA code calls on psychological scientists to respect the dignity and welfare of human subjects. People must participate voluntarily and must know enough about the study to make an intelligent decision about participating, a doctrine known as *informed consent.* Researchers must also protect participants from physical and mental harm, and if any risk exists, they must warn the subjects in advance and give them an opportunity to withdraw at any time. (In the case of the nicotine study used as an example in this chapter, we would have to use only people who were already smokers; exposing nonsmokers to the risks associated with smoking—a risk they would ordinarily not choose to run—would be unethical.)

However, the policy of informed consent sometimes clashes with an experimenter's need to deceive subjects about the true purpose of the study. In such cases, if the purpose were revealed in advance, the results would be ruined because the participants would not behave naturally. In social psychology, especially, a study's design sometimes calls for an elaborate deception. For example, a confederate might playact a person who is having a seizure. The researcher can then find out whether bystanders—the uninformed subjects—will respond to a person who needs help. If the subjects knew that the confederate was only acting, obviously they would not bother to intervene or call for assistance.

Sometimes people have been misled about procedures intentionally designed to make them uncomfortable, angry, guilty, ashamed, or anxious so that researchers can learn what people do when they feel this way. In anxiety studies, for instance, participants have been led to believe, falsely, that they failed a test or were going to get a painful shock. In studies of embarrassment and anger, people have been made to look clumsy in front of others, or been called names, or been told they were incompetent. In studies of dishonesty, participants have been entrapped into cheating, and then confronted with evidence of their guilt.

Debate about the morality of deception escalated during the 1970s (Korn, 1998). Today, the APA's ethical guidelines require researchers to show that any deceptive procedures are justified by a study's potential value, to consider alternative procedures, and to thoroughly debrief participants about the true purpose and methods of the study afterward. But the issues raised by deception are still with us, and the APA is now revising its ethical code to deal with these issues in greater detail.

The Ethics of Studying Animals

Another ethical issue concerns the use and treatment of animals in research. Animals have always been used in only a small percentage of psychological studies, and in recent years, the number has declined further (Dewsbury, 1996; Plous, 1996). Nonetheless, in certain areas of psychological research, animals still play a crucial role. Usually they are not harmed (as in research on mating in hamsters, which is fun for the hamsters), but sometimes they are (as in research on vision in kittens, when part of the animals' visual systems must be surgically removed). Some studies require the animal's death, as when rats brought up in deprived or enriched environments are sacrificed so that their brains can be examined for any effects.

Psychologists study animals for many reasons:

■ To conduct basic research on a particular species: for example, to learn about the unusually lusty and cooperative lives of bonobo chimps.

■ To discover practical applications. For example, using principles that emerged from behavioral studies, farmers have been able to reduce crop destruction by birds and deer without resorting to their traditional method—shooting the animals.

Psychologists sometimes use animals to study learning, memory, emotion, and other topics. Here a rat learns to find food in a radial maze.

- To study issues that cannot be studied experimentally with human beings because of practical or ethical considerations—for example, the effects of maternal deprivation on emotional development.

- To clarify theoretical questions. For example, we might not attribute the longer life spans of women solely to "lifestyle" factors and health practices if we discover that a male–female difference exists in other mammals as well.

- To improve human welfare. Animal studies have helped researchers develop ways to reduce chronic pain; rehabilitate patients with neurological disorders; teach people to control high blood pressure; and understand the mechanisms underlying memory loss and senility—to name only a few benefits (Feeney, 1987; Greenough, 1991; N. Miller, 1985).

Animal research, however, has provoked angry disputes. Many animal-rights activists want to eliminate all research using animals (Plous, 1991), and some defenders of animal research have refused to acknowledge that confinement in laboratories can be psychologically and physically harmful for some species. This conflict has motivated psychologists to find ways to improve the treatment of animals needed in research. The APA's ethical code covering the humane treatment of animals has been made more comprehensive, and federal laws governing the housing and care of research animals have been strengthened. The difficult task is to balance the many benefits of animal research with an acknowledgment of past abuses and a compassionate attitude toward species other than our own.

Now that you have finished the first two chapters of this book, you are ready to explore more deeply what psychologists have learned about human behavior. The methods of science are designed not only to help us learn new things, however, but also to illuminate our errors and biases and help us seek knowledge with an open mind. Biologist Thomas Huxley put it well: The essence of science, he said, is "to sit down before the fact as a little child, be prepared to give up every preconceived notion, follow humbly wherever and to whatever abyss nature leads, or you shall learn nothing."

TAKING PSYCHOLOGY WITH YOU

THE GAMBLER'S FALLACY AND OTHER "INTUITIVE STATISTICS"

- What is the likelihood that a child who was abused will grow up to become an abusive parent?

- If black has come up three times in a row on the roulette wheel, would you be inclined to bet next on red or on black?

- Where are you more worried about safety, in a car or in an airplane?

Most people rely on "intuitive statistics" to answer these questions: Their answers are based on casual observations and "intuitive" notions about probabilities that may or may not be correct (Ross, 1977). Based on intuitive statistics, most people would say that red is "due" for a hit, that they worry more in planes than in cars, and that the like-lihood of an abused child growing up to be an abusive parent is very high—perhaps nearly inevitable. Yet, all three answers are unjustified. Intuitive statistics sometimes work, but often they lead to errors.

You can take Chapter 2 with you by watching out for common statistical mistakes in your own thinking. One of the most common errors people make is to notice when their predictions are successful ("I *knew* you were a Virgo! You are so well organized") while ignoring or explaining away those that fail ("OK, so you're not a Virgo, but it's because you have a Jupiter rising"). They violate the principle of falsifiability (see page 35) by paying attention only to events that seem to confirm their beliefs and overlooking *nonoccurrences*—events that *do not* happen even though, according to their beliefs, they should.

We all need to be aware of what nonoccurrences can tell us. The common belief in the "cycle of abuse," for example, is based on confirming cases only—on cases of abused children who become abusive parents. But clinicians and police officers are unlikely to encounter, in therapy or in prison, the many people who were abused but who did *not* become abusive themselves. These cases are "nonoccurrences" that contradict the hypothesis. When psychologists take these nonoccurrences into account, they find that although being abused is certainly a risk factor

for becoming an abusive parent, more than two-thirds of all abused children do not grow up to mistreat their own offspring (Kaufman & Zigler, 1987; Widom, 1989).

Other intuitive statistics can also trap us into drawing false conclusions. For example, in the question about the roulette wheel, it is not red's "turn" to win. Black and red are equally likely to win on the fourth play, just as they were on the first three (assuming that the wheel is fair). How could the probabilities change from one play to the other? A roulette wheel has no memory! The same is true for tossing coins. If you get three heads, the chance of a head on the fourth toss is still .50; the probability of a head or a tail does not change from toss to toss. People forget that it is perfectly normal, statistically, to get a run of heads or tails, though over the long run (if the coin is fair), heads and tails will balance out. They succumb to the *gambler's fallacy*, the erroneous belief that a run of one event alters the chances of that event occurring again.

What about the question about cars and airplanes? You may already know that airplanes are far safer than cars, even controlling for number of passenger miles traveled. Yet, most of us still feel safer in cars, because we overestimate the probability of an event when examples are readily available in memory (Tversky & Kahneman, 1973). A single vivid plane crash, which kills many people at once, lingers longer in memory than the many auto accidents reported every day. Thus, airplane fatalities seem more likely. On the other hand, driving *is* riskier for some people than others. Your age, driving habits, and seat-belt use, as well as the type of car you drive, all affect your risk of dying in a traffic accident.

These examples show how intuitions can be clouded by biases and fallacies despite people's best efforts to be rational. The scientific approach described in this chapter is not foolproof, but it is the psychologist's way of guarding against illusions, biases, wishful thinking—and the pitfalls of intuitive statistics.

SUMMARY

WHAT MAKES PSYCHOLOGICAL RESEARCH SCIENTIFIC?

1. Research methods provide a way for psychologists to separate well-supported conclusions from unfounded belief. An understanding of these methods can also help people think critically about psychological issues and become astute consumers of psychological findings and programs.

2. The ideal scientist states hypotheses and predictions precisely, is skeptical of claims that rest solely on faith or authority, relies on empirical evidence, complies with the *principle of falsifiability*, and is open about methods and results so that findings can be replicated. In contrast, pseudoscientists ignore these requirements. The public nature of science gives it a built-in system of checks and balances.

DESCRIPTIVE STUDIES: ESTABLISHING THE FACTS

3. *Descriptive methods* allow psychologists to describe and predict behavior but not necessarily to choose one explanation over others. Such methods include case studies, observational studies, psychological tests, and surveys, as well as correlational methods.

4. *Case studies* are detailed descriptions of individuals. They are often used by clinicians, and they can be valuable in exploring new research topics and addressing questions that would otherwise be difficult to study. But because the person under study may not be representative of people in general, case studies are typically sources rather than tests of hypotheses.

5. In *observational studies*, the researcher systematically observes and records behavior without interfering in any way with the behavior. *Naturalistic observation* is

used to find out how subjects behave in their natural environments. *Laboratory observation* allows more control and the use of special equipment; behavior in the laboratory, however, may differ in certain ways from behavior in natural contexts.

6. *Psychological tests* are used to measure and evaluate personality traits, emotional states, aptitudes, interests, abilities, and values. A good test is one that has been *standardized* and is both *valid* and *reliable*. Critics have questioned the reliability and validity of even some widely used tests.

7. *Surveys* are questionnaires or interviews that ask people directly about their experiences, attitudes, and opinions. Researchers must take precautions to obtain a sample that is representative of the larger population that the researcher wishes to describe and that yields results that are not influenced by a *volunteer bias*. Findings can also be affected by the fact that respondents sometimes lie, misremember, or misinterpret the questions.

CORRELATIONAL STUDIES: LOOKING FOR RELATIONSHIPS

8. In descriptive research, studies that look for relationships between phenomena are known as *correlational*. A *correlation* is a measure of the strength of a positive or negative relationship between two variables. A correlation does *not* show a causal relationship between the variables.

EXPERIMENTS: HUNTING FOR CAUSES

9. *Experiments* allow researchers to control the situation being studied, manipulate an *independent variable*, and assess the effects of the manipulation on a *dependent variable*. Experimental studies usually require a comparison or *control condition*. *Single-blind* and *double-blind* procedures can be used to prevent the expectations of the subjects or the experimenter from affecting the results. Because experiments allow conclusions about cause and effect, they have long been the method of choice in psychology. However, like laboratory observations, experiments create a special situation that may call forth behavior not typical in other environments.

EVALUATING THE FINDINGS

10. Psychologists use *descriptive statistics*, such as the *arithmetic mean*, to summarize data. They use *inferential statistics* to find out how impressive the data are. *Significance tests* tell the researcher how likely it is that the results of a study occurred merely by chance. The results are said to be *statistically significant* if this likelihood is very low. Statistically significant results allow psychologists to make predictions about human behavior, but, as in all sciences, probabilistic results do not tell us with any certainty what a particular individual will do in a situation.

11. Choosing among competing interpretations of a finding can be difficult, and care must be taken to avoid going beyond the facts. Sometimes the best interpretation does not emerge until a hypothesis has been tested in more than one way—for example, by using both *cross-sectional* and *longitudinal* methods.

12. Statistical significance does not always imply real-world importance because the amount of variation in the data accounted for by the independent variable may be small. Conversely, a result that does not quite reach significance may be potentially useful. Therefore, many psychologists are now turning to other inferential measures. The technique of *meta-analysis*, for example, reveals how much of the variation in scores across many different studies can be explained by a particular variable.

KEEPING THE ENTERPRISE ETHICAL

13. The APA's ethical code requires researchers to obtain the *informed consent* of human subjects, protect them from harm, and warn them in advance of any risks. Many studies require deceptive procedures. Concern about the morality of such procedures has led to guidelines to protect participants.

14. Psychologists study animals in order to gain knowledge about particular species, discover practical applications of psychological principles, study issues that cannot be studied with human beings for practical or ethical reasons, clarify theoretical questions, and improve human welfare. Debate over the use of animals in research has led to more comprehensive regulations governing their treatment and care.

KEY TERMS

theory 34

hypothesis 34

operational definition 35

principle of falsifiability 35

replicate 35

descriptive methods 38

case study 38

observational study 39

naturalistic observation 39

laboratory observation 40

psychological tests 41

standardization 41

LOOKING BACK

- Where do psychological scientists get their hypotheses? (p. 34)

- In what way are scientists risk-takers? (p. 35)

- Why is secrecy a big "no-no" in science? (p. 35)

- When are psychological case studies informative, and when are they useless? (pp. 38–39)

- Why do psychologists often observe people's behavior in laboratories instead of in everyday situations? (p. 40)

- Why should you be skeptical about psychological tests you find in magazines and newspapers? (p. 42)

- What's the difference between a psychological survey and a poll of listeners by a radio DJ? (p. 43)

- If two things are "negatively" correlated, like grades and TV watching, what is the relationship between them? (p. 45)

- If depression and illness are correlated, does that mean depression causes illness? (p. 46)

- Why do psychologists rely so heavily on experiments? (p. 48)

- What, exactly, do control groups control for? (p. 50)

- In a double-blind experiment, who is "blind," and what aren't they supposed to "see"? (p. 51)

- In psychological studies, why are averages sometimes misleading? (p. 54)

- How can psychologists tell whether a finding is impressive or trivial? (pp. 54–55)

- Why are some findings significant statistically but unimportant in practical terms? (p. 57)

- Why do psychologists often lie to their subjects? (p. 59)

- Why do psychologists study nonhuman animals? (pp. 59–60)

EVOLUTION, GENES, AND BEHAVIOR

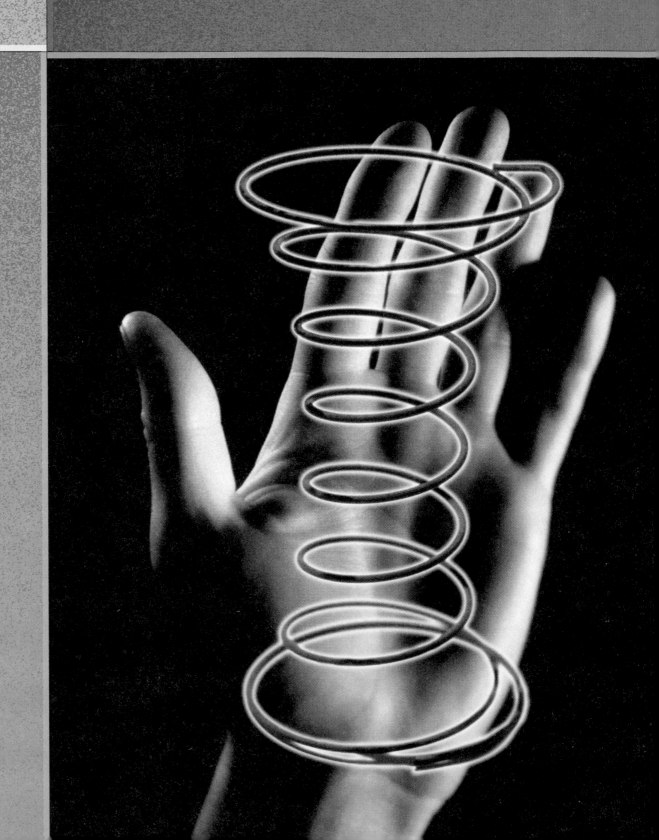

The tough-minded . . . respect difference.

Their goal is a world made safe for differences.

ANTHROPOLOGIST RUTH BENEDICT

Think of all the ways that human beings are alike. Everywhere, no matter what their backgrounds or where they live, people love, work, argue, dance, sing, complain, and gossip. They rear families, celebrate marriages, and mourn losses. They reminisce about the past and plan for the future. They help their friends and fight with their enemies. They smile with amusement, frown with displeasure, and glare in anger. *Where do all these commonalities come from?*

Think of all the ways that human beings differ. Some are extroverts, always ready to throw a party, make new friends, or speak up in a crowd; others are shy and introverted, preferring the safe and familiar. Some are trailblazers, ambitious and enterprising; others are placid, content with the way things are. Some take to book learning like a cat to catnip; others do not do so well in school but have lots of street smarts and practical know-how. Some are overwhelmed by even the most petty of problems; others, faced with severe difficulties, remain calm and resilient. *Where do all these differences come from?*

For many years, psychologists addressing these questions tended to fall into two camps. On one side were those who emphasized genes and inborn characteristics, or *nature;* on the other side were those who focused on learning and experience, or *nurture.* Edward L. Thorndike (1903), one of the leading psychologists of the early 1900s, staked out the first position when he claimed that "in the actual race of life . . . the chief determining factor is heredity." But in words that became famous, his contemporary, behaviorist John B. Watson (1925), insisted that experience could write virtually any message on the blank slate of human nature: "Give me a dozen healthy infants, well-formed, and my own specified world to bring them up in and I'll guarantee to take any one at random and train him to become any type of specialist I might select—doctor, lawyer, artist, merchant-chief and yes, even beggar-man and thief, regardless of his talents, penchants, tendencies, abilities, vocations, and race of his ancestors."

In this chapter, we focus mostly on the nature side of the debate, examining how heredity helps explain both our human commonalities and our individual differences, but we will also look at some environmental influences. You should keep in mind that today, no one argues in terms of nature *or* nurture; all scientists understand that heredity and environment interact to produce not only our psychological traits but even most physical ones. Children can inherit a tendency to be nearsighted, for instance, but whether nearsightedness actually develops may depend on whether a child reads a lot or sits for hours staring at a TV set or computer monitor (Gwiazda et al., 1993). A teenager with a natural aptitude for

The long and short of it: Human beings are similar and different.

sports may be more likely than other students to get on a school team and to get sports equipment as birthday presents, experiences that reward and encourage that aptitude.

● What does the chemical code in our genes encode *for*?
● What will a completed map of the human genes reveal—and not reveal?

UNLOCKING THE SECRETS OF GENES

Let's begin by looking at what genes are and how they operate. Genes, the basic units of heredity, are located on **chromosomes**, rod-shaped structures found in the center (nucleus) of every cell of the body. Each sperm cell and each egg cell (ovum) contains 23 chromosomes, so when a sperm and egg unite at conception, the fertilized egg and all the body cells that eventually develop from it (except for sperm cells and ova) contain 46 chromosomes, arranged in 23 pairs.

Chromosomes consist of threadlike strands of **DNA (deoxyribonucleic acid)** molecules, and genes consist of small segments of this DNA. Each human chromosome contains thousands of genes, each with a fixed location; collectively, the 140,000 or so human genes are referred to as the human genome. Many of these genes are found in other animals as well; others are uniquely human, setting us apart from chimpanzees, wasps, and plants. Some genes are inherited in the same form by everyone; others vary, contributing to our individuality.

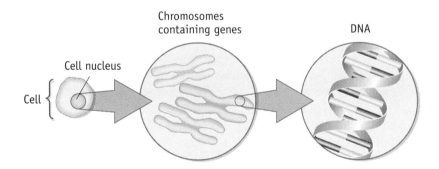

Within each gene, four basic chemical elements of DNA—identified by the letters A, T, C, and G, and numbering in the thousands or even tens of thousands—are arranged in a particular order: for example, ACGTCTCTATA. . . . This sequence forms a code that helps determine the synthesis of one of the many proteins that affect virtually every aspect of the body, from its structure to the chemicals that keep it running.

Identifying even a single gene is a daunting task; biologist Joseph Levine and geneticist David Suzuki (1993) compared it to searching for someone when all you know is that the person lives somewhere on earth. And because most human traits depend on more than one gene pair, tracking down the genetic contribution to a trait is even more difficult. Researchers must usually *clone* (produce copies of) several stretches of DNA on a chromosome, then use indirect methods to locate a given gene.

One method, which has been used to search for the genes associated with many physical and mental conditions, involves doing **linkage studies**. These studies take advantage of the tendency of genes lying close together on a chromosome to be

genes The functional units of heredity; they are composed of DNA and specify the structure of proteins.

chromosomes Within every body cell, rod-shaped structures that carry the genes.

DNA (deoxyribonucleic acid) The chromosomal molecule that transfers genetic characteristics by way of coded instructions for the structure of proteins.

genome The full set of genes in each cell of an organism (with the exception of sperm and egg cells).

linkage studies Studies that look for patterns of inheritance of genetic markers in large families in which a particular condition is common.

inherited together across generations. The researchers start out by looking for **genetic markers**, DNA segments that vary considerably among individuals and whose locations on the chromosomes are already known. They then look for patterns of inheritance of these markers in large families in which a condition is common, such as depression or impulsive violence. If a marker tends to exist only in the family members who have the condition, then it can be used as a genetic landmark: The gene involved in the condition is apt to be located nearby on the chromosome, so the researchers have some idea where to search for it.

The linkage method was used to locate the gene responsible for *Huntington's disease*, a fatal condition that usually strikes people in middle age, causing involuntary spasms and twisting movements of the body, facial grimacing, memory lapses, and sometimes paranoia and other psychological symptoms (Huntington's Disease Collaborative Research Group, 1993). Although only one gene was involved, the search took a decade of painstaking work.

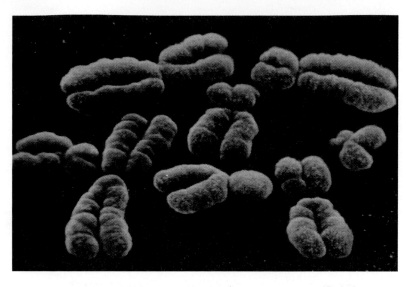

Human chromosomes, magnified almost 55,000 times.

An international collaboration of researchers has been hard at work to complete a map of the entire human genome—all 3 billion units of DNA (those As, Cs, Ts, and Gs). The Human Genome Project, as it is called, is working with new, high-tech methods to find out where the boundaries between genes are and how they are arranged on the chromosomes. This project has been enormously costly and time-consuming, but it reflects the view among many scientists that the twenty-first century will be the century of the gene.

It is important for people to understand that even when researchers locate a gene on a chromosome, they do not automatically know its role in physical or psychological functioning. Usually, locating a gene is just the first step in understanding what it does. Also, be wary of media reports implying that some gene is the *only* factor involved in a complex psychological ability or trait, such as intelligence or shyness. In 1998, for example, newspapers announced the discovery of a "worry gene." Don't worry about it. As we will see throughout this chapter, when it comes to psychological qualities, genetic and environmental influences are intertwined.

genetic marker A segment of DNA that varies among individuals, has a known location on a chromosome, and can function as a genetic landmark for a gene involved in a physical or mental condition.

GET ➡ INVOLVED

THUMBS UP!

Ask the members of your family, one person at a time, to clasp their hands together. Include aunts and uncles, grandparents—as many of your biological relatives as possible. Which thumb does each person put on top?

About half of all people fold the left thumb over the right, and about half fold the right thumb over the left, and these responses tend to run in families. Do your own relatives show one tendency over the other? (If your family is an adoptive one, of course, there is less chance of finding a trend.) Try the same exercise with someone else's family; do you get the same results? Even for behavior as simple as thumb folding, the details of how genes exert their effect remain uncertain (Jones, 1994).

WHAT'S AHEAD

● During evolution, why do some traits become more common and others less common?

● In the evolutionary view, why is the capacity to read faces innate, but not the capacity to read books?

● Why do so many people ignore signs saying "Don't touch"?

THE GENETICS OF SIMILARITY

How can we explain our human similarities—the experiences and behaviors that seem to be universal? Evolutionary psychologists, who apply the principles of evolution to human psychological qualities and behavior, believe the answer lies in genetic dispositions that developed during the long evolutionary history of our species. As British geneticist Steve Jones (1994) wrote, "Genetics is the key to the past. Every human gene must have an ancestor. . . . Each gene is a message from our forebears and together they contain the whole story of human evolution." Evolutionary psychologists try to read the genetic messages that might help explain commonalities in language learning, perception, memory, sexuality, decision making, emotion, and many other aspects of behavior (Barkow, Cosmides, & Tooby, 1992).

Evolution and Natural Selection

To understand evolutionary explanations of behavior, we must first understand the nature of evolution itself. Evolution is basically a change in gene frequencies within a population over many generations. As particular genes become more common in the population or less common, so do the characteristics they influence.

Why do gene frequencies in a population change? Why don't they stay put from one generation to another? Part of the reason is that if an error occurs in the copying of the original DNA sequence, genes can spontaneously change, or *mutate*, during the division of the cells that produce sperm and egg cells. In addition, during the formation of a sperm or egg, small segments of genetic material are apt to cross over (exchange places) between members of a chromosome pair before the final division. As genes spontaneously mutate and recombine during the production of sperm and eggs, new genetic variations—and therefore, potential new traits—keep arising.

But that is only part of the story. According to the principle of natural selection, first formulated in general terms by the British naturalist Charles Darwin in *On the Origin of Species* (1859/1964), the fate of these genetic variations depends on the environment. (Darwin did not actually know about genes, whose discovery had not yet been widely publicized; but he did know that a species' characteristics must somehow be transmitted from one generation to the next.)

If, in a particular environment, individuals with a genetically influenced trait tend to be more successful than other individuals at finding food, surviving the elements,

---

evolutionary psychology A field of psychology emphasizing evolutionary mechanisms that may help explain human commonalities in cognition, development, emotion, social practices, and other areas of behavior.

evolution A change in gene frequencies within a population over many generations; a mechanism by which genetically influenced characteristics of a population may change.

natural selection The evolutionary process in which individuals with genetically influenced traits that are adaptive in a particular environment tend to survive and to reproduce in greater numbers than do other individuals; as a result, their traits become more common in the population.

and fending off enemies—and therefore better at staying alive long enough to produce offspring—their genes will become more and more common in the population. Over many generations, these genes may even spread throughout the species. In contrast, individuals whose traits are not as adaptive in the struggle for survival will not be as "reproductively fit": They will tend to die before reproducing, and therefore their genes (and the traits influenced by those genes) will become less and less common and eventually may even become extinct.

Scientists debate how gradually or abruptly such changes occur and whether competition for survival is always the primary mechanism of change. But they agree on the basic processes of evolution, and evolutionary principles such as natural selection guide all the biological sciences.

Evolutionary biologists often start with an observation they want to explain, and then try to account for the observation in evolutionary terms. For example, why do male peacocks have such fabulous feathers whereas females look so woefully drab? Because during the evolution of peacocks, males with bright feathers could put on a flashy display that got the attention of females. These males therefore had a better chance of reproducing. In contrast, all females had to do was hang around and pick the guy with the fanciest feathers; they didn't even have to dress up.

Notice that this explanation, while plausible, is *after the fact*: It works backward from an observation to its possible cause. Some evolutionary psychologists take a different tack than the biologists do. They start by asking what sorts of challenges human beings might have faced in their prehistoric past—having to decide which foods were safe to eat, for example, or needing to size up a stranger's intentions quickly. Then they draw inferences about the behavioral tendencies that might have been selected because they helped our forebears solve these survival problems and enhanced reproductive fitness. (No assumption is made about whether the behavior is adaptive or intelligent in the *present* environment.) For example, our ancestors' need to avoid eating poisonous or rancid food might have led eventually to an innate dislike for bitter tastes and rotten smells. Similarly, it made good survival sense for our ancestors to develop an innate capacity for language and an ability to recognize

Many people at first ridiculed Darwin's notion that humans share a common ancestor with other primates. In this nineteenth-century cartoon, a monkeylike Darwin shows an ape how closely he resembles people. Today, evolutionary principles, which have long guided the biological sciences, are having a growing influence on psychological science as well.

Evolutionary changes sometimes occur rapidly because of sudden changes in the environment. Dark peppered moths, in contrast to light ones, were once rare, because they stood out against the lichen on trees and were apt to be eaten by predators before they could pass on their genes. In the nineteenth century, when pollution from coal-burning factories blackened the lichen (left), dark wings became adaptive and light ones maladaptive. By the late 1940s, 98 percent of all peppered moths were dark. Then pollution-control devices were installed and the trees lightened again (right). Since then, light-colored moths have made a comeback.

The Evolutionary View of the Mind

Not general-purpose computer

Specialized and independent "modules"

faces. In contrast, they would not have had much need for an innate ability to read or drive, inasmuch as books and cars did not yet exist (Pinker, 1994).

After drawing inferences about which behaviors might have evolved as responses to survival needs, evolutionary psychologists then do research, including cross-cultural studies, to see whether their inferences are correct. Their guiding assumption is that the human mind is not a general-purpose computer but instead developed as a collection of specialized and independent "modules" to handle specific survival problems (Buss, 1995; Cosmides, Tooby, & Barkow, 1992; Mealey, 1996). Culture and personal experience can affect which brain mechanisms actually get triggered, but everyone is born with the "wiring" for all of these mechanisms.

By drawing on many kinds of evidence, not only from psychology but from other disciplines as well, evolutionary psychologists believe they can distinguish behavior that has a biological origin from behavior that does not. For example, if a "mental module" for some behavior exists, then neuroscientists should eventually discover the brain circuits or subsystems associated with it (Pinker, 1994). Another clue is the difficulty or ease with which young children acquire certain skills: "When children solve problems for which they have mental modules," says Steven Pinker, "they should look like geniuses, knowing things they have not been taught; when they solve problems that their minds are not equipped for, it should be a long hard slog."

Innate Human Characteristics

Because of the way our species evolved, many abilities, tendencies, and characteristics are either present at birth in all human beings or develop rapidly as a child matures. These traits include not just the obvious ones, such as the ability to stand on two legs or to grasp objects with the forefinger and thumb, but also less obvious ones. Here are just a few examples:

1 **Infant reflexes.** Babies are born with a number of reflexes—simple, automatic responses to specific stimuli (see Chapter 14). For example, all infants will suck something put to their lips; by aiding nursing, this reflex enhances their chances of survival.

2 **An attraction to novelty.** Novelty is appealing to human beings and many other species. If a rat has had its dinner, it will prefer to explore an unfamiliar wing of a maze rather than the familiar wing where food is. Human babies reveal a surprising interest in looking at and listening to unfamiliar things—which, of course,

All primates, including human beings, are innately disposed to explore the environment, manipulate objects, play, and "monkey around."

includes most of the world. A baby will even stop nursing if someone new enters his or her range of vision.

3 *A desire to explore and manipulate objects.* All birds, mammals, and primates have this innate inclination. Primates, especially, like to "monkey" with things, taking them apart and scrutinizing the pieces, apparently for the sheer pleasure of it (Harlow, Harlow, & Meyer, 1950). Human babies shake rattles, bang pots, and grasp whatever is put into their tiny hands. For human beings, the natural impulse to handle interesting objects can be overwhelming, which may be one reason why the command "don't touch" is so often ignored by children, museum-goers, and shoppers.

4 *An impulse to play and fool around.* Think of kittens and lion cubs, puppies and pandas, and all young primates, who will play with and pounce on each other all day until hunger or naptime calls. Play and exploration may be biologically adaptive because they help members of a species find food and other necessities of life and learn to cope with their environments. Indeed, the young of many species enjoy *practice play*, behavior that will later be used for serious purposes when they are adults (Vandenberg, 1985). A kitten, for example, will stalk and attack a ball of yarn. In human beings, play teaches children how to get along with others and gives them a chance to practice their motor and linguistic skills (Pellegrini & Galda, 1993).

5 *Basic arithmetic skills.* Incredibly, by the age of only one week, infants show an understanding that a set of three items differs from a set of two items, indicating a rudimentary understanding of number. Of course, one-week-old babies cannot count! However, they will spend more time looking at a novel set of three items after getting used to a set of two items, or vice versa, which means that they can recognize the difference. By 18 months, infants know that four is more than three, which is more than two, which is more than one—suggesting that the brain is designed to understand "more than" and "less than" relationships for small numbers. Evolutionary psychologists believe that these fundamental arithmetic skills evolved because they were useful to our ancestors (Geary, 1995).

In other chapters, we consider the adaptive and evolutionary aspects of sensory and perceptual abilities (Chapter 6), learning (Chapter 7), emotion (Chapter 11), attachment (Chapter 12), and stress reactions (Chapter 15). For now, let us look more closely at two areas of great interest to evolutionary psychologists: the development of language and the nature of mating practices around the world.

QUICK QUIZ

How highly evolved is your understanding of evolutionary psychology?

1. Which is the *best* statement of the principle of natural selection? (a) Over time, the environment naturally selects some traits over others. (b) Particular genetic variations become more common over time if they are adaptive in a particular environment. (c) A species constantly improves as parents pass along their best traits to their offspring.

2. Evolutionary psychologists believe that the human mind evolved as (a) a collection of specialized modules to handle specific survival problems; (b) a general-purpose computer that adapts to any situation; (c) a collection of specific instincts for every human activity or capacity.

3. Which of the following is *not* part of our biological heritage? (a) a sucking reflex at birth; (b) a motive to explore and manipulate objects; (c) an avoidance of novel, unfamiliar objects; (d) a love of play

Answers:

1.b 2.a 3.c

WHAT'S AHEAD

- **What does language allow us to do that other animals can't do?**
- **What evidence suggests that evolution has equipped infants' brains with a module for acquiring language?**
- **How do parents help children acquire language?**

OUR HUMAN HERITAGE: LANGUAGE

Try reading this sentence aloud:

Kamaunawezakusomamanenohayawewenimtuwamaanasana.

Can you tell where one word begins and another ends? Unless you know Swahili, the syllables of this sentence will sound like gibberish.*

Well, to a baby learning its native tongue, *every* sentence must, at first, be gibberish. How, then, does an infant pick out discrete syllables and words from the jumble of sounds in the environment, much less figure out what the words mean and how to combine them? Is there something special about the human brain that allows a baby to discover how language works? Charles Darwin (1874) thought so: Language, he wrote, differs from other abilities, "for man has an instinctive tendency to speak." Many modern researchers think he was right.

The Nature of Language

To evaluate Darwin's claim, we must first appreciate that a **language** is not just any old communication system; it is a set of rules for combining elements that are inherently meaningless into utterances that convey meaning. The elements are usually sounds, but they can also be the gestures of American Sign Language (ASL) and other manual languages used by deaf and hearing-impaired people.

Some nonhuman animals are able to acquire aspects of language if they get help from their human friends (see Chapter 9). However, we seem to be the only species that acquires language naturally. Other primates use grunts, screeches, and gestures to warn each other of danger, attract attention, and express emotions, but the sounds are not combined to produce original sentences (at least, as far as anyone can tell). Bongo may make a sound of delight when he encounters food, but he cannot say, "The bananas in the next grove are a lot riper than the ones we ate last week and sure beat our usual diet of termites."

Whether spoken or signed, language allows us to express and comprehend an infinite number of novel utterances, created on the spot. This ability is critical because, except for a few fixed phrases ("How are you?" "Get a life!"), most of the utterances we produce or hear over a lifetime are new. For example, you will find few, if any, sentences in this book that you have read, heard, or spoken before in exactly the same form; yet you can understand what you are reading, and you can produce new sentences of your own about the material.

Human beings appear to have an inborn facility for acquiring language, even when they cannot hear speech. In North America, many hearing-impaired people use American Sign Language (ASL) to express not only everyday meanings but also poetic and musical ones. Deaf children learn to sign in ASL as easily as hearing children learn to speak.

---

*Kama unaweza kusoma maneno haya, wewe ni mtu wa maana sana, in Swahili means, "If you can read these words, you are a remarkable person."

The Innate Capacity for Language

At one time, most psychologists assumed that children acquired these dazzling abilities by imitating adults and paying attention when adults corrected their mistakes. Then along came linguist Noam Chomsky (1957, 1980), who argued that language was far too complex to be learned bit by bit, as one might learn the world capitals.

Children, said Chomsky, must not only figure out which sounds or gestures form words; they must also take the *surface structure* of a sentence—the way the sentence is actually spoken or signed—and infer an underlying *deep structure* that contains meaning. For example, although "Mary kissed John" and "John was kissed by Mary" have different surface structures, any 5-year-old knows that the two sentences have essentially the same deep structure, in which Mary is the actor and John gets the kiss:

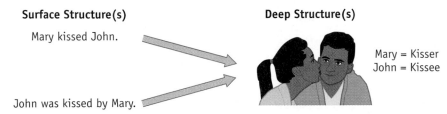

Surface Structure(s)

Mary kissed John.

John was kissed by Mary.

Deep Structure(s)

Mary = Kisser
John = Kissee

Conversely, "Bill heard the trampling of the hikers," a single surface structure, can have two different deep structures: one in which the hikers are actors doing the trampling, and one in which they are the objects getting trampled. Your ability to discern two different deep structures tells you that the sentence is ambiguous:

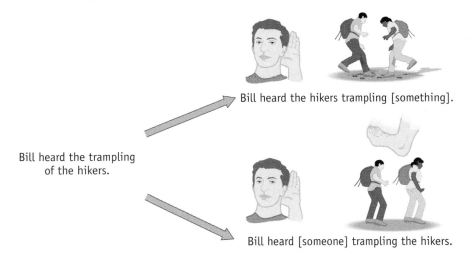

Bill heard the hikers trampling [something].

Bill heard the trampling of the hikers.

Bill heard [someone] trampling the hikers.

To transform surface structures into deep structures, said Chomsky, children must apply rules of grammar (*syntax*). These rules govern word order and other linguistic features that determine what role a word plays in a sentence (such as, say, kisser or kissee). Most people, even adults, cannot actually state the grammatical rules of their language (e.g., "Adjectives usually precede the noun they describe"), yet they are able to apply thousands of such rules without even thinking about it. No native speaker of English would say, "He threw the ball big."

No one actually teaches us grammar when we are toddlers. The human brain, Chomsky argued, must therefore contain a **language acquisition device**, an innate mental module that allows young children to develop language if they are exposed to an adequate sampling of conversation. Just as a bird is designed to fly, human beings are designed to use language. Over the years, linguists and *psycholinguists* (researchers who study the psychology of language) have gathered many types of evidence in support of this position (Crain, 1991; Pinker, 1994):

language A system that combines meaningless elements such as sounds or gestures to form structured utterances that convey meaning.

language acquisition device According to many psycholinguists, an innate mental module that allows young children to develop language if they are exposed to an adequate sampling of conversation.

1 *Children in different cultures* go through similar stages of linguistic development. For example, they will often form their first negatives simply by adding *no* or *not* at the beginning or end of a sentence ("No get dirty"); and at a later stage, they will use double negatives ("He don't want no milk"; "Nobody don't like me"), even when their language does not allow such constructions (Klima & Bellugi, 1966; McNeill, 1966). Cross-cultural similarities in sentence structure have even been reported for deaf children who have never learned a standard language, either signed or spoken, and have made up their *own* sign languages (Goldin-Meadow & Mylander, 1998). Such commonalities suggest that children are born with a *universal grammar,* which is another way of saying that the brain is disposed to notice the core features common to all languages (nouns and verbs, subjects and objects, constraints on phrase structures, and so forth). Even languages as seemingly different as Mohawk and English, or Okinawan and Bulgarian, share such features (Baker, 1999; Cinque, 1999; Pesetsky, 1999).

2 *Children combine words in ways that adults never would.* They reduce a parent's sentences ("Let's go to the store!") to their own two-word version ("Go store!") and make many charming errors that an adult would not ("The alligator goed kerplunk," "Daddy taked me," "Hey, Horton heared a Who") (Ervin-Tripp, 1964; Marcus et al., 1992). Such errors, which linguists call *overregularizations,* are not random; they show that the child has grasped a grammatical rule (e.g., add the *t* or *d* sound to make a verb past tense, as in *walked* or *hugged*) and is merely overgeneralizing it (*taked, goed*).

3 *Adults do not consistently correct their children's syntax,* yet children learn to speak or sign correctly. Learning explanations of language acquisition assume that children are rewarded for saying the right words and are punished for making errors. But parents do not stop to correct every error in their children's speech, so long as they can understand what the child is trying to say (Brown, Cazden, & Bellugi, 1969). Indeed, parents often *reward* children for incorrect statements! The 2-year-old who says "Want milk!" is likely to get it; most parents would not wait for a more grammatical (or polite) request.

Why is it that children have trouble learning the formal rules of "proper" language, yet by the time they start school they can apply the grammatical rules of their language to produce and understand new utterances?

"It's like learning a new language. You can't say 'ain't,' you don't end a sentence with a preposition, a sentence must have a subject and a predicate, you can't . . ."

4 *Even children who are profoundly retarded acquire language.* Indeed, they typically have a facility for language that exceeds by far their abilities in other areas (Bellugi et al., 1992; Smith, Tsimpli, & Ouhalla, 1993). This gap between general mental abilities and language abilities is especially dramatic in children with *Williams syndrome,* a rare genetic disorder (Harris et al., 1997). Children with Williams syndrome may be unable to tie their shoes, do a simple puzzle, or subtract 3 from 6, yet they often have extraordinary vocabularies (they can talk about newts and ibexes, not just dogs and cats), and they tell elaborate stories.

5 *Infants as young as 7 months can derive simple linguistic rules from a string of sounds.* If babies are repeatedly exposed to artificial "sentences" with an ABA pattern, such as *ga ti ga* or *li na li,* until they get bored, they will then prefer new sentences with an ABB pattern (such as *wo fe fe*) over new sentences with an ABA pattern (such as *wo fe wo*). (They indicate this preference by looking longer at a flashing light associated with the novel pattern than one associated with the familiar pattern.) Conversely, when the original sentences have an ABB structure, babies will prefer novel ones with an ABA structure. The babies' responses show that they can discriminate the different types of structures (Marcus et al., 1999). Astonishingly, this ability emerges even before they can understand or produce any words.

Chomsky's ideas so revolutionized thinking about language and human nature that some linguists refer to the initial publication of his ideas as The Event (Rymer, 1993).

Although Chomsky himself has avoided the evolutionary implications of his argument, others maintain that language evolved in human beings because it permitted our ancestors to convey precise information about time, space, objects, and events, and to negotiate alliances that were necessary for survival (Pinker, 1994).

The next logical step might be to identify the specific brain modules and genes that contribute to our ability to acquire language. One clue comes from a fascinating Canadian study of a large three-generation British family with a rare genetic disorder that prevents normal language acquisition (Gopnik, 1991; Gopnik & Goad, 1997; Matthews, 1994). Family members who are affected with this disorder have normal intelligence and perceptual abilities, but they have some pronunciation problems, and they cannot infer specific kinds of grammatical rules, including those for changing tenses or constructing plurals—rules that normal children learn easily and unconsciously. For example, they can learn the distinction between *mice* and *mouse* but they cannot learn the general rule about adding an *s, z,* or *iz* sound to make a noun plural, as in *bikes* (*s*), *gloves* (*z*), and *kisses* (*iz*). Instead, they must learn each plural as a separate item, and they make many errors. The pattern of inheritance seen in this study and others has provided clues to the specific genes involved in such disorders, which are often associated with abnormalities in brain structures (Kabani et al., 1997, 1998). For example, one team studying the same British family has found genetic markers associated with the affected members' pronunciation difficulties and grammatical deficits (Fisher et al., 1998).

GET →INVOLVED

A GRAMMAR TEST EVERYONE CAN PASS

How would you complete these sentences, spoken aloud?

This morning I saw one sik. Later I saw two more _____ .
This morning I saw one wug. Later I saw two more _____ .
This morning I saw one litch. Later I saw two more _____ .

Think about the sounds you added to these nonsense words; they differed, didn't they? In English, the plural form of most nouns depends on the last sound of the singular form. The precise rules are quite complicated, yet every speaker of English has an implicit knowledge of them, and will correctly add an *s* sound to *rat* to make *rats*, a *z* sound to *rag* to make *rags*, and an *iz* sound to *radish* to make *radishes*. (The only exceptions are people with a rare genetic disorder, as described in the text.) When 5- and 6-year-olds are asked for the plural versions of nonsense words, they easily apply the appropriate rules (Berko, 1958). Such evidence has helped to convince many psychologists that human beings have an innate ability to infer the rules of grammar.

Learning and Language

Despite the evidence for Chomsky's view, some theorists still give experience a greater role. Using computers, they have been able to design artificial *neural networks*, simplified models of the brain that can "learn" some aspects of language without assuming the existence of a language acquisition device. The success of these computer models, say these theorists, suggests that children, too, are able to acquire linguistic features without getting a head start from preprogrammed brain circuits

Although the capacity for language is innate, parents can foster their children's language development by talking and reading with them.

(Rumelhart & McClelland, 1987). Some theorists believe that instead of inferring grammatical rules, children learn the probability that any given word or syllable will follow another—something that infants as young as 8 months are able to do (Saffran, Aslin, & Newport, 1996; Seidenberg, 1997). In this view, infants are more like statisticians than grammarians.

Even theorists who emphasize an inborn grammatical capacity acknowledge that in any behavior as complex as language, both nature and nurture must play a role. Although there are commonalities in language acquisition around the world, there are also some differences. This means that language does not merely unfold biologically but also depends on the environment (Gopnik, Choi, & Baumberger, 1996; Slobin, 1985, 1991).

Further, although most children have the capacity to acquire language from mere exposure to it, parents help things along. They may not go around correcting their children's speech all day, but neither do they ignore their children's errors. For example, they are more likely to repeat verbatim a child's well-formed sentence than a sentence with errors ("That's a horse, mommy!" "Yes, that's a horse"). And when the child makes a mistake or produces a clumsy sentence, parents almost invariably respond by recasting it or expanding its elements ("Monkey climbing!" "Yes, the monkey is climbing the tree") (Bohannon & Stanowicz, 1988). In turn, children are more likely to imitate adult recasts and expansions, suggesting that they are learning from them (Bohannon & Symons, 1988). They also imitate their parents' accents, inflections, and tone of voice, and they will repeat some words that the parent tries to teach ("This is a ball, Erwin." "Baw").

It is likely, therefore, that language development depends on both biological readiness and social experience. Some aspects of language imply a genetic capacity for acquiring grammatical rules; but children may also learn, from experience, the statistical patterns among words (Marcus, 1999; Pinker, 1997).

Whatever the mechanism, the early years appear to be "make or break" years for acquiring a first language. Children who are abandoned, abused, and not exposed to language until late childhood (such as Genie, whom we mentioned in Chapter 2) rarely speak normally. Such sad evidence suggests a *critical period* in language development during the first few years of life or possibly the first decade (Curtiss, 1977; Lenneberg, 1967; Tartter, 1986). During these years, children need exposure to language and opportunities to practice their emerging linguistic skills in conversation with others.

QUICK QUIZ

Use your human capacity for language to answer these questions.

1. What did Chomsky mean by a "language acquisition device"?
2. What five findings support the existence of an innate "universal grammar"?
3. Those who reject Chomsky's ideas believe that instead of figuring out grammatical rules when acquiring language, children learn _____ .

Answers:

1. An innate mental module that permits young children to develop language if they are exposed to an adequate sampling of conversation. 2. Children everywhere seem to go through similar stages of linguistic development; children combine words in ways that adults would not; adults do not consistently correct their children's syntax; even profoundly retarded children usually acquire language; very young infants can recognize different sentence structures. 3. the probability that any given word or syllable will follow another one

WHAT'S AHEAD

● How do evolutionary psychologists explain male–female differences in courtship and sexuality?

● What basic issue divides evolutionary psychologists and their critics?

OUR HUMAN HERITAGE: COURTSHIP AND MATING

Most psychologists agree that the evolutionary history of our species has made certain kinds of learning either difficult or easy. Most acknowledge that simple behaviors, such as smiling or having a preference for sweet tastes, resemble *instincts*, behaviors that are relatively uninfluenced by learning and that occur in all members of the species. And most agree that human beings inherit some of their cognitive, perceptual, emotional, and linguistic capacities. But social scientists disagree heartily about whether biology and evolution can help account for complex social customs, such as warfare, cooperation, and altruism (the willingness to help others). Nowhere is this disagreement more apparent than in debates over the origins of courtship and mating practices.

Evolution and Sexual Strategies

In 1975, one of the world's leading experts on ants, Edward O. Wilson, published a little book that had a big impact. It was titled *Sociobiology: The New Synthesis*, the "synthesis" being the application of biological principles to the social and sexual customs of both nonhuman animals and human beings. **Sociobiology** became a popular topic for researchers and the public, generating great controversy (Symons, 1979; Trivers, 1972).

Sociobiologists believe that male–female differences in courtship and mating evolved in response to survival needs. In many species, they argue, it is adaptive for males to compete with other males for access to young and fertile females, and to try to win and then inseminate as many females as possible. The more females a male mates with, the more genes he can pass along. (The human record in this regard was achieved by a man who fathered 899 children [Daly & Wilson, 1983].) But according to sociobiologists, females need to shop for the best genetic deal, as it were, because they can conceive and bear only a limited number of offspring. Having such a large biological investment in each pregnancy, they cannot afford to make mistakes. Besides, mating with a lot of different males would produce no more offspring than staying with just one. So females try to attach themselves to dominant males, who have resources and status and are likely to have "superior" genes.

sociobiology An interdisciplinary field that emphasizes evolutionary explanations of social behavior in animals, including human beings.

This Kenyan man has 40 wives and 349 children. Although he is unusual, in societies around the world it is far more common for men to have many wives than for women to have many husbands. Sociobiologists and evolutionary psychologists attribute this difference to the evolution of different sexual strategies in males and females.

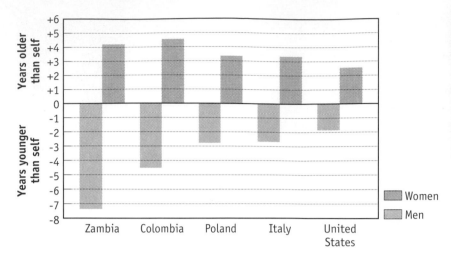

FIGURE 3.1

PREFERRED AGE IN A MATE

In most societies, men say they prefer to marry women younger than themselves, whereas women prefer men who are older (Buss, 1995). Evolutionary psychologists attribute these preferences to male concern with a partner's fertility and female concern with a partner's material resources and status. When the man is much older than the woman, people rarely comment, but when the woman is older, as in the case of actors Susan Sarandon and Tim Robbins, people take notice.

AVOID OVERSIMPLIFICATION

Sex differences in courtship and mating are common in cultures around the world and among nonhuman mammals as well. But human sexual behavior also varies in many ways. Do genes hold culture on a tight leash, a long and flexible one, or none at all?

The result of these two opposite sexual strategies, in this view, is that males generally want sex more often than females do; males are often fickle and promiscuous, whereas females are devoted and faithful; males are drawn to sexual novelty and even rape, whereas females want stability and security; males are relatively undiscriminating in their choice of partners, whereas females are cautious and choosy; and males are competitive and concerned about dominance, whereas females are less so.

Evolutionary psychologists generally agree with these conclusions, but they differ from sociobiologists in some respects. For example, sociobiologists tend to argue by analogy: If a male scorpion fly forces himself on a female, this behavior is analogous to human rape and thus human rape must have the same evolutionary origins (Thornhill, 1980). But even if human beings and other animals seem to behave in a similar fashion, this does not mean that the *origins* of the behavior must be the same in both species. In general, therefore, evolutionary psychologists rely less on comparisons with other species, instead focusing on the commonalities in human mating and dating practices around the world (Buss, 1994). Evolutionary psychologists and sociobiologists also disagree on some theoretical matters that are beyond the scope of our discussion here.

Nevertheless, both groups emphasize the evolutionary origins of many human sex differences that appear to be universal, or at least very common. In one massive project, 50 scientists studied 10,000 people in 37 cultures located on six continents and five islands (Buss, 1994). Around the world, they found, men are more violent than women and more socially dominant. They are more interested in the youth and beauty of their sexual partners (presumably because youth is associated with fertility) (see Figure 3.1). They are more sexually jealous and possessive (presumably because males can never be 100 percent sure that their children are really theirs genetically), quicker to have sex with partners they don't know well, and more inclined toward polygamy and promiscuity (presumably so that their sperm will be distributed as widely as possible). Women, in contrast, tend to emphasize the financial resources or prospects of a potential mate, his status, and his willingness to commit to a relationship (Bailey et al., 1994; Buss, 1994, 1996; Buunk et al., 1996; Daly & Wilson, 1983; Sprecher, Sullivan, & Hatfield, 1994).

Culture and the "Genetic Leash"

Sociobiological and evolutionary views of sex differences have become enormously popular. On a TV talk show, novelist Tom Wolfe explained that men are "genetically" wired to be promiscuous and women to be monogamous. *Time* magazine (August 15, 1994) made this idea into a cover story: "Infidelity:

It may be in our genes." The blurb at the start of the article read, "It is to a man's evolutionary advantage to sow his seeds far and wide. Women instead seek mates with the best genes and the most to invest in offspring. These strategies can put the sexes in conflict and undermine love."

But critics argue that evolutionary explanations of infidelity and monogamy are based on *stereotypes* of gender differences, not the actual behavior of human beings and other animals. When researchers put aside their expectations, they find that actual behavior often contradicts the image of the sexually promiscuous male and the coy, choosy female (Fausto-Sterling, 1997; Hrdy, 1988; Hubbard, 1990). In many species—birds, fish, mammals, and primates, including human beings—females are sexually ardent and often have many male partners. The female's sexual behavior does not seem to depend only on the goal of being fertilized by the male: Females have sex when they are not ovulating and even when they are already pregnant! And in many primate species, males do not just mate and run; they stick around, feeding the infants, carrying them on their backs, and protecting them against predators (Hrdy, 1988; Snowdon, 1997; Taub, 1984).

These findings have sent evolutionary theorists scurrying to figure out the evolutionary benefits of female promiscuity and male nurturance. Perhaps, in some species, females need sperm from several males in order to ensure conception by the healthiest sperm (Baker, 1996). Or perhaps females have many partners in order to increase the number of males who will help support the female's offspring. This motive could explain a custom of the Barí people of Venezuela: A man who impregnates a woman is considered the child's primary father; but a woman is permitted to take other lovers during her pregnancy, and these men are considered secondary fathers who must supply the child with extra food (Beckerman et al., 1998).

Critics of evolutionary theories, however, argue that all of these explanations, whether of female fidelity or female promiscuity, are inadequate when applied to primates, especially human beings. Human sexual behavior, they note, is amazingly varied and changeable. Cultures range from those in which women have many children to those in which they have very few; from those in which men are intimately involved in child rearing to those in which they do nothing at all; from those in which women may have many lovers to those in which women may be killed for having sex outside of marriage (Hatfield & Rapson, 1996). In some places, the chastity of a potential mate is much more important to men than to women; but in other places, it is important to both sexes—or to neither one (see Figure 3.2). Even within a culture, sexual attitudes and practices vary tremendously (Laumann et al., 1994). That is why critics of evolutionary analyses think that male and female sexual behavior—such as "promiscuous" behavior in one or both sexes—is best explained by economic and social factors, rather than by genes (see Chapter 12).

A basic assumption of evolutionary approaches to sexuality is that females across species have a greater involvement in child rearing than males do. But there are many exceptions. Female emperor penguins, for example, take off every winter, leaving behind males like this one to care for the kids.

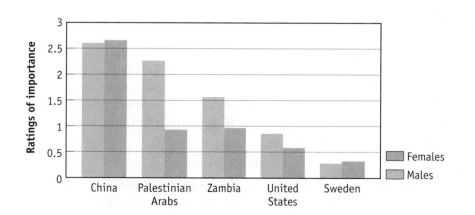

FIGURE 3.2
ATTITUDES TOWARD CHASTITY

In many places, men care more about a partner's chastity than women do, as evolutionary psychologists would predict. But culture has a powerful impact on these attitudes, as this graph shows. Notice that in China, both sexes prefer a partner who has not yet had intercourse, whereas in Sweden, chastity is a nonissue. (From Buss, 1995.)

Debate over these matters can get quite heated because of worries that evolutionary arguments will be used to justify social and political inequalities and violent behavior. For example, such arguments could be used to conclude that men, with less investment in child rearing and more interest in status and dominance, are destined to control business and politics. Edward O. Wilson (1975) thinks so. "Even with identical education and equal access to all professions [for both sexes]," he wrote, "men are likely to continue to play a disproportionate role in political life, business, and science." This is not a message that people who hope for gender equality welcome! In 1978, demonstrators at a meeting of the American Association for the Advancement of Science dumped water on Wilson's head, chanting "Wilson, you're all wet!" (though this was hardly a persuasive way to get him to change his mind).

Ultimately, what evolutionary scientists and their critics are quarreling about is the relative power of biology and culture. In *On Human Nature* (1978), Edward Wilson argued that genes hold culture on a leash. The big question, replied paleontologist Stephen Jay Gould (1987), is, how long and tight is that leash? Is it too tight to allow much change, or is it long enough to permit many possible customs? To sociobiologists, the leash is short and tight. To evolutionary psychologists, it is elastic enough to permit culture to modify evolved biological tendencies, although those tendencies can be pretty powerful (Kenrick & Trost, 1993). To critics of both sociobiology and evolutionary psychology, cultural variations mean that no single, genetically determined sexual strategy exists for human beings—the leash is long and flexible.

QUICK QUIZ

Males and females have evolved to be able to answer these questions.

1. Which of the following would an evolutionary psychologist expect to be more typical of males than of females? (a) promiscuity, (b) choosiness about sexual partners, (c) concern with dominance, (d) interest in young partners, (e) emphasis on physical attractiveness of partners

2. What major issue divides evolutionary theorists and their critics in debates over courtship and mating?

3. A friend of yours, who has read some sociobiology, tells you that men will *always* be more sexually promiscuous than women because during evolution, the best reproductive strategy for male primates has been to try to impregnate lots of females. What kind of evidence would you need to evaluate this claim?

Answers:

1. all but b   2. The relative influence of biology and culture   3. You would not want to look just for confirming evidence (recall the principle of falsifiability). You would want to look also for evidence of female promiscuity and male monogamy among humans and other species and changes in sexual customs in response to changing social conditions.

WHAT'S AHEAD

● If you have a highly heritable trait, does that mean you are stuck with it forever?
● What kinds of studies allow psychologists to estimate a trait's heritability?

THE GENETICS OF DIFFERENCE

We have been discussing where human similarities come from. Now let us turn to the second great issue in the nature–nurture debate: the origins of the differences among us. This issue is of special interest to developmental psychologists and to

behavioral geneticists, scientists who study the genetic bases of individual differences in behavior and personality.

We begin with a critical discussion of what it means to say that a trait is "heritable." Then, to illustrate how behavioral geneticists study differences that might be influenced by genes, we will examine two (unrelated!) topics: weight and intelligence. Behavioral-genetic findings on personality are discussed in Chapter 13, and on mental disorders in Chapter 16.

The Meaning of Heritability

Suppose you want to measure flute-playing ability in a large group of music students, so you have some independent raters assign each student a score, from 1 to 20. When you plot the scores, you find that some people are what you might call melodically disadvantaged and should forget about a musical career; others are flute geniuses; and the rest fall somewhere in between. What causes the variation in this group of students? Why are some so musically talented and others so inept? Are these differences primarily genetic, or are they the result of experience and motivation?

To answer these questions, behavioral geneticists compute a statistic called **heritability**, which gives an estimate of the *proportion of the total variance in a trait that is attributable to genetic variation within a group*. Because the heritability of a trait is expressed as a proportion, the maximum value it can have is 1.0. Height is highly heritable; that is, within a group of equally well-nourished individuals, most of the variation among them will be accounted for by their genetic differences. In contrast, table manners have low heritability because most variation among individuals is accounted for by differences in upbringing. Our guess is that flute-playing ability falls somewhere in the middle.

Many people hold completely mistaken ideas about heritability. But as genetic findings pour in, the public will need to understand this concept more than ever. You cannot understand the nature–nurture issue without understanding the following important facts about heritability:

1 *An estimate of heritability applies only to a particular group living in a particular environment,* and estimates may differ for different groups. Suppose that all the children in Community A are affluent, eat plenty of high-quality food, have kind and attentive parents, and go to the same top-notch schools. Because their environments are similar, any intellectual differences among them will have to be due largely to their genetic differences. In other words, mental ability in this group will be highly heritable. In contrast, the children in Community B are rich, poor, and in between. Some of them have healthy diets; others live on fatty foods and cupcakes. Some attend good schools; others go to inadequate ones. Some have doting parents, and some have unloving and neglectful ones. These children's intellectual differences could be due to their environmental differences, in which case the heritability of intelligence for this group will be low.

2 *Heritability estimates do not apply to individuals,* only to variations within a group. You inherited half your genes from your mother and half from your father, but your *combination* of genes has never been seen before and will never be seen again (unless you have an identical twin). You also have a unique history of family relationships, intellectual training, and life experiences. It is impossible to know just how your genes and your personal history have interacted to produce the person you are today.

For example, if you are a great flute player, no one can say whether your ability is mainly a result of inherited musical talent, living all your life in a family of devoted flute players, a private obsession that you acquired at age 6 when you saw

behavioral genetics An interdisciplinary field of study concerned with the genetic bases of behavior and personality.

heritability A statistical estimate of the proportion of the total variance in some trait that is attributable to genetic differences among individuals within a group.

THINKING CRITICALLY

DEFINE YOUR TERMS
What does it mean to say that some trait is "highly heritable"? If you want to improve your flute playing and someone tells you that musical ability is heritable, should you stop practicing?

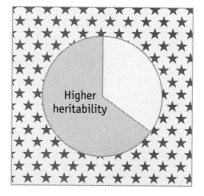

Similar Environments

Higher heritability

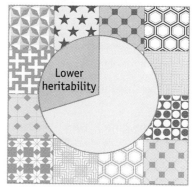

Diverse Environments

Lower heritability

the opera *The Magic Flute*—or a combination of all three. For one person, genes may make a tremendous difference in some aptitude or disposition; for another, the environment may be far more important. The best scientists can do is to try to explain the extent to which differences among people *in general* are explainable by their genetic differences.

3 ***Even highly heritable traits can be modified by the environment.*** Although height is highly heritable, malnourished children may not grow to be as tall as they would with sufficient food. Conversely, if children eat an extremely nutritious diet, they may grow to be taller than anyone thought they could. The same principle applies to psychological traits, although biological determinists often fail to realize this. They argue, for example, that because IQ is highly heritable, IQ and school achievement cannot be boosted much (Herrnstein & Murray, 1994). But even if the first part of the statement is true, the second part does not necessarily follow.

Computing Heritability

Scientists have no way to estimate the heritability of a trait or behavior directly, so they must *infer* it by studying people whose degree of genetic similarity is known. You might think that the simplest approach would be to compare blood relatives within families; everyone knows about families that are famous for some talent or trait. But family traits do not tell us much, because close relatives usually share environments, as well as genes. If Carlo's parents and siblings all love lasagna, that does not mean a taste for lasagna is heritable! The same applies if everyone in Carlo's family has a high IQ, is mentally ill, or is moody.

A better approach is to study adopted children (e.g., Loehlin, Horn, & Willerman, 1996; Plomin & DeFries, 1985). Such children share half their genes with each birth parent, but they grow up in a different environment, apart from their birth parents. On the other hand, they share an environment with their adoptive parents and siblings, but not their genes:

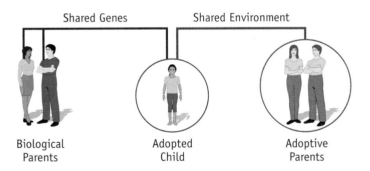

Shared Genes   Shared Environment

Biological   Adopted   Adoptive
Parents   Child   Parents

Researchers can compare correlations between the traits of adopted children and those of their biological and adoptive relatives and can use the results to estimate heritability.

Another approach is to compare **identical (monozygotic) twins** with **fraternal (dizygotic) twins**. Identical twins develop when a fertilized egg (zygote) divides into two parts that then develop into two separate embryos. Because the twins come from the same fertilized egg, they share all their genes. (Identical twins may be slightly different at birth, however, because of differences in the blood supply to the two fetuses or other chance factors.) In contrast, fraternal twins develop when a woman's ovaries release two eggs instead of one and each egg is fertilized by a different sperm. Fraternal twins are wombmates, but they are no more alike genetically than any other two siblings (they share, on average, only half their genes), and they may be of different sexes.

identical (monozygotic) twins Twins that develop when a fertilized egg divides into two parts that develop into separate embryos.

fraternal (dizygotic) twins Twins that develop from two separate eggs fertilized by different sperm; they are no more alike genetically than are any other pair of siblings.

Identical Twins

Single egg fertilized by single sperm, then splits in two

Fraternal Twins

Separate eggs fertilized by separate sperm

Womb

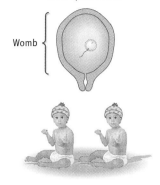

Share all of their genes

Share only about half their genes

Behavioral geneticists can estimate the heritability of a trait by comparing groups of same-sex fraternal twins with groups of identical twins. The assumption is that if identical twins are more alike than fraternal twins, then the increased similarity must be genetic.

Perhaps, however, identical twins are treated differently than fraternal twins. People may treat identical twins, well, identically—or they may go to the other extreme, emphasizing the twins' differences. To avoid these problems, investigators have studied identical twins who were separated early in life and reared apart. (Until recently, adoption policies and attitudes toward illegitimacy permitted such separations to occur.) In theory, separated identical twins share all their genes but not their environments. Any similarities between them should be primarily genetic and should permit a direct estimate of heritability.

Behavioral-genetics research is transforming our understanding of behavior that was once explained solely in psychological terms. Nowhere is this truer than in the study of body weight and shape, as we are about to see.

Separated at birth, the Mallifert twins meet accidentally.

QUICK QUIZ

Is test-taking ability a heritable trait or a matter of motivation? Either way, take this test.

1. Diane hears that basket-weaving ability is highly heritable. She assumes that her own low performance must therefore be due mostly to genes. What is wrong with her reasoning?

2. Bertram hears that basket-weaving ability is highly heritable. He concludes that schools should not bother trying to improve the skills of children who lack this talent. What is wrong with his reasoning?

3. Basket-weaving skills seem to run in Andy's family. Why shouldn't Andy conclude that his own talent is genetic?

4. Why do behavioral geneticists find it useful to study twins?

Answers:

1. Heritability applies only to differences among individuals within a group, not to particular individuals. 2. A trait may be highly heritable *and* still be susceptible to modification. 3. Family members share environments, as well as genes. 4. Identical twins growing up together share an environment, and so do fraternal twins, so if identical twins are more alike than fraternal twins, then the increased similarity is assumed to be genetic. In addition, identical twins reared apart share only their genes, not their environment, so similarities between them should be primarily genetic.

WHAT'S AHEAD

- **Is overweight usually a result of psychological problems?**
- **What genetic theory can help explain why you are thin or heavy?**
- **Why are Americans and people in many other countries getting fatter?**
- **Why are bright, academically motivated college women most vulnerable to eating disorders?**

OUR HUMAN DIVERSITY: BODY WEIGHT AND SHAPE

Some people are skinny; others are plump. Some people are shaped like string beans; others look more like pears. Some seem to eat anything they want without gaining an ounce; others struggle unsuccessfully their whole lives to shed pounds. Do genes have anything to do with how much we weigh and how those pounds are distributed?

THINKING CRITICALLY

ASK QUESTIONS

Obesity is caused mainly by psychological problems that drive people to overeat, isn't it? When researchers began to question this obvious assumption, they were in for a surprise.

Genes and Weight

At one time, most psychologists thought that being overweight was a sign of emotional disturbance. If you were fat, it was because you hated your mother, feared intimacy, or were trying to fill an emotional hole in your psyche by loading up on rich desserts. The evidence for psychological theories of overweight, however, came mainly from self-reports and from studies that were seriously flawed. Many studies lacked control groups and objective measures of how much people were actually eating (Allison & Heshka, 1993). When researchers did controlled experiments, they learned that fat people, on average, are no more and no less emotionally disturbed than average-weight people (Stunkard, 1980).

Even more surprising, studies showed that *heaviness is not always caused by overeating*. Many heavy people do eat large quantities of food, but so do some thin people. Many thin people eat very little, but so do some obese people. In one study that carefully monitored everything that subjects were eating, two 260-pound women maintained their weights while consuming only 1,000 calories a day (Wooley, Wooley, & Dyrenforth, 1979). In another study, which had volunteers gorge themselves for months, it was as hard for slender people to gain weight as it is for most heavy people to lose weight. The minute the study was over, the slender people lost weight as fast as dieters gained it back (Sims, 1974). A new theory was needed to explain such findings.

Is this man heavy because of his genes, his diet, or both? Does your answer affect how you feel about him—sympathetic, neutral, or contemptuous?

Set-point Theory. One approach that is widely accepted today holds that a biological mechanism keeps a person's body weight at a genetically influenced **set point**—the weight you stay at when you are not consciously trying to gain or lose (Lissner et al., 1991).

Everyone has a genetically programmed *basal metabolic rate*, the rate at which the body burns calories for energy, and a fixed number of *fat cells*, which store fat for energy and can change in size. According to set-point theory, a complex interaction of metabolism, fat cells, and hormones keeps people at the weight their bodies are designed to be, much in the way that a thermostat keeps a house at a preset temperature. When a heavy person diets, the body's metabolism slows down to conserve energy and fat reserves. When a thin person overeats, metabolism speeds up, burning energy. Set-point theory, which has been supported by dozens of studies of animals and human beings, explains why most people who go on restricted diets eventually gain their weight back: They are returning to their set-point weight (Leibel, Rosenbaum, & Hirsch, 1995; Levitan & Ronan, 1988).

Set-point theory predicts that the heritability of weight and body fat should be high. In twin and adoption studies, heritability estimates range widely, but most fall

set point The genetically influenced weight range for an individual, thought to be maintained by a biological mechanism that regulates food intake, fat reserves, and metabolism.

between .40 and .70, which is, indeed, quite high (Comuzzie & Allison, 1998). It seems clear, therefore, that genes contribute to size and weight differences among people. Consider some further evidence for the role of genes:

- In a study of Pima Indians in Arizona (see photo at right), two-thirds of the women and half of the men became obese over time, and the slower their metabolisms, the greater the weight gain. After adding anywhere from 20 to 45 pounds, however, the Pimas stopped gaining weight. Their metabolism rates rose, and their weights stabilized at the new, higher level (Ravussin et al., 1988). Many Pimas apparently have a set point for plumpness.

- In a study of 3-month-old infants, the babies of overweight mothers generated 21 percent less energy than the babies of normal-weight mothers, although the babies were all eating the same amount. By the age of 1 year, the lower-metabolism babies had become overweight (Roberts et al., 1988).

- Pairs of adult identical twins who grow up in different families are just as similar in body weight and shape as twins raised together. The early family environment has almost no effect at all on body shape, weight gain, or percentage of fat in the body (Stunkard et al., 1990).

- In a study of 12 pairs of adult male identical twins, the men were confined to a dormitory for 100 days, where they were forbidden to exercise and were given a diet that contained 1,000 extra calories a day. In each pair of twins, both members gained almost exactly the same amount of weight, but the differences *between* the pairs was astonishing. One pair of twins gained 9½ pounds, but another pair gained almost 30 pounds. Some pairs of twins gained weight on their hips and thighs; others gained weight around the waist (C. Bouchard et al., 1990).

Tracking Obesity Genes. Enormous progress has been made in identifying the genes involved in some types of obesity. The first step occurred when one team of researchers isolated a genetic variation that causes mice to become obese (Zhang et al., 1994). The usual form of the gene, called "obese," or *ob* for short, causes fat cells to secrete a protein, which the researchers named *leptin* (from the Greek *leptos*, "slender"). Leptin travels through the blood to a brain area called the *hypothalamus*, which is involved in the regulation of appetite. Rising and falling levels of leptin signal how large or small the body's fat cells are, so that the brain can maintain the animal's or person's set point by adjusting appetite and metabolism. Injecting leptin into mice reduces their appetites, speeds up their metabolisms, and makes them more active; as a result, the animals shed weight, even if they are not overweight to begin with (Halaas et al., 1995).

The role of leptin in human obesity is more complicated than it is in mice. (We are tempted to say "rats" to this news.) Some obese people may gain weight rapidly because their secretion of leptin is impaired (Ravussin et al., 1997). Other obese people may produce plenty of leptin but be insensitive to it, perhaps because of a gene that prevents brain cells from responding normally to leptin's signals (Chua et al., 1996; Considine et al., 1996; Maffei et al., 1995). But for most obese people, leptin probably does not play a major role (Comuzzie & Allison, 1998).

Still, genes are important: Dozens of other genes and many body chemicals besides leptin are thought to be involved in appetite, metabolic rates, and weight regulation.

Body weight and shape are strongly affected by genetic factors. Set-point theory helps explain why the Pimas of the American Southwest gain weight easily but lose it slowly, whereas the Bororo nomads of Nigeria (above) can eat a lot of food yet remain slender.

Both of these mice have a mutation in the *ob* gene, which usually makes mice chubby, like the one on the left. But when leptin is injected daily, the mice remain almost normal in weight, like the one on the right, because they eat less and burn more calories.

Genes that predispose individuals to obesity probably exist in our species because, in the past, starvation was all too often a real possibility, and a tendency to store calories in the form of fat provided a definite survival advantage. Unfortunately, evolution did not design a mechanism to prevent us from gaining weight when food is abundant, tasty, and cheap.

Environmental Influences on Weight

The discovery of genetic influences on body weight and shape may help to combat cultural prejudices toward obese individuals—and persuade normal-weight people to accept their bodies. But genes tell only part of the story. The other part has to do with what you eat, how active you are, and the culture you live in.

Diet and Exercise. If you consume the high-fat junk-food diet that so many North Americans love, and if you eat such food in the large quantities that most Europeans and Asians find excessive and alarming, you are likely to be heavier than if you eat a low-fat diet in moderate portions. It may not be only a matter of calories: A high-fat diet may actually change an individual's set point for body weight (Frederich et al., 1995). As one physician wrote to the *New York Times*, "Perhaps the flaw lies not so much in our mutations as in McDonald's."

Another nongenetic influence on weight is exercise, which boosts the body's metabolic rate and may lower its set point. When obese women are put on severely restricted diets, their metabolic rates drop sharply, as set-point theory would predict. But when they combine the diet with moderate physical activity—daily walking— they lose weight and their metabolic rates rise almost to previous levels (Wadden et al., 1990). This evidence suggests why changes in weight often accompany major changes in habits and activity levels. People start walking to work, or stop. They become lethargic after losing a job (and gain weight), or excited when they fall in love (and lose weight).

The results of rich diets and lack of exercise can be seen in the rising numbers of overweight people in North America. During the 1950s and 1960s, about 7 percent of American men and 14 percent of women were trying to lose weight, but over the years, the numbers rose steadily, until today about a quarter of all men and two-fifths of all women say they are dieting (Horm & Anderson, 1993; Serdula et al., 1993). Yet, all this dieting has not produced a thinner population. On the contrary: The prevalence of obesity has jumped dramatically in the past few decades—from 12.8 percent of the population in the early 1960s to 22.5 percent by the mid-1990s—and by government standards, half the adult population is now overweight. Increases have occurred in both sexes and all age groups, including children, and in many other countries as well (Taubes, 1998).

The reasons have little to do with the prevalence of obesity genes, which cannot have changed much in just a couple of decades. Instead, the likely culprits are an increased abundance of low-cost, high-fat foods, the habit of eating high-calorie food on the run rather than enjoying leisurely meals, the rise in energy-saving (fat-conserving) devices, the popularity of television over active hobbies, and "couch-potato" lifestyles (Brownell & Rodin, 1994; Hill & Peters, 1998).

Cultural Attitudes. Eating habits and activity levels, in turn, are shaped by your culture's customs and standards of what the ideal body should look like: fat, thin, muscular, soft, or gaunt. In many places around the world, especially in those where famine and crop failures are common, fat is taken as a sign of health in both sexes, affluence in men, and sexual desirability in women (Bennett & Gurin, 1982). In some

YES, THE KIDS WATCH THE TELETUBBIES ON T.V., I WATCH THE ONE IN FRONT OF THE T.V.

parts of Africa, marriage-age girls are even put in special "fattening huts" where they do nothing but eat, so as to become obese enough to attract a husband.

In North America, many whites regard fat as a sign of laziness, gluttony, and weakness of will, but blacks and Mexicans are generally more accepting of fat people and less concerned about their own weight (Crandall & Martinez, 1996; Hebl & Heatherton, 1998). We had a student who had spent several years in Tonga, where she said everyone worried that she was too thin and kept urging her to eat; in the United States, she said, all her friends kept urging her to diet.

As North Americans have grown heavier, the cultural ideal for white women has been getting thinner and thinner. The ideal of the voluptuously curvy woman, big breasted and big hipped, was popular before World War I and after World War II. But during the flapper era of the 1920s, and again starting in the 1970s, big breasts and hips became unfashionable. Why did these changes occur? One explanation is that men and women associate the curvy, big-breasted female body with femininity, nurturance, and motherhood (Bennett & Gurin, 1982). Hence, big breasts are fashionable in eras that celebrate women's role as mothers—such as after World War II, when women were encouraged to give up their wartime jobs and have many children.

Genes and evolution cannot explain cultural changes in attitudes toward the ideal female body. During the 1950s, actresses like Diana Dors embodied the post-war ideal: curvaceous, buxom, and "womanly." But by the late 1960s, women were struggling to look more like the aptly named model, Twiggy: boyish, angular, and nonmaternal.

Even women of wealth and influence are not immune to cultural pressures to be thin, and even they are vulnerable to the insecurities that can lead to an eating disorder. Singer Karen Carpenter eventually died of anorexia.

bulimia An eating disorder characterized by episodes of excessive eating (bingeing) following by forced vomiting or use of laxatives (purging).

anorexia nervosa An eating disorder characterized by fear of being fat, a distorted body image, radically reduced consumption of food, and emaciation.

But many people also, alas, associate femininity with incompetence. Thus, whenever women have entered traditionally male spheres of education and work, as they did in the 1920s and between the 1970s and the present, ambitious women have tried to look boyishly thin and muscular in order to avoid appearing feminine and dumb (Silverstein, Peterson, & Perdue, 1986). Lately, an even more unrealistic female ideal has appeared, possibly reflecting national ambivalence about whether women's proper role is domestic or professional: big breasted but narrow hipped.

Biology Meets Culture: The Problem of Eating Disorders

In cultures that value thinness, many women face a painful dilemma. Evolution has programmed them for a reserve of fat necessary for the onset of menstruation, healthy childbearing, nursing, and, after menopause, the production and storage of the hormone estrogen. The result of the battle between biological design and cultural norms is that many women are obsessed with weight and are continually dieting. A significant minority of women (and some men, too) develop serious eating disorders (Walsh & Devlin, 1998).

In **bulimia**, the person binges (eats vast quantities of rich food) and then purges by inducing vomiting or using laxatives. Individuals with bulimia are usually normal in weight, but they are obsessed with their weight and shape. In **anorexia nervosa**, the person eats hardly anything and therefore becomes dangerously thin because of a delusional belief that she or he is "too fat." Bulimia and anorexia are at least ten times more common in women than in men, and these eating disorders are most likely to begin in late adolescence, as girls' bodies are maturing. Although many people with these disorders recover, others damage their health permanently, or, in the case of anorexia, eventually die of self-starvation (Holmes, 1997).

Genetic vulnerabilities may play a role in the development of eating disorders (Allison & Faith, 1997). However, genetic dispositions clearly interact with a person's psychological needs and with cultural pressures for thinness. For example, given the cultural equation between slimness and masculine competence, psychologists predicted that women who value achievement, higher education, and careers—especially male-dominated careers—would be the ones most likely to be obsessed with being boyishly thin (and therefore most vulnerable to developing an eating disorder). Being thin allows them to identify with male competence and to distance themselves from female "softness." And that is just what research finds (Silverstein & Perlick, 1995).

College women who develop eating disorders are also often caught between their own desires to achieve and their parents' messages about "women's place"; for them, the body becomes a battleground to resolve this conflict. They are more likely than other women to say that their parents believe a woman's place is in the home, that their mothers are unhappy with their lives, that their fathers think their mothers are unintelligent, and that their fathers treat sons as being more intelligent than daughters (Silverstein & Perlick, 1995). Perhaps this is why women who develop eating disorders tend to be depressed and more self-critical than healthy eaters (Lehman & Rodin, 1989; Walsh & Devlin, 1998).

Findings on eating, weight, and eating disorders contain a lesson that applies to many other areas of behavior: Within a given environment, genes interact with cultural rules, psychological needs, and personal habits to shape—sometimes quite literally—who we are. In "Taking Psychology with You," we offer some suggestions on what you can do to maintain your healthiest personal weight while recognizing the limitations imposed by genetics.

QUICK QUIZ

Is all this information about eating making you hungry for knowledge?

1. *True or false:* Emotional problems explain why fat people are heavy.

2. Falling and rising levels of leptin help the brain regulate _____ and metabolism in order to maintain a person's genetically influenced _____ .

3. Rising rates of obesity can best be explained by (a) genetic changes over the past few decades, (b) a lack of will power, (c) an abundance of high-fat food and sedentary lifestyles, (d) the increase in eating disorders.

4. Bill, who is thin, reads in the newspaper that genes set the range of body weight and shape. "Oh, good," he exclaims, "now I can eat all the junk food I want; I was born to be skinny." What's wrong with Bill's conclusion?

Answers:

1. false   2. appetite, set point   3. c   4. Bill is right to recognize that there may be limits to how heavy he can become. But he may also be oversimplifying and jumping to conclusions. Even people who have a set point for leanness will gain some weight on fatty foods and excess calories, especially if they don't exercise; also, rich junk food is unhealthy for reasons that have nothing to do with overweight.

WHAT'S AHEAD

- To what extent is intelligence heritable?
- What error do many people make when arguing that one group is "genetically superior" to another in IQ?
- What sorts of environmental "nutrients" nurture mental ability?

OUR HUMAN DIVERSITY: ORIGINS OF INTELLIGENCE

Most people think that differences in body weight are due entirely to psychological factors, but, as we just saw, heredity is also involved. In contrast, many people think that variations in intelligence are due entirely to heredity, but, as we are about to see, psychology is also very much involved. Likewise, many people think that weight is easier to change than it is—and that IQ is harder to change than it is. In this section, we consider how biology and learning affect intelligence, just as they affect weight.

Genes and Individual Differences

In heritability studies, the usual measure of intellectual functioning is an **intelligence quotient,** or **IQ** score. Scores on an IQ test reflect how a child has performed compared with other children of the same age, or how an adult has performed compared with other adults. The average score for each age group is arbitrarily set at 100. The distribution of scores in the population approximates a normal bell-shaped curve, with scores near the average (mean) most common and very high or very low scores rare. Two-thirds of all test-takers score between 85 and 115.

Most psychologists believe that IQ tests measure a general quality that affects all aspects of mental ability, but the tests have many critics. Some argue that intelligence

intelligence quotient (IQ) A measure of intelligence originally computed by dividing a person's mental age by his or her chronological age and multiplying the result by 100; it is now derived from norms provided for standardized intelligence tests.

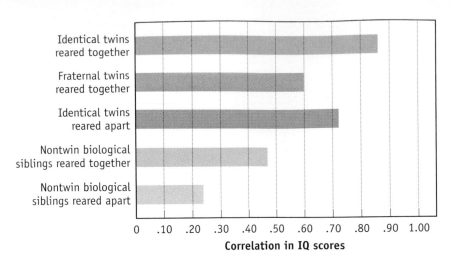

FIGURE 3.3

CORRELATIONS IN SIBLINGS' IQ SCORES

The IQ scores of identical twins are highly correlated, even when they are reared apart. The figures represented in this graph are based on average correlations across many studies (Bouchard & McGue, 1981).

comes in many varieties, more than are captured by the IQ score. Others argue that IQ tests are culturally biased, and that heritability estimates are biased because they are usually based on the scores of white people living in middle-class environments. We discuss the measurement of intelligence and debates surrounding this concept more fully in Chapter 9. For now, keep in mind that most heritability estimates apply only to those mental skills that affect IQ test scores, and that these estimates are likely to be more valid for some groups than for others.

Nonetheless, it is clear that the kind of intelligence that produces high IQ scores is highly heritable. For children and adolescents, heritability estimates average around .50; that is, about half of the variance in IQ scores is explainable by genetic differences (Chipuer, Rovine, & Plomin, 1990; Devlin, Daniels, & Roeder, 1997; Plomin, 1989). For adults, the estimates are higher—in the .60 to .80 range (Bouchard, 1995; McGue et al., 1993; McClearn et al., 1997).

In studies of twins, the scores of identical twins are always much more highly correlated than those of fraternal twins, a difference that reflects the influence of genes. In fact, the scores of identical twins reared *apart* are more highly correlated than those of fraternal twins reared *together*, as you can see in Figure 3.3. In adoption studies, the scores of adopted children are more highly correlated with those of their birth parents than with those of their biologically unrelated adoptive parents; the higher the birth parents' scores, the higher the child's score is likely to be. As adopted children grow into adolescence, the correlation between their IQ scores and those of their biologically unrelated family members diminishes; and in adulthood, the correlation falls to *zero* (Bouchard, 1997b; Scarr, 1993; Scarr & Weinberg, 1994).

Recently, a research team led by psychologist Robert Plomin identified the first marker for a gene that might influence performance on IQ tests (Chorney et al., 1998). DNA analysis showed that one form of the gene occurred twice as often in a group of children whose scores averaged 136 than in a group whose scores averaged 103, and a similar difference occurred when groups averaging 160 and 101 were compared. But the gene accounted for less than 2 percent of the variance among individuals, which translates to about 4 IQ points. No one knows yet how the gene might exert this small influence, or what other genes might be involved in IQ performance, and the basic finding still has to be replicated.

Overall, the research on the heritability of IQ-test performance is pretty impressive. But remember: If heredity accounts for only part of why people differ in their IQ scores, then the environment (and random errors in measurement) must account for the rest.

The Question of Group Differences

If genes influence individual differences in intelligence, do they also help account for differences between groups, as many people assume? Unfortunately, the history of this issue has been marred by ethnic, class, and gender prejudice. As Stephen Jay Gould (1981/1996) noted, genetic research has often been bent to support the belief that some groups are destined by "the harsh dictates of nature" to be subordinate to others. Because this issue has enormous political and social importance, we are going to examine it closely.

Most of the focus has been on black–white differences in IQ, because African-American children score, on average, some 10 to 15 points lower than do white children. (We are talking about *averages*; the distributions of scores for black children and white children overlap considerably.) A few psychologists have proposed a genetic explanation of this difference (Jensen, 1969, 1981; Rushton, 1988). In their much-discussed book *The Bell Curve: Intelligence and Class Structure in American Life* (1994), the late psychologist Richard Herrnstein and conservative political theorist Charles Murray cited heritability studies to imply that the gap in IQ scores between the average white and the average black child can never be closed.

You can see why heritability research provokes much more controversy than does research on, say, the sex lives of sea lions. Racists have used theories of genetic differences between groups to justify their own hatreds, and politicians have used them to argue for cuts in programs that would benefit blacks and other minorities. Herrnstein and Murray themselves concluded that there was little point in spending money trying to raise the IQs of low-scoring children.

Genetic explanations, however, have a fatal flaw: They use heritability estimates based mainly on white samples to estimate the role of heredity in *group* differences, a procedure that is not valid. This problem sounds pretty technical, but it is not really too difficult to understand, so stay with us.

Consider, first, not people but tomatoes. (Figure 3.4 will help you visualize the following mental experiment.) Suppose you have a bag of tomato seeds that vary genetically; all things being equal, some will produce tomatoes that are puny and tasteless, and some will produce tomatoes that are plump and delicious. Now you take a bunch of these seeds in your left hand and another bunch from the same bag in your right hand. Though one seed differs genetically from another, there is no *average* difference between the seeds in your left hand and those in your right. You plant the left hand's seeds in pot A, with some enriched soil that you have doctored with nitrogen and other nutrients, and you plant the right hand's seeds in pot B, with miserable, depleted soil from which you have extracted nutrients. You sing to pot A and put it in the sun; you ignore pot B and leave it in a dark corner.

When the tomato plants grow, they will vary *within* each pot in terms of height, the number of tomatoes produced, and the size of the tomatoes, purely because of genetic differences. But there will also be an average difference between the plants in pot A and those in pot B: The plants in pot A will be healthier and bear more tomatoes. This difference *between* pots is due entirely to the different soils and the care that's been given to them—even though the heritability of the *within*-pot differences is 100 percent (Lewontin, 1970).

The principle is the same for people as it is for tomatoes. Although intellectual differences *within* groups are at least partly genetic in origin, that does not mean differences *between* groups are genetic. Blacks and whites do not grow up, on the average, in the same "pots" (environments). Because of a long legacy of racial discrimination and de facto segregation, black children (as well as Latino and other minority children) often receive far fewer nutrients—literally, in terms of food, and figuratively, in terms of education, encouragement by society, and intellectual opportunities. Ethnic groups also differ in countless cultural ways that affect their performance on IQ tests (see Chapter 9).

Doing good research on the origins of group differences in IQ is extremely difficult in the United States, where racism affects the lives of even affluent, successful African-Americans (Cose, 1994; Parker, 1997; Staples, 1994). However, the handful of studies that have overcome past methodological problems fail to reveal any

EXAMINE ASSUMPTIONS

Behavioral-genetics studies, on the average, show the heritability of intelligence to be high. A popular book argues that heredity must play a similarly large role in average IQ differences between ethnic groups. What's wrong with the assumption behind that reasoning?

FIGURE 3.4

THE TOMATO PLANT EXPERIMENT

In the hypothetical experiment described in the text, even if the differences among plants within each pot were due entirely to genetics, the average differences *between* pots could be environmental. The same general principle applies to individual and group differences among human beings.

genetic differences between blacks and whites in whatever it is that IQ tests measure (Flynn, 1999). For example:

■ Children fathered by black and white American soldiers in Germany after World War II and reared in similar German communities by similar families did not differ significantly in IQ (Eyferth, 1961).

■ Degree of African ancestry (which can be roughly estimated from skin color, blood analysis, and genealogy) is not related to measured intelligence, as a genetic theory of black–white differences would predict (Scarr et al., 1977).

■ When white and black infants are given a test that measures their preference for novel stimuli, a predictor of later IQ scores, they do equally well (Fagan, 1992).

An intelligent reading of the research on intelligence, therefore, does not direct us to conclude that differences among cultural, ethnic, or national groups are permanent, genetically determined, or signs of any group's innate superiority. On the contrary, the research suggests that we should make sure that all children grow up in the best possible soil, with room for the smartest and the slowest to find a place in the sun.

The Environment and Intelligence

By now you may be wondering what kinds of experiences hinder intellectual development and what kinds of environmental "nutrients" promote it. Here are some of the influences associated with reduced mental ability:

■ *Poor prenatal care.* If a pregnant woman is malnourished, contracts infections, takes certain drugs, smokes, drinks excessively, or is heavily exposed to pollutants, her child is at risk of having learning disabilities and a lower IQ.

■ *Malnutrition.* The average IQ gap between severely malnourished and well-nourished children can be as high as 20 points (Stoch & Smythe, 1963; Winick, Meyer, & Harris, 1975).

■ *Exposure to toxins.* Lead, for example, can damage the nervous system, producing attention problems, lower IQ scores, and poorer school achievement (Needleman et al., 1996). Nearly 9 percent of all children in the United States ages 1 to 5 are exposed to dangerous levels of lead from lead paint and old lead pipes, and for black children ages 1 and 2, the percentage rises to 21.6 (Brody et al., 1994).

■ *Large family size.* The average IQ in a family tends to decline as the number of children rises (Belmont & Marolla, 1973). Birth order also makes a difference: IQ tends to decline slightly in each successive child (Zajonc & Markus, 1975). The reason seems to be that the more children parents have, the less time they can spend with each one.

■ *Stressful family circumstances.* Factors that predict reduced intellectual competence include a father who does not live with the family, a mother with a history of mental illness, limited parental work skills, and a history of stressful events during the child's early life (Sameroff et al., 1987). On average, each risk factor reduces a child's IQ score by 4 points. Children with no risk factors score more than *30 points higher* than those with seven risk factors.

The children of migrant workers (left) often spend long hours in backbreaking field work and may miss out on the educational opportunities and intellectual advantages available to middle-class children (right).

In contrast, a healthy and stimulating environment can raise mental performance, sometimes dramatically (Guralnick, 1997; Ramey & Ramey, 1998). In one longitudinal study called the Abecedarian Project, inner-city children who got lots of mental enrichment at home and in childcare or school, starting in infancy, had higher IQs and much better school achievement throughout childhood than did children in a control group (Campbell & Ramey, 1994, 1995). (In Chapter 9 we discuss specific ways that parents and teachers can affect children's mental development.)

Perhaps the best evidence for the importance of environmental influences on intelligence is the fact that IQ scores in developed countries have been climbing steadily for at least three generations (Flynn, 1987, 1999) (see Figure 3.5). Just as "obesity genes" cannot possibly have changed enough to account for increases in obesity, "intelligence genes" cannot possibly have changed enough to account for this rise in IQ scores. The causes are still being debated; suggested explanations have included improvements in education, urbanization, an increasing emphasis on skills required by technology, and better nutrition (Neisser, 1998).

In sum, although heredity may provide the range of a child's intellectual potential—a Forrest Gump can't ever become an Einstein—many other factors affect where in that range the child will fall.

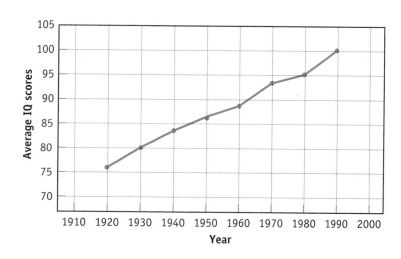

FIGURE 3.5

CLIMBING IQ SCORES

Raw scores on IQ tests have been rising in developed countries for many decades, at a rate much too steep to be accounted for by genetic changes. Because test norms are periodically readjusted to set the average score at 100, most people are unaware of the increase. On this graph, average scores are calibrated according to 1989 norms. As you can see, performance was much lower in 1918 than in 1989. (Adapted from Horgan, 1995.)

QUICK QUIZ

Are you thinking intelligently about intelligence?

1. On average, behavioral-genetics studies estimate the heritability of intelligence to be (a) about .90, (b) low at all ages, (c) about .50 for children and adolescents.

2. *True or false:* If a trait such as intelligence is highly heritable within a group, then differences between groups must also be due mainly to heredity.

3. The available evidence (does/does not) show that ethnic differences in average IQ scores are due to genetic differences.

4. Name five environmental factors associated with reduced mental ability.

Answers:

1. c 2. false 3. does not 4. poor prenatal care, malnutrition, exposure to toxins, large family size, stressful family circumstances

IN PRAISE OF HUMAN VARIATION

This chapter opened with two questions: What makes us alike as human beings, and why do we differ? Today, a prevalent, but greatly oversimplified, answer is: It's all in our genes. You either "have" a gene for smartness, musical ability, math genius, friendliness, or any other trait, or you don't. When researchers announced that they might have found a gene involved in mouse intelligence, *Time* magazine lost no time in putting the news on its cover, with the headline "The IQ gene?" (September 13, 1999). In this climate, many people who believe in the importance of learning, opportunities, and experience feel that they must take an equally oversimplified position: Genes don't matter much at all; it's all in our environments.

As we have seen, however, heredity and environment always interact to produce the unique mixture of qualities that make up a human being. And once genetic and environmental influences become a part of us, they blend and become indistinguishable. We can no more speak of genes, or of the environment, "causing" personality or intelligence than we can speak of butter, sugar, or flour individually causing the taste of a cake (Lewontin, Rose, & Kamin, 1984). Many people do speak that way, however, out of a desire to make things clearer than they actually are, and sometimes to justify prejudices about culture, ethnicity, gender, or class.

An unstated assumption in many debates about nature and nurture is that the world would be a better place if certain kinds of genes prevailed. This assumption overlooks the fact that Nature loves genetic diversity, not similarity. The ability of any species to survive depends on such diversity. If every penguin, porpoise, or person had exactly the same genetic strengths and weaknesses, these species could not survive changes in the environment—a new virus, or a change in weather, would wipe out the entire group. With diversity, at least some penguins, porpoises, or people have a good chance of making it.

When we see the world through an evolutionary lens, we realize that psychological diversity is adaptive, too. Each of us has something valuable to contribute, whether it is artistic talent, academic ability, creativity, social skill, athletic prowess, a sense of humor, mechanical aptitude, practical wisdom, a social conscience, or the energy to get things done. In our complicated, fast-moving world, all of these qualities are needed. The challenge, for any society, is to promote the potential of each of its members.

THINKING CRITICALLY

TOLERATE UNCERTAINTY

Many people would like to specify precisely how much genes and the environment independently contribute to human qualities. But is this goal achievable? Is a human being like a jigsaw puzzle, made up of separate components, or more like a cake, with blended ingredients that interact to produce its unique taste?

TAKING PSYCHOLOGY WITH YOU

HOW TO LOSE WEIGHT—AND WHETHER YOU SHOULD

While many normal-weight women are dieting because they want to achieve the cultural ideal of slimness, many seriously overweight men and women are trying to lose weight for the sake of their health. Health professionals are worried about the increasing rates of obesity in many industrialized nations, because obesity is associated with a higher risk of heart disease, stroke, hypertension, diabetes, some cancers, and other problems. Should seriously overweight people try to fight their set points, or should they instead fight society's prejudices? Does the genetic research mean that trying to lose weight is hopeless?

Physicians and psychologists disagree about the best course of action for overweight people. Some believe that dieting is unhealthy and may even contribute to medical problems and eating disorders (Garner & Wooley, 1991). Others believe that weight loss can help reduce the health risks associated with overweight; they note that even modest losses have medical benefits, such as lowered blood pressure and reduced risk of diabetes (Brownell & Rodin, 1994).

So what is an overweight person to do? Research offers some suggestions:

■ *Be realistic about your need to diet.* Dieting and a 10 percent reduction in weight may be of benefit to an obese older man with high blood pressure but unhealthy for a girl who is going through the normal changes of puberty and thinks she is fat (Brownell & Rodin, 1994).

■ *Avoid fad diets* that restrict you to only a few foods or put you on starvation rations. People on these diets often become obsessed with food, get depressed and anxious when they slip off the diet, and ultimately binge, which restores the lost weight—plus some. It is far better to permanently alter your eating habits by reducing fat intake and eating more grains, fruits, and vegetables.

■ *Get more exercise,* which may raise your metabolic rate and which, when combined with a low-fat diet, is associated with more weight loss than dieting alone (Foreyt et al., 1993). You do not have to become a marathon runner, but you can increase your activity level—for example, by walking instead of driving to work or school.

■ *Avoid yo-yo dieting,* in which you repeatedly lose and gain weight. Yo-yo dieting is linked to a higher-than-normal risk of cardiovascular disease, hypertension, and other chronic diseases (Brownell & Rodin, 1994).

■ *Find ways to nurture and reward yourself other than eating.* When you are feeling tired or blue, instead of heading for the refrigerator, try a soothing bath, a nice massage, a day off, or your favorite music.

■ *Avoid amphetamines and other diet pills,* which can be far more dangerous to your health than a few pounds and can become addictive. Diet pills raise the metabolic rate only as long as you take them. When you stop taking them, the pounds return.

■ *Seek treatment if you have an eating disorder.* If you are mistakenly trying to control weight by frequent vomiting and abuse of laxatives, or by starving yourself, you can break this harmful pattern by joining an eating-disorders program; school counselors and health clinics can direct you to suitable programs.

Remember that the biological disposition to gain weight varies from person to person, and that even with exercise, genetic factors limit how much you can change. Think carefully and critically about the reasons you are dieting. Are you truly overweight? Are you trying to look like a real person or like a magazine model? Whose standards are you following, and why?

SUMMARY

UNLOCKING THE SECRETS OF GENES

1. Genes can help us understand the qualities that unite human beings as a species and the qualities that differentiate us as individuals. However, all scientists understand that heredity and environment interact to produce our psychological traits and even most physical ones.

2. *Genes,* the basic units of heredity, are located on *chromosomes,* which consist of strands of *DNA.* Within each gene, a sequence of four elements of DNA constitutes a chemical code that helps determine the synthesis of a particular protein. In turn, proteins affect virtually all the structural and biochemical characteristics of the organism.

3. Most human traits depend on more than one gene pair, which makes tracking down the genetic contributions to

a trait extremely difficult. One method for doing so involves the use of *linkage studies*.

THE GENETICS OF SIMILARITY

4. *Evolutionary psychologists* believe that the mind is not a general-purpose computer but instead evolved as a collection of specialized mental modules to handle specific survival problems. They argue that many fundamental human similarities can be traced to the evolutionary workings of *natural selection*, including inborn reflexes, an attraction to novelty, a motive to explore and manipulate objects, an impulse to play, and the capacity for simple arithmetic operations.

OUR HUMAN HERITAGE: LANGUAGE

5. Human beings are the only species that uses language to express and comprehend an infinite number of novel utterances. Noam Chomsky argued that the ability to take the *surface structure* of any utterance and apply rules of *syntax* to infer its underlying *deep structure* must depend on an innate faculty for language, a *language acquisition device*. Many findings support this view: Children from different cultures go through similar stages of language development; children's language is full of *overregularizations* reflecting grammatical rules; adults do not consistently correct their children's syntax; even profoundly retarded children usually acquire language; and young infants can derive linguistic rules from strings of sounds. An innate capacity for language may have evolved in humans because it enhanced the chances of survival.

6. Some scientists, however, have devised models of language acquisition that do not assume an innate capacity. Moreover, it seems clear that parental practices, such as repeating correct sentences verbatim and recasting incorrect ones, aid in language acquisition. Biological readiness and experience probably interact in the development of language. Whatever the mechanism, case studies of children deprived of exposure to language suggest that a *critical period* exists for acquiring a first language.

OUR HUMAN HERITAGE: COURTSHIP AND MATING

7. *Sociobiologists* and evolutionary psychologists argue that males and females have evolved different sexual and courtship strategies in response to survival problems faced in the distant past. In this view, it has been adaptive for males to be promiscuous, to be attracted to young partners, and to want sexual novelty, and for females to be monogamous, to be choosy about partners, and to prefer security to novelty.

8. Cross-cultural studies support some evolutionary predictions about courtship and mating, but critics argue that human sexual behavior is too varied and changeable to fit a single evolutionary explanation, and many take exception to the entire line of evolutionary reasoning.

THE GENETICS OF DIFFERENCE

9. *Behavioral geneticists* study differences among individuals, often by using studies of twins and adopted children to estimate the *heritability* of traits and abilities—the extent to which differences in a trait or ability within a group of individuals are accounted for by genetic differences.

10. Heritability estimates do not apply to specific individuals or to differences between groups; they apply only to differences within a particular group living in a particular environment. Even highly heritable traits can often be modified by the environment.

OUR HUMAN DIVERSITY: BODY WEIGHT AND SHAPE

11. Genetic research is altering our understanding of body weight and shape. Genes influence body shape, distribution of fat, and whether the body will convert excess calories into fat. According to *set-point theory*, hunger, weight, and eating are regulated by a complex set of bodily mechanisms that keep people within a genetically influenced weight range. For example, rising and falling levels of *leptin* enable the brain to regulate appetite and metabolism. Some obese people have low levels of, or are insensitive to, leptin, although most are probably affected more by other factors.

12. Weight is also influenced by cultural notions of the ideal body, eating habits, and exercise, which may raise metabolism and lower a person's set point. Despite widespread dieting, people in many countries are becoming heavier on the average, because of high-fat diets and sedentary lifestyles.

13. Genetic predispositions and cultural and psychological needs interact to cause eating disorders such as *anorexia* and *bulimia*. These disorders are far more common in women than in men. They are often associated with a desire for a boyish body and a conflict between the desire to achieve and parental messages about "women's place."

OUR HUMAN DIVERSITY: ORIGINS OF INTELLIGENCE

14. Heritability estimates for intelligence (as measured by IQ tests) average about .50 for children and adolescents and .60 to .80 for adults. Identical twins are more similar in IQ-test performance than are fraternal twins, and adopted children's scores correlate more highly with those of their biological parents than with those of their nonbiological relatives. These results do not mean that genes determine

intelligence; the remaining variance in IQ scores must be due largely to environmental influences.

15. It is not valid to draw conclusions about *group* differences from heritability estimates based on differences *within* a group. The available evidence fails to support genetic explanations of ethnic differences in performance on IQ tests.

16. Environmental factors such as poor prenatal care, malnutrition, exposure to toxins, large family size, and stressful family circumstances are associated with lower performance on intelligence tests; and a healthy and stimulating environment can raise performance.

IN PRAISE OF HUMAN VARIATION

17. Neither nature nor nurture can entirely explain people's similarities or differences. Genetic and environmental influences blend and become indistinguishable in the development of any individual.

KEY TERMS

genes 66

chromosomes 66

DNA (deoxyribonucleic acid) 66

genome 66

linkage studies 66

genetic markers 66

evolutionary psychology 68

evolution 68

mutate 68

natural selection 68

Charles Darwin 68

language 72

surface structure/deep structure 73

syntax 73

language acquisition device 73

psycholinguists 73

universal grammar 74

overregularizations 74

neural networks 75

critical period (for language acquisition) 76

sociobiology 77

behavioral genetics 81

heritability 81

identical (monozygotic) twins 82

fraternal (dizygotic) twins 82

set point 84

leptin 85

bulimia 88

anorexia nervosa 88

intelligence quotient (IQ) 89

LOOKING BACK

- What does the chemical code in our genes encode *for*? (p. 66)

- What will a completed map of the human genes reveal— and not reveal? (p. 67)

- During evolution, why do some traits become more common and others less common? (p. 69)

- In the evolutionary view, why is the capacity to read faces innate, but not the capacity to read books? (p. 70)

- Why do so many people ignore signs saying "Don't touch"? (p. 71)

- What does language allow us to do that other animals can't? (p. 72)

- What evidence suggests that evolution has equipped infants' brains with a module for acquiring language? (p. 74)

- How do parents help children acquire language? (p. 76)

- How do evolutionary psychologists explain male–female differences in courtship and sexuality? (pp. 77–78)

- What basic issue divides evolutionary psychologists and their critics? (p. 80)

- If you have a highly heritable trait, does that mean you are stuck with it forever? (p. 82)

- What kinds of studies allow psychologists to estimate a trait's heritability? (pp. 82–83)

- Is overweight usually a result of psychological problems? (p. 84)

- What genetic theory can help explain why you are thin or heavy? (pp. 84–85)

- Why are Americans and people in many other countries getting fatter? (p. 86)

- Why are bright, academically motivated college women most vulnerable to eating disorders? (p. 88)

- To what extent is intelligence heritable? (p. 90)

- What error do many people make when arguing that one group is "genetically superior" to another in IQ? (p. 91)

- What sorts of environmental "nutrients" nurture mental ability? (pp. 92–93)

4 NEURONS, HORMONES, AND THE BRAIN

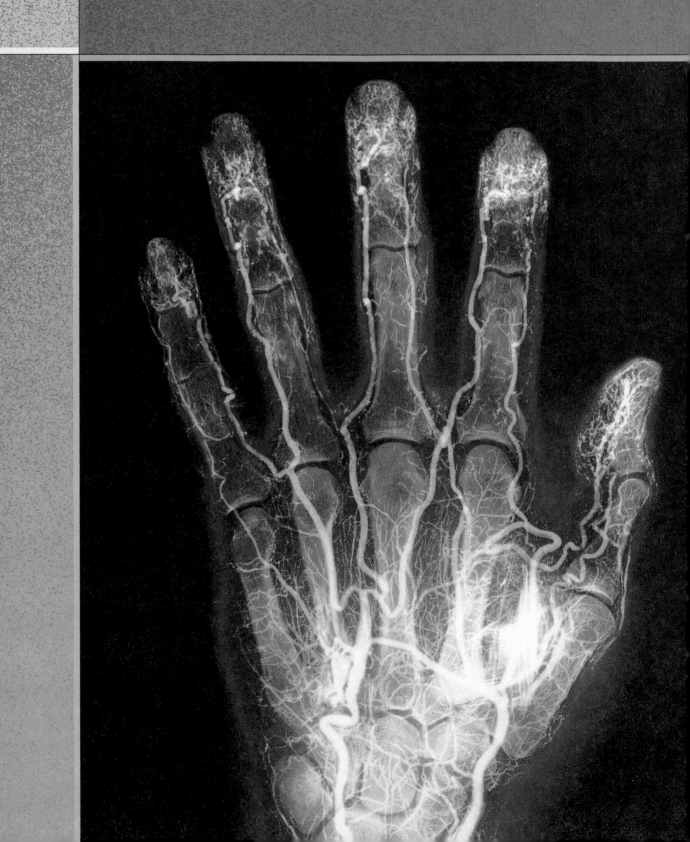

It's amazing to think that the body feeds the brain sugar and amino acids, and what comes out is poetry and pirouettes.

NEUROLOGIST ROBERT COLLINS

Emily D., a former English teacher and poet, had a tumor in a part of the brain that processes the expressive qualities of speech, such as rhythm and intonation. Although she could understand words and sentences perfectly well, she could not tell whether a speaker was indignant, cheerful, or dejected unless she carefully analyzed the person's facial expressions and gestures. Emily D.'s brain damage had left her entirely deaf to the emotional nuances of speech, the variations of tone and cadence that can move a listener to laughter, tears, or outrage. But she had one skill that many people lack. Because she could not be swayed by verbal theatrics or tone of voice, she could easily spot a liar.

Dr. P., a cultured and charming musician of great repute, suffered damage in a part of the brain that handles visualization. Although his vision remained sharp and his reasoning abilities keen, he could no longer recognize people or objects, or even dream in visual images. He would pat the heads of water hydrants and parking meters, thinking they were children, or chat with pieces of furniture and wonder why they did not reply. He could spot a pin on the floor but did not know his own face in the mirror. Once, when looking around for his hat, he thought his wife's head was the hat and tried to lift it off. Neurologist Oliver Sacks (1985), who studied Dr. P., came to call him "the man who mistook his wife for a hat."

These two fascinating cases, reported by Sacks, show us that the brain is the bedrock of behavior. Neuropsychologists, along with neuroscientists from other disciplines, excavate the bedrock by analyzing the brain and the rest of the nervous system. Among their many interests are the biological foundations of consciousness (Chapter 5), perception (Chapter 6), memory (Chapter 10), emotion (Chapter 11), stress (Chapter 15), and mental disorders (Chapter 16). In this chapter, we will examine the structure of the brain and the rest of the nervous system as background for our later discussions.

At this very moment, your own brain, assisted by other parts of your nervous system, is busily taking in these words. Whether you are excited, curious, or bored, your brain is registering some sort of emotional reaction. As you continue reading, your brain will (we hope) store away much of the information in this chapter. Later your brain may enable you to smell a flower, climb the stairs, greet a friend, solve a personal problem, or chuckle at a joke. But the brain's most startling accomplishment is its knowledge that it is doing all these things. This self-awareness makes brain research different from the study of anything else in the universe. Scientists must use the cells, biochemistry, and

The mysterious brain.

circuitry of their own brains to understand the cells, biochemistry, and circuitry of brains in general.

Because the brain is the site of consciousness, people disagree about what language to use in describing it. If we say that "your brain" stores events or registers emotions, we imply a separate "you" that is "using" that brain. But if we leave "you" out of the picture and just say "the brain" does these things, we risk implying that brain mechanisms alone explain behavior (which is untrue), and we lose sight of the person. No one has ever resolved this dilemma to everyone's satisfaction.

William Shakespeare called the brain "the soul's frail dwelling house." Actually, this miraculous organ is more like the main room in a house filled with many alcoves and passageways—the "house" being the nervous system as a whole. Before we can understand the windows, walls, and furniture of this house, we need to become acquainted with the overall floor plan. It's a pretty technical plan, which means that you will be learning many new terms, but you will need to know these terms in order to understand how biological psychologists go about explaining psychological topics.

WHAT'S AHEAD

- Why do you automatically pull your hand away from something hot, "without thinking"?
- Is it possible to consciously control your heartbeat or blood pressure?
- If you have to deal with a sudden emergency, which part of your nervous system whirls into action?

THE NERVOUS SYSTEM: A BASIC BLUEPRINT

The function of a nervous system is to gather and process information, produce responses to stimuli, and coordinate the workings of different cells. Even the lowly jellyfish and the humble worm have the beginnings of such a system. In very simple organisms that do little more than move, eat, and eliminate wastes, the "system" may be no more than one or two nerve cells. In human beings, who do such complex things as dance, cook, and take psychology courses, the nervous system contains billions of cells. Scientists divide this intricate network into two main parts—the central nervous system and the peripheral (outlying) nervous system (see Figure 4.1).

The Central Nervous System

The **central nervous system (CNS)** receives, processes, interprets, and stores incoming sensory information—information about tastes, sounds, smells, color, pressure on the skin, the state of internal organs, and so forth. It also sends out messages destined for muscles, glands, and internal organs. The CNS is usually conceptualized as having two components: the brain, which we will consider in detail later, and the spinal cord. The spinal cord is actually an extension of the brain. It runs from the base of the brain down the center of the back, protected by a column of bones (the spinal column), and it acts as a bridge between the brain and the parts of the body below the neck.

The spinal cord produces some behaviors on its own, without any help from the brain. These *spinal reflexes* are automatic, requiring no conscious effort. For example, if you accidentally touch a hot iron, you will immediately pull your hand away, even before the brain has had a chance to register what has happened. Nerve impulses bring a message to the spinal cord (hot!), and the spinal cord immediately sends out a command via other nerve impulses, telling muscles in your arm to contract and to pull your hand away from the iron. (Reflexes above the neck, such as sneezing and blinking, involve the lower part of the brain, rather than the spinal cord.)

central nervous system (CNS) The portion of the nervous system consisting of the brain and spinal cord.

spinal cord A collection of neurons and supportive tissue running from the base of the brain down the center of the back, protected by a column of bones (the spinal column).

The neural circuits underlying many spinal reflexes are linked to other neural pathways that run up and down the spinal cord, to and from the brain. Because of these connections, reflexes can sometimes be influenced by thoughts and emotions. An example is erection in men, a spinal reflex that can be inhibited by anxiety or distracting thoughts, and initiated by erotic thoughts. Some reflexes can be brought under conscious control. If you concentrate, you may be able to keep your knee from jerking when it is tapped, as it normally would. Similarly, most men can learn to voluntarily delay ejaculation, another spinal reflex.

The Peripheral Nervous System

The peripheral nervous system (PNS) handles the central nervous system's input and output. It contains all portions of the nervous system outside the brain and spinal cord, right down to nerves in the tips of the fingers and toes. A brain that could not collect information about the world by means of a peripheral nervous system would be like a radio without a receiver. In the peripheral nervous system, *sensory nerves* carry messages from special receptors in the skin, muscles, and other internal and external sense organs to the spinal cord, which sends them along to the brain. These nerves put us in touch with both the outside world and the activities of our own bodies. *Motor nerves* carry orders from the central nervous system to muscles, glands, and internal organs. They enable us to move our bodies, and they cause glands to contract and to secrete substances, including chemical messengers called *hormones.*

Scientists further divide the peripheral nervous system into two parts: the somatic (bodily) nervous system and the autonomic (self-governing) nervous system. The somatic nervous system, sometimes called the *skeletal nervous system*, consists of nerves that are connected to sensory receptors and to the skeletal muscles that permit voluntary action. When you sense the world around you, or when you turn off a light or write your name, your somatic system is active. The autonomic nervous system regulates the functioning of blood vessels, glands, and internal (visceral) organs such as the bladder, stomach, and heart. When you see someone you have a crush on, and your heart starts to pound, your hands get sweaty, and your cheeks feel hot, you can blame your autonomic nervous system.

The autonomic nervous system works more or less automatically, without a person's conscious control. However, some people can learn to heighten or suppress their autonomic responses intentionally. In India, some yogis can slow their heartbeats and metabolisms so dramatically that they can survive in a sealed booth long after most of us would have died of suffocation. During the 1960s and 1970s, Neal Miller and his colleagues showed that many other people can also learn to control their visceral responses, by taking advantage of a technique called **biofeedback** (Miller, 1978).

In biofeedback, monitoring devices track the bodily process in question and produce a signal, such as a light or a tone, whenever a person makes the desired response. The person may either use a prearranged method to produce the desired response or simply try to increase the signal's frequency in any way that he or she chooses. Using biofeedback, some people have learned to control such autonomic responses as blood pressure, blood flow, heart rate, and skin temperature. Some clinicians are therefore using biofeedback training to treat high blood pressure, asthma, and migraine headaches,

peripheral nervous system (PNS) All portions of the nervous system outside the brain and spinal cord; it includes sensory and motor nerves.

somatic nervous system The subdivision of the peripheral nervous system that connects to sensory receptors and to skeletal muscles; sometimes called the *skeletal nervous system.*

autonomic nervous system The subdivision of the peripheral nervous system that regulates the internal organs and glands.

biofeedback A method for learning to control bodily functions, including ones usually thought to be involuntary, by attending to feedback from an instrument that monitors the function and signals changes in it.

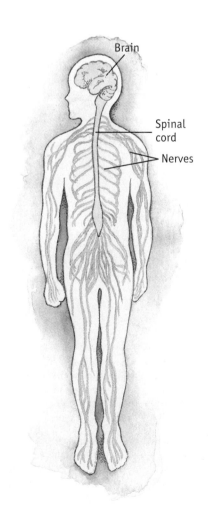

Brain

Spinal cord

Nerves

FIGURE 4.1

THE CENTRAL AND PERIPHERAL NERVOUS SYSTEMS

The central nervous system, shown here in yellow, includes the brain and the spinal cord. The peripheral nervous system, shown in red, consists of 43 pairs of nerves that transmit information to and from the central nervous system. Twelve pairs of cranial nerves in the head enter the brain directly; 31 pairs of spinal nerves enter the spinal cord at the spaces between the vertebrae of the spine.

Some patients with spinal cord injuries lose consciousness when they sit upright because their blood pressure plunges. Here, Neal Miller, a pioneer in biofeedback research, trains a patient to control her blood pressure at will, using biofeedback techniques.

although there is controversy about success rates and about what, exactly, is being controlled—the actual autonomic responses, or responses that can be voluntarily produced, such as breathing, which then in turn affect the autonomic system.

The autonomic nervous system is itself divided into two parts: the **sympathetic nervous system** and the **parasympathetic nervous system**. These two parts work together, but in opposing ways, to adjust the body to changing circumstances (see Figure 4.2). The sympathetic system acts like the accelerator of a car, mobilizing the body for action and an output of energy. It makes you blush, sweat, and breathe more deeply, and it pushes up your heart rate and blood pressure. As we will see in Chapter 15, when you are in a situation that requires you to fight, flee, or cope with stress, the sympathetic nervous system whirls into action. The parasympathetic system is more like a brake. It does not stop the body, but it does tend to slow things down or keep them running smoothly. It enables the body to conserve and store energy. If you have to jump out of the way of a speeding motorcyclist, sympathetic nerves increase your heart rate. Afterward, parasympathetic nerves slow it down again and keep its rhythm regular.

FIGURE 4.2
THE AUTONOMIC NERVOUS SYSTEM

In general, the sympathetic division of the autonomic nervous system prepares the body to expend energy, and the parasympathetic division restores and conserves energy. Sympathetic nerve fibers exit from areas of the spinal cord shown in purple in this illustration; parasympathetic fibers exit from the base of the brain and from spinal cord areas shown in green.

sympathetic nervous system The subdivision of the autonomic nervous system that mobilizes bodily resources and increases the output of energy during emotion and stress.

parasympathetic nervous system The subdivision of the autonomic nervous system that operates during relaxed states and that conserves energy.

Sympathetic Division

Dilates pupils
Weakly stimulates salivation
Stimulates sweat glands
Accelerates heartbeat
Dilates bronchial tubes in lungs
Inhibits digestion
Increases epinephrine,
 norepinephrine secretion
 by adrenal glands
Relaxes bladder wall
Decreases urine volume
Stimulates glucose release by liver
Stimulates ejaculation in males

Parasympathetic Division

Constricts pupils
Stimulates tear glands
Strongly stimulates salivation
Slows heartbeat
Constricts bronchial tubes in lungs
Activates digestion
Inhibits glucose release by liver

Contracts bladder wall
Stimulates genital erection (both
 sexes) and vaginal lubrication
 (females)

QUICK QUIZ

Pause now to test your memory by mentally filling in the missing parts of the nervous system "house."
Then see whether you can briefly describe what each part of the system does.

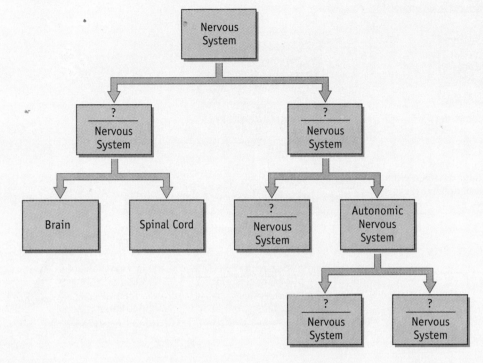

Answers:

Check your answers against Figure 4.3 on the next page. If you had difficulty, or if you could label the parts but forgot what they do, review the preceding section and try again.

Check your answers against Figure 4.3 on the next page.

WHAT'S AHEAD

● **Which cells are the nervous system's "communication specialists," and how do they "talk" to each other?**

● **How do learning and experience alter the brain's circuits?**

● **Why do neural impulses travel more slowly in babies than in adults?**

● **What happens when levels of brain chemicals called neurotransmitters are too low or too high?**

● **What substances in the brain mimic the effects of morphine by dulling pain and promoting pleasure?**

● **Do the sexes have different "sex hormones"?**

COMMUNICATION IN THE NERVOUS SYSTEM

The blueprint we have just described provides only a general idea of the nervous system's structure. Now we turn to the details.

The nervous system is made up in part of **neurons**, or *nerve cells*. These neurons are held in place by **glial cells** (from the Greek for "glue"). Glial cells, which greatly outnumber neurons, also provide the neurons with nutrients, insulate the neurons, and remove cellular debris when the neurons die. Many neuroscientists suspect that

neuron A cell that conducts electrochemical signals; the basic unit of the nervous system; also called a *nerve cell*.

glial cells Nervous-system cells that aid the neurons by providing them with nutrients, insulating them, and removing cellular debris when they die.

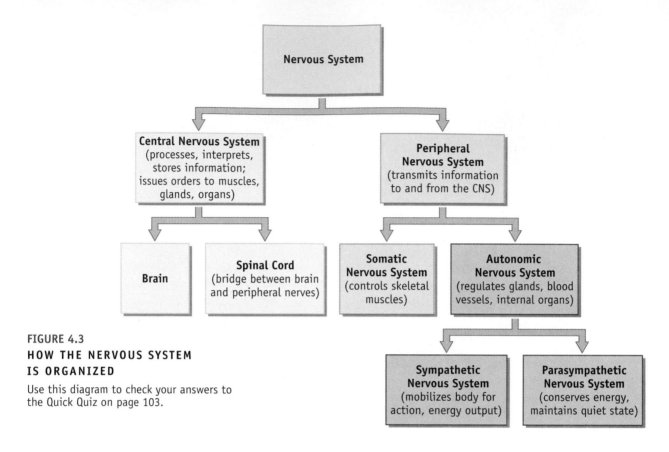

FIGURE 4.3
HOW THE NERVOUS SYSTEM IS ORGANIZED

Use this diagram to check your answers to the Quick Quiz on page 103.

glial cells carry electrical or chemical signals between parts of the nervous system, and that these signals somehow influence the activity of neighboring neurons. It is the neurons, however, that are the communication specialists, transmitting signals to, from, or within the central nervous system.

Although neurons are often called the building blocks of the nervous system, in structure they are more like snowflakes than blocks, exquisitely delicate and differing from one another greatly in size and shape (see Figure 4.4). In the giraffe, a neuron that runs from the spinal cord down the animal's hind leg may be nine feet long! In the human brain, neurons are microscopic. No one is sure how many neurons the human brain contains, but a typical estimate is 100 billion, about the same number as there are stars in our galaxy—and some estimates go much higher.

FIGURE 4.4
DIFFERENT KINDS OF NEURONS

Neurons vary in size and shape, depending on their location and function. More than 200 types of neurons have been identified in mammals.

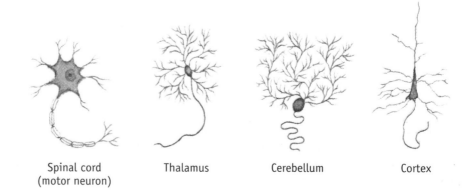

Spinal cord (motor neuron) Thalamus Cerebellum Cortex

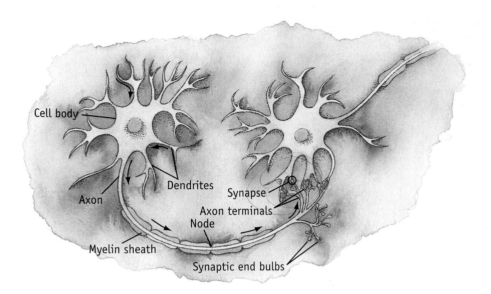

FIGURE 4.5
THE STRUCTURE OF A NEURON
Incoming neural impulses are received by the dendrites of a neuron and are transmitted to the cell body. Outgoing signals pass along the axon to terminal branches.

The Structure of the Neuron

As you can see in Figure 4.5, a neuron has three main parts: *dendrites*, a *cell body*, and an *axon*. The **dendrites** look like the branches of a tree; indeed, the word *dendrite* means "little tree" in Greek. Dendrites act like antennas, receiving messages from as many as 10,000 other nerve cells and transmitting these messages toward the cell body. The **cell body**, which is shaped roughly like a sphere or a pyramid, contains the biochemical machinery for keeping the neuron alive. As we will see later, it also determines whether the neuron should "fire"—that is, transmit a message to other neurons—based on the number of inputs it has received. The **axon** (from the Greek for "axle") transmits messages away from the cell body to other neurons or to muscle or gland cells. Axons commonly divide at the end into branches, called *axon terminals*. In adult human beings, axons vary from only 4 thousandths of an inch to a few feet in length. Dendrites and axons give each neuron a double role: As one researcher put it, a neuron is first a catcher, then a batter (Gazzaniga, 1988).

Many axons, especially the larger ones, are insulated by a surrounding layer of fatty material called the **myelin sheath**, which is derived from glial cells. This covering is divided into segments that make it look a little like a string of link sausages (see Figure 4.5 again). One purpose of the myelin sheath is to prevent signals in adjacent cells from interfering with each other. Another, as we will see shortly, is to speed up the conduction of neural impulses. In individuals with multiple sclerosis, loss of myelin causes erratic nerve signals, leading to loss of sensation, weakness or paralysis, lack of coordination, or vision problems.

In the peripheral nervous system, the fibers of individual neurons (axons and sometimes dendrites) are collected together in bundles called **nerves**, rather like the lines in a telephone cable. The human body has 43 pairs of peripheral nerves; one nerve from each pair is on the left side of the body, and the other is on the right. Most of these nerves enter or leave the spinal cord, but the 12 pairs that are in the head—the *cranial nerves*—connect directly to the brain. In Chapter 6, we will discuss three cranial nerves involved in sensory processing: the *olfactory nerve*, involved in smell; the *auditory nerve*, involved in hearing; and the *optic nerve*, involved in vision.

Until recently, neuroscientists thought that neurons in the central nervous system could not reproduce (multiply) or regenerate (grow back) after being injured. The

dendrites A neuron's branches that receive information from other neurons and transmit it toward the cell body.

cell body The part of the neuron that keeps it alive and determines whether it will fire.

axon A neuron's extending fiber that conducts impulses away from the cell body and transmits them to other neurons.

myelin sheath A fatty insulation that may surround the axon of a neuron.

nerves Bundles of neural fibers (axons and sometimes dendrites) in the peripheral nervous system.

Contrary to what scientists once thought, the brain produces new neurons throughout life. In an area associated with learning and memory, new cells develop from immature "precursor" cells, and physical and mental stimulation promotes their production and survival. These mice, who have toys to play with, tunnels to explore, wheels to run on, and other mice to share their cage with, will grow more cells than mice living in standard cages.

In 1998, in the operation shown here, surgeons attempted for the first time to treat a stroke victim by injecting specially prepared precursor cells into her brain. Scientists will soon learn how effective such experimental treatments are.

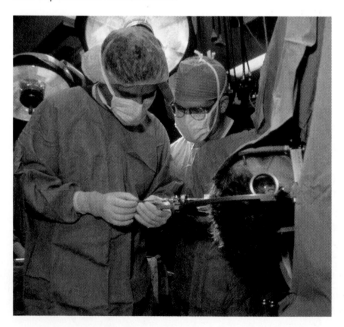

assumption was that no new CNS neurons arose after infancy, and that if cells in the brain or spinal cord were damaged, nothing could be done. But then the conventional wisdom got overthrown. Animal studies showed that severed axons in the spinal cord *can* regrow if you treat them with certain nervous-system chemicals (Schnell & Schwab, 1990). And Canadian neuroscientists working with mice discovered that immature cells, called *precursor cells*, will give birth to new neurons (a process called *neurogenesis*) when immersed in a growth-promoting protein in the laboratory. The new neurons will then continue to divide and multiply (Reynolds & Weiss, 1992). One of the researchers, Samuel Weiss, said that this result was hard to believe at first: "It challenged everything I had read; everything I had learned when I was a student" (quoted in Barinaga, 1992).

Since then, scientists have learned that the human brain also contains precursor cells (sometimes called *progenitor* or *stem cells*), and that these cells, too, give rise to new neurons when treated in the laboratory (Kirschenbaum et al., 1994). Even more astonishing, in rodents and monkeys, precursor cells in an area associated with learning and memory continue to divide and mature throughout adulthood (Gage et al., 1998; Gould et al., 1998). Researchers recently studied the brains of 5 elderly people who had died of cancer and found evidence of the very same process in human beings (Eriksson et al., 1998). Animal studies indicate that we have some control over that process, because physical and mental exercise promote the production and survival of these new cells (Gould et al., 1999; Kempermann, Brandon, & Gage, 1998; van Praag, Kempermann, & Gage, 1999). One of the researchers, psychologist Elizabeth Gould, commented, "It is a classic case of 'use it or lose it'" (quoted in the *Los Angeles Times*, February 23, 1999). On the other hand, stress can inhibit the production of new cells (Gould et al., 1998) and nicotine can kill precursor cells (Berger, Gage, & Vijayarqhavan, 1998).

Each year brings ever more findings that only a short time ago would have seemed like science fiction. Animal research is raising hopes that regenerated axons will someday enable people with spinal-cord injuries to use their limbs again. Researchers also hope that transplanted precursor cells from embryos or adults will someday help people recover from brain damage. The results from animal studies have been encouraging. And in 1998, the first attempt to use such cells in a human being took place: Specially prepared precursor cells extracted from a young man's tumor were implanted into the brain of a woman whose right side had been paralyzed by a stroke (Fackelmann, 1998). Since then, several similar surgeries have been performed. The results are still uncertain, but daring experiments like this one will continue. Eventually, treatments inspired by basic research on neurons may be among the most stunning contributions of biological research.

How Neurons Communicate

Neurons do not directly touch each other, end to end. Instead, they are separated by a minuscule space called the *synaptic cleft*, where the axon terminal of one neuron nearly touches a dendrite or the cell body of another. The entire site—the axon terminal, the cleft, and the covering membrane of the receiving dendrite or cell body—is called a **synapse**. Because a neuron's axon may have hundreds or even thousands of terminals, a single neuron may have synaptic connections with a great many others. As a result, the number of communication links in the nervous system runs into the trillions or perhaps even the quadrillions.

When we are born, most of these synapses have not yet formed. Throughout life, axons and dendrites continue to grow, and tiny bumplike projections on dendrites, called *spines*, increase in both size and number. As a result, synaptic connections among the brain's nerve cells become more complex. Just as new learning and stimulating environments promote the production of new neurons, they also produce the greatest increases in synaptic complexity (Diamond, 1993; Greenough & Anderson, 1991; Greenough & Black, 1992; Rosenzweig, 1984). At the same time, some unused synaptic connections are lost as cells or their branches die and are not replaced. Thus, the brain's circuits are continually changing in response to information, challenges, and changes in the environment. This remarkable *plasticity* (flexibility) helps explain why people with brain damage sometimes experience amazing recoveries—why individuals who cannot recall simple words after a stroke may be speaking normally within a matter of months, and why patients who cannot move an arm after a head injury may regain full use of it after physical therapy. Their brains have rewired themselves to adapt to the damage!

Neurons speak to one another, or in some cases to muscles or glands, in an electrical and chemical language. When a nerve cell is stimulated, a change in electrical potential occurs between the inside and the outside of the cell. The physics of this process involves the sudden, momentary inflow of positively charged sodium ions across the cell's membrane, followed by the outflow of positively charged potassium ions. The result is a brief change in electrical voltage—an *action potential*—which produces an electric current or impulse.

If an axon is unmyelinated, the action potential at each point in the axon gives rise to a new action potential at the next point; thus, the action potential travels down the axon somewhat as fire travels along the fuse of a firecracker. But in myelinated axons, the process is a little different. Conduction of a neural impulse beneath the sheath is impossible, in part because sodium and potassium ions cannot cross the cell's membrane except at the breaks (nodes) between the myelin's "sausages." Instead, the action potential "hops" from one node to the next. (More specifically, positively charged ions flow down the axon at a very fast rate, causing regeneration of the action potential at each node.) This arrangement allows the impulse to travel faster than it could if the action potential had to be regenerated at every point along the axon. Nerve impulses travel more slowly in babies than in older children and adults because when babies are born, the myelin sheaths on their axons are not yet fully developed.

When a neural impulse reaches the axon terminal's buttonlike tip, it must get its message across the synaptic cleft to another cell. At this point, *synaptic vesicles*, tiny sacs in the tip of the axon terminal, open and release a few thousand molecules of a chemical substance called a **neurotransmitter**. Like sailors carrying a message from one island to another, these molecules then diffuse across the synaptic cleft (see Figure 4.6 on the next page).

When they reach the other side, the neurotransmitter molecules bind briefly with *receptor sites*, special molecules in the membrane of the receiving neuron, fitting these sites much as a key fits a lock. Changes occur in the receiving neuron's membrane, and the ultimate effect is either *excitatory* (a voltage shift in a positive direction) or *inhibitory* (a voltage shift in a negative direction), depending on which receptor sites have been activated. If the effect is excitatory, the probability that the receiving neuron will fire increases; if it is inhibitory, the probability decreases. Inhibition in the nervous system is extremely important. Without it, we could not sleep or coordinate our movements. Excitation of the nervous system would be overwhelming, producing convulsions.

synapse The site where a nerve impulse is transmitted from one nerve cell to another; it includes the axon terminal, the synaptic cleft, and receptor sites in the membrane of the receiving cell.

neurotransmitter A chemical substance that is released by a transmitting neuron at the synapse and that alters the activity of a receiving neuron.

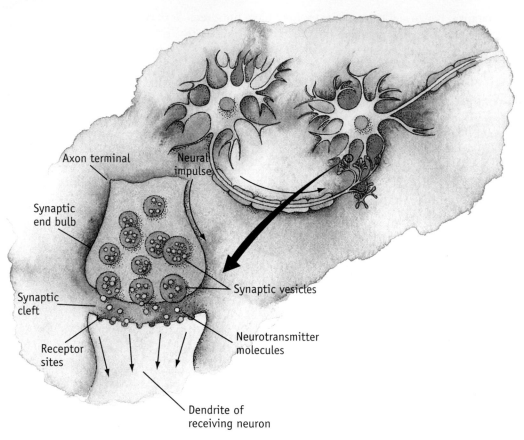

Axon terminal

Neural impulse

Synaptic end bulb

Synaptic vesicles

Synaptic cleft

Receptor sites

Neurotransmitter molecules

Dendrite of receiving neuron

FIGURE 4.6

NEUROTRANSMITTER CROSSING A SYNAPSE

Neurotransmitter molecules are released into the synaptic cleft between two neurons from vesicles (chambers) in the transmitting neuron's axon terminal. The molecules then bind to receptor sites on the receiving neuron. As a result, the electrical state of the receiving neuron changes, and the neuron becomes either more or less likely to fire an impulse, depending on the type of transmitter substance.

What any given neuron does at any given moment depends on the net effect of all the messages being received from other neurons. Only when the cell's voltage reaches a certain threshold will it fire. Thousands of messages, both excitatory and inhibitory, may be coming into the cell. Essentially, the neuron must average them. But how it does this, and how it "decides" whether to fire, is still not well understood. The message that reaches a final destination depends on the rate at which individual neurons are firing, how many are firing, what types of neurons are firing, and where the neurons are located. It does *not* depend on how strongly the neurons are firing, however, because a neuron always either fires or it doesn't. Like the turning on of a light switch, the firing of a neuron is an *all-or-none* event.

Chemical Messengers in the Nervous System

The nervous-system "house" would remain forever dark and lifeless without chemical couriers such as the neurotransmitters. Let's look more closely now at these substances, and at two other types of chemical messengers: endorphins and hormones.

Neurotransmitters: Versatile Couriers. As we have seen, neurotransmitters make it possible for one neuron to excite or inhibit another. Hundreds of substances are known or suspected to be neurotransmitters, and the number keeps growing. Each substance binds only to specific types of receptor sites. This means that if some of those "sailors" we mentioned (the neurotransmitter molecules) get off course and reach the wrong "islands" (receiving neurons), their messages will not be heard (no binding will occur). The existence of different neurotransmitters and receptor sites ensures that messages go where they are supposed to go.

Neurotransmitters exist not only in the brain, but also in the spinal cord, the peripheral nerves, and certain glands. Through their effects on specific nerve circuits, these substances can affect mood, memory, and well-being. The nature of the effect depends on the level of the neurotransmitter and its location. Here are a few of the better understood neurotransmitters and some of their known or suspected effects:

■ *Serotonin* affects neurons involved in sleep, appetite, sensory perception, temperature regulation, pain suppression, and mood.

■ *Dopamine* affects neurons involved in voluntary movement, learning, memory, and emotion.

■ *Acetylcholine* affects neurons involved in muscle action, cognitive functioning, memory, and emotion.

■ *Norepinephrine* affects neurons involved in increased heart rate and the slowing of intestinal activity during stress, and neurons involved in learning, memory, dreaming, waking from sleep, and emotion.

■ *GABA* (gamma-aminobutyric acid) functions as the major inhibitory neurotransmitter in the brain.

Harmful effects can occur when neurotransmitter levels are too high or too low. Low levels of serotonin and norepinephrine have been associated with severe depression. Abnormal GABA levels have been implicated in sleep and eating disorders and in convulsive disorders, including epilepsy (Bekenstein & Lothman, 1993). Elevated levels of serotonin, along with other biochemical and brain abnormalities, have been implicated in childhood autism (du Verglas, Banks, & Guyer, 1988). People with *Alzheimer's disease*, a devastating condition that leads to memory loss, personality changes, and eventual disintegration of all physical and mental abilities, lose brain cells responsible for producing acetylcholine, and this deficit may help account for their memory problems.

The degeneration of brain cells that produce and use another neurotransmitter, dopamine, appears to cause the symptoms of *Parkinson's disease*, a condition characterized by tremors, muscular spasms, and increasing muscular rigidity. Patients with advanced Parkinson's may "freeze" for minutes or even hours. Injections of dopamine do not help, because dopamine molecules cannot cross the *blood–brain barrier*, a system of densely packed capillary and glial cells whose function is to prevent potentially harmful substances from entering the brain. Symptoms can be lessened by the administration of levodopa (L-dopa), which is a building block of dopamine, but patients must take larger and larger doses to achieve the desired result. After a while, adverse effects from the medication—including depression, confusion, and even episodes of psychosis—may be worse than the disease itself.

During the 1990s, surgeons pioneered a dramatic new approach to treating Parkinson's disease and potentially other diseases as well. They grafted dopamine-producing brain tissue from aborted fetuses into the brains of Parkinson's patients and patients who developed Parkinson's-like symptoms after using a botched synthetic mood-altering drug that killed their dopamine-producing cells (Freed et al., 1993; Lindvall et al., 1994; Uchida & Toya, 1996; Widner et al., 1993). Not all patients improved, but some who were virtually helpless before the operation can now move

Fetal brain-tissue transplants have allowed some Parkinson's patients to perform daily tasks of living for the first time in years (Redmond et al., 1993). Before the procedure, the woman in these video images could not pick up a glass of water (left), but one year later, she had no trouble (right).

St. John's Wort (hypericum perforatum).

endorphins [en-DOR-fins] Chemical substances in the nervous system that are similar in structure and action to opiates; they are involved in pain reduction, pleasure, and memory, and they are known technically as *endogenous opioid peptides*.

freely and even dress and feed themselves. Although the long-term risks and benefits of brain-tissue transplants are not yet certain, and although the technique is not currently feasible on a large scale, this work has generated a lot of excitement.

We want to warn you, however, that pinning down the relationship between neurotransmitter abnormalities and behavioral abnormalities is extremely difficult. Each neurotransmitter plays multiple roles, and the functions of different substances often overlap. Further, it is always possible that something about a disorder leads to abnormal neurotransmitter levels, instead of the other way around. Although drugs that boost or decrease levels of particular neurotransmitters are sometimes effective in treating disorders, that does not necessarily mean that abnormal neurotransmitter levels are *causing* the disorders. After all, aspirin can relieve a headache, but headaches are not caused by a lack of aspirin!

Many of us do things that affect our own neurotransmitters, usually without knowing it. For example, most recreational drugs produce their effects by blocking or enhancing the actions of neurotransmitters. So do some herbal remedies. St. John's Wort, which many people take for depression, prevents the cells that release serotonin from reabsorbing excess molecules that have remained in the synaptic gap. As a result, serotonin levels rise. Even ordinary foods can influence the availability of neurotransmitters in the brain, as we discuss in "Taking Psychology with You."

Endorphins: The Brain's Natural Opiates. Another intriguing group of chemical messengers is known collectively as *endogenous opioid peptides*, or more popularly as **endorphins**. Endorphins have effects similar to those of natural opiates; that is, they reduce pain and promote pleasure. They are also thought to play a role in appetite, sexual activity, blood pressure, mood, learning, and memory. Some endorphins function as neurotransmitters, but most act primarily as *neuromodulators*, which alter the effects of neurotransmitters—for example, by limiting or prolonging those effects.

Endorphins were first identified in the early 1970s. Candace Pert and Solomon Snyder (1973) were doing research on morphine, a pain-relieving and mood-elevating opiate derived from heroin, which is made from poppies. They found that morphine works by binding to receptor sites in the brain. This seemed odd. As Snyder later recalled, "We doubted that animals had evolved opiate receptors just to deal with certain properties of the poppy plant" (quoted in Radetsky, 1991). Pert and Snyder reasoned that if opiate receptors exist, then the body must produce its own internally generated, or *endogenous*, morphinelike substances, which they named "endorphins." Soon they and other researchers confirmed this hypothesis.

Endorphin levels seem to shoot up when an animal or a person is afraid or under stress. This is no accident; by making pain bearable in such situations, endorphins give a species an evolutionary advantage. When an organism is threatened, it needs to do something fast. Pain, however, can interfere with action: A mouse that pauses to lick a wounded paw may become a cat's dinner; a soldier who is overcome by an injury may never get off the battlefield alive. But, of course, the body's built-in system of counteracting pain is only partly successful, especially when painful stimulation is prolonged.

A link may also exist between endorphins and the pleasures of social contact. When young puppies, guinea pigs, and chicks are injected with low doses of morphine or endorphins, the animals show much less distress than usual after separation from their mothers. (In all other respects, they behave normally.) The morphine seems to provide a biochemical replacement for the mother, or, more precisely, for the endorphin surge presumed to occur during contact with her. Conversely, when young guinea pigs and chicks receive a chemical that *blocks* the effects of opiates, their crying increases

(Panksepp et al., 1980). These findings suggest that endorphin-stimulated euphoria may be a child's initial motive for seeking affection and cuddling—that, in effect, a child attached to a parent is a child addicted to love.

Hormones: Long-Distance Messengers. **Hormones,** which make up the third class of chemical messengers, are produced primarily in **endocrine glands** and are released directly into the bloodstream, which carries them to organs and cells that may be far from their point of origin. Hormones have dozens of jobs, from promoting bodily growth to aiding digestion to regulating metabolism.

Neurotransmitters and hormones are not always chemically distinct; the two classifications are like clubs that admit some of the same members. A particular chemical, such as norepinephrine, may belong to more than one classification, depending on where it is located and what function it is performing. Nature has been efficient, giving some substances more than one task to perform.

The following hormones, among others, are of particular interest to psychologists:

1 **Melatonin,** which is secreted deep within the brain by the *pineal gland*, helps to regulate daily biological rhythms and promotes sleep, as we will discuss further in Chapter 5.

2 **Adrenal hormones,** which are produced by the *adrenal glands* (organs that are perched above the kidneys), are involved in emotion and stress. These hormones also rise in response to nonemotional conditions, such as heat, cold, pain, injury, burns, and physical exercise, and in response to some drugs, such as caffeine and nicotine. The outer part of each adrenal gland produces *cortisol*, which increases blood-sugar levels and boosts energy. The inner part produces *epinephrine* (popularly known as adrenaline) and *norepinephrine*. When adrenal hormones are released in your body, they activate the sympathetic nervous system, which in turn increases your arousal level and prepares you for action. Adrenal hormones also enhance memory, as we will see in Chapter 10.

3 **Sex hormones,** which are secreted by tissue in the gonads (testes in men, ovaries in women), and also by the adrenal glands, actually occur in both sexes, but in differing amounts and proportions in males and females after puberty. *Androgens* (the most important of which is *testosterone*) are masculinizing hormones produced mainly in the testes but also in the ovaries and the adrenal glands. Androgens set in motion the physical changes males experience at puberty—for example, a deepened voice and facial and chest hair—and cause pubic and underarm hair to develop in both sexes. Testosterone also influences sexual arousal in both sexes. *Estrogens* are feminizing hormones that bring on the physical changes females experience at puberty, such as breast development and the onset of menstruation, and that influence the course of the menstrual cycle. *Progesterone* contributes to the growth and maintenance of the uterine lining in preparation for a fertilized egg, among other functions. Estrogens and progesterone are produced mainly in the ovaries but also in the testes and the adrenal glands.

Researchers are now studying the involvement of sex hormones in behavior not directly related to sex and reproduction, such as memory and mental functioning. For example, estrogens appear to promote the growth of spines on dendrites, and thus the formation of synapses, in certain brain areas, and many researchers believe that estrogens contribute to improved learning and memory (Sherwin, 1998a; Wickelgren, 1997). However, the most common belief about the nonsexual effects of sex hormones—that fluctuating levels of estrogen and progesterone make many women "emotional" before menstruation—has not been borne out by research, as we will see in Chapter 5.

Review 4.1 summarizes the three types of brain chemicals we have discussed, and their effects.

hormones Chemical substances, secreted by organs called *glands,* that affect the functioning of other organs.

endocrine glands Internal organs that produce hormones and release them into the bloodstream.

melatonin A hormone, secreted by the pineal gland, that is involved in the regulation of daily biological rhythms.

adrenal hormones Hormones that are produced by the adrenal glands and that are involved in emotion and stress; they include cortisol, epinephrine, and norepinephrine.

sex hormones Hormones that regulate the development and functioning of reproductive organs and that stimulate the development of male and female sexual characteristics; they include androgens, estrogens, and progesterone.

REVIEW 4.1

NERVOUS-SYSTEM CHEMICALS AND THEIR EFFECTS

Type	Function	Effects	Where produced	Examples
Neurotransmitters	Enable neurons to excite or inhibit each other	Diverse, depending on which circuits are activated or suppressed	Brain, spinal cord, peripheral nerves, certain glands	Serotonin, dopamine, norepinephrine
Endorphins	Usually modulate the effects of neurotransmitters	Reduce pain, promote pleasure; also linked to learning, memory, and other functions	Brain, spinal cord	(Several varieties, not discussed in this text)
Hormones	Affect functioning of target organs and tissues	Dozens, ranging from promotion of digestion to regulation of metabolism	Primarily in endocrine glands	Epinephrine, norepinephrine, estrogens, androgens

QUICK QUIZ

You can activate your neurotransmitters by taking this quiz.

A. Which word in parentheses best fits each of the following definitions?

1. Basic building blocks of the nervous system (*nerves/neurons*)
2. Cell parts that receive nerve impulses (*axons/dendrites*)
3. Site of communication between neurons (*synapse/myelin sheath*)
4. Opiatelike substance in the brain (*dopamine/endorphin*)
5. Chemicals that make it possible for neurons to communicate (*neurotransmitters/hormones*)
6. Hormone closely associated with emotional excitement (*epinephrine/estrogen*)

B. Imagine that you are depressed, and you hear about a treatment for depression that affects the levels of several neurotransmitters thought to be involved in the disorder. Based on what you have learned, what questions would you want to ask before deciding whether to try the treatment?

Answers:

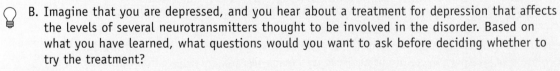

A. 1. neurons 2. dendrites 3. synapse 4. endorphin 5. neurotransmitters 6. epinephrine B. You might want to ask, among other things, about side effects (each neurotransmitter has several functions, all of which might be affected by the treatment); about evidence that the treatment works; and about whether there is any reason to believe that your own neurotransmitter levels are abnormal or whether there may be other reasons for your depression.

- Why are patterns of electrical activity in the brain called "brain waves"?
- What scanning techniques allow psychologists to view changes in brain activity while people listen to music or solve math problems?

MAPPING THE BRAIN

We come now to the main room of the nervous-system "house": the brain. A disembodied brain stored in a formaldehyde-filled container is a putty-colored, wrinkled glob of tissue that looks a little like a walnut whose growth has gotten out of hand. It takes an act of imagination to envision this modest-looking organ writing *Hamlet*, discovering radium, or inventing the paper clip.

In a living person, of course, the brain is encased in a thick, protective vault of bone. How, then, can scientists study it? One approach is to study patients who have had a part of the brain damaged or removed because of disease or injury. Another, called the *lesion method*, involves damaging or removing sections of brain in animals, then observing the effects.

The brain can also be probed with devices called *electrodes*. Some electrodes are coin-shaped and are simply pasted or taped onto the scalp. They detect the electrical activity of millions of neurons in particular regions of the brain and are widely used in research and medical diagnosis. The electrodes are connected by wires to a machine that translates the electrical energy from the brain into wavy lines on a moving piece of paper or visual patterns on a screen. That is why electrical patterns in the brain are known as "brain waves." Different wave patterns are associated with sleep, relaxation, and mental concentration, as we will see in Chapter 5.

A brain-wave recording is called an **electroencephalogram** (EEG). A standard EEG is useful but not very precise, because it reflects the activities of many cells at once. "Listening" to the brain with an EEG machine is like standing outside a sports stadium: You know when something is happening, but you cannot be sure what it is or who is doing it. Fortunately, computer technology can be combined with EEG technology to get a clearer picture of brain-activity patterns associated with specific events and mental processes; the computer suppresses all the background noise, leaving only the pattern of electrical response to the event being studied.

For even more precise information, researchers use *needle electrodes*, very thin wires or hollow glass tubes that can be inserted into the brain, either directly in an exposed brain or through tiny holes in the skull. Only the skull and the membranes covering the brain need to be anesthetized; paradoxically, the brain itself, which processes all sensation and feeling, feels nothing when it is touched. Therefore, a human patient or an animal can be awake and not feel pain during the procedure. Needle electrodes can be used both to record electrical activity from the brain and to stimulate the brain with weak electrical currents. Stimulating a given area often results in a specific sensation or movement. *Microelectrodes* are so fine that they can be inserted into single cells.

Electroencephalograms (EEGs) use electrodes to produce an overall picture of electrical activity in different areas of the brain.

electroencephalogram (EEG) A recording of neural activity detected by electrodes.

This microelectrode is being used to record the electrical impulses generated by a single cell in the brain of a monkey.

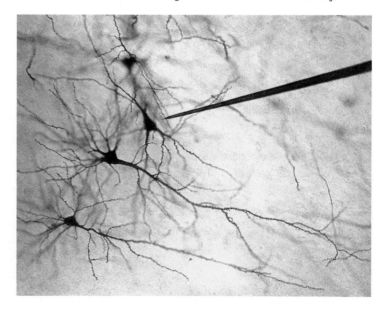

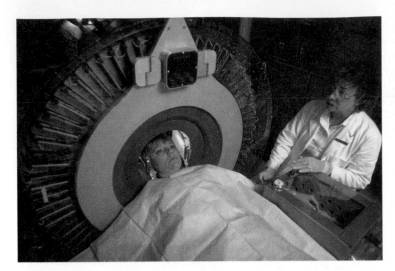

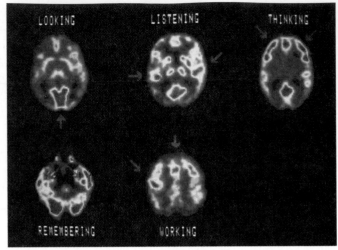

FIGURE 4.7

PET SCANS OF METABOLIC ACTIVITY IN THE BRAIN

On the left, a woman lies with her head in a PET scanner, which will detect biochemical activity in specific brain areas. In the scans on the right, red indicates areas of highest activity and violet indicates areas of lowest activity. Clockwise starting from the upper left, the arrows point to regions that are most active when the person looks at a complicated visual scene, listens to a sound, performs a mental task, moves the right hand, or recalls stories heard previously.

Since the mid-1970s, even more amazing doors to the brain have opened. The **PET scan (positron-emission tomography)** goes beyond anatomy to record biochemical changes in the brain as they are happening. One type of PET scan takes advantage of the fact that nerve cells convert glucose, the body's main fuel, into energy. A researcher can inject a patient with a substance that mimics glucose and contains a harmless radioactive element. This substance accumulates in brain areas that are particularly active and are therefore consuming glucose rapidly. The substance emits radiation, which is a telltale sign of activity, like cookie crumbs on a child's face. The radiation is detected by a scanning device, and the result is a computer-processed picture of biochemical activity on a display screen, with different colors indicating different activity levels (see Figure 4.7). Other kinds of PET scans measure blood flow or oxygen consumption, which also reflect brain activity.

PET scans, which were originally designed to diagnose abnormalities, have produced evidence that certain brain areas in people with emotional disorders are either unusually quiet or unusually active. But PET technology can also show which parts of the brain are active during ordinary activities and emotions. It lets researchers see which areas are busiest when a person hears a song, recalls a sad memory, works on a math problem, or shifts attention from one task to another.

Another technique used in both medical diagnosis and brain research, **MRI (magnetic resonance imaging)**, allows the exploration of "inner space" without injecting chemicals. Powerful magnetic fields and radio frequencies are used to produce vibrations in the nuclei of atoms making up body organs, and the vibrations are then picked up as signals by special receivers. A computer analyzes the signals and converts them into a high-contrast picture of the organ (see Figure 4.8). A new, ultrafast version of MRI ("functional MRI") detects blood flow by picking up magnetic signals from blood that has given up its oxygen to active brain cells. It can capture brain changes many

PET scan (positron-emission tomography) A method for analyzing biochemical activity in the brain, using injections of a glucoselike substance containing a radioactive element.

MRI (magnetic resonance imaging) A method for studying body and brain tissue, using magnetic fields and special radio receivers.

times a second as a person performs a task, such as reading a sentence or solving a puzzle. Other scanning techniques are becoming available with each passing year.

Review 4.2 summarizes methods used by psychologists to study the brain. A word of caution, though: After researchers find out which brain areas are active during a task, they still have to figure out precisely what is happening inside the person's head, both mentally and physiologically. Enthusiasm for new technology has produced a mountain of findings, but uncritical interpretation of these findings has often led to unwarranted conclusions. One scientist (cited in Wheeler, 1998) drew this analogy: A researcher scans the brains of gum-chewing volunteers, finds out which parts of their brains are active, and concludes that he or she has found the brain's "gum-chewing center"!

Descriptive studies using brain scans, then, are just a first step in understanding brain processes. Nonetheless, they are an important and exciting first step. We will be reporting many findings from PET-scan, MRI, and functional-MRI research throughout this book—findings on memory, sex differences, depression, schizophrenia, and even how psychotherapy affects brain activity. The brain can no longer hide from researchers behind the fortress of the skull. It is now possible to get a clear visual image of our most enigmatic organ without so much as lifting a scalpel.

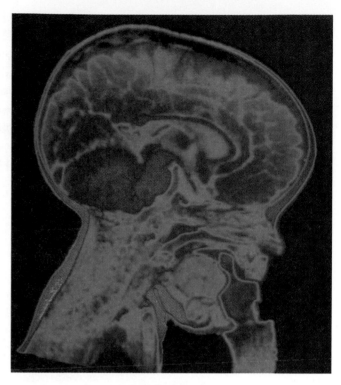

FIGURE 4.8
MRI OF A CHILD'S BRAIN

This MRI shows a child's brain—and the bottle he was drinking from while the image was obtained.

REVIEW 4.2

WINDOWS ON THE BRAIN

Method	What Is Learned
Case studies of persons with brain damage	How damage to or loss of neural circuits affects behavior and cognition
Lesion studies with animals	How damage to or loss of neural circuits affects behavior
EEGs	Patterns of electrical activity in the brain
Needle electrodes and microelectrodes	More precise information about electrical activity in small groups of neurons or even single neurons
PET scans	Visually displayed information about areas that are active or quiet during an activity or response, and about changes associated with disorders
MRI	Images of brain structure
Functional MRI	Visually displayed information about areas that are active or quiet during an activity or response, and about changes associated with disorders

- Which brain part acts as a "traffic officer" for incoming sensations?
- Which brain part is the "gateway to memory"—and what cognitive catastrophe occurs when it is damaged?
- Why is it a good thing that the outer covering of the human brain is so wrinkled?
- How did a bizarre nineteenth-century accident illuminate the role of the frontal lobes?

A TOUR THROUGH THE BRAIN

All modern brain theories assume that the major brain parts perform different (though overlapping) tasks. This concept, which is known as **localization of function**, goes back at least to Joseph Gall (1758–1828). Gall was the Austrian anatomist who thought that personality traits were reflected in the development of specific areas of the brain (see Chapter 1). Gall's theory of *phrenology* was completely wrong-headed (so to speak), but his general notion of specialization in the brain had merit.

To learn about what the various brain structures do, we are going to take an imaginary stroll through the brain. Pretend, now, that you have shrunk to a microscopic size and that you are wending your way through the "soul's frail dwelling house," starting at the lower part, just above the spine. Figure 4.9 shows the major structures we will encounter along our tour; you may want to refer to it as we proceed.

localization of function Specialization of particular brain areas for particular functions.

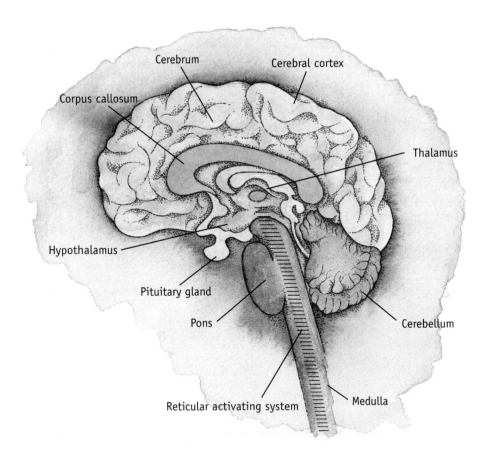

FIGURE 4.9
THE HUMAN BRAIN

This cross section depicts the brain as if it were split in half. The view is of the inside surface of the right half, and shows the structures described in the text.

The Brain Stem

We begin at the base of the skull with the **brain stem**, which began to evolve some 500 million years ago in segmented worms. The brain stem looks like a stalk rising out of the spinal cord. Pathways to and from upper areas of the brain pass through its two main structures, the **medulla** and the **pons**. The pons is involved in (among other things) sleeping, waking, and dreaming. The medulla is responsible for bodily functions that do not have to be consciously willed, such as breathing and heart rate. Hanging has long been used as a method of execution because when it breaks the neck, nervous pathways from the medulla are severed, stopping respiration.

Extending upward from the core of the brain stem is the **reticular activating system (RAS)**. This dense network of neurons, which extends above the brain stem into the center of the brain and has connections with higher areas, screens incoming information and arouses the higher centers when something happens that demands their attention. Without the RAS, we could not be alert or perhaps even conscious.

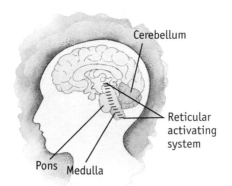

The Cerebellum

Standing atop the brain stem and looking toward the back part of the brain, we see a two-lobed structure about the size of a small fist. It is the **cerebellum**, or "lesser brain," which contributes to a sense of balance and coordinates the muscles so that movement is smooth and precise. If your cerebellum were damaged, you would probably become exceedingly clumsy and uncoordinated. You might have trouble using a pencil, threading a needle, riding a bike, or even walking. In addition, this structure is involved in remembering certain simple skills and acquired reflexes (Krupa, Thompson, & Thompson, 1993; Thompson, 1986). Some researchers think that the cerebellum is a lot less "lesser" than previously thought—that it also plays a role in such higher-order processes as analyzing sensory information, solving problems, and understanding words (Fiez, 1996; Gao et al., 1996; Müller, Courchesne, & Allen, 1998).

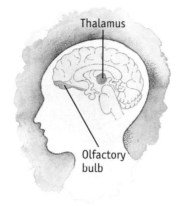

The Thalamus

Deep in the brain's interior, we can see the **thalamus**, the busy traffic officer of the brain. The thalamus relays motor impulses from higher centers to the spinal cord. And conversely, as sensory messages come into the brain, the thalamus directs them to higher centers. For example, the sight of a sunset sends signals that the thalamus directs to a visual area, and the sound of an oboe sends signals that the thalamus sends on to an auditory area. The only sense that completely bypasses the thalamus is the sense of smell, which has its own private switching station, the *olfactory bulb*. The olfactory bulb lies near areas involved in emotion. Perhaps that is why particular odors—the smell of fresh laundry, gardenias, a steak sizzling on the grill—often rekindle memories of important personal experiences.

The Hypothalamus and the Pituitary Gland

Beneath the thalamus sits a structure called the **hypothalamus** (*hypo* means "under"). It is involved in drives associated with the survival of both the individual and the species—hunger, thirst, emotion, sex, and reproduction. It regulates body temperature by triggering sweating or shivering, and it controls the complex operations of the autonomic nervous system.

brain stem The part of the brain at the top of the spinal cord, consisting of the medulla and the pons.

medulla [muh-DUL-uh] A structure in the brain stem responsible for certain automatic functions, such as breathing and heart rate.

pons A structure in the brain stem involved in, among other things, sleeping, waking, and dreaming.

reticular activating system (RAS) A dense network of neurons found in the core of the brain stem; it arouses the cortex and screens incoming information.

cerebellum A brain structure that regulates movement and balance, and that is involved in the learning of certain kinds of simple responses.

thalamus A brain structure that relays sensory messages to the cerebral cortex.

hypothalamus A brain structure involved in emotions and drives vital to survival, such as fear, hunger, thirst, and reproduction; it regulates the autonomic nervous system.

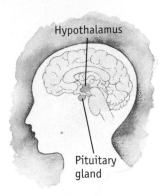

Hypothalamus

Pituitary gland

Hanging down from the hypothalamus, connected to it by a short stalk, is a cherry-sized endocrine gland called the **pituitary gland**. The pituitary is often called the body's "master gland" because the hormones it secretes affect many other endocrine glands. The master, however, is really only a supervisor. The true boss is the hypothalamus, which sends chemicals to the pituitary that tell it when to "talk" to the other endocrine glands. The pituitary, in turn, sends hormonal messages out to these glands.

The Limbic System

The hypothalamus has many connections to a set of loosely interconnected structures called the **limbic system**, shown in Figure 4.10. (*Limbic* comes from the Latin for "border": These structures form a sort of border between the higher and lower parts of the brain.) Some anatomists include the hypothalamus and parts of the thalamus in the limbic system. Although the usefulness of speaking of the limbic system as an integrated set of structures is now in dispute (LeDoux, 1996), it is clear that structures in this region are heavily involved in emotions, such as rage and fear, that we share with other animals (MacLean, 1993).

Many years ago, James Olds and Peter Milner reported finding "pleasure centers" in the limbic system (Olds, 1975; Olds & Milner, 1954). Olds and Milner trained rats to press a lever in order to get a buzz of electricity delivered through tiny electrodes to the limbic system. Some rats would press the bar thousands of times an hour, for 15 or 20 hours at a time, until they collapsed from exhaustion. When they revived, they went right back to the bar. When forced to make a choice, the hedonistic rodents opted for electrical stimulation over such temptations as

pituitary gland A small endocrine gland at the base of the brain, which releases many hormones and regulates other endocrine glands.

limbic system A group of brain areas involved in emotional reactions and motivated behavior.

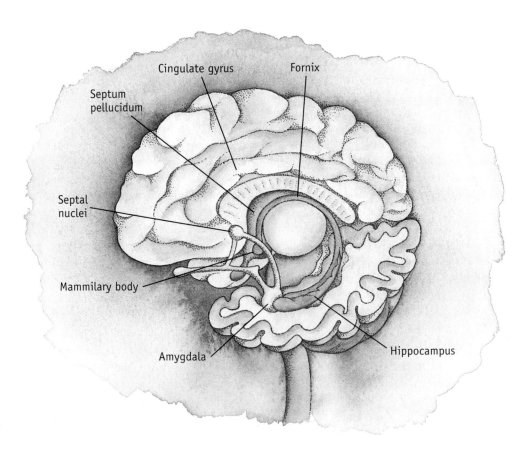

Cingulate gyrus

Fornix

Septum pellucidum

Septal nuclei

Mammilary body

Amygdala

Hippocampus

FIGURE 4.10
THE LIMBIC SYSTEM

Structures of the limbic system play an important role in memory and emotion. The text describes two of these structures, the amygdala and the hippocampus.

water, food, and even an attractive rat of the other sex that was making provocative gestures. Today, however, researchers believe that brain stimulation activates neural pathways rather than discrete "centers," and that changes in neurotransmitter or neuromodulator levels are involved.

The Amygdala. One limbic structure that especially concerns psychologists is the **amygdala**, which appears to be responsible for evaluating sensory information, quickly determining its emotional importance, and contributing to the initial decision to approach or withdraw from a person or situation (see Chapter 11). The amygdala also plays an important role in mediating anxiety and depression; PET scans find that depressed and anxious patients show increased neural activity in this structure (Schulkin, 1994).

The Hippocampus. Another important limbic area is the **hippocampus**, which has a shape that must have reminded someone of a sea horse, for that is what its name means. One of its tasks seems to be to compare sensory messages with what the brain has learned to expect about the world. When expectations are met, the hippocampus tells the reticular activating system, the brain's arousal center, to "cool it." It wouldn't do to be highly aroused in response to *everything*. What if neural alarm bells went off every time a car went by, a bird chirped, or you felt your saliva trickling down the back of your throat?

The hippocampus has also been called the "gateway to memory" because, along with adjacent brain areas, it enables us to form new memories, in particular memories about events—the kind of information you need to tell someone about your vacation trip or what you had for lunch. The information is then stored in the cerebral cortex, which we will be discussing shortly; but without the hippocampus, the information would never get to its ultimate destination in the cortex (Mishkin et al., 1997; Squire & Zola-Morgan, 1991).

We know about this function of the hippocampus in part from research on brain-damaged patients with severe memory problems. The case of one man, known to researchers as H. M., is probably the most intensely studied in the annals of medicine (Corkin, 1984; Corkin et al., 1997; Milner, 1970; Ogden & Corkin, 1991). In 1953, when H. M. was 27, surgeons removed most of his hippocampus, along with part of the amygdala. The operation was a last-ditch effort to relieve H. M.'s severe and life-threatening epilepsy. People who have epilepsy, a neurological disorder that has many causes and takes many forms, often have seizures. Usually, the seizures are brief, mild, and controllable by drugs, but in H. M.'s case, they were unrelenting and uncontrollable.

The operation did achieve its goal: Afterward, the young man's seizures were milder and could be managed with medication. His memory, however, had been affected profoundly. Although H. M. continued to recall most events that had occurred before the operation, he could no longer remember new experiences for much longer than 15 minutes; they vanished like water down the drain. With sufficient practice, H. M. could acquire new manual or problem-solving skills, such as playing tennis, but he could not remember the training sessions in which he learned these skills. He would read the same magazine over and over without realizing it. He could not recall the day of the week, the year, or even his last meal. Most scientists attribute these deficits to an inability to form new memories for long-term storage.

Today, many years later, H. M. will occasionally recall an unusually emotional event, such as the assassination of someone named Kennedy. He sometimes remembers that both his parents are dead, and he knows he has memory problems (which he describes as "like waking from a dream"). But, according to Suzanne

amygdala [uh-MIG-dul-uh] A brain structure involved in the arousal and regulation of emotion and the initial emotional response to sensory information.

hippocampus A brain structure involved in the storage of new information in memory.

Corkin, who has studied H. M. extensively, these "islands of remembering" are the exceptions in a vast sea of forgetfulness. This good-natured man still does not know the scientists who have studied him for decades. He thinks he is much younger than he is, and he can no longer recognize a photograph of his own face; he is stuck in a time warp from the past. (We will meet H. M. again when we discuss memory in Chapter 10.)

The Cerebrum

At this point in our tour, the largest part of the brain still looms above us. It is the cauliflower-like **cerebrum**, where the higher forms of thinking take place. The complexity of the human brain's circuitry far exceeds that of any computer in existence, and much of its most complicated wiring is packed into this structure. Compared with many other creatures, we humans may be ungainly, feeble, and thin-skinned, but our well-developed cerebrum enables us to overcome these limitations and creatively control our environment (and, some would say, to mess it up).

The cerebrum is divided into two separate halves, or **cerebral hemispheres**, connected by a large band of fibers called the **corpus callosum**. In general, the right hemisphere is in charge of the left side of the body and the left hemisphere is in charge of the right side of the body. As we will see shortly, the two hemispheres also have somewhat different tasks and talents, a phenomenon known as **lateralization**.

The Cerebral Cortex. Working our way right up through the top of the brain, we find that the cerebrum is covered by several thin layers of densely packed cells known collectively as the **cerebral cortex**. Cell bodies in the cortex, as in many other parts of the brain, produce a grayish tissue; hence the term *gray matter*. In other parts of the brain (and in the rest of the nervous system), long, myelin-covered axons prevail, providing the brain's *white matter*. Although the cortex is only about 3 millimeters thick, it contains almost three-fourths of all the cells in the human brain. The cortex has many deep crevasses and wrinkles, which enable it to contain its billions of neurons without requiring us to have the heads of giants—heads that would be too big to permit us to be born. In other mammals, which have fewer neurons, the cortex is less crumpled; in rats, it is quite smooth.

Lobes of the Cortex. On each cerebral hemisphere, deep fissures divide the cortex into four distinct regions, or lobes (see Figure 4.11):

■ The **occipital lobes** (from the Latin for "in back of the head") are at the lower back part of the brain. Among other things, they contain the *visual cortex*, where visual signals are processed. Damage to the visual cortex can cause impaired visual recognition or blindness.

■ The **parietal lobes** (from the Latin for "pertaining to walls") are at the top of the brain. They contain the *somatosensory cortex*, which receives information about pressure, pain, touch, and temperature from all over the body. The areas of the somatosensory cortex that receive signals from the hands and the face are disproportionately large because these body parts are particularly sensitive.

■ The **temporal lobes** (from the Latin for "pertaining to the temples") are at the sides of the brain, just above the ears and behind the temples. They are involved in memory, perception, and emotion, and they contain the *auditory cortex*, which processes sounds. An area of the left temporal lobe known as *Wernicke's area* is involved in language comprehension.

---

cerebrum [suh-REE-brum] The largest brain structure, consisting of the upper part of the brain. Divided into two hemispheres, it is in charge of most sensory, motor, and cognitive processes. (From the Latin for "brain.")

cerebral hemispheres The two halves of the cerebrum.

corpus callosum [CORE-puhs cah-LOW-suhm] The bundle of nerve fibers connecting the two cerebral hemispheres.

lateralization Specialization of the two cerebral hemispheres for particular operations.

cerebral cortex A collection of several thin layers of cells covering the cerebrum; it is largely responsible for higher mental functions. (*Cortex* is Latin for "bark" or "rind.")

occipital [ahk-SIP-uh-tuhl] lobes Lobes at the lower back part of the brain's cerebral cortex; they contain areas that receive visual information.

parietal [puh-RYE-uh-tuhl] lobes Lobes at the top of the brain's cerebral cortex; they contain areas that receive information on pressure, pain, touch, and temperature.

temporal lobes Lobes at the sides of the brain's cerebral cortex, just above the ears; they contain areas involved in hearing, memory, perception, emotion, and (in the left lobe, typically) language comprehension.

frontal lobes Lobes at the front of the brain's cerebral cortex; they contain areas involved in short-term memory, higher-order thinking, initiative, social judgment, and (in the left lobe, typically) speech production.

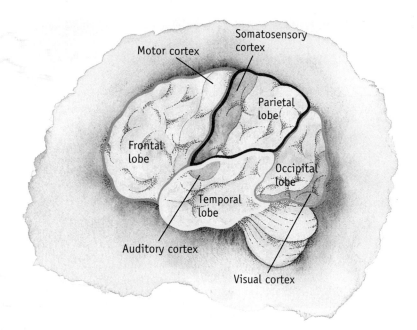

FIGURE 4.11
LOBES OF THE CEREBRUM
Deep fissures divide the cortex of each cerebral hemisphere into four regions.

■ The **frontal lobes**, as their name indicates, are located toward the front of the brain, just under the skull in the area of the forehead. They contain the *motor cortex*, which issues orders to the 600 muscles of the body that produce voluntary movement. In the left frontal lobe, a region known as *Broca's area* is involved in speech production. During short-term memory tasks, areas in the frontal lobes are especially active (Goldman-Rakic, 1996). The frontal lobes are also involved in the ability to make plans, think creatively, and take initiative.

Experiences at different times of your life can affect how areas in these lobes are organized. For example, functional MRI studies show that bilingual people who learned both of their languages in early childhood tend to use a single, uniform Broca's area when generating complex sentences in the two languages (see Figure 4.12). But in people who learned a second language during adolescence, Broca's area is divided into two distinct regions, one for each language (Kim et al., 1997). The explanation may be that the brain's wiring process for language production occurs differently in childhood than it does later on. The fact that children pick up a language naturally whereas adolescents and adults usually have to study it may also help account for these differences.

Despite some differences in organization based on experience, however, the lobes of the cerebral cortex do have characteristic tasks and respond in characteristic ways when stimulated. If a surgeon applied electrical current to the somatosensory cortex in your parietal lobes, for example, you would probably feel a tingling in the skin or a sense of being gently touched. If your visual cortex in the occipital lobes were electrically stimulated, you might report a flash of light or swirls of color. And, eerily, there are many areas of your cortex which, if stimulated, would do nothing at all; the areas are "silent."

The "silent" areas are sometimes called the *association cortex* because they are involved in higher mental processes. Psychologists are especially interested in the forwardmost part of the frontal lobes, the *prefrontal cortex*. This area barely exists in mice and rats and takes up only 3.5 percent of the cerebral cortex in cats, about 7 percent in dogs, and 17 percent in chimpanzees. In human beings, it accounts for fully 29 percent of the cortex.

FIGURE 4.12
THE BILINGUAL BRAIN
While having a functional MRI done, bilingual people were asked to think about what they had done the day before, first in one language and then the other. In those who learned both of their languages in childhood, a single region in Broca's area (which manages speech production) was active. But in those who learned a second language later in life, different parts of Broca's area were activated for the two languages (Kim et al., 1997).

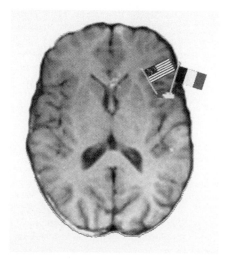

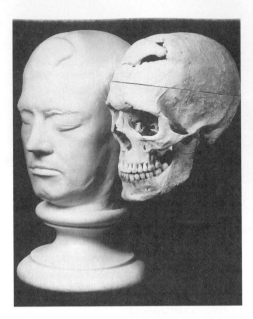
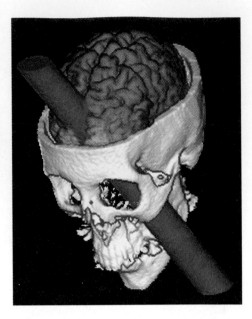

FIGURE 4.13

A FAMOUS SKULL

On the left is Phineas Gage's skull and a cast of his head. You can see where an iron rod penetrated his skull, altering his behavior and personality dramatically. The exact location of the brain damage remained controversial for almost a century and a half, until Hanna and Antonio Damasio and their colleagues (1994) used measurements of Gage's skull and MRIs of normal brains to plot possible trajectories of the rod. The reconstruction on the right shows that the damage occurred in an area of the prefrontal cortex associated with emotional processing and rational decision making.

Scientists have long known that the frontal lobes, and the prefrontal cortex in particular, must have something to do with personality. The first clue appeared in 1848, when a bizarre accident drove an inch-thick, 3½-foot-long iron rod clear through the head of a young railroad worker named Phineas Gage. As you can see in Figure 4.13, the rod (which is still on display at Harvard University, along with Gage's skull) entered beneath the left eye and exited through the top of the head, destroying much of the prefrontal cortex (H. Damasio et al., 1994). Miraculously, Gage survived this trauma and retained the ability to speak, think, and remember. But his friends complained that he was "no longer Gage." In a sort of Jekyll-and-Hyde transformation, he had changed from a mild-mannered, friendly, energetic, and efficient worker into a foul-mouthed, ill-tempered, undependable lout who could not hold a steady job or stick to a plan. His employers had to let him go, and he was reduced to exhibiting himself as a circus attraction.

This sad case and others suggest that parts of the frontal lobes are involved in social judgment, rational decision making, and the ability to set goals and to make and carry through plans (Klein & Kihlstrom, 1998). As neurologist Antonio Damasio (1994) wrote, "Gage's unintentional message was that observing social convention, behaving ethically, and, in general, making decisions advantageous to one's survival and progress, require both knowledge of rules and strategies *and* the integrity of specific brain systems." Interestingly, the mental deficits that characterize damage to these areas are accompanied by a flattening out of emotion and feeling, which suggests that normal emotions are necessary for everyday reasoning and the ability to learn from mistakes.

The frontal lobes also govern the ability to do a series of tasks in the proper sequence and to stop doing them at the proper time. The pioneering Soviet psychologist Alexander Luria (1980) studied many cases in which damage to the frontal lobes disrupted these abilities. One man observed by Luria kept trying to light a match after it was already lit. Another planed a piece of wood in the hospital carpentry shop until it was gone, and went on to plane the workbench!

Review 4.3 summarizes the parts of the brain and their primary functions. When you think you have mastered this material, pause to see how your own brain is working by taking the Quick Quiz.

REVIEW 4.3

FUNCTIONS ASSOCIATED WITH THE MAJOR BRAIN STRUCTURES

The functions listed here are just some of those that have been linked with these structures.

Structure	Function(s)
Brain stem	
Pons	Sleeping, waking, dreaming
Medulla	Automatic functions such as breathing, heart rate
Reticular activating system (RAS) (extends into center of the brain)	Screening of incoming information, arousal of higher centers, consciousness
Cerebellum	Balance, muscular coordination, memory for simple skills and learned reflexes, possible involvement in more complex mental tasks
Thalamus	Relay of impulses from higher centers to the spinal cord and of incoming sensory information (except for olfactory sensations) to other brain centers
Hypothalamus	Behaviors necessary for survival, such as hunger, thirst, emotion, reproduction; regulation of body temperature; control of autonomic nervous system
Pituitary gland	Under direction of the hypothalamus, secretion of hormones that affect other glands
Limbic system	Emotions related to survival
Amygdala	Initial evaluation of sensory information to determine its importance; mediation of anxiety and depression
Hippocampus	Comparison of sensory information with expectations, modulation of the RAS; formation of new memories about facts and events
Cerebrum (including cerebral cortex)	Higher forms of thinking
Occipital lobes	Visual processing
Parietal lobes	Processing of pressure, pain, touch, temperature
Temporal lobes	Memory, perception, emotion, hearing, language comprehension
Frontal lobes	Movement, short-term memory, planning, setting goals, creative thinking, initiative, social judgment, rational decision making, speech production

QUICK QUIZ

Match each description on the left with a term on the right.

1. Filters out irrelevant information
2. Known as the "gateway to memory"
3. Controls the autonomic nervous system; involved in drives associated with survival
4. Consists of two hemispheres
5. Wrinkled outer covering of the brain
6. Site of the motor cortex; associated with planning and taking initiative

a. reticular activating system
b. cerebrum
c. hippocampus
d. cerebral cortex
e. frontal lobes
f. hypothalamus

Answers:

1.a 2.c 3.f 4.b 5.d 6.e

WHAT'S AHEAD

- If the two cerebral hemispheres were out of touch, would they feel different emotions and think different thoughts?
- Why do researchers often refer to the left hemisphere as "dominant"?
- Should you sign up for a program that promises to perk up the right side of your brain?

THE TWO HEMISPHERES OF THE BRAIN

We have seen that the cerebrum is divided into two hemispheres that control opposite sides of the body. Although similar in structure, these hemispheres have some separate talents, or areas of specialization.

Split Brains: A House Divided

In a normal brain, the two hemispheres communicate with one another across the corpus callosum, the bundle of fibers that connects them. Whatever happens in one side of the brain is instantly flashed to the other side. What would happen, though, if the two sides were cut off from one another?

In 1953, Ronald E. Myers and Roger W. Sperry took the first step toward answering this question by severing the corpus callosum in cats. They also cut parts of the nerves leading from the eyes to the brain. Normally, each eye transmits messages to both sides of the brain. After this procedure, a cat's left eye sent information only to the left hemisphere and its right eye sent information only to the right hemisphere.

At first, the cats did not seem to be affected much by this drastic operation. But Myers and Sperry showed that something profound had happened. They trained the cats to perform tasks with one eye blindfolded. For example, a cat might have to push a panel with a square on it to get food but ignore a panel with a circle. Then the researchers switched the blindfold to the cat's other eye and tested the animal again. Now the cats behaved as if they had never learned the trick. Apparently, one side of the brain did not know what the other side was doing. It was as if the animals had two minds in one body. Later studies confirmed this result with other species, including monkeys (Sperry, 1964).

In all the animal studies, ordinary behavior, such as eating and walking, remained normal. Encouraged by this finding, a team of surgeons decided in the early 1960s to try cutting the corpus callosum in patients with debilitating, uncontrollable epilepsy. In severe forms of this disease, disorganized electrical activity spreads from an injured area to other parts of the brain. The surgeons reasoned that cutting the connection between the two halves of the cerebrum might stop the spread of electrical activity from one side to the other. As in the case of H. M., operating was a last resort.

The results of this *split-brain surgery* generally proved successful. Seizures were reduced and sometimes disappeared completely. As an added bonus, these patients gave scientists a chance to find out what each half of the brain can do when it is quite literally cut off from the other. It was already known that the two hemispheres are not mirror images of each other. In most people, language is largely handled by the left hemisphere; thus, a person who suffers brain damage because of a stroke—a blockage in or rupture of a blood vessel in the brain—is much more likely to have language problems if the damage is in the left side than if it is in the right. How would splitting the brain affect language and other abilities?

In their daily lives, split-brain patients did not seem much affected by the fact that the two sides of their brains were incommunicado. Their personalities and general intelligence remained intact; they could walk, talk, and in general lead normal lives. Apparently, connections in the undivided lower parts of the brain kept body movements normal. But in a series of ingenious studies, Sperry and his colleagues (and later other researchers) showed that perception and memory had been affected, just as they had been in earlier animal research. In 1981, Sperry won a Nobel Prize for his work.

To understand this research, you must know how nerves connect the eyes to the brain. (The human patients, unlike Myers and Sperry's cats, did not have these nerves cut.) If you look straight ahead, everything in the left side of the scene before you—the left *visual field*—goes to the right half of your brain, and everything in the right side of the scene goes to the left half of your brain. This is true for *both* eyes (see Figure 4.14 on the next page).

The procedure was to present information only to one or the other side of the subjects' brains. In one early study the researchers took photographs of different faces, cut them in two, and pasted different halves together (Levy, Trevarthen, & Sperry, 1972). The reconstructed photographs were then presented on slides. The person was told to stare at a dot on the middle of the screen, so that half the image fell to

---

GET ➡ INVOLVED

TAP, TAP, TAP

Have a right-handed friend tap on a paper with a pencil held in the right hand, for one minute. Then have the person do the same with the left hand, using a fresh sheet of paper. Finally, repeat the procedure, having the person talk at the same time as tapping. For most people, talking will decrease the rate of tapping—but more for the right hand than for the left, probably because both activities involve the same hemisphere, and there is "competition" between them for the left side's "attention." (Left-handed people vary more in terms of which hemisphere is dominant for language, so the results for them will be more variable.)

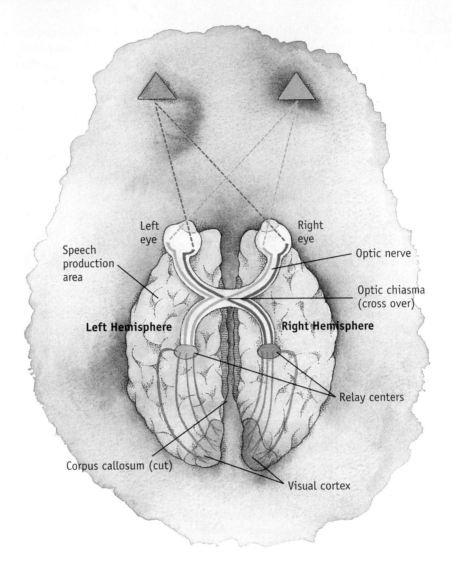

FIGURE 4.14
VISUAL PATHWAYS

Each cerebral hemisphere receives information from the eyes about the opposite side of the visual field. Thus, if you stare directly at the corner of a room, everything to the left of the juncture is represented in your right hemisphere and vice versa. This is so because half the axons in each optic nerve cross over (at the optic chiasma) to the opposite side of the brain. Normally, each hemisphere immediately shares its information with the other one, but in split-brain patients, severing the corpus callosum prevents such communication.

the left of this point and half to the right. Each image was flashed so quickly that the person had no time to move his or her eyes. When the subjects were asked to say what they had seen, they named the person in the right part of the image (which would be the little boy in Figure 4.15). But when they were asked to *point* with their left hands to the face they had seen, they chose the person in the left side of the image (the mustached man in the figure). Further, they claimed they had noticed nothing unusual about the original photographs! Each side of the brain saw a different half-image and automatically filled in the missing part. Neither side knew what the other side had seen.

Why did the patients name one side of the picture but point to the other? Speech centers are in the left hemisphere. When the person responded with speech, it was the left side of the brain doing the talking. When the person pointed with the left hand, which is controlled by the right side of the brain, the right hemisphere was giving *its* version of what the person had seen.

In another study, the researchers presented slides of ordinary objects and then suddenly flashed a slide of a nude woman. Both sides of the brain were amused, but because only the left side has speech, the two sides responded differently. When the picture was flashed to her left hemisphere, one woman laughed and identified it as a nude. When it was flashed to her right hemisphere, she said nothing but began to

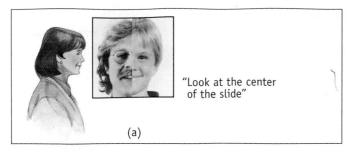

"Look at the center of the slide"

(a)

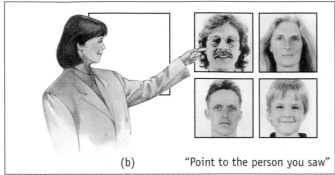

(b) "Point to the person you saw"

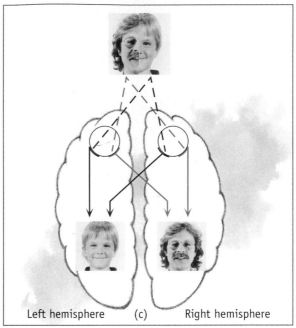

Left hemisphere (c) Right hemisphere

FIGURE 4.15
DIVIDED BRAIN, DIVIDED VIEW

When split-brain patients were shown composite photographs (a) and were then asked to pick out the face they had seen from a series of intact photographs (b), they said they had seen the face on the right side of the composite—yet they pointed with their left hands to the face that had been on the left. Because the two cerebral hemispheres could not communicate, the verbal left hemisphere was aware of only the right half of the picture, and the relatively mute right hemisphere was aware of only the left half (c).

chuckle. Asked what she was laughing at, she said, "I don't know . . . nothing . . . oh—that funny machine." The right hemisphere could not describe what it had seen, but it reacted emotionally, just the same (Gazzaniga, 1967).

A Question of Dominance

Dozens of people have undergone the split-brain operation since the mid-1960s, and research on left-right differences has also been done with people whose brains are intact (Springer & Deutch, 1998). Electrodes and brain scans have been used to gauge activity in the left and right hemispheres while people perform different tasks. The results confirm that nearly all right-handed people and a majority of left-handers process language mainly in the left hemisphere. The left side is also more active during some logical, symbolic, and sequential tasks, such as solving math problems and understanding technical material. Because of its cognitive talents, many researchers refer to the left hemisphere as *dominant*. They believe that the left hemisphere usually exerts control over the right hemisphere. One well-known split-brain researcher, Michael Gazzaniga (1983), has argued that without help from the left side, the right side's mental skills would probably be "vastly inferior to the cognitive skills of a chimpanzee." He and others also believe that a mental "module" in the left hemisphere is constantly trying to explain actions and emotions generated by brain parts whose workings are nonverbal and outside of awareness.

You can see in split-brain patients how the left brain concocts such explanations. In one classic example, a picture of a chicken claw was flashed to a patient's left hemisphere, a picture of a snow scene to his right. The task was to point to a related image

"Mama and I fixed a lovely dinner. I used the right side of my brain, and she used the left side of her brain."

for each picture from an array, with a chicken the correct choice for the claw and a shovel for the snow scene. The patient chose the shovel with his left hand and the chicken with his right. When asked to explain why, he responded (with his left hemisphere) that the chicken claw went with the chicken, and the shovel was for cleaning out the chicken shed. The left hemisphere had seen the left hand's response but did not know about the snow scene, so it interpreted the response by using the information it did have (Gazzaniga, 1988). In people with intact brains, says Gazzaniga, the left side's interpretations account for the sense of a unified, coherent identity.

Other researchers, including Roger Sperry (1982), have rushed to the right hemisphere's defense. The right side, they point out, is no dummy. It is superior in problems requiring spatial-visual ability, the ability you use to read a map or follow a dress pattern, and it excels in facial recognition and the ability to read facial expressions. (Dr. P. and Emily D., described at the beginning of this chapter, both had damage in the right hemisphere.) It is active during the creation and appreciation of art and music. It recognizes nonverbal sounds, such as a dog's barking. The right hemisphere also has some language ability. Typically, it can read a word briefly flashed to it and can understand an experimenter's instructions. In a few split-brain patients, the right hemisphere's language ability has been quite well developed.

Some researchers have credited the right hemisphere with having a cognitive style that is intuitive and holistic (in which things are seen as wholes), in contrast to the left hemisphere's more rational and analytic mode. However, many researchers are concerned about popular misinterpretations of this conclusion. Books and programs that promise to make you more "right-brained" tend to oversimplify and exaggerate hemispheric differences. Individuals differ in the degree of lateralization for different tasks. Further, the differences between the two sides are relative, not absolute—a matter of degree. In most real-life activities, the two hemispheres cooperate naturally, with each making a valuable contribution (Kinsbourne, 1982; J. Levy, 1985). "The left-right dichotomy," Sperry (1982) himself once noted, "is an idea with which it is very easy to run wild."

QUICK QUIZ

Use as many parts of your brain as necessary to answer these questions.

1. Keeping in mind that both sides of the brain are involved in most activities, see whether you can identify which of the following is (are) most closely associated with the left hemisphere: (a) enjoying a musical recording; (b) wiggling the left big toe; (c) giving a speech in class; (d) balancing a checkbook; (e) recognizing a long-lost friend

2. Over the past decades, thousands of people have taken courses and bought tapes that promise to develop the "creativity" and "intuition" of their right hemispheres. What characteristics of human thought might explain the eagerness of some people to glorify "right-brainedness" and disparage "left-brainedness" (or vice versa)?

Answers:

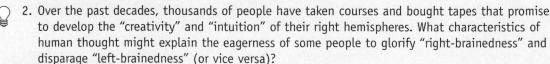

1. c, d   2. One possible answer: Human beings like to make sense of the world, and one easy way to do that is to divide humanity into opposing categories. This kind of either-or thinking can lead to the conclusion that fixing up one of the categories (e.g., making left-brained types more right-brained) will make individuals happier and the world a better place. If only it were that simple!

WHAT'S AHEAD

- **Why do some brain researchers think a unified "self" is an illusion?**
- **Do men talk about sports and women about feelings because their brains are different?**

TWO STUBBORN ISSUES IN BRAIN RESEARCH

If you have mastered the definitions and descriptions in this chapter, you are prepared to read popular accounts of advances in neuropsychology. But many mysteries remain about how the brain works, and we will end this chapter with two of them.

Where Is the Self?

When we think about the remarkable blob of tissue in our heads that allows us to remember, to dream, and to think—the blob that can make our existence a hideous nightmare when it is diseased—we are led, inevitably, to a question that has been pondered for thousands of years: Where, exactly, is the self?

When you say, "I am feeling unhappy," your amygdala, your serotonin receptors, your endorphins, and all sorts of other brain parts and processes are active, but who, exactly, is the "I" doing the feeling? When you say, "I've decided to have a hot dog instead of a hamburger" who is the "I" doing the choosing? When you say, "My mind is playing tricks on me," who is the "me" watching your mind play those tricks, and who is it that's being tricked? Isn't the self observing itself a little like a finger pointing at its own tip?

Most religions resolve the problem by teaching that an immortal self or soul exists entirely apart from the mortal brain. But modern brain scientists usually consider mind to be a matter of matter. They may have personal religious convictions about a soul, but most assume that what we call "mind," "consciousness," "self-awareness," or "subjective experience" can be explained in physical terms as a product of the cerebral cortex.

Our conscious sense of a unified self may even be an illusion. Neurologist Richard Restak (1983, 1994) has noted that many of our actions and choices occur without any direction by a conscious self. He concludes that "the brains of all creatures are probably organized along the lines of multiple centers and various levels." Cognitive scientist Daniel Dennett (1991) suggests that the brain or mind consists of independent parts that deal with different aspects of thought and perception, constantly conferring with each other and revising their "drafts" of reality. Likewise, Michael Gazzaniga (1985, 1998) proposes that the brain is organized as a loose confederation of independent modules, or mental systems, all working in parallel. Most of these modules operate without our conscious awareness. The sense of a unified self occurs, he says, because one verbal module, an "interpreter" (usually in the left hemisphere), is constantly coming up with theories to explain the actions, moods, and thoughts of the other modules.

Interestingly, the idea that the brain consists of modules and that the self is an illusion is consistent with the teachings of many Eastern spiritual traditions. Buddhism, for example, teaches that the self is not a unified "thing" but rather a collection of thoughts, perceptions, concepts, and feelings that shift and change from moment to moment. To Buddhists, the unity and the permanence of the self are a mirage. Such notions are contrary, of course, to what most people in the West, including psychologists, have always believed about their "selves."

TOLERATE UNCERTAINTY

We all have a sense of being a conscious "self," and brain research shows that consciousness arises from our brains. But if that is the case, where in the brain is this self located? Can this age-old question be answered?

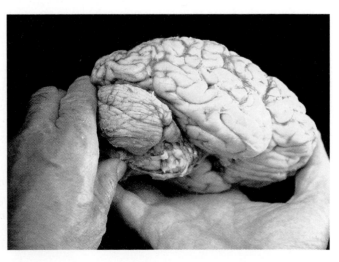

Where in the brain is the sense of self?

"THEN IT'S AGREED—YOU CAN'T HAVE A MIND WITHOUT A BRAIN, BUT YOU CAN HAVE A BRAIN WITHOUT A MIND."

The mind-brain puzzle has plagued philosophers for thousands of years. Even in these days of modern technology, details about the neural system or systems responsible for our sense of self remain hazy. Many researchers believe that the frontal lobes play a critical role. But no one understands yet how the inner life of the mind, or our sense of subjective experience, is linked to the physical processes of the brain. Nor does anyone know how our judgments about our selves are related to these brain processes. Some brain-injured patients who, like H. M., are unable to store new memories about their experiences can nonetheless describe what kind of person they have been since the brain damage occurred (Klein & Kihlstrom, 1998). Where in the brain does this capacity to reflect on one's own personality reside?

Over a century ago, William James (1890, 1950) described the "self-as-knower," the subjective sense we all have of being a distinct person who thinks, feels, and acts. Psychologists, neuroscientists, cognitive scientists, and philosophers all hope to learn more about how our brains and nervous systems give rise to the self-as-knower. What do *you* think about the existence and location of your "self" . . . and who, by the way, is doing the thinking? Think about it!

Are There "His" and "Hers" Brains?

A second stubborn issue concerns the existence of sex differences in the brain. Historically, findings on male-female brain differences have often flip-flopped in a most suspicious manner, a result of the biases of the observers rather than the biology of the brain (Shields, 1975). For example, in the 1960s, scientists speculated that women were more "right-brained" and men were more "left-brained," which supposedly explained why men were "rational" and women "intuitive." Then, when the virtues of the right hemisphere were discovered, such as creativity and ability in art and music, some researchers decided that *men* were more right-brained. But it is now clear that the abilities popularly associated with the two sexes do not fall neatly into the two hemispheres of the brain. The left side is more verbal (presumably a "female" trait), but it is also more mathematical (presumably a "male" trait). The right side is more intuitive ("female"), but it is also more spatially talented ("male").

To evaluate the issue of sex differences in the brain intelligently, we need to ask two questions: Do male and female brains differ physically? And if so, what, if anything, do these differences have to do with behavior?

Let's consider the first question. Many anatomical and biochemical sex differences have been found in animal brains, especially in areas related to reproduction, such as the hypothalamus (McEwen, 1983). Human sex differences, however, have been more elusive. Of course, we would expect to find male-female brain differences that are related to the regulation of sex hormones and other aspects of reproduction. But many researchers want to know whether there are differences that affect how men and women think or behave—and here, the picture is murkier.

For example, in 1982, two anthropologists autopsied 14 human brains and reported an average sex difference in the size and shape of the *splenium*, a small section at the end of the corpus callosum, the bundle of fibers dividing the cerebral hemispheres (de Lacoste-Utamsing & Holloway, 1982). The researchers concluded that women's

EXAMINE THE EVIDENCE

Perhaps no topic in brain research generates as much muddy thinking and as many premature conclusions as that of sex differences in the brain. Does the existing evidence tell us much about men's and women's behavior in their everyday lives?

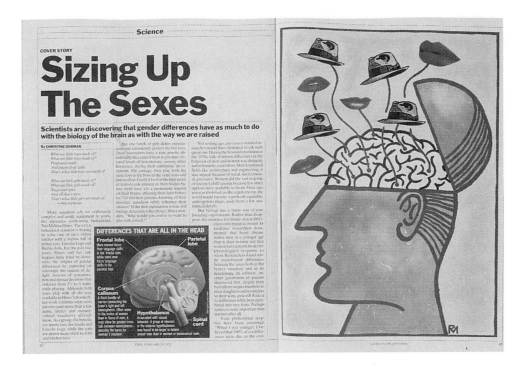

The press has been quick to run stories on differences in male and female brains. Many articles, such as this one from *Time,* conclude from interesting but tentative findings that gender differences in behavior must be biologically based. Is this conclusion justified? Why do you think the media give so much less attention to studies reporting similarities between the sexes?

brains are less lateralized for certain tasks than men's are—that men rely more heavily on one or the other side of the brain, whereas women tend to use both sides. This conclusion quickly made its way into newspapers, magazines, and even textbooks as a verified sex difference.

Today, however, the picture has changed. In a review of the available studies, neuroscientist William Byne (1993) found that only the 1982 study reported the splenium to be larger in women. Two very early studies (in 1906 and 1909) found that it was larger in men, and 21 later studies found no sex difference at all. Moreover, a Canadian analysis of 49 studies found only trivial differences between the two sexes, differences that paled in comparison with the huge individual variations *within* each sex (Bishop & Wahlsten, 1997). Most people are unaware of these findings because studies that find no differences rarely make headlines.

Researchers are now looking for other sex differences in the brain, such as in the density of neurons in specific areas. One team, examining nine brains from autopsied bodies, found that the women had an average of 11 percent more cells in areas of the cortex associated with the processing of auditory information; all of the women had more of these cells than did any of the men (Witelson, Glazer, & Kigar, 1994).

Other researchers are searching for sex differences in the brain areas that are active when people work on a particular task. In one study (Shaywitz et al., 1995), 19 men and 19 women were asked to say whether pairs of nonsense words rhymed, a task that required them to process and compare sounds. MRI scans showed that in both sexes an area at the front of the left hemisphere was activated. But in 11 of the women and none of the men, the corresponding area in the right hemisphere was also active (see Figure 4.16). These findings are further evidence for a sex difference in lateralization, at least for this one type of language function. Such a difference could help explain why left-hemisphere damage is less likely to cause language problems in women than in men after a stroke (Inglis & Lawson, 1981; McGlone, 1978).

FIGURE 4.16
GENDER AND THE BRAIN
These MRIs show that the brains of men and women tended to function differently during a task requiring them to compare sounds. (Because of the orientation of the images, the left hemisphere is seen on the right and vice versa.) During the first step in the task, the sounding out of words, Broca's area was active in all of the men's brains (a) and in 8 of the 19 women's brains. However, the MRIs of the other 11 women showed activity in both hemispheres (b). In spite of these brain differences, the two sexes performed equally well on the task. The researchers concluded that nature has provided the brain with different routes to the same ability (Shaywitz et al., 1995).

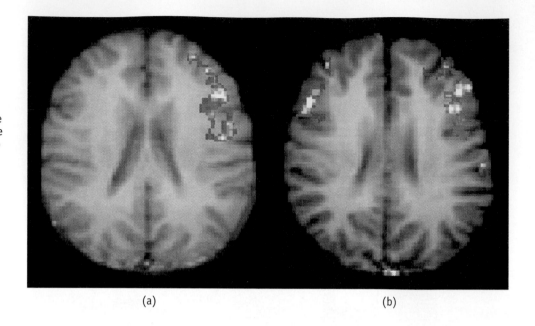

(a)   (b)

Over the next few years, research may reveal additional anatomical and information-processing differences in the brains of males and females. But even if such differences exist, we must then ask our second question: *What do the differences mean for the behavior of men and women in real life?*

Some popular writers have been quick to assume that brain differences explain, among other things, women's allegedly superior intuition, women's love of talking about feelings and men's love of talking about sports, women's greater verbal ability, men's edge in math ability, and why men won't ask for directions when they are lost. But there are at least three problems with these conclusions:

1 *These supposed gender differences in behavior are stereotypes;* the overlap between the sexes is greater than the difference between them. Although some differences may be statistically significant, most are small in practical terms.

2 *A biological difference does not necessarily have behavioral implications.* In the rhyme-judgment study, for example, men and women performed equally well, despite the differences in their MRIs—so what do those brain differences actually mean in practical terms? When it comes to explaining how brain differences are related to more general abilities, speculations are as plentiful as ants at a picnic, but at present they remain just that—speculations (Blum, 1997; Hoptman & Davidson, 1994). To know whether sex differences in the brain translate into significant behavioral differences, we would need to know much more about how brain organization and chemistry affect human abilities and traits.

3 *Sex differences in the brain could be the result rather than the cause of behavioral differences.* Remember that experiences in life are constantly sculpting the circuitry of the brain, affecting the way brains are organized and how they function—and males and females often have different experiences.

Thus, the answer to our second question, whether physical differences are linked to behavior, is "No one really knows." It is important to keep an open mind about new findings on sex differences in the brain, but because the practical significance of these findings (if any) is not clear, it is also important to be cautious and aware of how such results might be exaggerated and misused.

QUICK QUIZ

If you can locate your self, ask it what it thinks about sex differences in the brain.

1. Many brain researchers and cognitive scientists believe that the self is not a unified "thing" but a collection of _____.

2. A new study reports that in a sample of 11 brains, 4 of the 6 women's brains but only 2 of the 5 men's brains had enlarged chocolate receptors. (Note: We made this up; there's no such thing as a chocolate receptor!) The researchers conclude that their findings explain why so many women are addicted to chocolate. What concerns should a critical thinker have about this study?

Answers:

1. independent modules, mental systems, or brain parts, working together 2. It was based on only a few brains and has not yet been replicated. The differences may seem impressive, but may turn out to be trivial, or just a fluke. And differences *within* each sex may turn out to be more significant than those between them. Finally, perhaps eating chocolate affects chocolate receptors in the brain instead of the other way around.

In this chapter, we have seen that the more we know about our physical selves, the better we understand our psychological selves. The study of our most miraculous organ, the brain, illuminates the abilities and powers that we all share as human beings—thought, language, memory, emotion. And it also illuminates the ways in which each of us is unique. The proportion of brain cells found in any part of the brain varies considerably from person to person because of experience. As Roger Sperry (1982) once noted, "the individuality inherent in our brain networks makes that of fingerprints or facial features gross and simple by comparison."

Nevertheless, analyzing a human being in terms of physiology alone is like analyzing the Taj Mahal solely in terms of the materials that were used to build it. Even if we could monitor every cell and circuit of the brain, we would not know how we come to be who we are. We would still need to understand the circumstances, thoughts, and cultural rules that affect whether we are gripped by hatred, consumed by grief, lifted by love, or transported by joy.

TAKING PSYCHOLOGY WITH YOU

FOOD FOR THOUGHT: DIET AND NEUROTRANSMITTERS

Vitamin improves sex! Mineral boosts brainpower! Chocolate chases the blues! Claims such as these have long given nutritional theories of behavior a bad reputation. In the late 1960s, when Nobel laureate Linus Pauling proposed that some mental disorders be treated with massive doses of vitamins, few researchers listened. Mainstream medical authorities classified Pauling's vitamin therapy with such infamous cure-alls as snake oil and leeches.

Today, most mental-health professionals remain skeptical of nutritional cures for mental illness. But the underlying premise of nutritional treatments, that diet affects the brain and therefore behavior, is getting a second look. Claims that sugar or common food additives lead to undesirable behavior in otherwise normal people remain doubtful, but in some cases of disturbance, diet may make a difference. In one double-blind study, researchers asked depressed patients to abstain from refined sugar and caffeine. Over a three-month period, these patients showed significantly more improvement in their symptoms than did another group of patients who refrained from eating red meat and using artificial sweeteners instead (Christensen & Burrows, 1990).

Some of the most exciting work on diet and behavior has looked at the role played by nutrients in the synthesis of neurotransmitters, the brain's chemical messengers. *Tryptophan*, an amino acid found in protein-rich foods (dairy products, meat, fish, and poultry), is a building block of serotonin. *Tyrosine*, another amino acid found in proteins, is a building block of norepinephrine, epinephrine, and dopamine. *Choline*, a component of the lecithin found in egg yolks, soy products, peanuts, and liver, is a precursor of acetylcholine, which plays an important role in learning and memory.

In the case of tryptophan, the path between the dinner plate and the brain is indirect. Tryptophan leads to the production of serotonin, which reduces alertness, promotes relaxation, and hastens sleep. Because tryptophan is found in protein, you might think that a high-protein meal would make you drowsy and that carbohydrates (sweets, bread, pasta, potatoes) would leave you relatively alert. Actually, the opposite is true. High-protein foods contain several amino acids, not just tryptophan, and they all compete for a ride on carrier molecules headed for brain cells.

Because tryptophan occurs in foods in small quantities, it doesn't stand much of a chance *if* all you eat is protein. It is in the position of a tiny child trying to push aside a crowd of adults for a seat on the subway.

Carbohydrates, however, stimulate the production of the hormone insulin, and insulin causes all the other amino acids to be drawn out of the bloodstream while having little effect on tryptophan. So carbohydrates increase the odds that tryptophan will make it to the brain (Wurtman, 1982). Paradoxically, then, a high-carbohydrate, no-protein meal is likely to make you relatively calm or lethargic and a high-protein one is likely to promote alertness, all else being equal (Spring, Chiodo, & Bowen, 1987; Wurtman & Lieberman, 1982–1983).

How else might nutrition affect mental and physical performance? In a report commissioned by the U.S. Army, the National Academy of Sciences reviewed existing animal and human studies on this question (Marriott, 1994). Some of the highlights:

■ Tyrosine can reduce symptoms that occur in extreme cold and at high altitudes, such as fuzzy thinking, headache, and nausea.

■ Carbohydrates can prolong endurance under stressful conditions, increase fine-motor coordination,

improve mood, and help people sleep.

■ Choline can enhance memory and strengthen muscles and the immune system.

■ Caffeine improves alertness and mental performance, although in high doses it can cause anxiety and insomnia.

Keep in mind, though, that many other factors also influence mood and behavior, that the effects of nutrients are subtle, and that some of these effects depend on your age, the circumstances, and even the time of day. Further, nutrients interact with each other in complex ways. If you do not eat protein, you will not get enough tryptophan, but if you go without carbohydrates, the tryptophan found in protein will be useless. Many people try to rev themselves up with nutritional supplements, but in the United States, herbal remedies and other "dietary supplements" are currently exempt from regulation by the Food and Drug Administration. Brands vary enormously in quality and in the amount of the active ingredient contained in each pill (Angell & Kassirer, 1999).

The moral of the story is simple: If you are looking for brain food, you are most likely to find it in a well-balanced diet.

SUMMARY

1. The brain is the bedrock of consciousness, perception, memory, emotion, and reasoning. People debate how to speak about this organ: For example, where is the "you" that is using "your brain"?

THE NERVOUS SYSTEM: A BASIC BLUEPRINT

2. The function of the nervous system is to gather and process information, produce responses to stimuli, and

coordinate the workings of different cells. Scientists divide it into the *central nervous system (CNS)* and the *peripheral nervous system (PNS)*. The CNS, which includes the brain and *spinal cord*, receives, processes, interprets, and stores information and sends messages destined for muscles, glands, and organs. The PNS transmits information to and from the CNS by way of *sensory* and *motor nerves*.

3. The peripheral nervous system consists of the *somatic nervous system*, which permits sensation and voluntary actions, and the *autonomic nervous system*, which

regulates blood vessels, glands, and internal (visceral) organs. The autonomic system usually functions without conscious control, although some people can learn to heighten or suppress autonomic responses, using *biofeedback* techniques.

4. The autonomic nervous system is divided into the *sympathetic nervous system*, which mobilizes the body for action, and the *parasympathetic nervous system*, which conserves energy.

COMMUNICATION IN THE NERVOUS SYSTEM

5. *Neurons* are the basic units of the nervous system; they are held in place, nourished, and insulated by *glial cells*. Each neuron consists of *dendrites*, a *cell body*, and an *axon*. In the peripheral nervous system, axons (and sometimes dendrites) are collected together in bundles called *nerves*. Many axons are insulated by a *myelin sheath* that speeds up the conduction of neural impulses and prevents signals in adjacent cells from interfering with one another. Recent research has challenged the old assumption that neurons in the human central nervous system cannot be induced to regenerate or multiply. Scientists have also learned that *precursor cells* in brain areas associated with learning and memory continue to divide and mature throughout adulthood. A stimulating environment enhances this process of *neurogenesis*.

6. Communication between two neurons occurs at the *synapse*. Many synapses have not yet formed at birth. During development, axons and dendrites continue to grow as a result of both physical maturation and experience with the world, and throughout life, new learning results in new synaptic connections in the brain. Thus, the brain's circuits are not fixed and immutable but are continually changing in response to information, challenges, and changes in the environment.

7. When a wave of electrical voltage (*action potential*) reaches the end of a transmitting axon, *neurotransmitter* molecules are released into the *synaptic cleft*. When these molecules bind to *receptor sites* on the receiving neuron, that neuron becomes either more or less likely to fire. The message that reaches a final destination depends on how frequently particular neurons are firing, how many are firing, what types are firing, and where they are located.

8. Through their effects on neural circuits, neurotransmitters play a critical role in mood, memory, and psychological well-being. Abnormal levels of neurotransmitters have been implicated in several disorders, including depression, childhood autism, Alzheimer's disease, and Parkinson's disease.

9. *Endorphins*, which act primarily as *neuromodulators* that affect the action of neurotransmitters, reduce pain and promote pleasure. Endorphin levels seem to shoot up when an animal or person is afraid or is under stress. Endorphins may also be linked to the pleasures of social contact.

10. *Hormones*, produced mainly by the *endocrine glands*, affect and are affected by the nervous system. Psychologists are especially interested in *melatonin*, which appears to regulate daily biological rhythms; *adrenal hormones* such as *epinephrine* and *norepinephrine*, which are involved in emotions and stress; and the *sex hormones*, which are involved in the physical changes of puberty, the menstrual cycle (estrogens and progesterone), sexual arousal (testosterone), and some non-reproductive functions—including, many researchers believe, mental functioning.

MAPPING THE BRAIN

11. Researchers study the brain by observing patients with brain damage; by using the *lesion method* with animals; and by using such techniques as electroencephalograms (*EEGs*), positron-emission tomography (*PET scans*), and magnetic resonance imaging (*MRI*).

A TOUR THROUGH THE BRAIN

12. All modern brain theories assume *localization of function*. In the lower part of the brain, the *brain stem* controls automatic functions such as heartbeat and breathing, and the *reticular activating system (RAS)* screens incoming information and is responsible for alertness. The *cerebellum* contributes to balance and muscle coordination and may also play a role in some higher mental operations.

13. The *thalamus* directs sensory messages to appropriate higher centers. The *hypothalamus* is involved in emotion and in drives associated with survival. It also controls the operations of the autonomic nervous system and sends out chemicals that tell the *pituitary gland* when to "talk" to other endocrine glands.

14. The *limbic system* is involved in emotions that we share with other animals, and it contains pathways involved in pleasure. Within this system, the *amygdala* is responsible for evaluating sensory information and quickly determining its emotional importance, and for the initial decision to approach or withdraw from a person or situation. The *hippocampus* has been called the "gateway to memory" because it plays a critical role in the formation of long-term memories for facts and events.

15. Much of the brain's circuitry is packed into the *cerebrum*, which is divided into two *hemispheres* and is covered by

thin layers of cells known collectively as the *cerebral cortex*. The *occipital, parietal, temporal,* and *frontal lobes* of the cortex have specialized (but partially overlapping) functions. The *association cortex* appears to be responsible for higher mental processes. The frontal lobes, particularly areas in the *prefrontal cortex*, are involved in social judgment, the making and carrying out of plans, and decision making.

THE TWO HEMISPHERES OF THE BRAIN

16. Studies of *split-brain* patients, who have had the *corpus callosum* cut, show that the two cerebral hemispheres have somewhat different talents, a phenomenon known as *lateralization*. In most people, language is processed mainly in the left hemisphere, which generally is specialized for logical, symbolic, and sequential tasks. The right hemisphere is associated with spatial-visual tasks, facial recognition, and the creation and appreciation of art and music. However, in most mental activities, the two hemispheres cooperate as partners, with each making a valuable contribution.

TWO STUBBORN ISSUES IN BRAIN RESEARCH

17. One of the oldest questions in the study of the brain is where the "self" resides. Many brain researchers and cognitive scientists believe that a unified self may be something of an illusion. The brain, they argue, operates as a collection of independent modules or mental systems, perhaps with one of them functioning as an "interpreter." But much remains to be learned about the relationship between the brain and the mind.

18. Sex differences have been observed in anatomical and biochemical studies of animal brains. Sex differences in human brains, however, have been more elusive, and there is controversy about their existence and their meaning. Biological differences do not necessarily explain behavioral ones, and sex differences in experience could affect brain organization rather than the other way around.

19. The study of the brain helps us understand both the abilities we all share and our uniqueness as individuals. But physiological research alone does not explain human behavior.

KEY TERMS

central nervous system 100

spinal cord 100

spinal reflexes 100

peripheral nervous system 101

sensory nerves 101

motor nerves 101

somatic nervous system 101

autonomic nervous system 101

biofeedback 101

sympathetic nervous system 102

parasympathetic nervous system 102

neuron 103

glial cells 103

dendrites 105

cell body 105

axon 105

axon terminals 105

myelin sheath 105

nerves 105

precursor cells 106

neurogenesis 106

synaptic cleft 106

synapse 107

plasticity 107

action potential 107

synaptic vesicles 107

neurotransmitter 107

receptor sites 107

blood–brain barrier 109

endorphins 110

neuromodulators 110

hormones 111

endocrine glands 111

melatonin 111

adrenal hormones 111

adrenal glands 111

cortisol 111

epinephrine 111

norepinephrine 111

sex hormones (androgens, estrogens, progesterone) 111

electrodes 113

electroencephalogram (EEG) 113

PET scan (position-emission tomography) 114

MRI (magnetic resonance imaging) 114

localization of function 116

brain stem 117

medulla 117

pons 117

reticular activating system (RAS) 117

cerebellum 117

thalamus 117

olfactory bulb 117

hypothalamus 117

pituitary gland 118

limbic system 118

amygdala 119

hippocampus 119

cerebrum 120

cerebral hemispheres 120

corpus callosum 120

LOOKING BACK

- Why do you automatically pull your hand away from something hot, "without thinking"? (p. 100)

- Is it possible to consciously control your heartbeat or blood pressure? (p. 101)

- If you have to deal with a sudden emergency, which part of your nervous system whirls into action? (p. 102)

- Which cells are the nervous system's "communication specialists," and how do they "talk" to each other? (pp. 104, 107–108)

- How do learning and experience alter the brain's circuits? (p. 107)

- Why do neural impulses travel more slowly in babies than in adults? (p. 107)

- What happens when levels of brain chemicals called neurotransmitters are too low or too high? (p. 109)

- What substances in the brain mimic the effects of morphine by dulling pain and promoting pleasure? (p. 110)

- Do the sexes have different "sex hormones"? (p. 111)

- Why are patterns of electrical activity in the brain called "brain waves"? (p. 113)

- What scanning techniques allow psychologists to view changes in brain activity while people listen to music or solve math problems? (p. 114)

- Which brain part acts as a "traffic officer" for incoming sensations? (p. 117)

- Which brain part is the "gateway to memory"—and what cognitive catastrophe occurs when it is damaged? (p. 119)

- Why is it a good thing that the outer covering of the human brain is so wrinkled? (p. 120)

- How did a bizarre nineteenth-century accident illuminate the role of the frontal lobes? (p. 122)

- If the two cerebral hemispheres were out of touch, would they feel different emotions and think different thoughts? (pp. 125–127)

- Why do researchers often refer to the left hemisphere as "dominant"? (p. 127)

- Should you sign up for a program that promises to perk up the right side of your brain? (p. 128)

- Why do some brain researchers think a unified "self" is an illusion? (p. 129)

- Do men talk about sports and women about feelings because their brains are different? (p. 132)

5

BODY RHYTHMS AND MENTAL STATES

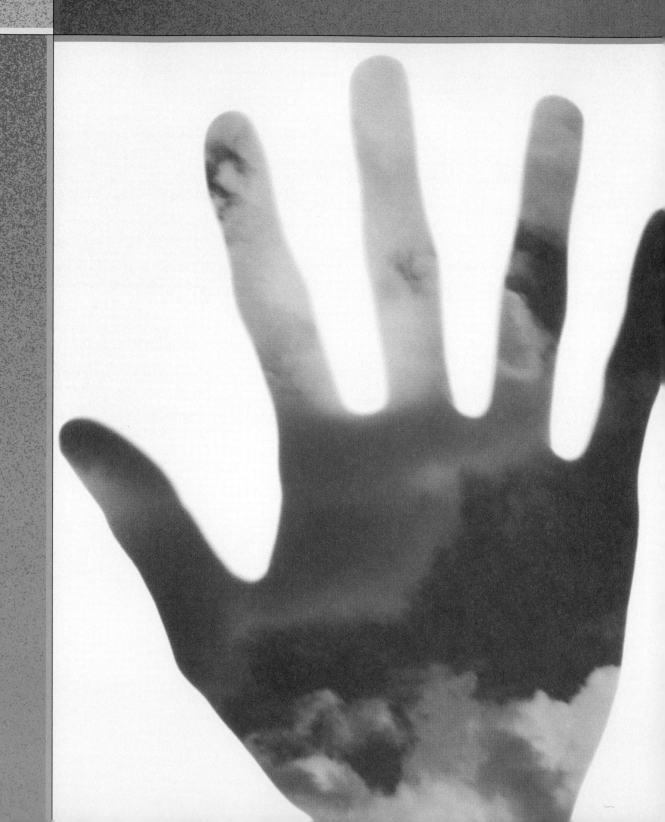

Like a bird's life, [consciousness] seems to be made

of an alternation of flights and perchings.

PSYCHOLOGIST WILLIAM JAMES

In Lewis Carroll's immortal story *Alice's Adventures in Wonderland,* the ordinary rules of everyday life keep dissolving in a sea of logical contradictions. First Alice shrinks to within only a few inches of the ground, then she shoots up taller than the treetops. The strange antics of Wonderland's inhabitants make her smile one moment and shed a pool of tears the next. "Dear dear!" muses the harried heroine. "How queer everything is today! . . . I wonder if I've been changed in the night? Let me think: *was* I the same when I got up this morning? I almost think I can remember feeling a little different. But if I'm not the same, the *next* question is, 'Who in the world am I?' Ah, *that's* the great puzzle!"

In a way, we all live in a sort of Wonderland. For a third of our lives, we reside in a realm where the ordinary rules of logic and experience are suspended: the dream world of sleep. Throughout the day, mood, alertness, efficiency, and *consciousness* itself—our awareness of ourselves and the environment—are in perpetual flux, sometimes shifting as dramatically as Alice's height. We are constantly moving in and out of different *states of consciousness*, as we experience distinct patterns of perception, thought, memory, and feeling. Sometimes, for example, we feel hyperalert and attentive to everything around us, and to our own feelings and sensations. At other times, as when we are daydreaming or "graying out" on a long drive, consciousness of our surroundings and of our own internal states fades.

Starting from the assumption that mental and physical states are as intertwined as sunshine and shadow, psychologists, along with other scientists, are exploring the links between these fluctuations in subjective experience and changes in brain activity and hormone levels. They have come to view changing states of consciousness as part of the rhythmic ebb and flow of experience over time. For example, dreaming, traditionally classified as a state of consciousness, is also part of a 90-minute cycle of brain activity.

Examining a person's ongoing rhythmic cycles is like watching a motion picture of consciousness. Studying the person's distinct states of consciousness is more like looking at separate snapshots. In this chapter, we will first run the motion picture, to see how functioning and consciousness vary predictably over time. Then we will zoom in on one specific "snapshot"—the world of dreams—and examine it in some detail. Finally, we will turn to two techniques that have been used in efforts to "retouch the film" by deliberately altering consciousness: the use of recreational drugs and the induction of hypnosis.

WHAT'S AHEAD

● **Do popular "biorhythm" charts tell you anything about what scientists call biological rhythms?**
● **Why do you feel "out of sync" when you fly across time zones or change shifts at work?**
● **How are researchers learning to reset the biological clock that governs our daily cycles?**
● **Does "PMS" cause most women to feel depressed or irritable before their periods?**

BIOLOGICAL RHYTHMS: THE TIDES OF EXPERIENCE

biological rhythm A periodic, more or less regular fluctuation in a biological system; may or may not have psychological implications.

entrainment The synchronization of biological rhythms with external cues, such as fluctuations in daylight.

Have you ever seen an advertisement for "biorhythm charts" that promise to predict, solely on the basis of the time and date of your birth, how your mood, alertness, and physical performance will fluctuate over your lifetime? Pseudoscientific ideas about biorhythms have been around for more than a century. Purveyors of biorhythm charts claim they can foresee your good days and tell when you will be susceptible to accidents, errors, and illness. Whenever researchers have taken the trouble to test such claims scientifically—for example, by examining occupational accidents in light of the charts' predictions—they have found the charts to be completely useless (e.g., Hines, 1998). Yet, biorhythm charts continue to be marketed, notably on the Internet; apparently, one human characteristic that does not fluctuate much is gullibility!

It *is* true, however, that the human body changes over the course of a day, a week, a year. We all experience dozens of periodic, fairly regular ups and downs in physiological functioning. A biological clock in our brains governs the waxing and waning of hormone levels, urine volume, blood pressure, and even the responsiveness of brain cells to stimulation. Such physiological fluctuations are what scientists mean by **biological rhythms.**

Biological rhythms are typically synchronized with external events, such as changes in clock time and daylight—a process called **entrainment.** But many of these rhythms continue to occur even in the absence of external time cues; they are *endogenous,* or generated from within. These rhythms fall into three categories:

1 **Circadian rhythms** *occur approximately every 24 hours.* The best-known circadian rhythm is the sleep–wake cycle, but there are hundreds of others that affect physiology and performance. For example, body temperature fluctuates about 1 degree centigrade each day, peaking, on average, in the late afternoon and hitting a low point, or trough, in the wee hours of the morning.

2 **Infradian rhythms** *occur less often than once a day*—say, once a month, or once a season. In the animal world, infradian rhythms are common. Birds migrate south in the fall, bears hibernate in the winter, and marine animals become active or inactive, depending on bimonthly changes in the tides. In human beings, the female menstrual cycle, which occurs every 28 days on the average, is an example of an infradian rhythm.

3 **Ultradian rhythms** *occur more often than once a day,* frequently on about a 90-minute schedule. The best-studied ultradian rhythm occurs during sleep, but many other physiological changes and behaviors also follow an ultradian pattern when social customs do not intervene. They include stomach contractions, hormone levels, susceptibility to visual illusions, verbal and spatial performance, brain-wave responses during cognitive tasks, alertness, and daydreaming (Escera, Cilveti, & Grau, 1992; Klein & Armitage, 1979; Kripke, 1974; Lavie, 1976).

Many psychologists used to regard the study of biological rhythms as a quirky subject on the fringe of mainstream psychology, but today this topic is one of the

BIOLOGICAL RYTHMS

Circadian

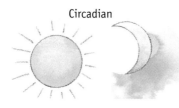

Infradian

Ultradian

hottest areas in biology and biological psychology. It turns out that biological rhythms affect everything from the effectiveness of medicines taken at different times of the day to alertness and performance on the job. With a better understanding of these internal tempos, we may be able to design our days to take better advantage of our bodies' natural rhythms. Let's look more closely at how these cycles operate.

Circadian Rhythms

Circadian rhythms exist in plants, animals, insects, and human beings. They reflect the adaptation of organisms to the many changes associated with the rotation of the earth on its axis, such as changes in light, air pressure, and temperature.

Usually our bodies adapt to a strict 24-hour schedule. External time cues abound, and our biological rhythms become entrained to them. To identify endogenous circadian rhythms, therefore, scientists must isolate volunteers from sunlight, clocks, environmental sounds, and all other cues to time. Some hardy souls have spent weeks or even months alone in caves and salt mines, linked to the outside world only by a one-way phone line and a cable transmitting physiological measurements to the surface. More often, volunteers live in specially designed rooms equipped with stereo systems, comfortable furniture, and temperature controls.

In some studies, participants have been allowed to sleep, eat, and work whenever they wished, free of the tyranny of the timepiece. Under these circumstances, a few people have lived a "day" that is much shorter or longer than 24 hours. When people are allowed to take daytime naps, however, most soon settle into a day that averages

circadian [sur-CAY-dee-un] rhythm
A biological rhythm with a period (from peak to peak or trough to trough) of about 24 hours; from the Latin *circa*, "about," and *dies*, "a day."

infradian [in-FRAY-dee-un] rhythm
A biological rhythm that occurs less frequently than once a day; from the Latin for "below a day."

ultradian [ul-TRAY-dee-un] rhythm
A biological rhythm that occurs more frequently than once a day; from the Latin for "beyond a day."

Stefania Follini (left) spent 4 months in a New Mexico cave (below), 30 feet underground, as part of an Italian study on biological rhythms. Her only companions were a computer and two friendly mice. In the absence of clocks, natural light, or changes in temperature, she tended to stay awake for 20 to 25 hours and then sleep for 10. Because her days were longer than usual, when she emerged she thought she had been in the cave for only 2 months.

suprachiasmatic [soo-pruh-kie-az-MAT-ick] nucleus (SCN) An area of the brain containing a biological clock that governs circadian rhythms.

melatonin A hormone secreted by the pineal gland; it is involved in the regulation of circadian rhythms.

internal desynchronization A state in which biological rhythms are not in phase (synchronized) with one another.

about 24.3 hours (R. Moore, 1997). And when people are put on an artificial 28-hour "day," in an environment free of all time cues, then their body temperature and certain hormone levels follow a cycle that is very close to 24 hours—24.18 hours to be precise (Czeisler et al., 1999). These rhythms are remarkably similar from one person to the next.

The Body's Clock. Circadian rhythms are controlled by a biological clock, or overall coordinator, located in a tiny teardrop-shaped cluster of cells in the hypothalamus called the **suprachiasmatic nucleus (SCN)**. Neural pathways from the back of the eye to the SCN allow the SCN to respond to changes in light and dark. It then sends out messages that cause the brain and body to adapt to these changes. Other clocks may also exist, scattered around the body, but the SCN seems to be the master pacemaker.

The SCN regulates fluctuating levels of hormones and neurotransmitters, and they in turn provide feedback that affects the SCN's functioning. For example, during the dark hours, one hormone regulated by the SCN, **melatonin,** is secreted by the pineal gland, deep within the brain. When you go to sleep in a darkened room, your melatonin level falls; when you wake up in the morning to a lightened room, it rises. Melatonin appears to help keep the biological clock in phase with the light–dark cycle (Haimov & Lavie, 1996; Lewy et al., 1992).

Melatonin also seems to directly promote sleep. Interestingly, in many (though not all) blind people who lack light perception, the normal melatonin cycle is absent. As a result, their circadian rhythms are disrupted, and insomnia and other sleep problems occur (Czeisler et al., 1995; Tabandeh et al., 1998). Melatonin treatments have been used to synchronize the disturbed sleep–wake cycles of such people (Sack & Lewy, 1997). Melatonin supplements can also help some sighted people who suffer from chronic insomnia, especially older people, who often show a decline in the hormone (Haimov & Lavie, 1996; Lewy & Sack, 1997).

Melatonin supplements that are sold over the counter, however, should be used with caution. Because they are classified in the United States as a dietary supplement rather than a drug, there are no federal standards for quality, dosage, and when to take them (and timing can be critical). Also, the long-term safety of such treatments is not yet known.

When the Clock Is Out of Sync. Under normal conditions, the rhythms governed by the SCN are synchronized, just as wristwatches can be synchronized. Their peaks may occur at different times, but they occur in phase with one another; thus, if you know when one rhythm peaks, you can predict when another will. But when your normal routine changes, your circadian rhythms may be thrown out of phase with one another. Such **internal desynchronization** often occurs when people take airplane flights across several time zones. Sleep and wake patterns usually adjust quickly, but temperature and hormone cycles can take several days to return to normal. The resulting jet lag affects energy level, mental skills, and motor coordination.

Internal desynchronization also occurs when workers must adjust to a new shift. Efficiency drops, the person feels tired and irritable, accidents become more likely, and sleep disturbances and digestive disorders may occur. For people such as police officers, emergency-room personnel, airline pilots, truck drivers, and nuclear-power-plant operators, the consequences can be serious—even a matter of life and death. A National Commission on Sleep Disorders concluded that lack of alertness in night-shift equipment operators may have contributed to the 1989 Exxon

Travel can be exhausting, and jet lag makes it worse.

MEASURING YOUR ALERTNESS CYCLES

For at least two days, except when you are sleeping, keep an hourly record of your mental alertness level, using this five-point scale: 1 = extremely drowsy or mentally lethargic; 2 = somewhat drowsy or mentally lethargic; 3 = moderately alert; 4 = alert and efficient; 5 = extremely alert and efficient. Does your alertness level appear to follow an ultradian or circadian rhythm? If so, when does it tend to peak and plummet? Is this cycle the same on weekends as during the week? Most important, how well does your schedule mesh with your natural fluctuations in alertness?

Valdez oil spill off the coast of Alaska and disastrous accidents during the 1980s at the Three Mile Island and Chernobyl nuclear-power plants.

Night work itself is not necessarily a problem: With a schedule that always stays the same (even on weekends), people can often adapt. However, many swing- and night-shift assignments are made on a rotating basis, so circadian rhythms never have a chance to resynchronize. Ideally, a rotating work schedule should follow circadian principles by switching workers as infrequently as possible.

Researchers are now studying ways to hasten recovery from jet lag and ease people's adjustment to new work shifts. One approach is to use bright lights to "reset" the clock in the SCN, just as you would reset a mechanical or electronic clock forward or backward (Dawson, Lack, & Morris, 1993; Martin & Eastman, 1998). Another approach is to give people small amounts of melatonin on a controlled schedule, or to combine melatonin with light treatments (Arendt et al., 1997; Lewy, Ahmed, & Sack, 1995). However, procedures that seem promising in the laboratory do not always work well in the real world, where people are exposed to many natural and artificial time cues (Gallo & Eastman, 1993).

We want to emphasize that circadian rhythms are not perfectly regular and can be affected by illness, stress, fatigue, excitement, exercise, drugs, and ordinary daily experiences. Further, circadian rhythms differ greatly from individual to individual, in part because of genetic differences. Some people are early birds, bouncing out of bed at the crack of dawn, whereas others are night owls who do their best work late at night and can't be pried out of bed until noon. (Schools are not designed to accommodate night owls.) You may be able to learn about your own personal pulses through careful self-observation, and you may want to try putting that information to use when planning your daily schedule.

Moods and Long-term Rhythms

According to Ecclesiastes, "To every thing there is a season, and a time for every purpose under heaven." Modern science agrees: Long-term (infradian) cycles have been observed in everything from the threshold for tooth pain to conception rates. Folklore holds that our moods follow infradian cycles, too—particularly in response to seasonal changes and, in women, menstrual changes. But do they?

Does the Season Affect Moods? Clinicians report that some people become depressed every winter, when periods of daylight are short, and improve in mood each spring, as daylight increases—a pattern that has come to be known as *seasonal affective disorder (SAD)* (Rosenthal, 1998). During the winter months, such patients report feeling sad, lethargic, and drowsy, having an increased appetite, and craving carbohydrates. To counteract the presumed effects of sunless days, some physicians and therapists have been treating "SAD" patients with phototherapy, having them sit in front of special, extremely bright fluorescent lights at specific times of the day.

Evaluating the actual prevalence of SAD and treatments for it is difficult, however. Information on SAD comes mainly from clinical case reports rather than controlled studies, and, as we saw in Chapter 2, case studies have many drawbacks. Many clinicians, extrapolating from patients who believe they suffer from SAD, think the disorder is quite common—that as many as 20 percent of the population might have it. But a recent survey suggests that in the United States, the lifetime prevalence of major seasonal depression is only 0.4 percent, and the prevalence of major or minor seasonal depression is only 1 percent (Blazer, Kessler, & Swartz, 1998).

As for the light treatments, research on this question, too, has unfortunately been flawed. A meta-analysis of SAD studies found that phototherapy produces a better outcome than no light treatment (Lee et al., 1997). But most studies have not used control groups, and it has therefore been impossible to rule out placebo effects when "SAD" patients cheer up.

Better research, though, is finally being done, and this research may throw some light on the subject, so to speak. In two well-controlled studies, patients had daily sessions of (a) bright light, (b) exposure to high levels of negative ions, (c) exposure to low levels of negative ions, or (d) placebo sessions in which they sat in front of a machine that they thought was generating negative ions but was not. Exposure to light and also, unexpectedly, to the high levels of negative ions, was effective in alleviating the patients' symptoms, but the other two conditions were not (Eastman et al., 1998; Terman, Terman, & Ross, 1998). The effectiveness of the light treatment suggests that true SAD patients have some deficiency in the secretion of melatonin. Indeed, in another study, morning light treatments advanced the onset of daily melatonin secretion in SAD patients by nearly two hours but did not have this effect in control subjects (Lewy et al., 1998).

These young Norwegian women are receiving light therapy for "seasonal affective disorder (SAD)." This type of treatment is becoming increasingly popular, but fewer people actually have SAD than is commonly thought.

Nonetheless, people should be cautious about diagnosing themselves as having SAD, or laying out hundreds of dollars for a light-treatment lamp. Even if depression does rise and fall in some people with the passing of the seasons, the reason is still not clear. True cases of SAD may have a biological basis, but the evidence is inconsistent (Checkley et al., 1993). Many people may get the winter blues because they hate sleet, ice, and cold weather; because they become less physically active; or because the winter holidays depress them.

Does the Menstrual Cycle Affect Moods? Controversy has also raged about another infradian rhythm, the female *menstrual cycle,* which occurs, on average, every 28 days. During the first half of this cycle, an increase in the hormone estrogen causes the lining of the uterus to thicken in preparation for a possible pregnancy. At midcycle, the ovaries release a mature egg, or ovum. Afterward, the ovarian sac that contained the egg begins to produce progesterone, which helps prepare the uterine lining to receive the egg. Then, if conception does not occur, estrogen and progesterone levels fall, the uterine lining sloughs off as the menstrual flow, and the cycle begins again.

The interesting question for psychologists is whether these physical changes are correlated with emotional or intellectual changes, as folklore and tradition would have us believe. Most people certainly think so. Since the 1970s, a vague cluster of symptoms associated with the days preceding menstruation—including fatigue, headache, irritability, and depression—has come to be thought of as an illness and has been given a label: "premenstrual syndrome" ("PMS"). Some popular books have asserted, without any evidence whatsoever, that most women suffer from "PMS."

This "syndrome," however, is an ill-defined hodgepodge of physical and emotional symptoms, and the emotional symptoms, the evidence shows, are *not* reliably and universally tied to the menstrual cycle. Just as with "SAD," more people claim to have symptoms than actually do. Of course, many women do have *physical* symptoms associated with menstruation, including cramps, breast tenderness, and water retention (although women vary tremendously in this regard). And of course these physical symptoms can make some women feel grumpy or unhappy, just as pain can make men feel grumpy or unhappy. But emotional symptoms associated with menstruation are rare, which is why we put "PMS" in quotes. In fact, less than 5 percent of all women have such symptoms predictably over their cycles (Brooks-Gunn, 1986; Reid, 1991).

If true "PMS" is so uncommon, then why do so many women think they have it? One possibility is that they tend to notice feelings of depression or irritability when these moods happen to occur premenstrually but overlook times when such moods are *absent* premenstrually. Or they may label symptoms that occur before a period as "PMS" and attribute the same symptoms at other times of the month to a stressful day or a low grade on an English paper. A woman's perceptions of her own emotional ups and downs can also be influenced by cultural attitudes and myths about menstruation. Although women all over the world report having menstrual cramps, the concept of a special *pre*menstrual package of symptoms is uniquely Western (Parlee, 1994).

Even the name of the questionnaire used in a study can reflect cultural biases and can thereby affect a woman's self-report. The "Menstrual Distress Questionnaire," which asks primarily about negative symptoms, elicits more negative responses when it is given alone than when it is preceded by a "Menstrual Joy

EXAMINE THE EVIDENCE

Many women say they become more irritable or depressed premenstrually. Does the evidence support their self-reports? How might attitudes and expectations be affecting these accounts? What happens when people of both sexes report their daily moods and feelings without knowing that menstruation is being studied?

"PMS" remedies line the shelves of drugstores, and most people think the "syndrome" is common—but is it?

Questionnaire" that asks about positive changes such as "high spirits" and "vibrant activity" (Chrisler et al., 1994).

To get around these problems, psychologists have polled women about their psychological and physical well-being *without revealing the true purpose of the study* (e.g., Alagna & Hamilton, 1986; AuBuchon & Calhoun, 1985; Burke, Burnett, & Levenstein, 1978; Englander-Golden, Whitmore, & Dienstbier, 1978; Gallant et al., 1991; Hardie, 1997; Parlee, 1982; Rapkin, Chang, & Reading, 1988; Slade, 1984; Vila & Beech, 1980). Using double-blind procedures, they have had women report symptoms for a single day and have then gone back to see what phase of the menstrual cycle the women were in; or they have had women keep daily records over an extended period of time. Some studies have included a control group that is usually excluded from research on hormones and moods: men! Here are some of the major findings:

■ *No gender differences exist in mood.* Overall, women and men do not differ significantly in the emotional symptoms they report or the number of mood swings they experience over the course of a month, as you can see in Figure 5.1 (McFarlane, Martin, & Williams, 1988).

■ *No relation exists between stage of the menstrual cycle and emotional symptoms.* Most women do not have the typical "PMS" symptoms even when they firmly believe they do (Hardie, 1997; McFarlane & Williams, 1994). They may recall their moods as having been more unpleasant before or during menstruation, but, as you can also see in Figure 5.1, their own daily reports fail to bear them out.

■ *No consistent "PMS" pattern exists across menstrual cycles.* Even when women know that menstruation is being studied, most do not consistently report negative (or positive) psychological changes from one cycle to the next. Their moods and emotions vary far more in degree and direction than we would expect if predictable hormone fluctuations were the main reason for these changes (Walker, 1994).

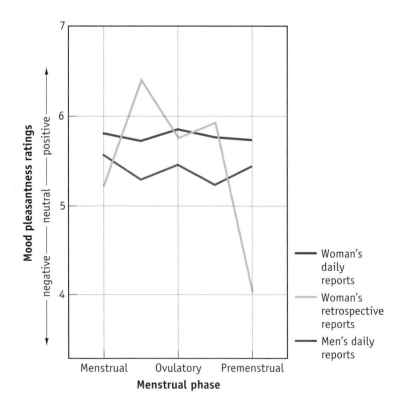

FIGURE 5.1

MOOD CHANGES IN MEN AND WOMEN

In a study that challenged popular stereotypes about "PMS," college women and men recorded their moods daily for 70 days without knowing the purpose of the study. When the women were asked to recall their moods, they said their moods had been more negative premenstrually (green line)—but their daily diaries did not bear this out (purple line). Both sexes experienced only moderate mood changes, and there were no significant differences between women and men at any time of the month (McFarlane, Martin, & Williams, 1988).

GET →INVOLVED

A CLOSER LOOK AT "PMS" REMEDIES

Go to your local drugstore and find the over-the-counter medications for menstrual symptoms. Do the containers mention only physical symptoms, such as water retention and cramps, or do they also mention emotional symptoms, such as "mood swings"? Do they refer to "PMS" or "premenstrual tension" as an illness? Are the active ingredients in these products unique to them, or are they generic painkillers such as ibuprofen? What kinds of claims are made for these remedies, and how would you evaluate those claims based on the information in this chapter?

■ *No connection exists between "PMS" and behavior.* There is no relationship between stage of the menstrual cycle and work efficiency, problem solving, motor performance, memory, college exam scores, creativity, or any other behavior that matters in real life (Golub, 1992; Richardson, 1992). In the workplace, men, premenstrual women, postmenstrual women, and nonmenstrual women all report similar levels of stress, wellness, and work performance (Hardie, 1997).

These results are unknown to most people and have usually been ignored by doctors, therapists, and the media. As a result, since the 1970s, premenstrual symptoms have come to be defined almost solely in medical and psychiatric terms (Parlee, 1994). So entrenched is the belief that "most women suffer from PMS" that we have occasionally been accused of "bias" for reporting the psychological studies that call this belief into question. In 1994, over the objections of many psychologists, the American Psychiatric Association included "premenstrual dysphoric disorder" (PMDD) in the *Diagnostic and Statistical Manual of Mental Disorders,* the official bible of psychiatric diagnosis; its characteristics do not differ much from those of "PMS."

Critics believe that the acceptance of "PMS" as a widespread problem and a psychiatric diagnosis has more to do with politics than with facts. The notion that hormones impair mood and performance, they point out, is rarely extended to men—even though the masculinizing hormone testosterone fluctuates daily in all men, usually reaching a peak in the morning, and also follows a longer, infradian cycle in some men, varying in length from one man to another (Doering et al., 1974). Indeed, almost no work has been done on correlations between testosterone cycles and psychological changes.

Researchers *have* compared men who have relatively high levels of testosterone with those who have relatively low ones. High levels have been linked to a long (and sometimes contradictory) list of behaviors and traits, including criminal violence, delinquency, rambunctiousness, restlessness, elation, sadness, moodiness, sociability, aloofness—and being a trial lawyer (Dabbs et al., 1995; Dabbs, Alford, & Fielden, 1998; Dabbs, Hargrove, & Heusel, 1996; Dabbs, Strong, & Milun, 1997; Mazur & Lamb, 1980; Susman et al., 1987). But researchers have been careful to point out that behavior affects testosterone levels, as well as the reverse. For example, testosterone tends to rise after a man behaves aggressively,

"Fill'er up with testosterone."

not before he does, and it also rises after he watches a favorite team win an exhilarating sports victory (Bernhardt et al., 1998; Sapolsky, 1997). Moreover, no researcher has suggested that men are victims of hormone fluctuations or that high testosterone levels constitute a syndrome calling for treatment.

We are not suggesting that, either! We raise the issue of testosterone to illustrate cultural biases in thinking about hormones and behavior—biases that cause people to reduce women's behavior to hormones but not men's. In reality, few people of either sex are likely to undergo personality shifts because of their hormones, except in rare cases of hormonal abnormalities. In most instances, the body only provides the clay for people's symptoms; learning and culture mold that clay, by teaching us which symptoms are important or worrisome and which are not. The impact of any bodily change—whether it is circadian, ultradian, or infradian—depends on how we interpret it and how we respond to it.

QUICK QUIZ

There are no hormonal excuses for avoiding this quiz.

1. The functioning of the biological clock governing circadian rhythms is affected by the hormone _____.

2. Jet lag occurs because of _____.

3. Which term describes the menstrual cycle? (a) circadian, (b) infradian, (c) ultradian

4. For most women, the days before menstruation are reliably associated with (a) depression, (b) irritability, (c) elation, (d) creativity, (e) none of these, (f) a and b.

5. A researcher tells male subjects that testosterone usually peaks in the morning and that it probably causes hostility. She then asks them to fill out a "HyperTestosterone Syndrome Hostility Survey" in the morning and again at night. Based on menstrual cycle findings, what results might she get? How could she improve her study?

Answers:

1. melatonin 2. internal desynchronization 3. b 4. e 5. Because of the expectations that the men now have about testosterone, they may be biased to report more hostility in the morning. It would be better to keep them in the dark about the hypothesis, use a neutral title on the questionnaire (say, "Health and Mood Checklist"), and measure their actual hormone levels at different points in the day, because individuals vary in their biological rhythms. Also, a control group of women could be added, to see whether their hostility levels vary in the same way that men's do.

WHAT'S AHEAD

- Why do we sleep?
- What happens when we go too long without enough sleep?
- Why are you likely to be dreaming when the alarm goes off in the morning?

THE RHYTHMS OF SLEEP

Perhaps the most perplexing of all our biological rhythms is the one governing sleep and wakefulness. Sleep, after all, puts us at risk: Muscles that are usually ready to respond to danger relax, and senses grow dull. As the late British psychologist Christopher Evans (1984) once noted, "The behavior patterns involved in sleep are glaringly, almost insanely, at odds with common sense." Then why is sleep such a profound necessity?

Why We Sleep

One obvious function of sleep is to provide a time-out period, so that the body can eliminate waste products from muscles, repair cells, strengthen the immune system, or recover abilities lost during the day. When we do not get enough sleep, our bodies operate abnormally; for example, levels of hormones that are necessary for normal muscle development and proper immune-system functioning decline (Leproult et al., 1997).

Although most people can still get along reasonably well after a day or two of sleeplessness, sleep deprivation that lasts for four days or longer is quite uncomfortable. In animals, forced sleeplessness leads to infections and eventually death (Rechtschaffen et al., 1983), and the same may be true for people. There is a case on record of a man who, at age 51, abruptly began to lose sleep. After sinking deeper and deeper into an exhausted stupor, he developed a lung infection and died. An autopsy showed that he had lost almost all the large neurons in two areas of the thalamus that have been linked to sleep and hormonal circadian rhythms (Lugaresi et al., 1986).

Sleep is also necessary for normal mental functioning. After the loss of even a single night's sleep, mental flexibility, attention, and creativity all suffer. In chronic sleep deprivation, high levels of cortisol, a stress hormone, may damage or impair the brain cells that are necessary for learning and memory (Leproult et al., 1997). After several days of staying awake, people may even begin to have hallucinations and delusions (Dement, 1978). Not surprisingly, when people are sleepy, traffic and work accidents become far more likely (Coren, 1996; Maas, 1998). In 1995 the National

Whatever your age, sometimes the urge to sleep is irresistible—especially because in fast-paced modern societies, many people do not get as much sleep as they need.

A SURVEY OF SLEEP PATTERNS

Get an idea of the variation in people's sleep patterns by asking some friends and relatives what time they typically go to sleep and what time they get up, and whether they routinely take daytime naps. Ask them, too, whether this pattern is their natural one or is simply required by their schedule (e.g., having to be at school or the office by 9:00 A.M.). Do people sleep longer on weekends, and if so, what does this fact suggest about the adequacy of their sleep during the week?

Transportation Safety Board reported that tired truck drivers who fall asleep at the wheel are responsible for up to 1,500 road deaths a year; driver fatigue is a greater safety problem than the use of alcohol or other drugs.

Because sleep is so vital to physical and mental well-being, many researchers are worried about the growing number of sleep-deprived people in modern societies. American students, for example, get only about six hours of sleep a night on average, even though most people need at least eight or nine hours for optimal performance, and adolescents typically need ten. According to sleep researcher James Maas (1998), many students therefore "drag themselves through high school and college like walking zombies . . . moody, lethargic, and unprepared or unable to learn." In the general population, two-thirds of all Americans get fewer than the recommended eight hours. Some people stay in bed long enough, but they suffer from insomnia or broken sleep. (For advice on how to get a better night's sleep, see "Taking Psychology with You" at the end of this chapter.)

The Realms of Sleep

Until the early 1950s, little was known about the physiology of sleep. Then a breakthrough occurred in the laboratory of physiologist Nathaniel Kleitman, who at the time was the only person in the world who had spent his entire career studying sleep. Kleitman had given one of his graduate students, Eugene Aserinsky, the tedious task of finding out whether the slow, rolling eye movements that characterize the onset of sleep continue throughout the night. To both men's surprise, eye movements did indeed occur, but they were rapid, not slow (Aserinsky & Kleitman, 1955). Using the electroencephalograph to measure the brain's electrical activity (see Chapter 4), these researchers, along with another of Kleitman's students, William Dement, were able to correlate the rapid eye movements with changes in sleepers' brain-wave patterns (Dement, 1992). Adult volunteers were soon spending their nights sleeping in laboratories while scientists measured changes in their brain activity, muscle tension, breathing, and other physiological responses.

As a result of this research, today we know that during sleep, periods of **rapid eye movement (REM)** alternate with periods of fewer eye movements, or *non-REM (NREM)*, in an ultradian cycle that recurs about every 90 minutes or so. The REM periods last from a few minutes to as long as an hour, averaging about 20 minutes in length. Whenever they begin, the pattern of electrical activity from the sleeper's brain changes to resemble that of alert wakefulness. Non-REM periods are themselves divided into shorter, distinct stages, each associated with a particular brain-wave pattern (see Figure 5.2).

rapid eye movement (REM) sleep Sleep periods characterized by eye movement, loss of muscle tone, and dreaming.

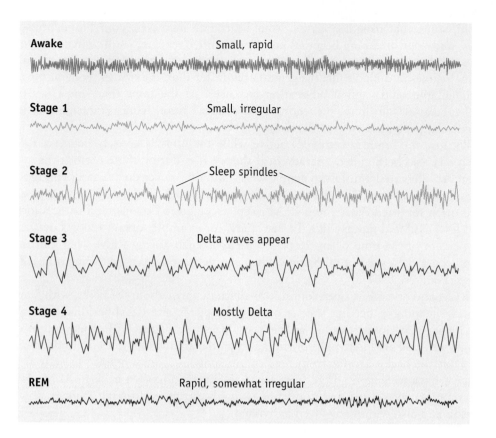

FIGURE 5.2
BRAIN-WAVE PATTERNS DURING WAKEFULNESS AND SLEEP
Most types of brain waves are present throughout sleep, but different ones predominate at different stages.

When you first climb into bed, close your eyes, and relax, your brain emits bursts of *alpha waves*. On an EEG recording, alpha waves have a regular, slow rhythm and a high amplitude (height). Gradually, these waves slow down even further, and you drift into the Land of Nod, passing through four stages, each deeper than the previous one:

■ *Stage 1.* Your brain waves become small and irregular, and you feel yourself drifting on the edge of consciousness, in a state of light sleep. If awakened, you may recall fantasies or a few visual images.

■ *Stage 2.* Your brain emits occasional short bursts of rapid, high-peaking waves called *sleep spindles*. Minor noises probably won't disturb you.

■ *Stage 3.* In addition to the waves characteristic of Stage 2, your brain occasionally emits *delta waves,* very slow waves with very high peaks. Your breathing and pulse have slowed down, your muscles are relaxed, and you are hard to arouse.

■ *Stage 4.* Delta waves have now largely taken over, and you are in a deep sleep. It will probably take vigorous shaking or a loud noise to awaken you. Oddly, though, if you talk or walk in your sleep, this is when you are likely to do so. (The causes of sleepwalking, which occurs more often in children than adults, are unknown.)

This sequence of stages takes about 30 to 45 minutes. Then you move back up the ladder from Stage 4 to 3 to 2 to 1. At that point, about 70 to 90 minutes after the onset of sleep, something peculiar happens. Stage 1 does not turn into drowsy wakefulness, as one might expect. Instead, your brain begins to emit long bursts of very

Because cats sleep so much—up to 80 percent of the time—it's easy to catch them in the various stages of slumber. A cat in non-REM sleep (top) remains upright, but during the REM phase (bottom), its muscles go limp and it flops onto its side.

rapid, somewhat irregular waves. Your heart rate increases, your blood pressure rises, and your breathing becomes faster and more irregular. Small twitches in your face and fingers may occur. In men, the penis becomes somewhat erect as vascular tissue relaxes and blood fills the genital area faster than it exits. In women, the clitoris enlarges and vaginal lubrication increases. At the same time, most of your skeletal muscles go limp, preventing your aroused brain from producing physical movement. You have entered the realm of REM.

Because the brain is extremely active while the body is entirely inactive, REM sleep has also been called "paradoxical sleep." It is during these periods that you are most likely to dream. Even people who claim they never dream at all will report dreams if awakened in a sleep laboratory during REM sleep. But dreaming is also often reported during non-REM sleep, though the dreams tend to be shorter and less vivid and fantasy-like. In one study, for example, dream reports occurred 82 percent of the time when sleepers were awakened during REM sleep, but they also occurred 51 percent of the time when people were awakened during non-REM sleep (Foulkes, 1962).

REM and non-REM sleep continue to alternate throughout the night, with Stages 3 and 4 tending to become shorter or even disappear, and REM periods tending to get longer and closer together as the hours pass (see Figure 5.3). This pattern explains why you are likely to be dreaming when the alarm clock goes off in the morning. But the cycles are far from regular. An individual may bounce directly from Stage 4 back to Stage 2, or go from REM to Stage 2 and then back to REM. Also, the time between REM and non-REM is highly variable, differing from person to person and also within any given individual.

The purpose of REM sleep is still a matter of debate, but clearly it does have a purpose. If you wake people up every time they lapse into REM sleep, nothing dramatic will happen. When finally allowed to sleep normally, however, they will spend a much longer time than usual in the REM phase, and it will be hard to rouse them. Electrical brain activity associated with REM may burst through into quiet sleep and even into wakefulness. The subjects will seem to be making up for something they were deprived of. Many people think that in adults, at least, this "something" is connected with dreaming, to which we now turn.

FIGURE 5.3
A TYPICAL NIGHT'S SLEEP FOR A YOUNG ADULT

In this graph, the thin horizontal red bars represent time spent in REM sleep. REM periods tend to lengthen as the night wears on; but Stages 3 and 4, which dominate during non-REM sleep early in the night, may disappear as morning approaches. (From Kelly, 1981.)

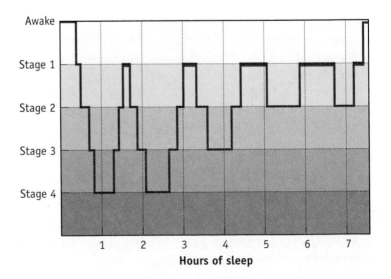

QUICK QUIZ

Wake up and take this quiz!

A. Match each term with the appropriate phrase.

1. REM periods
2. alpha
3. Stage 4 sleep
4. Stage 1 sleep

a. delta waves and talking in one's sleep
b. irregular brain waves and light sleep
c. relaxed but awake
d. active brain but inactive muscles

B. Sleep is necessary for normal (a) physical and mental functioning; (b) mental functioning but not physical functioning; (c) physical functioning but not mental functioning.

C. *True or false*: Most people can get by fine with six hours of sleep a night.

Answers:

A.1 d 2. c 3. a 4. b B. a C. false

WHAT'S AHEAD

● **Why did Freud call dreams the "royal road to the unconscious"?**
● **How might dreams be related to your current problems and concerns?**
● **How does a disruption of REM sleep affect memory?**
● **Could dreams be caused by meaningless brain-stem signals?**

EXPLORING THE DREAM WORLD

Every culture has its theories about dreams. In some cultures, dreams are thought to occur when the spirit leaves the body to wander the world or speak to the gods. In others, dreams are thought to reveal the future. A Chinese Taoist of the third century B.C. pondered the possible reality of the dream world. He told of dreaming that he was a butterfly flitting about. "Suddenly I woke up and I was indeed Chuang Tzu. Did Chuang Tzu dream he was a butterfly, or did the butterfly dream he was Chuang Tzu?"

In dreaming, the focus of attention is inward, though occasionally an external event, such as the sound of a siren, can influence the dream's content. While a dream is in progress, it may be vivid or vague, terrifying or peaceful. It may also seem to make perfect sense—until you wake up. Then it is often recalled as illogical, bizarre, and disjointed.

Although most of us are unaware of our bodies or where we are while we are dreaming, some people report having **lucid dreams,** in which they know they are dreaming and feel as though they are conscious. A few even say that they can control the action in these dreams, much as a scriptwriter decides what will happen in a movie (LaBerge, 1986; LaBerge & Levitan, 1995). In one case, a young woman was reportedly taught to use lucid dreaming to modify her frequent nightmares and make them less frightening (Abramovitch, 1995). Some researchers, however, are skeptical that most people can learn to control the contents of their dreams (Squier & Domhoff, 1998).

lucid dream A dream in which the dreamer is aware of dreaming.

One issue that has bothered sleep researchers for years, and is still the topic of much debate, is whether the eye movements of REM sleep correspond to events and actions in a dream. Are the eyes tracking these images? Some researchers believe that in adult dreamers, eye movements do resemble those of waking life, when the eyes and head move in synchrony as the person moves about and shifts his or her gaze (J. H. Herman, 1992). But others think that eye movements are no more related to dream content than are inner-ear muscle contractions, which also occur during REM sleep. Every mammal studied, except the spiny anteater, the bottlenose dolphin, and the porpoise, experiences REM sleep, as do human fetuses—but we might not want to credit mice, opossums, or human fetuses with what we ordinarily call dreams. Moles, which can hardly move their eyes at all, nonetheless show EEG patterns associated with REM sleep.

Why do the images in dreams arise at all? Why doesn't the brain just rest, switching off all thoughts and images and launching us into a coma? Why, instead, do we spend our nights flying through the air, battling monsters, or having weird conversations in the fantasy world of our dreams? Many explanations have been proposed; here we will cover four of them.

Dreams as Unconscious Wishes

One of the first psychological theorists to take dreams seriously was Sigmund Freud, the founder of psychoanalysis. After analyzing many of his patients' dreams and some of his own, Freud concluded that our nighttime fantasies provide insight into desires, motives, and conflicts of which we are unaware—a "royal road to the unconscious." In dreams, said Freud (1900/1953), we are able to express wishes and desires, often sexual or violent in nature, that have been forced into the unconscious part of the mind. If we did not dream, energy invested in these deep-seated wishes and desires would build up to intolerable levels, threatening our very sanity.

According to Freud, every dream is meaningful, no matter how absurd the images might seem. But if a dream's message arouses anxiety, the rational part of the mind must disguise and distort it. Otherwise, the dream would intrude into consciousness and waken the dreamer. In dreams, therefore, one person may be represented by another—for example, a father by a brother—or even by several different characters. Similarly, thoughts and objects are translated into symbolic images. A penis may be disguised as a snake, umbrella, or dagger; a vagina, as a tunnel or cave; and the human body, as a house.

To understand a dream, said Freud, we must distinguish its *manifest content*, the aspects of it that we consciously experience during sleep and may remember upon wakening, from its *latent* (hidden) *content*, the unconscious wishes and thoughts being expressed symbolically. Freud warned against the simpleminded translation of symbols, however. Each dream had to be analyzed in the context of the dreamer's waking life, as well as the person's associations to the dream's contents. Not everything in a dream is symbolic. Sometimes, Freud cautioned, "A cigar is only a cigar."

Most psychologists today accept Freud's notion that dreams are more than incoherent ramblings of the mind, that they have psychological meaning (Fisher & Greenberg, 1996). However, many find Freudian interpretations far-fetched. They point out that there are no reliable rules for interpreting the supposedly latent content of dreams, and there is no objective way to know whether a particular interpretation is correct. Popular books and newspaper columns that try to tell you what your dreams mean may be fun to read, but they are only the writer's personal hunches.

To a psychoanalyst, this image, if it's in a dream, has nothing to do with travel; it is more likely to have an unconscious sexual meaning.

Dreams as Reflections of Current Concerns

Another explanation holds that dreams reflect the ongoing *conscious* preoccupations of waking life, such as concerns over relationships, work, sex, or health (Siegel, 1991; Webb & Cartwright, 1978). In this *problem-focused approach to dreaming,* the symbols and metaphors in a dream do not disguise its true meaning; they convey it. For example, psychologist Gayle Delaney told of a woman who dreamed she was swimming underwater. The woman's 8-year-old son was on her back, his head above the water. Her husband was supposed to take a picture of them, but for some reason he wasn't doing it, and she was starting to feel as if she were going to drown. To Delaney, the message was obvious: The woman was "drowning" under the responsibilities of child care, and her husband wasn't "getting the picture" (Dolnick, 1990).

Dreams are, in fact, more likely to contain material related to a person's current concerns than chance would predict (Domhoff, 1996). For example, among college students, who are often anxious about grades and tests, "examination dreams" are common: The dreamer is unprepared for or unable to finish an exam, or shows up for the wrong exam, or can't find the room where the exam is being given (Halliday, 1993; Van de Castle, 1994). (Sound familiar?) Traumatic experiences can also affect people's dreams. In one cross-cultural study that had children keep dream diaries for a week, Palestinian children living in neighborhoods under threat of violence reported more themes of persecution and aggression than

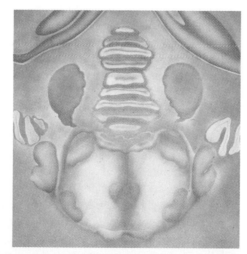

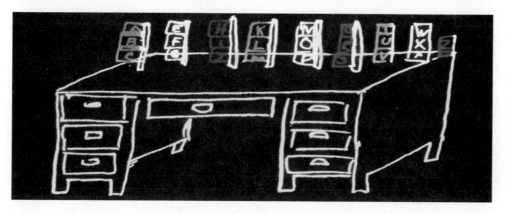

These drawings from dream journals show that the images in dreams can be either abstract or literal. The two fanciful paintings at the top represent the dreams of a person who worked all day long with brain tissue, which the drawings rather resemble. The desk was sketched in 1939 by a scientist to illustrate his dream about a mechanical device for instantly retrieving quotations—a sort of early desktop computer.

did Finnish or Palestinian children living in peaceful environments (Punamaeki & Joustie, 1998).

Do men and women have different dreams? Because they often have different concerns, we might expect the content of their dreams to differ—and until recently, at least, that has been true. Typically, women are more likely than men to dream about children, family members, familiar characters, friendly interactions, household objects, clothes, and indoor events. Men are more likely than women to dream about strangers, weapons, violence, sexual activity, achievement, and outdoor events (Domhoff, 1996; Hall et al., 1982). But as the lives and concerns of the two sexes have become more similar, so have their dreams. In one recent study of college students, only two differences showed up: Men were more likely to dream about behaving aggressively, and women were more likely to dream about their anxieties, especially about failing exams. Otherwise, a person's sex was not a good predictor of dream content (Bursik, 1998).

Some psychologists believe that dreams not only reflect our waking concerns, but also provide us with an opportunity to resolve them. Rosalind Cartwright has been investigating this hypothesis for many years. Among people suffering from the grief of divorce, she finds, recovery is related to a particular pattern of dreaming: The first dream of the night often comes sooner than it ordinarily would, lasts longer, and is more emotional and storylike (Cartwright, 1990, 1996). Depressed people's dreams tend to get less negative and more positive as the night wears on, and this pattern, too, predicts recovery (Cartwright et al., 1998). Cartwright concludes that getting through a crisis or a rough period in life takes "time, good friends, good genes, good luck, and a good dream system."

Skeptics of this view doubt people's ability to work out their problems or conflicts while sound asleep (Blagrove, 1996; Squier & Domhoff, 1998). Dreams, they say, merely give expression to our problems. The insights that people seem to gain could be occurring after they wake up and have a chance to think about what is troubling them.

Dreams as a By-product of Mental Housekeeping

A third approach explains dreams in entirely physiological terms: Dreams are a by-product of a process of mental housekeeping, in which unnecessary neural connections are eliminated and important ones are strengthened (Evans, 1984).

According to this explanation, the brain must periodically shut out sensory input so that it can process and assimilate new data and update what has already been stored. It divides new information into "wanted" and "unwanted" categories, makes new associations, and—to use a computer analogy—revises old "programs" in light of the day's experiences. The data the brain sifts through include not only recent events, but also ideas, obsessions, worries, wishes, and thoughts about the past. What we recall as dreams are really only brief snippets from an ongoing process of scanning and sorting that occurs most intensely during REM sleep but possibly throughout the night. Because these snippets give us only a glimpse of the night's mental activity, they naturally seem odd and nonsensical when recalled.

Several variations on this theme have been proposed. For example, Francis Crick and Graeme Mitchison (1995) emphasize only the weakening of unused synaptic connections in the brain's vast memory network. In their view, during REM sleep a sort of "reverse learning" occurs, making memory more efficient and accurate and protecting us from becoming obsessed by unwanted thoughts and images. Dreams are merely mental garbage, and there is no point in trying to remember them or analyze them for their "meanings," whether hidden or obvious.

Other dream and sleep researchers emphasize the strengthening of synaptic connections associated with recently stored memories. When people learn a perceptual task and are allowed to get normal REM sleep, their memory for the task is better the next day, even when they have been awakened during non-REM periods; but when they are deprived of REM sleep, their memories are impaired (Karni et al., 1994). The same thing happens with rats (Smith, 1995). REM sleep therefore seems to be associated with *consolidation,* a process by which the synaptic changes associated with a recently stored memory become durable and stable (see Chapter 10).

Information-processing approaches to dreaming might explain why REM sleep occurs not only in adult human beings but also in fetuses, babies, and other mammals. They, too, need to sort things out. Newborns, in fact, spend about 50 percent of their sleeping hours in REM sleep, versus only 20 percent for adults. Because everything that is happening to them is new, perhaps they have to do more writing, revising, and consolidating of "programs." But what does this tell us about dreaming itself? As we noted, it is hard to credit fetuses, babies, and other mammals with what we normally mean by dreaming. And "mental housekeeping" does not explain why some dreams are so storylike, or why some dreams recur periodically for years. Information-processing theories therefore seem to tell us more about REM sleep than they do about dreams.

"MENTAL HOUSEKEEPING" VIEW OF DREAMS

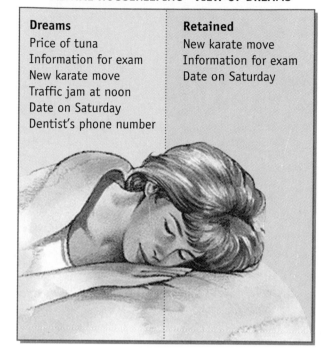

Dreams	Retained
Price of tuna	New karate move
Information for exam	Information for exam
New karate move	Date on Saturday
Traffic jam at noon	
Date on Saturday	
Dentist's phone number	

Dreams as Interpreted Brain Activity

A fourth approach to dreaming, the **activation-synthesis theory,** also draws heavily on physiological research. According to this explanation, proposed by Allan Hobson (1988, 1990), dreams are not "children of an idle brain," as Shakespeare called them. Rather, they are the result of neurons firing spontaneously in the lower part of the brain, in the pons, during REM sleep. These neurons control eye movement, gaze, balance, and posture, and they send messages to sensory and motor areas of the cortex responsible during wakefulness for visual processing and voluntary action.

According to the activation-synthesis theory, the signals originating in the pons have no psychological meaning in themselves. But the cortex tries to make sense of them by *synthesizing,* or integrating, them with existing knowledge and memories to produce some sort of coherent interpretation. (This is just what the cortex would do if the signals had come from sense organs during ordinary wakefulness.) When neurons fire in the part of the brain that handles balance, for instance, the cortex may generate a dream about falling. When signals occur that would ordinarily produce running, the cortex may manufacture a dream about being chased. Because the signals from the pons occur randomly, the cortex's interpretation—the dream—is likely to be incoherent and confusing. And because the cortical neurons that control the initial storage of new memories are turned off during sleep, we typically forget our dreams upon waking unless we write them down or immediately recount them to someone else.

Wishes, in this view, do not cause dreams; brain-stem mechanisms do. But that does not mean dreams are meaningless. Hobson (1988) argued that the brain "is so inexorably bent upon the quest for meaning that it attributes and even creates

activation-synthesis theory The theory that dreaming results from the cortical synthesis and interpretation of neural signals triggered by activity in the lower part of the brain.

ACTIVATION-SYNTHESIS THEORY OF DREAMS

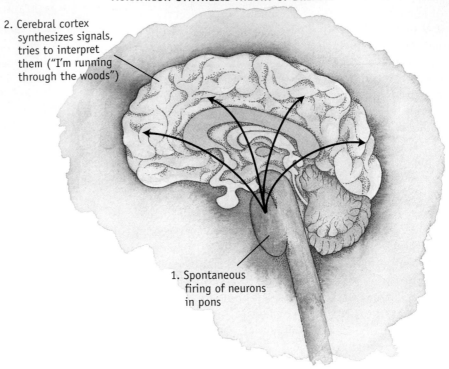

2. Cerebral cortex synthesizes signals, tries to interpret them ("I'm running through the woods")

1. Spontaneous firing of neurons in pons

meaning when there is little or none to be found in the data it is asked to process." By studying these attributed meanings, you can learn about your unique perceptions, conflicts, and concerns—not by trying to dig below the surface of the dream, as Freud would, but by examining the surface itself. Or you can relax and enjoy the nightly entertainment that dreams provide.

By now you won't be surprised to learn that this theory, like all the others, has come under fire (Squier & Domhoff, 1998). Not all dreams are as disjointed or as bizarre as the theory predicts; some tell a coherent (if fanciful) story. Moreover, the theory does not explain dreaming that goes on outside of REM sleep.

How are we to evaluate these attempts to explain dreaming? All four approaches account for some of the evidence, and each one has its drawbacks (see Review 5.1).

GET → INVOLVED

KEEP A DREAM DIARY

It can be fun to record your dreams. Keep a notebook or a tape recorder by your bedside. As soon as you wake up in the morning (or if you awaken during the night while dreaming), record everything you can about your dreams—even short fragments. After you have collected several dreams, see which theory or theories discussed in this chapter seem to best explain them. Do your dreams contain any recurring themes? Do they provide any clues to your current problems, activities, or concerns?

REVIEW 5.1

FOUR DREAM THEORIES COMPARED

Theory	Purpose of Dreaming	Weaknesses
Psychoanalytic	To express unconscious wishes, thoughts, and conflicts	Interpretations are often far-fetched; there is no reliable way to interpret "latent" meanings accurately
Problem-focused	To express ongoing concerns of waking life and/or resolve current concerns and problems	Some theorists are skeptical about the ability to resolve problems during sleep
Mental housekeeping	By-product of a process of either eliminating or strengthening neural connections in the brain	Says more about REM sleep than about dreaming; does not explain storylike or recurrent dreams
Activation-synthesis	None; dreams occur because of random brain-stem signals, though cortical interpretations may reflect concerns and conflicts	Does not explain coherent, storylike dreams or non-REM dreams

Perhaps it will turn out that different kinds of dreams have different purposes and origins. We all know from experience that some of our dreams seem to be related to daily problems, some are vague and incoherent, and some are anxiety dreams that occur when we are tense and worried. For the time being, we are going to have to live with uncertainty about what those fascinating stories and images in our sleeping brains really mean. Clearly, much remains to be learned about the functions of dreaming and even of sleep itself.

QUICK QUIZ

In his dreams, Andy is an infant crawling through a dark tunnel looking for something he has lost. Which theory of dreams would be most receptive to each of the following explanations?

1. Andy recently misplaced a valuable watch but eventually found it.
2. While Andy was sleeping, neurons in his pons that would ordinarily stimulate leg-muscle movement were active.
3. Andy has repressed an early sexual attraction to his mother; the tunnel symbolizes her vagina.
4. Andy has broken up with his lover and is working through the emotional loss.

Answers:

1. the mental-housekeeping (information-processing) approach (the dreamer is processing information about a recent experience) 2. the activation-synthesis theory 3. psychoanalytic theory 4. the problem-focused approach

WHAT'S AHEAD

- In its physiological effects, is alcohol a downer or an upper?
- How do recreational drugs affect the brain?
- Why can a glass of wine make you feel tired at one time but sociable and pepped up at another?

CONSCIOUSNESS-ALTERING DRUGS

■ In Jerusalem, hundreds of Hasidic men celebrate the completion of the annual reading of the holy Torah by dancing for hours in the streets. For them, dancing is not a diversion; it is a path to religious ecstasy.

■ In South Dakota, several Lakota (Sioux) adults sit naked in the darkness of the sweat lodge, a circular hut covered with hides and blankets. When their leader throws water on a pit of red-hot rocks, a crushing wave of heat envelops them. For the Lakota, the reward will be euphoria, the transcendence of pain, and possible connection with the Great Spirit of the Universe.

■ Deep in the Amazon jungle, a young man training to be a shaman, a religious leader, has been starving himself. Aided by a whiff of hallucinogenic snuff made from the bark of the virola tree, he prepares to enter a trance and communicate with animals, spirits, and supernatural forces.

These three rituals, although seemingly quite different, are all aimed at release from the confines of ordinary consciousness. Cultures around the world have devised such practices, often as part of their religions. Because attempts to alter mood and consciousness appear to be universal, some writers believe they reflect a human need, as basic as the needs for food and water (Siegel, 1989).

William James (1902/1936), who was fascinated by alterations in consciousness, would have agreed. After inhaling nitrous oxide ("laughing gas"), he wrote, "Our normal waking consciousness, rational consciousness as we call it, is but one special type of consciousness, whilst all about it, parted from it by the filmiest of screens, there lie potential forms of consciousness entirely different." James hoped that psychologists would study these other forms of consciousness, but for half a century, few took his words seriously. Then, during the 1960s, attitudes changed. During that decade of social upheaval, millions of people began to seek ways of deliberately producing *altered states of consciousness*, especially through the use of psychoactive drugs.

All cultures have found ways to alter consciousness. The Maulavis of Turkey (left), the famous whirling dervishes, spin in an energetic but controlled manner in order to achieve religious rapture. People in many cultures meditate (center) as a way to quiet the mind and achieve spiritual enlightenment. And in some cultures, psychoactive drugs are used for religious or artistic inspiration; the weaving on the right, made by the Huichol Indians of western Mexico, represents a peyote-induced hallucination of a tree.

Researchers became interested in the psychology, as well as the physiology, of such drugs. The "filmy screen" described by James finally began to lift.

Classifying Drugs

A **psychoactive drug** is a substance that alters perception, mood, thinking, memory, or behavior by changing the body's biochemistry. Around the world and throughout history, the most widely used drugs have been tobacco, alcohol, marijuana, opium, cocaine, peyote—and, of course, tea and coffee. The reasons for taking such drugs vary: to alter consciousness, as part of a religious ritual, for recreation, or for psychological escape. But human beings are not the only species that likes to get high on occasion; so do many other animals. Baboons ingest tobacco, elephants love the alcohol in fermented fruit, and reindeer and rabbits seek out intoxicating mushrooms (Siegel, 1989).

Most drugs can be classified as *stimulants, depressants, opiates,* or *psychedelics,* depending on their effects on the central nervous system and their impact on behavior and mood (see Table 5.1). (Chapter 17 reviews drugs that are used in the treatment of mental and emotional disorders.)

psychoactive drug A drug capable of influencing perception, mood, cognition, or behavior.

TABLE 5.1   Some Psychoactive Drugs and Their Effects

Class of Drug	Type	Common Effects	Results of Abuse/Addiction
Amphetamines	Stimulant	Wakefulness, alertness, raised metabolism, elevated mood	Nervousness, headaches, loss of appetite, high blood pressure, delusions, psychosis, heart damage, convulsions, death
Cocaine	Stimulant	Euphoria, excitation, boost of energy, suppressed appetite	Excitability, sleeplessness, sweating, paranoia, anxiety, panic, depression, heart damage, heart, failure, injury to nose if sniffed
Tobacco (nicotine)	Stimulant	Varies from alertness to calmness, depending on mental set, setting, and prior arousal; decreases appetite for carbohydrates	*Nicotine:* heart disease, high blood pressure, impaired circulation, erectile problems in men *Tar:* lung cancer, emphysema, mouth and throat cancer, many other health risks
Caffeine	Stimulant	Wakefulness, alertness, shortened reaction time	Restlessness, insomnia, muscle tension, heartbeat irregularities, high blood pressure
Alcohol (1–2 drinks)	Depressant	Depends on setting, mental set; tends to act like a stimulant because it reduces inhibitions, anxiety	
Alcohol (several/many drinks)	Depressant	Slowed reaction time, tension, depression, reduced ability to store new memories or to retrieve old ones, poor coordination	Blackouts, cirrhosis of the liver, other organ damage, mental and neurological impairment, psychosis, possibly death
Tranquilizers (e.g., Valium); barbiturates (e.g., phenobarbital)	Depressant	Reduced anxiety and tension, sedation	Increased dosage needed for effects; impaired motor and sensory functions, impaired permanent storage of new information, withdrawal symptoms; possibly convulsions, coma, death (especially when taken with other drugs)
Opium, heroin, morphine	Opiate	Euphoria, relief of pain	Loss of appetite, nausea, constipation, withdrawal symptoms, convulsions, coma, possibly death
LSD, psilocybin mescaline	Psychedelic	Exhilaration, visions and hallucinations, insightful experiences	Psychosis, paranoia, panic reactions
Marijuana	Mild psychedelic (classification controversial)	Relaxation, euphoria, increased appetite, reduced ability to store new memories, other effects depending on mental set and setting	Throat and lung irritation, lung damage (if smoked), impaired immunity; long-term effects not well established

1 Stimulants—such as cocaine, amphetamines ("uppers"), methamphetamine hydrochloride ("crank"), nicotine, and caffeine—speed up activity in the central nervous system. In moderate amounts, they tend to produce feelings of excitement, confidence, and well-being or euphoria. In large amounts, they make a person anxious, jittery, and hyperalert. In very large doses, they may cause convulsions, heart failure, and death.

Amphetamines are synthetic drugs usually taken in pill form. Cocaine ("coke") is a natural drug, derived from the leaves of the coca plant. Rural workers in Bolivia and Peru chew coca leaf every day, without apparent ill effects. In North America, the drug is usually inhaled ("snorted"), injected, or smoked in the highly refined form known as crack. These methods give the drug a more immediate, powerful, and dangerous effect than when coca leaf is chewed. Amphetamines and cocaine make users feel peppy but do not actually increase energy reserves. Fatigue, irritability, and depression may occur when the effects of these drugs wear off.

2 Depressants—such as alcohol, tranquilizers, and barbiturates, and most of the common chemicals inhaled by some people ("huffing")—slow down activity in the central nervous system. They usually make a person feel calm or drowsy, and they may reduce anxiety, guilt, tension, and inhibitions. In large amounts, they may produce insensitivity to pain and other sensations. Like stimulants, in very large doses they can cause irregular heartbeats, convulsions, and death.

People are often surprised to learn that alcohol is a central nervous system depressant. Paradoxically, in small amounts, alcohol has some of the effects of a stimulant, not because it *is* a stimulant but because it suppresses activity in parts of the brain that normally inhibit impulsive behavior, such as loud laughter and clowning around. Like barbiturates and opiates, alcohol can be used as an anesthetic; if you drink enough, you will eventually pass out. Extremely large amounts of alcohol can kill, by inhibiting the nerve cells in the brain areas that control breathing and heartbeat. (Every so often the news reports the death of a college student who had large amounts of alcohol "funneled" into him as part of an initiation or competition.)

On the other hand, *moderate* social drinking—a drink or two of wine or liquor a day—is associated with a variety of health benefits, especially for men, including a reduction in the risk of heart attacks and increased longevity (Gaziano & Hennekens, 1995; Gronbaek et al., 1995; Locher, Suter, & Vetter, 1998; Thun et al., 1997).

3 Opiates include opium, derived from the opium poppy; morphine, a derivative of opium; heroin, a derivative of morphine; and synthetic drugs such as methadone. All of these drugs relieve pain, mimicking the action of endorphins, and most have a powerful effect on the emotions. When injected, they may produce a sudden feeling of euphoria, called a "rush." They may also decrease anxiety and motivation, although the effects vary.

4 Psychedelic drugs alter consciousness by disrupting the normal perception of time and space, as well as normal thought processes. Sometimes, psychedelics produce hallucinations, especially visual ones. Some psychedelics, such as lysergic acid diethylamide (LSD), are made in the laboratory. Others, such as mescaline (from the peyote cactus) and psilocybin (from certain species of mushrooms), are natural substances. Emotional reactions to psychedelics vary from person to person, and from one time to another for any individual. A "trip" may be mildly pleasant or unpleasant, a mystical revelation or a nightmare.

Two commonly used drugs, anabolic steroids and marijuana, fall outside these four classifications. *Anabolic steroids,* which have legitimate medical uses, are synthetic derivatives of testosterone that are taken in pill form or by injection. Because they are thought to increase muscle mass and strength when they are combined with weight-bearing exercise, athletes and bodybuilders often use them illegally. As reports of use by high school and even junior high school athletes have increased, concern about

---

stimulants Drugs that speed up activity in the central nervous system.

depressants Drugs that slow down activity in the central nervous system.

opiates Drugs, derived from the opium poppy, that relieve pain and commonly produce euphoria.

psychedelic drugs Consciousness-altering drugs that produce hallucinations, change thought processes, or disrupt the normal perception of time and space.

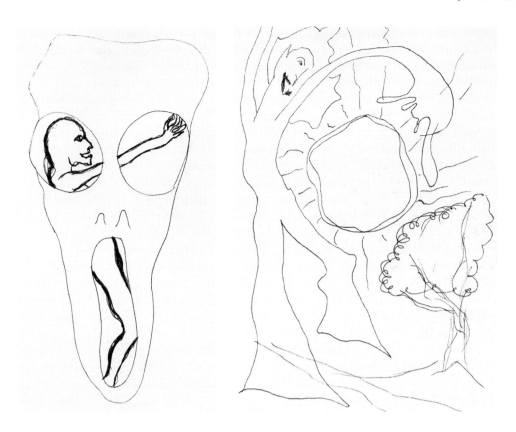

An LSD "trip" may be a ticket to agony or ecstasy. Both of these drawings were done under the influence of the drug.

these drugs has grown. Steroids have been implicated in numerous physical problems, including heart and liver disease, decreased testicular size, and erection difficulties in men (Pope & Katz, 1992). Whether anabolic steroids are psychoactive, however, is still an open question. Some people claim the drugs have positive psychological effects (e.g., increased sex drive, increased confidence, and reduced fatigue during training); others report negative effects (e.g., increased aggression, irritability, anxiety, and even psychosis). But because most studies have used questionable samples or have relied on unverified self-reports, no firm conclusions can yet be drawn about the psychological effects of these drugs.

Marijuana ("pot," "grass," "weed"), which is smoked or, less commonly, eaten in foods such as brownies, is probably the most widely used illicit drug in North America and Europe. Some researchers classify it as a mild psychedelic, but others feel that its chemical makeup and its psychological effects place it outside the major classifications. The active ingredient in marijuana is tetrahydrocannabinol (THC), derived from the hemp plant, *Cannabis sativa*. In some respects, THC appears to be a mild stimulant, increasing heart rate and making tastes, sounds, and colors seem more intense. But users often report reactions ranging from mild euphoria to relaxation, or even sleepiness. Time often seems to go by slowly. In moderate doses, marijuana can interfere with the transfer of information to long-term memory, a characteristic it shares with alcohol. In large doses, it can cause hallucinations and a sense of unreality. Sometimes the drug impairs coordination, concentration, visual perception, and reaction times, though it is not clear how long these effects last.

The Physiology of Drug Effects

Psychoactive drugs produce their effects primarily by acting on brain neurotransmitters, the substances that carry messages from one nerve cell to another. They may increase or decrease the release of neurotransmitters at the synapse; prevent the reabsorption of excess neurotransmitter molecules by the cells that have released them; block the effects of a neurotransmitter on a receiving nerve cell; or bind to receptors that would ordinarily be triggered by a neurotransmitter or a neuromodulator. Figure 5.4 shows how one drug, cocaine, increases the amount of norepinephrine and dopamine in the brain by blocking the reabsorption of these substances. Cocaine may also increase the transmission of serotonin (Rocha et al., 1998).

Such biochemical changes in the brain can have cognitive and emotional effects. For example, because of alcohol's effect on parts of the brain involved in judgment, drinkers often are unable to gauge their own competence. Just a couple of drinks can affect perception, response time, coordination, and balance, despite the drinker's own impression of unchanged or even improved performance. Liquor also affects memory, possibly by interfering with the work of serotonin. Information stored before a drinking session remains intact during the session but is retrieved more slowly (Stempel, Beckwith, & Petros, 1986). The ability to store new memories for later use also suffers, after the consumption of only two or three drinks (Parker, Birnbaum, & Noble, 1976). Consuming small amounts does not seem to affect *sober* mental performance, but even occasional heavy drinking impairs later abstract thought. In other words, a Saturday night binge is potentially more dangerous than a daily drink.

Animal studies suggest that repeated use of certain drugs, including *designer drugs* (easily synthesized variations of other drugs), can cause permanent brain damage. For example, the drug "Ecstasy" (MDMA) may permanently damage cells that produce serotonin (Ricaurte et al., 1988). The dosages given to animals, however, have been huge, and generalizing such findings to human beings remains highly controversial. There is no evidence that *light* or *moderate* use of recreational drugs can damage the human brain enough to affect cognitive functioning, although all researchers agree that heavy or frequent use of any drug is another matter (see Chapter 16, where we discuss abuse and addiction).

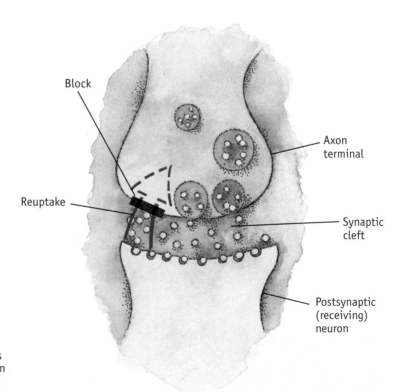

FIGURE 5.4
COCAINE'S EFFECT ON THE BRAIN

Cocaine blocks the brain's reabsorption ("reuptake") of the neurotransmitters dopamine and norepinephrine, so levels of these substances rise. The result is overstimulation of certain brain circuits and a brief euphoric high. Then, when the drug wears off, a depletion of dopamine may cause the user to "crash" and become sleepy and depressed.

The use of some psychoactive drugs, such as heroin and tranquilizers, can lead to **tolerance:** Over time, more and more of the drug is needed to get the same effect. When habitual heavy users stop taking a drug (whether it causes tolerance or not), they may suffer severe **withdrawal symptoms,** such as nausea, abdominal cramps, muscle spasms, depression, and sleep problems, depending on the drug.

The Psychology of Drug Effects

People often assume that the effects of a drug are automatic, the inevitable result of the drug's chemistry ("I couldn't help what I said; the booze made me do it"). But reactions to a psychoactive drug involve more than the drug's chemical properties. They also depend on a person's physical condition, experience with the drug, environmental setting, and mental set.

1 *Physical factors* include body weight, metabolism, initial state of emotional arousal, and physical tolerance for the drug. For example, women generally get drunker than men on the same amount of alcohol because women are smaller, on average, and their bodies metabolize alcohol differently (Fuchs et al., 1995). Similarly, many Asians have a genetically determined adverse reaction to even small amounts of alcohol, which can cause severe headaches, facial flushing, and diarrhea (Cloninger, 1990). For individuals, a drug may have one effect after a tiring day and a different one after a rousing quarrel, or the effect may vary with the time of day because of the body's circadian rhythms.

2 *Experience with the drug* refers to the number of times a person has used the drug. Trying a drug—a cigarette, an alcoholic drink, a stimulant—for the first time is often a neutral or unpleasant experience. But reactions typically change once a person has become familiar with the drug's effects.

3 *Environmental setting* greatly affects the response to a drug. A person might have one glass of wine at home alone and feel sleepy but have three glasses of wine at a party and feel full of energy. Someone might feel happy and high drinking with good friends but fearful and nervous drinking with strangers. In one study of reactions to alcohol, most of the drinkers became depressed, angry, confused, and unfriendly. Then it dawned on the researchers that anyone might become depressed, angry, confused, and unfriendly if asked to drink bourbon at 9:00 A.M. in a bleak hospital room, which was the setting for the experiment (Warren & Raynes, 1972).

4 *Mental set* refers to expectations about the drug's effects, and reasons for taking the drug. Some people drink to become more sociable, friendly, or seductive; some drink to try to reduce feelings of anxiety or depression; and some drink in

tolerance Increased resistance to a drug's effects accompanying continued use; as tolerance develops, larger doses are required to produce effects once brought about by smaller ones.

withdrawal symptoms Physical and psychological symptoms that occur when someone addicted to a drug stops taking it.

CONSIDER OTHER INTERPRETATIONS
One person takes a drink and flies into a rage. Another has a drink and "mellows out." What qualities of the user rather than the drug might account for this difference?

The motives for using a drug, expectations about its effects, and the setting in which it is used all contribute to a person's reactions to the drug.

order to have an excuse for abusiveness or violence. Addicts use drugs to escape from the real world; people living with chronic pain use the same drugs in order to function in the real world (Portenoy, 1994).

Expectations about a drug can be more powerful than the drug itself. In one imaginative study, researchers compared people who were drinking liquor (vodka and tonic) with those who *thought* they were drinking liquor but were actually getting only tonic and lime juice. (Vodka has a subtle taste, and most people could not tell the real and phony drinks apart.) The experimenters found a *"think-drink" effect:* Men behaved more belligerently when they thought they were drinking vodka than when they thought they were drinking plain tonic water, regardless of the actual content of the drinks. Both sexes reported feeling sexually aroused when they thought they were drinking vodka, whether they actually got vodka or not (Abrams & Wilson, 1983; Marlatt & Rohsenow, 1980).

Because so many violent crimes and marital arguments occur when the participants have been drinking, alcohol is often assumed to "release" anger and aggression. According to cognitive researchers, however, the real source of aggression is not in the alcohol but in the mind of the drinker. About half of all men arrested for assaulting their wives claim to have been drinking at the time. Yet, most of these men do not have enough alcohol in their bloodstreams to qualify as legally intoxicated, and many have not been drinking immediately prior to being violent (Gelles & Straus, 1988). This finding suggests that alcohol did not make the men violent, but rather that *their use of alcohol provided an excuse to behave violently.* The link between alcohol and aggression weakens when people believe they will be held responsible for their actions while drunk (Critchlow, 1983).

Expectations and beliefs about drugs are, in turn, shaped by the culture in which you live. Many people start their day with a cup of coffee because it increases alertness, but when coffee was first introduced in Europe, people protested against it. Women said it suppressed their husbands' sexual performance and made men inconsiderate—and maybe it did! In the nineteenth century, Americans regarded marijuana as a mild sedative with no "mind-altering" properties. They did not expect it to give them a high, and it didn't; it merely put them to sleep (Weil, 1972/1986). Today, motives for using marijuana have changed, and these changes have no doubt affected how people respond to it.

Cultural attitudes toward drugs vary with the times. Before it was banned in the United States in the 1920s, cocaine was widely touted as a cure for everything from toothaches to timidity. It was used in teas, tonics, throat lozenges, and even soft drinks (including, briefly, Coca-Cola, which derived its name from the coca plant). Similarly, until recent decades, cigarette smoking was promoted as healthy and glamorous.

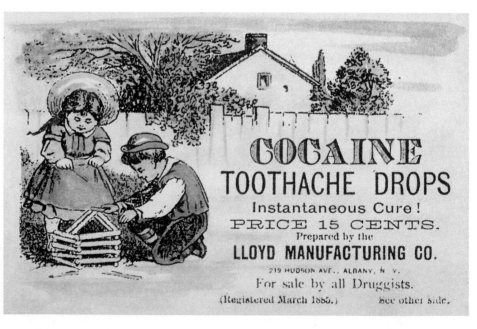

None of this means that alcohol and other drugs are merely placebos; drugs do have physiological effects, many of them quite powerful. Smoking cigarettes, for example, is seriously hazardous to your health, no matter how cool you think they are or what you expect them to do for you. But an understanding of the psychological factors involved in drug use (and abuse) may help us think critically about the ongoing national debates about which drugs, if any, should be legal.

The Drug Debate

Because the consequences of drug *abuse* are so devastating to individuals and to society, people often have trouble thinking critically about drug *use*. At one extreme, some people cannot accept evidence that their favorite drug—be it coffee, tobacco, alcohol, or marijuana—might have harmful effects. At the other extreme, some cannot accept the evidence that their most hated drug—whether it is alcohol, morphine, marijuana, or the coca leaf—might not be dangerous in all forms or amounts, and might even have some beneficial effects. Both sides often confuse potent drugs with others that have only subtle effects, and confuse light or moderate use of a drug with heavy or excessive use.

Once a drug is declared illegal, many people assume it is deadly, even though some legal drugs are more dangerous than illegal ones. Nicotine, which of course is legal, is as addictive as heroin and cocaine, which are illegal. And tobacco use contributes to more than 400,000 deaths in the United States every year, about 20 times the number of deaths from all other forms of drug use combined (McGinnis & Foege, 1993). Yet, most people have a far more negative view of heroin and cocaine than of nicotine.

Emotions have run especially high in debates over marijuana. Heavy, prolonged use of marijuana poses some physical dangers, including lung damage when the drug is smoked (Barsky et al., 1998). But marijuana also has some medical benefits: It reduces the nausea and vomiting that often accompany chemotherapy treatment for cancer and AIDS; it reduces the physical tremors, loss of appetite, and other symptoms caused by multiple sclerosis; it helps reduce the frequency of seizures in some patients with epilepsy; and it alleviates the retinal swelling caused by glaucoma (Grinspoon & Bakalar, 1993; Zimmer & Morgan, 1997). In the United States, voters in several states have approved the medical use of marijuana, yet the federal government has nonetheless continued its opposition to such use. In 1998, when a World Health Organization report concluded that marijuana, used in moderation, was safer than cigarettes and alcohol, United Nations officials suppressed the finding. In 1999, when a scientific panel commissioned by the U.S. government called for scientific trials on marijuana's medical benefits, government officials either ignored or repudiated the recommendation.

Some people are committed to the eradication of all illegal drugs, and some think that all drugs should be decriminalized. Others would legalize narcotics for people who are in chronic pain and marijuana for recreational and medicinal use, but they would ban tobacco. Still others think that instead of punishing or incarcerating people who use drugs, society would be better off regulating where drugs are used (never at work, for example), providing treatment for addicts, and educating people about the benefits and hazards of drug use—the current approach to cigarette smoking.

Where, given the research findings, do you stand in the drug debate? Which psychoactive drugs, if any, should be prohibited? Can we create mental sets and environmental settings that promote safe recreational use of some drugs, minimize the likelihood of drug abuse, and permit the medicinal use of beneficial drugs? What do you think?

THINKING CRITICALLY

AVOID EMOTIONAL REASONING

In arguments over legalizing drugs, emotion runs so high that individuals and governments alike are unable to think rationally. What kinds of evidence should we be considering when deciding whether to ban or permit certain drugs?

QUICK QUIZ

A. See whether you can name the following:

1. An illegal stimulant

2. Two drugs that interfere with the formation of new long-term memories

3. Three types of depressant drugs

4. A legal recreational drug that acts as a depressant on the central nervous system

5. Four factors that influence a person's psychological reactions to a drug

 B. A bodybuilder who has been taking anabolic steroids says the drugs make him more aggressive. What are some other possible interpretations?

Answers:

A. 1. cocaine; also some amphetamines   2. marijuana and alcohol   3. barbiturates, tranquilizers, and alcohol   4. alcohol   5. the person's physical condition, prior experience with the drug, mental set, and the environmental setting   B. The bodybuilder's increased aggressiveness may be due to his expectations (a placebo effect); bodybuilding itself may increase aggressiveness; the culture of the bodybuilding gym may encourage aggressiveness; other influences in his life or other drugs he is taking may be making him more aggressive; or he may only think he is more aggressive, and his behavior may contradict his self-perceptions.

WHAT'S AHEAD

● **Can a hypnotist force you to do things against your will?**

● **Can hypnosis help you remember the past more accurately?**

● **What are the legitimate uses of hypnosis in psychology and medicine?**

● **Are hypnotized persons merely faking or playacting?**

THE RIDDLE OF HYPNOSIS

In England a few years ago, a wave of panic followed reports of a stage hypnotist who was allegedly inducing people to do dangerous things, such as jump off the stage and hurt themselves. For many years now, stage hypnotists, "past-lives channelers," and some psychotherapists have been reporting "age regression" of hypnotized people to earlier years or even earlier centuries. And a few therapists claim that hypnosis has helped their patients recall alleged abductions by extraterrestrials. What are we to make of all this?

The Division of Psychological Hypnosis of the APA defines **hypnosis** as a procedure in which a practitioner suggests changes in the sensations, perceptions, thoughts, feelings, or behavior of the subject (Kirsch & Lynn, 1995). Other definitions, however, put the emphasis not on the practitioner but on the hypnotized person. In this view, hypnosis is a process in which people try to call up certain cognitive abilities in order to alter their normal cognitive functioning in accordance with suggestions from a therapist or experimenter (Nash & Nadon, 1997).

Hypnotic suggestions typically involve performance of an action ("Your arm will slowly rise"), an inability to perform an act ("You will be unable to bend your arm"), or a distortion of normal perception or memory ("You will feel no pain," "You will forget being hypnotized until I give you a signal"). People usually report that their compliance with these suggestions feels involuntary.

To induce hypnosis, the hypnotist typically suggests that the person being hypnotized feels relaxed, is getting sleepy, and feels the eyelids getting heavier and heavier. In a singsong or monotonous voice, the hypnotist assures the subject that he or she is sinking "deeper and deeper." Sometimes the hypnotist has the person concentrate

SPECIAL GUEST

BRUNDAGE MORNALD, OF BATTLE CREEK, MONTANA

UNDER HYPNOSIS, MR. MORNALD RECOVERED LONG-BURIED MEMORIES OF A PERFECTLY NORMAL, HAPPY CHILDHOOD.

hypnosis A procedure in which the practitioner suggests changes in the sensations, perceptions, thoughts, feelings, or behavior of the subject.

on a color or a small object, or on certain bodily sensations. People who have been hypnotized report that the focus of attention turns outward, toward the hypnotist's voice. They sometimes compare the experience to being totally absorbed in a good book, play, or favorite piece of music.

Because hypnosis has been used for everything from parlor tricks and stage shows to medical and psychological treatments, it is important to understand just what this procedure can and cannot achieve. We will begin with a general look at the findings on hypnosis; then we will consider two leading explanations of these findings.

The Nature of Hypnosis

Since the late 1960s, nearly 5,000 articles on hypnosis have appeared. Based on controlled laboratory and clinical research studies, most researchers agree on the following points (Kirsch & Lynn, 1995; Nash & Nadon, 1997):

1 *The hypnotic state is not sleep.* Whereas sleep is associated with predictable changes in brain waves and other physiological responses, comparable changes during hypnosis have not been reliably identified (Nash & Nadon, 1997). The hypnotized person almost always remains fully aware of what is going on and remembers the experience later, unless explicitly instructed to forget it. Even then, the memory can be restored by a prearranged signal.

2 *Hypnotic responsiveness depends more on the efforts and qualities of the person being hypnotized than on the skill of the hypnotist.* Some people are more responsive to hypnosis than others, and this responsiveness is stable over time. Surprisingly, however, hypnotic susceptibility is unrelated to general personality traits, such as gullibility, trust, submissiveness, or conformity (Nash & Nadon, 1997). People who are easily hypnotized do tend to have the ability to become easily absorbed in their activities and involved in the world of imagination (J. R. Hilgard, 1979; Nadon et al., 1991). But even this ability is only weakly related to hypnotic susceptibility (Council, Kirsch, & Grant, 1996; Nash & Nadon, 1997).

3 *Hypnotized people cannot be forced to do things against their will.* Like psychoactive drugs, hypnosis can be used to justify letting go of inhibitions ("I know this looks silly, but after all, I'm hypnotized"). And it's true that hypnotized individuals may comply with a suggestion to do something that looks embarrassing or dangerous. But the individual is choosing to turn responsibility over to the hypnotist and to cooperate with the hypnotist's suggestions (Lynn, Rhue, & Weekes, 1990). There is no evidence that hypnotized people will do anything that actually goes against their morals or that constitutes a real threat (Laurence & Perry, 1988). (In the case of the British hypnotist that opened this section, worry over his "magic powers" eventually evaporated, as did complaints of injury.)

4 *Hypnotic inductions increase suggestibility but only to a modest degree; people will accept suggestions with and without hypnosis.* Hypnotic suggestions sometimes lead to feats of great strength, pain reduction, hallucinations, and even the disappearance of warts. But suggestion alone, without the special procedures of hypnosis, can usually produce similar results as long as people are motivated, believe they can succeed, and are encouraged to relax, concentrate, and do their best (e.g., Chaves, 1989; Spanos, Stenstrom, & Johnson, 1988).

Amazing, right? Or maybe not. This stage hypnotist's audience believes that the man he is standing on can support his weight without flinching because he's hypnotized, but most unhypnotized people can do the same thing. The only way to find out whether hypnosis produces unique results is to do research with control groups.

"THE WITNESS HAS BARKED, MEOWED AND GIVEN US FIVE MINUTES OF BABY TALK. I'D SAY HYPNOSIS IS NOT THE ANSWER."

5 *Hypnosis does not increase the accuracy of memory.* Many people assume that hypnosis can enhance the recall of forgotten experiences. Sometimes hypnosis *can* be used successfully to jog the memories of crime victims. After the 1976 kidnapping of a busload of schoolchildren in Chowchilla, California, a breakthrough in the case occurred when the bus driver, under hypnosis, was able to recall all but one of the license-plate numbers on the kidnappers' cars. But in other cases, hypnotized witnesses, despite feeling confident about their memories, have been completely mistaken. Although hypnosis does sometimes boost the amount of information recalled, it also increases *errors*, perhaps because hypnotized people are more willing than others to guess, or because they mistake vividly imagined possibilities for actual memories (Dinges et al., 1992; Kihlstrom, 1994). Because pseudomemories and errors are so common in hypnotically induced recall, the American Psychological Association and the American Medical Association oppose the use of "hypnotically refreshed" testimony in courts of law.

6 *Hypnosis does not produce a literal reexperiencing of long-ago events.* When Michael Yapko (1994), a clinical psychologist who uses hypnosis in his own practice, surveyed 869 members of the American Association of Marriage and Family Therapists, he discovered that more than half believed that "hypnosis can be used to recover memories from as far back as birth." This belief is just dead wrong. When people are regressed to an earlier age, their mental and moral performance remains adultlike (Nash, 1987). Their brain-wave patterns and reflexes do not become childish; they do not reason as children do or show child-sized IQs. They may use baby talk or report that they feel 4 years old again, but the reason is not that they *are* 4; they are just willing to play the role. They will do the same when they are hypnotically *progressed* ahead—say, to age 70 or 80—or regressed to "past lives." Their belief that they are 7 or 70 or 7,000 years old may be sincere and convincing, but it is based on elaborate fantasy and role playing.

7 *Hypnotic suggestions have been used effectively for many medical and psychological purposes.* Although hypnosis is not of much use for finding out what happened in the past, it can be useful in the treatment of psychological and medical problems. Hypnotic suggestions have been used to reduce stress and anxiety; anesthetize people undergoing dental work, surgery, or childbirth; eliminate unwanted habits such as smoking or nail biting; improve study skills; reduce nausea in cancer patients undergoing chemotherapy; pump up the confidence of athletes; and reduce severe, chronic pain (Kirsch, Montgomery, & Sapirstein, 1995; Stam, 1989).

Theories of Hypnosis

Over the years, people have proposed many explanations of what hypnosis is and how it produces its effects. One early notion that hypnosis is a "trance state" was eventually rejected by most researchers. Today, two competing theories predominate, with many, if not most, scientists taking a position somewhere in the middle ground between them.

Dissociation Theories. One leading approach was originally proposed by Ernest Hilgard (1977/1986), who argued that hypnosis, like lucid dreaming and even simple distraction, involves **dissociation,** a split in consciousness in which one part of the mind operates independently of the rest of consciousness. In many hypnotized persons, said Hilgard, while most of the mind is subject to hypnotic suggestion, one part is a *hidden observer,* watching but not participating. Unless given special instructions, the hypnotized person remains unaware of the observer.

dissociation A split in consciousness in which one part of the mind operates independently of others.

In his research, Hilgard attempted to question the hidden observer directly. In one procedure, hypnotized volunteers had to submerge an arm in ice water for several seconds, an experience that is normally excruciating. They were told that they would feel no pain, but that the nonsubmerged hand would be able to signal the level of any hidden pain by pressing a key. In this situation, many people said they felt little or no pain— yet at the same time, their free hand was busily pressing the key. After the session, these people continued to insist that they had been pain-free, unless the hypnotist asked the hidden observer to issue a separate report.

A related theory holds that during hypnosis, dissociation occurs between an executive-control system in the brain (probably in the frontal lobes) and other brain systems that are involved in thinking and acting (Woody & Bowers, 1994). The result is an altered state of consciousness similar to that found in patients with frontal-lobe disorders. Because the dissociated systems are freed from control by the executive, they are more easily influenced by suggestions from the hypnotist.

A person whose arm is immersed in ice water ordinarily feels intense pain. But Ernest Hilgard, a pioneer in hypnosis research, found that when hypnotized people are told the pain will be minimal, they report little or no discomfort. Like the young woman shown here in one of Hilgard's studies, they seem unperturbed.

DISSOCIATION THEORIES OF HYPNOSIS

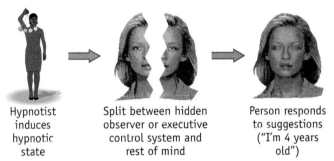

Hypnotist induces hypnotic state

Split between hidden observer or executive control system and rest of mind

Person responds to suggestions ("I'm 4 years old")

Explanations based on dissociation fit in well with recent research on nonconscious mental processing (see Chapters 9 and 10). They are also consistent with modern brain theories, which propose that one part of the brain operates as an interpreter and reporter of activities carried out unconsciously by other brain parts. Nevertheless, many psychologists believe that there is less to dissociation and the hypnotic state than meets the eye. Some flat-out reject the idea that hypnosis differs from normal consciousness. They point out that when a hypnotist suggests that a person hold an arm out rigidly and the person does so, all this really tells us is that the person is suggestible and willing to go along (Barber, 1979; Weitzenhoffer, 1996). Moreover, the definition of a hypnotized "state" is circular: How do you know when people are in that state? Because they go along with the suggestions. And why do they go along? Because they are in a hypnotic state!

The Sociocognitive Approach. The second major approach to hypnosis, the *sociocognitive explanation,* holds that the effects of hypnosis result from an interaction between the social influence of the hypnotist (the "socio" part) and the abilities, beliefs, and expectations of the subject (the "cognitive" part) (Kirsch, 1997; Sarbin, 1991; Spanos, 1991). The hypnotized person is basically playing a role, one that has analogies in ordinary life, where we willingly submit to the suggestions

SOCIOCOGNITIVE THEORIES OF HYPNOSIS

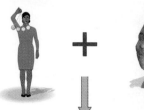

Social influence of hypnotist ("You're going back in time")

Person's own cognitions ("I believe in age regression")

Person conforms to suggestions ("I'm 4 years old")

of parents, teachers, doctors, therapists, and television commercials. Even the "hidden observer" is simply a reaction to the social demands of the situation and the suggestions of the hypnotist—an "experimental creation" (Kirsch & Lynn, 1998).

The hypnotized person is not merely faking or play-acting, however. A person who has been instructed to fool an observer by faking a hypnotic state will tend to overplay the role and will stop playing it as soon as the observer leaves the room. In contrast, hypnotized subjects continue to follow the hypnotic suggestions even when they think they are not being watched (Kirsch et al., 1989; Spanos et al., 1993). Like many social roles, the role of "hypnotized person" is so engrossing and involving that actions required by the role may occur without the person's conscious intent.

Sociocognitive views explain why some people under hypnosis report spirit possession or "memories" of alien abductions (Baker, 1992; Spanos, 1996). Such persons may have a need to "escape the self" by turning control over to someone else (Newman & Baumeister, 1994). Often, the hypnotist readily assumes such control, shaping the person's story by giving subtle and not-so-subtle hints about what the person should say. Here is an exchange between one therapist who believes in UFO abductions and a supposed abductee who has been hypnotized (quoted in Newman & Baumeister, 1994):

Dr. Fiore: Now I'm going to ask you a few questions at this point. You will remember everything because you want to remember. When you were being poked everywhere, did they do any kind of vaginal examination?

Sandi: I don't think they did.

Dr. Fiore: Now you're going to let yourself know if they put a needle in any part of your body, other than the rectum.

Sandi: No. They were carrying needles around, big ones, and I was scared for a while they were going to put one in me, but they didn't. [*Body tenses.*]

Dr. Fiore: Now just let yourself relax. At the count of three you're going to remember whether they did put one of those big needles in you. If they did, know that you're safe, and it's all over, isn't it? And if they didn't, you're going to remember that too, at the count of three. One . . . two . . . three.

Sandi: They did.

The sociocognitive view can also explain apparent cases of past-life regression. In a fascinating program of research, Nicholas Spanos and his colleagues (Spanos et al., 1991) directed hypnotized Canadian university students to regress past their own births to previous lives. About a third of the students reported being able to do so. But when they were asked, while supposedly reliving a past life, to name the leader of their country, say whether the country was at peace or at war, or describe the money used in their community, the students could not do it. (One young man, who thought he was Julius Caesar, said the year was 50 A.D. and he was emperor of Rome. But Caesar died in 44 B.C. and was never crowned emperor, and dating years as A.D. or B.C. did not begin until several centuries later.) Instead, the students tried to fulfill the

THINKING CRITICALLY

CONSIDER OTHER INTERPRETATIONS

Under hypnosis, Jim describes the chocolate cake at his fourth birthday and Joan remembers a former life as a twelfth-century French peasant. But lemon cake was served at Jim's party and Joan can't speak twelfth-century French. What explanation best accounts for these vivid but incorrect memories?

requirements of the role by weaving events, places, and persons from their present lives into their accounts, and by picking up cues from the experimenter. The researchers concluded that the act of "remembering" another self involves the construction of a fantasy that accords with the rememberer's own beliefs and also the beliefs of others—in this case, the authoritative hypnotist (Spanos et al., 1991).

Psychologists who think hypnosis is a special state of consciousness involving dissociation and those who emphasize sociocognitive explanations agree on many issues. They agree, for example, that hypnosis does *not* create a unique state in which people can do extraordinary things, memories become sharper, or early experiences can be replayed with perfect accuracy. And many psychologists feel that both approaches have something to offer (Kihlstrom, 1998; Woody & Sadler, 1998). Whatever hypnosis is, by studying it, psychologists are learning much about human suggestibility, the power of imagination, and the way we perceive the present and remember the past.

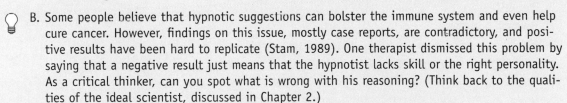

QUICK QUIZ

A. *True or false*:

1. A hypnotized person is usually aware of what is going on and remembers the experience later.
2. Hypnosis gives us special powers that we do not ordinarily have.
3. Hypnosis reduces errors in memory.
4. Hypnotized people play no active part in their behavior and thoughts.
5. According to Hilgard, hypnosis is a state of consciousness involving a "hidden observer."
6. Sociocognitive theorists view hypnosis as mere faking or conscious playacting.

B. Some people believe that hypnotic suggestions can bolster the immune system and even help cure cancer. However, findings on this issue, mostly case reports, are contradictory, and positive results have been hard to replicate (Stam, 1989). One therapist dismissed this problem by saying that a negative result just means that the hypnotist lacks skill or the right personality. As a critical thinker, can you spot what is wrong with his reasoning? (Think back to the qualities of the ideal scientist, discussed in Chapter 2.)

Answers:

A. 1. true 2. false 3. false 4. false 5. true 6. false B. The therapist's argument violates the principle of falsifiability. If a result is positive, he counts it as evidence. But if a result is negative, he refuses to count it as counterevidence ("Maybe the hypnotist just wasn't good enough"). With this kind of reasoning, there is no way to tell whether the hypothesis is right or wrong.

As we have seen in this chapter, fluctuations and changes in consciousness, though interesting in and of themselves, also show us how people's expectations and explanations of their own mental and physical states affect what they do and how they feel. Controversy still exists about some very basic issues: the prevalence of "SAD" and "PMS," the purpose of sleep, the meaning of dreams, the dangers and benefits of drugs, and the best explanation of hypnosis. But the scientific scrutiny of biological rhythms, dreams, drug-induced states, and hypnotic suggestion—phenomena once thought beyond the pale of science—can deepen our understanding of the intimate relationship between body and mind.

HOW TO GET A GOOD NIGHT'S SLEEP

You hop into bed, turn out the lights, close your eyes, and wait for slumber. An hour later, you're still waiting. Finally you drop off, but at 3:00 A.M. you're awake again. By the time the rooster crows, you have put in a hard day's night.

Insomnia affects most people at one time or another, and many people most of the time. No wonder that sleeping pills are a multimillion-dollar business. Yet, most over-the-counter pills are almost worthless for inducing sleep, and some prescription drugs can actually make matters worse. Barbiturates greatly suppress REM sleep, a result that eventually causes wakefulness, and they also suppress Stages 3 and 4, the deeper stages of sleep. Melatonin supplements help some people, but no one knows what dosages are safe and effective, and the optimal time for taking it depends on your individual circadian cycles. Most physicians prescribe sleeping remedies for only very short periods of time. Sleep research suggests better alternatives:

- **Be sure you actually have a sleep problem.** Many people only *think* they don't sleep well. People who complain of insomnia, for instance, often overestimate how long it takes them to doze off and underestimate how much sleep they are getting. When they are observed in the laboratory, they usually fall asleep in less than 30 minutes and are awake for only very short periods during the night (Bonnet, 1990; Carskadon, Mitler, & Dement, 1974).

  The amount of time spent sleeping is not a good criterion of insomnia in any case. As we saw in this chapter, most people need at least the standard eight hours of sleep (Maas, 1998). Some people, however, get by on as little as five or six hours. As people age, they typically sleep more lightly, and they often break up sleep into nighttime slumber and an afternoon nap. Young people, too, can benefit from napping, which many researchers feel is biologically beneficial (Lavie, 1996). The real test for diagnosing a sleep deficit is how you feel during the day. Do you doze off without intending to? Do you feel drowsy at meetings or in class? If you function well with less sleep than most people get, you probably shouldn't worry.

- **Get a correct diagnosis of the sleep problem.** Disruption of sleep can result from psychological disturbances, such as depression, and from physical disorders. In *sleep apnea,* breathing periodically stops for a few moments, causing the person to choke and gasp. Breathing may cease hundreds of times a night, often without the person knowing it, and chronic apnea may lead to high blood pressure or irregular heartbeat. Sleep apnea has several causes, from blockage of air passages to failure of the brain to control respiration correctly. In *narcolepsy,* another serious disorder, an individual is subject to irresistible and unpredictable daytime attacks of sleepiness lasting from 5 to 30 minutes. A quarter of a million people in the United States alone suffer from this condition, many without knowing it.

- **Avoid excessive use of alcohol or other drugs.** Many drugs interfere with sleep. For instance, coffee, tea, cola, and chocolate all contain caffeine, which is a stimulant; alcohol suppresses REM sleep; and tranquilizers such as Valium and Librium reduce Stage 4 sleep.

- **Don't associate the bedroom with wakefulness.** When environmental cues are repeatedly associated with some behavior, they can come to trigger the behavior. If you don't want your bedroom to trigger wakefulness, avoid reading, studying, and watching TV there. Also avoid lying awake for hours waiting for sleep; your frustration will cause arousal that can be associated with the bedroom (Lavie, 1996). If you can't sleep, get up and do something else, preferably something dull and relaxing, in another room. When you feel drowsy, try sleeping again.

- **Take care of your health.** As your grandmother probably told you, good health habits are important for good sleep. Nutrition is one area to watch. The amino acid tryptophan promotes the onset of sleep, and other dietary elements may also influence alertness and relaxation. Exercise during the day also enhances sleep, but it should be avoided right before bedtime because in the short term it heightens alertness.

Finally, when insomnia is related to anxiety and worry, it makes sense to get to the source of your problems. Woody Allen once said, "The lamb and the lion shall lie down together, but the lamb will not be very sleepy." Like a lamb trying to sleep with a lion, you cannot expect to sleep well with stress hormones pouring through your bloodstream and worries crowding your mind. In an evolutionary sense, sleeplessness is an adaptive response to danger and threat. When your anxieties decrease, so may your sleepless nights.

SUMMARY

BIOLOGICAL RHYTHYMS: THE TIDES OF EXPERIENCE

1. *Consciousness* is the awareness of oneself and the environment. *States of consciousness*, which are distinct patterns of consciousness, are often associated with *biological rhythms*—periodic fluctuations in physiological functioning. These rhythms are typically *entrained* (synchronized) to external cues, but many are also *endogenous*, generated from within. *Circadian* fluctuations occur about once a day; *infradian* rhythms are longer; and *ultradian* rhythms are shorter, often occurring on about a 90-minute cycle.

2. When people live in isolation from all time cues, they tend to live a day that is just slightly longer than 24 hours. Circadian rhythms are governed by a biological "clock" in the *suprachiasmatic nucleus (SCN)* of the hypothalamus. The SCN is affected by the hormone *melatonin*, which is responsive to changes in light and dark, and which increases during the dark hours. When a person's normal routine changes, the person may experience *internal desynchronization*, in which the usual circadian rhythms are thrown out of phase with one another.

3. Folklore holds that moods follow infradian cycles. Some people do show a recurrence of depression every winter, in a pattern that has been labeled *seasonal affective disorder (SAD)*, but serious seasonal depression is rare. The causes of SAD are not yet clear, and it has been difficult to rule out placebo effects in the most common treatment, phototherapy. However, recent research does suggest that light treatments can be effective, especially if administered in the morning.

4. Another infradian rhythm is the menstrual cycle, during which various hormones rise and fall. Physical symptoms associated with the cycle usually have a biological cause, but well-controlled, double-blind studies on *"PMS"* do not support claims that emotional symptoms are reliably and universally tied to the menstrual cycle. Overall, women and men do not differ in the emotional symptoms they report or in the number of mood swings they experience over the course of a month. Expectations and learning affect how we interpret bodily and emotional changes. Few people of either sex are likely to undergo dramatic monthly mood swings or personality changes because of hormones.

THE RHYTHMS OF SLEEP

5. Sleep, which recurs on a circadian rhythm, is necessary not only for bodily restoration but also for normal mental functioning. During sleep, periods of *rapid eye movement*, or *REM*, alternate with non-REM sleep in an ultradian rhythm. *Non-REM sleep* is divided into four stages on the basis of characteristic brain-wave patterns. During REM sleep, the brain is active, and there are other signs of arousal, yet most of the skeletal muscles are limp; dreams are reported most often during REM sleep.

EXPLORING THE DREAM WORLD

6. Dreams are often recalled as illogical and bizarre. Some people say they have *lucid dreams*, in which they know they are dreaming. Researchers disagree about whether the eye movements of REM sleep are related to events and actions in dreams.

7. The *psychoanalytic explanation of dreams* is that they allow us to gratify forbidden or unrealistic wishes and desires that have been forced into the unconscious part of the mind. In dreams, according to Freud, thoughts and objects are disguised as symbolic images. Most psychologists today accept the notion that dreams are more than incoherent ramblings of the mind, but many psychologists quarrel with specific psychoanalytic interpretations.

8. Another approach holds that dreams express current concerns or help us solve current problems by working through emotional issues, especially during times of crisis. Findings on recurrent and traumatic dreams, gender differences in dreams, and the dreams of divorced people support this *problem-focused explanation*.

9. A third view holds that dreams are the by-product of *mental housekeeping*. According to this information-processing approach, dreams are merely random snippets from an ongoing process that is otherwise inaccessible to consciousness. During sleep, the brain may scan and sort through new data, or unneeded synaptic associations in the brain may be weakened. REM sleep has also been associated with the consolidation of memories, during which the synaptic changes associated with a recently stored memory become durable and stable.

10. The *activation-synthesis theory* of dreaming holds that dreams occur when the cortex tries to make sense of spontaneous neural firing initiated in the pons. The resulting interpretation, or synthesis, of the signals with existing knowledge and memories, is the dream. In this view, dreams do not disguise unconscious wishes, but they can reveal a person's perceptions, conflicts, and concerns.

CONSCIOUSNESS-ALTERING DRUGS

11. In all cultures, people have found ways to produce *altered states of consciousness*. For example, *psychoactive drugs* alter cognition and emotion by acting on

neurotransmitters in the brain. Most psychoactive drugs are classified as *stimulants, depressants, opiates,* or *psychedelics,* depending on their central nervous system effects and their impact on behavior and mood. However, two common drugs, *anabolic steroids* and *marijuana,* fall outside these categories. The use of some psychoactive drugs leads to *tolerance,* in which increasing dosages are needed for the same effect, and *withdrawal symptoms* if an addict tries to quit.

12. Reactions to a psychoactive drug are influenced not only by its chemical properties but also by the user's physical condition, prior experience with the drug, environmental setting, and *mental set*—the person's expectations and motives for taking the drug. Expectations can be even more powerful than the drug itself, as shown by the *"think-drink"* effect. Expectations and beliefs about drugs are in turn affected by a person's culture. People often find it difficult to distinguish abuse from use and to think critically about research findings on drug effects.

THE RIDDLE OF HYPNOSIS

13. *Hypnosis* is a procedure in which the practitioner suggests changes in the sensations, perceptions, thoughts, feelings, or behavior of the subject. Hypnotic responsiveness depends more on the efforts and qualities of the person being hypnotized than on the skill of the hypnotist. Although hypnosis has been used successfully for many medical and psychological purposes, it does not produce special abilities. Hypnosis can sometimes improve memory for facts about real events, but it also results in confusion between facts and vividly imagined possibilities. Therefore, "hypnotically refreshed" accounts are often full of errors and pseudomemories.

14. A leading explanation of hypnosis and its effects is that hypnosis involves *dissociation,* a split in consciousness. In one version of this approach, the split is between a part of consciousness that is hypnotized and a *hidden observer* that watches but does not participate. In another version, the split is between an executive-control system in the brain and other brain systems responsible for thinking and acting.

15. Another leading approach, the *sociocognitive explanation,* regards hypnosis as a product of normal social and cognitive processes. In this view, hypnosis is a form of role playing in which the hypnotized person uses active cognitive strategies, including imagination, to comply with the hypnotist's suggestions. The role is so engrossing that the person interprets it as real. Sociocognitive processes can account for the apparent age and past-life "regressions" of people under hypnosis and their reports of alien abductions; these individuals are simply playing a role based on fantasy, imagination, and suggestion.

KEY TERMS

LOOKING BACK

- Do popular "biorhythm" charts tell you anything about what scientists call biological rhythms? (p. 140)

- Why do you feel "out of sync" when you fly across time zones or change shifts at work? (p. 142)

- How are researchers learning to reset the biological clock that governs our daily cycles? (p. 143)

- Does "PMS" cause most women to feel depressed or irritable before their periods? (pp. 145–147)

- Why do we sleep? (p. 149)

- What happens when we go too long without enough sleep? (pp. 149–150)

- Why are you likely to be dreaming when the alarm goes off in the morning? (p. 152)

- Why did Freud call dreams the "royal road to the unconscious"? (p. 154)

- How might dreams be related to your current problems and concerns? (pp. 155–156)

- How does a disruption of REM sleep affect memory? (p. 157)

- Could dreams be caused by meaningless brain-stem signals? (pp. 157–158)

- In its physiological effects, is alcohol a downer or an upper? (p. 162)

- How do recreational drugs affect the brain? (pp. 162–164)

- Why can a glass of wine make you feel tired at one time but sociable and pepped up at another? (p. 165)

- Can a hypnotist force you to do things against your will? (p. 169)

- Can hypnosis help you remember the past more accurately? (p. 170)

- What are the legitimate uses of hypnosis in psychology and medicine? (p. 170)

- Are hypnotized persons merely faking or playacting? (p. 172)

6

SENSATION AND PERCEPTION

Nothing we use or hear or touch can be expressed

in words that equal what is given by the senses.

SOCIAL HISTORIAN HANNAH ARENDT

When Shirl Jennings was only three years old, an illness put him into a coma. He finally emerged, but his eyesight had faded, and within a few years, all he could see was light and dark. As he grew into adulthood, Shirl adjusted well to his disability; he studied massage therapy, went to work as a masseur for the YMCA, and led an independent life.

Then, in his forties, he fell in love and got married. Before the wedding, his fiancée asked him to see her ophthalmologist, who found that Shirl had dense cataracts (clouding of the lenses of the eyes). In 1991, at the age of 51, Shirl had the cataracts removed and regained his long-lost sight. But oddly, although Shirl's eyes now functioned well, he had no clue about what he was seeing; to identify objects, he had to touch or smell them. His own shadow confused him. His depth perception was poor, so he kept tripping. He could not read facial expressions well. And when he returned to work, his clients' bodies began to disgust him! He found himself living not in a happier, brighter world, but in one that was strange and frightening.

In the years that followed, Shirl's eyesight deterioriated once again, and today he can only make out vague shapes. Yet, he is untroubled; in fact, although he feels grateful for his short period of sight, he is rather relieved to be losing it again. "It's really more easy to be blind than see," he says.

Shirl's story (which inspired the 1999 movie *At First Sight*) is, of course, an unusual one, but it contains important lessons for us all. Like Shirl Jennings, we all depend on our senses for our everyday understanding of physical reality, and also like Shirl, we have only a partial perception of that reality. Even with normal eyesight and hearing, we are blind to most of the electromagnetic energy waves around us and deaf to most of the pressure waves that fill the air. And because of expectations shaped by our experiences, even with normal sensory abilities we may look but not see, listen but not hear.

Sensation is the detection of physical energy emitted or reflected by physical objects. The cells that do the detecting are located in the *sense organs*—the eyes, ears, tongue, nose, skin, and internal body tissues. The receptors for the senses of smell, pressure, pain, and temperature are extensions (dendrites) of sensory neurons. The receptors for vision, hearing, and taste are distinct cells that are separated from sensory neurons by synapses.

Sensory processes produce an immediate awareness of sound, color, form, and other building blocks of consciousness. They tell us what is happening, both inside our bodies and in the world that exists beyond our own skins. Without sensation, we would lose touch—literally—with reality. But to make sense of the world impinging on our senses, we also need perception, a set of processes that organize sensory

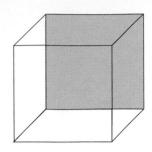

If you stare at the cube, the surface on the outside and front will suddenly be on the inside and back or vice versa, because your brain can interpret the sensory image in two different ways. The purple and white drawing can also be perceived in two ways, one involving a word. Do you see it?

impulses into meaningful patterns. Our sense of vision produces a two-dimensional image on the back of the eye, but we *perceive* the world in three dimensions. Our sense of hearing brings us the sound of a C, an E, and a G played simultaneously on the piano, but we *perceive* a C-major chord. Sometimes, a single sensory image produces two alternating perceptions, as illustrated by the examples in the margin.

Sensation and perception are the foundation of learning, thinking, and acting, and findings on these topics can often be put to practical use—for example, in the design of hearing aids and industrial "robots." These findings have also been used to improve the training of flight controllers, astronauts, and others who must make crucial decisions based on what they sense and perceive. In this chapter, you will learn why our sensory and perceptual processes are usually astonishingly accurate—and why sometimes, they are not.

WHAT'S AHEAD

● **What kind of code in the nervous system helps explain why a pinprick and a kiss feel different?**
● **Why does your dog hear a "silent" doggie whistle when you can't?**
● **What kind of bias can influence whether you think you hear the phone ringing when you're in the shower?**
● **What happens when people are deprived of all external sensory stimulation?**

OUR SENSATIONAL SENSES

At some point you probably learned there are five senses, corresponding to five sense organs: vision (eyes), hearing (ears), taste (tongue), touch (skin), and smell (nose). This way of categorizing the senses has existed for thousands of years. But actually, there are more than five senses, though scientists disagree about the exact number. The skin, which is the organ of touch or pressure, also senses heat, cold, and pain, not to mention itching and tickling. The ear, which is the organ of hearing, also contains receptors that account for a sense of balance. The skeletal muscles contain receptors responsible for a sense of bodily movement.

All of our senses evolved to help us survive. Even pain, which causes so much human misery, is an indispensable part of our evolutionary heritage, for it alerts us to illness and injury. In rare cases, people have been born without the ability to feel any of the hurts and aches that plague most people. That sounds like it would be great, but it's not. Because they feel none of pain's warnings, these people frequently burn, bruise, and cut themselves. One young woman developed inflamed joints because she failed to turn over in her sleep or to shift her weight while standing, acts that people with normal pain sensation do automatically. At the age of only 29, she died from massive infections, due in part to skin and bone injuries (Melzack, 1973).

Sensory experiences contribute immeasurably to the quality of life, even when they are not directly helping us stay alive. They entertain us, amuse us, soothe us, stimulate us, inspire us. If we really pay attention to our senses, said poet William Wordsworth, we can "see into the life of things" and hear "the still, sad music of humanity."

The Riddle of Separate Sensations

Sensation begins with the sense receptors, cells located in the sense organs. When these receptors detect an appropriate stimulus—light, mechanical pressure, or chem-

sensation The detection of physical energy emitted or reflected by physical objects; it occurs when energy in the external environment or the body stimulates receptors in the sense organs.

perception The process by which the brain organizes and interprets sensory information.

sense receptors Specialized cells that convert physical energy in the environment or the body to electrical energy that can be transmitted as nerve impulses to the brain.

ical molecules—they convert the energy of the stimulus into electrical impulses that travel along nerves to the brain. Sense receptors are like military scouts who scan the terrain for signs of activity. The scouts cannot make many decisions on their own. They must transmit what they learn to field officers—sensory nerves in the peripheral nervous system. The field officers in turn must report to generals at a command center—the cells of the brain. The generals are responsible for analyzing the reports, combining information brought in by different scouts, and deciding what it all means.

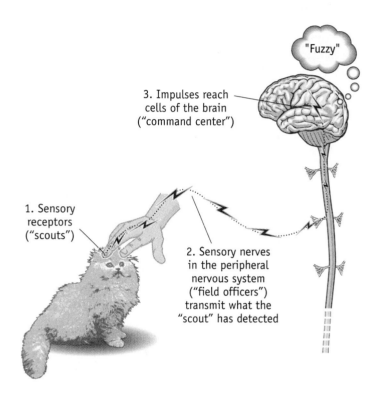

The "field officers" in the sensory system all use exactly the same form of communication, a neural impulse. It is as if they must all send their messages on a bongo drum and can only go "boom." How, then, are we able to experience so many different kinds of sensations? The answer is that the nervous system *encodes* the messages. One kind of code, which is *anatomical,* was described in 1826 by the German physiologist Johannes Müller, in his **doctrine of specific nerve energies.** According to this doctrine, different sensory modalities (such as vision and hearing) exist because signals received by the sense organs stimulate different nerve pathways leading to different areas of the brain. Signals from the eye cause impulses to travel along the optic nerve to the visual cortex. Signals from the ear cause impulses to travel along the auditory nerve to the auditory cortex. Light and sound waves produce different sensations because of these anatomical differences.

The doctrine of specific nerve energies implies that what we know about the world ultimately reduces to what we know about the state of our own nervous system. Therefore, if sound waves could stimulate nerves that end in the visual part of the brain, we would "see" sound. In fact, a similar sort of crossover does occur when you close your right eye, press lightly on the right side of the lid, and "see" a flash of light seemingly coming from the left. The pressure produces an impulse that travels up the optic nerve to the visual area in the right side of the brain, where it is interpreted as coming from the left side of the visual field.

doctrine of specific nerve energies
The doctrine that different sensory modalities, such as vision and hearing, exist because signals received by the sense organs stimulate different nerve pathways leading to different areas of the brain.

Anatomical encoding, however, does not completely solve the riddle of separate sensations, because it does not explain sensory variations *within* a particular sense—the sight of pink versus red, the sound of a piccolo versus the sound of a tuba, or the feel of a pinprick versus the feel of a kiss. An additional kind of code is therefore necessary. This second kind of code has been called *functional* (Schneider & Tarshis, 1986).

Functional codes rely on the fact that sensory receptors and neurons fire, or are inhibited from firing, only in the presence of specific sorts of stimuli. At any particular moment, then, some cells in the nervous system are firing, and some are not. Information about *which* cells are firing, *how many* cells are firing, the *rate* at which cells are firing, and the *patterning* of each cell's firing constitutes a functional code. You might think of such a code as the neurological equivalent of the Morse code. Functional encoding may occur all along a sensory route, starting in the sense organs and ending in the brain. As we will see, much remains to be learned about how functional encoding allows us to form an overall perception of an object.

Measuring the Senses

Just how sensitive are our senses? The answer comes from the field of *psychophysics*, which is concerned with how the physical properties of stimuli are related to our psychological experience of them. Drawing on principles from both physics and psychology, psychophysicists have studied how the strength or intensity of a stimulus affects the strength of sensation in an observer.

Absolute Thresholds. One way to find out how sensitive the senses are is to show people a series of signals that vary in intensity and ask them to say which signals they can detect. The smallest amount of energy that a person can detect reliably is known as the **absolute threshold**. The word *absolute* is a bit misleading because people detect borderline signals on some occasions and miss them on others. "Reliable" detection is said to occur when a person can detect a signal 50 percent of the time.

If you were having your absolute threshold for brightness measured, you might be asked to sit in a dark room and look at a wall or screen. You would then be shown flashes of light varying in brightness, one flash at a time. Your task would be to say whether you noticed a flash. Some flashes you would never see. Some you would always see. And sometimes you would miss seeing a flash, even though you had noticed one of equal brightness on other trials. Such errors seem to occur in part because of random firing of cells in the nervous system, which produces fluctuating background noise, something like the background noise in a stereo system.

By studying absolute thresholds, psychologists have found that our senses are very sharp indeed. If you have normal sensory abilities, you can see a candle flame on a clear, dark night from 30 miles away. You can hear a ticking watch in a perfectly quiet room from 20 feet away. You can taste a teaspoon of sugar diluted in two gallons of water, smell a drop of perfume diffused through a three-room apartment, and feel the wing of a bee falling on your cheek from a height of 1 centimeter (Galanter, 1962).

Yet, despite these impressive sensory skills, our senses are tuned in to only a narrow band of physical energies. For example, we are visually sensitive to only a tiny fraction of all electromagnetic energy; we do not see radio waves or microwaves (see Figure 6.1). Other species can pick up signals that we cannot: Dogs can detect high-frequency sound waves that are beyond our range, as you know if you have ever called your pooch with a "silent" doggie whistle; birds and many other creatures sense magnetic fields; and bees can see ultraviolet light, which merely gives human

absolute threshold The smallest quantity of physical energy that can be reliably detected by an observer.

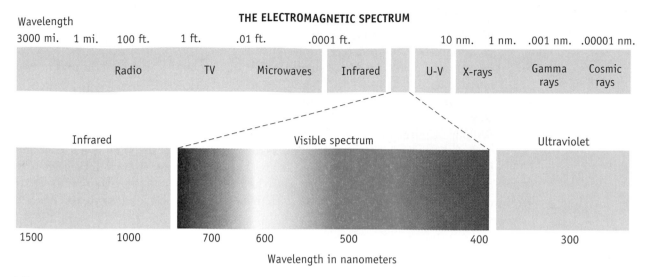

THE ELECTROMAGNETIC SPECTRUM

Wavelength

3000 mi. | 1 mi. | 100 ft. | 1 ft. | .01 ft. | .0001 ft. | | 10 nm. | 1 nm. | .001 nm. | .00001 nm.

| Radio | TV | Microwaves | Infrared | | U-V | X-rays | Gamma rays | Cosmic rays |

Infrared   Visible spectrum   Ultraviolet

1500   1000   700   600   500   400   300

Wavelength in nanometers

FIGURE 6.1
THE VISIBLE SPECTRUM OF ELECTROMAGNETIC ENERGY
Our visual system detects only a small fraction of the electromagnetic energy around us.

beings a sunburn. Because our sense organs evolved for particular purposes, our sensory windows on the world are partly shuttered. Fortunately, by using ingenuity, technology, and science, we can pry open those shutters and measure forms of energy that our senses cannot detect directly.

Difference Thresholds. Psychologists also study sensory sensitivity by having people compare two stimuli and judge whether they are the same or different. For example, a person might be asked to compare the weight of two blocks, the brightness of two lights, or the saltiness of two liquids. The smallest difference in stimulation that a person can detect reliably (again, half of the time) is called the **difference threshold**, or *just noticeable difference (jnd)*. When you compare two stimuli, A and B, the difference threshold will depend on the intensity or size

difference threshold The smallest difference in stimulation that can be reliably detected by an observer when two stimuli are compared; also called the *just noticeable difference (jnd)*.

Different species sense the world differently. The flower on the left was photographed in normal light. The one on the right, photographed under ultraviolet light, is what a butterfly might see, because butterflies have ultraviolet receptors. The hundreds of tiny bright spots are nectar sources.

of A. The larger or more intense A is, the greater the change must be before you can detect a difference. If you are comparing the weights of two pebbles, you might be able to detect a difference of only a fraction of an ounce, but you would not be able to detect such a subtle difference if you were comparing two massive boulders.

In everyday life, we may sometimes think we can detect a difference between stimuli when we cannot. Years ago, as a class project, undergraduate students at Williams College offered tasters three glasses of cola, two of one leading brand and one of the other (or vice versa), and asked them which drink they liked most and least. Each taster was given three trials. Most of the tasters were inconsistent in their preferences, indicating that they had trouble telling the two brands apart (Solomon, 1979). Apparently, the difference between the two tastes exceeded the students' difference thresholds.

Signal-Detection Theory. Despite their usefulness, the procedures we have described have a serious limitation: Measurements for any given individual may be affected by the person's general tendency, when uncertain, to respond, "Yes, I noticed a signal (or a difference)" or "No, I didn't notice anything." Some people are habitual yeasayers, willing to gamble that the signal was really there; others are habitual naysayers, cautious and conservative. In addition, alertness, motives, and expectations can influence how a person responds on any given occasion. If you are in the shower and you are expecting an important call, you may think you heard the telephone ring when it didn't. In laboratory studies, when observers want to impress the experimenter, they may lean toward a positive response.

Fortunately, these problems of *response bias* can be overcome. According to **signal-detection theory,** an observer's response in a detection task can be divided into a *sensory process,* which depends on the intensity of the stimulus, and a *decision process,* which is influenced by the observer's response bias. Methods are available for separating these two components. For example, the researcher can include some trials in which no stimulus is present and others in which a weak signal is present. Under these conditions, four kinds of responses are possible: The person (1) detects a signal that was present (a "hit"); (2) says the signal was present when it wasn't (a "false alarm"); (3) fails to detect the signal when it was present (a "miss"); or (4) correctly says the signal was absent when it was absent (a "correct rejection"):

RESPONSES IN SIGNAL DETECTION

signal-detection theory A psychophysical theory that divides the detection of a sensory signal into a sensory process and a decision process.

Yeasayers will have more hits than naysayers, but they will also have more false alarms because they are too quick to say "Yup, it was there." Naysayers will have more correct rejections than yeasayers, but they will also have more misses, because they are too quick to say "Nope, nothing was there." This information can be fed into a mathematical formula that yields separate estimates of a person's response bias and sensory capacity. The individual's true sensitivity to a signal of any particular intensity can then be predicted.

The old method of measuring thresholds assumed that a person's ability to detect a stimulus depended solely on the stimulus. Signal-detection theory assumes that there is no single "threshold," because at any given moment, a person's sensitivity to a stimulus depends on a decision that he or she actively makes. Signal-detection methods have many real-world applications, from screening applicants for jobs requiring keen hearing to training air-traffic controllers, whose decisions about the presence or absence of a blip on a radar screen may mean the difference between life and death.

sensory adaptation The reduction or disappearance of sensory responsiveness that occurs when stimulation is unchanging or repetitious.

Sensory Adaptation

Variety, they say, is the spice of life. It is also the essence of sensation, for our senses are designed to respond to change and contrast in the environment. When a stimulus is unchanging or repetitious, sensation often fades or disappears. Receptors or nerve cells higher up in the sensory system get "tired" and fire less frequently. The resulting decline in sensory responsiveness is called **sensory adaptation**. Such adaptation is usually useful because it spares us from having to respond to unimportant information; for example, most of the time you have no need to feel your watch sitting on

---

GET ➔ INVOLVED

NOW YOU SEE IT, NOW YOU DON'T

Sensation depends on change and contrast in the environment. Hold your hand over one eye and stare steadily at the dot in the middle of the circle on the right. You should have no trouble maintaining an image of the circle. However, if you do the same with the circle on the left, the image will fade. The gradual change from light to dark does not provide enough contrast to keep the visual receptors in your eyes firing at a steady rate. The circle reappears only if you close and reopen your eye or you shift your gaze to the X.

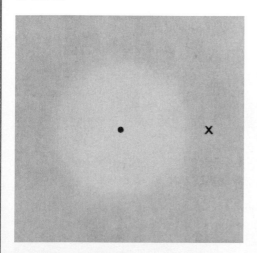 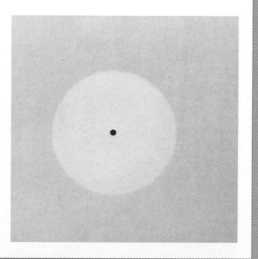

your wrist. Sometimes, however, adaptation can be hazardous, as when you no longer smell a gas leak that you noticed when you first entered the kitchen.

We never completely adapt to extremely intense stimuli—a terrible toothache, the odor of ammonia, the heat of the desert sun. And we rarely adapt completely to visual stimuli, whether they are weak or intense. Eye movements, voluntary and involuntary, cause the location of an object's image on the back of the eye to keep changing, so that visual receptors never have a chance to "fatigue." But in the laboratory, researchers can stabilize the image of a simple pattern, such as a line, at a particular point on the back of a person's eye. They use an ingenious device consisting of a tiny projector mounted on a contact lens. Although the eyeball moves, the image of the object stays focused on the same receptors. In minutes, the image begins to disappear.

What would happen if our senses adapted to *most* incoming stimuli? Would we sense nothing, or would the brain substitute its own images for the sensory experiences no longer available by way of the sense organs? In early research on **sensory deprivation,** researchers studied this question by isolating male volunteers from all patterned sight and sound. Vision was restricted by a translucent visor; hearing by a U-shaped pillow and noise from an air conditioner and fan; and touch by cotton gloves and cardboard cuffs. The volunteers took brief breaks to eat and use the bathroom, but otherwise, they lay in bed, doing nothing. The results were dramatic. Within a few hours, many of the men felt edgy. Some were so disoriented that they quit the study the first day. Those who stayed longer became confused, restless, and grouchy. Many reported bizarre visions, such as a squadron of marching squirrels or a procession of marching eyeglasses. Few were willing to remain in the study for more than two or three days (Heron, 1957).

But the notion that sensory deprivation is unpleasant or even dangerous turned out to be an oversimplification (Suedfeld, 1975). In many of the studies, the experimental procedures themselves probably aroused anxiety: Participants were told about "panic buttons" and were asked to sign "release from legal liability" forms. Later research, using better methods, showed that hallucinations are less dramatic and less disorienting than was believed at first. In fact, many people enjoy time-limited periods of deprivation, and some perceptual and intellectual abilities actually improve. The response to sensory deprivation is affected by your expectations and interpretations of what is happening. Reduced sensation can be scary if you are locked in a

DON'T OVERSIMPLIFY

You are in a dark room, isolated from sight, sound, smell, and taste. Will you hallucinate and beg to be released, or will you find the experience restful and soothing? What might affect your reaction?

room for an indefinite period, but relaxing if you have retreated to that room voluntarily for a little time out—or if you are paying cash money for a session in a "relaxation chamber."

Still, it is clear that the human brain requires a minimum amount of sensory stimulation in order to function normally. This need may help explain why people who live alone often keep the radio or television set running continuously and why prolonged solitary confinement is used as a form of punishment or even torture.

Sensory Overload

If too little stimulation can be bad for you, so can too much, because it can lead to fatigue and mental confusion. If you have ever felt exhausted, nervous, and headachy after a day crammed with hectic activities and deadlines, you know firsthand about sensory overload.

When people find themselves in a state of overload, they often cope by blocking out unimportant sights and sounds and focusing only on those they find interesting or useful. Psychologists have dubbed this the "cocktail party phenomenon" because at a cocktail party, a person typically focuses on just one conversation, ignoring other voices, the clink of ice cubes, music, and bursts of laughter across the room. The competing sounds all enter the nervous system, enabling the person to pick up anything important—even the person's own name, spoken by someone several yards away. Unimportant sounds, though, are not fully processed by the brain.

The capacity for **selective attention** protects us in daily life from being overwhelmed by all the sensory signals impinging on our receptors. The brain is not forced to respond to everything the sense receptors send its way. The "generals" in the brain can choose which "field officers" get past the command center's gates. Those that do not seem to have anything important to say are turned back.

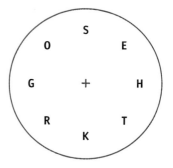

You can exercise selective attention even without moving your eyes. While staring at the cross in the center of this figure, read the letters one at a time, starting at the top, without moving your eyes. As you shift your attention to each letter, notice how your awareness of it is enhanced relative to the other letters (from Kanwisher & Downing, 1998).

selective attention The focusing of attention on selected aspects of the environment and the blocking out of others.

QUICK QUIZ

If you are not overloaded, try answering these questions.

1. Even on the clearest night, some stars cannot be seen by the naked eye because they are below the viewer's _____ threshold.

2. If you jump into a cold lake, but moments later the water no longer seems so cold, sensory _____ has occurred.

3. If you are immobilized in a hospital bed, with no roommate and no TV or radio, and you feel edgy and disoriented, you may be suffering the effects of _____.

4. During a break from your job as a waiter, you decide to read. For 20 minutes, you are so engrossed that you fail to notice the clattering of dishes or orders being called out to the cook. This is an example of _____.

5. In real-life detection tasks, is it better to be a "naysayer" or a "yeasayer"?

Answers:

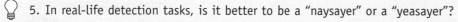

1. absolute 2. adaptation 3. sensory deprivation 4. selective attention 5. Neither; it depends on the consequences of a "miss," or "false alarm," and the probability of an event occurring. You might want to be a "yeasayer" if you are just out the door, you hear the phone ringing, and you are expecting a call about a job interview. You might want to be a "naysayer" if you are just out the door, you think you hear the phone, and you are on your way to a job interview and don't want to be late.

WHAT'S AHEAD

- How does the eye differ from a camera?
- Why can we describe a color as bluish green but not as reddish green?
- If you were blind in one eye, why might you misjudge the distance of a painting on the wall but not of buildings a block away?
- As a friend approaches, her image on your retina grows larger; why do you continue to see her as the same size?
- Why are perceptual illusions so valuable to psychologists?

VISION

Vision is the most frequently studied of all the senses, and with good reason. More information about the world comes to us through our eyes than through any other sense organ. (Perhaps that is why people say "I see what you mean" instead of "I hear what you mean.") Because we are most active in the daytime, we are "wired" to take advantage of the sun's illumination. Animals that are active at night tend to rely more heavily on hearing.

What We See

The stimulus for vision is light; even cats, raccoons, and other creatures famous for their ability to get around in the dark need *some* light to see. Visible light comes from the sun and other stars and from lightbulbs, and is also reflected off objects. Light travels in the form of waves, and three aspects of our visual world depend on the characteristics of these waves: hue, brightness, and saturation.

1 **Hue,** the dimension of visual experience specified by color names, is related to the *wavelength* of light—that is, to the distance between the crests of a light wave. Shorter waves tend to be seen as violet and blue, and longer ones as orange and red. (We say "tend to" because other factors also affect color perception, as we will see later.) The sun produces white light, a mixture of all the visible wavelengths. Sometimes, drops of moisture in the air act like a prism: They separate the sun's white light into the colors of the visible spectrum, and we are treated to a rainbow.

2 **Brightness** is the dimension of visual experience related to the amount, or *intensity,* of the light an object emits or reflects. Intensity corresponds to the amplitude (maximum height) of the wave. Generally speaking, the more light an object reflects, the brighter it appears. However, brightness is also affected by wavelength: Yellows appear brighter than reds and blues when physical intensities are actually equal. (For this reason, some fire departments have switched from red engines to yellow ones.)

3 **Saturation** (colorfulness) is the dimension of visual experience related to the *complexity* of light—that is, to how wide or narrow the range of wavelengths is. When light contains only a single wavelength, it is said to be "pure," and the resulting color is said to be completely saturated. At the other extreme is white light, which lacks any color and is completely unsaturated. In nature, pure light is extremely rare. Usually, we sense a mixture of wavelengths, and we see colors that are duller and paler than completely saturated ones.

Hue, brightness, and saturation are all *psychological* dimensions of visual experience, whereas wavelength, intensity, and complexity are all *physical* properties of the visual stimulus, light.

hue The dimension of visual experience specified by color names and related to the wavelength of light.

brightness Lightness or luminance; the dimension of visual experience related to the amount of light emitted from or reflected by an object.

saturation Vividness or purity of color; the dimension of visual experience related to the complexity of light waves.

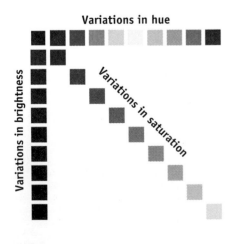

Variations in hue

Variations in saturation

Variations in brightness

An Eye on the World

Light enters the visual system through the eye, a wonderfully complex and delicate structure. As you read this section, examine Figure 6.2. Notice that the front part of the eye is covered by the transparent *cornea*. The cornea protects the eye and bends incoming light rays toward a *lens* located behind it. A camera lens focuses incoming light by moving closer to or farther from the shutter opening. However, the lens of the eye works by subtly changing its shape, becoming more or less curved to focus light from objects that are close by or far away. The amount of light that gets into the eye is controlled by muscles in the *iris*, the part of the eye that gives it color. The iris surrounds the round opening, or *pupil,* of the eye. When you enter a dim room, the pupil widens, or dilates, to let more light in. When you emerge into bright sunlight, the pupil gets smaller, contracting to allow in less light. You can see these changes by watching your eyes in a mirror as you change the lighting.

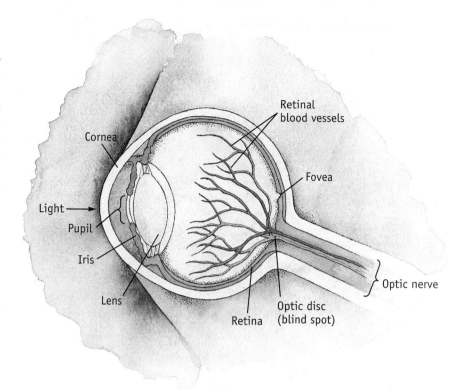

FIGURE 6.2
MAJOR STRUCTURES OF THE EYE
Light passes through the pupil and lens and is focused on the retina at the back of the eye. The point of sharpest vision is at the fovea.

The visual receptors are located in the back of the eye, or **retina**. In a developing embryo, the retina forms from tissue that projects out from the brain, not from tissue destined to form other parts of the eye; thus the retina is actually an extension of the brain. As Figure 6.3 shows, when the lens of the eye focuses light on the retina, the result is an upside-down image (which can actually be seen with an instrument used by eye specialists). Light from the top of the visual field stimulates light-sensitive receptor cells in the bottom part of the retina, and vice versa. The brain interprets this upside-down pattern of stimulation as something that is right side up.

About 120 to 125 million receptors in the retina are long and narrow and are called **rods**. Another 7 or 8 million receptors are cone-shaped and are called, appropriately enough, **cones**. The center of the retina, or *fovea*, where vision is sharpest, contains only cones, clustered densely together. From the center to the periphery, the ratio of rods to cones increases, and the outer edges contain virtually no cones.

Rods are more sensitive to light than cones are. They enable us to see in dim light and at night. (Cats see well in dim light in part because they have a high proportion

retina Neural tissue that lines the back of the eyeball's interior and contains the receptors for vision.

rods Visual receptors that respond to dim light but that are not involved in color vision.

cones Visual receptors involved in color vision.

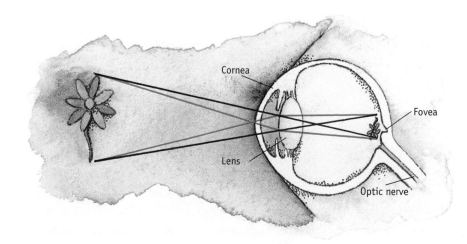

FIGURE 6.3
THE RETINAL IMAGE

When we look at an object, the light pattern on the retina is upside down. René Descartes was probably the first person to demonstrate this fact. He cut a piece from the back of an ox's eye and replaced the piece with paper. When he held the eye up to the light, he saw an upside-down image of the room on the paper!

dark adaptation A process by which visual receptors become maximally sensitive to dim light.

ganglion cells Neurons in the retina of the eye that gather information from receptor cells (by way of intermediate bipolar cells); their axons make up the optic nerve.

feature detectors Cells in the visual cortex that are sensitive to specific features of the environment.

of rods.) Because rods occupy the outer edges of the retina, they also handle peripheral (side) vision. That is why you can sometimes see a star from the corner of your eye even though it is invisible to you when you gaze straight at it. But rods cannot distinguish different wavelengths of light and therefore are not sensitive to color. As a result, it is often hard to distinguish colors clearly in dim light. The cones, on the other hand, are differentially sensitive to specific wavelengths of light and allow us to see colors. However, the cones need much more light than rods do to respond. They do not help us much when we are trying to find a seat in a darkened movie theater. (For a summary of these differences, see Review 6.1.)

We have all noticed that our eyes take time to adjust fully to dim illumination. This process of **dark adaptation** involves chemical changes in the rods and cones and occurs in two stages. The cones adapt quickly, within 10 minutes or so, but never become very sensitive to the dim illumination. The rods adapt more slowly, taking 20 minutes or longer, but are ultimately much more sensitive. After the first phase of adaptation, you can see better but not well; after the second phase, your vision is as good as it ever will get.

Rods and cones are connected by synapses to *bipolar neurons*, which in turn communicate with neurons called **ganglion cells** (see Figure 6.4). The axons of the ganglion cells converge to form the *optic nerve,* which carries information out through the back of the eye and on to the brain. Where the optic nerve leaves the eye, at the *optic disc*, there are no rods or cones. The absence of receptors produces a blind spot in the field of vision. Normally, we are unaware of the blind spot because (1) the image projected on the spot is hitting a different, "nonblind" spot in the other eye; (2) our eyes move so fast that we can pick up the complete image; and (3) the brain tends to fill in the gap. You can find your blind spot by following the instructions in the Get Involved exercise on the next page.

Why the Visual System Is Not a Camera

Although the eye is often compared with a camera, the visual system, unlike a camera, is not a passive recorder of the external world. Instead of simply registering spots of light and dark, as in a photograph, neurons in the visual system build up a picture of the world by detecting its meaningful features.

Ganglion cells and neurons in the thalamus of the brain respond to simple features in the environment, such as spots of light and dark. In mammals, special **feature-detector** cells in the visual cortex respond to more complex features. This fact was

DIFFERENCES BETWEEN RODS AND CONES

	Rods	Cones
How many?	120–125 million	7–8 million
Where most concentrated?	Periphery of retina	Center (fovea) of retina
How sensitive?	High sensitivity	Low sensitivity
Sensitive to color?	No	Yes

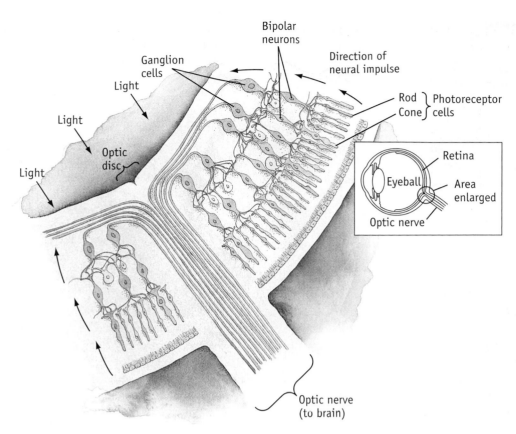

FIGURE 6.4
THE STRUCTURES OF THE RETINA

For clarity, all cells in this drawing are greatly exaggerated in size. In order to reach the receptors for vision (the rods and cones), light must pass through the ganglion cells and bipolar neurons as well as the blood vessels that nourish them (not shown). Normally, we do not see the shadow cast by this network of cells and blood vessels because the shadow always falls on the same place on the retina, and such stabilized images are not sensed. But when an eye doctor shines a moving light into your eye, the treelike shadow of the blood vessels falls on different regions of the retina and you may see it—a rather eerie experience.

first demonstrated by David Hubel and Torsten Wiesel (1962, 1968), who painstakingly recorded impulses from individual cells in the brains of cats and monkeys. (In 1981, they received a Nobel Prize for their work.) Hubel and Wiesel found that different neurons were sensitive to different patterns projected on a screen in front of the animals' eyes. Most cells responded maximally to moving or stationary lines that were oriented in a particular direction and located in a particular part of the visual

GET ➜ INVOLVED

FIND YOUR BLIND SPOT

A blind spot exists where the optic nerve leaves the back of your eye. Find the blind spot in your left eye by closing your right eye and looking at the magician. Then slowly move the book toward and away from you. The rabbit should disappear when the book is between 9 and 12 inches from your eye.

Cases of brain damage support the idea that particular systems of brain cells are highly specialized. One man's injury left him unable to identify ordinary objects, which he said often looked like "blobs." Yet, he had no trouble with faces, even when they were inverted, incomplete, or in cartoons. When shown this painting, he could easily see the face, but he could not see the vegetables comprising it (Moscovitch, Winocur, & Behrmann, 1997).

field. One type of cell might fire most rapidly in response to a horizontal line in the lower right part of the visual field, another to a diagonal line at an angle in the upper left part of the visual field. In the real world, such features make up the boundaries and edges of objects.

Since this pioneering work was done, scientists have found other cells in the visual system with more complex kinds of specialties. For example, in primates, the visual cortex contains cells that respond maximally to bull's-eyes, spirals, or concentric circles (Gallant, Braun, & Van Essen, 1993). Even more intriguing, some cells in the temporal and frontal lobes respond maximally to *faces* (Ó Scalaidhe, Wilson, & Goldman-Rakic, 1997; Young & Yamane, 1992). That might help explain why a person with brain damage may continue to recognize faces even after losing the ability to recognize other objects. In one case (Moscovitch, Winocur, & Behrmann, 1997), a man could recognize a face made up entirely of vegetables but could not recognize the vegetables! (See the photograph on the left.)

The brain's job is to take fragmentary information about lines, angles, shapes, motion, brightness, texture, and patterns, and come up with a unified view of what and where things are. How on earth does it do this? We saw in Chapter 4 that as neurons converge at a synapse, their overall pattern of firing determines whether the neuron on the other side of the synapse is excited or inhibited. The firing (or inhibition) of that neuron, then, actually conveys information to the *next* neuron along the sensory route about what was happening in many other cells. Eventually, a single cell in the cortex of the brain may receive information that was originally contained in the firing of thousands of different visual receptors. The perception of a visual stimulus may ultimately depend on the activation of many cells in far-flung parts of the brain, and on the overall pattern and rhythm of their activity (Bower, 1998).

How We See Colors

For 300 years, scientists have been trying to figure out why we see the world in living color. It turns out that different processes explain different stages of color vision.

The Trichromatic Theory. The **trichromatic theory** (also known as the *Young-Helmholtz theory*), applies to the first level of processing, which occurs in the retina of the eye. The retina contains three basic types of cones. One type responds maximally to blue (or more precisely, to a range of wavelengths near the short end of the spectrum, which give rise to the experience of blue), another to green, and a third to red. The hundreds of colors we see result from the combined activity of these three types of cones.

We may not all see exactly the same hues, however; researchers have discovered that subtypes of the basic cone types exist, and that men with different subtypes for red see the color red somewhat differently (Neitz & Neitz, 1995). Such variations may explain why people argue about how the color on the TV set should be adjusted!

Total color blindness is usually due to a genetic variation that causes cones of the retina to be absent or malfunctional. The visual world then consists of black, white, and shades of gray. Many species of animals are totally color-blind, but the condition is extremely rare in human beings. Most "color-blind" people are actually *color deficient*. Usually, the person is unable to distinguish red and green; the world is painted in shades of blue, yellow, brown, and gray. In rarer instances, a person may be blind to blue and yellow and may see only reds, greens, and grays. Color deficiency

trichromatic theory A theory of color perception that proposes three mechanisms in the visual system, each sensitive to a certain range of wavelengths; their interaction is assumed to produce all the different experiences of hue.

is found in about 8 percent of white men, 5 percent of Asian men, and 3 percent of black men and Native American men (Sekuler & Blake, 1994). Because of the way the condition is inherited, it is very rare in women.

The Opponent-Process Theory. The **opponent-process theory** applies to the second stage of color processing, which occurs in ganglion cells in the retina and in neurons in the thalamus and visual cortex of the brain. These cells, known as *opponent-process cells,* either respond to short wavelengths but are inhibited from firing by long wavelengths, or vice versa (DeValois & DeValois, 1975). Some opponent-process cells respond in opposite fashion to red and green; that is, they fire in response to one and turn off in response to the other. Others respond in opposite fashion to blue and yellow. (A third system responds in opposite fashion to white and black and thus yields information about brightness.) The net result is a color code that is passed along to the higher visual centers. Because this code treats red and green, and also blue and yellow, as antagonistic, we can describe a color as bluish green or yellowish green but not as reddish green or yellowish blue.

Opponent-process cells that are *inhibited* by a particular color seem to produce a burst of firing when the color is removed, just as they would if the opposing color were present. Similarly, cells that *fire* in response to a color will stop firing when the color is removed, just as they would if the opposing color were present. These facts explain why we are susceptible to *negative afterimages* when we stare at a particular hue—why we see, for instance, red after staring at green (see the Get Involved exercise on this page). A sort of neural rebound effect occurs: The cells that switch on or off to signal the presence of "green" send the opposite signal ("red") when the green is removed—and vice versa.

> **opponent-process theory** A theory of color perception, which assumes that the visual system treats pairs of colors as opposing or antagonistic.

GET ➜ INVOLVED

A CHANGE OF HEART

Opponent process cells that switch on or off in response to green send an opposite message—"red"—when the green is removed, producing a negative afterimage. Stare at the black dot in the middle of this heart for at least 20 seconds. Then shift your gaze to a white piece of paper or a white wall. Do you get a "change of heart"? You should see an image of a red heart with a blue border.

FIGURE 6.5
COLOR IN CONTEXT

The way you perceive a color depends on the colors around it. In this work by Joseph Albers, the adjacent Xs in each pair are actually the same color, but against different backgrounds they look different.

FIGURE 6.6
FIGURE AND GROUND

Do you see the goblins or angels? The woodcut *Heaven and Hell* by M. C. Escher shows both, depending on whether you see the black or white sections as figure or ground.

Color in Context. The perceived color of an object also depends on the wavelengths reflected by *everything around it*—a fact well known to artists and interior designers (see Figure 6.5). Thus, you never see a good, strong red unless other objects in the surroundings reflect the green and blue part of the spectrum. Edwin Land (1959), inventor of the Polaroid camera, worked out precise rules that predict exactly how an object will appear, given the wavelengths reflected by all the objects in a scene, and the brain may use similar rules.

Constructing the Visual World

We do not see a retinal image; that image is merely grist for the mill of the mind, which actively interprets the image and constructs the world from the often fragmentary data of the senses. In the brain, sensory signals that give rise to vision, hearing, taste, smell, and touch are combined from moment to moment to produce a unified model of the world. This is the process of perception.

Form Perception. To make sense of the world, we must know where one thing ends and another begins. In vision, for example, we must separate the teacher from the lectern; in hearing, we must separate the piano solo from the orchestral accompaniment; and in taste, we must separate the marshmallow from the hot chocolate. This process of dividing up the world occurs so rapidly and effortlessly that we take it completely for granted—until we must make out objects in a heavy fog or words in the rapid-fire conversation of someone speaking a foreign language.

The *Gestalt psychologists,* who belonged to a movement that began in Germany and was influential in the 1920s and 1930s, were among the first to study how people organize the world visually into meaningful units and patterns. In German, *gestalt* means "pattern" or "configuration." The Gestalt psychologists' motto was "The whole is more than the sum of its parts." They observed that when we perceive something, properties emerge from the whole configuration that are not found in any particular component. When you watch a movie, for example, the motion you "see" is nowhere in the film, which consists of separate static frames projected at 24 frames per second.

The Gestalt psychologists noted that we always organize the visual field into *figure* and *ground*. The figure stands out from the rest of the environment (see Figure 6.6). Some things stand out as figure by virtue of their intensity or size; it is hard to ignore the blinding flash of a camera or a tidal wave approaching your piece of beach. Unique objects also stand out, such as a banana in a bowl of oranges. Moving objects in an otherwise still environment, such as a shooting star, will usually be seen as figure. Indeed, it is hard to ignore a sudden change of any kind in the environment because our brains are geared to respond to change and contrast. However, selective attention, the ability to concentrate on some stimuli and to filter out others, gives us some control over what we perceive as figure and ground.

Here are some other **Gestalt principles** that describe how the visual system groups sensory building blocks into perceptual units:

1 *Proximity.* Things that are near each other tend to be grouped together. Thus, you perceive the dots on the left as three groups of dots, not as 12 separate, unrelated ones. Similarly, you perceive the pattern on the right as vertical columns of dots, not as horizontal rows:

2 *Closure.* The brain tends to fill in gaps in order to perceive complete forms. This is fortunate because we often need to decipher less-than-perfect images. The following figures are easily perceived as a triangle, a face, and the letter *e*, even though none of the figures are complete:

3 *Similarity.* Things that are alike in some way (for example, in color, shape, or size) tend to be perceived as belonging together. In the figure on the left, you see the circles as forming an *x*. In the one on the right, you see horizontal bars rather than vertical columns because the horizontally aligned stars share the same color:

4 *Continuity.* Lines and patterns tend to be perceived as continuing in time or space. You perceive the figure on the left as a single line partially covered by an oval rather than as two separate lines touching an oval. In the figure on the right, you see two lines, one curved and one straight, instead of two curved and two straight lines, touching at one focal point:

Consumer products are sometimes designed with little thought for visual principles such as those formulated by the Gestalt psychologists—which is why it can be a major challenge to find the pause button on the remote control for your VCR (Norman, 1988). Good design requires, among other things, that crucial distinctions be visually obvious. For instance, knobs and switches with different functions should be distinguished by color, texture, or shape, and they should stand out as "figure."

Gestalt principles Principles that describe the brain's organization of sensory building blocks into meaningful units and patterns.

binocular cues Visual cues to depth or distance requiring two eyes.

convergence The turning of the eyes inward, which occurs when they focus on a nearby object.

retinal disparity The slight difference in lateral separation between two objects, as seen by the left eye and the right eye.

monocular cues Visual cues to depth or distance, which can be used by one eye alone.

Depth and Distance Perception. Ordinarily we need to know not only what something is, but also where it is. Touch gives us this information directly, but vision does not, so we must *infer* an object's location by estimating its distance or depth.

To perform this remarkable feat, we rely in part on **binocular cues**—cues that require the use of two eyes. One is **convergence**, the turning of the eyes inward, which occurs when they focus on a nearby object. The closer the object, the greater the convergence (as you know if you have ever tried to "cross" your eyes by looking at your own nose). As the angle of convergence changes, the corresponding muscular changes provide the brain with information about distance.

The two eyes also receive slightly different retinal images of the same object. You can prove this by holding a finger about 12 inches in front of your face and looking at it with only one eye at a time. Its position will appear to shift when you change eyes. Now hold up two fingers, one closer to your nose than the other. Notice that the amount of space between the two fingers appears to change when you switch eyes. The slight difference in lateral (sideways) separation between two objects as seen by the left eye and the right eye is called **retinal disparity**. Because retinal disparity increases as the distance between two objects increases, the brain can use it to infer depth and calculate distance.

Binocular cues help us estimate distances up to about 50 feet. For objects farther away, we need only **monocular cues**, cues that do not depend on using both eyes. One such cue is *interposition:* When an object is interposed between the

MONOCULAR CUES TO DEPTH

Most cues to depth do not depend on having two eyes. Some monocular (one-eyed) cues are shown here.

INTERPOSITION

An object that partly blocks or obscures another one must be in front of the other one and is therefore seen as closer.

LIGHT AND SHADOW

Both of these attributes give objects the appearance of three dimensions.

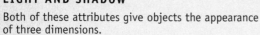

MOTION PARALLAX

When an observer is moving, objects appear to move at different speeds and in different directions. The closer an object, the faster it seems to move; and close objects appear to move backward, whereas distant ones seem to move forward.

viewer and a second object, partly blocking the view of the second object, the first object is perceived as being closer. Another monocular cue is *linear perspective:* When two lines known to be parallel appear to be coming together or converging, they imply the existence of depth. For example, if you are standing between rail-road tracks, they appear to converge in the distance. These and other monocular cues are illustrated on these pages.

Visual Constancies: When Seeing Is Believing. Your perceptual world would be a confusing place without another important perceptual skill. Lighting conditions, viewing angles, and the distances of stationary objects are all continually changing as we move about, yet we rarely confuse these changes with changes in the objects themselves. This ability to perceive objects as stable or unchanging even though the sensory patterns they produce are constantly shifting is called **perceptual constancy**. The best-studied constancies are visual, and they include the following:

1 *Shape constancy.* We continue to perceive objects as having a constant shape even though the shape of the retinal image produced by an object changes when our point of view changes. If you hold a Frisbee directly in front of your face, its image on the retina will be round. When you set the Frisbee on a table, its image becomes elliptical, yet you continue to identify the Frisbee as round.

perceptual constancy The accurate perception of objects as stable or unchanged despite changes in the sensory patterns they produce.

RELATIVE SIZE
The smaller an object's image on the retina, the farther away the object appears.

TEXTURE GRADIENTS
Distant parts of a uniform surface appear denser; that is, its elements seem spaced more closely together.

RELATIVE CLARITY
Because of particles in the air—from dust, fog, or smog—distant objects tend to look hazier, duller, or less detailed.

LINEAR PERSPECTIVE
Parallel lines will appear to be converging in the distance; the greater the apparent convergence, the greater the perceived distance. This cue is often exaggerated by artists to convey an impression of depth.

When size constancy fails.

2 *Location constancy.* We perceive stationary objects as remaining in the same place, even though the retinal image moves about as we move our eyes, heads, and bodies. As you drive along the highway, telephone poles and trees fly by—on your retina. But you know that these objects do not move on their own, and you also know that your body is moving, so you perceive the poles and trees as staying put.

3 *Size constancy.* We continue to see an object as having a constant size even when its retinal image becomes larger or smaller as we get closer to or farther from it. A friend approaching on the street does not seem to be growing; a car pulling away from the curb does not seem to be shrinking. Size constancy depends in part on familiarity with objects; you *know* people and cars do not change size from moment to moment. It also depends on the apparent distance of an object. When you move your hand toward your face, your brain registers the fact that the hand is getting closer, and you correctly perceive its unchanging size. There is, then, an intimate relationship between perceived size and perceived distance.

4 *Brightness constancy.* We continue to see objects as having a relatively constant brightness, even though the amount of light they reflect changes as the overall level of illumination changes. Snow remains white even on a cloudy day. We are not fooled, though, because the brain registers the total illumination in the scene, and we automatically take this information into account in the perception of any particular object's brightness.

5 *Color constancy.* We see an object as maintaining its hue despite the fact that the wavelength of light reaching our eyes from the object may change somewhat as the illumination changes. For example, outdoor light is "bluer" than indoor light, and objects outdoors therefore reflect more "blue" light than those indoors. Conversely, indoor light from a lamp is rich in long wavelengths and is therefore "yellower." Yet, objects usually look the same color in both places. The explanation involves sensory adaptation, which we discussed earlier. Outdoors, we quickly adapt to short-wavelength (bluish) light, and indoors, we adapt to long-wavelength light. As a result, our visual responses are similar in the two situations. Also, as we saw earlier, the brain takes into account all the wavelengths in the visual field when computing the color of a particular object. If a lemon is bathed in bluish light, so, usually, is everything else around it. The increase in blue light reflected by the lemon is "canceled" in the visual cortex by the increase in blue light reflected by the lemon's surroundings, and so the lemon continues to look yellow.

Visual Illusions: When Seeing Is Misleading. Perceptual constancies allow us to make sense of the world. Occasionally, however, we can be fooled, and the result is a **perceptual illusion**. For psychologists, illusions are valuable because they are *systematic* errors that provide hints about the perceptual strategies of the mind.

Although illusions can occur in any sensory modality, visual illusions have been studied more than other kinds. Visual illusions sometimes occur when the strategies that normally lead to accurate perception are overextended to situations where they do not apply. Compare the lengths of the two vertical lines in Figure 6.7a. If you are like most people, you perceive the line on the right as slightly longer than the one on the left—yet they are exactly the same length. This is the Müller-Lyer illusion, named after the German sociologist who first described it in 1889.

One explanation for the Müller-Lyer illusion is that the branches on the lines serve as perspective cues that normally suggest depth (Gregory, 1963). The line on the left is like the near edge of a building; the one on the right is like the far corner of a room (see part b of the figure). Although the two lines produce the same-sized retinal image, the one with the outward-facing branches suggests greater distance. We are fooled into perceiving it as longer because we automatically apply a rule about the relationship between size and distance that is normally useful: When two

perceptual illusion An erroneous or misleading perception of reality.

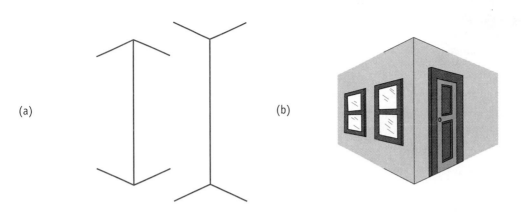

(a)

(b)

objects produce the same-sized retinal image and one is farther away, the farther one is larger. The problem, in this case, is that there is no actual difference in the distance of the two lines, so the rule is inappropriate.

Just as there are size, shape, location, brightness, and color constancies, so there are size, shape, location, brightness, and color illusions. Some illusions are simply a matter of physics. Thus, a chopstick in a half-filled glass of water looks bent because water and air refract light differently. Other illusions occur due to misleading messages from the sense organs, as in sensory adaptation. Still others, like the Müller-Lyer illusion, seem to occur because the brain misinterprets sensory information. Figure 6.8 shows other startling illusions.

In everyday life, most illusions are harmless, or even useful or entertaining. Occasionally, however, an illusion interferes with the performance of some skill. In baseball, two types of pitches that drive batters batty are the rising fastball, in which the ball seems to jump a few inches when it reaches home plate, and the breaking curveball, in which the ball seems to loop toward the batter and then fall at the last moment; both of these pitches are physical impossibilities. According to one explanation, they are illusions that occur when batters misestimate a ball's speed and momentarily shift their gaze to where they think it will cross home plate (Bahill & Karnavas, 1993). Illusions may also lead to industrial and automobile accidents. For example, because large objects often appear to move more slowly than small ones, drivers sometimes underestimate the speed of onrushing trains at railroad crossings and think they can "beat" the train, with tragic results.

FIGURE 6.7
THE MÜLLER-LYER ILLUSION

The two lines in (a) are exactly the same length. (If you don't believe it, measure them!) We are probably fooled into perceiving them as different because the brain interprets the one with the outward-facing branches as farther away, as if it were the far corner of a room, and the one with the inward-facing branches as closer, as if it were the near edge of a building (b).

FIGURE 6.8
FOOLING THE EYE

Although perception is usually accurate, we can be fooled. In (a) the cats as drawn are all the same size; in (b) the diagonal lines are all parallel. To see the illusion depicted in (c), hold your index fingers 5 to 10 inches in front of your eyes as shown, then focus straight ahead. Do you see a floating "fingertip frankfurter"? Can you make it shrink or expand?

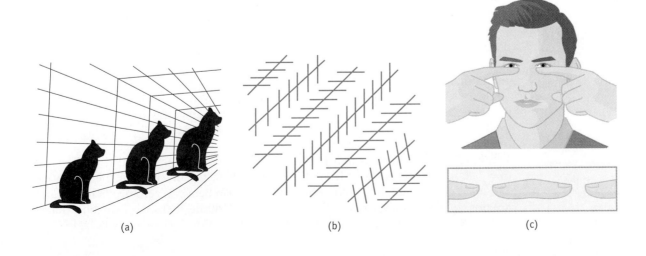

(a)

(b)

(c)

QUICK QUIZ

Can you accurately perceive these questions?

1. How can two Gestalt principles help explain why you can make out the Big Dipper on a starry night?

2. *True or false:* Binocular cues help us locate objects that are very far away.

3. Hold one hand about 12 inches from your face and the other one about 6 inches away. (a) Which hand will cast the smaller retinal image? (b) Why don't you perceive that hand as smaller?

Answers:

1. *Proximity* of certain stars encourages you to see them as clustered together to form a pattern; *closure* allows you to "fill in the gaps" and see the contours of a "dipper."   2. false   3. (a) The hand that is 12 inches away will cast a smaller retinal image. (b) Your brain takes the differences in distance into account in estimating size; also, you know how large your hands are.

WHAT'S AHEAD

- Why does a note played on a flute sound different from the same note on an oboe?
- If you habitually listen to loud music through headphones, what kind of hearing impairment are you risking?
- To locate the source of a sound, why does it sometimes help to turn or tilt your head?

HEARING

Like vision, the sense of hearing, or *audition*, provides a vital link with the world around us. Because relationships with others rely so heavily on hearing, when people lose their hearing they sometimes come to feel socially isolated. That is why many hearing-impaired people feel strongly about teaching deaf children American Sign Language (ASL) or other gestural systems, which allow them to communicate with and forge close relationships with other signers.

What We Hear

The stimulus for sound is a wave of pressure created when an object vibrates (or, sometimes, when compressed air is released, as in a pipe organ). The vibration (or release of air) causes molecules in a transmitting substance to move together and apart. This movement produces variations in pressure that radiate in all directions. The transmitting substance is usually air, but sound waves can also travel through water and solids, as you know if you have ever put your ear to the wall to hear voices in the next room.

As with vision, psychological aspects of our auditory experience are related in a predictable way to physical characteristics of the stimulus—in this case, a sound wave:

1 **Loudness** is the dimension of auditory experience related to the *intensity* of a wave's pressure. Intensity corresponds to the amplitude, or maximum height, of the wave. The more energy contained in the wave, the higher it is at its peak. Perceived loudness is also affected by *pitch*—how high or low a sound is. If low and high sounds produce waves with equal amplitudes, the low sound may seem quieter.

Sound intensity is measured in units called *decibels* (dB). A decibel is one-tenth of a *bel*, a unit named for Alexander Graham Bell, the inventor of the telephone. The average absolute threshold of hearing in human beings is zero decibels. Decibels are not equally distant, as inches on a ruler are. A 60-decibel sound (such as that of

loudness The dimension of auditory experience related to the intensity of a pressure wave.

a sewing machine) is not 50 percent louder than a 40-decibel sound (such as that of a whisper); it is 100 times louder. Table 6.1 shows the intensity in decibels of some common sounds.

2 **Pitch** is the dimension of auditory experience related to the frequency of the sound wave and, to some extent, its intensity. *Frequency* refers to how rapidly the air (or other medium) vibrates—that is, the number of times per second the wave cycles through a peak and a low point. One cycle per second is known as 1 *hertz* (Hz). The healthy ear of a young person normally detects frequencies in the range of 16 Hz (the lowest note on a pipe organ) to 20,000 Hz (the scraping of a grasshopper's legs).

3 **Timbre** is the distinguishing quality of a sound. It is the dimension of auditory experience related to the *complexity* of the sound wave—to the relative breadth of the range of frequencies that make up the wave. A pure tone consists of only one frequency, but in nature, pure tones are extremely rare. Usually what we hear is a complex wave consisting of several subwaves with different frequencies. A particular combination of frequencies results in a particular timbre. Timbre is what makes a note played on a flute, which produces relatively pure tones, sound different from the same note played on an oboe, which produces very complex sounds.

pitch The dimension of auditory experience related to the frequency of a pressure wave; height or depth of a tone.

timbre The distinguishing quality of a sound; the dimension of auditory experience related to the complexity of the pressure wave.

TABLE 6.1   Sound Intensity Levels in the Environment

The following decibel levels apply at typical working distances. Each ten-point increase represents a tenfold increase in sound intensity over the previous level. Even some everyday noises can be hazardous to hearing if exposure goes on for too long a time.

Typical Level (Decibels)	Examples	Dangerous Time Exposure
0	Lowest sound audible to human ear	
30	Quiet library, soft whisper	
40	Quiet office, living room, bedroom away from traffic	
50	Light traffic at a distance, refrigerator, gentle breeze	
60	Air conditioner at 20 feet, conversation, sewing machine	
70	Busy traffic, noisy restaurant (constant exposure)	Critical level begins
80	Subway, heavy city traffic, alarm clock at 2 feet, factory noise	More than 8 hours
90	Truck traffic, noisy home appliances, shop tools, lawn mower	Less than 8 hours
100	Chain saw, boiler shop, pneumatic drill	Less than 2 hours
120	Rock concert in front of speakers, sandblasting, thunderclap	Immediate danger
140	Gunshot blast, jet plane at 50 feet	Any length of exposure time is dangerous
180	Rocket launching pad	Hearing loss inevitable

Source: Reprinted with permission from the American Academy of Otolaryngology—Head and Neck Surgery, Washington, D.C.

cochlea [KOCK-lee-uh] A snail-shaped, fluid-filled organ in the inner ear, containing the receptors for hearing.

When many frequencies are present but are not in harmony, we hear noise. When all the frequencies of the sound spectrum occur, they produce a hissing sound called *white noise*. White noise is named by analogy to white light. Just as white light includes all wavelengths of the visible light spectrum, so white noise includes all frequencies of the audible sound spectrum.

An Ear on the World

As Figure 6.9 shows, the ear has an outer, a middle, and an inner section. The soft, funnel-shaped outer ear is well designed to collect sound waves, but hearing would still be quite good without it. The essential parts of the ear are hidden from view, inside the head.

A sound wave passes into the outer ear and through an inch-long canal to strike an oval-shaped membrane called the *eardrum*. The eardrum is so sensitive that it can respond to the movement of a single molecule! A sound wave causes it to vibrate with the same frequency and amplitude as the wave itself. This vibration is passed along to three tiny bones in the middle ear, the smallest bones in the human body. These bones, known informally as the "hammer," the "anvil," and the "stirrup," move one after the other, which has the effect of intensifying the force of the vibration. The innermost bone, the stirrup, pushes on a membrane that opens into the inner ear.

The actual organ of hearing, the *organ of Corti,* is a chamber inside the **cochlea**, a snail-shaped structure within the inner ear. The organ of Corti plays the same role in hearing that the retina plays in vision. It contains the all-important receptor cells, which in this case look like bristles and are called hair cells, or *cilia*. Exposure to extremely loud noise for a brief period, or more moderate levels of noise for a sustained period, can damage these fragile cells (see Table 6.1 again). They flop over

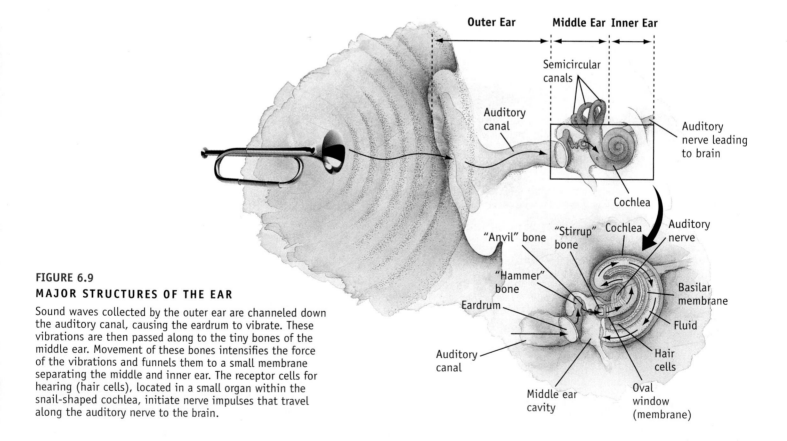

FIGURE 6.9
MAJOR STRUCTURES OF THE EAR

Sound waves collected by the outer ear are channeled down the auditory canal, causing the eardrum to vibrate. These vibrations are then passed along to the tiny bones of the middle ear. Movement of these bones intensifies the force of the vibrations and funnels them to a small membrane separating the middle and inner ear. The receptor cells for hearing (hair cells), located in a small organ within the snail-shaped cochlea, initiate nerve impulses that travel along the auditory nerve to the brain.

like broken blades of grass, and if the damage reaches a critical point, hearing loss occurs. In modern society, with its ubiquitous office machines, automobiles, power saws, leaf blowers, jackhammers, and stereos (often played at full blast through headphones), such impairment is common. Many college students already have impaired hearing because of damage to the cilia.

The hair cells of the cochlea are embedded in the rubbery *basilar membrane,* which stretches across the interior of the cochlea. When pressure reaches the cochlea, it causes wavelike motions in fluid within the cochlea's interior. These motions push on the basilar membrane, causing it to move in a wavelike motion, too. Just above the hair cells is yet another membrane. As the hair cells rise and fall, their tips brush against it, and they bend. This causes the hair cells to initiate a signal that is passed along to the *auditory nerve,* which then carries the message to the brain. The particular pattern of hair-cell movement is affected by the manner in

The spiraled interior of a guinea pig's cochlea, shown here, is almost identical to that of a human cochlea.

which the basilar membrane moves. This pattern determines which neurons fire and how rapidly they fire, and the resulting code in turn determines the sort of sound we hear. For example, we discriminate high-pitched sounds largely on the basis of where activity occurs along the basilar membrane; activity at different sites leads to different neural codes. We discriminate low-pitched sounds largely on the basis of the frequency of the basilar membrane's vibration; again, different frequencies lead to different neural codes.

Could anyone ever imagine such a complex and odd arrangement of bristles, fluids, and snail shells if it did not already exist?

Constructing the Auditory World

Just as we do not see a retinal image, so we do not hear a chorus of brushlike tufts bending and swaying in the dark recesses of the cochlea. Just as we do not see a jumbled collection of lines and colors, so we do not hear a chaotic collection of disconnected pitches and timbres. Instead, we use our perceptual powers to organize patterns of sound and to construct a meaningful auditory world.

For example, in class, your psychology instructor hopes you will perceive his or her voice as *figure* and the hum of a passing airplane, cheers from the athletic field, or distant sounds of a construction crew as *ground.* Whether these hopes are realized will depend, of course, on where you choose to direct your attention. Other Gestalt principles can also be applied to hearing. The *proximity* of notes in a melody tells you which notes go together to form phrases; *continuity* helps you follow a melody on one violin when another violin is playing a different melody; *similarity* in timbre and pitch helps you pick out the soprano voices in a chorus and hear them as a unit; *closure* helps you understand a radio announcer's words even when static makes some of the individual sounds unintelligible.

Besides needing to organize sounds, we also need to know where they are coming from. We can estimate the *distance* of a sound's source by using loudness as a cue. For example, we know that a train sounds louder when it is 20 yards away than when it is a mile off. To locate the *direction* a sound is coming from, we depend in part on the fact that we have two ears. A sound arriving from the right reaches the right ear a fraction of a second sooner than it reaches the left ear, and vice versa. The sound may also provide a bit more energy to the right ear (depending on its frequency) because it has to get around the head to reach the left ear. Localizing sounds that are coming from directly in back of you or from directly above your head is hard because such sounds reach both ears at the same time. When you turn or cock your head, you are actively trying to overcome this problem. Many animals do not have to do this; they can move their ears independently of their heads.

Scientists know far less about the physiology of sound perception than they do about visual perception, but they are starting to see some similarities. For example, just as cells in the visual system are sensitive to specific features of the visual environment, so cells in the brain's auditory system seem sensitive to specific features of sound, such as its frequency, timing, or location (deCharms, Blake, & Merzenich, 1998; Konishi, 1993).

QUICK QUIZ

How well can you detect the answers to these questions on hearing?

1. Which psychological dimensions of hearing correspond to the intensity, frequency, and complexity of the sound wave?

2. Tom Petty has a nasal voice, and Bob Dylan has a gravelly voice. Which psychological dimension of hearing describes the difference?

3. An extremely loud or sustained noise can permanently damage the _____ of the ear.

4. During a lecture, a classmate draws your attention to a buzzing fluorescent light that you had not previously noticed. What will happen to your perception of figure and ground?

Answers:

1. loudness, pitch, timbre   2. timbre   3. hair cells (cilia)   4. The buzzing sound will become figure, and the lecturer's voice will become ground, at least momentarily.

WHAT'S AHEAD

- Why do saccharin and caffeine taste bitter to some people but not to others?
- Why do you have trouble tasting your food when you have a cold?
- Why do people often continue to "feel" limbs that have been amputated?

THE OTHER SENSES

Psychologists have been particularly interested in vision and audition because of the importance of these senses to human survival. However, research on the other senses is growing dramatically, as awareness of how they contribute to our lives increases and new ways are found to study them.

Taste: Savory Sensations

Taste, or *gustation*, occurs because chemicals stimulate thousands of receptors in the mouth. These receptors are located primarily on the tongue, but some are also found in the throat, inside the cheeks, and on the roof of the mouth. If you look at your tongue in a mirror, you will notice many tiny bumps; they are called **papillae** (from the Latin for "pimple"), and they come in several forms. In all but one form, **taste buds** line the sides of each papilla (see Figure 6.10). The buds, which up close look a little like a segmented orange, are commonly referred to, mistakenly, as the receptors for taste. The actual receptor cells are *inside* the buds, 15 to 50 to a bud. These cells send

papillae [pa-PILL-ee] Knoblike elevations on the tongue, containing the taste buds. (Singular: *papilla*.)

taste buds Nests of taste-receptor cells.

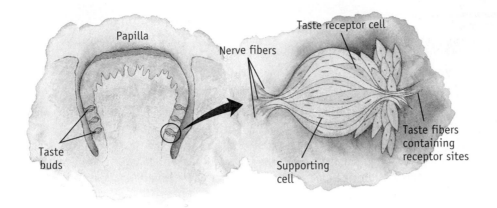

FIGURE 6.10
TASTE RECEPTORS

The illustration on the left shows taste buds lining the sides of a papilla on the tongue's surface. The illustration on the right shows an enlarged view of a single taste bud.

tiny fibers out through an opening in the bud; the receptor sites are on these fibers. The receptor cells are replaced by new cells about every 10 days. After age 40 or so, however, the total number of taste buds (and therefore receptors) declines, which is probably why older people can often enjoy strong tastes that children may detest.

Most researchers believe that there are four basic tastes: *salty, sour, bitter,* and *sweet,* each produced by a different type of chemical. Until a few years ago, nearly all textbooks included a "tongue map," showing areas supposedly most sensitive to these tastes. But then physiological psychologist Linda Bartoshuk (1993) found that the map was based on a misleading graph published in 1942—and it was simply wrong. The four basic tastes can be perceived at any spot on the tongue that has receptors, and differences among the areas are small. Interestingly, the center of the tongue contains no taste buds, and so it cannot produce *any* sort of taste sensation. But, as in the case of the eye's blind spot, you will not usually notice the lack of sensation because the brain fills in the gap.

When you bite into an egg or a piece of bread or an orange, its unique flavor is composed of some combination of the four basic taste types. The physiological details are still not well understood, and there is even uncertainty about whether distinct tastes are associated with different types of nerve fibers. A team of researchers recently reported finding two possible taste receptors in rats, one for sweet tastes and the other for bitter (Hoon et al., 1999). But this work is still preliminary, and may or may not apply to human beings.

Some taste preferences, such as a liking for sweets, are universal, a part of our evolutionary heritage (Bartoshuk & Beauchamp, 1994). Others are a matter of culture. For example, many North Americans who enjoy raw oysters, raw smoked salmon, and raw herring are nevertheless put off by other forms of raw seafood that are popular in Japan, such as sea urchin and octopus. Individual tastes also vary; within a given culture, some people will greedily gobble up a dish that makes others turn green. These differences are due in part to learning (see Chapter 7). But they are also related to genetic differences in the density of taste buds; human tongues can have as few as 500 or as many as 10,000 taste buds (Miller & Reedy, 1990).

Because of genetic differences in sensitivity to particular tastes, people live in different "taste worlds" (Bartoshuk, 1993, 1998). For example, about 25 percent of people in the United States are "supertasters," who find saccharin, caffeine, broccoli, and many other substances to be unpleasantly bitter; 50 percent are "tasters" who detect less bitterness; and 25 percent (most of them white) are "nontasters" who detect no bitterness at all. (Former President George Bush, famous for hating broccoli, may be a supertaster; and women are more likely than men to be in this group.) Supertasters also perceive sweet tastes as sweeter and salty tastes as saltier than other people do, and they feel more "burn" from substances like ginger, pepper, and hot chiles (Bartoshuk

ARE YOU A SUPERTASTER?

Get some blue food coloring at the grocery store and dab some on the front of your tongue with a cotton swab. Mushroom-shaped papillae will show up as pink circles against a blue background. Make a hole in waxed paper with a paper punch—or get one of those hole reinforcers used for notebook paper. Place the side of the hole so it just touches the midline of your tongue, as far toward the tip as possible. Then count the papillae falling more than halfway into the hole, using a flashlight and a magnifying glass to get a better view. Nontasters will have only a few; supertasters will have 25 or more; and most people will fall in the middle (Bartoshuk, 1998).

If you are a supertaster, might you be avoiding some healthful fruits and vegetables because of your sensitivity to bitterness? If so, try adding a little salt (not too much) to the food; salt sometimes neutralizes a bitter taste.

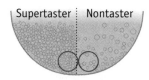

FIGURE 6.11
TASTE TEST

The red bars show the percentages of people who could identify a substance dropped on the tongue when they were able to smell it. The blue bars show the percentage who could identify the substance when they were prevented from smelling it. (From Mozell et al., 1969.)

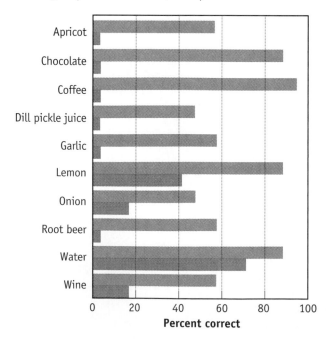

et al., 1998; Lucchina et al., 1998). The reasons for these differences are found on the tongue: Supertasters have more taste buds, and certain papillae are smaller, are more densely packed, and look different than those in nontasters (Reedy et al., 1993).

The attractiveness of a food can be affected by its temperature and texture. As Goldilocks found out, a bowl of cold porridge isn't nearly as delicious as one that is properly heated. And any peanut butter fan will tell you that chunky and smooth peanut butters just don't taste the same. Even more important is a food's odor. Subtle flavors such as chocolate and vanilla would have little taste if we could not smell them (see Figure 6.11). The dependence of taste on smell explains why you have trouble tasting your food when you have a stuffy nose. Most people who chronically have trouble tasting things have a problem with smell, not taste per se.

Smell: The Sense of Scents

The great author and educator Helen Keller, who was blind and deaf from infancy, once called smell "the fallen angel of the senses." Yet, our sense of smell, or *olfaction,* although seemingly crude when compared to a bloodhound's, is actually quite good—and is far more useful than most people realize.

The receptors for smell are specialized neurons embedded in a tiny patch of mucous membrane in the upper part of the nasal passage, just beneath the eyes (see Figure 6.12). Millions of receptors in each nasal cavity respond to chemical molecules in the air. When you inhale, you pull these molecules into the nasal cavity, but they can also enter from the mouth, wafting up the throat like smoke up a chimney. These molecules trigger responses in the receptors that combine to yield the yeasty smell of freshly baked bread or the spicy fragrance of

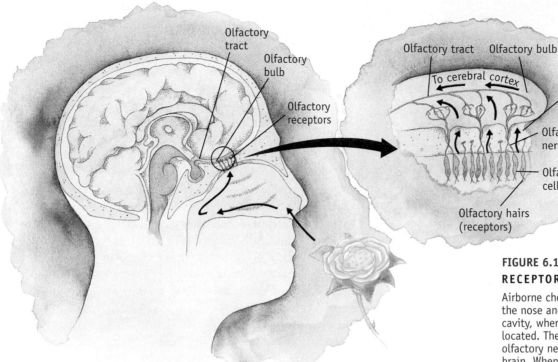

FIGURE 6.12
RECEPTORS FOR SMELL

Airborne chemical molecules (vapors) enter the nose and circulate through the nasal cavity, where the smell receptors are located. The receptors' axons make up the olfactory nerve, which carries signals to the brain. When you sniff, you draw more vapors into the nose and speed their circulation. Vapors can also reach the nasal cavity through the mouth by way of a passageway from the throat.

a eucalyptus tree. Signals from the receptors are carried to the brain's olfactory bulb by the *olfactory nerve,* which is made up of the receptors' axons. From the olfactory bulb, they travel to a higher region of the brain.

Figuring out the neural code for smell has been a real challenge. Of the 10,000 or so smells we detect (rotten, burned, musky, fruity, spicy, flowery, resinous, putred, . . .) none seems to be more basic than any other. Moreover, a thousand kinds of receptors exist, each kind responding to a part of an odor molecule's structure (Axel, 1991; Buck & Axel, 1991). This complicated system is quite different from the one involved in color vision, which uses only three basic receptor types, or in taste, which seems to use only four. But researchers are making progress; they have discovered that distinct odors activate unique *combinations* of receptor types, and they have succeeded in identifying some of those combinations (Malnic et al., 1999). Soon we may know the neural codes for all of the world's smells.

Although smell is less vital for human survival than for the survival of other animals, it is still important. We sniff out danger by smelling smoke, food spoilage, or poison gases. Thus, a deficit in the sense of smell is nothing to turn up your nose at. Such a loss can come about because of infection or disease, and smokers are nearly twice as likely as nonsmokers to show impaired ability to detect common odors. A person who has smoked two packs a day for 10 years must abstain from cigarettes for 10 more years before this ability will return to normal (Frye, Schwartz, & Doty, 1990).

Folklore tells us that smells also contribute to positive and negative "chemistry" between people. In many species, airborne chemicals called *pheromones* convey messages from one individual to another: A female cat in heat will attract, through scent, all the unneutered tomcats in the neighborhood; a female moth entices male suitors who are miles away by giving off pheromones; wolves and many other mammals post an olfactory "keep out" notice by urinating around the borders of their territory. For years, scientists have looked for similar chemical messages in human beings, with little success. Recently, however, two researchers showed that pheromones may affect

Smell has not only evoutionary but also cultural significance. These pilgrims in Japan are purifying themselves with holy incense for good luck and health. Incense has always been an important commodity; in the New Testament, the gifts of the Magi included frankincense and myrrh.

women's menstrual cycles (Stern & McClintock, 1998). If a woman sniffs cotton material that has absorbed the underarm sweat of another woman who is ovulating, the sniffer's menstrual cycle is likely to lengthen; if the other woman is in the preovulation phase, the sniffer's cycle is likely to get shorter. This effect may explain why the menstrual cycles of women living together in close quarters often become synchronized. The odor of sweat is not a factor, however; in their study, the researchers disguised the odor of the women's sweat by dousing the cotton material with alcohol.

Odors, of course, can have psychological effects on us, which is why we buy perfumes and sniff flowers. Perhaps because olfactory centers in the brain are linked to areas that process memories and emotions, specific smells often evoke vivid, emotionally colored memories (Herz & Cupchik, 1995; Vroon, 1997). The smell of hot chocolate may trigger fond memories of cozy winter mornings from your childhood; the smell of rubbing alcohol may remind you of an unpleasant trip to the hospital.

Odor preferences, like taste preferences, vary considerably. In some societies, people use rancid fat as a hair pomade, but anyone in North America who did so would quickly have a social problem. Within a particular culture, context and experience are all-important. The very same chemicals that contribute to unpleasant body odors and bad breath also contribute to the pleasant bouquet and flavor of cheese.

Senses of the Skin

The skin's usefulness is more than just skin deep. Besides protecting our innards, our 2 square yards of skin help us identify objects and establish intimacy with others. By providing a boundary between ourselves and everything else, the skin also gives us a sense of ourselves as distinct from the environment.

The basic skin senses include *touch* (or pressure), *warmth, cold,* and *pain.* Within these four types are such variations as itch, tickle, and painful burning. Although certain spots on the skin are particularly sensitive to the four basic skin sensations, scientists have had difficulty finding distinct receptors for these sensations, except in the case of pressure. Swedish researchers, however, have reported a new kind of nerve fiber that may be responsible for at least some types of itching (Schmelz et al., 1997). These fibers may have gone unnoticed in the past because they are very thin and have no myelin sheath (see Chapter 4). Perhaps other specialized fibers will also be discovered for other skin sensations.

In the meantime, many aspects of touch continue to baffle science—for example, why lightly touching adjacent pressure spots in rapid succession produces tickle; and why simultaneously stimulating warm and cold spots produces not a lukewarm sensation but the sensation of heat. Decoding the neural messages of the skin senses will eventually tell us how we are able to distinguish sandpaper from velvet and glue from grease.

The Mystery of Pain

Pain, which is both a skin sense and an internal sense, differs from other senses in an important way: When the stimulus producing pain is removed, the sensation may continue—sometimes for years. Chronic pain disrupts lives, puts stress on the body, keeps people from their jobs, and causes depression and despair. (For ways of coping with pain, see "Taking Psychology with You.")

The face of pain is unmistakable.

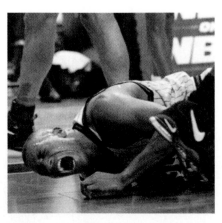

The Gate-Control Theory of Pain. For many years, the leading explanation of pain has been the **gate-control theory**, which was first proposed by Canadian psychologist Ronald Melzack and British physiologist Patrick Wall (1965). According to this theory, the experience of pain depends partly on whether certain nerve impulses get past a "gate" in the spinal cord. The gate is not an actual structure, but rather a pattern of neural activity that either blocks pain messages coming from the skin, muscles, and internal organs or lets those signals through. Normally, the gate is kept shut, either by impulses coming into the spinal cord from large fibers that respond to pressure and other kinds of stimulation or by signals coming down from the brain itself. But when body tissue is injured, impulses from smaller pain fibers open the gate. According to the gate-control theory, pain occurs when disease, infection, or injury damages the fibers that ordinarily close the gate, and pain messages are able to reach the brain unchecked.

Because the gate-control theory emphasizes the role of the brain in controlling the gate, it correctly predicts that thoughts and feelings can influence our reactions to pain. When we dwell on our pain, focusing on it and talking about it constantly rather than acting in spite of it, we often intensify our experience of it (Sullivan, Tripp, & Santor, 1998). Conversely, when we are distracted from our pain, we may not feel it the way we ordinarily would—as gymnast Kerri Strug demonstrated in 1996, when she won an Olympic gold medal despite having a sprained ankle.

The gate-control theory also correctly predicts that mild pressure, as well as other types of stimulation, can interfere with severe or protracted pain by closing the spinal gate, either directly or by means of signals sent from the brain. When we vigorously rub a banged elbow, or apply ice packs, heat, or stimulating ointments to injuries, we are applying this principle.

The Neuromatrix Theory of Pain. In its general outlines, the gate-control theory has been extremely useful, but it does not completely explain pain. Pain is now known to be far more complex than scientists thought when the gate-control theory was first proposed. For example, pain due to tissue damage involves the release of several chemicals at the site of the damage and in the spinal cord and brain.

Moreover, the gate-control theory has trouble explaining the many instances of severe, chronic pain that occur without any sign of injury or disease whatsoever. In one typical case, a Boston architect fractured his shoulder at a construction site. The injury was fixed by surgery, but the architect continued to be tormented by unbearable spasms of back pain and had to give up his business. Years later, incapacitating pain still keeps him from standing in a line, climbing stairs, or sleeping for more than four hours in a row, yet doctors can find nothing physically wrong with him (Gawande, 1998).

The gate-control theory also has trouble accounting for the strange phenomenon of *phantom pain,* in which a person continues to feel pain that seemingly comes from an amputated limb, or from an organ that has been surgically removed. Although sense receptors that used to be in the body part no longer exist, phantom pain can nonetheless be excruciating. An amputee may feel the same aching, burning, or sharp pain from gangrenous ulcers, calf cramps, throbbing toes, surgical wounds, or even ingrown toenails that he or she endured before the surgery. Even amputees who have a completely severed spinal cord often continue to report phantom pain from areas below the break. There are no nerve impulses for the spinal-cord gate to block or let through—so why is there pain?

These puzzles have led Ronald Melzack (1992, 1993) to propose the **neuromatrix theory** of pain. According to this theory, the brain not only responds to incoming signals from sensory nerves but is also capable of *generating* pain (and other sensations) entirely on its own. An extensive network of neurons in the brain—Melzack calls it a

THE GATE-CONTROL THEORY OF PAIN

"Gate" closed by incoming impulses from large fibers or from the brain; opened by impulses from smaller fibers

If "gate" is open, then pain impulses reach the brain

gate-control theory The theory that the experience of pain depends in part on whether pain impulses get past a neurological "gate" in the spinal cord and thus reach the brain.

neuromatrix theory The theory that a matrix of neurons in the brain is capable of generating pain (and other sensations) in the absence of signals from sensory nerves.

THE NEUROMATRIX THEORY OF PAIN

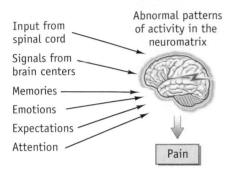

Input from spinal cord

Signals from brain centers

Memories

Emotions

Expectations

Attention

Abnormal patterns of activity in the neuromatrix

Pain

neuromatrix—gives us a sense of our own bodies and body parts. When these neurons produce abnormal patterns of activity, the result is pain. Such activity can occur not only because of input from peripheral nerves, but also as a result of memories, emotions, expectations, or signals from diverse brain centers. Real pain can therefore occur even without any external stimulation.

Melzack believes that the neuromatrix exists from birth, because even people who were born without an arm or leg sometimes "feel" the missing limb (Melzack et al., 1997). Phantom pain may occur, according to Melzack, when a lack of sensory stimulation, or efforts to move a nonexistent limb, produce abnormal patterns of activity in the neuromatrix, resulting in burning, cramping, or other unpleasant sensations. Evidence that brain areas associated with a missing limb continue to function in its absence is consistent with this view (Davis et al., 1998).

Pain is one of the most fascinating psychological mysteries of our time. It can rise and fall in epidemics, like the flu—as national outbreaks of back pain or whiplash or repetitive motion injuries reveal (Gawande, 1998). The people who suffer during such epidemics are not faking it, and their pain is not just "in their heads." But it may be in their brains.

The Environment Within

We usually think of our senses as pipelines to the "outside" world, but two senses keep us informed about the movements of our own bodies. **Kinesthesis** tells us where our body parts are located and lets us know when they move. This information is provided by pain and pressure receptors located in the muscles, joints, and tendons (tissues that connect muscles to bones). Without kinesthesis, you could not touch your finger to your nose with your eyes shut. In fact, you would have trouble with any voluntary movement. Think of how hard walking is when your leg has "fallen asleep" or how clumsy chewing is when a dentist has numbed your jaw with novocaine.

Equilibrium, or the sense of balance, gives us information about our bodies as a whole. Along with vision and touch, it lets us know whether we are standing upright or on our heads and tells us when we are falling or rotating. Equilibrium relies primarily on three **semicircular canals** in the inner ear (see Figure 6.9 on page 202). These thin tubes are filled with fluid that moves and presses on hairlike receptors whenever the head rotates. The receptors initiate messages that travel through a part of the auditory nerve that is not involved in hearing.

Normally, kinesthesis and equilibrium work together to give us a sense of our own physical reality, something we take utterly for granted but should not. Oliver Sacks (1985) told the heartbreaking story of a young British woman named Christina, who suffered irreversible damage to her kinesthetic nerve fibers because of a mysterious inflammation. At first, Christina was as floppy as a rag doll; she could not sit up, walk, or stand. Then, slowly, she learned to do these things, relying on visual cues and sheer willpower. But her movements remained unnatural; she had to grasp a fork with painful force or she would drop it. More important, despite her remaining sensitivity to light touch on the skin, she could no longer experience herself as physically embodied: "It's like something's been scooped right out of me, right at the centre. . . . "

With equilibrium, we come, as it were, to the end of our senses. Every second, millions of sensory signals reach the brain, which combines and integrates them to produce a model of reality from moment to moment. How does it know how to do this? Are our perceptual abilities inborn, or must we learn them? We turn next to this issue.

kinesthesis [KIN-es-THEE-sis] The sense of body position and movement of body parts; also called *kinesthesia.*

equilibrium The sense of balance.

semicircular canals Sense organs in the inner ear, which contribute to equilibrium by responding to rotation of the head.

On the left, Olympic gold medalist Greg Louganis executes a winning dive that requires precise positioning of each part of his body. "I have a good kinesthetic awareness," Louganis once said, with considerable understatement. "I am aware of where I am in space." On the right is famed dancer and choreographer Martha Graham, who turned her kinesthetic talents into artistry.

QUICK QUIZ

Can you make some sense out of the following sensory problems?

1. April always has trouble tasting foods, especially those with subtle flavors. What is the most likely reason for her difficulty?
2. May has chronic shoulder pain. How might the gate-control theory explain it?
3. June, a rock musician, does not hear as well as she used to. What is a likely explanation?

Answers:

1. An impaired sense of smell, possibly due to disease, illness, or cigarette smoking.   2. Nerve fibers that normally close the pain "gate" may have been damaged.   3. Hearing impairment has many causes, but in June's case, we might suspect that prolonged exposure to loud music has damaged the hair cells of her cochlea.

WHAT'S AHEAD

- Do babies see the world the way adults do?
- Why does one person think a cloud is a cloud, and another think it's a spaceship?

PERCEPTUAL POWERS: ORIGINS AND INFLUENCES

What happens when babies first open their eyes? Do they see the same sights, hear the same sounds, smell the same smells, taste the same tastes? Are their strategies for organizing the world wired into their brains from the beginning? Or is an infant's

FIGURE 6.13
VISION AND EARLY EXPERIENCE

Cats were reared in darkness for five months after birth, but for several hours each day were put in a special cylinder that permitted them to see only vertical or horizontal lines, and nothing else. Later on, cats who were exposed only to vertical lines had trouble perceiving horizontal ones, and those exposed only to horizontal lines had trouble perceiving vertical ones (Blakemore & Cooper, 1970).

world, as William James once suggested, only a "blooming, buzzing confusion," waiting to be organized by experience and learning? The truth lies somewhere between these two extremes.

Inborn Abilities and Perceptual Lessons

One way to study the origins of perceptual abilities is to see what happens when the usual perceptual experiences of early life fail to take place. To do so, researchers study animals whose sensory and perceptual systems are similar to our own, such as cats. What they find is that without certain experiences during critical periods of development, perception develops abnormally.

Researchers studying vision, for example, have discovered that when newborn animals are reared in total darkness for weeks or months, or are fitted with translucent goggles that permit only diffuse light to get through, or are allowed to see only one visual pattern and no others, visual development is impaired. In one famous study, kittens were exposed to either vertical or horizontal black and white stripes. Special collars kept them from seeing anything else, even their own bodies (see Figure 6.13). After several months, the kittens exposed only to vertical stripes seemed blind to all horizontal contours; they bumped into horizontal obstacles and ran to play with a bar that an experimenter held vertically but not to a bar held horizontally. In contrast, those exposed only to horizontal stripes bumped into vertical obstacles and ran to play with horizontal bars but not vertical ones (Blakemore & Cooper, 1970).

Kittens are actually born with the ability to detect horizontal and vertical lines, and other orientations as well; at birth, their brains are equipped with the same kinds of feature-detector cells that adult cats have. But when kittens are kept from seeing horizontal lines or vertical lines during a critical period in their development, as in the study we described, the cells sensitive to those orientations deteriorate or change, and perception suffers (Crair, Gillespie, & Stryker, 1998; Hirsch & Spinelli, 1970). Similar critical periods may exist in human beings as well.

Many visual skills besides the ability to detect orientations are also present at birth, at least in rudimentary form, or they develop quite early, given normal experiences. For example, human infants are probably born with the ability to detect and discriminate the edges and angles of objects. They can discriminate sizes and colors very early, possibly at birth. They can distinguish contrasts, shadows, and complex patterns after only a few weeks. Even some depth perception may be present from the beginning.

Testing an infant's perception of depth requires considerable ingenuity. One clever procedure that was used for decades was to place infants on a device called a *visual cliff* (Gibson & Walk, 1960). The "cliff" is a pane of glass covering a shallow surface and a deep one (see Figure 6.14). Both surfaces are covered by a checkerboard pattern. The infant is placed on a board in the middle, and the child's mother tries to lure the baby across either the shallow or the deep side. Babies as young as 6 months of age will crawl across the shallow side but will refuse to crawl out over the "cliff." Their hesitation shows that they have depth perception.

Of course, by 6 months of age, a baby has had quite a bit of experience with the world. But infants younger than 6 months, even though they are unable to crawl, can also be tested on the visual cliff. At only 2 months of age, babies show a drop in heart rate when placed on the deep side of the cliff, but no change when they are placed on the shallow side. A slowed heart rate is usually a sign of increased attention. Thus, although these infants may not be frightened the way an older infant would be, it seems they can perceive the difference between the "shallow" and "deep" sides of the cliff (Banks & Salapatek, 1984).

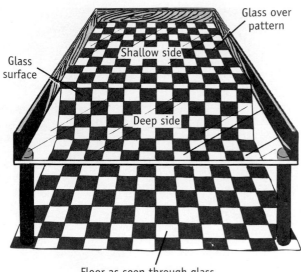

Glass over pattern

Shallow side

Glass surface

Deep side

Floor as seen through glass

FIGURE 6.14
A CLIFF-HANGER

Infants as young as 6 months usually hesitate to crawl past the apparent edge of a visual cliff, which suggests that they are able to perceive depth.

We have been talking only about vision, but other sensory abilities are also inborn or develop very early, as we saw in Chapter 3. Infants can distinguish salty from sweet and can discriminate among odors. They can distinguish a person's voice from other kinds of sounds. And they will startle to a loud noise and turn their heads toward its source, showing that they perceive sound as being localized in space. Because neurological connections in their brains and sensory systems are not completely formed, their senses are less acute than an adult's. However, an infant's world is far from the blooming, buzzing confusion that William James took it to be.

Psychological and Cultural Influences on Perception

The fact that some perceptual processes appear to be innate does not mean that all people perceive the world in the same way. A camera doesn't care what it "sees." A tape recorder doesn't ponder what it "hears." A robot arm on a factory assembly line holds no opinion about what it "touches." But because we human beings care about what we see, hear, taste, smell, and feel, psychological factors can influence what we perceive and how we perceive it. Here are a few of them:

1 *Needs.* When we need something, have an interest in it, or want it, we are especially likely to perceive it. For example, hungry individuals are faster than others at seeing words related to hunger when the words are flashed briefly on a screen (Wispé & Drambarean, 1953).

2 *Beliefs.* What we hold to be true about the world can affect the interpretation of ambiguous sensory signals. Suppose you spot a round object hovering high in the sky. If you believe that extraterrestrials occasionally visit the earth, you may "see" the object as a spaceship. But if you think such beliefs are hogwash, you are more likely to see a weather balloon or a cloud. Images that remind people of a crucified Jesus have been reported on walls, dishes, and food items, causing great excitement among those who are ready to believe that divine messages can be found on everyday objects. In California, an image of Jesus on a garage door drew large crowds; it turned out to be caused by two streetlights that merged the shadows of a bush and a "For Sale" sign in the yard.

3 *Emotions.* Emotions also influence our interpretation of sensory information. A small child afraid of the dark may see a ghost instead of a robe hanging on the

People often see what they want to see. A man in Nashville bought a cinnamon bun at a coffee shop and thought he saw a likeness of Mother Theresa in it. The bun was shellacked and enshrined at the coffee shop, and hundreds traveled to see it.

door, or a monster instead of a beloved doll. Pain, in particular, is affected by emotion. Soldiers who are seriously wounded often deny being in much pain, even though they are alert and are not in shock. Their relief at being alive may offset the anxiety and fear that contribute so much to pain (although other explanations are also possible). Conversely, negative emotions such as anger, fear, sadness, or depression can prolong and intensify a person's pain (Fernandez & Turk, 1992; Fields, 1991).

4 *Expectations.* Previous experiences often affect how we perceive the world (Lachman, 1996). The tendency to perceive what you expect is called a **perceptual set.** Perceptual sets can come in handy; they help us fill in words in sentences, for example, when we haven't really heard every one. But perceptaul sets can also cause misperceptions. In Center Harbor, Maine, local legend has it that veteran newscaster Walter Cronkite was sailing into port one day when he heard a small crowd on shore shouting, "Hello, Walter . . . Hello, Walter." Pleased, he waved and took a bow. Only when he ran aground did he realize what they had really been shouting: "Low water . . . low water."

By the way, the previous paragraph has a misspelled word. Did you notice it? If not, probably it was because you expected all the words in this book to be spelled correctly.

Our needs, beliefs, emotions, and expectations are all affected, in turn, by the culture we live in. Different cultures give people practice with different environments. In a classic study done in the 1960s, researchers found that members of some African tribes were much less likely to be fooled by the Müller-Lyer illusion and other geometric illusions than were Westerners. In the West, the researchers observed, people live in a "carpentered" world, full of rectangular structures built with the aid of saws, planes, straight edges, and carpenter's squares. Westerners are also used to interpreting two-dimensional photographs and perspective drawings as representations of a three-dimensional world. Therefore, they interpret the kinds of angles used in the Müller-Lyer illusion as right angles extended in space—just the sort of habit that would increase susceptibility to the illusion. The rural Africans in the study, living in a less carpentered environment and in round huts, seemed more likely to take the lines in the figures literally, as two-dimensional, which could explain why they were less susceptible to the illusion (Segall, Campbell, & Herskovits, 1966).

perceptual set A habitual way of perceiving, based on expectations.

This research was followed by a flurry of replications in the 1970s, showing that it was indeed culture that produced the differences between groups (Segall, 1994; Segall et al., 1999). Since then, there has been little further work on the fascinating intersection of culture and visual illusions. However, culture affects perception in many other ways: by shaping our stereotypes, directing our attention, and telling us what is important to notice and what is not.

QUICK QUIZ

Direct your perceptual attention now to this quiz.

1. Animal studies suggest that newborns and infants (a) have few perceptual abilities, (b) need visual experiences during a critical period for vision to develop normally, (c) see as well as adults.

2. On the visual cliff, 6-month-old babies (a) go right across because they cannot detect depth until age 1, (b) cross even though they cannot detect depth, (c) are afraid to cross because they can detect depth, (d) cry or get bored.

3. "Have a nice . . . " says Dewey, but then he gets distracted and doesn't finish the thought. Yet, Clarence was sure he heard Dewey wish him a nice *day*. Why?

Answers:

1. b 2. c 3. perceptual set due to expectations

WHAT'S AHEAD

- Can "subliminal perception" tapes help you lose weight or reduce your stress?
- Why are most psychologists skeptical about ESP?

PUZZLES OF PERCEPTION

We come, finally, to two intriguing questions about perception that have captured the public's imagination for years. First, can we perceive what is happening in the world without being conscious of doing so? Second, can we pick up signals from the world or from other people without using our usual sensory channels at all?

Subliminal Perception

As we saw earlier in our discussion of the "cocktail party phenomenon," even when people are oblivious to speech sounds, they are processing and recognizing those sounds at some level. But these sounds would be *above* the absolute threshold if a person were consciously attending to them. Is it also possible to perceive and respond to messages that are *below* the threshold—too quiet to be consciously heard (in the case of hearing) or too brief or dim to be consciously seen (in the case of vision)? Perhaps you have seen ads for products that will allow you to take advantage of such "subliminal perception." Or perhaps you have heard that subliminal perception does not really exist. What are the facts?

Perceiving Without Awareness. First, a simple visual image *can* affect your behavior even when you are unaware that you saw it. In one study, people subliminally exposed to a face tended to prefer the face over one they did not "see" in this way (Bornstein, Leone, & Galley, 1987). In other studies, researchers have flashed words subliminally in the periphery of a person's visual field while the person focuses on the middle of a display field. When the words are related to some personality trait, such as honesty, people are more likely later on to judge someone they read about as having that trait. They have been "primed" to evaluate the person that way (Bargh, 1999).

Findings such as these have convinced many psychologists that people often know more than they know they know. In fact, nonconscious processing appears to occur not only in perception, but also in memory, thinking, and decision making (see Chapters 9 and 10). However, the real-world implications of subliminal perception are not as dramatic as you might think. Even in the laboratory, where researchers have considerable control, the phenomenon is hard to demonstrate. The strongest evidence comes from studies using simple stimuli (faces or single words, like "bread"), rather than complex stimuli such as sentences ("Eat whole-wheat bread, not white bread"). And even with single words, the influence of the subliminal stimulus is usually short-lived (Greenwald, Draine, & Abrams, 1996).

Perception Versus Persuasion. While *subliminal perception* may occur under certain conditions, subliminal *persuasion,* the subject of many popular books and magazine articles, is quite another matter. Empirical research finds no basis whatsoever for believing that advertisers can seduce us into buying soft drinks or voting for political candidates by slipping subliminal slogans and images into television and magazine ads. Nor can anyone corrupt young minds with subliminal images or messages slipped into animated movies or rock songs.

What about those subliminal tapes that promise to help you lose weight, stop smoking, relieve stress, read faster, boost your motivation, lower your cholesterol, stop biting your nails, overcome jet lag, or stop taking drugs—all without any effort on your part? In study after study, "placebo" tapes—tapes that do not contain any messages even though participants think they do—are just as "effective" as subliminal tapes (Eich & Hyman, 1992; Greenwald et al., 1991; Merikle & Skanes, 1992; Moore, 1992, 1995).

In one typical study, some 200 college students and other adults listened every day to commercially available tapes that claimed to improve memory or boost self-esteem. Some people thought they were using memory tapes, but they were actually using self-esteem tapes; for others, the reverse was true. Still others listened to correctly labeled tapes. These people had all volunteered; they all wanted the tapes to work. At the end of a month, about half reported improvement in the area corresponding to the label they had received, *whether the label was correct or not.* In reality, there were no improvements beyond a placebo effect due to expectations alone (Greenwald et al., 1991).

In sum, if advertisers want you to buy something, they would do better to spend their money on *above*-threshold messages. And if you want to improve yourself or your life, we encourage you to do so—but you will probably have to do it the old-fashioned way: by working at it.

Zits

Reprinted with permission of King Features Syndicate.

QUICK Q U I Z

Suppose you hear about a study that appeared to find evidence of "sleep learning"—the ability to perceive and retain material played on an audiotape while a person sleeps. What would you want to know about this research before deciding to tape this chapter and play it by your bedside all night instead of studying it in the usual way?

Answer:

You might ask about the kinds of stimuli used (in studies of other kinds of nonconscious perception, positive results have usually been obtained with very simple stimuli, not whole sentences); whether the results were large enough to have practical consequences; and most important, how it was determined that the subjects were really asleep while the tape was playing. When brain-wave measurements are used to verify that subjects are actually sleeping, no "sleep learning" takes place. So if you want to learn the material in this chapter, you'll have to stay awake!

Extrasensory Perception: Reality or Illusion?

Eyes, ears, mouth, nose, skin—we rely on these organs for our experience of the external world. Some people, however, claim they can send and receive messages about the world without relying on the usual sensory channels, by using *extrasensory perception (ESP)*.

Reported ESP experiences (also known as *Psi,* a shortening of "psychic phenomena") fall into four general categories: (1) *Telepathy* is direct communication from one mind to another without the usual visual, auditory, and other sensory signals. If you try to guess what number someone is thinking or what card a person is holding, you are attempting telepathy. (2) *Clairvoyance* is the perception of an event or fact without normal sensory input. If a man suddenly "knows" that his wife has just died, yet no one has informed him of the death, he might be called clairvoyant. (3) *Precognition* is the perception of an event that has not yet happened. Fortune-tellers make their livings by claiming to read the future in tea leaves or in a person's palm. (4) *Out-of-body experiences* involve the perception of one's own body from "outside," as an observer might see it. Such experiences are often reported by persons who have been near death, but some people say they can bring them on at will.

Normal perception depends on the ability to detect changes in energy in the physical world. Claims for most forms of extrasensory perception, however, challenge everything we currently know to be true about the way the world and the universe operate. Precognition, for example, contradicts our usual assumptions about time and space. If precognition exists, then tomorrow is as real as today, and future events can be known even though they have not yet caused any physical changes in the environment.

Evidence—or Just Coincidence? Much of the "evidence" for extrasensory perception comes from anecdotal accounts. Unfortunately, people are not always reliable reporters of their own experiences. They often embellish and exaggerate or recall only part of what happened. They also tend to forget incidents that don't fit their beliefs, such as "premonitions" of events that fail to occur. Many ESP experiences could merely be unusual coincidences that are memorable because they are dramatic. What passes for telepathy, clairvoyance, or precognition could also be based on what a person knows or deduces through ordinary means. If Joanne's father has had two heart attacks, her premonition that her father will die shortly (followed, in fact, by her father's death) may not be so impressive.

THE FAR SIDE By GARY LARSON

For the most part, the meeting was quite successful. Only a slight tension filled the air, stemming from the unforeseen faux pas of everyone wearing the same dress.

EXAMINE THE EVIDENCE

ESP would certainly be useful before a tough exam or a blind date. But it's one thing to wish ESP existed and another to conclude that it does. What kind of evidence would convince you that ESP is real, and what kind is only wishful thinking?

The scientific way to establish a phenomenon is to produce it under controlled conditions. Extrasensory perception has been studied extensively by researchers in the field of **parapsychology**. In a typical study, a person might be asked to guess which of five symbols will appear on a card presented at random. A "sender" who has already seen the card tries to transmit a mental image of the symbol to the person. Although most people do no better than chance at guessing the symbols, in some studies, a few people have consistently done somewhat better than chance. But ESP studies have often been poorly designed, with inadequate precautions against fraud and improper statistical analysis. When skeptical researchers try to repeat the studies, they get negative results. After an exhaustive review, the National Research Council concluded that there was "no scientific justification" for the existence of parapsychological phenomena (Druckman & Swets, 1988).

The issue did not go away, however. A few years ago, social psychologist Daryl Bem made waves in the psychological community when he reported a series of ESP studies carried out with the late Charles Honorton, a British parapsychologist. Bem and Honorton (1994) studied telepathy (they called it the "anomalous process of information transfer"). A "sender" sat in a soundproof room and concentrated on a picture or video clip selected at random by a computer. A "receiver" sat in another soundproof room. At the end of the transmission period, the receiver was shown four pictures or video clips and was asked to pick out the one that most closely matched his or her mental imagery during the transmission period. If the receiver selected the stimulus that was "sent," that trial was counted as a "hit." Bem and Honorton reported an overall hit rate of about 33 percent, whereas chance would predict only 25 percent.

Of course, these findings have been the subject of much critical interpretation. Critics pointed out that although the methods used by Bem and Honorton were better than those used by previous researchers, possible flaws existed in the way the pictures and video clips were randomized and selected (Hyman, 1994). A recent meta-analysis of 30 studies using methods as rigorous as Bem and Honorton's found no evidence of telepathy whatsoever (Milton & Wiseman, 1999).

The history of research on psychic phenomena has been one of initial enthusiasm followed by disappointment when results cannot be replicated, and the thousands of studies done over the past 50 years have failed to make a convincing case for ESP.

Lessons from a Magician. Despite the lack of evidence for ESP, about half of all Americans say they believe in it. Perhaps you yourself have had an experience that seemed to involve ESP or have seen a convincing demonstration by someone else. Surely you can trust the evidence of your own eyes—or can you? We will answer with a true story that contains an important lesson, not only about ESP but about ordinary perception as well.

During the 1970s, Andrew Weil (who is now known for his efforts to promote alternative medicine) set out to investigate the claims of a self-proclaimed psychic named Uri Geller (Weil, 1974a, 1974b). Geller seemed able to bend keys without touching them, start broken watches, and guess the nature of simple drawings hidden in sealed envelopes. Although he had performed as a stage magician in Israel, his native country, he denied using trickery. His powers, he said, came from energy from another universe.

Weil, who believed in telepathy, felt that ESP might be explained by principles of modern physics and was receptive to Geller's claims. When he met Geller at a private gathering, he was not disappointed. Geller correctly identified a cross and a Star of David sealed inside separate envelopes. He made a stopped watch start

parapsychology The study of purported psychic phenomena such as ESP and mental telepathy.

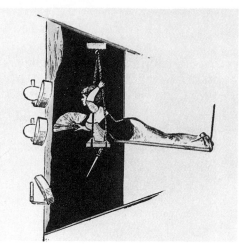

running and a ring sag into an oval shape, apparently without touching them. He made keys change shape in front of Weil's very eyes. Weil came away a convert. What he had seen with his own eyes seemed impossible to deny . . . until he met The Amazing Randi.

James Randi ("The Amazing Randi") is a famous magician who is dedicated to educating the public about psychic deception. To Weil's astonishment, Randi was able to duplicate much of what Geller had done. He, too, could bend keys and guess the contents of sealed envelopes. But Randi's feats were tricks, and he was willing to show Weil exactly how they were done. Weil suddenly experienced "a sense of how strongly the mind can impose its own interpretations on perceptions; how it can see what it expects to see, but not see the unexpected."

Weil was dis-illusioned—literally. He was forced to admit that the evidence of one's own eyes is not always reliable. Even when he knew what to look for in a trick, he could not catch The Amazing Randi doing it. Weil learned that our sense impressions of reality are not the same as reality. Our eyes, our ears, and especially our brains can play tricks on us.

The great Greek philosopher Plato once said that "knowledge is nothing but perception." But in fact, simple perception is *not* always the best path to knowledge. As we have seen throughout this chapter, we do not passively register the world "out there"; we mentally construct it. The truth about human behavior, then, is most likely to emerge if we are aware of how our beliefs and assumptions shape and alter our perceptions.

"Seeing is believing," goes the saying, but is it? The engraving on the left shows a "living half-woman," seemingly swinging in mid-air. The sketch on the right shows how the illusion is produced. The woman reclines on an artificial bust, her body supported by another swing and hidden by black curtains. Due to a trick of lighting, the viewer sees only the swing, the face, the necklace, and the sword beneath the swing. The moral: Be skeptical about paranormal claims, even if you "saw it with your own eyes."

TAKING PSYCHOLOGY WITH YOU

LIVING WITH PAIN

Temporary pain is an unpleasant but necessary part of life, a warning of disease or injury. Chronic pain is another matter, a serious problem in itself. Back injuries, arthritis, migraine headaches, serious illnesses such as cancer—all can cause unrelieved misery to pain sufferers and their families. Chronic pain can also impair the immune system, putting patients at risk of further complications from their illnesses (Page et al., 1993).

At one time, the only way to fight pain was with drugs or surgery, which were not always effective. Today, we know that the experience of pain is affected by attitudes, actions, emotions, and circumstances, and that treatment must therefore take psychological factors into account. Social roles, too, can influence a person's response to pain. For example, although women tend to report more intense pain than men do, a real-world study of people who were in pain for more than six months found that men suffered more psychological distress than women did, possibly because the male role made it hard for them to admit their pain (Snow et al., 1986).

Many pain-treatment programs encourage patients to manage their pain themselves instead of relying entirely on health-care professionals. Usually, these programs combine several strategies:

■ *Painkilling medication.* Doctors often worry that patients will become addicted to painkillers or will develop a tolerance to the drugs. The physicians will therefore give a minimal dose, then wait until the effects wear off and the patient is once again in agony before giving more. This approach is ineffective in reducing and controlling a patient's pain. And it is based on outdated notions about addiction; in reality, people who take painkillers to control their pain rarely become addicted (see Chapter 16).

The method now recommended by experts (although doctors and hospitals do not always follow the advice) is to give pain sufferers a continuous dose of painkiller in whatever amount is necessary to keep them pain-free, and to allow them to do this for themselves when they leave the hospital. This strategy leads to *reduced* dosages rather than larger ones and does

not lead to drug dependence (Hill et al., 1990; Portenoy, 1994).

■ *Involvement by family members and friends.* When a person is in pain, friends and relatives understandably tend to sympathize and to excuse the sufferer from regular responsibilities. The sufferer takes to bed, avoids physical activity, and focuses on the pain. As we discuss in Chapter 7, attention from others is a powerful reinforcer of whatever behavior produces the attention. Also, focusing on pain tends to increase it, and inactivity can lead to shortened muscles, muscle spasms, and fatigue. So sympathy and attention can sometimes backfire and may actually prolong the ordeal (Flor, Kerns, & Turk, 1987).

For this reason, many pain experts now encourage family members to resist rewarding or reinforcing the pain and to reward activity, exercise, and wellness instead. This approach, however, must be used carefully, preferably under the direction of a professional, because a patient's complaints about pain are an important diagnostic tool for the physician.

■ *Self-management.* When patients learn to identify how, when, and where their pain occurs, this knowledge helps them determine whether the pain is being maintained by external events. Just having a sense of control over pain can have a powerful pain-reducing effect. In one study, students who monitored their pain while one hand was submerged in freezing water showed more rapid recovery from the pain than did students who had tried to suppress their awareness of pain sensations or distract themselves, apparently because the monitoring students

had a sense of control (Cioffi & Holloway, 1993).

■ *Relaxation techniques, hypnosis, biofeedback, and acupuncture.* In 1996, a blue-ribbon panel of experts concluded that relaxation techniques, such as meditating or focusing on reducing tension in specific muscle groups, can help reduce chronic pain from a variety of medical conditions; that hypnosis is effective in reducing pain due to cancer and may help in other conditions; and that moderate evidence exists for the effectiveness of biofeedback in relieving many types of chronic pain (NIH Technology Assessment Panel, 1996).

There has also been a lot of interest in acupuncture, with some studies finding that it, too, helps in reducing some kinds of pain, possibly by stimulating the release of endorphins (Holden, 1997). Unfortunately, the best-designed studies of acupuncture are the least likely to find an effect, so many medical experts remain skeptical.

■ *Cognitive-behavioral techniques.* Cognitive-behavioral strategies teach people how to recognize the connections among thoughts, feelings, and pain; substitute adaptive thoughts for negative ones; and use coping strategies such as distraction, relabeling of sensations, and imagery to alleviate suffering (see Chapter 17). These techniques increase feelings of control and reduce feelings of inadequacy.

For further information, you can contact pain clinics or services in teaching hospitals and medical schools. There are many reputable clinics around the country, some specializing in specific disorders, such as migraines or back injuries. But take care: There are also many untested therapies and quack practitioners who only prey on people's pain.

SUMMARY

1. *Sensation* is the detection and direct experience of physical energy as a result of environmental or internal events. *Perception* is the process by which sensory impulses are organized and interpreted.

OUR SENSATIONAL SENSES

2. Sensation begins with the *sense receptors*, which convert the energy of a stimulus into electrical impulses that travel along nerves to the brain. Separate sensations can be accounted for by *anatomical codes* (as set forth by the *doctrine of specific nerve energies*) and *functional codes* in the nervous system.

3. Psychologists specializing in *psychophysics* have studied sensory sensitivity by measuring *absolute* and *difference thresholds*. *Signal-detection theory*, however, holds that responses in a detection task consist of both a sensory process and a decision process and will vary with the person's motivation, alertness, and expectations.

4. Our senses are designed to respond to change and contrast in the environment. When stimulation is unchanging, *sensory adaptation* occurs. Too little stimulation can cause *sensory deprivation*, and too much stimulation can cause *sensory overload*, which is why we exercise *selective attention*.

VISION

5. Vision is affected by the wavelength, frequency, and complexity of light, which produce the psychological dimensions of visual experience—*hue, brightness*, and *saturation*. The visual receptors, *rods* and *cones*, are located in the *retina* of the eye. Rods are responsible for vision in dim light; cones are responsible for color vision.

6. Specific aspects of the visual world, such as lines and angles, are detected by *feature-detector cells* in the visual areas of the brain. Some cells respond maximally to complex patterns such as concentric circles—and even faces. The brain takes in fragmentary information about lines, angles, shapes, motion, brightness, texture, and other features of what we see, and comes up with a unified view of the world.

7. The *trichromatic* and *opponent-process* theories of color vision apply to different stages of processing. In the first stage, three types of cones in the retina respond selectively to different wavelengths of light. In the second, *opponent-process cells* in the retina and the thalamus respond in opposite fashion to short and long wavelengths of light.

8. Perception involves the active construction of a model of the world from moment to moment. The *Gestalt principles* (e.g., *figure and ground, proximity, closure, similarity*, and *continuity*) describe visual strategies used by the brain to perceive forms.

9. We localize objects in visual space by using both *binocular* and *monocular cues* to depth. Binocular cues include *convergence* and *retinal disparity*. Monocular cues include interposition and linear perspective. *Perceptual constancies* allow us to perceive objects as stable despite changes in the sensory patterns they produce. *Perceptual illusions* occur when sensory cues are misleading or when we misinterpret cues.

HEARING

10. Hearing (*audition*) is affected by the intensity, frequency, and complexity of pressure waves in the air or other transmitting substance, corresponding to the experience of *loudness, pitch*, and *timbre* of the sound. The receptors for hearing are hair cells (cilia) embedded in the *basilar membrane*, in the interior of the *cochlea*. The sounds we hear are determined by patterns of hair-cell movement, which produce different neural codes. When we localize sounds, we use as cues subtle differences in how pressure waves reach our ears.

THE OTHER SENSES

11. Taste (*gustation*) is a chemical sense. Elevations on the tongue, called *papillae*, contain many *taste buds*. There are four basic tastes—salty, sour, bitter, and sweet. Responses to a particular taste depend on culture, genetic differences among individuals (for example, some people are "supertasters"), the texture and temperature of the food, and, above all, the food's smell.

12. Smell (*olfaction*) is also a chemical sense. Research on the neural code for smell has been complicated, because no basic odors have been identified, and as many as a thousand different receptor types exist. But researchers have discovered that distinct odors activate unique combinations of receptor types, and they have started to identify those combinations. Cultural and individual differences also affect people's responses to particular odors.

13. The skin senses include touch (pressure), warmth, cold, and pain, and variations such as itch and tickle. Until recently, no simple correspondence seemed to exist between the various senses and different types of receptors (except in the case of pressure). Recently, however, researchers reported a receptor for at least one kind of itching.

14. Pain is both a skin sense and an internal sense. According to the *gate-control theory,* the experience of pain depends on whether neural impulses get past a "gate" in the spinal cord and reach the brain. A more recent theory, the *neuromatrix theory,* holds that a matrix of neurons in the brain can generate pain even in the absence of signals from sensory neurons; this theory may help explain the puzzling phenomenon of phantom pain.

15. *Kinesthesis* tells us where our body parts are located, and *equilibrium* tells us the orientation of the body as a whole. Together, these two senses provide us with a feeling of physical embodiment.

PERCEPTUAL POWERS: ORIGINS AND INFLUENCES

16. Studies of animals and human infants suggest that many fundamental perceptual skills are inborn or acquired shortly after birth. By using the *visual cliff,* for example, psychologists have learned that babies have depth perception by the age of 6 months and possibly even earlier. However, without certain experiences early in life, cells in the nervous system deteriorate or change, and perception is impaired.

17. Psychological influences on perception include needs, beliefs, emotions, and expectations. These influences are affected by culture, which gives people practice with certain kinds of experiences. Because psychological factors affect the way we construct the perceptual world, the evidence of our senses is not always reliable.

PUZZLES OF PERCEPTION

18. In the laboratory, simple visual subliminal messages can influence behavior, at least briefly. However, there is no evidence that complex behaviors can be altered by commercial "subliminal-perception" tapes or other subliminal techniques.

19. *Extrasensory perception (ESP)* refers to paranormal abilities such as telepathy, clairvoyance, precognition, and out-of-body experiences. Believers in ESP tend to overlook disconfirming evidence. Years of research have not produced convincing evidence for ESP. Many so-called psychics take advantage of people's desire to believe in ESP, but what they do is no different from the tricks of any good magician. The story of ESP illustrates a central fact about human perception: It does not merely capture objective reality but also reflects our needs, biases, and beliefs.

KEY TERMS

sensation 179

perception 179

sense receptors 180

anatomical codes 181

doctrine of specific nerve energies 181

functional codes 182

psychophysics 182

absolute threshold 182

difference threshold 183

signal-detection theory 184

sensory adaptation 185

sensory deprivation 186

selective attention 187

hue 188

brightness 188

saturation 188

complexity of light 188

retina 189

rods 189

cones 189

dark adaptation 190

ganglion cells 190

optic nerve 190

feature detectors 190

trichromatic theory 192

opponent-process theory 193

negative afterimage 193

figure and ground 194

Gestalt principles 195

binocular cues 196

convergence 196

retinal disparity 196

monocular cues 196

perceptual constancy 197

perceptual illusion 198

audition 200

loudness 200

pitch 201

frequency (of a sound wave) 201

timbre 201

cochlea 202

basilar membrane 203

auditory nerve 203

gustation 204

papillae 204

taste buds 204

olfaction 206

gate-control theory 209

phantom pain 209

neuromatrix theory 209

kinesthesis 210

equilibrium 210

semicircular canals 210

visual cliff 212

perceptual set 214

subliminal perception 215

extrasensory perception (ESP) 217

parapsychology 218

- What kind of code in the nervous system helps explain why a pinprick and a kiss feel different? (p. 182)

- Why does your dog hear a "silent" doggie whistle when you can't? (p. 182)

- What kind of bias can influence whether you think you hear the phone ringing when you're in the shower? (p. 184)

- What happens when people are deprived of all external sensory stimulation? (p. 186)

- How does the eye differ from a camera? (p. 190)

- Why can we describe a color as bluish green but not as reddish green? (p. 193)

- If you were blind in one eye, why might you misjudge the distance of a painting on the wall but not of buildings a block away? (p. 196)

- As a friend approaches, her image on your retina grows larger; why do you continue to see her as the same size? (p. 198)

- Why are perceptual illusions so valuable to psychologists? (p. 198)

- Why does a note played on a flute sound different from the same note on an oboe? (p. 201)

- If you habitually listen to loud music through headphones, what kind of hearing impairment are you risking? (p. 203)

- To locate the source of a sound, why does it sometimes help to turn or tilt your head? (p. 204)

- Why do saccharin and caffeine taste bitter to some people but not to others? (p. 205)

- Why do you have trouble tasting your food when you have a cold? (p. 206)

- Why do people often continue to "feel" limbs that have been amputated? (p. 209)

- Do babies see the world the way adults do? (p. 212)

- Why does one person think a cloud is a cloud, and another think it's a spaceship? (p. 213)

- Can "subliminal perception" tapes help you lose weight or reduce your stress? (p. 216)

- Why are most psychologists skeptical about ESP? (p. 218)

7

LEARNING AND CONDITIONING

Reward and punishment . . . are the spur and reins

whereby all mankind are set on work, and guided.

PHILOSOPHER JOHN LOCKE

I t's January 1, a brand-new year. The sins and lapses of the old year are behind you; the slate is clean, and you're ready for a fresh start. Optimistically, you sit down to record your New Year's resolutions: to eat more healthfully, study harder, control your temper, get more exercise, manage your spending, . . . (you can fill in the rest). How likely are you to achieve these goals? Within weeks, days, or even hours, many people find themselves reverting to their old habits ("Well, maybe just one *small* dish of double chocolate ice cream"). They may decide that trying to mend their ways is pointless because they lack the willpower or brains or courage to do it. But in this chapter, we will see that willpower, brains, and courage often have little to do with a person's ability to alter bad habits.

Once you understand the laws of learning, you realize that behavior *can* change for the better—and you understand why it often does not. In ordinary speech, learning usually refers to classroom activities, such as memorizing the facts of geography, or to the acquisition of practical skills, such as carpentry or sewing. But to psychologists, **learning** is *any* relatively permanent change in behavior that occurs because of experience (except for changes due to fatigue, injury, or disease). Experience is the great teacher, providing the essential link between the past and the future, enabling an organism to adapt to changing circumstances in order to survive and thrive.

Research on learning has been heavily influenced by **behaviorism,** the school of psychology that accounts for behavior in terms of observable acts and events, without reference to mental entities, such as "mind" or "will." Behaviorists focus on a basic kind of learning called **conditioning,** which involves associations between environmental stimuli and responses. That is why behaviorism is sometimes referred to informally as stimulus-response ("S-R") psychology. Behaviorists have shown that two types of conditioning—*classical conditioning* and *operant conditioning*—can explain much of human behavior. But other approaches, known as *social-cognitive learning theories,* hold that omitting mental processes from explanations of human learning is like omitting passion from descriptions of sex: You may explain the form, but you miss the substance. To social-cognitive theorists, learning is not so much a change in behavior as a change in *knowledge* that has the potential for affecting behavior.

WHAT'S AHEAD

- Why would a dog salivate when it sees a light bulb or hears a buzzer, even though it can't eat these things?
- How can classical conditioning help explain prejudice?
- If you have learned to fear collies, why might you also be scared of sheepdogs?

CLASSICAL CONDITIONING

At the turn of the century, the great Russian physiologist Ivan Pavlov (1849–1936) was studying salivation in dogs, as part of a research program on digestion. His work would shortly win him the Nobel Prize in physiology and medicine. One of Pavlov's procedures was to make a surgical opening in a dog's cheek and insert a tube that conducted saliva away from the animal's salivary gland so that the saliva could be measured. To stimulate the reflexive flow of saliva, Pavlov placed meat powder or other food in the dog's mouth. This procedure was later refined by others (see Figure 7.1).

learning A relatively permanent change in behavior (or behavioral potential) due to experience.

behaviorism An approach to psychology that emphasizes the study of observable behavior and the role of the environment as a determinant of behavior.

conditioning A basic kind of learning that involves associations between environmental stimuli and the organism's responses.

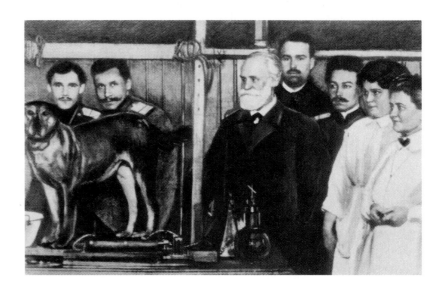

FIGURE 7.1

A MODIFICATION OF PAVLOV'S METHOD

In the apparatus on the right, which was based on Pavlov's techniques, saliva from a dog's cheek flowed down a tube and was measured by the movement of a needle on a revolving drum. In the photo above, you can see Ivan Pavlov himself in the center, flanked by his students and a canine subject.

Pavlov was a truly dedicated scientific observer; many years later, as he lay dying, he even dictated his sensations for posterity! And he imbued his students with the same kind of attention to detail. During the salivation studies, one of these students noticed something that most people would have overlooked or dismissed as trivial. After a dog had been brought to the laboratory a number of times, it would start to salivate *before* the food was placed in its mouth. The sight or smell of the food, the dish in which the food was kept, even the sight of the person who delivered the food each day or the sound of the person's footsteps were enough to start the dog's mouth watering. This new salivary response clearly was not inborn, so it had to have been acquired through experience.

At first, Pavlov treated the dog's drooling as just an annoying secretion. But he quickly realized that his student had stumbled onto an important phenomenon, one that Pavlov came to believe was the basis of a great deal of learning in human beings and other animals. He called that phenomenon a "conditional" reflex—conditional because it depended on environmental conditions. Later, an error in the translation of his writings transformed "conditional" into "conditioned," the word most commonly used today.

Pavlov soon dropped what he had been doing and turned to the study of conditioned reflexes, to which he devoted the last three decades of his life. Why were his dogs salivating to things other than food?

New Reflexes from Old

At first, Pavlov speculated about what his dogs might be thinking and feeling to make them drool before getting their food. Was the doggy equivalent of "Oh boy, this means chow time" going through their minds? Eventually, however, he decided that speculating about his dogs' mental abilities was pointless (Todes, 1997). Instead, he focused on analyzing the environment in which the conditioned reflex arose. The original salivary reflex, according to Pavlov, consisted of an **unconditioned stimulus (US)**, food, and an **unconditioned response (UR)**, salivation. By an *unconditioned stimulus,* Pavlov meant an event or thing that elicits a response automatically or reflexively. By an *unconditioned response,* he meant the response that is automatically produced:

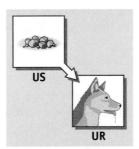

Learning occurs, said Pavlov, when a neutral stimulus is regularly paired with an unconditioned stimulus:

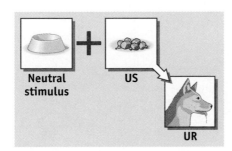

unconditioned stimulus (US) The classical-conditioning term for a stimulus that elicits a reflexive response in the absence of learning.

unconditioned response (UR) The classical-conditioning term for a reflexive response elicited by a stimulus in the absence of learning.

conditioned stimulus (CS) The classical-conditioning term for an initially neutral stimulus that comes to elicit a conditioned response after being associated with an unconditioned stimulus.

conditioned response (CR) The classical-conditioning term for a response that is elicited by a conditioned stimulus; it occurs after the conditioned stimulus is associated with an unconditioned stimulus.

classical conditioning The process by which a previously neutral stimulus acquires the capacity to elicit a response through association with a stimulus that already elicits a similar or related response.

extinction The weakening and eventual disappearance of a learned response; in classical conditioning, it occurs when the conditioned stimulus is no longer paired with the unconditioned stimulus.

The neutral stimulus then becomes a **conditioned stimulus (CS)**, which elicits a learned or **conditioned response (CR)** that is usually similar to the original, unlearned one. In Pavlov's laboratory, the sight of the food dish, which had not previously elicited salivation, became a CS for salivation:

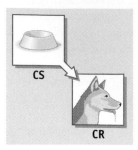

The procedure by which a neutral stimulus becomes a conditioned stimulus became known as **classical conditioning**, also called *Pavlovian* or *respondent conditioning*. Pavlov and his students went on to show that all sorts of things can become conditioned stimuli for salivation if they are paired with food: the ticking of a metronome, the musical tone of a bell or tuning fork, the vibrating sound of a buzzer, a triangle drawn on a large card, even a pinprick or an electric shock. (Figure 7.2 summarizes the steps involved in classical conditioning.) And since Pavlov's day, many automatic, involuntary responses besides salivation have been classically conditioned—for example, heartbeat, stomach secretions, blood pressure, reflexive movements, blinking, and muscle contractions. The optimal interval between the presentation of the neutral stimulus and the presentation of the US depends on the kind of response involved; in the laboratory, the interval is often less than a second.

Principles of Classical Conditioning

Classical conditioning occurs in all species, from worms to *Homo sapiens*. Let us look more closely at how four of the most important classical-conditioning processes work: extinction, higher-order conditioning, and stimulus generalization and discrimination.

Extinction. Conditioned responses do not necessarily last forever. If, after conditioning, the conditioned stimulus is repeatedly presented without the unconditioned stimulus, the conditioned response eventually disappears, and **extinction** is said to have occurred (see Figure 7.3). Suppose that you train your dog Milo to salivate to the sound of a bell, but then you ring the bell every five minutes and do *not* follow it with food. Milo will salivate less and less to the bell and will soon stop salivating altogether; salivation will have been extinguished. However, if you come back the

FIGURE 7.2

STEPS IN CLASSICAL CONDITIONING

Before conditioning, the unconditioned stimulus elicits an unconditioned response (left). During conditioning, a neutral stimulus (in this drawing, a dish) is repeatedly presented before the unconditioned stimulus (center). After conditioning, the neutral stimulus elicits a conditioned response, one that is usually similar to the unconditioned response (right); the neutral stimulus has therefore become a conditioned stimulus.

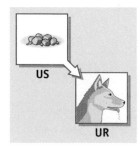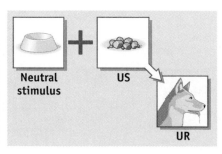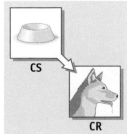

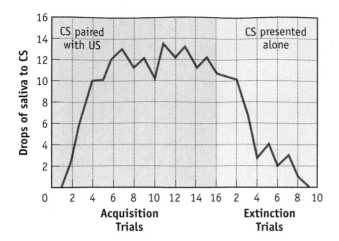

FIGURE 7.3

ACQUISITION AND EXTINCTION OF A SALIVARY RESPONSE

A neutral stimulus that is consistently followed by an unconditioned stimulus for salivation will become a conditioned stimulus for salivation. But when this conditioned stimulus is then repeatedly presented without the unconditioned stimulus, the conditioned salivary response will weaken and eventually disappear; it has been extinguished.

next day and ring the bell, Milo may salivate again for a few trials. The reappearance of the response, called **spontaneous recovery**, explains why completely eliminating a conditioned response usually requires more than one extinction session.

Higher-Order Conditioning. Sometimes a neutral stimulus can become a conditioned stimulus by being paired with an already established CS, a procedure known as **higher-order conditioning**. Say Milo has learned to salivate to the sight of a food dish. Now you flash a bright light before you present the dish. With repeated pairings of the light and the dish, Milo may learn to salivate to the light. The procedure for higher-order conditioning is illustrated in Figure 7.4.

Higher-order conditioning may explain why some words trigger emotional responses in us—why they can inflame us to anger or evoke warm, sentimental feelings. When words are paired with objects or other words that already elicit some emotional response, they, too, may come to elicit that response (Chance, 1999; Staats & Staats, 1957). For example, a child may learn a positive response to the word *birthday* because of its association with gifts and attention. Conversely, the child may learn a negative response to ethnic or national labels, such as *Swede, Turk,* or *Jew,* if those words are paired with words that the child has already learned are disagreeable, such as *dumb* or *dirty.* Higher-order conditioning, in other words, may contribute to the formation of prejudices.

Stimulus Generalization and Discrimination. After a stimulus becomes a conditioned stimulus for some response, other, similar stimuli may produce a similar reaction—a phenomenon known as **stimulus generalization**. For example, if you condition your patient pooch Milo to salivate to middle C on the piano, Milo may also salivate to D, which is one tone above C, even though you did not pair D with food. Stimulus generalization is described nicely by an old English proverb: "He who hath been bitten by a snake fears a rope."

spontaneous recovery The reappearance of a learned response after its apparent extinction.

higher-order conditioning In classical conditioning, a procedure in which a neutral stimulus becomes a conditioned stimulus through association with an already established conditioned stimulus.

stimulus generalization After conditioning, the tendency to respond to a stimulus that resembles one involved in the original conditioning; in classical conditioning, it occurs when a stimulus that resembles the CS elicits the CR.

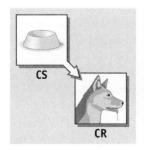
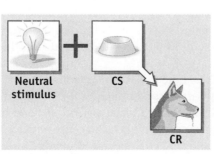
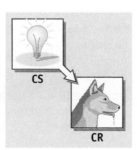

FIGURE 7.4

HIGHER-ORDER CONDITIONING

In this illustration of higher-order conditioning, the food dish is a previously conditioned stimulus for salivation (left). When the light, a neutral stimulus, is paired with the dish (center), the light, too, becomes a conditioned stimulus for salivation (right).

CONDITIONING AN EYE-BLINK RESPONSE

Try out your behavioral skills by conditioning an eye-blink response in a friend, using classical-conditioning procedures. You will need a drinking straw and something to make a ringing sound—a spoon tapped on a water glass works well. Tell your friend that you are going to blow air in his or her eye through the straw, but don't say why. Immediately before each puff of air, make the ringing sound. Repeat this procedure ten times. Then make the ringing sound but *don't* puff. Your friend will probably blink anyway, and may continue to do so for one or two more repetitions of the sound before the response extinguishes. Can you identify the US, the UR, the CS, and the CR in this exercise?

The mirror image of stimulus generalization is **stimulus discrimination**, in which *different* responses are made to stimuli that resemble the conditioned stimulus in some way. Suppose that you have conditioned Milo to salivate to middle C on the piano by repeatedly pairing the sound with food. Now you play middle C on a guitar, *without* following it by food (but you continue to follow C on the piano by food). Eventually, Milo will learn to salivate to a C on the piano and not to salivate to the same note on the guitar; that is, he will discriminate between the two sounds. If you keep at this long enough, you could train Milo to be a pretty discriminating drooler.

What Is Actually Learned in Classical Conditioning?

For classical conditioning to be most effective, the stimulus to be conditioned should *precede* the unconditioned stimulus rather than follow it or occur simultaneously with it. This makes sense, because in classical conditioning, the conditioned stimulus becomes a kind of signal for the unconditioned stimulus. It enables the organism to prepare for an event that is about to happen. In Pavlov's studies, for instance, a bell or a buzzer was a signal that meat was coming, and the dog's salivation was preparation for digesting food.

Today, therefore, many psychologists contend that what an animal or person actually learns in classical conditioning is not merely an association between two paired stimuli that occur close together in time, but rather *information* conveyed by one stimulus about another: e.g., "If a tone sounds, food is likely to follow" (Davey, 1992). This view is supported by the research of Robert Rescorla (1988), who showed, in a series of imaginative studies, that the mere pairing of an unconditioned stimulus and a neutral stimulus is not enough to produce learning. To become a conditioned stimulus, the neutral stimulus must reliably signal, or *predict*, the unconditioned stimulus. If food occurs just as often without a preceding tone as with it, the tone is unlikely to become a conditioned stimulus for salivation—because the tone does not provide any information about the probability of getting food.

In everyday life, too, a potential CS may sometimes predict an unconditioned stimulus and sometimes not, so conditioning is less certain than when the CS and US always occur together in the laboratory. A friend of ours, behaviorist Paul Chance, gave us this example: Suppose you work in an office where you are allowed to receive calls only from other employees; you may take outside calls only in emergencies. One

stimulus discrimination The tendency to respond differently to two or more similar stimuli; in classical conditioning, it occurs when a stimulus similar to the CS fails to evoke the CR.

day, your lover calls to jilt you; the police call to report that your new car was stolen; and your landlord calls to tell you that a broken water pipe has flooded your apartment. If these were the only calls you got, the next time you heard the phone ring (the CS), you might freak out (the CR). But if they occurred randomly among 50 routine business calls, the phone's ringing would probably not upset you because it would not necessarily signal another disaster.

Rescorla (1988) concluded that "Pavlovian conditioning is not a stupid process by which the organism willy-nilly forms associations between any two stimuli that happen to co-occur. Rather, the organism is better seen as an information seeker using logical and perceptual relations among events, along with its own preconceptions, to form a sophisticated representation of its world." Not all learning theorists agree with this conclusion; an orthodox behaviorist would say that it is silly to talk about the preconceptions of a rat. The important point, however, is that concepts such as "information seeking," "preconceptions," and "representations of the world" open the door to a more cognitive view of classical conditioning.

QUICK QUIZ

Classical-conditioning terms can be hard to learn, so be sure to take this quiz before going on.

A. Name the unconditioned stimulus, unconditioned response, conditioned stimulus, and conditioned response in these two situations.

1. Five-year-old Samantha is watching a storm from her window. A huge bolt of lightning is followed by a tremendous thunderclap, and Samantha jumps at the noise. This happens several more times. There is a brief lull and then another lightning bolt. Samantha jumps in response to the bolt.

2. Gregory's mouth waters whenever he eats anything with lemon in it. One day, while reading an ad that shows a big glass of lemonade, Gregory notices his mouth watering.

B. In the view of many learning theorists, pairing a neutral and unconditioned stimulus is not enough to produce classical conditioning; the neutral stimulus must _____ the unconditioned stimulus.

Answers:

1. US = the thunderclap; UR = jumping elicited by the noise; CS = the sight of the lightning; CR = jumping elicited by the lightning. 2. US = the taste of lemon; UR = salivation elicited by the taste of lemon; CS = the picture of a glass of lemonade; CR = salivation elicited by the picture. B. signal or predict

WHAT'S AHEAD

- Why do advertisers often include pleasant music and gorgeous scenery in ads for their products?
- How would a classical-conditioning theorist explain your irrational fear of heights or mice?
- If you eat licorice and then happen to get the flu, how might your taste for licorice change?
- How can sitting in a doctor's office make you feel sick?

CLASSICAL CONDITIONING IN REAL LIFE

If a dog can learn to salivate to the ringing of a bell, so can you. In fact, you probably have learned to salivate to the sound of a lunch bell, not to mention the phrase *hot fudge sundae,* "mouth-watering" pictures of food in magazines, and a voice calling out "Dinner's ready!" But the role of classical conditioning goes far

John Watson (1878–1958)

beyond the learning of simple reflexive responses; conditioning affects us every day in many ways.

One of the first psychologists to recognize the real-life implications of Pavlovian theory was John B. Watson, who founded American behaviorism and enthusiastically promoted Pavlov's ideas. Watson believed that the whole rich array of human emotion and behavior could be accounted for by conditioning principles. For Watson, learning to love a parent or a lover was no different from learning to salivate to the sound of a bell. It was just a matter of pairing unconditioned stimuli (stroking, cuddling, kissing) with the person doing the stroking and cuddling. (Watson, who was married five times, apparently tried many different pairings.)

Watson turned out to be wrong about love, which is a lot more complicated than he thought (see Chapter 12). But he was right about the power of classical conditioning to affect our emotions, preferences, and tastes.

Learning to Like

Classical conditioning plays a big role in our emotional responses to objects, symbols, events, and places. It can explain why sentimental feelings sweep over us when we see a school mascot, a national flag, or the logo of the Olympic games. We have learned to experience these emotions because these objects have been associated in the past with positive feelings.

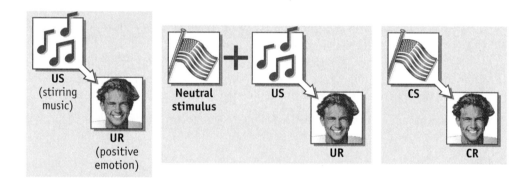

Many Madison Avenue techniques for getting us to like clients' products are also based on the principles first demonstrated by Pavlov, whether advertising executives realize it or not. In one study, college students looked at slides of either a beige pen or a blue pen. During the presentation, half of the students heard a song from a recent American musical film, and half heard a selection of traditional music from India. (The experimenter made the reasonable assumption that the American music would be more appealing to the young Americans in the study.) Later the students were allowed to choose one of the pens. Almost three-fourths of those who heard the popular music chose a pen that was the same color as the one they had seen in the slides. An equal number of those who heard the Indian music chose a pen that *differed* in color from the one they had seen (Gorn, 1982).

In classical-conditioning terms, the music in this study was an unconditioned stimulus for internal responses associated with pleasure or displeasure, and the pens became conditioned stimuli for similar responses. You can see why television commercials often pair their products with music, attractive people, or other appealing sounds and images.

Learning to Fear

As we already saw in some of our previous examples of conditioning, positive emotions are not the only ones that can be classically conditioned; so can dislikes and negative emotions such as fear. A person can learn to fear just about anything if it is paired with something that elicits pain, surprise, or embarrassment. But human beings are biologically primed to acquire some fears more easily than others. It is far easier to establish a conditioned fear of spiders, snakes, and heights than of butterflies, flowers, and toasters; the former can be dangerous to your health, and in the process of evolution, human beings therefore acquired a tendency to be wary of them.

When fear of an object or situation becomes irrational and interferes with normal activities, it qualifies as a *phobia*. To demonstrate how a phobia might be learned, John Watson and Rosalie Rayner (1920) deliberately established a rat phobia in an 11-month-old boy named Albert. For ethical reasons, no psychologist today would do such a thing to a child. Nevertheless, the study remains a classic, and its main conclusion, that fears can be conditioned, is still well accepted.

"Little Albert" was a placid child who rarely cried. When Watson and Rayner gave him a furry white rat to play with (a live one, not a toy), Albert showed no fear; in fact, he was delighted. However, like most children, Albert was afraid of loud noises. When the researchers made a loud noise behind his head by striking a steel bar with a hammer, he would jump and fall sideways onto the mattress he was sitting on. The noise made by the hammer was an unconditioned stimulus for the unconditioned response of fear.

Having established that Albert liked rats, Watson and Rayner set about teaching him to fear them. Again they offered him a rat, but this time, as Albert reached for it, one of the researchers struck the steel bar. Startled, Albert fell onto the mattress. The researchers repeated this procedure several times. Albert began to whimper and tremble. Finally, they held out the rat to him without making the noise. Albert fell over, cried, and crawled away as fast as he could; the rat had become a conditioned stimulus for fear.

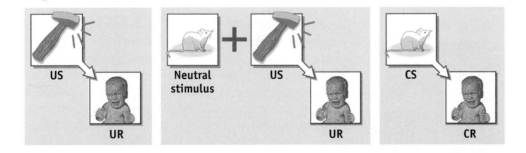

Tests done five days later showed that Albert's fear had generalized to other hairy or furry objects, including white rabbits, cotton wool, a Santa Claus mask, and even John Watson's hair.

Unfortunately, Watson and Rayner lost access to Little Albert and so were unable to reverse the conditioning. A few years later, however, Watson and Mary Cover Jones did reverse a child's conditioned fear—one that was, as Watson put it, "home-grown" rather than psychologist induced (Jones, 1924).

Three-year-old Peter was deathly afraid of rabbits. Watson and Jones eliminated his fear with a method called **counterconditioning**, in which a conditioned stimulus is paired with some other stimulus that elicits a response incompatible

counterconditioning In classical conditioning, the process of pairing a conditioned stimulus with a stimulus that elicits a response that is incompatible with an unwanted conditioned response.

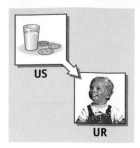

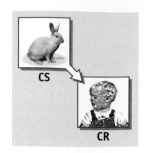

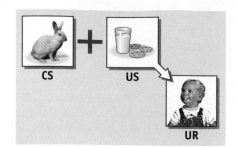

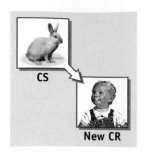

with the unwanted response. In this case, the rabbit (the CS) was paired with a snack of milk and crackers, and the snack produced pleasant feelings that were incompatible with the conditioned response of fear. (See illustration above.) At first, the researchers kept the rabbit some distance from Peter, so that his fear would remain at a low level. Otherwise, Peter might have learned to fear milk and crackers! But gradually, over several days, they brought the rabbit closer and closer. Eventually, Peter was able to sit with the rabbit in his lap, playing with it with one hand while he ate with the other. A variation of this procedure, called *systematic desensitization,* was later devised for treating phobias in adults (see Chapter 17).

Accounting for Taste

Classical conditioning can also explain how we learn to like and dislike many foods and odors. In the laboratory, researchers have taught animals to dislike foods or odors by pairing them with drugs that cause nausea or other unpleasant symptoms. One researcher trained slugs to associate the smell of carrots, which slugs normally like, with a bitter-tasting chemical that they detest. Soon the slugs were avoiding the smell of carrots. The researcher then demonstrated higher-order conditioning by pairing the smell of carrots with the smell of potato. Sure enough, the slugs began to avoid the smell of potato, as well (Sahley, Rudy, & Gelperin, 1981).

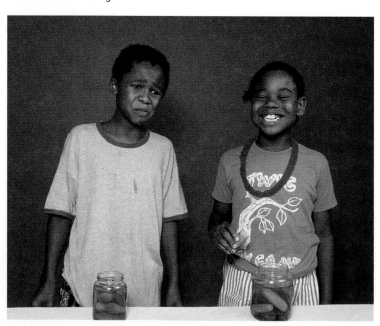

Whether we say "yum" or "yuk" to a food may depend on a past experience involving classical conditioning.

Many people have learned to dislike a food after eating it and then falling ill, even when the two events were unrelated. The food, previously a neutral stimulus, becomes a conditioned stimulus for nausea or other symptoms produced by the illness. Psychologist Martin Seligman once told how he himself was conditioned to hate béarnaise sauce. One night, shortly after he and his wife ate a delicious filet mignon with béarnaise sauce, he came down with the flu. Naturally, he felt wretched. His misery had nothing to do with the béarnaise sauce, of course, yet the next time he tried it, he found he disliked the taste (Seligman & Hager, 1972).

Notice that unlike conditioning in the laboratory, Seligman's aversion to the sauce occurred after only one pairing of the sauce with illness and with a considerable delay between the conditioned and unconditioned stimuli. Further, neither Seligman's wife nor his dinner plate became conditioned stimuli for nausea, even though they, too, had been paired with illness.

Apparently, many animals (including psychologists) are biologically primed to associate sickness with taste more readily than with sights or sounds (Garcia & Koelling, 1966; Seligman & Hager, 1972). Like the tendency to acquire certain fears, this biological tendency enhances the species' survival: Eating bad food is more likely to be followed by illness than are particular sights or sounds.

Reacting to Medical Treatments

Because of classical conditioning, medical treatments can create unexpected misery or relief from symptoms, for reasons that are entirely unrelated to the treatment itself.

For example, unpleasant reactions to a treatment generalize to a wide range of other stimuli. This is a particular problem for cancer patients. The nausea and vomiting resulting from chemotherapy often generalize to the place where the therapy takes place, the waiting room, the sound of a nurse's voice, or the smell of rubbing alcohol. The drug treatment is an unconditioned stimulus for nausea and vomiting, and through association, the other, previously neutral stimuli become conditioned stimuli for these responses. Even *mental images* of the sights and smells of the clinic may become conditioned stimuli for nausea (Dadds et al., 1997; Redd et al., 1993).

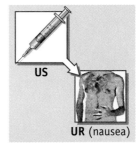

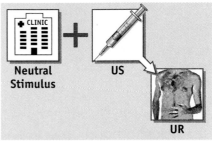

Some cancer patients also acquire a classically conditioned anxiety response to anything associated with their chemotherapy. In one study, patients who drank lemon-lime Kool-Aid before their therapy sessions developed an anxiety response to the drink—an example of higher-order conditioning. They continued to feel anxious even when the drink was offered in their homes rather than at the clinic (Jacobsen et al., 1995).

On the other hand, patients may have *reduced* pain and anxiety when they take *placebos*—pills and injections with no active ingredients. The bottle containing the drug, the room in which the medication is given, the doctor's white coat, and the pill or injection itself may all become conditioned stimuli for relief from symptoms, because these stimuli have been associated in the past with *real* drugs (Ader, 1997). The real drugs are the unconditioned stimuli, the relief they bring is the unconditioned response, and the placebos acquire the ability to elicit similar reactions (conditioned responses).

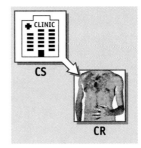

QUICK QUIZ

We hope you haven't acquired a classically conditioned fear of quizzes. See whether you can supply the correct term to describe the outcome in each of these situations:

1. After a child learns to fear spiders, he also responds with fear to ants, beetles, and other crawling bugs.

2. A toddler is afraid of the bath, so her father puts just a little water in the tub and gives the child a lollipop to suck on while she is being washed. Soon, the little girl loses her fear of the bath.

3. A factory worker notices that his mouth waters whenever a noontime bell signals the beginning of his lunch break. One day, the bell goes haywire and rings every half hour. By the end of the day, the worker has stopped salivating to the bell.

Answers:

1. stimulus generalization   2. counterconditioning   3. extinction

WHAT'S AHEAD

● What do praise and ceasing to nag have in common?
● How can operant principles account for superstitious rituals?
● What is the best way to discourage a friend from interrupting you while you're studying?
● How do trainers teach guide dogs to perform the amazing services they do for their owners?

OPERANT CONDITIONING

At the end of the nineteenth century, in the first known scientific study of anger, G. Stanley Hall (1899) asked people to describe angry episodes they had experienced or observed. One person told of a 3-year-old girl who broke out in furious, seemingly uncontrollable sobs when she was punished by being kept home from a ride. In the middle of her tantrum, the child suddenly stopped crying and asked her nanny in a perfectly calm voice if her father was in. Told no, she immediately resumed her sobbing.

Children, of course, cry for many valid reasons—pain, discomfort, fear, illness, fatigue—and these cries deserve an adult's sympathy and attention. The child in Hall's study, however, was crying for a different reason. She had learned, from prior experience, that an outburst of sobbing would bring her attention and possibly the ride she wanted. Her behavior, though some might call it "naughty," was perfectly understandable, because it followed one of the most basic laws of learning: *Behavior becomes more likely or less likely, depending on its consequences.*

An emphasis on environmental consequences is at the heart of **operant conditioning** (also called *instrumental conditioning*), the second type of conditioning studied by behaviorists. In classical conditioning, it does not matter whether an animal's or person's behavior has consequences; in Pavlov's procedure, for example, the dog got food whether it salivated or not. But in operant conditioning, the organism's response (the little girl's sobbing, for example) *operates* or produces effects on the environment. These effects, in turn, influence whether the response will occur again.

Classical and operant conditioning also tend to differ in the types of responses they involve. In classical conditioning, the response is reflexive, an automatic reaction to something happening in the environment, such as the sight of food or the sound of a bell. Generally, responses in operant conditioning are complex and are not reflexive—for instance, riding a bicycle, writing a letter, climbing a mountain, . . . or throwing a tantrum.

the neighborhood. Jerry Van Amerongen

An instantaneous learning experience.

The Birth of Radical Behaviorism

Operant conditioning has been studied since the start of the twentieth century, although it was not called that until later. Edward Thorndike (1898), then a young doctoral candidate, set the stage by observing cats as they tried to escape from a complex "puzzle box" to reach a scrap of fish located just outside the box. At first, the cat would scratch, bite, or swat at parts of the box in an unorganized way. Then, after a few minutes, it would chance on the successful response (loosening a bolt, pulling a string, or hitting a button) and rush out to get the reward. Placed in the box again, the cat now took a little less time to escape, and after several trials, the animal immediately made the correct response. According to Thorndike, this response had been "stamped in" by its satisfying results (getting the food). In contrast, annoying or unsatisfying results "stamped out" behavior. Behavior, said Thorndike, is controlled by its consequences.

This general principle was elaborated and extended to more complex forms of behavior by B. F. (Burrhus Frederick) Skinner (1904–1990). Skinner called his approach "radical behaviorism" to distinguish it from the behaviorism of John Watson, who

operant conditioning The process by which a response becomes more or less likely to occur, depending on its consequences.

emphasized classical conditioning. Skinner argued that to understand behavior we should focus on the external causes of an action and the action's consequences. Skinner avoided terms that Thorndike used, such as "satisfying" and "annoying," which reflect assumptions about what an organism feels and wants. To explain behavior, he said, we should look outside the individual, not inside.

The Consequences of Behavior

In Skinner's analysis, which has inspired an immense body of research, a response ("operant") can lead to three types of consequences:

1 *A neutral consequence does not alter the response.* That is, it neither increases nor decreases the probability that the response will recur. If a door handle squeaks each time you turn it, but you ignore the sound and it has no effect on your door-opening behavior, the squeak is considered a neutral consequence. We will not be concerned further with neutral consequences.

2 Reinforcement *strengthens the response or makes it more likely to recur.* When your dog begs for food at the table, and you give her the lamb chop off your plate, her begging is likely to increase:

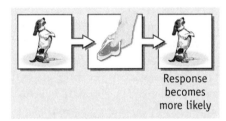

Response becomes more likely

Reinforcers are roughly equivalent to rewards, and many psychologists use *reward* and *reinforcer* as approximate synonyms. However, strict behaviorists avoid the word *reward,* because it implies that something has been earned that results in happiness or satisfaction. To a behaviorist, a stimulus is a reinforcer if it strengthens the preceding behavior, whether or not the organism experiences pleasure or a positive emotion. Conversely, no matter how pleasurable a stimulus is, it is not a reinforcer if it does not increase the likelihood of a response. It is pleasurable to get a paycheck, but if you get paid regardless of the effort you put into your work, the money will not reinforce "hard-work behavior."

3 Punishment *weakens the response or makes it less likely to recur.* Any aversive (unpleasant) stimulus or event may be a *punisher.* If your dog begs for food from the table, and you shout "No!" in a loud voice, her begging is likely to decrease (as long as you don't feel guilty and then give her the lamb chop anyway).

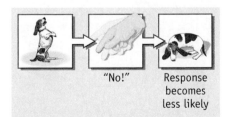

"No!"   Response becomes less likely

In general, the sooner a reinforcer or punisher follows a response, the greater its effect; you are likely to respond more reliably when you do not have to wait too long for a paycheck, a smile, or a grade. When there is a delay, other responses occur in the interval, and the connection between the desired or undesired response and the consequence may not be made.

reinforcement The process by which a stimulus or event strengthens or increases the probability of the response that it follows.

punishment The process by which a stimulus or event weakens or reduces the probability of the response that it follows.

primary reinforcer A stimulus that is inherently reinforcing, typically satisfying a physiological need; an example is food.

primary punisher A stimulus that is inherently punishing; an example is electric shock.

secondary reinforcer A stimulus that has acquired reinforcing properties through association with other reinforcers.

secondary punisher A stimulus that has acquired punishing properties through association with other punishers.

positive reinforcement A reinforcement procedure in which a response is followed by the presentation of, or increase in intensity of, a reinforcing stimulus; as a result, the response becomes stronger or more likely to occur.

negative reinforcement A reinforcement procedure in which a response is followed by the removal, delay, or decrease in intensity of an unpleasant stimulus; as a result, the response becomes stronger or more likely to occur.

Skinner argued that parents, employers, and governments resort to reinforcers and punishers all the time—to get their kids to behave, their employees to work harder, and their constituents to pay taxes. But they do not always use them effectively.

Primary and Secondary Reinforcers and Punishers. Food, water, light stroking of the skin, and a comfortable air temperature are naturally reinforcing because they satisfy biological needs. They are therefore known as **primary reinforcers**. Similarly, pain and extreme heat or cold are inherently punishing and are therefore known as **primary punishers**. Primary reinforcers and punishers can be very powerful, but they have some drawbacks, both in real life and in research. For one thing, a primary reinforcer may be ineffective if an animal or person is not in a deprived state; a glass of water is not much of a reward if you just drank three glasses. Also, for obvious ethical reasons psychologists cannot go around using primary punishers (say, by hitting their subjects) or taking away primary reinforcers (say, by starving their subjects).

Fortunately, behavior can be controlled just as effectively by **secondary reinforcers** and **secondary punishers**, which are learned. Money, praise, applause, good grades, awards, and gold stars are common secondary reinforcers. Criticism, demerits, catcalls, scoldings, fines, and bad grades are common secondary punishers. Most behaviorists believe that secondary reinforcers and punishers acquire their ability to influence behavior by being paired with primary reinforcers and punishers. (If that reminds you of classical conditioning, reinforce your excellent thinking with a pat on the head! Indeed, secondary reinforcers and punishers are often called *conditioned* reinforcers and punishers.) Money has considerable power over most people's behavior because it can be exchanged for primary reinforcers such as food and shelter. It is also associated with other secondary reinforcers, such as praise and respect.

Positive and Negative Reinforcers and Punishers. Reinforcement and punishment may seem pretty straightforward, but they are not always simple. Consider, first, reinforcement. In our example of the begging dog, something pleasant (getting the lamb chop) followed the dog's begging response, so the response increased. Similarly, if a good grade follows your studying, your efforts to study are likely to continue or increase. This kind of process, in which a pleasant consequence makes a response more likely, is known as **positive reinforcement**. But there is another type of reinforcement, **negative reinforcement**, which involves the *removal* of something *unpleasant*. For example, if someone nags you all the time to study, but stops nagging when you comply, your studying is likely to increase—because you will then avoid the nagging:

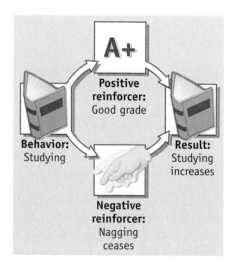

The positive-negative distinction can also be applied to punishment: Something unpleasant may occur following some behavior (positive punishment), or something *pleasant* may be *removed* (negative punishment). For example, if your friends tease you for being an egghead (positive punishment) or if studying makes you lose time with your friends (negative punishment), you may stop studying:

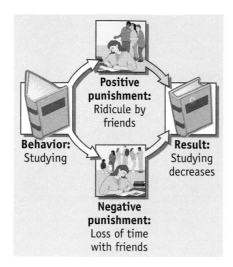

The distinction between positive and negative reinforcement and punishment has been a source of confusion for generations of students, turning strong people into quivering heaps. (We can assure you that if we had been around when these terms were coined, we would have complained loudly.) You will master these terms more quickly if you understand that "positive" and "negative" have nothing to do with "good" or "bad." They refer to *procedures*—giving something or taking something away.

In the case of reinforcement, think of a positive reinforcer as something that is added or obtained, and a negative reinforcer as avoidance of, or escape from, something unpleasant. *With either positive or negative reinforcement, a response becomes more likely.* Do you recall what happened when Little Albert learned to fear rats through a process of classical conditioning? After he acquired this fear, crawling away was negatively reinforced by escape from the now-fearsome rodent. The negative reinforcement that results from escaping or avoiding something unpleasant explains why so many fears are long-lasting. When you avoid a feared object or situation, you also cut off all opportunities for extinguishing your fear.

Understandably, people often confuse negative reinforcement with positive punishment, because both involve an unpleasant stimulus. With punishment, though, you are subjected to the unpleasant stimulus, and with negative reinforcement, it is taken away. To keep these terms straight, remember that *punishment—whether positive or negative—decreases the likelihood of a response, whereas reinforcement—positive or negative—increases* it. In real life, punishment and negative reinforcement often go hand in hand. If you use a choke collar to teach your dog to heel, a yank on the collar *punishes* the act of walking; release of the collar *negatively reinforces* the act of standing by your side.

You can positively reinforce your studying of this material by taking a refreshment break. As you master the material, a decrease in your anxiety will negatively reinforce studying. But we hope you won't punish your efforts by telling yourself "I'll never get it" or "It's too hard"!

QUICK QUIZ

What kind of consequence will follow if you can't answer these questions?

1. A child nags her father for a cookie; he keeps refusing, but finally, unable to stand the nagging any longer, he hands over the cookie. For him, the ending of the child's pleas is a _____. For the child, the cookie is a _____.

2. An able-bodied driver is careful not to park in a handicapped space anymore after paying a large fine for having done so. The loss of money is a _____.

3. Which of the following are secondary reinforcers: quarters spilling from a slot machine, a winner's blue ribbon, a piece of candy, an A on an exam, frequent-flyer miles.

4. During late-afternoon "happy hours" in bars and restaurants, drinks are sold at a reduced price and appetizers are often free. What undesirable behavior may be rewarded by this practice?

Answers:

1. negative reinforcer; positive reinforcer 2. punisher—or more precisely, a negative punisher (because something desirable was taken away) 3. All but the candy are secondary reinforcers. 4. One possible answer: The reduced prices, free appetizers, and cheerful atmosphere all reinforce heavy alcohol consumption just before the commuter rush hour, thus possibly contributing to drunk driving (Geller & Lehman, 1988).

Principles of Operant Conditioning

Thousands of operant conditioning studies have been done, many using animals. A favorite experimental tool is the *Skinner box*, a cage equipped with a device that delivers food into a dish when an animal makes a desired response (see Figure 7.5). In the original version, a machine connected to the cage automatically recorded each response and produced a graph on a piece of paper, showing the cumulative number of responses across time; nowadays, computers are used.

Early in his career, Skinner (1938) used the Skinner box for a classic demonstration of operant conditioning. A rat that had previously learned to eat from the pellet-releasing device was placed in the box. Because no food was present, the animal proceeded to do typical ratlike things, scurrying about the box, sniffing here and there, and randomly touching parts of the floor and walls. Quite by accident, it happened to press a lever mounted on one wall, and immediately, a pellet of tasty rat food fell into the food dish. The rat continued its movements and again happened to press the bar, causing another pellet to fall into the dish. With additional repetitions of bar pressing followed by food, the animal began to behave less randomly and to press the bar

FIGURE 7.5
THE SKINNER BOX

When a rat in a Skinner box presses a bar, a food pellet or drop of water is automatically released. The photo shows Skinner demonstrating one of the boxes.

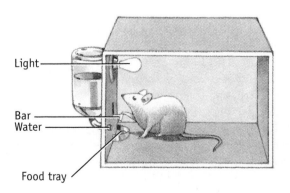

Light

Bar
Water

Food tray

more consistently. Eventually, Skinner had the rat pressing the bar as fast as it could. Since then, behavioral researchers have used the Skinner box and similar devices to discover many techniques and applications of operant conditioning.

Extinction. In operant conditioning, as in classical, **extinction** is a procedure that causes a previously learned response to stop. In operant conditioning, extinction takes place when the reinforcer that maintained the response is removed or is no longer available. At first, there may be a spurt of responding, but then the responses gradually taper off and eventually cease. Suppose you put a coin in a vending machine and get nothing back. You may throw in another coin, or perhaps even two, but then you will probably stop trying. The next day, you may put in yet another coin, an example of *spontaneous recovery.* Eventually, however, you will give up on that machine. Your response will have been extinguished.

"Boy, do we have this guy conditioned. Every time I press the bar down he drops a pellet in."

Stimulus Generalization and Discrimination. In operant conditioning, as in classical, **stimulus generalization** may occur. That is, responses may generalize to stimuli that were not present during the original learning situation but that resemble the original stimuli. For example, a pigeon that has been trained to peck at a picture of a circle may also peck at a slightly oval figure. But if you wanted to train the bird to discriminate between the two shapes, you would present both the circle and the oval, giving reinforcers whenever the bird pecked at the circle and withholding reinforcers when it pecked at the oval. Eventually, **stimulus discrimination** would occur.

Sometimes an animal or human being learns to respond to a stimulus only when some other stimulus, called a **discriminative stimulus**, is present. The discriminative stimulus signals whether a response, if made, will pay off. In a Skinner box containing a pigeon, a light may serve as a discriminative stimulus for pecking at a circle. When the light is on, pecking brings a reward; when it is off, pecking is futile.

Human behavior is controlled by many discriminative stimuli, both verbal ("Store hours are 9 to 5") and nonverbal (traffic lights, doorbells, the ring of a telephone, the facial expressions of others). Learning to respond correctly when such stimuli are present is an essential part of a person's socialization. In a public place, if you have to go to the bathroom, the words *Women* and *Men* are discriminative stimuli for entering one door or the other. One word tells you the response will be rewarded by the opportunity to empty a full bladder, the other that it will be punished by the jeers or protests of other people.

Learning on Schedule. When a response is first acquired, learning is usually most rapid if the response is reinforced each time it occurs; this procedure is called **continuous reinforcement**. However, once a response has become reliable, it will be more resistant to extinction if it is rewarded on an **intermittent (partial) schedule of reinforcement**, which involves reinforcing only some responses, not all of them. Skinner (1956) happened on this fact when he ran short of food pellets for his rats and was forced to deliver reinforcers less often. (Not all scientific discoveries are planned!)

Intermittent reinforcement helps explain why people often get attached to "lucky" hats, charms, and rituals. A batter touches his gold chain and pulls his earlobe, and gets a home run; thereafter he always touches his chain and pulls his earlobe before a pitch. A student takes an exam with a purple pen and gets an A, and won't take any other exam without a purple pen. These rituals persist because *sometimes* they are followed by a reinforcer—a hit, a good grade.

Skinner (1948) actually created eight "superstitious" pigeons in his laboratory. He rigged their cages so that food was delivered every 15 seconds, even if the birds didn't lift a feather. Pigeons are often in motion, so when the food

extinction The weakening and eventual disappearance of a learned response; in operant conditioning, it occurs when a response is no longer followed by a reinforcer.

stimulus generalization In operant conditioning, the tendency for a response that has been reinforced (or punished) in the presence of one stimulus to occur (or be suppressed) in the presence of other, similar stimuli.

stimulus discrimination In operant conditioning, the tendency of a response to occur in the presence of one stimulus but not in the presence of other, similar stimuli that differ from it on some dimension.

discriminative stimulus A stimulus that signals when a particular response is likely to be followed by a certain type of consequence.

continuous reinforcement A reinforcement schedule in which a particular response is always reinforced.

intermittent (partial) schedule of reinforcement A reinforcement schedule in which a particular response is sometimes but not always reinforced.

THINKING CRITICALLY

CONSIDER OTHER INTERPRETATIONS

People cling to superstitious rituals because they seem to work. Could this "effectiveness" be an illusion, explainable in terms of operant principles?

fixed-ratio schedule An intermittent schedule of reinforcement in which reinforcement occurs only after a fixed number of responses.

variable-ratio schedule An intermittent schedule of reinforcement in which reinforcement occurs after a variable number of responses.

came, each animal was likely to be doing *something*. That something was then reinforced by delivery of the food. The behavior, of course, was reinforced entirely by chance, but it still became more likely to occur, and thus to be reinforced again. Within a short time, six of the pigeons were practicing some sort of consistent ritual—turning in counterclockwise circles, bobbing their heads up and down, or swinging their heads to and fro. None of these activities had the least effect on the delivery of the reinforcer; the birds were behaving "superstitiously." It was as if they thought their movements were responsible for bringing the food. (The moral is, If you don't want to be a pigeon, examine how intermittent rewards might be perpetuating your own superstitions.)

Many kinds of intermittent schedules have been studied. *Ratio schedules* deliver a reinforcer after a certain number of responses have occurred. *Interval schedules* deliver a reinforcer if a response is made after the passage of a certain amount of time since the last reinforcer. The number of responses that must occur or the amount of time that must pass before the payoff may be *fixed* (constant) or *variable*. Combining the ratio/interval patterns and fixed/variable patterns yields four types of intermittent schedules (see Figure 7.6). These variations in how the reinforcers are delivered have characteristic effects on the rate, form, and timing of behavior—effects that most people are not aware of.

1 *On* fixed-ratio schedules, *reinforcement occurs after a fixed number of responses.* Fixed-ratio schedules produce very high rates of responding. In the laboratory, a rat may rapidly press a bar several hundred times to get a single reward. Outside the laboratory, fixed-ratio schedules are often used by employers to increase productivity. Both a salesperson who must sell a specific number of items before getting a commission and a factory worker who must produce a specific number of products before earning a given wage (a system known as "piecework") are on fixed-ratio schedules. An interesting feature of fixed-ratio schedules is that performance sometimes drops off just after reinforcement. If a writer must complete four chapters before getting a check, interest and motivation will sag right after the check is received.

2 *On* variable-ratio schedules, *reinforcement occurs after some average number of responses, but the number varies from reinforcement to reinforcement.* For example, a reinforcer might be delivered on the average after every fifth response but sometimes after one, two, six, or seven responses, or any other number, as long as the average was five. Variable-ratio schedules produce extremely high, steady rates of responding. The responses are more resistant to extinction than when a fixed-ratio schedule is used. The prime example of a variable-ratio schedule is delivery of payoffs by a slot machine. The player knows that the average number of responses necessary

FIGURE 7.6
REINFORCEMENT SCHEDULES AND BEHAVIOR

In this figure, each star represents the delivery of a reinforcer. As you can see, different schedules produce different learning curves (patterns of responding over time). A fixed-ratio schedule produces a very fast rate of responding. When a fixed-interval schedule is used, responses drop off immediately after reinforcement, resulting in a scalloped curve. (Adapted from Skinner, 1961.)

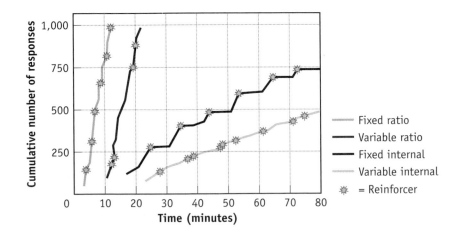

to win is set at a level that makes money for the house. Hope springs eternal, though. The gambler takes a chance on being in front of the machine during one of those lucky moments when fewer responses bring a payoff.

3 On fixed-interval schedules, *reinforcement of a response occurs only if a fixed amount of time has passed since the previous reinforcer.* For example, a rat might get a food pellet the first time it presses a bar after passage of a 10-second interval. Pressing the bar earlier does not hasten the reward. Animals on fixed-interval schedules seem to develop a sharp sense of time. After a pellet is delivered, they often stop responding altogether. Then as the end of the interval approaches, responding again picks up, reaching a maximum rate right before reinforcement. Similarly, if you get an e-mail message from your true love every morning at around ten, you might start checking as the hour approaches, then not check again until the next day.

4 On variable-interval schedules, *reinforcement of a response occurs only if a variable amount of time has passed since the previous reinforcer.* For example, the interval might average 10 seconds but will vary from reinforcement to reinforcement. Because the animal or person cannot predict when a reward will come, responding is relatively low but steady. That is why, if your true love's e-mail messages come at unpredictable intervals, you might check your e-mail at a steady, but slow rate—perhaps once every two or three hours. You never know when you will be rewarded with the message "You have mail!"

A basic principle of operant conditioning is that if you want a response to persist after it has been learned, you should reinforce it intermittently, not continuously. If you are continuously giving Harry, your hamster, a treat for pushing a ball with his nose, and then you suddenly stop the reinforcement, Harry will soon stop pushing that ball. Because the change in reinforcement is large, from continuous to none at all, Harry will easily discern the change. But if you have been reinforcing Harry's behavior only every so often, the change will not be so dramatic, and your hungry hamster will keep responding for quite a while. Pigeons, rats, and people on intermittent schedules of reinforcement have responded in the laboratory thousands of times without reinforcement before throwing in the towel, especially when the timing of the reinforcer varies. Animals will sometimes work so hard for an unpredictable, infrequent bit of food that the energy they expend is greater than that gained from the reward; theoretically, they could actually work themselves to death!

It follows that if you want to get rid of a response, you should be careful *not* to reinforce it intermittently. If you are going to extinguish undesirable behavior by ignoring it—a child's tantrums, a friend's midnight phone calls, a parent's unasked-for advice—you must be absolutely consistent in withholding reinforcement (your attention). Otherwise, you will probably only make matters worse. The other person will learn that if he or she keeps up the screaming, calling, or advice giving long enough, it will eventually be rewarded. One of the most common errors people make, from a behavioral point of view, is to reward intermittently the very responses that they would like to eliminate.

Shaping. For a response to be reinforced, it must first occur. But suppose you want to train Harry the hamster to pick up a marble, a child to use a knife and fork properly, or a friend to play terrific tennis. Such behaviors, and most others in everyday life, have almost no probability of appearing spontaneously. You could grow old and gray waiting for them to occur so that you could reinforce them. The operant solution to this dilemma is a procedure called **shaping**.

In shaping, you start by reinforcing a tendency in the right direction, then you gradually require responses that are more and more similar to the final, desired response.

fixed-interval schedule An intermittent schedule of reinforcement in which a reinforcer is delivered for the first response made after a fixed period of time has elapsed since the last reinforcer.

variable-interval schedule An intermittent schedule of reinforcement in which a reinforcer is delivered for a response made after a variable period of time has elapsed since the last reinforcer.

shaping An operant-conditioning procedure in which successive approximations of a desired response are reinforced.

Animals can learn to do some surprising things, with a little help from humans and the use of shaping techniques. Here Marian Breland Bailey, who pioneered the application of operant conditioning principles to animal training, teaches a chicken to peck at a marked cup. She uses an electric feeder to deliver a secondary reinforcer (the sound of food being delivered) and a primary reinforcer (the food). Eventually, the chicken will learn to select the marked cup from a row of identical but unmarked cups.

successive approximations In the operant-conditioning procedure of shaping, behaviors that are ordered in terms of increasing similarity or closeness to the desired response.

The responses that you reinforce on the way to the final one are called **successive approximations**. In the case of Harry and the marble, you might deliver a food pellet if the hamster merely turned toward the marble. Once this response was well established, you might then reward the hamster for taking a step toward the marble. After that, you could reward it for approaching the marble, then for touching the marble, then for putting both paws on the marble, and finally for holding it. With the achievement of each approximation, the next one would become more likely, making it available for reinforcement.

Using shaping and other techniques, Skinner was able to train pigeons to play Ping-Pong with their beaks and to "bowl" in a miniature alley, complete with a wooden ball and tiny bowling pins. Animal trainers routinely use shaping to teach dogs to act as the "eyes" of the blind and to act as the "limbs" of people with spinal-cord injuries by turning on light switches, opening refrigerator doors, and reaching for boxes on supermarket shelves.

Biological Limits on Learning. All principles of operant conditioning, like those of classical conditioning, are limited by an animal's genetic dispositions and physical characteristics; a fish cannot be trained to climb a ladder. That is why operant and classical conditioning procedures always work best when they capitalize on inborn tendencies.

Years ago, two psychologists who became animal trainers, Keller and Marian Breland (1961), learned what happens when you ignore biological constraints on learning. They found that their animals were having trouble learning tasks that should have been easy. For example, a pig was supposed to drop large wooden coins in a box. Instead, the pig would drop the coin, push at it with its snout, throw it in the air, and push at it some more. This odd behavior actually delayed delivery of the reinforcer (food, which is *very* reinforcing to a pig), so it was hard to explain in terms of operant principles. The Brelands finally realized that the pig's rooting instinct—using its snout to uncover and dig up edible roots—was keeping it from learning the task. The Brelands called such a reversion to instinctive behavior *instinctive drift.*

GET ➔ INVOLVED

THE WELL-BEHAVED PET

If you have a pet, you can use operant conditioning to teach your animal something you'd like it to do. Choose something simple. One student we know taught her cat to willingly enter the garage for the night by feeding the animal a special treat there each evening at the same time. Soon the cat was "asking" to get into the garage at bedtime! Another student taught her pastured horse to come to her and submit willingly to the halter by rewarding the animal's occasional approach with a carrot. Soon the horse was approaching regularly and could be put on an intermittent schedule of reinforcement. Be creative, and see whether you can make your pet better behaved or more cooperative in some way.

An animal's natural responses can sometimes interfere with operant learning. For example, it is hard for pigs to learn to drop wooden coins into a "piggy bank" because the animals have a rooting instinct that causes them to lower their snouts and throw the coin in the air. Keller and Marian Breland were able to get around this problem by making the coins heavier so that the pigs could not easily toss them around.

In human beings, too, operant learning is affected by genetics, biology, and the evolutionary history of our species. As we saw in Chapter 3, human children are biologically disposed to learn language without much effort, and they may be disposed to learn some arithmetic operations, as well. Further, temperaments and other inborn dispositions may set limits on how we respond to rewards and punishments. Some researchers, for example, think that people with "antisocial personality disorder" (popularly called "sociopaths") have an inborn nervous-system condition that prevents them from responding to punishment the way other people do, as we will discuss further in Chapter 16.

Skinner: The Man and the Myth

Because of his groundbreaking work on operant conditioning, B. F. Skinner has often been called the greatest of American psychologists. Certainly he is one of the best known—and also one of the most misunderstood. For example, many people (even some psychologists) think that Skinner denied the existence of human consciousness and the value of studying it. In reality, Skinner (1972, 1990) maintained that we *can* study private, internal events—what we call perceptions, emotions, and thoughts—by observing our own sensory responses, the verbal reports of others, and the conditions under which such events occur. Internal events, he said, are as real as any others. But he insisted that thoughts and feelings cannot *explain* behavior; these components of "consciousness," he said, are themselves simply behaviors that occur because of reinforcement and punishment.

Skinner aroused strong passions in both his supporters and his detractors. Perhaps the issue that most provoked and angered people was his insistence that "free will" is an illusion. In contrast to humanist and some religious doctrines that human beings have the power to shape their own destinies, his philosophy promoted the *determinist* view that we are shaped by our environments and our genetic heritage. Skinner

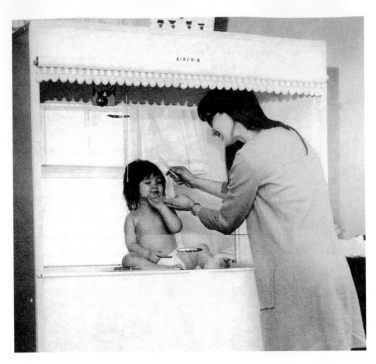

B. F. Skinner invented the Air Crib to provide a more comfortable, less restrictive infant bed than the traditional crib with its bars and blankets. The baby in this Air Crib is Skinner's granddaughter Lisa, with her mother, Julie.

refused to credit personal traits (such as curiosity and perseverance) or mental events (such as goals and motives) for anyone's accomplishments, including his own. Indeed, he regarded himself not as a "self" but as a "repertoire of behaviors" resulting from an environment that encouraged looking, searching, and investigating (Bjork, 1993).

Because Skinner thought the environment should be manipulated to alter behavior, some critics have portrayed him as cold-blooded. One famous controversy regarding Skinner occurred when he invented an enclosed "living space," the Air Crib, for his younger daughter Deborah when she was an infant. This "baby box," as it came to be known, had temperature and humidity controls to eliminate the usual discomforts suffered by babies: heat, cold, wetness, and confinement by blankets and clothing. Skinner believed that to reduce a baby's cries of physical distress and make infant care easier for the parents, you should fix the environment. But people imagined, incorrectly, that the Skinners were leaving their child in the baby box all the time without cuddling and holding her, and rumors later circulated that Deborah had gone insane or killed herself. Actually, both of Skinner's daughters turned out to be perfectly normal and very successful.

Skinner, who was a kind and mild-mannered man, felt that it would be unethical *not* to try to improve human behavior by applying behavioral principles. He practiced what he preached, proposing many ways to improve society and reduce human suffering. In old age, he wrote a book showing how behavioral principles can help the elderly cope with mental and physical losses. At the height of public criticism of Skinner, in 1972, the American Humanist Association recognized his efforts on behalf of humanity by honoring him with its Humanist of the Year Award.

QUICK QUIZ

Can you apply the principles of operant conditioning? In each of the following situations, choose the best alternative, and give your reason for choosing it:

1. You want your 2-year-old to ask for water with a word instead of a grunt. Should you give him water when he says "wa-wa" or wait until his pronunciation improves?

2. Your roommate keeps interrupting your studying even though you have asked her to stop. Should you ignore her completely or occasionally respond for the sake of good manners?

3. Your father, who rarely writes to you, has finally sent a letter. Should you reply quickly or wait a while so he will know how it feels to be ignored?

Answers:

1. You should reinforce "wa-wa," an approximation of *water,* because complex behaviors need to be shaped. 2. From a behavioral view, you should ignore her completely because intermittent reinforcement (attention) could cause her interruptions to persist. 3. If you want to encourage letter writing, you should reply quickly because immediate reinforcement is more effective than delayed reinforcement.

WHAT'S AHEAD

- Why do efforts to "crack down" on wrongdoers often go awry?
- What's the best way to discourage a child from throwing a tantrum?
- Why does paying children for good grades sometimes backfire?

OPERANT CONDITIONING IN REAL LIFE

Operant principles can clear up many mysteries about why people behave as they do, and why, in spite of all the well-meaning motivational seminars they attend or resolutions they make, they have trouble changing when they want to. If life at work and at home remains full of the same old reinforcers, punishers, and discriminative stimuli (a grumpy boss, an unresponsive spouse, a refrigerator stocked with high-fat goodies), any new responses that have been acquired may fail to generalize.

To help people change unwanted, dangerous, or self-defeating habits, behaviorists have carried operant principles out of the laboratory and into the wider world of the classroom, athletic field, prison, mental hospital, nursing home, rehabilitation ward, child-care center, factory, and office. The use of operant techniques (and classical ones) in such real-world settings is called **behavior modification.**

Behavior modification has had some enormous successes. Behaviorists have taught parents to toilet-train their children in only a few sessions (Azrin & Foxx, 1974). They have taught autistic children who have never before spoken to use a vocabulary of several hundred words (Lovaas, 1977). They have trained disturbed and mentally retarded adults to communicate, dress themselves, mingle socially with others, and earn a living (Lent, 1968; McLeod, 1985). They have taught brain-damaged patients to control inappropriate behavior, focus their attention, and improve their language abilities (McGlynn, 1990). And they have helped ordinary folk get rid of unwanted habits, such as smoking and nail biting, or acquire wanted ones, such as practicing the piano or studying.

Behavioral principles have many practical applications. Monkeys like this one have been trained to assist their paralyzed owners by performing such everyday tasks as picking up objects, opening doors, helping with feeding, and turning the pages of books.

Yet when people try to apply the principles of conditioning to commonplace problems, their efforts sometimes miss the mark. Both punishment and reinforcement have their pitfalls, as we are about to see.

The Pros and Cons of Punishment

In his novel *Walden Two* (1948, 1976), Skinner imagined a utopia in which reinforcers were used so wisely that people rarely misbehaved. Unfortunately, we do not live in a utopia; bad habits and antisocial acts abound, and we are faced with how to get rid of them.

An obvious approach might seem to be punishment. Most Western countries have banned the physical punishment of schoolchildren by principals and teachers, but in many parts of the United States, schools still permit it for disruptiveness, vandalism, and other misbehavior. The United States is also far more likely than any other developed country to jail its citizens for nonviolent crimes such as drug

behavior modification The application of conditioning techniques to teach new responses or to reduce or eliminate maladaptive or problematic behavior.

use and to enact the ultimate punishment—the death penalty—for violent crimes. And of course in daily life, people punish one another constantly, by yelling, scolding, fining, and sulking. Does all this punishment work?

When Punishment Works. Sometimes punishment is unquestionably effective. Some highly disturbed children have been known to chew their own fingers to the bone, stick objects in their eyes, or tear out their hair. You cannot ignore such behavior because the children will seriously injure themselves. You cannot respond with concern and affection because you may unwittingly reward the behavior. But immediately punishing the self-destructive behavior eliminates it (Lovaas, 1977; Lovaas, Schreibman, & Koegel, 1974). Mild punishers, such as a spray of water in the face or even a firm "No!", are often just as effective as strong ones, such as electric shock.

Punishment can also deter some young criminals from repeating their offenses. Patricia Brennan and Sarnoff Mednick (1994) examined data on all Danish men born between 1944 and 1947 (nearly 29,000 men), focusing on repeat arrests (recidivism) through age 26. After any given arrest, punishment reduced rates of subsequent arrests for both minor and serious crimes (though recidivism still remained fairly high). Contrary to the researchers' expectations, however, the severity of punishment made no difference: Fines and probation were about as effective as jail time. What mattered most was the *consistency* of the punishment. This is understandable: When punishment is inconsistent—when lawbreakers sometimes get away with their crimes—their behavior is intermittently reinforced and therefore becomes resistant to extinction.

These results show that punishment can reduce recidivism, but they also show why harsh sentencing laws and simplistic efforts to "crack down" on wrongdoers often fail or even backfire. Despite its high incarceration rates, the United States has a far higher rate of violent crime than other developed countries do; and crime rates in the various states show no consistent correlation with rates of incarceration (Currie, 1998). Why? Brennan and Sarnoff point out that in the United States, young offenders are punished far less consistently than they are in Denmark, often because prosecutors, juries, and judges do not want to condemn them to mandatory prison terms. Because the courts have no other options for punishment, they may merely admonish the offenders and set them free. Ironically, then, policies that mandate severe punishment can actually lead to ineffective punishment—or to no punishment at all.

When Punishment Fails. What about punishment that occurs every day, in families, schools, and workplaces? Laboratory and field studies find that it, too, often fails, for several reasons:

1 *People often administer punishment inappropriately or mindlessly.* They swing in a blind rage or shout things they don't mean, applying punishment so broadly that it covers all sorts of irrelevant behaviors. And even when people are not carried away by anger, they often misunderstand the proper application of punishment. One student told us his parents used to punish their children before leaving them alone for the evening because of all the naughty things they were *going* to do. Naturally, the children did not bother to behave like angels.

2 *The recipient of punishment often responds with anxiety, fear, or rage.* Through a process of classical conditioning, these emotional side effects may then generalize to the entire situation in which the punishment occurs—the place, the person

EXAMINE THE EVIDENCE

The response to wrongdoing is often punishment. People assume that fines, long prison terms, yelling, and spanking are good ways to get rid of undesirable behavior. What does the evidence show?

Many harried parents habitually resort to physical punishment without being aware of its many negative consequences for themselves and their children. Based on your reading of this chapter, what alternatives does this mother have?

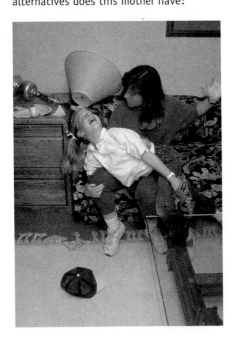

delivering the punishment, and the circumstances. These negative emotional reactions can create more problems than the punishment solves. A teenager who has been severely punished may strike back or run away. A spouse who is constantly abused will feel bitter and resentful and is likely to retaliate with small acts of hostility. Being physically punished in childhood is a risk factor for depression, low self-esteem, violent behavior, and many other problems (Barrish, 1996; Straus & Kantor, 1994; Weiss et al., 1992).

3 *The effectiveness of punishment is often temporary, depending heavily on the presence of the punishing person or circumstances.* All of us can probably remember some transgressions of childhood that we never dared commit when our parents were around but that we promptly resumed as soon as they were gone. All we learned was not to get caught.

4 *Most misbehavior is hard to punish immediately.* Punishment, like reward, works best if it quickly follows a response. But outside the laboratory, rapid punishment is often hard to achieve, and during the delay, the behavior may be reinforced many times. For example, if you punish your dog when you get home for getting into the doggie treats and eating them all up, the punishment will not do any good: Your pet's misbehavior has already been reinforced by all those delicious goodies.

5 *Punishment conveys little information.* If it immediately follows the misbehavior, punishment may tell the recipient what *not* to do. But it does not communicate what the person (or animal) *should* do. For example, spanking a toddler for messing in her pants will not teach her to use the potty chair, and scolding a student for learning slowly will not teach him to learn more quickly.

6 *An action intended to punish may instead be reinforcing because it brings attention.* Indeed, in some cases, angry attention may be just what the offender is after. If a mother yells at a child who is throwing a tantrum, the very act of yelling may give him what he wants—a reaction from her. In the school-room, teachers who scold children in front of other students, thus putting them in the limelight, often unwittingly reward the very misbehavior they are trying to eliminate.

Why do so many people ignore warning and threats of punishment?

Because of these drawbacks, most psychologists believe that punishment, especially severe punishment, is a poor way to eliminate unwanted behavior in most situations. When punishment must be used, these guidelines should be kept in mind: (1) It should avoid physical abuse; for example, parents can use "time-outs" and loss of privileges instead of hitting; (2) it should be accompanied by information about what kind of behavior would be appropriate; and (3) it should be followed, whenever possible, by the reinforcement of desirable behavior.

Fortunately, a good alternative to punishment exists: extinction of the responses you want to discourage. Of course, the simplest form of extinction—ignoring the behavior—is often hard to carry out. It is not easy to ignore a child nagging for a cookie before dinner, a roommate interrupting your concentration, or a dog barking its lungs out. And ignoring the behavior is not always appropriate. A teacher cannot ignore a child who is hitting a playmate. The dog owner who ignores Fido's backyard barking may soon hear "barking" of another sort from the neighbors. A parent whose child is a video-game addict cannot ignore the behavior, because playing video games is rewarding to the child. One solution: Combine extinction of undesirable acts with reinforcement of alternative ones. For example, the parent of a video-game addict might ignore the child's pleas for "just one more game" and at the same time praise the child for doing something else that is incompatible with video-game playing, such as reading or playing basketball.

The Problems with Reward

So far, we have been praising the virtues of reinforcement. But like punishers, rewards do not always work as expected. Let's look at two complications that arise when people try to use them.

DON'T OVERSIMPLIFY

Because reinforcers increase desirable behavior, some teachers give out high grades whether students deserve them or not. Does this practice improve the students' performance or self-esteem? What do these rewards actually reinforce?

Misuse of Rewards. Suppose you are a fourth-grade teacher, and a student has just turned in a paper full of grammatical and punctuation errors. This child has little self-confidence and is easily discouraged. What should you do?

Many people think you should give the paper a high mark anyway, in order to bolster the child's self-esteem. Indeed, teachers everywhere are handing out lavish praise and high grades in hopes that students' academic performance will improve as they learn to "feel good about themselves." One obvious result has been grade inflation at all levels of education. In many colleges and universities, Cs, which once meant "average" or "satisfactory," are nearly extinct.

The problem, from a behavioral point of view, is that to be effective, rewards *must be tied to the behavior you are trying to increase.* When rewards are dispensed indiscriminately, they become meaningless because they no longer reinforce desired behavior. As behavioral principles would predict, when teachers or parents praise mediocre work, that is just what they get (Kohn, 1993). Lillian Katz (1993), a professor of early childhood education, argues that real self-esteem does not come from "cheap success in a succession of trivial tasks," or from phony flattery, good stars, or happy faces drawn by the teacher. It emerges from effort, persistence, and the gradual acquisition of skills, and it is nurtured by a teacher's genuine appreciation of the *content* of the child's work (Damon, 1995). In the case of the child who turned in a poorly written paper, the teacher can praise its strengths but

I CAN'T ACTUALLY 'READ' IT—BUT I'M TOLD IT MAKES SPECIFIC REFERENCE TO MY OUTSTANDING ACHIEVEMENT IN 'SELF-ESTEEM STUDIES'...

GABLE
THE GLOBE AND MAIL
Toronto
CANADA

should also give feedback on the paper's weaknesses and show the child how to correct them. (In Chapter 12, we discuss how this approach increases work motivation, and in Chapter 13, how it increases a person's feelings of competence.)

Why Rewards Can Backfire. A little girl we know came home from school one day in a huff after her teacher announced that good work would be rewarded with play money that could later be exchanged for privileges. "Doesn't she think I can learn without being bribed?" the child asked her mother indignantly.

This child's reaction illustrates another problem in the use of reinforcers. Most of our examples of operant conditioning have involved **extrinsic reinforcers**, which come from an outside source and are not inherently related to the activity being reinforced. Money, praise, gold stars, applause, hugs, and thumbs-up signs are all extrinsic reinforcers. But people (and probably some other animals, too) also work for **intrinsic reinforcers**, such as enjoyment of the task and the satisfaction of accomplishment. As psychologists have applied operant conditioning in real-world settings, they have found that extrinsic reinforcement sometimes becomes too much of a good thing: If you focus on it exclusively, it can kill the pleasure of doing something for its own sake.

Consider what happened when psychologists gave nursery-school children the chance to draw with felt-tipped pens (Lepper, Greene, & Nisbett, 1973). The children already liked this activity and readily took it up during free play. First, the researchers recorded how long each child spontaneously played with the pens. Then they told some of the children that if they would draw with felt-tipped pens for a man who had come "to see what kinds of pictures boys and girls like to draw with Magic Markers," they would get a prize, a "Good Player Award" complete with gold seal and ribbon. After drawing for six minutes, each child got the award, as promised. Other children did not expect a reward and were not given one.

A week later, the researchers again observed the children's free play. Those children who had expected and received a reward were spending much less time with the pens than they had before the start of the experiment. In contrast, children who were not given an award continued to show as much interest in playing with the pens as they had initially, as you can see in Figure 7.7. Similar results occurred when older children were or were not rewarded for working on academic tasks.

Because promised rewards (otherwise known as bribes) can be effective in the short term and can sometimes increase test scores by boosting students' motivation, some educators advocate using more of them. But motivation to do well on a test is not the same thing as motivation to learn. In a study of 9-year-olds and their mothers, half of the mothers were told to encourage learning for the intrinsic pleasure of it, and half were told to reward high grades and punish low ones. A year later, those in the first group had higher motivation and better school performance. For those in the second group, however, extrinsic rewards and punishments actually seemed to impede academic achievement (Gottfried, Fleming, & Gottfried, 1994).

Why should extrinsic rewards undermine the pleasure of doing something for its own sake? One possibility is that when we are paid for an activity, we interpret it as work. It is as if we say to ourselves, "I'm doing this because I'm being paid for it. Since I'm being paid, it must be something I wouldn't do if I didn't have to." When the reward is withdrawn, we refuse to "work" any longer. Or perhaps, because we regard extrinsic rewards as controlling, they reduce our sense of autonomy and choice

extrinsic reinforcers Reinforcers that are not inherently related to the activity being reinforced, such as money, prizes, and praise.

intrinsic reinforcers Reinforcers that are inherently related to the activity being reinforced, such as enjoyment of the task and the satisfaction of accomplishment.

FIGURE 7.7
TURNING PLAY INTO WORK

Extrinsic rewards can sometimes reduce the intrinsic pleasure of an activity. When preschoolers were promised a prize for drawing with felt-tipped pens, the behavior temporarily increased. But after the children got their prizes, they spent less time with the pens than they had before the study began.

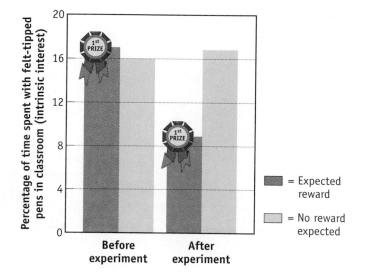

= Expected reward

= No reward expected

GET → INVOLVED

WHAT'S REINFORCING YOUR BEHAVIOR?

Which of your actions are controlled by extrinsic reinforcers and which by intrinsic ones? Fill in this checklist:

Activity	Reinforcers mostly extrinsic	Reinforcers mostly intrinsic	Reinforcers about equally extrinsic and intrinsic
Studying	————	————	————
Housework	————	————	————
Worship	————	————	————
Grooming	————	————	————
Job	————	————	————
Dating	————	————	————
Attending class	————	————	————
Reading unrelated to school	————	————	————
Sports	————	————	————
Cooking	————	————	————

Is there an area of your life in which you would like intrinsic reinforcement to play a larger role? What can you do to make that happen?

"That is the correct answer, Billy, but I'm afraid you don't win anything for it."

("I guess I should just do what I'm told to do—and *only* what I'm told to do") (Deci & Ryan, 1987). A third, more behavioral explanation is that extrinsic reinforcement sometimes raises the rate of responding above some optimal, enjoyable level. Then the activity really does become work.

However, extrinsic rewards do not always weaken the impact of intrinsic ones. If you get money, a high grade, or a trophy for doing a task *well*, rather than for just doing it, your intrinsic motivation is not likely to decline (Dickinson, 1989; Eisenberger & Cameron, 1996, 1998). If you have always been crazy about reading or playing the banjo, you will probably keep reading or playing even when you are not getting a grade or applause for doing so (Mawhinney, 1990).

So, what is the take-home message about extrinsic rewards? First, that sometimes they are necessary: Few people would trudge off to work every morning if they never got paid; and in the classroom, teachers may need to offer incentives to unmotivated students. Second: We should use extrinsic rewards sparingly, so that intrinsic pleasure in an activity can blossom. As one mother wrote in *Newsweek,* children need to discover for themselves "the joy of music from songs, the power of mathematics from counting and all of human wisdom from reading" (Skreslet, 1987). And finally, educators and employers can avoid the trap of either-or thinking by recognizing that most people do their best when they get tangible rewards *and* when they have interesting, challenging, and varied kinds of work to do.

Effective behavior modification, as you can see, is not only a science but an art. In "Taking Psychology with You," we offer additional guidelines for mastering that art.

QUICK QUIZ

A. According to behavioral principles, what is happening here?

1. An adolescent whose parents have hit him for minor transgressions since he was small runs away from home.

2. A young woman whose parents paid her to clean her room while she was growing up is a slob when she moves to her own apartment.

3. Two parents scold their young daughter every time they catch her sucking her thumb. The thumb sucking continues anyway.

B. In a fee-for-service system of health care, doctors are paid for each visit by a patient or for each service performed; the longer the visit, the higher the fee. In contrast, some health maintenance organizations (HMOs) pay their doctors a fixed amount per patient for an entire year. If the amount spent is less, the physician gets a bonus, and in some systems, if the amount spent is more, the physician must pay a penalty. Given what you know about operant conditioning, what are the advantages and disadvantages of each system?

Answers:

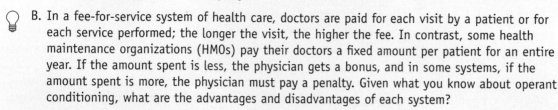

A. 1. The physical punishment was painful, and through a process of classical conditioning, the situation in which it occurred also became unpleasant. Because escape from an unpleasant stimulus is negatively reinforcing, the boy ran away. 2. Extrinsic reinforcers are no longer available, and room-cleaning behavior has been extinguished. Also, extrinsic rewards may have dis-placed the intrinsic satisfaction of having a tidy room. 3. Punishment has failed, possibly because it rewards thumb sucking with attention or because thumb sucking still brings the child pleasure whenever the parents are not around. B. In a fee-for-service system, the doctor is likely to provide the attention and tests that ill patients need. However, this system also rewards doctors for unnecessary tests and patient visits, contributing to the explosion in health-care costs. The policies of the HMOs help contain these costs, but because doctors are rewarded for reducing costs and in some cases penalized for running up charges, some patients may not get the attention or services they need.

WHAT'S AHEAD

- **How might watching violence on TV make (some) people more aggressive?**
- **Why do two people often learn different lessons from exactly the same experience?**

SOCIAL-COGNITIVE THEORIES

For half a century, most American learning theories held that learning could be explained by specifying the behavioral "ABCs"—*antecedents* (events preceding behavior), *behaviors,* and *consequences.* Yet even during the early glory years of behaviorism, a few behaviorists rebelled against explanations of behavior that relied solely on conditioning principles.

In the 1940s, two social scientists proposed a modification they called *social-learning theory* (Dollard & Miller, 1950). Most human learning, they argued, is acquired by observing other people in a social context, rather than through standard conditioning procedures. By the 1960s and 1970s, social-learning theory was in full bloom, and a new element had been added: the human capacity for higher-level cognitive processes. Its proponents agreed with behaviorists that human beings, along with the rat and the rabbit, are subject to the laws of operant and classical conditioning. But they added that human beings, unlike the rat and the rabbit, are full of attitudes, beliefs, and expectations that affect the way they acquire information, make decisions, reason, and solve problems. These mental processes affect what individuals will do at any given moment and also, more generally, the personality traits they develop.

Because of this emphasis on mental processes, one leading theorist, Walter Mischel, has called his approach *cognitive social-learning theory* (Mischel, 1973; Mischel & Shoda, 1995); and another, Albert Bandura, calls his *social-cognitive theory* (Bandura, 1986). We will use the general term **social-cognitive theories** to include all modern social-learning approaches (Barone, Maddux, & Snyder, 1997).

Learning by Observing

Late one night, a friend who lives in a rural area was awakened by a loud clattering and banging. Her whole family raced outside to find the source of the commotion. A raccoon had knocked over a "raccoon-proof" garbage can and seemed to be demonstrating to an assembly of other raccoons how to open it: If you jump up and down on the can's side, the lid will pop off.

According to our friend, the observing raccoons learned from this episode how to open stubborn garbage cans, and the observing humans learned how smart raccoons can be. In short, they all benefited from **observational learning**: learning by watching what others do and what happens to them for doing it.

Behaviorists have always acknowledged the importance of observational learning, which they call *vicarious conditioning*, and have tried to explain it in stimulus-response terms. But social-cognitive theorists believe that in human beings, observational learning cannot be fully understood without taking into account the thought processes of the learner (Meltzoff & Gopnik, 1993). They emphasize the knowledge that results when a person sees a model—another person—behaving in certain ways and experiencing the consequences (Bandura, 1977).

None of us would last long without observational learning. We would have to learn to avoid oncoming cars by walking into traffic and suffering the consequences or learn to swim by jumping into a deep pool and flailing around. Learning would be not only dangerous but inefficient. Parents and teachers would be busy 24 hours a day shaping children's behavior. Bosses would have to stand over their employees' desks, rewarding every little link in the complex behavioral chains we call typing, report writing, and accounting.

Many years ago, Albert Bandura and his colleagues showed just how important observational learning is, especially for children who are learning the rules of social behavior (Bandura, Ross, & Ross, 1963). The researchers had nursery-school children watch a short film of two men, Rocky and Johnny, playing with toys. (Apparently, the children did not think this behavior was the least bit odd.) In the film, Johnny refuses to share his toys, and Rocky responds by clobbering him. Rocky's actions are rewarded because he winds up with all the toys. Poor Johnny sits dejectedly in the corner, while Rocky marches off with a sack full of his loot and a hobbyhorse under his arm. After viewing the film, each child was left alone for 20 minutes in a playroom full of toys, including some of the items shown in the film. Watching through a one-way mirror, the researchers found that the children were much more aggressive in their play than a control group that had not seen the film. Some children imitated Rocky almost exactly. At the end of the session, one little girl even asked the experimenter for a sack!

Of course, children imitate positive activities, too. Matt Groening, the creator of the TV cartoon show *The Simpsons*, decided it would be funny if the Simpsons' 8-year-old daughter Lisa played the baritone sax. Sure enough, across the country, little girls began imitating her. Cynthia Sikes, a saxophone teacher in New York, told *The New York Times* (January 14, 1996) that "When the show started, I got an influx of girls

social-cognitive theories Theories that emphasize how behavior is learned and maintained through observation and imitation of others, positive consequences, and cognitive processes such as plans, expectations, and beliefs.

observational learning A process in which an individual learns new responses by observing the behavior of another (a model) rather than through direct experience; sometimes called *vicarious conditioning*.

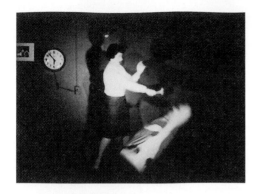

Adults and children alike learn through observation. In studies by Albert Bandura and his colleagues, children watched films of an adult kicking, punching, and hammering on a big rubber doll (top). Later, the children imitated the adult's behavior, some of them almost exactly.

coming up to me saying, 'I want to play the saxophone because Lisa Simpson plays the saxophone.'" And Groening says his mail regularly includes photos of girls holding up their saxophones.

Behavior and the Mind

Early behaviorists liked to compare the mind to an engineer's hypothetical "black box," a device whose workings must be inferred because they cannot be observed directly. To them, the box contained irrelevant wiring; it was enough to know that pushing a button on the box would produce a predictable response.

But even as early as the 1930s, a few behaviorists could not resist peeking into that black box. Edward Tolman (1938) committed virtual heresy at the time by noting that his rats, when pausing at turning points in a maze, seemed to be *deciding* which way to go. Moreover, the animals sometimes seemed to be learning even without any reinforcement. What, he wondered, was going on in their little rat brains that might account for this puzzle?

In a classic experiment, Tolman and C. H. Honzik (1930) placed three groups of rats in mazes and observed their behavior each day for more than two weeks. The rats in Group 1 always found food at the end of the maze. Group 2 never found food. Group 3 found no food for ten days but then received food on the eleventh. The Group 1 rats, which had been reinforced with food, quickly learned to head straight for the end of the maze without going down blind alleys, whereas Group 2 rats did not learn to go to the end. But the Group 3 rats were different. For ten days they appeared to follow no particular route. Then, on the eleventh day, when food was introduced, they quickly learned to run to the end of the maze. By the next day, they were doing as well as Group 1, which had been rewarded from the beginning (see Figure 7.8).

FIGURE 7.8
LATENT LEARNING

In a classic experiment, rats that always found food in a maze made fewer and fewer errors in reaching the food (green curve). Rats that never received food showed little improvement (purple curve). Rats in a third group got no food for ten days, and then were given food on the eleventh. These animals showed rapid improvement from then on, quickly equaling the performance of the rats that had received food from the start. This result suggests that learning involves cognitive changes that can occur in the absence of reinforcement and that may not be acted on until a reinforcer becomes available (Tolman & Honzik, 1930).

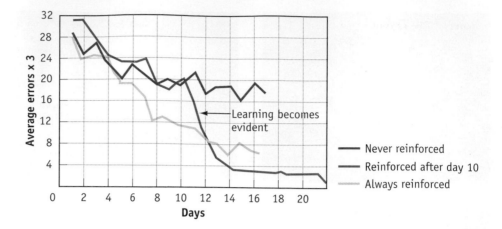

Group 3 had demonstrated **latent learning**, learning that is not immediately expressed. A great deal of human learning also remains latent until circumstances allow or require it to be expressed. A driver finds her way to Fourth and Kumquat Streets using a new route she has never used before. A little boy observes a parent setting the table or tightening a screw but does not act on this learning for years; then he finds he knows how to do these things, even though he has never done them before.

Latent learning not only occurs without any obvious reinforcer; it also raises questions about what, exactly, is learned during learning. In the Tolman and Honzik study, the rats who did not get any food until the eleventh day seemed to have acquired a mental representation of the maze. Similarly, the driver taking a new route can do so because she already knows how the city is laid out. More generally, according to social-cognitive theories, what we learn in both observational and latent learning is not a specific response, but *knowledge* about responses and their consequences. We learn how the world is organized, which paths lead to which places, and which actions can produce which payoffs. This knowledge permits us to be creative and flexible in reaching our goals.

Social-cognitive theories also emphasize the importance of people's *perceptions* in what they learn: perceptions of the models they observe and also perceptions of themselves (Bandura, 1994). Because people differ in their attitudes, expectations, and perceptions, they can live through the same event and come away with entirely different lessons from it. All siblings know this. One may regard being grounded by their father as evidence of his all-around meanness, and another may see the same behavior as evidence of his care and concern for his children.

Individual differences in perceptions and interpretations help explain why violent television programs do not have the same impact on all children. As the Rocky and Johnny findings would predict, some children do imitate the incessant aggression they observe on television and in movies (APA Commission on Violence and Youth, 1993; Eron, 1995). But not all of them do; some just are not interested and others find violence too scary or stupid to watch.

Behaviorists would say that we acquire habitual ways of behaving because they have been rewarded over a lifetime. Social-cognitive theorists, however, maintain that our learned habits and beliefs eventually acquire a life of their own, coming to exert their own effects on behavior (see Chapter 13). In fact, internalized beliefs, perceptions, and goals may have a greater impact than external rewards and punishers, as when people sacrifice money and love for the sake of a great ambition or persist in the quest of a life's dream in spite of constant setbacks and losses.

latent learning A form of learning that is not immediately expressed in an overt response; it occurs without obvious reinforcement.

Today, most psychologists accept the social-cognitive emphasis on mental processes, believing that people act as they do in part because of their beliefs, expectations, and perceptions. To the true behaviorist, however, cognitive explanations are misleading fictions, and nothing is to be gained by using them; people act as they do because of reinforcers and punishers in the environment. As behaviorist William Baum (1994) wrote, "I no more have a mind than I have a fairy godmother. I can talk to you about my mind or about my fairy godmother; that cannot make either of them less fictional. No one has ever seen either one . . . such talk is no help in a science."

The debates between behaviorists and cognitive psychologists over the nature of learning promise to continue. In practice, however, behavioral and cognitive approaches are often combined. Many therapists, for example, combine behavioral principles with cognitive findings to treat people in psychotherapy (see Chapter 17).

QUICK QUIZ

How latent is your learning?

1. After watching her teenage sister put on some lipstick, a little girl takes a lipstick and applies it to her own lips. She has acquired this behavior through a process of _____.

2. Your friend asks you to meet her at a new restaurant across town. You have never been to this specific address, but you find your way there anyway because you have experienced _____ learning.

3. To a social-cognitive theorist, the phenomenon of latent learning shows that we learn not specific responses but rather _____.

Answers:

1. observational learning   2. latent   3. knowledge about responses and their consequences

The behavioral and social-cognitive approaches to learning share a fundamental optimism about the possibilities of change for individuals and societies. To modify self-defeating, inappropriate, or dangerous behavior, these approaches suggest, we can do more than just sit around hoping that people will magically have a change of heart. Instead, we can focus on changing the reinforcers, role models, and media messages that affect people's attitudes and actions. To improve ourselves and the communities we live in, we can use learning principles to fashion better environments for ourselves, our families, and our fellow human beings.

For example, why are so many affluent people in developed nations bored and depressed, even though they have every material comfort? Toward the end of his life, Skinner (1987) offered one reason: The pleasures of consumerism—shopping, watching television, buying a nice car—tend to drive out the intrinsic satisfactions of personal accomplishment. "People look at beautiful things, listen to beautiful music, and watch exciting entertainments," he wrote, "but the only behavior reinforced is looking, listening, and watching." Too rarely, said Skinner, are reinforcers given for creativity, risk, or active participation. Too rarely do people get an opportunity to take pride in the products of their work, or to exercise initiative in their choice of pleasures.

In Skinner's science-fiction novel *Walden Two*, the main character, Frazier, exclaims. "The one fact that I would cry from every housetop is this: The Good Life is waiting for us—here and now! We have the necessary techniques, both material and psychological, to create a full and satisfying life for everyone." Frazier was overstating his case, which was his prerogative as a character in a utopian novel. But his take-home message was right: that research on the principles of learning can have a powerful effect on our lives, if we use those principles wisely.

TAKING PSYCHOLOGY WITH YOU

SHAPE UP!

Operant conditioning can seem deceptively simple—a few rewards here, a bit of shaping there, and you're done. In practice, though, behavior modification can be full of unwanted surprises, even in the hands of experts. Here are a few things to keep in mind if you want to modify someone's behavior.

■ *Accentuate the positive.* Most people notice bad behavior more than good and therefore miss opportunities to use reinforcers. Parents, for example, often scold a child for bedwetting but fail to give praise for dry sheets in the morning; or they punish a child for poor grades but fail to reward studying.

■ *Reinforce small improvements.* A common error is to withhold reinforcement until behavior is perfect (which may be never). Has your child's grade in math improved from a D to a C? Has your favorite date, who is usually an awful cook, managed to serve up a half-decent omelette? Has your messy roommate left some dirty dishes in the sink but vacuumed the rug? It's probably time for a reinforcer. On the other hand, you don't want to overdo praise or give it insincerely. Gushing about every tiny step in the right direction will cause your praise to lose its value, and soon nothing less than a standing ovation will do.

■ *Find the right reinforcers.* You may have to experiment a bit to find which reinforcers a person (or animal) actually wants. In general, it is good to use a variety of reinforcers because the same one used again and again can get boring. Reinforcers, by the way, do not have to be *things*. You can also use valued activities, such as going out to dinner, to reinforce other behavior.

■ *Always examine what you are reinforcing.* It is easy to reinforce undesirable behavior just by responding to it. Suppose someone is always yelling at you at the slightest provocation, and you want the shouting to stop. If you respond to it at all, whether by crying, apologizing, or yelling back, you are likely to reinforce it. An alternative might be to explain in a calm voice that you will henceforth not respond to complaints unless they are communicated without yelling—and then, if the yelling continues, walk away. When the person does speak civilly, you can reward this behavior with your attention and goodwill.

■ *Analyze the reasons for a person's undesirable behavior before responding to it.* A child screaming in a supermarket may be saying, "I'm going out of my head with boredom. Help!" A lover who sulks may be saying, "I'm not sure you really care about me; I'm frightened." Once you understand the purpose of someone's behavior, you may be more effective in dealing with it.

These guidelines apply to your own behavior, as well. Assume, for example, that you want to get yourself to study more. Here are some behavioral strategies for increasing the time you spend with your books:

■ *Analyze the situation.* Are there circumstances that keep you from studying, such as a friend who is always pressuring you to go out or a rock band that practices next door? If so, you need to change the discriminative stimuli in your environment during study periods. Try to find a comfortable, cheerful, quiet, well-lit place. Not only will you concentrate better, but you may also have positive emotional responses to the environment that may generalize to the activity of studying.

■ *Set realistic goals.* Goals should be demanding but achievable. If a goal is too vague, as in "I'm going to work harder," you don't know what behavioral changes are necessary to reach it or how to know when you have done so (what does "harder" mean?). If your goal is focused, as in "I am going to study two hours every evening instead of one" or "I will read 25 pages instead of 15," you have specified both a course of action and a goal you can achieve (and reward).

■ *Keep records.* Chart your progress in some way, perhaps by making a graph. This will keep you honest, and the progress you see on the graph will serve as a secondary reinforcer.

■ *Don't punish yourself.* If you did not study enough last week, don't brood about it or berate yourself with self-defeating thoughts, such as "I'll never be a good student" or "I'm a failure." Think about the coming week instead.

Above all, be patient. Shaping behavior is a creative skill that takes time to learn. Like Rome, new habits cannot be built in a day.

SUMMARY

1. Research on *learning* has been heavily influenced by *behaviorism*, which accounts for behavior in terms of observable events, without reference to such hypothetical mental entities as "mind" or "will." Behaviorists have focused on two types of *conditioning*: classical conditioning and operant conditioning.

CLASSICAL CONDITIONING

2. *Classical conditioning* was first studied by Russian physiologist Ivan Pavlov. In this type of learning, when a neutral stimulus is paired with an *unconditioned stimulus (US)* that elicits some reflexive *unconditioned response (UR)*, the neutral stimulus comes to elicit a similar or related response. The neutral stimulus is then called a *conditioned stimulus (CS)*, and the response it elicits, a *conditioned response (CR)*. Nearly any kind of involuntary response can become a CR.

3. In *extinction*, the conditioned stimulus is repeatedly presented without the unconditioned stimulus, and the conditioned response eventually disappears. In *higher-order conditioning*, a neutral stimulus becomes a conditioned stimulus by being paired with an already established conditioned stimulus. In *stimulus generalization*, after a stimulus becomes a conditioned stimulus for some response, other, similar stimuli may produce the same reaction. In *stimulus discrimination*, different responses are made to stimuli that resemble the conditioned stimulus in some way.

4. Many theorists believe that what an animal or person learns in classical conditioning is not just an association between the unconditioned and conditioned stimulus, but information conveyed by one stimulus about another. They cite evidence that the neutral stimulus does not become a CS unless it reliably signals or predicts the US.

CLASSICAL CONDITIONING IN REAL LIFE

5. Classical conditioning may account for positive emotional responses to particular objects and events; fears and phobias; the acquisition of likes and dislikes; and reactions to medical treatments and placebos. John Watson showed how fears may be learned and then unlearned through a process of *counterconditioning*.

OPERANT CONDITIONING

6. In *operant conditioning*, behavior becomes more likely to occur or less so, depending on its consequences. Responses are generally not reflexive and are more complex than in classical conditioning. Research in this area is closely associated with B. F. Skinner, who called his approach "radical behaviorism."

7. In the Skinnerian analysis, a response ("operant") can lead to neutral, reinforcing, or punishing consequences. *Reinforcement* strengthens or increases the probability of a response. *Punishment* weakens or decreases the probability of a response. Immediate consequences usually have a greater effect on a response than do delayed consequences.

8. Reinforcers are called *primary* when they are naturally reinforcing (e.g., because they satisfy a biological need) and *secondary* when they have acquired their ability to strengthen a response through association with other reinforcers. A similar distinction is made for punishers.

9. Reinforcement (and punishment) may be positive or negative, depending on whether the consequence involves a stimulus that is presented, or one that is removed or avoided. In *positive reinforcement*, something pleasant follows a response; in *negative reinforcement*, something unpleasant is removed. In *positive punishment*, something unpleasant follows the response; in *negative punishment*, something pleasant is removed.

10. Behaviorists have shown that *extinction, stimulus generalization,* and *stimulus discrimination* occur in operant as well as in classical conditioning.

11. The pattern of responding in operant conditioning depends in part on the *schedule of reinforcement*. *Continuous reinforcement* leads to the most rapid learning, but *intermittent*, or *partial, reinforcement* makes a response resistant to extinction (and therefore helps account for the persistence of superstitious rituals). Intermittent schedules deliver a reinforcer after a given amount of time has passed since the last reinforcer (*interval schedules*) or after a given number of responses are made (*ratio schedules*). Such schedules may be *fixed* or *variable*. One of the most common errors people make is to reward intermittently the responses they would like to eliminate.

12. *Shaping* is used to train behaviors with a low probability of occurring spontaneously. Reinforcers are given for *successive approximations* of the desired response, until the desired response is achieved.

13. Biology places limits on what an animal or person can learn through operant conditioning.

OPERANT CONDITIONING IN REAL LIFE

14. *Behavior modification*, the application of conditioning principles, has been used successfully in many settings, but reinforcement and punishment both have their pitfalls.

15. Punishment, when used properly, can be effective in discouraging undesirable behavior, including criminal behavior. But it is often misused and may have unintended consequences. It is often administered inappropriately because of the emotion of the moment; it may produce rage and fear; its effects are often only temporary; it is hard to administer immediately; it conveys little information about the kind of behavior that is desired; and it may provide attention that is rewarding. Extinction of undesirable behavior, combined with reinforcement of desired behavior, is generally preferable to the use of punishment.

16. Reinforcers can also be misused. Rewards that are given out indiscriminately, as in efforts to raise children's self-esteem, do not reinforce desirable behavior. An exclusive reliance on *extrinsic reinforcement* can sometimes undermine the power of *intrinsic reinforcement*. But money and praise do not usually interfere with intrinsic pleasure when a person is rewarded for succeeding or making progress rather than for merely participating in an activity, or when a person is already highly interested in the activity.

SOCIAL-COGNITIVE THEORIES

17. The 1960s and 1970s saw the increased influence of *social-cognitive theories* of learning, which focus on observational learning and the role played by beliefs, interpretations of events, and other cognitions. In *observational learning*, the learner imitates the behavior of a model. In *latent learning*, no obvious reinforcer may be present during learning, and a response is not expressed until later. Social-cognitive theorists argue that in these types of learning, knowledge, rather than a specific response, is acquired. Because people differ in their perceptions and beliefs, they may learn different lessons from the same event or situation.

KEY TERMS

learning 225

behaviorism 225

conditioning 225

unconditioned stimulus (US) 227

unconditioned response (UR) 227

conditioned stimulus (CS) 228

conditioned response (CR) 228

classical conditioning 228

extinction (in classical conditioning) 228

spontaneous recovery 229

higher-order conditioning 229

stimulus generalization (in classical conditioning) 230

stimulus discrimination (in classical conditioning) 230

phobia 233

counterconditioning 233

operant conditioning 236

reinforcement/reinforcers 237

punishment/punishers 237

primary reinforcers/punishers 238

secondary reinforcers/punishers 238

positive and negative reinforcement and punishment 238

Skinner box 240

extinction (in operant conditioning) 241

stimulus generalization (in operant conditioning) 241

stimulus discrimination (in operant conditioning) 241

discriminative stimulus 241

continuous reinforcement 241

intermittent (partial) schedule of reinforcement 241

fixed-ratio schedule 242

variable-ratio schedule 242

fixed-interval schedule 243

variable-interval schedule 243

shaping 243

successive approximations 244

instinctive drift 244

free will vs. determinism 245

behavior modification 247

extrinsic/intrinsic reinforcers 251

behavioral "ABCs" 253

social-cognitive theories 254

observational (vicarious) learning 254

latent learning 256

LOOKING BACK

- Why would a dog salivate when it sees a light bulb or hears a buzzer, even though it can't eat these things? (pp. 227–228)

- How can classical conditioning help explain prejudice? (p. 229)

- If you have learned to fear collies, why might you also be scared of sheepdogs? (p. 229)

- Why do advertisers often include pleasant music and gorgeous scenery in ads for their products? (p. 232)

- How would a classical-conditioning theorist explain your irrational fear of heights or mice? (p. 233)

- If you eat licorice and then happen to get the flu, how might your taste for licorice change? (p. 234)

- How can sitting in a doctor's office make you feel sick? (p. 235)

- What do praise and ceasing to nag have in common? (pp. 238–239)

- How can operant principles account for superstitious rituals? (p. 241)

- What is the best way to discourage a friend from interrupting you while you're studying? (p. 243)

- How do trainers teach guide dogs to perform the amazing services they do for their owners? (p. 244)

- Why do efforts to "crack down" on wrongdoers often go awry? (pp. 248–249)

- What's the best way to discourage a child from throwing a tantrum? (p. 250)

- Why does paying children for good grades sometimes backfire? (pp. 251–252)

- How might watching violence on TV make (some) people more aggressive? (p. 254)

- Why do two people often learn different lessons from exactly the same experience? (p. 256)

8

BEHAVIOR IN SOCIAL AND CULTURAL CONTEXT

I cannot and will not cut my conscience to fit this year's fashion.

WRITER LILLIAN HELLMAN

In a quiet suburb of Baton Rouge, Louisiana, Yoshihiro Hattori, a 16-year-old Japanese exchange student, went along with his friend Webb Haymaker to a Halloween party. They mistakenly stopped in front of a house covered in Halloween decorations and rang the bell. Hearing no answer, Yoshi went to see whether the party might be in the backyard. The home owner, Bonnie Peairs, opened the front door, saw Webb in a Halloween costume and then saw Yoshi running back toward her waving an object (which turned out to be a camera). She panicked and called for her husband to get his gun. Rodney Peairs grabbed a .44 Magnum and shouted, "Freeze." Yoshi, not understanding the word, did not stop. Peairs shot him in the heart, killing him instantly.

When Rodney Peairs' case came to trial, the jury acquitted him of manslaughter after only three hours of deliberation. The Japanese were appalled at this verdict. To them, it illustrated everything that is wrong with America, a nation rife with guns and violence, still growing out of its Wild-West past. The Japanese cannot imagine a country that would permit private individuals to keep guns, and the murder rate in Japan is a tiny percentage of what it is in America. In contrast, the citizens of Baton Rouge were surprised that the case came to trial at all. What is more right and natural, they asked, than protecting your family from intruders? A local man, puzzled that Peairs had even been arrested, said, "It would be to me what a normal person would do under those circumstances."

But what is normal? The shooting of Yoshihiro Hattori is a dramatic example of how external circumstances can affect behavior, and how notions of what a "normal person" would do in one culture may be considered wildly abnormal in others. In this chapter, we will see again and again that people's behavior often depends more on the situations they are in, and on the values and rules of their society and culture, than on their individual personality traits. Even acts of courage and cowardice are more often affected by circumstances than by whether a person is inherently "good" or "bad."

The fields of *social psychology* and *cultural psychology* examine the powerful influence of the social and cultural environment on the actions of individuals and groups. We report findings from these fields throughout this book: for example, in our discussions of love and sexuality, how the environmental setting affects people's responses to drugs, how emotions communicate, why friends are necessary for health, and the nature of social influence in psychotherapy. Here we will focus on the foundations of social psychology: roles, attitudes, and groups, and the conditions under which people conform or dissent. Then we will consider some of the social and cultural reasons for prejudice and conflict between groups.

WHAT'S AHEAD

● How do social rules regulate behavior—and what is likely to happen when you violate them?
● Do you have to be mean or disturbed to inflict pain on someone just because an authority tells you to?
● How can ordinary college students be transformed into sadistic prison guards?
● How can people be "entrapped" into violating their moral principles?

ROLES AND RULES

"We are all fragile creatures entwined in a cobweb of social constraints," social psychologist Stanley Milgram once said. The constraints he referred to are social **norms**, rules about how we are supposed to act, enforced by threats of punishment if we violate them and by promises of reward if we follow them (Kerr, 1995). Norms are the conventions of everyday life that make interactions with other people predictable and orderly; like a cobweb, they are often as invisible as they are strong. Every society has norms for just about everything in human experience: for conducting courtships, raising children, making decisions, behaving in public places. Some norms are enshrined in law, such as, "A person may not beat up another person, except in self-defense." Some are unspoken cultural understandings, such as, "A man may beat up another man who insults his masculinity." And some are tiny, unspoken regulations that people learn to follow unconsciously, such as, "You may not sing at the top of your lungs on a public bus."

In every society, people also fill a variety of social **roles**, positions that are regulated by norms about how people in those positions should behave. Gender roles define the proper behavior for a man and a woman. Occupational roles determine the correct behavior for a manager and an employee, a professor and a student. Family roles

norms (social) Rules that regulate human life, including social conventions, explicit laws, and implicit cultural standards.

role A given social position that is governed by a set of norms for proper behavior.

Many roles in modern life require us to give up individuality, as conveyed by this dazzling image of referees at the Seoul Olympics. If each referee behaved out of role, the games could not continue. When is it appropriate to suppress your personal desires for the sake of the role, and when not?

set tasks for parent and child, husband and wife. Certain aspects of every role must be carried out or there will be penalties—emotional, financial, professional. As a student, for instance, you know just what you have to do to pass your psychology course (or you should by now!).

The requirements of a social role are in turn shaped by the culture you live in. **Culture** can be defined as a program of shared rules that govern the behavior of people in a community or society, and a set of values and beliefs shared by most members of that community and passed from one generation to another (Lonner, 1995). You learn most of your culture's rules and values the way you learn your culture's language—without thinking about it.

For example, cultures differ in their rules for *conversational distance*: how close people normally stand to one another when they are speaking (Hall, 1959, 1976). Arabs like to stand close enough to feel your breath, touch your arm, and see your eyes—a distance that makes white Americans, Canadians, and northern Europeans uneasy, unless they are talking intimately with a lover. The English and the Swedes stand farthest apart when they converse; southern Europeans stand closer; and Latin Americans and Arabs stand the closest (Keating, 1994; Sommer, 1969). Knowing another culture's rules, though, does not make it any easier to change your own. Caroline Keating (1994), an American cultural psychologist, told about walking with a Pakistani colleague. The closer he moved toward her, seeking the closeness he was comfortable with, the more she moved away, seeking the distance *she* was comfortable with. "I would suddenly disappear from his view, having fallen into the street," she reported, "perhaps not 'the ugly American,' but a clumsy one!"

The same discomfort occurs when people violate a role requirement, intentionally or unintentionally; they are likely to feel uncomfortable—or other people will try to make them feel uncomfortable. For instance, in your family, whose job is it to buy gifts for parents, send greeting cards to friends, organize parties and prepare the food, remember an aunt's birthday, and call friends to see how they're doing? Chances are you are thinking of a woman. These activities are considered part of the woman's role in most cultures, and women are usually blamed if they do not carry them out (di Leonardo, 1987; Lott & Maluso, 1993).

Likewise, in your culture what are the role requirements of a "real man"? According to studies conducted with a widely used measure, the Male Role Norms Scale, traditional male norms require a man to be strong (e.g., "A man should never back down in the face of trouble"); reject qualities associated with women (e.g., "It bothers me when a man does something that I consider 'feminine'"); keep his problems to himself (e.g., "Nobody respects a man very much who frequently talks about his worries, fears, and problems"); and behave aggressively if threatened (e.g., "Fists are sometimes the only way to get out of a bad situation") (Fischer et al., 1998).

What is likely to happen to men who break these norms, for example, by revealing their fears and worries? They are frequently regarded by both sexes as being "too feminine" and poorly adjusted (Peplau & Gordon, 1985; Taffel, 1990). However,

Arabs stand much closer in conversation than Westerners do, close enough to feel one another's breath and "read" one another's eyes. Most Westerners would feel "crowded" standing so close, even talking to a friend.

culture A program of shared rules that govern the behavior of members of a community or society, and a set of values, beliefs, and attitudes shared by most members of that community.

In most cultures, men are required to take on the dangerous, life-threatening roles . . . but it's not always easy to get all of them to do it.

the norms of the male role, like those for females, are changing rapidly in Western cultures, as we discuss in Chapter 11. Today many men think it is normal and beneficial to express their feelings; male politicians and athletes even cry in public.

Naturally, people bring their own personalities and interests to the roles they play. Just as two actors will play James Bond differently although they are reading from the same script, you will have your own "reading" of how to play the role of student, friend, parent, or employer. Nonetheless, the requirements of a social role are pretty strong, so strong that they may even cause you to behave in ways that shatter your fundamental sense of the kind of person you are, as we will see next.

The Obedience Study

A man was on trial for murder, although he personally had never killed anyone. Six psychiatrists examined him and pronounced him sane. His family life was normal and he had deep feelings of love for his wife, children, and parents. Two observers, after reviewing transcripts of his 275-hour interrogation, described him as "an average man of middle class origins and normal middle class upbringing, a man without identifiable criminal tendencies" (Von Lang & Sibyll, 1984).

The man was Adolf Eichmann, a high-ranking officer of the Nazi SS, an elite military unit of storm troopers. Eichmann supervised the deportation and death of millions of Jews during World War II. He was proud of his efficiency at his work and his ability to resist feeling pity for his victims. But when the Israelis captured him and put him on trial in 1961, he insisted that he was not anti-Semitic: He had had a Jewish mistress, and he personally arranged for the protection of his Jewish half-cousin—two dangerous crimes for an SS officer. Shortly before his execution by hanging, Eichmann said, "I am not the monster I am made out to be. I am the victim of a fallacy" (R. Brown, 1986).

The fallacy to which Eichmann referred was the widespread belief that a person who does monstrous deeds must be a monster, someone sick and evil. Is that true? In the early 1960s, Stanley Milgram (1963, 1974) designed a study that would become world famous; it was, in effect, a test of Eichmann's claim of normality.

Design and Findings. Milgram wanted to know how many people would obey an authority figure when directly ordered to violate their own ethical standards. Participants in the study, however, thought they were part of an experiment on the effects of punishment on learning. Each was assigned, apparently at random, to the role of "teacher." Another person, introduced as a fellow volunteer, was the "learner."

Adolf Eichmann at his trial. Was he a "monster"?

Whenever the learner, seated in an adjoining room, made an error in reciting a list of word pairs he was supposed to have memorized, the teacher had to give him an electric shock by depressing a lever on a machine (see Figure 8.1). With each error, the voltage (marked from 0 to 450) was to be increased by another 15 volts. The shock levels on the machine were labeled from SLIGHT SHOCK to DANGER—SEVERE SHOCK and, finally, ominously, XXX. In reality, the learners were confederates of Milgram and did not receive any shocks, but none of the teachers ever realized this during the study. The actor-victims played their parts convincingly: As the study continued, they shouted in pain and pleaded to be released, all according to a prearranged script.

Before doing this study, Milgram asked a number of psychiatrists, students, and middle-class adults how many people they thought would "go all the way" to XXX on orders from the researcher. The psychiatrists predicted that most people would refuse to go beyond 150 volts, when the learner first demanded to be freed, and that only one person in a thousand, someone who was disturbed and sadistic, would administer the highest voltage. The nonprofessionals agreed with this prediction, and all of them said that they personally would disobey early in the procedure.

That is not the way the results turned out, however. Every single person administered some shock to the learner, and about two-thirds of the participants, of all ages and from all walks of life, obeyed to the fullest extent. Many protested to the experimenter, but they backed down when he merely asserted, "The experiment requires that you continue." They obeyed no matter how much the victim shouted for them to stop and no matter how painful the shocks seemed to be. They obeyed even when they themselves were anguished about the pain they believed they were causing. As Milgram (1974) noted, participants would "sweat, tremble, stutter, bite their lips, groan, and dig their fingernails into their flesh"—but still they obeyed.

More than 1,000 people at several American universities eventually went through replications of the Milgram study. Most of them, men and women equally, inflicted what they thought were dangerous amounts of shock to another person (Blass, 1993). Researchers in other countries have also found high percentages of obedience, ranging to more than 90 percent in Spain and the Netherlands (Meeus & Raaijmakers, 1995; Smith & Bond, 1993, 1994).

Milgram and his team subsequently set up several variations of the study to determine the circumstances under which people might disobey the experimenter. They found that virtually nothing the victim did or said changed the likelihood of compliance—even when the victim said he had a heart condition, screamed in agony, or stopped responding entirely as if he had collapsed.

 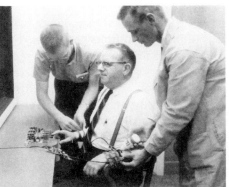

FIGURE 8.1
THE MILGRAM OBEDIENCE EXPERIMENT

On the left is Milgram's original shock machine; in 1963, it looked pretty ominous. On the right, the "learner" is being strapped into his chair by the experimenter and the "teacher."

Copyright 1965 by Stanley Milgram. From the film Obedience, *distributed by Penn State Media Sales.*

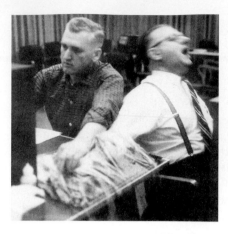

In Milgram's study, when the "teacher" had to administer shock directly to the learner, most subjects refused—but this one continued to obey.

However, people *were* more likely to disobey under the following conditions:

- *When the experimenter left the room.* Many people then subverted authority by giving low levels of shock but reporting that they had followed orders.
- *When the victim was right there in the room,* and the teacher had to administer the shock directly to the victim's body.
- *When two experimenters issued conflicting demands* to continue the experiment or to stop at once. In this case, no one kept inflicting shock.
- *When the person ordering them to continue was an ordinary man,* apparently another volunteer, instead of the authoritative experimenter.
- *When the subject worked with peers who refused to go further.* Seeing someone else rebel gave subjects the courage to disobey.

Obedience, Milgram concluded, was more a function of the situation than of the particular personalities of the participants. "The key to [their] behavior," Milgram (1974) summarized, "lies not in pent-up anger or aggression but in the nature of their relationship to authority. They have given themselves to the authority; they see themselves as instruments for the execution of his wishes; once so defined, they are unable to break free."

Evaluating the Obedience Study. The Milgram study has had its critics. Some consider it unethical because people were kept in the dark about what was really happening until the session was over (of course, telling them in advance would have invalidated the study) and because many suffered emotional pain (Milgram countered that they would not have felt pain if they had simply disobeyed the instructions). Others question the conclusion that personality traits always have less influence on behavior than the demands of the situation; certain traits, such as hostility and rigidity, do increase obedience to authority in real life (Blass, 1993).

Some psychologists also object to the parallel Milgram drew between the behavior of the study's participants and the brutality of the Nazis and others who have committed acts of barbarism in the name of duty. As John Darley (1995) noted, the people in Milgram's study obeyed only when the experimenter was hovering right there, and many of them felt enormous discomfort and conflict. In contrast, the Nazis acted without direct supervision by authorities, without external pressure, and without feelings of anguish.

Nevertheless, this study has had a tremendous influence on public awareness of the dangers of uncritical obedience. As Darley himself observed, "Milgram shows us the beginning of a path by means of which ordinary people, in the grip of social forces, become the origins of atrocities in the real world."

The Prison Study

Imagine that one day, as you are walking home from school, a police car pulls up. Two uniformed officers get out, arrest you, and take you to a prison cell. There you are stripped of your clothes, sprayed with a delousing fluid, assigned a prison uniform, photographed with your prison number, and put behind bars. You feel a little queasy but you are not panicked; you have agreed to play the part of prisoner for a two-week study, and your arrest is merely part of the script. Your prison cell, while apparently authentic, is located in the basement of a university building. So began an effort to discover what happens when ordinary college students take on the roles of prisoners and guards (Haney, Banks, & Zimbardo, 1973).

Design and Findings. The young men who volunteered for this experience were paid a nice daily fee. They were randomly assigned to be prisoners or guards, but other than that, they were given no instructions about how to behave. The results were dramatic. Within a short time, the prisoners became distressed, helpless, and panicky. They developed emotional symptoms and physical ailments. Some became apathetic; others became rebellious. After a few days, half of the prisoners begged to be let out. They were more than willing to forfeit their pay to gain an early release.

Within an equally short time, the guards adjusted to their new power. Some tried to be nice, helping the prisoners and doing little favors for them. Some were "tough but fair," holding strictly to "the rules." But about a third became tyrannical. Although they were free to use any method they liked to maintain order, they almost always chose to be harsh and abusive, even when the prisoners were not resisting in any way. One guard, unaware that he was being observed by the researchers, paced the corridor while the prisoners were sleeping, pounding his nightstick into his hand. Another put a prisoner in solitary confinement (a small closet) and tried to keep him there all night. He concealed this information from the researchers, who, he thought, were "too soft" on the prisoners. Not one of the less actively cruel guards, by the way, ever intervened or complained about the behavior of their more abusive peers.

Prisoners and guards quickly learn their respective roles, which usually have more influence on their behavior than their personalities do.

The researchers, who had not expected such a speedy and terrifying transformation of mentally healthy students, ended this study after only six days. The prisoners were relieved by this decision, but most of the guards were disappointed. They had enjoyed their short-lived authority.

Evaluating the Prison Study. Critics maintain that you cannot learn much from such an artificial setup. They argue that the volunteers already knew, from movies, TV, and games, how they were supposed to behave. The guards acted their parts to the hilt in order to have fun and please the researchers. Their behavior was no more surprising than if they had been dressed in football gear and had then been found to be willing to bruise each other in a game. The prison study made a great story, say some critics, but it wasn't *research*. That is, the researchers did not carefully investigate relationships between factors; for all the study's drama, it provided no new information (Festinger, 1980).

Craig Haney and Philip Zimbardo, who designed the prison study, respond that this dramatization illustrated the power of roles in a way that no ordinary lab experiment ever could. If the guards were just having fun, why did they lose sight of the "game" and behave as if it were a real job? Twenty-five years after the prison study was done, Haney and Zimbardo (1998) noted how much it contributed to understanding the behavior of real prisoners and guards in prisons, and also to increasing public awareness of how situations can outweigh personality and private values in influencing behavior.

The Power of Roles

The two imaginative studies we have described vividly demonstrate the power of social roles and obligations to influence the behavior of individuals. When people in the Milgram study believed they had to follow the legitimate orders of authority, most of them put their private values and personality traits aside. The behavior of the prisoners and guards varied—some prisoners were more rebellious than others, some guards were more abusive than others—but ultimately what the students did depended on the roles they were assigned.

Obedience, of course, is not always harmful or bad. A certain amount of routine compliance with rules is necessary in any group, and obedience to authority has many benefits for individuals and society. A nation could not operate if all its citizens ignored traffic signals, cheated on their taxes, dumped garbage wherever they chose, or assaulted each other. An organization could not function if its members came to work only when they felt like it. But obedience also has a darker aspect. Throughout history, the plea "I was only following orders" has been offered to excuse actions carried out on behalf of orders that were foolish, destructive, or illegal. The writer C. P. Snow once observed that "more hideous crimes have been committed in the name of obedience than in the name of rebellion."

Most people follow orders because of the obvious consequences of disobedience: They can be suspended from school, fired from their jobs, or arrested. They may also obey because of what they hope to gain: being liked, getting certain advantages or promotions from the authority, learning from the authority's greater knowledge or experience. Primarily, though, people obey because they are deeply convinced of the authority's legitimacy—that is, they obey not in hopes of gaining some tangible benefit, but because they like and respect the authority and value the relationship (Tyler, 1997).

But what about all those obedient people in Milgram's study who felt they were doing wrong and who wished they were free, but who could not untangle themselves from the cobweb of social constraints? Why do people obey when it is not in their interests, or when obedience requires them to ignore their own values or even commit a crime?

To answer this question, Herbert Kelman and Lee Hamilton (1989) studied "crimes of obedience," ranging from military massacres of civilians in the Vietnam War to political crimes committed by American presidents, such as Watergate (in which Richard Nixon and his advisers tried to cover up the attempted theft of files from Democratic headquarters) and the Iran-Contra scandal (in which Ronald Reagan's administration illegally sold arms to Iran in order to unlawfully fund the Contra forces in Nicaragua). They and other researchers draw our attention to several factors that cause people to obey when they would rather not:

1 *Investing the authority, rather than oneself, with responsibility* allows people to absolve themselves of accountability for their own actions. In Milgram's study, many of those who administered the highest levels of shock relinquished responsibility to the experimenter. A 37-year-old welder explained that the experimenter was responsible for any pain the victim might suffer "for the simple reason that I was paid for doing this. I had to follow orders." In contrast, individuals who refused to give high levels of shock took responsibility for their actions and refused to grant the authority legitimacy. "One of the things I think is very cowardly," said a 32-year-old engineer, "is to try to shove the responsibility onto someone else. See, if I now turned around and said, 'It's your fault . . . it's not mine,' I would call that cowardly" (Milgram, 1974).

2 *Routinization* is the process of defining the activity in terms of routine duties and roles so that the behavior becomes normalized, a job to be done, with little opportunity to raise doubts or ethical questions. In the Milgram study, some people became so fixated on the "learning task" that they shut out any moral concerns about the learner's demands to be let out of the experiment. Routinization is typically the mechanism by which governments enlist citizens to aid and abet programs of genocide. German bureaucrats

The routinization of torture allows people to commit or collaborate in atrocities. More than 16,000 political prisoners were tortured and killed at Tuol Sleng prison by Cambodia's Khmer Rouge, during the genocidal regime of Pol Pot. Prison authorities kept meticulous records and photos of each victim in order to make their barbarous activities seem mundane and normal. This man, Ing Pech, one of only seven survivors, was spared because he had skills useful to his captors. He now runs a museum at the prison.

kept meticulous records of every Nazi victim, and in Cambodia the Khmer Rouge recorded the names and histories of the millions of victims they tortured and killed. "I am not a violent man," said Sous Thy, one of the clerks who recorded these names, to a reporter from the *New York Times*. "I was just making lists."

3 *The rules of good manners* protect people's feelings and make relationships and civilization possible. But once people are caught in what they perceive to be legitimate roles and are obeying a legitimate authority, good manners ensnare them into further obedience. Most people do not like to rock the boat, appear to doubt the experts, or be rude, because they know they will be disliked for doing so (Collins & Brief, 1995).

Most people learn the language of manners ("please," "thank you," "I'm sorry for missing your birthday"), but they literally lack the words to justify disobedience and rudeness toward an authority they respect. In the Milgram study, many people could not find the words to justify walking out, so they stayed. One woman kept apologizing to the experimenter, trying not to offend him with her worries for the victim: "Do I go right to the end, sir? I hope there's nothing wrong with him there." (She did go right to the end.) A man repeatedly protested and questioned the experimenter, but he, too, obeyed, even when the victim had apparently collapsed in pain. "He thinks he is killing someone," Milgram (1974) commented, "yet he uses the language of the tea table."

4 *Entrapment* is a process in which individuals escalate their commitment to a course of action in order to justify their investment in it (Brockner & Rubin, 1985) The first steps of entrapment pose no difficult choices, but one step leads to another, and before you realize it, you have become committed to a course of action that poses problems. In Milgram's study, once subjects had given a 15-volt shock, they had committed themselves to the experiment. The next level was "only" 30 volts. Because each increment was small, before they knew it most people were administering what they believed were dangerously strong shocks. At that point, it was difficult to explain a sudden decision to quit. Participants who resisted early in the study, questioning the procedure, were less likely to become entrapped by it and more likely to eventually disobey (Modigliani & Rochat, 1995).

Everyone, individuals and nations alike, is vulnerable to the sneaky process of entrapment. You start dating someone you like moderately; before you know it, you have been together so long that you can't break up, although you don't want to become committed, either. Government leaders start a war they think will end quickly. Years later, the nation has lost so many soldiers and so much money that the leaders believe they cannot retreat without losing face.

A chilling study of entrapment was conducted with 25 men who had served in the Greek military police during the authoritarian regime that ended in 1974 (Haritos-Fatouros, 1988). A psychologist who interviewed the men identified the steps used in training them to use torture when questioning prisoners. First, the men were ordered to stand guard outside the interrogation and torture cells. Then, they stood guard in the detention rooms, where they observed the torture of prisoners. Then, they "helped" beat up prisoners. Once they had obediently followed these orders and became actively involved, the torturers found their actions easier to carry out.

Many people expect solutions to moral problems to fall into two clear categories, with right on one side and wrong on the other. Yet in everyday life, as in the Milgram study, people often set out on a path that is morally ambiguous, only to find that they have traveled a long way toward violating their own principles. From Greece's torturers to the Khmer Rouge's dutiful clerks, from Milgram's well-meaning volunteers to all of us in our everyday lives, people face the difficult task of drawing a line beyond which they will not go. For many, the demands of the external role defeat the inner voice of conscience.

Entrapment is the reason that casinos win millions. A person vows to spend only a few dollars, but, after losing them, says, "Well, maybe another couple of tries" or "I've spent so much, now I really have to win something to get back my loss."

entrapment A gradual process in which individuals escalate their commitment to a course of action to justify their investment of time, money, or effort.

QUICK QUIZ

Step into your role as student to answer these questions.

1. About what percentage of the people in Milgram's obedience study administered the highest levels of shock? (a) two-thirds, (b) one-half, (c) one-third, (d) one-tenth

2. Which of the following actions by the "learner" reduced the likelihood of being shocked by the "teacher" in Milgram's study? (a) protesting noisily, (b) screaming in pain, (c) complaining of having a heart ailment, (d) nothing he did made a difference

3. A friend of yours, who is moving, asks you to bring over a few boxes. Since you are there anyway, he asks you to fill them with books. Before you know it, you have packed up his entire kitchen, living room, and bedroom. What social-psychological process is at work here?

Answers:

1. a 2. d 3. entrapment

WHAT'S AHEAD

- **What is one of the most common mistakes people make when they explain the behavior of others?**
- **Why would a person blame victims of rape or torture for having brought their misfortunes on themselves?**
- **What is the "Big Lie," and why does it work so well?**
- **What is the difference between ordinary techniques of persuasion and the coercive techniques used by cults?**

SOCIAL INFLUENCES ON BELIEFS

Social psychologists are interested not only in what people do in social situations, but also in what goes on in their heads while they are doing it. Researchers in the area of **social cognition** examine how the social environment influences people's thoughts, beliefs, and memories, and how people's perceptions of themselves and others affect their relationships (A. Fiske & Haslam, 1996). We will consider two important topics in this area: explanations about behavior and the formation of attitudes.

Attributions

People read detective stories to find out *who* did the dirty deed, but in real life we also want to know *why* people do things—was it because of a terrible childhood, a mental illness, possession by a demon, or what? According to **attribution theory,** the explanations we make of our behavior and the behavior of others generally fall into two categories. When we make a *situational attribution*, we are identifying the cause of an action as something in the situation or environment: "Joe stole the money because his family is starving." When we make a *dispositional attribution*, we are identifying the cause of an action as something in the person, such as a trait or a motive: "Joe stole the money because he is a born thief."

When people are trying to find reasons for someone else's behavior, they reveal a common bias: They tend to overestimate personality traits and underestimate the influence of the situation (Forgas, 1998; Nisbett & Ross, 1980). In terms of attribution theory, they tend to ignore situational attributions in favor of dispositional ones. This tendency has been called the **fundamental attribution error.** Were the hundreds

---

social cognition An area in social psychology concerned with social influences on thought, memory, perception, and other cognitive processes.

attribution theory The theory that people are motivated to explain their own and other people's behavior by attributing causes of that behavior to a situation or a disposition.

fundamental attribution error The tendency, in explaining other people's behavior, to overestimate personality factors and underestimate the influence of the situation.

of people who obeyed Milgram's experimenters sadistic by nature? Were the student guards in the prison study sadistic and the prisoners cowardly? Those who think so are committing the fundamental attribution error.

People are especially likely to overlook situational attributions when they are in a good mood and not inclined to think about other people's motives critically, or when they are distracted and preoccupied and don't have time to stop and ask themselves, "Why, exactly, *is* Aurelia behaving like a dork today?" (Forgas, 1998). Instead, they leap to the easiest attribution, which is dispositional: Aurelia simply has a dorky personality.

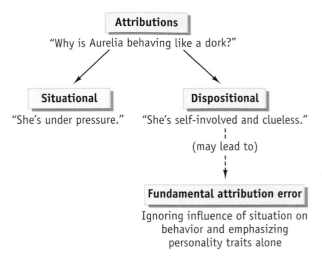

The fundamental attribution error is especially prevalent in Western nations, where middle-class people tend to believe that individuals are responsible for their own actions. In countries such as India, where everyone is embedded in caste and family networks, and in Japan, China, and Hong Kong, where people are more group oriented than in the West, people are more likely to be aware of situational constraints on behavior (Choi, Nisbett, & Norenzayan, 1999; Morris & Peng, 1994). Thus, if someone is behaving oddly, makes a mistake, or plays badly in a soccer match, a person from India or China, unlike a Westerner, is more likely to make a situational attribution of the behavior ("He's under pressure") than a dispositional one ("He's incompetent").

Westerners do not always prefer dispositional attributions, however. When it comes to explaining their *own* behavior, they often reveal a **self-serving bias:** They tend to choose attributions that are favorable to them, taking credit for their good actions (a dispositional attribution) but letting the situation account for their bad or embarrassing actions. For instance, most Westerners, when angry, will say, "I am furious for good reason—this situation is intolerable." They are less likely to say, "I am furious because I am an ill-tempered grinch." On the other hand, if they do something admirable, such as donating to charity, they are likely to attribute their

self-serving bias The tendency, in explaining one's own behavior, to take credit for one's good actions and rationalize one's mistakes.

Children learn the value of self-serving attributions at an early age.

just-world hypothesis The notion that many people need to believe that the world is fair and that justice is served; that bad people are punished and good people rewarded.

motives to a personal disposition ("I'm so generous") instead of the situation ("That guy on the phone pressured me into it").

People's attributions are also affected by the need to believe that the world is fair, that good people are rewarded and bad guys punished. According to the **just-world hypothesis,** the belief in a just world helps people make sense out of senseless events and feel safe in the presence of threatening events (Lerner, 1980). Unfortunately, this belief also leads to a dispositional attribution called *blaming the victim.* If a friend loses his job, if a woman is raped, if a prisoner is tortured, it is reassuring to think that they all must have done something to deserve what happened or to provoke it. This kind of attribution was apparent in the Milgram study, when many of the "teachers" made comments such as, "[The learner] was so stupid and stubborn he deserved to get shocked" (Milgram, 1974).

Of course, sometimes dispositional (personality) attributions do explain a person's behavior. The point to remember is that attributions, whether they are accurate or not, have tremendously important consequences for emotions and actions, for legal decisions, and for everyday relations. Happy couples, for example, tend to attribute their partners' occasional lapses to something in the situation ("Poor Harold is under a lot of stress at work"), whereas unhappy couples tend to make dispositional attributions ("Harold is just a selfish skunk")(Fincham & Bradbury, 1993; Karney et al., 1994). Your attributions about your partner, your parents, and your friends will make a big difference in how you get along with them—and how long you will put up with their failings.

QUICK QUIZ

To what do you attribute your success in answering these questions?

1. What kind of attribution is being made in each case, situational or dispositional? (a) A man says, "My wife has sure become a grouchy person." (b) The same man says, "I'm grouchy because I've had a bad day at the office." (c) A woman reads that unemployment is high in inner-city communities. "Well, if those people weren't so lazy, they would find work," she says.

2. What principles of attribution theory are suggested by the items in the preceding question?

Answers:

1. a. dispositional   b. situational   c. dispositional   2. Item *a* illustrates the fundamental attribution error; *b,* the self-serving bias; and *c,* blaming the victim, possibly because of the just-world hypothesis.

Attitudes

People hold attitudes about all sorts of things—politics, people, food, children, movies, sports heroes, you name it. An *attitude* is a relatively stable opinion containing both a cognitive element (perceptions and beliefs about the topic) and an emotional element (feelings about the topic, which can range from negative and hostile to positive and warm).

THINKING CRITICALLY

CONSIDER OTHER EXPLANATIONS

Are all your attitudes a result of clear reasoning? What are some other origins of attitudes, and why is it important for critical thinkers to be aware of them?

Most people think that their attitudes are based on thinking, a result of reasoned conclusions about how things work. Sometimes, of course, that's true! But some attitudes are a result of not thinking at all. They are a result of conformity, habit, rationalization, economic self-interest, and many subtle social and environmental influences. For example, some attitudes arise because of the shared experiences of an age group or generation. Each generation has its own defining social and political events, economic interests, job and marital opportunities, and other shared concerns, and therefore its own characteristic attitudes. (That is why

Your generational identity consists of the psychological attitudes and values arising from the shared experiences of your generation. Many people who came of age during the political protests of the 1960s, such as the couple on the left, have continued their political activism throughout their lives. But what, if any, are the defining experiences of Generation X and of those in their early 20s today? The news media keep trying to identify them!

people speak of the Depression generation, the Baby Boomers, and "Generation X.") The ages of 16 to 24 appear to be critical for the formation of a "generational identity" that lasts throughout adulthood; the experiences that occur during these years make deeper impressions and exert more lasting influence than those that happen later in life (Inglehart, 1990; Schuman & Scott, 1989). For example, Americans who were young adults during the Depression (1930s), World War II (1940s), the civil-rights movement (1950s–1960s), the Vietnam War (1965–1973), or the rebirth of the women's rights movement (1970s) regard these events as major influences on their political philosophy, values, attitudes, and ambitions. What do you think might be the critical generational events affecting the attitudes of your generation?

Attitudes and behavior influence each other. Often, attitudes dispose people to behave in certain ways; if you have a positive attitude toward martial-arts movies, you'll go to as many as you can, and if you hate them, you'll stay away from them. But new behavior can also change attitudes. Suppose your friend drags you unwillingly to a Jackie Chan movie, and you discover that you like it. Your attitude toward martial-arts movies will change accordingly.

Attitudes also change because of the need for consistency. In Chapter 9, we discuss *cognitive dissonance,* the uncomfortable feeling that occurs when two attitudes, or an attitude and behavior, are in conflict (are dissonant). Cognitive dissonance will occur, for example, if you learn that a male athlete you admire has been arrested for rape. To restore consistency, you will need to lose your admiration for the man, rationalize his behavior, or decide that his accuser is lying.

Our attitudes are also influenced constantly by other people. Sometimes people persuade us to change our minds using reasoned argument; sometimes they use subtle manipulation; and sometimes they use outright coercion.

Friendly Persuasion. All around you, every day, advertisers, politicians, and friends are trying to influence your attitudes. One weapon they use is the drip, drip, drip of a repeated idea. Repeated exposure even to a nonsense syllable such as *zug* is enough to make a person feel more positive toward it (Zajonc, 1968).

The more familiar things are, the more we tend to like them. The Oreo name on these cereal boxes takes advantage of the fact that Oreo cookies have been advertised since 1912.

The effectiveness of familiarity has long been known to politicians and advertisers: Repeat something often enough, even the basest lie, and eventually the public will believe it—which is why Hitler's propaganda minister, Joseph Goebbels, called this technique the "Big Lie." Its formal name is the **validity effect**.

In a series of experiments, Hal Arkes and his associates demonstrated how the validity effect operates (Arkes, 1993; Arkes, Boehm, & Xu, 1991). In a typical study, people read a list of statements, such as "Mercury has a higher boiling point than copper" or "Over 400 Hollywood films were produced in 1948." They had to rate each statement for its validity, on a scale of 1 (definitely false) to 7 (definitely true). A week or two later, they again rated the validity of some of these statements and also rated others that they had not seen previously. The result: Mere repetition increased the perception that the familiar statements were true. The same effect also occurred for other kinds of statements, including unverifiable opinions (e.g., "At least 75 percent of all politicians are basically dishonest"), opinions that subjects initially felt were true, and even opinions they initially felt were false. "Note that no attempt has been made to persuade," said Arkes (1993). "No supporting arguments are offered. We just have subjects rate the statements. Mere repetition seems to increase rated validity. This is scary."

Another effective technique for influencing people's attitudes is to have arguments presented by someone who is considered admirable, knowledgeable, or beautiful; this is why advertisements are full of sports heroes, experts, and fashion models (Cialdini, 1993). Persuaders may also try to link their message with a good feeling. In one classic study, students who were given peanuts and Pepsi while listening to a speaker's point of view were more likely to be convinced by it than were students who listened to the same words without the pleasant munchies and soft drinks (Janis, Kaye, & Kirschner, 1965). This finding has been replicated many times (Pratkanis & Aronson, 1992) and may explain why so much business is conducted over lunch, and so many courtships over dinner!

In sum, here are three good ways to influence attitudes:

EFFECTIVE WAYS TO INFLUENCE ATTITUDES

Repetition of an idea or assertion (the validity effect)

Endorsement by an admired or attractive person

Association of the message with a good feeling

In contrast, the emotion of fear can cause people to resist arguments that are in their own best interest (Pratkanis & Aronson, 1992). Fear tactics are often used to try to persuade people to quit smoking or abusing other drugs, drive only when sober, use condoms, check for signs of cancer, and prepare for earthquakes. However, fear works only if people become moderately anxious, not scared to death, *and* if the message also provides information about how to avoid the danger (Leventhal & Nerenz, 1982).

validity effect The tendency of people to believe that a statement is true or valid simply because it has been repeated many times.

When messages about a future disaster are too terrifying and when people believe that they can do nothing to avoid it, they tend to deny the danger. (This finding makes us curious about how the recent antismoking ads will do—the ones that inform men that smoking is a leading cause of impotence. Do you think they will work?)

Coercive Persuasion. Some manipulators use harsher tactics, not just hoping that people will change their minds but attempting to force them to. These tactics are sometimes referred to as *brainwashing,* a term first used during the Korean War to describe techniques used on American prisoners of war to get them to collaborate with their Chinese Communist captors and to endorse anti-American propaganda. Most psychologists, however, prefer the phrase *coercive persuasion.* "Brainwashing" implies that a person has a sudden change of mind and is unaware of what is happening; it sounds mysterious and powerful. In fact, the methods involved are neither mysterious nor unusual. The difference between "persuasion" and "brainwashing" is often only a matter of degree and the observer's bias, just as a group that is a crazy cult to one person may be a group of devoutly religious people to another.

How, then, might we distinguish coercive persuasion from its more benign form? Persuasion techniques become coercive when they suppress an individual's ability to reason, think critically, and make choices in his or her own best interests. Studies of religious, political, and other cults have identified some of the key processes of coercive persuasion (Galanter, 1989; Mithers, 1994; Ofshe & Watters, 1994; Singer, Temerlin, & Langone, 1990; Zimbardo & Leippe, 1991):

1 *The person is put under physical or emotional distress.* The individual may not be allowed to eat, sleep, or exercise; may be isolated in a dark room with no stimulation or food; or may be induced into a trancelike state through repetitive chanting, hypnosis, or fatigue.

2 *The person's problems are reduced to one simple explanation, which is repeatedly emphasized.* There are as many simplistic explanations as there are cults, but here are some real examples: Are you afraid or unhappy? It all stems from the pain of being born. Are you worried about homeless earthquake victims? It's not your problem; victims are responsible for everything that happens to them. Are you struggling financially? It's your fault for not fervently wanting to be rich. Members may also be taught to blame their problems on particular enemies: Jews, blacks, whites, nonbelievers.

3 *The leader offers unconditional love, acceptance, and attention.* The new recruit may be given a "love bath" from the group—constant praise, support, applause, and affection. Euphoria and well-being are intense because they typically follow exhaustion and fatigue. In exchange, the leader demands everyone's adoration and obedience.

4 *A new identity based on the group is created.* The recruit is told that he or she is part of the chosen, the elite, or the saved. To foster this new identity, many cults require their members to wear special clothes or eat special diets, and they assign each member a new name. All members of

New State TV Ads Link Smoking to Impotence in Men

By DAN MORAIN
TIMES STAFF WRITER

SACRAMENTO—What Viagra may give, tobacco taketh away. So says the California Department of Health Services.

State health officials, trying to pound their anti-tobacco message through to young men, unveiled new television commercials Monday making the point that smoking is a leading cause of impotence.

The new ad, part of the state's $22-million-a-year anti-smoking campaign, portrays a black-tie

Associated Press
Ad portrays smoking's effect on sexual potency.

These members of the Aum Shinrikyo ("Supreme Truth") sect in Japan, wearing masks of their leader's face, take the uniformity of cult identity to an extreme. The group's founder instructed his devotees to place a nerve gas in a Japanese subway, which killed 10 and sickened thousands of other passengers. One former member said of the sect, "Their strategy is to wear you down and take control of your mind. They promise you heaven, but they make you live in hell."

the Philadelphia group MOVE were given the last name "Africa"; all members of the Church of Armageddon took the last name "Israel."

5 *The person is subjected to entrapment.* At first, the new member agrees only to do small things, but gradually the demands increase: for example, to spend a weekend with the group, then another weekend, then take weekly seminars, then advanced courses. During the Korean War, the Chinese first got the American POWs to agree with mild remarks, such as "The United States is not perfect." Then the POWs had to add their own examples of American imperfections. At the end, they were signing their names to anti-American broadcasts (Schein, Schneier, & Barker, 1961).

6 *The person's access to information is severely controlled.* As soon as a person is a committed believer or follower, the group limits the person's choices, denigrates critical thinking, makes fun of doubts, and insists that any private distress is due to lack of belief in the group. Total conformity is demanded. The person may be physically isolated from the outside world and thus from antidotes to the leader's ideas. In many groups, members are encouraged or required to break all ties with their parents, who are the most powerful link to the members' former world and thus the greatest threat to the leader's control.

You could see these strategies in operation in the Heaven's Gate cult, which made the news a few years ago when its leader, Marshall Applewhite, and all 38 of his followers committed suicide. Applewhite had offered members a new identity (extraterrestrials in human bodies) and a simplistic solution to their problems (suicide would free them to travel to heaven in a spaceship hiding in the tail of a comet). He encouraged members to sever their relationships with friends and relatives, had them dress alike, and censored all dissenting opinions. Applewhite entrapped his followers in an escalating series of obligations and commitments. He never said to new recruits, "If you follow me, you will eventually give up your marriages, your homes, your children, and your lives"; but by the end, that is just what they did.

Some people may be more vulnerable than others to coercive tactics. But these techniques are powerful enough to overwhelm even strong individuals; by all accounts, Applewhite's followers were pleasant people without serious mental disorders, and many were well educated. The first step in increasing people's resistance to coercive persuasion, therefore, is to dispel their illusion of invulnerability to these tactics (Sagarin, Cialdini, & Rice, 1998).

QUICK QUIZ

Now, how can we persuade you to take this quiz without using coercive techniques?

1. Candidate Carson spends 3 million dollars to make sure his name is seen and heard frequently, and to repeat unverified charges that his opponent is a thief. What psychological process is he relying on to win?

2. Your best friend urges you to join a "life-renewal" group called "The Feeling Life." Your friend has been spending increasing amounts of time with her fellow Feelies, and you have some doubts about them. What questions would you want to have answered before joining up?

Answers:

1. the validity effect   2. A few things to consider: Is there an autocratic leader who tolerates no dissent or criticism, while rationalizing this practice as a benefit for members? ("Doubt and disbelief are signs that your feeling side is being repressed.") Have long-standing members cut off ties with their families and given up their interests and ambitions for this group? Does the leader offer simple but unrealistic promises to repair your life and all that troubles you? Are members required to make extreme personal sacrifices and donate large amounts of money to the group?

WHAT'S AHEAD

- Why do people in groups often go along with the majority even when the majority is dead wrong?
- How can "groupthink" lead to bad, even catastrophic, decisions?
- In an emergency, are you more likely to get help when there are lots of strangers in the area or only a few?
- What enables some people to disagree with a group, take independent action, or blow the whistle on wrongdoers?

INDIVIDUALS IN GROUPS

In March 1998, a man named Larry Froistad admitted to his Internet support group that he had killed his 5-year-old daughter, Amanda, three years earlier. "When she was asleep," he wrote on e-mail, he got drunk, set the house on fire, "listened to her scream twice, climbed out the window and set about putting on a show of shock and surprise and grief to remove culpability from myself." Of the more than 200 members of his online support group, only 3 called the police; Froistad was arrested and pleaded guilty. When members learned that the matter had been reported to the police, many of them became enraged—not at the man who had cold-bloodedly murdered his child, but at the "meddlesome rat fink" who turned him in. "Frankly, I'm offended," wrote one. "This is a SUPPORT group."

The members of Froistad's group were caught between two sets of norms and values: You are supposed to report a murderer to the police, but you are also supposed to be loyal to members of your "support" group. If you were in such a situation, what do you think you would do?

As we will see, all of us act differently when we are with a bunch of other people than when we are on our own, regardless of whether the group has convened to solve problems and make decisions, has gathered to have fun, consists of anonymous bystanders or anonymous members of an Internet chat room, or is just a loose collection of individuals waiting around in a room. The decisions we make and the actions we take, in groups, often depend less on our personal desires than on the structure and dynamics of the group itself.

Conformity

One thing people in groups do is conform, taking action or adopting attitudes as a result of real or imagined group pressure.

Suppose that you are required to appear at a psychology laboratory for an experiment on perception. You join seven other students seated in a room. You are shown a 10-inch line and asked which of three other lines is identical to it:

Test line   A   B   C

The correct answer, line A, is obvious, so you are amused when the first person in the group chooses line B. "Bad eyesight," you say to yourself. "He's off by 2 whole inches!" The second person also chooses line B. "What a dope," you think. But by the time the fifth person has chosen line B, you are beginning to doubt yourself.

The sixth and seventh students also choose line B, and now you are worried about *your* eyesight. The experimenter looks at you. "Your turn," he says. Do you follow the evidence of your own eyes or the collective judgment of the group?

This was the design for a series of famous studies of conformity conducted by Solomon Asch (1952, 1965). The seven "nearsighted" students were actually Asch's confederates. Asch wanted to know what people would do when a group unanimously contradicted an obvious fact. He found that when people made the line comparisons on their own, they were almost always accurate. But in the group, only 20 percent of the students remained completely independent on every trial, and often they apologized for not agreeing with the group. One-third conformed to the group's incorrect decision more than half the time, and the rest conformed at least some of the time. Whether they conformed or not, the students often felt uncertain of their decision. As one participant later said, "I felt disturbed, puzzled, separated, like an outcast from the rest."

Asch's experiment has been replicated many times over the years, in the United States and other countries. According to a meta-analysis of 133 studies, conformity in America has declined since the 1950s, when Asch first did his work, suggesting that conformity rises or falls according to changing social norms. Conformity also reflects cultural norms. People in individual-oriented cultures, such as the United States, are less conformist than are people in group-oriented cultures, where social harmony is considered more important than individual assertiveness. But regardless of culture, we are all more likely to conform when the group consists of people like us—in age, sex, and ethnicity—and as the group's size increases (Bond & Smith, 1996).

People conform for all sorts of reasons. Some do so because they identify with group members and want to be like them in dress, attitudes, or behavior. Some want to be liked and know that disagreeing with a group can make them unpopular. Some believe the group has knowledge that is superior to their own. And some conform out of pure self-interest, to keep their jobs, win promotions, or win votes. For their part, groups are often uncomfortable with nonconformists, and their members will try to persuade a rebel to conform. If pleasant persuasion fails, the group may punish, isolate, or reject the person altogether (Moscovici, 1985).

Like obedience, conformity has both its positive and its negative sides. Society runs more smoothly when people know how to behave in a given situation and when they share the same attitudes. But conformity can also suppress critical thinking and creativity. In a group, many people will deny their private beliefs, agree with silly notions, and violate their own values (Cialdini, 1993).

Sometimes people like to conform in order to feel part of the group . . . and sometimes, like this rebellious bride, they like to assert their individuality.

Groupthink

Close, friendly groups usually work well together. But they face the problem of getting the best ideas and efforts of their members while avoiding an extreme form of conformity called **groupthink,** the tendency to think alike and suppress dissent. According to Irving Janis (1982, 1989), groupthink occurs when a group's need for total agreement overwhelms its need to make the wisest decision. The symptoms of groupthink include:

- *An illusion of invulnerability.* The group believes it can do no wrong and is 100 percent correct in its decisions.
- *Self-censorship.* Dissenters decide to keep quiet rather than rock the boat, offend their friends, or risk being ridiculed.
- *Direct pressure on dissenters to conform.* The leader teases or humiliates dissenters or otherwise pressures them to go along.
- *An illusion of unanimity.* By discouraging dissent, leaders and group members create an illusion of consensus. They may even explicitly deny suspected dissenters the chance to say what they think.

Throughout history, groupthink has led to disastrous decisions in military and civilian life. One example occurred in 1961, when President John F. Kennedy, after meeting with his advisers, approved a CIA plan to invade Cuba at the Bay of Pigs and overthrow the government of Fidel Castro; the invasion was a humiliating defeat. Another occurred in the mid–1960s, when President Lyndon Johnson and his cabinet escalated the war in Vietnam in spite of obvious signs that further bombing and increased troops were not bringing the war to an end. And a third example occurred in 1986, when NASA officials made the fatal decision to launch the space shuttle *Challenger,* which exploded shortly after take off. Apparently, they insulated themselves from the objections of dissenting engineers who tried to warn them that the rocket was unsafe (Moorhead, Ference, & Neck, 1991).

Groupthink can occur in any setting, even in hospitals. For example, throughout the 1990s, psychiatrists at mental hospitals in Texas, Illinois, and elsewhere persuaded many patients that they were victims of ritual abuse by satanic cults despite a complete absence of evidence that the cults even existed (Kaczynski, 1997). The psychiatrists favoring this interpretation of their patients' problems refused to consider alternative explanations from "outsiders" and suppressed dissent from staff nurses and other physicians. It took a wave of successful malpractice suits to break this epidemic of psychiatric groupthink.

Janis (1982) examined the records of historical military decisions and identified typical features of groups that are vulnerable to groupthink: Their members feel that they are part of a tightly connected team; they are isolated from other viewpoints; they feel under pressure from outside forces; and they have a strong, directive leader. (Do you notice the similarities between these conditions and those of coercive cults?)

Fortunately, groupthink can be counteracted by creating conditions that explicitly encourage and reward the expression of doubt and dissent and by basing decisions on majority rule instead of unanimity (Kameda & Sugimori, 1993). President Kennedy apparently learned this lesson from the Bay of Pigs decision. In his next political crisis, provoked by missiles placed in Cuba by the then–Soviet Union in 1962, Kennedy brought in outside experts to advise his inner circle, often absented himself from the group so as not to influence their discussions, and encouraged free debate between

groupthink In close-knit groups, the tendency for all members to think alike for the sake of harmony and to suppress disagreement.

the "hawks" and the "doves" (Aronson, Wilson, & Akert, 1999). The crisis, one of the most dangerous in post–World War II history, was resolved peacefully.

Of course, it is easy to see after the fact how conformity contributed to a bad decision or open debate to a good one, as Janis did. Predicting whether a group will make good or bad decisions *in the future* is far more complicated; you have to know a lot more about the history, structure, and purpose of the group (Aldag & Fuller, 1993). Nevertheless, according to many laboratory studies and analyses of historical events, Janis put his finger on a phenomenon that many of us have experienced: individual members of a group suppressing their real opinions and doubts so as to be good team players.

The Anonymous Crowd

If you were in trouble—say, being mugged or having a sudden appendicitis attack—on a city street or in another public place, do you think you would be more likely to get help if (1) one other person was passing by, (2) several other people were in the area, or (3) dozens of people were in the area?

Diffusion of Responsibility. Most people think that the more people who are available to help, the more likely it is that someone will step forward. But that is not how people operate. On the contrary, the more people there are around you, the *less* likely it is that one of them will come to your aid. The reason has to do with a common group process called the **diffusion of responsibility,** in which responsibility for an outcome is diffused, or spread, among many people. In crowds, individuals often fail to take action because they believe that someone else will do so.

The many reports of *bystander apathy* in the news reflect the diffusion of responsibility. When others are near, people fail to call the police when they see a woman being attacked on the street, they fail to report that a child in their neighborhood is being neglected and beaten by a parent, or they stand frozen to the spot as a store clerk is robbed and beaten by an assailant—even after the assailant flees. People are more likely to come to a stranger's aid if they are the only ones around to help, because responsibility cannot be diffused (see Figure 8.2).

In work groups, the diffusion of responsibility sometimes takes the form of *social loafing:* Each member of a team slows down, letting others work harder (Karau & Williams, 1993; Latané, Williams, & Harkins, 1979). Social loafing occurs when individual group members are not accountable for the work they do; when people feel that working harder would only duplicate their colleagues' efforts; when workers feel that others are getting a "free ride"; or when the work itself is uninteresting (Shepperd, 1995). When the challenge of the job is increased or when

FIGURE 8.2

WHEN WILL BYSTANDERS HELP?

When people believed they were the only one hearing a student having an epileptic seizure in the next room, most of them went to help him immediately; and all of them did so within a few minutes. When they believed another bystander also heard the need for help, however, they were less likely to intervene. And when they believed that four other bystanders were listening, they were even less likely to help (from Darley & Latané, 1968).

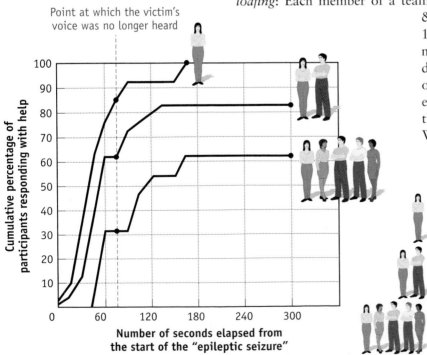

Point at which the victim's voice was no longer heard

Number of seconds elapsed from the start of the "epileptic seizure"

Cumulative percentage of participants responding with help

Participants who believed they were the only bystander

Participants who believed there was one other bystander besides themselves

Participants who believed there were four other bystanders besides themselves

People in crowds often seem to "forget themselves" and do destructive things they would never dream of doing on their own. When the Chicago Bulls won the National Basketball Association Championship several years ago, thousands of fans rioted, overturning cars and destroying property.

each member of the group has a different, important job to do, the sense of individual responsibility rises and social loafing declines (Harkins & Szymanski, 1989; Williams & Karau, 1991).

Deindividuation. The most extreme instances of the diffusion of responsibility occur in large, anonymous mobs or crowds—whether they are cheerful ones, such as sports spectators, or angry ones, such as rioters. In situations like these, people often lose all awareness of their individuality and seem to "hand themselves over" to the mood and actions of the crowd, a state called **deindividuation** (Festinger, Pepitone, & Newcomb, 1952). You are more likely to feel deindividuated in a large city, where no one recognizes you, than in a small town, where it is hard to hide. Sometimes organizations actively promote the deindividuation of their members in order to enhance conformity and allegiance to the group. This is an important function of uniforms or masks, which eliminate each member's distinctive identity.

Deindividuation has long been considered a prime reason for mob violence. According to this explanation, because deindividuated people in crowds "forget themselves" and do not feel accountable for their actions, they are more likely to violate social norms and laws than they would on their own: breaking store windows, looting, getting into fights, rioting at a sports event. Their usual inhibitions against aggressiveness are weakened.

Many studies have indeed found that deindividuation increases a person's willingness to harm a stranger, cheat, or break the law (Aronson, Wilson, & Akert, 1999). Deindividuation even eliminates gender differences in aggressiveness, in spite of the common belief that women are "naturally" less aggressive than men. In two

diffusion of responsibility In organized or anonymous groups, the tendency of members to avoid taking responsibility for actions or decisions because they assume that others will do so.

deindividuation In groups or crowds, the loss of awareness of one's own individuality.

GET ➔ INVOLVED

LOSING YOURSELF

For this exercise in deindividuation, choose two situations: one in which you are one of many people, perhaps hundreds (as in a large classroom or a concert audience); and one in which you are one of a few (as in a small discussion group). In both situations, close your eyes and pretend to fall asleep. Is this easier to do in one context than the other? Why? In each case, what is the reaction of other people around you?

studies, men behaved more aggressively than women in a competitive video war game when they were individuated—that is, when their names and background information about them were spoken aloud, heard by all participants, and recorded publicly by the experimenter. But when the men and women believed they were anonymous to their fellow students and to the experimenter—that is, when they were deindividuated—they did not differ in how aggressively they played the game (Lightdale & Prentice, 1994).

But deindividuation does not always make people more combative. Sometimes it makes them more friendly; think of all the chatty, anonymous people on buses and planes who reveal things to their seatmates they would never tell anyone they knew. What really seems to be happening when people are in large crowds or anonymous situations is not that they become mindless or uninhibited, but that they are simply more likely to conform to the norms of the *specific situation* (Postmes & Spears, 1998). College students who go on wild sprees during spring break may be violating the local laws and norms of Palm Springs or Key West, not because their "aggressiveness" has been released but because they are conforming to the "let's party!" norms of their fellow students.

Wearing a uniform or disguise can increase deindividuation and mindlessness.

Two classic experiments illustrate the power of the situation to influence what deindividuated people will do. In one, women who wore Ku Klux Klan–like disguises that completely covered their faces and bodies (see photo) delivered twice as much apparent electric shock to another woman as did women who were not only undisguised but also wore large name tags (Zimbardo, 1970). In a second, women who were wearing nurses' uniforms gave *less* shock than did women in regular dress (Johnson & Downing, 1979). Evidently, the KKK disguise was a signal to behave aggressively; the nurses' uniforms were a signal to behave nurturantly.

In real life, too, members of crowds, conforming to the goals and norms of the situation, can be induced to take part in either collective violence or collective kindness. Peer pressure and conformity to an angry mob can induce people to commit hate crimes, such as violence against gay men or lesbians, lynchings or attacks on black people or Jews, and the rape of women by gangs of civilians or soldiers (Franklin, 1998; Green, Glaser, & Rich, 1998). On the other hand, when collective norms are positive, anonymous members of a community will behave in constructive ways. When Swissair Flight 111 crashed over Halifax, Nova Scotia, in 1998, killing 229 people, the entire community—which holds a group norm about the importance of helping one another in that tough terrain—turned out to join in the rescue effort and comfort families in distress.

Anonymity and Responsibility. Deindividuation has important legal as well as psychological implications. Should individuals in a crowd be held accountable for their harmful "deindividuated" behavior? Consider a trial held in South Africa in the late 1980s, in which six black residents of an impoverished township were accused of murdering an 18-year-old black woman who was having an affair with a hated black police officer. The woman was "necklaced"—a tire was placed around her neck and set afire—during a community protest against the police. The crowd danced and sang as she burned to ashes.

The six men were convicted of murder, but their sentence was commuted to 20 months of prison when a British social psychologist, Andrew Colman (1991), testified that deindividuation should reduce the "moral blameworthiness" of their behavior.

The young men were swept up in the mindless behavior of the crowd, he argued, and hence not fully responsible for their actions. Do you agree? An African social scientist, Pumla Gobodo-Madikizela (1994), did not. She interviewed some of the men accused of the necklacing and found they were not so mindless after all. Some were tremendously upset, were well aware of their actions, had debated the woman's guilt, thought about running away, and consciously tried to rationalize their behavior. Moreover, she argued, we must remember that in every crowd, some people do not go along; they remain mindful of their own values and norms.

And so, should the deindividuation excuse, like the "I was only following orders" excuse, exonerate a person of responsibility for looting, rape, or murder? If so, to what degree? What do you think?

EXAMINE THE EVIDENCE

How mindless are "mindless" crowds? Should deindividuation be a legitimate excuse for people who loot, rape, or commit murder because the mob is doing it?

QUICK QUIZ

On your own, take responsibility for identifying which phenomenon discussed in the previous section is illustrated in the following situations:

1. The president's closest advisers are afraid to disagree with his views on arms negotiations.

2. You are at a Halloween party wearing a silly gorilla suit. When you see a chance to play a practical joke on the host, you do it.

3. Walking down a busy street, you see that fire has broken out in a store window. "Someone must have called the fire department," you say.

Answers:

1. groupthink 2. deindividuation 3. diffusion of responsibility

Disobedience and Dissent

We have seen how social roles, norms, and pressures to obey authority and conform to one's group can cause people to behave in ways they might not otherwise do. Yet, throughout history, men and women have disobeyed orders they believed to be immoral and have gone against prevailing cultural beliefs; their actions have changed the course of history. In 1956 in Montgomery, Alabama, Rosa Parks refused to give up her seat and move to the back of a bus, as the segregation laws of the time required. She was arrested, fingerprinted, and convicted of breaking the law. Her calm defiance touched off a boycott in which black citizens refused to ride city buses. It took them over a year, but they won—and the civil rights movement began.

Dissent and *altruism*, the willingness to take selfless or dangerous action on behalf of others, are in part a matter of personal convictions and conscience. However, just as there are situational reasons for obedience and conformity, so there are situational influences on a person's decision to speak up for an unpopular opinion, choose conscience over conformity, or help a stranger in trouble. Here are some of the steps involved in deciding to "rock the boat," and some social and cultural factors involved in them (Aronson, Wilson, & Akert, 1999):

1 *You perceive the need for intervention or help.* It may seem obvious, but before you can take independent action, you must realize that such action is necessary. Sometimes people willfully blind themselves to wrongdoing to justify their own inaction ("I'm just minding my business here"). But blindness to the need for action

Rosa Parks being fingerprinted on the day she was arrested.

also occurs when people have too many demands on their attention. Workers who must juggle many pressures from work and family cannot stop to make a fuss about every problem or bureaucratic misdeed they notice. Likewise, residents of densely populated cities cannot stop to offer help to everyone who seems to need it; they would never do anything else (Levine et al., 1994).

Whether you even interpret a situation as requiring your aid also depends on cultural rules (see Figure 8.3). In northern European nations and in the United States, husband-wife disputes are considered strictly private; neighbors intervene at their peril. In one field study, bystanders observed a (staged) fight between a man and a woman. When the woman yelled, "Get away from me; I don't know you!" two-thirds of the bystanders went to help her. When she shouted, "Get away from me; I don't know why I ever married you!" only 19 percent tried to help (Shotland & Straw, 1976). In Mediterranean and Latin cultures, however, a dispute between any two people is considered fair game for anyone who is passing by. In fact, two people in a furious dispute might even rely on bystanders to intervene (Hall & Hall, 1990).

2 *You decide to take responsibility.* When you are in a large crowd of observers or in a large organization, it is easy to avoid action because of the diffusion of responsibility. Even when you might like to help a stranger in trouble, in some places it is impossible to help everyone who needs it, as in cities where homeless persons number in the thousands. The decision to take responsibility also depends on the degree of risk involved. It is easier to be a whistle-blower or to protest a company policy when you know you can find another job, but what if jobs in your field are scarce and you have a family to support?

3 *You decide that the costs of doing nothing outweigh the costs of getting involved.* The cost of helping or protesting might be embarrassment and wasted time or, more seriously, lost income, loss of friends, and even physical danger. The cost of not helping or remaining silent might be guilt, blame from others, loss of honor, or, in some tragic cases, the injury or death of others. Three employees of Rockwell International weighed these two sets of costs and ended up trying to convince NASA that the space shuttle *Challenger* was unsafe. The NASA authorities (perhaps influenced by groupthink, as we noted earlier) weighed the costs differently, and refused

FIGURE 8.3
CULTURE AND THE OBLIGATION TO HELP

Community-oriented Hindus in India believe that people are obligated to help anyone who needs it—parent, friend, or stranger—even if the need is minor. In contrast, individualistic Americans do not feel as strongly obligated to help friends and strangers, or even parents who merely have "minor" needs. People in both cultures, however, share a sense of obligation to help anyone in a life-threatening situation (Miller, Bersoff, & Harwood, 1990).

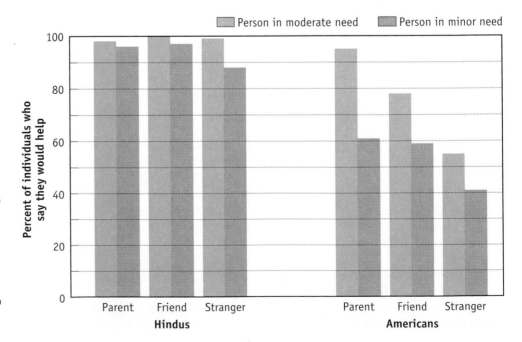

Many people retain their individuality and courage even at risk to themselves. On the left, Terri Barnett and Gregory Alan Williams are honored for rescuing white people during violence that erupted in Los Angeles following the acquittal of white police officers who had beaten a black motorist. On the right is Christophe Meili, a young watchman at a Swiss bank, who blew the whistle on Swiss banks that had illegally confiscated hundreds of millions of dollars belonging to Holocaust survivors. As a result of Meili's leaking secret bank documents to the media, Jewish survivors—such as Estelle Sapir, shown with him here—were able to get the money that had been stolen from their families during the war. Meili was fired.

to postpone the launch. The price of their decision was an explosion that caused the deaths of the entire crew.

4 **You have an ally.** In Asch's conformity experiment, the presence of one other person who gave the correct answer was enough to overcome agreement with the majority. In Milgram's experiment, the presence of a peer who disobeyed the experimenter's instruction to shock the learner sharply increased the number of people who also disobeyed. One dissenting member of a group may be viewed as a troublemaker, but several are a coalition. An ally reassures a person of the rightness of the protest, and their combined efforts may eventually persuade the majority (Wood et al., 1994).

5 **You become entrapped.** Once having taken the initial step of getting involved, most people will increase their commitment. In one study, nearly 9,000 federal employees were asked whether they had observed wrongdoing at work, whether they had told anyone about it, and what had happened if they had told. About half of the sample had observed some serious cases of wrongdoing, such as stealing federal funds, accepting bribes, or creating a situation that was dangerous to public safety. Of that half, 72 percent had done nothing at all, but the other 28 percent had reported the problem to their immediate supervisors. Once they had taken that step, a majority of the whistle-blowers eventually took the matter to higher authorities (Graham, 1986).

As you can see, certain social and cultural factors make altruism, disobedience, and dissent more likely to occur, just as other factors suppress them. This is why people are so often inconsistent across situations: A woman may be forthright about her opinions on her job, yet conform to the opinions of others when she serves on a jury; a man might leap into a frozen river on Tuesday to rescue a child, yet keep silent on Wednesday when his employer orders him to ignore worker-safety precautions at a factory because they are too expensive. How do you think you would behave if you were faced with a conflict between social pressure and conscience? Would you call 911 if you saw someone being injured in a fight or voice your true opinion in class even though everyone else seemed to disagree with you? What aspects of the situation and your culture's norms would influence your responses?

WHAT'S AHEAD

- **How difficult is it to create "us-them" thinking?**
- **How do stereotypes benefit us, and how do they distort reality?**
- **Is prejudice more likely to be a *cause* of competition and war or a *result* of them?**
- **Why do well-meaning people sometimes get caught up in a "cycle of distrust" with other ethnic groups?**
- **Why isn't mere contact between cultural groups enough to reduce prejudice between them? What does work?**

GROUP CONFLICT AND PREJUDICE

So far, we have been discussing the effects of groups on their members. But a lot of human mischief and misery occurs when groups compete and conflict with one another, and especially when groups are operating on the basis of different cultural rules. Most of us take our own rules and norms for granted, and assume they are logical, normal, and right. The trouble starts when we assume that other people's customs are irrational, peculiar, and wrong.

Ethnocentrism, the belief that one's own culture or ethnic group is superior to all others, is universal, probably because it aids survival by making people feel attached to their own group and willing to work on the group's behalf. Ethnocentrism is even embedded in some languages: The Chinese word for China means "the center of the world" and the Navajo and the Inuit both call themselves simply "The People." But does the fact that we feel good about our own culture, nationality, gender, or school mean that we have to regard other groups as inferior? Social and cultural psychologists strive to identify the conditions that promote harmony or conflict, understanding or prejudice, between groups.

Group Identity: Us Versus Them

ethnocentrism The belief that one's own ethnic group, nation, or religion is superior to all others.

social identity The part of a person's self-concept that is based on his or her identification with a nation, culture, or ethnic group or with gender or other roles in society.

Each of us develops a personal identity that is based on our particular traits and unique history. But we also develop **social identities** based on the groups we belong to, including our national, ethnic, religious, and occupational groups (Brewer & Gardner, 1996; Hogg & Abrams, 1988; Tajfel & Turner, 1986). Social identities are important because they give us a feeling of place and position in the world. Without them, most of us would feel like loose marbles rolling around in an unconnected universe.

Being in a group confers an immediate social identity: Us. As soon as people have created a category called "us," however, they invariably perceive everybody else as "not-us." This in-group solidarity can be manufactured in a minute in a laboratory, as Henri Tajfel and his colleagues (1971) first demonstrated in a classic experiment with British schoolboys. Tajfel showed the boys slides with varying numbers of dots on them and asked the boys to guess how many dots there were. The boys were arbitrarily told they were "overestimators" or "underestimators" and were then asked to work on another task. In this phase, they had the chance to award points to other boys identified as overestimators or underestimators. Although each boy worked alone in his own cubicle, almost every single one assigned far more points to boys he thought were like him, an overestimator or an underestimator. As the boys emerged from their rooms, they were asked, "Which were you?"—and the answers received a mix of cheers and boos from the others.

Us-them social identities are strengthened when two groups compete with one another. Competition can be great fun, of course; during an exciting basketball game or Olympic event, participants and spectators alike are exhilarated. Moreover, competition in business and science can lead to better services and products and new inventions. Yet, competition has psychological hazards. It often decreases work motivation; it makes people feel insecure and anxious, even if they win; it makes people angry and frustrated if they lose; it fosters jealousy and hostility. After reviewing the huge number of studies on its effects, Alfie Kohn (1992) concluded that "the phrase *healthy competition* is a contradiction in terms."

Years ago, Muzafer Sherif and his colleagues used a natural setting, a Boy Scout camp called Robbers Cave, to demonstrate the effects of competition on hostility and conflict between groups (Sherif, 1958; Sherif et al., 1961). Sherif randomly assigned 11- and 12-year-old boys to two groups, the Eagles and the Rattlers. To build a sense of in-group identity and team spirit, he had each group work together on projects such as making a rope bridge and building a diving board. Sherif then put the Eagles and Rattlers in competition for prizes. During fierce games of football, baseball, and tug-of-war, the boys whipped up a competitive fever that soon spilled off of the playing fields. They began to raid each other's cabins, call each other names, and start fistfights. No one dared to have a friend from the rival group. Before long, the Rattlers and the Eagles were as hostile toward each other as any two gangs fighting for turf or any two nations fighting for dominance. Their hostility continued even when they were just sitting around together watching movies.

Then Sherif decided to try to undo the hostility he had created and make peace between the Eagles and Rattlers. He and his associates set up a series of predicaments in which both groups needed to work together to reach a desired goal. The boys had to cooperate to get the water supply system working. They had to pool their resources to get a movie they all wanted to see. When the staff truck "accidentally" broke down on a camping trip, they all had to join forces to pull the truck up a steep hill and get it started again.

This policy of *interdependence in reaching mutual goals* was highly successful in reducing the boys' competitiveness and hostility; the boys eventually made friends with their former enemies (see Figure 8.4). Interdependence has a similar effect in adult groups. The reason is that cooperation causes people to think of themselves as members of one big group instead of two opposed groups, *us* and *them* (Gaertner et al., 1990).

Stereotypes

If you are like most people, you can think of a million ways that members of your family vary—Harold is stodgy, Ruth is prissy, Fatima is outgoing. But if you have never met a person from Turkey or Tibet, you are likely to *stereotype* Turks and Tibetans. A **stereotype** is a summary impression of a group of people in which all

**FIGURE 8.4
THE EXPERIMENT AT
ROBBERS CAVE**

In this study, competitive games fostered hostility between the Rattlers and the Eagles. Few boys had a best friend from the other group (top). But after the boys had to cooperate to solve various problems, the percentage who made friends across "enemy lines" shot up (bottom) (Sherif et al., 1961).

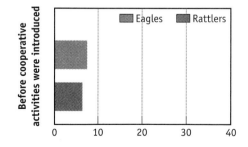

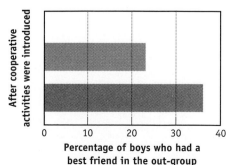

Percentage of boys who had a
best friend in the out-group

stereotype A summary impression of a group, in which a person believes that all members of the group share a common trait or traits (positive, negative, or neutral).

Which woman is the chemical engineer and which is the assistant? The Western stereotype holds that women are not engineers in the first place, but if they are, they are Western. Actually, the engineer at this refinery is the Kuwaiti woman on the left.

members of the group are viewed as sharing a common trait or traits. Stereotypes may be negative, positive, or neutral. There are stereotypes of people who drive Jeeps or BMWs, of men who wear earrings and of women who wear business suits, of engineering students and art students, of feminists and fraternity members.

Stereotypes play an important role in human thinking. They help us quickly process new information and retrieve memories. They allow us to organize experience, make sense of differences among individuals and groups, and predict how people will behave. They are, as some psychologists have called them, useful "tools in the mental toolbox"—energy-saving devices that allow us to make efficient decisions (Macrae, Milne, & Bodenhausen, 1994).

Although stereotypes reflect real differences among people, however, they also distort that reality in three ways (Judd et al., 1995). First, *they exaggerate differences between groups*, making the stereotyped group seem odd, unfamiliar, or dangerous, not like "us." Second, *they produce selective perception*; people tend to see only the evidence that fits the stereotype and reject any perceptions that do not fit. Third, *they underestimate differences within other groups*. People realize that their own groups are made up of all kinds of individuals, but stereotypes create the impression that all members of other groups (say, all Texans or all teenagers) are the same.

Some stereotypes stem from a person's cultural values. For example, as discussed in Chapter 3, white Americans tend to have strongly negative stereotypes about fat people because of a cultural ideology that individuals are responsible for what happens to them and for how they look. In contrast, Mexicans (in Mexico and the United States) and African-Americans are significantly more accepting of heavy people (Crandall & Martinez, 1996; Hebl & Heatherton, 1998).

Cultural values also affect how people evaluate a particular action (Taylor & Porter, 1994). For example, Chinese students in Hong Kong, where communalism and respect for elders are valued, think that a student who comes late to class or argues with a parent about grades is being selfish and disrespectful of adults. But Australian students, who value individualism, think that the same behavior is perfectly appropriate (Forgas & Bond, 1985). You can see how the Chinese might form negative stereotypes of "disrespectful" Australians, and how the Australians might form negative stereotypes of the "spineless" Chinese. And it is a small step from negative stereotypes to prejudice.

Prejudice

A *prejudice* consists of a negative stereotype and a strong, unreasonable dislike or hatred of a group or its individual members. Feelings of prejudice violate the spirit of critical thinking because they resist rational argument and evidence. In his classic book *The Nature of Prejudice*, Gordon Allport (1954/1979) described the responses characteristic of a prejudiced person when confronted with evidence contradicting his or her beliefs:

Mr. X: The trouble with Jews is that they only take care of their own group.

Mr. Y: But the record of the Community Chest campaign shows that they give more generously, in proportion to their numbers, to the general charities of the community, than do non-Jews.

Mr. X: That shows they are always trying to buy favor and intrude into Christian affairs. They think of nothing but money; that is why there are so many Jewish bankers.

Mr. Y: But a recent study shows that the percentage of Jews in the banking business is negligible, far smaller than the percentage of non-Jews.

Mr. X: That's just it; they don't go in for respectable business; they are only in the movie business or run night clubs.

Notice that Mr. X does not respond to Mr. Y's evidence; he just moves along to another reason for his dislike of Jews. That is the slippery nature of prejudice. It is based on faulty generalizations about an entire group; it is not grounded in the prejudiced person's direct experience with that group; and, unlike mere misconceptions about a group that can be modified with information, it is resistant to change (Herek, 1998).

The Origins of Prejudice. Prejudice is a universal human experience because it has so many sources—psychological, social, economic, and cultural.

Psychologically, prejudice often serves to ward off feelings of doubt and fear. Prejudiced persons may transfer their worries onto the target group; thus, a person who has doubts or anxieties about his own sexuality may develop a hatred of gay people. Prejudice also allows people to use the target group as a scapegoat: "Those people are the source of all my troubles." And, as research from many nations has confirmed, prejudice is a tonic for low self-esteem: People puff up their own low self-worth by disliking or hating groups they see as inferior (Islam & Hewstone, 1993; Stephan et al., 1994; Tajfel & Turner, 1986).

Not all prejudices have deep-seated psychological roots, however. Some prejudices are acquired through groupthink and social pressures to conform to the views of friends, relatives, or associates. Some prejudices are passed along mindlessly from one generation to another, as when parents communicate to their children that "We don't associate with people like that." And some are acquired uncritically from advertising, TV shows, and news reports that contain derogatory images and stereotypes of certain groups.

Prejudice also has important economic functions. It makes official forms of discrimination seem legitimate, by justifying the majority group's dominance, status, or greater wealth (Sidanius, Pratto, & Bobo, 1996). Historically, for example, white men in positions of power have justified their exclusion of women, blacks, and other minorities from the workplace and politics by claiming that those minorities were inferior, irrational, and incompetent (Gould, 1996). But any majority group—of any ethnicity, gender, or nationality—that discriminates against a minority will call upon prejudice to legitimize its actions (Islam & Hewstone, 1993).

Although it is widely believed that prejudice is the primary cause of conflict and war, prejudice is actually more often a *result* of conflict and war; it *legitimizes* them. When any two groups are in direct competition for jobs, or when people are worried about their incomes and the stability of their communities, prejudice between them increases (Doty, Peterson, & Winter, 1991). Social psychologist Elliot Aronson (1999b) traced the rise and fall of attitudes toward Chinese immigrants in the United States in the nineteenth century, as reported in newspapers of the time. When the Chinese were working in the gold mines and potentially taking jobs from white laborers, whites described them as depraved, vicious, and bloodthirsty. Just a decade later, when the Chinese began working on the transcontinental railroad—doing difficult and dangerous jobs that few white men wanted—prejudice against them declined. Whites described them as hardworking, industrious, and law-abiding.

Then, after the railroad was finished and the Chinese had to compete with Civil War veterans for scarce jobs, white attitudes changed again. Whites now considered the Chinese to be "criminal," "crafty," "conniving," and "stupid" (Aronson, 1999b). (The white newspapers did not report the attitudes of the Chinese.)

Finally, prejudice toward other groups also serves cultural purposes, bonding people to their own ethnic or national group and its ways; indeed this may be a major evolutionary reason for the universal persistence of prejudice (Fishbein, 1996). In this respect, prejudice is the flip side of ethnocentrism; it is not only that we are good, but also that they are bad, lazy, or dumb.

When two nations are at war, prejudice toward the enemy allows each side to continue feeling righteous about its cause. As you can see in Figure 8.5, each side portrays the other in stereotyped ways to demonize and dehumanize the enemy, making it seem that the enemy deserves to be killed (Aronson, 1999b). Fomenting prejudice against the perceived enemy—calling them traitors, heathens, vermin, subhuman, baby-killers, brutes, or monsters—legitimizes the attackers' motives for war.

Review 8.1 summarizes the many sources of prejudices and the many functions prejudices serve for those who hold them.

FIGURE 8.5
FACES OF THE ENEMY

In every country, propaganda posters stereotype "them," the enemy, as ugly, aggressive, brutish, and greedy, and usually not quite human. These examples show the Soviet view of the United States in the 1930s as a greedy capitalist; an American depiction of the German enemy in World War I as a "mad brute"; an IRA poster of bloodthirsty "English pigs"; and a Jordanian caricature of George Bush as a golf-playing monkey.

REVIEW 8.1

SOURCES OF PREJUDICE

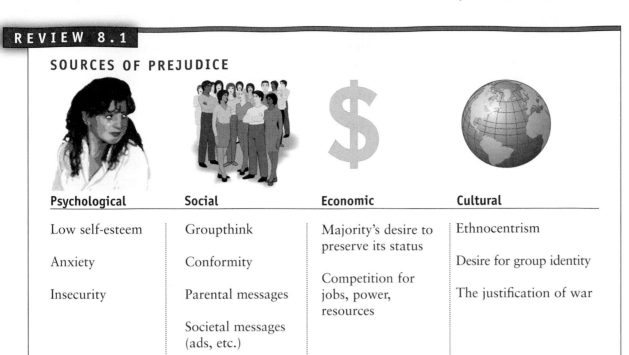

Psychological	Social	Economic	Cultural
Low self-esteem	Groupthink	Majority's desire to preserve its status	Ethnocentrism
Anxiety	Conformity		Desire for group identity
Insecurity	Parental messages	Competition for jobs, power, resources	The justification of war
	Societal messages (ads, etc.)		

The Varieties of Prejudice. If you ask people directly about their attitudes, you may conclude that prejudice in the United States and Canada is declining. White attitudes toward integration have become steadily more favorable, and the belief that blacks are inferior to whites has become much less prevalent (Plant & Devine, 1998). Men and women are also more likely to endorse gender equality; the number of men openly expressing prejudice toward women executives declined from 41 percent in 1965 to only 5 percent in 1985 (Tougas et al., 1995), and between 1970 and 1995 antiwoman attitudes in general dropped sharply (Twenge, 1997).

However, some social scientists believe that these statistics are misleading. Overt attitudes, they say, are not necessarily an accurate measure of prejudice, because many people know they should not admit their prejudices (Bell, 1992; Plant & Devine, 1998). These observers maintain that racial animosity and sexism are undiminished. Prejudice toward blacks, they argue, lurks behind a mask of *symbolic racism*, in which whites focus not on dislike of black individuals but on issues such as "reverse discrimination," "hard-core criminals," or "welfare abuse." In this view, such issues have become code words for the continuing animosity that many whites feel toward blacks.

The way to measure racism, according to this argument, is by using unobtrusive measures rather than direct attitude questionnaires. One method is to observe people's unconscious behavior when they are with a possible object of prejudice. Do they sit farther away than they normally would; reveal involuntary, negative facial expressions; or have other signs of physical tension (Fazio et al., 1995; Vanman et al., 1997)? In such cases, however, it is difficult to say whether you are identifying "real" prejudice or merely discomfort and unfamiliarity with the target.

Another method is to observe how people who say they are unprejudiced actually behave when they are emotionally upset (Jones, 1991). In one such experiment,

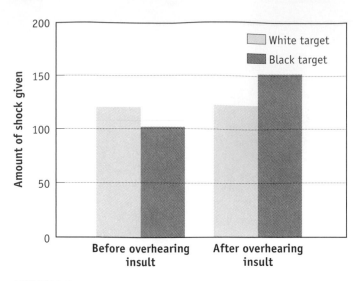

FIGURE 8.6
PROVOCATION AND PREJUDICE

When white students were insulted, they gave much higher levels of shock to blacks than they did when not angry (Rogers & Prentice-Dunn, 1981). Studies of the majority's behavior toward other minorities, such as Jews, gays, and French Canadians, find the same results.

students thought they were giving shock to other subjects in a study of biofeedback. White students initially showed *less* aggression toward blacks than toward whites. But as soon as the white students were angered by overhearing derogatory remarks about themselves, they showed *more* aggression toward blacks than toward whites (Rogers & Prentice-Dunn, 1981). (See Figure 8.6.)

In another study, English-speaking Canadians who had been put through a frustrating experience with failure rated members of the out-group (French-speaking Canadians) more negatively than did those who had not been frustrated (Meindl & Lerner, 1985). And in studies with non-Jewish students and heterosexuals, students who had received a blow to their self-esteem evaluated Jews or gay men more harshly than other students did (Fein & Spencer, 1997). Findings like these imply that people are willing to control negative feelings toward their customary targets of prejudice under normal conditions. But as soon as they are angry, frustrated, provoked, or suffer a loss of self-esteem, their real prejudice reveals itself.

One complication in measuring prejudice is that not all people are prejudiced in the same way. Some people are unapologetically racist, sexist, or antigay; others have a patronizing sense of superiority over other groups but are not explicitly hostile toward them; still others feel guilty about harboring negative feelings toward other groups. Gordon Allport (1954/1979) observed that "defeated intellectually, prejudice lingers

THE MANY TARGETS OF PREJUDICE

Prejudice has a long history, everywhere in the world. Why do new prejudices keep emerging and why do some old ones persist? In the 1920s (photo at left) and during World War II, anti-Japanese feelings ran high, and returned during America's economic competition with Japan in the early 1990s. Prejudice toward gay men and lesbians has often erupted in virulent protest, anger, and violence. Antisemitism is one of the world's oldest prejudices, and still erupts among those who make Jews the scapegoats for their problems.

GET ➜ INVOLVED

PROBING YOUR PREJUDICES

Are you prejudiced toward a specific group of people? Is it a group defined by gender, ethnicity, sexual orientation, nationality, religion, physical appearance, or political views? Write down your deepest thoughts and feelings about this group. Take as long as you want, and do not censor yourself or say what you think you ought to say. Now reread what you have written. Which of the many sources of prejudice discussed in the text might be contributing to your views? Do you feel that your attitudes toward the group are legitimate, or are you uncomfortable about having them?

emotionally." That is, a person might realize that a prejudice is unwarranted, yet still feel uncomfortable with members of certain groups. Should we put this person in the same category as one who is an outspoken bigot or who actively discriminates against others because of their sex, culture, sexual orientation, weight, disability, or skin color? What if a person is ignorant of another culture and mindlessly blurts out a remark that reflects that ignorance? Does that count as prejudice or mere thoughtlessness? Can women be sexist and blacks be racist, or do "sexism" and "racism" apply only to institutional practices by those in power? Because people differ in their definitions of *racist*, *sexist*, and *prejudiced*, their conclusions about prejudice will also differ.

During the economic recession of the early 1990s, Iranians and other immigrants became targets of American hostility. Native Americans have been objects of hatred since Europeans first arrived on the continent. Segregated facilities for blacks were legal until the 1950s, and even today many neighborhoods and schools remain separate and unequal. And anti-female prejudice continues.

Efforts to Reduce Prejudice

Given the many sources and definitions of prejudice, no one method of reducing it is likely to work in all situations (Monteith, 1996). That is why social and cultural psychologists have designed different programs to try to reduce misunderstanding and prejudice, depending on the origins of a given conflict and the factors that are supporting it.

For example, according to Patricia Devine (1995), different strategies should be used with people who are trying to break their "prejudice habit" than with people who are comfortable with their bigotry. She has been working with people who are making an effort to put old prejudices aside, but who are unfamiliar or uncomfortable with members of another group. In such situations, a "cycle of distrust" and animosity can emerge even when individuals start off with the best intentions to get along. Some majority group members, although highly motivated to work well with minorities, may be self-conscious and anxious about doing the wrong thing. Their anxiety makes them behave awkwardly; for instance, by blurting out dumb remarks and avoiding eye contact with minority-group members. The minority members, based on their own history of discrimination, may interpret the majority-group members' behavior as evidence of hostility and respond with withdrawal, aloofness, or anger. The majority members, not understanding that their own anxieties have been interpreted as evidence of prejudice, regard the minority members' behavior as unreasonable or mysterious, so they reciprocate the hostility or withdraw. This behavior confirms the minority members' suspicions about the majority's true feelings and prejudices (Devine, Evett, & Vasquez-Suson, 1996).

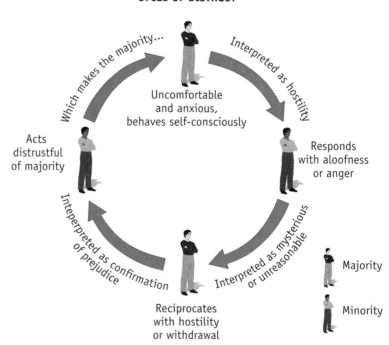

CYCLE OF DISTRUST

Which makes the majority... Uncomfortable and anxious, behaves self-consciously

Interpreted as hostility → Responds with aloofness or anger

Interpreted as mysterious or unreasonable → Reciprocates with hostility or withdrawal

Interpreted as confirmation of prejudice → Acts distrustful of majority

Majority

Minority

By understanding this cycle, Devine argues, people can learn to break it. Majority members can become aware of the discrepancy between their intentions and their actual behavior. They can learn to reduce their discomfort with people unlike themselves and acquire the skills that will lessen their anxiety. But minorities must become part of the solution too—for example, by recognizing their possible biases in seeing the majority members' behavior only in a negative light. Both sides, Devine (1995) emphasizes, should remember that reducing prejudice is a *process* and does not happen overnight.

It is important, she argues, to reward people who are making an effort to change their biases, instead of condemning them for not being perfect.

What happens, however, when two groups really do bear enormous animosity toward each other? How then might their conflicts be reduced? Sociocultural researchers emphasize the importance of changing people's circumstances, rather than waiting around for individuals to undergo a moral or psychological conversion. They have identified four conditions that must be met before conflict and prejudice between groups can be overcome (Dovidio, Gaertner, & Validzic, 1998; Fishbein, 1996; Fisher, 1994; Pettigrew, 1997; Rubin, 1994; Staub, 1996):

QUESTION ASSUMPTIONS
"If only people got to know each other, they could get along." What is wrong with this popular assumption?

1 *Both sides must have equal legal status, economic opportunities, and power.* This requirement is the spur behind efforts to change laws that permit discrimination. Integration of public facilities in the American South would never have occurred if civil-rights advocates had waited for segregationists to have a change of heart. Women would never have gotten the right to vote, attend college, or do "men's work" without persistent challenges to the laws that permitted gender discrimination. Laws, however, do not necessarily change attitudes if all they do is produce unequal contact between groups or if competition for jobs continues.

2 *The larger culture—authorities and community institutions—must endorse egalitarian norms and thereby provide moral support and legitimacy for both sides.* The larger culture must establish norms of equality and support them in the actions of its officials—teachers, employers, the judicial system, government officials, and the police.

3 *Both sides must have opportunities to work and socialize together, formally and informally.* According to the *contact hypothesis,* prejudice declines when people have the chance to get used to one another's rules, food, music, customs, and attitudes. By making friends with one another, people of different groups and cultures can discover their shared interests and shared humanity (Pettigrew, 1997).

The contact hypothesis has been supported by many studies in the laboratory and in the real world. Researchers have examined newly integrated housing projects in the American South during the 1950s and 1960s; relationships between German and immigrant Turkish children in German schools; young people's attitudes toward and contact with the elderly; healthy people's attitudes toward the mentally ill; nondisabled children's attitudes toward the disabled; and straight people's prejudices toward gay men and lesbians (Fishbein, 1996; Herek, 1998; Herek & Capitanio, 1996; Pettigrew, 1997; Wilner, Walkley, & Cook, 1955). These studies confirm that when people make friends with members of another group, they tend to become less prejudiced toward the group as a whole.

Nevertheless, contact and friendship alone are not enough to reduce prejudice and achieve harmony between groups (Fishbein, 1996). This is sadly apparent at multi-ethnic high schools, where ethnic groups often form cliques and gangs, fighting other groups and defending their own ways.

4 *Both sides must cooperate, working together for a common goal,* an enterprise that reduces us-them thinking and creates an encompassing social identity ("We're all in this together"). This fourth key to reducing prejudice is one of the most powerful (Fishbein, 1996). Researchers learned this by setting up cooperative situations in schools, businesses, and communities, requiring formerly antagonistic groups to work together for a common goal—the Eagles and the Rattlers solution.

In schools, psychologists have experimented with variations on *cooperative learning,* in which the success of any individual child rests on the success of the whole group. For example, years ago, researchers were able to reduce ethnic conflict among white, Chicano, and black children in Texas elementary schools by designing a "jigsaw method" to build cooperation (Aronson et al., 1978). Classes were divided into groups of six students of mixed ethnicity, and every group worked together on a task that was broken up like a jigsaw puzzle. Each child needed the contributions of the others to put the assignment together; for instance, each child might be given one paragraph of a six-paragraph biography and be asked to learn the whole story. The cooperative students, in comparison to classmates in regular classes, had greater self-esteem, liked their classmates better, showed a decrease in stereotyping and prejudice, and improved their grades.

These findings, and studies of other kinds of cooperative learning, have been replicated in many classrooms (Aronson & Patnoe, 1997; Vanman et al., 1997; Wolfe & Spencer, 1996). However, cooperation does not work when members of a group have unequal status, blame one another for loafing or "dropping the ball," or perceive that their teachers or employers are playing favorites.

Each of these four approaches to reducing prejudice is important, but none is sufficient on its own. Perhaps one reason that group conflicts are so persistent is that all four conditions are rarely met at the same time.

QUICK QUIZ

Try to overcome your prejudice against quizzes by taking this one.

A. Which concept—ethnocentrism, stereotyping, or prejudice—is illustrated by each of the following statements?

1. Juan believes that all Anglos are uptight and cold, and he won't listen to any evidence that contradicts his belief.

2. John knows and likes the Mexican minority in his town, but he privately believes that Anglo culture is superior.

3. Jane believes that Honda owners are thrifty and practical. June believes that Honda owners are stingy and dull.

B. What strategy does the Robbers Cave study suggest for reducing hostility between groups?

 C. Surveys find that large percentages of African-Americans, Asian-Americans, and Latinos hold negative stereotypes of one another and resent other minorities, too. What are some reasons that people who have themselves been victims of stereotyping and prejudice would hold the same attitudes toward others?

Answers:

A. 1. prejudice 2. ethnocentrism 3. stereotyping B. fostering interdependence in reaching mutual goals C. their own insecurity and low self-esteem; socialization by parents and messages in the larger society; conformity with relatives and friends who share these prejudices; competition for jobs; ethnocentrism

WHAT'S AHEAD

● Are "age-old tribal hatreds" the best explanation for war and genocide?
● What is the "banality of evil," and what does it tell us about human nature?

THE QUESTION OF HUMAN NATURE

In 1942, Wladyslaw Misiuna, a Polish teenager, was ordered by the Germans to supervise inmates at a concentration camp. One day, an inmate named Devora Salzberg came to see him about an infection that had covered her arms with open lesions. Misiuna knew that he could never get a doctor to the camp to treat her.

So he infected himself with her blood, contracted the lesions himself, and went to a doctor. Then he shared with Devora the medication he was given. Both were cured, and both survived the war (Fogelman, 1994).

Heroes like Misiuna represent the greatest good in humanity. In contrast, the Nazis have come to symbolize the evil in human nature, because they systematically exterminated millions of Jews, Gypsies, homosexuals, disabled people, and anyone else not deemed to be of the "pure" Aryan "race." But the Nazis were not a strange historical oddity; torture, genocide, and massacres are all too common in history. Americans and Canadians slaughtered native peoples in North America, Turks slaughtered Armenians, the Khmer Rouge slaughtered millions of fellow Cambodians, the Spanish conquistadors slaughtered native peoples in Mexico and South America, Idi Amin waged a reign of terror against his own people in Uganda, the Japanese slaughtered Koreans and Chinese, Iraqis slaughtered Kurds, despotic political regimes in Argentina and Chile killed thousands of dissidents and rebels. In recent years in Rwanda, hundreds of thousands of Tutsis have been shot or hacked to death with machetes by members of the rival Hutu tribe; and in the former Yugoslavia, Bosnian Serbs have massacred Bosnian Muslims in the name of "ethnic cleansing."

Many people believe that these outbreaks of horrifying violence are a result of inner aggressive drives or, in the case of Rwanda and Yugoslavia, "age-old tribal hatreds." But in fact, policies of genocide against a perceived outside enemy are almost always generated by governments that feel weakened and vulnerable (Smith, 1998; Staub, 1996). Governments then rely on the social psychological processes discussed in this chapter—including obedience to authority, conformity, rationalization, groupthink, deindividuation, and prejudice—to carry out their policies.

That is why, from the standpoint of social and cultural psychology, all human beings, like all cultures, contain the potential for good *and* bad; how most of us actually behave in a given situation depends more on human social organization than on human nature. The philosopher Hannah Arendt (1963), who covered the trial of Adolf Eichmann, used the phrase *the banality of evil* to describe how it was possible for Eichmann and other ordinary people in Nazi Germany to commit the monstrous acts they did. (*Banal* means "commonplace" or "unoriginal.")

The compelling evidence for the banality of evil is, perhaps, the hardest lesson in psychology. Most people want to believe that only evil people, who are bad down to their bones, do harm others; or that only evil cultures, which do not have one good custom to recommend them, start wars. It is reassuring to divide the world into those who are good or bad, kind or cruel, moral or immoral. But research from social and cultural psychology knocks us off our ethnocentric pedestal. No culture can claim to be wholly virtuous, and no culture is entirely villainous either. Throughout history, as circumstances have changed, societies have changed from being warlike to being peaceful, and vice versa.

Of course, some people do stand out as being unusually heroic or unusually sadistic. But as we have seen, good people can do terribly disturbing things when norms and roles encourage or require them to do so—when the situation takes over and they do not stop to think critically. Otherwise healthy people may join self-destructive cults, inflict pain on others if ordered to, and go along with a violent crowd.

The research discussed in this chapter suggests that ethnocentrism and prejudice will always be with us, as long as differences exist among groups. But it can also help us formulate realistic yet nonviolent ways of living in a diverse world. By identifying the conditions that create the banality of evil, perhaps we can create others that foster the "banality of virtue"—everyday acts of kindness, selflessness, and generosity.

THINKING CRITICALLY

DON'T OVERSIMPLIFY
Many people like to divide individuals and nations into those that are "good" and those that are "evil." What is wrong with thinking this way?

Many people think in simplistic terms about good and evil, expecting the good guys to "blow away" the bad guys once and for all.

TAKING PSYCHOLOGY WITH YOU

TRAVELS ACROSS THE CULTURAL DIVIDE

A French salesman worked for a company that was bought by Americans. When the new American manager ordered him to step up his sales within the next three months, the employee quit in a huff, taking his customers with him. Why? In France, it takes years to develop customers; in family-owned businesses, relationships with customers may span generations. The American wanted instant results, as Americans often do, but the French salesman knew this was impossible and quit. The American view was, "He wasn't up to the job; he's lazy and disloyal, so he stole my customers." The French view was, "There is no point in explaining anything to a person who is so stupid as to think you can acquire loyal customers in three months" (Hall & Hall, 1987).

Both men were committing the fundamental attribution error: assuming the other person's behavior was due to personality rather than the situation—in this case, a situation governed by cultural rules. Many corporations now realize that such rules are not trivial and that success in a global economy depends on understanding them. You, too, can benefit from the psychological research on cultures, whether you plan to do business abroad, visit as a tourist, or just want to get along better in your own society.

■ *Be sure you understand the other culture's rules, manners, and customs.* If you find yourself getting angry over something a person from another culture is doing, try to find out whether your expectations and perceptions of that person's behavior are appropriate. For example, Koreans typically do not shake hands when greeting strangers, whereas most North Americans and Europeans do. People who shake hands as a gesture of friendship and courtesy are likely to feel insulted if another person refuses to do the same unless they understand this cultural difference.

Here is another example: Suppose you are shopping in the Middle East or Latin America. If you are not used to bargaining, the experience is likely to be exasperating. Because you do not know the unstated rules, you will not know whether you got taken or got a great buy. On the other hand, if you are from a culture where people bargain for everything, you will feel just as exasperated if a seller offers you a flat price. "Where's the fun in this?" you'll say. "The whole human transaction of shopping is gone!" It will help to find a cultural translator who can show you the ropes.

■ *When in Rome, do as the Romans do—as much as possible.* Most of the things you really need to know about a culture are not to be found in the guidebooks or travelogues. To learn the unspoken rules of a culture, look, listen, and observe. What is the pace of life like? Do people regard brash individuality as admirable or embarrassing? When customers enter a shop, do they greet and chat with the shopkeeper or ignore the person as they browse?

Remember, though, that even when you know the rules, you may find it difficult to carry them out, as we noted in discussing conversational distance. For exam-

ple, cultures differ in their tolerance for prolonged gazes (Keating, 1994). In the Middle East, two men will look directly at one another as they talk, but such direct gazes would be deeply uncomfortable to most Japanese and a sign of insult or confrontation to some African-Americans. Knowing this fact about gaze rules can help people accept the reality of different customs, but most of us will still feel uncomfortable trying to change our own ways.

■ *Avoid stereotyping.* Try not to let your awareness of cultural differences cause you to overlook individual variations within cultures. During a dreary Boston winter, social psychologist Roger Brown (1986) went to the Bahamas for a vacation. To his surprise, he found the people he met unfriendly, rude, and sullen. He decided that the reason was that Bahamians had to deal with spoiled, demanding foreigners, and he tried out this hypothesis on a cab driver. The cab driver looked at Brown in amazement, smiled cheerfully, and told him that Bahamians don't mind tourists—just *unsmiling* tourists.

And then Brown realized what had been going on. "Not tourists generally, but this tourist, myself, was the cause," he wrote. "Confronted with my unrelaxed wintry Boston face, they had assumed I had no interest in them and had responded noncommittally, inexpressively. I had created the Bahamian national character. Everywhere I took my face it sprang into being. So I began smiling a lot, and the Bahamians changed their national character. In fact, they lost any national character and differentiated into individuals."

Wise travelers can use their knowledge of cultural differences to expand their understanding of human behavior, while avoiding the trap of stereotyping. Sociocultural research teaches us to appreciate the countless explicit and implicit cultural rules that govern our behavior, values, and attitudes, and those of others. Yet, we should not forget Roger Brown's lesson that every human being is an individual: one who not only reflects his or her culture, but also shares the common concerns of all humanity.

SUMMARY

ROLES AND RULES

1. *Social psychology* is the study of people in social context, including the influence of *norms*, *roles*, and groups on behavior and cognition. Roles and norms are affected by one's *culture*.

2. Two classic studies illustrate the power of roles to affect individual actions. In Milgram's obedience study, most people in the role of "teacher" inflicted what they thought was extreme shock on another person because of the authority of the experimenter. In Zimbardo's prison study, college students quickly fell into the role of "prisoner" or "guard."

3. Obedience to authority contributes to the smooth running of society, but obedience can also lead to actions that are deadly, foolish, or illegal. People obey orders because they can be punished if they do not, out of respect for authority, and to gain advantages. Even when they would rather not obey, they may do so because they believe the authority is *legitimate*; because the role is *routinized* into duties that are performed mindlessly; because they are embarrassed to break the rules of good manners and lack the words to protest; or because they have been *entrapped*.

SOCIAL INFLUENCES ON BELIEFS

4. According to *attribution theory*, people are motivated to search for causes to which they can attribute their own and other people's behavior. Their attributions may be *situational or dispositional*. The *fundamental attribution error* occurs when people overestimate personality traits as a cause of behavior and underestimate the influence of the situation. A *self-serving bias* allows people to excuse their mistakes by blaming the situation yet also take credit for their good deeds. According to the *just-world hypothesis*, most people need to believe that the world is fair and that people get what they deserve. To preserve this belief, they may blame victims of abuse or injustice for provoking or deserving it, instead of blaming the perpetrators.

5. People hold many *attitudes*, which include cognitions and feelings about a subject. One important influence on attitudes is the shared experiences of a person's age group or generation. Another influence is the *validity effect*: Simply hearing a statement over and over again makes it seem more believable. Techniques of attitude change include associating a product or message with someone who is famous, attractive, or expert; and linking the product with good feelings. Fear tactics tend to backfire.

6. Some methods of attitude change are intentionally manipulative. Tactics of *coercive persuasion* include putting a person under extreme distress, defining problems simplistically, offering the appearance of unconditional love and acceptance in exchange for unquestioning loyalty, creating a new identity for the person, using entrapment, and controlling access to outside information.

INDIVIDUALS IN GROUPS

7. In groups, individuals often behave differently than they would on their own. They may conform to social pressure because they identify with a group, trust the group's judgment or knowledge, hope for personal gain, or wish to be liked. But they also may conform mindlessly and self-destructively, violating their own preferences and values because "everyone else is doing it."

8. Groups that are strongly cohesive, are isolated from other views, are under outside pressure, and have strong leaders are vulnerable to *groupthink*, the tendency of group members to think alike, censor themselves, actively suppress disagreement, and feel that their decisions are invulnerable. Groupthink often produces faulty decisions because group members fail to seek disconfirming evidence for their ideas. However, groups can be structured to counteract groupthink.

9. *Diffusion of responsibility* in a group can lead to inaction on the part of individuals, such as *bystander apathy* or, in work groups, *social loafing*. The diffusion of

responsibility is especially likely to occur under conditions that promote *deindividuation*, the loss of awareness of one's individuality. Deindividuation increases when people feel anonymous, as in a large group or crowd, or when they are wearing masks or uniforms. In some situations, crowd norms lead deindividuated people to behave aggressively, but in others, crowd norms foster helpfulness and *altruism*.

10. The willingness to speak up for an unpopular opinion, blow the whistle on illegal or immoral practices, or help a stranger in trouble is partly a matter of personal belief and conscience. But several social and situational factors are also important. These include seeing a need for help, deciding to take responsibility, deciding that the costs of not doing anything are greater than the costs of getting involved, having an ally, and becoming entrapped in a commitment to help or to dissent.

GROUP CONFLICT AND PREJUDICE

11. *Ethnocentrism*, the belief that one's own group or nation is superior to all others, promotes *"us-them" thinking*. People develop *social identities* based on their group affiliations, including nationality, ethnicity, religion, and other social memberships. As soon as people see themselves as "us" (members of an in-group), they tend to define anyone different as "them." Dividing the world into us and them is often fueled by competition. Conflict and hostility between groups can be reduced by teamwork and by *interdependence* in working for mutual goals.

12. *Stereotypes* help people rapidly process new information, organize experience, and predict how others will behave. But they distort reality by (1) emphasizing differences between groups, (2) underestimating the differences within groups, and (3) producing selective perception. Cultural values and rules determine how people from different cultures see and interpret the same event.

13. A *prejudice* is an unreasonable negative feeling toward a category of people. People acquire prejudices through childhood socialization, media images, and conformity and groupthink. Prejudice wards off feelings of anxiety and doubt, provides a simple explanation of complex problems, and bolsters self-esteem when a person feels threatened. Prejudice also justifies a majority group's economic interests and dominance, and, in extreme cases, legitimizes group conflict and war. During times of economic insecurity and competition for jobs, prejudice rises significantly.

14. Prejudice occurs in many varieties and degrees. As a result, people disagree about how to define racism, sexism, and other prejudices, and on whether racism and other prejudices are declining or have merely taken new forms (such as *symbolic racism*).

15. Efforts to reduce prejudice and group conflict must take into account the origins of the conflict and the factors that support it. In groups where members of majority and minority groups are unfamiliar with one another's ways, it is important to break the *cycle of distrust*, by not inferring prejudice or hostility when none is intended.

16. Four important conditions are required for reducing prejudice and conflict between groups: Both sides must have equal legal status, economic standing, and power; both sides must have the legal and moral support of authorities and the larger culture; both sides must have opportunities to work and socialize together (the *contact hypothesis*); and both sides must work together for a common goal.

THE QUESTION OF HUMAN NATURE

17. Although many people believe that only bad people do bad deeds, the principles of social and cultural psychology show that under certain conditions, good people are often induced to do bad things too. All of us, depending on circumstances, are susceptible to obedience and conformity, bystander apathy, groupthink, deindividuation, ethnocentrism, stereotyping, and prejudice. All of us are subject to the same social and cultural forces that foster tolerance or animosity, conformity or dissent, courage or cowardice.

KEY TERMS

LOOKING BACK

- How do social rules regulate behavior—and what is likely to happen when you violate them? (pp. 264–265)

- Do you have to be mean or disturbed to inflict pain on someone just because an authority tells you to? (pp. 267–268)

- How can ordinary college students be transformed into sadistic prison guards? (p. 269)

- How can people be "entrapped" into violating their moral principles? (p. 271)

- What is one of the most common mistakes people make when they explain the behavior of others? (p. 272)

- Why would a person blame victims of rape or torture for having brought their misfortunes on themselves? (p. 274)

- What is the "Big Lie," and why does it work so well? (p. 276)

- What is the difference between ordinary techniques of persuasion and the coercive techniques used by cults? (pp. 277–278)

- Why do people in groups often go along with the majority even when the majority is dead wrong? (p. 280)

- How can "groupthink" lead to bad, even catastrophic, decisions? (p. 281)

- In an emergency, are you more likely to get help when there are lots of strangers in the area or only a few? (p. 282)

- What enables some people to disagree with a group, take independent action, or blow the whistle on wrongdoers? (pp. 285–287)

- How difficult is it to create "us-them" thinking? (p. 289)

- How do stereotypes benefit us, and how do they distort reality? (p. 290)

- Is prejudice more likely to be a *cause* of competition and war or a *result* of them? (p. 291)

- Why do well-meaning people sometimes get caught up in a "cycle of distrust" with other ethnic groups? (p. 296)

- Why isn't mere contact between cultural groups enough to reduce prejudice between them? What does work? (p. 297)

- Are "age-old tribal hatreds" the best explanation for war and genocide? (p. 299)

- What is the "banality of evil," and what does it tell us about human nature? (p. 299)

9

THINKING AND INTELLIGENCE

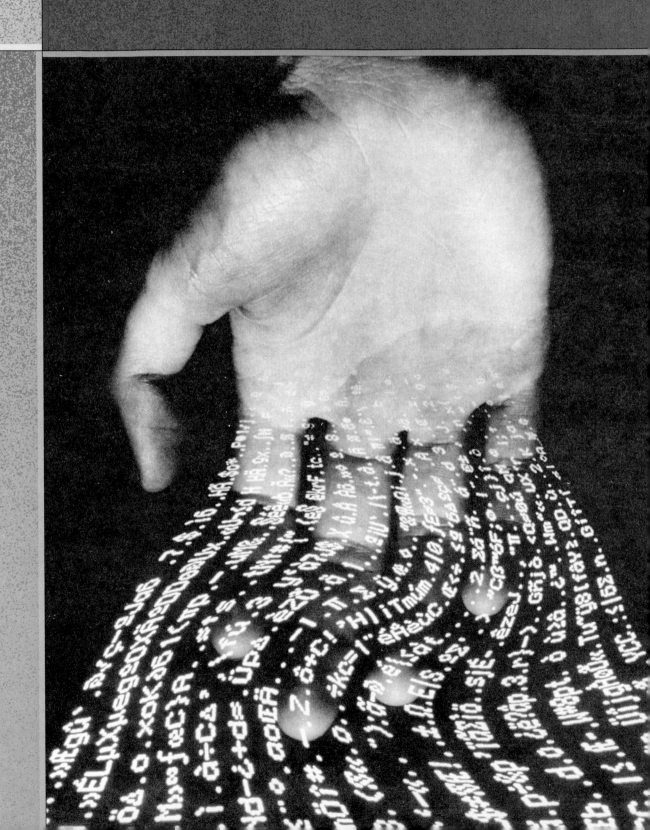

A great many people think they are thinking when

they are merely rearranging their prejudices.

PSYCHOLOGIST WILLIAM JAMES

Think about what *thinking* does for you. It frees you from the confines of the immediate present: You can think about a trip taken three years ago, a party next Saturday, or the War of 1812. It carries you beyond the boundaries of reality: You can imagine unicorns and utopias, Martians and magic. Because you think, you do not need to grope your way blindly through your problems but, with some effort and knowledge, can solve them intelligently and creatively.

Descartes' famous declaration, "I think, therefore I am," could just as well have been reversed: "I am, therefore I think." Each day, in the course of ordinary living, we all make plans, draw inferences, construct explanations, analyze relationships, and organize and reorganize our mental world. Our impressive powers of thought and intelligence so inspired our forebears that they gave our species the immodest name *Homo sapiens*, Latin for wise or rational man. But just how "sapiens" are we, really? Consider:

- As children, we all learn how clocks arbitrarily divide time into hours, minutes, and seconds. Yet every spring, when daylight savings time begins, some people fret about tampering with "God's time." One woman in Colorado complained to a local newspaper that the "extra hour of sunlight" was burning up her front lawn!
- Many people seem convinced that fictional characters in novels, movies, and soap operas are real. After *Forrest Gump* became a hit film, people began showing up at Gump's supposed alma mater, the University of Alabama, demanding to see his football trophies.
- A few years ago, the pilots of an Air Florida flight were going over a pretakeoff checklist. When the de-icer was mentioned, a crew member automatically responded "off." After all, it's always warm in Florida, isn't it? Unfortunately, on this occasion the weather happened to be icy, and the plane crashed, killing 74 people.

The human mind, which has managed to come up with poetry, penicillin, and pantyhose, is a truly miraculous thing, but the human mind has also managed to come up with traffic jams, junk mail, and war. To better understand why the same species that figured out how to get to the moon is also capable of breathtaking bumbling here on Earth, this chapter will look at how people reason, solve problems, and grow in intelligence, as well as some sources of their mental shortcomings.

Thought: Using What We Know

The Elements of Cognition
How Conscious Is Thought?

Reasoning Rationally

Formal Reasoning
Informal Reasoning
Reflective Judgment

Barriers to Reasoning Rationally

Exaggerating the Improbable
Avoiding Loss
The Confirmation Bias
Biases Due to Mental Sets
The Hindsight Bias
The Need for Cognitive Consistency
Overcoming Our Cognitive Biases

Measuring Intelligence: The Psychometric Approach

The Invention of IQ Tests
Can IQ Tests be "Culture Free"?
Beyond the IQ Test

Dissecting Intelligence: The Cognitive Approach

The Triarchic Theory
The Theory of Multiple Intelligences
Thinking Critically About Intelligence(s)
Motivation and Intellectual Success

Animal Minds

Animal Intelligence
Animals and Language
Thinking About the Thinking of Animals

Taking Psychology with You

Becoming More Creative

WHAT'S AHEAD

- When you think of a bird, why are you more likely to recall a robin than a penguin?
- How are visual images similar to images on a computer screen?
- What is happening mentally when you mistakenly take your geography notes to your psychology class?

THOUGHT: USING WHAT WE KNOW

To explain our mental abilities, many cognitive psychologists liken the human mind to an information processor, somewhat analogous to a computer but far more complex. Information-processing approaches capture the fact that the brain does not passively record information but actively alters and organizes it. When we take action, we physically manipulate the environment; when we think, we *mentally* manipulate internal representations of objects, activities, and situations.

The Elements of Cognition

One type of mental representation, or unit of thought, is the **concept**, a mental category that groups objects, relations, activities, abstractions, or qualities having common properties. The instances of a concept are seen as roughly similar. For example, *golden retriever, cocker spaniel,* and *border collie* are instances of the concept *dog,* and *anger, joy,* and *sadness* are instances of the concept *emotion.* Concepts simplify and summarize information about the world so that it is manageable, and so that we can make decisions quickly and efficiently. You may never have seen a *basenji* or eaten *escargots,* but if you know that the first is an instance of *dog* and the second an instance of *food,* you will know, roughly, how to respond (unless you do not like to eat snails, which is what escargots are).

Basic concepts have a moderate number of instances and are easier to acquire than those that have either few or many instances (Rosch, 1973). What is the object pictured in the margin? You will probably call it an apple. The concept *apple* is more basic than *fruit,* which includes many more instances and is more abstract. It is also more basic than *McIntosh apple,* which is quite specific. Similarly, *book* is more basic than either *printed matter* or *novel.* Children seem to learn basic-level concepts earlier than others, and adults use them more often than others, because basic concepts convey an optimal amount of information in most situations.

The qualities associated with a concept do not necessarily all apply to every instance: Some apples are not red; some dogs do not bark; some birds do not fly or perch on trees. But all the instances of a concept do share a "family resemblance." When we need to decide whether something belongs to a concept, we are likely to compare it to a **prototype**, a representative example of the concept (Rosch, 1973). For instance, which dog is doggier—a golden retriever or a chihuahua? Which fruit is more fruitlike—an apple or a pineapple? Which activity is more representative of sports—football or weight lifting? Most people within a culture can easily tell you which instances of a concept are most representative, or *prototypical.*

Concepts are the building blocks of thought, but they would be of limited use if we merely stacked them up mentally. We must also represent their relationships to one another. One way we accomplish this may be by storing and using **propositions**, units of meaning that are made up of concepts and that express a unitary idea. A proposition can express nearly any sort of knowledge (*Hortense raises basenjis*) or belief (*basenjis are beautiful*). Propositions, in turn, are linked together in complicated networks of

What is this?

---

concept A mental category that groups objects, relations, activities, abstractions, or qualities having common properties.

basic concepts Concepts that have a moderate number of instances and that are easier to acquire than those having few or many instances.

prototype An especially representative example of a concept.

proposition A unit of meaning that is made up of concepts and expresses a single idea.

 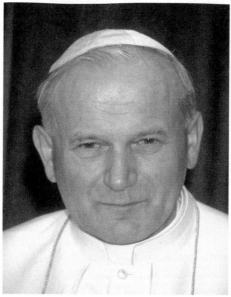 

knowledge, associations, beliefs, and expectations. These networks, which psychologists call **cognitive schemas**, serve as mental models of aspects of the world. For example, gender schemas represent a person's beliefs and expectations about what it means to be male or female (see Chapter 14). People also have schemas about cultures, occupations, animals, geographic locations, and many other features of the social and natural environment.

Some instances of a concept are more representative, or prototypical, than others. For example, Hollywood heartthrob Leonardo diCaprio clearly qualifies as a "bachelor," an unmarried man (at least, as of 1999). But is the Pope a bachelor? What about Robert Redford, who is divorced and has not remarried?

Mental images—especially visual images, pictures in the mind's eye—are also important in thinking and in the construction of cognitive schemas. Although no one can directly "see" another person's visual images, psychologists are able to study them indirectly. One method is to measure how long it takes people to rotate an image in their imaginations, scan from one point to another in an image, or read off some detail from an image. The results suggest that visual images are much like images on a computer screen: We can manipulate them, they occur in a mental "space" of a fixed size, and small ones contain less detail than larger ones (Kosslyn, 1980; Shepard & Metzler, 1971).

Most people also report auditory images (for instance, a song, slogan, or poem you can hear in your "mind's ear"), and many report images in other sensory modalities as well—touch, taste, smell, or pain. Some even report kinesthetic images, imagined feelings in the muscles and joints. Athletes often imagine themselves performing a skill, such as diving or sprinting, and this visual and kinesthetic rehearsal seems to improve actual performance (Druckman & Swets, 1988). Brain scans show that mental practice of this sort activates most of the brain circuits involved in the activity itself (Stephan et al., 1995).

Here, then, is a visual summary of the elements of cognition:

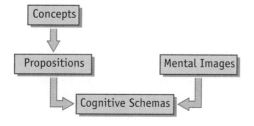

cognitive schema An integrated mental network of knowledge, beliefs, and expectations concerning a particular topic or aspect of the world.

mental image A mental representation that mirrors or resembles the thing it represents; mental images can occur in many and perhaps all sensory modalities.

How Conscious Is Thought?

When we think about thinking, we usually have in mind those mental activities, such as solving problems or making decisions, that are carried out in a deliberate way with a conscious goal in mind. However, a great deal of mental processing occurs without conscious awareness.

Subconscious and Nonconscious Thinking. **Subconscious processes** lie outside of awareness but can be brought into consciousness when necessary. These processes allow us to handle more information and to perform more complex tasks than if we depended entirely on conscious thought, and they enable us to perform more than one task simultaneously (Kahneman & Treisman, 1984). Consider all the automatic routines performed "without thinking," though they might once have required careful, conscious attention: knitting, typing, driving a car, decoding the letters in a word in order to read it. Because of the capacity for automatic processing, people can, with proper training, even learn to perform simultaneously such complex tasks as reading and taking dictation (Hirst, Neisser, & Spelke, 1978).

Nonconscious processes, in contrast, remain outside of awareness. For example, you have no doubt had the odd experience of having a solution to a problem "pop into mind" after you have given up trying to find one. With sudden insight, you see how to solve an equation, assemble a cabinet, or finish a puzzle, without quite knowing how you managed to find the solution. Similarly, people will often say they rely on "intuition"—hunches and gut feelings—rather than conscious reasoning to make decisions.

Insight and intuition probably involve two stages of mental processing (Bowers et al., 1990). In the first stage, clues in the problem automatically activate certain memories or knowledge, and you begin to see a pattern or structure in the problem, although you cannot yet say what it is. This nonconscious process guides you toward a hunch or a hypothesis. Then, in the second stage, your thinking becomes conscious, and you become aware of a possible solution. This stage may feel like a sudden revelation ("Aha, I've got it!"), but considerable nonconscious mental work has already occurred.

Imagine that you are given four decks of cards and are told that you will win or lose money depending on which cards you turn over. Unbeknownst to you, two of the decks are stacked so that they will produce payoffs at first but will make you lose in the long run, whereas the other two pay less at first but cause you to win in the long run. Every so often, someone stops you and asks whether you have figured out the best strategy for winning. Most people, when presented with this problem, start to show physiological signs of anxiety before picking cards from the losing decks and begin avoiding those decks *before* they consciously realize which decks are riskier. And some learn to make good choices without *ever* consciously discovering the rules for winning. Interestingly, people with damage in part of the prefrontal cortex have trouble learning that two of the decks are stacked against them; they seem to lack the sort of intuition that most people take for granted (Bechara et al., 1997).

Mindlessness. Usually, of course, much of our thinking is conscious, but we may not be thinking very *hard*. Like the pilots who left the de-icer off, we may act, speak, and make decisions out of habit, without stopping to analyze what we are doing or why we are doing it. This sort of mental inertia, which Ellen Langer (1989) has called *mindlessness*, keeps people from recognizing when a change in context requires a change in behavior.

Some well-learned tasks do not require much conscious thought, so this mother is able to do several things at once. There's even a word for this now: "multi-tasking."

subconscious processes Mental processes occurring outside of conscious awareness but accessible to consciousness when necessary.

nonconscious processes Mental processes occurring outside of and not available to conscious awareness.

In one study by Langer and her associates, a researcher approached people as they were about to use a photocopier and made one of three requests: "Excuse me, may I use the Xerox machine?" "Excuse me, may I use the Xerox machine, because I have to make copies?" or "Excuse me, may I use the Xerox machine, because I'm in a rush?" Normally, people will let someone go before them only if the person has a legitimate reason, as in the third request. In this study, however, people also complied when the reason sounded like an authentic explanation but was actually meaningless ("because I have to make copies"). They heard the form of the request, but not its content, and they mindlessly stepped aside (Langer, Blank, & Chanowitz, 1978).

The mindless processing of information has benefits: If we stopped to think twice about everything we did, we would get nothing done ("I'm reaching for my toothbrush; now I'm putting toothpaste on it; now I'm brushing my upper-right molars"). But mindlessness can also lead to errors and mishaps, ranging from the trivial (putting the butter in the dishwasher or locking yourself out of your apartment) to the serious (driving carelessly while on "automatic pilot").

Jerome Kagan (1989) has argued that fully conscious awareness is needed only when we must make a deliberate choice, when events happen that cannot be handled automatically, and when unexpected moods and feelings arise. "Consciousness," he says, "can be likened to the staff of a fire department. Most of the time, it is quietly playing pinochle in the back room; it performs [only] when the alarm sounds." That may be so, but most of us would probably benefit if our mental firefighters paid a little more attention to their jobs. Cognitive psychologists have, therefore, devoted a great deal of study to mindful, conscious thought and the capacity to reason.

"This CD player costs less than players selling for twice as much."

This salesman knows all about mindlessness.

QUICK QUIZ

Think consciously about this quiz.

1. Stuffing your mouth with cotton candy, licking a lollipop, and chewing on a piece of beef jerky are all instances of the _____ *eating.*

2. Which concept is most basic: *furniture, chair,* or *high chair?*

3. Which example of the concept *chair* is most prototypical: *high chair, rocking chair, dining-room chair?*

4. In addition to concepts and images, _____, which express a unitary idea, have been suggested as a basic form of mental representation.

5. Peter's mental representation of *Thanksgiving* includes associations (e.g., to turkeys), attitudes ("It's a time to be with relatives"), and expectations ("I'm going to gain weight from all that food"). They are all part of his _____ for the holiday.

6. Zelda discovers that she has dialed her boyfriend's number instead of her mother's, as she intended. Her error can be attributed to _____.

Answers:

1. concept 2. chair 3. a plain, straight-backed dining-room chair will be prototypical for most people 4. propositions 5. cognitive schema 6. mindlessness

- Mentally speaking, why is making a cake, well, a piece of cake?
- Why can't logic solve all our problems?
- What kind of reasoning do juries need to be good at?
- When people say that all opinions and claims are equally valid, what error are they making?

REASONING RATIONALLY

Reasoning is purposeful mental activity that involves operating on information in order to reach conclusions. Unlike impulsive or nonconscious responding, reasoning requires us to draw specific inferences from observations, facts, or assumptions.

Formal Reasoning: Algorithms and Logic

In *formal reasoning problems*—the kind you might find, say, on an intelligence test or a college-entrance exam—the information needed for drawing a conclusion or reaching a solution is specified clearly, and there is a single right (or best) answer.

In some formal problems and well-defined tasks, all you have to do is apply an **algorithm**, a set of procedures guaranteed to produce a solution even if you do not really know how it works. To solve a problem in long division, for example, you just apply a series of operations that you learned in elementary school. To make a cake, you apply an algorithm called a *recipe*.

For other formal problems, the rules of formal logic are crucial tools to have in your mental toolbox. One such tool is **deductive reasoning**, which involves drawing conclusions from a set of observations or propositions (*premises*). In deductive reasoning, if the premises are true, then the conclusion *must* also be true. For example, if the premises "All human beings are mortal" and "I am a human being" are true, then the conclusion "I am mortal" must necessarily follow:

DEDUCTIVE REASONING

We all use deductive reasoning all the time, although many of our premises are implicit rather than explicitly spelled out: "I never have to work on Saturday. Today is Saturday. Therefore, I don't have to work today." But the ability to apply deductive reasoning to abstract problems that are divorced from everyday life does not come naturally; it depends on experience, culture, and schooling (Segall et al., 1999). And even in everyday life, almost everyone has trouble thinking deductively in some situations.

For example, suppose the premises are "All rich people live in big fancy houses" and "Sheila lives in a big fancy house." Does it follow that Sheila is rich? Many people think so, but they are wrong. Sheila may well be rich, but the conclusion does not follow from the premises. Perhaps she inherited that big fancy house, or perhaps she bought it 30 years ago when it was inexpensive. Errors of this type occur because people mentally reverse a premise. In this case, they convert "All rich people live in big fancy houses" to "All people who live in big fancy houses are rich." The reversed premise may seem plausible, but it is not the one that was given. Reversed premises

reasoning The drawing of conclusions or inferences from observations, facts, or assumptions.

algorithm A problem-solving strategy guaranteed to produce a solution even if the user does not know how it works.

deductive reasoning A form of reasoning in which a conclusion follows necessarily from certain premises; if the premises are true, the conclusion must be true.

Zits

Reprinted with special permission of King Features Syndicate.

can have serious consequences for people's expectations and even their relationships. One of our male students worried about the effects of confusing "All rapists are men" with "All men are rapists."

Another important form of logical thinking is **inductive reasoning** in which the conclusion *probably* follows from the premises but could conceivably be false:

INDUCTIVE REASONING

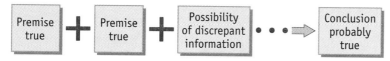

People often mistakenly think of inductive reasoning as the drawing of general conclusions from specific observations, as when you generalize from past experience: "I had three good meals at that restaurant; they sure have great food." But an inductive argument can also have premises that are stated as general statements (Copi & Burgess-Jackson, 1992). If your premises are that all cows are mammals and have lungs, all whales are mammals and have lungs, and all humans are mammals and have lungs, you might reasonably conclude that probably all mammals have lungs. Inductive arguments can also have specific conclusions: If your premises are that most people with season tickets to the concert love music and that Jeannine has season tickets to the concert, you might conclude that Jeannine probably loves music.

Science depends heavily on inductive reasoning because scientists make careful observations and then draw conclusions that they think are probably true. But in inductive reasoning, no matter how much supporting evidence you gather, it is always possible that new information will turn up to show you are wrong. For example, you might discover that the three good meals you ate at that restaurant were not typical—that, in fact, all the other dishes on the menu are awful. Or you might learn that Jeannine bought season tickets to the concert not because she loves music but because she wanted to impress a friend. In science, too, new information may show that previous conclusions were faulty and must therefore be revised.

Informal Reasoning: Heuristics and Dialectical Thinking

Useful as they are, algorithms and logical reasoning cannot solve all of life's problems. In *informal reasoning problems*, there may be no clearly correct solution; many approaches, viewpoints, or possible solutions may compete, and you may have to

inductive reasoning A form of reasoning in which the premises provide support for a conclusion, but it is still possible for the conclusion to be false.

Whether you are chess champion Garry Kasparov, pondering his next move against the computer known as Deep Blue, or just an ordinary person solving ordinary problems, you need to use heuristics, rules of thumb that help you decide on a reasonable strategy.

decide which one is most reasonable, based on what you know. Further, the information at your disposal may be incomplete, or people may disagree on what the premises should be. Your position on the controversial issue of abortion, for example, will depend on your premises about when meaningful human life begins, what rights an embryo has, and what rights a woman has to control her own body. People on opposing sides of this issue even disagree on how the premises should be phrased because they have different emotional reactions to terms such as "rights," "meaningful life," and "control over one's body."

The differences between formal and informal reasoning problems are summarized in Table 9.1. These two kinds of problems typically call for different approaches. Whereas formal problems can often be solved with an algorithm, informal problems often call for a **heuristic**—a rule of thumb that suggests a course of action without guaranteeing an optimal solution. Anyone who has ever played chess or a card game such as Bridge or Hearts is familiar with heuristics (e.g., "Get rid of high cards first"). In these games, working out all the possible sequences of moves would take too long and be too difficult. Heuristics are also useful to an investor trying to predict the stock market, a renter trying to decide whether to lease an apartment, a doctor trying to determine the best treatment for a patient, and a factory owner trying to boost production: All are faced with incomplete information on which to base a decision and may therefore resort to rules of thumb that have proven effective in the past.

In thinking about real-life problems, a person must also be able to use **dialectical reasoning**, the process of comparing and evaluating opposing points of view in order to resolve differences. Philosopher Richard Paul (1984) has described dialectical reasoning

heuristic A rule of thumb that suggests a course of action or guides problem solving but does not guarantee an optimal solution.

dialectical reasoning A process in which opposing facts or ideas are weighed and compared, with a view to determining the best solution or to resolving differences.

TABLE 9.1 Two Kinds of Reasoning

In formal reasoning, we apply rules of logic to solve well-specified problems. In informal, everyday reasoning, we must solve problems that are less clearly defined. Here are some differences between the two modes of thought:

Formal	Informal
All premises are supplied.	Some premises are implicit, and some are not supplied at all.
There is typically one correct answer.	There are typically several possible answers that vary in quality.
Established methods often exist for solving the problem.	Established procedures of inference that apply to the problem rarely exist.
You usually know when the problem is solved.	It is often unclear whether the current solution is good enough.
The problem often has limited real-world interest.	The problem is often of personal relevance.
Problems are often solved as a means of achieving other goals.	Problems are solved for their own sake.

Source: Adapted from Galotti, 1989.

as movement "up and back between contradictory lines of reasoning, using each to critically cross-examine the other":

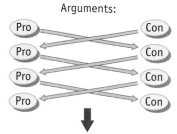

DIALECTAL REASONING

Arguments:

Pro → Con
Pro → Con
Pro → Con
Pro → Con

↓

Most reasonable conclusion based on evidence and logic

"I'm going to ask the jury to hold its applause until all the evidence has been introduced."

Dialectical reasoning is what juries are supposed to do to arrive at a verdict: consider arguments for and against the defendant's guilt, point and counterpoint. It is also what voters are supposed to do when thinking about whether the government should raise taxes or lower them or about the best way to improve public education.

Reflective Judgment

Unfortunately, many adults have trouble thinking dialectically. Evidence comes from the research of Karen Kitchener and Patricia King, who over a period of many years asked adolescents and adults of all ages and occupations to explain where they stood on issues such as nuclear power, the safety of food additives, and the objectivity of the news media. Kitchener and King did not care how much people knew about these issues, or even how they felt about them; they just wanted to know how their respondents had reached their conclusions. More specifically, they wanted to know whether people use *reflective judgment* in thinking about everyday problems (King & Kitchener, 1994; Kitchener & King, 1990). Reflective judgment is basically what we have called critical thinking: the ability to question assumptions, evaluate and integrate evidence, relate that evidence to a theory or opinion,

---

GET ➜ INVOLVED

PRACTICE YOUR DIALECTICAL REASONING

Choose a controversial topic, such as whether marijuana should be legalized or whether the right to abortion should be revoked. First, list all the arguments you can to support your own position. Then list all the arguments you can on the *other side* of the issue. You do not have to agree with these arguments; just list them. Do you feel a mental block or emotional discomfort while doing this? Can you imagine how opponents of your position would answer your arguments? Having strong opinions is fine; you should have an (informed) opinion on matters of public interest. But does that opinion get in the way of even imagining a contrary point of view, or of altering your view if the evidence warrants?

consider alternative interpretations, and reach conclusions that can be defended as reasonable or plausible, while standing ready to reassess those conclusions in the face of new information.

The researchers first provided their interviewees with statements that described opposing viewpoints on various topics. Then the interviewer asked, What do you think about these statements? How did you come to hold that point of view? On what do your base your position? Can you ever know for sure that your position is correct? Why do you suppose disagreement exists about this issue?

Based on the responses, King and Kitchener were able to identify seven cognitive stages on the road to reflective thought, some occurring in childhood and others unfolding throughout adolescence and adulthood. At each stage, people make different assumptions about how things are known and use different ways of justifying or defending their beliefs. Each stage builds on the skills of the prior one and lays a foundation for successive ones.

We will not be concerned here with the details of these stages, but only with their broad outlines. In general, people in the two early, *prereflective* stages assume that a correct answer always exists and that it can be obtained directly through the senses ("I know what I've seen") or from authorities ("They said so on the news"; "That's what I was brought up to believe"). If authorities do not yet have the truth, prereflective thinkers tend to reach conclusions on the basis of what "feels right" at the moment. They do not distinguish between knowledge and belief, or between belief and evidence, and they do not see any reason for justifying a belief (King & Kitchener, 1994):

Pre-reflective judgment

"I was brought up to believe..."
"I just know what I know."

> *Interviewer:* Can you ever know for sure that your position [on evolution] is correct?
>
> *Respondent:* Well, some people believe that we evolved from apes, and that's the way they want to believe. But I would never believe that way, and nobody could talk me out of the way I believe because I believe the way that it's told in the Bible.

During the three *quasi-reflective* stages, people recognize that some things cannot be known with absolute certainty, but they are not sure how to deal with these situations. They realize that judgments should be supported by reasons, but they pay attention only to evidence that fits what they already believe. They know that there are alternative viewpoints, but they seem to think that because knowledge is uncertain, any judgment about the evidence is purely subjective. Quasi-reflective thinkers will defend a position by saying that "We all have a right to our own opinion," as if all opinions are created equal. Here is the response of a college student who uses quasi-reflective reasoning:

Quasi-reflective judgment

"Knowledge is purely subjective."
"We all have a right to our opinion."

> *Interviewer:* Can you say you will ever know for sure that chemicals [in foods] are safe?
>
> *Student:* No, I don't think so.
>
> *Interviewer:* Can you tell me why you'll never know for sure?
>
> *Student:* Because they test them in little animals, and they haven't really tested them in humans, as far as I know. And I don't think anything is for sure.
>
> *Interviewer:* When people differ about matters such as this, is it the case that one opinion is right and one is wrong?
>
> *Student:* No. I think it just depends on how you feel personally because people make their decisions based on how they feel and what research they've seen. So what one person thinks is right, another person

might think is wrong. . . . If I feel that chemicals cause cancer and you feel that food is unsafe without it, your opinion might be right to you and my opinion is right to me.

In the last two stages, a person becomes capable of reflective judgment. He or she understands that although some things can never be known with certainty, some judgments are more valid than others because of their coherence, their fit with the evidence, their usefulness, and so on. People at these stages are willing to consider evidence from a variety of sources and to reason dialectically. At the very highest stage, they are able to defend their conclusions as representing the most complete, plausible, or compelling understanding of an issue, based on currently available evidence. This interview with a graduate student illustrates reflective thinking:

Reflective judgment

"Based on the evidence, I believe..."
"Here are the reasons for my conclusions..."

Interviewer: Can you ever say you know for sure that your point of view on chemical additives is correct?

Student: No, I don't think so. . . . [but] I think that we can usually be reasonably certain, given the information we have now, and considering our methodologies.

Interviewer: Is there anything else that contributes to not being able to be sure?

Student: Yes . . . it might be that the research wasn't conducted rigorously enough. In other words, we might have flaws in our data or sample, things like that.

Interviewer: How then would you identify the "better opinion"?

Student: One that takes as many factors as possible into consideration. I mean one that uses the higher percentage of the data that we have and, perhaps, that uses the methodology that has been most reliable.

Interviewer: And how do you come to a conclusion about what the evidence suggests?

Student: I think you have to take a look at the different opinions and studies that are offered by different groups. Maybe some studies offered by the chemical industry, some studies by the government, some private studies. . . . You wouldn't trust, for instance, a study funded by the tobacco industry that proved that cigarette smoking is not harmful . . . you have to try to interpret people's motives, and that makes it a more complex soup to try to strain out.

Most people do not show evidence of reflective judgment until their middle or late twenties, if at all. And most undergraduates, regardless of age, tend to score at only Stage 3 during their first year of college. But here's the good news: When students get support for thinking reflectively and have opportunities to practice, their thinking tends to become more complex, sophisticated, and well grounded (Kitchener et al., 1993). Moreover, higher education gradually moves people closer to reflective judgment: By their senior year, students typically score at Stage 4; most graduate students score at Stage 4 or 5; and many advanced doctoral students perform consistently at Stage 6 (King & Kitchener, 1994). Longitudinal studies show that these differences do not occur only because lower-level thinkers are more likely to drop out along the way.

The gradual development of thinking skills among college students, said Barry Kroll (1992), represents an abandonment of "ignorant certainty" in favor of "intelligent confusion." It may not seem so, but this is a big step forward! You can see why, in this book, we emphasize thinking about and evaluating psychological findings, and not just memorizing them.

QUICK QUIZ

Put on your thinking cap to answer these questions.

1. Most of the holiday gifts Mervin bought this year cost more than they did last year, so he concludes that inflation is increasing. Is he using inductive, deductive, or dialectical reasoning?

2. Yvonne is arguing with Henrietta about whether real estate is a better investment than stocks. "You can't convince me," says Yvonne. "I just know I'm right." Yvonne needs training in _____ reasoning.

3. Seymour thinks the media have a liberal political bias, and Sophie thinks they are too conservative. "Well," says Seymour, "I have my truth and you have yours. It's purely subjective." Which of King and Kitchener's levels of thinking is Seymour at?

4. What kind of evidence might resolve the issue that Seymour and Sophie are arguing about?

Answers:

1. inductive 2. dialectical 3. quasi-reflective 4. Researchers might have raters watch a random sample of TV news shows and measure the time devoted to conservative and liberal viewpoints. Or raters could read a random sample of newspaper editorials from all over the country and evaluate the editorials as liberal or conservative. You may be able to think of other strategies as well. However, subjective ratings of *entire* TV programs or newspapers as liberal or conservative might not be informative because often people perceive only what they want or expect to perceive.

WHAT'S AHEAD

● Why do people worry about dying in an airplane crash but ignore dangers that are far more likely?

● How might your physician's choice of words about alternative treatments for your illness affect which one you choose?

● When "Monday morning quarterbacks" say they knew all along who would win Sunday's big game, what bias might they be showing?

● Why will a terrible hazing make you more loyal to the group that hazed you?

BARRIERS TO REASONING RATIONALLY

Although most people have the capacity to think logically, reason dialectically, and make judgments reflectively, it is abundantly clear that they don't always do so. One obstacle is the need to be right; if your self-esteem depends on being right all the time, you will find it hard to listen with an open mind to competing views. Another obstacle is mental laziness. Many social critics think such laziness is on the rise because television watching is replacing reading. Reading requires you to sit still and follow extended arguments; it gives you the opportunity to examine connections among statements and to spot contradictions, and you can always go back a page and reread something you missed. When you read a book, therefore, you are usually mindfully engaged in its argument. But television programs often provide sound bites instead of fully developed arguments, encouraging viewers to form quick, impulsive opinions instead of carefully considered ones. As writer Mitchell Stephens (1991) noted, "All television demands is our gaze."

Human thought processes are also tripped up by many predictable biases and errors. Psychologists have studied dozens of these cognitive pitfalls; here we describe just a few of them.

TELEVISION IS VERY USEFUL IN OCCUPYING TIME THAT MIGHT OTHERWISE BE USED FOR THINKING!

Exaggerating the Improbable

One common bias is the inclination to exaggerate the probability of very rare events—a bias that helps explain why so many people enter lotteries and buy airline disaster insurance.

As we saw in Chapter 2, people are especially likely to exaggerate the likelihood of a rare event if its consequences are catastrophic. One reason is the **availability heuristic**, the tendency to judge the probability of an event by how easy it is to think of examples or instances (Tversky & Kahneman, 1973). Catastrophes and shocking accidents stand out in our minds and are therefore more "available" mentally than are other kinds of negative events. In one study, people overestimated the frequency of deaths from tornadoes and underestimated the frequency of deaths from asthma, which occur 20 times as often but do not make headlines. These same people estimated deaths from accidents and disease to be equally frequent, even though 16 times as many people die each year from disease as from accidents (Lichtenstein et al., 1978).

Many of us overestimate the chances of dying in a plane crash and underestimate the chances of dying in a car crash. As the text explains, one reason is the availability heuristic: Although airline disasters are rare, we remember them better than the automobile accidents that take place every day.

People will sometimes work themselves into a froth about unlikely events such as dying in an airplane crash, yet they will irrationally ignore dangers to human life that are harder to visualize, such as a growth in skin cancer rates due to depletion of the ozone layer in the Earth's atmosphere. Similarly, parents are often more frightened about real but unlikely threats to their children, such as being kidnapped by a stranger or dying from a routine immunization shot (both horrible but extremely rare), than they are about problems more common in children, such as depression, delinquency, and poor grades, or dangers that are far more likely, such as auto accidents or accidental drownings.

Avoiding Loss

In general, people try to avoid or minimize risks and losses when they make decisions. So when a choice is framed in terms of the risk of losing something, they will respond more cautiously than when the *same* choice is framed in terms of gain. They will, for example, choose a ticket that has a 10 percent chance of winning a raffle to one that has a 90 percent chance of losing! Or they will rate a condom as effective when they are told it has a 95 percent success rate in protecting against the AIDS virus, but not when they are told it has a 5 percent failure rate—which is logically the same thing (Linville, Fischer, & Fischhoff, 1992).

Here's another example. Suppose you had to choose between two health programs to combat a disease expected to kill 600 people. Which would you prefer: a program that will definitely save 200 people or one with a one-third probability of saving all 600 people and a two-thirds probability of saving none? (Figure 9.1a on the next page illustrates this choice.) When asked this question, most people, including physicians, say they would prefer the first program. In other words, they reject the riskier though potentially more rewarding solution in favor of a sure gain. However, people *will* take a risk if they see it as a way to *avoid loss*. Suppose now that you have to choose between a program in which 400 people will definitely die and a program in which there is a one-third probability of nobody dying and a two-thirds probability that all 600 will die. If you think about it, you will see that the alternatives are exactly the same as in the first problem; they are merely worded differently (see Figure 9.1b). Yet this time, most people choose the second solution. They reject risk when they think of the outcome in terms of lives saved, but they accept risk when they think of the outcome in terms of lives lost (Tversky & Kahneman, 1981).

availability heuristic The tendency to judge the probability of a type of event by how easy it is to think of examples or instances.

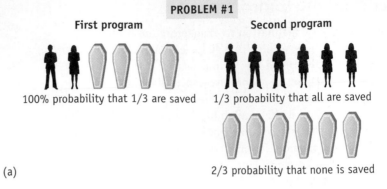

PROBLEM #1

First program

100% probability that 1/3 are saved

Second program

1/3 probability that all are saved

2/3 probability that none is saved

(a)

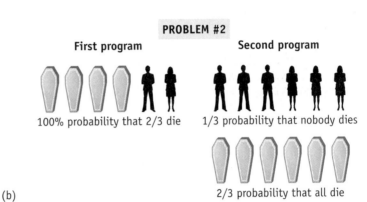

PROBLEM #2

First program

100% probability that 2/3 die

Second program

1/3 probability that nobody dies

2/3 probability that all die

(b)

FIGURE 9.1
A MATTER OF WORDING

The decisions we make depend on how the alternatives are framed. When asked to choose between the two programs in choice *a*, which are described in terms of lives saved, most people choose the first program. When asked to choose between the programs in choice *b*, which are described in terms of lives lost, most people choose the second program. Yet the alternatives in *a* are actually identical to those in *b*.

Few of us will have to face a decision involving hundreds of lives, but we may have to choose between different medical treatments for ourselves or a relative. Our decision may be affected by whether the doctor frames the choice in terms of chances of surviving or chances of dying.

The Confirmation Bias

When people want to make the most accurate judgment possible, they will usually try to consider all of the relevant information. But when they are thinking about an issue they already feel strongly about, they tend to give in to the **confirmation bias**, paying attention only to evidence that confirms their belief and finding fault with evidence or arguments that point in a different direction (Edwards & Smith, 1996; Kunda, 1990; Nickerson, 1998). You rarely hear someone say, "Oh, thank you for explaining to me why my lifelong philosophy of child raising is wrong. I'm so grateful for the facts!" The person usually says, "Oh, buzz off, and take your cockamamie ideas with you."

We see the confirmation bias all around us. Politicians, for example, are likely to accept economic news that confirms their philosophies and dismiss counterevidence as biased or unimportant. Police officers who are convinced of a suspect's guilt are likely to take anything the suspect says or does as evidence that confirms it. The confirmation bias also affects jury members. In one study, people listened to an audiotaped reenactment of an actual murder trial and then said how they would have voted and why. Instead of considering and weighing possible verdicts against the evidence, many people quickly constructed a story about what had happened and then considered only the evidence that supported their version of events. These

confirmation bias The tendency to look for or pay attention only to information that confirms one's own belief.

GET ➔ INVOLVED

CONFIRMING THE CONFIRMATION BIAS

Suppose someone deals out four cards, each with a letter on one side and a number on the other. You can see only one side of each card:

Your job is to find out whether the following rule is true: "If a card has a vowel on one side, then it has an even number on the other side." Which two cards do you need to turn over to find out?

The vast majority of people say they would turn over the E and the 6, but they are wrong. You do need to turn over the E (a vowel), because if the number on the other side is even, it confirms the rule, and if it's odd, the rule is false. However, the card with the 6 tells you nothing. The rule does not say that a card with an even number must always have a vowel on the other side. So it doesn't matter whether the 6 has a vowel or a consonant on the other side. The card you do need to turn over is the 7, because if it has a vowel on the other side, that fact disconfirms the rule.

People do poorly on this problem because they are biased to look for confirming evidence and because they ignore the possibility of disconfirming evidence. Don't feel too bad if you missed it. Most judges, lawyers, and people with doctorates do, too. On the other hand, everyone does better when the problem is more realistic. Try this one (from Griggs & Cox, 1982):

Rule: If a person is drinking beer, then the person is over 19 years of age.

Which two cards must you turn over? The correct answer is on page 344.

same people were the most confident in their decisions and were most likely to vote for an extreme verdict (Kuhn, Weinstock, & Flaton, 1994).

The confirmation bias can also affect how you react to what you are learning. When students read about scientific findings that dispute one of their own cherished beliefs or that challenge the wisdom of their own actions, they tend to acknowledge but minimize the strengths of the research. In contrast, when a study supports their view, they will acknowledge any flaws (such as a small sample or a reliance on self-reports) but will give these flaws less weight than they would otherwise (Sherman & Kunda, 1989). Psychologists do the same thing! In thinking critically, it seems, people apply a double standard: They think most critically about results they dislike.

mental set A tendency to solve problems using procedures that worked before on similar problems.

Biases Due to Mental Sets

Another roadblock on the way to rational decision making and problem solving is the development of a **mental set**, a tendency to attack new problems by using the same heuristics, strategies, and rules that worked in the past on similar problems. Mental sets make learning and problem solving efficient; because of them, we do not have to keep reinventing the wheel. But they are *not* helpful when a problem calls for fresh insights and methods. They cause us to cling rigidly to the same old assumptions and strategies, blinding us to better or more rapid solutions. (For an illustration of this point, try the "Get Involved" exercise on this page.)

One common mental set is the tendency to find meaningful patterns in events. This tendency is adaptive because it helps us understand and exert some control over what happens in our lives. But it also leads us to see meaningful patterns even when they don't exist. For example, many people with arthritis think that their symptoms follow a pattern dictated by the weather. They suffer more, they say, when the barometric pressure changes or when it is damp or humid. Yet when researchers followed 18 arthritis patients for 15 months, *no* association whatsoever emerged between weather conditions and the patients' self-reported pain levels, their ability to function in daily life, or a doctor's evaluation of their joint tenderness (Redelmeier & Tversky, 1996). Did the patients say, "Oh, thank you for pointing out that my belief was unfounded! How incredibly interesting"? No, they adamantly refused to believe the results.

The Hindsight Bias

Would you have predicted, beforehand, that the movie *Shakespeare in Love* would win the 1999 Oscar for best movie, instead of the heavily favored *Saving Private Ryan*? When people learn the outcome of an event or the answer to a question, they are often sure that they "knew it all along." Armed with the wisdom of hindsight, they see the outcome that actually occurred as inevitable, and they overestimate the probability that they could have predicted what happened. Compared

---

GET ➔ INVOLVED

CONNECT THE DOTS

Copy the following figure, and see whether you can connect the dots by using no more than four straight lines, without lifting your pencil or pen. A line must pass through each point. Can you do it?

Most people have difficulty with this problem because they have a mental set to interpret the arrangement of dots as a square. Once having done so, they then assume that they can't extend a line beyond the "boundaries" of the square. Now that you know this, you might try again if you haven't yet solved the puzzle. Some possible solutions are given on page 344.

with judgments made *before* an event takes place, their after-the-fact judgments about their own ability to have predicted the event are inflated (Fischhoff, 1975; Hawkins & Hastie, 1990).

This **hindsight bias** is common in political assessments ("I always knew my candidate would win"), medical judgments ("I could have told you that mole was cancerous"), and military opinions ("The generals should have known that Pearl Harbor would be attacked"). And when investors buy a stock, and then it goes up in price, they are apt to think, in hindsight, that they were more confident about their purchase at the time they made it than they really were (Louie, 1999).

Like mental sets, the hindsight bias may be adaptive. When we try to predict the future, we consider many possible scenarios, but when we try to make sense of the past, we focus on explaining just one outcome—the one that actually occurred. This strategy is efficient, because explaining outcomes that did not take place can be a waste of time. As Scott Hawkins and Reid Hastie (1990) wrote, "Hindsight biases represent the dark side of successful learning and judgment." They are the dark side because when we are sure that we knew something "all along," we are also less willing to find out what we need to know in order to make accurate predictions in the future. In medical conferences, for example, when doctors are told what the post-mortem findings were for a patient who died, they tend to think the case was easier to diagnose than it actually was ("I would have known it was a brain tumor"), and so they learn less from the case than they should (Dawson et al., 1988).

Perhaps you feel that we are not telling you anything new because you have always known about the hindsight bias. But then, you may just have a hindsight bias about the hindsight bias!

The Need for Cognitive Consistency

As the twentieth century rolled to an end, predictions of doomsday—the end of the world—escalated. (We assume that if you are reading this paragraph, the world did not in fact end.) One cult of true believers from Colorado traveled all the way to Israel at the start of 1999, hoping to set up camp with a good view to await Armageddon; the Israelis sent them home. There have been lots of similar doomsday predictions throughout history. Do you ever wonder what happens to true believers when their prophecy fails? How come they never seem to say, "Boy, what a jerk I was"?

According to the theory of **cognitive dissonance**, people will resolve such conflicts in predictable, though not always obvious, ways (Festinger, 1957). *Dissonance*, the opposite of consistency (*consonance*), is a state of tension that occurs when you simultaneously hold either two cognitions (beliefs, thoughts, attitudes) that are psychologically inconsistent or a belief that is incongruent with your behavior. This tension is uncomfortable, so you will be motivated to reduce it. You may do this by rejecting or modifying one of those inconsistent beliefs, changing your behavior, denying the evidence, or rationalizing (Harmon-Jones et al., 1996):

hindsight bias The tendency to overestimate one's ability to have predicted an event once the outcome is known; the "I knew it all along" phenomenon.

cognitive dissonance A state of tension that occurs when a person simultaneously holds two cognitions that are psychologically inconsistent, or when a person's belief is incongruent with his or her behavior.

ASK QUESTIONS
Time and again, doomsday predictions fail. Have you ever wondered why people who wrongly predict a devastating earthquake or the end of the world don't feel embarrassed when their forecasts flop?

COGNITIVE DISSONANCE

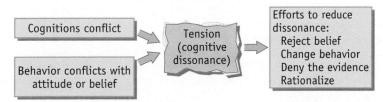

Many years ago, in a famous and clever field study, Leon Festinger and two associates explored people's reactions to failed prophecies by infiltrating a group of people who thought the world would end on December 21 (Festinger, Riecken, & Schachter, 1956). The group's leader, whom the researchers called Marian Keech, promised that the faithful would be picked up by a flying saucer and whisked to safety at midnight on December 20. Many of her followers quit their jobs and spent all their savings, waiting for the end. What would they do or say, Festinger and his colleagues wondered, to reduce the dissonance between "The world is still muddling along on the 21st" and "I predicted the end of the world and sold all my worldly possessions"?

The researchers predicted that believers who had made no public commitment to the prophecy, who awaited the end of the world by themselves at home, would simply lose their faith. But those who had acted on their conviction by selling their property and waiting with Keech for the spaceship would be in a state of dissonance. They would, said the researchers, have to *increase* their religious belief to avoid the intolerable realization that they had behaved foolishly and others knew it. That is just what happened. At 4:45 A.M., long past the appointed hour of the saucer's arrival, the leader had a new vision. The world had been spared, she said, because of the impressive faith of her little band.

Cognitive-dissonance theory predicts that in more ordinary situations, too, people will resist or rationalize information that conflicts with their existing ideas. For example, if you are a cigarette smoker, your behavior is dissonant with your awareness that smoking causes illness. You might try to reduce the dissonance by trying to quit; by rejecting the evidence that smoking is bad; by persuading yourself that you will quit later on ("after these exams"); by emphasizing the benefits of smoking ("A cigarette helps me relax"); or by deciding that you don't want a long life, anyhow ("It will be shorter, but sweeter"). Likewise, cigarette manufacturers are good at reducing the dissonance between "this job makes a lot of money for the company and for me" and "cigarette smoking kills 400,000 people a year." When the president of one tobacco company was told that smoking during pregnancy increases the chances of having a low-birthweight baby, he replied, "Some women would prefer having smaller babies" (quoted in Kluger, 1996).

Here are three conditions under which you are particularly likely to try to reduce dissonance (Aronson, Wilson, & Akert, 1999):

1 *When you need to justify a choice or decision that you freely made.* All car dealers know about "buyer's remorse": The second that people buy a car, they worry that they made the wrong decision, spent too much, or got a lemon. This is called *postdecision dissonance,* and cognitive-dissonance theory predicts that you will try to resolve it. Probably, you will decide that the car, toaster, house, or spouse that you chose is really, truly the best in the world. However, if someone else made your decision for you, you will not feel much dissonance if it proves misguided. There is no dissonance between "The Army drafted me; I had no choice about being here" and "I hate basic training."

2 *When your actions violate your self-concept.* If you are in a political discussion and you pretend to agree with the majority's position for the sake of harmony, you will experience dissonance only if you have a concept of yourself as honest and true to your convictions. If you lie frequently and you know it (and don't care), you will not feel dissonance, even if your words contradict your beliefs (Aronson, 1999a; Thibodeau & Aronson, 1992).

3 *When you put a lot of effort into a decision, only to find the results less than you hoped for.* The harder you work to reach a goal, or the more you suffer for it, the more you will try to convince yourself that you value the goal, even if the goal itself is not so great after all (Aronson & Mills, 1959). This explains why hazing, whether in social clubs or in the military, turns new recruits into loyal members. You might think that people would hate the group that hazed them. But the cognition "I went through a lot of awful stuff to join this group" is dissonant with the cognition " . . . only to find I hate the group." Therefore people must decide either that the hazing was not so bad or that they really like the group. This mental reevaluation is called the **justification of effort,** and it is one of the most popular methods of reducing dissonance.

Cognitive-dissonance theory predicts the "justification of effort." The more you must endure to reach a goal, the more you will value it—which may be one reason fraternities often subject pledges to disgusting, frightening, or even dangerous hazing. These initiates, blindfolded and forced to wear vomit-drenched T-shirts, were also covered with molasses and were urinated on by their new fraternity brothers. They probably became extremely devoted members.

Cognitive-dissonance theory has its limitations. It can be hard to know when two cognitions are inconsistent: What feels dissonant to you may be neutral or pleasingly paradoxical to another. Further, some people do not have a strong need for consistency, and so they are less subject than others to cognitive dissonance (Cialdini, Trost, & Newsom, 1995). And some people are secure enough to own up to their mistakes instead of rationalizing them. Still, there is vast evidence of a motive for cognitive consistency under certain conditions, and this motive can lead to irrational decisions and actions.

Overcoming Our Cognitive Biases

The fact that our decisions and judgments, and the feelings of regret or pleasure that follow, are not always logical or rational has enormous implications for decision makers in the legal system, business, medicine, government—in fact, in all areas. But before you despair about the human ability to think clearly and rationally, we should tell you that the situation is not hopeless. For one thing, people are not equally irrational in all situations. When they are doing things they have some expertise in, or are making decisions that have serious consequences, their cognitive biases often diminish. Accountants who audit companies' books, for example, are less subject to the confirmation bias than are undergraduates in psychology experiments, perhaps because auditors can be sued if they overestimate a firm's profitability or economic health (Smith & Kida, 1991).

Further, once we understand a bias, we may be able to reduce or eliminate it. As we have seen, doctors are vulnerable to the hindsight bias if they already know what caused a patient's death. But Hal Arkes and his colleagues (1988) were able to reduce a similar bias in neuropsychologists. The psychologists were given a case study and asked to state one reason why each of three possible diagnoses—alcohol withdrawal, Alzheimer's disease, and brain damage—might have been applicable. This procedure forced the psychologists to consider all the evidence, not just evidence that supported the correct diagnosis. The hindsight bias evaporated, presumably because the psychologists realized that the correct diagnosis had not been so obvious at the time the patient was being treated.

Some people, of course, seem to think more rationally than others all the time; we call them "intelligent." But just what is intelligence, and how can we measure and improve it? We take up that question next.

justification of effort The tendency of individuals to increase their liking for something that they have worked hard or suffered to attain; a common form of dissonance reduction.

QUICK QUIZ

Think rationally to answer these questions.

1. Stu takes a study break and meets a young woman at the cafeteria. They hit it off, start to see each other regularly, and eventually get married. Says Stu, "I knew that day, when I headed for the cafeteria, that something special was about to happen." What cognitive bias is affecting his thinking, charmingly romantic though it is?

2. In a classic study of cognitive dissonance, students did some boring, repetitive tasks and then had to tell another student, who was waiting to participate in the study, that the work was interesting and fun (Festinger & Carlsmith, 1959). Half the students were offered $20 for telling this lie and the others only $1. Which students who lied decided later on that the tasks had been fun after all?

Answers:

1. the hindsight bias   2. The students who got only $1. They were in a state of dissonance, because "the task was as dull as dishwater" is dissonant with "I said I enjoyed it—and for a mere dollar, at that." Those who got $20 could rationalize that the large sum (which was *really* large in 1956) justified the lie.

WHAT'S AHEAD

- Why do psychologists debate whether a single thing called "intelligence" even exists?
- How did the original purpose of intelligence testing change when IQ tests came to America?
- Is it possible to design intelligence tests that are not influenced by culture?
- Why do some psychologists defend traditional intelligence testing and others oppose it?

MEASURING INTELLIGENCE: THE PSYCHOMETRIC APPROACH

Educator Sylvia Ashton-Warner once called intelligence "the tool to find the truth—a tool that must be kept sharpened." Yet much as we all desire to possess this tool, it is hard to agree on just what it is. Some psychologists equate it with the ability to reason abstractly, others with the ability to learn and profit from experience in daily life. Some emphasize the ability to think rationally, others the ability to act purposefully. These qualities are all probably part of what most people mean by **intelligence**, but theorists weigh them differently.

One of the longest-running debates in psychology is whether a global quality called "intelligence" even exists. A typical intelligence test asks you to do several things: provide a specific bit of information, notice similarities between objects, solve arithmetic problems, define words, fill in the missing parts of incomplete pictures, arrange pictures in a logical order, arrange blocks to resemble a design, assemble puzzles, use a coding scheme, or judge what behavior would be appropriate in a particular situation. Researchers use a statistical method called **factor analysis** to try to identify which basic abilities underlie performance on the various items. This procedure identifies clusters of correlated items that seem to be measuring some common ability, or factor. A majority of scientists believe that a general ability, or **g factor**, underlies the specific abilities and talents measured by intelligence tests (Herrnstein & Murray, 1994; Spearman, 1927; Wechsler, 1955). But others dispute the existence of a g factor on the grounds that a person can excel in some tasks yet do poorly in others (Gould, 1994; Guilford, 1988). Disagreements over how to define intelligence have led some writers to agree with Edward Boring, who in 1903 quipped that intelligence is "whatever intelligence tests measure."

---

intelligence An inferred characteristic of an individual, usually defined as the ability to profit from experience, acquire knowledge, think abstractly, act purposefully, or adapt to changes in the environment.

factor analysis A statistical method for analyzing the intercorrelations among various measures or test scores; clusters of measures or scores that are highly correlated are assumed to measure the same underlying trait, ability, or aptitude (factor).

g factor A general intellectual ability assumed by some theorists to underlie specific mental abilities and talents.

The traditional approach to intelligence, the **psychometric** approach, focuses on how well people perform on standardized mental tests. The tests you take in your courses are called **achievement tests**, because they are designed to measure skills and knowledge you have already learned. **Aptitude tests**, in contrast, are designed to measure the ability to acquire skills or knowledge in the future. For example, vocational aptitude tests can help you decide whether you will do better as a mechanic or a musician, and IQ tests do a pretty good job of predicting school performance. But all mental tests are in some sense achievement tests because they assume past learning or experience with particular objects, words, or situations. The difference between achievement and aptitude tests is one of degree and intended use.

A psychologist gives a student an intelligence test.

The Invention of IQ Tests

The first intelligence test was devised in 1904, when the French Ministry of Education asked psychologist Alfred Binet (1857–1911) to find a way to identify children who were slow learners and who therefore would benefit from remedial work. The ministry was reluctant to let teachers identify such children, because the teachers might have prejudices about poor children or might assume that shy or disruptive children were mentally impaired. They wanted a more objective approach.

Binet's Brainstorm. Wrestling with the problem, Binet had a great insight: In the classroom, the responses of "dull" children resembled those of ordinary children of younger ages. Bright children, on the other hand, responded like children of older ages. The thing to measure, then, was a child's **mental age (MA)**, or level of intellectual development relative to other children's. Then instruction could be tailored to the child's capabilities.

The test devised by Binet and his colleague, Theophile Simon, measured memory, vocabulary, and perceptual discrimination. Items ranged from those that most young children could do easily to those that only older children could handle, as determined by the testing of large numbers of children. A scoring system developed later by others used a formula in which the child's mental age was divided by the child's chronological age to yield an **intelligence quotient**, or **IQ** (a quotient is the result of division). Thus, a child of 8 who performed like the average 10-year-old would have a mental age of 10 and an IQ of 125 (10 divided by 8, times 100). All average children, regardless of age, would have an IQ of 100 because mental age and chronological age would be the same.

This method of figuring IQ had serious flaws. At one age, scores might cluster tightly around the average, whereas at another age, they might be more dispersed. As a result, the score necessary to be in the top 10 or 20 or 30 percent of your age group varied, depending on your age. Also, the IQ formula did not make sense for adults; a 50-year-old who scores like a 30-year-old does not have low intelligence! Today, therefore, intelligence tests are scored differently. The average is usually set arbitrarily at 100, and tests are constructed so that about two-thirds of all people score between 85 and 115. Individual scores are computed from tables based on established norms. These scores are still informally referred to as "IQs," and they still reflect how a person compares with other people, either children of a particular age or adults in general. At all ages, the distribution of scores approximates a normal (bell-shaped) curve, with scores near the average (mean) most common and very high or very low scores rare (see Figure 9.2).

psychometrics The measurement of mental abilities, traits, and processes.

achievement tests Tests designed to assess skills and knowledge that have been learned.

aptitude tests Tests designed to assess the ability to acquire skills and knowledge in the future.

mental age (MA) A measure of mental development expressed in terms of the average mental ability at a given age; for instance, a child with a mental age of 8 performs on a test of mental ability at the level of the average 8-year-old.

intelligence quotient (IQ) A measure of intelligence originally computed by dividing a person's mental age by his or her chronological age and multiplying by 100; now derived from norms provided for standardized intelligence tests.

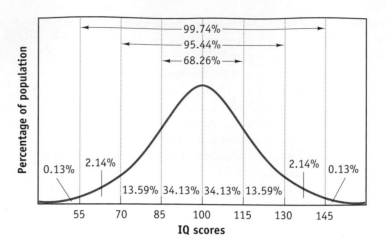

FIGURE 9.2
EXPECTED DISTRIBUTION OF IQ SCORES

In a large population, IQ scores tend to be distributed on a normal (bell-shaped) curve. On most tests, about 68 percent of all people will score between 85 and 115; about 95 percent will score between 70 and 130; and about 99.7 percent will score between 55 and 145. In any actual sample, however, the distribution will depart somewhat from the theoretical ideal.

The IQ Test Comes to America. In the United States, Stanford psychologist Lewis Terman revised Binet's test and established norms for American children. His version, the Stanford-Binet Intelligence Scale, was first published in 1916 and has been updated several times since. (For some sample items, see Table 9.2.) Two decades later, David Wechsler designed another test expressly for adults, which became the Wechsler Adult Intelligence Scale (WAIS). It was followed by the Wechsler Intelligence Scale for Children (WISC). Although the Wechsler tests produce a general IQ score, they also provide specific scores for different kinds of ability. Verbal items test a person's vocabulary, arithmetic abilities, immediate memory span, ability to recognize similarities (e.g., "How are books and movies alike?"), and general knowledge and comprehension (e.g., "Who was Thomas Jefferson?" "Why do people who want a divorce have to go to court?"). Performance items test a range of nonverbal skills (see Figure 9.3).

Binet had emphasized that his test merely *sampled* intelligence and did not measure everything covered by that term. A test score, he said, could be useful, along with

---

TABLE 9.2   Sample Items from the Stanford-Binet Intelligence Test, Form L–M

The older the test-taker is, the more the test requires in the way of verbal comprehension and fluency.

Age	Task
4	Fills in the missing word when asked, "Brother is a boy; sister is a _____." Answers correctly when asked, "Why do we have houses?"
9	Answers correctly when examiner says, "In an old graveyard in Spain, they have discovered a small skull which they believe to be that of Christopher Columbus when he was about 10 years old." What is foolish about that? Examiner presents folded paper; child draws how it will look unfolded.
12	Completes "The streams are dry . . . there has been little rain." Tells what is foolish about statements such as "Bill Jones's feet are so big that he has to put his trousers on over his head."
Adult	Can describe the difference between *misery* and *poverty*, *character* and *reputation*, *laziness* and *idleness*. Explains how to measure 3 pints of water with a 5-pint and a 2-pint can.

Source: From Lewis M. Terman & Maud A. Merrill, *Stanford-Binet Intelligence Scale* (1972 norms ed.). Boston: Houghton Mifflin, 1973. (Currently published by The Riverside Publishing Company.) Items are copyright 1916 by Lewis M. Terman, 1937 by Lewis M. Terman and Maud A. Merrill, © 1960, 1973 by The Riverside Publishing Company. Reproduced or adapted by permission of the publisher.

Picture arrangement
(Arrange the panels to make a meaningful story)

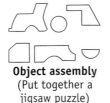

Object assembly
(Put together a jigsaw puzzle)

Code

Test

Digit symbol
(Using the key at the top, fill in the appropriate symbol beneath each number)

Picture completion
(Supply the missing feature)

Block design
(Copy the design shown, using another set of blocks)

FIGURE 9.3

PERFORMANCE TASKS ON THE WECHSLER TESTS

Nonverbal items such as these are particularly useful for measuring the abilities of those who have poor hearing, are not fluent in the tester's language, have limited education, or resist doing classroom-type problems. A large gap between a person's verbal score and performance score on a Wechsler test sometimes indicates a specific learning problem. (Object assembly, digit symbol, and picture completion adapted from Cronbach, 1990.)

other information, for predicting school performance, but it should not be confused with intelligence itself. The tests were designed to be given to each child individually, so the test-giver could see whether a child was ill or nervous, had poor vision, or was not trying. The purpose was to identify children with learning problems, not to rank normal children.

But when intelligence testing was brought from France to the United States, its original purpose got lost at sea. In America, IQ tests became widely used not to bring slow learners up to the average, but to categorize people in school and in the armed services according to their presumed "natural ability." The testers overlooked the fact that in America, with its many ethnic groups, people did not all share the same background and experience (Gould, 1981/1996).

Can IQ Tests Be "Culture Free"?

Intelligence tests developed between World War I and the 1960s for use in schools favored city children over rural ones, middle-class children over poor ones, and white children over nonwhite children. One item, for example, asked whether the Emperor Concerto was written by Beethoven, Mozart, Bach, Brahms, or Mahler. (The answer is Beethoven.) Critics soon complained that the tests did not measure the kinds of knowledge and skills that are intelligent in a minority neighborhood or in the hills of Appalachia (Scarr, 1984). They feared that because teachers thought IQ scores revealed the limits of a child's potential, low-scoring children would not get the educational attention or encouragement they needed. As a result of these concerns, in the 1970s, school boards and employers were sued for restricting the opportunities of low scorers, and some states prohibited the use of group tests.

Test-makers responded by trying to construct tests that were *culture free*. Such tests were usually nonverbal; in some, instructions were even pantomimed. Psychologists also tried to design tests that were *culture fair*. Their aim was not to eliminate the influence of culture, but to find items that incorporate knowledge and skills common to many different cultures. But both approaches were less successful than originally hoped because cultural values affect just about *everything* to do with taking a test: a person's

CONSIDER OTHER EXPLANATIONS

When tests find IQ differences between groups of children, many people assume that the children who score lower are inherently less intelligent. What other explanations are possible?

attitude toward tests, comfort in the settings required for testing, motivation, rapport with the test-giver, competitiveness, and experience in solving problems independently rather than with others (Anastasi & Urbina, 1997; López, 1995).

Cultures also differ in the problem-solving strategies they emphasize (Serpell, 1994). In the West, white, middle-class children typically learn to classify things by category—to say that an apple and a peach are similar because they are both fruits, and that a saw and a rake are similar because they are both tools. But children who are not trained in middle-class ways of sorting things may classify objects according to their function. They will say that an apple and a peach are similar because they taste good. That's a charming and innovative answer, but it is one that test-givers interpret as less intelligent (Miller-Jones, 1989).

Expectations, Stereotypes, and IQ Scores. People's performance on IQ tests also depends on their own expectations about how they will do. Those expectations, in turn, are shaped by cultural stereotypes about the abilities of people of their particular ethnicity, age, gender, or socioeconomic class. Stereotypes that portray members of certain groups as unintelligent can actually depress the test performance of people in these groups. You might think that a woman would say, "So sexists think women are dumb at math? I'll show *them*" or that an African-American would say, "So racists believe that blacks aren't as smart as whites? Just give me that exam." But often that is not what happens.

On the contrary, such individuals commonly feel a burden of doubt about their abilities that Claude Steele (1992, 1997) has labeled **stereotype threat**. The threat occurs because they believe that if they do not do well, they will confirm the stereotypes about their group. Their anxiety may then worsen their performance. Or they may cope by "disidentifying" with the test, saying to themselves, in effect, "The outcome of this test has no bearing on how I feel about myself" (Major et al., 1998). As a result, they may not be motivated to do well.

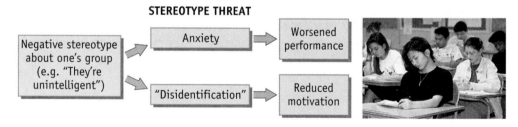

STEREOTYPE THREAT

Stereotype threat has been shown to affect the test performance of many African-Americans, low-income people, women, and elderly people—all of whom perform better on tests when they are not feeling self-conscious about themselves as members of negatively stereotyped groups (Brown & Josephs, 1999; Croizen & Claire, 1998; Levy, 1996; Steele & Aronson, 1995). But white men, too, can be affected by stereotype threat. White male athletes who are self-conscious about the stereotype that "white men can't jump" actually do *not* jump as high in the presence of a black experimenter as in the presence of a white one (Garcia, Helms, & Garcia, in preparation)!

Positive stereotypes, in contrast, can *improve* performance. When Asian women answered a questionnaire about their ethnicity, they then performed better on a math test than did Asian women who did not answer the questionnaire. Apparently, the positive stereotype—"Asians are good at math"—had been activated, and the women tried to live up to it. But when Asian women answered a questionnaire about their *gender* and then took the test, they did worse than the control group! In this

stereotype threat A burden of doubt a person feels about his or her performance, due to negative stereotypes about his or her group's abilities.

case, a negative stereotype—"women are bad at math"—had been activated (Shih, Pittinsky, & Ambady, 1999).

The Dilemma of Differences. So, what can be done to reduce differences in IQ test scores between ethnic groups and to reduce the stereotype threat that results from them? In theory, it should be possible to establish test norms that are not based on white urban children by throwing out items on which such children get higher scores than others. A similar strategy was actually used years ago to eliminate sex differences in IQ. On early tests, girls scored higher than boys at every age (Samelson, 1979). No one was willing to conclude that males were intellectually inferior, so in the 1937 revision of the Stanford-Binet test, Lewis Terman simply deleted the items on which boys had done poorly. Poof! No sex differences.

But few people seem willing to do for cultural differences what Terman did for sex differences, and the reason reveals a dilemma at the heart of intelligence testing. Intelligence tests put some groups of children at a disadvantage, yet they also measure skills and knowledge useful in the classroom. How can educators recognize and accept cultural differences and, at the same time, require students to demonstrate mastery of the skills, knowledge, and attitudes that will help them succeed in school and in the larger society? How can they eliminate bias from tests, while preserving the purpose for which the tests were designed?

Beyond the IQ Test

Some social scientists believe that it is important for society to keep using IQ tests. The tests predict school performance fairly well, and they identify not only the mentally retarded, but also gifted students who have not previously considered higher education. To these scientists, concealing the effects of cultural disadvantage by rejecting conventional tests is "equivalent to breaking a thermometer because it registers a body temperature of 101" (Anastasi, 1988). When the tests reveal group differences, the pro-test camp maintains, the solution is to give special help to children who need it so they can do better. But other social scientists feel that conventional mental tests do more harm than good. Sociologist Jane Mercer (1988) tried for years to get testers to understand that children can be *ignorant* of information required by IQ tests without being *stupid*, but she finally gave up, resolving instead to "kill the IQ test."

The resolution of this debate may depend on whether test-users can learn to use intelligence tests more intelligently. In many schools, a child's placement in a special-education program now depends not only on an IQ score, but also on tests of specific abilities, medical data, and the child's demonstrated inability to get along in the family and community. And many schools are returning to Binet's original concept: using the tests to identify a child's weaknesses so that teachers can design individualized programs that will boost the child's performance. This change in emphasis reflects an increasing awareness that the intellect—and IQ scores—can be improved, even in the mentally retarded (Butterfield & Belmont, 1977; Feuerstein, 1980; Sternberg, 1986).

But critics of IQ tests point out that standardized tests tell us nothing about *how* a person goes about answering questions and solving problems. Nor do they explain why people with low scores on IQ tests often behave intelligently in real life—making smart consumer decisions, winning at the racetrack, and making wise personal choices (Ceci, 1996). Some researchers, therefore, have rejected the psychometric approach to the study and measurement of intelligence in favor of a cognitive approach, as we will discuss next.

Children with Down syndrome, who score low on standard IQ tests, are accomplishing more academically than anyone once thought they could—showing that intellectual performance is not as unchangeable as many people assume.

WHAT'S AHEAD

- **What kind of intelligence allows you to master the unspoken rules for academic success?**
- **What is "EQ" and why is it as important as IQ?**
- **Why do Asian children preform so much better in school than American students do, even though Asian classes are larger, with poorer facilities?**

DISSECTING INTELLIGENCE: THE COGNITIVE APPROACH

Cognitive psychologists, thinking critically, have questioned prevailing assumptions about the very meaning of intelligence and the best way to measure it. In contrast to the psychometric approach to intelligence, which is concerned with how many answers a person gets right on a test, the *cognitive approach* emphasizes the *strategies* people use when thinking about problems and arriving at a solution.

The Triarchic Theory

One leading cognitive theory, Robert Sternberg's *triarchic* (three-part) *theory of intelligence* (1988), distinguishes three aspects of intelligence:

1 *Componential intelligence* refers to the information-processing strategies that go on inside your head when you are thinking intelligently about a problem. These mental "components" include recognizing the problem, selecting a method for solving it, mastering and carrying out the strategy, and evaluating the result.

Some of these operations require **metacognition**, the knowledge or awareness of your own cognitive processes and the ability to monitor and control those processes. Metacognition is associated with a sense of control and strong academic performance (Landine & Stewart, 1998). Students who are weak in metacognition fail to notice when a passage in a textbook is especially difficult or they haven't understood it. As a result, they spend too little time on difficult material and too much time on material they already know (Nelson & Leonesio, 1988). In contrast, students who are strong in metacognition check their comprehension by restating what they have read, backtracking when necessary, and questioning what they are reading (Bereiter & Bird, 1985). (If they are reading this textbook, they also take the Quick Quizzes!)

2 *Experiential intelligence* refers to how well you transfer skills to new situations. People with experiential intelligence cope well with novelty and learn quickly to make new tasks automatic; those who are lacking in this area perform well only under a narrow set of circumstances. For example, a student may do well in school,

metacognition The knowledge or awareness of one's own cognitive processes.

ARE YOU A SAVVY STUDENT?

How good is your tacit knowledge about how to be a student? List as many strategies for success as you can think of. Consider what the successful student does when listening to lectures, participating in class discussions, communicating with professors, preparing for exams, writing term papers, and dealing with an unexpectedly low grade. Many of these strategies are never explicitly taught. You may want to do this exercise with a friend and compare lists. Are there some strategies that one of you thought of and the other didn't?

where assignments have specific due dates and feedback is immediate, but be less successful after graduation if her job requires her to set her own deadlines and her employer doesn't tell her how she is doing.

tacit knowledge Strategies for success that are not explicitly taught but that instead must be inferred.

3 *Contextual intelligence* refers to the practical application of intelligence, which requires you to take into account the different contexts in which you find yourself. People who are strong in contextual intelligence know when to adapt to the environment (you are in a dangerous neighborhood, so you become more vigilant); when to change environments (you had planned to be a teacher but discover that you dislike working with kids, so you switch to accounting); and when to fix the situation (your marriage is rocky, so you and your spouse go for counseling).

Without contextual intelligence, you will not acquire **tacit knowledge**—practical, action-oriented strategies for achieving your goals that usually are not formally taught but must instead be inferred from observing others (Sternberg et al., 1995). In studies of college professors, business managers, and salespeople, tacit knowledge is a strong predictor of effectiveness on the job (Sternberg, Wagner, & Okagaki, 1993). In college students, tacit knowledge about how to be a good student actually predicts academic success as well as entrance exams do (Sternberg & Wagner, 1989).

The Theory of Multiple Intelligences

Other psychologists, too, are expanding our understanding of what it means to be intelligent. Howard Gardner (1983, 1993, 1995), in his *theory of multiple intelligences*, has proposed that intelligence takes many distinct forms besides the verbal, spatial, and mathematical aptitudes measured by conventional tests. Among them, he says, are musical aptitude, kinesthetic intelligence (the bodily grace and physical self-awareness of athletes and dancers), and the capacity to understand yourself, others, or the natural world.

Some theorists who argue for an expanded definition of intelligence would say that a surveyor has spatial intelligence, a compassionate friend has emotional intelligence, and a singer has musical intelligence.

People with emotional intelligence are skilled at reading nonverbal emotional cues. Which of these boys do you think feels the most confident and relaxed, which one is shyest, and which feels most anxious? What cues are you using to answer?

These intelligences, Gardner argues, are relatively independent, and each may even have its own neural structures. People with brain damage often lose one without losing their competence in the others. Some autistic and retarded individuals with *savant syndrome* (*savant* means "learned" in French) have exceptional talents in one area—such as music, art, or rapid mathematical computation—despite poor functioning in all others.

Two of Gardner's "intelligences," the abilities to understand yourself and others, overlap with what some psychologists call **emotional intelligence:** the ability to identify your own and other people's emotions accurately, express your emotions clearly, and regulate emotions in yourself and others (Goleman, 1995; Mayer & Salovey, 1997). People with high emotional intelligence—popularly known as "EQ"—use their emotions to motivate themselves, to spur creative thinking, and to deal empathically with others. People who are low in emotional intelligence are often unable to identify their own emotions; they may insist that they are not depressed when a relationship ends, for example, but meanwhile they start drinking too much, become extremely irritable, and stop going out with friends. They express emotions inappropriately, such as by acting violently or impulsively when they are angry or worried. And they misread nonverbal signals from others; for example, they will give a long-winded account of all their problems even when the listener is obviously bored.

Studies of brain-damaged adults suggest a biological basis for emotional intelligence. Neuroscientist Antonio Damasio (1994) has studied patients with prefrontal-lobe damage that makes them incapable of experiencing strong feelings. Although they score in the normal range on conventional mental tests, these patients persistently make "dumb," irrational decisions in their lives because they cannot assign values to different options or read emotional cues from others. As we will see again in Chapter 11, feeling and thinking are not necessarily incompatible processes, as many people assume.

Thinking Critically About Intelligence(s)

Not everyone is enthusiastic about the proliferation of new "intelligences." Some argue that emotional intelligence is not a special cognitive ability, but a collection of personality traits, such as empathy and extroversion, and nothing is gained by

emotional intelligence The ability to identify your own and other people's emotions accurately, express your emotions clearly, and regulate emotions in yourself and others.

REVIEW 9.1

THE PSYCHOMETRIC AND COGNITIVE APPROACHES TO INTELLIGENCE, COMPARED

	Psychometric	Cognitive
Main focus	How well people perform on standardized tests	Strategies people use when solving problems
Nature of intelligence	A general intellectual ability captured by IQ scores; or a range of specific verbal and nonverbal abilities	Many different skills and talents, in addition to intellectual ones
Deals with emotional intelligence?	No	Yes
Deals with practical intelligence?	No	Yes
Uses well validated standardized tests?	Yes	Tests currently being developed

giving "EQ" its own trendy new label (Davies, Stankov, & Roberts, 1998). Others maintain that abilities such as Gardner's musical and kinesthetic intelligences are better thought of as talents, or else the very concept of intelligence loses all meaning. What is to prevent someone from adding "handicraft intelligence" or "financial intelligence" or "farming intelligence"?

Broadening the notion of intelligence, however, has been useful for several reasons. It has forced us to think more critically about what we mean by intelligence. It has inspired a promising (though still unproven) new type of mental testing, called *dynamic* testing, in which the test-giver provides ongoing feedback to the test-taker during the test so that the person can learn from the experience and improve his or her performance (Grigorenko & Sternberg, 1998). And it has led to a focus on teaching children other kinds of "smarts" that improve their abilities in reading, writing, homework, and test-taking: for example, how to manage their time so they don't procrastinate, how to apply different strategies when studying for multiple-choice and essay exams, and how to make a persuasive case for their ideas (Sternberg et al., 1995).

Most important, new approaches to intelligence encourage us to overcome the mental set of assuming that the only kind of intelligence necessary for a successful life is the kind captured by IQ tests. (For a summary of the differences between the psychometric and cognitive approaches, see Review 9.1.)

Motivation and Intellectual Success

Even with a high IQ, emotional intelligence, talent, and a knowledge of "the ropes," you still might get nowhere at all. Talent, unlike cream, does not inevitably rise to the top; success also depends on drive and determination.

The Lesson of the Termites. Consider a finding from one of the longest-running psychological studies ever conducted. Since 1921, researchers at Stanford University have been following more than 1,500 people with childhood IQ scores in the top 1 percent of the distribution. As boys and girls, these subjects were nicknamed "Termites," after Lewis Terman, who originally directed the research. The Termites started out bright, physically healthy, sociable, and well adjusted. As they entered adulthood, most became successful in the traditional ways of the times: men in careers and women as homemakers (Sears & Barbee, 1977; Terman & Oden, 1959). However, some gifted men failed to live up to their early promise, dropping out of school or drifting into low-level work. When the researchers compared the 100 most successful men in the Stanford study with the 100 least successful, they found that motivation made the difference. The successful men were ambitious, were socially active, had many interests, and were encouraged by their parents. The least successful drifted casually through life. There was *no* average difference in IQ between the two groups.

Cultural Attitudes and Motivation. Motivation to work hard at intellectual tasks depends in turn on your beliefs about the origins of intelligence and your feelings about achievement. Cultural values have an influence on these beliefs and feelings.

For many years, Harold Stevenson and his colleagues have been studying attitudes toward achievement in Asia and the United States. The researchers began in 1980 by comparing large samples of first- and fifth-grade children, their parents, and their teachers in Minneapolis, Sendai (Japan), and Taipei (Taiwan). In another project, they compared children from 20 schools in Chicago and 11 schools in Beijing (Stevenson & Stigler, 1992). In 1990, Stevenson, along with Chuansheng Chen and Shin-ying Lee (1993), revisited the original schools to collect new data on fifth-graders, and they also retested many of the children who had been in the 1980 study and who were now in the eleventh grade. Their results have much to teach us about the cultivation of intellect.

In 1980, the Asian children far outperformed the American children on a broad battery of mathematical tests. (A similar gap existed between the Chinese and American children on reading tests.) On computations and word problems, there was virtually no overlap between schools, with the lowest-scoring Beijing schools doing better than the highest-scoring Chicago schools. By 1990, the gap between the Asian and American children had grown even greater (see Figure 9.4). Only 4 percent of the Chinese children and 10 percent of the Japanese children had scores as low as those of the *average* American child. These differences could not be accounted for by educational resources: The Chinese had worse facilities and larger classes than the Americans, and on average, the Chinese parents were poorer and less educated than the American parents. Nor did it have anything to do with intellectual abilities in general; the American children were just as knowledgeable and capable as the Asian children on tests of general information.

But, this research found Asians and Americans are worlds apart in their attitudes, expectations, and efforts:

FIGURE 9.4

MATHEMATICAL PERFORMANCE OF ASIAN AND AMERICAN CHILDREN

In 1980 and again in 1990, the math performance of fifth-graders in Taiwan and Japan far outstripped that of children in the United States. This graph shows the gap on one of the tests given (Stevenson, Chen, & Lee, 1993). The performance differences were associated with differences in attitudes, standards, and effort.

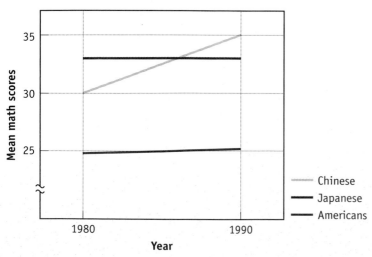

■ *Beliefs about intelligence.* American parents, teachers, and children are far more likely than Asians to believe that mathematical ability is innate. They think that if you "have it," you don't have to work hard, and if you don't have it, there's no point in trying (see Figure 9.5).

■ *Standards.* American parents have far lower standards for their children's performance; they are satisfied with scores barely above average on a 100-point test. In contrast, Chinese and Japanese parents are happy only with very high scores.

■ *Conflicts.* American students have more stressful, conflicting demands on their time than their Asian counterparts do. Chinese and Japanese students are expected to devote themselves to their studies, but American students are expected to be "well-rounded"—to have after-school jobs, active social lives, and time for sports and other activities.

■ *Values.* American students do not value education as much as Asian students do and they are more complacent about mediocre work. When asked what they would wish for if a wizard could give them anything they wanted, more than 60 percent of the Chinese fifth-graders named something related to their education. Can you guess what the American children wanted? A majority said money or possessions.

The moral is clear: When it comes to intellect, it's not just what you've got that counts, but what you do with it. Complacency, fatalism, or low standards can prevent people from recognizing what they don't know and can reduce their efforts to learn.

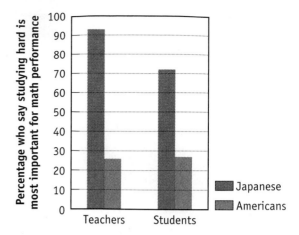

FIGURE 9.5
WHAT'S THE SECRET OF MATH SUCCESS?

Japanese school teachers and students are much more likely than their American counterparts to believe that the secret to doing well in math is working hard. Americans tend to think that you either have mathematical intelligence or you don't.

QUICK QUIZ

Are you feeling complacent about your quiz performance?

1. What goals do cognitive theories of intelligence have that psychometric theories do not?

2. Logan understands the material in his statistics class, but on tests, he plans his time poorly, spending the entire period on the most difficult problems and never even getting to the problems he can solve easily. According to the triarchic theory of intelligence, which aspect of intelligence does he need to improve?

3. Tracy does not have an unusually high IQ, and she was not an A student in school, but at work, she was quickly promoted because she knows how to set priorities, communicate with management, and make others feel valued. Tracy has _____ knowledge about how to succeed on the job.

4. What is wrong with defining intelligence as "whatever intelligence tests measure"?

Answers:

1. to understand people's strategies for solving problems and to use this information to improve mental performance 2. componential intelligence (which involves metacognition) 3. tacit 4. This definition implies that a low score must be entirely the scorer's fault rather than the test's. But the test-taker may be intelligent in ways that the test fails to measure, and the test may be measuring traits other than intelligence. (And by the way, the definition is also circular: How do we know someone is intelligent? Because he or she scored high on an intelligence test. Why did the person score high? Because the person is intelligent!)

WHAT'S AHEAD

● Why do some researchers think that animals can think, whereas others remain skeptical?

● People love to talk to their pets—but can their pets learn to talk back?

ANIMAL MINDS

A green heron swipes some bread from a picnicker's table and scatters the crumbs on a nearby stream. When a minnow rises to the bait, the heron strikes, swallowing its prey before you can say "hook, line, and sinker." A sea otter, floating calmly on its back, bangs a mussel shell against a stone that is resting on its stomach. When the shell cracks apart, the otter devours the tasty morsel inside, tucks the stone under its flipper, and dives for another shell, which it will open in the same way. Incidents such as these, summarized in Donald Griffin's *Animal Minds* (1992), have convinced some biologists, psychologists, and ethologists that we are not the only animals with cognitive abilities—that "dumb beasts" are far smarter than we may think.

Animal Intelligence

In the 1920s, Wolfgang Köhler (1925) put chimpanzees in situations in which some tempting bananas were just out of reach, then watched to see what the apes would do. Most did nothing, but a few turned out to be quite clever. If the bananas were outside the cage, the animal might pull them in with a stick. If they were hanging overhead, and there were boxes in the cage, the chimpanzee might pile up the boxes and climb on top of them to reach the fruit. Often the solution came after the animal had been sitting quietly for a while. It appeared as though the chimp had been thinking about the problem and was struck by a sudden insight.

Behaviorists, as you might imagine, felt that this seemingly impressive behavior could be accounted for perfectly well by the standard principles of operant learning

How smart is this otter?

In an early study of animal intelligence, Sultan, a talented chimpanzee studied by Wolfgang Köhler, was able to figure out how to reach a cluster of bananas by stacking some boxes and climbing on top of them.

(see Chapter 7). Because of their influence, for years, any scientist who claimed that animals could think was likely to get laughed at, or worse. Today, however, the study of animal intelligence is enjoying a resurgence, especially in the interdisciplinary field of **cognitive ethology** (Gould & Gould, 1995; Ristau, 1991). (*Ethology* is the study of animal behavior, especially in natural environments.) Cognitive ethologists argue that some animals can anticipate future events, make plans, and coordinate their activities with those of their comrades—that they are, indeed, capable of thought.

When we think about animal cognition, though, we must be cautious, because even complex behavior might be genetically prewired and automatic. The assassin bug of South America catches termites by gluing nest material on its back as camouflage, but it is hard to imagine how the bug's tiny dab of brain tissue could enable it to plan this strategy consciously. Even many cognitive ethologists are cautious about how much cognition they are willing to read into an animal's behavior. An animal could be aware of its environment and know some things, they say, without knowing that it knows and without being able to think about its own thoughts as human beings do—in short, without having metacognition (Budiansky, 1998; Crook, 1987).

Yet explanations of animal behavior that leave out any sort of consciousness at all and that attribute animals' actions entirely to instinct do not seem to account for some of the amazing things that animals can do. Like the otter who uses a stone to crack mussel shells, many animals are capable of using objects in the natural environment as rudimentary tools. For example, mother chimpanzees occasionally show their young how to use stone tools to open hard nuts (Boesch, 1991).

In the laboratory, too, nonhuman primates have accomplished some surprising things. In one study, chimpanzees compared two pairs of food wells containing chocolate chips. One pair might contain, say, five chips and three chips, the other four chips and three chips. Allowed to choose which pair they wanted, the chimps almost always chose the one with the higher combined total, showing some sort of summing ability (Rumbaugh, Savage-Rumbaugh, & Pate, 1988). Other chimps have learned to use numerals to label quantities of items and simple sums (Boysen & Berntson, 1989; Washburn & Rumbaugh, 1991). Two rhesus monkeys, named Rosencrantz and Macduff, learned to order groups of one to four symbols according to the number of symbols in each group (e.g., one square, two trees, three ovals, four flowers). Later, when presented with pairs of symbol groups containing five to nine symbols, they were able to point to the group with more symbols, without any further training (Brannon & Terrace, 1998) (see Figure 9.6). This is not exactly algebra, but it does suggest that monkeys have a rudimentary sense of number.

Animals and Language

A primary ingredient in human cognition is *language*, the ability to combine elements that are themselves meaningless into an infinite number of utterances that convey meaning. Language is often regarded as the last bastion of human uniqueness, a result of evolutionary forces that produced our species (see Chapter 3). Do animals have anything comparable? Many people have wished they could ask their pet what it's like to be a dog, or a cat, or a horse. If only animals could speak!

To qualify as a language, a communication system must meet certain criteria (Hockett, 1960). It must use combinations of sounds, gestures, or symbols that are *meaningful*, not random. It must permit *displacement*, communication about objects and events that are not present here and now but rather are displaced in time or space; merely pointing to things is not language. And it must have a grammar (syntax) that permits *productivity*, the ability to produce and comprehend an infinite number of new utterances.

cognitive ethology The study of cognitive processes in nonhuman animals.

FIGURE 9.6
CAN MONKEYS COUNT?

Two rhesus monkeys learned to put pictures, each consisting of 1 to 4 elements, in the correct order. Later, when shown pairs of pictures selected from those below, the monkeys were able to touch the pictures in the correct order, even when they had not seen the quantities before (e.g., 5 before 7).

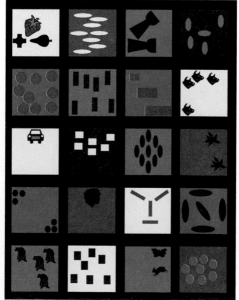

By these criteria, no nonhuman species has its own language. Of course, animals do communicate, using gestures, body postures, facial expressions, vocalizations, and odors. And some of these signals have highly specific meanings. For example, vervet monkeys seem to have separate calls to warn about leopards versus eagles versus snakes (Cheney & Seyfarth, 1985). But vervets cannot combine these sounds to produce entirely novel utterances, as in "Look out, Harry, that eagle-eyed leopard is a real snake-in-the-grass."

Perhaps, however, some animals could acquire language if they got a little help from their human friends. Dozens of researchers have tried to provide chimpanzees with just such help. Because the vocal tract of an ape does not permit speech, since the 1960s, most of these researchers have tried innovative approaches that rely on gestures or visual symbols. In one project, chimpanzees learned to use as words geometric plastic shapes arranged on a magnetic board (Premack & Premack, 1983). In another, they learned to punch symbols on a computer-monitored keyboard (Rumbaugh, 1977). In yet another, they learned hundreds of signs from American Sign Language (ASL) (Fouts & Rigby, 1977; Gardner & Gardner, 1969).

All of these animals learned to follow instructions, answer questions, and make requests. More important, they combined individual signs or symbols into longer utterances that they had never seen before. Before long, accounts of the apes' abilities were causing quite a stir. The animals were apparently using their newfound skills to apologize for being disobedient, scold their trainers, and even talk to themselves. Koko, a lowland gorilla, reportedly used signs to say that she felt happy or sad, to refer to past and future events, to mourn for her dead pet kitten, and to convey her yearning for a baby. She even lied on occasion, when she did something naughty (Patterson & Linden, 1981).

AVOID EMOTIONAL REASONING

It's hard not to fall in love with apes who use symbols to request food, apologize, or lie. But emotion can sometimes get in the way of objectivity. What does objective research actually show about the ability of animals to use language?

The animals in these studies were lovable, the findings appealing—so it was easy for emotional reasoning to prevail over critical thinking. But soon skeptics and some of the researchers themselves began to point out serious problems (Seidenberg & Petitto, 1979; Terrace, 1985). In their desire to talk to the animals and their affection for their primate friends, researchers had not always been objective. They had overinterpreted the animal's utterances, reading all sorts of meanings and intentions into a single sign or symbol, and unwittingly giving nonverbal cues that might enable the apes to respond correctly. Further, the animals appeared to be stringing signs and symbols together in no particular order, instead of using grammatical rules to produce novel utterances; "Me eat banana" seemed to be no different for them than "Banana eat me."

These problems still plague some projects. In 1998, America Online sponsored a live chat with Koko. Her trainer, Francine Patterson, used sign language to relay questions from the audience to the gorilla. Critics felt Patterson read much too much into Koko's "replies":

Question: Koko, are you going to have a baby in the future?

    Koko: Pink

Patterson: Koko was commenting on the color of my shirt. We had an earlier discussion about colors today.

    Q: Do you like to chat with people?

    Koko: Fine nipple.

Patterson: Nipple rhymes with people, she doesn't sign people per se, she was trying to do a "sounds like. . . . "

    Q: Koko, do you feel love from the humans who have raised you?

    Koko: Lips, apple give me.

Patterson: People give her favorite foods.

Kanzi, a bonobo with the most advanced linguistic skills yet acquired by a nonhuman primate, answers questions and makes requests by punching symbols on a specially designed computer keyboard. He also understands short English sentences. He is shown here with researcher Sue Savage-Rumbaugh.

Today, however, most researchers have taken the criticisms to heart and have greatly improved their procedures. They have shown that with careful training, chimps can indeed acquire the ability to use symbols to refer to objects. Some animals have even spontaneously used signs to converse with each other, suggesting that they are not merely imitating or trying to get a reward (Van Cantfort & Rimpau, 1982). Bonobos (sometimes misleadingly called "pygmy chimps") are even more adept at language than are chimpanzees. One bonobo named Kanzi has learned to understand English words, short sentences, and keyboard symbols *without formal training* (Savage-Rumbaugh & Lewin, 1994; Savage-Rumbaugh, Shanker, & Taylor, 1998). Kanzi responds correctly to commands such as "Put the key in the refrigerator" and "Go get the ball that is outdoors," even when he has never heard the words combined in that particular way before. He picked up language as children do—by observing others using it and through normal social interaction. He has also learned, with training, to manipulate keyboard symbols to request favorite foods or activities (games, TV, visits to friends) and to announce his intentions.

You do not even have to be a primate to acquire some aspects of language. In Hawaii, Louis Herman and his colleagues have taught dolphins to respond to requests made in two artificial languages, one consisting of computer-generated whistles and another of hand and arm gestures (Herman, 1987; Herman, Kuczaj, & Holder, 1993; Herman & Morrel-Samuels, 1996). To interpret a request correctly, the dolphins must take into account both the meaning of the individual symbols in a string of whistles or gestures and the order of the symbols (syntax). For example, they must understand the difference between "To left Frisbee, right surfboard take" and "To right surfboard, left Frisbee take."

In another fascinating project, Irene Pepperberg (1990, 1994) has taught an African gray parrot named Alex to count, classify, and compare objects by vocalizing English words. When the bird is shown up to six items and is asked how many there are, he responds with spoken (squawked?) English phrases, such as "two cork(s)" or "four key(s)." He can even respond correctly to questions about items specified on two dimensions, as in "How many blue key(s)?" Alex also makes requests ("Want pasta") and answers simple questions about objects ("What color [is this]?" "Which is bigger?"). When presented with a blue cork and a blue key and asked "What's the same?" he will correctly respond "Color." He actually scores slightly better with new objects than with familiar ones, suggesting that he is not merely memorizing a set of stock phrases.

Alex is one clever bird—but how clever? His abilities raise intriguing questions about the intelligence of animals and their capacity for specific aspects of language.

"It's always 'Sit,' 'Stay,' 'Heel'—never 'Think,' 'Innovate,' 'Be yourself.'"

Thinking About the Thinking of Animals

These results on animal language and cognition are impressive, but scientists are still divided over just what the animals in these studies are doing. Do they have true language? Are they "thinking," in human terms?

On one side are those who worry about *anthropomorphism*, the tendency to falsely attribute human qualities to nonhuman beings. They tell the story of Clever Hans, a "wonder horse" at the turn of the century, who was said to possess mathematical and other abilities (Spitz, 1997). For example, Clever Hans would answer math problems by stamping his hoof the appropriate number of times. But a little careful experimentation by a psychologist, Oskar Pfungst (1911/1965), revealed that when Hans was prevented from seeing his questioners, his "powers" left him. It seems that questioners were staring at the horse's feet and leaning forward expectantly after stating the problem, then lifting their eyes and relaxing as soon as he completed the right number of taps. Clever Hans was indeed clever, but not at math or other human skills. He was merely responding to nonverbal signals that people were inadvertently providing. (Perhaps he had a high EQ.)

On the other side are those who warn against *anthropocentrism*, the tendency to think, mistakenly, that human beings have nothing in common with other animals (de Waal, 1997; Fouts, 1997). The need to see our own species as unique, they say, may keep us from recognizing that other species, too, have cognitive abilities, even if not as intricate as our own. Those who take this position point out that most modern researchers have gone to great lengths to avoid the Clever Hans problem.

The outcome of this debate is bound to have an effect on how we view ourselves and our place among other species. As Donald Griffin (1992) wrote, "Cognitive ethology presents us with one of the supreme scientific challenges of our times, and it calls for our best efforts of critical and imaginative investigation."

QUICK QUIZ

Regrettably, your pet beagle can't help you answer this quiz.

1. *True or false:* Many animals use objects in the environment as rudimentary tools.

2. A honeybee performs a little dance that communicates to other bees the direction and distance of food. Because the bee can "talk" about something that is located elsewhere, its communication system shows _____. But because the bee can create only utterances that are genetically wired into its repertoire, its communication system lacks _____.

3. In thinking about animal language and cognition, it is important to avoid both _____ and _____.

Answers:

1. true 2. displacement, productivity 3. anthropomorphism, anthropocentrism

We human beings are used to thinking of ourselves as the smartest species around because of our astounding ability to adapt to change, come up with novel solutions to problems, invent endless new gizmos, and use language to create everything from puns to poetry. Yet, as this chapter has shown, we are not quite as wise in our thinking as we might think. We can, however, boast of one crowning accomplishment: *We are the only species that tries to understand its own misunderstandings.* We want to know what we don't know; we are motivated to overcome our mental shortcomings. This capacity for self-examination is probably the best reason to remain optimistic about our cognitive capacities.

TAKING PSYCHOLOGY WITH YOU

BECOMING MORE CREATIVE

Take a few moments to answer these items from the Remote Associates Test. Your task is to come up with a fourth word that is associated with each item in a set of three words (Mednick, 1962). For example, an appropriate answer for the set *news-clip-wall* is *paper*. Got the idea? Now try these (the answers are given on page 344):

1. piggy-green-lash
2. surprise-line-birthday
3. mark-shelf-telephone
4. stick-maker-tennis
5. blue-cottage-cloth

Associating elements in new ways by finding a common connection among them is an important component of creativity. People who are uncreative rely on *convergent thinking*, following a particular set of steps that they think will converge on one correct solution. Once they solve a problem, they tend to develop a mental set and approach future problems the same way.

Creative people, in contrast, exercise *divergent thinking;* instead of stubbornly sticking to one tried-and-true path, they explore side alleys and generate several possible solutions. They come up with new hypotheses, imagine other interpretations, and look for connections that may not be immediately obvious. They can think of many uses for familiar objects, such as, say, unneeded CD-ROM disks (which can be used as mobiles, Christmas decorations, coasters, . . .). Creative thinking can be found in the auto mechanic who invents a new tool, the mother who designs and makes her children's clothes, or the office manager who devises a clever way to streamline work flow (Richards, 1991).

Interestingly, high IQ does not guarantee creativity. Personality characteristics seem more important, especially these three (MacKinnon, 1962, 1968; McCrae, 1987; Schank, 1988):

1. *Nonconformity.* Creative individuals are not overly concerned about what others think of them. They are willing to risk ridicule by proposing ideas that may initially appear foolish or off the mark. Geneticist Barbara McClintock's research was ignored or belittled by many for nearly 30 years. But she was sure she could show how genes move around and produce sudden changes in heredity. In 1983, McClintock won the Nobel Prize. The judges called her work the second greatest genetic discovery of our time, after the discovery of the structure of DNA.

2. *Curiosity.* Creative people are open to new experiences; they notice when reality contradicts expectations, and they are curious about the reason. For example, Wilhelm Roentgen, a German physicist, was studying cathode rays when he noticed a strange glow on one of his screens. Other people had seen the glow, but they ignored it because it didn't jibe with their understanding of cathode rays. Roentgen studied the glow, found it to be a new kind of radiation, and thus discovered X rays (Briggs, 1984).

3. *Persistence.* This is perhaps the most important attribute of the creative person. After that imaginary lightbulb goes on over your head, you still have to work hard to make the illumination last. Or, as Thomas Edison, who invented the real lightbulb, reportedly put it, "Genius is one-tenth inspiration and nine-tenths perspiration." No invention or work of art springs forth full-blown from a person's head. There are many false starts and painful revisions along the way.

In addition to traits that foster creativity, there are *circumstances* that do. One is the encouragement of *intrinsic* rather than *extrinsic* motivation. Intrinsic motives include a sense of accomplishment, intellectual fulfillment, the satisfaction of curiosity, and the sheer love of the activity. Extrinsic motives include a desire for money, fame, and attention, or the wish to avoid punishment. In one study, artworks created for extrinsic reasons (they were commissioned by art collectors) were judged to be less creative than works done by the same artists for the intrinsic pleasure of creation—and this was true even when the person commissioning the work allowed the artist complete freedom (Amabile, Phillips, & Collins, 1993). As Robert Frost once said, "One should never write a poem to pay a gas bill." But this does not mean that writers and artists should work for free! When people have been trained to think divergently, and when extrinsic rewards are tied explicitly to creative effort (and not just to doing the job), then rewards can promote further creativity (Eisenberger, Armeli, & Pretz, 1998).

Creativity also flourishes when people have control over how to perform a task or solve a problem; are evaluated unobtrusively, instead of being constantly observed and judged; and are able to work independently (Amabile, 1983). Organizations encourage creativity when they let people take risks, give them plenty of time to think about problems, and welcome innovation.

In sum, if you hope to become more creative, there are two things you can do. One is to cultivate the personal qualities that lead to creativity. The other is to seek out the kinds of situations that permit you to express them.

SUMMARY

THOUGHT: USING WHAT WE KNOW

1. *Thinking* is the mental manipulation of information. Our mental representations simplify and summarize information from the environment.

2. A *concept* is a mental category that groups objects, relations, activities, abstractions, or qualities that share certain properties. *Basic concepts* have a moderate number of instances and are easier to acquire than concepts with few or many instances. *Prototypical* instances of a concept are more representative than others. *Propositions* are made up of concepts and express a unitary idea. They may be linked together to form *cognitive schemas*, which serve as mental models of aspects of the world. *Mental images* also play a role in thinking.

3. Not all mental processing is conscious. *Subconscious processes* lie outside of awareness but can be brought into consciousness when necessary. *Nonconscious processes* remain outside of awareness but nonetheless affect behavior and are involved in what we call "intuition" and "insight." Conscious processing may be carried out in a mindless fashion if we overlook changes in context that call for a change in behavior.

REASONING RATIONALLY

4. *Reasoning* is purposeful mental activity that involves drawing inferences and conclusions from observations, facts, or assumptions (premises).

5. *Formal reasoning problems* can often be solved by applying an *algorithm*, a set of procedures guaranteed to produce a solution, or by using logical processes, such as *deductive* and *inductive reasoning*.

6. In *informal reasoning problems*, there may be no clearly correct solution. Disagreement may exist about basic premises, information may be incomplete, and many viewpoints may compete. Such problems may call for the application of *heuristics*, rules of thumb that suggest a course of action without guaranteeing an optimal solution. They may also require *dialectical thinking* about opposing points of view.

7. Studies of *reflective judgment* show that many people have trouble thinking dialectically. People in the *pre-reflective* stages assume that a correct answer always exists; they do not distinguish between knowledge and belief, or between belief and evidence. Those in the *quasi-reflective* stages think that because knowledge is sometimes uncertain, any judgment about the evidence is purely subjective. Those who think *reflectively* understand that although some things cannot be known with certainty, some judgments are more valid than others, depending on their coherence, usefulness, fit with the evidence, and so on. Higher education moves people gradually closer to reflective judgment.

BARRIERS TO REASONING RATIONALLY

8. The need to be right can be an obstacle to rational thinking, as can mental laziness, which many commentators think has increased because of the replacement of reading by television watching.

9. The ability to reason clearly and rationally is also affected by many *cognitive biases*. People tend to exaggerate the likelihood of improbable events, in part because of the *availability heuristic;* to be swayed in their choices by the desire to *avoid loss;* to attend mostly to evidence that confirms what they want to believe (the *confirmation bias*); to be mentally rigid, forming *mental sets* and seeing patterns where none exists; and to overestimate their ability to have made accurate predictions (the *hindsight bias*). The theory of *cognitive dissonance* holds that people are also motivated to reduce the tension that exists when two cognitions are in conflict—by rejecting or changing a belief, changing their behavior, or rationalizing. People are not always rational, but once we understand a bias, we may be able to reduce or eliminate it.

MEASURING INTELLIGENCE: THE PSYCHOMETRIC APPROACH

10. Although we all wish to think intelligently, *intelligence* is hard to define. Some theorists believe that a general ability (a *g factor*) underlies the many specific abilities tapped by intelligence tests, whereas others do not.

11. The traditional approach to intelligence, the *psychometric approach*, focuses on how well people perform on standardized mental tests. The *intelligence quotient*, or *IQ*, represents how a person has done on an intelligence test, compared to other people. Alfred Binet designed the first widely used intelligence test for the purpose of identifying children who could benefit from remedial work. But in the United States, people assumed that intelligence tests revealed "natural ability," and they used the tests to categorize people in school and in the armed services.

12. IQ tests have been criticized for being biased in favor of white, middle-class people. However, efforts to construct *culture-free* and *culture-fair tests* have been disappointing. Culture affects nearly everything to do with taking a test, including attitudes, expectations, problem-solving

strategies, and comfort level. Negative stereotypes about a person's ethnicity, gender, or age may cause the person to suffer *stereotype threat,* a burden of doubt about his or her own abilities, which can lead to anxiety or "disidentification" with the test.

13. Many social scientists consider IQ tests useful for predicting school performance and diagnosing learning difficulties, as long as test scores are combined with other information and used "intelligently." But some critics would like to dispense with IQ tests because they are so often misused or misinterpreted.

DISSECTING INTELLIGENCE: THE COGNITIVE APPROACH

14. In contrast to the psychometric approach, *cognitive approaches* to intelligence emphasize the strategies people use to solve problems, not just whether they get the right answers.

15. Sternberg's *triarchic theory of intelligence* proposes three aspects of intelligence: *componential* (including *metacognition*), *experiential,* and *contextual.* Most intelligence tests do not measure experiential and contextual intelligence, or people's *tacit knowledge,* yet these help determine a person's personal and occupational success.

16. Howard Gardner's *theory of multiple intelligences* holds that there are actually several "intelligences" besides those usually considered, including musical and kinesthetic intelligence, and the capacity to understand the natural world, yourself, or others. The latter two overlap with what some psychologists call *emotional intelligence.* The traits associated with emotional intelligence are related to personal, academic, and occupational success.

17. Intellectual achievement also depends on motivation and attitudes. Cross-cultural work shows that beliefs about the origins of mental abilities, parental standards, and attitudes toward education can help account for differences in academic performance.

ANIMAL MINDS

18. Some researchers, especially those in *cognitive ethology,* argue that nonhuman animals have greater cognitive abilities than is usually thought. Some animals can use objects as rudimentary tools. Chimpanzees have learned to use numerals to label quantities of items and symbols to refer to objects. Several researchers have used visual symbol systems or American Sign Language (ASL) to teach primates language skills, and some animals (even some nonprimates) seem able to use simple grammatical ordering rules to convey or comprehend meaning. However, scientists are still divided as to how to interpret these findings.

KEY TERMS

Answer to the Get Involved problem on page 319:

You need to turn over the cards that say "Drinking beer" and "16 years old."

Answers to the creativity test on page 341:

back, party, book, match, cheese

Some solutions to the nine-dot problem in the Get Involved exercise on page 320 (from Adams, 1986):

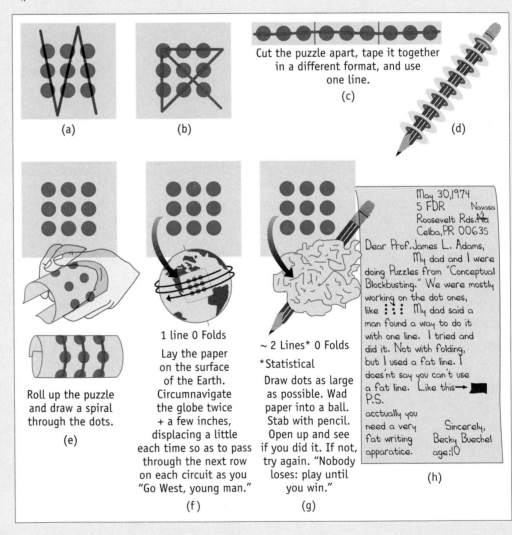

(a)

(b)

Cut the puzzle apart, tape it together in a different format, and use one line.

(c)

(d)

Roll up the puzzle and draw a spiral through the dots.

(e)

1 line 0 Folds

Lay the paper on the surface of the Earth. Circumnavigate the globe twice + a few inches, displacing a little each time so as to pass through the next row on each circuit as you "Go West, young man."

(f)

~ 2 Lines* 0 Folds

*Statistical

Draw dots as large as possible. Wad paper into a ball. Stab with pencil. Open up and see if you did it. If not, try again. "Nobody loses: play until you win."

(g)

May 30, 1974
5 FDR   Nayasa
Roosevelt Rds. Na
Ceiba, PR 00635

Dear Prof. James L. Adams,
   My dad and I were doing Puzzles from "Conceptual Blockbusting." We were mostly working on the dot ones, like ⋮⋮⋮ My dad said a man found a way to do it with one line. I tried and did it. Not with folding, but I used a fat line. It does'nt say you can't use a fat line. Like this→ ▬
P.S.
acctually you need a very fat writing apparatice.

                 Sincerely,
                 Becky Buechel
                 age:10

(h)

LOOKING BACK

- When you think of a bird, why are you more likely to recall a robin than a penguin? (p. 306)

- How are visual images similar to images on a computer screen? (p. 307)

- What is happening mentally when you mistakenly take your geography notes to your psychology class? (pp. 308–309)

- Mentally speaking, why is making a cake, well, a piece of cake? (p. 310)

- Why can't logic solve all our problems? (pp. 311–312)

- What kind of reasoning do juries need to be good at? (p. 313)

- When people say that all opinions and claims are equally valid, what error are they making? (p. 314)

- Why do people worry about dying in an airplane crash but ignore dangers that are far more likely? (p. 317)

- How might your physician's choice of words about alternative treatments for your illness affect which one you choose? (p. 318)

- When "Monday morning quarterbacks" say they knew all along who would win Sunday's big game, what bias might they be showing? (p. 321)

- Why will a terrible hazing make you more loyal to the group that hazed you? (p. 323)

- Why do psychologists debate whether a single thing called "intelligence" even exists? (p. 324)

- How did the original purpose of intelligence testing change when IQ tests came to America? (p. 327)

- Is it possible to design intelligence tests that are not influenced by culture? (pp. 327–328)

- Why do some psychologists defend traditional intelligence testing and others oppose it? (p. 329)

- What kind of intelligence allows you to master the unspoken rules for academic success? (pp. 330–331)

- What is "EQ" and why is it as important as IQ? (p. 332)

- Why do Asian children perform so much better in school than American students do, even though Asian classes are larger, with poorer facilities? (pp. 334–335)

- Why do some researchers think that animals can think, whereas others remain skeptical? (p. 337)

- People love to talk to their pets—but can their pets learn to talk back? (pp. 338–339)

10 MEMORY

Better by far that you should forget and smile

than that you should remember and be sad.

POET CHRISTINA ROSSETTI

In 1990, a California jury convicted retired firefighter George Franklin of murder on the basis of his adult daughter's recovered memory. The daughter, Eileen Franklin Lipsker, testified that while she was playing with her young daughter, a shocking memory had suddenly returned. Her daughter reminded her of a close childhood friend who had been slain 21 years earlier, at the age of 8. The case had never been solved, but in that moment Eileen remembered who had killed her friend because she remembered being there: It was her own father. A few months later, she also remembered that he had molested her for years, starting when she was 3.

Other cases involving recovered memories, mostly of sexual abuse, were soon being reported across North America, leading to a wave of criminal charges and lawsuits. In one typical case, a woman named Laura B. sued her father, claiming that he had molested her from the ages of 5 to 23 and had raped her just days before her wedding. Laura B. said she had no memories of these events until they emerged during therapy.

A bitter controversy has raged for years now about whether such accusations should be believed, and whether they provide sufficient evidence, in the absence of corroboration, to convict the alleged perpetrators. One side—we'll call it the *recovered-memory school*—believes that false memories are rare, that traumatic memories are commonly blocked from consciousness, and that people who raise doubts about recovered memories of trauma or abuse are inadvertently betraying victims and abetting child molesters (Freyd, 1996; Pope, 1996). The other side—we'll call it the *pseudomemory school*—argues that although real abuse occurs, many false memories of victimization are being encouraged by naïve or uninformed therapists (Lindsay & Read, 1994; Loftus & Ketcham, 1994). Emotions run high because much is at stake: finding justice for true victims by punishing perpetrators of abuse and other crimes, while also protecting adults from false charges that can destroy their lives.

At the end of this chapter we will see what finally happened in the Franklin case and the Laura B. case. But first, let's consider the reliability of memories in general. Of course, we all forget a great deal: We watch the evening news and half an hour later can't recall the main story; we enjoy a meal and forget what we ate by the next day; we study our heads off for an exam, only to find that some of the information is missing when we need it most. Do we also "remember" things that never happened? Are we likely to forget traumatic events that *did* happen? Are memory malfunctions the exception to the rule, or could they be the norm? And if memory is not always reliable, how can any of us hope to know the story of our own lives? How can we hope to understand the past?

WHAT'S AHEAD

- What's wrong with thinking of memory as a mental movie camera?
- If you have a strong emotional reaction to a remembered event, does that mean your memory is accurate?
- Why do "flashbulb memories" of surprising or shocking events sometimes have less wattage than we assume?
- Can the question someone asks you about a past event affect what you remember about it?

RECONSTRUCTING THE PAST

Memory refers to the capacity to retain and retrieve information, and also to the structures that account for this capacity. Human beings are capable of astonishing feats of memory. Most of us can easily remember who fought whom in World War II, the tune of our national anthem, how to use an automated teller machine, the most embarrassing experience we ever had, and hundreds of thousands of other bits of information, without hesitation. A mathematician once calculated that over the course of a lifetime, we store 500 times as much information as there is in the entire *Encyclopædia Britannica* (Griffith, in Horn & Hinde, 1970).

Memory confers competence; without it we would be as helpless as newborns, unable to carry out even the most trivial of our daily tasks. Memory also confers a sense of personal identity; we are each the sum of our personal recollections, which is why we feel so threatened when others challenge our memories. Individuals and cultures alike rely on a remembered history for a sense of coherence and meaning; memory gives us our past and guides our future.

The Manufacture of Memory

In ancient times, philosophers compared memory to a soft wax tablet that would preserve anything that chanced to make an imprint on it. Then, with the advent of the printing press, they began to think of memory as a gigantic library, storing specific events and facts for later retrieval. Today, in the audiovisual age, many people compare memory to a tape recorder or a movie camera, automatically recording each and every moment of their lives.

Popular and appealing though this belief about memory is, however, it is utterly wrong. Not everything that happens to us or impinges on our senses is tucked away for later use; memory is selective. If it were not, our minds would be cluttered with mental junk—the temperature at noon Thursday, the price of turnips two years ago, a phone number needed only once. Moreover, recovering a memory is not at all like replaying a videotape of an event; it is more like watching a few unconnected frames and then figuring out what the rest of the scene must have been like.

One of the first scientists to make this point was the British psychologist Sir Frederic Bartlett (1932). Bartlett

Films and novels reflect and influence popular notions about memory. When Alfred Hitchcock made *Spellbound* in 1945, psychoanalytic ideas held sway. In the film, amnesia patient Gregory Peck is suspected of murder, and the clues to the identity of the real killer appear in a dream he has. The surrealistic dream sequences, designed by artist Salvador Dali, conveyed the idea that painful memories are never forgotten but are merely locked away in the unconscious with all the details intact, waiting to be recovered—a notion that modern research has questioned.

asked people to read lengthy, unfamiliar stories from other cultures and then tell the stories back to him. As the volunteers tried to recall the stories, they made interesting errors: They often eliminated or changed details that did not make sense to them, and they added other details to make the story coherent, sometimes even adding a moral. Memory, Bartlett concluded, must therefore be largely a *reconstructive* process. (Psychologists today sometimes call this process *confabulation*.) We may reproduce some kinds of simple information by rote, said Bartlett, but when we remember complex information, we typically alter it in ways that help us make sense of the material, based on what we already know, or think we know. Since Bartlett's time, hundreds of studies have found this to be true for everything from stories to conversations to personal experiences (Schacter, 1996).

If these children remember their vacation later in life, their reconstruction may include information picked up from family photographs, videos, and stories. Because of source amnesia, they will probably be unable to distinguish their actual memories from information they got elsewhere.

In reconstructing their memories, people often draw on many sources. Suppose, for example, that someone asks you to describe one of your early birthday parties. You may have some direct recollection of the event, but you may also incorporate information from family stories, photographs, or home videos, and even from accounts of other people's birthdays and re-enactments of birthdays on television. You take all these bits and pieces and build one integrated account. Later, you may not be able to separate your original experience from what you added after the fact—a phenomenon called **source amnesia**, or *source misattribution*.

A dramatic instance of reconstruction once occurred in the sad case of H. M., whom we described briefly in Chapter 4. Ever since 1953, when much of H. M.'s hippocampus and the adjacent cortex were surgically removed, he has been unable to form lasting memories for new events, facts, songs, stories, or faces, and so he does not remember much of anything that has happened since his operation (Hilts, 1995; Ogden & Corkin, 1991). To cope with his devastating condition, H. M. will sometimes resort to confabulation. On one occasion, after eating a chocolate Valentine's Day heart, H. M. stuck the shiny red wrapping in his shirt pocket. Two hours later, while searching for his handkerchief, he pulled out the paper and looked at it in puzzlement. When a researcher asked why he had the paper in his pocket, he replied, "Well, it could have been wrapped around a big chocolate heart. It must be Valentine's Day!" The researcher could hardly contain her excitement about H. M.'s possible recall of a recent episode. But a short time later, when she asked him to take out the paper again and say why he had it in his pocket, he replied, "Well, it might have been wrapped around a big chocolate rabbit. It must be Easter!"

Sadly, H. M. *had* to reconstruct the past; his damaged brain could not recall it in any other way. But those of us with normal memory abilities also reconstruct, far more often than we realize.

The Conditions of Confabulation

False memories of events or experiences, or misremembering of the particulars of an event, are especially likely to occur under the following circumstances (Garry, Manning, & Loftus, 1996; Hyman & Pentland, 1996; Johnson, 1995):

1 *You have thought about the imagined event many times.* Suppose that at family gatherings you keep hearing about the time that Uncle Sam scared everyone at a New Year's party by pounding a hammer into the wall with such force that

source amnesia The inability to distinguish what you originally experienced from what you heard or were told about an event later.

NEVER FORGETS   SOMETIMES FORGETS   ALWAYS FORGETS

the wall collapsed. The story is so colorful that you can practically see Uncle Sam in your mind's eye. The more you think about this event, the more likely you are to believe that you were actually there, even if you were sound asleep in another house.

2 *The image of the event contains a lot of details.* Ordinarily, we can distinguish an imagined event from a real one by the amount of detail we recall; real events tend to produce more details. However, the longer you think about an imagined event, the more details you are likely to add—what Sam was wearing, the fact that he'd had too much to drink, the crumbling plaster, people standing around in party hats—and these details may in turn persuade you that the event really happened and that you have a direct memory of it.

3 *The event is easy to imagine.* If forming an image of an event takes little effort (as does visualizing a man pounding a wall with a hammer), then we tend to think that our memory is real. In contrast, when we must make an effort to form an image—for example, of being in a place we have never seen or doing something that is utterly foreign to us—our cognitive efforts apparently serve as a cue that the event did not really take place, or that we were not there when it did.

4 *You focus on your emotional reactions to the event rather than on what actually happened.* Emotional reactions to an imagined event can resemble those that would have occurred in response to a real event, and so they can mislead us. This means that your feelings about an event, no matter how strongly you hold them, are no guarantee that the event really happened. Consider again our Sam story, which happens to be true. A woman we know believed for years that she had been present in the room as an 11-year-old child when her uncle destroyed the wall. Because the story was so vivid and upsetting to her, she felt angry at him for what she thought was his mean and violent behavior, and she assumed that she must have been angry at the time as well. Then, as an adult, she learned that she was not at the party at all but had merely heard about it repeatedly over the years; and that Sam had not pounded the wall in anger, but as a joke—to inform the assembled guests that he and his wife were about to remodel their home. Nevertheless, our friend's family has had a hard time convincing her that her "memory" of this event is entirely wrong, and they are not sure she believes them yet.

As the Sam story illustrates, and as laboratory research verifies, false memories can be as stable over time as true ones (Brainerd, Reyna, & Brandse, 1995; Poole, 1995; Roediger & McDermott, 1995). Yet many people still believe that memories are permanently stored in the brain with perfect accuracy. They may cite cases of apparently superb recall under hypnosis, or cases in which electrical brain stimulation prior to surgery has seemed to evoke memories of events thought by the patient to be long forgotten (Penfield & Perot, 1963). Hypnotically induced memories, however, are as vulnerable to confabulation and error as are any other memories (see Chapter 5). And the "memories" that result from brain stimulation are usually fragmentary reconstructions that draw in part on actual memories and in part on current thoughts or bits of conversation heard just before the operation (Loftus, 1980).

The Fading Flashbulb

Of course, some unusual, shocking, or tragic events, such as earthquakes or accidents, do seem to hold a special place in memory, especially when we were personally involved. Such events seem frozen in time, with all the details intact. Years ago, Roger Brown and James Kulik (1977) labeled these vivid recollections of emotional events "flashbulb memories" because that term captures the surprise, illumination, and seemingly photographic detail that characterize them. Brown and Kulik speculated that the capacity for flashbulb memories may have evolved because such memories had survival value. Remembering the details of a surprising or dangerous experience could have helped our ancestors avoid similar situations.

Despite their intensity, however, even flashbulb memories are not always complete or accurate records of the past (Wright, 1993). For example, many people over the age of 25 say that they know exactly where they were and what they were doing when they learned of the 1986 explosion of the space shuttle *Challenger*, as well as who told them the news and what their own reactions were. But research done after the explosion occurred showed that memories like these grow dimmer with time. In one study, college students, on the morning after the *Challenger* tragedy, reported how they had heard the news. Three years later, when they again recalled how they learned of the incident, not one student was entirely correct and a third of them were *completely wrong*, although they felt confident that they were remembering accurately (Neisser & Harsch, 1992).

What about emotionally arousing *positive* events, like a first romantic kiss? These events, too, sometimes have the qualities of a flashbulb memory. Lovers who were highly excited by their first kiss report more details about the experience than people who were not very excited. Some say they can recall what the other person was wearing, the exact hour and day of the kiss, and the first words that were uttered afterward. Yet time takes a toll on these memories as well, with recall best within two years of the event (Fisher et al., 1999).

Do you recall where you were and what you were doing on April 20, 1999, when you learned of the shooting rampage at Columbine High School? If so, you may have a "flashbulb" memory of that event. But even vivid flashbulb memories are not always complete or accurate, and they often change over time.

Even with flashbulb memories, then, facts tend to get mixed with a little fiction. The conclusion is inescapable: Remembering is an *active* process, one that involves not only dredging up stored information but also putting two and two together to reconstruct the past.

The Eyewitness on Trial

The reconstructive nature of memory helps the mind work efficiently. Instead of cramming our brains with zillions of specific details, we can store the essentials of an experience, then use our knowledge of the world to figure out the specifics when we need them. But sometimes the same process gets us into hot water, and this raises some thorny problems in legal cases that involve eyewitness testimony.

Without the accounts of eyewitnesses, many guilty people would go free. But because memory is reconstructive, eyewitness testimony is not always reliable, even when the witness is certain about the accuracy of his or her report (Bothwell, Deffenbacher, & Brigham, 1987; Sporer et al., 1995). As a result, convictions based solely or mostly on such testimony occasionally turn out to be tragic mistakes. When researchers looked into 40 cases of wrongful imprisonment in which DNA evidence eventually established the innocence of the accused person, they found that 90 percent of the cases had involved a false identification by one or more eyewitnesses (Wells et al., 1998). Errors by eyewitnesses are especially likely to occur when the suspect's ethnicity differs from that of the witness, perhaps because prejudices or unfamiliarity prevent people from attending to the distinctive features of members of other groups, or because ethnic stereotypes affect people's reconstructions of what happened (Brigham & Malpass, 1985; Chance & Goldstein, 1995; Sherman & Bessenoff, 1999).

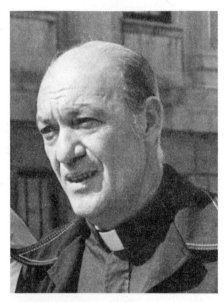

The legal system relies on the memories of eyewitnesses, but sometimes witnesses make mistakes. Seven people identified Father Bernard Pagno (top) as having committed a series of armed robberies, but Robert Clouser (bottom) later confessed to the crimes.

The Power of Suggestion. To complicate matters further, eyewitness accounts are heavily influenced by the way in which questions are put to the witness and by suggestive comments made during an interrogation. In a classic study of *leading questions*, Elizabeth Loftus and John Palmer (1974) showed people short films depicting car collisions. Afterward, the researchers asked some of the viewers, "About how fast were the cars going when they hit each other?" Other viewers were asked the same question, but with the verb changed to *smashed, collided, bumped,* or *contacted.* Estimates of how fast the cars were going varied, depending on which word was used. *Smashed* produced the highest average speed estimates (40.8 mph), followed by *collided* (39.3 mph), *bumped* (38.1 mph), *hit* (34.0 mph), and *contacted* (31.8 mph).

In a similar study, the researchers asked some participants, "Did you see a broken headlight?" but asked of others "Did you see the broken headlight?" (Loftus & Zanni, 1975). The question with *the* presupposes a broken headlight and merely asks whether the witness saw it, whereas the question with *a* makes no such presupposition. People who received questions with *the* were far more likely to report having seen something that had not really appeared in the film than were those who received questions with *a*. If a tiny word like *the* can lead people to "remember" what they never saw, you can imagine how the leading questions of police detectives and lawyers might influence a witness's recall.

Leading questions and suggestive comments affect people's memories for their own experiences, as well as events they have merely witnessed. In a number of studies, researchers have induced people to "recall" complicated events from early in life that never actually happened at all, such as getting lost in a shopping mall,

Misleading information can profoundly affect recall. Students saw the face of a young man with straight hair, then heard a description of the face supposedly written by another witness—one that wrongly mentioned light, curly hair. When they reconstructed the face using a kit of facial features, a third of their reconstructions contained the misleading detail, whereas only 5 percent contained it when curly hair was not mentioned. On the left is one person's reconstruction in the absence of the misleading information; on the right is another person's reconstruction of the same face after exposure to the misleading information (Loftus & Greene, 1980).

being hospitalized for a high fever, being harassed by a bully, or spilling punch all over the mother of the bride at a wedding (Hyman & Pentland, 1996; Loftus & Pickrell, 1995; Mazzoni et al., 1999). The more often people tell the story, the more details about these "events" they recall.

Children's Testimony. The power of suggestion can affect anyone, but many people are especially concerned about its impact on children being questioned about possible sexual abuse. For many decades most adults believed that children's memories could not be trusted—that children confuse fantasy with reality and tend to say whatever adults expect. Then, as the issue of child abuse came to public attention in the 1970s and 1980s, some people began to argue that no child would ever lie about or misremember such a traumatic experience. Resolving this debate became critical as accusations of child abuse in daycare centers across the United States skyrocketed. Dozens of children, after being interviewed by therapists and police investigators, were claiming that their teachers had molested them in terrible ways: hanging them in trees, putting handcuffs on them, even forcing them to eat feces.

After carefully reviewing the research on this issue, Stephen Ceci and Maggie Bruck (1993, 1995) concluded that both of these extreme positions—"children always lie" and "children never lie"—are wrong. Ceci and Bruck found that most young children *do* recollect accurately most of what they have observed or experienced, including potentially embarrassing experiences such as genital examinations at a doctor's office. More specifically, most children do not report that their genitals were touched if they were not touched, even when the children are asked leading questions (Goodman et al., 1990; Saywitz et al., 1991). This finding is important, because without a few leading questions, some young children who have been abused will not volunteer information that they feel is embarrassing or shameful. On the other hand, some children *will* say that something happened when it did not. Like adults, they can be influenced to report an event in a certain way, depending on the frequency of the suggestions and the insistence of the person making them.

Therefore, instead of asking "Are children suggestible?" or "Are children's memories accurate?", Ceci and Bruck (1995) suggest asking a more useful question:

THINKING CRITICALLY

DON'T OVERSIMPLIFY

Some people claim that children's memories of sexual abuse are always accurate; others claim that children can't distinguish fantasy from reality. How can we avoid either-or thinking on this emotional issue? Is the question "Are children's memories accurate?" even the right one to ask?

"Under what conditions are children apt to be suggestible?" One such condition is age. Preschoolers' memories are more vulnerable to suggestive questions than are those of school-age children and adults. Preschoolers are also more likely to have source amnesia, failing to remember whether they actually saw or experienced something themselves or heard about it from an adult. And the boundary between reality and fantasy may blur for very young children, especially in emotionally charged situations, making it more likely that their accounts will include confabulations of imagined events.

In addition, children's memories, just like adults' memories, can be influenced by pressure to conform to the interviewer's expectations and by the desire to please the interviewer (Poole & Lamb, 1998). In one revealing experiment (Garven et al., 1999), a young man visited children at their preschool, read them a story, and handed out treats. The man did nothing that was aggressive, socially inappropriate, or surprising. A week later the experimenter questioned the children about the man's visit. She asked children in one group leading questions ("Did he shove the teacher? Did he throw a crayon at a kid who was talking?"). She asked a second group the same questions, but also used influence techniques that have been used by interrogators in cases of daycare workers accused of child abuse: for example, telling the children what "other kids" had supposedly said, expressing disappointment if answers were negative, and praising children for making allegations.

In the first group, children said "yes, it happened" to about 15 percent of the false allegations about the man's visit. This finding alone refutes the notion that children never lie, misremember, or make things up. In the second group, the 3-year-olds, on average, said "yes" to over *80 percent* of the false allegations suggested to them, and the 4- to 6-year-olds said yes to about half the allegations (see Figure 10.1). Note that the interviews in this study lasted only five to 10 minutes, whereas in actual investigations, interviewers often question children repeatedly over many weeks.

In sum, children, like adults, can be accurate in what they report; and, also like adults, they can distort, forget, fantasize, and be misled. As research shows, their memory processes are only human.

FIGURE 10.1
SOCIAL PRESSURE AND CHILDREN'S FALSE ALLEGATIONS

When researchers asked a group of preschoolers whether a visitor to their classroom had committed aggressive acts—acts that had not actually occurred—many said that yes, he had. And when the researchers interviewed another group of children using social influence techniques taken from real-life child-abuse investigations, most of the children said yes. As you can see, the younger the children, the more likely they were to agree with the interviewer's leading questions (Garven et al., 1998).

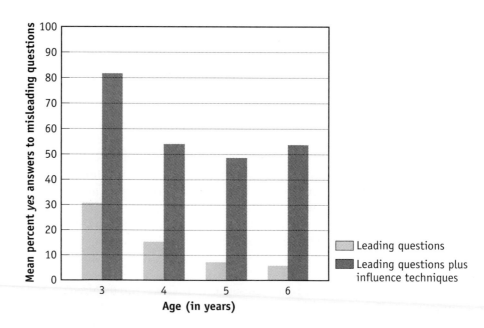

QUICK QUIZ

See whether you can reconstruct what you have read in order to answer these questions.

1. Memory is like (a) a wax tablet, (b) a giant file cabinet, (c) a video recorder, (d) none of these.

2. In the children's game "telephone," one person tells another person a story, the second person relates the story to a third, and so on. By the end of the game, the story will have changed considerably, which illustrates the principle that memory is _____.

3. *True or false:* Like other memories, flashbulb memories are vulnerable to distortion.

 4. In psychotherapy, hundreds of people have claimed to recall long-buried memories of having taken part in satanic rituals involving animal and human torture and sacrifice. Yet law-enforcement investigators and psychologists have been unable to confirm any of these reports (Goodman et al., 1995). Based on what you have learned so far, how might you explain such "memories"?

Answers:

1. d 2. reconstructive 3. true 4. Therapists who uncritically assume that satanic abuse cults are widespread may ask leading questions and make leading comments to their patients. Patients, who are susceptible to their therapists' interpretations, may then confabulate and "remember" experiences that did not happen, borrowing details from fictionalized accounts or from other traumatic experiences in their lives (Ganaway, 1991; Ofshe & Watters, 1994). If the therapist continues to probe for more details and emotions associated with the alleged experience, the result may be source amnesia and the mistaken conviction on the part of the patient that the memory is real.

WHAT'S AHEAD

- In general, which is easier, a multiple-choice item or a short-answer essay item—and why?
- Can you know something without knowing that you know it?
- Why is the computer often used as a metaphor for the mind?

IN PURSUIT OF MEMORY

Now that we have seen how memory *doesn't* work—namely, like a tape recorder, an infallible filing system, or a journal written in indelible ink—we turn to studies of how it *does* work. The ability to remember is not an absolute talent; it depends on the type of performance being called for. Students who express a preference for multiple-choice, essay, or true-false exams already know this.

Measuring Memory

Conscious recollection of an event or an item of information is called **explicit memory**. It is usually measured using one of two methods. The first method tests for **recall**, the ability to retrieve and reproduce information encountered earlier. Essay and fill-in-the-blank exams and memory games such as Trivial Pursuit or Jeopardy require recall. The second method tests for **recognition**, the ability to identify information you have previously observed, read, or heard about. The information is given to you, and all you have to do is say whether it is old or new, or perhaps correct or incorrect, or pick it out of a set of alternatives. The task, in other words, is to compare the information you are given with the information stored in your memory. True-false and multiple-choice tests call for recognition.

explicit memory Conscious, intentional recollection of an event or of an item of information.

recall The ability to retrieve and reproduce from memory previously encountered material.

recognition The ability to identify previously encountered material.

GET →INVOLVED

RECALLING RUDOLPH'S FRIENDS

You can try this test of recall if you are familiar with the poem *'Twas the Night Before Christmas* or the song *Rudolph the Red-Nosed Reindeer*. Rudolph had eight reindeer friends; name as many of them as you can. After you have done your best, turn to the Get Involved exercise on page 358 for a recognition test on the same information.

Recognition tests can be tricky, especially when false items closely resemble correct ones. Under most circumstances, however, recognition is easier than recall. Recognition for visual images is particularly impressive. If you show people 2,500 slides of faces and places, and later you ask them to identify which ones they saw out of a larger set, they will be able to identify more than 90 percent of the original slides accurately (Haber, 1970).

The superiority of recognition over recall was once demonstrated in a study of people's memories of their high-school classmates (Bahrick, Bahrick, & Wittlinger, 1975). The participants, ages 17 to 74, first wrote down the names of as many class-mates as they could remember. Recall was poor; even when prompted with yearbook pictures, the youngest people failed to name almost a third of their classmates, and the oldest failed to name most of them. Recognition, however, was far better. When asked to look at a series of cards, each of which contained a set of five photographs, and to say which picture in each set showed a former classmate, recent graduates were right 90 percent of the time—and so were people who had graduated 35 years earlier! The ability to recognize names was nearly as impressive.

How many of your high school classmates can you recall by name? Would you do better at recognizing than recalling their pictures or their names?

Sometimes information encountered in the past affects our thoughts and actions even though we do not consciously or intentionally remember it—a phenomenon known as **implicit memory** (Graf & Schacter, 1985; Schacter, Chiu, & Ochsner, 1993). To get at this subtle sort of knowledge, researchers must rely on indirect methods, instead of the direct ones used to measure explicit memory. One common method, **priming**, asks you to read or listen to some information and then tests you later to see whether the information affects your performance on another type of task.

For example, suppose that you had to read a list of words, some of which began with the letters *def* (such as *define, defend,* or *deform*). Later you might be asked to complete word stems (such as *def-*) with the first word that comes to mind. Even if you could not recognize or recall the original words very well, you would be more likely to complete the word fragments with words from the list than you would be if you had not seen the list. In this procedure, the original words "prime" certain responses on the word-completion task (that is, make them more available), showing that people can retain more knowledge about the past than they realize. They know more than they know that they know (Richardson-Klavehn & Bjork, 1988; Roediger, 1990).

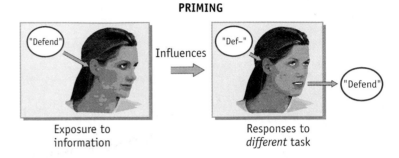

PRIMING

"Defend" Influences "Def–" → "Defend"

Exposure to information | Responses to *different* task

Another method of measuring implicit memory, the **relearning method**, or *savings method*, straddles the boundary between implicit and explicit memory tests. Devised by Hermann Ebbinghaus (1885/1913) over a century ago, the relearning method requires you to relearn information or a task that you learned earlier. If you master it more quickly the second time around, you must be remembering something from the first experience. One eminent memory researcher told us that he considers the relearning method to be a test of explicit memory. But another maintained that it can function as a test of implicit memory if the learner is unaware that the material being relearned was ever learned earlier.

Models of Memory

Although people usually refer to memory as a single faculty, as in "I must be losing my memory" or "He has a memory like an elephant's," the term *memory* actually covers a complex collection of abilities and processes. If tape recorders or video cameras are not accurate metaphors for capturing these diverse components of memory, then what metaphor would be better?

As we saw in Chapter 9, many cognitive psychologists liken the mind to an information processor, along the lines of a computer, though more complex. They have constructed *information-processing models* of cognitive processes, liberally borrowing computer-programming terms such as *input, output, accessing,* and *information retrieval*. When you type something on your computer's keyboard, the machine encodes the information into an electronic language, stores it on a disk, and retrieves it when you need to use it. Similarly, in information-processing models of memory, we *encode* information (convert it to a form that the brain can process and use), *store* the information (retain it over time), and *retrieve* the information (recover it for use). In storage, the information may be represented as concepts, propositions, images, or *cognitive schemas*—mental networks of knowledge, beliefs, and expectations concerning particular topics or aspects of the world. (If you can't retrieve these terms, see Chapter 9, pages 306–307.)

implicit memory Unconscious retention in memory, as evidenced by the effect of a previous experience or previously encountered information on current thoughts or actions.

priming A method for measuring implicit memory in which a person reads or listens to information and is later tested to see whether the information affects performance on another type of task.

relearning method A method for measuring retention that compares the time required to relearn material with the time used in the initial learning of the material.

GET ➔ INVOLVED

RECOGNIZING RUDOLPH'S FRIENDS

If you took the recall test in the Get Involved exercise on page 356, now try a recognition test. From the following list, see whether you can identify the correct names of Rudolph the Red-Nosed Reindeer's eight reindeer friends. The answers are at the end of this chapter—but no fair peeking!

Blitzen	Dander	Dancer	Masher
Cupid	Dasher	Prancer	Comet
Kumquat	Donder	Flasher	Pixie
Bouncer	Blintzes	Trixie	Vixen

Which was easier, recall or recognition? Can you speculate on the reason?

BASIC MEMORY PROCESSES

Retrieval — Shakespeare wrote Hamlet.

Storage

Encoding

FIGURE 10.2
THREE MEMORY SYSTEMS

In the "three-box model" of memory, information that does not transfer out of sensory memory or short-term memory is assumed to be forgotten forever. Once in long-term memory, information can be retrieved for use in analyzing incoming sensory information or performing mental operations in short-term memory.

In most information-processing models, storage takes place in three interacting memory systems. *Sensory memory* retains incoming sensory information for a second or two, until it can be processed further. *Short-term memory (STM)* holds a limited amount of information for a brief period of time, perhaps up to 30 seconds or so, unless a conscious effort is made to keep it there longer. *Long-term memory (LTM)* accounts for longer storage—from a few minutes to decades (Atkinson & Shiffrin, 1968, 1971). Information can pass from sensory memory to short-term memory and in either direction between short-term and long-term memory, as illustrated in Figure 10.2.

This model, which is often informally called the "three-box model," has dominated research on memory since the late 1960s. However, some psychologists argue that just one system exists, with different mental processes called on for different tasks. Critics of the three-box model also note that the human brain does not operate like your average computer. Most computers process instructions and data sequentially, and so the three-box model has emphasized sequential operations; but the human brain performs many operations simultaneously, in parallel. It recognizes patterns all at once rather than as a sequence of information bits, and it perceives new information, produces speech, and searches memory all at the same time. It can do this because millions of neurons are active at once, and each neuron communicates with thousands of others, which in turn communicate with millions more.

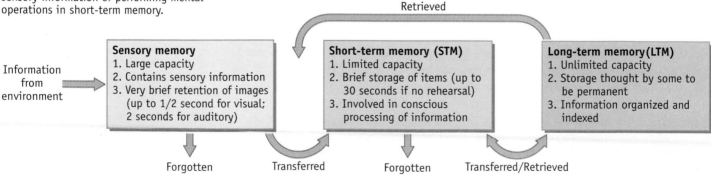

Retrieved

Sensory memory	Short-term memory (STM)	Long-term memory (LTM)
1. Large capacity	1. Limited capacity	1. Unlimited capacity
2. Contains sensory information	2. Brief storage of items (up to 30 seconds if no rehearsal)	2. Storage thought by some to be permanent
3. Very brief retention of images (up to 1/2 second for visual; 2 seconds for auditory)	3. Involved in conscious processing of information	3. Information organized and indexed

Information from environment

Forgotten   Transferred   Forgotten   Transferred/Retrieved

Because of these differences between human beings and machines, some cognitive scientists prefer a **parallel distributed processing (PDP)**, or *connectionist*, model. Instead of representing information as flowing from one system to another, a PDP model represents the contents of memory as connections among a huge number of interacting processing units, distributed in a vast network and all operating in parallel—just like the neurons of the brain (McClelland, 1994; Rumelhart, McClelland, & the PDP Research Group, 1986). As information enters the system, the ability of these units to excite or inhibit each other is constantly adjusted to reflect new knowledge.

Memory researchers are still arguing about which model of memory is most useful. In this chapter, we emphasize the three-box model, but keep in mind that the computer metaphor which inspired the model could one day be as outdated as the metaphor of memory as a camera.

QUICK QUIZ

How well have you encoded what you just learned?

1. Alberta solved a crossword puzzle a few days ago. She no longer recalls the words in the puzzle, but while playing a game of Scrabble with her brother, she unconsciously tends to form words that were in the puzzle, showing that she has _____ memories of some of the words.

2. The three basic memory processes are _____, storage, and _____.

3. Do the preceding two questions ask for recall, recognition, or relearning? (And what about *this* question?)

4. One objection to traditional information-processing theories of memory is that unlike most computers, the brain performs many independent operations _____.

Answers:

1. implicit 2. encoding, retrieval 3. The first two questions both measure recall; the third question measures recognition. 4. simultaneously, or in parallel

WHAT'S AHEAD

● **Why is short-term memory like a leaky bucket?**
● **When a word is on the tip of your tongue, what errors are you likely to make in recalling it?**
● **What's the difference between "knowing how" and "knowing that"?**

THE THREE-BOX MODEL OF MEMORY

The information model of three separate memory systems—sensory, short-term, and long-term—remains the leading approach because it offers a convenient way to organize the major findings on memory, does a good job of accounting for these findings, and is consistent with biological facts about memory, which we will describe shortly. Let us now peer more closely into each of the "boxes."

Sensory Memory: Fleeting Impressions

In the three-box model, all incoming sensory information must make a very brief stop in **sensory memory**, the entryway of memory. Sensory memory includes a number of separate subsystems, as many as there are senses. Visual images remain in a visual

parallel distributed processing (PDP) An alternative to the information-processing model of memory, in which knowledge is represented as connections among thousands of interacting processing units, distributed in a vast network, and all operating in parallel.

sensory memory A memory system that momentarily preserves extremely accurate images of sensory information.

GET ➔ INVOLVED

YOUR SENSORY MEMORY AT WORK

Go into a dark room or closet and swing a flashlight rapidly in a circle. You will see an unbroken circle of light instead of a series of separate points. The reason: The successive images remain briefly in sensory memory.

subsystem for a maximum of half a second. Auditory images remain in an auditory subsystem for a slightly longer time, by most estimates up to two seconds or so.

Sensory memory acts as a holding bin, retaining information until we can select items for attention from the stream of stimuli bombarding our senses. It gives us a brief time to decide whether information is extraneous or important; not everything detected by our senses warrants our attention. *Pattern recognition*, the preliminary identification of a stimulus on the basis of information already contained in long-term memory, occurs during the transfer of information from sensory memory to short-term memory. Information that does not go on to short-term memory vanishes forever, like a message written in disappearing ink.

Images in sensory memory are fairly complete. How do we know that? In a clever experiment, George Sperling (1960) briefly showed people visual arrays of letters that looked like this:

$$
\begin{array}{cccc}
X & K & C & Q \\
N & D & X & G \\
T & F & R & J
\end{array}
$$

In previous studies, subjects had been able to recall only four or five letters, no matter how many they initially saw. Yet many people insisted that they had actually seen more items. Some of the letters, they said, seemed to slip away from memory before they could retrieve and report them. To overcome this problem, Sperling devised a method of "partial report." He had people report the first row of letters when they heard a high tone, the middle row when they heard a medium tone, and the third row when they heard a low tone:

$$
\begin{array}{cccc}
X & K & C & Q \\
N & D & X & G \\
T & F & R & J
\end{array}
$$

← High tone
← Medium tone
← Low tone

If the tone occurred right after they saw the array, people could recall about three letters from a row. Because they did not know beforehand which row they would have to report, they therefore must have had most of the letters in sensory memory right after viewing them. However, if the tone occurred after a delay of even one second, people remembered little of what they had seen. The letters had slipped away. In normal processing, too, sensory memory needs to clear quickly to prevent sensory "double exposures."

Short-term Memory: Memory's Scratch Pad

Like sensory memory, **short-term memory (STM)** retains information only temporarily—for up to about 30 seconds by most estimates, although some researchers think that the maximum interval may extend to a few minutes. In short-term memory, the material is no longer an exact sensory image but is an encoding of one, such as a word or a phrase. This material either transfers into long-term memory or decays and is lost forever.

Cases of brain injury such as H. M.'s demonstrate the importance of transferring new information from short-term memory into long-term memory. H. M., you will recall, can store information on a short-term basis; he can hold a conversation and he appears normal when you first meet him. He also retains implicit memories. However, for the most part, H. M. cannot retain explicit information about new facts and events for longer than a few minutes. His terrible memory deficits involve a problem in transferring explicit memories from short-term storage into long-term storage. With a great deal of repetition and drill, H. M. can learn some new visual information, retain it in long-term memory, and recall it normally (McKee & Squire, 1992). But usually information does not get into long-term memory in the first place.

Working Memory. Besides retaining new information for brief periods while we are learning it, short-term memory holds information that has been retrieved from long-term memory for temporary use, providing the mental equivalent of a scratch pad. Thus, short-term memory functions in part as a *working memory.* When you do an arithmetic problem, your working memory contains the numbers and the instructions for doing the necessary operations ("Add the right-hand column, carry the 2"), plus the intermediate results from each step. The ability to bring information from long-term memory into working memory is not disrupted in patients such as H. M. They can do arithmetic, converse, relate events that predate their injury, and do anything else that requires retrieval of information from long-term into short-term memory. Their problem is with the flow of information in the other direction, from short-term memory to long-term.

The Leaky Bucket. People such as H. M. fall at the extreme end on a continuum of forgetfulness, but even those of us with normal memories know from personal experience how frustratingly brief short-term retention can be. We look up a telephone number, are distracted for a moment, and find that the number has vanished from our minds. We meet someone at a meeting and two minutes later find ourselves groping unsuccessfully for the person's name. Is it any wonder that short-term memory has been called a "leaky bucket"?

According to most memory models, if the bucket did not leak it would quickly overflow, because at any given moment, short-term memory can hold only so many items. Years ago, George Miller (1956) estimated its capacity to be "the magical number 7 plus or minus 2." Five-digit zip codes and 7-digit telephone numbers fall conveniently in this range; 16-digit credit-card numbers do not. Some researchers have questioned whether Miller's magical number is so magical after all; estimates of

If the visual sensory register did not clear quickly, multiple images might interfere with the accurate perception and encoding of information.

short-term memory (STM) In the three-box model of memory, a limited-capacity memory system involved in the retention of information for brief periods; it is also used to hold information retrieved from long-term memory for temporary use.

If you do not play chess, you probably will not be able to recall the positions of these chess pieces after looking away. But experienced chess players, in the middle of a game, can remember the position of every piece after glancing only briefly at the board. They are able to "chunk" the pieces into a few standard configurations, instead of trying to memorize where each piece is located.

STM's capacity have ranged from 2 items to 20. Everyone agrees, however, that the number of items that short-term memory can handle at any one time is small.

If this is so, then how do we remember the beginning of a spoken sentence until the speaker reaches the end? After all, most sentences are longer than just a few words. According to most models of memory, we overcome this problem by grouping small bits of information into larger units, or **chunks**. The real capacity of STM, it turns out, is not a few bits of information but a few chunks. A chunk may be a word, a phrase, a sentence, or even a visual image, and it depends on previous experience. For most of us, the acronym *FBI* is one chunk, not three, and the date *1492* is one chunk, not four. In contrast, the number *9214* is four chunks and *IBF* is three—unless your address is 9214 or your initials are IBF. To take a more visual example: If you are unfamiliar with football and look at a field full of players, you probably won't be able to remember their positions when you look away. But if you are a fan of the game, you may see a single chunk of information—say, a wishbone formation—and be able to retain it.

Even chunking cannot keep short-term memory from eventually filling up. Fortunately, much of the information we take in during the day is needed for only a few moments. If you are multiplying two numbers, you need to remember them only until you have the answer. If you are talking to someone, you need to keep the person's words in mind only until you have understood them. But some incoming information is needed for longer periods and must be transferred to long-term memory. Items that are particularly meaningful, have an emotional impact, or relate to something already in long-term memory may enter long-term storage easily, with only a brief stay in STM. The destiny of other items depends on how soon new information displaces them in short-term memory. Material in short-term memory is easily displaced unless we do something to keep it there, as we will discuss shortly.

Long-term Memory: Final Destination

The third box in the three-box model of memory is **long-term memory (LTM)**. The capacity of long-term memory seems to have no practical limits. The vast amount of information stored there enables us to learn, get around in the environment, and build a sense of identity and a personal history.

Organization in Long-term Memory. Because long-term memory contains so much information, it must be organized in some way, so that we can find the particular items we're looking for. One way to organize words (or the concepts they represent) is by the *semantic categories* to which they belong. *Chair*, for example, belongs to the category *furniture*. In a classic study, people had to memorize 60 words that came from four semantic categories: animals, vegetables, names, and professions. The words were presented in random order, but when people were allowed to recall the items in any order they wished, they tended to recall them in clusters corresponding to the four categories (Bousfield, 1953). This finding has been replicated many times.

Evidence on the storage of information by semantic category also comes from cases of people with brain damage. In one such case, a patient called M. D. appeared to have made a complete recovery after suffering several strokes, with one odd exception: He had trouble remembering the names of fruits and vegetables. M. D. could easily name

chunk A meaningful unit of information; it may be composed of smaller units.

long-term memory (LTM) In the three-box model of memory, the memory system involved in the long-term storage of information.

a picture of an abacus or a sphinx but he drew a blank when he saw a picture of an orange or a carrot. He could sort pictures of animals, vehicles, and other objects into their appropriate categories but did poorly with pictures of fruits and vegetables. On the other hand, when M. D. was *given* the names of fruits and vegetables, he immediately pointed to the corresponding pictures (Hart, Berndt, & Caramazza, 1985). Apparently, M. D. still had information about fruits and vegetables, but his brain lesion prevented him from using their names to get to the information when he needed it, unless the names were provided by someone else. This evidence suggests that information about a particular concept (such as *orange*) is linked in some way to information about the concept's semantic category (such as *fruit*).

Indeed, many models of long-term memory represent its contents as a vast network of interrelated concepts and propositions (Anderson, 1990; Collins & Loftus, 1975). In these **network models,** a small part of a conceptual network for *animals* might look something like the one in Figure 10.3. The way people use these networks, however, depends on experience and education. For example, studies of rural children in Liberia and Guatemala have shown that the more schooling children have, the more likely they are to use semantic categories in recalling lists of objects (Cole & Cole, 1993). This makes sense, because in school, children must memorize a lot of information in a short time, and semantic grouping can help. Unschooled children, having less need to memorize lists, do not cluster items and do not remember them as well. But this does not mean that unschooled children have poor memories. When the task is meaningful to them—say, recalling objects that were in a story or a village scene—they remember extremely well (Mistry & Rogoff, 1994).

We organize information in long-term memory not only by semantic groupings but also in terms of the way words sound or look. Have you ever tried to recall some word that was on the "tip of your tongue"? Nearly everyone experiences such *tip-of-the-tongue (TOT) states,* especially when trying to recall the names of acquaintances

network models Models of long-term memory that represent its contents as a vast network of interrelated concepts and propositions.

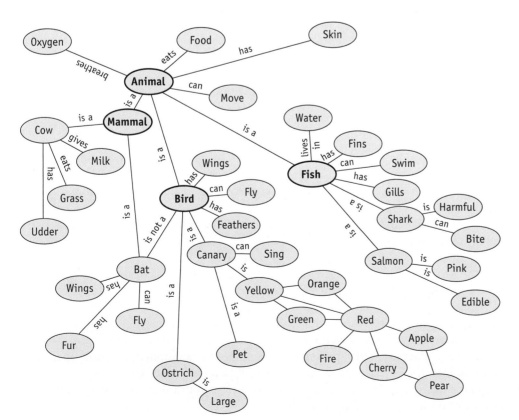

FIGURE 10.3
PART OF A CONCEPTUAL GRID IN LONG-TERM MEMORY

Many models of memory represent the contents of long-term semantic memory as an immense network or grid of concepts and the relationships among them. This illustration shows part of a hypothetical grid for *animals*.

Culture affects the encoding, storage, and retrieval of information in long-term memory. Navajo healers, who use stylized, symbolic sand paintings in their rituals, must commit to memory dozens of intricate visual designs because no exact copies are made and the painting is destroyed after each ceremony.

or famous persons, the names of objects and places, or the titles of movies or books (Burke et al., 1991). TOT states are reported even by users of sign language, who call them tip-of-the-finger states!

One way to study this frustrating experience is to have people record tip-of-the-tongue episodes in daily diaries. Another is to give people the definitions of uncommon words and ask them to supply the words. When a word is on the tip of the tongue, people tend to come up with words that are similar in meaning to the right one before they finally recall it. For example, for "patronage bestowed on a relative, in business or politics" a person might say "favoritism" rather than the correct response, "nepotism." But verbal information in long-term memory also seems to be indexed by sound and form, and it is retrievable on that basis. Thus, incorrect guesses often have the correct number of syllables, the correct stress pattern, the correct first letter, or the correct prefix or suffix (A. Brown, 1991; R. Brown & McNeill, 1966). For example, for the target word *sampan* (an Asian boat), a person might say "Siam" or "sarong."

Information in long-term memory may also be organized by its familiarity, relevance, or association with other information. The method used in any given instance probably depends on the nature of the memory; you would no doubt store information about the major cities of Europe differently from information about your first date. To understand the organization of long-term memory, then, we must know what kinds of information can be stored there.

The Contents of Long-term Memory. Most theories of memory distinguish skills or habits ("knowing how") from abstract or representational knowledge ("knowing that"). **Procedural memories** are memories of knowing how—for example, knowing how to comb your hair, use a pencil, solve a jigsaw puzzle, knit a sweater, or swim. Conditioned responses (see Chapter 7) also fall into this category. Some researchers consider procedural memories to be implicit, because once skills and habits are well learned, they do not require much conscious processing. **Declarative memories**, on the other hand, are memories of "knowing that," and they are usually assumed to be explicit.

procedural memories Memories for the performance of actions or skills ("knowing how").

declarative memories Memories of facts, rules, concepts, and events ("knowing that"); they include semantic and episodic memories.

Declarative memories, in turn, come in two varieties, semantic memories and episodic memories (Tulving, 1985). **Semantic memories** are internal representations of the world, independent of any particular context. They include facts, rules, and concepts—items of general knowledge. On the basis of your semantic memory of the concept *cat*, you can describe a cat as a small, furry mammal that typically spends its time eating, sleeping, prowling, and staring into space, even though a cat may not be present when you give this description, and you probably won't know how or when you first learned it. **Episodic memories** are internal representations of personally experienced events. When you remember how your cat once surprised you in the middle of the night by pouncing on your face as you slept, you are retrieving an episodic memory.

You might draw on procedural memories to ride a bike, semantic memories to identify a bird, and episodic memories to recall your wedding. The following diagram summarizes these distinctions. Can you come up with other examples for each memory type?

semantic memories Memories of general knowledge, including facts, rules, concepts, and propositions.

episodic memories Memories of personally experienced events and the contexts in which they occurred.

serial-position effect The tendency for recall of the first and last items on a list to surpass recall of items in the middle of the list.

Long-term memory

```
                    Long-term memory
                    /              \
       Procedural memories        Declarative memories
        ("Knowing how")            ("Knowing that")
                                   /            \
                        Semantic memories    Episodic memories
                      (General knowledge)  (Personal recollections)
```

From Short-term to Long-term Memory: A Riddle. The three-box model of memory is often invoked to explain an interesting phenomenon called the **serial-position effect**. If you are shown a list of items and are then asked immediately to recall them, your retention of any particular item will depend on its position in the list (Glanzer & Cunitz, 1966). Recall will be best for items at the beginning of the list (the *primacy effect*) and at the end of the list (the *recency effect*). When retention of all the items is plotted, the result will be a U-shaped curve, as shown in Figure 10.4. A serial-position effect occurs when you are introduced to a lot of people at a party and find you can recall the names of the first few people you met and the last, but almost no one in between.

According to the three-box model, the first few items on a list are remembered well because short-term memory was relatively "empty" when they entered, so these items did not have to compete with others to make it into long-term memory. They were thoroughly processed, so they remain memorable. The last few items are remembered for a different reason: At the time of recall, they are still sitting in short-term memory. The items in the middle of a list, however, are not so well retained because by the time they get into short-term memory, it is already crowded. As a result, many of these items drop out of short-term memory before they can be stored in long-term memory.

FIGURE 10.4
THE SERIAL-POSITION EFFECT

When people try to recall a list of similar items immediately after learning it, they tend to remember the first and last items best and the ones in the middle worst.

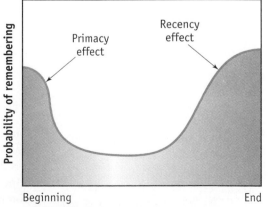

This explanation makes sense except for one thing: Under some conditions, the last items on a list are well remembered even when the test is delayed past the time when short-term memory has presumably been "emptied" and filled with other information (Greene, 1986). In other words, the recency effect occurs even when, according to the three-box model, it should not. At present, then, the serial-position curve remains something of a puzzle.

QUICK QUIZ

Find out whether the findings just discussed have transferred from your short-term memory to your long-term memory.

1. _____ memory holds images for a fraction of a second.

2. For most people, the abbreviation *U.S.A.* consists of _____ informational chunk(s).

3. Suppose you must memorize a long list of words that includes the following: *desk, pig, gold, dog, chair, silver, table, rooster, bed, copper,* and *horse*. If you can recall the words in any order you wish, how are you likely to group them in recall? Why?

4. When you roller-blade, are you relying on procedural, semantic, or episodic memory? How about when you recall the months of the year? Or when you remember falling while roller-blading on an icy January day?

5. If a child is trying to memorize the alphabet, which sequence should present the greatest difficulty: *abcdefg, klmnopq,* or *tuvwxyz*? Why?

Answers:

1. sensory 2. one 3. *Desk, chair, table,* and *bed* would probably form one cluster; *pig, dog, rooster,* and *horse* a second; and *gold, silver,* and *copper* a third. Concepts tend to be organized in long-term memory in terms of semantic categories, such as *furniture, animals,* and *metals.* 4. procedural; semantic; episodic 5. *klmnopq,* because of the serial-position effect

WHAT'S AHEAD

- **What's wrong with trying to memorize in a rote fashion when you're studying—and what's a better strategy?**
- **Memory tricks are fun, but are they always useful?**

HOW WE REMEMBER

Once we understand how memory works, we can use that understanding to encode and store information so that it "sticks" and will be there when we need it. What are the best strategies to use?

Effective Encoding

Our memories, as we have seen, are not exact replicas of experience. Sensory information is summarized and encoded—for example, as words or images—almost as soon as it is detected. When you hear a lecture, for example, you may hang on every word (we hope you do!), but you do not memorize those words verbatim. You extract the main points and encode them.

To remember information well, you have to encode it accurately in the first place. With some kinds of information, accurate encoding takes place automatically, without effort. Think about where you usually sit in your psychology class. When were you last there? You can probably provide this information easily, even though you never made a deliberate effort to encode it. In general, people automatically encode their location in space and time and the frequency with which they do certain things (Hasher & Zacks, 1984). But other kinds of information require *effortful encoding*. To retain such information, you might have to select the main points, label concepts, associate the information with personal experiences or with material you already know, or rehearse it until it is familiar. A friend of ours tells us that in her ballet class, she knows exactly what to do when asked to perform a *pas de bourrée*, yet she often has trouble recalling the term itself. Because she rarely uses it, she probably has not bothered to encode it well.

Encoding classroom material for later recall usually takes a deliberate effort. Which of these students do you think will remember best?

Unfortunately, people sometimes count on automatic encoding when effortful encoding is needed. For example, some students wrongly assume that they can encode the material in a textbook as effortlessly as they encode where they sit in the classroom. Or they assume that the ability to remember and perform well on tests is innate and that effort will not make any difference (Devolder & Pressley, 1989). As a result, they wind up in trouble at test time. Experienced students know that most of the information in a college course requires effortful encoding and therefore hard work.

Rehearsal

An important technique for keeping information in short-term memory and increasing the chances of long-term retention is *rehearsal*, the review or practice of material while you are learning it. When people are prevented from rehearsing, the contents of their short-term memories quickly fade.

In an early study of this phenomenon, people had to memorize meaningless groups of letters. Immediately afterward, they had to start counting backward by threes from an arbitrary number; this counting prevented them from rehearsing the letter groups. Within only 18 seconds, the subjects forgot most of the items (see Figure 10.5 on the next page). But when they did not have to count backward, their performance was much better, probably because they were rehearsing the items to themselves (Peterson & Peterson, 1959). You are taking advantage of rehearsal when you look up a telephone number and then repeat it over and over in order to keep it in short-term memory until you no longer need it.

A dramatic and poignant demonstration of the power of rehearsal once occurred during a session with H. M. (Ogden & Corkin, 1991). The experimenter gave H. M. five digits to repeat and remember, but then she was unexpectedly called away. When she returned after more than an hour, H. M. was able to repeat the five digits correctly. He had been rehearsing them the entire time!

Short-term memory holds many kinds of information, including visual information and abstract meanings. But most people—or at least most hearing people—seem to favor speech for encoding and rehearsing the contents of short-term memory. The

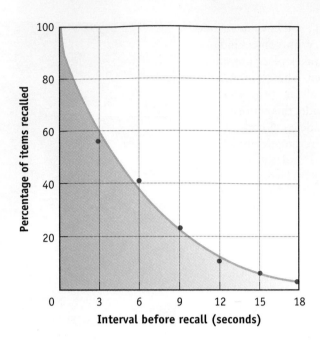

FIGURE 10.5
GOING, GOING, GONE

As this graph shows, without rehearsal the ability to recall information in short-term memory quickly falls off. (From Peterson & Peterson, 1959.)

speech may be spoken aloud or to oneself. When people make errors on short-term memory tests that use letters or words, they often confuse items that sound the same or similar, such as *d* and *t*, or *bear* and *bare*. These errors suggest that they have been rehearsing verbally.

Elaborative Rehearsal. Some strategies for rehearsing are more effective than others. **Maintenance rehearsal** involves merely the rote repetition of the material. This kind of rehearsal is fine for keeping information in STM, but it will not always lead to long-term retention. A better strategy if you want to remember for the long haul is **elaborative rehearsal**, also called *elaboration of encoding* (Cermak & Craik, 1979; Craik & Tulving, 1975). Elaboration involves associating new items of information with material that has already been stored or with other new facts. It can also involve analyzing the physical, sensory, or semantic features of an item.

Suppose, for example, that you are studying the hypothalamus in Chapter 4. Simply rehearsing the definition of the hypothalamus in a rote manner is unlikely to help much. Instead, when going over (rehearsing) the concept, you could encode the information in Figure 10.6. The more you elaborate the concept of the hypothalamus, the better you will remember it.

Deep Processing. A related strategy for prolonging retention is **deep processing**, or the processing of meaning. If you process only the physical or sensory features of a stimulus, such as how the word *hypothalamus* is spelled and how it sounds, your processing will be shallow even if it is elaborated. If you recognize patterns and assign labels to objects or events ("The hypothalamus is below the thalamus"), your processing will be somewhat deeper. If you fully analyze the meaning of what you are trying to remember (for example, by encoding the functions and importance of the hypothalamus), your processing will be deeper yet.

Sometimes, shallow processing is useful; when you memorize a poem, for instance, you will want to pay attention to (and elaborately encode) the sounds of the words and the patterns of rhythm in the poem, and not just the poem's meaning. Usually, however,

maintenance rehearsal Rote repetition of material in order to maintain its availability in memory.

elaborative rehearsal Association of new information with already stored knowledge and analysis of the new information to make it memorable.

deep processing In the encoding of information, the processing of meaning rather than simply the physical or sensory features of a stimulus.

IMPOVERISHED ENCODING
(poor retention)

Brain part ———— "Hypo-thalamus" ———— Involved in emotion

ELABORATE ENCODING
(good retention)

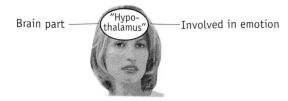

Brain part
Connections with limbic system
Involved in emotion
Located under the thalamus
(hypo = under)
Probably active when I'm mad or afraid

Involved in survival drives like hunger and thirst
Regulates body temperature
Sends messages to pituitary gland
Controls autonomic nervous system

FIGURE 10.6
ELABORATION OF ENCODING

In elaborated encoding, you encode the features of an item and its associations with other items in memory. When you studied the hypothalamus in Chapter 4, was your encoding elaborated or impoverished?

deep processing is more effective. Unfortunately, students often try to memorize information that has little or no meaning for them, which explains why the information doesn't stick.

Mnemonics

In addition to using elaborative rehearsal and deep processing, people who want to give their powers of memory a boost sometimes use **mnemonics** [neh-MON-iks], formal strategies and tricks for encoding, storing, and retaining information. (Mnemosyne—neh-MOZ-eh-nee—was the ancient Greek goddess of memory.) Some mnemonics take the form of easily memorized rhymes (e.g., "Thirty days hath September / April, June, and November . . . "). Others use formulas (e.g., "Every **g**ood **b**oy **d**oes **f**ine" for remembering which notes are on the lines of the treble clef in musical notation). Still others use visual images or word associations.

The best mnemonics force you to encode material actively and thoroughly. They may also reduce the amount of information by chunking it (as in the phone number 466-3293, which corresponds to the letters in GOOD-BYE—appropriate, perhaps, for a travel agency). Or they may make the material meaningful and thus easier to store and retrieve; facts and words are often more memorable, for example, if they are woven into a coherent story (Bower & Clark, 1969). If you needed to remember the parts of the digestive system for a physiology course, you could construct a narrative about what happens to a piece of food after it enters a person's mouth, then repeat the narrative aloud to yourself or to a study partner.

Some stage performers with amazing recall rely on more complicated mnemonics. We are not going to spend time on them here, because for ordinary memory tasks, such tricks are often no more effective than rote rehearsal, and sometimes they are actually worse (Wang, Thomas, & Ouellette, 1992). Most memory researchers do not use such mnemonics themselves (Park, Smith, & Cavanaugh, 1990). After all, why bother to memorize a grocery list using a fancy mnemonic when you can write down what you need to buy? The fastest route to a good memory is to follow the principles suggested by the findings in this section and by research reviewed in "Taking Psychology with You."

"YOU SIMPLY ASSOCIATE EACH NUMBER WITH A WORD, SUCH AS 'TABLE' AND 3,476,029."

mnemonics Strategies and tricks for improving memory, such as the use of a verse or a formula.

VERY QUICK QUIZ

Camille is furious with her history professor. "I read the chapter three times, but I still failed the exam," she fumes. "The test must have been unfair." What's wrong with Camille's reasoning, and what are some other possible explanations for her poor performance, based on principles of critical thinking and what you have learned so far about memory?

Answers:

Camille is reasoning emotionally and is not examining the assumptions underlying her explanations. Perhaps she relied on automatic rather than effortful encoding, used maintenance instead of elaborative rehearsal, and used shallow instead of deep processing when she studied. She may also have tried to encode everything, instead of being selective.

WHAT'S AHEAD

● **What changes occur in your neurons when you store a long-term memory?**
● **Where in the brain are memories for facts and events stored?**
● **Which hormones can improve your memory?**

THE BIOLOGY OF MEMORY

We have been discussing memory solely in terms of information processing, but what is happening in the brain while all that processing is going on? In work on this question, researchers draw on many of the concepts already covered in this chapter and in Chapter 4. (It might help you to encode the following information in your own memory if you review the material in Chapter 4 first.)

Changes in Neurons and Synapses

Forming a memory involves chemical and structural changes at the level of neurons, and these changes differ for short-term memory and long-term memory.

In short-term memory, changes within neurons temporarily alter the neurons' ability to release neurotransmitters, the chemicals that carry messages from one cell to another. Evidence comes from studies with sea snails, sea slugs, and other organisms that have small numbers of easily identifiable neurons (Alkon, 1989; Kandel & Schwartz, 1982). These primitive animals can be taught simple conditioned responses, such as withdrawing or not withdrawing parts of their bodies in response to a light touch. When the animal retains the skill for only the short term, the neuron or neurons involved temporarily show an increase or decrease in readiness to release neurotransmitter molecules, depending on the kind of response being learned.

In contrast, long-term memory involves lasting structural changes in the brain. To mimic what they think may happen during the formation of a long-term memory, researchers apply brief, high-frequency electrical stimulation to groups of neurons in the brains of animals. In various areas, especially the hippocampus, this stimulation increases the strength of synaptic responsiveness, a phenomenon known as **long-term potentiation** (McNaughton & Morris, 1987). In other words, some synaptic pathways become more excitable. Long-term potentiation seems to involve (1) an increase in the release of the neurotransmitter glutamate from transmitting neurons, and (2) chemical reactions in the glutamate receptors of receiving neurons, which make these neurons more receptive to the next signal that comes along (Bliss & Collingridge, 1993). It is a little like increasing the diameter of a funnel's neck to permit more flow through the funnel.

long-term potentiation A long-lasting increase in the strength of synaptic responsiveness, thought to be a biological mechanism of long-term memory.

Other changes also occur in long-term potentiation. For example, dendrites grow and branch out, and certain types of synapses increase in number (Greenough, 1984). At the same time, some neurons become *less* responsive than they were previously (Bolshakov & Siegelbaum, 1994). These changes all take time, which may explain why long-term memories remain vulnerable to disruption for a while after they are stored—why, for example, a blow to the head may disrupt new memories even though old ones are unaffected. Just as concrete takes time to set, the neural and synaptic changes in the brain that underlie long-term memory take time to develop. Memories therefore undergo a gradual period of **consolidation**, or stabilization, before they "solidify" and become stable. Consolidation can continue for weeks in animals and for several years in human beings.

Locating Memories

In 1996 a little study made big headlines: Researchers had their first clue that true memories might actually be located in a different part of the brain from false memories. PET scans showed that false and true memories for words in a list triggered different patterns of brain activity. Only true memories produced activity in left-hemisphere areas involved in processing sounds and speech; only false memories activated frontal-lobe areas thought to be involved in conscious attempts to remember information (Schacter et al., 1996). Some writers wondered whether these results would lead to a "litmus test" for distinguishing real memories from phony ones. (Think of all the family quarrels that could finally be resolved, such as the one about whether Sam's niece was really at that New Year's party!)

Such a test is a long way off and may never be possible. Nevertheless, this research illustrates one of the most important developments in the study of memory: the ability to use microelectrodes, brain-scan technology, and other techniques to identify the brain structures responsible for the formation and location of specific types of memories.

Work in this area shows that during short-term memory tasks, areas in the frontal lobes of the brain are especially active (Goldman-Rakic, 1996). And in the formation of long-term declarative memories (memory for facts and events, or "knowing that"), the hippocampus and adjacent parts of the temporal-lobe cortex play a critical role (Squire & Zola-Morgan, 1991). The hippocampus is especially important: Damage that is limited to this structure results in amnesia for facts and events (Press, Amaral, & Squire, 1989).

In contrast, the formation of procedural memories (memory for skills and habits) seems to involve other brain structures and pathways. For example, in work with rabbits, Richard Thompson (1983, 1986) showed that one kind of procedural memory—a simple, classically conditioned response to an unpleasant stimulus—is associated with specific changes in the cerebellum. When rabbits are conditioned to blink their eyes in response to a tone, changes in electrical activity occur in parts of the cerebellum. If the affected brain tissue is removed or destroyed, the animals immediately forget the response and cannot relearn it. Moreover, if you deaden a part of the cerebellum during initial conditioning, the rabbits will not learn the response in the first place (Krupa, Thompson, & Thompson, 1993). Human patients with damage in the cerebellum are also incapable of this type of conditioning (Daum & Schugens, 1996).

The formation of declarative and procedural memories in different brain areas could explain a curious finding about patients like H. M. Despite their inability to form new declarative memories, such patients can, with sufficient practice, acquire new procedural memories that enable them to solve a puzzle, read mirror-reversed words, or play tennis—although they do not recall the training sessions in which they learned these skills. Apparently, the parts of the brain involved in acquiring new procedural memories have remained intact.

consolidation The process by which a long-term memory becomes durable and stable.

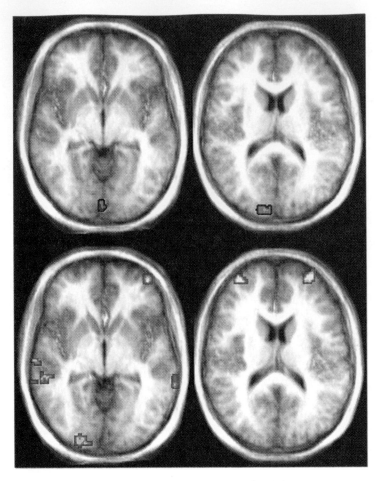

FIGURE 10.7

BRAIN ACTIVITY IN EXPLICIT AND IMPLICIT MEMORY

As these composite functional MRI scans show, patterns of brain activity differ depending on the type of memory task involved. When people had an explicit memory for dot patterns they had seen earlier, areas in the visual cortex, temporal lobes, and frontal lobes (indicated by orange in the lower photos) were more active. When people's implicit memories were activated, areas in the visual cortex (blue in the upper photos) were relatively inactive (Reber, Stark, & Squire, 1998).

Patients such as H. M. also retain some implicit memory for verbal material, as measured by priming tasks. For example, if H. M. sees the word *define* on a list and later has to complete the stem "*def-*" with the first word that comes to mind, he is more likely to say *define* than some other word, just as people with normal memories are (Keane, Gabrieli, & Corkin, 1987). Some psychologists conclude that there must therefore be separate systems in the brain for implicit and explicit tasks. As Figure 10.7 shows, this view has been bolstered by brain scans, which reveal differences in the location of brain activity when normal subjects perform explicit versus implicit memory tasks (Reber, Stark, & Squire, 1998; Squire et al., 1992).

The brain circuits that take part in the *formation* of long-term memories, however, are not the same as those involved in long-term *storage* of those memories. The role of the hippocampus, for example, appears to be only temporary, and the ultimate destinations of declarative memories seem to lie in parts of the cerebral cortex, possibly in the same cortical areas that were involved in the original perception of the information (Mishkin & Appenzeller, 1987).

The typical "memory" is a complex cluster of information. When you recall meeting a man yesterday, you remember his greeting, his tone of voice, how he looked, and where he was. Even a single concept, such as "shovel," includes a lot of information (about length, material, uses . . .). These different pieces of information are probably processed separately and stored at different locations that are distributed across wide areas of the brain, with all the sites participating in the representation of the event or concept as a whole (Damasio et al., 1996; Squire, 1987). The role of the hippocampus may be to somehow bind together the diverse aspects of a memory at the time it is formed, so that even though these aspects are stored in different cortical sites, the memory can be retrieved as one coherent entity (Squire & Zola-Morgan, 1991).

Figure 10.8 shows the structures that we have mentioned as important in the formation, storage, and retrieval of memories. But we have given you just a few small nibbles from the smorgasbord of findings now available. Researchers are learning more and more about where memories are located; they have even been able to relate the encoding of different types of material, such as words and scenes, to specific areas in the frontal and temporal lobes (Schacter, 1999). Someday, neuroscientists may be able to describe the entire stream of events in the brain that occur from the moment you say to yourself "I must remember this" to the moment you actually do remember (or find that you can't).

Hormones and Memory

Have you ever smelled fresh cookies and recalled a tender scene from your childhood? Do you have a vivid memory of the first time you fell in love? Emotional memories such as these are often especially intense, and the explanation resides partly in our hormones.

The Adrenaline Connection. Hormones released by the adrenal glands during stress and emotional arousal, including epinephrine (adrenaline) and certain steroids, enhance memory. If you give people a drug that prevents their adrenal glands from producing these hormones, they will remember less about emotional

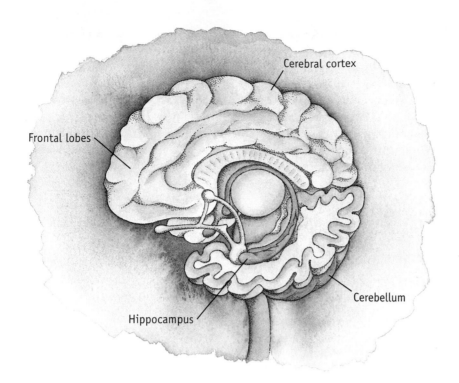

Cerebral cortex

Frontal lobes

Cerebellum

Hippocampus

**FIGURE 10.8
BRAIN AREAS CRITICAL
FOR MEMORY**

The labeled regions are particularly important in the formation or storage of memories.

stories they heard than control subjects will (Cahill et al., 1994). Conversely, if you give epinephrine to animals right after learning, their memories will improve (McGaugh, 1990). The link between emotional arousal and memory makes evolutionary sense: Arousal tells the brain that an event or piece of information is important enough to encode and store for future use.

In real life, the hormones that flood our bodies during an upsetting experience may actually make the event *too* memorable. For example, high levels of epinephrine and other hormones during a traumatic experience may help explain the persistent flashbacks suffered by people with posttraumatic stress disorder (see Chapter 16). Work is now underway to find out whether administering drugs that block these hormones immediately after a traumatic event will help prevent the later development of these troubling symptoms (McGaugh, 1999).

The effects of hormones on ordinary learning, however, differs from their effects on memory for a single, striking experience. When animals are given very high dosages of adrenal hormones, their memories for learned tasks suffer instead of improving; a moderate dose is optimal. Similarly, if you are trying to encode, integrate, and remember information for a psychology exam, very high hormone levels could actually interfere with memory. If you want to remember such information well, you should aim for an arousal level somewhere between "hyper" and "laid back."

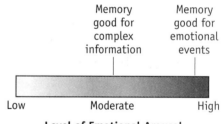

Memory good for complex information

Memory good for emotional events

Low   Moderate   High
Level of Emotional Arousal

Sweet Memories. How can hormones produced in the adrenal glands affect storage of information in the brain? One possibility is that epinephrine causes the level of glucose (a sugar) to rise in the bloodstream. Although epinephrine does not readily enter the brain from the bloodstream, glucose does. Once in the brain, glucose may enhance memory either directly or by altering the effects of neurotransmitters (Gold, 1987).

This "sweet memories" effect occurs both in aged rats and mice and in elderly human beings. In one fascinating study, healthy older people fasted overnight, drank a glass of lemonade sweetened with either glucose or saccharin, and then took two memory tests. The saccharine-laced drink had no effect on their performance, but lemonade with glucose greatly boosted their ability to recall a taped passage 5 or 40 minutes after hearing it (Manning, Hall, & Gold, 1990). Glucose also enhances the ability of Alzheimer's patients to recognize words, prose passages, and faces (Manning, Ragozzino, & Gold, 1993).

However, the exact mechanisms involved in the hormone-memory link remain unclear and controversial. In this area, as in others in the biology of memory, many findings are still provisional, and we have much to learn. No one knows yet exactly how the brain actually stores information, how different memory circuits link up with one another, or how a student is able to locate and retrieve information at the drop of a multiple-choice item. And there is as much to be learned about why we forget as about how we remember.

QUICK QUIZ

Find out whether your brain has recorded what you just read.

1. Is long-term potentiation associated with (a) increased responsiveness of a receiving neuron to a transmitting neuron, (b) a decrease in receptors on a receiving neuron, or (c) reaching your true potential?

2. The cerebellum has been associated with _____ memories; the hippocampus has been associated with _____ memories.

3. *True or false:* Hormone research suggests that if you want to remember well, you should be as relaxed as possible while learning.

4. After reading about glucose and memory, should you immediately start gulping down lemonade? Why or why not?

Answers:

1. a 2. procedural, declarative 3. false 4. You probably should not pig out on sugar yet. Results from elderly people, using measures of memory on which older people show deficits, may not generalize to younger people with normal memories. Even if the results do generalize, you would need to know how much glucose is effective; in the elderly, there is an optimal dose (Parsons & Gold, 1992). Also, in some people, frequent glucose consumption may have adverse health consequences that would outweigh the benefits.

WHAT'S AHEAD

● How might new information "erase" old memories?
● What theory explains why you keep dialing an old area code instead of the one that has replaced it?
● Why is it easier to recall experiences from elementary school if you see pictures of your classmates?

WHY WE FORGET

Have you ever, in the heat of some deliriously happy moment, said to yourself, "I'll never forget this, never, *never*, NEVER"? Do you find that you can more clearly remember saying those words than the deliriously happy moment itself? Sometimes you encode an event, you rehearse it, you analyze its meaning, you tuck it away in long-term storage—and still you forget it. Is it any wonder that most of us have wished, at one time or another, for a "photographic memory"?

Actually, having a perfect memory is not the blessing that you might suppose. The Russian psychologist Alexander Luria (1968) once told of a journalist, S., who could reproduce giant grids of numbers both forward and backward, even after the passage of 15 years. S. also remembered the exact circumstances under which he had originally learned the material. To accomplish his astonishing feats, he used mnemonics, especially the formation of visual images. But you should not envy him, for he had a serious problem: He could not forget even when he wanted to. Along with the diamonds of experience, he kept dredging up the pebbles. Images he had formed in order to remember kept creeping into consciousness, distracting him and interfering with his ability to concentrate. At times he even had trouble holding a conversation because the other person's words would set off a jumble of associations. In fact, Luria called him "rather dullwitted." Eventually, unable to work at his profession, S. took to supporting himself by traveling from place to place, demonstrating his mnemonic abilities for audiences.

Like remembering, then, a certain degree of forgetting contributes to our survival and our sanity. (Think back; would you really want to recall every angry argument, every embarrassing episode, every painful moment in your life? Could it be that self-confidence and optimism depend on locking some follies and grievances in a back drawer of memory?) Nonetheless, most of us forget more than we would like to, and we would like to know why.

Over a century ago, in an effort to measure pure memory loss independent of personal experience, Hermann Ebbinghaus (1885/1913) memorized long lists of nonsense syllables, such as *bok*, *waf*, or *ged*, and then tested his retention over a period of several weeks. Most of his forgetting occurred soon after the initial learning and then leveled off (see Figure 10.9). Ebbinghaus's method of studying memory was adopted by generations of psychologists, even though it did not tell them much about the kinds of memories that people care about most.

A century later, Marigold Linton decided to find out how people forget real events rather than nonsense syllables. Like Ebbinghaus, she used herself as a subject, but she charted the curve of forgetting over years rather than days. Every day for 12 years she recorded on a 4- × 6-inch card two or more things that had happened to her that day. Eventually, she accumulated a catalogue of thousands of discrete events, both trivial ("I have dinner at the Canton Kitchen: delicious lobster dish") and significant ("I land at Orly Airport in Paris"). Once a month, she took a random sampling of all the cards accumulated to that point, noted whether she could remember the events on them, and tried to date the events. Linton (1978) later told how she had expected the kind of rapid forgetting reported by Ebbinghaus. Instead, as you can see in Figure 10.9b, she found that long-term forgetting was slower and proceeded at a much more constant pace, as details gradually dropped out of her memories.

FIGURE 10.9

TWO KINDS OF FORGETTING CURVES

When Hermann Ebbinghaus tested his own memory for nonsense syllables, forgetting was rapid at first and then tapered off (a). In contrast, when Marigold Linton tested her own memory for personal events over a period of several years, her retention was excellent at first, but then it fell off at a gradual but steady rate (b).

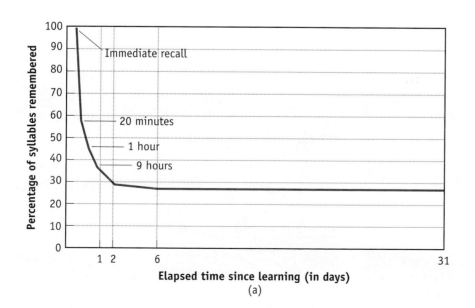

(a)

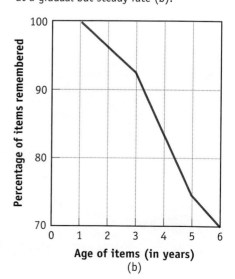

(b)

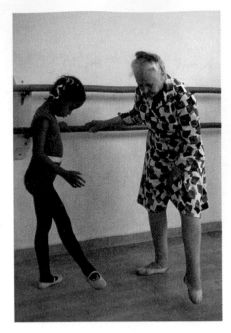

Motor skills, which are stored as procedural memories, can last a lifetime.

Of course, some memories, especially those that mark important transitions (marriage, getting a first job), are more memorable than others. But why did Marigold Linton, like the rest of us, forget so many details? Psychologists have proposed five mechanisms to account for forgetting: decay, replacement of old memories by new ones, interference, motivated forgetting, and cue-dependent forgetting.

The Decay Theory

One commonsense view, the **decay theory**, holds that memory traces fade with time if they are not "accessed" now and then. We have already seen that decay occurs in sensory memory and that it occurs in short-term memory as well, unless we rehearse the material. However, the mere passage of time does not account so well for forgetting in long-term memory. People commonly forget things that happened only yesterday while remembering events from many years ago. Indeed, some memories, both procedural and declarative, remain accessible for a lifetime. If you learned to swim as a child, you will still know how to swim at age 30, even if you have not been in a pool or lake for 22 years. We are also happy to report that some lessons learned in school have great staying power. In one study, people did well on a Spanish test as long as 50 years after taking Spanish in high school, even though most had hardly used Spanish at all in the intervening years (Bahrick, 1984). Decay alone, although it may play some role, cannot entirely explain lapses in long-term memory.

New Memories for Old

Another theory holds that new information entering memory can wipe out old information, just as rerecording on an audiotape or videotape will obliterate the original material. In one study supporting this view, researchers showed people slides of a traffic accident and used leading questions to get them to think that they had seen a stop sign when they had really seen a yield sign, or vice versa. People in a control group who were not misled in this way were able to identify the sign they had actually seen. Later, all the participants were told the purpose of the study and were asked to guess whether they had been misled. Almost all of those who had been misled continued to insist that they had *really, truly* seen the sign whose existence had been planted in their minds (Loftus, Miller, & Burns, 1978). The researchers interpreted these findings to mean that the subjects had not just been trying to please them, and that people's original perceptions had in fact been "erased" by the misleading information.

When people who saw a car with a yield sign (left) were later asked if they had seen "the stop sign" (a misleading question), many said they had. Likewise, when those shown a stop sign were asked if they had seen "the yield sign," many said yes. These false memories persisted even after the participants were told about the misleading questions, suggesting that misleading information had erased their original mental representations of the signs (Loftus, 1980).

Interference

A third theory holds that forgetting occurs because similar items of information interfere with one another in either storage or retrieval; the information may get into memory, but it becomes confused with other information. Such interference, which occurs in both short- and long-term memory, is especially common when you have to recall isolated facts—names, addresses, personal identification numbers, access numbers, area codes, and the like.

Suppose you are at a party and you meet someone named Julie. A little later you meet someone named Judy. You go on to talk to other people, and after an hour, you again bump into Julie, but by mistake you call her Judy. The second name has interfered with the first. This type of interference, in which new information interferes with the ability to remember old information, is called **retroactive interference:**

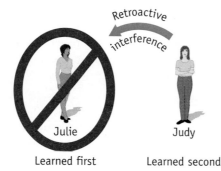

Retroactive interference is sometimes illustrated by a story about an absent-minded professor of ichthyology (the study of fish) who complained that whenever he learned the name of a new student, he forgot the name of a fish.

Because new information is constantly entering memory, we are all vulnerable to the effects of retroactive interference—or at least *most* of us are. H. M. is an exception; his memories of childhood and adolescence are unusually detailed, clear, and unchanging. H. M. can remember actors who were famous when he was a child, the films they were in, and who their costars were. He also knows the names of friends from the second grade. Presumably, these early declarative memories were not subject to interference from memories acquired since the operation because H. M. could not acquire any new memories!

Interference also works in the opposite direction. Old information (such as the Spanish you learned in high school) may interfere with the ability to remember new information (such as the French you are trying to learn now). This type of interference is called **proactive interference:**

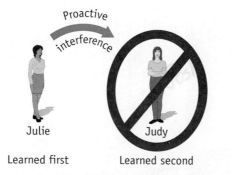

Over a period of weeks, months, and years, proactive interference may cause more forgetting than retroactive interference does, because we have stored up so much information that can potentially interfere with anything new.

decay theory The theory that information in memory eventually disappears if it is not accessed; it applies more to short-term than to long-term memory.

retroactive interference Forgetting that occurs when recently learned material interferes with the ability to remember similar material stored previously.

proactive interference Forgetting that occurs when previously stored material interferes with the ability to remember similar, more recently learned material.

motivated forgetting Forgetting that occurs because of a desire to eliminate awareness of painful, embarrassing, or otherwise unpleasant experiences.

cue-dependent forgetting The inability to retrieve information stored in memory because of insufficient cues for recall.

state-dependent memory The tendency to remember something when the rememberer is in the same physical or mental state as during the original learning or experience.

Charlie Chaplin's film *City Lights* provides a classic illustration of state-dependent memory. After Charlie saves the life of a drunken millionaire, the two spend the rest of the evening in boisterous merrymaking. But the next day, after sobering up, the millionaire fails to recognize Charlie and gives him the cold shoulder. Then, once again, the millionaire gets drunk—and once again he greets Charlie as a pal.

Motivated Forgetting

Sigmund Freud maintained that people forget because they block from consciousness those memories that are too threatening or painful to live with, and he called this self-protective process *repression* (see Chapter 13). Today, many psychologists prefer a more general term, **motivated forgetting**, and they argue that people might be motivated to forget events for many reasons, including embarrassment, guilt, shock, and a desire to protect their own pride. (In Chapter 16 we will discuss *dissociative amnesia*, in which people selectively forget a stressful or traumatic experience that is threatening to the self.)

The concepts of repression and motivated forgetting are based mostly on clinical reports of people in psychotherapy who appear to recall long-buried memories, typically of traumatic events in childhood—as in the cases of Eileen Franklin Lipsker and Laura B. Only rarely, however, have such memories been corroborated by objective evidence, so it is difficult and often impossible to determine their accuracy. It is also difficult to distinguish "repression" from other kinds of forgetting or from a simple refusal to think about an upsetting experience.

Cue-dependent Forgetting

Often, when we need to remember, we rely on *retrieval cues*, items of information that can help us find the specific information we're looking for. For example, if you are trying to remember the last name of an actor, it might help to know the person's first name or the name of a recent movie the actor starred in.

When we lack retrieval cues, we may feel as if we have lost the call number for an entry in the mind's library. In long-term memory, this type of memory failure, called **cue-dependent forgetting**, may be the most common type of all. Willem Wagenaar (1986), who, like Marigold Linton, recorded critical details about events in his life, found that within a year, he had forgotten 20 percent of those details, and after five years, he had forgotten 60 percent. However, when he gathered cues from witnesses about ten events that he thought he had forgotten, he was able to recall something about all ten, which suggests that some of his forgetting was cue dependent.

Cues that were present when you learned a new fact or had an experience are apt to be especially useful later as retrieval aids. That may explain why remembering is often easier when you are in the same physical environment as you were when an event occurred: Cues in the present context match those from the past. Some people have suggested that the overlap between present and past cues may also lead to a *false* sense of having been in exactly the same situation before; this is the eerie phenomenon of *déjà vu* (which means "already seen" in French). Ordinarily, however, contextual cues help us remember the past more accurately.

Your mental or physical state may also act as a retrieval cue, evoking a **state-dependent memory**. For example, if you are intoxicated when something happens, you may remember it better when you once again have had a few drinks than when you are sober. (This is not an endorsement of drunkenness!

Your memory will be best if you are sober during both encoding and recall.) Likewise, if your emotional arousal is especially high or low at the time of an event, you may remember that event best when you are once again in the same emotional state. When victims of violent crimes have trouble recalling details of the experience, it may be in part because they are far less emotionally aroused than they were at the time of the crime (Clark, Milberg, & Erber, 1987).

You may also be better able to retrieve a memory when your mood is the same as it was when you first stored the memory, presumably because mood serves as a retrieval cue. But what matters even more is the match between your current mood and the *kind of material* you are trying to remember. You are likely to remember happy events better when you are feeling happy than when you are sad (Mayer, McCormick & Strong, 1995). Similarly, you are likely to remember unhappy events better and remember more of them when you are feeling unhappy, especially if you dwell on your bleak feelings without doing anything constructive about them. The more unhappy memories you recall, the more depressed you feel, and the more depressed you feel, the more unhappy memories you recall . . . so you stay stuck in your depression and make it even worse (Lyubomirsky, Caldwell, & Nolen-Hoeksema, 1998; McFarland & Buehler, 1998). You can avoid this vicious cycle by acknowledging your depressed feelings and by purposely focusing on memories of happy events instead of unpleasant ones.

QUICK QUIZ

If you have not repressed what you just read, try these questions.

1. Ever since she read *Even Cowgirls Get the Blues* many years ago, Wilma has loved the novels of Tom Robbins. Later, she developed a crush on actor Tim Robbins, but every time she tried to recall his name she called him "Tom." Why?

2. When a man at his twentieth high-school reunion sees his old friends, he recalls incidents he had thought were long forgotten. Why?

Answers:

1. proactive interference 2. The sight of his friends provides retrieval cues for the incidents.

WHAT'S AHEAD

- Why are the first few years of life a mental blank?
- Which periods of life tend to stand out in memory?

AUTOBIOGRAPHICAL MEMORIES

Memory provides each of us with a sense of identity that evolves and changes as we build up a store of episodic memories about events we have experienced firsthand. For most of us, the memories we have of our own lives—our *autobiographical memories*—are by far the most fascinating. We use them as entertainment ("Did I ever tell you about the time . . . ?"); we manipulate them—some people even publish them—in order to create an image of ourselves; we analyze them to learn more about who we are.

AVOID EMOTIONAL REASONING

Many people get upset at the idea that their earliest experiences are lost to memory and angrily insist that memories from the first two years must be true. How can research help us think clearly about this issue?

Psychologists have devised ingenious methods to measure memory in infants. This infant, whose leg is attached by a string to a colorful mobile, will learn within minutes to kick in order to make the mobile move. A week later, when tested without the string, she may still remember the trick—an example of procedural memory (Rovee-Collier, 1993). However, when she is older she will not remember the experience itself. Like the rest of us, she will fall victim to childhood amnesia.

childhood (infantile) amnesia
The inability to remember events and experiences that occurred during the first two or three years of life.

Childhood Amnesia: The Missing Years

A curious aspect of autobiographical memory is that most adults cannot recall any events from earlier than the third or fourth year of life. A few people apparently can recall momentous experiences that occurred when they were as young as 2 years old, such as the birth of a sibling, but not earlier (Usher & Neisser, 1993). As adults, we cannot remember being fed in infancy by our parents, taking our first steps, or uttering our first halting sentences. We are victims of **childhood amnesia** (sometimes called *infantile amnesia*).

There is something disturbing about childhood amnesia—so disturbing that some people adamantly deny it, claiming to remember events from the second or even the first year of life. But like other false memories, these recollections are merely reconstructions based on photographs, family stories, and imagination. The "remembered" event may not even have taken place. Swiss psychologist Jean Piaget (1951) once reported a memory of nearly being kidnapped at the age of 2. Piaget remembered sitting in his pram, watching his nurse as she bravely defended him from the kidnapper. He remembered the scratches she received on her face. He remembered a police officer with a short cloak and white baton who finally chased the kidnapper away. But when Piaget was 15, his nurse wrote to his parents confessing that she had made up the entire story. Piaget noted, "I therefore must have heard, as a child, the account of this story . . . and projected it into the past in the form of a visual memory, which was a memory of a memory, but false."

Of course, we all retain procedural memories from the toddler stage, when we first learned to use a fork, drink from a cup, and pull a wagon. We also retain semantic memories acquired early in life: the rules of counting, the names of people and things, knowledge about objects in the world. Further, toddlers who are only 1 to 2 years old can often remember past experiences, and some 4-year-olds can remember experiences that occurred before age 2½ (Bauer & Dow, 1994; McDonough & Mandler, 1994). The mystery is why our early episodic memories do not survive into later childhood or adulthood.

Sigmund Freud thought that childhood amnesia was due to repression. Today, however, some biological researchers argue that repression has nothing to do with it; childhood amnesia, they say, occurs because brain areas involved in the formation or storage of events are not well developed until a few years after birth (McKee & Squire, 1993; Nadel & Zola-Morgan, 1984). And other psychologists have proposed cognitive explanations for the amnesia of the first years. These include:

1 *Lack of a sense of self.* In one view, we cannot have an autobiographical memory of our*selves* until we have a self to remember. Indeed, autobiographical memories do not begin until the emergence of a self-concept, an event that occurs at somewhat different ages for different children, but not before the age of 2 (Howe, Courage, & Peterson, 1994).

2 *Impoverished encoding.* Preschoolers probably encode experiences far less elaborately than adults do. Young children have not yet mastered the social conventions for reporting events; they do not know what is important and interesting to others. Instead, they tend to rely on adults' questions to provide retrieval cues ("Where did we go for breakfast?" "Who did you go trick-or-treating with?"), and this dependency on adults may prevent them from building up a stable core of remembered material that will be available when they are older (Fivush & Hamond, 1991).

ANALYZE A CHILDHOOD MEMORY

Write down as much as you can about an incident in your childhood that stands out in your memory. Now ask a friend or family member who was present at the time to write a description of the same event. Do your accounts differ? If so, why? What does this exercise tell you about the nature of memory—and about your own personality or present concerns?

3 *A focus on the routine.* Preschoolers tend to focus on the routine, familiar aspects of an experience, such as eating lunch or playing with toys, rather than the distinctive aspects that will provide retrieval cues and make an event memorable in the long run (Fivush & Hamond, 1991; White & Pillemer, 1979).

4 *Differences between early and later cognitive schemas.* Cognitive schemas—networks of knowledge, beliefs, and expectations about particular aspects of the world—provide people with cues for retrieving and reconstructing past experiences. For example, your schema about junior high—knowledge of the subjects taught, sports activities, field trips, and so forth—might help you recall the time your 7th-grade class visited the planetarium. But the schemas used by older children and adults are very different from those used by preschoolers, because preschoolers' linguistic and cognitive abilities are still limited. Only after starting school do children learn to think like adults do. Once that happens, new, more adultlike schemas replace the earlier ones—and these new schemas are not useful for recalling earlier experiences, so memories of those experiences are lost (Howe & Courage, 1993).

Whatever the explanation for childhood amnesia, our first memories, even when they are not accurate, may provide some useful insights into our personalities, basic concerns, ambitions, and attitudes toward life (Kihlstrom & Harackiewicz, 1982). The early psychologist Lloyd Morgan once wrote that an autobiography "is a story of oneself in the past, read in the light of one's present self." That is just what our private memories are.

Memory and Narrative: The Stories of Our Lives

Communications psychologist George Gerbner (1988) once observed that our species is unique because we tell stories—and live by the stories we tell. This view of human beings as the "storytelling animal" has had a huge impact in cognitive psychology. The *narratives* we compose to simplify and make sense of our lives have a profound influence on us: Our plans, memories, love affairs, hatreds, ambitions, and dreams are all guided by plot outlines.

Thus we say, "I am this way because, as a small child, this happened to me, and then my parents. . . ." We say, "Let me tell you the story of how we fell in love." We say, "When you hear what happened, you'll understand why I felt entitled to take such cold-hearted revenge." These stories are not necessarily fictions, as in the child's meaning of "tell me a story." Rather, they are attempts to provide a unifying theme that organizes and gives meaning to the events of our lives. But because these narratives rely heavily on memory, and because memories are reconstructed and are constantly shifting in response to present needs, beliefs, and experiences, our stories are also, to some degree, works of interpretation and imagination. Adult memories thus reveal as much about the present as they do about the past.

The completeness of our autobiographical narratives depends on many of the processes we have discussed in this chapter. For example, elaborative encoding and deep processing, in addition to helping us remember academic information, also help us retain memories about our own lives. This fact may explain why girls and women tend to remember more childhood events than boys and men do, especially when the memories are emotional (Davis, 1999; Seidlitz & Diener, 1998). The two sexes are equally motivated to remember past events, equally likely to rehearse details about these events, and equally verbal in describing the events—and the incidents they remember have the same degree of emotional intensity. But females may encode more details, and such details may provide them with retrieval cues that enhance their recall.

Once we have formulated a story's central theme or gist ("My parents opposed my occupational plans," "My lover was domineering"), that theme may then serve as a cognitive schema that guides what we remember and what we forget (Schank & Abelson, 1995). The story's theme may also influence our judgments of events and people in the present (McGregor & Holmes, 1999). If you have a fight with your lover, for example, the central theme in your story about the fight might be negative ("He was a jerk") or neutral ("It was a mutual misunderstanding"). This theme may bias you to blame or forgive your partner long after you have forgotten what the conflict was all about or who said what. You can see that the "spin" you give a story is critical—so be careful about the stories you tell!

Human beings construct and preserve the past in many imaginative ways. The Hmong of Laos have created needlework narratives that depict life in their former villages and tell of their long, dangerous flight from their homeland in the early 1970s, at the end of the war in Southeast Asia. If you had the sewing skills of the Hmong, what tapestry would you create of your own life?

As we age, certain periods of our lives tend to stand out. Old people remember more from adolescence and early adulthood than from midlife, a phenomenon known as the *reminiscence bump* (MacKavey, Malley, & Stewart, 1991). Perhaps the younger years are especially memorable because they are full of significant milestones and transitions: going off to college, graduating, getting a first job, falling in love, marrying or forming a committed relationship. Or perhaps people are especially likely to weave events from their youth into a coherent story and thus remember them better ("After I graduated from college I met the love of my life, who dumped me in the most cruel and heartless fashion, and before I knew it . . . ")

Yet, as we have seen throughout this chapter, many details about events, even those landmarks we are sure we remember clearly, are probably distorted, forgotten, or added after the fact (see Review 10.1). By now, you should not be surprised that memory can be as fickle as it can be accurate. As cognitive psychologists have shown repeatedly, we are not merely actors in our personal life dramas; we also write the scripts.

REVIEW 10.1

MEMORY'S SEVEN BASIC SINS

The problems of memory discussed in this chapter can be summarized by the following categories, which Daniel Schacter (1999) calls memory's "seven basic sins." The first three problems involve forgetting; the second three involve distortion; and the last involves unwanted remembering.

Problem	Description	Example
Transience	Information becomes less accessible over time.	You forget a phone number you just looked up.
Poor encoding	Inattention or shallow processing results in weak storage.	You do poorly on an exam because you didn't concentrate while studying.
Blocking	Retrieval problems cause temporary inaccessibility.	You have a name you know on the tip of your tongue.
Misattribution	A recollection or idea is attributed to the wrong source (source amnesia).	You "remember" your first day in kindergarten when your memory is really based on what your mother told you.
Suggestibility	Leading questions or comments implant a memory that did not previously exist.	A witness "remembers" a suspect's face after being questioned in a leading manner.
Bias	Current knowledge and beliefs distort memory of the past.	Current resentments toward a parent cause you to overestimate the parent's past harshness towards you.
Persistence	A person is unable to forget information or events despite wanting to do so.	An assault victim has persistent "flashbacks" to the event.

QUICK QUIZ

You did not learn the answers to these questions in childhood, so you can't blame childhood amnesia if you get them wrong.

1. Name four possible cognitive reasons for childhood amnesia.

2. When older people look back on their lives, which periods constitute the "reminiscence bump"?

Answers:

1. lack of a sense of self in early childhood; differences between earlier and later cognitive schemas; impoverished encoding in early childhood; the tendency of preschoolers to focus on routine rather than distinctive aspects of an experience   2. adolescence and early adulthood

EXAMINE THE EVIDENCE

Some people think recovered memories of traumatic experiences should always be trusted and some think they should not. How can we draw on research findings when evaluating someone's claim to have recovered a memory that was long buried?

MEMORIES AND MYTHS

We are now ready to reconsider the story that opened this chapter (which we hope you still remember!). Eileen Franklin Lipsker claimed that a long-buried memory had returned in a flash, with perfect accuracy: her friend's murder at the hands of George Franklin. But as we have seen, research disputes the belief that memories can be preserved for years in a pristine, uncontaminated state of "repression"; most memories, even of shocking experiences, are vulnerable to distortion, error, and influence by others. Leading questions and suggestive interrogation methods can encourage memories for events that never happened. And, unfortunately, a person's confidence in his or her memory is not always a reliable guide to its accuracy.

The recovered-memory school argues that these findings do not apply to memories of something as horrible as murder or incest. Yet the Franklin case, which launched the recovered-memory phenomenon, eventually fell apart. George Franklin's conviction was reversed on the grounds that Eileen's testimony could have been based on information she read in the newspapers rather than on her own memories, which provided no new details or incriminating evidence. It also turned out that Eileen's "memories" had emerged under hypnosis during psychotherapy, not spontaneously as she initially claimed. And her accusations escalated: After accusing her father of murdering her friend, she "remembered" that he murdered two other girls. An investigation completely exonerated him.

In an important ruling in the case of Laura B., the woman who said she had repressed the memory of 18 years of molestation by her father, the judge wrote that her recovered memories would not be admissible evidence because "the phenomenon of memory repression, and the process of therapy used in these cases to recover the memories, have not gained general acceptance in the field of psychology; and are not scientifically reliable" (*State of New Hampshire v. Joel Hungerford*, May 23, 1995). Many other courts across the country have reached similar decisions.

Of course, all psychologists realize that people can and do forget troubling, embarrassing, and painful experiences, and that with the right cues, these memories may return. Obviously, then, not all "recovered" memories are false. How, then, should we respond to an individual's claim to have recovered memories of abuse or other traumas? Based on the research in this chapter, we should be skeptical if the person says that, thanks to therapy, he or she now has memories from the first year or two of life. We should be skeptical if, over time, the person's memories become more and more implausible—for instance, the person says that sexual abuse continued day and night for 15 years without ever being remembered and without anyone else in the household noticing anything amiss. And we should hear alarm bells go off if a therapist used suggestive techniques and leading questions to "help" a patient recall the alleged abuse.

In contrast, a person's recollections are more likely to be trustworthy if there is corroborating evidence from medical records or the recollections of other family members; if the person revealed signs of trauma, such as nightmares and disturbed behavior, at the time the remembered event is said to have occurred; and if the person spontaneously recalled the event without pressure from others or the use of suggestive techniques in therapy.

In many ways, we are our memories: What we remember, and what we choose to forget, are the hallmarks of our personalities. Shared memories—real or distorted—bind families and sometimes destroy them. Private memories—real or distorted—make up the narratives that guide our lives. Psychological research on this hugely complex and fascinating topic can give us greater respect for our ability to remember and greater humility when we fail to remember accurately.

TAKING P S Y C H O L O G Y WITH YOU

HOW TO . . . UH . . . REMEMBER

Someday in the near future, drugs may be available to help people with memory deficiencies and to increase normal memory performance. For the time being, however, those of us who hope to improve our memories must rely on mental strategies. Some simple mnemonics can be useful, but complicated ones are often more bother than they are worth. A better approach is to follow some general guidelines based on the principles in this chapter:

■ *Pay attention!* It seems obvious, but often we fail to remember because we never encoded the information in the first place. For example, which of these is the real Lincoln penny?

Most Americans have trouble recognizing the real penny because they have never attended to the details of a penny's design (Nickerson & Adams, 1979). We are not advising you to do so, unless you happen to be a coin collector or a counterfeiting expert. Just keep in mind that when you do have something to remember, such as the material in this book, you will do better if you encode it well. (The real penny, by the way, is the left one in the bottom row.)

■ *Encode information in more than one way.* The more elaborate the encoding of information, the more memorable it will be. Use your imagination! For instance, in addition to remembering a telephone number by the sound of the individual digits, you might note the spatial pattern they make as you punch them in on the telephone.

■ *Add meaning.* The more meaningful the material, the more likely it is to link up with information already in long-term memory. Meaningfulness also reduces the number of chunks of information you have to learn. Common ways of adding meaning include making up a story about the material (fitting the material into a cognitive schema) and forming visual images. (Some people find that the odder the image, the better.) If your

license plate happens to be 236MPL, you might think of 236 maples. If you are trying to remember the concept of procedural memory from this chapter, you might make the concept meaningful by thinking of an example from your own life, such as your ability to ride a mountain bike, and then imagine a "P" superimposed on an image of yourself on your bike.

■ *Take your time.* Leisurely learning, spread out over several sessions, usually produces better results than harried cramming (although *reviewing* material just before a test can be helpful). In terms of hours spent, "distributed" (spaced) learning sessions are more efficient than "massed" ones; in other words, three separate one-hour study sessions may result in better consolidation and more retention than one session of three hours.

■ *Take time out.* If possible, minimize interference by using study breaks for rest or recreation. Sleep is the ultimate way to reduce interference. In a classic study, students who slept for eight hours after learning lists of nonsense syllables retained them better than students who went about their usual business (Jenkins & Dallenbach, 1924). Sleep is not always possible, of course, but periodic mental relaxation usually is.

■ *Overlearn.* You cannot remember something that you never learned well in the first place. Overlearning—studying information even after you think you already know it—is one of the best ways to ensure that you'll remember it.

■ *Monitor your learning.* By testing yourself frequently, rehearsing thoroughly, and reviewing periodically, you will have a better idea of how you are doing. Don't just evaluate your learning immediately after reading the material, though; because the information is still in short-term memory, you are likely to feel a false sense of confidence about your ability to recall it later. If you delay making a judgment for at least a few minutes, your evaluation will probably be more accurate (Nelson & Dunlosky, 1991).

Whatever strategies you use, you will find that active learning produces more comprehension and better retention than does passive reading or listening. The mind does not gobble up information automatically; you must make the material digestible. Even then, you should not expect to remember everything you read or hear. Nor should you want to: Piling up facts without distinguishing the important from the trivial is just confusing. Popular books and tapes that promise a "perfect," "photographic" memory, or "instant recall" of everything you learn, fly in the face of what psychologists know about how the mind operates. Our advice: Forget them.

SUMMARY

RECONSTRUCTING THE PAST

1. Unlike a tape recorder or video camera, human *memory* is highly selective and is *reconstructive:* People confabulate, adding, deleting, and changing elements in ways that help them make sense of information and events. They often have *source amnesia,* the inability to distinguish information stored during an event from information added later. Sometimes they confuse imagined events with actual ones, especially when they have thought about the imagined event many times, the image of the event contains many details, the event is easy to imagine, and the focus of attention is on emotional reactions to the event.

2. People who hold the mistaken belief that all memories are permanently stored with perfect accuracy often cite cases of recall under hypnosis and electrical brain stimulation, but confabulation also occurs under these conditions. Even *flashbulb memories,* emotionally powerful memories that seem particularly vivid, are often embellished or distorted, and tend to change over time.

3. The reconstructive nature of memory raises problems in legal cases involving eyewitness testimony. Errors are especially likely when the suspect's ethnicity differs from that of the witness and when leading questions are put to witnesses.

4. Findings on memory help clarify the issues in the debate about whether children are capable of making up accounts of sexual abuse. Children, like adults, are often able to remember the essential aspects of an important event with great accuracy. However, like adults, they can also be suggestible, especially when they are very young, are in emotionally charged situations that blur the line between fantasy and reality, are asked leading questions, or have a desire to please the interviewer or conform to what other kids have supposedly said.

IN PURSUIT OF MEMORY

5. The ability to remember depends in part on the type of performance called for. In tests of *explicit memory* (conscious recollection), *recognition* is usually better than *recall.* In tests of *implicit memory,* which is measured by indirect methods such as *priming,* past experiences may affect current thoughts or actions even when these experiences are not consciously and intentionally remembered. The *relearning method* seems to straddle the boundary between explicit and implicit tests of memory.

6. In *information-processing models,* memory involves the *encoding, storage,* and *retrieval* of information. In the *three-box model,* there are three interacting systems: sensory memory, short-term memory, and long-term memory. Some cognitive scientists prefer a *parallel distributed processing (PDP)* or *connectionist model,* which represents knowledge as connections among numerous interacting processing units, distributed in a vast network and all operating in parallel. But the three-box model continues

to offer a convenient way to organize the major findings on memory.

THE THREE-BOX MODEL OF MEMORY

7. In the three-box model, incoming sensory information makes a brief stop in *sensory memory*, which momentarily retains it in the form of literal sensory images. *Pattern recognition* occurs during the transfer of information from sensory memory to short-term memory. Sensory memory gives us a little time to decide whether information is important enough to warrant further attention.

8. *Short-term memory (STM)* retains new information for up to 30 seconds by most estimates (unless rehearsal takes place) and also serves as a *working memory* for the processing of information retrieved from long-term memory for temporary use. The capacity of STM is extremely limited but can be extended if information is organized into larger units by *chunking*. Items that are meaningful, have an emotional impact, or link up to something already in long-term memory may enter long-term storage easily, with only a brief stay in STM.

9. *Long-term memory (LTM)* contains an enormous amount of information that must be organized to make it manageable. For example, words (or the concepts they represent) seem to be organized by *semantic categories*. *Network models* of LTM represent its contents as a network of interrelated concepts. The way people use these networks depends on experience and education. Research on *tip-of-the-tongue states* shows that words are also indexed in LTM in terms of sound and form.

10. *Procedural memories* ("knowing how") are memories for how to perform specific actions; *declarative memories* ("knowing that") are memories for abstract or representational knowledge. Declarative memories include *semantic memories* (general knowledge) and *episodic memories* (memories for personally experienced events).

11. The three-box model is often invoked to explain the *serial-position effect* in memory, but it cannot explain why a *recency effect* sometimes occurs even when it should not.

HOW WE REMEMBER

12. In order to remember material well, we must encode it accurately in the first place. Some kinds of information, such as material in a college course, require effortful, as opposed to automatic, encoding.

13. Rehearsal of information keeps it in short-term memory and increases the chances of long-term retention. *Elaborative rehearsal* is more likely to result in transfer to long-term memory than is *maintenance rehearsal*, and *deep processing* is usually a more effective retention strategy than *shallow processing*.

14. *Mnemonics* can also enhance retention by promoting elaborative encoding and making material meaningful, but for ordinary memory tasks, complex memory tricks are often ineffective or even counterproductive.

THE BIOLOGY OF MEMORY

15. Short-term memory appears to involve temporary changes within neurons that alter their ability to release neurotransmitters, whereas long-term memory involves lasting structural changes in neurons and synapses. *Long-term potentiation*, an increase in the strength of synaptic responsiveness, seems to be an important mechanism of long-term memory. Neural changes associated with long-term potentiation take time to develop, which helps explain why long-term memories require a period of *consolidation*.

16. Areas of the prefrontal cortex are especially active during short-term memory tasks. The hippocampus and adjacent areas play a critical role in the formation of long-term declarative memories. Other areas, such as the cerebellum, are crucial for the formation of procedural memories. Studies of patients with amnesia suggest that different brain systems are active during explicit and implicit memory tasks. The long-term storage of declarative memories may take place in cortical areas that were active during the original perception of the information or event. The various components of a memory are probably stored at different sites, with all of these sites participating in the representation of the event as a whole.

17. Hormones released by the adrenal glands during stress or emotional arousal, including epinephrine and some steroids, enhance memory. This fact helps explain why emotional events are particularly memorable and sometimes are hard to forget even when we want to. Epinephrine causes the level of glucose to rise in the bloodstream, and glucose may enhance memory directly or by altering the effects of neurotransmitters. But very high hormone levels can interfere with the retention of complex information or tasks; a moderate level is optimal.

WHY WE FORGET

18. Forgetting can occur for several reasons. Information in sensory and short-term memory appears to *decay* if it does not receive further processing. New information may "erase" old information in long-term memory. *Proactive* and *retroactive interference* may take place. Some lapses in memory may be due to *motivated forgetting*, although it is difficult to confirm the validity of "repressed" memories that are then "recovered." Finally, *cue-dependent forgetting* may occur when retrieval cues are inadequate. The most effective retrieval cues are those that were present at the time of the initial experience. A person's mood or physical state may also act as a retrieval cue, evoking a *state-dependent memory*.

AUTOBIOGRAPHICAL MEMORIES

19. Most people cannot recall any events from earlier than the third or fourth year of life. The reason for such *childhood amnesia* may be partly biological. Cognitive explanations include the lack of a sense of self until the age of 2 or 3, young children's impoverished encoding of their experiences, their focus on routine rather than distinctive aspects of an experience, and changes after the early years in the cognitive schemas used to retrieve and reconstruct past events.

20. A person's *narrative* or "life story" organizes the events of his or her life and gives them meaning. Narratives change as people build up a store of episodic memories, and life stories are, to some degree, works of interpretation and imagination. The central themes of our stories can guide recall and influence our judgments of people and events. Older people remember more from adolescence and young adulthood than from midlife, a phenomenon known as the *reminiscence bump*.

MEMORIES AND MYTHS

21. Findings on memory suggest caution in evaluating claims of recovered memories of past trauma, especially when such memories emerge after suggestive techniques have been used in therapy, when the memories are for events that allegedly occurred very early in life, and when the memories become increasingly implausible over time.

KEY TERMS

memory 348

reconstruction in memory
 (confabulation) 349

source amnesia 349

flashbulb memories 351

leading questions 352

explicit memory 355

recall 355

recognition 355

implicit memory 357

priming 357

relearning method 357

information-processing models 357

encoding, storage, and retrieval 357

"three-box model" 358

parallel distributed processing (PDP)
 models 359

sensory memory 359

pattern recognition 360

short-term memory (STM) 361

working memory 361

chunks 362

long-term memory (LTM) 362

semantic categories 362

network models 363

tip-of-the-tongue states 363

procedural memories 364

declarative memories 364

semantic memories 365

episodic memories 365

serial-position effect 365

primacy and recency effects 365

effortful versus automatic encoding
 367

maintenance rehearsal 368

elaborative rehearsal 368

deep versus shallow processing 368

mnemonics 369

long-term potentiation 370

consolidation 371

decay theory 376

retroactive interference 377

proactive interference 377

motivated forgetting 378

retrieval cues 378

cue-dependent forgetting 378

state-dependent memory 378

autobiographical memories 379

childhood (infantile) amnesia 380

narratives 381

reminiscence bump 383

LOOKING BACK

- What's wrong with thinking of memory as a mental movie camera? (pp. 348–349)

- If you have a strong emotional reaction to a remembered event, does that mean your memory is accurate? (p. 350)

- Why do "flashbulb memories" of surprising or shocking events sometimes have less wattage than we assume? (pp. 351–352)

- Can the question someone asks you about a past event affect what you remember about it? (p. 352)

- In general, which is easier, a multiple-choice item or a short-answer essay item—and why? (p. 356)

- Can you know something without knowing that you know it? (p. 357)

- Why is the computer often used as a metaphor for the mind? (p. 357)

- Why is short-term memory like a leaky bucket? (p. 361)

- When a word is on the tip of your tongue, what errors are you likely to make in recalling it? (p. 364)

- What's the difference between "knowing how" and "knowing that"? (p. 364)

- What's wrong with trying to memorize in a rote fashion when you're studying—and what's a better strategy? (p. 368)

- Memory tricks are fun, but are they always useful? (p. 369)

- What changes occur in your neurons when you store a long-term memory? (pp. 370–371)

- Where in the brain are memories for facts and events stored? (p. 372)

- Which hormones can improve your memory? (p. 372)

- How might new information "erase" old memories? (p. 376)

- What theory explains why you keep dialing an old area code instead of the one that has replaced it? (p. 377)

- Why is it easier to recall experiences from elementary school if you see pictures of your classmates? (p. 378)

- Why are the first few years of life a mental blank? (pp. 380–381)

- Which periods of life tend to stand out in memory? (p. 383)

Answers to the Get Involved exercises on pages 356 and 358: Rudolph's eight friends were Dasher, Dancer, Prancer, Vixen, Comet, Cupid, Donder, and Blitzen.

11

EMOTION

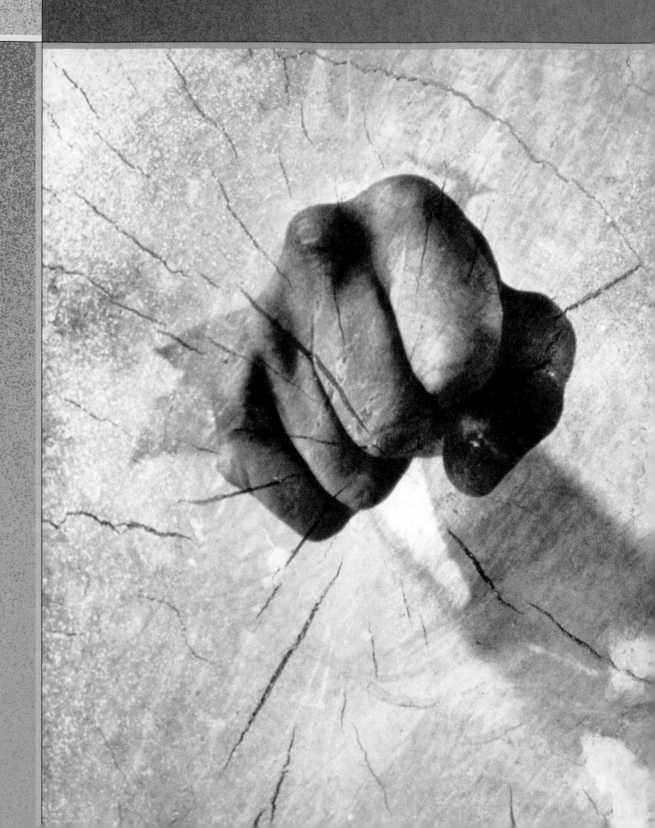

The beauty of the world has two edges, one of laughter,

one of anguish, cutting the heart asunder.

WRITER VIRGINIA WOOLF

For the first seven years of her life, Chelsea Thomas was a happy, cheerful, normal child with an unusual problem. Chelsea had been born with Möbius syndrome, in which a nerve that transmits commands from the brain to the facial muscles is missing. As a result, the child had a perpetually grumpy look. She could not convey delight at being given a present, amusement at watching a favorite TV show, or happiness at meeting a friend. Then surgeons transplanted nerves from Chelsea's leg to both sides of her mouth, and today Chelsea can do what most people in the world take for granted—smile.

Temple Grandin (1996) is a successful scientist and writer in spite of having a neurological disorder, a form of autism that can be extremely debilitating. Grandin's emotions differ in quality and kind from those of most other people: She can feel the anguish of animals, but not of human beings. She has never known romantic love or been moved by the beauty of a sunset. Unable to feel the array of normal emotions, she is unable to read the emotions of others; she is out of tune with the rest of humanity.

Cases like these are poignant reminders of how important it is to feel and express emotions. Emotions are the heart and soul of human experience. If you lacked emotion, you would never again worry about a test result, a job interview, or a first date, and you would never be riled by injustice. But you would also be unmoved by the magic of music. You would never feel the grief of losing someone you love, not only because you wouldn't know sadness but also because you wouldn't know love. You would never laugh because nothing would strike you as funny.

Yet, people often curse their emotions, wishing to be freed from anger, jealousy, shame, guilt, grief, and unrequited love. The paradox of emotions is that we can't live with them, and we can't live without them. Phineas Gage, whom we met in Chapter 4, suffered frontal-lobe damage that made him ill-tempered and undependable, and "flattened out" the emotions necessary for him to organize and plan his life. In Chapter 9, we discussed the problems faced by people who lack emotional intelligence, the ability to identify their own and other people's feelings. And in Chapter 16, we will look at the problems that occur when people suffer emotions they cannot seem to control, such as unrelenting anxiety or depression, and when they lack such socially important emotions as empathy and guilt.

For many centuries, emotion was regarded as the opposite of thinking, and an inferior opposite at that. The heart (emotion) was said to go its own way, in spite of what the head (reason) wanted. This distinction between thinking and feeling has

Emotions are the heart and soul of human experience.

led to some of the longest-running either-or debates in intellectual history. Are emotions and cognitions two separate processes that often conflict with each other, or are they inextricably connected? Can we control our emotions, or do they control us? Is thinking always "rational" and emotion "irrational"?

Psychologists have made great strides in answering these questions. They are learning that the full experience of **emotion** involves three influences: *physiological* changes in the face, brain, and body, *cognitive* processes such as interpretations of events, and *cultural* influences that shape the experience and expression of emotion. If we compare human emotions to a tree, the biological capacity for emotion is the trunk and root system; thoughts and explanations create the many branches; and culture is the gardener that shapes the tree and prunes it, cutting off some limbs and cultivating others. We will begin with the trunk.

WHAT'S AHEAD

- Which facial expressions of emotion do people recognize the world over?
- Which side of your brain is most active when you are feeling elated—or overcome by despair?
- Which little structure in the brain sees to it that you cross the street fast when a truck is headed toward you?
- Which two hormones can make you "too excited to eat"?
- What do "lie detectors" actually detect?

ELEMENTS OF EMOTION 1: THE BODY

Centuries ago, philosophers thought that our personalities derived from blends of four basic body fluids, or "humors": blood, phlegm, choler, and bile. If you were an angry, irritable sort of person, you supposedly had an excess of choler; even now, the word *choleric* describes a hothead. If you were slow-moving and unemotional, you supposedly had an excess of phlegm; the word for such people is *phlegmatic*. *Bilious* (from bile) still describes a peevish person, and *sanguine* (from the Latin word for blood) describes an optimistic or cheerful one.

The theory of the four humors was far-fetched, and yet the questions it was trying to answer remain with us. What is the physiology of emotion? Where in the body do emotions occur? Armed with high-tech methods, psychologists have explored the contributions to emotion of facial expressions, brain processes, and the autonomic nervous system.

The Face of Emotion

The most obvious place to look for emotion is on the face, where its expression is usually most visible. "There are characteristic facial expressions which are observed to accompany anger, fear, erotic excitement, and all the other passions," wrote Aristotle (384–322 B.C.). Two thousand years later, scientists were still pondering the origins and purpose of facial expressions. In *The Expression of the Emotions in Man and Animals*, Charles Darwin (1872/1965) argued that human facial expressions—the smile, the frown, the grimace, the glare—are as "wired in" as the wing flutter of a frightened bird, the purr of a contented cat, and the snarl of a threatened wolf. Such expressions evolved, he said, because they allowed our forebears to tell at a glance the difference between a friendly stranger and a hostile one.

emotion A state of arousal involving facial and bodily changes, brain activation, cognitive appraisals, subjective feelings, and tendencies toward action.

**FIGURE 11.1
SOME UNIVERSAL
EXPRESSIONS**

Can you tell what feelings are being conveyed here? Most people around the world can readily identify expressions of surprise, disgust, happiness, sadness, anger, fear, and contempt—no matter what the age, culture, sex, or historical epoch of the person conveying the emotion.

Universal Expressions of Emotion. Modern psychologists have supported Darwin's evolutionary explanation by confirming that certain emotional expressions are recognized the world over (see Figure 11.1). For example, Paul Ekman and his colleagues have gathered abundant evidence for the universality of seven basic facial expressions of emotion: anger, happiness, fear, surprise, disgust, sadness, and contempt (Ekman, 1994; Ekman & Heider, 1988; Ekman et al., 1987). In every culture they have studied—in Brazil, Chile, Estonia, Germany, Greece, Hong Kong, Italy, Japan, New Guinea, Scotland, Sumatra, Turkey, and the United States—a large majority of people recognize the emotional expressions portrayed by those in other cultures. Even most members of isolated groups that have never watched a movie or read *People* magazine, such as the Foré of New Guinea or the Minangkabau of West Sumatra, can recognize the emotions expressed in pictures of people who are entirely foreign to them, and we can recognize theirs.

These findings do not mean, however, that everybody in a society can recognize the same expressions in all situations. Ekman (1994) called his theory *neurocultural* to emphasize that two factors are involved in facial expression: a universal neurophysiology in the facial muscles associated with certain emotions, and culture-specific variations in the expression of emotion. Thus, while most people in most cultures do recognize basic emotions as portrayed in photographs, sometimes a large minority does not. Across 20 studies of Western cultures, for example, fully 95 percent of the participants agreed in their judgments of happy faces, but only 78 percent agreed on expressions of sadness and anger. And across 11 non-Western societies, 88 percent recognized happiness, but only 74 percent agreed on sadness and 59 percent on anger (Ekman, 1994).

One emotion that nicely illustrates the neurocultural approach to facial expression is disgust. Make an expression of disgust and notice what you are doing: You are probably wrinkling your nose, dropping the corners of your mouth, or retracting your upper lip. These universal reactions may have originated in the "distaste" response of infants to bitter flavors and may serve as a warning against eating tainted food. But the *content* of what produces disgust changes as the infant matures, and it varies from culture to culture. In the course of growing up, people may acquire feelings of disgust in response to particular foods (e.g., meat if they are vegetarian, or pork if they are Muslims or orthodox Jews), bugs, unfamiliar sexual practices, gore, dirt, and death. Some feel disgust if they are "contaminated" by contact with strangers—even a simple handshake. Some feel disgust when their culture's moral rules are broken, such as the taboos against incest or sex with children (Rozin, Lowery, & Ebert, 1994).

Of course, people do not always display their emotions on their faces. Most of us do not go around scowling and clenching our jaws whenever we are angry. We can grieve and feel enormously sad without weeping. We can feel worried and tense, yet put on a happy face. People use facial expressions, in short, to lie about their feelings, as well as to express them.

To get around the human ability to mask emotions, Ekman and his associates developed a way to peek under the mask. They developed a special coding system to analyze and identify each of the nearly 80 muscles of the face, as well as the combinations of muscles associated with various emotions. When people try to hide their real emotions, they use different groups of muscles. For example, when people try to pretend that they feel grief, only 15 percent manage to get the eyebrows, eyelids, and forehead wrinkle exactly right, mimicking the way grief is expressed spontaneously. Authentic smiles last only two seconds; false smiles may last ten seconds or more (Ekman, 1994; Ekman, Friesen, & O'Sullivan, 1988).

The Functions of Facial Expressions. Facial expressions not only express internal states; they also help us communicate to others and evoke a response from them. You can see this even in infants. A baby's expressions of misery, angry frustration, happiness, or disgust are apparent to most parents, who respond by soothing an uncomfortable baby, cuddling a happy one, and feeding a hungry, grumpy one (Izard, 1994b; Stenberg & Campos, 1990).

Facial expressions do not always convey the emotion being felt. A posed, social smile like Gloria Vanderbilt's (left) may have nothing to do with true feelings of happiness. Conversely, you would never know from the apparently anguished face of Oksana Baiul (right) that she was actually feeling jubilant over winning an Olympic medal for figure skating.

Babies, in turn, react to the facial expressions of their parents, especially when their parents are happy. American, German, Greek, Japanese, Trobriand Island, and Yanomamo mothers all "infect" their babies with happy moods by displaying happy expressions (Keating, 1994). Babies even seem primed to respond to happy facial expressions. Tiny newborns will suck longer on a pacifier if it produces a happy face than if it produces a face with a neutral or negative expression (Walker-Andrews, 1997). (If you become a parent, remember this!)

Starting at the end of their first year, babies begin to alter their own behavior in reaction to their parents' facial expressions of emotion, and this ability has survival value. Do you recall the visual-cliff studies described in Chapter 6 (see pp. 212–213)? These studies were originally designed to test for depth perception, which emerges early in infancy. But in one experiment, 1-year-old babies were put on a more ambiguous visual cliff that did not drop off sharply and thus did not automatically evoke fear, as the original cliff did. In this case, 74 percent of the babies crossed the cliff when their mothers put on a happy, reassuring expression, but not a single one crossed when their mothers showed an expression of fear (Sorce et al., 1985). If you have ever watched a toddler take a tumble and then look at his or her parent before deciding whether to cry or to forget it, you will understand the influence of parental facial expressions.

Interestingly, facial expressions may help us communicate not only with others, but also with ourselves, so to speak, by helping us to identify our own emotions. In the process of **facial feedback**, the facial muscles send messages to the brain about the basic emotion being expressed: A smile tells us that we're happy, a frown that we're angry or perplexed (Izard, 1990). When people are told to smile and look pleased or happy, their positive feelings increase; when they are told to look angry, displeased, or disgusted, positive feelings decrease (Kleinke, Peterson, & Rutledge, 1998).

Facial feedback affects emotional states even when people are not specifically requested to imitate an emotion, but are just asked to alter their facial muscles. For example, when people are told to contract the facial muscles involved in smiling (though not actually instructed to smile) and are then shown cartoons, they find the cartoons funnier than if they are contracting their muscles in a way that is incompatible with smiling (Strack, Martin, & Stepper, 1988). And when they are asked to contort their facial muscles into patterns associated with anger, that is often the emotion they feel. As one young man put it, "When my jaw was clenched and my brows down, I tried not to be angry but it just fit the position" (Laird, 1974). The reason seems to be that facial expressions affect the sympathetic nervous system. If you put on an "angry" face, your heart rate will rise faster than if you put on a "happy" face (Levenson, Ekman, & Friesen, 1990).

Facial Expressions in Social Context. When you are at home by yourself, you are unlikely to walk around smiling or frowning. You may be feeling perfectly

Great moms have always understood the importance of facial feedback.

facial feedback The process by which the facial muscles send messages to the brain about the basic emotion being expressed.

GET ➔ INVOLVED

PUT ON A HAPPY FACE

See whether facial feedback works for you. The next time you are feeling sad or afraid, try purposely smiling, even if no one is around. Keep smiling. Does your facial expression affect your mood? Is it true, as Anna sings in *The King and I,* that when we fool the people we meet—by wearing a happy smile or whistling a happy tune to disguise fear—we fool ourselves as well?

happy, but you probably won't actually smile unless you are recalling a particularly delicious memory or watching a funny TV show. You will save your smiles until you have an audience. A study of 22 Olympic gold medalists, observed as they stood on the podium during the awards ceremonies, found that the athletes smiled only when they were interacting with officials or the public, not when they were standing alone—though presumably they were equally happy the whole time (Fernández-Dols & Ruiz-Belda, 1995). And when people do put on public expressions of emotion, they can convey very different things. A smile, for example, might not mean "I'm happy," but rather "I'm trying to be pleasant" or "Don't be mad at me" or even "I was right and you were wrong."

Because facial expressions occur primarily in a social context, and because they can have different meanings depending on that context, some psychologists take issue with the view that basic facial expressions have universal meanings. How you interpret someone else's expression, they maintain, always depends on the circumstance in which it occurs (Fridlund, 1994). For example, look at the photograph of the woman in the margin; what emotion would you say she is feeling? Most people will say that her staring eyes and open mouth are signs of fear. But suppose we tell you that she has been waiting for a table at a ritzy restaurant, in spite of having made reservations months earlier. Trendy-looking couples are being seated immediately, but she has been told she will have to wait another hour. Now what emotion do you think she is expressing? Given this information, most people will say that her staring eyes and open mouth are signs of anger. Conversely, people who see an "angry" face in a situation that would normally provoke fear tend to say that the person is afraid (Carroll & Russell, 1996).

Facial expressions are important clues to a person's emotions, therefore, but they are only part of the emotional picture. Even Ekman, who has been studying them for years, concludes, "There is obviously emotion without facial expression and facial expression without emotion." In Shakespeare's play *Henry VI*, the villain who will become the evil King Richard III says,

> *Why, I can smile, and murder while I smile;*
> *And cry content to that which grieves my heart;*
> *And wet my cheeks with artificial tears,*
> *And frame my face to all occasions.*

The Brain and Emotion

Another line of physiological research seeks to identify parts of the brain responsible for the many components of emotional experience: recognizing another person's emotion, feeling an emotion, expressing an emotion, and acting on an emotion. Many of these components are quite specifically localized in the brain.

The Two Hemispheres. The right hemisphere is especially important for processing incoming emotional information and for expressing the emotions you feel. People with damage in a particular part of the right hemisphere have trouble understanding jokes or getting the emotions portrayed in films and stories. And if you ask them to express emotions, for instance, by repeating sentences in happy, sad, or angry tones of voice, they cannot do it very well (Heller, Nitschke, & Miller, 1998).

The two cerebral hemispheres also play different roles in the experience of positive and negative emotions. Regions of the left hemisphere appear to be specialized for the processing of positive emotions like happiness, whereas regions of the right hemisphere are specialized for negative emotions like fear and sadness. People with damage to the left hemisphere often lose the capacity for joy and instead report

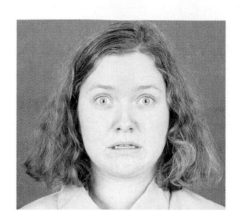

What emotion is this woman expressing?

excessive anger or depression. Conversely, people with damage to the right hemisphere may feel excessively manic and euphoric. Even in people without brain damage, those who are clinically depressed have less activation in the left frontal regions than nondepressed people do (Davidson, 1992, 1995).

Hemispheric specialization seems related to another aspect of emotion, as well: acting on it. When you feel an emotion, you will generally feel motivated to do something specific: embrace or approach the person who instills joy in you, withdraw or flee from a person or situation that frightens you (Brehm, 1999). Left-hemisphere activation is associated with tendencies to approach other people, whereas right-hemisphere activation is associated with tendencies to withdraw (Harmon-Jones & Allen, 1998). These hemispheric differences occur even in infants. In one study, 10-month-old babies were briefly separated from their mothers, then monitored during the happy reunion. The babies smiled, their "happy" left hemispheres were active, and they reached out to their moms. But when the babies were only smiling socially at strangers, their left hemispheres showed no increased activation, and the babies did not reach out (Fox & Davidson, 1988). Even a baby brain feels the difference between the warm happiness of a love smile and the cooler pleasure of a social one.

The Amygdala and the Cortex. In recent years psychologists have discovered that the *amygdala,* a small structure in the brain's limbic system, plays a key role in emotion (see Chapter 4). The amygdala is responsible for evaluating sensory information, quickly determining its emotional importance, and making the initial decision to approach or withdraw from a person or situation (LeDoux, 1994, 1996). For example, the amygdala quickly assesses danger or threat, which is a good thing, because otherwise you could be standing in the street asking, "Is it wise to cross

---

GET ➔ INVOLVED

TURN ON YOUR RIGHT HEMISPHERE

These faces have expressions of happiness on one side and sadness on the other. Look at the nose of each face; which face looks happier? Which face looks sadder?

(a)

(b)

You are likely to see face (b) as the happier one and face (a) as the sadder one. The likely reason is that in most people the left side of a picture is processed by the right side of the brain, where recognition of emotional expression primarily occurs (Oatley & Jenkins, 1996).

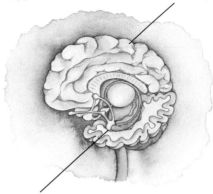

2. The cerebral cortex generates a more complete picture; it can override signals sent by the amygdala ("It's only Mike in a down coat").

1. The amygdala scrutinizes information for its emotional importance ("It's a bear! Be afraid! Run!").

now, while that very large truck is coming toward me?" The amygdala's initial response may then be overridden by a more accurate appraisal from the *cerebral cortex* (LeDoux, 1996). This is why you jump with fear when you suddenly feel a hand on your back in a dark alley, and why your fear evaporates when the cortex registers that the hand belongs to a friend whose lousy idea of humor is to scare you in a dark alley.

If either the amygdala or critical areas of the cortex are damaged, emotional abnormalities result. A rat with a damaged amygdala "forgets" to be afraid when it should be. Likewise, people with damage to the amygdala often have difficulty recognizing fear in themselves or others (Damasio, 1994). In contrast, rats or people with damage to critical areas of the cortex often lose the capacity to put aside their initial fear when the emotion is no longer necessary or appropriate. The result can be constant, irrational feelings of impending doom or anxiety or obsessive thoughts of danger, as we discuss in more detail in Chapter 16 (Schulkin, 1994; Schwartz et al., 1996).

Hormones and Emotion

A third line of physiological research focuses on hormones, which produce the energy of emotion in response to the alarm signals from the amygdala. In particular, the inner part of the adrenal gland sends out two hormones, *epinephrine* and *norepinephrine* (see Chapter 4). These chemical messengers activate the sympathetic division of the autonomic nervous system and produce a state of arousal and alertness. The pupils dilate, widening to allow in more light; the heart beats faster; breathing speeds up; and blood sugar rises, providing the body with more energy to act. Digestion slows down, so that blood flow can be diverted from the stomach and intestines to the muscles and surface of the skin. (This is why, when you are excited, scared, furious, or wildly in love, you may not want to eat.) The ultimate purpose of all these physiological changes is to prepare the body to respond quickly to danger or threat, excitement or opportunity (Frijda, 1988; Lang, 1995).

The adrenal glands produce epinephrine and norepinephrine in response to many challenges in the environment. These hormones will surge if you are laughing at a funny movie, playing a video game, worrying about an exam, cheering at a sports event, or driving on a hot day in terrible traffic. Epinephrine in particular provides the energy of an emotion—that familiar tingle, excitement, and sense of animation. At high levels, it can create the sensation of being "seized" or "flooded" by an emotion that is out of your control. In a sense, the release of epinephrine does cause us to lose control, because few people can consciously alter their heart rates, blood pressures,

Road rage is a widespread problem, a result in part of physiological arousal from the stress of driving.

and digestive tracts. However, people *can* learn to control their actions when they are under the sway of an emotion (as we discuss in "Taking Psychology with You"). And no emotion, no matter how urgent or compelling, lasts forever. As arousal subsides, a "hot" emotion turns into its "cool" counterpart. Anger may pale into annoyance, ecstasy into contentment, fear into worry, past emotional whirlwinds into calm breezes.

Although epinephrine and norepinephrine are released during many emotional states, emotions also differ from one another biochemically. The brain has a variety of chemical messengers at its disposal—neurotransmitters, hormones, and neuromodulators—and these play different roles in different emotions (Oatley & Jenkins, 1996). Fear, disgust, anger, sadness, surprise, and happiness are also associated with somewhat different patterns of autonomic nervous system activity, as measured by heart rate, electrical conductivity of the skin (*galvanic skin response* or *GSR*), and finger temperature (Levenson, 1992; Levenson, Ekman, & Friesen, 1990). These distinctive patterns may explain why people say they feel "hot and bothered" when they are angry, but "cold and clammy" when they are afraid: These metaphors capture what is going on in their bodies.

In sum, the physiology of emotion involves characteristic facial expressions; activity in specific parts of the brain, notably the amygdala and specialized parts of the two cerebral hemispheres; and sympathetic nervous system activity that prepares the body for action.

Detecting Emotions: Does the Body Lie?

Because physiological arousal and brain activation are associated with emotional states, many societies have tried to use physiological measurements to detect what a person is feeling and whether the person is lying about it. For example, in Asia the "rice method" of lie detection was once commonly used on people accused of a crime. The suspect had to chew on a handful of dry rice and then spit it out. The belief was that an innocent person would be able to do this easily, whereas a guilty person would have grains of rice stuck to the tongue and the roof of the mouth.

The theory behind the rice method is similar to that of the modern *polygraph machine*, commonly called the lie detector. Both methods are based on the assumption that a person who is guilty and fearful will have increased activity in the autonomic nervous system. In the case of the guilty rice-eater, such arousal should dry the saliva in the mouth and cause grains to stick to the tongue. In the case of the guilty suspect taking a polygraph test, a lie should be revealed by increased heart rate, respiration rate, and GSR as the person responds to incriminating questions.

A few psychologists still lobby enthusiastically on behalf of the polygraph, arguing that it is both a reliable and a valid way to identify a liar (Raskin, Honts, & Kircher, 1997). However, they represent a minority view. Most researchers regard polygraph tests as invalid, because *no physiological patterns of responses are specific to lying* (Iacono & Lykken, 1997; Lilienfeld, 1993; Saxe, 1994). Machines cannot tell whether you are feeling guilty, angry, nervous, amused, or revved up from an exciting day. Innocent people may be tense and nervous about the whole procedure. They may react to the word *bank* not because they robbed a bank, but because they recently bounced a check. In either case, the machine will record a "lie." The reverse mistake is also common. Some suave, practiced liars can lie without flinching, and others learn to "beat the machine" by tensing muscles or thinking about an exciting experience during neutral questions (Lykken, 1981).

In experiments in which federal employees were given knowledge of acts of mock espionage and told to try to hide this knowledge from investigators, many of the "guilty" respondents were able to pass polygraph tests with flying colors (Honts, 1994). This happens in real life, too. Aldrich Ames, a high-level CIA official, was convicted of spying for the former Soviet Union and selling national secrets. During the investigation, Ames passed two polygraph tests designed to detect his treasonous acts.

The polygraph is also unreliable. The people who administer the test often make many errors in reading the results and disagree with one another's judgments. Worst of all, they are more likely to accuse the innocent of lying than to let the guilty go free (Kleinmuntz & Szucko, 1984; Saxe, 1994). Because of such findings, the U.S. Congress passed a law prohibiting employers from using lie detectors to screen job applicants or randomly test employees, and most courts do not admit polygraph evidence in trials. However, most police

THINKING CRITICALLY

EXAMINE ASSUMPTIONS

Many people assume that because physiological changes, such as elevated heart rate, are involved in emotional states, physiological measurements can tell us whether someone is afraid, guilty—or lying. Is this assumption valid? What evidence does it overlook?

"WE CAN'T DETERMINE IF YOU'RE TELLING THE TRUTH, BUT YOU SHOULD HAVE A DOCTOR CHECK YOUR PRESSURE."

departments continue to use them, not so much for their accuracy as to try to induce suspects to confess—by telling them that they failed the test.

Other efforts to measure physiological signs of emotional reactivity and lying continue. Some researchers are using measures of brain activity to see whether they can infer whether a person possesses guilty knowledge of a crime or is lying (Bashore & Rapp, 1993). But because of the normal variability among people in their autonomic and brain reactivity, innocent but highly reactive people are still likely to be misdiagnosed as "guilty" by these tests.

The case of the lie detector illustrates some of the limitations of biological approaches to emotion. As powerful as the physical changes involved in emotion are, they are not a sure guide to what a person is feeling. You cannot know just from measuring someone's hormones or heart rate whether he or she is feeling thrilled or frightened, sick or just in love. Nor can biology alone explain why, of two students about to take an exam, one feels psyched up and the other feels overwhelmed by anxiety. To understand emotions, you must also know what is going on in a person's mind.

QUICK QUIZ

Smile as you take this quiz, and see whether that makes you feel better.

1. A 3-year-old sees her dad dressed as a gorilla and runs away in fear. What brain structure is probably involved in her reaction?

2. Casey is watching *Hatchet Murders in the Dorm: Sequel XVII*. Which hormones cause his heart to pound and his palms to sweat when the murderer stalks an unsuspecting victim?

3. Melissa is watching an old Laurel and Hardy film, which makes her chuckle and puts her in a good mood. Which hemisphere of her brain is likely to be activated?

Answers:

1. the amygdala   2. epinephrine, norepinephrine   3. the left

WHAT'S AHEAD

● In a competition, who is likely to be happier, the third-place winner or the second-place winner?

● Why can't an infant feel shame or guilt?

● What is wrong with thinking that thinking is rational and emotion is irrational?

ELEMENTS OF EMOTION 2: THE MIND

Two friends of ours returned from a mountain-climbing trip to Nepal. One said, "It was wonderful! The crystal-clear skies, the millions of stars, the friendly people, the majestic mountains, the harmony of the universe!" The other said, "It was horrible! The bedbugs and fleas, the lack of toilets, the yak-butter tea, the awful food, the unforgiving mountains!" Can you guess which traveler was ecstatic while traveling and which was unhappy?

Same trip, two different reactions to it. Why? As we saw in Chapter 1, in the first century A.D., the Stoic philosophers suggested an answer: People do not become angry or sad or anxious because of actual events, but because of their explanations of those events. Modern psychologists have been verifying the Stoics' ideas experimentally and identifying the cognitive processes involved in emotions.

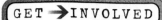

GET ➔ INVOLVED

GOING DOTTY

Put your finger on the dot below, and smile.

How do you feel at this moment, amused or irritated? If you followed our instructions and touched the dot, you probably feel more amused than angry. You may be laughing at yourself for doing such a silly thing, and that will make you feel happy. If you didn't put your finger on the dot, you probably feel more irked than amused. "Why are the authors of this book asking me to play stupid games?" you may be asking yourself. Notice that it is not our request that produced your emotion; it is your interpretation of what we asked you to do. Such interpretations are critical to all emotions.

How Thoughts Create Emotions

In 1924, a Spanish physician named Gregorio Marañon wondered whether he could generate emotions in his subjects simply by injecting them with epinephrine (Cornelius, 1991). He got a curious result. Nearly 30 percent of the people in his research reported feeling genuine emotions. But more than 70 percent merely reported physical changes ("My heart is beating fast," "My throat feels tight") or what Marañon called "as if" emotions: "I feel *as if* I were angry," "I feel *as if* I were happy."

What caused the difference between the two groups? Marañon was able to induce genuine emotions by asking the first group to think about their sick children or their deceased parents. In short, the people who reported genuine emotions had a reason for them! Marañon concluded that emotions involve a *physical* component, consisting of the bodily changes that accompany arousal, and a psychological or *mental* component, consisting of the interpretation the individual gives them, within the context in which those changes occur.

Marañon's findings were completely ignored until the 1960s, when Stanley Schachter and Jerome Singer (1962) advanced similar ideas with their **two-factor theory of emotion**. Like Marañon, they argued that bodily changes are necessary to experience an emotion, but they are not enough. Emotion, they said, depends on two factors: *physiological arousal* and the *cognitive interpretation* of that arousal. Your body may be churning away in high gear, but unless you can interpret, explain, and label those changes, you will not feel a true emotion.

Schachter and Singer's own experiments testing their hypothesis were not successfully replicated by others. But their ideas launched scores of studies designed to investigate how emotions are created or influenced by beliefs, perceptions of the situation, expectations, and *attributions*—the explanations that people make of their own and other people's behavior (see Chapter 8). Human beings, after all, are the only species that can say, "The more I thought about it, the madder I got." That common remark shows that we can think ourselves into an emotion, and, by implication, that we can think ourselves out of it.

two-factor theory of emotion The theory that emotions depend on both physiological arousal and a cognitive interpretation of that arousal.

Attributions and Emotions. Perceptions and attributions are involved in all kinds of emotions, from joy to sadness. To see how, imagine that you have had a crush for weeks on a fellow student in your history class. Finally you get up the nerve to start a conversation. Heart pounding, palms sweating, you manage to say, "Hi, there!" Before you can continue, the object of your passion has walked past you without even a nod. How do you feel? Angry? Sad? Embarrassed? Your answer will depend on how you explain the student's behavior:

Angry: "What a rude thing to do, to ignore me like that!"

Sad: "I knew it; I'm no good. No one will ever like me."

Embarrassed: "Oh, no! Everyone saw how I was humiliated!"

And of course if you say, "Whew, that was a close call; I didn't want to get involved, anyway," you will feel relief. Notice that it is not the student's behavior, but your interpretation of it, that generates your emotional response—or lack of one.

Here is another example: Imagine that you get an A on your psychology midterm; how will you feel? Or perhaps you get a D on that exam; how will you feel then? Most people assume that success brings happiness and failure brings unhappiness, but the emotions you feel will depend more on how you *explain* your grade than on what you actually get. Do you attribute your grade to your own efforts (or lack of them) or to the teacher, fate, or luck? In one series of experiments, students who believed they did well because of their own efforts tended to feel proud, happy, and satisfied. Those who believed they did well because of a lucky fluke or chance tended to feel gratitude, surprise, or guilt ("I don't deserve this"). Those who believed their failures were their own fault tended to feel regretful, guilty, or resigned. And those who blamed others tended to feel—can you guess?—angry (Weiner, 1986).

Surprisingly, third-place winners tend to be happier about their performance than those who come in second. Certainly, Olympic fencing bronze medalist Jean-Michel Henry of France (left) is happier than silver medalist Pavel Kolobkov of the Unified Team (right). (Eric Strecki, center, won the gold for France.)

Here is still another fascinating example of how thoughts affect emotions. Of two Olympic finalists, one who wins a second-place silver medal and one who wins a third-place bronze medal, which will feel happier? Won't it be the silver medalist? Nope. In a study of athletes' reactions to placing second and third in the 1992 Olympics and the 1994 Empire State games, the bronze medalists were happier than the silver medalists (Medvec, Madey, & Gilovich, 1995). Apparently, the athletes were comparing their performance to "what might have been." The second-place winners, comparing themselves to the gold medalists, were unhappy that they didn't get the gold. But the third-place winners, comparing themselves to those who did worse than they, were happy that they had earned a medal at all! Over a century ago, William James commented on the paradox of an athlete who is "shamed to death" because he is merely the second best in the whole world: "That he is able to beat the whole population of the globe minus one is nothing; he has 'pitted' himself to beat that one; and as long as he doesn't do that nothing else counts."

People are constantly appraising the events that befall them for their personal implications: Do I care about what is happening? Is it good or bad for me? Can I do anything about it? Is this matter going to get better or worse? These appraisals determine the degree of emotional "heat" in our encounters (C. Smith et al., 1993). If you decide that being

EXAMINING YOUR EMOTIONS AFTER AN EXAM

After your next psychology test, write down the reasons you think you got the grade you did. Do you attribute the reasons to your own efforts, or perhaps a lack of effort? If you did not do as well as you hoped, do you blame yourself, or the teacher? If you did do well, do you take credit, or do you think your success was a lucky fluke? How are these explanations related to your feelings about your grade?

stuck in a traffic jam is trivial and you can't do anything about it anyway, you may take it calmly. If you are on the way to, say, your best friend's wedding, and you see that the traffic is getting worse, and being late is *really* going to be bad for you, you are likely to feel hopping mad at those stupid cars that are blocking your way.

The cognitions involved in emotion range from your immediate perceptions of a specific event to your general philosophy of life. If you believe that winning is everything and trying your best counts for nothing, you may feel depressed rather than happy if you "only" come in second (like those silver medalists). If you think a friend's criticism is intentionally mean rather than well meaning, you may respond with anger rather than gratitude. This is why cognitive appraisals—including the *meanings* that people attribute to events—are an essential part of the experience of emotion (Frijda, 1988; Lazarus, 1991; Oatley & Jenkins, 1996).

The Case of Shame and Guilt. To see how particular thoughts and perceptions can generate different emotions, consider the examples of shame and guilt. Both of these emotions occur when you do something you know is wrong, but they differ in the cognitions that provoke them and in the behavior they motivate (Lewis, 1971; Tangney et al., 1996). In shame, the focus is on the bad *self* ("How could I be such a horrible person?"). The shamed person regards his or her failure or bad behavior as evidence of a global and enduring personality defect; he or she feels small, worthless, and powerless. The resulting motive is to hide or sink into the floor.

In guilt, the focus is on the bad *behavior* ("How could I have done such a horrible thing?"). The guilty person knows that what he or she did was wrong but sees it as just that— a bad act but one that does not affect the overall worthiness of the self. The resulting motive is to apologize and make amends. You may be surprised to learn that shame is related to anger, resentment, and blame, but guilt is not (Tangney et al., 1996). Guilty people tend to think about their behavior this way: "Gee, I did such a bad thing; I really should try to fix it." But shamed people make cognitive appraisals that lead to blaming the person who they feel shamed them: "Gee, I did that bad thing because I'm so horrible. And how could you have put me in such a bind and made me feel so terrible, you skunk?"

Studies of the cognitive element in emotion suggest that people can learn how their thinking affects their emotions and change their thinking accordingly. (As we will see in

Some people think that shaming is the right punishment for illegal or immoral behavior. For centuries, locking people in stocks was a common punishment in England and America, a method of exposing offenders to public derision. This British conscientious objector was put in the stocks in 1915 because he refused to fight in World War I. But as the text explains, publicly shaming and humiliating a person often backfires. Why?

Chapter 17, cognitive therapy is based on this assumption.) They can ask themselves what the evidence is for their belief that the world will collapse if they get a C in biology, that no one loves them, or that they will be lonely forever. In such cases, notice that it is not emotional reasoning that prevents critical thinking, it is the failure to think critically that creates the emotion!

Reason and Emotion: Opposites or Allies?

Research has moved us a long way from the old notion that emotion and cognition are opposite, unrelated processes. It is true that some emotions require only minimal or primitive cognitions. A conditioned sentimental response to a patriotic symbol, a conditioned disgust response to an ugly bug, or a warm fuzzy feeling toward a familiar object all involve simple, nonconscious reactions (Izard, 1994a; Murphy, Monahan, & Zajonc, 1995). And infants display primitive emotions but do not yet have much mental sophistication. Their "cognitions" are fairly basic: "Hey, I'm mad because no one is feeding me!" or "I'm really miserable because I've got colic!"

Many emotions, however, require higher cognitive capacities. Infants do not feel shame or guilt, for example, because these "self-conscious" emotions require the emergence of a sense of self and the perception that one has behaved badly and has let down another person (Baumeister, Stillwell, & Heatherton, 1994; Tangney et al., 1996). Only when the baby's cerebral cortex develops can cognitive appraisals, and therefore emotions, become more complex (Malatesta, 1990; Oatley & Jenkins, 1996).

Moreover, just as cognitions affect emotions, so too do emotional states influence our cognitions. For example, blaming others for your woes can make you feel angry, but once you are angry, you may be more inclined to think that other people are letting you down (Lerner, Goldberg, & Tetlock, 1998).

THE INTERACTION OF THOUGHTS AND EMOTIONS

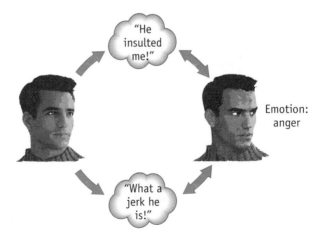

An understanding of the reciprocal interaction between thinking and feeling is dissolving the historical distinction between reason (our "rational" human abilities) and emotion (our "irrational" mammalian heritage). As we discuss in the chapters on thinking (Chapter 9) and memory (Chapter 10), human cognition is not always rational. It involves many biases, including the confirmation bias, biases due to cognitive dissonance, and biases in the construction of memories. Conversely, emotions are not always irrational. They bind people together, regulate relationships, and motivate people to achieve their goals (Oatley, 1990). Without the capacity to feel emotion, people have difficulty making ethical decisions and planning for the future (Damasio, 1994). When you are faced with a decision between two appealing and justifiable career alternatives, for example, your sense of which one "feels right" emotionally may help you make the best choice.

An individual's experience of emotion, then, combines mind and body. Yet, there is still one part of the emotional "tree" missing. Thoughts may influence emotion, but where do these thoughts come from? When people feel that it is shameful for a woman to walk down a street with her arms and legs uncovered, where do their ideas about shame originate? You may feel angry enough to punch the walls, but where do you learn what to do when you are that enraged? To answer these questions, we turn to the third major aspect of emotional experience: the role of culture.

QUICK QUIZ

Are your thoughts about quizzes affecting your feelings about taking this one?

1. What were the two factors in Schachter and Singer's two-factor theory of emotion?

2. Given that shame and guilt tend to motivate people differently, which emotion should you prefer your best friend to feel if she or he behaves badly toward you, and why?

3. At a party, a stranger is flirting with your date. You are flooded with jealousy. What cognitions might be causing this emotion? *Be specific.* What alternative thoughts might reduce your jealousy?

Answers:

1. Physiological arousal and a cognitive interpretation of that arousal. 2. Guilt, because your friend is likely to be motivated to apologize and make amends rather than become angry and blame you, as shamed people tend to do. 3. Possible thoughts causing jealousy are "My date finds other people more attractive," "That person is trying to steal my date," or "My date's behavior is humiliating me." But you could be saying, "It's a compliment to me that other people find my date attractive" or "It pleases me that my date is getting such deserved attention."

WHAT'S AHEAD

● Are the "basic" emotions basic everywhere?

● Do Germans, Japanese, and Americans always mean the same thing when they smile at others?

● Why do people show sadness at funerals even when they are not feeling sad?

ELEMENTS OF EMOTION 3: THE CULTURE

A young wife leaves her house one morning to draw water from the local well as her husband watches from the porch. On her way back from the well, a male stranger stops her and asks for some water. She gives him a cupful and then invites him home to dinner. He accepts. The husband, wife, and guest have a pleasant meal together. The husband, in a gesture of hospitality, invites the guest to spend the night—with his wife. The guest accepts. In the morning, the husband leaves early to bring home breakfast. When he returns, he finds his wife again in bed with the visitor.

The question is, at what point in this story does the husband feel angry? The answer is, it depends on the culture to which he belongs (Hupka, 1981, 1991). A North American husband would feel rather angry at a wife who had an extramarital affair, and a wife would feel rather angry at being offered to a guest as if she were a lamb chop. But these reactions are not universal. A Pawnee husband of the nineteenth century would be enraged at any man who dared ask his wife for water.

An Ammassalik Inuit husband finds it perfectly honorable to offer his wife to a stranger, but only once. He would be angry to find his wife and the guest having a second encounter. And a Toda husband at the turn of the century in India would not be angry at all because the Todas allowed both husband and wife to take lovers. Both spouses might feel angry, though, if one of them had a *sneaky* affair, without announcing it publicly.

As you can see, although people in most cultures feel angry in response to insult and the violation of social rules, they often disagree about what an insult is or what the correct rule should be. In this section, we will explore how culture influences the emotions we feel and the ways in which we express them.

Cultural Influences on Emotion

No one disputes that cultures determine much of what people feel angry, sad, lonely, happy, ashamed, or disgusted about. Among the Bedouins, shame is produced by violations of a code of honor; on Bali, shame results from perceived challenges to one's status (Mesquita & Frijda, 1992). But do the Bedouins and the Balinese experience the same feeling, regardless of its different causes? Are all emotions universal, or are some of them specific to culture?

Language and Emotion. One problem in studying the question of universality is that some languages have words for emotional states that other languages lack (Mesquita & Frijda, 1992). The Germans have *schadenfreude*, a feeling of joy at another's misfortune. The Japanese can feel *hagaii*, helpless anguish tinged with frustration. *Litost* is a Czech word that combines grief, sympathy, remorse, and longing; the Czech writer Milan Kundera used it to describe "a state of torment caused by a sudden insight into one's own miserable self."

Conversely, some languages lack words for emotions that seem universal. For example, Tahitians lack the Western concept of and word for sadness. If you ask a Tahitian who is grieving over the loss of a lover what is wrong, he will say, "A spirit has made me ill." In contrast, Tahitians have a word for an emotion that most Westerners do not experience: *Mehameha* refers to "a sense of the uncanny," a trembling sensation that Tahitians feel when ordinary categories of perception are suspended—at twilight, in the brush, watching fires glow without heat. To Westerners, an event that cannot be identified is usually greeted with fear. Yet, *mehameha* does not describe what Westerners call fear or terror (Levy, 1984).

Do these interesting linguistic differences mean that Germans are more likely than others actually to feel *schadenfreude*, the Japanese to feel *hagaii*, the Czechs to feel *litost*, and the Tahitians to feel *mehameha*? Or are they just more willing to give these emotions a single name? Do Tahitians experience sadness the way Westerners do even though they identify it as illness?

The Search for Primary Emotions. Many psychologists believe that it is possible to identify a number of **primary emotions** that are experienced universally. Depending on the method of measuring emotion, the list of the primary ones varies somewhat, but it typically includes fear, anger, sadness, joy, surprise, disgust, and contempt. Some lists also include love, on the grounds that infant-parent love and the devotion of lovers are universal and unmistakably reflected in the "gaze of love" (Smith, Keltner, & Gonzaga, 1998). In contrast, **secondary emotions** are culture-specific. They include cultural variations such as *schadenfreude* or *hagaii*; blends of emotions such as *litost* or *mehameha*; and degrees of intensity and nuance that some cultures recognize or emphasize and others do not.

Those who argue on behalf of the universality of primary emotions draw on four lines of evidence:

primary emotions Emotions considered to be universal and biologically based; they generally include fear, anger, sadness, joy, surprise, disgust, and contempt.

secondary emotions Emotions that some cultures recognize or emphasize and others apparently do not, including blends of feeling or variations in intensity and nuance.

There is no mistaking how these babies feel! The fact that babies throughout the world show similar facial expressions and gestures of emotion persuades many researchers that certain emotions are primary and universal.

1 *Physiological research on the brain and central nervous system,* which suggests that primary emotions are linked with specific survival tendencies, such as running from something fearful. Some physiological researchers argue that we should distinguish these hard-wired emotions from "feelings," which include all the higher-level varieties influenced by cognition and culture (LeDoux, 1996). Around the world, people's physical descriptions of basic emotions are similar, such as feeling hot in response to anger and having a "lump in the throat" in response to sadness (Mesquita & Frijda, 1992; Oatly & Duncan, 1994).

2 *The existence of facial expressions that seem to be recognizable all over the world.* As we have seen, these expressions first appear, without learning, in infancy, and they correspond to the emotions most often identified as primary.

3 *The existence of similar emotion prototypes in most languages.* A *prototype* is a typical representative of a class of things (see Chapter 9). Primary emotions would be those that people everywhere consider the core examples of the concept *emotion:* For example, most people will say that "anger" and "sadness" are more representative of an emotion than "irritability" and "nostalgia" are. Prototypical emotions are reflected in the emotion words that young children learn first: *happy, sad, mad,* and *scared.* As children develop, they begin to draw emotional distinctions that are less prototypical and more specific to their language and culture, such as *ecstatic, depressed, hostile,* or *anxious* (Russell, 1991; Russell & Fehr, 1994; Shaver, Wu, & Schwartz, 1992).

4 *The fact that certain emotions are evoked by the same experiences everywhere.* A massive cross-cultural project, involving 37 countries on five continents, found remarkable commonalities in people's reported experiences with fear, anger, joy, sadness, disgust, shame, and guilt. Everywhere, sadness follows perception of loss, fear follows perception of threat and bodily harm, anger follows perception of insult or injustice, and so forth (Scherer, 1997).

Other psychologists, however, think that the effort to find primary, universal emotions is futile. They point out that most people do not think of surprise, disgust, or contempt as true emotions, although all three are registered on the face (Ortony & Turner, 1990; Shaver et al., 1987). Conversely, they add, many true emotions are missing from the "primary" list, including shame, guilt, pride, pity, embarrassment, and empathy. These are as much a part of human

TOLERATE UNCERTAINTY

There is persuasive evidence for a few central, universal "primary emotions"—and persuasive evidence that the effort to identify primary emotions may be fruitless. Why is this issue so hard to resolve?

The father on the left is clearly proud of his family, and the husband on the right is clearly showing the affectionate "gaze of love" to his wife. But pride and love are not on most lists of primary emotions. Should they be, or are they just variations of happiness?

emotional experience as sadness and anger, but they fail to make the list of primary emotions because they cannot always be measured in the brain or identified on the face (Keltner & Buswell, 1997; Roseman, Wiest, & Swartz, 1994).

Critics of the universalist argument emphasize the profound influence of culture on every aspect of emotional experience, starting with which feelings a culture even considers "primary." For example, anger is regarded as a primary emotion by Western psychologists, who tend to come from cultures that emphasize independence and personal rights. But anger is caused and experienced quite differently in community-oriented cultures, such as those throughout Asia and the Middle East, where shame and loss of face are more central emotions (Kitayama & Markus, 1994).

On the tiny Micronesian atoll of Ifaluk, everyone would say that *fago* is the most fundamental emotion. *Fago*, translated as "compassion/love/sadness," reflects the sad feeling one has when a loved one is absent or in need, and the pleasurable sense of compassion in being able to care and help (Lutz, 1988). What, then, would theories of primary emotions look like from a non-Western perspective? They might start with shame and *fago*, which are just blips on the radar screen of Western emotion research.

As you can see, answers to the question "Are emotions universal?" depend on whether researchers are focusing on the common elements in all emotions or on cultural differences.

The Communication of Emotion

On Sunday, April 25, in the year 1227, a knight named Ulrich von Lichtenstein disguised himself as the goddess Venus. Wearing an ornate white gown, waist-length braids, and heavy veils, Ulrich traveled from Venice to Bohemia, challenging all local warriors to a duel. By his own count (which may have been exaggerated), Ulrich broke 307 lances, unhorsed four opponents, and completed his five-week journey with an undefeated record. The reason for Ulrich's knightly performance was his passion for a princess, nameless to history, who barely gave poor Ulrich the time of day. Ulrich trembled in her presence, suffered in her absence, and constantly endured feelings of longing, misery, and melancholy—a state of love that apparently made him very happy (M. Hunt, 1959, 1967).

We will have a lot more to say about love in the next chapter, but for the moment consider only Ulrich's *expression* of his passion. If someone tried to win your heart by performing a modern version of such acts of bravery, would you be charmed, irritated, or alarmed?

What some of us do for love: Ulrich von Lichtenstein disguised as Venus.

Display Rules. Your feelings about Ulrich will depend in part on what your culture has taught you about the **display rules** that govern how and when emotions may be expressed (Ekman et al., 1987). In some cultures, people would find Ulrich's extravagant demonstration of love exciting and touching; in others, they would find it weird and lunatic—they would be suspicious of Ulrich's real motives. Likewise, in some cultures, grief is expressed by noisy wailing and weeping; in others, by tearless resignation; and in still others, by merry dance, drink, and song. Once you feel an emotion, how you express it is rarely a simple matter of "I say what I feel."

Even the smile, which seems a straightforward signal of friendliness, has many meanings and uses that are not universal. Americans smile more frequently than Germans, not because Americans are friendlier but because they differ in their notions of when a smile is appropriate. After a German-American business session, Americans often complain that the Germans are cold and aloof. For their part, Germans often complain that Americans are excessively cheerful, hiding their real feelings under the mask of a smile (Hall & Hall, 1990). The Japanese smile even more than Americans, to disguise negative emotions whose public display is considered rude and incorrect.

Just as people can speak without knowing the rules of grammar, most people express or suppress their emotions without being aware of the rules they are following (Hall & Hall, 1990; Keating, 1994). When they try to communicate across cultures, however, not knowing the other person's display rules of emotion can lead to major misunderstandings, hostilities, and, in extreme cases, even war.

Here is a tragic example (Triandis, 1994): On January 9, 1991, the Foreign Minister of Iraq, Tariq Aziz, met with the American Secretary of State, James Baker, to discuss Iraq's invasion of Kuwait. Seated next to Aziz was the half-brother of Iraq's president, Saddam Hussein. Baker said, "If you do not move out of Kuwait we will attack you." A clear statement, right? But his *nonverbal* language was that of an American diplomat—moderate and restrained. He did not shout, stamp his feet, or wave his hands. Saddam Hussein's brother, for his part, behaved like a normal Iraqi. He paid attention to Baker's nonverbal language, which he considered the important form of communication. He reported to Saddam Hussein that Baker

CONSIDER OTHER EXPLANATIONS

A European who behaves in a way that conveys good manners and dignified restraint may seem cold to the average American. An American who smiles effusively may seem superficial and childish to the average European. How might each of them explain the other's behavior more constructively?

---

display rules Social and cultural rules that regulate when, how, and where a person may express (or must suppress) emotions.

Around the world, the cultural rules for expressing emotions (or suppressing them) differ. The display rule for a formal Japanese wedding portrait is "no expressions of emotion"—but not every member of this family has learned that rule yet.

As much as words do, arms and hands communicate interest, emphasis, and feeling. But a gesture that is harmless or fun in one culture, such as the sign of the Texas Longhorns, can be insulting in another—so be careful!

Smiling to convey friendliness is part of the job description for flight attendants, whether they are male or female—but not necessarily for the passengers they serve.

was "not at all angry. The Americans are just talking, and they will not attack." Saddam therefore instructed Aziz to be inflexible and to yield nothing. This misunderstanding contributed to the outbreak of a bloody war in which thousands of people died.

Body Language. Fiorello LaGuardia, who was mayor of New York from 1933 to 1945, was fluent in three languages: English, Italian, and Yiddish. LaGuardia knew more than the words of those languages; he also knew the gestures that went along with each one. Researchers who studied films of his speeches could tell which language he was speaking with the sound turned off! They could do so by reading his *body language,* the nonverbal signals of body movement, posture, gesture, and gaze that people constantly express (Birdwhistell, 1970). Italians and Jews embellish their speech with circular movements of their arms and hands, and by measuring the radius of those movements you can often predict whether a speaker is of Italian or Jewish descent: The larger the radius, the more likely the speaker is Italian (Keating, 1994).

Some signals of body language, like some facial expressions, seem to be "spoken" universally. Across cultures, people generally recognize body movements that reveal pleasure or displeasure, liking or dislike, tension or relaxation, high status or low status, grief and anger (Buck, 1984; Matsumoto, 1996). When people are depressed, it shows in their walk, stance, and head position. However, most aspects of body language are specific to particular spoken languages and cultures, which makes even the simplest gesture subject to misunderstanding and offense. The sign of the University of Texas football team, the Longhorns, is to extend the index finger and the pinkie. In Italy and other parts of Europe, this gesture means a man's wife has been unfaithful to him—a serious insult.

When people are talking to each other, a mismatch of body languages will make their conversation feel "out of sync"; they may feel as confused and emotionally upset as if they had had a verbal misunderstanding. The ability to synchronize moods through body language is crucial to smooth interaction and rapport between people (Bernieri et al., 1996; Hatfield, Cacioppo, & Rapson, 1994). When people are in synchrony, their moods, as expressed through body language, can literally be contagious (see Figure 11.2). Have you ever been in a cheerful mood, had lunch with a depressed friend, and come away feeling vaguely depressed yourself? Have you ever stopped to have a chat with a friend who was nervous about an upcoming exam, and ended up feeling panicked yourself? That's *emotional contagion* at work.

People who live together are especially vulnerable to emotional contagion. For example, in a study of 96 pairs of college roommates, roommates of depressed students became more depressed themselves over the course of the three-week study, even when the researchers statistically controlled for upsetting life events that might be affecting them (Joiner, 1994). And people who work together in close teams, such as nurses, are more likely to be infected by their colleagues' moods than are those who work more independently (Totterdell et al., 1998). If you are starting to feel gloomy and pessimistic at school or work, perhaps you should check out your friends' or co-workers' moods before you decide that *you* are the one who is depressed!

Emotion Work. Display rules tell us not only what to do when we *are* feeling an emotion, but also how and when we should show an emotion we do *not* feel. Acting out an emotion we do not really feel, or trying to create the right emotion for the

FIGURE 11.2
THE CONTAGION OF EMOTION

These volunteers, videotaped in a study of conversational synchrony, are obviously "in sync" with one another, even though they have just met. The degree to which two people's gestures and expressions are synchronized affects the rapport they feel with one another. Such synchrony can also create a "contagion" of moods (Bernieri et al., 1991).

occasion, is called **emotion work.** Most people are expected to demonstrate sadness at funerals, happiness at weddings, and affection toward relatives. If they do not really feel such emotions, they may playact to convince others that they do.

Sometimes emotion work is actually a job requirement. Flight attendants must outwardly convey cheerfulness, even if they are privately angry about a rude or drunken passenger. Bill collectors must put on a stern face to convey threat, even if they are feeling sorry for the poor person in debt (Hochschild, 1983). Other employees do emotion work when they express agreement with an employer's infuriating decision or friendliness to annoying customers. One possible benefit of this kind of emotion work—if you remember what you read about facial feedback—is that the effort to display feelings of warmth and friendliness toward others may generate positive feelings in the sender as well as the receiver.

emotion work Expression of an emotion, often because of a role requirement, that the person does not really feel.

QUICK QUIZ

Please use verbal communication to answer these questions.

1. In Western theories of emotion, anger would be called a _____ emotion, whereas *fago* would be called a _____ emotion.

2. In a class discussion, a student says something that embarrasses a student from another culture. The second student smiles to disguise his discomfort; the first student, thinking he is not being taken seriously, gets angry. These students' misunderstanding reflects their different _____ for the expression of embarrassment and anger.

3. Maureen is working in a fast-food restaurant and becoming irritated with a customer who isn't ordering fast enough. "Hey, whaddaya want to order, slowpoke?" she snaps at him. To keep her job, and her temper, Maureen needs practice in _____.

Answers:

1. primary, secondary 2. display rules 3. emotion work

- Do women experience emotions more often than men do?
- What factors other than your sex predict how well you can "read" someone's emotional state?
- What factors other than your sex predict how emotionally expressive you are?

PUTTING THE ELEMENTS TOGETHER: EMOTION AND GENDER

"Women are too emotional," men often complain. "Men are too uptight," women often reply. People hold strong beliefs about gender differences in emotion and about whether the male or female style is better. But what do they mean by "emotional"?

THINKING CRITICALLY

DEFINE YOUR TERMS

People say that women are the emotional sex, but they often fail to define their terms. What, for example, does *emotional* mean? Why is it "arguing" when he does it but "getting emotional" when she does it?

If we define emotionality as the ability to feel the everyday emotions of life, men and women do not differ much (Baumeister, Stillwell, & Wotman, 1990; Fischer et al., 1993; Kring & Gordon, 1998; Oatley & Duncan, 1994; Shields, 1991). Both sexes are equally likely to feel anxious in new situations; to feel love and loneliness; to feel angry when they believe they have been insulted or treated unfairly; to feel embarrassed when they make goofy mistakes; and to grieve when attachments break up. (However, around the world women *are* more likely than men to suffer from severe depression, a mood disorder we discuss in Chapter 16.) So we must look elsewhere for evidence that one sex is "more emotional" than the other and the conditions under which such differences might occur.

Physiology. If we define emotionality in terms of reactivity to provocation, men are often more emotional than women. Studies of hundreds of married couples have found that conflict is physiologically more upsetting for men than for women, which may be why many men try to avoid conflict entirely (Gottman, 1994). In studies of actual quarrels between married couples, men's heart rates, unlike women's, often soar as soon as signs of conflict begin and stay high longer. Moreover, husbands tend to feel more negative and hostile the more agitated they are, but wives do not (Levenson, Carstensen, & Gottman, 1994).

One possible explanation for these differences is that the male's autonomic nervous system is generally more sensitive and reactive than the female's. When men are under stress or in a competitive situation, many show a more pronounced elevation in blood pressure, heart rate, and epinephrine than women do (Polefrone & Manuck, 1987; T. Smith et al., 1996). But an alternative explanation is that men are more likely than women to rehearse angry thoughts, such as "I don't have to take this" or "It's all her fault." These thoughts prolong and intensify the physiological reactions involved in anger (Rusting & Nolen-Hoeksema, 1998). (Women, in contrast, are more likely than men to ruminate about, and thus prolong, feelings of depression and sadness.)

"Can you just give me a synopsis of your rage so we can move on from there?"

Many men try to avoid angry confrontations with their partners. Some researchers think the reason is physiological.

Cognitions. If a male teacher compliments a female student on her appearance, is that a sign of flattery or harassment? If a woman touches a male friend on his arm, is she signaling affection or sexual interest? Men and women often differ in their perceptions of the same event (Lakoff, 1990; Stapley & Haviland, 1989). Their different interpretations, in turn, can create different emotional responses to the event.

For example, although men and women often feel angry in response to betrayal and injustice, they sometimes differ in the kinds of everyday events that provoke their anger. Women are more likely than men to become angry over things they perceive as signs of a partner's disregard, such as forgetting a birthday; men are more likely to become angry about damage to their property or affronts by a stranger (Fehr et al., 1999). When your partner blows up over something you think is trivial, it is easy to conclude that he or she is being "too emotional"! ("Your silly *birthday*?" "Your stupid *fender*?")

Sensitivity to Other People's Emotions. Sometimes women are considered more emotional because of their supposed sensitivity to other people's emotional states. On a test that measures the ability to detect emotions revealed in tones of voice, movements of the body, and facial expressions, women have indeed scored slightly better than men (Blum, 1998; J. Hall, 1987). But sensitivity to another person's emotions depends far more on the *context* in which the two people are interacting than on their gender. In particular, the ability to "read" emotional signals depends on the following factors:

Does this woman's touch signify affection, dominance, harassment, sexual interest, or simple friendliness? How do you think the man is reacting? Men and women often disagree on the meaning of another's touch. Depending on their perceptions, they may respond with anger, happiness, disgust, fear, or desire.

1 *The sex of the sender and of the receiver.* Most people are better at reading the emotional signals, facial expressions, and gestures of members of their own sex than those of the other sex (Buck, 1984).

2 *How well the sender and receiver know each other.* Fortunately, affection improves cross-gender accuracy. Dating and married couples can interpret each other's facial expressions and other emotional signs better than strangers can (Hatfield, Cacioppo, & Rapson, 1994; Smith, Keltner, & Gonzaga, 1998).

3 *How expressive the sender is.* The receiver's gender and sensitivity to other people are less important than the sender's expressiveness. In other words, women are no better at reading the emotions of a "strong, silent" type than men are. Even among intimate couples, the best predictor of communication accuracy is the expressiveness of the sender; the sensitivity of the receiver counts for much less (Snodgrass, Hecht, & Ploutz-Snyder, 1998).

4 *Who has the power.* In any relationship in which one person has more power or authority than the other—such as parent and child, boss and employee, or teacher and student—the less powerful person is motivated to learn to read the powerful person's nonverbal signals (Fiske, 1993; Henley, 1995; Lakoff, 1990). Is mommy upset today, or will she play with me? Is Mr. Hepworth in a mood to give me a raise? Is Professor Postlethwaite mad at us for blowing the midterm?

Many supposed gender differences in the ability to read emotions actually reflect power differences. As one psychologist put it, "women's intuition" is really "subordinate's intuition" (Snodgrass, 1985). In male–female pairs in which one person was randomly assigned to be the leader and the other the follower, the subordinate was more sensitive to the leader's nonverbal signals than the leader was to the follower's cues. This difference occurred whether a man or a woman was the leader or the follower (Snodgrass, 1985, 1992).

Expressiveness. The one gender difference that undoubtedly contributes most to the stereotype that women are "more emotional" than men—their status and power being equal—is women's greater willingness to express their feelings, nonverbally and verbally. In North America, women on average do smile more than men do, gaze at their listeners more, have more emotionally expressive faces, use more expressive hand and body movements, and tend to touch others more and be touched more

Both sexes feel emotionally attached to friends and loved ones, but often they express their affections differently. From childhood on, girls tend to prefer "face to face" friendships, based on shared feelings; boys tend to prefer "side by side" friendships, based on shared activities.

(DePaulo, 1992; Kring & Gordon, 1998). Women also talk about their emotions more than men do. They are far more likely than men to cry, and to acknowledge emotions that reveal vulnerability and weakness, such as "hurt feelings," fear, sadness, loneliness, shame, and guilt (Grossman & Wood, 1993; Smith & Reise, 1998; Timmers, Fischer, & Manstead, 1998).

In contrast, most North American men express only one emotion more freely than women: anger to strangers, especially other men, when they believe they have been challenged or insulted. Otherwise, men are expected to control and mask negative feelings. When they are angry, worried, or afraid, they are more likely than women to say they feel moody, irritable, frustrated, or "on edge" (Fehr et al., 1999; Smith & Reise, 1998). If they express supposedly unmanly emotions at all, they will usually do so only to their intimate partners, and rarely to casual male friends. Many men fear, often correctly, that women and other men will reject or dislike them if they seem emotionally weak (Borys & Perlman, 1985).

An unfortunate consequence of the social taboo on male expressiveness may be a difficulty in recognizing when men are seriously unhappy. Many boys and men fail to be diagnosed as depressed because the tests for depression are based on typically female reactions—crying and talking about their unhappiness (Riessman, 1990; Stapley & Haviland, 1989). But most North American men do not express grief this way. Instead, they try to distract themselves, work harder or quit working altogether, bury their feelings in alcohol or other drugs, or, in extreme cases, become violent. Because the sexes tend to have different ways of expressing grief, some people wrongly infer that men suffer less than women when relationships end or that men are incapable of deep feeling.

Even gender differences in emotional expressiveness, however, are strongly affected by three important factors:

1 *Gender roles.* Women *and* men who are untraditional in their gender roles are more emotionally expressive—verbally and nonverbally—than traditionalists (Kring & Gordon, 1998). Perhaps they feel freer to express their "true selves" because they do not feel obligated to play the proper male or female role.

2 *Family and cultural norms.* Expressive people, male or female, tend to come from families or cultures in which expressiveness is the rule (Kring & Gordon, 1998). Italian, French, Spanish, and Middle Eastern men can have entire conversations using highly expressive hand gestures and facial expressions, and you won't find gender differences in nonverbal expressiveness in their cultures. In contrast, in Asian cultures, both sexes are taught to control emotional expression (Matsumoto, 1996; Mesquita & Frijda, 1992). Cultures also determine which emotions men and women express most freely. Israeli and Italian men are more likely than women

 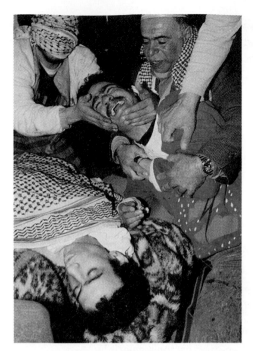

Israeli parents (left) and a Palestinian father (right) react to the death of their children in the Middle Eastern conflict. Notice that the men are following different cultural display rules for the expression of grief, rules that govern whether they should "let it out" or "keep a stiff upper lip." Your own culture's rules may affect your reactions to these scenes: Is the Israeli father "cold and uptight" or "mature and manly"? Is the Palestinian father being "hysterical" or "humanly expressive"?

to mask feelings of sadness, but British, Spanish, Swiss, and German men are *less* likely than their female counterparts to inhibit this emotion (Wallbott, Ricci-Bitti, & Bänninger-Huber, 1986).

3 *The specific situation.* As we saw in the case of "subordinate's intuition," the influence of a particular situation often determines whether you will express your feelings or inhibit them, regardless of your gender or culture. An American man will be as likely as an American woman to control his temper when the target of anger is someone with higher status or power; few people, no matter how angry, will readily sound off at a professor, police officer, or employer. And you won't find many gender differences in emotional expressiveness at a football game.

Emotion Work. Both sexes know the experience of having to hide emotions they feel and to show emotions they do not feel. Yet their emotion work, on the job and at home, is often different. On the whole, women tend to be involved in the flight-attendant side of emotion work, persuading others that they are friendly, happy, and warm, and making sure others are happy (DePaulo, 1992). Men tend to be involved in the bill-collection side, persuading others that they are stern, aggressive, and unemotional.

Again, the major reason for this difference has to do with gender roles and status. Attentiveness to other people's feelings is typically part of the female role (Fischer, 1993; Grossman & Wood, 1993). Thus, many North American women smile more often than men do as part of their emotion work—to pacify others, smooth over conflicts, or convey deference (Hecht & LaFrance, 1998). If women do *not* smile when others expect them to, they are often disliked, even if they are actually smiling as often as men would. Girls learn this lesson early; 6- to 10-year-olds show a steady increase in knowledge about when they should disguise their true feelings and put on a "polite smile"—for instance, when they are given a gift they don't like. Boys are much less likely to mask their negative feelings with a polite smile (Davis, 1995; Saarni, 1989).

In summary, the answer to "which sex is more emotional?" is—sometimes men, sometimes women, and sometimes neither. "Being emotional" can refer to feeling an emotion, being highly reactive physiologically, being inclined to perceive events in an emotion-generating way, being sensitive to other people's emotional states, being emotionally expressive, or feeling obligated to do "emotion work." Everyone feels emotions, but cultural norms and gender roles shape the expression of these emotions in countless ways.

QUICK QUIZ

A. If you aren't feeling too emotional, indicate whether each of these descriptions applies (a) more to men than to women, (b) more to women than to men, or (c) to both sexes equally.

   1. Does "emotion work" to make other people feel good.

   2. Finds it difficult to express anger to a superior.

   3. Expresses anger to a stranger.

   4. Feels grief when a relationship ends.

   5. Admits feeling scared to death.

   6. Can read another person's emotions.

B. Question #6 was sneaky, because the ability to identify another person's emotions is affected by factors other than the perceiver's sex. What are they?

Answers:

A. 1. b 2. c 3. a 4. c 5. b 6. b, but the difference is very small, for the reasons listed in Part B. B. Sensitivity to another person's emotions is enhanced when the sender and receiver are the same sex; the two people know each other; the sender is expressive; and the receiver is in a subordinate position in relation to the sender.

As we have seen in this chapter, the full experience and expression of emotion involve physiology, cognitive processes, and cultural rules. The case of gender and emotion shows that if we look at just one component, we come up with an incomplete or misleading picture. And it shows, too, that emotions have many purposes: They allow us to establish close bonds, threaten and warn, get help from others, reveal or deceive. The many varieties and expressions of emotion suggest that although we feel emotions physically, we use them socially. As we explore further issues in the study of motivation, personality, development, well-being, and mental disorders, we will see again and again how emotions involve thinking and feeling, perception and action—head and heart.

TAKING PSYCHOLOGY WITH YOU

"LET IT OUT" OR "BOTTLE IT UP"? THE DILEMMA OF ANGER

What do you do when you feel angry? Do you tend to brood and sulk, collecting your righteous complaints like acorns for the winter, or do you erupt, hurling your wrath upon anyone or anything at hand? Do you discuss your feelings when you have calmed down? Does "letting anger out" get rid of it for you, or does it only make it more intense? The answer is crucial for how you get along with your family, neighbors, employers, and strangers.

Chronic feelings of anger and an inability to control anger can be as emotionally devastating and unhealthy as chronic problems with depression, panic, or anxiety (see Chapter 15). In contrast to much pop-psych advice, research shows that expressing anger does not always get it "out of your system"; often, people feel worse after an angry confrontation, both physically and mentally (Bushman, Baumeister, & Stack, 1999; Tavris, 1989). When people talk about their anger or act on that feeling, they tend to rehearse their grievances, create a hostile disposition, and pump up their blood pressure. Conversely, when people learn to control their tempers and express anger constructively, they usually feel better, not worse; calmer, not angrier (Deffenbacher et al., 1996). Charles Darwin (1872/1965) observed this fact more than a century ago. "The free expression by outward signs of an emotion intensifies it," he wrote. "On the other hand, the repression, as far as this is possible, of all outward signs softens our emotions. He who gives way to violent gestures will increase his rage."

When people are feeling angry, they have a choice of doing any number of things. They can write letters, play the piano, jog, bake bread, try to solve the problem that is causing their anger, abuse their friends or family, hit a punching bag, or yell. If a particular action soothes their feelings or gets the desired response from others, they are likely to acquire a habit. Soon that habit feels "natural," as if it could never be changed; indeed, many people justify their violent tempers by saying, "I just couldn't help myself." But they can. If you have learned an abusive or aggressive habit, the research in this chapter offers practical suggestions for relearning constructive ways of managing anger:

■ *Don't sound off in the heat of anger; let bodily arousal cool down.*

Whether your arousal comes from background stresses such as heat, crowds, or loud noise, or from conflict with another person, take time to relax. Time allows you to decide whether you are really angry or just tired and tense. This is the reason for that sage old advice to count to 10, count to 100, or sleep on it. Other cooling-off strategies include taking a time-out in the middle of an argument, meditating or relaxing, and calming yourself with a distracting activity.

■ *Check your perception that you have been insulted for its accuracy.* Could there be another reason for the behavior you find offensive? People who are quick to feel anger tend to interpret other people's actions as intentional offenses. People who are slow to anger tend to give others the benefit of the doubt, and they are not as focused on their own injured pride. Empathy ("Poor guy, he's feeling rotten") is usually incompatible with anger, so practice seeing the situation from the other person's perspective (Miller & Eisenberg, 1988). Also, be sure you understand another person's nonverbal communication before you decide that you have been insulted and get angry. In Stockton, California, a driver used a hand signal to alert a car behind him at a stoplight that his headlights were off. The driver of the second car interpreted this gesture as a sign of disrespect, shot at the first car—and killed a passenger.

■ *If you decide that expressing anger is appropriate, be sure you use the right verbal and nonverbal language to make yourself understood.* Because different cultures have different display rules, be sure the recipient of your anger understands what you are feeling and what complaint you are trying to convey. If your way of expressing anger is to

sulk, expecting everyone else to read your mind and make amends to you, you are not likely to be communicating clearly!

■ *Think carefully about how to express anger so that you will get the results you want.* What do you want your anger to accomplish? Do you just want to make the other person feel bad, or do you want the other person to understand your concerns and make amends? Shouting "You turkey! You dimwit! How *could* you be so stupid!" might accomplish the former goal, but it's not too likely to get the person to apologize—let alone to change his or her behavior. If your goal in expressing anger is to restore your rights, persuade the other person to change in some way, improve a bad situation, or achieve justice, then learning how to express anger so the other person will listen is essential. People who have been the targets of injustice have learned that outbursts of anger may draw society's attention to a problem, but real change requires sustained political effort, challenges to unfair laws, and the use of tactics that persuade rather than alienate the opposition.

Of course, if you just want to blow off steam, go right ahead; but you risk becoming a hothead.

SUMMARY

1. The complex experience of *emotion* involves physiological changes in the brain, face, and autonomic nervous system; cognitive processes; and cultural norms and regulations.

ELEMENTS OF EMOTION 1: THE BODY

2. Some basic facial expressions—anger, fear, sadness, happiness, disgust, surprise, contempt—are widely recognized across cultures. Distinctive facial expressions are apparent in infancy, and infants recognize adult expressions of fear, anger, and happiness. But culture interacts with physiology (according to the *neurocultural theory*) to influence when and how emotions are displayed, as the example of disgust illustrates. Moreover, the interpretation of any expression depends on the context in which it is expressed.

3. Facial expressions probably evolved to foster communication and help us survive, and, as studies of *facial feedback* show, they also help us to identify our own emotional states. Because people can disguise their emotions, however, facial expressions do not always communicate accurately.

4. Many aspects of emotion are associated with specific parts of the brain. Regions of the right hemisphere specialize in recognizing facial expressions and expressing emotions. The right hemisphere seems to be specialized for the experience of negative emotions, the left hemisphere for positive emotions. The *amygdala* is responsible for initially evaluating the emotional importance of incoming sensory information. The *cerebral cortex* provides the cognitive ability to override this initial appraisal.

5. During the experience of any emotion, *epinephrine* and *norepinephrine* produce a state of physiological arousal to prepare the body for an output of energy. But different emotions are also associated with different biochemical responses and different patterns of autonomic nervous system activity.

6. Many efforts have been made to detect guilt and lies by measuring changes in physiological arousal or brain activity. The most popular method is the *polygraph machine*, or "lie detector," but this method has low reliability and validity because there are no patterns of physiological responses specific to lying.

ELEMENTS OF EMOTION 2: THE MIND

7. The *two-factor theory of emotion* held that emotions result from arousal and the labeling or interpretation of that arousal. Research spurred by this theory has investigated the cognitive processes involved in emotion, such as the *attributions* people make about others' behavior and the way people interpret and evaluate events. For example, shame and guilt can be distinguished by the perceptions and beliefs that generate them.

8. Emotion and thinking are not separate, independent processes. Some primitive emotions and conditioned emotional responses can occur without much cognition, but many emotions, such as shame and guilt, depend on higher cognitive processes. Thoughts and emotions also operate reciprocally, each influencing the other. Both processes can be rational or irrational, and both are necessary for making plans and wise decisions.

ELEMENTS OF EMOTION 3: THE CULTURE

9. Some researchers distinguish *primary emotions*, which are thought to be universal, from *secondary emotions*, which include blends and variations that are specific to cultures. The list of primary emotions typically includes fear, anger, sadness, joy, surprise, disgust, and contempt, and sometimes also love. Evidence supporting the existence of primary emotions comes from findings on brain physiology, facial expressions, *emotion prototypes*, and the similarity of situations, the world over, that evoke particular emotions.

10. Other psychologists question efforts to find primary emotions. They doubt that surprise and disgust are true emotions, and they argue that the list of primary emotions omits such universal feelings as empathy, shame, guilt, embarrassment, and pride, which are often difficult to measure through facial expressions or brain activity. Critics of the primary/secondary distinction argue that culture affects every aspect of emotional experience, including which emotions are considered primary.

11. Cultures determine what people feel emotional about, what people do when they feel an emotion, and the *body language* as well as words that they use to express their feelings. The ability to synchronize moods through body language is important for smooth interactions, but may create *emtional contagion*. Cultural *display rules* regulate how, when, and where a person may express or must suppress an emotion. *Emotion work* is the effort a person makes to display an emotion he or she does not feel but feels obliged to convey. Cultural differences in body language, display rules, and emotion work can lead to misunderstandings.

PUTTING THE ELEMENTS TOGETHER: EMOTION AND GENDER

12. Women and men are equally likely to feel a wide array of emotions, from love to anger. Many men seem to be

more physiologically reactive to conflict than women are, however, and the sexes sometimes differ in the perceptions and attributions that generate emotion and emotional intensity. Although women are thought to be better than men at reading another person's emotional state, gender is less important than other factors: whether the two individuals are of the same sex, how well they know each other, the sender's expressiveness, and which person has more power in the situation.

13. Men and women differ primarily in the display rules they follow for expressing emotions, both verbally and nonverbally. In North America, women are more likely to cry and to reveal feelings of fear, sadness, guilt, and loneliness than men are; men are more likely to deny or mask such feelings. These gender differences are in turn affected by gender roles, cultural norms, and the influence of a particular situation. Gender role requirements also often specify different emotion work for the two sexes.

14. The example of gender and emotion shows that to understand the full experience and expression of emotion, we must understand biology, cognitive attributions and perceptions, and cultural rules. Examining just one component gives an incomplete picture.

KEY TERMS

emotion 392

neurocultural theory 393

facial feedback 395

amygdala 397

cerebral cortex 398

epinephrine 398

norepinephrine 398

galvanic skin response (GSR) 399

polygraph ("lie detector") 399

two-factor theory of emotion 401

attributions 402

primary emotions 406

secondary emotions 406

prototypes of emotion 407

display rules 409

body language 410

emotional contagion 410

emotion work 411

LOOKING BACK

- Which facial expressions of emotion do people recognize the world over? (p. 393)

- Which side of your brain is most active when you are feeling elated—or overcome by despair? (pp. 396–397)

- Which little structure in the brain sees to it that you cross the street fast when a truck is headed toward you? (pp. 397–398)

- Which two hormones can make you "too excited to eat"? (p. 398)

- What do "lie detectors" actually detect? (pp. 399–400)

- In a competition, who is likely to be happier, the third-place winner or the second-place winner? (p. 402)

- Why can't an infant feel shame or guilt? (p. 404)

- What is wrong with thinking that thinking is rational and emotion is irrational? (pp. 404–405)

- Are the "basic" emotions basic everywhere? (pp. 406–408)

- Do Germans, Japanese, and Americans always mean the same thing when they smile at others? (p. 409)

- Why do people show sadness at funerals even when they are not feeling sad? (pp. 410–411)

- Do women experience emotions more often than men do? (p. 412)

- What factors other than your sex predict how well you can "read" someone's emotional state? (p. 413)

- What factors other than your sex predict how emotionally expressive you are? (pp. 414–415)

12

MOTIVATION

Just don't give up trying to do what you really want to do.

Where there is love and inspiration, I don't think you can go wrong.

SINGER ELLA FITZGERALD

The movie *Titanic* was a titanic success, partly because many of its loyal viewers saw it more than once. One man told the *Los Angeles Times* that he saw the movie twice and cried both times. "If you didn't," he said, "you may not have a pulse." A 23-year-old teacher, having seen the film a third time, said, "That's the kind of love I want for myself. Now that I know it exists, I'm going to wait for exactly the right man."

Sergeant Major Gene C. McKinney was accused of 18 counts of sexual misconduct and harassment by six servicewomen who had been under his command. McKinney was acquitted of the basic charges; he was reprimanded and demoted one rank but allowed to retain his pension.

All Dian Fossey ever wanted to do was study mountain gorillas. She lived in the wilderness with her beloved gorillas, fought fiercely against the human poachers who were paid to kill or capture the animals, and endured countless hardships and physical assaults. Fossey was eventually murdered by unknown assailants.

What attracts so many women and men to the love story in *Titanic*? What are the reasons for the misunderstandings and sometimes outright war between men and women about sex? And what in the world would motivate a young woman to choose a career that required her to live in a remote mountain world, forgoing all comforts, family, and human love? These are the kinds of questions that motivate psychologists who study motivation.

The word *motivation*, like the word *emotion*, comes from the Latin root meaning "to move," and the psychology of motivation is indeed the study of what moves us, why we do what we do. Emotions move us, but so do many other psychological states. To psychologists, **motivation** refers to any process that causes a person or animal to move *toward* a goal or *away* from an unpleasant situation. The goal may be anything from trying to discover a vaccine for AIDS to escaping a scorpion.

For many decades, the study of motivation was dominated by a focus on biological *drives*, states of tension resulting from the deprivation of physical needs, such as those for food and water. An organism in such a deprived state is motivated to satisfy the need, for example, by eating or drinking. Human beings, however, have only a few primary, unlearned drives, including the need to reduce hunger and thirst and avoid cold and pain. Drive theory could not account for the complexity and variety of human motivations, most of which are psychological or social in nature rather than biological— such as the pursuit of fame or perfect love, the desire to study mountain gorillas, or the determination to be the first to row across the Atlantic Ocean in a dinghy.

Today, therefore, motivation researchers emphasize the fact that people are conscious creatures who think and plan ahead, set goals for themselves, and plot strategies to reach

motivation A process within a person or animal that causes movement toward a goal or away from an unpleasant situation.

need for affiliation The motive to associate with other people, as by seeking friends, companionship, or love.

those goals. In this chapter, we will examine three central areas of human motivation: love, sex, and work. Then we will look at the overall importance of the motives that guide our lives. We will see how happiness, health, and overall well-being are affected by the kinds of goals we set for ourselves, by whether we believe we are able to achieve our goals, and by how we cope when our goals conflict.

WHAT'S AHEAD

● **Why is cuddling so important for infants (and adults, too)?**

● **If you have a 1-year-old, why shouldn't you worry if your baby cries when left with a new babysitter?**

● **Why are some people secure in their love relationships, while others are always anxious and worried that their lovers will abandon them?**

● **Do men and women differ in the ability to love?**

● **How are your beliefs about love affected by your income?**

THE SOCIAL ANIMAL: MOTIVES FOR LOVE

Everybody needs somebody; even Batman has Robin. One of the deepest and most universal of human motives is the **need for affiliation**, the need to be with others, make friends, cooperate, love. Human survival depends on the child's ability to form attachments and learn from others, and on the adult's ability to form relationships with partners, family, friends, and colleagues.

The Need for Attachment

In human beings and other primates, *attachment*—the deep emotional tie to, and sense of almost physical connection with, a loved one—is important all through life. The mother is usually the first and primary object of attachment for an infant, but in many cultures (and other species), babies become just as attached to their fathers, siblings, and grandparents.

Contact Comfort. Emotional attachment begins with physical touching and cuddling between infant and parent. Babies who are given adequate food, water, and warmth, but who are completely deprived of **contact comfort**, the pleasure of being touched and held, develop abnormally and often have serious emotional problems (Bowlby, 1969, 1973). Adults who are "undertouched," such as the sick and the

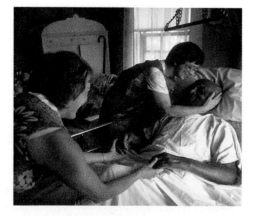

Human beings respond to contact comfort, whether from a cherished pet or the reassuring touch of a caregiver.

 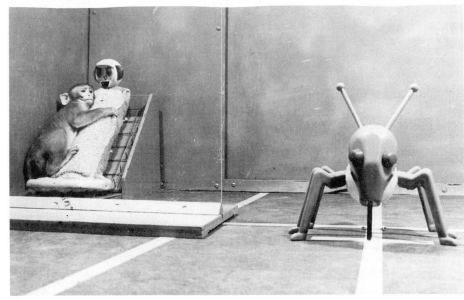

FIGURE 12.1
THE COMFORT OF CONTACT
Infants need cuddling as much as they
need food. In Margaret and Harry Harlow's
studies, infant rhesus monkeys were reared
with a cuddly terry cloth "mother" and
with a bare wire "mother" that provided
milk (left). The infants would cling to the
terry mother when they weren't being fed,
and when they were frightened (as by a
toy spider, right), it was the terry mother
they ran to.

aged, also suffer emotional and physical symptoms. In hospital settings, even the mildest touch by a nurse or physician on the arm, forehead, or shoulder of a sick person reassures and comforts (Field, 1998; Lynch, 1985).

Margaret and Harry Harlow first demonstrated the primate need for contact comfort by raising infant rhesus monkeys with two kinds of artificial mothers (Harlow, 1958; Harlow & Harlow, 1966). The first was a forbidding construction of wires and warming lights, with a milk bottle connected to it. The second was constructed of wire and covered in foam rubber and cuddly terry cloth (see Figure 12.1). At the time, psychologists thought that babies become attached to their mothers because mothers provide food and warmth. But the Harlows' baby monkeys ran to the terry cloth "mother" when they were frightened or startled, and cuddling up to it calmed them down. Human children, too, often seek contact comfort when they are in an unfamiliar situation, are scared by a nightmare, or fall and hurt themselves.

Separation and Security. Once babies are emotionally attached to the mother or other caregiver, separation can be a wrenching experience. Between 7 and 9 months of age, most babies become wary or fearful of strangers. They wail if they are put in an unfamiliar setting or are left with an unfamiliar person. And they show **separation anxiety** if the primary caregiver temporarily leaves them. This reaction usually continues until the middle of the second year, but many children show signs of distress at parental separation until they are about 3 years old. Virtually all children go through this phase, though cultural child-rearing practices influence how strongly the anxiety is felt and how long it lasts (see Figure 12.2).

To determine the nature of the attachment between mothers and babies, Mary Ainsworth (1973, 1979) devised an experimental method called the *Strange Situation.* A mother brings her baby into an unfamiliar room containing lots of toys. After a while a stranger comes in and attempts to play with the child. The mother leaves the baby with the stranger. She then returns, plays with the child, and the stranger leaves. Finally, the mother leaves the baby alone for three minutes and returns. In each case, observers carefully note how the baby behaves with the mother, with the stranger, and when the baby is alone.

contact comfort In primates (including humans), the innate pleasure derived from close physical contact; it is the basis of an infant's first attachment.

separation anxiety The distress that most children develop, at about 7 to 9 months of age, when their primary caregivers temporarily leave them with strangers or in a new situation; it varies according to cultural practices.

FIGURE 12.2
THE RISE AND FALL OF SEPARATION ANXIETY

At around 8 months of age, many babies show separation anxiety when the person who is their main source of attachment tries handing them over to someone else or leaves the room. This anxiety typically peaks at about a year of age and then steadily declines. But the proportion of children responding this way varies across cultures, from a high among rural African children to a low among children raised in a communal Israeli kibbutz, where children become attached to many adults (Kagan, Kearsley, & Zelazo, 1978).

[Graph: Percentage of children who cried following mother's departure (y-axis, 0–100) vs. Age (months) (x-axis, 5–35). Lines for: Rural African (n=25), Antigua, Guatemala (n=36), Israeli kibbutz (n=122), Guatemalan Indian (n=34).]

STYLES OF ATTACHMENT

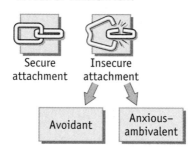

Ainsworth divided children into three categories on the basis of their reactions to the Strange Situation. Some babies are *securely attached*: They cry or protest if the parent leaves the room; they welcome her back and then play happily again; they are clearly more attached to the mother than to the stranger. Other babies are *insecurely attached*, and this insecurity can take two forms. The child may be *avoidant*, not caring if the mother leaves the room, making little effort to seek contact with her on her return, and treating the stranger about the same as the mother. Or the child may be *anxious or ambivalent*, resisting contact with the mother at reunion but protesting loudly if she leaves. Anxious or ambivalent babies may cry to be picked up and then demand to be put down, or they may behave as if they are angry with the mother and resist her efforts to comfort them.

Insecure attachment is an important concern to psychologists because it may lead to emotional and behavioral problems in childhood and even throughout life (Mickelson, Kessler, & Shaver, 1997; Shaw, Keenan, & Vondra, 1994; Speltz, Greenberg, & Deklyen, 1990). What causes it?

What Causes Insecure Attachment? Ainsworth believed that the difference between secure, avoidant, and anxious attachment lies primarily in the way mothers treat their babies in the first year. Mothers who are sensitive and responsive to their babies' needs, she said, create securely attached infants; mothers who are uncomfortable with or insensitive to their babies create insecurely attached infants. To many, the implication was that babies needed the "right kind" of mothering from the very first in order to become securely attached, and that putting a child in daycare would retard or impede this development. Many psychologists agreed with Ainsworth that the mother's treatment of the child is the most important factor in causing secure or insecure attachment—a notion that has caused considerable insecurity among mothers about whether they are doing the right thing!

But the popularized notion that it is entirely up to mothers to create securely attached children turned out to be incorrect. It is true that *extreme* neglect, abuse, and deprivation affect a child's attachment (Bowlby, 1973). However, today we know that differences in *normal* parental child-rearing practices do not affect a child's attachment style; about two-thirds of all children become securely attached under a wide range of parental practices. Maternal "sensitivity" is an important but not even a primary condition of attachment security (De Wolff & van Ijzendoorn, 1997). It does not much matter whether babies are exposed to many adults, either in extended families or in daycare centers, or to few. German babies are frequently left on their own for a few hours at a stretch by mothers who believe that even babies should become self-reliant (Kagan, 1998b). Among the Efe of Africa, babies spend about half their time away from their mothers, in the care of older children and other adults (Tronick, Morelli, & Ivey, 1992). Efe children do not experience the one-on-one intense attachment that Western children do, and they develop a sense of self that is tied more closely to other people and the larger group. Yet, German and Efe children are not insecure and develop normally.

Likewise, time spent in daycare has little or no effect on attachment. In a major study that tracked more than 1,000 children from birth to age 7, children who were in child care 30 hours or more a week, from age 3 months to age 15 months, were compared with children who spent less than 10 hours a week in child care. The two groups did not differ on any measure of attachment (NICHD Early Child Care Research Network, 1997; see also McKim et al., 1999).

Longitudinal studies repeatedly find that good daycare does not affect the security of children's attachments, and indeed often produces many social and cognitive benefits (NICHD Early Child Care Research Network, 1997).

In short, babies develop secure attachments to their caregivers under a wide assortment of conditions and parental practices. What factors, then, other than serious neglect and rejection, *are* related to the development of insecure attachment?

- *The child's temperament and genetic disposition.* Some babies are fearful, insecure, and prone to crying from birth, as we discuss in Chapter 13 (Belsky, Hsieh, & Crnic, 1996; Fox, 1992). In a study of infants in their homes, the children's secure or insecure behavior in the Strange Situation was unrelated to the mother's degree of sensitivity; but it was strongly related to the child's temperament—easygoing or fearful (Seifer et al., 1996).

- *The child's family circumstances.* Infants and young children are likely to shift from secure to insecure attachment if their families are undergoing a period of chronic stress or illness (Belsky et al., 1996).

- *Later stressful events in childhood.* According to a large longitudinal study that followed children from age 1 year to age 18, parental divorce in later childhood was strongly related to insecure attachment and anxiety at age 18; but degree of security in infancy was not (Lewis, 1997).

Insecure attachment, therefore, may result from a child's temperament, family experiences, stressful events, or rejection by parents. Whatever its cause, insecure children are likely to grow into adults who are anxious or avoidant in their own close relationships, as we will see next.

QUICK QUIZ

Are you feeling secure, anxious, or avoidant about quizzes?

1. Melanie is playing happily on a jungle gym at her daycare center when she falls off and badly scrapes her knee. She runs to her caregiver for a consoling cuddle. Melanie seeks _____.

2. A baby left in the Strange Situation does not protest when his mother leaves the room, and he seems to ignore her when she returns. This behavior is said to reflect insecure attachment, but what else could be causing the child's reaction?

Answers:

1. contact comfort 2. the child's own temperament; the child's frequent exposure to other adults; the child's familiarity with being left alone temporarily

Beautiful inside and out, SWF, 35, slender, professional, bright, communicative, sensitive, loving, seeks emotionally and financially secure SMW, 35-45, to share affection, honesty, laughter, friendship, love. Note/Phone/Photo. **(A)**

Successful, attractive, sexy, published/produced writer (books, TV, Village Voice, Playboy), 38, not secretly yearning to be a director. Likes Don Mattingly, KCRW, making waffles and staying out late. Wants successful, interesting and well-read guy who enjoys his career, for dinner dates during world series & possible post season play. Please tell me about yourself. Photo optional. **(B)**

Looking for a permanent best friend/lover, 25-35, with a 3 digit IQ, big heart, skinny legs. Race unimportant. But **MUST** be honest, kind, witty, sensuous, confident, compassionate, adventurous, competent, reliable, and looking for a future with love, sincerity, children and time zone changes. Letter/photo/phone. **(C)**

DESPERATELY SEEKING SUSAN, or Mary, or Evelyn, or Nancy or Lorraine or? **(D)**

Seeking an ugly, overweight, short woman lacking style, intelligence & humor. Hopefully she smokes, is in lousy shape & wouldn't know sensitive if it bit her on the butt. I'm dumpy, balding unattractive & not in my early 30's. I don't work out. I'm stuck in a deadend job, smoke like a chimney & I'm a compulsive liar. Note, photo & phone not necessary. **(E)**

Personals columns show that people define love in many ways. Some have very specific requirements, some are old-fashioned romantics, some just want to fool around, and some will take whatever they can get.

The Varieties of Love

Do you have a favorite love story? Is it one where the couple falls madly in love at first sight, and, after a couple of silly misunderstandings, lives happily ever after (or, as in the case of *Titanic*, one of them dies)? Or is your ideal love story captured by Rhett Butler's concluding remark to Scarlett in *Gone with the Wind*: "Frankly, my dear, I don't give a damn"?

While the need for attachment is universal, the meanings and experiences of love—that most intense of attachments—are more diverse. "How do I love thee? Let me count the ways," wrote Elizabeth Barrett Browning in a love sonnet to Robert Browning. Social scientists have also counted the ways of loving, although not as lovingly as Browning did. Perhaps the oldest distinction is that between *passionate ("romantic") love*, characterized by a turmoil of intense emotions and sexual passion, and *companionate love*, characterized by affection, trust, and stability (Hatfield & Rapson, 1996). But most psychologists who study love—a tough job, but someone's got to do it—think that love comes in more varieties than two. Here are three leading theories about what they are.

The Six Styles of Love. After surveying hundreds of people, John Alan Lee (1973, 1988) proposed that there are six distinct kinds of love, which he labeled with Greek names. Psychologists have empirically validated Lee's work by administering a Love Attitudes Scale to thousands of adults in such ethnically diverse cities as Miami (Hendrick & Hendrick, 1992, 1997) and Toronto (Dion & Dion, 1993). The six "styles" of love that Lee described are:

■ *Eros* (romantic, passionate love). People who score high on eros believe in love at first sight and instant chemistry. They would agree, for example, that "My lover and I were attracted to each other immediately after we first met."

■ *Ludus* (game-playing love). Those who score high on ludic love like to play the game of love with several partners at once. They enjoy the chase more than the catch, agreeing that "I try to keep my lover a little uncertain about my commitment to him or her."

■ *Storge* [STOR-gay] (affectionate, friendly love). Those who score high on storge believe that true love grows out of friendship. They value companionship and trust, and agree that "It is hard for me to say exactly when our friendship turned into love."

■ *Pragma* (logical, pragmatic love). Pragmatic lovers choose partners on the basis of a shopping list of compatible traits. For example, they agree that "I considered what my lover was going to become in life before I committed myself to him or her."

■ *Mania* (possessive, dependent, "crazy" love). People who score high on mania yearn desperately for love but suffer from jealousy and worry when they find it. "When things aren't right with my lover and me," they would agree, "my stomach gets upset."

■ *Agape* [ah-GAH-pay] (unselfish love). Those who score high on agape think of love as a selfless, almost spiritual form of giving to the partner. They will say, "I always try to help my lover through difficult times."

The Triangle Theory of Love. Robert Sternberg (1997) argues that the three ingredients of love are *passion* (euphoria and sexual excitement), *intimacy* (feeling free to talk about anything, feeling close to and understood by the loved one), and

WHAT IS THIS THING CALLED LOVE?

What qualities do you look for in a partner in a close relationship? Write down five qualities that matter most to you: intelligence, looks, sexiness, abilities, background, values, income, whatever. Now examine your list. What does it tell you about your own style of love, according to the theories discussed in the text? If you have a current partner—and have the nerve—ask the person which five qualities he or she regards as most important. Do your lists match?

commitment (needing to be with the other person, being loyal). In this view, varieties of love occur because of the ways people combine the three elements. *Liking* is intimacy alone; *companionate love* is intimacy plus commitment, without passion; *romantic love* is intimacy plus passion, without commitment; *infatuation* is passion alone; *fatuous* (illusory or shallow) *love* is passion plus commitment, without intimacy—like the whirlwind celebrity courtships that end in marriage but generally don't last; and *empty love* is commitment alone, without passion or intimacy. In Sternberg's view, the ideal or *consummate* form of love combines all three elements: passion, closeness, and the secure attachment that comes from commitment.

When people are asked to define the key ingredients of love, most do agree that love is a mix of passion, intimacy, and commitment (Aron & Westbay, 1996). However, in most relationships, over the years, romantic passion subsides and intimacy increases. Intimacy is based on deep knowledge of the other person, which accumulates gradually and thus needs time to reach a maximum degree of closeness; but passion is based on emotion, which is generated by novelty and change. That is why passion is usually highest at the beginning of a relationship, when two people begin to disclose things about themselves to each other, and lowest when knowledge of the other person's beliefs and habits is at its maximum—when it seems that there is nothing left to learn about your beloved. The negative correlation between passion and intimacy explains why passion is often reawakened when a couple is separated or unexpected crises occur, or when the couple is discovering fresh sources of intimacy, such as new shared activities and exciting experiences (Baumeister & Bratslavsky, 1999).

The Attachment Theory of Love. The theory that has generated the most research and interest, by far, is one that relates adult styles of love to types of infant attachment. According to Phillip Shaver and Cindy Hazan (1993), adults, just like

JUMP START reprinted by permission of United Feature Syndicate, Inc.

babies, can be secure, avoidant, or anxious-ambivalent in their attachments. Securely attached lovers are, well, secure: They are rarely jealous or worried about being abandoned. Anxious or ambivalent lovers are always fretting about their relationships; they want to be close but worry that their partners will leave them. Other people often describe them as "clingy," which may be why they are more likely than secure lovers to suffer from unrequited love (Aron, Aron, & Allen, 1998). Avoidant people distrust and avoid intimate attachments.

In this view, people acquire their attachment styles in large part from how their parents cared for them. Starting in infancy and childhood, people form internal, "working models" of relationships: Can I trust others? Am I worthy of being loved? Will my beloved leave me? If a child's parents were cold and rejecting and provided little or no contact comfort, that is how the child learns to expect other relationships will be. If children form secure attachments to trusted parents, they become more trusting of others (Levy, Blatt, & Shaver, 1998).

"My preference is for someone who's afraid of closeness, like me."

An avoidant lover in action.

According to a large, nationally representative survey of American adults, the distribution of the three basic styles of attachment among adults is very similar to that found for infants: about 59 percent secure, 25 percent avoidant, and 11 percent anxious. Further, the kind of relationships that people have as adults is strongly related to their reports of how their parents treated them (Mickelson, Kessler, & Shaver, 1997). Securely attached adults report having had warm, close relationships with their parents. Although they recognize their parents' flaws, they describe their parents as having been more benevolent and kind than insecurely attached people do. Anxious-ambivalent people report feeling more ambivalence toward their parents, especially their mothers, and also describe their parents ambivalently—as having been both punitive and kind. And people with an avoidant attachment style describe their parents in almost entirely negative terms, as having been punitive and malevolent (Levy, Blatt, & Shaver, 1998). Avoidant individuals are most likely to report having had cold, rejecting parents, extended periods of separation from their mothers, or childhood environments that prevented them from forming close ties with others (Feeney & Noller, 1990; Hazan & Shaver, 1994).

Childhood attachment styles carry over into adulthood and remain quite stable. The avoidant style is particularly resistant to change, because people who are busy avoiding one another never learn to trust someone long enough to become securely attached. In a longitudinal study that followed a sample of women from ages 21 to 52, avoidant women had a history of troubled and unstable relationships. They tended to be defensive, distrustful, and emotionally distant from others (Klohnen & Bera, 1998). However, even avoidant or anxiously attached people can have successful, stable relationships if they find securely attached partners who will put up with their insecurities (Kirkpatrick & Davis, 1994; Koski & Shaver, 1997).

Keep in mind, however, that people's self-reports about their parents or childhoods may be influenced more by their *current* perceptions of their parents rather than by how the parents actually treated them. Also, as we noted earlier, the child's own temperament may account for the consistency of attachment styles, as well as for the "working models" of relationships that the child forms. Certainly some parents are cold, punitive, and rejecting. But a temperamentally fearful and avoidant child may reject even a kind parent's efforts to console and cuddle, and eventually come to believe that all relationships are untrustworthy.

Gender, Culture, and Love

Gender stereotypes tell us that men are more ludic and avoidant than women, and that women are more romantic and anxious than men; but like all stereotypes, these oversimplify. What are the true gender differences—and similarities?

Gender Differences. To begin with, neither sex loves more than the other in terms of "love at first sight," manic (possessive) love, erotic (passionate) love, selfless love, or companionate love over the long haul (Dion & Dion, 1993; Fehr, 1993; Hatfield & Rapson, 1996). Both sexes suffer when a love relationship ends, if they did not want it to.

However, women and men do differ, on average, in how they *express* love. Males in many cultures learn early that revelations of affection can be construed as evidence of vulnerability and weakness, which are considered unmasculine (see Chapter 11). Thus, men often develop ways of expressing love that differ from women's. In contemporary Western societies, many women express feelings of love in words, whereas many men express these feelings in actions—doing things for the partner, supporting the family financially, or just sharing the same activity, such as watching TV or a basketball game together (Baumeister & Bratslavsky, 1999; Cancian, 1987; Gilmore, 1990). Similarly, many women tend to define "intimacy" as shared revelations of feelings; but many men define intimacy as being together comfortably.

Cultural Origins of Gender Differences. Gender differences in ways of expressing love and intimacy do not just pop up from nowhere; they reflect social, economic, and cultural forces. For example, for many years Western men were more romantic than women in their choice of partner, and women in turn were far more pragmatic than men. One reason was that a woman did not just marry a man; she married a standard of living. Therefore, she could not afford to marry someone "unsuitable" or waste her time in a relationship that was "not going anywhere," even if she loved him. In contrast, a man could afford to be sentimental in his choice of partner. In the 1960s, two-thirds of a sample of college men said they would not marry someone they did not love, but only one-fourth of the women ruled out the possibility (Kephart, 1967).

As women entered the workforce and as two incomes became necessary in most families, however, the gender difference in romantic love waned and so did pragmatic reasons for marriage, *all over the world.* Nowadays, in every developed and developing nation, east and west, only tiny numbers of women and men would consider marrying someone who had all the "right" qualities if they were not in love with the person. Pragmatic reasons for marriage persist only in economically underdeveloped countries, such as India and Pakistan, where the extended family still controls the rules of marriage (Hatfield & Rapson, 1996).

As you can see, our beliefs about love, and the kind of love we feel, are influenced by the culture we live in, the historical era that shapes us, and something as unromantic as economic self-sufficiency. How do these influences affect your own style of love?

Love Stories and Their Consequences

The three theories of love that we have described use different terms, but all agree that people define and experience love in diverse ways (see Review 12.1). Perhaps, then, when someone says "I love you," you should ask, "What, exactly, do you mean by that?" We are kidding, but only half

DEFINE YOUR TERMS
In popular culture, people often define love as a "Titanic" romantic passion. What are the consequences of defining love that way? What other definitions might lead to greater satisfaction in a relationship over time?

THEORIES OF LOVE COMPARED

 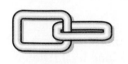 

	The Six Styles of Love	Attachment Theory	Triangle Theory
Definitions of love	A philosophy or an experience	An expression of the need for attachment that begins in infancy	Passion, intimacy, and commitment, in varying combinations
Types of love	Romantic (eros)	—	Romantic (passion + intimacy)
	Game-playing (ludus)	Avoidant	Infatuation (passion only)
	Possessive (mania)	Anxious-ambivalent	Fatuous (passion + commitment)
	Affectionate (storge)	Secure	Companionate (intimacy + commitment)
	Pragmatic (pragma)	Secure	Empty (commitment only)
	Unselfish (agape)	Secure	Liking (intimacy only)
	—	—	Consummate (passion + intimacy + commitment)

kidding. No one wants to interrogate a person who has just made a heartfelt declaration of love. Yet, as research on the motives for love repeatedly finds, the way we define love, and the love stories we choose to guide our lives, deeply affect our satisfaction with relationships—and even whether relationships last. For example, if you believe that love "just happens," that you have no control over it, that love is defined exclusively by sexual passion and emotion, then you may decide you are "out of love" when the initial passion fades.

Many people assume that critical thinking and love are mutually exclusive: If you are thinking critically about love, you kill the emotion; and if you are in love, you stop thinking altogether! But many psychologists and philosophers believe that the best kind of love depends on thinking critically. Philosopher Robert Solomon (1994) has argued that "We conceive of [love] falsely—as a feeling, as novelty, as bound up with youth and beauty. . . . We expect an explosion at the beginning powerful enough to fuel love through all of its ups and downs instead of viewing love as a process over which we have control, a process that tends to increase with time rather than wane."

"Love is blind" so poets say,
But love was wide awake to-day,
For he stole my heart away.

Many people think that love strikes like Cupid's arrow—suddenly and mysteriously, out of the blue. What are the benefits and drawbacks of this popular view of love?

Yet, the most popular love stories in Western culture are almost always about the initial "explosion" and not the ensuing, sustaining affection and intimacy. What would have happened to the young couple in *Titanic* if the ship had not gone down? Would they have been as happy clearing the table together and diapering the kids as they were in the swanky salons of a luxury liner? Would the original flame of passion have left a satisfying afterglow, or burned to ashes? Perhaps a little critical thinking about the long-term nature of love, far from killing it, can make it a truer and richer experience.

QUICK QUIZ

Are you passionately committed to quizzes yet?

1. Of Lee's six styles of loving, which kind does each of the following examples illustrate?
   a. The nineteenth-century historian Thomas Carlyle and his friend Jane Welsh enjoy exchanging ideas and confidences for years before realizing they love each other.
   b. In choosing his last four wives, Henry VIII makes sure they are likely to bear children and are of suitably high status for his court.
   c. Romeo and Juliet think only of each other and hate to be separated for even an hour.
   d. Casanova tries to seduce every woman he meets for the thrill of the conquest.

2. Tiffany is wildly in love with Timothy, and he with her, but she can't stop worrying about him and doubting his love. She wants to be with him constantly, but often she feels jealous and pushes him away. According to the attachment theory of love, which style of attachment does Tiffany have? In terms of the six styles of love, which style does she have?

Answers:

1. a. friendship (storge)   b. pragmatic love (pragma)   c. romantic, passionate love (eros)   d. game-playing love (ludus)
2. anxious-ambivalent; mania

WHAT'S AHEAD

- Which part of the anatomy do psychologists think is the "sexiest sex organ"?
- How do the sexual rules for heterosexual couples foster misunderstandings?
- Can psychological theories about "smothering mothering" or absent fathers explain why some men are gay?

THE EROTIC ANIMAL: MOTIVES FOR SEX

Most people believe that sex is a matter of doing what comes naturally, a biological drive like hunger. In fact, people often use the same words in describing food and sex: "She has a strong sexual appetite," someone will say, or "I'm lusting for a hamburger." But social scientists do not agree on whether human sexuality is a primary drive or even whether it is a drive at all. After all, a person will not live long without food and water, but people can survive their whole lives without sex.

In lower species, sexual behavior is genetically programmed. Without instruction, a male stickleback fish knows exactly what to do with a female stickleback, and a whooping crane knows when to whoop. But as sex researcher Leonore Tiefer (1995) has observed, for human beings "sex is not a natural act." People have to learn from experience and culture what they are supposed to do with their sexual desires and how they are expected to behave sexually (Laumann & Gagnon, 1995). Human sexuality is a blend of biological, psychological, and cultural factors.

The Biology of Desire

How much of sexual motivation is influenced by physiology? Some, although not as much as you may think. Nevertheless, biological researchers have made a major contribution to our understanding of sexual motivation by sweeping away the cobwebs of superstition and ignorance about how the body works. They have disproved the idea that the sexes are physically opposite and have documented the capacity for sexual arousal, orgasm, and pleasure in both sexes.

Hormones and Sexual Response. One biological factor that seems to promote sexual desire in both sexes is the hormone testosterone. The role of testosterone has been documented in studies of male sex offenders who have been given synthetic hormones that suppress the production of testosterone; of men who have abnormally low testosterone levels; of women who have taken androgens after having their ovaries removed; and of women who kept diaries of their sexual activity while also having their hormone levels periodically measured (Bradford & Pawlak, 1993; Carani et al., 1992; Sherwin, 1988, 1998b).

However, hormones do not "cause" sexual behavior, or any other behavior, in a simple, direct way, even though some pop-psych books claim they do. Testosterone may be of benefit to women who have unusually low levels of it, as might occur if their ovaries were removed, but for most women psychological factors influence sexual desire far more than hormone levels do (Bancroft et al., 1991). Conversely, sex offenders who are chemically castrated when they take a medication that suppresses production of testosterone do not

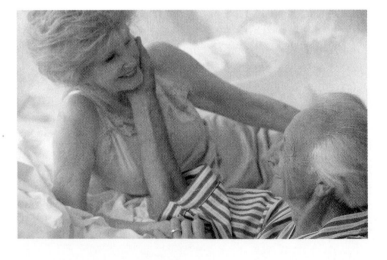

Desire and sensuality are lifelong pleasures.

always lose their sexual desires. Moreover, hormones and behavior are a two-way street: Testosterone contributes to sexual arousal, but sexual activity also produces higher levels of testosterone (Sapolsky, 1997).

Arousal and Orgasm. Physiological research has dispelled a lot of nonsense written about female sexuality. Freud, for example, believed that when women reach puberty, their locus of sexual sensation shifts from the "childish" clitoris to the "mature" vagina, and women can then have healthy "vaginal" orgasms instead of immature "clitoral" orgasms. (Freud's theory was at least an improvement on the Victorian notion, still held in some cultures, that normal or "good" women don't have orgasms at all.) Freudian ideas caused countless women to worry that they were mentally disturbed or sexually repressed if they were not having the correct kind of orgasm (Ehrenreich, 1978).

The first modern attack on these beliefs came from Alfred Kinsey and his associates (1948, 1953), in their pioneering books on male and female sexuality. In *Sexual Behavior in the Human Female*, they observed that "males would be better prepared to understand females, and females to understand males, if they realized that they are alike in their basic anatomy and physiology." For example, the penis and the clitoris develop from the same embryonic tissues; they differ in size, of course, but not in sensitivity.

The idea that men and women are sexually similar was extremely shocking and progressive in 1953. At that time many people believed that women were not as sexually motivated as men, that orgasm was not as important to women, that female sexuality was more "diffuse" than male sexuality, and that women cared more about affection than sexual satisfaction. Yet, Kinsey also tended to attribute the sex differences he did find, such as in frequency of masturbation and orgasm, primarily to biology—specifically, to women's supposedly lesser sexual capacity. Although he acknowledged throughout his books that women are taught to avoid, dislike, or feel ambivalent about sex, he did not connect these psychological messages with women's physiological responses.

Kinsey's survey findings were replicated and expanded in the 1960s in the laboratory research of physician William Masters and his associate Virginia Johnson (1966). In studies of physiological changes during sexual arousal and orgasm, they confirmed that male and female arousal and orgasms are indeed remarkably similar and that all orgasms are physiologically the same, regardless of the source of stimulation. But Masters and Johnson disagreed with Kinsey's assertion that women have a lesser sexual capacity than men. On the contrary, they argued, women's capacity for sexual response "infinitely surpasses that of men" because a woman, unlike most men, is physiologically able to have repeated orgasms until exhaustion or a persistent telephone makes her stop.

Masters and Johnson's work, like Kinsey's, had limitations (Tiefer, 1995). Perhaps the most serious one was that Masters and Johnson did not do research to learn how sexual response might vary among individuals according to age, experience, and culture. They accepted as research subjects only those volunteers who met their predetermined notions of normalcy—for instance, who were readily orgasmic. But not all women, or even all men, are easily orgasmic, let alone multiply orgasmic.

In addition, Masters and Johnson assumed that a person's *physiological* responses would be indications of the *subjective* experience of desire and arousal, but this is not always the case (Irvine, 1990). For example, vaginal lubrication is not always a sign of arousal; it is sometimes a response to nervousness, excitement, disgust, or fear. Similarly, a man's erection is not always due to sexual stimulation; a man can also have an erection as a response to fear, anger, or exercise.

Thus, sexual desire and behavior cannot be reduced simply to the physiological responses of the body. Nonetheless, research on human sexual physiology has swept away a lot of superstitions and myths about sex.

The Psychology of Desire

Psychologists are fond of observing that the sexiest sex organ is the brain, where perceptions begin. People's values, expectations, fantasies, and beliefs profoundly affect sexual desire and behavior. That is why a touch on the knee by an exciting new date feels terrifically sexy, but the same touch by a creepy stranger on a bus feels disgusting. It is why a distracting thought can kill sexual arousal in a second, and a fantasy can be more erotic than reality. And it is why people who are "thinking too much" during sex play—for example, who are worrying about how they look or whether they are doing the wrong thing—may have difficulty letting go and yielding to sexual sensations.

The Many Motives for Sex.　To most people, the primary motives for sex are pretty obvious: to enjoy the pleasure of it, to express love and intimacy, or to make babies. But there are other motives too, not all of them so positive. In a series of studies of several hundred college students and more than 1,500 older adults, psychologists identified six factors underlying the many reasons that people give for having sex (Cooper, Shapiro, & Powers, 1998). These factors are:

- *Enhancement:* having sex for the emotional satisfaction or physical pleasure of it.
- *Intimacy:* having sex to feel emotionally close to the partner.
- *Coping:* having sex to cope with negative emotions and disappointments.
- *Self-affirmation:* having sex to be reassured of one's attractiveness or desirability.
- *Partner approval:* having sex to please or appease one's partner (e.g., to avoid the partner's anger or rejection).
- *Peer approval:* having sex to impress one's friends, be part of the group, and conform to what "everyone else" seems to be doing.

There are many motivations for sex, including financial gain and physical lust, intimacy and love, and joyful playfulness.

In this research, men and women did not differ in their motives for intimacy, but men more strongly endorsed all the other motives, especially peer approval. The older that people were, the more likely they were to have sex for intimacy and for self-enhancement (pleasure), and the less likely they were to have sex for peer or partner approval. White adolescents more strongly endorsed intimacy motives than black adolescents did, and black teenagers more strongly endorsed coping and peer-pressure motives.

People's motives for having sex affect many aspects of their sexual behavior, including whether they engage in sex in the first place, whether they enjoy it, whether they have unprotected or otherwise risky sex, and whether they have few or many partners. Coping and approval motives are most strongly associated with risky sexual behavior, including having many partners and not using effective birth control, and also with having more unplanned pregnancies (Cooper, Shapiro, & Powers, 1998).

Many studies of college students find that large numbers of women *and* men are having sex not for pleasure or intimacy, but because of feelings of inadequacy or peer pressure. In one survey of nearly a thousand college students, fully two-thirds of the men reported having had unwanted intercourse (Muehlenhard & Cook, 1988). The main reasons for doing so, the men said, were peer pressure, inexperience, a desire for popularity, and a fear of seeming homosexual or "unmasculine." Women too said they "gave in," but for different reasons: because it was easier than having an argument; because they didn't want to lose the relationship; because they felt obligated, once the partner had spent time and money on them; or because the partner made them feel guilty.

Sexual Coercion and Rape. One of the most persistent differences in the sexual experiences of women and men has to do with their perceptions of, and experiences with, sexual coercion. In a nationally representative survey of more than 3,000 Americans ages 18 to 59, nearly one-fourth of the women said that a man—usually a husband or boyfriend—had forced them to do something sexually that they did not want to do (Laumann et al., 1994). But only about 3 percent of the men said they had ever forced a woman into a sexual act. Obviously, what many women regard as coercion is not always seen as coercive by men. Among Canadian and American university students, too, men are far more likely than women to admit coercing a partner into sex—using alcohol or other drugs, or threats of physical force (O'Sullivan, Byers, & Funkelman, 1988). Such men tend to have a set of attitudes and misperceptions that justify their behavior: They misperceive women's behavior in social situations, equate feelings of power with sexuality, regard women as being entirely responsible for whatever happens to them, and tend to have coercive sexual fantasies (Drieschner & Lange, 1999).

The most extreme form of sexual coercion, of course, is rape. Although the public image of the rapist tends to be one of a menacing stranger, in most cases the rapist is known to the victim. They may have dated once or a few times; they may have been friends for years; they may even be married (Koss, 1993; Russell, 1990). According to a representative survey of more than 4,000 women in the United States, 14 percent of all American women have been the victims of forcible rape at least once in their lives, most by men they knew; only 22 percent of rape victims were assaulted by strangers (National Victim Center, 1992). The survey did not include men; children and teenagers under age 18; women in college residences, prisons, or the military; or homeless women. So the percentage of people who have been raped is undoubtedly even higher (Koss, 1993; Merrill et al., 1998).

What motivates some men to rape? For many, the answer is peer approval. College men who have physically coerced their dates into having sex have often been

Many people define "rape" as an act of sexual violence committed by a stranger, but more often the perpetrator is a woman's husband, boyfriend, or casual date. Many colleges are taking steps to educate students about acquaintance rape, for example, by producing posters like this one for women. What kind of poster would you write, directed to men?

Women don't cause acquaintance rape. Rapists do.

But there are things you can do to reduce the risks of being raped by someone you know.

1 STAY away from men who: put you down a lot, talk negatively about women, think that "girls who get drunk should know what to expect," drink or use drugs heavily, are physically violent, don't respect you or your decisions.

2 SET sexual limits and intentions. Communicate them early and firmly.

3 DON'T pretend you don't want to have sex if you really do.

4 STAY sober.

5 DON'T make men guess what you want. Tell them.

6 REMAIN in control. Pay your own way. Make some of the decisons.

7 LISTEN to your feelings.

8 FORGET about being a "nice girl" as soon as you feel threatened.

9 LEARN self-defense. Know how to yell. Take assertiveness training.

10 TAKE care of yourself. Don't assume others will.

For more information, please phone 893-3778. A service of the Women's Center and Police Department, University of California, Santa Barbara.

pressured by male friends, since early adolescence, to prove their masculinity by "scoring" (Kanin, 1985). For other men who rape, the motive is anger, revenge, or a desire to dominate; by its very nature, rape is an act of hostility that reflects a devaluing and dehumanizing of the victim. Sexually aggressive males are characterized by a cluster of traits: insecurity, defensiveness, hostility toward women and a wish to control them, and a preference for promiscuous, impersonal sex (Drieschner & Lange, 1999; Malamuth et al., 1995). Convicted rapists have a mixture of even more disturbed motives: anger at women or the world, a need for power, contempt for women, a desire to act out a sexual fantasy, and sometimes sexual sadism (Knight, Prentky, & Cerce, 1994).

The argument that rape is primarily an act of dominance and aggression is also supported by the widespread evidence of soldiers who rape captive women during war, and then often kill them (Olujic, 1998). These motives also occur in the rape of men by other men, usually by anal penetration (King & Woollett, 1997). This form of rape typically occurs in youth gangs, where the intention is to humiliate rival gang members, and in prison, where again the motive is to conquer and degrade the victim.

Perhaps you can see that the answer to the question "Why do people have sex?" is not obvious after all, and by no means a simple matter of biology. In addition to intimacy, pleasure, procreation, and love, psychological motives include intimidation and dominance, insecurity, appeasing the partner, need for reassurance, and approval from peers.

The Culture of Desire

Think about kissing. Westerners like to think about kissing, and to do it, too. But if you think kissing is natural, try to remember your first serious kiss—and all you had to learn about noses, breathing, and position of teeth and tongue. The sexual kiss is so complicated that some cultures have never even gotten around to it. They think that kissing another person's mouth—the very place that food enters!—is disgusting (Tiefer, 1995). Others have elevated the sexual kiss to high art; why do you suppose one version is called "French" kissing?

Cultural Variations in Sexuality. As the kiss illustrates, having the physical equipment to perform a sexual act is not all there is to sexual behavior. People have to learn, from cultural norms, peers, and parental lessons, what is supposed to "turn them on" (and off), which parts of the body and which activities are erotic (or repulsive), and even how to have sexual relations (Laumann & Gagnon, 1995).

The range of cultural variations in sexuality is remarkable. To men of the Victorian era, the sight of an ankle, let alone an entire leg, was highly arousing; to men of the modern era, an ankle doesn't do it. In some cultures, oral sex is regarded as a bizarre sexual deviation; in others, it is not only considered normal but also supremely desirable. And in some cultures, sex is seen as something joyful and beautiful, an art to be cultivated as one might cultivate the skill of gourmet cooking; in others, it is considered ugly and dirty, an act to be "gotten through" as quickly as possible.

Sexual Scripts. How do cultures transmit their rules and requirements about sex to their members? During childhood and adolescence, people learn their culture's *gender roles*—collections of rules that determine the proper attitudes and behavior for men and women, sexual and otherwise (see Chapter 8). Just as an actor in the role of Hamlet needs a script to learn his part, a person following a gender role needs

ANALYZE ASSUMPTIONS

Many people assume that sex is a matter of "doing what comes naturally"—that all sexual behavior, including kissing, is caused by a simple physiological drive. What evidence disputes this common assumption?

Kissing is a learned skill—one that some people start practicing earlier than others.

IS THE DOUBLE STANDARD STILL ALIVE?

Think of all the words you know to describe a sexually active woman, and then think of words for a sexually active man. Is one list longer than the other? Are the two lists equally negative or positive in their connotations? What does this exercise tell you about the survival of the double standard and your culture's sexual scripts?

a **sexual script** that teaches men and women how to behave in sexual matters (Gagnon & Simon, 1973; Laumann & Gagnon, 1995). Are women supposed to be sexually adventurous and assertive or sexually modest and passive? Are old people supposed to be sexually active or "past all that"? The answers differ from culture to culture, as members act in accordance with the sexual scripts for their gender and age.

In many parts of the world, boys acquire their attitudes about sex in a competitive atmosphere where the goal is to impress other males, and they talk and joke about masturbation and other sexual experiences with their friends (Laumann & Gagnon, 1995). While boys are learning to value physical sex, however, many girls are learning to value relationships and to make themselves attractive. They learn that their role is to be sexually desirable (which is good), but not to indulge in their own sexual pleasures (which would be bad). One psychologist summarized the different sexual scripts that boys and girls learn as "'Nice women' don't say yes and 'real men' don't say no" (Muehlenhard, 1988). Does this describe the script your own culture has written for you? If not, what are your culture's sexual rules?

In North America, the sexual scripts for heterosexual couples are almost guaranteed to create conflicting motives for sexuality and misreadings of one another's behavior. For example, what is a sexual signal? How do you know whether a person is conveying sexual interest in you? Men and women often answer these questions differently (Baumeister & Bratslavsky, 1999). A woman might dress in tight clothes and a short skirt with the intention of looking attractive, but a man may interpret her dress and demeanor as indicating sexual interest. In a study of 400 teenagers ages 14 to 17, boys generally thought that almost *everything* was a sexual signal! They were more likely to regard tight clothing, situations such as being alone in a room, and affectionate actions (such as a girl's playing with her date's hair or gazing into his eyes) as signs of willingness for sex. The girls were more likely to regard tight clothing as a sign of being fashionable, and being alone with a date or behaving affectionately as signs of—well, affection (Zellman & Goodchilds, 1983).

Gay men and lesbians follow sexual scripts, too. In terms of number of sexual partners, sexual behavior, and acceptance of casual sex, gay men are generally similar to heterosexual men and lesbians are similar to heterosexual women. But lesbians and gay men tend to be more innovative than heterosexuals in establishing rules for their relationships. Their scripts are more open and flexible than heterosexual dating and sexual scripts, because neither partner is clearly the pursuer or the pursued or the one who makes the sexual overtures (Peplau & Spalding, 2000; Rose, Zand, & Cini, 1993).

The Origins of Sexual Attitudes. Finally, where do sexual scripts and gender differences in sexual motives and behavior come from? As we saw in Chapter 3, evolutionary psychologists and sociobiologists think that evolutionary processes such as

Is she dressing provocatively or comfortably? Boys and girls often disagree on the answer.

sexual scripts Scenarios that specify proper sexual behavior for a person in a given situation, varying with the person's age, culture, and gender.

Economic and social changes are transforming gender roles in all developed nations. But marriage for financial security is still the only option for many women from impoverished nations—like this bride, whose husband chose her from a mail-order catalogue.

natural selection best account for gender differences in courtship and mating practices. These processes, they say, explain why men often pressure women for sex, women tend to reject casual sex, and women "give in" and men "make a move" when they do not really want to (Buss, 1994; Oliver & Hyde, 1993). Certainly, one key biological difference has always affected sexual attitudes and behavior: the fact that only one sex gets pregnant.

Social and cultural psychologists, however, maintain that most of the differences between women and men are a result of gender roles, which in turn reflect a culture's economic and social arrangements. When those arrangements change, so do people's attitudes and behavior, as we saw in the case of love. Throughout history and across cultures, whenever women have needed marriage to ensure their social and financial security, they have regarded sex as a bargaining chip, an asset to be rationed rather than an activity to be enjoyed for its own sake (Hatfield & Rapson, 1996). A woman cannot afford to casually seek and enjoy sex if that means risking an unwanted pregnancy, the security of marriage, her reputation in society, or her physical safety. When women become self-supporting and able to control their own fertility, however, they are more likely to want sex for pleasure rather than as a means to another goal.

All over the world, as industrialization and modernization are transforming gender roles, the sexual behavior of women and men is indeed becoming more alike (Laumann et al., 1994). Although this transformation is slow and uneven, and although change always brings protest and confusion in its wake, social scientists have documented a growing endorsement, worldwide, of birth control, sexual freedom in general, and of the entitlement of both sexes to love and sexual pleasure (Hatfield & Rapson, 1996).

The Riddle of Sexual Orientation

Why do some people become heterosexual, others homosexual, and still others bisexual? Although same-sex sexual behavior has existed throughout history, the words *homosexual* and *heterosexual* were not even invented until the late nineteenth century (Katz, 1995). Only then did homosexuality become a "problem" to be studied, an entity distinct from heterosexuality.

Psychological Versus Biological Explanations. Many social scientists believe that sexual orientation must have a biological basis because exclusively *psychological* theories of homosexuality (or heterosexuality) have never been supported. Homosexuality is not a result of having a "smothering mother," an absent father, or emotional problems, as was once thought. It is not caused by same-sex sexual play in childhood or adolescence, which is actually quite common.

Nor is sexual orientation related to parental practices or role models. Most gay men recall that they rejected the typical "boy" role and boys' toys and games from a very early age, in spite of enormous pressures from their parents and peers to conform to the traditional male role (Bailey & Zucker, 1995). Conversely, the overwhelming majority of children of gay parents do not become gay (Bell, Weinberg, & Hammersmith, 1981; Patterson, 1992). In a study of 82 adult sons of 55 gay men, more than 90 percent of the sons were heterosexual, and gay and heterosexual sons did not differ in the length of time they had lived with their fathers, or in any other childhood experiences (Bailey et al., 1995).

Many researchers believe that sexual orientation is largely determined by genetics or prenatal exposure to androgens, which in turn affect certain neural structures in the brain (Bailey & Pillard, 1995; Gladue, 1994). The evidence so far, however, is inconclusive. A few studies of gay men have reported associations between sexual orientation and very specific areas of the brain (Allen & Gorski, 1992; LeVay, 1991). These studies got lots of press, but they have not been replicated (Byne, 1995). Other studies have suggested that female babies who were accidentally exposed in the womb to masculinizing hormones—androgens or other chemicals—are more likely than other girls to become bisexual or lesbian (Collaer & Hines, 1995; Meyer-Bahlburg et al., 1995). However, the vast majority of "androgenized" women are not more likely to become lesbians, and most lesbians were not exposed to atypical prenatal hormones (Peplau et al., 2000).

There is some evidence that sexual orientation is moderately heritable, particularly in men (Bailey & Pillard, 1995; Whitam, Diamond, & Martin, 1993). Two genetic linkage studies of gay brothers found a shared stretch of DNA on the X chromosome in most of these pairs, a rate significantly above what one would expect in siblings by chance (Hamer et al., 1993; Hu et al., 1995). However, a later study of 52 pairs of gay brothers did not replicate this finding (Rice et al., 1999). In addition, the vast majority of gay men and lesbians do *not* have a close gay relative, and their siblings, including twins, are overwhelmingly likely to be heterosexual (Peplau et al., 2000). So we are left with a real puzzle.

One problem with trying to find "the" origin of sexual orientation is that sexual identity and behavior take many different forms. Many people are neither exclusively homosexual nor exclusively heterosexual; others are heterosexual in behavior but have homosexual fantasies (Baumrind, 1995; Byne, 1995). In some cultures, boys go through a homosexual phase that they do not define as homosexual and that does not affect their future relations with women. In the Sambian society of Papua New Guinea, for example, adolescent males are required to engage in oral sex with older men as part of their initiation into manhood; it is believed that a boy cannot mature unless he ingests another man's semen for several years. But all Sambian boys eventually marry women (Herdt, 1984). In Lesotho, in Africa, women have intimate relations with other women, including passionate kissing and oral sex, but the women do not define these acts as sexual, as they do when a man is the partner (Kendall, 1999).

Genetics cannot account for such customs, nor can genetics explain the flexible sexual histories of most lesbians. Some lesbians do have an exclusively same-sex orientation their whole lives, but many others have sex with the person they fall in love with, regardless of his or her gender, rather than loving someone only of one sex (Kitzinger & Wilkinson, 1995; Peplau et al., 2000).

In most relationships, whether gay or straight, people seek the pleasures of love, family, and companionship.

At present, therefore, the most reasonable conclusions may be that sexual identity and behavior involve an interaction of biology, cultural norms, and experiences; that the routes to homosexual orientation are likely to be different for males and females; and that the origins of sexual orientation may differ among individuals (Gladue, 1994; Patterson, 1995).

Homosexuality and Politics. What is your response to these findings? Your reactions are probably affected by your feelings about homosexuality and gay rights. Many gay men and lesbians welcome biological research on the grounds that it supports what they have been saying all along: Sexual orientation is not a matter of choice, but a fact of nature. Others fear that people who are prejudiced against homosexuals will use this research to argue that gay people have a biological "defect" that should be eradicated or "corrected." But people who are hostile to homosexuals will use any theory, biological or psychological, to justify their wish to eliminate homosexuality (Burke, 1996). For example, they have used learning theories to argue, mistakenly, that "if it's learned, it can be unlearned."

In any case, the *scientific* question of the origins of sexual orientation is logically unrelated to *political and moral* questions of the rights of gay men and lesbians (Strickland, 1995). In a democracy, civil rights do not depend on whether one's beliefs or practices are a matter of choice, nor do they depend on how popular those beliefs are. A person's religion is not biologically inherited, yet America and Canada guarantee freedom of religion to everyone—whether your religion is shared by 75 percent of the population or 2 percent.

Research on sexuality can be used for many contradictory purposes and political goals, depending on the values and attitudes of the popular culture in which such findings emerge. As long as a society is uncomfortable about homosexuality, preconceptions and prejudice are likely to cloud its reactions to anything that psychologists learn about it.

THINKING CRITICALLY

AVOID EMOTIONAL REASONING

Many people, straight and gay, have strong emotional reactions (pro and con) to biological research on homosexuality. Why? How do people's emotions and attitudes toward homosexuality affect their interpretations of this research?

QUICK QUIZ

Were you motivated to learn about sexual motivation?

1. Biological research finds that (a) male and female sexual responses are physiologically very different, (b) vaginal orgasms are healthier than clitoral ones, (c) testosterone is related to sexual desire in both sexes, (d) all women have multiple orgasms.

2. Keith and Brandy have been married a few years, and Keith finds himself wishing that once in a while she would make a sexual overture instead of waiting for him to always be the initiator. Brandy wishes that Keith would be more assertive sexually than he is. This couple has a conflict about the proper _____ for their gender.

3. Research on the motives of rapists finds that rape is usually (a) a result of thwarted sexual desire, (b) the result of hostility or a need for power, (c) a matter of crossed signals.

4. Under what conditions are women most likely to use sex as a "bargaining chip"? (a) when they are employed and thus have their own money to bargain with, (b) when they don't know how to play cards, (c) when they are using birth control, (d) when they are financially dependent

5. *True or false:* Exclusively psychological theories of the origins of homosexuality have not been supported.

Answers:

1. c 2. sexual scripts 3. b 4. d 5. true

WHAT'S AHEAD

- How do psychologists measure a person's motives for achievement or power?
- Which aspects of the job are more important than money in increasing people's work satisfaction and involvement?
- How is the *desire* to achieve affected by the *opportunity* to achieve?

THE COMPETENT ANIMAL: MOTIVES TO WORK

Almost every adult works. Most people spend more time at work than they do at play or with their families. "Work" does not mean only paid employment. Students work at studying. Homemakers work, often more hours than salaried employees, at running a household. Artists, poets, and actors work, even if they are paid erratically. What keeps everybody doing it?

Psychologists, particularly those in the field of *industrial/ organizational psychology*, have studied work motivation in the laboratory, where they have measured internal motives such as the desire for achievement, and in organizations, where they study the conditions that influence productivity and satisfaction.

The Effects of Motivation on Work

Most people are motivated to work, of course, to meet the basic needs for food and shelter. Yet, survival does not explain what motivates LeRoy to work for caviar on his table and Duane to work for peanut butter on his. It does not explain why some people want to do their work well and others want just to get it done. It does not explain the difference between Aristotle's view ("All paid employments absorb and degrade the mind") and Noël Coward's ("Work is more fun than fun"). What psychological factors might account for these variations in the motivation to work?

Expectations and Values. How hard you work for something depends, first, on what you expect to accomplish. If you are fairly certain of success, you will work much harder to reach your goal than if you are fairly certain of failure.

A classic experiment showed how quickly experience affects these expectations. Young women were asked to solve 15 anagram puzzles. Before working on each one, they had to estimate their chances of solving it. Half of the women started off with 5 very easy anagrams, but half began with 5 insoluble ones. Sure enough, those who started with the easy ones increased their estimates of success on later ones. Those who began with the impossible ones decided they would all be impossible. These expectations, in turn, affected the young women's ability to actually solve the last 10 anagrams, which were the same for everyone. The higher the expectation of success, the more anagrams the women solved (Feather, 1966).

How hard you work for something also depends on how much you want it, which in turn depends on your general value system (Feather, 1982). A *value* is a central motivating belief, reflecting a person's fundamental goals and ideals: freedom, beauty, equality, friendship, fame, wisdom, and so on (Rokeach & Ball-Rokeach, 1989).

The values that motivate people can themselves have psychological consequences. For example, American culture puts a high value on wealth and financial success. But the pursuit of material wealth for its own sake has a dark side. According to studies conducted in both America (an affluent nation) and Russia (a struggling nation), people who are primarily motivated to get rich have poorer psychological adjustment and lower well-being than do people whose primary values are self-acceptance, affiliation with others, or wanting to make the world a better place (Kasser & Ryan, 1996; Ryan et al., 1999). This is especially true when the reasons for striving for money are external (something you feel obligated to do, or a way of earning the

need for achievement A learned motive to meet personal standards of success and excellence in a chosen area (abbreviated *nAch*).

Thematic Apperception Test (TAT) A personality test that asks respondents to interpret a series of drawings showing ambiguous scenes of people; usually scored for various motives such as the needs for affiliation, power, and achievement.

respect of others) rather than internal (because it is satisfying or a means of assuring freedom to do what you want) (Carver & Baird, 1998).

Needs for Achievement and Power. In the early 1950s, David McClelland and his associates (1953) speculated that some people have a **need for achievement** (abbreviated *nAch*) that motivates them as much as hunger motivates people to eat. To measure the strength of this motive, McClelland used the **Thematic Apperception Test (TAT)**, which requires the test-taker to make up a story about each scene in a set of ambiguous pictures. A standardized scoring system permits the test to be scored for the need for achievement, power, affiliation, and other motives. The strength of these internal motives, said McClelland (1961), is captured in the fantasies the test-taker reveals. "In fantasy anything is at least symbolically possible," he explained. "A person may rise to great heights, sink to great depths, kill his grandmother, or take off for the South Sea Islands on a pogo stick."

Needless to say, people with high achievement motivation do not fantasize about taking off for the South Seas or sinking to great depths. They tell stories about working hard, becoming rich and famous, and clobbering the opposition with their wit and brilliance; if they don't succeed, they foresee devastation. For example, here is what two people wrote in response to a neutral illustration of a man named George, who is sitting at his desk (McClelland, 1985):

■ *High need for achievement:* George is an engineer who wants to win a competition in which the man with the most practicable drawing will be awarded the contract to build a bridge. He is taking a moment to think how happy he will be if he wins. He has been baffled by how to make such a long span strong, but remembers to specify a new steel alloy of great strength, submits his entry, but does not win and is very unhappy.

THE MANY MOTIVES OF ACCOMPLISHMENT

PRODUCTIVITY

ISAAC ASIMOV
(1920–1992)
Scientist, writer

"If my doctor told me I had only six minutes to live, I wouldn't brood. I'd type a little faster."

KNOWLEDGE

HELEN KELLER
(1880–1968)
Blind/deaf author and lecturer

"Knowledge is happiness, because to have knowledge— broad, deep knowledge—is to know true ends from false, and lofty things from low."

JUSTICE

MARTIN LUTHER KING, JR.
(1929–1968)
Civil rights activist

"I have a dream . . . that my four little children will one day live in a nation where they will not be judged by the color of their skin but the content of their character."

AUTONOMY

GEORGIA O'KEEFFE
(1887–1986)
Artist

"[I] found myself saying to myself—I can't live where I want to, go where I want to, do what I want to . . . I decided I was a very stupid fool not to at least paint as I wanted to."

- *High need for affiliation:* George is an engineer who is working late. He is worried that his wife will be annoyed with him for neglecting her. She has been objecting that he cares more about his work than his wife and family. He seems unable to satisfy both his boss and his wife, but he loves her very much, and will do his best to finish up fast and get home to her.

When high achievers are in situations that arouse their competitiveness and desire to succeed—when, for example, they are told that the TAT measures their intelligence and leadership ability—their achievement-related themes shoot up (Atkinson, 1958). In the laboratory and real life, people who score high on the need for achievement consistently differ from those who score low. High scorers are more likely, for example, to start their own businesses. They set high personal standards. They prefer to work with capable colleagues who can help them succeed rather than with co-workers who are merely friendly (McClelland, 1987).

The TAT has also been used to identify people motivated by a **need for power,** the desire to dominate others and to influence people (McClelland, 1975). Men and women who score high on this motive may try to win power by being aggressive and manipulative or by being inspirational and charismatic (Winter, 1993). They seek prestige and visibility, enter powerful careers, and run for office. In innovative research linking individual motives to national events, David Winter (1993) has measured power and achievement motivation in secret government documents and official speeches by leaders. His work suggests that power motivation may be a crucial psychological cause of war. "When it rises," Winter reports, "war is likely; when it falls, war is less likely and ongoing wars are likely to end." The affiliation motive works in just the opposite fashion: When it rises, wars are averted.

As this study suggests, achievement, power, and affiliation motives can actually be measured on a national scale as well as an individual one. Researchers have scored

need for power A learned motive to dominate or influence others.

POWER
HENRY KISSINGER
(b. 1923)
Former Secretary of State

"Power is the ultimate aphrodisiac."

DUTY
ELEANOR ROOSEVELT
(1884–1962)
Humanitarian, lecturer, stateswoman

"As for accomplishments, I just did what I had to do as things came along."

EXCELLENCE
FLORENCE GRIFFITH JOYNER
(1959–1998)
Olympic gold medalist

"When you've been second best for so long, you can either accept it, or try to become the best. I made the decision to try and be the best."

GREED
IVAN BOESKY
(b. 1937)
Financier, convicted of insider trading violations

"Greed is all right . . . I think greed is healthy. You can be greedy and still feel good about yourself."

WHAT DO YOU VALUE?

Rank the following values in terms of their importance to you, with 1 the most important and 18 the least, being as honest as you can. If something you value is missing, be sure to add it. How does your ranking affect your ambitions and life goals? Are any of your key values in conflict, and if so, does that conflict motivate you to change in any way? (From Rokeach and Ball-Rokeach, 1989.)

_____ A world at peace

_____ Family security

_____ Freedom

_____ Happiness

_____ Self-respect

_____ Wisdom

_____ Equality

_____ Salvation

_____ A comfortable life

_____ Accomplishment

_____ True friendship

_____ National security

_____ Inner harmony

_____ Mature love

_____ A world of beauty

_____ Social recognition

_____ Pleasure

_____ An exciting life

_____ Other

these motives using a variety of imaginative measures, including historical documents, speeches, popular books, and indicators of achievement such as number of new patents, businesses, and discoveries. Their work raises fascinating questions. What causes power, achievement, and affiliation motives to rise and fall within a society? Do we have any control over them? Historical events can change people's motivations, but people's motivations can also change the course of history.

The Effects of Work on Motivation

Psychologists who study achievement motivation ask, "How does having an internal motive to achieve affect a person's chances of success?" But others reverse the question, asking, "How does a person's chances of success affect the motive to achieve?" Achievement, they find, does not depend solely on internal expectations, values, and motives—that is, on enduring, unchanging qualities of the individual. It also depends on conditions of the work you do.

Working Conditions. Several specific aspects of the work environment are known to increase job involvement, work motivation, and job satisfaction (S. Brown, 1996; Kohn & Schooler, 1983):

■ The work provides a sense of meaningfulness.

■ Employees have control over many aspects of their work—for example, they can set their own hours and make decisions.

■ Tasks are varied rather than repetitive.

■ The company maintains clear and consistent rules for its workers.

THINKING CRITICALLY

ASK QUESTIONS

Americans tend to ask, "How does the internal motive to achieve affect a person's chances of success?" What other questions would lead to different answers about people's motivation to do well at work?

- Employees have supportive relationships with their superiors and co-workers.
- Employees receive useful feedback about their work, so they know what they have accomplished and what they need to do to improve.
- The company offers opportunities for its employees' growth and development.

Companies that foster these conditions tend to have more productive and satisfied employees, and this is true in countries as diverse as the Netherlands, Hungary, and Bulgaria (Roe et al., 1998). Workers tend to become more creative in their thinking and feel better about themselves and their work than they do if they feel stuck in routine, boring jobs that give them no control or flexibility over their daily tasks (Karasek & Theorell, 1990; Locke & Latham, 1990). Conversely, when people with high power or achievement motivation are put in situations that frustrate their desire and ability to express these motives, they become dissatisfied and stressed, and their power and achievement motives decline (Jenkins, 1994).

Like employees, students can have poor working conditions that affect their motivation. They may have to study in crowded quarters or may have small siblings who interrupt and distract them.

Did you notice anything missing from that list of beneficial working conditions? Where is money, supposedly the great motivator? Actually, work motivation is related not to the amount of money you get, but to how and when you get it. The strongest motivator is *incentive pay*, bonuses that are given upon completion of a goal rather than as an automatic raise (Locke et al., 1981). Incentive pay increases people's feelings of competence and accomplishment ("I got this raise because I deserved it"). This doesn't mean that people should accept low pay so they will like their jobs better, or that they should never demand cost-of-living raises!

Opportunities to Achieve. One of the most important working conditions that affects achievement, however, is having the *opportunity* to achieve. When someone does not do well at work, others are apt to say it is the individual's own fault because he or she lacks the internal drive to "make it." But what the person may really lack is a fair chance to make it, and this is especially true for those who have been subjected to systematic discrimination, such as women and ethnic minorities. At one time, for example, women were said to be less successful than men in the workplace because women had an internalized "fear of success." Yet, as opportunities for women improved and sex discrimination was made illegal, this apparent "motive" vanished.

Similarly, when the proportion of men and women in an occupation changes, so do people's motivations to work in that field (Kanter, 1977/1993). Many occupations are still highly segregated by gender; there are few male secretaries or female auto mechanics. As a result, many people form gender stereotypes of the requirements of such careers: "Female" jobs require kindness and nurturance, "male" jobs require strength and smarts. These stereotypes, in turn, stifle people's aspirations to enter a nontraditional career (Cejka & Eagly, 1999). As job segregation breaks down, however, people's motivations change. When law and bartending were almost entirely male professions, few women aspired to become lawyers or bartenders. Now that women make up a large percentage of both occupations, their motivation to become lawyers or bartenders has changed rapidly.

Once in a career, people may become more or less motivated to advance up the ladder, depending on how many rungs they are permitted to climb. Men and women who work in dead-end jobs with no prospect of promotion tend to play down the importance of achievement, fantasize about quitting, and emphasize the social benefits of their jobs instead of the intellectual or financial benefits (Kanter, 1977/1993). Consider the comments of a man who realized in his mid-30s that he was never going to be promoted to top management and who scaled down his ambitions accordingly (Scofield, 1993). As organizational psychologists would predict, he began to emphasize the benefits of not achieving: "I'm freer to speak my mind," "I can choose not to play office politics," and "I don't volunteer for lousy assignments." He had time, he learned, for coaching Little League and could stay home when the kids were sick. "Of course," he wrote, "if I ever had any chance for upward corporate mobility it's gone now. I couldn't take the grind. Whether real or imagined, that glass ceiling has become an invisible shield."

Women and members of minority groups are especially likely to encounter a "glass ceiling" in management—a barrier to promotion that is so subtle as to be transparent, yet strong enough to prevent advancement. For example, in a study of the banking industry, the three most significant problems that African-Americans reported were not being "in the network," and therefore not being told what was going on; racism; and an inability to find a mentor (Irons & Moore, 1985). When a company has a glass ceiling, a minority person's educational level, work experience, and professional accomplishments do not predict advancement as they do for white men (Cabezas et al., 1989; Graham, 1994; Valian, 1998).

The U.S. Department of Labor launched a Glass Ceiling Initiative to determine how various industries fill their middle- and upper-management positions. It found that most companies have a level beyond which few women or minorities advance, although the level differs across companies, and white women often get farther than minorities of either sex do (Smither, 1998). Male managers typically believe that women and minorities quit or fail to be promoted because of their lack of ambition or commitment to the company, but research does not confirm this belief (Snyder, 1993; Valian, 1998). When minorities reach the glass ceiling, many leave for better jobs or to find more congenial environments.

As you can see, work motivation and satisfaction depend on the right fit between qualities of the individual and conditions of the work. Increasingly, in a global economy dependent on an ethnically diverse workforce, companies face the challenge of how best to structure the work environment so that employees will be productive and satisfied, rather than feeling apathetic, resentful, or burned out.

QUICK QUIZ

Work on your understanding of work motivation.

1. Which of these factors significantly increase work motivation? (a) incentive pay, (b) regular pay, (c) feedback, (d) job predictability, (e) being told what to do, (f) being able to make decisions, (g) having a chance of promotion, (h) having routine work

2. Phyllis works at an umbrella company. Her work is competent, but she rarely arrives on time, doesn't seem as motivated to do well as others, and has begun to take an unusual number of sick days. This behavior is irritating her boss, who is thinking of firing her. What guidelines of critical thinking is the boss overlooking, and what research should the boss consider before taking this step?

Answers:

1. a, c, f, g 2. The boss is jumping to the conclusion that Phyllis has low achievement motivation. This may be true, but because her work is competent, the boss should consider other explanations and examine the evidence. Perhaps the work conditions are unsatisfactory: There may be few opportunities for promotion; she may get no feedback; perhaps the company does not provide child care, so Phyllis arrives late because she has child-care obligations. What other possible explanations come to mind?

WHAT'S AHEAD

- Why is "doing your best" an ineffective goal to set for yourself?
- Does it matter whether you are pursuing a goal that you *do* want or avoiding an outcome that you *don't* want?
- When you are learning a new skill, should you concentrate on mastering it or on performing it well in front of others?
- What kind of conflict do you have when you want to study for a big exam but you also want to go out partying?
- Do you have to satisfy basic needs for security and belonging before you can become "self-actualized"?

MOTIVES, GOALS, AND WELL-BEING

Throughout this chapter we have been looking at the specific motives involved in love, sex, and work. But modern motivation research has identified some themes that are common to all aspirations, whether you want to be the best rodeo rider in the world, run a marathon, get through school, or have a huge, happy family. Life satisfaction and well-being are affected by the way you think about the goals you set for yourself and by how you resolve motivational conflicts.

The Importance of Goals

One of the strongest findings about motivation is the importance of having goals, but not just any old goals. Goals are most likely to improve performance—whatever the performance is—when three conditions are met (Cooper, Shapiro, & Powers, 1998; Higgins, 1998; Locke & Latham, 1990; Smither, 1998). First, the goal must be *specific*. Defining a goal as "doing your best" is as ineffective as having no goals at all. You need to be specific about what you are going to do and when you are going to do it: "I will write four pages of this paper today."

Second, the goal must be *challenging but achievable*. You are apt to work harder for tough but realistic goals that make you feel gratified when you reach them, than for easy goals that pose no challenge or impossible goals that can never be attained.

And third, the goal should be framed in terms of *getting what you want rather than avoiding what you do not want*. *Approach goals* are positive experiences that you seek directly, such as "trying to be smarter" or "learning to scuba dive." *Avoidance goals* are unpleasant experiences that you hope to avoid, such as "trying not to make a fool of myself" or "trying to avoid being dependent."

People who frame their goals in approach terms (e.g., "I'm going to lose weight by jogging three times a week") feel better about themselves, feel more competent, are more optimistic and less depressed, and even have fewer colds and other physical symptoms than people who frame the same goals in avoidance terms (e.g., "I'm going to lose weight by staying away from rich foods"). Can you guess why? Approach goals allow you to focus on what you can actively do to accomplish them, whereas avoidance goals make you focus on what you have to give up (Coats, Janoff-Bulman, & Alpert, 1996; Elliot & Sheldon, 1998).

Performance Versus Mastery Goals. Defining goals is only the first step on the road to success; next you need to know what to do when you hit a pothole. Some people give up when a goal becomes difficult or they are faced with a setback, whereas others become even more determined to succeed. Talent or ambition alone

performance goals Goals framed in terms of performing well in front of others, being judged favorably, and avoiding criticism.

mastery (learning) goals Goals framed in terms of increasing one's competence and skills.

FIGURE 12.3
MASTERY AND MOTIVATION

Children praised for "being smart" rather than for "working hard" tend to lose the pleasure of learning and focus on how well they are doing. Nearly 70 percent of fifth graders who were praised for intelligence later chose performance goals (doing "problems that aren't too hard, so I don't get many wrong") rather than learning goals (doing "problems that I'll learn a lot from, even if I won't look so smart")— compared to fewer than 10 percent of children who were praised for their efforts. Children praised for intelligence were also far more likely to lie to their classmates about how many problems they had solved (Mueller & Dweck, 1998).

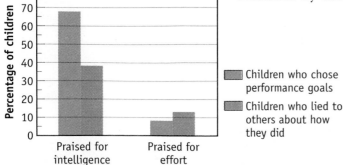

Children who chose performance goals

Children who lied to others about how they did

does not predict who will push on and who will give up. The crucial factor is whether their main motivation is to perform well in front of others or to learn the task for the satisfaction of it (Utman, 1997).

People who are motivated by **performance goals** are concerned with doing well, being judged favorably, and avoiding criticism (Dweck, 1992; Dweck & Sorich, 1999). When such people are focused on how well they are performing and then do poorly, they often decide the fault is theirs and they stop trying to improve. Because their goal is to demonstrate their abilities, they set themselves up for grief when they temporarily fail—as all of us must if we are to learn anything new.

In contrast, those who are motivated by **mastery (learning) goals** are concerned with increasing their competence and skills. Therefore, they regard failure as a source of useful information that will help them improve. Failure and criticism do not discourage them because they know that learning takes time. In addition, people who focus on mastery rather than performance usually feel greater intrinsic pleasure in the task they are doing or the goal they are pursuing. (However, there is an exception to this rule for highly ambitious, performance-driven people, such as great athletes and musicians. For them, focusing on specific ways of improving their performance raises their intrinsic motivation and satisfaction [Elliot & Harackiewicz, 1994].)

Children acquire learning or mastery goals early, from the actions adults praise them for and from what they observe in their environments. For example, many parents believe in the importance of praising their child's intelligence and ability when the child does well ("Wow, Katie, are you smart!"). Yet, surprisingly, such praise can backfire. In several studies, children who were praised for their intelligence and ability later cared more about performance goals and less about learning goals than did children who were praised for their *efforts* (see Figure 12.3). And after these "smart" children failed a problem-solving game, they tended to give up on subsequent ones, enjoyed them less, lied to other kids about how well they had done, and actually performed less well than children who had been praised for their efforts (Mueller & Dweck, 1998). The reason seems to be that most American children regard intelligence and ability as fixed traits that you can't do anything about. Therefore, if you fail, you might as well give up. But effort is subject to improvement; you can always try again, and that is the key to mastery. As one learning-oriented child said, "Mistakes are our friends" (Dweck & Sorich, 1999).

Choice, Duty, and Satisfaction. "Freedom," wrote Thomas Jefferson, "is the right to choose: the right to create for oneself the alternatives of choice." Decades of research in Western cultures amply confirm his observation. People who feel that their motives and goals are freely chosen and self-directed are better off in many ways than people who feel their goals and motives are externally controlled by social pressures and demands. Self-directed people have greater intrinsic satisfaction in the goals they pursue, persist longer in reaching them, perform better, and are happier (Higgins, 1998; Sheldon & Elliot, 1999).

Notions about freedom and the right to choose, however, are deeply affected by culture. As we discuss in Chapter 13, many cultures, such as those throughout Asia, value the group and social relations more than the self and individual "rights." In studies of fifth-grade children in San Francisco, Anglo-American and Asian-American children were given an assortment of anagram puzzle games. Some children were

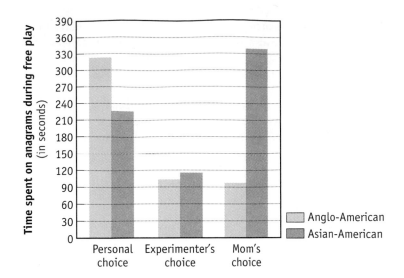

FIGURE 12.4
CULTURE, CHOICE, AND MOTIVATION
The "freedom to choose" is not a universal value or universally motivating. When white children were permitted to choose which anagram puzzles they wanted to solve, their intrinsic motivation in playing the game increased (as measured by the amount of time they later spent on anagrams during free play). But for Asian-American children, intrinsic motivation was highest when their mothers had made the choice for them (Iyengar & Lepper, 1999).

allowed to decide for themselves which puzzle to solve; some were told which one to select by the experimenter; and some were told what to choose by their mothers. As you can see in Figure 12.4, the results for white and Asian children were very different. Anglo children showed greater intrinsic motivation—as measured by the amount of time they later voluntarily spent with the puzzles—when they could make their own choices than when the experimenter or their mothers decided for them. But Asian children did not care as much about making their own choices, and they were far more intrinsically motivated when the choice was made for them by their mothers (Iyengar & Lepper, 1999).

Thus, culture not only influences which goals will guide your life, but also whether you believe that your happiness rests on choosing goals for yourself or loyally following the choices made for you by others.

When Motives Conflict

The many motives of human life rarely coexist in perfect harmony. How we combine them, and how we resolve them when they conflict, are critically important to well-being and satisfaction with life.

Kinds of Motivational Conflicts. Two motives are in conflict when the satisfaction of one leads to the inability to act on the other—when, that is, you want to eat your cake and have it, too. There are four basic kinds of motivational conflicts (Lewin, 1948):

1 *Approach-approach conflicts* occur when you are equally attracted to two or more possible activities or goals. For example, you would like to go out with Tom, Dick, *and* Harry, all at the same time; you would like to be a veterinarian *and* a rock singer; you would like to go out with friends (an affiliation motive) *and* study like mad for an exam (an achievement motive).

2 *Avoidance-avoidance conflicts* require you to choose between the lesser of two evils because you dislike both alternatives. Novice parachute jumpers, for example, must choose between the fear of jumping and the fear of losing face if they don't jump.

THE FAR SIDE By GARY LARSON

DAMNED if you do

DAMNED if you don't

7-10

© 1984 FarWorks, Inc. All Rights Reserved

"C'mon, c'mon—it's either one or the other."

A classic avoidance-avoidance conflict.

3 *Approach-avoidance conflicts* occur when one activity or goal has both a positive and a negative aspect. For example, you want to be a powerful executive but you worry about losing your friends if you succeed. You want power and yet you fear it at the same time. In culturally diverse nations, differing cultural values produce many approach-avoidance conflicts. Our students have offered many examples. A Chicano student said he wants to succeed and do well in the mainstream culture, but his parents, valuing the family's closeness, worry that if he goes to college and graduate school, he will become too independent and eventually leave them behind. An African-American student from a poor neighborhood is in college on a prestigious scholarship. He is torn between wanting to leave his background behind him forever and returning to help the community that supported him. And a white student wants to be a marine biologist, but her friends tell her that only nerdy guys and dweebs go into science.

In approach-avoidance conflicts, both attraction and repulsion are typically strongest when you are nearest the goal. The closer you are to something appealing, the stronger your desire to approach it; the closer you are to something unpleasant, the stronger your desire to flee. However, as you step away from the goal, the two motives change in strength. The attractive aspects of the goal still seem appealing, but the negative ones seem less unpleasant. This may be one reason people often have trouble resolving their ambivalence: When they leave a situation that has some benefits but many problems and observe it from a distance, they see its benefits and overlook the problems. So they approach it again. Up close, the problems appear more clearly, motivating them to avoid the situation once more.

4 *Multiple approach-avoidance conflicts* occur in situations that offer several choices, each with advantages and disadvantages. For example, you want to marry while you are still in school, and you think you have found the right person. On the other hand, you also want to establish a career and have some money in the bank, and lately you and the right person have been quarreling a lot.

Conflicts like these are inevitable, part of the price and pleasure of living. But if they remain unresolved, they can take an emotional toll. In students, high levels of conflict and ambivalence are associated with anxiety, depression, headaches and other symptoms, and more visits to the health center (Emmons & King, 1988). In contrast, students who are "true to themselves," who strive for goals that are consistent with the qualities they value most, have greater self-integrity and a stronger sense of meaning and purpose in life than do those who are pursuing goals discrepant with their core values (McGregor & Little, 1998).

Can Motives Be Ranked? Another way of thinking about the competing motives in our lives comes from a theory proposed by humanist psychologist Abraham Maslow (1970). Maslow envisioned people's motives as forming a pyramid, a *hierarchy of needs* ranked by their importance for survival. At the bottom level of the pyramid were basic *survival needs,* for food, sleep, and water; at the next level were *security needs,* for shelter and protection against danger; at the third level were *social needs,* for belonging and affection; at the fourth level were *esteem needs,* for self-respect and the respect of others; and at the top were *needs for self-actualization* and "self-transcendence." Maslow argued that your needs must be met at each level before you can even think

THINKING CRITICALLY

EXAMINE THE EVIDENCE

Maslow argued that motives can be ranked from basic physical needs to higher psychological ones. This theory is intuitively appealing, but does the evidence support it? Do people's motives always form a progressive hierarchy, from lower to higher?

of the matters posed by the level above it. You can't worry about achievement if you are hungry, cold, and poor. You can't become self-actualized if you haven't satisfied your needs for self-esteem and love. Human beings behave badly, he argued, only when their lower needs are frustrated.

This theory, which is intuitively logical and optimistic about human progress, became immensely popular, but it has not been well supported by research (Smither, 1998). People have *simultaneous* needs for comfort and safety and for attachments, self-esteem, and competence. Individuals who have met their "lower" needs do not inevitably seek "higher" ones, nor is it the case that people behave badly only when their lower needs are frustrated. Higher needs may even take precedence over lower ones. History is full of examples of people who would rather starve than be humiliated; who would rather die of torture than sacrifice their convictions; who would rather explore, risk, or create new art than be safe and secure at home.

QUICK QUIZ

Do you wish to approach or avoid this quiz?

1. Horatio wants to earn a black belt in karate. Which way(s) of thinking about this goal are most likely to help him reach it? (a) "I should do the best I can," (b) "I should be sure not to lose many matches," (c) "I will set specific goals that are tough but attainable," (d) "I will set specific goals that I know I can reach easily," (e) "I will strive to achieve key milestones on the way to my goal."

2. Ramon and Ramona are learning to ski. Every time she falls, Ramona says, "This is the most humiliating experience I've ever had! Everyone is watching me behave like a clumsy dolt!" When Ramon falls, he says, "&*!!@$#! I'll show these dratted skis who's boss!" Why is Ramona more likely than Ramon to give up? (a) She *is* a clumsy dolt; (b) she is less competent at skiing; (c) she is focused on learning; (d) she is focused on performance.

3. A Pakistani student says she desperately wants an education and a career as a pharmacist, but she also does not want to be disobedient to her parents, who have arranged a marriage for her back home. Which kind of conflict does she have?

Answers:

1. c, e   2. d   3. approach-avoidance

Psychology can teach us a great deal about the many motives of human life, including the meanings of love, the mysteries of sex, and the conditions that enhance or suppress the pursuit of achievement. It has revealed some of the consequences to our well-being of choosing some goals or values over others.

Of course, psychology cannot tell us which motives, goals, and values to choose in the first place: love, wealth, security, passion, freedom, fame, the desire to improve the world, or anything else. But repeatedly it does find that people who are motivated by the intrinsic satisfaction of an activity—whatever the activity is—are happier and healthier than those motivated solely by the pursuit of wealth, luxury, or other external rewards (Kasser & Ryan, 1999). In a commencement address some years ago, Mario Cuomo, the former governor of New York, had these words of wisdom for the graduating students: "When you've parked the second car in the garage, and installed the hot tub, and skied in Colorado, and wind-surfed in the Caribbean, when you've had your first love affair and your second and your third, the question will remain: Where does the dream end for me?"

TAKING PSYCHOLOGY WITH YOU

GET MOTIVATED!

Why are you in school? What do you hope to accomplish in your life? Are you motivated primarily by the intrinsic goals of a job well done and the pleasure of your work or by extrinsic goals such as getting a job and a big salary? Do you have a burning ambition, or are you burned out? If you are feeling unmotivated these days, research on work motivation suggests some steps you might take.

■ *Seek activities that are intrinsically pleasurable,* even if they don't "pay off." If you really, really want to study Swahili or Swedish even though these languages are not in your prelaw requirements, try to find a way to do it. If you are not enjoying your major or your job, consider finding a career that would be more intrinsically pleasurable; or at least make sure you have other projects and activities that you do enjoy for their own sake.

■ *Set specific goals that have a target date.* Remember to be as specific as you can in what you hope to achieve; "do my best" is too vague. If you know you have to meet a goal by a specific date, you are more likely to succeed than if you give yourself an indefinite amount of time ("by next year").

■ *Focus on learning goals* rather than on performance goals. In general,

you will be better able to cope with setbacks if your goal is to learn rather than to show off how good you are. Regard failure as a chance to learn rather than as a sign of incompetence. The more you are able to focus on improvement, the better your performance will be.

■ *Get accurate feedback* on your performance. Once you have specified a goal, continued motivation depends in part on getting feedback about your performance. Edward Koch, the former mayor of New York, used to go around asking people, "How'm I doing?" We all need to know how we are doing and what steps we can take to do better. If you are not getting enough feedback, ask for it—and then remember that criticism is useful too.

■ *Assess your working conditions.* Are you getting support from co-workers, employers, or instructors? Do you have opportunities to develop ideas and vary your routine, or are you expected to toe the line and do the same thing day after day? Do you perceive a glass ceiling that might limit your advancement in your chosen field, and are your perceptions accurate? If you have entered school or a job with enthusiasm, optimism, and expectations of

success, only to have these feelings slowly dwindle and dissipate, you might consider whether your working conditions are causing your burnout. And then you might see whether changing some of those conditions could recharge your batteries.

■ *Take steps to resolve motivational conflicts.* Many students in an approach-avoidance conflict tend to think a great deal about their conflicts but not do anything to resolve them. A student in one study, for instance, remained unhappily stuck between his goal of achieving independence and his desire to be cared for by his parents (Emmons & King, 1988). The reconciliation of conflicts like these is important for your well-being.

Abraham Maslow may have been wrong about a universal hierarchy of motives, but perhaps each of us develops our own hierarchy as we grow from childhood to old age. For some people, needs for love, security, and safety will dominate. For others, the need for achievement or power will rule. Some of us will wrestle with conflicting motives; for others, one consuming ambition will hold sway over all others. The motives and goals that inspire us, and the choices we make in their pursuit, are what give our lives passion, color, and meaning.

SUMMARY

1. *Motivation* refers to a process within a person or animal that causes that organism to move toward a goal—satisfy a biological need or achieve a psychological ambition—or away from an unpleasant situation. A few primary motivating *drives* are based on physiological

needs, but most human motives are psychological or social in nature.

THE SOCIAL ANIMAL: MOTIVES FOR LOVE

2. All human beings have a *need for affiliation* with others. Babies' survival depends on physical and emotional

attachment to their caregivers. Their innate need for *contact comfort* gives rise to attachment to their caregivers, and by the age of 7 to 9 months, they begin to feel *separation anxiety* when the primary caregiver temporarily leaves. Studies of the *Strange Situation* have identified three styles of infant attachment: *secure, avoidant,* and *anxious-ambivalent.* Insecurely attached children often develop long-term emotional and behavioral problems.

3. Styles of attachment are relatively unaffected by the normal range of child-rearing practices, including whether babies spend time in daycare. Insecure attachment may be caused by the child's own fearful, insecure temperament; by stressful family situations; by upsetting events in later childhood (such as parental divorce); and by parents who are extremely neglectful or rejecting of their babies.

4. Three leading theories describe the varieties of love. One describes *six styles of love* (romantic, game-playing, affectionate, pragmatic, possessive, and selfless). In the *triangle theory of love,* love consists of different combinations of passion, intimacy, and commitment. And the *attachment theory of love* views adult love relationships, like those of infants, as being secure, avoidant, or anxious-ambivalent. Adults' attachment styles tend to be stable from childhood throughout adulthood and affect their own close relationships.

5. Men and women are equally likely to feel love and need attachment, but *gender roles* affect how they experience and express love. In turn, economic and cultural factors, such as whether women are economically self-sufficient, affect gender roles and whether people regard love in pragmatic or romantic terms.

THE EROTIC ANIMAL: MOTIVES FOR SEX

6. Biological research finds that testosterone influences sexual desire in both sexes, although hormones do not "cause" sexual behavior in a simple, direct way. Kinsey and later Masters and Johnson showed that physiologically, male and female sexuality are more similar than different, that there is no "right" kind of orgasm for women to have, and that both sexes are capable of sexual arousal and response.

7. Psychological, social, and cultural approaches to sexual motivation emphasize the ways that values, beliefs, perceptions, and fantasies affect sexual desire and response. Men and women have sex to satisfy many different psychological motives, including pleasure, intimacy, coping, self-affirmation, the partner's approval, or peer approval. Coping and approval motives are associated with risky sexual behavior. Both sexes may agree to intercourse for nonsexual reasons: Men sometimes feel obligated to "make a move" to prove their masculinity, and women sometimes feel obliged to "give in" to preserve the relationship.

8. A major gender difference in sexual experience has to do with rape and perceptions of sexual coercion: What women regard as coercion or pressure is not always seen as such by men. Men who rape do so for diverse reasons, including peer pressure, insecurity, hostility toward women, and sometimes sadism.

9. Cultures differ widely in determining what parts of the body people learn are erotic, which sexual acts are erotic or repulsive, and whether sex itself is good or bad. Cultures transmit these ideas through *gender roles* and *sexual scripts,* which specify appropriate behavior during courtship and sex, depending on a person's gender, age, and sexual orientation. Scripts for heterosexual women and men often lead to different sexual goals and to misunderstandings over the meaning of sexual signals. As in the case of love, gender differences (and growing similarities) in sexuality are affected by cultural and economic factors.

10. The origins of sexual orientation are still unknown. Traditional psychological explanations do not account for why some people become homosexual despite strong social pressures for heterosexuality. Genetic and hormonal factors may be involved, although the evidence is stronger for gay men than for lesbians, whose sexuality seems more varied and flexible. Biology, culture, learning, and circumstance interact in complex ways to produce a given person's orientation. Research on this issue is sensitive because people often confuse scientific questions about the origins of homosexuality with political and moral questions about the rights of gays and lesbians.

THE COMPETENT ANIMAL: MOTIVES TO WORK

11. The motivation to work depends on a person's expectations of success and on the *value* the person places on the goal. People who are motivated by a high *need for achievement* set their own standards for success and excellence. People who are motivated by a *need for power* seek to dominate and influence others.

12. Work motivation also depends on circumstances of the job itself. Key working conditions that promote motivation and satisfaction are those that provide workers with a sense of meaningfulness, control, variation in tasks, clear rules, supportive relationships, feedback, and opportunities for advancement and learning. *Incentive pay* is more effective than predictable raises

in elevating work motivation. For women, one factor in the motivation to enter a career is its gender ratio. The motivation to achieve also depends on having the opportunity to be promoted, in contrast to hitting a "glass ceiling."

MOTIVES, GOALS, AND WELL-BEING

13. Motivation is powerfully affected by the goals that people set for themselves. Goals tend to improve performance when they are specific, challenging but achievable, and framed in terms of getting what you want rather than avoiding what you do not want.

14. Success or failure depend not only on ability, but also on whether people set *mastery (learning) goals*, in which the focus is on learning the task well, or *performance goals*, in which the focus is on performing for others. Mastery goals lead to persistence in the face of failures and setbacks; performance goals often lead to giving up. Cultural norms regarding individual rights or loyalty to others affect whether people want to choose their own goals or strive for goals set for them by others they admire.

15. Human motives often conflict. In an *approach-approach conflict*, a person is equally attracted to two goals. In an *avoidance-avoidance conflict*, a person is equally repelled by two goals. An *approach-avoidance conflict* is the most difficult to resolve, because the person is both attracted to and repelled by the same goal. Prolonged conflict can lead to physical symptoms and reduced well-being.

16. Abraham Maslow believed that human motives could be ranked along a *hierarchy of needs*, from basic biological needs for survival to higher psychological needs for self-actualization. This popular theory has not been supported. People can have simultaneous motives; "higher" motives can outweigh "lower" ones; and people do not always become kinder or more self-actualized when their "lower" needs are met.

KEY TERMS

motivation 421

drives 421

need for affiliation 422

contact comfort 422

separation anxiety 423

the Strange Situation 423

kinds of attachment 424

   secure 424

   avoidant 424

   anxious-ambivalent 424

passionate and companionate love 426

six styles of love 426

triangle theory of love 426

attachment theory of love 427

gender roles 436

sexual scripts 437

values 441

need for achievement (nAch) 442

Thematic Apperception Test (TAT) 442

need for power 443

incentive pay 445

"glass ceiling" 446

performance goals 448

mastery (learning) goals 448

approach and avoidance conflicts 449

   approach-approach 449

   avoidance-avoidance 449

   approach-avoidance 450

Maslow's hierarchy of needs 450

LOOKING BACK

- Why is cuddling so important for infants (and adults, too)? (p. 422)

- If you have a 1-year-old, why shouldn't you worry if your baby cries when left with a new babysitter? (p. 423)

- Why are some people secure in their love relationships, while others are always anxious and worried that their lovers will abandon them? (p. 428)

- Do men and women differ in the ability to love? (p. 429)

- How are your beliefs about love affected by your income? (p. 429)

- Which part of the anatomy do psychologists think is the "sexiest sex organ"? (p. 434)

- How do the sexual rules for heterosexual couples foster misunderstandings? (p. 437)

- Can psychological theories about "smothering mothering" or absent fathers explain why some men are gay? (p. 438)

- How do psychologists measure a person's motives for achievement or power? (p. 442)

- Which aspects of the job are more important than money in increasing people's work satisfaction and involvement? (pp. 444–445)

- How is the *desire* to achieve affected by the *opportunity* to achieve? (pp. 445–446)

- Why is "doing your best" an ineffective goal to set for yourself? (p. 447)

- Does it matter whether you are pursuing a goal that you *do* want or avoiding an outcome that you *don't* want? (p. 447)

- When you are learning a new skill, should you concentrate on mastering it or on performing it well in front of others? (p. 448)

- What kind of conflict do you have when you want to study for a big exam but you also want to go out partying? (p. 449)

- Do you have to satisfy basic needs for security and belonging before you can become "self-actualized"? (p. 451)

13 THEORIES OF PERSONALITY

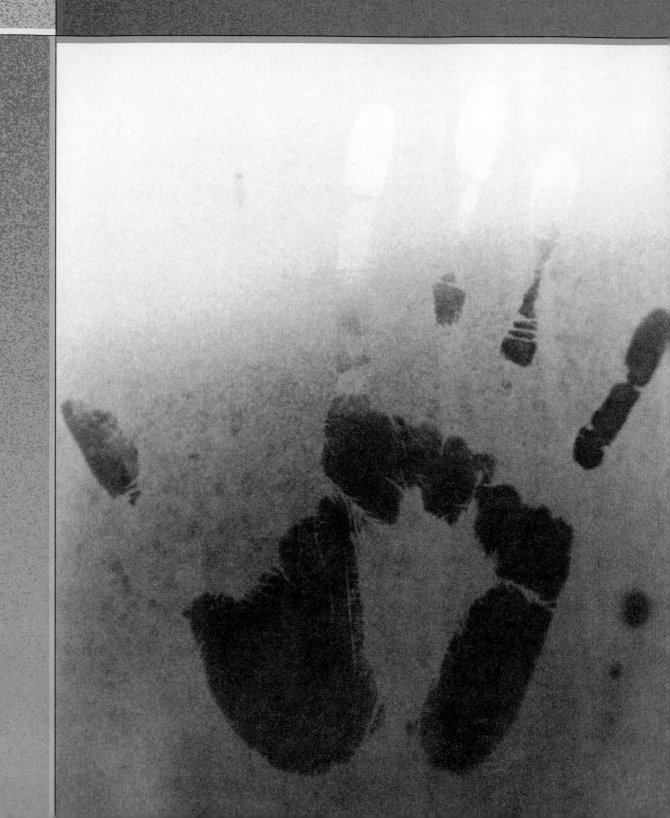

"People often say that this or that person has not yet found himself.

But the self is not something that one finds.

It is something that one creates."

PSYCHIATRIST THOMAS SZASZ

Dennis ("the Worm") Rodman, the controversial basketball player, has quite a "personality"—but what is it? Some people love his attention-grabbing behavior—his drag-queen clothes and makeup, his ever-changing hair colors and tattoos, his defiant and unpredictable behavior on the court—and some people hate it. After Rodman kicked a cameraman in the groin for no apparent reason and got himself suspended for 11 games, his own coach compared his actions to those of a 4-year-old who has had his toys taken away. Rodman's former teammate Scottie Pippen said, "I'm not sure he's capable of learning any lessons from his suspensions. I don't expect him ever to change because if he did, he wouldn't be the Worm, the personality he has invented for himself."

Can Dennis Rodman change? Was he born to be an outlandish exhibitionist, or is that merely a persona he cleverly created to make himself famous? Which personality traits best describe him: hardworking, street smart, and effective, or outlandish, childish, and silly? Do his actions stem from some deep-seated, perhaps unconscious aspect of his personality, or is he just being playful? Who is the "real" Dennis Rodman? Is there a real one?

In psychology, "personality" is not just a general everyday term, as in "She's got a great personality" or "He needs a personality transplant." **Personality** refers to a distinctive pattern of behavior, thoughts, motives, and emotions that characterizes an individual over time. Personality consists of specific **traits**, habitual ways of behaving, thinking, and feeling: shy, brave, reliable, friendly, hostile, confident, and so on. But psychologists differ in the traits they consider most important or central, and in their views of the origins and stability of those traits.

In this chapter, we will describe five major approaches to personality. The first three are part of the modern, empirical tradition in psychology: the *behavioral genetic, social-cognitive,* and *cultural* approaches. We will then turn to *psychodynamic* and *humanist* theories, whose proponents regard the objective measurement of traits as too fragmented and incomplete a way of capturing personality. Instead, they propose global explanations, using subjective methods to describe the development of the whole person. As you read, ask yourself what your own defining qualities might be, how stable you think they are, and where you think they came from. Is your "public" self the same as your "private," internal self?

● How do psychologists identify the elements of your personality?
● How can psychologists tell which personality traits "clump together"?
● Which five dimensions of personality seem to describe people the world over?

MEASURING PERSONALITY

Psychological tests provide information about specific aspects of personality, such as needs, values, interests, typical ways of responding to situations, and mental disorders. Using these tests, psychologists have identified a broad array of traits, from sensation seeking (the enjoyment of risk) to "erotophobia" (the fear of sex).

Testing for Traits

Personality researchers and clinical psychologists generally rely on two kinds of personality tests. *Projective tests*, which we will discuss later in this chapter, are based on the psychodynamic assumption that the test-taker will transfer ("project") unconscious conflicts and motivations onto an ambiguous test stimulus. *Objective tests*, or **inventories**, are standardized questionnaires that require written responses, typically to multiple-choice or true-false items. For example, the Beck Depression Inventory is widely used to measure the severity of depression and distress, and the Taylor Manifest Anxiety Scale assesses the level of a person's anxiety. Objective tests have better reliability (they are more consistent over time) and validity (they are more likely to measure what they say they measure) than do projective tests or the subjective judgment of clinicians (Anastasi, 1988; Dawes, 1994).

The most famous and widely used objective test of personality is the **Minnesota Multiphasic Personality Inventory (MMPI)**. The MMPI was developed in the 1930s by two psychiatrists who wanted a way to screen people with psychological disorders. They administered 1,000 potential test items to 200 people with various mental disorders and to a control group of 1,500 people who were not in treatment; the two groups differed in their answers to 550 items, and these items were retained. The items were then assigned to ten clinical categories, or *scales*, that identified such problems as depression, paranoia, schizophrenia, and introversion. Four *validity scales* indicated whether a test-taker was likely to be lying, defensive, or evasive while answering the items. For example, if you tried to present a favorable but unrealistic image of yourself on nearly every item, your score on the lie scale would be high.

Since the original MMPI was devised, hundreds of additional scales have been added, and thousands of books and articles have been written on the test. In 1989, a major revision of the MMPI was released, the MMPI-2, with norms based on a sample that was more representative in terms of region, ethnicity, age, and gender (Butcher et al., 1989).

Despite its popularity, the MMPI has many critics. Some have observed that the test's standards of "normalcy" do not take into account cultural differences. For example, Mexican, Puerto Rican, and Argentine respondents score differently from non-Hispanic Americans, on average, on the Masculinity-Femininity Scale (Lucio et al., 1998). Latinos tend to be more traditional in their sex-role attitudes than non-Hispanic Americans and Canadians, but this reflects cultural values, not personality problems. In addition, norms for the MMPI-2 were based on samples in which minorities, the elderly, the poor, and the poorly educated were still underrepresented (Edwards & Edwards, 1991; Helmes & Reddon, 1993).

personality A distinctive and relatively stable pattern of behavior, thoughts, motives, and emotions that characterizes an individual throughout life.

trait A characteristic of an individual, describing a habitual way of behaving, thinking, and feeling.

inventories Standardized objective questionnaires requiring written responses; they typically include scales on which people are asked to rate themselves.

Minnesota Multiphasic Personality Inventory (MMPI) A widely used objective personality test.

One review concluded that the MMPI is adequate if the test is used *only* to identify people with emotional problems (Parker, Hanson, & Hunsley, 1988); cross-culturally, the MMPI-2 does reliably identify people with psychiatric disorders (Butcher, Lim, & Nezami, 1998). Yet in practice, the MMPI is often used in business, industry, and education for inappropriate reasons by persons who are not well trained in testing.

In research, well-validated personality inventories can identify key traits that accurately predict how people will behave (Paunonen, 1998). But consumers should be wary of tests that claim to capture personality "types" and to predict how people will do on a job, whether they will get along with others, or whether they will succeed as leaders. One such test, the Myers-Briggs Type Indicator, is very popular in business and motivational seminars. But many researchers have failed to confirm the test's premise that knowledge of a person's alleged "type" can reliably predict behavior (Barbuto, 1997; Pittenger, 1993). In "Taking Psychology with You," we discuss other personality tests to watch out for.

The four basic personality types

Identifying Central Traits

One of the most influential personality theorists was Gordon Allport (1897–1967). Allport (1937, 1961) recognized that not all traits have equal weight and significance in people's lives. Most of us have five to ten *central traits* that reflect a characteristic way of behaving, dealing with others, and reacting to new situations. For instance, some people see the world as a hostile, dangerous place, whereas others see it as a playpen. *Secondary traits*, in contrast, are more changeable aspects of personality, such as music preferences, habits, casual opinions, and the like.

Another influential personality theorist, Raymond B. Cattell, essentially confirmed Allport's idea that traits vary in their "centrality" to the individual. Cattell advanced the study of personality by applying a statistical method called **factor analysis**. Performing a factor analysis is like adding water to flour: It causes the material to clump up into little balls. When applied to personality traits, this procedure identifies clusters of correlated items that seem to be measuring some common, underlying factor. For example, the traits of assertiveness, willingness to tell jokes in large groups, and pleasure in meeting new people might share the common factor of extroversion.

Using questionnaires, life descriptions, and observations, Cattell (1965, 1973) measured dozens of personality traits in thousands of people, including humor, intelligence, creativity, dominance, and emotional disorders. Out of these he developed the 16 Personality Factors (PF) Questionnaire. Later in his career, he noted that only 6 of the 16 factors measured by the questionnaire had been repeatedly confirmed, but the 16 PF test has nonetheless remained popular (Digman, 1996).

By the mid-1980s, the evidence for a small cluster of fundamental personality traits had become overwhelming. Although researchers are still debating exactly how many traits belong to this inner group—some say three, others say as many as nine—most personality researchers agree on the centrality of five key traits, called the *Big Five* for short (Digman, 1996; Jang et al., 1998; McCrae & Costa, 1996; Wiggins, 1996):

1 *Introversion versus extroversion* describes the extent to which people are outgoing or shy. It includes such traits as being talkative or silent, sociable or reclusive, adventurous or cautious, eager to be in the limelight or inclined to stay in the shadows. Extroversion is associated with the tendency to be enthusiastic, lively, and cheerful.

factor analysis A statistical method for analyzing the intercorrelations among various measures or test scores; clusters of measures or scores that are highly correlated are assumed to measure the same underlying trait or ability.

Extroversion is one of the "Big Five" personality factors. Not every politician would be moved to get up and dance with a rock band, as the extroverted Boris Yeltin did during the Russian presidential campaign of 1996.

2 *Neuroticism,* or *negative emotionality,* includes such traits as anxiety, an inability to control impulses, and a tendency to feel negative emotions such as anger, guilt, scorn, and resentment. Neurotic individuals are worriers, complainers, and defeatists, even when they have no major problems. They complain about different things at different ages, but they are always ready to see the sour side of life and none of its sweetness.

3 *Agreeableness* describes the extent to which people are good-natured or irritable, gentle or headstrong, cooperative or abrasive, secure or suspicious and jealous. It reflects the tendency to have friendly relationships or hostile ones.

4 *Conscientiousness* describes the degree to which people are responsible or undependable, persevering or quick to give up, steadfast or fickle, tidy or careless.

5 *Openness to experience* describes the extent to which people are original, imaginative, questioning, artistic, and capable of creative thinking, or are conforming, unimaginative, and predictable.

Evidence for the Big Five has turned up in studies of many thousands of children and adults all over the world—with, among others, Chinese, Dutch, Japanese, Spanish, Filipino, Hawaiian, German, Portuguese, Israeli, Korean, Russian, and Australian samples (Benet-Martínez & John, 1998; Digman & Shmelyov, 1996; Katigbak, Church, & Akamine, 1996; McCrae & Costa, 1997; Yang & Bond, 1990).

The Big Five traits are remarkably stable over a lifetime, especially once a person hits 30 (Costa & McCrae, 1994). But there is some good news for crabby neurotics, especially young ones. Studies of thousands of people, ages 16 to over 80, in 10 countries, find that young people, ages 16 to 21, are the most neurotic (emotionally

GET ➡ INVOLVED

RATE YOUR TRAITS

Using the Big Five, rate your own personality traits along a five-point scale (refer to the text for the description of traits that make up each dimension). For example:

introverted _____/_____/_____/_____/_____ extroverted

neurotic _____/_____/_____/_____/_____ emotionally stable

agreeable _____/_____/_____/_____/_____ stubborn

conscientious _____/_____/_____/_____/_____ undependable

open to experience _____/_____/_____/_____/_____ prefer the familiar

Now ask a friend or relative to rate you on the Big Five. How close does this rating match your own? If there's a discrepancy, what might be the reason for it?

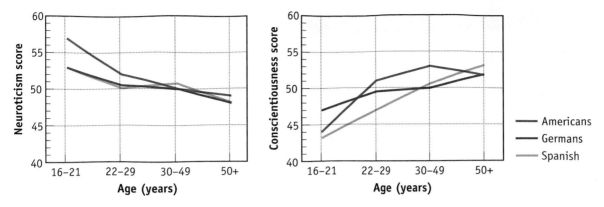

FIGURE 13.1

CONSISTENCY AND CHANGE IN PERSONALITY OVER THE LIFE SPAN

Studies of thousands of people in many different cultures in Europe, North America, and Asia find that although the Big Five traits remain fairly stable, changes occur over the life span. As you can see here, neuroticism (negative emotionality) is highest among young adults, and then declines; conscientiousness is lowest among young adults, and then steadily increases. These changes probably reflect common experiences that occur as young people leave home and grow up (Costa et al., 1999).

negative) and the least agreeable and conscientious. By age 30, however, perhaps as a result of the new responsibilities of adulthood, they become more agreeable and conscientious and less negative and bitter (see Figure 13.1). Unfortunately, in later adulthood older people also tend to become less extroverted and less open to new experiences. Because these changes have been found in so many different countries, they seem to reflect common maturational changes, especially those of early adulthood, rather than changes due to culture or generation (Costa et al., 1999; McCrae et al., 1999).

The Big Five do not represent all of the traits that make up personality, but they do seem to capture its essential dimensions. The logical next question is, where do these traits come from?

QUICK QUIZ

1. What is the advantage of inventories, compared with clinical judgment and projective tests, in measuring personality?
2. Raymond Cattell advanced the study of personality with his method of (a) case-study analysis, (b) factor analysis.
3. Which of the following traits are *not* among the Big Five traits in personality? (a) introversion, (b) agreeableness, (c) psychoticism, (d) openness to experience, (e) intelligence, (f) neuroticism, (g) conscientiousness
4. Which trait among the Big Five typically decreases by age 30? (a) agreeableness, (b) extroversion, (c) openness to experience, (d) neuroticism

Answers:

1. In general, they have better reliability and validity. 2. b 3. c, e 4. d

WHAT'S AHEAD

- Is it possible to be born irritable or easygoing?
- To what extent are personality differences among people influenced by their genetic differences?
- Are people who have highly heritable personality traits stuck with them forever?

THE GENETIC CONTRIBUTION

A mother we know was describing her two children. "My daughter has always been emotionally intense and a little testy," she said, "but my son is the opposite, placid and good-natured. They came out of the womb that way." Did they? What aspects of personality might have an inherited component?

Psychologists who take a biological view of personality try to answer these questions in two ways: by studying temperaments in children and by doing heritability studies of adult twins. They hope that the genes underlying temperaments and the apparently universal Big Five traits will one day be discovered (Plomin et al., 1998). One research team believes it has already found one of several genes involved in neuroticism, pessimism, and anxiety (Lesch et al., 1996). This finding is still tentative, but the search for genes involved in aspects of personality is moving ahead rapidly, and you will be hearing lots more about genetic discoveries in the coming years.

Heredity and Temperament

Even in the first weeks after birth, infants differ in activity level, mood, responsiveness, soothability, and attention span (Belsky, Hsieh, & Crnic, 1996; Kagan, 1994). Some are irritable and cranky; others are placid and sweet-natured. Some will cuddle up in an adult's arms and snuggle; others squirm and fidget, as if they cannot stand being held. Some smile easily; others fuss and cry. Because such differences appear so early—even when you control for possible prenatal influences such as the mother's nutrition, drug use, or problems with the pregnancy—most psychologists believe they have a genetic basis. These **temperaments** are physiological dispositions to respond to the environment in relatively stable, typical ways, and they may later form the basis of specific personality traits, such as extroversion.

Jerome Kagan (1994, 1998a, b) has been studying two temperamental styles, which he calls "reactive" and "nonreactive." About 20 percent of all children are at one extreme or the other; the rest fall somewhere in between. Highly reactive infants, even at four months of age, are excitable and nervous; they overreact to any little thing. If you put a colorful picture in front of them, they get aroused and upset. At 14 and 21 months, they tend to be wary and fearful of new things—toys that make noise, odd-looking robots—even when their moms are right there with them. At 5 years, many of these children are still timid and uncomfortable in new situations. And at 7 years, many still have symptoms of anxiety. They are afraid of being kidnapped, they need to sleep with the light on, they are afraid of sleeping in an unfamiliar house—even if they have never been traumatized.

Shyness and fear of new situations tend to be stable aspects of temperament. Children who are extremely shy can learn to become more sociable, but they rarely become extroverts.

In contrast, nonreactive infants, Kagan (1998a) says, are "California, laid-back babies." They lie there; they never cry; they babble happily. A year later, they are outgoing and curious about new toys and events. They continue to be easygoing and extroverted throughout childhood.

Children with these temperaments have distinctive physiological patterns. When reactive children are doing mildly stressful mental tasks, they are more likely than non-reactive children to show signs of activity in the sympathetic nervous system, indicating physiological arousal—increased heart rate, dilation of the pupils, heightened brain activity, and high levels of two stress hormones, norepinephrine and cortisol. Interestingly, Stephen Suomi (1987, 1991) has found exactly the same physiological attributes in shy, anxious infant rhesus monkeys. Starting early in life, these "uptight" monkeys respond with anxiety to novelty and challenge, just as Kagan's overreacting children do. They too have high heart rates and elevated levels of cortisol. When uptight rhesus monkeys grow up, they usually continue to be anxious when challenged, and, like Kagan's children, they act traumatized even though nothing bad has ever happened to them (Higley et al., 1991).

Biologically based temperaments, then, seem to influence later personality traits. However, they do not provide an unchangeable blueprint for personality. Consistency in a given temperament depends in part on how extreme that trait is in infancy. Kagan, who has been following reactive and nonreactive children for many years, put it this way: What proportion of extremely reactive babies remain extremely shy and fearful as older children? About 15 percent. What proportion become average, neither extremely shy nor extremely outgoing? The rest. What proportion become vivacious, fearless, and extroverted? Zero. "The environment acts on fearful children to move them toward health, toward the center," Kagan (1998a) explains, "but it's really hard to move them to the other end."

Whether extremely fearful infants shift toward the center depends on how parents and others respond to them. Even a highly reactive infant monkey can overcome its timidity if it is reared by an extremely nurturant foster mother (see Figure 13.2). In human beings, the fit between a child's nature and the parents' reactions is critical. Imagine a high-strung parent with a baby who is fearful, quick to cry, and slow to be consoled. The parent may begin to feel desperate, angry, or rejected. Over time, the parent may withdraw from the child or use excessive punishment, which in turn makes the child even more timid and withdrawn. In contrast, a more easygoing parent may have a calming effect on a frightened child, leading the child to become more outgoing.

temperaments Physiological dispositions to respond to the environment in certain ways; they are present in infancy and are assumed to be innate.

FIGURE 13.2
DON'T BE SHY

On the left, a timid infant rhesus monkey cowers behind a friend in the presence of an outgoing stranger. This extreme fearfulness, typical of 10 to 15 percent of monkeys and human beings, seems to be biologically based (Kagan, 1994; Suomi, 1989). But a nurturant foster mother (center) can help an infant overcome its timidity. At first, the infant clings to her, but a few days later (right) the same young monkey has become more adventurous.

Identical twins Gerald Levey (left) and Mark Newman were separated at birth and raised in different cities. When they were reunited at age 31, they discovered some astounding similarities. Both were volunteer firefighters, wore mustaches, and were unmarried. They were exactly the same height and weight. Both liked to hunt, watch old John Wayne movies, and eat Chinese food. They drank the same brand of beer, held the can with the little finger curled around it, and crushed the can when it was empty. The challenge is to figure out which of these traits and behaviors are influenced strongly by heredity, and which result mainly from environmental factors such as social class and upbringing.

heritability A statistical estimate of the proportion of the total variance in some trait within a group that is attributable to genetic differences among individuals within the group.

Heredity and Traits

Another way to study genetic contributions to personality is to estimate the **heritability** of specific traits within groups of children or adults. As we saw in Chapter 3, heritability estimates are based on *behavioral-genetic* studies of adopted children and of identical and fraternal twins reared apart and together. (If you need to review these methods and how they are used to estimate the role of genetics, see pages 84–85.) Findings from adoption and twin studies have been consistent and remarkable. For example, identical twins reared apart will often have unnerving similarities in gestures, mannerisms, and moods; if one tends to be optimistic, glum, or excitable, the other will probably be that way too (Braungert et al., 1992). Their personalities often seem as similar as their physical features.

In behavioral-genetic studies, the heritability of an enormous range of personality traits—including the Big Five, selflessness, aggression, and overall happiness and well-being—is typically between .40 and .60 (Bouchard, 1997a; Loehlin, 1992; Lykken & Tellegen, 1996; Waller et al., 1990). This means that within a group of people, 40 to 60 percent of the variation in such traits is attributable to genetic differences among the individuals in the group. These findings have been replicated in many countries. For example, a study of Canadian and German twin samples found the same high heritability of the Big Five traits (Jang et al., 1998).

Some researchers have even reported high heritability for such specific activities as getting divorced (McGue & Lykken, 1992) and watching a lot of television in childhood (Plomin et al., 1990)! These results are astounding; how can divorce and TV watching be heritable? Our prehistoric ancestors didn't get married, let alone divorced, and they certainly didn't watch TV. What could be the personality traits or temperaments underlying these behaviors?

Here is an even more startling finding: In numerous behavioral–genetic studies, the only environmental contribution to personality differences comes from having unique experiences *not shared* with other family members, such as being in Mrs. Miller's class in the fourth grade or winning the lead in the school play (Bouchard, 1997a; Hur, McGue, & Iacono, 1998; Loehlin, 1992). Shared environment—the family you grew up with and the experiences you shared with your siblings and parents—seems to have no significant effect on your personality. (We are speaking only of your personality traits, though; of course your family experiences affect your feelings toward, and relationships with, your parents and siblings.)

Understandably, behavioral geneticists are excited about these findings, which have huge implications for the age-old debate over the contributions of "nature" (genetic dispositions) and "nurture" (upbringing and environment) to the development of personality. "It will doubtless seem incredible to many readers that variables such as social class, educational opportunities, religious training, and parental love and discipline have no substantial influence on adult personality," wrote Robert McCrae and Paul Costa (1988), "but imagine for a moment that it is correct. What will it mean for research in developmental psychology? How will clinical psychology and theories of therapy be changed?"

Good questions! What *do* these findings mean for education, for raising children, or for psychotherapy and the treatment of personality problems? Does the environment count for nothing?

Evaluating Genetic Research

Although the findings on the heritability of personality traits are impressive, genes are not the whole story. If heredity accounts for about half of the explanation of why people differ in their traits, then the environment (and errors in measurement) must account for the other half. As Robert Plomin (1989), a leading behavioral geneticist, observed, "The wave of acceptance of genetic influence on behavior is growing into a tidal wave that threatens to engulf the second message of this research: These same data provide the best available evidence for the importance of environmental influences." Let's consider some reasons not to jump to the conclusion that "genes are everything":

THINKING CRITICALLY

CONSIDER OTHER EXPLANATIONS
Some personality traits, such as shyness, are highly heritable. Does that mean that a shy 5-year-old will inevitably grow up to become a wallflower? What is a better way to think about the impact of heredity on personality?

1 *Not all traits are equally heritable or unaffected by shared environment.* Religious orthodoxy, intellectual interests, feelings of inadequacy, and adherence to traditional notions of masculinity and femininity are some of the traits that are strongly affected by a child's shared environment and culture (Beer, Arnold, & Loehlin, 1998).

2 *Even traits that are highly heritable are not rigidly fixed;* experience can strengthen or diminish them. As we noted, temperamentally fearful children can learn, from parents and peers, to control the inclination to avoid unfamiliar people, large dogs, or new experiences (Kagan, 1998b). And even the Big Five, as we saw, change somewhat over the life span.

3 *The relative influence of genes versus the environment can change over a person's lifetime.* For some traits, experiences at certain periods in life become particularly influential and therefore heritability decreases. For example, an analysis of data from nearly 15,000 Finnish twins, ages 18 to 59, found that the heritability of extroversion decreases (and thus the impact of the environment *increases*) from the late teens and early 20s to the late 20s—a time when people are leaving home and establishing independent lives (Viken et al., 1994).

Behavioral-genetic research has the potential to be used wisely or foolishly. Some psychotherapists believe that one wise use is to help people in therapy realize that they cannot transform their personalities, but that they can learn to cope with their existing temperamental dispositions and limits (Efran, Greene, & Gordon, 1998). For example, a shy man won't become Robin Williams and a timid woman won't become Whoopi Goldberg, but they can both learn to become more comfortable and sociable in new situations. Another wise result of behavioral–genetic research might be to unburden parents of the sole responsibility for how their children turn out—a controversial idea we discuss in the next chapter (Harris, 1998).

However, behavioral-genetic research can easily be misused and misunderstood, especially when people oversimplify. When people believe that "genes are everything," they overlook the role of the environment in modifying traits. As a result, they may assume that personality problems that have a genetic component are hopeless—that someone is "born to be bad" or born to be a miserable grump forever. Likewise, they may mistakenly assume that if a problem, such as depression, has "genetic" origins, it will respond only to medication, and there is no point trying other solutions (we discuss this fallacy in Chapter 17).

The most important lesson from behavioral-genetic research is that a genetic *predisposition* does not imply genetic *inevitability* (Sapolsky, 1998). Biology and experience, and genetics and culture, are inextricably intertwined.

"THERE'S ANOTHER HEREDITARY DISEASE THAT RUNS IN THE ROYAL FAMILY. YOUR GRANDFATHER WAS A STUBBORN FOOL, YOUR FATHER WAS A STUBBORN FOOL, AND _YOU_ ARE A STUBBORN FOOL."

QUICK QUIZ

We hope the trait of conscientiousness will motivate you to take this quiz.

1. What two broad lines of research support the hypothesis that personality differences are due in part to genetic differences?

2. In behavioral-genetic studies, the heritability of personality traits, including the Big Five, is typically about (a) .40 to .60, (b) .90, (c) .10 to .20, (d) zero.

3. Diane hears that timidity is an inherited temperament. She tells her roommate that her own fear of meeting people and going to parties must be due mostly to genes and that there is nothing she can do about it. What's wrong with her reasoning?

4. A newspaper headline announces, "Couch Potatoes Born, Not Made: Kids' TV habits May Be Hereditary." Why is this headline misleading? What other explanations of the finding are possible? What aspects of TV watching *could* have a hereditary component?

Answers:

1. Research on temperaments and on heritability.   2. a   3. Diane could be shy for any number of reasons, but even if her extreme shyness is inherited, it could be modified by experience.   4. The headline implies that there is a "TV-watching gene," but the writer is failing to consider other explanations. Perhaps some temperaments dispose people to be sedentary or passive, and this disposition can lead to a tendency to watch a lot of television.

WHAT'S AHEAD

● Why do some people always expect to do poorly while others are confident of success?

● What is the difference between people who think they control their own destiny and those who think destiny controls them?

THE SOCIAL-COGNITIVE CONTRIBUTION

Whenever a news story appears about someone who murdered his wife and children, embezzled thousands of dollars from her employer, or shot a neighbor in the midst of a furious dispute, what do friends and family always say about the accused? "Gosh, he was such a nice guy." "Gee, she was always honest with me." "I can't believe my son would shoot anyone—I never saw him even lose his temper."

Social-cognitive theories account for such apparent contradictions by emphasizing the *social situations* that affect behavior and personality. In the social-cognitive view, a person may be cheerful and friendly at work but hostile and obnoxious at home, or vice versa. Personality traits can change, depending on the demands of the situation (see Chapter 8) and on how people perceive and interpret those situations.

In the social-cognitive view, we acquire our characteristic ways of behaving and our reactions to situations in part because of how we were rewarded and punished as we were growing up (see Chapter 7). But these habits, behaviors, and cognitions in turn influence how we respond to others, whom we associate with, and the situations we seek out (Bandura, 1986, 1990; Cervone, 1997; Mischel & Shoda, 1995). Environmental influences, cognitions, and behavior affect each other in a process of **reciprocal determinism** that shapes our distinctive personalities.

Thus, in the social-cognitive view, if you want to understand why some people are conscientious—prompt to pay bills and good at making plans—you don't learn much by assuming that "conscientiousness" is an internal, consistent trait that sits inside you like a kidney (Cervone, 1997). Instead, you need to observe people in different

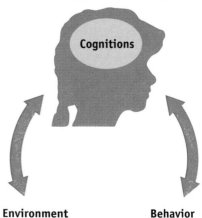

RECIPROCAL DETERMINISM

Cognitions

Environment   Behavior

situations: Do they behave the same way in school and at home? What aspects of the situation, rather than their own preferences, might be affecting their behavior? You also need to know how people perceive and interpret each situation: as one in which they feel *capable* of behaving conscientiously, or one that swamps their ability to modify their actions?

To illustrate the social-cognitive approach to personality, we will consider two important psychological qualities that researchers in this tradition have investigated: self-efficacy and the sense of control over one's life.

Self-efficacy

From childhood, Jim Abbott wanted to play professional baseball. He succeeded in his ambition and has had a brilliant career as a pitcher in the majors. But Jim Abbott had a problem that might have squelched the ambitions of most young athletes: He has no right hand. What gave him the belief that he could succeed anyway?

Jim Abbott clearly had a sense of **self-efficacy**, the conviction that you can accomplish what you set out to do. People who have a strong sense of self-efficacy are quick to cope with problems that befall them, spend effort striving for their goals, and sustain that effort even in the face of setbacks and failures. Research in North America, Europe, and Russia has found that self-efficacy has a positive effect on just about every aspect of people's lives: how well they do on a task, how persistently they pursue their goals, the kind of career choices they make, their ability to solve complex problems, their motivation to work for political and social goals, their health habits, and even their chances of recovery from heart attack (Bandura, 1994; Ewart, 1995; Maddux, 1995; Stajkovic & Luthans, 1998).

According to Albert Bandura (1994, 1995), self-efficacy is acquired from four sources:

Talk about self-efficacy! Aimee Mullins was born without the bones that connect the knee to the ankle, and her legs were amputated below the knee on her first birthday. Mullins learned to ski, and also set records for the 100m, 200m, and long jump at the 1996 Paralympics. In 1998 she became a professional model, dazzling the fashion world by modeling an outfit complete with high-heeled wood prostheses carved to look like boots. "[People] relate to what I'm doing, which is challenging the norm," says Mullins.

1 *Having experiences in mastering new skills and overcoming obstacles.* Occasional failures may not be much fun, but they are necessary for self-efficacy. Without them, people learn to expect quick results and tend to be easily discouraged by normal difficulties.

2 *Having successful and competent role models.* By observing the competence of people you identify with, you learn that a task is possible. For example, if an African-American boy learns that the inventor of the traffic light, Garrett Morgan, was also African-American, his belief that he too could be an engineer might be strengthened. Negative role models, on the other hand, can undermine self-efficacy: If other people in your group have not succeeded, you may come to doubt that you can make it.

3 *Getting feedback and encouragement from others.* Self-efficacy increases when other people give you helpful feedback about your performance, and when they reward your efforts and do not subject you to repeated put-downs and discouragement.

4 *Learning how to read and manage your own physiological state.* You will feel more competent when you are calm and relaxed than when you are tense or under stress. But people with self-efficacy are even able to use nervousness productively. For example, instead of interpreting normal feelings of stage fright as evidence that they are going to make fools of themselves when they give a talk, they regard these jitters as a source of energy that will help them perform better.

social-cognitive theories (of personality) Theories that emphasize how personality traits are learned and maintained depending on the specific situation and the individual's cognitive processes.

reciprocal determinism In social-cognitive theories, the two-way interaction between the environment and the individual in determining and shaping personality factors.

self-efficacy A person's belief that he or she is capable of producing desired results, such as mastering new skills and reaching goals.

RECIPROCAL DETERMINATION IN SELF-EFFICACY

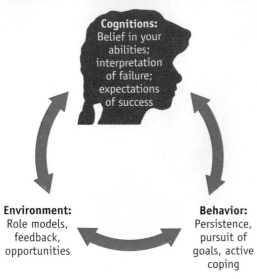

Cognitions: Belief in your abilities; interpretation of failure; expectations of success

Environment: Role models, feedback, opportunities

Behavior: Persistence, pursuit of goals, active coping

As you can see, some of the sources of self-efficacy lie in your situation (does it provide feedback, role models, opportunities to succeed?) and some in your perceptions (how do you interpret your own responses and your experiences with success or failure?). That is why, as social-cognitive theory would predict, self-efficacy varies across situations. A person may feel highly competent and able to change the world in one domain (say, sports), but feel like an inadequate nincompoop in another (say, love relationships) (Cervone, 1997).

Fortunately, self-efficacy can be acquired through programs and experiences that provide skills, mastery, and role models, and that teach people to think of failure as a temporary detour and an opportunity to learn, rather than as a hopeless sign of incompetence (Maddux, 1995). You can see how self-efficacy illustrates reciprocal determinism: Your beliefs affect what happens to you, and what happens to you affects your beliefs.

Perceptions of Control

Another important example of how reciprocal determinism shapes personality is the extent to which people believe they have control over their lives.

Much of the original research on this topic was done by Julian Rotter, who started out as a behaviorist. Rotter was both a psychotherapist and a researcher, trying to treat his patients' persistent, self-defeating actions according to behavioral principles (Hunt, 1993). But these methods weren't working, and Rotter, thinking critically, came up with a better, alternative explanation for his clients' behavior. He saw that his clients had formed entrenched attitudes as a result of their lifetimes of experience, and that these attitudes were affecting their decisions and actions (Rotter, 1982, 1990).

Over time, Rotter concluded, people learn that some acts will be rewarded and others punished, and thus they develop general expectations about whether or not their efforts will be successful. A child who studies hard and gets good grades, attention from teachers, admiration from friends, and praise from parents will come to expect that hard work in other situations will also pay off. A child who studies hard and gets poor grades, is ignored by teachers and parents, and is rejected by friends for being a grind will come to expect that working hard isn't worth it. Once acquired, these expectations often create a **self-fulfilling prophecy** (Merton, 1948): The person's expectations lead to behavior that makes the expectation come true. You expect to succeed, so you work hard—and succeed. Or you expect to fail, so you don't do much work, and as a result you do poorly. Self-fulfilling prophecies also occur in love affairs: People who expect to be rejected ("No one could love a schlub like me") often behave in ways that cause their partners to eventually reject them ("OK, you convinced me; you *are* a schlub") (Downey et al., 1998).

Rotter and his colleagues demonstrated the power of expectancies in many experiments. At the same time, both in his private practice and in his research, Rotter was observing people whose expectations of success never went up even when they were actually successful. "Oh, that was just a fluke," they would say, or "I was lucky; it will never happen again."

Rotter concluded that people's feelings or beliefs about the forces that govern their behavior are as important as anything that actually happens to them. He chose the term **locus of control** to refer to people's beliefs about whether the results of their actions are under their own control. People who have an *internal locus of control* ("internals") tend to believe that they are responsible for what happens to them, that they control their own destiny. People who have an *external locus of control* ("externals") tend to believe that their lives are controlled by luck, fate, or other people.

self-fulfilling prophecy An expectation that comes true because of the tendency of the person holding it to act in ways to bring it about.

locus of control A general expectation about whether the results of a person's actions are under her or his control (internal locus) or beyond the person's control (external locus).

To measure these traits, Rotter developed an Internal/External (I/E) Scale consisting of pairs of statements. You have to choose the statement in each pair with which you most strongly agree, as in these two items:

1. a. Many of the unhappy things in people's lives are partly due to bad luck.
   b. People's misfortunes result from mistakes they make.

2. a. Becoming a success is a matter of hard work; luck has little or nothing to do with it.
   b. Getting a good job depends mainly on being in the right place at the right time.

Research on locus of control took off like a shot, and over the years more than 2,000 studies based on the I/E scale (including a version for children) have been published, with people of all ages and many different ethnic groups. An internal locus of control emerges at an early age and is associated with many aspects of life—including health, academic achievement, and political activism (Nowicki & Strickland, 1973; Strickland, 1989).

But, as social-cognitive theory would again predict, your locus of control can change, depending on your experiences in society and your perceptions of them. During the 1960s, when the civil-rights movement was gathering steam in America, civil-rights activists and black student leaders were more likely to score at the "internal" end of the scale than were their counterparts who were uninvolved in civil-rights efforts (Gore & Rotter, 1963). By the 1970s, however—after the assassinations of Martin Luther King, Jr., and John and Robert Kennedy, and after the United States had become embroiled in the Vietnam War—scores on the locus-of-control scale changed. Civil-rights leaders and college students became less

These members of the Communication Workers Union have an internal locus of control, motivating them to protest their city's budget cuts. What social forces and events might promote an internal locus of control, and which ones might reduce it?

GET ➜ INVOLVED

WHO'S IN CONTROL?

Think back to the last time you did well on a test or on some task. Which of the following phrases best describes how you explained your success to yourself?

■ I'm really competent (or smart, skillful, etc.).
■ I worked hard, and it paid off.
■ I was lucky.
■ The test (or task) was pretty easy.
■ I did well, but only because someone else helped me.

Now think about a time you did *not* do well on a test or task. Which phrase best describes how you accounted for your disappointing performance?

■ I'm just not good at this.
■ I didn't work (or try) hard enough.
■ I was unlucky.
■ I did poorly, but the test (or task) wasn't fair.
■ I did poorly, but only because I got bad instruction or too little help.

What do your answers tell you about your own locus of control? Do you tend to be internal or external for success? What about for failure? Do your beliefs about the results of your actions motivate you to further effort, or discourage you?

RECIPROCAL DETERMINISM IN LOCUS OF CONTROL

internal—that is, less confident that they, as individuals, could improve social conditions (Strickland, 1989).

Today, many Americans seem to have an external locus of control, reflected in the rising numbers who do not vote and who believe their fates are predetermined by the stars or by destiny. Where would you place your own locus of control? How do you think it influences your actions? How does it affect your beliefs about the possibility of changing yourself or improving the world?

Evaluating Social-Cognitive Approaches

Social-cognitive theorists have made important contributions to the study of personality by drawing our attention to how traits are learned over time, and by explaining why traits sometimes vary across situations. Drawing on basic principles of learning (Chapter 7), social psychology (Chapter 8), and cognition (Chapter 9), social-cognitive theorists show that many personality traits are largely acquired through experience and can change, depending on the demands of the situation and on how we are interpreting it.

One problem with the social-cognitive emphasis on reciprocal determinism, however, is that for any given trait, it is hard to tell just how "reciprocal" the person and situation actually are. Behavioral geneticists, for instance, believe that when you have a certain biologically influenced trait or temperament, you will be disposed to seek out situations that let you express it, or in which you feel comfortable. Social-cognitive theorists account for this phenomenon by saying you will seek situations in which you *believe* you can behave a certain way. Which comes first, the biology or the belief?

The social-cognitive view reminds us of the many interacting factors in our lives that shape our personality and behavior, as we saw in the case of the four complex factors that promote self-efficacy. When so many factors *can* have an influence,

Celebrities and media stars can be powerful role models, as the popularity of "look-alike" contests reveals. These Elvis Presley impersonators are entrants in the annual Elvis Day Parade in Kansas City, Mo.

Calvin and Hobbes

by Bill Watterson

As social-cognitive theories would predict, not everyone is influenced by television to the same degree.

however, it can be frustratingly hard to show that any one thing actually *is* having an influence. It's like trying to grab a fistful of fog; you know it's there, but it keeps getting away from you.

For example, how strongly do role models in the media influence what personality traits the sexes value and which they cultivate in themselves? Does watching Jennifer Lopez play a ruthless FBI agent in "Out of Sight" give women a sense of self-efficacy? Does watching Bruce Willis or Wesley Snipes blow away the bad guys make men more aggressive? As social-cognitive theorists would be the first to agree, not everyone perceives the same images in the same way. Some men admire action heroes, while others regard them as foolish cartoon figures. Some women might think that if Lopez could be an FBI agent, so could they, whereas others would no more want to join the FBI than jump off a building. Thus, it is difficult to specify *which* media images are having an effect, and on whom. And it is difficult to disentangle the effects of the media from all the other events and factors that influence people's ideas about men and women, or their sense of self-efficacy.

Despite these problems, the social-cognitive approach has shown that personality is shaped in part by the environment, experience, beliefs, and expectations. Thus, to understand both the stability and the flexibility of traits, we need to know not only about people's genetics, but also about their minds, their learning histories, and, as we will see next, their culture.

QUICK QUIZ

Do you have a general expectation of answering these questions correctly?

1. Which of the following are associated with acquiring a sense of self-efficacy? (a) occasional failure, (b) experiences of success, (c) feedback about your performance, (d) a high income, (e) positive role models, (f) not having to work under stress

2. Anika usually takes credit for doing well on her work assignments and blames her failures on lack of effort. Benecia attributes her successes to luck and blames her failures on the fact that she is an indecisive Gemini. Anika has an _____ locus of control whereas Benecia has an _____ locus.

Answers:

1. all but d and f   2. internal; external

● Why are risk-taking, aggressiveness, and punctuality more than just individual personality traits?

● How does belonging to an individualist or collectivist culture influence your personality—and even whether you think you have a stable "self"?

THE CULTURAL CONTRIBUTION

Are you the kind of person who likes taking risks—say, by smoking cigarettes, driving 100 mph on the highway without a seat belt, or having unprotected sex with a stranger? Are you the kind of person who wants to smack someone who calls you a rude word, or are you more likely to laugh it off?

Most Western psychologists regard risk-taking and quickness to anger as personality traits that are embedded in an individual, either because of a genetic predisposition or a history of rewarded experiences. But those in the *cultural tradition* are interested in how cultures affect people's behavior, attitudes, and the traits they value or disdain. *Culture* is a program of shared rules that govern the behavior of people in a community or society, and a set of values and beliefs shared by most members of that community and passed from one generation to another (Lonner, 1995; see Chapter 8).

Cultural values, for example, affect people's feelings about risk. People in the Netherlands and Britain are more likely than Germans and Austrians to take risks and less likely to favor rules and regulations that promote public safety, such as the requirement to carry citizen identification cards (Cvetkovich & Earle, 1994). The reason is that Germany and Austria (among other societies) place a high value on avoiding uncertainty and thus welcome laws that reduce danger to individuals and communities.

Likewise, the readiness to get riled up when you are insulted is deeply affected by your culture. In "cultures of honor"—including those throughout the Middle East and South America, Southern Europe, and the American South and West—men are often raised to take insults and threats to their reputations very seriously, responding with violence if necessary to restore their sense of honor (Cohen, 1998; Nisbett, 1993). Compared to other regions in the United States, for example, the South and West have the highest rates of honor-related homicides (such as murder to avenge a perceived family insult) and support for guns and vengeful social policies (such as the death penalty) (see Figure 13.3). In a clever experiment in which college men were called an offensive name, those raised in the North tended to respond calmly; they thought it was funny. But many Southerners were immediately inflamed. They felt that their masculine reputations were threatened; their stress hormones and testosterone levels shot up; and they were more likely to retaliate aggressively than Northerners were (Cohen et al., 1996).

Until recently, most psychologists were uninterested in the influence of culture on individuals. In contrast to biology, which they treated as real and tangible, they regarded culture as merely a light veneer on human behavior, or perhaps a source of amusing information for tourist travel ("In Spain, people eat dinner after 10 P.M."). As a result, students and teachers knew little about the psychological characteristics of people living in other societies, and they assumed that they could generalize from studies of people in their own culture to people everywhere (Matsumoto, 1996; Segall, Lonner, & Berry, 1998).

FIGURE 13.3

VIOLENCE AND "CULTURES OF HONOR"

This map of the United States shows that "argument-related" homicide rates—deaths caused by fights to restore status and honor among men—are five times higher in Southern and Western states, which foster "cultures of honor," than in Northern and Eastern states. The rates are per 100,000 white males ages 15 to 39, and occur independently of the general crime rate, poverty, or community instability. (Study excluded Washington, D.C., Alaska, and Hawaii.)

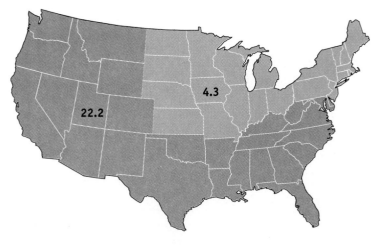

Today many psychologists recognize that culture is just as powerful an influence on personality and behavior as any biological process. In this section, we will consider some contributions of the cultural approach to the understanding of personality.

Culture and Personality

It can be hard to see the influence of cultural rules on our personality traits, but here is a demonstration. Who are you? Take as much time as you like to complete this sentence: "I am _____."

Your response to the "who am I?" test will be influenced by your cultural background, particularly whether your culture emphasizes individualism or community (Hofstede & Bond, 1988; Markus & Kitayama, 1991; Triandis, 1995, 1996). In **individualist cultures**, the independence of the individual takes precedence over the needs of the group, and the self is often defined as a collection of personality traits ("I am outgoing, agreeable, and ambitious") or in occupational terms ("I am a psychologist"). In **collectivist cultures**, group harmony takes precedence over the wishes of the individual, and the self is defined in the context of relationships and the community ("I am the son of a farmer, descended from three generations of storytellers on my mother's side and five generations of farmers on my father's side . . . ").

As Table 13.1 shows, individualist and collectivist ways of defining the self influence many aspects of life, including which personality traits we value, how we express emotions, and how much we value having relationships or maintaining freedom (Campbell et al., 1996; Kashima et al., 1995). Individualist and collectivist outlooks even affect whether we believe that personality is stable across situations. In a revealing study comparing Japanese and Americans, the Americans reported that their sense of self changes only 5 to 10 percent in different situations, whereas the Japanese said that 90 to 99 percent of their sense of self changes (de Rivera, 1989). For the group-oriented Japanese, it is important to enact *tachiba*, to perform your social roles correctly so that there will be harmony with others. Americans, in contrast, tend to value "being true to your self" and having a "core identity." Thus, even basic ideas of what personality means and whether it is consistent across situations are deeply affected by culture.

individualist cultures Cultures in which the self is regarded as autonomous, and individual goals and wishes are prized above duty and relations with others.

collectivist cultures Cultures in which the self is regarded as embedded in relationships, and harmony with one's group is prized above individual goals and wishes.

TABLE 13.1	Some Average Differences Between Individualist and Collectivist Cultures	
Members of individualist cultures	**Members of collectivist cultures**
Define the self as autonomous, independent of groups	Define the self as an interdependent part of groups
Give priority to individual, personal goals	Give priority to the needs and goals of the in-group
Value independence, leadership, achievement, "self-fulfillment"	Value group harmony, duty, obligation, security
Give more weight to an individual's attitudes and preferences than to group norms as explanations of behavior	Give more weight to group norms than to individual attitudes as explanations of behavior
Attend to the benefits and costs of relationships; if costs exceed advantages, a person is likely to drop a relationship	Attend to the needs of group members; if a relationship is beneficial to the group but costly to the individual, the individual is likely to stay in the relationship

Source: Triandis, 1996.

Collectivist Chinese workers in Beijing do their morning T'ai Chi exercises in identical, harmonious fashion. Individualistic Americans exercise by running, walking, bicycling, and skating, all in different directions and wearing different clothes.

When people fail to understand the power of culture on behavior, they often attribute another person's mysterious or annoying actions to personality rather than to cultural norms. Take cleanliness. How often do you bathe—once a day, once a week? Do you regard baths as healthy and invigorating or as a disgusting wallow in dirty water? How often, and where, do you wash your hands—or feet? A person who might seem obsessively clean in one culture might seem an appalling slob in another (Fernea & Fernea, 1994).

Or consider tardiness. Individuals differ in whether they try to be places "on time" or are always late, but cultural norms affect how individuals regard time in the first place. In **monochronic cultures**, such as those of Northern Europe, Canada, and the United States, time is organized into linear segments in which people do one thing "at a time" (Hall, 1983; Hall & Hall, 1990). The day is divided into appointments, schedules, and routines, and because time is a precious commodity, people don't like to "waste" time or "spend" too much time on any one activity. In such cultures, therefore, it is considered the height of rudeness (or high status) to keep someone waiting. But in the southern parts of Europe, in South America, and in Africa, you are likely to find **polychronic cultures**, where time is organized along parallel lines. People do many things at once, and the needs of friends and family supersede mere appointments. People in Latin America and the Middle East think nothing of waiting all day, or even a week, to see someone. The idea of having to be somewhere "on time," as if time were more important than a person, is unthinkable.

In culturally diverse North America, the two time systems keep bumping into each other. Business, government, and other institutions are organized monochronically, but Native Americans, Latinos, African-Americans, and others tend to operate on polychronic principles. The result is repeated misunderstandings. An Anglo judge in Miami got into hot water when he observed that "Cubans always show up two hours late for weddings"—late in his culture's terms, that is. The judge was accurate in his observation; the problem was his implication that something was wrong with Cubans for being "late." And "late" compared to what, by the way? The Cubans were perfectly on time for Cubans.

Evaluating Cultural Influences

monochronic cultures Cultures in which time is organized sequentially; schedules and deadlines are valued over people.

polychronic cultures Cultures in which time is organized horizontally; people tend to do several things at once and value relationships over schedules.

A woman we know, originally from England, married a Lebanese man. They were happy together but had the usual number of marital misunderstandings and squabbles. After a few years, they visited his home town in Lebanon, where she had never been before. "I was stunned," she told us. "All the things I thought he did because of his *personality* turned out to be because he's *Lebanese*! Everyone there was just like him!"

Our friend's reaction illustrates both the contributions and the limitations of cultural studies of personality. She was right in recognizing that some of her husband's behavior was attributable to his culture—for example, his Lebanese notions of time were very different from her English notions. But she would be wrong to infer that the Lebanese are all "like him": Individuals are affected by their culture, but they vary within it.

Cultural psychologists face the problem of how to describe cultural influences on personality without stereotyping (Church & Lonner, 1998). As one student of ours put it, "How come when we students speak of 'the' Japanese or 'the' blacks or 'the' whites or 'the' Latinos, it's called stereotyping, and when you do it, it's called 'cross-cultural psychology'?" This question shows excellent critical thinking! The study of culture does not rest on the assumption that all members of a culture behave the same way or have the same personality traits. As we have already seen in this chapter, individuals vary according to their temperaments, beliefs, and learning histories, and this variation occurs within every culture. But the fact that individuals vary within a culture does not negate the existence of cultural rules that, on the average, make Swedes different from Bedouins or Cambodians different from Italians.

Cultural theories of personality remind us, therefore, that what we value, how we behave, and the qualities we like and dislike in ourselves and others start with the culture in which we are raised.

THINKING CRITICALLY

DON'T OVERSIMPLIFY

People often speak of "the" German personality or "the" British character. How can we think about the cultural factors that do influence personality traits without stereotyping?

QUICK QUIZ

Are you from a culture that values taking quizzes?

1. Cultures whose members regard the "self" as a collection of stable personality traits are (individualist/collectivist).

2. Cultures whose members do many things at once and value relationships over schedules and appointments are (monochronic/polychronic).

3. Which of the terms in Items 1 and 2 apply to the majority culture in the United States and Canada?

Answers:

1. individualist 2. polychronic 3. individualist, monochronic

WHAT'S AHEAD

- How do psychologists regard Freud today—as a genius or a fraud?
- In Freud's theory of personality, why are the id and the superego always at war?
- When people say you're being "defensive," what defenses might they be thinking of?
- What would Carl Jung have had to say about Darth Vader?
- What are the "objects" in the object-relations approach to personality?

THE PSYCHODYNAMIC TRADITION

Of all the theories of personality, the psychodynamic approach is the one most embedded in popular culture. A man apologizes for "displacing" his frustrations at work onto his family. A woman suspects that she is "repressing" a childhood trauma. An alcoholic reveals that he is no longer "in denial" about his drinking.

Sigmund Freud (1856–1939).

A teacher informs a divorcing couple that their 8-year-old child is "regressing" to immature behavior. All of this language—about displacing, repressing, denying, and regressing—can be traced to the first psychodynamic theory of personality, Sigmund Freud's theory of **psychoanalysis**.

Freud's theory is called **psychodynamic** because it emphasizes the movement of psychological energy within the person, in the form of attachments, conflicts, and motivations. Today many psychodynamic theories exist, differing from Freudian theory and from one another, but they all share five general elements:

- *An emphasis on unconscious **intrapsychic** dynamics*, the movement of mental (psychic) energy within the mind.

- *A belief in the primacy of the first 5 years*—i.e., an assumption that adult personality and ongoing problems are formed primarily by experiences in early childhood.

- *A belief that psychological development occurs in fixed stages*, during which predictable mental events occur and unconscious issues or crises must be resolved.

- *A focus on fantasies and symbolic meanings of events* as the unconscious mind perceives them, rather than on actual experiences, as the main influences on behavior.

- *A reliance on subjective rather than objective methods* of getting at the truth of a person's life—for example, through analysis of dreams, myths, folklore, symbols, and, most of all, the revelations uncovered in psychotherapy.

No one disputes the profound influence that Sigmund Freud had on the twentieth century. But there is enormous dispute about the lasting value of his work. Freud saw himself as one of the great geniuses of history, and many people agree with that assessment. But many modern scientists think he was a flat-out fraud whose ideas have not stood the test of time—a "dinosaur in the history of ideas" (Medawar, 1982). In this section, we will introduce you to Freud's ideas, and to two of the many psychodynamic theories that followed his. We will try to show you why attitudes toward Freud today range from reverence to contempt, and why he evokes such controversy.

Freud and Psychoanalysis

To enter the world of Sigmund Freud is to enter a realm of unconscious motives, passions, guilty secrets, unspeakable yearnings, and conflicts between desire and duty. These unseen forces, Freud believed, have far more power over us than our conscious intentions do. The unconscious reveals itself, said Freud, in dreams, jokes, apparent accidents, and slips of the tongue. The British member of Parliament who referred to the "honourable member from Hell" when he meant to say "from Hull," said Freud (1920/1960), was revealing his actual, unconscious appraisal of his colleague.

The Structure of Personality. In Freud's theory, personality consists of three major systems: the id, the ego, and the superego (see Review 13.1). Any action we take or problem we have results from the interaction and degree of balance among these systems (Freud, 1905b, 1920/1960, 1923/1962).

The **id**, which is present at birth, is the reservoir of unconscious psychological energies and the motives to avoid pain and obtain pleasure. The id contains two competing instincts: the life, or sexual, instinct (fueled by psychic energy called the **libido**) and the death, or aggressive, instinct. As energy builds up in the id, tension results. The id may discharge this tension in the form of reflex actions, physical symptoms, or uncensored mental images and unbidden thoughts.

psychoanalysis A theory of personality and a method of psychotherapy developed by Sigmund Freud; it emphasizes unconscious motives and conflicts.

psychodynamic theories Theories that explain behavior and personality in terms of unconscious energy dynamics within the individual.

intrapsychic Within the mind (psyche) or self.

id In psychoanalysis, the part of personality containing inherited psychic energy, particularly sexual and aggressive instincts.

libido [luh-BEE-do] In psychoanalysis, the psychic energy that fuels the life or sexual instincts of the id.

R E V I E W   1 3 . 1

SUMMARY OF FREUD'S MODEL OF THE MIND

	Id	Ego	Superego
What it does	Expresses sexual and aggressive instincts; follows the pleasure principle	Mediates between desires of the id and demands of the superego; follows the reality principle; uses defense mechanisms to ward off unconscious anxiety	Represents conscience and the rules of society; follows internalized moral standards
How conscious it is	Entirely unconscious	Partly conscious, partly unconscious	Partly conscious, mostly unconscious
When it develops	Present at birth	Emerges after birth, with early formative experiences	Last system to develop; becomes internalized after the Oedipal stage
Example	"I'm so mad I could kill you" (felt unconsciously)	Might make a conscious choice ("Let's talk about this") or resort to an unconscious defense mechanism, such as denial ("What, me angry? Never.")	"Thou shalt not kill."

The **ego**, the second system to emerge, is a referee between the needs of instinct and the demands of society. It bows to the realities of life, putting a rein on the id's desire for sex and aggression until a suitable, socially appropriate outlet for them can be found. The ego, said Freud, is both conscious and unconscious, and it represents "reason and good sense."

The **superego**, the last system of personality to develop, represents morality, the rules of parents and society, and the power of authority; it includes the conscience, the inner voice that says you did something wrong. The superego, which is partly conscious but largely unconscious, judges the activities of the id, handing out good feelings (pride, satisfaction) when you do something well and handing out miserable feelings (guilt, shame) when you break the rules.

According to Freud, the healthy personality must keep all three systems in balance. Someone who is too controlled by the id is governed by impulse and selfish desires. Someone who is too controlled by the superego is rigid, moralistic, and bossy. Someone who has a weak ego is unable to balance personal needs and wishes with social duties and realistic limitations.

If a person feels anxious or threatened when the wishes of the id conflict with social rules, the ego has weapons at its command to relieve the tension. These unconscious strategies, called **defense mechanisms**, deny or distort reality, but they protect us from conflict and the stresses of reality. They become unhealthy only when they cause self-defeating behavior and emotional problems. Freud described 17 defense mechanisms; later, other psychoanalysts revised his list. Here are some of the primary defenses identified by Freud's daughter Anna (1967), who became a psychoanalyst herself, and by most contemporary psychodynamic psychologists (Vaillant, 1992):

"VERY WELL, I'LL INTRODUCE YOU. EGO, MEET ID. NOW GET BACK TO WORK."

ego In psychoanalysis, the part of personality that represents reason, good sense, and rational self-control.

superego In psychoanalysis, the part of personality that represents conscience, morality, and social standards.

defense mechanisms Methods used by the ego to prevent unconscious anxiety or threatening thoughts from entering consciousness.

"I'm sorry, I'm not speaking to anyone tonight. My defense mechanisms seem to be out of order."

1 *Repression* occurs when a threatening idea, memory, or emotion is blocked from consciousness. A woman who had a frightening childhood experience that she cannot remember, for example, is said to be repressing her memory of it.

2 *Projection* occurs when a person's own unacceptable or threatening feelings are repressed and then attributed to someone else. A person who is embarrassed about having sexual feelings toward members of a different ethnic group, for example, may project this discomfort onto them, saying, "Those people are dirty-minded and oversexed."

3 *Displacement* occurs when people direct their emotions (especially anger) toward things, animals, or other people that are not the real object of their feelings. A boy who is forbidden to express anger toward his father, for example, may "take it out" on his toys or his younger sister. When displacement serves a higher cultural or socially useful purpose, as in the creation of art or inventions, it is called *sublimation*. Freud argued that society has a duty to help people sublimate their unacceptable impulses for the sake of civilization. Thus, aggressive impulses might be displaced in sports competition instead of directly expressed in war.

4 *Reaction formation* occurs when a feeling that produces unconscious anxiety is transformed into its opposite in consciousness. A woman who is afraid to admit to herself that she fears her husband may instead cling to the belief that she loves him deeply. A person who is aroused by erotic images may angrily assert that pornography is disgusting. How does such a transformed emotion differ from a true emotion? In reaction formation the professed feeling is excessive, and the person is extravagant and compulsive about demonstrating it. ("Of course I love him! I *never* have any bad thoughts about him! He's perfect!")

5 *Regression* occurs when a person reverts to a previous phase of psychological development. An 8-year-old boy who is anxious about his parents' quarreling may regress to earlier habits of thumb sucking or clinging. Adults may regress to immature behavior when they are under pressure—for example, by having temper tantrums if they don't get their way.

6 *Denial* occurs when people refuse to admit that something unpleasant is happening, such as mistreatment by a partner; that they have a problem, such as drinking too much; or that they are feeling a forbidden emotion, such as anger. Denial protects a person's self-image and preserves the illusion of invulnerability ("It can't happen to me").

The Development of Personality. Freud thought that personality develops in a series of *psychosexual stages*, in which sexual energy takes different forms as the child matures. Each new stage produces a certain amount of frustration, conflict, and anxiety. If these become too great, normal development may be interrupted, and the child may remain *fixated*, or stuck, at the current stage.

For example, said Freud, people who remain fixated at the *oral stage*, in the first year of life (when babies experience the world through their mouths), may seek oral gratification in smoking, overeating, nail biting, or chewing on pencils; or they may become clinging and dependent, like a nursing child. Those who remain fixated at the *anal stage*, ages 2 to 3 (when toilet training and control of bodily wastes are the key issues), may become "anal retentive," holding everything in, obsessive about neatness and cleanliness. Or they become just the opposite, "anal expulsive"—messy and disorganized.

For Freud, however, the most crucial stage for the formation of personality was the *phallic (Oedipal) stage*, which lasts roughly from age 3 to age 5 or 6. During this stage, said Freud, the child unconsciously wishes to possess the parent of the other sex and to get rid of the parent of the same sex. Children often announce proudly, "I'm going to marry Daddy (or Mommy) when I grow up," and they reject the same-sex "rival." Freud (1924a, 1924b) labeled this phenomenon the **Oedipus complex**, after the Greek legend of King Oedipus, who unwittingly killed his father and married his mother.

Boys and girls, Freud believed, go through the Oedipal stage differently. Boys are discovering the pleasure and pride of having a penis, so when they see a naked girl for the first time, they are horrified. Their unconscious exclaims (in effect), "Her penis has been cut off! Who could have done such a thing to her? Why, it must have been her powerful father. And if he could do it to her, my father could do it to me!" This realization, said Freud, causes the boy to repress his desire for his mother and identify with his father. He accepts his father's authority and the father's standards of conscience and morality; the superego has emerged.

Freud admitted that he did not know what to make of girls, who, lacking the penis, could not go through the same steps. He speculated that a girl, upon discovering male anatomy, would panic that she had only a puny clitoris instead of a stately penis. She would conclude, said Freud, that she already had lost her penis. As a result, girls do not have the powerful motivating fear that boys do to give up their Oedipal feelings and develop a strong superego; they have only a lingering sense of "penis envy."

By about age 5 or 6, when the Oedipus complex is resolved, said Freud, the child's personality patterns are fundamentally formed. The child settles into a supposedly nonsexual *latency* stage in later childhood, in preparation for the stage of mature *genital sexuality* in adulthood. (He was wrong. Modern research shows that most "latency"-age children are curious about sex and experiment with sexual play [Friedrich, 1998]).

In Freud's view, then, your adult personality is shaped by how you progressed through the early psychosexual stages, which defense mechanisms you have learned to use to reduce anxiety, and whether your ego is strong enough to balance the conflict between the id (what you would like to do) and the superego (your conscience).

As you might imagine, Freud's ideas were not exactly received with yawns. Sexual feelings in 5-year-olds! Repressed longings in respectable adults! Unconscious meanings in dreams! Penis envy! This was strong stuff in the early years of the twentieth century, and before long psychoanalysis had captured the public imagination in Europe and America. But it also produced a sharp rift with the emerging schools of empirical psychology (Hornstein, 1992).

This rift continues to divide psychologists. Many revere Freud as a hero who battled public censure and ridicule in his unwavering pursuit of truth (Gay, 1988). Others acknowledge that some of Freud's ideas have proved faulty, but they believe that the

A Freudian would say that this woman's smoking and nail-biting are signs of an oral fixation.

Oedipus complex In psychoanalysis, a conflict in which a child desires the parent of the other sex and views the same-sex parent as a rival.

overall framework of his theory is timeless and brilliant (Westen, 1998). Others think psychoanalytic theory is nonsense, with little empirical support (Cioffi, 1998). Citing evidence from long unpublished papers, these critics argue that Freud was not the brilliant theoretician, impartial scientist, or even successful clinician that he claimed to be. On the contrary, Freud often pressured his patients into accepting his explanations of their symptoms, and he ignored all evidence disconfirming his ideas (Crews, 1998; Powell & Boer, 1994, 1995; Sulloway, 1992; Webster, 1995).

Consider the story of Freud's 18-year-old patient "Dora" (Freud, 1905a). Dora had been spurning the sexual advances made by her father's friend, "Herr K," since she was 14 (Lakoff & Coyne, 1993). Dora's father wanted her to accept Herr K, perhaps because he himself was having an affair with Herr K's wife; so he sent her off to Freud, who attempted to cure Dora of her "hysterical" refusal to have sex with Herr K. Freud tried to convince Dora that it was not the ugly situation involving her father and his friend that was distressing her, but her own repressed desires for sex. He actually advised Herr K to "press his suit with a passion" and ignore Dora's slaps and repeated rejections. Dora angrily left treatment after three months, and Freud never accepted her "obstinate" rejection of his analysis of her symptoms.

On the positive side, Freud welcomed women into the profession of psychoanalysis, wrote eloquently about the devastating results for women of society's suppression of their sexuality, and argued, ahead of his time, that homosexuality was neither a sin nor a perversion but a "variation of the sexual function" and "nothing to be ashamed of" (Freud, 1961). Freud was thus a mixture of intellectual vision and blindness, sensitivity and arrogance. His provocative ideas left a powerful legacy to psychology—one that others began to tinker with immediately.

QUICK QUIZ

Which Freudian concepts do these events suggest?

1. A 4-year-old girl wants to snuggle on Daddy's lap but refuses to kiss her mother.
2. A celibate priest writes poetry about sexual passion.
3. A man who is angry at his boss shouts at his kids for making noise.
4. A woman who was molested by her stepfather for many years assures her friends that she adores him and thinks he is perfect.
5. A racist justifies segregation by saying that black men are only interested in sex with white women.
6. A 9-year-old boy who moves to a new city starts having tantrums.

Answers:

1. Oedipus complex 2. sublimation 3. displacement 4. reaction formation 5. projection 6. regression

Other Psychodynamic Approaches

Some of Freud's followers stayed in the psychoanalytic tradition and modified Freud's theories from within. Women, you might imagine, were not too pleased about "penis envy." Clara Thompson (1943/1973) and Karen Horney [HORN-eye] (1926/1973) argued that it was insulting philosophy and bad science to claim that half the human race is dissatisfied with its anatomy. When women feel inferior to men, they said, we should look for explanations in the disadvantages that women live with and their second-class status. In fact, Horney added, if anyone has an envy problem, it is men. Men have "womb envy": They envy women's ability to bear children.

Others broke away from Freud, or were actively rejected by him, and went off to start their own schools. Today, there are many psychodynamic approaches, but two are especially popular: those of Carl Jung and of the object-relations theorists.

Jungian Theory. Carl Jung (1875–1961) was originally one of Freud's closest friends, but by 1914 he had left Freud's inner circle. His greatest difference with Freud concerned the nature of the unconscious. In addition to the individual's own unconscious, said Jung (1967), there is a **collective unconscious** shared by all human beings, containing universal memories, symbols, and images that are the legacy of human history. In his studies of myths, art, and folklore in cultures all over the world, Jung identified a number of these common themes, which he called **archetypes**.

An archetype, he said, can be a picture, such as the "magic circle," called a *mandala* in Eastern religions, which Jung thought symbolizes the unity of life and "the totality of the self." Or it can be a figure found in fairy tales, legends, and popular stories, such as the Hero, the Nurturing Mother, the Powerful Father, or the Wicked Witch. It can even be an aspect of the self. For example, he said, the *shadow* archetype reflects the prehistoric fear of wild animals and represents the sinister, evil side of human nature.

Many of Jung's ideas were more suited to mysticism and philosophy than to empirical psychology, which may be why so many Jungian ideas are popular with New Age movements today. But psychologists have found that some basic archetypes, such as the Hero and the Earth Mother, do appear in the stories and images of virtually every society, taking different forms (Campbell, 1949, 1968; Neher, 1996). Jung would recognize dragons, Darth Vader, and Dracula as expressions of the shadow archetype.

Two of the most important archetypes, in Jung's view, are those of men and women themselves. Jung (like Freud) recognized that "masculine" and "feminine" qualities exist in both sexes. The *anima* represents the feminine archetype in men; the *animus* represents the masculine archetype in women. Problems can arise, however, if a person tries to repress his or her internal, opposite archetype—that is, if a man totally denies his softer "feminine" side or if a woman denies her "masculine" aspects. People also create problems in relationships when they expect the partner to behave like the ideal archetypal man or woman, instead of a real human being who has both sides (Young-Eisendrath, 1993).

Although Jung shared with Freud a fascination with the unconscious side of the personality, he (along with several other dissenters from Freudian orthodoxy) had confidence in the positive, forward-moving strengths of the ego. He believed that people are motivated not only by past conflicts, but also by their future goals and their desire to fulfill themselves.

Jungians today are interested in how universal images and stories affect the way people see their own lives. When Dan McAdams (1988) asked 50 people to tell their life stories in a two-hour session, he found that people tended to reveal a common archetype, a mythic character, at the

To Jung, this magnificent Tibetan mandala, made of sand, is an archetype representing the unity of life.

collective unconscious To Carl Jung, the universal memories and experiences of humankind, represented in the unconscious images and symbols of all people.

archetypes [AR-ki-tipes] Universal, symbolic images that appear in myths, art, stories, and dreams; to Carl Jung, they reflect the collective unconscious.

Jungians believe that Dracula can never be killed because he represents the shadow archetype, the evil side of human nature. You can't kill Dracula movies, either!

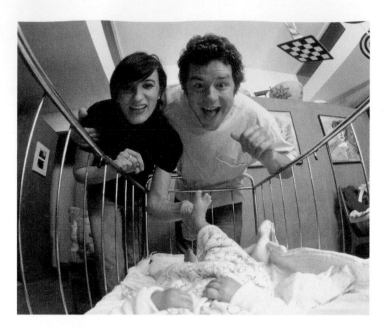

According to object-relations theory, a baby constructs unconscious representations of his or her parents, which will influence the child's relations with others throughout life.

heart of their life narratives. For example, many individuals told stories that could be symbolized by the myth of the Greek god Dionysus, the pleasure seeker who escapes responsibility. Archetypes, says McAdams, represent "the main characters in the life stories we construct as our identities."

The Object-Relations School. Freud essentially regarded the baby as if it were an independent, greedy little organism ruled by its own instinctive desires; other people were relevant only insofar as they gratified the infant's drives or blocked them. But by the 1950s, increased awareness of the importance of human attachments led to the emergence of the **object-relations school**, developed in Great Britain by Melanie Klein, D. W. Winnicott, and others (Horner, 1991; Hughes, 1989).

To object-relations theorists, the central problem in life is to find a balance between the need for independence and the need for others. This balance requires constant adjustment to separations and losses: small ones that occur during quarrels, moderate ones such as leaving home for the first time, and major ones such as divorce or death. The way we react to these separations, according to object-relations analysts, is largely determined by our experiences in the first year or two of life.

Whereas Freud emphasized the child's fear of the powerful father, object-relations analysts emphasize the child's need for the powerful mother, who is usually the baby's caregiver in the first critical years. The reason for the clunky word "object" in object-relations (instead of the warmer words "mother" or "parent") is that the infant's attachment is not only to the actual mother but also to the infant's evolving perception of her. The child creates a *representation* of the mother—someone who is kind or fierce, protective or rejecting—that is not literally the same as the woman herself. The child's representations of important adults, whether realistic or distorted, unconsciously affect personality throughout life, influencing how the person relates to others: with trust or suspicion, acceptance or criticism (Westen, 1998).

The object-relations school also departs from Freudian theory regarding the nature of male and female development (Sagan, 1988; Winnicott, 1957, 1990). In the object-relations view, children of both sexes identify first with the mother. Girls, who are the same sex as the mother, do not need to separate from her; the mother treats a daughter as an extension of herself. But boys, if they are to develop a masculine identity, must break away from the mother; the mother encourages a son to be independent and separate. Thus, men develop more rigid boundaries between themselves and other people than women do.

The result, in the object-relations view, is that men are less secure than women because their identity is based on *not* being like women. Later in life, the typical psychological problem for women is how to increase their autonomy and assert their own needs in close relationships. In contrast, the typical problem for men is how to permit close attachments (Gilligan, 1982). Some object-relations theorists believe that this gender difference is inevitable because women are biologically suited to be the primary nurturers. Others argue that if men played a greater role in nurturing infants and small children, the sex difference in the need for separation from the mother would fade, and so would men's need to be "opposite" from women (Chodorow, 1978, 1992).

Psychodynamic Measures of Personality

Psychodynamic concepts have been very influential, not only for theories of personality and behavior, but also in the creation of personality tests. For example, the concept of projection led to the development of **projective tests** that attempt to measure unconscious motives, feelings, and conflicts—aspects of personality that may not be apparent in a person's overt behavior. The tests present ambiguous pictures, patterns, or stories for the test-taker to interpret or complete. You might be asked to draw a person, a house, or other object, or to complete a sentence (such as "My mother . . . " or "Women are . . . "). The assumption behind such tests is that your unconscious thoughts and feelings will be "projected" onto the test materials and revealed in your responses.

Clinicians who like projective techniques maintain that they are a rich source of information because test-takers cannot fake answers or lie as easily as on objective tests. The tests can help a clinician establish rapport with a client and encourage a person to open up about anxieties, conflicts, and problems. Very young children may reveal feelings in their play or drawings that they cannot express verbally (Anastasi, 1988). And the tests may help clinicians determine when someone is defensively attempting to hide worries or mental problems (Shedler, Mayman, & Manis, 1993).

But although projective tests may be helpful for doing therapy, the evidence is clear that they are too unreliable to be used, as they often currently are, for assessing personality traits or diagnosing disorders (Lilienfeld, 1999). (For example, these tests are often used, inappropriately, to determine whether a parent has a personality problem that would make him or her "unfit" in some way.) Different clinicians often interpret the same person's scores differently, depending on their own biases. The tests also have low validity—that is, they often do not measure what they claim to measure. One reason is that your response to a projective test is significantly affected by sleepiness, hunger, drugs, worry, verbal ability, the clinician's instructions about how to take the test, the clinician's own personality (friendly and warm, or cool and remote), and events in your life that day (Anastasi, 1988).

projective tests Psychological tests used to infer a person's motives, conflicts, and unconscious dynamics on the basis of the person's interpretations of ambiguous stimuli.

GET ➡ INVOLVED

TEST THIS PROJECTIVE TEST

This drawing was made by a young man who bludgeoned his girlfriend with a hammer in a jealous rage. A psychologist has interpreted the drawing as follows: The upraised hands represent aggression and readiness to strike; the short legs represent feelings of inadequacy, possibly of sexual inadequacy; and the red shirt represents passion, violence, and impulsivity. Rank the plausibility of this analysis, on the following scale:

Very high _____/_____/_____/_____/_____ Very low

When you have finished, turn the page—but not before!

TEST THIS PROJECTIVE TEST (*continued*)

Suppose now we tell you that the drawing on the previous page was made by a young man hospitalized following a suicide attempt. A psychologist has interpreted the drawing as follows: The upraised hands represent helplessness and loss; the short legs represent diminished stature, an inability to "measure up"; and the red shirt represents anger turned toward himself. Rank the plausibility of this analysis, on the following scale:

Very high _____/_____/_____/_____/_____ Very low

What does this exercise, combined with the one on the previous page, tell you about how prior knowledge about a person might affect the interpretation of the person's performance on a projective test, such as the Rorschach Inkblot Test?

A Rorschach inkblot. What do you see in it?

EXAMINE THE EVIDENCE

Projective tests like the Rorschach are very popular, but does the evidence support claims of their reliability and validity in diagnosing disorders and sexual abuse?

Rorschach Inkblot Test A projective personality test that asks respondents to interpret abstract, symmetrical inkblots.

All of these problems are apparent in the **Rorschach Inkblot Test**, devised by Swiss psychiatrist Hermann Rorschach in 1921. It consists of ten cards with symmetrical abstract patterns, originally formed by spilling ink on paper and folding the paper in half (you can see a similar inkblot in the margin). You report what you see in the inkblots, and the clinician interprets your answers according to the symbolic meanings emphasized by psychodynamic theories.

Although the Rorschach is enormously popular among many clinicians, efforts to confirm its reliability and validity have repeatedly failed, despite more than 2,000 publications about the test (Dawes, 1994). In recent years, a different scoring method, called the Comprehensive System, has become widely used (Exner, 1993). But there are significant problems with this method too. Many scores are of questionable validity; again, they do not measure the personality traits they claim to measure, particularly in contrast to objective tests like the MMPI (Garb, Florio, & Grove, 1998; Lilienfeld, 1999). And claims of the system's success come from Rorschach workshops where clinicians are taught how to use the method, which is not an impartial way of assessing it (Wood, Nezworski, & Stejskal, 1996).

The critical assessment of projective methods is important because their use has spilled over from clinical evaluation into the legal arena. Many innocent people have been convicted of sexually abusing children, for example, based on how the children played with anatomically detailed dolls. Supposedly, children project their unconscious feelings onto the doll, but this test has proved entirely unreliable in diagnosing abuse, as we discuss in Chapter 17 (Ceci & Bruck, 1995; Poole & Lamb, 1998).

The reverse error, letting guilty people go free, has also occurred. James Wood, who is both a clinician and a researcher, told us about a woman who reported to Child Protection Services (CPS) that her ex-husband was molesting their 4-year-old son. CPS thought that the mother was perhaps "deranged" in making this accusation, so they had her tested by a psychologist who administered the Rorschach. The mother said that one blot looked like "a Thanksgiving turkey already eaten"—and the psychologist, ignoring the fact that the test was being given shortly after Thanksgiving, scored this "food response" as evidence of the woman's dependency. CPS, accepting the psychologist's conclusion that the mother had emotional problems, refused to investigate her claims. A year later the boy was brought to the emergency room after a visit with his father. This time, semen was found in his rectum.

Evaluating Psychodynamic Theories

Although modern psychodynamic theorists differ in many ways, they share a general belief that the way to understand personality is by exploring its unconscious dynamics. Many psychologists in other fields, however, regard psychodynamic ideas as literary metaphors that can never be tested, rather than as scientific hypotheses (Cioffi, 1998; Crews, 1998).

Problems with Psychodynamic Theories. Critics argue that psychodynamic theories are guilty of three scientific failings:

1 *Violating the principle of falsifiability.* As we saw in Chapter 2, a theory that is impossible to disconfirm in principle is not scientific. Many psychodynamic ideas about unconscious motivations are, in fact, impossible to confirm or disconfirm. If your experience seems to support these ideas, it is taken as evidence of their correctness. But if you doubt them or offer disconfirming evidence, you must be "defensive," lack observational skills, or (a favorite accusation) be "in denial." This way of responding to criticism is neither scientific nor fair!

2 *Drawing universal principles from the experiences of a few atypical patients.* Freud and most of his followers generalized from a few individuals, often patients in therapy, to all human beings. Of course, the problem of overgeneralizing from small samples occurs in other areas of psychology too, and sometimes valid insights about human behavior can be obtained from case studies. The problem occurs when the observer fails to confirm these observations by studying other samples and incorrectly infers that what applies to some individuals applies to all. For example, to confirm Freud's ideas about penis envy, you would need to observe or talk to many young children. Freud himself did not do this; however, when research psychologists interview preschool-age children, they typically find that many children of *both* sexes envy one another. In one charming study of 65 preschool-age boys and girls, 45 percent of the girls had fantasized about having a penis or being male in other ways—and 44 percent of the boys had fantasized about being pregnant (Linday, 1994).

3 *Basing theories of personality development on the fallible memories and retrospective accounts of patients.* Most psychodynamic theorists have not observed random samples of children at different ages, as modern child psychologists do, to construct their theories of development. Instead they have worked backward, creating theories based on themes in adults' recollections of childhood.

The analysis of memories can be an illuminating way to achieve insights about our lives; in fact, it is the only way we can think about our own lives! But memory is often inaccurate, influenced as much by what is going on currently in our lives as by what happened in the past (see Chapter 10). If you are currently not getting along with your mother, you may remember all the times in the past when she was hard on you and forget the counterexamples of her kindness.

Retrospective analysis has another problem: It creates an *illusion of causality* between events. People often assume that if A came before B, then A must have caused B. For example, if your mother spent three months in the hospital when you were 5 years old and today you feel shy and insecure in college, an object-relations analyst

Some psychodynamic ideas can be tested empirically. For example, Freud thought that aggressive sports "displace" aggressive energy into socially accepted activities, and hence reduce it. But behavioral research repeatedly finds that violent sports actually stimulate increased hostility and violence among players and fans.

would probably draw a connection between the two facts. But a lot of other things could be causing your shyness and insecurity, as we have already seen—your temperament, your learning history, or something in your college environment. When psychologists conduct longitudinal studies, following people from childhood to adulthood, they often get a very different picture of causality from the one that emerges by looking backward (see Chapter 14).

Contributions of Psychodynamic Approaches. In response to the concerns of critics, some psychodynamic psychologists are turning to empirical methods and research findings to reformulate and refine their theories and clinical assessments (Westen, 1998). For example, some have developed objective tests of defense mechanisms to find out how these strategies protect self-esteem and reduce anxiety (Margo et al., 1993; Plutchik et al., 1988). Psychologists in other fields, especially cognitive psychology, are also investigating psychodynamic concepts, such as nonconscious processes in thought and memory (Epstein, 1994; Kihlstrom, Barnhardt, & Tataryn, 1992) and the influence of mental representations (Blatt, Auerbach, & Levy, 1997). Such research highlights the contributions of psychodynamic theories. People are indeed often unaware of the motives behind their own puzzling actions. Rational thoughts and behavior can be distorted by guilt, anxiety, and shame. The mind does defend itself against information that is threatening, unpleasant, or shocking. Prolonged emotional conflict may indeed play itself out in physical symptoms, immature habits, and self-defeating actions. And unconscious expectations, such as those about how mothers and fathers should behave, often do affect adult relationships.

Moreover, despite their scientific shortcomings, psychodynamic theories have encouraged researchers to tackle large, fascinating questions, such as why some symbols are universal, why men and women often regard each other with envy and animosity rather than love, and why many people are drawn to horror movies and ghost stories. Psychodynamic psychologists have also made imaginative use of qualitative sources of information, such as rituals, literature, fairy tales, jokes, and art. Psychodynamic approaches have thus enriched psychology in many respects.

QUICK QUIZ

Find out whether the correct response to these questions is in the conscious part of your mind.

1. A Jungian and a social-cognitive theorist are arguing about horror movies. Which one is likely to think such movies are healthy, which to think they are potentially harmful, and why?

2. Which statement about the Rorschach Inkblot test is *true*? The test (a) has high reliability, (b) has high validity, (c) can be best used to help people in therapy reveal their feelings, (d) can be used to accurately diagnose sexual abuse.

3. In the 1950s and 1960s, many psychoanalysts, observing unhappy gay men who had sought therapy, concluded that homosexuality was a mental illness. What violation of the scientific method were they committing?

Answers:

1. The Jungian will say that horror images are inevitable and benign because they reflect universal archetypes of evil; the social-cognitive theorist is likely to worry about the effects on children of modeling violent images and actions. 2. c 3. The analysts were drawing inappropriate conclusions from atypical patients in therapy, failing to test these conclusions with gay men who were not in therapy or with heterosexuals. When such research was done, it turned out that gay men were not more mentally disturbed or depressed than heterosexuals (Hooker, 1957).

- How does the humanist vision of human nature differ from the visions of behaviorism and psychoanalysis?
- In the humanist view, what's wrong with saying to a child, "I love you because you've been good"?

THE HUMANIST CONTRIBUTION

A final way to look at personality starts with the person's own view of the world—his or her subjective interpretation of what is happening right now. Psychologists who take a *humanist* approach to personality believe that personality is influenced less by our genes, past learning, or unconscious conflicts than by our uniquely human capacity to shape our own futures. It is defined, they say, by the human abilities that separate us from other animals: freedom of choice and free will.

The Inner Experience

Humanist psychology was launched as a movement within psychology in the early 1960s. Humanists rejected the psychoanalytic emphasis on hostility, instincts, and conflict. They also rejected behaviorism, with its emphasis on reinforcers and punishment as determinants of behavior. The movement's chief leaders—Abraham Maslow (1908–1970), Carl Rogers (1902–1987), and Rollo May (1909–1994)—argued that it was time for a "third force" in psychology, one that would draw a fuller picture of human potential.

Abraham Maslow. The trouble with psychology, said Maslow (1970, 1971), was that it had forgotten many of the positive aspects of human life, such as joy, laughter, love, happiness, and *peak experiences* (rare moments of rapture caused by the attainment of excellence or the drive toward higher values). The traits that Maslow thought most important to personality were not the Big Five, but rather the qualities of the *self-actualized person*—the person who strives for a life that is meaningful, challenging, and productive.

For Maslow, personality development could be viewed as a gradual progression toward a state of self-actualization. He thought that most psychologists had a lopsided view of human nature, a result of their emphasis on studying negative traits (such as neuroticism or insecurity) and people's emotional problems. In contrast, Maslow (1971) wrote, "When you select out for careful study very fine and healthy people, strong people, creative people . . . then you get a very different view of mankind. You are asking how tall can people grow, what can a human being become?"

Carl Rogers. Rogers, like Freud, derived many of his ideas from observing his clients in therapy. As a clinician, Rogers (1951, 1961) was interested not only in why some people cannot function well, but also in what he called the fully functioning individual. How you behave depends on your subjective reality, Rogers said, not on the external reality around you. Fully functioning people experience *congruence*, or harmony, between the image they project to others and their true feelings and wishes. They are trusting, warm, and open, rather than defensive or intolerant. Their beliefs about themselves are realistic.

Abraham Maslow regarded self-actualization as a lifelong process, one you are never too old to begin. Hulda Crooks, shown here at age 91 climbing Mt. Fuji, took up mountain climbing at 54. "It's been a great inspiration for me," she said. "When I come down from the mountain, I feel like I can battle in the valley again." She died at the age of 101.

humanist psychology A psychological approach that emphasizes personal growth and the achievement of human potential rather than the scientific understanding and assessment of behavior.

Existential psychologists remind us of the inevitable struggles of human existence, such as the fight against loneliness and alienation.

DEFINE YOUR TERMS

Unconditional positive regard sounds like a good thing, but what does it mean, exactly? Does it mean giving loved ones your total support and approval, no matter what they do? Does it permit setting limits and offering constructive criticism?

unconditional positive regard To Carl Rogers, love or support given to another person with no conditions attached.

To become fully functioning people, Rogers maintained, we all need **unconditional positive regard**, love and support for the people we are, without strings (conditions) attached. This doesn't mean that Charlotte should be allowed to kick her brother when she is angry with him or that Wilbur may throw his dinner out the window because he doesn't like pot roast. In these cases, a parent can correct the child's behavior without withdrawing love from the child. The child can learn that the behavior, not the child, is what is bad. "House rules are 'no violence,' Charlotte," is a very different message from "You are a horrible person, Charlotte."

Unfortunately, Rogers observed, many children are raised with *conditional* positive regard. The condition is "I will love you if you behave well, and I won't love you if you behave badly." Adults often treat each other this way, too. People treated with conditional regard begin to suppress or deny feelings or actions that they believe are unacceptable to those they love. The result, said Rogers, is the sensation of being "out of touch with your feelings," of not being true to your "real self." The suppression of feelings and parts of oneself produces low self-regard, defensiveness, and unhappiness. The result is an individual who scores high on neuroticism—bitter and negative.

Rollo May. May shared with the humanists a belief in free will and freedom of choice. But he also emphasized some of the inherently difficult and tragic aspects of the human condition, including loneliness, anxiety, and alienation.

May, author of such books as *Love and Will* and *The Meaning of Anxiety*, brought to American psychology elements of the European philosophy of *existentialism*, which holds that free will confers on us responsibility for our actions. Freedom, and its burden of accountability, carries a price in anxiety and despair. This is why so many people try to escape from freedom into narrow certainties and blame others for their misfortunes. For May, our personalities reflect the ways we cope with the inevitable struggles of life: to find meaning in existence, to use our freedom wisely, and to face suffering and death bravely. May popularized the humanist idea that we can choose to make the best of ourselves because of inner resources such as love and courage, but he added that we can never escape the harsh realities of life and death.

Evaluating Humanist Theories

As with psychodynamic theories, the major criticism of humanist psychology is that many of its assumptions are untestable. Freud looked at humanity and saw destructive drives, selfishness, and lust. Maslow and Rogers looked at humanity and saw cooperation, selflessness, and love. May looked at humanity and saw fear of freedom, loneliness, and the struggle for meaning. These differences, say the critics, may tell us more about the observers than about the observed.

Many humanist concepts, although intuitively appealing, are hard to define operationally. How can we know whether a person is self-fulfilled or self-actualized? How can we tell whether a woman's decision to quit her job and become a professional rodeo rider represents an "escape from freedom" or a freely made choice? And what exactly is unconditional positive regard? If it is interpreted as unquestioned support of a child's efforts at mastering a new skill, or as assurance that the child is loved in spite of his or her mistakes, then it is clearly a good idea. But in the popular culture, it has often been interpreted as an unwillingness ever to say "no" to a child, offer constructive criticism, or set limits—all of which children need.

Despite such concerns, humanist psychologists have added balance to the study of personality. Influenced in part by the humanists, psychologists in other perspectives are studying many positive human traits, such as courage, helpfulness to others, the motivation to excel, and self-confidence. Stress researchers have discovered the healing powers of humor and hope. Developmental psychologists are studying ways to foster children's empathy and creativity. And the humanist argument that we have the power to choose our own destinies, even when fate delivers us into tragedy, has fostered a new appreciation of human resilience in the face of adversity.

QUICK QUIZ

Exercise your free will, and choose to take this quiz.

1. According to Carl Rogers, a man who loves his wife only when she is looking her best is giving her positive regard that is (a) conditional or (b) unconditional.

2. The humanist who described the importance of having peak experiences was (a) Abraham Maslow, (b) Rollo May, (c) Carl Rogers.

3. A humanist and a psychoanalyst are arguing about human nature. What underlying assumptions about psychology and human potential are they likely to bring to their discussion, and what do their assumptions overlook?

Answers:

1. a 2. a 3. The analyst assumes that human nature is basically selfish and destructive; the humanist, that it is basically loving and life-affirming. Their assumptions overlook the facts that human beings have both capacities, and the situation often determines which capacity is expressed.

THE PUBLIC AND PRIVATE PERSONALITY

Now that you have read about the five major approaches to personality, how would you "explain" Dennis Rodman? What are the reasons for his outrageous behavior? (For a summary of how the five personality theories would answer, see Review 13.2 on the next page.)

One way to integrate these different theories may lie in recognizing that personality has two dimensions. Each of us has a "public personality" that we present to the world, consisting of our characteristic habits and temperaments and our basic traits. This is the personality that biological, learning, and cultural theories address. But we also have a "private personality" that reflects our interior sense of self, consisting of our subjective experience of emotions, memories, dreams, wishes, and worries (Singer, 1984). This is the personality that psychodynamic and humanist theories address.

Each of us weaves these two dimensions of personality together in the narratives we tell to explain our lives, our inconsistencies across situations, our failures and successes—to explain, in short, why we are the way we are. Genetic influences, learned habits, cultural norms, unconscious fears and conflicts, and visions of possibility, filtered through our interior sense of self and our life story, give each of us the stamp of our personality . . . one that is as distinctive as a fingerprint.

Personality includes our public "faces" and the inner sense of self that exists beneath the external masks we present to the world.

THEORIES OF PERSONALITY CONTRASTED

	Basic Method of Inquiry	Explanation of Personality Traits	Possibility of Personal Change	Probable Explanation of Dennis Rodman's Personality
Biological theories	Empirical	Temperaments are inborn and many traits are highly influenced by genes.	Limited by biology, but partly modifiable by experience.	He has a genetic disposition to be extroverted.
Social-cognitive theories	Empirical	Situational demands and a person's cognitions interact in a process of reciprocal determinism.	Good, because people can change their situations and beliefs.	He has learned to expect rewards and attention for his flamboyance in public; he might be different in private.
Cultural theories	Empirical	Cultural rules and values determine which traits are encouraged.	Depends on whether a culture values personal change or stability.	American culture values celebrity, and rewards outrageous and aggressive acts.
Psychodynamic theories	Subjective	Unconscious dynamics stemming from childhood experiences produce adult defenses, inner conflicts, and motives.	Limited by unconscious processes and the difficulty of overcoming early formative experiences.	His provocative behavior may mask inner feelings of insecurity, inadequacy, and need for approval.
Humanist theories	Subjective	A person's subjective reality and ability to determine his or her life shape decisions and behavior.	Good, if the person exercises free will and takes responsibility for change.	Rodman chooses to behave as he does—or perhaps he is seeking unconditional positive regard from the public!

TAKING PSYCHOLOGY WITH YOU

GRAPHOLOGY, HOROSCOPES, AND THE "BARNUM EFFECT"

How well does the following paragraph describe you?

Some of your aspirations tend to be pretty unrealistic. At times you are extroverted, affable, sociable, while at other times you are introverted, wary, and reserved. You pride yourself on being an independent thinker and do not accept others' opinions without satisfactory proof. You prefer a certain amount of change and variety, and you become dissatisfied when hemmed in by restrictions and limitations. At times you have serious doubts as to whether you have made the right decision or done the right thing.

When people believe that this description was written just for them—the result of a personalized horoscope or handwriting analysis— they all say the same thing: "It's me! It describes me *exactly*!" The magician James Randi often gives audiences of college students a similar "personalized profile" and asks them to rate it for its accuracy. Students invariably rate their profiles as highly accurate—until Randi asks them to exchange profiles with a neighbor, and they realize that all the descriptions are identical.

The reason that everyone thinks this description is accurate is that it is vague enough to apply to almost everyone, and it is flattering (don't we all consider ourselves to be "independent thinkers"?). And if people pay money for a profile, take the time to write away for it, or give detailed information about themselves, they are even more likely to believe that the profile is eerily correct.

This is why many psychologists worry about the "Barnum effect" (Snyder & Shenkel, 1975). P. T. Barnum was the great circus impresario who said, "There's a sucker born every minute." He knew that the formula for success was to "have a little something for everybody"—and that is just what unscientific personality profiles, horoscopes, and handwriting tests have in common. The Barnum effect refers to susceptibility to pseudoscientific explanations that have "a little something for everybody" and hence are nonfalsifiable.

For example, graphologists claim that they can identify your personality traits from the form and distribution of your handwriting (Beyerstein, 1996). Wide spacing between words means you feel isolated and lonely. If you crowd your words together, you are desperate for companionship. If your lines drift upward, you are an "uplifting" optimist, and if your lines droop downward, you are a gloomy pessimist who feels you are being "dragged down." If you make large capital I's, you have a large ego. And if you put large loops on your g's, y's and other letters that dangle provocatively below the lines, you have a strong sex drive.

Graphologists are not the same as handwriting experts, who are trained to determine, say, whether a document was really written by Hitler or is a forgery. (Most of these experts are as unhappy at being confused with a graphologist as an astronomer would be if mistaken for an astrologer.) Graphologists are not trained in the scientific method; they typically learn their "art" from popular books, correspondence schools, or unaccredited night-school classes. There are more than 30 graphological societies in the United States alone, and their methods often conflict. For example, according to one system, a certain way of crossing t's reveals a vicious, sadistic temperament; according to another, it reveals a practical joker (Beyerstein, 1996).

Pseudosciences such as graphology fail the basic test of science: They are nonfalsifiable. Pesky, disconfirming facts are simply explained away after the fact. For example, when one graphologist learned that Mohandas Gandhi did not display the large writing she said was typical of great leaders, she explained that his writing showed that he was modest and preferred to lead from a position of inferiority.

Further, whenever graphology *has* been tested empirically, it has failed. A meta-analysis of 200 published studies found no validity or reliability to graphology in predicting work performance, aptitudes, or personality. No school of graphology fared better than any other, and no graphologist was able to perform better than untrained amateurs making guesses from the same materials (Dean, 1992; see also Klimoski, 1992).

Unfortunately, handwriting analysis is not just an amusing pastime; it can have harmful consequences. Graphologists have been hired by companies to

"Handwriting analysis has revealed that Spencer is not in fact my husband."

predict a person's leadership ability, attention to detail, willingness to be a good team player, and more. They pass judgment on people's honesty, generosity, jealousy, and criminal tendencies (Beyerstein, 1996). How would you feel if you were turned down for a job because some graphologist said your handwriting indicated you might become violent? How would you feel if you were branded a thief because you have "desire-for-possession hooks" on your S's?

"The Barnum effect is so powerful," says one psychologist who has investigated graphology and other pseudoscientific personality tests (Beyerstein, 1996), is that most people won't believe you if you tell them about it (as we are telling you!). People actually need to see for themselves that they have been hoodwinked into agreeing with a personality profile that was given to everyone—the demonstration that Randi does. Otherwise, we automatically "read into" personality profiles what we want to see, in order to make them fit our own sense of ourselves. The smartest people, says Beyerstein, are often the best at making these connections! That is why critical thinkers will be aware of the need to control for

the Barnum Effect—the false sense of accuracy these "profiles" provide.

If you do not want to be taken in by graphology or other methods that rely on the Barnum effect, research offers this advice:

■ *Beware of all-purpose descriptions that could apply to anyone.* Sometimes you doubt your decisions; who among us has not? Sometimes you feel outgoing and sometimes shy; who does not? Do you "have sexual secrets that you are afraid of confessing"? The fact that they are secret is the reason few people share them—but they are actually extremely common.

■ *Beware of your own selective perceptions.* Most of us are so impressed when a horoscope, psychic, or graphologist gets something right that we overlook all the descriptions that are plain wrong. Be aware of the confirmation bias, your tendency to "explain away" anything that doesn't fit or confirm your own impression of yourself.

■ *Resist flattery.* This is undoubtedly the hardest suggestion to follow. It is easy to reject a profile that describes you as being selfish, stupid, or un-

original. Watch out for the ones that tell you how wonderful and smart you are, what a great leader you will be, or how modest you are about your abilities. Watch out for the fortune-tellers who predict with certainty that you *will* one day be wealthy, happy, in love, successful, and able to run marathons in record time. (A nice prediction, but don't pay money for it.)

■ *Ask questions about the reliability and validity of the test you are taking.* This will protect you against all the pop-psych tests that, like Barnum, offer "a little something for everybody." Does the test accurately predict specific behaviors ("you have an aptitude for journalism"), or is it too general and vague to be useful ("you get along with people")? Does the test measure traits consistently over time? Does it measure what it says it does?

If you keep your critical faculties with you, you won't end up paying hard cash for soft answers, and you will be able to protect yourself from being the victim of unvalidated personality tests in the workplace.

SUMMARY

1. *Personality* refers to an individual's distinctive and relatively stable pattern of behavior, motives, thoughts, and emotions. Personality is made up of many different *traits*, characteristics that describe a person across situations.

MEASURING PERSONALITY

2. Personality researchers typically use *objective tests*, or *inventories*, such as the *MMPI*, to identify and study personality traits and disorders.

3. Gordon Allport argued that people have a few *central traits* that are key to their personalities, and a greater

number of *secondary traits* that are less fundamental. Raymond Cattell used *factor analysis* to identify clusters of traits that he considered the basic components of personality. Today there is strong evidence for the *Big Five* dimensions of personality: extroversion versus introversion, neuroticism (negative emotionality), agreeableness, conscientiousness, and openness to experience.

THE GENETIC CONTRIBUTION

4. Individual differences in *temperaments* or ways of reacting to the environment emerge early in life and can influence subsequent personality development. Temperamental differences in extremely reactive and nonreactive children

(and monkeys) may be due to variations in the responsiveness of the sympathetic nervous system to change and novelty. Experience can help extremely shy children and monkeys to become less shy and timid in new situations, but it cannot make them extroverts.

5. *Behavioral-genetic* data from twin and adoption studies suggest that the *heritability* of many adult personality traits is around .40 to .60, with the remaining variation accounted for by a person's unique experiences, rather than ones shared with other family members. But genes tell only half the story. Not all traits are equally heritable or unaffected by shared environment; even traits that are highly heritable are not rigidly fixed (many are modifiable by experience); and the relative influence of genes versus the environment can change over a lifetime. In some cases, the effects of genes diminish over time.

THE SOCIAL-COGNITIVE CONTRIBUTION

6. *Social-cognitive theorists* focus on the situation a person is in and on the person's expectations, habits, and beliefs. This approach holds that the environment, cognitions, and a person's behavior all influence each other in a complex pattern of *reciprocal determinism*. We acquire ways of reacting to situations in part because of rewards and punishers, but once acquired, our habits, behaviors, and cognitions in turn influence how we respond to others, whom we associate with, and the situations we seek out.

7. One important personality trait that illustrates reciprocal determinism is *self-efficacy*, the sense of being able to achieve results and reach goals. Self-efficacy comes from experience in mastering new skills, having successful role models, receiving encouragement from others, and making constructive interpretations of your emotional state. Another example of reciprocal determinism is *locus of control*, a general expectation about whether you have control over your life. Expectations of success or failure, control over events or lack of control, may create a *self-fulfilling prophecy*, in which your expectations lead to behavior that makes the expectation come true. Self-efficacy and an internal locus of control are associated with many benefits, such as health, achievement, and social activism.

8. Critics of social-cognitive approaches to personality argue that reciprocal determinism is difficult to demonstrate in real life, and because so many factors influence people's behavior, it can be hard to single out the impact of any one of them.

THE CULTURAL CONTRIBUTION

9. Many qualities that Western psychologists treat as individual personality traits, such as risk-taking and quickness to become angry over perceived insults, are heavily influenced by *culture*. Men in "cultures of honor" are more likely to behave aggressively to restore their sense of honor than are men from other cultures. People from *individualist cultures* define themselves in different terms than those from *collectivist cultures*, and they perceive their "selves" as more stable across situations. People from *monochronic cultures* are more concerned with punctuality and doing things "one at a time" than are people from *polychronic cultures*, who value relationships above time schedules.

10. Cultural theories of personality face the problem of describing broad cultural differences and their influences on personality without fostering stereotypes.

THE PSYCHODYNAMIC CONTRIBUTION

11. Sigmund Freud was the founder of *psychoanalysis*, which was the first *psychodynamic* theory. Modern psychodynamic theories share an emphasis on (a) *intrapsychic* dynamics, (b) the formative role of childhood experiences and conflicts, (c) the idea that psychological development occurs in stages, (d) the importance of a person's unconscious perceptions of events rather than actual ones, and (e) subjective methods of understanding a person's life and personality.

12. To Freud, the personality consists of the *id* (the source of sexual energy, which he called the *libido*, and the aggressive instinct); the *ego* (the source of reason); and the *superego* (the source of conscience). *Defense mechanisms* protect the ego from unconscious anxiety. They include, among others, repression, projection, displacement (one form of which is sublimation), reaction formation, regression, and denial.

13. Freud believed that personality develops in a series of *psychosexual stages*, with the *phallic (Oedipal) stage* most crucial. During this stage, Freud believed, the *Oedipus complex* occurs, in which the child desires the parent of the other sex and feels rivalry with the same-sex parent. When the Oedipus complex is resolved, the child identifies with the same-sex parent, but females retain a lingering sense of inferiority and "penis envy"—a notion contested by female psychoanalysts like Clara Thompson and Karen Horney.

14. Carl Jung believed that people share a *collective unconscious* that contains universal memories and images, or

archetypes. Personality includes many archetypes, including the shadow (evil) and the anima and animus.

15. The *object-relations school* emphasizes the importance of the first two years of life, rather than the Oedipal phase; the infant's relationships to important figures, especially the mother, rather than sexual needs and drives; and the problem in male development of breaking away from the mother.

16. Psychodynamic theories have generated subjective tests of personality called *projective tests* (including the *Rorschach Inkblot Test*). These can be useful in doing therapy, but they often have poor reliability and validity, which causes problems when they are used in the legal arena or in employment or other settings.

17. Psychodynamic approaches have been criticized on several scientific grounds: for violating the principle of falsifiability; for overgeneralizing from atypical patients to everyone; and for basing theories on the unreliable memories and retrospective accounts of patients, rather than on prospective studies. But some psychodynamic ideas, especially about nonconscious processes and defenses, are being studied empirically and have made an important contribution to psychology.

THE HUMANIST CONTRIBUTION

18. *Humanist psychologists* focus on a person's subjective sense of self and free will to change. They emphasize human potential and the strengths of human nature, as in Abraham Maslow's concepts of *peak experiences* and *self-actualization*. Carl Rogers stressed the importance of *unconditional positive regard* in creating a "fully functioning" person. Rollo May brought *existentialism* into psychology, emphasizing some of the inherent dilemmas of human existence that result from having free will, such as the search for meaning in life. Critics observe that these ideas are subjective and difficult to measure, but they have added depth to the study of personality.

THE PUBLIC AND PRIVATE PERSONALITY

19. Biological, social-cognitive, and cultural theories of personality tend to emphasize the public personality that we present to the world; psychodynamic and humanist theories emphasize the private, interior sense of self. Together these approaches portray a complex vision of human personality.

KEY TERMS

personality 457

trait 457

inventories 458

Minnesota Multiphasic Personality Inventory (MMPI) 458

Gordon Allport 459

central and secondary traits 459

Raymond Cattell 459

factor analysis 459

"Big Five" personality traits 459–460

temperaments 462

heritability 464

behavioral genetics 464

social-cognitive theories (of personality) 466

reciprocal determinism 466

self-efficacy 467

self-fulfilling prophecy 468

locus of control 468

culture 472

individualist 473

collectivist cultures 474

monochronic 476

polychronic cultures 476

Sigmund Freud 476

psychoanalysis 476

psychodynamic theories 476

intrapsychic 476

id 476

libido [luh-BEE-do] 476

ego 477

superego 477

defense mechanisms 478

  repression 478

  projection 478

  displacement and sublimation 478

  reaction formation 478

  regression 478

  denial 478

psychosexual stages 479

phallic (Oedipal) stage 479

Oedipus complex 479

Clara Thompson and Karen Horney 480

Carl Jung 481

collective unconscious 481

archetypes [AR-Ki-types] 481

object-relations school 482

projective tests 483

Rorschach Inkblot Test 484

humanist psychology 487

Abraham Maslow 487

peak experiences 487

self-actualization 487

Carl Rogers 487

unconditional positive regard 488

Rollo May 488

existentialism 488

LOOKING BACK

- How do psychologists identify the elements of your personality? (p. 458)

- How can psychologists tell which personality traits "clump together"? (p. 459)

- Which five dimensions of personality seem to describe people the world over? (pp. 459–460)

- Is it possible to be born irritable or easygoing? (pp. 462–463)

- To what extent are personality differences among people influenced by their genetic differences? (p. 464)

- Are people who have highly heritable personality traits stuck with them forever? (p. 465)

- Why do some people always expect to do poorly while others are confident of success? (pp. 467–468)

- What is the difference between people who think they control their own destiny and those who think destiny controls them? (pp. 468–469)

- Why are risk-taking, aggressiveness, and punctuality more than just individual personality traits? (p. 472)

- How does belonging to an individualist or collectivist culture influence your personality—and even whether you think you have a stable "self"? (p. 473)

- How do psychologists regard Freud today—as a genius or a fraud? (p. 476)

- In Freud's theory of personality, why are the id and the superego always at war? (pp. 476–477)

- When people say you're being "defensive," what defenses might they be thinking of? (p. 478)

- What would Carl Jung have had to say about Darth Vader? (p. 481)

- What are the "objects" in the object-relations approach to personality? (p. 482)

- How does the humanist vision of human nature differ from the visions of behaviorism and psychoanalysis? (p. 487)

- In the humanist view, what's wrong with saying to a child, "I love you because you've been good"? (p. 488)

14

DEVELOPMENT OVER THE LIFE SPAN

Time is a dressmaker specializing in alterations.

NOVELIST FAITH BALDWIN

A few years ago, a 63-year-old woman, Arceli Keh, gave birth to a healthy baby girl. The child was conceived through in vitro ("test tube") fertilization, with sperm from the woman's 60-year-old husband and an egg donated by a younger woman. The woman's family was delighted, but some fertility experts and ethicists had misgivings. Dr. Mark Sauer, who pioneered the use of donor eggs in older women, said, "I lose my comfort level after 55 because I have to believe that there are quality-of-life issues involved in raising a child at [the parent's] age. When [the baby] is 5, her mother will be 68. And I have to believe that a 78-year-old dealing with a teenager may have some problems."

How do *you* react to the idea of a 63-year-old woman having a baby? Would it make any difference if the mother were "only" 55 years old, or 50, or 45? How do you feel about actor Tony Randall fathering a baby when he was 76? Do you feel the same about older fathers as you do about older mothers? Is there some "right" time to become a parent? For that matter, is there a "right" time to do anything in life—go to school, get married, retire . . . die?

During the first half of the twentieth century, social and economic changes occurring in developed countries led to the notion that life unfolds in a progression of distinct stages. Childhood came to be seen as a special time, when "formative" experiences determine what kind of adult the child will become. Adolescence, the years between the physical changes of puberty and the social markers of adulthood, became longer and longer, and its defining characteristics were said to be turmoil and turbulence. Adulthood was conceptualized as a series of predictable stages from marriage and parenthood to retirement. Elderly people were increasingly separated from the rest of society on the grounds that they could not keep up with the fast-moving world.

Today, we are undergoing another revolution in the way we think about the universal human journey from birth to death. Because of improvements in health care, a changing economy, a high divorce rate, and advances in reproductive technology, events over the life span are no longer as predictable as they were just a few decades ago. Many individuals still have their first child in their 20s, but others become first-time parents in their 40s. Most college students are still in their late teens or their twenties, but many are older. A person might marry or start a career at 25, and do so again at 55.

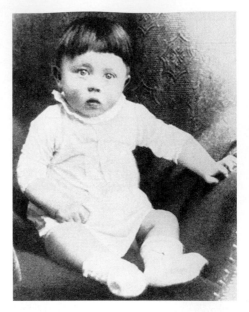

Development over the life span depends on the genetic hand you are dealt at birth, the resources and opportunities your parents provide for you, experiences that happen to you, and the unexpected events of history. What future might you imagine for these three children? Later in this chapter, you'll see who they are.

Developmental psychologists study universal aspects of life-span development and also cultural and individual variations. Many of them study **socialization,** the psychological and social processes by which children learn the rules and behavior expected of them by their society. In this chapter, we will explore the highlights of development, starting at the very beginning, with the period from conception to birth, and continuing through adulthood into old age.

WHAT'S AHEAD

- **How can a pregnant woman reduce the risk of damage to the embryo or fetus?**
- **Given a choice, what do newborns prefer to look at?**
- **How does culture affect how a baby matures physically and socially?**
- **Do the experiences of the first years of life affect a child forever?**

FROM CONCEPTION TO THE FIRST YEAR

A baby's development, before and after birth, is a marvel of *maturation*, the sequential unfolding of genetically influenced behavior and physical characteristics. In only 9 months of a mother's pregnancy, a cell grows from a dot this big (.) to a squalling bundle of energy that looks just like Aunt Sarah. In another 15 months, that bundle of energy grows into a babbling toddler who is curious about everything. No other time in human development brings so many changes, so fast.

Prenatal Development

socialization The processes by which children learn the behaviors, attitudes, and expectations required of them by their society or culture.

Prenatal development is divided into three stages: the germinal, the embryonic, and the fetal. The *germinal stage* begins at conception, when the male sperm unites with the female ovum (egg). A day or so after conception, the fertilized egg, or *zygote,* begins to divide into two parts, and in 10 to 14 days it attaches itself to the wall of the uterus. The outer portion of the zygote will form part of the placenta and umbilical cord, and the inner portion becomes the embryo. The placenta, connected to the embryo by the umbilical cord, serves as the growing embryo's link for food from the mother; it allows nutrients to enter and wastes to exit, and it screens out some, but not all, harmful substances.

Once implantation of the zygote is completed, about two weeks after conception, the *embryonic stage* begins, lasting until the eighth week after conception. The embryo develops webbed fingers and toes, a tail, eyes, ears, a nose, a mouth, a heart and circulatory system, and a spinal cord—although at 8 weeks, the embryo is only 1½ inches long. During the fourth to eighth week, the male hormone testosterone is secreted by the rudimentary testes in embryos that are genetically male; without this hormone, the embryo will develop to be anatomically female.

After 8 weeks, the *fetal stage* begins. The organism, now called a *fetus*, further develops the organs and systems that existed in rudimentary form in the embryonic stage. By 28 weeks, the nervous and respiratory systems are developed enough to allow most fetuses to live if born prematurely. (Technological advances allow many to survive if born even earlier, but the risks are much higher.) The greatest gains in brain and nervous-system development occur during the last 12 weeks of a full-term pregnancy.

Although the womb is a fairly sturdy protector of the growing embryo or fetus, some harmful influences can cross the placental barrier. These influences, which are particularly damaging during the embryonic stage, include the following:

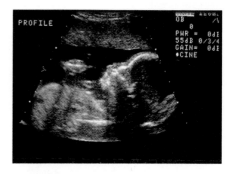

The first picture that many parents have of their offspring is a fetal sonogram, like this one taken during the twenty-third week of pregnancy.

1 *German measles* (rubella), especially early in the pregnancy, can affect the fetus's eyes, ears, and heart. The most common consequence is deafness. Rubella is preventable if the mother has been vaccinated, which can be done in adulthood, up to three months before pregnancy.

2 *X-rays or other radiation, or toxic chemicals* such as lead, can cause fetal abnormalities and deformities. Exposure to lead is also associated with attention problems and lower IQ scores.

3 *Sexually transmitted diseases* can cause mental retardation, blindness, and other physical disorders. Genital herpes affects the fetus only if the mother has an outbreak at the time of delivery, which exposes the newborn to the virus as the baby passes through the birth canal. (This risk can be avoided by having a cesarean section.) The AIDS virus too can be transmitted to the fetus and is usually fatal, though not all babies of HIV-infected mothers become infected; estimates range from 13 to 30 percent (Bee, 1997).

4 *Cigarette smoking* during pregnancy increases the likelihood of miscarriage, premature birth, abnormal fetal heartbeat, and an underweight baby. The negative effects may last long after birth, showing up in increased rates of infant sickness, sudden infant death syndrome (SIDS), and, in later childhood, hyperactivity and learning difficulties. Cigarette smoking is actually more dangerous to the fetus than cocaine use (Slotkin, 1998).

5 *Having more than two alcoholic drinks every day* significantly increases the risk of a baby having *fetal alcohol syndrome (FAS)*. FAS infants are smaller than normal and have smaller brains, have facial deformities, are uncoordinated, and are mentally retarded. Even when babies do not have FAS, frequent exposure to alcohol during pregnancy can impair their later mental abilities, attention span, and academic achievement (Streissguth et al., 1999). The most dangerous stage is the first trimester (12 weeks). But the consequences of lighter drinking—a drink or two every so often—are not as clear. Some longitudinal studies find no effects, whereas others find small intellectual deficits (Forrest et al., 1991; Hunt et al., 1995).

6 *Drugs other than alcohol* can be harmful to the fetus, whether they are illicit ones such as morphine, cocaine, and heroin, or commonly used legal substances such as antibiotics, antihistamines, tranquilizers, acne medication, and diet pills. Fathers' drug use can also cause fetal defects; cocaine, for example, does so by binding to sperm (Yazigi, Odem, & Polakoski, 1991). Longitudinal studies of children exposed to cocaine in the womb have dispelled the myth of the "crack baby" who is supposedly brain damaged for life (Newman & Buka, 1991). Nonetheless, cocaine can cause small, subtle impairments in children's cognitive and language abilities (Lester, LaGasse, & Seifer, 1998).

The lesson is clear. A pregnant woman does well to abstain from smoking completely, to avoid alcohol or drink very little of it, and to take no other drugs of any kind unless they are medically necessary and have been adequately tested for safety—and then to accept the fact that her child will never be properly grateful for all that sacrifice!

The Infant's World

Newborn babies could never survive on their own, but they are far from being passive and inert. Many abilities, tendencies, and characteristics are universal in human beings and are present at birth or develop very early, given certain experiences.

Physical Abilities. Newborns begin life with several *motor reflexes*, automatic behaviors that are necessary for survival (see Table 14.1). They will grasp tightly a finger pressed on their tiny palms. They will turn their heads toward a touch on the cheek or corner of the mouth and search for something to suck on, a handy "rooting reflex" that allows them to find the breast or bottle. Many of these reflexes eventually disappear, but others—such as the knee-jerk, eye-blink, and sneeze reflexes—remain.

Babies are also equipped with a set of inborn perceptual abilities. They can see, hear, touch, smell, and taste (bananas and sugar water are in, rotten eggs are out).

TABLE 14.1	Reflexes of the Newborn Baby
Reflex	**Description**
Rooting	An infant touched on the cheek or corner of the mouth will turn toward the touch and search for something to suck on.
Sucking	An infant will suck on anything suckable, such as a nipple or finger.
Swallowing	An infant can swallow, though this reflex is not yet well coordinated with breathing.
Moro or "startle"	In response to a loud noise or a physical shock, an infant will throw its arms outward and arch back.
Babinski	In response to a touch on the bottom of the foot, the infant's toes will splay outward and then curl in. (In adults, the toes just curl in.)
Grasp	In response to a touch on the palm of the hand, an infant will grasp.
Stepping	If held so that the feet just touch the ground, an infant will show "walking" movements, alternating the feet in steps.

A newborn's visual focus range is only about 8 inches, the average distance between the baby and the face of the person holding the baby, but visual ability develops rapidly. Newborns open their eyes wide to investigate what is around them, even in the dark. They can distinguish contrasts, shadows, and edges. They can discriminate their mother or other primary caregiver on the basis of smell, sight, or sound almost immediately. Within a couple of months, they show evidence of depth perception (see Chapter 6).

Social Skills. Newborns are sociable from the start. At birth, they are primed to respond to human faces. Babies who are only *9 minutes old* will turn their heads to watch a drawing of a face if it moves in front of them, but they will not turn if the "face" consists of scrambled features or is only the outline of a face (Goren, Sarty, & Wu, 1975; Johnson et al., 1991). By the age of 4 to 6 weeks, babies are smiling regularly, even when they haven't the foggiest notion of whom they are smiling at.

Babies also have rudimentary "conversations" with those who tend them. Like many social exchanges, a baby's first "conversation" with its mother or primary caregiver often takes place over a good meal: During nursing, babies and their mothers often play little games with each other, exchanging nonverbal signals in a rhythmic pattern. This rhythmic dialogue illustrates a crucial aspect of all human exchanges: *synchrony*, the adjustment of one person's nonverbal behavior to coordinate with another's (Bernieri et al., 1994; Condon, 1982). Just as adults unconsciously modify their rhythms of speech and gestures to be "in sync" with those of a person they are speaking to (see Chapter 11), newborns synchronize their behavior and attention to adult speech but not to other sounds, such as street noise or tapping. Parents in turn coordinate their movements and rhythms with those of their baby.

Culture and Maturation. Although infants everywhere develop according to the same maturational sequence, many aspects of their development depend on cultural customs that govern how their parents hold, touch, feed, and talk to them (Super & Harkness, 1994). For example, in the United States, babies are expected to sleep for eight uninterrupted hours by the age of 4 or 5 months. This milestone is considered a sign of neurological maturity, although many babies wail when the parent puts them in the crib at night and leaves the room. But among Mayan Indians, rural Italians, African villagers, and urban Japanese, this nightly clash of wills never occurs because the infant sleeps with the mother for the first few years of life, waking and nursing about every four hours. Although many North American mothers constantly worry about the "right" or "wrong" way of caring for an infant, neither custom is better than the other. These differences in babies'

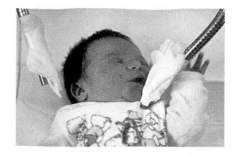

Researchers use imaginative methods to study the remarkable abilities of newborn babies. One study found that infants as young as three days old are calmer when they get a whiff of gauze worn by their mothers than when they smell gauze worn by other women (Montagner, 1985).

This mother and infant, exchanging giggles, gestures, coos, and smiles, illustrate synchrony in action.

Most Navaho babies calmly accept being strapped to a cradle board (left), whereas white babies will often protest vigorously (right). Yet despite cultural differences in such practices, babies everywhere eventually sit, crawl, and walk.

EXAMINE ASSUMPTIONS

Some experts advise parents to give their infants constant mental stimulation so the babies' brains will develop many synapses in the crucial first year of life. What assumptions are the experts making about the importance of the first year, and is their advice always warranted?

sleep arrangements reflect cultural and parental values. Mayan mothers believe it is important to sleep with the baby in order to forge a close bond with the child; many North American and German parents believe it is important to foster the child's independence as soon as possible (Kagan, 1998b; Morelli et al., 1992).

Cultural customs even influence the rate of physical development. Infants in many African cultures, such as the Kipsigis, surpass white American infants in their rate of learning to sit and to walk. Parents in these cultures routinely bounce babies on their feet, exercise the newborn's walking reflex, prop young infants in sitting positions, and discourage crawling. In contrast, infants of the Ache people, who live in the rain forest of South America, are physically restricted in their first year, as it is too dangerous for them to venture far from their mothers. Ache children begin walking at about 23 months, nearly a year later than children in North America (Feldman, 1997). Eventually, though, healthy children everywhere are able to crawl, sit, and walk.

How Critical Are the Early Years?

Many psychologists believe that the first one to three years of life are crucial to healthy child development, largely because of the rapid growth of the brain during this time. During the baby's first 15 months, there is an explosion of connections between neurons in the brain (see Figure 14.1). In fact, too many interconnecting synapses are produced. As the brain integrates and consolidates early experience, it prunes away unnecessary synapses, leaving behind an efficient neural network.

Some psychologists and popular writers have interpreted these facts to mean that infants need maximum stimulation in order to develop a maximum number of synapses. They fear that if a baby does not start out well or get "enough" mental stimulation, the baby's whole life may be influenced for the worse. This is true in the sad cases of infants completely deprived of contact comfort, love, and attention, or whose developing brains are damaged by abuse.

But children do not need a constant bombardment of games and visual stimulation in order to develop normally. As we saw in Chapter 4 and will see again later in this chapter, the brain is not formed, once and for all, at any critical time in life. The process of synapse formation and "pruning" continues all through childhood, and even into the later years (Greenough, Cohen, & Juraska, 1999). Although the first few years are very important for cognitive development, they are not the whole story. In fact, study after study shows that a child's early environment does not necessarily have permanent effects.

FIGURE 14.1
GETTING CONNECTED

Neurons in a newborn's brain are widely spaced, but they immediately begin to form connections. These drawings show the marked increase in the number of connections from birth to age 15 months.

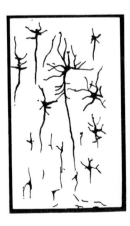
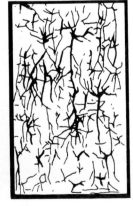

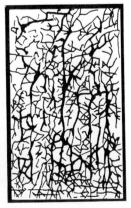

In Holland, for example, many middle-class mothers place their tightly swaddled infants in bedrooms with closed doors and no toys, because they believe that such an austere environment will give their children strong characters. At one year, these infants are somewhat less socially mature than Dutch children not reared this way. By age 5, however, there are no psychological differences between them (described in Kagan, 1998b).

Even infants who start off with illness or other biological vulnerabilities will eventually thrive if treated well. Researchers who followed the development of hundreds of biologically vulnerable children from birth to age 32 found that supportive home environments totally overcame any initial problems. "As we watched these children grow from babyhood to adulthood," the researchers reported, "we could not help but respect the self-righting tendencies within them that produced normal development under all but the most persistently adverse circumstances" (Werner, 1989).

Given adequate stimulation, attention, and nourishment, most healthy babies, and even those with physical difficulties, will develop normally. And "adequate" covers a lot of territory. Babies get along fine on cradle boards or unbound, sleeping with their parents or in a crib, being cared for at home or in good child-care centers (NICHD Early Child Care Research Network, 1997; Scarr, 1997).

By the end of the first year, infants everywhere have made tremendous progress in their physical abilities. Now the story becomes even more interesting.

QUICK QUIZ

Is your understanding of early development developing normally?

1. Name as many potentially harmful influences on fetal development as you can.

2. A mother coos and rocks her baby, who smiles and giggles back at her. Their "conversation" shows
_____.

3. *True or false:* To develop normally, infants must sleep apart from their mothers.

Answers:

1. German measles early in pregnancy; exposure to radiation or toxic chemicals; sexually transmitted diseases; the mother's use of cigarettes, alcohol, or other drugs 2. synchrony 3. false

WHAT'S AHEAD

● How are a toddler's first word combinations similar to the language in a telegram?
● What important accomplishment are infants revealing when they learn to play peekaboo?
● Why will most 5-year-olds choose a tall, narrow glass of lemonade over a short, fat one containing the same amount?
● According to a leading theory, why is moral reasoning based on law, justice, and duty *not* the pinnacle of moral development?
● When reasoning about moral dilemmas, are women more compassionate and caring than men are?

COGNITIVE DEVELOPMENT

Our friend Joel reports how thrilled he was when his 13-month-old daughter Alison looked at him one day and said, for the first time, "Daddy!" His delight was deflated somewhat, though, when the doorbell rang and she ran to the door, calling, "Daddy!" Later Joel learned that there was a 2-year-old child in Alison's daycare group whose father would ring the doorbell when he picked her up. Alison acquired her friend's enthusiasm for doorbells but didn't quite get the hang of "Daddy." She will soon enough, though. She will also be able to reason and see the world from Daddy's viewpoint. And soon, too, she will be able to understand what her daddy means when he praises her for being a "good girl"—or calls her a naughty one.

Language

In Chapter 3 we saw that the ability to use language is an evolutionary adaptation of the human species. In only a few years, children are able to understand thousands of words; use rules of syntax to string them together in meaningful sentences; and produce and understand an endless number of new word combinations.

The acquisition of language begins in the first few months. Infants can only cry and coo, but they are already responsive to the pitch, intensity, and sound of language, and they react to the emotions and rhythms in people's voices (Fernald & Mazzie, 1991). When most people speak to babies, their pitch is higher and more varied than usual and their intonation is more exaggerated. Adult use of "baby talk"—researchers call it "parentese"—has been documented all over the world, including France, Russia, Sweden, Italy, Japan, rural South Africa, Britain, Canada, the United States, and China. Parentese helps babies learn the "melody" and rhythm of their native language (Kuhl et al., 1997). Babies as young as 2 days old prefer to hear adults talk this way.

By 4 to 6 months, babies know many of the key consonant and vowel sounds (phonemes) of their native language and can distinguish such sounds from those of other languages (Kuhl et al., 1992). They can also recognize their own names and other words that are regularly spoken with emotion, such as "mommy" and "daddy." Over time, exposure to the baby's native language reduces his or her ability to perceive speech sounds in other languages. Thus, Japanese infants can hear the difference between the English sounds "la" and "ra," but older Japanese children and adults cannot. Because this contrast does not exist in their language, they become insensitive to it.

Between 6 months and 1 year, infants become increasingly familiar with the sound structure of their native language. They are able to distinguish words from the flow of speech. They will listen longer to words that violate their expectations of what words should sound like and even what a sentence structure should be (Jusczyk, 1997; Marcus et al., 1999). They start to babble, making many "ba-ba" and "goo-goo" sounds, endlessly repeating sounds and syllables. Then, at about a year of age (although the timing varies considerably), children start to name things. They already have some concepts in their minds for familiar people and objects, and their first words represent these concepts ("mama," "doggie," "truck").

Starting at about 11 months, babies develop a repertoire of symbolic gestures, another important tool of communication. They gesture to refer to objects (e.g., sniffing to indicate "flower"), to request something (smacking the lips for "food"), to describe objects (blowing or waving a hand for "hot"), and to reply to questions (opening the palms or shrugging the shoulders for "I don't know"). They clap in response to pictures they like—from Teletubbies to baseball games. Parents who encourage their babies to use gestures like these actually spur their child's language learning. Their babies acquire larger vocabularies, have better comprehension, are better listeners, and are less frustrated in their efforts to communicate than babies who are not encouraged to use gestures (Goodwyn & Acredolo, 1998).

Between the ages of 18 months and 2 years, toddlers begin to produce words in two- or three-word combinations ("Mama here," "go 'way bug," "my toy"). The

Say out loud, "Where is your eye?" Now repeat the question as if you were this mother talking to her baby. Chances are that your voice will shift to "parentese," becoming more singsong, rhythmic, and higher in pitch. The melodic rhythms of "baby talk" help babies learn their native language.

child's first combinations of words have a common quality in most languages: They are **telegraphic**. When people had to pay for every word in a telegram, they quickly learned to drop unnecessary articles (*a, an,* or *the*) and auxiliary verbs (*is* or *are*), but they still conveyed the message. Similarly, the two-word sentences of toddlers omit articles, word endings, auxiliary verbs, and other parts of speech, but are remarkably accurate in conveying meaning. Children use two-word "telegrams" to locate things ("there toy"), make demands ("more milk"), negate actions ("no want," "all-gone milk,"), describe events ("Bambi go," "hit ball"), describe objects ("pretty dress"), show possession ("Mama dress"), and ask questions ("where Daddy?") (Slobin, 1985). Pretty good for a little kid, don't you think?

At about this age, children reveal another impressive talent: the rapid acquisition of new words. They absorb new words as they hear them, forming a quick impression of the likely meaning of the word by using their knowledge of grammatical contexts and the rules for formulating words. The process of absorbing and understanding thousands of new words continues throughout childhood.

Thinking

As anyone who has ever observed a young child knows, children do not think the way adults do. At age 2, they may call all large animals by one name (say, *horsie*) and all small animals by another (say, *bug*). At 4, they may protest that a sibling has "more" fruit juice when it is only the shapes of the glasses that differ, not the amount of juice.

In the 1920s, Swiss psychologist Jean Piaget [Zhan Pee-ah-ZHAY] (1896–1980) proposed a theory of cognitive development to explain these childish mistakes. Piaget was to child development what Freud was to psychoanalysis and Skinner to behaviorism: a figure of towering influence (Flavell, 1996). His keen observations of children caused a revolution in thinking about how thinking develops, and they inspired thousands of studies by investigators all over the world. Piaget's great insight was that children's errors are as interesting as their correct responses. Children will say things that seem cute or wildly illogical to adults. But the *strategies* that children use to think and solve problems, said Piaget, are not random or meaningless. They reflect a predictable interaction between the child's maturational stage and the child's experience in the world.

Piaget's Theory of Cognitive Stages. According to Piaget (1929/1960, 1952a, b, 1984), as children develop, they must make constant mental *adaptations* to new observations and experiences. Adaptation takes two forms: assimilation and accommodation.

Assimilation is what you do when you fit new information into your present system of knowledge and beliefs or into your mental *schemas* (networks of associations, beliefs, and expectations about categories of things and people). Suppose that little Harry learns a schema for "dog" by playing with the family spaniel. If he then sees the neighbor's German shepherd and says "doggie!", he has assimilated the new information about the neighbor's pet into his schema for dogs. **Accommodation** is what you

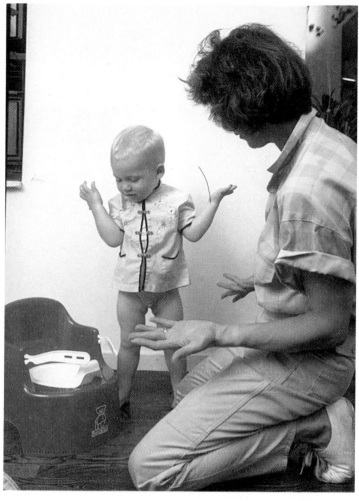

Symbolic gestures emerge early! This mother and her son are clearly having a "conversation."

telegraphic speech A child's first word combinations, which omit (as a telegram does) unnecessary words.

assimilation In Piaget's theory, the process of absorbing new information into existing cognitive structures.

accommodation In Piaget's theory, the process of modifying existing cognitive structures in response to experience and new information.

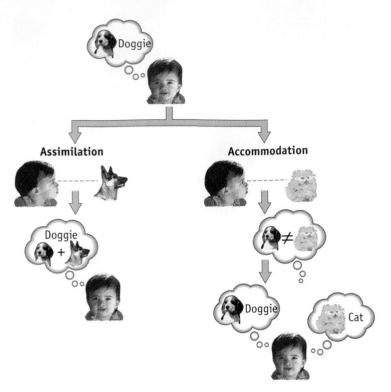

do when, as a result of undeniable new information, you must change or modify your existing schemas. If Harry sees the neighbor's Persian cat and still says "doggie!", his parents are likely to laugh and correct him. Harry will have to modify his schema for *dogs* to exclude cats, and he will have to create a schema for *cats*. In this way, he accommodates the new information that a Persian cat is not a dog.

Using these concepts, Piaget proposed that all children go through four stages of cognitive development.

1 *The sensorimotor stage (birth to age 2).* In this stage, the infant learns through concrete actions: looking, touching, hearing, putting things in the mouth, sucking, grasping. "Thinking" consists of coordinating sensory information with bodily movements. Gradually, these movements become more purposeful, as the child explores the environment and learns that specific movements will produce specific results. Swatting a cloth away will reveal a hidden toy; letting go of a fuzzy toy duck will cause it to drop out of reach; banging on the table with a spoon will produce dinner (or Mom, taking the spoon away).

A major accomplishment at this stage, said Piaget, is **object permanence**, the understanding that something continues to exist even when you can't see it or touch it. In the first few months, he observed, infants seem to follow the motto "out of sight, out of mind." They will look intently at a little toy, but if you hide it behind a piece of paper they will not look behind the paper or make an effort to get the toy. By about 6 months of age, however, infants begin to grasp the idea that a toy exists and the family cat exists, whether or not they can see the toy or the cat. If a baby of this age drops a toy from her playpen, she will look for it; she also will look under a cloth for a toy that is partially hidden. By 1 year of age, most babies have developed an awareness of the permanence of (some) objects—even if a toy is covered by a cloth, it must be under there. This is when they love to play peekaboo.

Object permanence, said Piaget, represents the beginning of the child's capacity to use mental imagery and other symbolic systems. The child is able for the first time to hold a concept in mind, to learn that the word *fly* represents an annoying, buzzing creature, and that *Daddy* represents a friendly, playful one.

2 *The preoperational stage (ages 2 to 7).* During this stage, the use of symbols and language accelerates. A 2-year-old is able to pretend, for instance, that a large box is a house, table, or train. But Piaget described this stage largely in terms of what (he thought) the child cannot do. Although children can think, said Piaget, they cannot reason, and they lack the mental abilities necessary for understanding abstract principles or cause and effect. Piaget called these missing abilities **operations**, by which he meant reversible actions that the child performs in the mind. An operation is a sort of "train of thought" that can be run backward or forward. Multiplying 2 times 6 to get 12 is an operation; so is the reverse operation, dividing 12 by 6 to get 2.

Piaget also believed (mistakenly, as we will see) that preoperational children cannot take another person's point of view because their thinking is **egocentric**. They see the world only from their own frame of reference and cannot imagine that others see things differently.

Further, said Piaget, preoperational children cannot grasp the concept of **conservation**, the notion that physical properties do not change when their forms or appearances

object permanence The understanding that an object continues to exist even when you cannot see it or touch it.

operations In Piaget's theory, mental actions that are cognitively reversible.

egocentric thinking Seeing the world from only your own point of view; the inability to take another person's perspective.

conservation The understanding that the physical properties of objects—such as the number of items in a cluster or the amount of liquid in a glass—can remain the same even when their form or appearance changes.

FIGURE 14.2
PIAGET'S PRINCIPLE OF CONSERVATION

In a typical test for conservation of number (left), the child must say whether one of the sets of blocks has "more." His answer shows whether he understands that the two sets contain the same number, even though the larger blocks in one set take up more space. In a test for conservation of quantity (right), the child is shown two short, fat glasses with equal amounts of liquid. Then the contents of one glass are poured into a tall, narrow beaker, and the child is asked whether one container now has more. Her answer shows whether she understands that pouring liquid from a short, fat glass into a tall, narrow one leaves the amount of liquid unchanged.

change. Children at this age are unable to understand that an amount of liquid, a number of pennies, or a length of rope remains the same even if you pour the liquid from one glass to another, stack the pennies, or coil the rope (see Figure 14.2). If you pour liquid from a short, fat glass into a tall, narrow glass, preoperational children will say there is more liquid in the second glass. They attend to the appearance of the liquid (its height in the glass) to judge its quantity, and so are misled.

3 *The concrete operations stage (ages 7 to 12).* In this stage, Piaget said, children's thinking is still grounded in *concrete* experiences and concepts, rather than in abstractions or logical deductions. However, the nature and quality of their thought processes change significantly. Children come to understand the principles of conservation, reversibility, and cause and effect. They learn mental operations, such as addition, subtraction, multiplication, and division. They learn to categorize things (e.g., oaks as trees) and to order things serially from smallest to largest, lightest to darkest, and shortest to tallest. And they understand the nature of *identity*; for example, they know that a girl does not turn into a boy by wearing a boy's hat, and that a brother will always be a brother, even if he grows up.

4 *The formal operations stage (age 12 through adulthood).* In this last stage, teenagers become capable of abstract reasoning. They understand that ideas can be compared and classified, just as objects can. They are able to reason about situations they have not experienced firsthand, and they can think about future possibilities.

GET ➔ INVOLVED

A TEST OF CONSERVATION

If you know any young children, try one of Piaget's conservation experiments. A simple one is to make two rows of seven buttons or pennies, aligned identically. Ask the child whether one row has more. Now simply spread out the buttons in one row, and ask the child again whether one has more. If the child says "Yes," ask which one, and why. Try to do this experiment with a 3-year-old and a 7- or 8-year-old. You will probably see a big difference in their answers.

They are able to search systematically for answers to problems. They are able to draw logical conclusions from premises common to their culture and experience. (Review 14.1 summarizes Piaget's stages of cognitive development.)

Evaluating Piaget. Piaget transformed the field of developmental psychology, providing an entirely new vision of the nature of children. However, modern research has challenged certain key aspects of Piaget's view of cognitive development.

1 *The changes from one stage to another are neither as clear-cut nor as sweeping as Piaget implied.* Cognitive abilities develop in overlapping waves rather than discrete steps (Siegler, 1996). At any given age, a child may use several different strategies to solve a problem, some more complex or accurate than others. Moreover, children's reasoning ability often depends on the circumstances—who is asking them questions, the specific words used, the materials used, and what they are reasoning *about*—not only on the stage they are in.

2 *Children can understand far more than Piaget gave them credit for.* Taking advantage of the fact that infants look longer at novel or surprising stimuli than at familiar ones, psychologists have designed delightfully imaginative methods of testing what babies know. As we discuss in Chapter 3, these methods reveal that babies may be born with "mental modules" that help them make sense of the world. At only 4 months of age, they even seem to understand some basic principles of physics! Babies that young will look longer at a ball if it seems to roll through a solid barrier, leap between two platforms, or hang in midair than they do when the ball obeys the laws of physics—suggesting that the unusual event is surprising to them. And infants as young as 2½ to 3½ months are aware that objects continue to exist even when masked by other objects, a form of object permanence that Piaget never imagined possible in babies so young (Baillargeon, 1994).

Children also advance rapidly in their symbolic abilities earlier than Piaget thought. Between the ages of 2½ and 3, toddlers become able to think of a miniature model of a room in two ways at once: as a room in its own right and as a symbol

---

REVIEW 14.1

SUMMARY OF PIAGET'S STAGES OF COGNITIVE DEVELOPMENT

	Stage	Major Accomplishments
 "Ball"	Sensorimotor (0–2)	Object permanence Beginning of capacity to use mental images and symbols
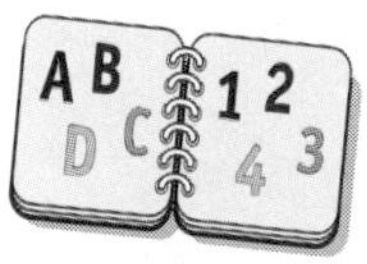 A B C D 1 2 3 4	Preoperational (2–7)	Accelerated use of symbols and language
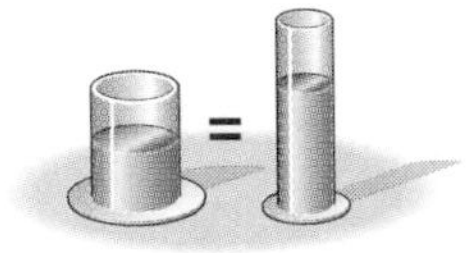 (beakers)	Concrete operations (7–12)	Understanding of conservation Understanding of identity Understanding of serial ordering
 "if x then y"	Formal operations (12–)	Abstract reasoning Ability to compare and classify ideas

This 3-year-old was asked to place the doll where the policeman could not find him. According to Piaget, she should be "egocentric" and therefore hide the doll from herself as well (left). On several occasions, however, she placed the doll where she, but not the policeman, could see him, suggesting that she was able to take the policeman's point of view (right).

of the larger room it represents (DeLoache, 1995). This ability is a big step toward adult symbolic thought, in which anything can stand for anything else: a flag for a country, a logo for a company.

3 *Preschoolers are not as egocentric as Piaget thought.* Most 3- and 4-year-olds *can* take another person's perspective (Flavell, 1993). When 4-year-olds play with 2-year-olds, for example, they modify and simplify their speech so the younger children will understand (Shatz & Gelman, 1973). Even very young children are capable of touching acts of empathy, understanding when another child or adult is sad and offering comfort. In one study, a toddler of only 13 months offered her beloved doll to a grieving adult (Hoffman, 1990).

By about age 4 to 5, children begin to figure out that another person might see things differently than they do. One 5-year-old we know showed her teacher a picture she had drawn of a cat and an unidentifiable blob. "The cat is lovely," said the teacher, "but what is this thing here?" "That has nothing to do with you," said the child. "That's what the *cat* is looking at."

This shift in perspective-taking is part of a broader change in how the child understands appearance and reality (Flavell, 1992, 1993). Two- and 3-year-olds judge by appearance: If you put a dog mask on a cat, they will say it's a dog. By age 5, children know it's still a cat. Even more important, they understand that someone else might be fooled into thinking it's a dog and even act on that false belief. More generally, they understand that you cannot predict what a person will do just by observing a situation or knowing the "facts"; you have to know what the person is feeling and thinking—the person might even lie. They start asking why other people behave as they do ("Why is Johnny so mean?"). In short, they are developing a **theory of mind**, a system of beliefs about how their own and other people's minds work and how people are affected by their beliefs (Flavell, Green, & Flavell, 1990; Jenkins & Astington, 1996; Lillard, 1998).

Thus, the accumulating evidence shows that Piaget was wrong in assuming that children of this age are egocentric and literal-minded. They are capable of forms of logic and inference about other people's behavior that Piaget thought impossible.

4 *Cognitive development depends on the child's education and culture.* Traditional nomadic hunting peoples, such as the Inuit of Canada and the Aborigines of Australia, do not quantify things and do not need to (Dasen, 1994). The Aborigines have number words only up to five; after that, all quantities are described as "many." In such cultures, understanding the conservation of quantity develops late, if at all. But nomadic hunters excel in spatial abilities, because spatial orientation is crucial

theory of mind A system of beliefs about the way your own mind and other people's minds work, and of how people are affected by their beliefs and feelings; emerges at age 4 or 5.

Experience and culture influence cognitive development. Children who work with clay, wood, and other materials, such as this young potter in India, tend to understand the concept of conservation sooner than children who have not had this kind of experience.

for finding water holes and successful hunting routes. In contrast, children who live in settled agricultural communities, such as the Baoulé of the Ivory Coast, develop rapidly in the ability to quantify and much more slowly in spatial reasoning. In all cultures, however, education affects cognitive abilities: Many unschooled children of the Wolof, a rural group in Senegal, do not understand conservation, as do their peers who attend school, but brief training can speed its development (Greenfield, 1976).

5 *Just as Piaget underestimated the cognitive skills of young children, he overestimated those of many adults.* As we discuss in Chapter 9, not all adolescents and adults develop the ability for formal reasoning and reflective judgment. Some never develop the capacity for formal operations, and others think concretely unless a specific problem requires abstract thought.

These findings have altered our understanding of children's abilities. Nevertheless, most psychologists accept Piaget's major point, that new reasoning abilities depend on the emergence of previous ones—you cannot learn algebra before you can count, and you cannot learn philosophy before you understand logic. Perhaps the most enduring legacy of Piaget's work is his emphasis on the fact that children are not passive vessels into which education and experience are poured. Children actively interpret their worlds, using their developing schemas and abilities to assimilate new information and figure things out.

QUICK QUIZ

Please use language and thought to answer these questions.

1. "More cake!" and "Mommy come" are examples of _____ speech.

2. Understanding that two rows of six pennies are equal in number, even if one row is flat and the other is stacked up, is an example of _____.

3. Understanding that a toy exists even after Mom puts it in her purse is an example of _____, which develops during the _____ stage.

4. A 5-year-old who tells his dad that "Sally said she saw a bunny but she was lying" has developed a _____.

5. List five findings that challenge aspects of Piaget's theory.

Answers:

1. telegraphic 2. conservation 3. object permanence, sensorimotor 4. theory of mind 5. The changes from one stage to another are not as clear as Piaget implied; children know more and know it earlier than Piaget thought; they are less egocentric than Piaget thought; their cognitive development is affected by their culture; and not all adolescents and adults achieve the ability for formal operations.

Moral Reasoning

Piaget (1932) pioneered in the study of another important aspect of cognitive development: moral reasoning, which changes according to a child's cognitive maturity. A young child, he observed, will say that a child who breaks a vase by accident is as naughty as one who breaks it intentionally. Older children, because of their maturing cognitive abilities, are able to evaluate moral behavior in terms of a person's intentions and motives.

In the 1960s, Lawrence Kohlberg (1964), inspired by Piaget's work, outlined a stage theory of moral reasoning that became highly influential. Your moral stage, said Kohlberg, can be determined by the answers you give to hypothetical dilemmas. Suppose a man's wife is dying and needs a special drug. The man cannot afford the drug and the druggist refuses to lower his price. Should the man steal the drug? What if he no longer loves his wife? If the man is caught, should the judge be lenient? To Kohlberg, as to Piaget, the reasoning behind the answers was more important than the decisions themselves.

Kohlberg (1964, 1976, 1984) proposed that children progress through three levels of moral development, each consisting of two stages:

■ *Preconventional morality.* Very young children obey rules because they fear being punished if they disobey and later because they think it is in their best interest to obey. Their moral reasoning is hedonistic, self-centered, and lacking in empathy; what is "right" is what feels good.

■ *Conventional morality.* At about ages 10 or 11, according to Kohlberg, children shift to the conventional morality of adult society, which is based at first on conformity and loyalty to others and later on an understanding of law and justice.

According to Kohlberg, Mohandas Gandhi (the "Mahatma," or wise one) reached the highest level of morality because of his commitment to nonviolence and peaceful change. But research finds that people's moral behavior is not the same in every situation or relationship. Gandhi, for example, was aloof from his family and followers, whom he often treated in a harsh and callous manner.

■ *Postconventional ("principled") morality.* Some adults, said Kohlberg, realize that certain laws—such as those that legitimize the mistreatment of minorities—are themselves immoral. They realize that people hold different values and standards, and that laws are important but can be changed. Very few postconventional individuals develop a moral standard based on universal human rights. When faced with a conflict between law and conscience, they follow conscience, even at great personal risk.

Kohlberg's theory of moral reasoning generated much discussion, and research has confirmed the general shift from preconventional to conventional morality in many cultures. However, the theory has three significant limitations:

1 *Kohlberg's theory tends to overlook educational and cultural influences on moral reasoning.* College-educated people tend to give "higher-level" explanations of moral decisions than people who have not attended college, but all that shows, say Kohlberg's critics, is that college-educated people are more verbally sophisticated and have learned to think in legalistic terms (Eckensberger, 1994). Moreover, cultural factors play a major role in how children make moral decisions (Shweder, Mahapatra, & Miller, 1990; Wygant, 1997). In Iceland and Germany, for example, even very young children reveal a moral sense based on concern for others. In countries such as China, moral decisions and values based on social harmony and devotion to parents often conflict with Kohlberg's notion that "higher" moral reasoning is based on analytic, individualistic thinking (Dien, 1982).

2 *People's moral reasoning is often inconsistent across situations.* The kind of moral reasoning that people do depends on the situation and on the nature of the dilemma (Wygant, 1997). For example, you might show conventional morality by overlooking a racial slur at a dinner party because you do not want to upset anyone, but reveal postconventional reasoning by protesting a governmental policy you regard as immoral. In one study using Kohlberg's dilemmas, most of the participants gave responses spanning three to six substages; only one young man based all his judgments on the same stage (Wark & Krebs, 1996).

THINKING CRITICALLY

DON'T OVERSIMPLIFY

People go through stages of moral reasoning as their cognitive abilities mature. But is moral reasoning all there is to morality? Does it ensure moral behavior? Are people consistent in their moral reasoning, or does it vary according to the situation?

"It all depends on how you define 'chop.'"

A child or adult may show verbally sophisticated moral reasoning, and still do the wrong thing.

3 *Moral reasoning is often unrelated to moral behavior.* Moral reasoning ability increases during the school years, but so do cheating, lying, cruelty, and the cognitive ability to rationalize these actions (Kagan, 1993). College students usually draw on lofty principles of justice and fair play to justify moral decisions, yet about one third of American and Canadian college men say they would force a woman into sexual acts if they could get away with it—the lowest form of moral reasoning (Malamuth & Dean, 1990). As Thomas Lickona (1983) wryly summarized, "We can reach high levels of moral reasoning, and still behave like scoundrels."

Another popular approach to moral reasoning was offered in the early 1980s by Carol Gilligan (1982). Gilligan argued that men tend to base their moral choices on abstract principles of law and justice, asking questions such as "Whose rights should take precedence here?" whereas women tend to base their moral decisions on principles of compassion and caring, asking questions such as "Who will be hurt least?" Some studies have supported Gilligan's view, but most find no gender differences, especially when people are allowed to rank all the reasons behind their moral judgments (Clopton & Sorell, 1993; Cohn, 1991; Friedman, Robinson, & Friedman, 1987; Thoma, 1986). Both sexes usually say that they base their moral decisions on compassion *and* on principles of justice; that they worry about feelings *and* fairness.

The main problem with Gilligan's theory, as with Kohlberg's, is that it implies that "moral reasoning" is fixed and consistent, depending either on your stage or your gender. But moral reasoning at any age depends on what people are reasoning about—abstract dilemmas that have no relevance to their lives or personal dilemmas they care deeply about (Wygant, 1997). Both sexes tend to use justice-based reasoning when they are thinking about highly abstract ethical dilemmas, and care-based reasoning when they are thinking about intimate dilemmas in their own lives (Clopton & Sorell, 1993; Walker, deVries, & Trevethan, 1987).

The child's emerging ability to understand right from wrong depends not only on reasoning skills, but also on the emergence of conscience and "moral emotions" such as shame, guilt, and empathy (Hoffman, 1990). The capacity for moral feeling, like that for language, seems to be inborn. As Jerome Kagan (1984) wrote, "Without this fundamental human capacity, which nineteenth-century observers called a *moral sense*, the child could not be socialized." The moral sense can be nurtured or extinguished, however, by experiences in a child's life, as we will see later.

QUICK QUIZ

Do you have a moral sense about taking this quiz?

1. Margo says she pays her taxes because she believes in obeying the law; Manny pays because he is afraid of getting caught. According to Kohlberg, what level of moral reasoning has each of them achieved?

2. Two psychologists noted that in Kohlberg's system, the cruelest lawyer could get a higher moral-reasoning score than the kindest 8-year-old (Schulman & Mekler, 1994). What did the psychologists mean?

Answers:

1. Margo is at a conventional level; Manny at a preconventional level.   2. The lawyer's score reflects verbal sophistication and education and does not indicate whether he or she actually behaves in a kind and moral way; people's moral reasoning and their behavior are often unrelated.

WHAT'S AHEAD

- How would a biologically oriented psychologist explain why most little boys and girls are so "sexist" in their choice of toys?
- If one 2-year-old girl can distinguish males from females and another cannot, which one is most likely to behave as aggressively as her brother?
- How do teachers unintentionally reinforce aggressiveness in boys?

GENDER DEVELOPMENT

No parent ever excitedly calls a relative to exclaim, "It's a baby! It's a 7½-pound, black-haired baby!" The baby's sex is the first thing everyone notices. Most babies, unless they have rare abnormalities, are born unambiguously male or female, an anatomical distinction. But how do children learn the rules of masculinity and femininity, the things that boys do that are supposedly different from what girls do? Why, as one psychologist we know put it, do most preschool children act like the Gender Police—insisting, say, that boys can't be nurses and girls can't be doctors?

To distinguish what is anatomically given from what is learned, many psychologists distinguish *sex* from *gender* (Deaux, 1985; Lott, 1997). *Sex* is used to refer to the physiological or anatomical attributes of the sexes; thus, we might speak of a "sex difference" in the frequency of baldness or color blindness. *Gender* is used to refer to the cultural and psychological attributes that children learn are appropriate for the sexes; thus we might speak of a "gender difference" in sexual attitudes, dishwashing, and fondness for romance novels.

Toddlers can label themselves as boys or girls, but it is not until the age of 4 or 5 that most children develop a secure **gender identity**, a fundamental sense of maleness or femaleness that exists regardless of what they wear or how they behave. Only then do they understand that what boys and girls do or wear does not necessarily indicate what sex they are: A girl remains a girl even if she can climb a tree, and a boy remains a boy

gender identity The fundamental sense of being male or female; it is independent of whether the person conforms to the social and cultural rules of gender.

Mary Read op Jamaica in de Gevangeniſſe Overleden.

A person's anatomical sex and the culturally assigned duties of gender do not always correspond. Throughout history, some men have chosen the roles and dress of women, sometimes with the approval of their communities. In the photo on the left, taken about 1885, We-Wha, a Zuni Indian man, wears the traditional dress and decoration of a woman. Likewise, some women have worn the dress and taken on the roles of men, as did the eighteenth-century pirate Mary Read (right).

gender typing The process by which children learn the abilities, interests, personality traits, and behaviors associated with being masculine or feminine in their culture.

gender schema A mental network of knowledge, beliefs, metaphors, and expectations about what it means to be male or female.

even if he has long hair. In contrast, **gender typing** reflects society's ideas about which abilities, interests, traits, and behaviors are appropriately "masculine" or "feminine." A person can have a strong gender identity and not be gender typed: A man may be confident in his maleness and not feel threatened by doing "unmasculine" things such as needlepointing a pillow; a woman may be confident in her femaleness and not feel threatened by doing "unfeminine" things such as serving in combat.

Influences on Gender Development

Developmental psychologists study the biological, learning, and cognitive factors involved in the emergence of gender identity, gender differences in behavior, and gender typing.

Biological Factors. Starting in the preschool years, boys and girls congregate primarily with other children of their sex and prefer the toys and games of their own sex (Maccoby, 1998). Boys and girls will play together if required to, though it is often "side by side" play in which each does something different. But given their druthers, they immediately choose to play with friends of their own sex. This same-sex preference occurs all over the world, almost regardless of how adults treat children—whether they encourage boys and girls to play together or separate them (Lytton & Romney, 1991; Maccoby, 1998). Many parents lament that they try to give their boys and girls the same toys, but it makes no difference; their sons want trucks and their daughters want dolls.

Biological researchers and some psychologists conclude that these toy and play preferences must have a biological basis, perhaps in prenatal hormones, genes, or brain organization. They point out that girls who were exposed to prenatal androgens (masculinizing hormones) in the womb are later more likely than nonexposed girls to prefer "boys' toys" such as cars, fire engines, and Lincoln logs (Berenbaum & Snyder, 1995). And in all primate species, young males are more likely than females to go in for physical roughhousing (Maccoby, 1998).

However, biological explanations have limitations. For one thing, young boys and girls have the same hormones. For another, boys do not have a greater activity level, as commonly believed; they are not more physically active than girls when children are playing on their own. But when boys play with other boys they become more excited and aroused than girls do, and by different things: threats, challenges, and competition. High rates of male physical activity are therefore a *consequence* of male-male play, not a cause (Maccoby, 1998). Similarly, preschool girls play as independently and assertively as boys when they are in all-girl groups. However, when boys are in the room, girls become more passive, letting the boys monopolize the toys. The reason, it seems, is that when a boy and girl compete for a toy, the boy tends to dominate unless an adult is around (Maccoby, 1990). So there is something about being *in a group* that causes male roughhousing and dominance, but no one yet knows what it might be or how biological factors might account for it (Maccoby, 1998).

Look familiar? In a scene typical of many nursery schools and homes, the boy builds a gun out of anything he can, and the girl dresses up in any pretty thing she can find. Psychologists (and parents) debate whether such gender typing is biologically based or a result of subtle reinforcements and the emergence of gender schemas.

Gender Schemas. Cognitive psychologists explain the mystery of children's gender segregation and toy preferences not in terms of biology but in terms of the child's own unfolding cognitive abilities. As children mature, they develop a **gender schema**, a mental network of beliefs, metaphors, and expectations about what it means to be male or female (Bem, 1993; Fagot, 1985; Spence, 1985). As soon as children have a gender schema, they change their behavior to conform to it.

Before you can have a gender schema, of course, you have to be able to recognize that there are two genders. This ability begins to emerge even before children can speak. By the age of 9 months, most babies can discriminate male and female faces (Fagot & Leinbach, 1993), and they can match female faces with female voices (Poulin-Dubois et al., 1994). But it takes a couple of years before children label themselves and others consistently as being a "boy" or "girl." Once they can do that, they begin to prefer same-sex playmates and sex-traditional toys, without being explicitly taught to do so. They become more gender typed in their toy play, games, aggressiveness, and verbal skills than children who still cannot consistently label males and females. Most notably, girls stop behaving aggressively (Fagot, 1993). It is as if they go along, behaving like boys, until they know they are girls. At that moment, but not until that moment, they seem to decide, "Girls don't do this; I'm a girl; I'd better not either."

Gender schemas eventually expand to include all sorts of meanings, metaphors, and associations. For example, after age 4, children of both sexes will usually say that rough, spiky, black, or mechanical things are "male" and that soft, pink, fuzzy, or flowery things are "female" (Fagot & Leinbach, 1993).

One mystery of gender development is that virtually all over the world, boys' gender schemas are more rigid than girls' are. That is, boys express stronger preferences for "masculine" toys and activities than girls do for "feminine" ones, and boys are harsher on themselves and other boys who fail to behave in gender-typed ways (Maccoby, 1998; see Figure 14.3). One reason may be that most societies value masculine occupations and traits more than feminine ones, and in general give males higher status. So when boys behave like (or play with) girls they lose status, and when girls behave like boys they gain status (Serbin, Powlishta, & Gulko, 1993).

With increasing experience and cognitive sophistication, older children construct their own standards of what boys and girls may or may not do. Eventually, they become aware of exceptions to their gender schemas; they understand that women can be engineers and men can be cooks. From middle childhood on, many people become more flexible about gender rules, especially if they have friends of the other sex and if their families, jobs, or cultures encourage such flexibility (Katz & Ksansnak, 1994). Other people retain rigid gender schemas throughout their lives, feeling uncomfortable with or angry about the prospect of a male nurse or female drill sergeant. How flexible are your own gender schemas?

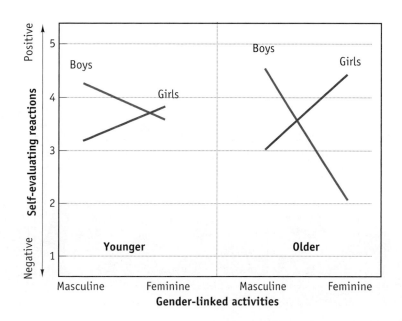

FIGURE 14.3
THE INTERNALIZATION OF GENDER RULES

In a study of how gender rules become internalized over time, 3-year-old-children did not expect to feel very different about themselves if they played with "masculine" or "feminine" toys (left graph). But 4-year-olds, especially boys, anticipated feeling much better about playing with toys associated with their own sex than those associated with the other sex (right graph). These self-evaluations accurately predicted which toys the children actually played with (Bussey & Bandura, 1992).

GET → INVOLVED

CAN YOU IMAGINE BEING THE OTHER SEX?

If you woke up tomorrow and found that you had been transformed into a member of the other sex, how would your life change, if at all? Would anything be different about your attitudes, behavior, habits, experiences, choices, preferences, and feelings? Write down your first reactions, and then ask a few of your male and female friends the same question. If possible, ask young children, too. Do their answers differ depending on their sex? If so, how? What does this exercise reveal about gender typing and gender development?

Learning Influences. A third influence on gender typing is the child's environment, which is full of many subtle and not-so-subtle reinforcers and societal messages about what girls do and what boys do. Behavioral and social-learning theorists emphasize the process of gender socialization that instills these messages in children (Yoder, 1999). Socialization begins at the moment of birth, when the newborn is enveloped in the clothes, colors, and toys the parents think are appropriate for its sex.

Learning theorists dispute adults' claims that they treat boys and girls equally or that "my little girl was just naturally feminine but my boy was born feisty." Adults will respond to the same baby differently, depending on whether the child is dressed as a boy or a girl (Stern & Karraker, 1989). Parents even describe their newborn babies stereotypically, describing girls as being more feminine and delicate than boys, and boys as more athletic and strong than girls—although it is hard to know how "athletic" a newborn boy could be, and all newborns are pretty "delicate" (Karraker, Vogel, & Lake, 1995). Adults respond to boys and girls differently *even when the children are behaving the same way.* For example, one observational study found that 12- to 16-month-old boys and girls did not differ in the frequency of assertive acts (such as efforts to get an adult's attention) and efforts to communicate (Fagot et al., 1985). Yet teachers responded far more often to assertive boys than to shy ones, and to verbal girls than to less verbal ones. When the researchers observed the same children a year later, a gender difference was now apparent, with boys behaving more assertively and girls talking more to teachers.

Parents, teachers, and other adults convey their beliefs and expectations about gender even when they are unaware of doing so. For example, when parents believe that boys are naturally better at math or sports and girls naturally better at English, the children get the message. The parents' beliefs are related to their children's interest in

cathy®   **by Cathy Guisewite**

these activities and feelings of competence in pursuing them—even among boys and girls who start out with equal abilities (Eccles, 1993; Frome & Eccles, 1998).

Gender over the Life Span

In today's fast-moving world, gender development has become a lifelong process, in which people's gender schemas, attitudes, and behavior shift as they have new experiences and as society changes. Although gender *identity*, the inner sense of being male or female, does not change, *gender-typed behavior* changes frequently, both over time and across situations.

Thus, although most people think of "feminine" and "masculine" qualities as stable aspects of personality, both sexes often behave in feminine ways *and* in masculine ways, depending on the situation (Deaux & Major, 1990; West & Zimmerman, 1991). Some situations, such as a date, evoke gender-typed behavior (or conscious efforts to change it): Which partner pays? Who asks whom out? Who makes the sexual overtures? In other situations, such as working on an assembly line or cooking dinner, gender is irrelevant.

Many notions about gender evolve over the life span, a result of people's experience in the workplace and in family relations. Gender differences in personality traits and motivations are greatest in childhood and adolescence, but they decline significantly among college-age adults and disappear entirely among older men and women (Cohn, 1991). By middle age, many people report a "gender crossover," as they explore aspects of their personalities and interests they had previously suppressed: Women often become more achievement oriented, men more nurturant and family oriented (Franz, 1997; James & Lewkowicz, 1997; Stewart & Ostrove, 1998).

In sum, 3-year-old children may behave like sexist piglets while they are trying to figure out what it means to be male or female; their behavior may be driven by genes, cognitive schemas, parental and social lessons, or a combination of all three factors. But their behavior as 3-year-olds has little to do with how they will behave at 23 or 43. Children can grow up in an extremely gender-typed family, and yet, as adults, find themselves in careers or relationships they would never have imagined for themselves (Maccoby, 1998). If 3-year-olds are the Gender Police, many adults end up breaking the law.

These images once had the power to startle or offend people; today, they are commonplace. Economic changes have required the participation of women in every kind of work, and the participation of men in family life.

QUICK QUIZ

Males and females are equally capable of taking this quiz.

1. Two-year-old Jeremy thinks that if he changed from wearing pants to wearing dresses he could become a girl. He still lacks a stable _____ .

2. Which statement about gender schemas is *false*? (a) They are present in early form by 1 year of age; (b) they are permanent conceptualizations of what it means to be masculine or feminine; (c) they eventually expand to include many meanings and associations to being male and female.

3. Herb hopes his 4-year-old daughter will be a doctor, but she refuses to play with the toy stethoscope he bought her and insists that only boys can be doctors. What conclusions about gender differences can Herb draw?

Answers:

1. gender identity 2. b 3. Not many. His daughter's rigid gender-typed behavior is typical when children are acquiring gender schemas, but it does not predict much of anything about what career she will choose as an adult.

- **What is wrong with "because I say so" as a way of getting children to behave?**
- **What three key factors set limits on how much parents can influence their children's personalities and behavior?**

PARENTS AND PEERS

Can parents determine how their children will turn out, as if their children were a batch of cookies? Are parents the strongest influence on their children's personalities, actions, moral behavior, and emotional problems? Until recently, most psychologists (and parents) would not have dreamed of even asking these questions. The answers, they would have said, are self-evident: Of course parents are the most important influence on their children's development. The question is not *whether* they influence children, but *how*.

In the past few years, however, some psychologists have begun to chip away at this widely held belief. Parents are important, they say, but other factors play an equally important role—maybe a more important role—in children's personality and behavior. We turn now to this lively debate.

The Influence of Parents

When you did something wrong as a child, did the adults in your family spank you, shout at you, punish you, ignore you, or explain the error of your ways? One of the most common methods used by parents to enforce moral standards is **power assertion**, which includes threats, physical punishment, depriving the child of privileges, and generally taking advantage of being bigger, stronger, and more powerful ("Do it because I say so"). Yet power assertion, which is based on the child's fear of punishment, is associated with a *lack* of moral feeling and behavior in children, poor self-control, and a failure to internalize moral values. When parents are verbally abusive—insulting and ridiculing the child—the results are particularly devastating for children (Moore & Pepler, 1998).

Longitudinal studies show how power assertion by parents can lead to aggressiveness and poor impulse control in children. Parents of aggressive children do a lot of shouting, scolding, and spanking, but they fail to clearly connect the punishment with the child's behavior. They do not state clear rules, require compliance, consistently punish violations, or praise good behavior. Instead, they nag and shout at the child, occasionally and unpredictably tossing in a slap or a loss of privileges. This combination of power assertion with a pattern of intermittent discipline causes the children's aggressiveness to increase and eventually get out of hand. The child becomes withdrawn, manipulative, and difficult to control, which causes the parents to try to assert their power even more forcefully, which makes the child angrier . . . and a vicious cycle is generated (Patterson, Reid, & Dishion, 1992; Snyder & Patterson, 1995).

A far more successful method for teaching moral behavior is **induction**, in which the parent appeals to the child's own resources, helpful nature, affection for others, and sense of responsibility. A parent using induction might explain to a misbehaving child that the child's actions could harm, inconvenience, or disappoint another person ("You made Doug cry; it's not nice to bite"; "You must never poke anyone's eyes because that could hurt them seriously"). Or the parent might appeal to the child's own helpful inclinations ("I know you're a person who likes to be good to others"), which is far more effective than citing external reasons to be good ("You'd better be nice or you won't get dessert") (Eisenberg, 1995). Children whose parents use induction tend to feel guilty if they hurt others. They internalize standards of

power assertion A method of child rearing in which the parent uses punishment and authority to correct the child's misbehavior.

induction A method of child rearing in which the parent appeals to the child's own resources, abilities, sense of responsibility, and feelings for others in correcting the child's misbehavior.

POWER ASSERTION

The parent uses threats, physical force, or other kinds of power to get the child to obey.

Example:
"Do it because I say so"; "Stop that right now."

Result:
The child obeys, but only when the parent is present; the child often feels resentful.

INDUCTION

The parent appeals to the child's good nature, empathy, love for the parent, and sense of responsibility to others, and offers explanations of rules.

Example:
"You're too grown up to behave like that"; "Fighting hurts your little brother."

Result:
The child tends to internalize reasons for good behavior.

right and wrong, confess rather than lie if they misbehave, accept responsibility for their misbehavior, and are thoughtful of others (Hoffman, 1994; Radke-Yarrow, Zahn-Waxler, & Chapman, 1983).

In a program of research spanning three decades, Diana Baumrind (1966, 1971, 1989, 1991), expanding on the concepts of induction and power assertion, has identified three overall styles of child rearing and their results.

1 *Authoritarian parents* exercise too much power and give too little nurturance. Communication is all one way: The parent issues orders ("Stop that!" "Do it because I say so!"), and the child is expected to listen and obey. The children of these parents tend to be less socially skilled than other children, have lower self-esteem, and do worse in school.

2 *Permissive parents* are nurturant, but they exercise too little control and don't make strong demands for mature and responsible behavior on the part of their children. They fail to state rules clearly and enforce them consistently, and they have poor communication with their kids. Their children, compared with the offspring of other kinds of parents, are likely to be impulsive, immature, irresponsible, and academically unmotivated.

3 *Authoritative parents* travel a middle road, knowing when and how to discipline their children. They set high but reasonable expectations and teach their children how to meet them. They also give their children emotional support and encourage two-way communication. Their children tend to have good self-control, high self-esteem, and high self-efficacy; to be independent yet cooperative; to do better than average in school; and to be socially mature, cheerful, thoughtful, and helpful.

Developmental psychologists have studied many specific child-rearing practices associated with these styles, trying to find which ones might be associated with emotional disorders, intelligence, achievement, self-esteem, aggressiveness, and just about any other outcome you can think of. Yet a key problem in this research is that few parents have a single child-rearing style that is consistent over time and with all their children. Parents are inconsistent from day to day and over the years, depending on their own stresses, moods, marital satisfaction, the child's age, and the like (Holden & Miller, 1999). As one child we know said to her exasperated mother, "Why are you so mean to me today, Mommy? I'm this naughty every day."

Even when parents are consistent in the way they treat their children, there may be little relation between what they do and how the children turn out. Some children of troubled and abusive parents are resilient and do not suffer lasting emotional damage; some children of the kindest and most nurturing parents succumb to drugs, mental illness, or gangs. Why?

How Much Do Parents Matter?

For psychodynamic theorists, parents are *the* most powerful influence in a child's life, even if much of that influence is unconscious. For many behavioral geneticists, parents make virtually no difference at all (see Chapters 3 and 13). Neither extreme is warranted, we think, but today it is undeniable that three factors do set limits on a parent's power to shape a child's personality, behavior, and future life: (1) the child's temperament and perceptions; (2) the child's peer group and experiences outside the home; and (3) the child's larger cultural environment.

Temperament and Perceptions.   Think again about the research on the effects of authoritarian, authoritative, and permissive parents. The findings make sense, but they imply that the direction of influence is all one way: from parent to child. Such research overlooks the child's own temperament and *interpretations* of the parent's actions (Grusec & Goodnow, 1994). A father may seem harsh and authoritarian to an outsider, but the child may perceive his strict rules as evidence of love and concern (Baumrind, 1991). A mother may insist authoritatively that her two sons do their homework; one son does so conscientiously, while the other complains that she is crushing his "freedom." And many parents become authoritarian because they are dealing with a difficult child who has been aggressive or disruptive from the outset (Harris, 1998; Henry et al., 1996).

In short, how children perceive their parents, and how parents treat their children, depends a great deal on the children themselves. Parents are more permissive with easygoing children and more punitive with defiant ones. They might use induction with a child who listens, and power assertion with a child who is rebellious (Harris, 1998). This is one reason that, as we saw in Chapter 13, behavioral geneticists have found no correlation—zero—between the personality traits of adopted children and their adoptive parents or other children in the home. If parental influences or home environment had a strong influence, there would be a correlation. Research has repeatedly shown that when it comes to personality traits, the influence of genetics is

Many parents nowadays fear they had better keep very close tabs on their children! But do parents have total control, even when they try to keep tabs on their kids?

very strong, and the influence of child-rearing practices and family life is weak to nonexistent (Cohen, 1999).

Peer Groups. Children, like adults, have two socializing environments: their homes and their world outside the home (Harris, 1998). Their behavior, like that of adults, depends on the situation they are in—a basic principle of social psychology that we have just seen at work in the case of gender development. Outside the home, most of the situations that children are in involve their peers.

Thus, children who are competitive with their siblings may be cooperative with friends. They can be honest at home and deceitful at school, or vice versa. At home, children learn how their parents want them to behave and what they can get away with; as soon as they leave home, they conform to the dress, habits, language, and rules of their peers. Children who were law-abiding in the fifth grade may start breaking the law in high school, if that is what it takes—or what they think it takes—to win the respect of their peers.

Parents lament the conformity of their children to their peer groups and worry about their kids falling into the "wrong clique," but, according to Judith Harris (1998), children's attachment to their peer groups is not irrational but essential. Identification with the peer group, not identification with the parent, Harris argues, is the key to survival of the next generation. That is why children have their own traditions, words, rules, and games, and why their culture often operates in opposition to adult rules. And it is why kids feel a powerful pressure "not to tell" on their friends who misbehave or need help.

It has been difficult to tease apart the effects of parents and peers, Harris observes, because children's environments often duplicate parental values, language, and customs. (Many parents see to it that they do!) To see which factors are strongest, therefore, we must look at situations in which these environments clash. For example, when parents value academic achievement and their child's peers do not, who wins? The answer is, typically peers.

In a study of 15,000 students at nine different American high schools, researchers sought reasons for the average difference in school performance of Asian-Americans, African-Americans, Latinos, and whites (Steinberg, Dornbusch, & Brown, 1992). Asian-American students, who had the highest grades on the average, reported having the highest level of peer support for academic achievement. They studied together in groups, cheered one another on, and praised one another's success. But many African-American students regarded academic success as a sign of selling out to the white establishment. High-achieving black students often said they had few black friends for this reason; they felt they had to choose between doing well in school and being popular with their peers. This dilemma affects students of *any* ethnicity or gender whose peer group thinks that academic success is only for nerds and sellouts (Arroyo & Zigler, 1995; Fordham, 1991).

Of course, some children have the resources, because of their temperaments or close family bonds, to resist peer pressure. But exceptions should not detract from the rule: that children, like adults, are oriented to their peers. Do *you* dress, think, speak, and behave more like others of your generation or more like your parents?

Culture. The third important influence on children is the larger culture. In the case of moral behavior, for example, parents may use induction to teach their children to be kind and considerate; peers in turn may endorse or contradict these home lessons; but the child will also acquire many ideas from what goes on in society.

The first day of day care can be a rude awakening for an only child raised at home.

Committed reprinted by permission of United Feature Syndicate, Inc.

In many cultures, children are expected to contribute to the family income and to take care of their younger siblings. These experiences encourage helpfulness and empathy.

Does a public figure commit an illegal or immoral act and then earn a fortune from movie deals? Does a sports hero get away with breaking the law because his team needs him to win and to keep earning big bucks for them?

One of the strongest influences on children's moral behavior comes from their cultural obligations and what others expect of them (Eisenberg, 1995; Segall et al., 1999). In a cross-cultural study of children in Kenya, India, Mexico, Okinawa, the Philippines, the United States, and five other cultures, researchers measured how often children behaved altruistically (offering help, support, or unselfish suggestions) or egoistically (seeking help and attention or wanting to dominate others) (Whiting & Edwards, 1988; Whiting & Whiting, 1975). American children were the least altruistic on all measures and the most egoistic. The most altruistic children came from societies in which children are assigned many tasks, such as caring for younger children and gathering and preparing food. These children knew that their work made a genuine contribution to the well-being or economic survival of the family. In cultures that value individual achievement and self-advancement, taking care of others has less importance.

Do Parents Matter? Clearly the answer to how much parents matter depends on how we define our terms: matter for what? Child-rearing techniques seem to have little impact on children's basic temperaments and traits, such as timidity or extroversion. But, as we saw in Chapter 13, child-rearing techniques can make a big difference in children's behavior, if the parents keep the children's temperaments in mind. For example, parents can't make inhibited children into extroverts, but they can help them become more sociable and less frightened of new situations.

Second, parents may not be able to control their children's behavior in peer groups, but they can help their children resist the appeal of delinquent or violent ones. Consider the factors that predict which boys at high risk of delinquency and crime will be less vulnerable: consistent parental discipline and close supervision, parental affection and close parent-child attachment, and high parental standards and expectations (McCord, 1992; Patterson et al., 1998; C. Smith et al., 1997).

Most of all, what parents do affects the quality of their relationship with their children—whether their children feel loved, secure, and valued, or humiliated, frightened, and worthless. Surely this is the most important way that parents "matter"! But once children leave home, starting in preschool, parental influence on children's behavior outside the home begins to wane. Peers and culture take over. The conflict a child might feel between parental values and allegiance to peers typically reaches its peak during adolescence, to which we now turn.

QUICK QUIZ

Would your peers encourage you to take this quiz?

1. Which method of parental discipline tends to create children who have internalized values of helpfulness and empathy? (a) induction, (b) punishment, (c) power assertion

2. Which cultural practice tends to create helpful children? (a) Every family member "does his or her own thing," (b) parents insist that children obey, (c) children contribute to the family welfare, (d) parents remind children often about the importance of being helpful.

3. Most developmental psychologists believe that what parents do affects children profoundly. Behavioral geneticists believe that most personality traits have a genetic component and emerge almost regardless of what parents do. How might these two positions be reconciled?

Answers:

1. a 2. c 3. We can avoid either-or thinking by asking which qualities may be due largely to temperament (such as timidity and extroversion) and which are strongly affected by parental lessons (such as aggressiveness and empathy). Also, we can recognize that how a child turns out depends on the interaction between a child's temperament and the parents' behavior.

WHAT'S AHEAD

- **What are the advantages and disadvantages of experiencing puberty earlier than most of your classmates do?**
- **During adolescence, are extreme turmoil and unhappiness the exception or the rule?**
- **When teenagers and their parents quarrel, what is it typically about?**
- **In what ways do teenagers balance their ethnic identity and their membership in the larger culture?**

ADOLESCENCE

Adolescence refers to the period of development between **puberty**, the age at which a person becomes capable of sexual reproduction, and adulthood. In some cultures, the time span between puberty and adulthood is only a few months; a sexually mature boy or girl is expected to marry and assume adult tasks. In modern Western societies, teenagers are not considered emotionally mature enough to assume the rights, responsibilities, and roles of adulthood. The long span of adolescence is new to this century. In the past, societies needed the labor of young people and could not afford to have them spend a decade in school or "self-discovery."

The Physiology of Adolescence

Until puberty, boys and girls produce roughly the same levels of "male" hormones (androgens) and "female" hormones (estrogens). At puberty, the brain's pituitary gland begins to stimulate hormone production in the adrenal and reproductive glands (see Chapter 4). From puberty on, boys have a higher level of androgens than girls do, and girls have a higher level of estrogens than boys do.

puberty The age at which a person becomes capable of sexual reproduction.

menarche [men-ARR-kee] The onset of menstruation.

In boys, the reproductive glands are the testes (testicles), which produce sperm; in girls, the reproductive glands are the ovaries, which release eggs, or ova. During puberty, these sex organs mature and the individual becomes able to reproduce. In girls, the onset of menstruation, called **menarche**, and the development of breasts are signs of sexual maturity. In boys, the signs are the onset of nocturnal emissions and the growth of the testes, scrotum, and penis. Hormones are also responsible for the emergence of *secondary sex characteristics*, such as a deepened voice and facial and chest hair in boys and pubic hair in both sexes.

Researchers used to think that sexual attraction and behavior followed the onset of puberty; now there is evidence that the age of first sexual attraction—whether heterosexual or homosexual—usually *precedes* puberty. Adrenal androgens begin to rise in both boys and girls as early as age 6, and the average age of first sexual attraction to another is about age 10, before a child's reproductive abilities have fully matured (McClintock & Herdt, 1996).

The Timing of Puberty. The onset of puberty depends on both genetic and environmental factors. Menarche, for example, depends on a female's having a critical level of body fat (necessary to sustain a pregnancy), as signaled by amounts of the protein leptin (Chehab et al., 1997). This is one reason that the onset of menstruation is affected by nutrition and exercise, and why chubbier girls often go through menarche earlier than very thin or athletic girls.

Better nutrition may help explain why the average age of menarche has been declining in Europe and North America for the past 150 years. A study of more than 17,000 girls found that almost 15 percent of white girls and about 48 percent of African-American girls now show signs of pubic hair or breast development by age 8 (Herman-Giddens et al., 1997). The onset of puberty seems to be occurring earlier for males, too. Decades ago, the average American man did not reach his maximum height until the age of 26; today this marker of the end of puberty occurs, on the average, at age 18.

The physical changes of puberty are part of the last "growth spurt" on the child's road to adulthood. For girls, the adolescent growth spurt begins, on the average, at age 10, peaks at 12 or 13, and stops at about age 16, by which time most girls are sexually mature. For boys, the average adolescent growth spurt starts at about age 12 and ends at about age 18. This difference in rates of development is often a source of misery to adolescents, for most girls mature sooner than most boys.

Children typically reach puberty at different times, often to their embarrassment. These girls are all the same age, but they differ considerably in physical maturity.

Early and Late Puberty. The figures we have given you are only averages; individuals vary enormously in the onset and length of puberty. If you entered puberty before most of your classmates, or if you matured much later than they did, you know that your experience of adolescence was different from that of the average teenager (whoever that is). Early-maturing boys generally have a more positive view of their bodies, and their relatively greater size and strength gives them a boost in sports and the prestige that being a good athlete brings young men. But they are also more likely to smoke, drink, use drugs, and break the law than later-maturing boys, and to have less self-control and emotional stability (Duncan et al., 1985).

Likewise, some early-maturing girls have the prestige of being socially popular. But, partly because others in their peer group regard them as being sexually precocious, they are also more likely to fight with their parents, drop out of school, have a negative body image, and have emotional problems (Caspi & Moffitt, 1991; Stattin & Magnusson, 1990). Early menarche itself does not cause these problems; rather, it tends to accentuate existing behavioral problems and family conflicts. Girls who go through puberty relatively late, in contrast, have a more difficult time at first, but by the end of adolescence many are happier with their appearance and more popular than their early-maturing classmates (Feldman, 1997).

The Psychology of Adolescence

The violence at Columbine High School in Littleton, Colorado, put adolescent suffering on full public display. In April 1999, two male teenagers, enraged at the popularity of school jocks and resentful about their own inadequacies, killed 12 classmates and a teacher in a coldly premeditated plan and then committed suicide. In the national self-scrutiny that followed these murders, hundreds of people—adolescents and adults—wrote to newspapers and called in to talk shows to describe the misery of being an unpopular teenager. They spoke of what it was like to be to be excluded, routinely bullied by the popular kids, and considered nerds or losers. How typical are these experiences? Are most teenagers angry and unhappy?

Turmoil and Adjustment. Feelings of insecurity, anger, and rejection are, in fact, common in adolescence, but they are not typical of all teenagers all the time. In studies of representative samples, only a minority are seriously troubled, angry, or unhappy. Most teenagers have supportive families, a sense of purpose and self-confidence, good friends, and the skill to cope with their problems. Extreme turmoil and unhappiness are the exception, not the rule (Steinberg, 1990). Nevertheless, three kinds of problems are more common during adolescence than during childhood or adulthood: conflict with parents, mood swings and depression, and higher rates of reckless, rule-breaking, and risky behavior (Arnett, 1999).

The years of adolescence can be difficult and challenging because teenagers are developing their own standards and values, often by trying on the styles, actions, and attitudes of their peers in contrast to those of their parents. This is one reason for the appeal of breaking adult rules. They don't do this just to annoy their parents. The peer group represents the values and style of the generation that the adolescent identifies with, the generation that will share psychological and cultural experiences as adults (Harris, 1998). That is why the peer group becomes especially important during adolescence.

Adolescent culture often consists of many different peer groups, organized by interests (jocks, nerds, musicians, artists), by ethnicity, or by status and popularity. Tragically, children and teenagers who are temperamentally fearful and shy, have few or no friends, or are physically unattractive or weak are more likely than other kids to be bullied, victimized, and rejected by their peers (Hodges & Perry, 1999). Peer acceptance is so important to children and adolescents that these experiences are often far more traumatic and memorable than is punitive treatment by parents. In one Canadian study, college students were asked, "What made you most unhappy when

Adolescence can be a time of turmoil and rebellion (left), but most teens feel good about themselves and their communities, as do the young people on the right who have volunteered to remove graffiti.

you were a child?" Only 9 percent mentioned their parents; 37 percent described humiliation or rejection by peers (Ambert, 1997).

Adolescents who are lonely, depressed, worried, or angry tend to express these concerns in ways characteristic of their sex. Boys are more likely than girls to *externalize* their emotional problems in acts of aggression and other antisocial behavior; the killers at Columbine High School were an extreme example of this kind of "acting out." Girls, in contrast, are more likely than boys to *internalize* their problems, for example by becoming depressed or developing eating disorders (Zahn-Waxler, 1996).

Separation and Connection. During the transition from childhood to adulthood, conflicts with adults typically focus on the adolescent's increased desire for autonomy. The Michigan Study of Adolescent Life Transitions followed 1,500 adolescents as they moved from the sixth to seventh grades. Some teenagers became less motivated to study and began to misbehave—not because of hormonal changes but because, in essence, they were still being treated like children. Their new teachers were not encouraging active classroom participation as their former teachers had

done in elementary school, but were instead requiring rote learning. And their parents, perhaps worried about their maturing children's sexuality and possible drug use, were using increasingly punitive measures of controlling them. Thus, the researchers concluded, just when adolescents' cognitive abilities are maturing to enable them to do more complex academic tasks and make responsible personal decisions, some teachers and parents are stifling these needs (Eccles et al., 1993).

When teenagers have conflicts with their parents over autonomy, they are usually trying to *individuate*, to develop their own opinions, values, and style of dress and look; they do not want to sever the connection entirely. In one typical study, adolescents described quarrels over issues like these: "Why my mother manipulates the conversation to get me to hate her"; "How much of a bastard my father is to my sister"; "How ugly my mom's taste is"; "How pig-headed my mom and dad are" (Csikszentmihalyi & Larson, 1984). But these fights—over what is important, who should set the rules, differences of opinion and taste, and the like—rarely reflected a true rift between parent and adolescent.

For young men and women in Western societies, then, quarrels with parents tend to signify a change from one-sided parental authority to a more reciprocal, adult relationship (Laursen & Collins, 1994). But in the many collectivist cultures around the world, such as India, adolescents would not dream of rebelling against their parents, to whom they feel they owe allegiance and loyalty, nor would the goal of autonomy be more important than family harmony (Arnett, 1999; Segall et al., 1999).

Ethnic Identity and Acculturation

One of the great psychological tasks for Western adolescents, as they prepare for entrance into adult responsibilities, centers on the formation of identity: Who am I? Where do I belong in the world? What can I become? Adolescents are formulating many aspects of their identities, including their sexuality, their goals and ambitions, their sense of themselves and the "possible selves" they strive to become (Oyserman & Saltz, 1993).

An important aspect of identity development, especially in societies that are ethnically diverse, has to do with finding a balance between **ethnic identity**, a close identification with one's religious or ethnic group, and **acculturation**, an identification with the dominant culture (Cross, 1971; Phinney, 1996; Segall et al., 1999). This process begins early in childhood and continues all through life. But the issues are often especially powerful in adolescence, when teenagers tend to cluster according to their own ethnic groups in school and struggle to find a balance between "loyalty to your own" and "making it" (or "selling out") in the larger world (Spencer & Dornbusch, 1990).

As Table 14.2 (on the next page) shows, there are four ways of balancing ethnic identity and acculturation, depending on whether ethnic identity is strong or weak, and whether identification with the larger culture is strong or weak (Berry, 1994; Phinney, 1990). People who are *bicultural* have strong ties both to their ethnicity and to the larger culture: They say, "I am proud of my ethnic heritage, but I identify just as much with my country." They can alternate easily between their culture of origin and the majority culture, slipping into the customs and language of each as circumstances dictate (LaFromboise, Coleman, & Gerton, 1993). People who choose *assimilation* have weak feelings of ethnicity but a strong sense of acculturation: Their attitude, for example, might be "I'm an American, period." *Ethnic separatists* have a strong sense of ethnic identity but weak feelings of acculturation: They may say, "My ethnicity comes first; if I join the mainstream, I'm betraying my

ethnic identity A person's identification with a racial, religious, or ethnic group.

acculturation The process by which members of minority groups come to identify with and feel part of the mainstream culture.

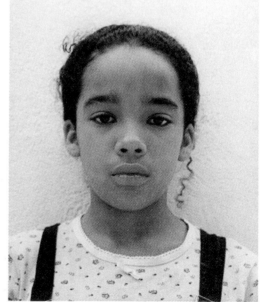

What is this girl's "ethnic identity"? For the growing number of multiethnic individuals, this question is hard to answer. This 10-year-old is African-American, Native American, and Mexican.

TABLE 14.2 **Patterns of Ethnic Identity and Acculturation**

		Ethnic identity is	
		Strong	**Weak**
Acculturation is	**Strong**	Bicultural	Assimilated
	Weak	Separatist	Marginal

origins." And some people feel *marginal*, connected to neither their ethnicity nor the dominant culture: They tend to feel that they do not belong anywhere. Adolescents may try out different choices, shifting from being a "100 percent (member of the dominant culture)" to a "devoutly loyal (member of the minority culture)."

The way a person balances ethnic identity and acculturation, however, may change in response to experiences and larger social and historical events. Thus, many immigrants arrive in North America with every intention of becoming "true" Canadians or Americans. If they encounter discrimination or setbacks, however, they may decide that acculturation is harder than they anticipated or that ethnic separatism offers greater solace. Moreover, acculturation is rarely a complete accommodation to mainstream culture. Most people pick and choose among customs of their own ethnicity and those of the dominant culture, or set limits on how far they want acculturation to go (Segall et al., 1999). You might become acculturated to another ethnic group's food and customs, but believe in the importance of marrying within your own group.

As groups develop a strong ethnic identity, they often reject the name that was imposed on them by the majority culture and choose their own. The Eskimos of Canada are now called the Inuit, their own name for themselves, and the Sioux are now the Lakota. A group's name reflects its history, status, and self-concept. The shift from Negro (a label based on racial categories) to black (based on skin color) to African-American (based on geographical origin) reflects the evolution of ethnic identity, psychological self-concept, and political strength (Cross, 1971, 1991; Fairchild, 1985). The tension over group names is likely to continue, as ethnic groups struggle to define their place, raise their status, and secure their identity in a medley of cultures.

GET ➜ INVOLVED

HOW ACCULTURATED ARE YOU?

Refer to Table 14.2, and locate yourself in the box that describes you best: bicultural, assimilated, an ethnic separatist, or marginal. Have you always felt this way, or has the balance between ethnic identity and acculturation in your own life changed in recent years? Ask five friends, relatives, or acquaintances—ideally from different ethnic groups—how they would respond. If you feel you do not have an "ethnicity," why is that? Would your parents and grandparents feel the same as you?

QUICK QUIZ

If you are not in the midst of adolescent turmoil, try these questions.

1. The onset of menstruation is called _____ .
2. *True or false*: The onset of puberty depends on genetic and environmental factors.
3. Extreme turmoil and rebellion in adolescence are (a) nearly universal, (b) the exception rather than the rule, (c) rare.
4. In Western societies, conflicts between teenagers and their parents are typically over issues of _____ .
5. Frank, an African-American college student, finds himself caught between two philosophies on his campus. One holds that blacks should move toward full integration into mainstream culture. The other holds that blacks should immerse themselves in the history, values, and contributions of African culture. The first group values _____ whereas the second emphasizes _____ .

Answers:

1. menarche 2. true 3. b 4. autonomy or individuation 5. acculturation, ethnic identity

WHAT'S AHEAD

- **What is wrong with thinking that life occurs in a series of predictable stages?**
- **What feelings are common when people fail to marry, start working, or have children at the "right" time?**
- **Does menopause make most women depressed or irrational?**
- **Do men experience a male version of menopause?**
- **What intellectual skills often decline in old age, and which ones do not?**

ADULTHOOD

According to ancient Greek legend, the Sphinx was a monster—half lion, half woman—who terrorized passersby on the road to Thebes. The Sphinx would ask each traveler a question and then murder those who failed to answer correctly. (The Sphinx was a pretty tough grader.) The question was this: What animal walks on four feet in the morning, two feet at noon, and three feet in the evening? Only one traveler, Oedipus, knew the solution to the riddle. The animal, he said, is Man, who crawls on all fours as a baby, walks upright as an adult, and limps in old age with the aid of a staff.

The Sphinx was the first life-span theorist. Since then, many philosophers, writers, and scientists have speculated on the course of adult development. Are the changes of adulthood predictable, like those of childhood? What are the major psychological issues of adult life? Is mental and physical deterioration in old age inevitable?

Stages and Ages

One of the first modern theorists to propose a life-span approach to psychological development was psychoanalyst Erik H. Erikson (1902–1994). Just as children progress through stages, he said, so do adults.

Erikson's Stage Theory. Erikson (1950/1963, 1982) wrote that all individuals go through eight stages in their lives, resolving an inevitable "crisis" at each one:

1 *Trust versus mistrust* is the crisis that occurs during the baby's first year, when the baby depends on others to provide food, comfort, cuddling, and warmth. If these needs are not met, the child may never develop the essential trust necessary to get along in the world, especially in relationships.

2 *Autonomy (independence) versus shame and doubt* is the crisis that occurs when the child is a toddler. The young child is learning to be independent and must do so without feeling too ashamed or doubtful of his or her actions.

3 *Initiative versus guilt* is the crisis that occurs as the preschooler develops. The child is acquiring new physical and mental skills, setting goals, and enjoying newfound talents, but must also learn to control impulses and energies. The danger lies in developing too strong a sense of guilt over his or her fantasies, growing abilities, and childish instincts.

4 *Competence versus inferiority* is the crisis for school-age children, who are learning to make things, use tools, and acquire the skills for adult life. Children who fail these lessons of mastery and competence risk feeling inadequate and inferior.

5 *Identity versus role confusion* is the crisis of adolescence, when teenagers must decide what they are going to be and what they hope to make of their lives. The term *identity crisis* describes what Erikson considered to be the primary conflict of this stage. Those who resolve this crisis will come out of this stage with a strong identity, ready to plan for the future. Those who do not will sink into confusion, unable to make decisions.

6 *Intimacy versus isolation* is the crisis of young adulthood. Once you have decided who you are, said Erikson, you must share yourself with another and learn to make commitments. No matter how successful you are in work, you are not complete until you are capable of intimacy.

7 *Generativity versus stagnation* is the crisis of the middle years. Now that you know who you are and have an intimate relationship, will you sink into complacency and selfishness, or will you experience generativity, the pleasure of creativity and renewal? Parenthood is the most common means for the successful resolution of this stage, but people can be productive, creative, and nurturant in other ways, in their work or their relationships with the younger generation.

8 *Ego integrity versus despair* is the crisis of old age. As they age, people strive to reach the ultimate goal—wisdom, spiritual tranquility, an acceptance of their lives. Just as the healthy child will not fear life, said Erikson, the healthy adult will not fear death.

According to Erik Erikson, children must resolve the crisis of competence and older adults must resolve the crisis of generativity. This child and her grandmother are certainly meeting their respective developmental tasks, but are the needs for competence and generativity confined to a particular stage of life?

Erikson recognized that cultural and economic factors affect psychological development. Some societies, for example, make the passage between stages relatively easy. If you know you are going to be a farmer like your parents and you have no alternative, then moving from adolescence into young adulthood is not a terribly painful step (unless you hate farming). If you have many choices, however, as adolescents in urban societies often do, the transition can become prolonged. Some people put off making choices and never resolve their "identity crisis." Similarly, cultures that place a high premium on independence and individualism will make it difficult for many of their members to resolve Erikson's sixth crisis, that of intimacy versus isolation.

Evaluating Erikson. Erikson showed that development is never finished; it is an ongoing process, and the issues of one period of life may be reawakened during another. His work was important because he placed adult development in the context of family and society, and he specified many of the essential concerns of adulthood: trust, competence, identity, generativity, and the ability to enjoy life and accept death.

However, Erikson's stages are far from universal, and the psychological concerns he identified do not necessarily occur at only one stage of life. Although in Western societies adolescence *is* often a time of confusion about identity and aspirations, as we saw, an identity crisis is not limited to the teen years. A man who has worked in one job all his life—and then is laid off and must find an entirely new career—may have an identity crisis too. Likewise, competence is not mastered once and for all in childhood. People learn new skills and lose old ones throughout their lives, and their sense of competence rises and falls accordingly. Moreover, people who are highly generative (in terms of being committed to helping the next generation) tend to be so throughout their lives, doing volunteer work or choosing occupations that allow them to help others, rather than at only one age (Mansfield & McAdams, 1996).

Finally, Erikson's stages do not occur in the same sequence for everyone. Erikson omitted women from his original work, and when they were later studied they seemed to be doing things out of order, for example, going through generativity by having families before they faced the matter of professional identity (Peterson & Stewart, 1993). Soon it became apparent that many people were grappling with such psychological issues "out of order." Stage theories, therefore, are no longer considered an adequate approach to capturing life development. As one psychologist summarized, "There is not one process of aging, but many; there is not one life course followed, but multiple courses. . . . The variety is as rich as the historic conditions people have faced and the current circumstances they experience" (Pearlin, 1982).

Remember the children pictured on p. 498? They grew up to be Adolf Hitler, Queen Elizabeth II, and Albert Einstein. The diverse lives of these three famous people illustrate the many directions that adult development can take.

The Transitions of Life

Today, theories of adult development emphasize the *transitions* and milestones that mark adult life (Baltes, 1983; Schlossberg, 1984). Having a child has strong effects on you and will affect your life in predictable ways, whether you become a parent for the first time at 16 or 46. Entering the workforce affects your self-confidence and ambition regardless of whether you start work at 18 or 48. Some experiences are hallmarks of major life transitions, notably getting a job, getting married or committed to a partner, having children, retiring, and becoming a grandparent. But as we will see, what affects most people psychologically about transitions is not whether they occur, but whether people feel that the transitions are expected or unexpected, and whether most other people of their gender and generation are sharing them.

Starting Out: The Social Clock. In all societies, people evaluate their transitions according to a *social clock* that determines whether they are "on time" for their age or "off time" (Helson & McCabe, 1993; Neugarten, 1979). Cultures have different social clocks that define the "right" time to marry, start work, and have children. In some societies young men and women are supposed to marry and start having children right after puberty, and work responsibilities come later. In others, a man may not marry until he has shown that he can support a family, which might not be until his 30s. Society's reactions to people who are "off time" vary as well, from amused tolerance ("Oh, when will he grow up?") to pity, scorn, and outright rejection.

Doing the right thing at the right time, compared to your friends and age-mates, is reassuring. When nearly everyone in your group goes through the same experience or enters a new role at the same time—going to school, driving a car, voting, marrying, having a baby, retiring—adjusting to these *anticipated transitions* is relatively easy. Conversely, if hardly anyone you know is doing these things, you will not feel out of step.

As we have noted, though, traditional social clocks in Western societies are changing. Increasingly, people face *unanticipated transitions*, the events that happen without warning, such as being fired from a job or becoming too ill to finish school.

What is your reaction to these two first-time mothers? Arceli Keh (left), whose story began this chapter, became a mother at the age of 63; but the mother on the right had a child as a young teen. Do you think that either or both of these women are "off time" for motherhood, and does your answer affect your feelings about them?

And many people have to deal with "*nonevent*" *transitions*, the changes they expect to happen that do not: for example, not getting married at the age they expected to; realizing that they cannot have children; not getting promoted; not being able to afford to retire (Schlossberg & Robinson, 1996).

One of the reasons that young adulthood is often the most stressful time in people's lives is that young adults are often making many rapid transitions at once: leaving home for college or a job, starting a career, finding a serious relationship. These transitions will be more difficult for those who feel they are not keeping up with their peers: "I'm a junior and haven't declared a major," "I'm almost 30 and not even in a serious relationship" (Helson & McCabe, 1993). Being freed of a cultural social clock can be liberating, but people who cannot do things "on time," for reasons out of their control, may feel depressed and anxious.

The Middle Years. Most people think that the most important issues of the middle years are, for women, the misery of menopause and the "empty nest" (when grown children leave home), and, for men, a corresponding "midlife crisis." But they are wrong.

Actually, according to a large-scale research project that has followed 8,000 Americans for 10 years, for most women and men the midlife years—between 35 and 65—are the prime of life (MacArthur Foundation, 1999). It is true that these years are often a time of reflection and reassessment, as people look back on what they have accomplished, take stock of what they regret not having done, and think about what they want to do with their remaining years (Stewart & Vandewater, 1999). But far from being a time of turmoil, midlife is typically a time of psychological well-being, good health, productivity, and community involvement. American women in their 50s today are more likely than those in any other age group to describe their lives as being "first-rate" and to report having a high quality of life (Mitchell & Helson, 1990). Midlife crises are the exception, and when they occur it is not for reasons related to aging but to specific events, such as the loss of a job or spouse. Another stereotype bites the dust!

But doesn't menopause make most midlife women depressed, irritable, and irrational? **Menopause,** which usually occurs between ages 45 and 55, is the cessation of menstruation after the ovaries stop producing estrogen and progesterone. Menopause does produce physical symptoms in many women, notably "hot flashes," as the vascular system adjusts to the decrease in estrogen. But only about 10 percent of all women have unusually severe physical symptoms.

The negative view of menopause as a syndrome that causes depression and other negative emotional reactions is based on women who have had an early menopause following a hysterectomy (removal of the uterus) or who have had a

menopause The cessation of menstruation and of the production of ova; usually a gradual process lasting up to several years.

Doonesbury   BY GARRY TRUDEAU

In the middle years, most parents are not unhappy to have an "empty nest." The real problem is the fledgling who leaves the nest—but then flies back.

lifetime history of depression. But these women are not typical. According to many surveys of thousands of healthy, randomly chosen women in the general population, most view menopause positively (with relief that they no longer have to worry about pregnancy or menstrual periods) or with no particular feelings at all. The vast majority have only a few, temporarily bothersome symptoms, and do not become depressed; only 3 percent even report regret at having reached menopause (MacArthur Foundation, 1999; Matthews et al., 1990; McKinlay, McKinlay, & Brambilla, 1987).

What about men? Although testosterone diminishes throughout life, it never drops as sharply in men as estrogen does in women, and men do not lose their fertility, although their sperm count may slowly diminish. In short, there is no "male menopause," and hormones do not cause a midlife crisis in men any more than in women. For both sexes, the physical changes of midlife do not predict how people will feel about aging or how they will respond to it (Ryff & Keyes, 1995).

Old Age

In Western youth-oriented cultures, old people are typically assumed to be forgetful, somewhat senile, and physically feeble. On television and in the movies, old people are usually portrayed as objects of amusement, sympathy, or scorn. But *gerontologists*—researchers who study aging and the old—have been challenging these stereotypes.

To begin with, when does old age start? Not long ago you would have been considered old in your 60s. Today, the fastest-growing segment of the population in North America consists of people over the age of 85. There were 4 million Americans age 85 or older in 2000, and the Census Bureau projects that there may be as many as 31 million by 2050 (Schneider, 1999). And there will be more than 600,000 Americans over the age of 100. How will these people function?

First, the Bad News. Various aspects of intelligence, memory, and other forms of mental functioning decline significantly with age; older adults score lower on tests of reasoning, spatial ability, and complex problem solving than do younger adults (Verhaeghen & Salthouse, 1997). As people age, they lose some of their sense of smell (which is why food often does not taste as appealing as it once did), hearing, and vision. It takes them longer to retrieve names, dates, and other information; in fact, the speed of cognitive processing in general slows down significantly (Bashore et al., 1997).

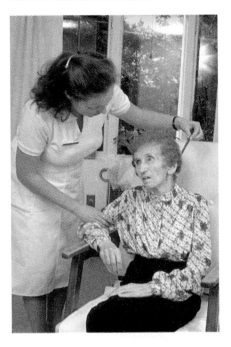

Many of the infirmities of old age, once thought inevitable, have turned out to be a result of illness, malnutrition, or overmedication. This elderly woman is a victim of Alzheimer's disease.

GET ➔ INVOLVED

"YOU'RE AS OLD AS YOU FEEL"

Ask five people—each about a decade apart in age, and one of whom is at least 70—how old they feel. (You may include yourself.) What is the gap, if any, between their chronological age and their psychological age? Is the gap larger among the older individuals? Ask why they perceive an "age gap" between their actual years and how old they feel.

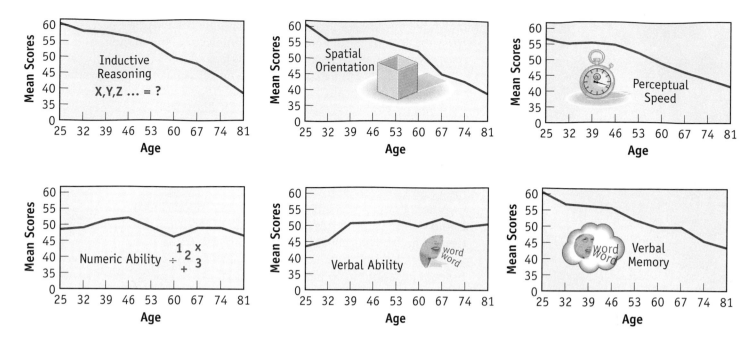

FIGURE 14.4
CHANGES IN INTELLECTUAL FUNCTIONING OVER THE LIFE SPAN

As these graphs show, some intellectual abilities tend to dwindle with age, whereas others remain relatively steady over the years.

But not all cognitive abilities get worse with age. Gerontologists distinguish two kinds of cognitive ability. The first is **fluid intelligence**, the capacity for deductive reasoning and the ability to use new information to solve problems (the kind of intelligence discussed in Chapters 3 and 9). Fluid intelligence is relatively independent of education and experience. It reflects an inherited predisposition, and it parallels other biological capacities in its growth and, in later years, decline (Baltes & Graf, 1996; Bosworth & Schaie, 1999).

In contrast, **crystallized intelligence** consists of the knowledge and skills that are built up over a lifetime—the kind of intelligence that gives us the ability to solve math problems, define words, or summarize the President's policy on the environment. Crystallized intelligence depends heavily on culture, education, and experience, and it tends to remain stable or even improve over the life span. This is why physicians, lawyers, teachers, farmers, musicians, insurance agents, politicians, psychologists, and people in many other occupations can continue working well into old age (Baltes & Graf, 1996).

Memory abilities too decrease with age but, again, the decline does not affect all abilities equally (see Figure 14.4). Older people do as well as younger ones on tests of *semantic memory* (recall of words and knowledge), but they do much less well on tests of *episodic memory* (recall of events and personal experiences). This decline occurs even when researchers control for education, health, and demographic factors (Nyberg et al., 1996; Verhaeghen & Salthouse, 1997).

Now the Good News. Fortunately, gerontologists have made great strides in separating conditions once thought to be an inevitable part of old age from those that are preventable or treatable. For example, osteoporosis (having extremely brittle bones), senility and mental confusion, and lesser insults such as wrinkles and "age spots" are often a result of malnutrition, overmedication, disease, or cellular damage from too much sun. Apparent senility in the elderly is often caused by prescription medications, harmful combinations of medications, and even by over-the-counter drugs (such as sleeping pills and antihistamines), all of which can be hazardous to old people. Other problems once thought to be

fluid intelligence The capacity for deductive reasoning and the ability to use new information to solve problems; it is relatively independent of education and tends to decline in old age.

crystallized intelligence Cognitive skills and specific knowledge of information acquired over a lifetime; it is heavily dependent on education and tends to remain stable over the lifetime.

Stereotypes about old people are breaking down as more and more people are living long, healthy, active lives.

inevitable in old age, such as depression and passivity, are not; they result from the loss of meaningful activity, intellectual stimulation, and control over events (Langer, 1989; Schaie, 1994).

Gerontologists estimate that only about 30 percent of the physical losses of old age are genetically based; the other 70 percent have to do with behavioral and psychological factors (Rowe & Kahn, 1998). The strongest predictors of a vigorous and healthy old age are remaining intellectually active and mentally stimulated, getting exercise (especially weight-bearing exercise to strengthen bones and muscles and prevent or offset physical deterioration), and cultivating psychological resilience—the ability to bounce back after life's losses and stresses.

A longitudinal Canadian study of 250 middle-aged and older adults found that those who remained involved in intellectually challenging activities did not show declines in cognitive ability (Hultsch et al., 1999). The researchers could not rule out the possibility that people with high cognitive functioning continue to pursue intellectual challenges because they are able to. But other research shows that mental stimulation does increase mental functioning in the elderly. Older adults can do as well on memory tests as people in their 20s, when given guidance and cues for retrieving memories—for example, when they are taught to use encoding strategies rather than making lists (Loewen, Shaw, & Craik, 1990). Short-term training programs for people between 60 and 80 produce gains in mental-test scores that are as large as the losses typical for that age group (Baltes, Sowarka, & Kliegl, 1989; Willis, 1987).

The popular notion that the aging brain sheds neurons the way hair sheds dandruff has been disproven by studies of women and men who continue to thrive into their 80s and 90s. In healthy brains, the loss of brain cells is quite modest and is unrelated to cognitive functioning (Morrison & Hof, 1997). As we noted in Chapter 4, physical exercise and mental stimulation promote the growth of synapses in the human brain, even well into old age (Kleim et al., 1998). Also, as people age, their brain seem to compensate for cognitive losses by recruiting areas that previously had not been involved in a given task. In a PET-scan study comparing young college students and people ages 62 to 73 on two kinds of memory tests, both groups performed equally well. But in the older people, both halves of their frontal lobes were activated, whereas in the younger ones, only one hemisphere was activated (Reuter-Lorenz et al., 1999; Reuter-Lorenz, Stanczak, & Miller, 2000).

Perhaps the best news is that as people get older, they get happier and their well-being improves. In a study of nearly 3,000 people ages 25 to 74, the young people were far more likely than the eldest to report feeling sad, nervous, hopeless, or worthless (Mroczek & Kolarz, 1998). As many people age, they learn to control negative feelings and emphasize the positive. Older couples, compared with younger couples, are less likely to express anger, belligerence, and whining when they quarrel (Carstensen & Charles, 1998). In this case, age really does bring wisdom!

Many researchers who study aging are therefore optimistic. From studies of healthy rats and of elderly people who live in stimulating, enriched environments, they conclude that brain function does not inevitably decay (Diamond, 1993; Kolb & Whishaw, 1998). In this view, people who have challenging occupations and interests, and who adapt flexibly to change, are likely to maintain their cognitive abilities. "Use it or lose it," they say. Other researchers are less optimistic. "When you've lost it, you can't use it," they reply. They are worried about the growing numbers of people living into their 90s and 100s, when rates of cognitive impairment and dementia rise dramatically (Baltes & Graf, 1996; Thomassen, van Schaick, & Blansjaar, 1998). The challenge for society is to make sure that the many people who will be living into their 90s can keep using their brains instead of losing them.

QUICK QUIZ

This quiz provides a nice transition to the last section of this chapter.

1. The key psychological issue during adolescence, said Erikson, is a(n) _____ crisis.
2. Ernie wants to go to law school but is failing his prelaw classes. Ernie is about to undergo a(n) _____ transition.
3. Most women react to menopause by (a) feeling depressed, (b) regretting the loss of femininity, (c) going a little crazy, (d) feeling relieved or neutral.
4. Almost overnight, your 80-year-old grandmother has become confused and delusional. Before concluding that old age has made her senile, what other explanations should you rule out?
5. Which of these statements about the decline of mental abilities in old age is *false*? (a) It can often be reversed with training programs; (b) it inevitably happens to all old people; (c) it is often a result of malnutrition or disease rather than aging; (d) it is slowed when people live in stimulating environments.

Answers:

1. identity 2. nonevent 3. d 4. You should rule out the possibility that she is taking too many medications, even nonprescription drugs, that can be hazardous in older people. 5. b

---

WHAT'S AHEAD

- **Do traumatic childhood experiences affect a person forever?**
- **Do most abused children become abusive parents?**

ARE ADULTS PRISONERS OF CHILDHOOD?

Most people take for granted that the path from childhood to adolescence to adulthood is a fairly straight line. We think of the lasting attitudes, habits, and values our parents taught us. We continue to have deep emotional attachments to our families, even when we are fighting with them. And many people carry with them the scars of emotional wounds they suffered as children.

Moreover, when children have been beaten or neglected, have been constantly subjected to verbal and physical abuse by their parents, or live in violent communities, they are more likely than other children to have emotional problems, become delinquent and violent themselves, commit crimes, have low IQs, drop out of school, or attempt suicide (Malinosky-Rummell & Hansen, 1993; Maxfield & Widom, 1996; Moore & Pepler, 1998). Yet studies that follow people from childhood to adulthood challenge the widespread assumption that childhood traumas always have specific and inescapable effects:

EXAMINE ASSUMPTIONS

Many people are convinced that childhood traumas almost always cause emotional problems in adulthood. Is this assumption correct?

With proper support and positive experiences, many children triumph over the adversity of their early lives. Although the actress Audrey Hepburn nearly starved to death in her native Belgium during the Nazi occupation in World War II, she ultimately became a happy and successful adult. Until the end of her life, she worked tirelessly on behalf of children suffering from the effects of illiteracy, famine, and war.

■ *Recovery from war.* After World War II, many European children, made homeless by the war, were adopted by American families. About 20 percent of the children had problems at first, but over the years they all made good progress in school; none had psychiatric problems; and all established happy, affectionate relationships with their new parents (Rathbun, DiVirgilio, & Waldfogel, 1958).

■ *Recovery from abusive or alcoholic parents.* Compared to children of healthy parents, more children of abusive or alcoholic parents become abusive or alcoholic themselves, but the majority do not (Cohen, 1999; Kaufman & Zigler, 1987; West & Prinz, 1987).

■ *Recovery from sexual abuse.* Children who have been sexually abused do have more emotional and behavioral symptoms than nonabused children, especially if the abuse is severe, repeated, and part of other chronically stressful experiences in a child's life. Yet the research shows, much to people's surprise, that by adulthood, most victims are as well adjusted as people in the general population. Meta-analyses of studies of nearly 37,000 college students and of more than 12,000 adults have found no overall link between childhood sexual abuse and later emotional disorders or unusual psychological problems (Rind & Tromovich, 1997; Rind, Tromovitch, & Bauserman, 1998).

Many clinicians have found these results difficult to accept because, by virtue of the work they do, they see the people who are having trouble coping with the effects of difficult or traumatic childhoods. They don't see the people in the general population who have overcome their pasts or vow not to repeat their parents' mistakes.

Because of these heartening discoveries, some psychologists are looking for the origins of *resilience* in the children of violent, neglectful, abusive, or alcoholic parents (Cowen et al., 1990; Garmezy, 1991). Many of these children have easygoing temperaments or personality traits, such as self-efficacy, that affect how they respond to adversity; they manage to withstand severe hardships. Other resilient children are rescued by love and attention from their siblings, peers, or caring adults other than their parents. And some have experiences outside the family—in schools, places of worship, or other organizations—that give them a sense of competence, moral support, solace, religious faith, and self-esteem (Masten & Coatsworth, 1998).

This optimistic news does not mean that it is easy to recover from childhood abuse and neglect, which are widespread problems (Emery & Laumann-Billings, 1998). Childhood experiences are not insignificant, and society cannot afford to be indifferent to children's welfare. Unlike Canada, Sweden, and most European nations, the United States places a low priority on child-care services and education; one in five American children lives in poverty, more than in any other industrialized nation.

But as children develop, they are subject to other influences, too. Perhaps the most powerful reason for the resilience of so many children, and for the changes that adults make throughout their lives, is that we are all constantly interpreting our experiences. We can decide to repeat the mistakes our parents made or to break free of them. We can decide to remain prisoners of childhood or to strike out in new directions at 20, 50, . . . or 80. Children and adults alike have minds of their own—which is why the link between childhood and adulthood is more like a dotted curve than a straight line.

TAKING PSYCHOLOGY WITH YOU

BRINGING UP BABY

How should you treat your children? Should you be strict or lenient, powerful or permissive? Should you require your child to stop having tantrums, to clean up his or her room, to be polite? Should you say, "Oh, nothing I do will matter, anyway?" Even granted the limitations of what parents can do, certain guidelines from research are clearly effective in teaching children to be confident, considerate, and helpful:

■ *Set high expectations that are appropriate to the child's age and temperament, and teach the child how to meet them* (Damon, 1995). Some parents make few demands on their children, either unintentionally or because they believe a parent should not impose standards. Others make many demands, such as requiring children to be polite, help with chores, control their anger, be thoughtful of others, and do well in school. The children of parents who make few demands tend to be aggressive, impulsive, and immature. The children of parents who have high expectations tend to be helpful and above average in competence and self-confidence. But the demands must be appropriate

for the child's age. You can't expect 2-year-olds to dress themselves, and before you can expect children to get up on time they have to know how to work an alarm clock.

■ *Explain, explain, explain.* Induction—telling a child why you have applied a rule—teaches a child to be responsible. Punitive methods ("Do it because I say so") may result in compliance, but the child will tend to disobey as soon as you are out of sight. Explanations also teach children how to reason and understand; they reward curiosity and open-mindedness. This does not mean you have to argue with a 4-year-old about the merits of table manners. But, while setting standards for your children, you can also allow them to express disagreements and feelings.

■ *Encourage empathy.* Call the child's attention to the effects of his or her actions on others, appeal to the child's sense of fair play and desire to be good, and teach the child to take another person's point of view. Vague orders, such as "Don't fight," are less effective than showing the child how fighting disrupts and hurts others. For boys especially, aggres-

sion and empathy are strongly and negatively related: the higher the one, the lower the other (Eisenberg et al., 1996).

■ *Notice, approve of, and reward good behavior.* Many parents tend to punish the behavior they dislike, a form of attention that may actually be rewarding to the child (see Chapter 7). It is much more effective to praise the behavior you do want, which teaches the child what is right.

Nevertheless, even the best parental practices cannot create the "ideal child," that is, one who is an exact replica of you. You can never control everything that happens to your child or everything about your child's personality. "The idea that we can make our children turn out any way we want is an illusion. Give it up," advises Judith Harris (1998). "You can neither perfect them nor ruin them. They are not yours to perfect or ruin: they belong to tomorrow." But, she adds, you do have the power to make their lives miserable or secure, and to affect the quality of the relationship you will have with them throughout your life: one filled with conflict and resentment, or one that is close and loving.

SUMMARY

1. Developmental psychologists study how people grow and change over the life span. They study *socialization*, the processes by which children learn the rules and behavior their society expects of them, and *maturation*, the unfolding of genetically influenced behavior and characteristics.

FROM CONCEPTION TO THE FIRST YEAR

2. Prenatal development consists of the *germinal, embryonic*, and *fetal* stages. Harmful influences that can adversely affect the fetus's development include German measles, radiation, toxic chemicals, some sexually transmitted diseases, cigarettes, alcohol (which in excess can cause *fetal alcohol syndrome*

and cognitive deficits), illegal drugs, and even over-the-counter medications.

3. Babies are born with *motor reflexes* and a number of perceptual abilities. Newborns are naturally attracted to human faces, and soon after birth they develop *synchrony* of pace and rhythm with their caregivers. Cultural practices affect the timing of physical milestones such as walking, but eventually all healthy children catch up.

4. The first few years of life are important for later cognitive development. But the brain develops all through life; and the events of the first years, unless they involve severe abuse or deprivation, do not necessarily have a lasting influence.

COGNITIVE DEVELOPMENT

5. Infants are responsive to the pitch, intensity, and sound of language, which may be why adults in many cultures speak to babies in *"parentese"*—using higher-pitched words and exaggerated intonation. At 4 to 6 months of age, babies begin to recognize the sounds of their own language; and they go through a "babbling phase" from age 6 months to 1 year. At about 1 year, they start saying single words and using symbolic gestures. At age 2, children speak in two- or three-word *telegraphic* sentences that convey a variety of messages.

6. Jean Piaget argued that cognitive development depends on an interaction between maturation and a child's experiences in the world. Children's thinking changes and adapts through *assimilation* and *accommodation*. Piaget proposed four stages of cognitive development: *sensorimotor* (birth to age 2), during which the child learns *object permanence; preoperational* (ages 2 to 7), during which language and symbolic thought develop, although the child remains *egocentric* in reasoning; *concrete operations* (ages 7 to 11), during which the child comes to understand *conservation* and identity; and *formal operations* (age 12 to adulthood), during which abstract reasoning develops.

7. Researchers have found that the changes from one stage to another are not as clear-cut as Piaget implied; that young children have more cognitive abilities, at earlier ages, than Piaget thought; and that young children are not always egocentric in their thinking. By the age of 4 or 5 they have developed a *theory of mind* to account for their own and other people's behavior. Cultural practices affect the pace and content

of cognitive development; and not all adults develop the ability for formal operations.

8. Lawrence Kohlberg's theory of moral development proposed three levels of moral reasoning: *preconventional morality* (based on rules, punishment, and self-interest), *conventional morality* (based on relationships and rules of justice and law), and *postconventional ("principled") morality* (based on higher principles of human rights). Carol Gilligan argued that women tend to base moral decisions on principles of compassion, whereas men tend to base theirs on abstract principles of justice; most research, however, finds no gender differences in moral reasoning.

9. Stage theories of moral reasoning have three limitations: They tend to overlook the influence of culture and education; moral reasoning is often inconsistent across situations; and moral reasoning and moral behavior are often unrelated.

GENDER DEVELOPMENT

10. Gender development includes the emerging awareness of *gender identity*, the cognitive understanding that a person is biologically male or female, regardless of what he or she does or wears, and *gender typing*, the process by which boys and girls learn what it means to be masculine or feminine in their culture.

11. Biological psychologists account for gender differences in behavior and gender typing in terms of genetics, hormones, and brain organization, observing that universally, young children tend to prefer same-sex toys and playing with other children of their own sex. Cognitive psychologists study how children develop *gender schemas* of "male" and "female" categories and qualities, which in turn shape their gender-typed behavior. Gender schemas tend to be inflexible at first but often assimilate new information as the child cognitively matures. Learning theorists study the direct and subtle reinforcers and social messages that foster gender typing.

12. Gender development changes over the life span, depending on people's experiences with work and family life, and on the gender composition of the situations they are in.

PARENTS AND PEERS

13. Parental methods of discipline have different consequences for a child's moral behavior. *Power assertion* is associated with children who have a sense of

external control, are aggressive and destructive, and show a lack of empathy and moral behavior. *Induction* is associated with children who develop empathy and internalized moral standards and who can resist temptation. In general, *authoritative* parents have better results with their children than do *authoritarian* or *permissive* parents.

14. Three factors limit the influence that parents have on their children: the child's own genetically influenced temperament, the child's peer groups, and the larger culture. Altruistic (helpful) children tend to come from cultures in which their families assign them many tasks that contribute to the family's well-being or economic survival. However, parents can modify their children's temperaments, and a strong parent-child relationship can buffer a child against antisocial peer groups.

ADOLESCENCE

15. *Adolescence* begins with the physical changes of *puberty*. In girls, puberty is signaled by *menarche* and the development of breasts; in boys, it begins with the onset of nocturnal emissions and the development of the testes and scrotum. Boys and girls who enter puberty early tend to have a more difficult adjustment than do those who enter puberty later than average. One reason may be that early puberty intensifies existing problems from childhood.

16. Most adolescents do not go through extreme emotional turmoil, anger, or rebellion. However, conflict with parents, mood swings and depression, and reckless behavior are more common in adolescence than in childhood or adulthood. The peer group becomes especially important for teenagers, and rejection by peers can lead to psychological problems. Boys tend to *externalize* their emotional problems in acts of aggression and other antisocial behavior; girls tend to *internalize* their problems by becoming depressed or developing eating disorders. One challenge of adolescence in Western cultures is *individuation*, breaking away enough from parents to develop autonomy and a more reciprocal relationship with them.

17. In culturally diverse societies, many adolescents face the problem of balancing their *ethnic identity* with *acculturation* into the larger society. Depending on whether ethnic identity and identification with the larger culture are strong or weak, a person may become bicultural, choose assimilation, become an ethnic separatist, or feel marginal. The way people balance ethnic identity and acculturation often changes over the life span.

ADULTHOOD

18. *Erik Erikson* proposed that life consists of eight stages, each with a unique psychological crisis that must be resolved, such as an *identity crisis* in adolescence. Erikson made an important contribution by recognizing the essential concerns of adulthood and by showing that development is a lifelong process. However, unlike stages of child development, adult stages are not universal and psychological issues or crises are not confined to particular chronological periods.

19. The *transitions* approach to development emphasizes the changes in people's lives regardless of when they occur. Adults often evaluate their development according to a *social clock* that determines whether they are "on time" or "off time" for a particular event. Transitions may be *anticipated*, *unanticipated*, and *"nonevent"* (expected changes that do not occur).

20. The middle years are generally not a time of turmoil or crisis, but the prime of most people's lives. In women, *menopause* begins in the late 40s or early 50s. Many women have temporary physical symptoms but most do not regret the end of fertility or become depressed and irritable. In middle-aged men, hormone production slows down, but fertility continues.

21. *Gerontologists* have revised our ideas about old age, now that people are living longer and healthier lives. The speed of cognitive processing slows down, and *fluid intelligence* parallels other biological capacities in its eventual decline. *Crystallized intelligence*, in contrast, depends heavily on culture, education, and experience, and it tends to remain stable or even improve over the life span. Many supposedly inevitable results of aging, such as osteoporosis, senility, and depression, are often the result of disease, inappropriate medication, poor nutrition, and lack of stimulation and control of one's environment.

ARE ADULTS PRISONERS OF CHILDHOOD?

22. Children who experience violence or neglect are at risk of many serious problems later in life. But the majority of children are resilient, able to overcome early traumas and even parental abuse. Psychologists now study the origins of children's resilience, as well as the consequences of childhoods of poverty and trauma.

KEY TERMS

socialization 498

maturation 498

germinal, embryonic, fetal stages 498–499

zygote 498

fetus 499

fetal alcohol syndrome 499

motor reflexes 500

synchrony 501

"parentese" 504

telegraphic speech 505

Jean Piaget 505

assimilation 505

accommodation 505

sensorimotor stage 506

object permanence 506

preoperational stage 506

operations 506

egocentric thinking 506

conservation 506

concrete operations stage 507

formal operations stage 507

theory of mind 509

levels of moral reasoning (Kohlberg) 511

   preconventional 511

   conventional 511

   postconventional 511

care-based versus justice-based types of moral reasoning (Gilligan) 512

gender identity 513

gender typing 514

gender schema 514

power assertion 518

induction 518

authoritarian, permissive, and authoritative parenting styles 519

puberty 523

menarche 524

secondary sex characteristics 524

ethnic identity 527

acculturation 527

Erik Erikson 529

identity crisis 530

social clock 532

transitions 532

   anticipated 532

   unanticipated 532

   "nonevent" 533

menopause 533

gerontology 534

fluid intelligence 535

crystallized intelligence 535

LOOKING BACK

- How can a pregnant woman reduce the risk of damage to the embryo or fetus? (pp. 499–500)

- Given a choice, what do newborns prefer to look at? (p. 501)

- How does culture affect how a baby matures physically and socially? (pp. 501–502)

- Do the experiences of the first years of life affect a child forever? (pp. 502–503)

- How are a toddler's first word combinations similar to the language in a telegram? (p. 505)

- What important accomplishment are infants revealing when they learn to play peekaboo? (p. 506)

- Why will most 5-year-olds choose a tall, narrow glass of lemonade over a short, fat one containing the same amount? (p. 507)

- According to a leading theory, why is moral reasoning based on law, justice, and duty *not* the pinnacle of moral development? (p. 511)

- When reasoning about moral dilemmas, are women more compassionate and caring than men are? (p. 512)

- How would a biologically oriented psychologist explain why most little boys and girls are so "sexist" in their choice of toys? (p. 514)

- If one 2-year-old girl can distinguish males from females and another cannot, which one is most likely to behave as aggressively as her brother? (p. 515)

- How do teachers unintentionally reinforce aggressiveness in boys? (p. 516)

- What is wrong with "because I say so" as a way of getting children to behave? (p. 518)

- What three key factors set limits on how much parents can influence their children's personalities and behavior? (p. 520)

- What are the advantages and disadvantages of experiencing puberty earlier than most of your classmates do? (p. 524)

- During adolescence, are extreme turmoil and unhappiness the exception or the rule? (p. 525)

- When teenagers and their parents quarrel, what is it typically about? (p. 527)

- In what ways do teenagers balance their ethnic identity and membership in the larger culture? (pp. 527–528)

- What is wrong with thinking that life occurs in a series of predictable stages? (p. 531)

- What feelings are common when people fail to marry, start working, or have children at the "right" time? (p. 532)

- Does menopause make most women depressed or irrational? (pp. 533–534)

- Do men experience a male version of menopause? (p. 534)

- What intellectual skills often decline in old age, and which ones do not? (p. 535)

- Do traumatic childhood experiences affect a person forever? (p. 538)

- Do most abused children become abusive parents? (p. 538)

15

HEALTH, STRESS, AND COPING

The process of living is the process of reacting to stress.

PSYCHOLOGIST STANLEY SARNOFF

Bill and his father have been battling for years. Bill feels that his father is always ready to criticize him for the slightest flaw. After Bill left home he gained some perspective on their relationship, but every time his father comes to visit, Bill breaks out in a rash.

Tanya lost her apartment and most of her possessions in a hurricane. Months later, she finds it difficult to talk about her continuing anxieties, sure that no one will understand or sympathize.

Vicente is working two jobs to make ends meet. His supervisor at one job is making his life miserable, but Vicente can't afford to offend him, so he says nothing. His blood pressure is high, and lately he's been having awful stomachaches, but he can't see a way of improving his situation.

Val gets caught in a massive traffic jam and is late for class. As she walks in the door, her instructor reprimands her for being late. Later, rushing to get her notes together for an overdue assignment, Val spills coffee all over herself and the papers. By noon she has a splitting headache and feels exhausted.

All of these people are certainly under "stress," but, as you see, their experiences are far from the same. People use the word *stress* to refer to recurring conflicts (Bill and his father), a traumatic experience that shatters your sense of safety (Tanya), continuing pressures that seem uncontrollable (Vicente), or small irritations that wear you down (Val). The question that most fascinates laypeople and professionals alike is what link, if any, exists between these events and illness? Can we, by controlling our stress, prevent illness and maintain good health?

In this chapter, we will explore these questions by looking at findings from *health psychology*, which is concerned with the psychological factors that influence how people stay healthy, why they become ill, and how they respond when they do get ill. Health psychologists study the sources of wellness and illness, to learn why some people succumb to stress and disease and others do not.

- What happens to your body when you try to cross a busy street against the light?
- Which stressors pose the greatest hazard to your health?
- Are you really more likely to get a cold when you are "stressed out"?
- Why is being "under stress" not enough to make you ill?

THE NATURE OF STRESS

Throughout history, "stress" has been one of those things, like love, that is hard to define, even though everyone has experienced it. Why has it been so difficult to agree on a definition of something all of us have felt? In this section, we will see how the concept of stress has changed as we have learned more about what stress is and how it operates in our lives.

The Physiology of Stress

The modern era of stress research began in 1956, when Canadian physician Hans Selye (1907–1982) published his book *The Stress of Life*. Environmental stressors such as heat, cold, noise, pain, and danger, Selye wrote, disrupt the body's normal equilibrium. The body then mobilizes its resources to fight off these stressors and restore normal functioning. Drawing on data from animal studies, Selye concluded that "stress" consists of a series of physiological reactions that occur in three phases:

1 *The alarm phase,* in which your body mobilizes to meet the immediate threat or other stressor. Physiological responses include a boost in energy, tense muscles, reduced sensitivity to pain, the shutting down of digestion (so that blood will flow more efficiently to the brain, muscles, and skin), a rise in blood pressure, and increased output of the adrenal hormones epinephrine (adrenaline), norepinephrine, and cortisol. These responses are pretty much the same, whether you are running from a tiger, about to take a test you haven't studied for, or trying to cross a busy street against the light.

Stress hormones elevated

Blood flow increases

Heart rate speeds up

Digestion slows

Muscles tense

2 *The resistance phase,* in which your body attempts to resist or cope with a stressor that cannot be avoided, but which persists over time. During this phase, the physiological responses of the alarm phase continue, but these very responses make the body more vulnerable to *other* stressors. For example, when your body has mobilized to fight off the flu, you may find you are more easily annoyed by minor frustrations. In most cases, the body will eventually adapt to the stressor and return to normal.

3 *The exhaustion phase,* in which persistent stress depletes the body of energy and therefore increases vulnerability to physical problems and eventually illness. The same reactions that allow the body to respond effectively in the alarm and resistance phases are unhealthy as long-range responses. Tense muscles can cause headache and neck pain. Increased blood pressure can become chronic hypertension. If normal digestive processes are interrupted or shut down for too long, digestive disorders may result.

Selye did not believe that people should aim for a stress-free life. Some stress is positive and productive, he said, even if it also requires the body to produce short-term energy: competing in an athletic event, falling in love, working hard on a project you enjoy. And some negative stress is simply unavoidable; it's called life. The goal, said Selye, is to minimize wear and tear on the system, not get rid of it entirely.

Selye recognized that psychological stressors, such as fighting with a loved one or grief over loss, can have as great an impact on health as do physical stressors, such as freezing weather and pain. He also observed that some factors act as buffers between the stressor and the stress. A comfortable climate or a nutritious diet, for example, can soften the impact of an environmental stressor such as pollution. But by and large, he concentrated on the biological responses that result from a person's or animal's attempt to adapt to environmental demands. A diagram of his view would look like this:

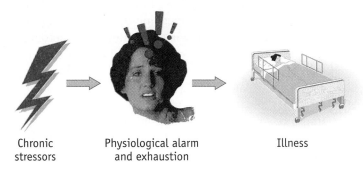

| Chronic stressors | Physiological alarm and exhaustion | Illness |

Selye's ideas spurred extensive research on the kinds of external stressors that might lead to illness. In one classic study, two identical groups of mice, both carrying a virus known to produce a type of breast cancer, were housed in two different conditions: a high-stress environment, characterized by crowding, noise, temperature fluctuations, frequent handling by the experimenters, and other stressful events; or a mouse-friendly, low-stress, comfortable environment. After 12 months, 92 percent of the stressed mice had developed cancerous tumors, compared with only 7 percent of the stress-free mice (Riley, Spackman, & Santisteban, 1975).

These were amazing results. Soon researchers were exploring the kinds of stressful environments that might pose dangers for human beings, too.

Common Sources of Stress

When people speak of being under stress, they are often thinking of everyday aggravations, such as traffic jams, bad weather, broken plumbing, lost keys, or a computer that crashes when a deadline is near. These daily "hassles" are certainly irritating, and psychologists once thought that they increased the risk of illness. Now we know that hassles do not pose much threat to health, except for highly strung, anxious individuals who are quick to overreact to any little thing (Kohn, Lafreniere, & Gurevich, 1991).

The risk of illness does increase, however, when stressors severely disrupt a person's life, when they are uncontrollable, or when they are chronic, lasting at least six months. For example, a brief burst of loud noise is not normally unhealthy—but noise that goes on day in and day out without relief *is* unhealthy. Children who live or go to school near noisy airports have higher blood pressure and higher levels of stress hormones, are more distractible, and have more learning and attention difficulties than do children in quieter environments (Cohen et al., 1980; Evans,

Work can sometimes feel overwhelming.

Bullinger, & Hygge, 1998). In adults, constant loud noise contributes to cardiovascular problems, irritability, fatigue, and aggressiveness, probably because of overstimulation of the autonomic nervous system (Staples, 1996).

The stressors most likely to affect human health are those related to the central activities and relationships of our lives: work-related problems, such as unemployment and tensions on the job; bereavement and loss of loved ones; and struggles to survive in the face of poverty and discrimination.

Work-Related Problems. Just about everyone has work-related troubles: finding a job, dealing with pressures once you get one, recovering when you lose one. Because work is central in most people's lives, the effects of unemployment or of a chronically stressful work environment can be severe. A Swedish study found that people who reported a history of severe workplace problems over the preceding decade had 5.5 times the risk of developing colon or rectal cancers, even when diet and other factors linked to these malignancies were taken into account (Courtney et al., 1993).

Work-related stress can also increase a person's vulnerability to more mundane illnesses, such as the common cold. Heroic volunteers in the war against winter colds were given either ordinary nose drops or nose drops containing a cold virus. Everyone was then quarantined for five days. The people most likely to get a cold's miserable symptoms were those who had been underemployed or unemployed for at least a month (see Figure 15.1). They were even more likely to get a cold than people who had been recently divorced or who were having ongoing conflicts with friends or family. The longer the work problems had lasted, the greater the likelihood of illness (Cohen et al., 1998).

Bereavement and Loss. One of life's most powerful stressors is the loss of a loved one, especially through divorce or death. In the two years following bereavement, widowed people are more susceptible to illness and physical ailments, and their mortality rate is higher than expected. Divorce can also take a long-term health toll: Divorced adults have higher rates of heart disease, pneumonia, and other diseases than married couples (Laudenslager, 1988). Bereaved and divorced people may be

FIGURE 15.1
STRESS AND THE COMMON COLD
Chronic stress lasting a month or more boosts the risk of catching a cold. The risk is increased among people undergoing problems with their friends or loved ones—and is highest among people who are out of work (Cohen et al., 1998).

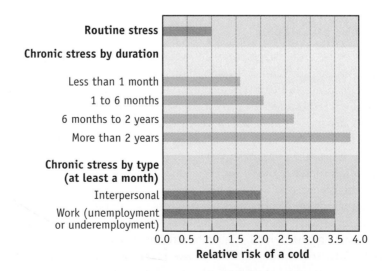

vulnerable to illness in part because, feeling unhappy, they don't sleep well, they stop eating properly, they smoke more, and they consume more alcohol and other drugs. But broken attachments also seem to affect the body at a cellular level, producing cardiovascular changes, a lowered number of white blood cells, and other abnormal responses of the immune system (Stroebe et al., 1996).

Poverty and Powerlessness. People at the lower rungs of the socioeconomic ladder have worse health and higher mortality rates for almost every disease and medical condition than do those at the top (Adler et al., 1994). One obvious reason is that poor people cannot afford good medical care, healthy food, and preventive examinations. Another reason, however, has to do with the continuous environmental stressors that low-income people often live with and feel powerless to change: higher crime rates, discrimination, fewer community services, run-down housing, fewer recreational facilities, and greater exposure to hazards such as chemical contamination (Taylor, Repetti, & Seeman, 1997; Wandersman & Nation, 1998).

In North America, these conditions affect urban blacks disproportionately and may help account for their relatively high incidence of hypertension (high blood pressure), which can lead to kidney disease, strokes, and heart attacks. Persistent racial discrimination is another factor: In a study of 4,000 workers, the anger and emotional stress brought on by racial discrimination were stronger predictors of hypertension than were diet and smoking (Krieger & Sidney, 1996). Many black North Americans also have a genetic tendency to retain salt, which can elevate blood pressure. The combination of having this genetic risk factor *and* living in a high-stress environment can lead to hypertension and heart disease (Weder & Schork, 1994).

Middle-class stress is a luxury to people whose health is chronically jeopardized by poverty, exposure to toxic materials, malnutrition, and lack of access to medical care.

The Stress-Illness Mystery

Before you try to persuade your instructors that the stress of chronic studying is bad for your health, consider this mystery: None of the chronic stressors we just discussed leads in a direct, simple way to illness or affects everyone in the same way. Some people's health is affected by bereavement, losing a job, poverty, or discrimination; yet most individuals living with these stressors do *not* get sick (Basic Behavioral Science Task Force, 1996; Taylor, Repetti, & Seeman, 1997). Some people exposed to a flu virus are sick all winter; others do not even get the sniffles. Some people in high-pressure careers wind up with heart disease; others work just as hard but remain healthy. Why do people differ so much in their susceptibility to stress and disease?

For many centuries, the answer has alternated between two extreme views: physiological explanations and psychological ones. Throughout much of the twentieth century, for example, psychoanalysts promoted the view that physical conditions such as rheumatoid arthritis, hypertension, asthma, ulcers, and migraine headaches are the result of unconscious conflicts and neurotic personality patterns. Although the word *psychosomatic* refers to the two-way interaction of mind (*psyche*) and body (*soma*), the public soon came to think of a "psychosomatic" illness as one that is due entirely to personality problems and thus is "all in your head."

Today, researchers recognize the complex relationships between mind and body. For example, peptic ulcers are not caused solely by suppressed anger and other personality problems; they are caused by a bacterium, *H. pylori*. However, many healthy people who have *H. pylori* in their stomach linings do not get ulcers.

A phagocyte, magnified many millions of times, looks more fantastical than any alien creature Hollywood could design. This one is about to engulf and destroy a cigarette-shaped parasite that causes a tropical disease.

The bacterium is necessary, but not sufficient; stress and psychological factors can also play a role (Levenstein et al., 1999).

To investigate the exact mechanisms that link mind and body, and to find out how stress gets "under the skin" and causes mischief, researchers have created an interdisciplinary specialty with the cumbersome name **psychoneuroimmunology**, or **PNI** for short. The "psycho" part stands for psychological processes such as emotions and perceptions; "neuro" for the nervous and endocrine systems; and "immunology" for the immune system, which enables the body to fight disease and infection (Andersen, Kiecolt-Glaser, & Glaser, 1994; Cohen & Herbert, 1996).

PNI researchers are especially interested in the white blood cells of the immune system, which are designed to recognize foreign substances (*antigens*), such as flu viruses, bacteria, and tumor cells, and then destroy or deactivate them. When an antigen invades the body, the immune system deploys different kinds of white blood cells as weapons, depending on the nature of the enemy. Chemicals produced by the immune cells are sent to the brain, and the brain in turn sends chemical signals to stimulate or restrain the immune system. Anything that disrupts this communication pathway—drugs, surgery, or stress—can weaken or suppress the immune system (Sternberg & Gold, 1997).

In their efforts to understand why prolonged stress makes trouble for some people but not others, PNI researchers have focused on three areas of investigation:

1 *Individual variations in the body's cardiovascular, digestive, endocrine, and immune systems.* Have you ever noticed how your classmates differ in their physical reaction to exams? Some seem tense and edgy, and others are as placid as cabbages. The reason is that some people respond to stressors with much greater increases in blood pressure, heart rate, and hormone levels than other individuals do (T. Smith et al., 1996; Uchino et al., 1995). Over time, these changes may result in disease or damage to organs.

Crowds can be fun or stressful, depending on whether you want to be in them and whether you feel you joined them voluntarily or are trapped against your will.

2 *Psychological factors, such as personality traits, perceptions, and emotions.* People's perceptions of an event play a big role in determining how stressful the event is. Losing a job, traveling to China, or having "too much" work is stressful to some people, whereas others might interpret these experiences as challenging opportunities.

Psychological factors explain why people, unlike mice, are not always stressed by environmental conditions. Take crowding. Mice get really nasty when they're crowded. But human beings show signs of stress not when they are *actually* crowded but when they *feel* crowded—trapped or forced to endure unwanted interactions with others (Evans, Lepore, & Schroeder, 1996; Taylor, 1995). These feelings are in turn affected by culture. In Tokyo, Japan, where the population density exceeds that of any North American city, residents are accustomed to the kind of crowding that would make even a New Yorker feel stressed; crowding in Japan is not associated with urban problems like crime or risks to health.

3 *How people behave under stress and how they manage it.* Some people under stress drink too much, drive recklessly, or fail to take care of themselves, actions that increase their risk of illness or accident. Others, in contrast, cope constructively and thereby reduce the effects of stress.

You can see that health researchers have come a long way from Selye's original physiological formulation of stress as the body's response to any environmental threat. To understand the links between stress and illness, they look not only at external stressors in your life, but also at qualities in you (such as how you perceive the stressor, your emotional state, and your personality traits) and whether you feel able to control or cope with the stressor. Thus a modern view of *psychological stress*—the interaction between external stressors and illness—looks like this:

psychoneuroimmunology (PNI) The study of the relationships among psychology, the nervous and endocrine systems, and the immune system.

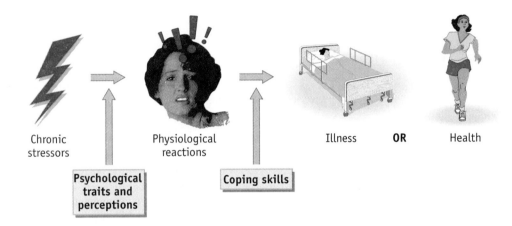

Chronic stressors → Physiological reactions → Illness **OR** Health

Psychological traits and perceptions

Coping skills

QUICK QUIZ

We hope these questions are not sources of stress for you.

1. Steve is unexpectedly called on in class. He hasn't the faintest idea of the answer, and he feels his heart start to pound and his palms sweat. According to Selye, he is in the _____ phase of his stress response.

2. Which of these statements is *true*? (a) Most people who suffer the death of a loved one become sick; (b) work problems and unemployment are not especially stressful because they are common experiences; (c) people with high incomes often have more stressful lives than poorer people; (d) daily hassles are stressful but not especially hazardous to health.

3. How does the modern view of the relationship between external stressors and illness differ from Selye's?

Answers:

1. alarm   2. d   3. It includes the individual's personality traits, perceptions, and emotions, and whether a person copes effectively with stressors.

WHAT'S AHEAD

- Which emotion may be most hazardous to your heart?
- Does chronic depression lead to physical illness?
- Is confession as healthy for the body as it is for the soul?
- When something bad happens that you can't control, is it better to fight back or "go with the flow"?
- Why do optimists tend to live longer than pessimists?

• PERSONALITY AND HEALTH

Some people seem to manufacture their own misery. Send them to a beach for a week to escape the pressures of civilization, and they bring along a suitcase full of worries and irritations. Others stay serene in the midst of chaos and conflict; send them to a tense family gathering, and they seem to bring along their own inner tranquilizer. We now turn to three aspects of personality that affect how people respond to stressors: their emotional responses, their degree of pessimism or optimism, and whether they feel in control of their lives.

Emotions and Illness

Perhaps you have heard people say things like "She was so depressed, it's no wonder she got cancer" or "He's always so angry he's going to give himself a heart attack one day." Are negative emotions—anger, anxiety, and depression—hazardous to your health?

There is good evidence that *once a person already has a virus or medical condition*, negative emotions are indeed influential in affecting the course of the illness. Feelings of anxiety and helplessness, for example, can delay the healing of wounds after surgery, whereas feeling optimistic and able to cope can speed healing significantly (Kiecolt-Glaser et al., 1998). Loneliness and worry can suppress the immune system and permit existing viruses, such as herpes, to erupt (Kiecolt-Glaser et al., 1985a). And depression following a heart attack significantly increases the risk of death from cardiac causes in the succeeding year, even controlling for severity of the disease and other risk factors. In a study that followed hundreds of women and men who had had heart attacks, 8.3 percent of the depressed women and 7 percent of the depressed men died within a year, compared to only about 2.5 percent of those who were not depressed (Frasure-Smith et al., 1999).

However, evidence for the popular idea that negative emotions can *cause* illness all on their own is much murkier. We wish we could give you a simple, clear answer, the kind so favored by news headlines. Unfortunately, we all will have to live with some uncertainty on this matter. Let's see why.

Hostility and Depression. One of the first modern efforts to link emotions and illness was research in the 1970s on the *Type A personality*, a set of qualities thought to be associated with heart disease (Friedman & Rosenman, 1974). Type A people are determined to achieve, have a sense of time urgency, are irritable, respond physiologically to threat and challenge very quickly, and are impatient at anyone who gets in their way. Type B people are calmer and less intense. It seemed logical that Type A's would be at greater risk of heart trouble than Type B's.

A classic Type A personality.

It turned out, however, that being highly reactive to stress and challenge is not in itself a risk factor in heart disease (Krantz & Manuck, 1984). Type A people do set themselves a fast work pace and a heavy workload, but many cope better than Type B people who have a lighter workload. Further, people who are highly involved in their jobs, even if they work hard, have a low incidence of heart disease. "There would be nothing wrong with us fast-moving Type A's," said a friend of ours, "if it weren't for all those slow-moving Type B's."

The next round of research uncovered what it was about the behavior of some Type A's that *is* dangerous to health: hostility. By "hostility" we do not mean the irritability or anger that everyone feels on occasion. The toxic kind is *cynical* or *antagonistic hostility*, which characterizes people who are mistrustful of others and ready to provoke mean, furious arguments (Marshall et al., 1994; T. Miller et al., 1996). As you can see in Figure 15.2, men who are chronically angry and resentful and who have a hostile attitude are five times as likely as nonhostile men to get heart disease, even when other risk factors, such as smoking and a poor diet, are eliminated (Ewart & Kolodner, 1994; Williams, Barefoot, & Shekelle, 1985). (The relationship between hostility and heart disease in women is less clear, in part because many studies have used only men as subjects.)

Can depression also lead to illness? In two studies that each followed more than 1,000 people for many years, those who had been clinically depressed at the outset were two to four times more likely to have a heart attack than nondepressed people were. This finding, too, held up even after the researchers controlled for high blood pressure and smoking (Pratt et al., 1996), and even when they controlled for obesity, amount of exercise, and family history of heart disease (Ford et al., 1998). Yet other studies get different results; for example, a large study of elderly people found no link between depression and heart disease (Mendes de Leon et al., 1998). Maybe the connection depends on the age or generation of the people being studied.

Evidence that depression is involved in other diseases, such as cancer and AIDS, is also conflicting. Some researchers find no links among depression, immune function, and cancer or outbreaks of illness among men with HIV (Lyketsos et al., 1993). Others report that chronic depression *is* associated with aberrations in the immune system and that it speeds the development of cancer and AIDS-related diseases (Burack et al., 1993; Herbert & Cohen, 1993; Penninx et al., 1998). All we can say at present, therefore, is that chronic depression may be a risk factor for heart disease and possibly other diseases as well. And, as we saw, severe depression affects the course of recovery from illness.

Emotional Inhibition. Now pay attention: *Don't think of a white bear.* Are you not thinking of it?

You might assume by now that the safest thing to do when you feel angry, depressed, or worried is to try to suppress the feeling. But anyone who has tried to banish an unwelcome thought, bitter memory, or pangs of longing for an unrequited lover knows how hard it can be to do this. In an actual study, people who were told not to think of a white bear mentioned it nine times in a five-minute stream-of-consciousness session (Wegner et al., 1987). When you are trying to avoid a thought, you are in fact processing the thought more frequently—rehearsing it. That is why, when you are obsessed with someone you were once romantically involved with, trying not to think of the person actually prolongs your emotional responsiveness to him or her (Wegner & Gold, 1995).

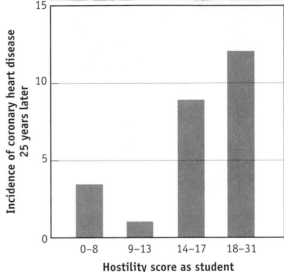

FIGURE 15.2

HOSTILITY AND HEART DISEASE

Anger is more hazardous to health than a heavy workload. Men who had the highest hostility scores as young medical students were the most likely to have coronary heart disease 25 years later (Williams, Barefoot, & Shekelle, 1985).

Everyone has secrets and private moments of sad reflection. But when you feel sad, anxious, or fearful for too long, keeping your feelings to yourself may increase your stress.

Most people try to suppress their feelings some of the time, but some people do so almost all of the time; they have a personality trait called *emotional inhibition* (Basic Behavioral Science Task Force, 1996). Suppressors tend to deny feelings of anxiety, anger, or fear and pretend that everything is fine. Yet, when they are in stressful or emotion-producing situations, their physiological responses, such as heart rate and blood pressure, rise sharply. Suppressors are at greater risk of becoming ill than people who can acknowledge their fears, and once they contract a serious disease, they may even die sooner (Cohen & Herbert, 1996).

Why should emotional inhibition increase the risk of health problems? One possibility is that the prolonged inhibition of thoughts and emotions requires physical effort that is stressful to the body (Pennebaker, 1995; Smyth & Pennebaker, 1999). The inability or unwillingness to confide important or traumatic events also seems to place continuing stress on the immune system. People who are able to express matters of great emotional importance to them show elevated levels of circulating white blood cells, whereas people who suppress such feelings tend to have decreased levels of these disease-fighting cells (Petrie, Booth, & Pennebaker, 1998).

Given these findings, then, divulging private thoughts and feelings that make you ashamed or depressed may be helpful, both psychologically and physically. It certainly was for one class of students going through a normal but stressful transition: starting college. Freshmen who wrote about their feelings about leaving home and being in college reported greater homesickness and anxiety in the short run, compared to students who wrote about trivial topics. But by the end of the school year they had had fewer bouts of flu and visits to the infirmary than the control group (Pennebaker, Colder, & Sharp, 1990).

Confession is also beneficial for people who feel they are carrying the burden of painful secrets. A group of college students were assigned to write about either a personal, traumatic experience or a neutral topic for 20 minutes a day for four days. Those who were asked to reveal their "deepest thoughts and feelings" about a traumatic event all had something to talk about. Many told stories of sexual coercion, physical beatings, humiliation, and parental abandonment. Yet most had never discussed these feelings with anyone. The researchers collected data on the students' physical symptoms, white blood cell counts, emotions, and visits to the health center. On every measure, the students who wrote about traumatic experiences were better off than those who did not (Pennebaker, Kiecolt-Glaser, & Glaser, 1988). Some of them showed short-term increases in anger and depression; writing about an unpleasant experience, after all, was disturbing. But over time, their health and well-being improved.

GET ➡ INVOLVED

TRUE CONFESSIONS

To see whether the research on the benefits of confession will benefit you, take a moment to jot down your "deepest thoughts and feelings" about being in college, your past, a secret, your future . . . anything you have never told anyone. Do this again tomorrow, and again for a few days in a row. Write down your feelings after writing, too. Are you upset? Troubled? Sad? Relieved? Does your account change over time? Research suggests that if you do this exercise now, you are likely to have fewer colds, headaches, and trips to the doctor next year.

Writing about the same experience for several days may be beneficial because it often produces insight and distance, and it ends the stressful repetition of obsessive thoughts and unresolved feelings (Lepore, 1997). One young woman, who had been molested at the age of 9 by a boy a year older, at first wrote about her feelings of embarrassment and guilt. By the third day, she was writing about how angry she felt at the boy. By the last day, she had begun to see the whole event differently; he was young, too, after all. When the study was over, she said, "Before, when I thought about it, I'd lie to myself. . . . Now, I don't feel like I even have to think about it because I got it off my chest. I finally admitted that it happened."

Emotion and Health: A Two-Way Street. How strong, overall, is the link between emotion and illness? Some researchers believe that the inhibition or expression of specific emotions can be tied to specific illnesses, such as cancer or heart disease (Eysenck, 1993). Others caution against exaggerating the role of emotional styles in health, arguing that we must not overlook the stronger influences of chronic stressors in the environment, the biology of the disease, and the individual's health habits, such as smoking (Jorgensen et al., 1996).

Both sides, however, agree that the links between emotions and illness should not be oversimplified. Living with unresolved negative emotions can be stressful to the body, but a life of constant stress also tends to foster negative emotions. Depression and anxiety may contribute to illness in some individuals, but illness also makes some people depressed or anxious. Emotional inhibition is hazardous to some people's health, but so is constant emotional ventilation, which violates social and cultural rules and can alienate others (Kelly & McKillop, 1996; Wellenkamp, 1995). Health psychology suggests a middle path: learning to identify, express, and deal with our negative emotions, without ruminating on them and letting them dominate our lives or erode our relationships.

THINKING CRITICALLY

TOLERATE UNCERTAINTY

Some research finds that negative emotions contribute to illness; other research, that it doesn't. Ventilating emotions can be unhealthy, but so can suppressing them. Given this uncertainty, how should we best think about the relationship between emotions and health?

Optimism and Pessimism

When something bad happens to you, what is your first reaction? Do you tell yourself not to panic, that you will somehow come through it okay, or do you gloomily mutter, "More proof that if something can go wrong for me, it will"?

These two responses to bad events reflect *pessimistic* and *optimistic explanatory styles*, and as far as health is concerned, optimism is a lot better for you (Carver & Scheier, 1999; Seligman, 1991). Pessimism is associated with lower achievement, more illness, and slower recovery from defeats and traumas. If you are a pessimist, you will probably protest that optimism is just a *result*, not a cause, of good health or good fortune; it's easy to think positively when you feel good. But optimism actually seems to produce good health. In one imaginative study of baseball Hall-of-Famers who had played between 1900 and 1950, 30 players were rated according to their explanatory style. A pessimist would attribute a bad performance to a permanent failing in himself, as in, "We didn't win because my arm is shot, and it'll never get better." An optimist would attribute the same performance to external and changing conditions, as in, "We didn't win because we got a couple of lousy calls, just bad luck in this game, but we'll be great tomorrow." The optimists were significantly more likely to have lived well into old age than were the pessimists (Seligman, 1991).

Optimists may have better health than pessimists in part because they take better care of themselves when they get sick, whether their ailment is a simple cold or a life-threatening disease like AIDS (Taylor, 1995). Pessimists, in contrast, often do self-destructive things, especially if they are male: They drink too much, smoke, fail to wear seat belts, drive too fast, refuse to take medication for illness. This may be why

THE PESSIMIST SEES A BARREN DESERT

THE OPTIMIST SEES A REALLY, REALLY, REALLY, REALLY LOW TIDE

Explanatory style—pessimism or optimism—may affect health and longevity. Zack Wheat, an outfielder for the Brooklyn Dodgers, had an optimistic explanatory style: "I'm a better hitter than I used to be because my strength has improved and my experience has improved." Wheat lived to be 83.

Walter Johnson, a star pitcher for the Washington Senators, had a pessimistic explanatory style: "I can't depend on myself to pitch well. I'm growing old. I've had my day." Johnson died at the age of 59.

they are more likely than optimists to die untimely deaths as a result of accidents or violence (Peterson et al., 1998). But optimism is also directly associated with better immune function, such as a rise in "natural killer" cells, a kind of white blood cell that fights infection (Räikkönen et al., 1999; Segerstrom et al., 1998).

Optimists are sometimes accused of being unrealistic. Yet health and well-being often depend on having some "positive illusions" about yourself and your circumstances. Optimist illusions, even in the face of tragedy, can literally be lifesaving (Taylor & Brown, 1994). For example, in one study of gay men with AIDS, those who had realistically accepted the likelihood of an early death actually lived 9 months less than did optimists who were unrealistic about their chances of survival. This result could not be accounted for by the time since the initial diagnosis, their use of the medication AZT, their age, or their use of alcohol and other drugs (Reed et al., 1994).

Positive illusions, however, are not the same as denial. Optimists do not deny their problems or avoid facing bad news. On the contrary, they are more likely than pessimists to be active problem solvers and to seek information that can help them (Aspinwall & Taylor, 1997). They do not give up at the first sign of a setback or escape into wishful thinking. They keep their senses of humor, plan for the future, and reinterpret the situation in a positive light (Aspinwall & Brunhart, 1996; Chang, 1998).

Can pessimists be "cured" of their gloomy outlook? Optimists, naturally, think so! In Chapter 17, we discuss cognitive therapy, which teaches pessimists to test their dim predictions against the evidence. There we also describe an effective intervention program that inoculates elementary-school children against pessimism and depression by teaching them optimistic explanatory styles (Gillham et al., 1995). Another method worked for psychologist Rachel Hare-Mustin, whose mother cured her budding childhood pessimism with humor. "Nobody likes me," Rachel lamented. "Don't say that," her mother said. "Everybody hasn't met you yet."

QUICK QUIZ

Write down your deepest thoughts and feelings about taking this quiz.

1. Which of the following aspects of Type A behavior seems most hazardous to men's health?
   (a) working hard, (b) being in a hurry, (c) cynical hostility, (d) high physical reactivity to work,
   (e) general grumpiness

2. Nguyen has many private worries about being in college that she is afraid to tell anyone. What might be the healthiest solution for her? (a) exercise, (b) writing down her feelings in a diary, (c) talking frequently to strangers who won't judge her, (d) expressing her hostility whenever she feels it

3. "I'll never find anyone else to love because I'm not good-looking; that one romance was a fluke" illustrates a(n) _____ explanatory style.

Answers:

1. c 2. b 3. pessimistic

The Sense of Control

Optimism is related to another important ingredient of psychological and physical health: having an internal locus of control (Chang, 1998; Marshall et al., 1994). **Locus of control,** described more fully in Chapter 13, refers to your general expectation about whether you can control the things that happen to you (Rotter, 1966). People who have an *internal* locus of control ("internals") tend to believe that they are responsible for what happens to them; those who have an *external* locus of control ("externals") tend to believe that they are the victims of circumstance.

The Benefits of Control. The greatest threat to health and well-being occurs when people feel unable to control their circumstances—when they feel caught in a situation they cannot escape. People can tolerate all kinds of stressors if they feel able to predict or control them. The crowd you choose to join for a football game is not as stressful as being trapped in a crowd on a busy street; the music you choose to play at ear-splitting volume is not as stressful as being forced to listen to your roommate's rotten choice of CDs. Feelings of control can reduce or even eliminate the relationship between stressors and health that we described earlier in this chapter, as these diverse examples illustrate:

- Among people exposed to cold viruses, those who feel in control of their lives are half as likely to actually develop colds as are people who feel that their lives are "unpredictable, uncontrollable, and overwhelming" (Cohen, Tyrrell, & Smith, 1993).

- Low-income people who have a strong sense of control and mastery over their lives are as healthy, and have as high levels of well-being, as people from higher-income groups (Lachman & Weaver, 1998).

- People who have the greatest control over their work pace and activities—that is, executives and managers—have fewer illnesses and stress symptoms than do employees who have little opportunity to exercise initiative and who feel trapped doing repetitive tasks (Karasek & Theorell, 1990).

- The women who are most at risk of heart disease are not supposedly "stressed-out executives" but clerical workers who feel they have no support from their bosses, who are stuck in low-paying jobs without hope of promotion, and who have financial problems at home (Haynes & Feinleib, 1980).

locus of control A general expectation about whether the results of your actions are under your own control (internal locus) or beyond your control (external locus).

Who has more "stress"—corporate managers in highly competitive jobs or assembly-line workers in routine and predictable jobs? Researchers find that "it is not the bosses but the bossed who suffer most from job stress"—especially if they cannot control many aspects of their work (Karasek & Theorell, 1990).

■ Black professionals who have the resources and confidence to fight discrimination, and who feel in control of their work lives, are at much lower risk of hypertension than are black workers who feel forced to accept racial hostility as a fact of life (Krieger & Sidney, 1996).

Feeling in control helps to reduce pain, improve adjustment to surgery and illness, and speed up recovery from some diseases (Shapiro, Schwartz, & Astin, 1996; E. Skinner, 1996). As with optimism, feeling in control makes people more likely to take action to improve their health when necessary. In a group of patients recovering from heart attacks, for example, those who thought their illness was due to bad luck or fate—factors outside their control—were less likely to generate active plans for recovery and more likely to resume their old unhealthy habits. In contrast, those who thought the heart attack occurred because they smoked, didn't exercise, or had a stressful job were more likely to change their bad habits and recover more quickly (Affleck et al., 1987; Ewart, 1995).

A sense of control actually affects the neuroendocrine and immune systems (Cohen & Herbert, 1996). This finding may explain why it is especially beneficial to old people, whose immune systems normally decline. When elderly residents of nursing homes are given more choices over their activities and environment and given more control over day-to-day events—even small but engrossing activities such as tending plants—the results are dramatic. They become more alert, more active, and happier, and they live longer (Langer, 1983).

Cultures differ in their degree of fatalism and in their beliefs about whether it is possible to take control of one's health. For example, in Germany, which has a highly structured social welfare system, people feel they have more psychological control over their health and work than Americans do (Staudinger, Fleeson, & Baltes, 1999). In some other cultures, people feel they have almost no control over their health and lives.

Might these cultural attitudes be related to mortality rates? The answer, remarkably, seems to be yes. In traditional Chinese astrology, certain birth years are considered unlucky, and people born in those years often fatalistically expect bad fortune. This expectation can become a self-fulfilling prophecy. In a study of many thousands of people matched by age and cause of death, Chinese-Americans who had been born in a year traditionally considered to be ill-fated died significantly earlier—one to five years earlier!—than whites who had been born in the same year and who had the same disease. The more strongly traditional the Chinese were, the more years of life they lost. These results held for nearly all causes of death studied, even when the researchers controlled for how well the patients took care of themselves and which treatments they were given (Phillips, Ruth, & Wagner, 1993).

The Limits of Control. Overall, then, a sense of control is a good thing. But the question must always be asked: control over what? It is surely not beneficial for people to believe they can control absolutely every aspect of their lives; some things, such as death, taxes, or being a random victim of a crime, are out of anyone's control. Health and well-being are not enhanced by self-blaming kinds of control ("Whatever goes wrong with my health is my fault") or the belief that all disease can be prevented by doing the right thing ("If I take vitamins and work out nine times a week, I'll never get sick").

Eastern and Western cultures tend to hold different attitudes toward the ability and desirability of controlling our own lives. In general, Western cultures celebrate **primary control**, in which people try to influence existing reality by trying to exert control over it: If you do not like a situation, you are supposed to change it, fix it, or fight it. The Eastern approach emphasizes **secondary control**, in which people try to accommodate to reality by changing their own aspirations or desires: If you have a problem, you are supposed to live with it or act in spite of it (Rothbaum, Weisz, & Snyder, 1982).

A Japanese psychologist once offered some examples of Japanese proverbs that teach the benefits of yielding to the inevitable (Azuma, 1984): *To lose is to win* (giving in, to protect the harmony of a relationship, demonstrates the superior trait of generosity); *Willow trees do not get broken by piled-up snow* (no matter how many problems pile up in your life, flexibility will help you survive them); and *The true tolerance is to tolerate the intolerable* (some "intolerable" situations are facts of life that no amount of protest will change). You can imagine how long "to lose is to win" would survive on an American football field, or how long most Americans would be prepared to tolerate the intolerable!

People who are ill or under stress can reap the benefits of both Western and Eastern forms of control by avoiding either–or thinking: for example, by taking responsibility for future actions, while not blaming themselves unduly for past ones. Those who do so adjust better than people who believe they can control everything—or nothing (Thompson, Nanni, & Levine, 1994). Among women coping with cancer, for instance, adjustment is related to a woman's belief that she is not to blame for getting sick but that she *is* in charge of taking care of herself from now on (Taylor, Lichtman, & Wood,

THINKING CRITICALLY

DEFINE YOUR TERMS

In general, it's good to feel in control of your life, but what does that mean exactly? Control over what? How much of your life? Can too much control ever be a bad thing?

primary control An effort to modify reality by changing other people, the situation, or events; a "fighting back" philosophy.

secondary control An effort to accept reality by changing your own attitudes, goals, or emotions; a "learn to live with it" philosophy.

Sometimes life serves up a disaster, as it has for many farm families who have lost their lands and livelihoods because of natural disasters or changes in the economy. When is it helpful to believe we can control everything that happens to us, and when is it harmful?

1984). "I felt that I had lost control of my body somehow," said a woman in one study, "and the way for me to get back some control was to find out as much as I could." This way of thinking allows you to avoid guilt and self-blame while retaining self-efficacy—the belief that you are basically in charge of your own life and can take steps to get better when you are sick.

Many problems require us to decide what we can change and accept what we cannot; perhaps the secret of healthy control lies in knowing the difference.

QUICK QUIZ

You can increase your sense of control over the material in this section by answering these questions.

1. Maria has worked as a file clerk for 17 years. Which aspect of the job is likely to be most stressful for her? (a) feeling trapped, (b) the predictable routine, (c) the speed of the work, (d) the daily demands from her boss

2. Adapting yourself to the reality that you are getting older is an example of (primary/secondary) control; joining a protest to make a local company clean up its hazardous wastes is an example of (primary/secondary) control.

3. On television, a self-described health expert explains that "no one gets sick if they don't want to be sick," because all of us can learn to take control of our bodies. As a critical thinker, how should you assess this claim?

Answers:

1. a 2. secondary, primary 3. Skeptically. First, how is the expert defining "control"? What kind of control are we talking about? People can control some things, such as the decision to exercise and quit smoking, and they can control some aspects of treatment once they become ill; but they do not have control over everything that happens to them. Second, this "expert" assumes that control is always a good thing, but the belief that we have total control over our lives could lead to depression and unwarranted self-blame when illness strikes.

WHAT'S AHEAD

- When you are feeling overwhelmed, what are some good ways to calm down?
- Why is it important to move beyond the emotions caused by a problem and deal with the problem itself?
- How can you rethink your problems?
- When do friends reduce your stress, and when do they just make matters worse?

COPING WITH STRESS

We have noted that most people who are under stress, even continuing, difficult situations, do not become ill. In addition to feeling optimistic and in control, and not wallowing around in negative emotions, how do they manage to cope?

Coping consists of all the things people do to control, tolerate, or reduce the effects of life's stressors—perceived threats, existing problems, or emotional losses (Aspinwall & Taylor, 1997; Lazarus & Folkman, 1984). Coping is not a single strategy that applies to all circumstances; people cope differently with hassles, deaths of loved ones, dangers, and challenges. And the techniques they use change over time and circumstance, depending on the nature of the stressor and the particular situation (Carver & Scheier, 1994; Terry, 1994).

The word *coping* implies that people are behaving in ways that barely help them keep their heads above water ("How are you doing?" "Oh, I'm coping"). But some people cope in ways that help them not only *survive* adversity, but actually *thrive*, by enabling them to learn from their experiences (see Figure 15.3). In this section, we will consider some of the most effective methods of coping with, living with, and learning from the troubles of life.

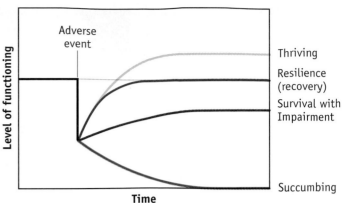

FIGURE 15.3
THE RANGE OF RESPONSES TO TRAUMA

As this graph illustrates, people may respond to tragedy and loss by giving up, surviving but with continuing impairment, recovering fully, or thriving—learning from the experience and coming out stronger because of it (Carver, 1998; O'Leary & Ickovics, 1994).

Cooling Off

The most immediate way to handle the physiological symptoms of stress, including high blood pressure, muscle tension, and rapid breathing, is to calm down. Techniques that reduce bodily arousal can help people cope not only with everyday stresses but also with serious, even terminal illnesses.

1 *Relaxation.* One of the simplest but most important ways of reducing stress symptoms is to relax. You might think that relaxing is easy—you just flop there on a sofa and tune out. But it takes practice to clear your mind of its buzz of distracting thoughts and worries. Try it for five minutes—a full five minutes—and you will see what we mean. Now try to do it for half an hour.

Relaxation training teaches you to alternately tense and relax your muscles, from your toes to your nose, while you are lying down quietly; or to meditate by clearing your mind of all thoughts and fantasies. Physical relaxation and meditation have beneficial effects on the body, lowering blood pressure, stress hormones, and pain due to tension (Taylor, 1995). Studies of many different groups, including elderly residents of retirement homes and women with first-stage breast cancer, find that people who reduce stress by using relaxation techniques show significantly improved immune activity (Gruber et al., 1993; Kiecolt-Glaser et al., 1985b). Relaxation and meditation also help people who are feeling angry or anxious, which is why these techniques are increasingly being used as part of psychotherapy (Kabat-Zinn, 1994).

2 *Massage and "contact comfort."* In Chapter 12 we noted that contact comfort is important to all human beings and other mammals. Our innate need for contact comfort probably explains why massage therapy is one of the oldest treatments in the world. The Chinese recommended it in the second century B.C. and Hippocrates observed its healing powers in medicine in 400 B.C. (Field, 1998). Wide-ranging studies have demonstrated the benefits of massage on human beings of every age, from premature infants to the very old, and on people with asthma and diabetes, adolescents with eating disorders, depressed elderly people, and children with attention deficit/hyperactivity disorder. Massage helps to reduce stress, depression, pain, and anxiety; improves immune function; and increases concentration and mental alertness (Field, 1998).

3 *Exercise.* After you have scheduled meditation and massage into your busy week, go for a walk! Inactivity is associated with decreased life expectancy for both sexes and contributes to the development of many chronic diseases (Dubbert, 1992). As you can see in Figure 15.4, when people are undergoing the same objective pressures, those who are physically fit have fewer health problems than people who are less fit. They also show less physiological arousal to stressors and pay fewer visits to the doctor (Brown, 1991). People who exercise regularly also tend to be less anxious, depressed, and irritable than couch potatoes, and they have fewer physical symptoms and colds (Hendrix et al., 1991). These benefits of exercise apply to adults, adolescents, and even preschoolers (Alpert et al., 1990).

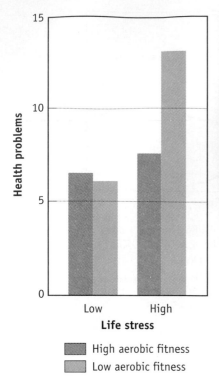

Health problems

15

10

5

0

Low   High
Life stress

■ High aerobic fitness
□ Low aerobic fitness

FIGURE 15.4
FITNESS AND HEALTH

Among people under low stress, aerobically fit individuals had about the same number of health problems as those who were less fit. But among people under high stress, fit individuals had fewer health problems (Roth & Holmes, 1985).

No one is quite sure how exercise works its wonders. Some researchers have argued that it does so by stimulating the production of endorphins (the brain's opiates), raising body temperature, or calming brain waves, but these theories have not been supported (McDonald, 1998). Another possibility is that exercise, like meditation, provides a distraction from stressful thoughts and problems. But whereas relaxation lowers blood pressure for only about 20 minutes afterward, exercise lowers it for several hours (Raglin & Morgan, 1987).

Exercise is not a cure-all, however. People who exercise in order to avoid solving their problems are not necessarily reducing their stress load; you can't jog away from everything. Exercise can help reduce the blues and the blahs, but not severe depression. And *excessive* exercise has been linked to infertility, damage to the immune system, premature aging, and higher levels of anxiety and other mood problems (Becker, 1993; Raglin, 1990).

Perhaps you can think of other ways to cool off when you are hot and bothered. Some people listen to soothing music, write in a journal, or bake bread. Such activities give the body a chance to recover from the "alarm phase" of its stress response and from the intensity of negative emotions. But none of them can change the fact that your house just burned down or that you need a serious operation. Sometimes other coping strategies are necessary.

Solving the Problem

A woman we know, whom we will call Nancy, was struck by tragedy when she was 22. She and her new husband were driving home one evening when a car ran out of control and crashed into them. When Nancy awoke in a hospital room, she learned that her husband had been killed and that she herself had permanent spinal injury and would never walk again. For many months, Nancy reacted with understandable rage and despair. "Get it out of your system," her friends said. "You need to get in touch with your feelings." "But I know I'm miserable," Nancy lamented. "What do I *do*?"

The advice Nancy's friends gave her and her reply illustrate the difference between *emotion-focused* and *problem-focused coping* (Lazarus & Folkman, 1984; Stanton & Franz, 1999). Emotion-focused coping concentrates on the emotions the problem has caused, whether anger, anxiety, or grief. For a period of time after any personal tragedy or traumatic natural disaster, it is normal to give in to these emotions and feel overwhelmed by them. In this stage, people often need to talk obsessively about the event in order to come to terms with it, make sense of it, and decide what to do about it (Lepore et al., 1996).

Eventually, though, most people are ready to move beyond their emotional state and concentrate on the problem itself. Over time, problem-focused strategies are associated with better adjustment than are emotion-focused ones (Carver, 1998; Terry & Hynes, 1998). The specific steps in problem-focused coping depend on the nature of the problem: whether it is a pressing but one-time decision; a continuing difficulty, such as living with a disability; or an anticipated event, such as having an operation.

Once the problem is identified, the coper can learn as much as possible about it from professionals, friends, books, and others in the same predicament (Clarke & Evans, 1998). In Nancy's case, she learned more about her medical condition and prognosis, how other accident victims had coped, and the occupations that were possible for her (which was most of them). Nancy stayed in school, remarried, got a Ph.D. in psychology, and now does research and counseling with disabled people.

Problem-focused coping tends to increase self-efficacy and reduce anger, anxiety, and physiological stress (D'Zurilla & Sheedy, 1991; Katz & Epstein, 1991). By requiring you to think critically—that is, to consider alternatives and resist emotional reasoning—it often leads to constructive solutions.

Rethinking the Problem

Some problems cannot be "solved"; these are the tragedies that occur out of the blue, or such unavoidable facts of life as an inability to have children. When you cannot fix a problem, however, you can change the way you think about it. Here are four effective cognitive coping methods.

Children are a famous source of delight—and stress. If you were in this weary mother's place, how would you cope with your children's behavior?

1 *Reappraising the situation.* Although you may not be able to get rid of a stressor (that nasty neighbor is unlikely to move; you cannot undo the fact that you lost your job), you can choose to think about it differently. The annoying behavior of difficult people may not be intentionally directed at you; maybe your neighbor is nasty because he suffers constant back pain or is deeply unhappy. Likewise, problems can be turned into challenges and losses into unexpected gains. Maybe that job you lost was pretty dismal but you were too afraid to quit to look for another; now you can.

As we saw in Chapter 11, the way you think about a situation or provocation affects the emotions you feel about it. Reappraisal is effective because it changes your emotional responses, turning anger into sympathy, worry into determination, or feelings of loss into feelings of opportunity. In contrast, efforts to suppress an emotion, without reappraising the thoughts that have caused it, simply lead to greater activation of the sympathetic nervous system, as we noted earlier (Gross, 1998).

2 *Learning from the experience.* Even when people suffer major losses, traumas, and serious illnesses, they can often find useful lessons in them. For example, a study of people with spinal-cord injuries found that two-thirds of them felt the disability had had positive side effects. They named such benefits as becoming a better person, seeing the value in other people, and gaining a new appreciation of "brain, not brawn" (Schulz & Decker, 1985).

Some people emerge from adversity with newfound or newly acquired skills, having been forced to learn something they had not known before—how to cope with the medical system, say, or how to manage a deceased parent's estate. Others discover sources of courage and strength they did not know they had. People who are able to draw lessons from the inescapable tragedies of life, or find meaning in them, are far better off psychologically than are people

The ultimate example of rethinking your problems.

GET →INVOLVED

RETHINK YOUR STRESSES

The next time you feel stressed by a situation you can't control, observe your thoughts. What are you saying to yourself? Are your thoughts adding to your stress ("That stupid driver just tried to kill me!")? Try to apply the lessons on "rethinking the problem" to your own situation. For example, can you think of another explanation for a family member's behavior? Can you think of something funny about your predicament—and will it make a good story later? Can you think of something good about the situation?

who cannot (Davis, Nolen-Hoeksema, & Larson, 1998; Tennen & Affleck, 1999). They are the ones who thrive as a result of adversity instead of simply surviving it (Janoff-Bulman, 1999).

3 *Making social comparisons.* In a difficult situation, successful copers often compare themselves to others who are (they feel) less fortunate. No matter how bad off they are, even if they have fatal diseases, they find someone who is worse off (Taylor & Lobel, 1989). One AIDS sufferer said in an interview, "I made a list of all the other diseases I would rather not have than AIDS. Lou Gehrig's disease, being in a wheelchair; rheumatoid arthritis, when you are in knots and in terrible pain. So I said, 'You've got to get some perspective on this, and where you are on the Great Nasty Disease List.'" Another said: "I really have an advantage in a sense over other people. I know there is a possibility that my life may not go on for as many years as other people's. I have the opportunity to look at my life, to make changes, and to deeply appreciate the time that I have" (Reed, 1990).

Sometimes successful copers also compare themselves to those who are doing *better* than they are (Collins, 1996). Such comparisons are beneficial when they provide a person with information about ways of coping or managing the illness, and when the person feels able to take advantage of such information (Clarke & Evans, 1998).

4 *Cultivating a sense of humor.* "A merry heart doeth good like a medicine," says Proverbs in the Old Testament, and so it does. A "sense of humor" includes the ability to see the humor in tense or even tragic situations, to appreciate humor and witty people, and to use humor in coping with stress.

People who can see the absurd or whimsical aspects of a bad situation are less prone to depression, anger, and physical tension than are people who give in to gloom, moping, and tears (P. Fry, 1995; Nezu, Nezu, & Blissett, 1988; Solomon, 1996). In people with serious illnesses, humor reduces distress, improves immune functioning, and hastens recovery from surgery (Carver et al., 1993; Martin & Dobbin, 1988). It may also stimulate the flow of endorphins, the painkilling chemicals in the brain (Fry, 1994). Laughter may have these effects because of its ability to reduce tension and emotional hostility. You have probably been in a tense group situation when someone suddenly made a remark that made everyone laugh and defused the mood.

Humor also has mental benefits. When you laugh at a problem, you are putting it in a new perspective—seeing its silly or ridiculous aspects—and gaining a sense of control over it (Dixon, 1980). Humor also allows you to express indirectly feelings that are risky to express directly, which is why it is so often the weapon of the powerless and of minorities. In Nazi Germany, no Jewish person would have dared to insult a Nazi to his face, but jokes let them do it. One tells of a Jewish man who

The actor Bert Lahr, shown here as the lovable Cowardly Lion in *The Wizard of Oz*, began using humor as a way to cope with the unhappiness of his early life.

accidentally bumped into a Nazi on a street. "Swine!" bellowed the Nazi. "And I'm Cohen," he replied, "pleased to meet you."

Having a sense of humor is not the same as smiling all the time or "putting on a happy face." For humor to be effective in coping with stress, you have to actually use it during a stressful situation—by noticing or inventing its funny or absurd aspects and laughing at them. For example, one therapist we know helps motorists reduce their stress and anger when they are caught in traffic jams by having them visualize other drivers as donkeys (a better technique than *calling* another driver a donkey). The humor must also be good-natured; vicious, rude jokes at another person's expense only create more tension and hostility.

Drawing on Social Support

So far we have been discussing individual coping strategies—things you can do for yourself. But often these individual strategies are not enough, and it is necessary to draw on the help and support of others in your network of family, friends, neighbors, and co-workers. Your health depends not only on what is going on in your body and mind, but also on what is going on in your relationships: what you take from them and what you give to them.

When Friends Help You Cope . . . Think of all the ways that other people help you. They offer concern and affection. They help you evaluate problems and plan a course of action. They offer resources and services such as loaning you money or the car, or taking notes in class for you when you are sick. Most of all, they are sources of attachment and connection, which everyone needs throughout life. Perhaps this is why old people who have dogs as companions visit medical clinics less often than their comparable peers who have no pets—or who have cats! Dogs provide companionship and attachment, the two ingredients of a truly best friend (J. Siegel, 1990).

Friends are not just a nice part of life; they can improve your health and even save your life. Remember the study we described earlier, showing that stress can increase your risk of getting a cold? Well, having a lot of friends and social contacts reduces that risk. In a group of nearly 300 volunteers, ages 18 to 55, all exposed to the same flu virus, those with the most friends were the least likely to get sick (Cohen et al., 1997). Social support is even more important for people who have extremely stressful jobs that require high cardiovascular responsiveness day after day, such as firefighters. Something about social support literally helps the heart rate return to normal more quickly after a stressful episode (Roy, Steptoe, & Kirschbaum, 1998).

People who live in a network of close connections actually live longer than those who do not. In two major studies that followed thousands of adults for 10 years, people who had many friends, social connections, or memberships in church and other groups were more likely to live longer than those who had few. The importance of having social networks was unrelated to physical health at the time the studies began, to socioeconomic status, and to risk factors like smoking (Berkman & Syme, 1979; House, Landis, & Umberson, 1988).

In some cases, social support can even extend the survival time of people with serious illnesses. In a study of older men and women who had had heart attacks, 58 percent of those who reported having no close contacts died within the year, compared with only 27 percent of those who said they had two or more people they could count on (Berkman, Leo-Summers, & Horwitz, 1992). And among women with terminal breast cancer, those who had cancer treatment plus weekly group therapy with other patients lived almost twice as long as those who had cancer treatment

Friends can be our greatest source of warmth, support, and fun . . .

alone (36.6 months to 18.9 months) (Spiegel et al., 1989). Even when social support does not lengthen the lives of people with terminal illnesses, it often lessens their suffering and pain.

As with all the other factors we have seen that are related to health, from locus of control to humor, social support may produce its benefits because of its effects on the immune system. Lonely people have poorer immune function than people who are not lonely; students in a network of friends have better immune function before, during, and after exam periods than students who are more solitary; and spouses of cancer patients, although under considerable stress themselves, do not show a drop in immune function if they have lots of social support (Uchino, Cacioppo, & Kiecolt-Glaser, 1996).

. . . And Coping with Friends. Of course, you don't have to be a psychologist to know that sometimes other people *aren't* helpful. Sometimes they themselves are the source of unhappiness, stress, and anger.

In close relationships, the same person who is a source of support can also become a source of stress, especially if the two parties are arguing all the time. Constant fights can elevate both partners' blood pressures and suppress the immune system, too. Married couples who argue in a hostile fashion—criticizing, interrupting, or insulting each other, and becoming angry and defensive—show significant elevations of stress hormones and impairments of immune function afterward. Couples who argue in a positive fashion—trying to find common ground, compromising, listening to each other's concerns, and using humor to defuse tension—do not show these impairments (Kiecolt-Glaser et al., 1993; Malarkey et al., 1994). As one student of ours observed, "This study gives new meaning to the accusation 'You make me sick'!" It also suggests that learning to argue fairly and constructively may have physical as well as psychological benefits.

In addition to being sources of conflict, friends and relatives may be unsupportive in times of disaster or illness simply out of ignorance or awkwardness. They may abandon you or say something stupid and hurtful. Sometimes they actively block your

. . . and also sources of exasperation, anger, and misery.

efforts to change bad health habits—say, to cut down on binge drinking or smoking—by making fun of you or pressuring you to conform to what "everyone" does. And sometimes, because they have never been in the same situation and don't know what to do to help, they offer the wrong kind of support. For example, they may try to cheer you up, saying "Everything will be fine," rather than let you talk about your fears or find solutions (Bolger et al., 1996). That is why support groups of people experiencing the same illness (such as breast cancer or AIDS), problem (such as a parent's alcoholism), or tragedy (such as the death of a child) are often more helpful than friends who haven't "been there" (see Chapter 17).

"Healing through helping others" is one of the most beneficial ways of coping with our own troubles. These volunteers are preparing and serving food to the homeless.

Healing Through Helping

A final way to cope with stress, loss, and tragedy is by reaching out to others. There are as many benefits to giving support as to receiving it. A psychologist who worked with Holocaust survivors, prisoners of war, hostages, refugees, and other survivors of catastrophe wrote that a key element in their recovery was compassion, "healing through helping." People gain strength, he said, by giving it to others (Segal, 1986). In fact, people who are empathic and cooperative are healthier and happier than those who are self-involved (Crandall, 1984).

Why should this be so? The ability to look outside oneself, to be concerned with helping others, is related to virtually all of the successful coping mechanisms we have discussed (summarized in Review 15.1). It stimulates optimism and a feeling of control over future events, since past ones can't be helped. It shifts your attention

REVIEW 15.1

SUCCESSFUL WAYS OF COPING WITH STRESS

	Category	Examples
	Physical strategies	Relaxation Meditation Massage Exercise
	Problem-oriented strategies	Emotion-focused coping to reduce negative emotions Problem-focused coping (e.g., gathering information)
	Cognitive strategies	Reappraising the problem Learning from the problem Making social comparisons Cultivating a sense of humor
	Social strategies	Relying on friends and family Helping others

from your own worries to others who are worse off than you. It encourages you to solve problems instead of blaming others; helps you reappraise a conflict by seeing it as others do, instead of taking it personally; and allows you to gain perspective on a problem instead of exaggerating its importance. Because of its elements of forgiveness, tolerance, and empathy, "looking outward" helps you live with situations that are facts of life.

QUICK QUIZ

Can you cope with these refresher questions?

1. Finding out what your legal and financial resources are when you have been victimized by a crime is an example of (a) problem-focused coping, (b) emotion-focused coping, (c) distraction, (d) reappraisal.

2. Learning deep-breathing techniques to reduce anxiety about having been victimized by a crime is an example of (a) problem-focused coping, (b) emotion-focused coping, (c) avoidance, (d) reappraisal.

3. You accidentally broke your glasses. Which response is an example of reappraisal? (a) "I am such a stupid clumsy idiot!" (b) "I never do anything right." (c) "What a shame, but I've been wanting new frames anyway." (d) "I'll forget about it in aerobics class."

4. "This class drives me crazy, but I'm better off than my friends who aren't in college" is an example of (a) distraction, (b) social comparison, (c) denial, (d) empathy.

5. Isabel has been diagnosed with diabetes. Her family is trying to be helpful, but they are reluctant to listen to her talk about her fears and worries. What lesson about social support is her family illustrating? And what might Isabel do about it?

6. Your roommate has turned your room into a garbage dump, filled with rotten leftover food and unwashed clothes. Assuming that you don't like living with rotting food and dirty clothes, what coping strategies described in this section might help you?

Answers:

1. a 2. b 3. c 4. b 5. Isabel's family is not offering her the right kind of support because they don't understand her worries and can't provide emotional comfort. She might seek a support group of other people with diabetes who can meet this need. 6. You might solve the problem by finding a compromise (clean the room together). You might reappraise the seriousness of the problem ("I only have to live with this person until the end of the term") or compare your roommate to others ("at least mine is generous and friendly"). You might try to find the humor in being so mismatched (the comedy "The Odd Couple" was about a slob and a neatness fanatic who shared an apartment). And you might mobilize some social support—offer your friends a pizza dinner if they help you clean up.

WHAT'S AHEAD

● **What are the three best things you can do to prolong your life?**
● **How can we think critically about mainstream and alternative approaches to health?**

HOW MUCH CONTROL DO WE HAVE OVER OUR HEALTH?

It should be clear by now that the line between stress and illness is not straightforward and direct. Many factors are links in the long chain that connects stressors and illness, including personality traits, biological vulnerabilities to certain diseases, emotional inhibition, explanatory styles, coping strategies, and social networks (see Review 15.2).

REVIEW 15.2

FACTORS THAT INCREASE THE RISK OF ILLNESS

	Factors	Examples
	Environmental	Uncontrollable noise, poverty, lack of access to health care, persistent discrimination
	Experiential	Bereavement or divorce, traumatic events, chronic and severe job stress, unemployment
	Biological	Viral or bacterial infections, disease, genetic vulnerability
	Psychological	Toxic hostility, possibly chronic depression; emotional inhibition, pessimism, external locus of control (fatalism); feeling powerless
	Behavioral	Smoking, high-fat diet, lack of exercise, abuse of alcohol and other drugs, lack of sleep
	Social	Lack of supportive friends and relatives, low involvement in groups

Yet to hear some people talk, health is almost entirely a matter of "mind over matter"; even the worst diseases, they say, can be cured with jokes, vitamins, and positive thinking. This attitude is actually quite recent, a result of medical advances that occurred over the past century. As industrialized societies conquered many of the environmental sources of infectious diseases, through innovations in water treatment, sewage disposal, and food storage, and through the discovery of antibiotics and vaccines, public attention turned to diseases that are affected by what we eat and how we live. Accordingly, the focus of health professionals shifted from changing the environment to changing individuals (Taylor, Repetti, & Seeman, 1997).

Clearly, people's behavior has a tremendous impact on their health. A study done at the Harvard School of Public Health found that smoking, a poor diet, and lack of exercise cause 65 percent of all deaths from cancer, while only 2 percent of deaths are due to environmental pollution and 10 percent to genetics (Trichopoulos, Li, & Hunter, 1996). People who do not smoke (or who quit smoking), who are not obese, and who exercise regularly live longer and have fewer disabilities in old age (Vita et al., 1998).

But the debate continues to rage over the extent to which *psychological* factors are involved in the onset or course of some illnesses. As we have seen, certain factors do play a significant role: long-lasting feelings of depression and hostile anger;

suppression of negative thoughts and feelings; pessimism and feelings of powerlessness; and lack of social support (Andersen, Kiecolt-Glaser, & Glaser, 1994; Cohen & Herbert, 1996). But such evidence does not mean that all illnesses have psychological causes. Many diseases, such as tuberculosis and ulcers, were once thought to be caused exclusively by emotional and personality factors, until the bacteria that actually do cause them were identified. Some physicians believe that the major killers today, including heart disease and cancer, may also prove to have viruses or other infectious agents at their source (Hooper, 1999).

All health professionals are worried about the rise of a "pop-health" industry that oversimplifies findings from health psychology, for example by encouraging people to believe that they are always to blame when they become ill (Becker, 1993). And they worry that the public is starting to think in either–or terms about medical treatment: *Either* you get traditional medical procedures to treat a disease *or* you get alternative psychological ones, such as visual imagery, meditation, and support groups. These are not opposite choices, of course. In fact, most physicians today, while endorsing traditional medical treatments, also recognize the role of psychological and social factors in their patients' recovery and well-being: the importance of an optimistic attitude, a good support system, and effective coping strategies. The danger is that people will put off medical procedures that they need in favor of relying exclusively on alternative treatments.

Psychologists and physicians are also concerned about the many unscrupulous marketers who prey on the public's worries by selling them worthless programs, pills, and devices (Angell & Kassirer, 1998). The health-care marketplace is overflowing with quacks who have meaningless but impressive-looking "credentials," often from unaccredited "universities" that offer mail-order degrees (Raso, 1996).

When it comes to taking control of our health, therefore, we need to avoid the traps of oversimplifying, either–or thinking, and emotional reasoning. If you are under stress at school because you are not doing as well as you hoped, learning to relax or splurging on massages might help, but ultimately you will have to decide what you can do to improve your grades. If you are under stress at home because you are constantly quarreling with your partner, joining a social-support group to talk about the problem might make you feel temporarily better, but ultimately you and your partner will have to figure out why you are fighting so much—and how you can argue without hostility.

Research in health psychology has produced many psychological and behavioral interventions that promote good health and many effective strategies for coping with problems. Keep in mind, however, that successful coping does not mean eliminating all stress. It does not mean constant happiness or a life without pain. The healthy person faces problems, deals with them, and gets beyond them, but

DON'T OVERSIMPLIFY

Mary and Maurie are arguing about alternative and traditional medicine. One thinks modern medicine is cold and too commercial. The other thinks alternative methods are silly and superstitious. How might they best resolve their differences about the two approaches to health?

Cathy © 1999 Cathy Guisewite. Reprinted with permission of Universal Press Syndicate. All rights reserved.

the problems are necessary if the person is to acquire coping skills that endure. To wish for a life without stress would be like wishing for a life without friends. The result might be calm, but it would be joyless and ultimately hazardous to your health. The stresses of life—the daily hassles and the occasional tragedies—force us to grow, and to grow up.

TAKING P S Y C H O L O G Y WITH YOU

HEALTH HABITS YOU CAN LIVE WITH

Findings from health psychology offer practical guidelines for maintaining good health and coping with stressors or illness when they occur. Here are some suggestions based on the research in this chapter:

- *Follow "good old-fashioned motherly advice" and practice those habits associated with health.* We bet you already know what they are: Do not smoke; do not drink excessively or in binges; eat a healthful diet; wear seat belts; walk or do other forms of regular exercise at least several times a week; and get enough sleep (Matarazzo, 1984; Vita et al., 1998). Healthful habits are important not only for prevention of illness, but also for its treatment. When people become ill, they often stop taking care of themselves. They drink too much, stop taking walks, misuse medication, and don't eat well, all of which can speed the course of the disease.

- *Take control of what you can, such as finding the best treatment for a medical problem or the best solution to a psychological one.* The effects of stress are worsened when you feel helpless. Many things happen that are out of your control: accidents, being born to particular parents, flu epidemics, natural disasters, and countless other events. But you do have control over how you cope with them. Building self-efficacy—by learning to monitor

the behavior you wish to change, setting incentives for success, and finding social support—can help you increase control over your health and emotional well-being (Bandura, 1992).

- *Remember that some ways of coping are better than others.* If the situation requires action, it is better to use problem-solving techniques than to wallow around indecisively or simply vent emotions. If the situation is a fact of life, people who can use humor, reappraisal, and constructive social comparisons will be better off than those who remain focused on their negative emotions.

- *Don't try to "go it alone"; get the social support you need.* Find individuals who understand your problems and those who can offer practical as well as moral support. Whether your stress results from a one-time upsetting event or a chronic situation, try to find people who have "been there" and who can advise you on the best ways to cope, without keeping you mired in self-defeating patterns.

- *Don't stay in a network that is not helpful; get rid of the "social support" you don't need.* Are your friends or colleagues encouraging you to maintain unhealthy practices that you would like to change? Are they preventing you from making improvements in your life? If so,

you may need to think about finding new friends or new ways of sticking to your changed habits in spite of your old friends' efforts.

- *Learn when and how to disclose your emotions and upsetting experiences.* One effective way to banish intrusive thoughts, resolve unfinished business, and control negative emotions is to write down your deepest thoughts and feelings about them (Lepore, 1997; Smyth & Pennebaker, 1999). (Talking into a tape recorder will also work.) This process can help you assimilate the experience and come to a sense of completion about it; it may help you see it in a new light and think about it differently. But confession must not turn to obsession. Confessing your deepest thoughts and feelings is not therapeutic if you keep rehearsing and confessing them endlessly to anyone who will listen (Nolen-Hoeksema, 1991).

These suggestions are only a few of the practical implications of health psychology. Perhaps you can find others mentioned in this chapter, such as the importance of maintaining primary control under some circumstances, of helping other people, and of modifying the environment when you can. But if you find that you are not perfectly able to control every stressor that comes your way, don't get upset. After all, that will only add to your stress.

SUMMARY

THE NATURE OF STRESS

1. Hans Selye argued that environmental stressors such as heat, pain, and danger cause the body to respond in three stages: *alarm, resistance,* and *exhaustion.* If a stressor persists, it may overwhelm the body's ability to cope, and fatigue and illness may result. The three chronic stressors that most increase the risk of illness are bereavement and loss, unemployment and work-related problems, and poverty and powerlessness.

2. Researchers in the field of *psychoneuroimmunology (PNI)* are studying how psychological factors, the nervous and endocrine systems, and the immune system interact to produce illness. Modern views of stress have moved beyond Selye's approach to include psychological factors (such as personality traits, emotions, and how the individual perceives the stressor) and how the individual copes with the stressor.

PERSONALITY AND HEALTH

3. Researchers have sought links between personality traits and illness. Having a competitive, impatient *Type A personality* is not itself related to heart disease, but *cynical hostility,* which is often part of the Type A pattern, is. Chronic depression seems to also be a risk factor in heart disease, but its link to other illnesses remains unclear.

4. People who are emotionally inhibited are at greater risk of illness than people who can acknowledge and cope with negative emotions. The effort to suppress thoughts, worries, secrets, and memories of upsetting experiences can paradoxically lead to obsessively ruminating on these thoughts and be stressful to the body.

5. Other important personality factors that affect health are having an *optimistic explanatory style* (in contrast to a *pessimistic* one) and a *sense of control.* Optimism and control increase a person's ability to tolerate pain, live with ongoing illness and stress, and recover from disease.

But people can sometimes have too strong a sense of control; the healthiest balance is to take responsibility for getting well without blaming oneself for getting sick.

6. Health and well-being may depend on the right combination of *primary control,* trying to change the stressful situation, and *secondary control,* learning to accept the stressful situation. Cultures differ in the kind of control they emphasize and value.

COPING WITH STRESS

7. *Coping* involves a person's active efforts to manage demands that he or she feels are stressful. Individual methods of coping include *cooling off* (relaxation and meditation, massage, and exercise); efforts to *solve the problem* (generally by using *problem-focused* rather than *emotion-focused coping*); and cognitive techniques involved in *rethinking the problem* (*reappraising* the situation to find other ways of interpreting it, learning from the experience, *comparing* oneself to others who are worse off, and seeing the humor in the situation).

8. Social forms of coping draw on friends, family, and other sources of social support, which are important in maintaining physical health and emotional well-being. Friends and relatives provide emotional solace, advice, financial help, companionship, and attachment. However, they can also be stressful—a source of conflicts, burdens, and betrayals—or offer the wrong kind of support. In close relationships, couples who fight in a hostile and negative way show impaired immune function. *Giving* social support, "healing through helping others," is also an important positive form of coping.

HOW MUCH CONTROL DO WE HAVE OVER OUR HEALTH?

9. Psychological factors and social networks are links in a long chain that connects stress and illness. Coping with stress does not mean trying to live without pain, problems, or losses. It means learning how to live with them.

KEY TERMS

health psychology 545

alarm/resistance/exhaustion phases of stress 546

psychoneuroimmunology (PNI) 550

psychological stress 551

Type A personality 552

cynical hostility 553

pessimistic and optimistic explanatory styles 555

locus of control (internal vs. external) 557

primary control 559

secondary control 559

coping 560

emotion-focused coping 562

problem-focused coping 562

reappraisal 563

social comparisons 564

LOOKING BACK

- What happens to your body when you try to cross a busy street against the light? (p. 546)

- Are you really more likely to get a cold when you are "stressed out"? (p. 548)

- Which stressors pose the greatest hazard to your health? (pp. 548–549)

- Why is being "under stress" not enough to make you ill? (pp. 550–551)

- Which emotion may be most hazardous to your heart? (p. 553)

- Does chronic depression lead to physical illness? (p. 553)

- Is confession as healthy for the body as it is for the soul? (p. 554)

- Why do optimists tend to live longer than pessimists? (pp. 555–556)

- When something bad happens that you can't control, is it healthier to fight back or "go with the flow"? (p. 559)

- When you are feeling overwhelmed, what are some good ways to calm down? (p. 561)

- Why is it important to move beyond the emotions caused by a problem and deal with the problem itself? (pp. 562–563)

- How can you rethink your problems? (pp. 563–565)

- When do friends reduce your stress, and when do they just make matters worse? (pp. 565–567)

- What are the three best things you can do to prolong your life? (p. 569)

- How can we think critically about mainstream and alternative approaches to health? (p. 570)

16

PSYCHOLOGICAL DISORDERS

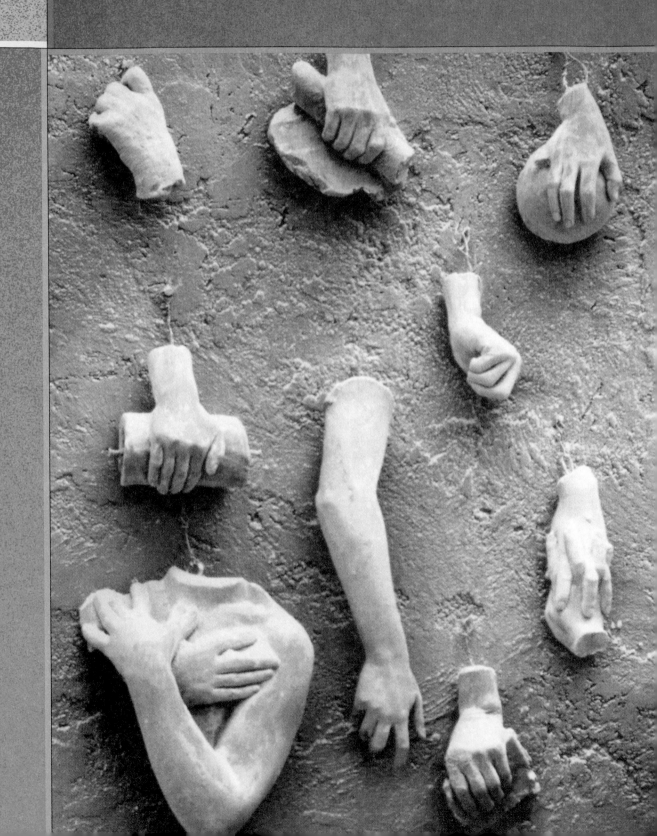

Who in the rainbow can draw the line where the violet tint ends and the orange tint begins? . . . So with sanity and insanity. In pronounced cases there is no question about them. But in [less obvious cases, few people are willing] to draw the exact line of demarcation . . . though for a fee some professional experts will.

NOVELIST HERMAN MELVILLE, IN "BILLY BUDD"

Margaret Mary Ray believed with all her heart that late-night talk-show host David Letterman was in love with her. Caught up in this delusion, she stalked Letterman day and night for a decade, writing him letters and repeatedly breaking into his house. She camped out on his tennis court and once stole his car. Her exploits were routinely reported in the tabloids, which treated her delusions as a running joke. Finally, she gave up. She wrote to her mother, "I'm all traveled out," and put herself in front of a coal train. She was killed instantly.

You don't have to be a psychologist to know that something was terribly wrong with Margaret Mary Ray. When people think of "mental illness," they usually think of individuals like her—people with delusions, people who behave in bizarre ways, or people who, like the Unabomber Theodore Kaczynski, plant bombs or commit random murders. Mental illness is frightening to many people because they associate it with irrational, dangerous, or uncontrollable behavior—from the lonely mutterings of some disturbed homeless people to the random violence committed by those who seem to have "run amok." But most psychological problems are far less dramatic and far more common. Some people go through episodes of complete inability to function, yet get along fine between those episodes. Others function adequately every day, yet suffer chronic feelings of melancholy (always feeling "below par" in happiness), anxiety, or panic. Some cannot control their worries or tempers.

One of the most common worries that people have is "Am I normal?" It is normal to fear being abnormal—especially when you are reading about psychological problems! As you will see, it is also normal to have problems. All of us on occasion have difficulties that seem too much to handle, that make us feel we cannot cope, and it is often difficult to pinpoint precisely when "normal" problems shade into "abnormal" ones on the spectrum of human behavior. In this chapter, you will learn how psychologists and psychiatrists define disorder and how they diagnose a wide range of psychological problems.

WHAT'S AHEAD

- Is insanity the same thing as having a mental disorder?
- What are three approaches to defining "mental disorder"?
- Why were slaves who dreamed of freedom once considered to be mentally ill?
- Why is the standard guide to the diagnosis of mental disorders controversial?

DILEMMAS OF DIAGNOSIS

Many people confuse *abnormal behavior*—behavior that deviates from the norm—with *mental disorder*, but the two are not the same. A person may behave in ways that are statistically rare (collecting ceramic pigs, being a genius at math, committing murder) without having a mental illness. Conversely, some mental disorders, such as depression and anxiety, are extremely common. If frequency of the problem is not a guide, how then should we define mental disorder?

Defining Mental Disorders

In the law, the definition of mental disorder rests primarily on whether a person is aware of the consequences of his or her actions and can control his or her behavior. If not, the person may be declared insane and therefore incompetent to stand trial. But *insanity* is a legal term only; psychologists and psychiatrists do not use the terms *sanity* or *insanity* in either research or diagnosis.

One problem with trying to define "mental disorder" is that the definition depends on whether we are taking society's point of view, the view of people who are personally affected by the behavior of the troubled individual, or the perspective of troubled individuals themselves:

1 *Mental disorder as a violation of cultural standards.* Every society sets up standards for its members to follow, and those who break the rules—say, by running around naked on campus—are usually considered deviant or disturbed. Many of these rules are specific to a particular time or group. For example, in most North American cultural groups, having visions of a deceased relative (though not uncommon) is considered abnormal; bereaved people tend to keep their hallucinations secret, for fear of being labeled "crazy" (Bentall, 1990). But the Chinese, the Hopi, and members of many other cultures regard such visions as perfectly normal.

Sometimes a society's notions of mental disorder serve the interests of those in power. In the early years of the nineteenth century, for instance, a physician named Samuel Cartwright argued that many slaves were suffering from *drapetomania*, an "irrational" urge to escape from slavery. As Hope Landrine (1988) noted, "Sanity for a slave was synonymous with submission, and protest and seeking freedom were the equivalent of psychopathology." Thus doctors could assure slave owners that a mental illness, not the intolerable condition of slavery, made slaves seek freedom. Today, of course, psychologists consider "drapetomania" foolish and cruel. But decisions about what should count as a mental disorder often still depend on the prevailing cultural climate, as we will see.

2 *Mental disorder as maladaptive or harmful behavior.* Another approach to defining mental disorder emphasizes the negative consequences of a person's behavior. Some behavior is harmful to the individual—for example, the behavior of a woman who is so afraid of crowds that she cannot leave her house, a man who drinks so much that he cannot keep a job, and a student who is so anxious that he cannot take exams. In other cases, the individual may report feeling fine and deny that anything is wrong, yet behave in ways that are disruptive or dangerous to the community, or

When Calista Flockhart won an Emmy for her portrayal of the TV character Ally McBeal, audiences were shocked at how gaunt she looked. But Flockhart denied that she is anorexic. What is the line between "normal" behavior (e.g., trying to achieve a cultural ideal of thinness) and an "abnormal" problem (e.g., having an eating disorder)?

People the world over paint their bodies, but what is normal for one person or one culture may not be to others. Hiromi Nakano (left), whose body has been completely tattooed, has taken body painting to an extreme rare in most societies, including her own. The Samburu tribesman of Kenya (center) has adorned his face in ways that seem odd to Westerners but that are typical of his culture. The tattoos of the American bikers (right) seem abnormal to most Americans but are perfectly normal in their biking subculture. Do you find these examples of body decoration to be beautiful, amusing, disgusting, or creepy? Your own cultural ideas of what is "normal" will affect your answers.

out of touch with reality—as when a child sets fires, a compulsive gambler loses the family savings, or a woman hears voices telling her to stalk a celebrity.

3 *Mental disorder as emotional distress.* A third approach identifies mental disorder in terms of a person's suffering. By this criterion, according to nationwide surveys, about 28 percent of all Americans in any given year have one or more mental disorders, including depression, anxiety, incapacitating fears, and problems with alcohol or other drugs (Kessler et al., 1994; Regier et al., 1993). This definition recognizes that a behavior that is unendurable or upsetting for one person, such as lack of interest in sex, may be acceptable and normal for another. But it does not cover the behavior of people who are clearly disturbed and dangerous to others, yet are not troubled about their actions.

In this chapter, we define **mental disorder** broadly, as any behavior or emotional state that causes an individual great suffering or worry, is self-defeating or self-destructive, or is maladaptive and disrupts either the person's relationships or the larger community. By this definition, many people will have some mental-health problem in the course of their lives, or their loved ones will.

Diagnosis: Art or Science?

Even armed with a broad definition of mental disorder, psychologists have found that agreeing on specific diagnoses is easier said than done. As George Albee (1985), a past president of the American Psychological Association, put it, "Appendicitis, a brain tumor and chicken pox are the same everywhere, regardless of culture or class; mental conditions, it seems, are not." In this section we will examine why it is often difficult to get psychologists to agree on what those mental conditions are.

Classifying Disorders: The DSM. The standard reference used to diagnose all mental disorders is the *Diagnostic and Statistical Manual of Mental Disorders* (DSM), published by the American Psychiatric Association. The first edition of the DSM, in 1952, was only 86 pages long and contained just nine basic categories, including brain disorders, "mental deficiency," and personality problems. The latest edition, the DSM-IV (1994), is nearly 900 pages long and contains more than 300 mental disorders. The DSM's primary aim is descriptive: to provide clear diagnostic categories, so that clinicians and researchers can agree on which disorders they are talking about, and then can study and treat these disorders. (For a list of the DSM's major categories, see Table 16.1.)

mental disorder Any behavior or emotional state that causes an individual great suffering or worry, is self-defeating or self-destructive, or is maladaptive and disrupts the person's relationships or the larger community.

TABLE 16.1   Major Diagnostic Categories in the DSM-IV

Disorders usually first diagnosed in infancy, childhood, or adolescence include mental retardation, attention deficit disorders (such as hyperactivity or an inability to concentrate), and developmental problems.

Delirium, dementia, amnesia, and other cognitive disorders are those resulting from brain damage, degenerative diseases such as syphilis or Alzheimer's, toxic substances, or drugs.

Substance-related disorders are problems associated with excessive use of or withdrawal from alcohol, amphetamines, caffeine, cocaine, hallucinogens, nicotine, opiates, or other drugs.

Schizophrenia and other psychotic disorders are disorders characterized by delusions, hallucinations, and severe disturbances in thinking and emotion.

Mood disorders include major depression, bipolar disorder (manic depression), and dysthymia (chronic depressed mood).

Anxiety disorders include generalized anxiety disorder, phobias, panic attacks with or without agoraphobia, posttraumatic stress disorder, and obsessive thoughts or compulsive rituals.

Eating disorders include anorexia nervosa (self-starvation because of an irrational fear of being or becoming fat) and bulimia nervosa (episodes of binge eating and vomiting).

Somatoform disorders involve physical symptoms (e.g., paralysis, heart palpitations, fatigue) for which no organic cause can be found. This category includes hypochondria (an extreme preoccupation with health and the unfounded conviction that one is ill) and conversion disorder (in which a physical symptom, such as a paralyzed arm or blindness, serves a psychological function).

Dissociative disorders include dissociative amnesia (in which important events cannot be remembered after a traumatic event) and dissociative identity disorder (formerly "multiple personality disorder"), characterized by the presence of two or more distinct identities or personalities.

Sexual and gender identity disorders include problems of sexual (gender) identity, such as transsexualism (wanting to be the other gender), problems of sexual performance (such as premature ejaculation or lack of orgasm), and paraphilias (unusual or bizarre imagery or acts that are necessary for sexual arousal, as in sadomasochism or exhibitionism).

Impulse-control disorders involve an inability to resist an impulse to perform some act that is harmful to the individual or to others, such as pathological gambling, stealing (kleptomania), setting fires (pyromania), or having violent rages.

Personality disorders are inflexible and maladaptive patterns that cause distress to the individual or impair the ability to function; they include paranoid, narcissistic, and antisocial personality disorders.

Additional conditions that may be a focus of clinical attention include "problems in living" such as bereavement, academic difficulties, spiritual problems, and acculturation problems.

The DSM lists the symptoms of each disorder and, wherever possible, gives information about the typical age of onset, predisposing factors, course of the disorder, prevalence of the disorder, sex ratio of those affected, and cultural issues that might affect diagnosis. In addition, clinicians are encouraged to evaluate each client according to five *axes*, or dimensions:

1. The primary clinical problem, such as depression;

2. Ingrained aspects of the client's personality that are likely to affect the person's ability to be treated, such as self-involvement or dependency;

3. Medical conditions that are relevant to the disorder, such as respiratory or digestive problems;

4. Social and environmental problems that can make the disorder worse, such as job and housing troubles or having recently left a network of close friends;

5. A global assessment of the client's overall level of functioning in work, relationships, and leisure time, including whether the problem is of recent origin or of long duration, and how incapacitating it is.

The DSM has had an extraordinary impact worldwide. Virtually all textbooks in psychiatry and psychology base their discussions of mental disorders on the DSM. Insurance companies require clinicians to assign their clients an appropriate DSM code number for the diagnosed disorder, which puts pressure on compilers of the manual to add more diagnoses so that physicians and psychologists will be compensated. Attorneys and judges often refer to the manual's list of mental disorders, even though the DSM warns that its categories "may not be wholly relevant to legal judgments."

Problems with the DSM. Because of the DSM's powerful influence, it is important to be aware of its limitations. Critics point to the following concerns about the very effort to classify and label mental disorders, and the DSM's efforts in particular:

1 **The danger of overdiagnosis.** "If you give a small boy a hammer," wrote Abraham Kaplan (1967), "it will turn out that everything he runs into needs pounding." In the same way, say critics, if you give mental-health professionals a diagnostic label, it will turn out that everyone they run into has the symptoms of it.

Consider "attention deficit/hyperactivity disorder" (ADHD), a diagnostic label given to children (and adults) who are impulsive, messy, restless, and easily frustrated, and who have trouble concentrating. Since ADHD was added to the DSM, it has become the fastest-growing disorder in America, where it is diagnosed at least ten times as often as it is in Europe. Many psychiatrists believe that ADHD results from neurological abnormalities, possibly in the prefrontal cortex of the brain (Barkley, 1997). But critics fear that parents, teachers, and mental-health professionals are overusing this diagnosis, especially on boys, who make up 80 to 90 percent of all ADHD cases. The critics argue that normal boy behavior—being rambunctious, refusing to nap, being playful, not listening to teachers in school—is being pathologized as a disorder (Panksepp, 1998).

2 **The power of diagnostic labels.** Being given a diagnosis reassures people who are seeking an explanation for their emotional symptoms or problems ("Whew! So *that's* what I've got!"). But it can also create a self-fulfilling prophecy: The client tries to conform to the assigned diagnosis, and the clinician interprets everything the client does as confirmation of the diagnosis (Maddux, 1996).

Moreover, once a person has been given a diagnosis, other people begin to see that person primarily in terms of the label; it sticks like lint. For example, when an impulsive, disobedient teenager is diagnosed as having "oppositional defiant disorder," people tend to see him as a Person with a Permanent Disorder rather than as a boy who is behaving badly at times. Observers tend to ignore changes in his behavior and the times when he is not being "defiant." They often fail to consider other explanations of his actions: Maybe he is defiant because he has been mistreated or his parents never listen to him.

ANALYZE ASSUMPTIONS AND BIASES

Many people assume that diagnosing mental disorders is as straightforward and objective as diagnosing appendicitis. What human biases are involved in creating and applying diagnoses of mental disorders?

What's the difference between a common life problem and a mental disorder? And does it make a difference which one people think they have?

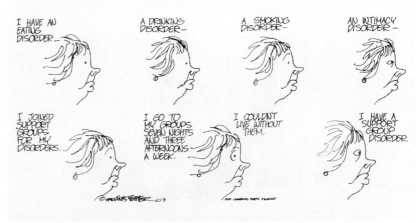

In a famous study, David Rosenhan (1973) demonstrated how rigid many people become when they are dealing with a person who has been given a psychiatric diagnosis. Eight healthy adults, including Rosenhan himself, appeared at different hospitals, claiming to have heard hazy voices that seemed to be saying "hollow," "empty," and "thud." Apart from this lie, they all gave honest personal histories. One was diagnosed as manic-depressive and the others as schizophrenic, and all eight were quickly admitted. At that point, the pseudopatients stopped faking any symptoms and behaved normally. Nonetheless, the hospital staff regarded everything they did as further confirmation of the diagnosis. For example, when the pseudopatients took notes on their experiences, several nurses recorded this act as if writing were an odd thing to do—one wrote "patient engages in writing behavior." Even when the pseudopatients were released, after a period ranging from 7 to 52 days, their diagnoses stuck. They were labeled as being "in remission" (without symptoms), rather than "recovered" or "well."

3 *Confusion of serious mental disorders with normal problems.* The DSM is not called "The Diagnostic and Statistical Manual of Mental Disorders and a Whole Bunch of Everyday Problems." Yet the compilers of the DSM keep adding everyday problems. The latest version actually contains "disorder of written expression" (having trouble writing clearly), "mathematics disorder" (not doing well in math), and "caffeine-induced sleep disorder" (which at least is easy to cure, by just laying off the coffee). Some critics fear that by lumping together such normal difficulties with true mental illnesses, such as schizophrenia, the DSM implies that everyday problems are comparable to disorders—and equally likely to require treatment (Kutchins & Kirk, 1997; Maddux, 1993).

4 *The illusion of objectivity.* Finally, some psychologists argue that the whole enterprise of the DSM is a vain attempt to impose a veneer of science on an inherently subjective process (Kutchins & Kirk, 1997; Maddux, 1993; Tiefer, 1995). Many decisions about what to include, say these critics, are based not on empirical evidence, but on group consensus. The problem is that group consensus often reflects prevailing attitudes and prejudices rather than objective evidence; physicians, in contrast, do not have to "vote" on whether diabetes is a disease.

Group consensus has sometimes led to self-correcting decisions. Over the years, psychiatrists have quite properly voted out many "disorders" that reflected cultural prejudices, such as lack of vaginal orgasm and childhood masturbation disorder (Wakefield, 1992). And in the 1970s, they voted to remove homosexuality, which until then had been classified as a mental illness despite research showing that homosexuals are no more disturbed than heterosexuals.

But as long as decisions about DSM categories are based on collective opinion, they will be subject to the biases and fads of their times, just as drapetomania was (Greenberg, 1997). Narcissism was voted out in 1968, and then voted back in 1980. Self-defeating personality disorder—which would have applied mainly to women who have the extreme self-sacrificing qualities required by the traditional female role—was adopted in 1987 and voted out in 1994. It is no longer a disorder to want to have sex too much, but it is if you do not want to have sex often enough ("hypoactive sexual desire disorder"). "Premenstrual dysphoric disorder" was added in 1987 and remains in an appendix to the DSM, even though, as we saw in Chapter 5, this alleged syndrome lacks an agreed-on definition. The point to underscore is that *as times change, so does the cultural consensus about what is normal—and thus what is abnormal.*

Harriet Tubman (on the left) poses with some of the people she helped to escape from slavery on her "underground railroad." Slaveholders welcomed the idea that Tubman and others who insisted on their freedom had a "mental disorder" called "drapetomania."

Benefits of the DSM. Defenders of the DSM point out that new studies are improving empirical support for its categories; and they argue that when the manual is used carefully and correctly, it improves the accuracy of diagnosis (Barlow, 1991; Spitzer & Williams, 1988; Wittchen et al., 1995). The DSM's labels, its supporters feel, help people identify the source of their unhappiness so they can get proper treatment (Kessler et al., 1994). Supporters recognize that there are biases in certain diagnoses, particularly those involving gender differences, but they believe these can be corrected with awareness and better research (Hartung & Widiger, 1998). As for the problem of subjectivity, advocates point out that not all diagnoses reflect society's biases (Wakefield, 1992). In cultures around the world, from the Inuit of Alaska to the Yorubas of Nigeria, some individuals have delusions, are severely depressed, or cannot control their behavior. In every culture, such individuals are considered to have mental illnesses (Butcher, Lim, & Nezami, 1998; Kleinman, 1988).

QUICK QUIZ

Your mental health will be enhanced if you can answer these questions.

1. Ruthie is afraid to leave her apartment unless she is with a close friend or relative, yet she says she feels fine and she angrily resists her friends' advice that she get help. What criterion of mental disorder does Ruthie's behavior meet?

2. The primary purpose of the DSM is to (a) provide descriptive criteria for diagnosing mental disorders, (b) help psychologists assess normal as well as abnormal behavior, (c) describe the causes of common disorders, (d) keep the number of diagnostic categories of mental disorders to a minimum.

3. List four criticisms of the DSM.

Answers:

1. maladaptive behavior   2. a   3. It can foster overdiagnosis; it fails to acknowledge the power of diagnostic labels on the perceptions of clinicians and the behavior of clients; it confuses normal problems in living with serious mental disorders; and it falsely implies that its diagnoses are always based on objective evidence.

WHAT'S AHEAD

- What is the difference between ordinary anxiety and an anxiety disorder?
- Why is the most disabling of all phobias known as the "fear of fear"?
- When is checking the stove before leaving home a sign of caution—and when does it signal a disorder?

ANXIETY DISORDERS

Anyone who is waiting for important news, or living in a situation that is unpredictable and uncontrollable, quite sensibly feels anxiety, a general state of apprehension or psychological tension. And anyone who is in a dangerous and unfamiliar situation, such as making a first parachute jump or being accosted by a hungry hippopotamus on the attack, quite sensibly feels flat-out fear. In the short run, these emotions are adaptive because they energize us to cope with danger. They ensure that we don't make that first jump without knowing how to operate the parachute, and that we get away from that hippo as fast as we can.

But in some individuals, fear and anxiety become detached from any actual danger, or they continue even when danger and uncertainty are past. Such individuals may be suffering from *chronic anxiety*, marked by long-lasting feelings of apprehension and doom; *panic attacks*, short-lived but intense feelings of spontaneous anxiety; *phobias*, excessive fears of specific things or situations; or *obsessive-compulsive disorder*, in which repeated thoughts and rituals are used to ward off anxious feelings.

Anxiety States

The chief characteristic of **generalized anxiety disorder** is continuous, uncontrollable anxiety or worry—a feeling of foreboding and dread—that occurs on a majority of days during a six-month period and that is not brought on by physical causes such as disease, drugs, or drinking too much coffee. Symptoms include restlessness or feeling keyed up, difficulty concentrating, irritability, muscle tension and jitteriness, sleep disturbance, and disturbing, unwanted, intrusive worries (McNally, 1996).

Some people suffer from generalized anxiety disorder without having lived through any specific anxiety-producing event. They may have a physiological tendency to experience anxiety symptoms—sweaty palms, a racing heart, shortness of breath—when they are in challenging or uncontrollable situations; as we saw in Chapter 13, temperamentally shy children are predisposed to react with anxiety in novel situations. Other chronically anxious people may have a history, starting in childhood, of being unable to control or predict their environments (Chorpita & Barlow, 1998).

Sometimes, however, chronic anxiety occurs in the aftermath of traumatic experiences. People who survive uncontrollable and unpredictable dangers—such as war, rape, torture, or natural disasters—may suffer from **posttraumatic stress disorder (PTSD)**. Typical anxiety symptoms in PTSD include reliving the trauma in recurrent, intrusive thoughts or dreams; "psychic numbing," a sense of detachment from others and an inability to feel happy or loving; and increased physiological arousal, reflected in insomnia, irritability, and impaired concentration. These symptoms can occur either immediately after a trauma or after a delay of many weeks or months; episodes may recur for months, years, or even decades (Kessler et al., 1995).

You may have heard about veterans of Vietnam and other wars who have suffered from PTSD for years. Most veterans, however, have PTSD symptoms for only a while, and then recover. Why do others continue to suffer? One possibility is that in some people, the stress hormones that are released when a person is coping with danger do not cease production when the danger is past. At chronically high levels, these hormones are literally toxic to parts of the brain, such as the hippocampus, which is involved in memory. Indeed, healthy Vietnam vets and those who still have PTSD differ significantly in the size of their hippocampi and in memory functioning (Shin et al., 1997). Perhaps stress caused these differences, or perhaps brain and memory impairments made it difficult for some vets to recover from the stress of combat. Psychologists are hot on the trail of the answer.

Panic Disorder

In **panic disorder**, a person has recurring attacks of intense fear or panic, with feelings of impending doom or death (Clark & Ehlers, 1993; McNally, 1998). These panic attacks may last from a few minutes to (more rarely) several hours. Symptoms

This grief-stricken soldier has just learned that the body bag on the flight with him contains the remains of a close friend who was killed in action. Understandably, soldiers like him suffer posttraumatic stress symptoms. But why do most eventually recover, whereas others have PTSD for many years?

generalized anxiety disorder A continuous state of anxiety marked by feelings of worry and dread, apprehension, difficulties in concentration, and signs of motor tension.

posttraumatic stress disorder (PTSD) An anxiety disorder in which a person who has experienced a traumatic or life-threatening event has symptoms such as psychic numbing, reliving of the trauma, and increased physiological arousal.

panic disorder An anxiety disorder in which a person experiences recurring *panic attacks,* periods of intense fear and feelings of impending doom or death, accompanied by physiological symptoms such as rapid breathing and pulse, and dizziness.

include trembling and shaking, dizziness, chest pain or discomfort, heart palpitations, feelings of unreality, hot and cold flashes, sweating, and, as a result of all these physical reactions, a fear of dying, going crazy, or losing control.

Although panic attacks seem to occur out of nowhere, they in fact usually occur in the aftermath of stress, prolonged emotion, exercise, specific worries, or frightening experiences (Beck, 1988; McNally, 1998). For example, a friend of ours was on a plane that was a target of a bomb threat—while airborne at 33,000 feet. He coped beautifully at the time, but two weeks later, seemingly out of nowhere, he had a panic attack.

Such delayed attacks after life-threatening scares are common. The essential difference between people who develop panic disorder and those who do not lies in *how they interpret their bodily reactions* (Clark & Ehlers, 1993; McNally, 1998). Healthy people who have occasional panic attacks see them correctly as a result of a passing crisis or period of stress, comparable to another person's migraines. But people who develop panic disorder regard the attack as a sign of illness or impending death, and they begin to live their lives in restrictive ways, trying to avoid future attacks.

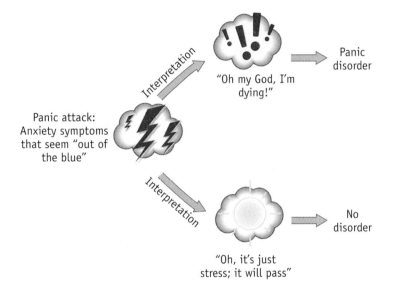

Panic attack: Anxiety symptoms that seem "out of the blue"

Interpretation → "Oh my God, I'm dying!" → Panic disorder

Interpretation → "Oh, it's just stress; it will pass" → No disorder

People who have panic disorder are found throughout the world, although culture influences the particular symptoms they experience (Barlow, Chorpita, & Turovsky, 1996). Feelings of choking or being smothered, numbness, and fear of dying are most common in Latin America and southern Europe; fear of public places is most common in northern Europe and America; and a fear of going crazy is more common in the Americas than in Europe. In Greenland, some fishermen suffer from "kayak-angst": a sudden attack of dizziness and fear that occurs while they are fishing in small, one-person kayaks (Amering & Katschnig, 1990).

Fears and Phobias

Are you afraid of bugs, snakes, or dogs? Are you so afraid that you can't stand to be around one, or are you just vaguely uncomfortable? A **phobia** is an exaggerated fear of a specific situation, activity, or thing. Some common phobias—such as fear of snakes and insects, heights (acrophobia), thunder (brontophobia), or closed spaces (claustrophobia)—may have evolved in human beings because these fears were adaptive for the species. Other, more idiosyncratic phobias, such as a fear of the color purple (porphyrophobia), may be acquired through classical conditioning, as we saw in Chapter 7. Still other phobias, such as fear of dirt and germs (mysophobia) or of the number 13 (triskaidekaphobia), reflect personality differences or cultural norms.

phobia An exaggerated, unrealistic fear of a specific situation, activity, or object.

If you hate to get up in public to make a speech, you are not alone! Fear of public speaking is one of the most common social phobias, probably because so many people have the "speaker's nightmare" that the audience will be bored to death or go to sleep.

agoraphobia A set of phobias, often set off by a panic attack, involving the basic fear of being away from a safe place or person.

obsessive-compulsive disorder (OCD) An anxiety disorder in which a person feels trapped in repetitive, persistent thoughts (obsessions) and repetitive, ritualized behaviors (compulsions) designed to reduce anxiety.

Whatever its source, a phobia is truly frightening and often incapacitating for its sufferer. It is not just a tendency to say "ugh" at tarantulas or skip the snake display at the zoo.

People who have a *social phobia* fear situations in which they will be observed by others. They worry that they will do or say something that will humiliate or embarrass them. Common social phobias are fears of speaking or performing in public, using public restrooms, eating in public, and writing in the presence of others. Again, these phobias are more severe forms of the occasional shyness and social anxiety that everyone experiences.

By far the most disabling fear disorder is **agoraphobia**, which accounts for more than half of the phobia cases for which people seek treatment. In ancient Greece, the *agora* was the social, political, business, and religious center of town, the public meeting place away from home. The fundamental fear in agoraphobia is of being alone in a public place, where escape might be difficult or where help might be unavailable. Individuals with agoraphobia report many specific fears—of public buses, driving in traffic or tunnels, eating in restaurants, or going to parties—but the underlying fear is of being away from a safe place, usually home, or a safe person, usually a parent or spouse.

Agoraphobia usually begins with a panic attack that seems to have no reason (Chambless, 1988; McNally, 1998). The attack is so unexpected and so scary that the agoraphobic-to-be begins to avoid situations that he or she thinks may provoke another one. For example, a woman we know had a panic attack while driving on a freeway. This was a perfectly normal posttraumatic response to the suicide of her husband a few weeks earlier. She pulled over and calmed down, but thereafter avoided freeways—as if the freeway, and not the suicide, had caused the attack. In extreme agoraphobia, the sufferer retreats to one safe haven, such as the home. But because so many of the actions associated with this phobia are designed to help the person avoid a panic attack, psychologists regard agoraphobia as a "fear of fear" rather than a fear of places.

Obsessions and Compulsions

Obsessive-compulsive disorder (OCD) is characterized by recurrent, persistent, unwished-for thoughts or images (*obsessions*) and by repetitive, ritualized, stereotyped behaviors that the person feels must be carried out to avoid disaster (*compulsions*).

GET → INVOLVED

WHAT SCARES YOU?

Everyone fears something. Stop for a moment to think about what you fear most. Is it heights? Snakes? Speaking in public? Ask yourself these questions: (1) How long have you feared this thing or situation? (2) How would you respond if you could not avoid this thing or situation? (3) How much would you be willing to rearrange your life to avoid this feared thing or situation?

After considering these questions, would you regard your fear as a full-blown phobia or merely a normal source of apprehension? What are your criteria for deciding?

Of course, many people have trivial compulsions and practice superstitious rituals; baseball players are famous for them. Obsessions and compulsions become a disorder when they become uncontrollable and interfere with a person's life.

Obsessive thoughts are often experienced as frightening or repugnant. For example, the person may have repetitive thoughts of killing a child, of becoming contaminated by shaking hands, or of having unknowingly hurt someone in a traffic accident. Obsessive thoughts take many forms, but they are alike in reflecting maladaptive ways of reasoning and processing information.

People who suffer from compulsions likewise feel they have no control over them. The most common compulsions are hand washing, counting, touching, and checking. A woman *must* check the furnace, lights, locks, oven, and fireplace three times before she can sleep; or a man *must* wash his hands and face precisely eight times before he leaves the house. Most sufferers of OCD do not enjoy such rituals and realize that the behavior is senseless. But if they try to forgo the ritual, they feel mounting anxiety that is relieved only by giving in to it. For one young man with OCD, stairs became a treadmill he could not get off: "At first I'd walk up and down the stairs only three or four times," he recalled. "Later I had to run up and down 63 times in 45 minutes. If I failed, I had to start all over again from the beginning" (quoted in King, 1989).

As with some cases of PTSD, some cases of obsessive-compulsive disorder may involve a brain abnormality. PET scans find that several parts of the brain are hyperactive in people with OCD. One area of the frontal lobes, the *orbital cortex* (which lies just above the eye sockets), apparently sends messages of impending danger to the *caudate nucleus*, an area involved in controlling the movement of the limbs, and to other structures involved in preparing the body to feel afraid and respond to external threats. Normally, once danger is past or a person realizes that there is no cause for fear, the caudate nucleus switches off the alarm signals. In people with OCD, however, the orbital cortex sends out repeated false alarms; then the emotional networks send out mistaken "fear!" messages, and the caudate nucleus fails to turn them off. The sufferer feels in a constant state of danger and tries repeatedly to reduce the resulting anxiety (Schwartz et al., 1996).

What is a normal concern with hygiene in one culture could seem an abnormal compulsion in another. This Lysol ad played on Americans' fear of disease by warning about the "unseen menace—more threatening, more fatal, more cruel than a million mad dogs— . . . the disease germ."

- How can you tell whether you have major depression or just the blues?
- What are the "poles" in bipolar disorder?
- How do some people think themselves into depression?

MOOD DISORDERS

In the DSM, "mood disorders" include disturbances in mood ranging from extreme depression to extreme mania. Of course, most people feel sad and blue from time to time, and also elated and joyful. And most people, at some time in their lives, will know the wild grief that accompanies tragedy and bereavement. These feelings, however, are a far cry from the clinical disorders described by the DSM.

Depression and Bipolar Disorder

The most widespread serious mood disorder is **major depression,** which has been called the common cold of psychiatric problems. Major depression involves emotional, behavioral, cognitive, and physical changes severe enough to disrupt a person's ordinary functioning for six months or longer. The writer William Styron, who fought and recovered from severe depression, used the beginning of Dante's classic poem, *The Divine Comedy,* to convey his suffering:

> *In the middle of the journey of our life*
> *I found myself in a dark wood.*
> *For I had lost the right path.*

"For those who have dwelt in depression's dark wood," wrote Styron in *Darkness Visible,* "and known its inexplicable agony, the return from the abyss is not unlike the ascent of the poet, trudging upward and upward out of hell's black depths and at last emerging into what he saw as 'the shining world.'"

People with major depression, like Styron, feel despairing and hopeless. They may think often of death or suicide. They lose interest or pleasure in their usual activities. They feel unable to get up and do things; it takes an enormous effort just to get dressed. Their thinking patterns feed their bleak moods. They exaggerate minor failings, ignore or discount positive events ("She didn't mean that compliment; she was only being polite"), and interpret any little thing that goes wrong as evidence that nothing will ever go right. Emotionally healthy people who are sad or grieving do not see themselves as completely worthless and unlovable, and they know at some level that their sadness or grief will pass. But depressed people interpret losses as signs of personal failure and conclude that they will never be happy again.

Depression is accompanied by physical changes as well. The depressed person may overeat or stop eating, have difficulty falling asleep or sleeping through the night, have trouble concentrating, and feel tired all the time. Some sufferers have other physical reactions, such as inexplicable pain or headaches.

About half of all those who go through a period of major depression will do so only once; others have recurrent bouts. Some people have episodes that are many years apart; others have clusters of depressive episodes over a few years. And some people suffer from constant but low-grade depression; they can do what they need to, but nearly always report their mood as sad or "down in the dumps." Alarmingly, depression and suicide rates among young people have increased rapidly in recent years (see "Taking Psychology with You").

At the opposite pole from depression is *mania,* an abnormally high state of exhilaration. You might think it's impossible to feel too good, but mania is not the

Even people who are rich, beautiful, and adored by millions can suffer from major depression. Marilyn Monroe committed suicide at the age of 36, a victim of depression and insecurity that no one could alleviate.

major depression A mood disorder involving disturbances in emotion (excessive sadness), behavior (loss of interest in one's usual activities), cognition (thoughts of hopelessness), and body function (fatigue and loss of appetite).

The great humorist Mark Twain (left) and brilliant jazz bassist Charles Mingus (right) had bipolar disorder. Bipolar disorder affects both sexes equally, and many great artists have suffered from it.

normal joy of being in love or winning the Pulitzer Prize. Someone in a manic state is expansive to an extent that is out of character. The symptoms are exactly the opposite of those in depression. Instead of feeling fatigued and listless, the person is full of energy. Instead of feeling hopeless and powerless, the person feels full of ambitions, plans, and power. The depressed person speaks slowly, monotonously, without inflection. The manic person speaks rapidly, dramatically, often with many jokes and puns. The depressed person has low self-esteem. The manic person has inflated self-esteem.

When people alternate between episodes of depression and one or more episodes of mania, they are said to have **bipolar disorder** (formerly called *manic-depressive disorder*), a much rarer problem than depression. The great humorist Mark Twain had bipolar disorder, which he described as "periodical and sudden changes of mood . . . from deep melancholy to half-insane tempests and cyclones." Other writers, artists, musicians, and scientists have suffered from this disorder too, including Charles Dickens and Isaac Newton. During the "highs" many of these artists create their best work, but the price of the "lows" is disastrous relationships, bankruptcy, and sometimes suicide (Barondes, 1998).

Although bipolar disorder occurs equally in both sexes, major depression occurs two or three times as often among women as among men, all over the world (Culbertson, 1997; McGrath et al., 1990). (See Figure 16.1.) Some psychologists think that women are truly more likely to become depressed than men are, but others think the difference is more apparent than real. Because the sexes often express feelings differently (see Chapter 11), and because women are much more likely than men to seek help for depression, depression in males may be overlooked or misdiagnosed. Men who are depressed often try to mask the feeling by denying their unhappiness, abusing drugs, or committing acts of violence (Canetto, 1992; Kessler et al., 1994).

Theories of Depression

Explanations of depression generally emphasize five possible causes: biological predispositions, social conditions, problems with close attachments, cognitive habits, or a combination of individual vulnerability and stress.

FIGURE 16.1

GENDER, AGE, AND DEPRESSION

Women are more likely than men to be diagnosed with depression. Yet after age 65, rates of depression drop sharply in both sexes.

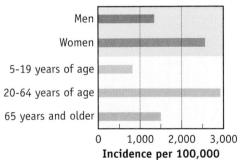

bipolar disorder A mood disorder in which episodes of both depression and mania (excessive euphoria) occur.

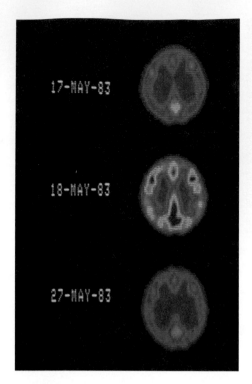

FIGURE 16.2
THE BIPOLAR BRAIN

These PET scans show changes in the metabolism of glucose, the brain's energy supply, in a patient with bipolar disorder. On May 17 and 27, the patient was depressed, and glucose metabolism throughout the brain was lower than normal. On May 18, the patient became manic, and metabolic activity increased to near normal levels. Keep in mind that such changes do not show the direction of cause and effect: A drop in glucose might bring on depression, but depression might also cause a drop in glucose levels.

1 *Biological explanations emphasize genetics and brain chemistry.* Studies of adopted children and twins support the notion that depression and bipolar disorder have a genetic component. But the precise gene or genes have yet to be identified (DiLalla et al., 1996; Nurnberger & Gershon, 1992). One investigator compares his search to tracking down an enemy spy who is carrying a radio transmitter. Searchers know roughly where he is—the city and neighborhood—but not his street and number (Barondes, 1998).

Genes may exert their influence by creating biochemical imbalances in neurotransmitters, which permit messages to be transmitted from one neuron to another in the brain. Two neurotransmitters that may be implicated in depressive disorders are serotonin and norepinephrine. In the view of some researchers, depression is caused by a deficient production of one or both of these neurotransmitters, and manic moods are caused by an excessive production (see Figure 16.2). Drugs that increase the levels of serotonin and norepinephrine sometimes alleviate symptoms of depression, and drugs that reduce norepinephrine sometimes alleviate those of mania. However, as we will see in the next chapter, these drugs do not help everyone.

Researchers are now using brain-scan technologies to identify changes that occur in the brain during depressive and manic episodes. In general, the brains of depressed people seem less active, especially the left frontal lobes, which are involved in positive emotions (see Chapter 11). However, brain scans alone do not tell us whether low activation in the brain causes depression, or whether depression changes the brain. It may work both ways, of course.

2 *Social explanations emphasize the stressful circumstances of people's lives.* In the social view, women are more likely than men to suffer from depression because they have less satisfying work and family lives, lower status than men in work and society, and higher rates of poverty and sexual victimization. Mothers are especially vulnerable to depression: The more children a woman has, the more likely she is to become depressed, especially if she is unemployed (McGrath et al., 1990). In contrast, men are more likely than women to be both married and working full time, a combination of activities that is strongly associated with mental health and low rates of depression (G. Brown, 1993; Culbertson, 1997). Violence is also a risk factor for depression: Inner-city adolescents of both sexes who are exposed to high rates of violence report higher levels of depression and more attempts to commit suicide than those who are not subjected to constant violence in their lives or communities (Mazza, Reynolds, & Grover, 1995).

Social analyses, however, fail to explain why *most* victims of violence, let alone most mothers and poor people, do not become clinically depressed. Nor do they explain why some people become depressed even though their lives are comfortable, safe, and secure.

3 *Attachment explanations emphasize problems with close relationships.* In this view, depression results from disturbed relationships; separations and losses, both past and present; and a history of insecure attachments (Klerman et al., 1984; Roberts, Gotlib, & Kassel, 1996). This explanation is supported by the fact that depressive episodes are frequently set off by disruption of a primary relationship.

However, it is not always clear whether a broken relationship caused depression, or the relationship dissolved because one partner was chronically depressed. Depressed people often seem demanding and "depressing" to family and friends, who in turn feel angry or sad when they cannot help the sufferer cheer up. Eventually, the depressed person's partner and friends may leave (Alloy et al., 1998; Coyne, 1990). One longitudinal study found that the direction of cause and effect may be different for husbands and wives: In general, for wives, marital problems made them depressed; for husbands, being depressed caused the marital problems (Fincham et al., 1997).

4 *Cognitive explanations emphasize particular habits of thinking and interpreting events.* In Chapter 11, we saw that particular attributional (explanatory) ways of thinking can create different emotions. Depression often involves three negative habits of thinking:

- *Internality.* Depressed people tend to believe that the reason for their misery is internal—something in them, an entrenched aspect of their personality. They will say, for example, "I'm unattractive and awkward; no wonder I'm not making friends." They rarely consider external explanations, such as "This school is so big and impersonal it's hard to meet new people" (Anderson et al., 1994).

- *Stability.* Depressed people tend to believe that their situation is permanent ("Nothing good will ever happen to me"; "I'll never fall in love"). Expecting nothing to get better, they do nothing to improve their lives, and therefore they remain unhappy.

- *Lack of control.* Depressed people tend to believe that they have no control over their emotions or the situations that caused those emotions ("I'm depressed because I'm ugly and horrible and I can't do anything about it").

Where do these ways of thinking come from? In the 1970s, the theory of *learned helplessness* held that people become depressed when their efforts to avoid pain or to control the environment consistently fail (Seligman, 1975). However, the fatal flaw with this theory was that not all depressed people have actually failed in their lives, and even living in painful or difficult situations does not make everyone depressed. The real problem for depressed people is their *belief* that nothing they do will make a difference. In short, they are not helpless, but hopeless. Because they have a *pessimistic explanatory style* (see Chapter 15), they believe that nothing good will ever happen to them, that the future is bleak and they are powerless to change it (Abramson, Metalsky, & Alloy, 1989; Seligman, 1991).

Another cognitive bad habit strongly associated with depression is brooding. People who ruminate endlessly about their negative feelings—who focus inward and stew about their unhappiness—tend to have longer and more intense periods of depression than do those who are able to distract themselves, look outward, and seek solutions to their problems. Women are more likely than men to develop a ruminating, introspective style, beginning in adolescence, and to rehearse the reasons for their unhappiness. This tendency may contribute both to longer-lasting depressions in women and to the sex difference in reported rates (Bromberger & Matthews, 1996; Nolen-Hoeksema, 1991; Nolen-Hoeksema & Girgus, 1994). The good news is that rumination tends to decline with age—and so does depression.

Of course, when you are already feeling sad, gloomy thoughts come more easily (Hilsman & Garber, 1995). But negative thinking is also an independent cause of depression. People with pessimistic, ruminating cognitive styles that foster hopelessness are at greater risk of developing full-blown, major depression than are people who think positively (Alloy & Abramson, 1998; Chorpita & Barlow, 1998).

5 *"Vulnerability–stress" explanations draw on all four explanations just discussed.* They hold that depression and other disorders result from an *interaction* between individual vulnerabilities—in personality traits, habits of thinking, and genetic predispositions—and environmental stress or sad events.

Depressed people feel not only helpless, but hopeless.

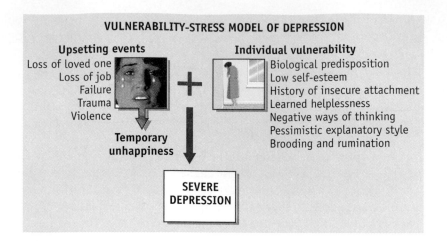

VULNERABILITY-STRESS MODEL OF DEPRESSION

Upsetting events
Loss of loved one
Loss of job
Failure
Trauma
Violence

Temporary unhappiness

Individual vulnerability
Biological predisposition
Low self-esteem
History of insecure attachment
Learned helplessness
Negative ways of thinking
Pessimistic explanatory style
Brooding and rumination

SEVERE DEPRESSION

Interaction models are an improvement over theories implying that everyone is equally vulnerable to depression, given a certain experience, gene, or biological disposition. These models try to specify which personality traits interact with which events to produce depression. For example, in one study, students who got worse grades than they expected reported feeling temporarily depressed (not a surprise). But depression persisted in those who *also* had a pessimistic explanatory style ("I'm stupid and always will be") *and* low self-esteem, resulting in hopelessness (Metalsky et al., 1993). (See Figure 16.3.)

DON'T OVERSIMPLIFY

Many people hope to find "the" cause of depression. What is wrong with framing the goal that way?

In assessing these different approaches critically, keep in mind that depression comes in varying degrees of intensity, and it may have different causes in different people. One person may have been abandoned in childhood and therefore feel insecurely attached in current relationships. Another may have a pessimistic explanatory style that fosters depressive interpretations of even happy events ("Yeah, yeah, I've met this great person but it will never last"). A third may have a biological predisposition to respond to stress with depression. And a fourth may lack satisfying work or love or may have been subjected to violence or other trauma.

This is why we should avoid either–or explanations of depression—it's biochemical *or* it's psychological. By understanding depression as an interaction among an individual's biology, personality, and experiences, we can see why the same precipitating event, such as a minor setback or even the loss of a loved one, might produce normal sadness in one person and extreme depression in another.

FIGURE 16.3
INTERACTING PATHS TO DEPRESSION

Students who failed an exam felt temporarily depressed but they "popped back" to normal by the third day—*unless* they were pessimistic and had low self-esteem, in which case they continued to feel depressed and hopeless. This finding illustrates how events interact with personality traits to determine how we respond to setbacks (Metalsky et al., 1993).

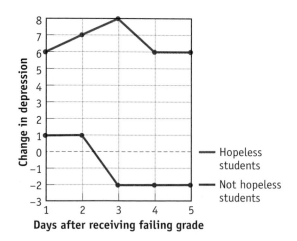

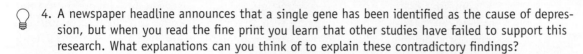

QUICK QUIZ

Don't let another quiz make you vulnerable to sadness.

1. In the view of some biological researchers, depression involves a deficit in the neurotransmitters _____ and/or _____ .

2. Depressed people tend to believe that the reasons for their unhappiness are (a) controllable, (b) temporary, (c) internal, (d) caused by the situation.

3. Vulnerability-stress theories attribute depression to an interaction between _____ and _____ .

4. A newspaper headline announces that a single gene has been identified as the cause of depression, but when you read the fine print you learn that other studies have failed to support this research. What explanations can you think of to explain these contradictory findings?

Answers:

1. serotonin, norepinephrine   2. c   3. individual vulnerabilities; environmental stress or sad events   4. The conflicting evidence may mean, among other possibilities, that if a genetic predisposition for depression exists, it is not due to a single specific gene, but involves several genes working in the context of environmental events. It may mean that the right gene has not yet been identified. Or it may mean that genes are not a factor in all forms of depression.

WHAT'S AHEAD

● **When does being self-centered become a disorder?**

● **What do a charming but heartless tycoon and a remorseless killer have in common?**

● **Why are some people seemingly incapable of feeling guilt and shame?**

PERSONALITY DISORDERS

Personality disorders involve rigid, maladaptive traits that cause great distress or an inability to get along with others. The DSM-IV describes such a disorder as "an enduring pattern of inner experience and behavior that deviates markedly from the expectations of the individual's culture [and] is pervasive and inflexible." That means it is not caused by depression, drugs, or a situation that temporarily induces a person to behave in ways that are out of character.

Problem Personalities

One personality disorder, **paranoid personality disorder**, involves pervasive, unfounded suspiciousness and mistrust of other people; irrational jealousy; secretiveness; and doubt about the loyalty of others. People with paranoid personalities have delusions of being persecuted by everyone from their closest relatives to government agencies, and their beliefs are immune to disconfirming evidence.

Another personality disorder, **narcissistic personality disorder**, involves an exaggerated sense of self-importance and self-absorption. Narcissism gets its name from the Greek myth of Narcissus, a beautiful young man who fell in love with his own image. Individuals who are narcissistic are preoccupied with fantasies of unlimited success, power, brilliance, or ideal love. They demand constant attention and admiration and feel entitled to special favors, without being willing to reciprocate. They fall in love quickly and out of love just as fast, when the beloved proves to have some human flaw.

Narcissus fell in love with his own image, and now he has a personality disorder named after him—just what a narcissist would expect!

personality disorders Rigid, maladaptive personality patterns that cause personal distress or an inability to get along with others.

paranoid personality disorder A disorder characterized by habitually unreasonable and excessive suspiciousness, jealousy, or mistrust; paranoid symptoms may also occur in schizophrenia and other psychoses.

narcissistic personality disorder A disorder characterized by an exaggerated sense of self-importance and self-absorption.

antisocial personality disorder A disorder (sometimes called psychopathy or sociopathy) characterized by antisocial behavior such as lying, stealing, manipulating others, and sometimes violence; a lack of guilt, shame, and empathy; and impulsivity.

Notice that although these descriptions evoke flashes of recognition ("I know that type!"), it is hard to know where value judgments end and a clear disorder begins (Maddux & Mundell, 1997). Cultures draw the line differently. For example, American society often encourages people to pursue dreams of unlimited success and ideal love, but such dreams might be considered signs of serious disturbance in a more group-oriented society. Where would you draw the line between having a narcissistic personality disorder and being a normal member of a group or culture that encourages "looking out for number one" and puts a premium on youth and beauty?

Antisocial Personality Disorder

Throughout history, societies have recognized and feared the few members in their midst who lack all human connection to anyone else—who can cheat, con, and kill without flinching. In the 1830s, these individuals were said to be afflicted with "moral insanity," and in the twentieth century they came to be called "psychopaths" or "sociopaths." The DSM, trying to avoid such emotionally charged terms, refers to **antisocial personality disorder (APD)**. By any name, this condition is fascinating and frightening because of the great harm these people inflict on their victims and on society.

Symptoms of APD. According to the DSM, people diagnosed with APD must meet at least three of seven criteria: (1) They repeatedly break the law; (2) they are deceitful, using aliases and lies to con others; (3) they are impulsive and unable to plan ahead; (4) they repeatedly get into physical fights or assaults; (5) they show reckless disregard for their own safety or that of others; (6) they are constantly irresponsible, failing to meet obligations to others; and (7) they lack remorse for actions that harm others.

Lacking conscience and remorse, people with APD can lie, seduce, and manipulate others and then drop them without a qualm. If caught in a lie or a crime, they may seem sincerely sorry and promise to make amends, but it is all an act. Some are sadistic, able to kill a pet, a child, or a random adult without a twinge of regret. Others direct their energies into con games or career advancement, abusing other people emotionally or economically rather than physically (Robins, Tipp, & Przybeck, 1991).

Some people with antisocial personalities use charm and elaborate con tricks to deceive others. Giovanni Vigliotto (right) married 105 women over 33 years, seized their assets, and then abandoned them. He was convicted of bigamy and fraud, and sentenced to 34 years in prison. But other people with APD are sadistic and violent, starting in childhood. At age 13, Eric Smith (left) bludgeoned and strangled a 4-year-old boy to death. He was tried as an adult and sentenced to a prison term of nine years to life.

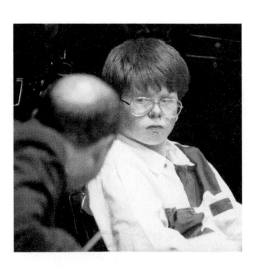

According to the DSM-IV, antisocial personality disorder occurs in about 3 percent of all males and less than 1 percent of all females. Yet people with APD may account for more than half of all serious crimes committed in the United States (Hare, 1993). Terrie Moffitt (1993), who observed the development of APD over time, reported that the remorselessness and law-breaking start early and take different forms at different ages: "biting and hitting at age 4, shoplifting and truancy at age 10, selling drugs and stealing cars at age 16, robbery and rape at age 22, and fraud and child abuse at age 30 . . . [people with APD] lie at home, steal from shops, cheat at school, fight in bars, and embezzle at work."

Causes of APD. Researchers studying APD, like those studying other mental disorders, are investigating possible biological and social factors that contribute to antisocial personalities:

1 *Abnormalities in the brain and central nervous system.* Antisocial individuals do not respond physiologically to punishments the way other people do; this may be why they can behave fearlessly in situations that would scare others to death. Normally, when a person is anticipating danger, pain, or punishment, the electrical conductance of the skin changes—a classically conditioned response that indicates anxiety or fear. But people with APD are slow to develop such responses, which suggests that they are unable to feel the anxiety necessary for learning that their actions will have unpleasant consequences (see Figure 16.4). Their inability to feel emotional arousal—empathy, guilt, fear of punishment, anxiety under stress—suggests some abnormality in the brain and central nervous system (Hare, 1965, 1993; Raine, 1996).

2 *Problems with impulse control.* People who are antisocial, hyperactive, addicted, or impulsive may share a common inherited disorder involving an inability to control responses to frustration and provocation (Luengo et al., 1994; Raine, 1996). The biological children of parents with antisocial personality disorder, substance-abuse problems, or impulsivity disorders are at greater than normal risk of developing these disorders themselves, even when these children are reared by others (Nigg & Goldsmith, 1994).

3 *Brain damage.* Another, more significant cause of the violent forms of antisocial behavior may be brain damage resulting from physical neglect, battering, and injury (Lewis, 1992; Milner & McCanne, 1991; Moffitt, 1993; Raine et al., 1998). Consider the results of a study that compared two groups of violent boys: those who had been arrested for vicious assault, rape, or murder, and those whose violence was limited to fistfights. More than three-fourths of the extremely violent boys had suffered head injuries as children, had a history of serious medical problems, or had been beaten savagely by their parents, compared with one-third of the others (Lewis, 1981).

4 *Vulnerability-stress explanations.* Brain damage or genetic predispositions alone are rarely enough to create a violent or antisocial individual. But according to the *vulnerability-stress model of APD,* when biological vulnerability is combined with physical abuse, parental neglect, lack of love and contact comfort, or other environmental stresses, individuals are far more likely to become impulsive and violent, often ending up in prison. A study of more than 4,000 boys, followed from birth

FIGURE 16.4

EMOTIONS AND ANTISOCIAL PERSONALITY DISORDER

In several experiments, people with antisocial personality disorder (APD) were slow to develop classically conditioned responses to anticipated danger, pain, or shock—responses that indicate normal anxiety (Hare, 1965). This deficit may be related to the ability of people with APD to behave in destructive ways without remorse or regard for the consequences (Hare, 1993).

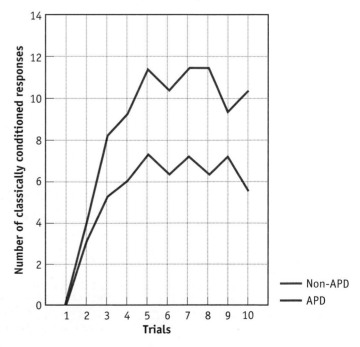

to age 18, found that many of those who became violent offenders had experienced two risk factors: birth complications that caused damage to the prefrontal cortex, and early maternal rejection. Their mothers had not wanted the pregnancy, and the babies were put in public institutional care for at least four months during their first year. Although only 4.4 percent of the boys had both risk factors, these boys accounted for 18 percent of all violent crimes committed by the sample as a whole (Raine, Brennan, & Mednick, 1994).

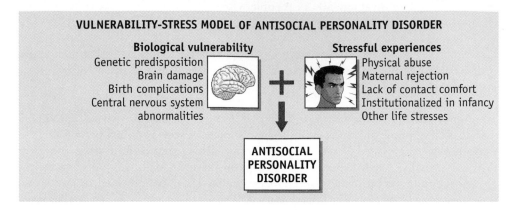

VULNERABILITY-STRESS MODEL OF ANTISOCIAL PERSONALITY DISORDER

Biological vulnerability
Genetic predisposition
Brain damage
Birth complications
Central nervous system abnormalities

+

Stressful experiences
Physical abuse
Maternal rejection
Lack of contact comfort
Institutionalized in infancy
Other life stresses

ANTISOCIAL PERSONALITY DISORDER

Remember, though, that not all persons with APD are violent, and not all violent individuals have APD. Some people who meet the criteria for APD are exploitative and unempathic, but they express these traits in professional ruthlessness rather than physical aggression. Some are charming con artists, who could steal your heart and your wallet in a minute. Conversely, people can commit antisocial *acts* without having antisocial *personalities*. Most antisocial crimes—such as homicide, rape, robbery, assault, and auto theft—are committed by young men who are "going along with the guys"; their criminal activities peak in late adolescence and drop off in their 20s. In some groups, such as violent gangs and organized-crime organizations, members are expected to kill without remorse and are rewarded for doing so; such individuals may otherwise show great loyalty and affection toward the people who matter to them.

QUICK QUIZ

A. Can you diagnose each of the following disorders?

1. Ann can barely get out of bed in the morning. She feels that life is hopeless and despairs of ever feeling good about herself.

2. Connie constantly feels a sense of impending doom; for many weeks, her heart has been beating rapidly and she can't relax.

3. Damon is totally absorbed in his own feelings and wishes.

4. Edna believes that everyone is out to get her and no one can be trusted.

 B. Suppose you read about an unusually brutal assault committed by a gang member during a robbery. Should you assume that he has an antisocial personality disorder? Why or why not?

Answers:

A. 1. major depression 2. generalized anxiety disorder 3. narcissistic personality disorder 4. paranoid personality disorder B. Behaving antisocially is not the same thing as having an antisocial personality disorder. Many factors could have contributed to this man's violence, including his perceptions of danger, feelings of anger and panic, or the demands and norms of his fellow gang members.

WHAT'S AHEAD

● Can people actually forget who they are?

● Why are many clinicians and researchers skeptical about multiple personality disorder?

DISSOCIATIVE DISORDERS

Have you ever been out driving on a highway and suddenly realized you have lost all track of time and distance? This is a small but common everyday example of *dissociation*, a split in awareness (see Chapter 5): Part of you is driving the car and attending to other drivers, and part of you is daydreaming. Dissociation also occurs when we must deal with stress or shock and we feel temporarily cut off from ourselves—strange, dazed, or "unreal."

In **dissociative disorders**, however, consciousness, behavior, and identity are more severely split or altered. The symptoms are intense, last a long time, and appear to be out of the individual's control. Like posttraumatic stress disorder, dissociative disorders often occur in response to shocking or harmful events. But whereas people with PTSD cannot get the trauma out of their minds and waking thoughts, people with dissociative disorders apparently escape the trauma by putting it out of their minds, erasing it from memory (Cardeña et al., 1994).

Amnesia and Fugue

Amnesia, according to the DSM-IV, is an inability to remember important personal information, usually of a traumatic or stressful nature, that cannot be explained by ordinary forgetfulness. Amnesia can result from organic conditions such as head injury. When no physical causes are apparent, and when the person forgets only information that is threatening to the self, the amnesia is considered to be *dissociative* or *psychogenic* (psychological in origin). Cases of dissociative amnesia have been

dissociative disorders Conditions in which consciousness or identity is split or altered.

amnesia (dissociative) When no organic causes are present, a dissociative disorder involving partial or complete loss of memory for threatening information or traumatic experiences.

This amnesia victim found himself on a Hawaiian beach with no memory of how he got there, what year it was, or where he was from. He said his name was William D'Souza, but a detective learned that his real name was Philip Cutajar and that he had been living in Maryland. Yet even after calls from his mother and brother, Cutajar was not sure who they were—or who he was. Here he is using the Internet to search for more information about his identity.

reported in the aftermath of criminal acts, devastating accidents, combat, and rape. The victim temporarily loses memory for details of the trauma; however, with the passage of time, the memory usually returns.

In the case of a related disorder called dissociative **fugue** (pronounced "fewg"), a person forgets his or her identity entirely and wanders far from home. (The word *fugue* comes from the Latin for "flight.") The person may take on a new name, remarry, get a new job, and live contentedly, sometimes for years, until he or she suddenly "wakes up"—puzzled and often with no memory of the fugue experiences.

Dissociative amnesia and fugue are controversial diagnoses among psychologists, who disagree about the mind's ability to "cut off" or "repress" traumatic memories (see Chapter 10). Many psychologists point out that amnesia and fugue are also easy to fake, especially when a person has a motive for "forgetting" bad or illegal behavior or for escaping situations that have become intolerable.

Dissociative Identity Disorder ("Multiple Personality")

The DSM-IV uses the term **dissociative identity disorder** to describe the appearance, within one person, of two or more distinct identities. In our discussion, however, we will retain the more commonly used term, *multiple personality disorder* (MPD). In this disorder, each identity appears to have its own memories, preferences, personality traits, and even medical problems.

The MPD Controversy. Cases of multiple personality portrayed on TV, in popular books, and in films such as *The Three Faces of Eve* and *Sybil* have captivated the public for years. Among mental-health professionals, however, two competing views of MPD exist. On one side are those who think that MPD is common, but often unrecognized or misdiagnosed. On the other side are those who believe that most cases of MPD are generated by clinicians themselves, knowingly or unknowingly, during their interactions with vulnerable and suggestible clients, and that if the condition exists at all, it is rare.

Those in the MPD-is-real camp believe that it originates in childhood, as a means of coping with unspeakable, repeated traumas, such as torture (Gleaves, 1996; Kluft, 1993; Ross, 1995). In this view, the trauma produces a mental "splitting"; one personality emerges to handle everyday experiences and another emerges to cope with the bad ones. MPD patients are frequently described as having lived for years with several personalities of which they were unaware, until hypnosis revealed them.

Those who are skeptical about MPD point out that before 1980, fewer than 200 cases of MPD had ever been diagnosed anywhere in the world; yet since 1980, *tens of thousands* of cases have been reported, virtually all of them in North America (see Table 16.2) (Nathan, 1994; Piper, 1997). Critics of MPD think such numbers are suspicious, a sign that the disorder is being wildly overdiagnosed by its proponents.

Research on MPD. Skeptics have shown that the evidence used to support the diagnosis of MPD is indeed highly questionable, for several reasons (Ganaway, 1995; Merskey, 1995; Piper, 1997; Spanos, 1996):

1 *Flaws in the research.* Claims have been made that MPD patients show different physiological responses (e.g., EEG patterns) for different personalities, but such claims rely mostly on anecdotes or on studies that lacked control groups (P. Brown, 1994). When researchers compare MPD patients with healthy people who are merely role-playing different personalities, they find differences in physiology between "personalities" in the *healthy* people, too (Miller & Triggiano, 1992;

fugue [FEWG] A dissociative disorder in which a person flees home and forgets his or her identity.

dissociative identity disorder A controversial disorder marked by the appearance within one person of two or more distinct personalities, each with its own name and traits.

TABLE 16.2	The Rise of Multiple Personality Disorder
1789	Early case of young German woman with several "personalities" (including a French woman and a little boy).
1816	First recorded case of "multiple personality" in America (Mary Reynolds).
1875	Condition renamed "multiple personality" in France.
1886	Robert Louis Stevenson's *Dr. Jekyll and Mr. Hyde* popularizes notion of "two personalities" in one body.
1800s–1960	**200 cases reported worldwide.**
1957	*The Three Faces of Eve* published.
1960–1970	**8 cases reported.**
1976	*Sybil* (movie) released.
1980	**DSM includes MPD diagnosis for first time.**
1980	*Michelle Remembers* published, which claims "Satanic ritual abuse" as cause of MPD.
1980–1991	Media coverage escalates in popular books and talk shows (*Oprah, Geraldo*) that feature MPD "victims."
1985	Richard Kluft claims to have treated 250 MPD patients.
By 1986	**6,000 cases reported in North America.**
1987	First MPD inpatient treatment unit established at Rush Presbyterian Hospital in Chicago; others follow across the country.
By 1992	**More than 25,000 cases reported in North America.**
1995	Dr. Diane Humenansky becomes first psychiatrist found guilty of malpractice for inducing multiple personalities in a vulnerable patient.
1996–present	Other successful lawsuits against major proponents of MPD diagnosis and treatment units in hospitals.

Sources: Kenny, 1986; Loftus, 1996; Nathan, 1994; Pendergrast, 1995; Piper, 1997.

Popular books and films about multiple personality, such as *The Three Faces of Eve* and *Sybil*, spawned countless imitators—and thousands of reported cases. Controversy exists about whether this increase is due to better diagnosis, or to unwitting therapist influence and sensational stories in the media.

Spanos, 1996). People can alter physiological measures such as brain-wave activity by changing their moods, energy levels, and concentration, so these measures are not a valid way to verify MPD.

2 *Pressure and suggestion by clinicians.* Some clinicians may actually be creating the disorder in their clients through the power of suggestion, sometimes bordering on coercion (McHugh, 1993a; Merskey, 1992, 1995; Spanos, 1996). For example, one prominent believer in MPD, Richard Kluft (1987), wrote that efforts to determine the presence of MPD—that is, to get the person to reveal a dissociated personality—may require "between 2½ and 4 hours of continuous interviewing. Interviewees must be prevented from taking breaks to regain composure. . . . In one recent case of singular difficulty, the first sign of dissociation was noted in the 6th hour, and a definitive spontaneous switching of personalities occurred in the 8th hour." But think about it: After eight hours of "continuous interviewing" without a single break, how many of us wouldn't do what the interviewer wanted?

Clinicians who conduct such interrogations argue that they are merely *permitting* other personalities to reveal themselves. However, in numerous malpractice cases across the country, courts have ruled, on the basis of the testimony of scientific experts in psychiatry and psychology, that it is more likely that these clinicians were actively *creating* personalities through suggestion and sometimes outright intimidation (Loftus, 1996; Spanos, 1996).

3 *The role of the media.* The media coverage of sensational MPD cases has played a major role in fostering MPD diagnoses. When Canadian psychiatrist Harold Merskey (1992) reviewed the published cases of MPD, including Sybil, he was unable to find a single one in which a patient developed MPD without being influenced by the therapist's suggestions or reports about the disorder in books and the media. Even the authors of *The Three Faces of Eve* were alarmed by the media hype and proliferation of questionable cases. Thirty years later, they reported that although in the intervening years they had had hundreds of referrals of patients believed to have MPD by their psychiatrists, they thought only one of these was a genuine multiple personality (Thigpen & Cleckley, 1984).

The Sociocognitive Explanation. No one disputes that some troubled, highly imaginative individuals can produce many different "personalities" when asked. The question is whether they are suffering from an actual disorder over which they have no control—one in which different personalities just pop up—or whether they are going along with the clinician's diagnosis and expectations.

The *sociocognitive explanation* of multiple personality disorder holds that it is simply an extreme form of the ability we all have to present different aspects of our personalities to others (Piper, 1997; Spanos, 1996). In this view, the diagnosis of MPD provides a culturally acceptable way for some troubled people to make sense of their problems (Kenny, 1986). It allows them to account for behavior that they now regret or find intolerably embarrassing. It allows some people to excuse criminal behavior as well, including murder; they can claim their "other personality did it." Therapists who are looking for MPD reward such patients with attention and praise for revealing more and more personalities (Ofshe & Watters, 1994). (These rewards would explain why the early cases of MPD involved only two or three personalities, whereas in recent years MPD patients have reported having hundreds and even thousands of them.) And of course, as the evidence of media involvement in the escalating numbers of MPD cases suggests, there can be big financial incentives for patients and therapists.

Of course, the fact that MPD is controversial and has little empirical evidence to support it does not mean that no legitimate cases exist. Each case must be examined on its own merits. But the story of MPD teaches us to think critically about disorders that suddenly become trendy: to consider other explanations, to examine assumptions and biases, and to demand good evidence.

THINKING CRITICALLY

CONSIDER OTHER EXPLANATIONS

On the *Oprah* show, a man came on to talk about his new book, in which he claims to have 24 personalities, including a 6-year-old boy, twin 4-year-old girls, and a 30-year-old seducer of women. The book immediately became a best-seller and was sold to the movies for more than $1 million. He says he developed this mental disorder as a result of severe sexual abuse as a child. What other explanations might explain how and why he developed "MPD"?

QUICK QUIZ

Suppose you are on a jury in which the defendant, who killed six prostitutes, claims he suffers from multiple personality disorder. He has no memory of committing the murders, he says, and his psychiatrist testifies that the man is a true case of MPD. As a critical thinker, what questions would you want to ask about this defense? (By the way, this is a real case.)

Answers:

Some possible questions to ask: Was the diagnosis of MPD made *before* the man committed murder—that is, did he have a history of MPD or any other mental disorder—or did he conveniently "discover" his other personalities after being arrested? Is the psychiatrist a believer in MPD or a skeptic? Did any other psychiatrist or psychologist interview the defendant? How were the interviews conducted?

WHAT'S AHEAD

- In what ways might genes contribute to alcoholism?
- Why is alcoholism more common in Ireland than in Italy?
- Why don't policies of abstinence from alcohol reduce problem drinking?
- If you take morphine to control chronic pain, does that mean you will become addicted to it?

DRUG ABUSE AND ADDICTION

Most people use drugs (legal, illegal, or prescription) in moderation and for short-lived effects, but some people depend too much on them, and others abuse drugs even at the cost of their own health. The DSM-IV defines *substance abuse* as "a maladaptive pattern of substance use leading to clinically significant impairment or distress." Symptoms of such impairment include the failure to hold a job, care for children, or complete schoolwork because of excessive drug use; use of the drug in hazardous situations (e.g., while driving a car or operating machinery); recurrent arrests for drug use; and frequent conflicts with others about use of the drug or as a result of using the drug.

Why, though, are some people able to use drugs moderately, whereas others abuse them? In this section, focusing on the example of alcoholism, we will consider the two dominant approaches to understanding addiction and drug abuse—the biological model and the learning model—and conclude with an effort to integrate the contributions of both.

Biology and Addiction

In 1960, a book was published that profoundly changed the way most people thought about alcoholics. In *The Disease Concept of Alcoholism*, E. M. Jellinek argued that alcoholism is a disease over which an individual has no control and from which he or

When does the social use of a drug turn into drug abuse? This is a "kegs and eggs" party that started at 7 a.m. at a bar near a New York college campus. The party will end when the beer runs out.

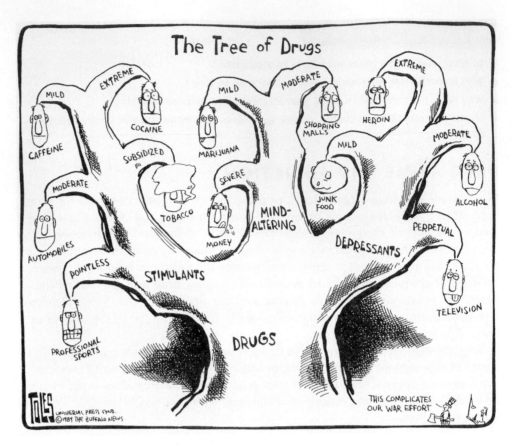

By poking fun at the things people do to make themselves feel better, this cartoon reminds us that many "addictions" are not biochemical.

she never recovers. Drunkenness is not an inevitable property of alcohol, he said, but a characteristic of some people who have an inborn vulnerability to liquor; for them, complete abstinence is the only solution. The disease theory of alcoholism transformed the moral condemnation of the addict as a bad and sinful person into concern for someone who is sick.

Today, many people continue to regard alcoholism as a disease, and the *biological model* of addiction is widely accepted by researchers and the public. The biological model holds that addiction, whether to alcohol or any other drug, is due primarily to a person's biochemistry, metabolism, and genetic predisposition. Twin and other family studies suggest that alcoholism may sometimes involve an inherited vulnerability (Cloninger, 1990; Goodwin et al., 1994; Schuckit & Smith, 1996). For alcoholics who begin heavy drinking in adulthood, genetic factors do not seem to be involved. But there may be a heritable component in the kind of alcoholism that begins in adolescence and is linked to impulsivity, antisocial behavior, and violent criminality (Bohman et al., 1987; McGue, Pickens, & Svikis, 1992).

Genes could contribute to alcoholism by contributing to traits or temperaments that predispose a person to become alcoholic. Or they may affect biochemical processes in the brain that make some people more susceptible to alcohol or cause them to respond to it differently than others do (Reich et al., 1998; Schuckit & Smith, 1996). For example, genes may affect the functioning of key neurotransmitters, such as dopamine, which researchers think is somehow related to addiction and other disorders (Noble et al., 1991). Genes may also affect how much a person needs to drink before feeling any effect. In an ongoing longitudinal study of 450 young men (half of whom had alcoholic fathers and half of whom did not), the men who at age 20 had to drink more than others to feel any reaction were at increased risk of becoming alcoholic within the decade. This was true regardless of their current drinking habits or family history (Schuckit, 1998; Schuckit & Smith, 1996).

Geneticists are trying to identify the key genes that might be involved in alcoholism. Virtually all agree that there is more than one, and that they interact in complex ways. As with so many other disorders, however, tracking down such genes has been difficult. When one research team finds a likely candidate (e.g., Noble, 1998; Noble et al., 1991), their work is promptly contradicted by others (e.g., Baron, 1993; Edenberg et al., 1998).

Moreover, although genes may influence alcoholism, it is also possible that alcoholism results, basically, from alcohol! Heavy drinking alters brain function, reduces the level of painkilling endorphins, produces nerve damage, shrinks the cerebral cortex, and damages the liver. In the view of some researchers, these changes then create biological dependence, an inability to metabolize alcohol, and psychological problems.

Learning, Culture, and Addiction

The biological model, popular though it is, has been challenged by another approach. According to the *learning model*, drug addiction is neither a sin nor a disease but "a central activity of the individual's way of life" that depends on learning and culture (Fingarette, 1988). Four arguments support this view:

1 *Addiction patterns vary according to cultural practices and the social environment.* Alcoholism is much more likely to occur in societies that forbid children to drink but condone drunkenness in adults (as in Ireland) than in societies that teach children how to drink responsibly and moderately but condemn adult drunkenness (as in Italy, Greece, and France). In cultures with low rates of alcoholism (except for those committed to a religious rule that forbids use of all psychoactive drugs), adults demonstrate correct drinking habits to their children, gradually introducing them to alcohol in safe family settings. Alcohol is not used as a rite of passage into adulthood, nor is it associated with masculinity and power (Peele & Brodsky, 1991; Vaillant, 1983). Abstainers are not sneered at and drunkenness is not considered charming, comical, or manly; it is considered stupid or obnoxious.

Within a particular country, addiction rates can rise or fall rapidly in response to cultural changes. In colonial America, the average person actually drank two to three times the amount of liquor consumed today, yet alcoholism was not the serious social problem it is now. Drinking was a universally accepted social activity; families drank and ate together. Alcohol was believed to produce pleasant feelings and relaxation. The Puritan minister Cotton Mather even called liquor "the good creature of God" (Critchlow, 1986). Then, between 1790 and 1830, when the American frontier was expanding, drinking came to symbolize masculine independence and toughness. The saloon became the place for drinking away from home, and, as the learning model would predict, alcoholism rates shot up.

Substance abuse and addiction problems increase not only when people fail to learn how to take drugs in moderation, but also when they move from their own culture of origin into another that has different drinking rules (Westermeyer, 1995). For example, in most Latino cultures, such as those of Mexico and Puerto Rico,

In cultures in which people drink moderately with meals and children learn the rules of social drinking from their families, alcoholism rates are much lower than in cultures in which drinking occurs mainly in bars, in binges, or in privacy.

For over a century, the temperance movement in the United States promoted total abstinence from alcoholic beverages as a way of reducing addiction and crime. For a brief period (1920–1933), Prohibition was the law of the land. But Prohibition was actually associated with *increased* rates of alcoholism and heavy drinking.

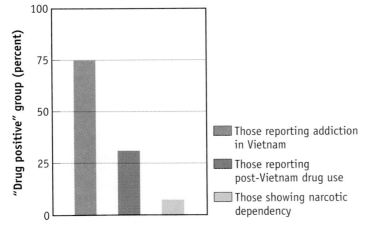

Those reporting addiction in Vietnam

Those reporting post-Vietnam drug use

Those showing narcotic dependency

FIGURE 16.5

DRUGS AND VIETNAM VETERANS: FAILURE OF THE ADDICTION PREDICTION

U.S. soldiers who tested "drug positive" when they were in Vietnam showed a dramatic drop in drug use when they returned to civilian life—contrary to what the disease model of addiction would predict (Robins, Davis, & Goodwin, 1974).

drinking and drunkenness are considered male activities. Thus, Latina women tend to drink little, if at all, and they have few drinking problems—until they move into an Anglo environment, when their rates of alcoholism rise (Canino, 1994).

2 *Policies of total abstinence tend to increase rates of addiction rather than reduce them.* In the United States, the temperance movement of the early twentieth century held that drinking inevitably leads to drunkenness, and drunkenness to crime. The solution it won for the Prohibition years (1920 to 1933) was national abstinence. But this victory backfired: As the learning model would predict, Prohibition actually *increased* rates of alcoholism. Because people were denied the opportunity to learn to drink moderately, they drank excessively when given the chance (McCord, 1989). Something similar happened in Canada with the Inuit and other native groups, who were prohibited from drinking alcohol—and would therefore drink as much as they could when they could get hold of it. In 1951, they were permitted to drink only in licensed bars and would therefore drink as much as they could while in a bar. Both policies were guaranteed to create drunkenness. (The 1951 law was repealed in 1960.)

3 *Not all addicts have withdrawal symptoms when they stop taking a drug.* When heavy users of a drug stop taking it, they often suffer such unpleasant symptoms as nausea, abdominal cramps, muscle spasms, depression, and sleep problems, depending on the drug. But these symptoms are far from universal. During the Vietnam War, nearly 30 percent of American soldiers were taking heroin in doses far stronger than those available on the streets of U.S. cities. These men believed themselves to be addicted, and experts predicted a drug-withdrawal disaster among the returning veterans. It never materialized; over 90 percent of the men simply gave up the drug, without significant withdrawal pain, when they came home to new circumstances (see Figure 16.5). Similarly, most people who are addicted to cigarettes, tranquilizers, or painkillers are able to stop taking these drugs without outside help and with-out severe withdrawal symptoms (Prochaska, Norcross, & DiClemente, 1994).

4 *Addiction does not depend on properties of the drug alone, but also on the reason for taking it.* Addicts use drugs to escape from the real world, but people living with chronic pain use some of the same drugs, including morphine and other opiates, in order to function in the real world—and they do not become addicted (Portenoy, 1994). In a study of 100 hospital patients who had been given strong doses of narcotics for postoperative pain, 99 had no withdrawal symptoms upon leaving the hospital (Zinberg, 1974). And of 10,000 burn patients who received narcotics as part of their hospital care, not one became an addict (Perry & Heidrich, 1982).

To understand why people abuse drugs, therefore, the learning model focuses on the reasons for taking them. In the case of alcohol, most people drink simply to be sociable, to conform to the group they are with, or to relax when they are stressed. But those who drink in order to disguise or suppress anxiety, depression, or fear have significantly more drinking problems than sociable drinkers do (Cooper et al., 1995). College students who feel uninvolved with their studies or their school are more likely to drink excessively in binges, with the intention of getting drunk (Flacks & Thomas, 1998). And although marijuana is relatively safe and is not chemically addictive at moderate doses (see Chapter 5), adolescents who are *already* troubled and antisocial quickly become dependent on marijuana after starting to use it and do show withdrawal symptoms when they try to stop (Crowley et al., 1998). In all of these

GET ➔ INVOLVED

TEST YOUR MOTIVES FOR DRINKING

If you drink, why? Check all of the motives that apply to you:

_____ to relax

_____ to be sociable

_____ to escape from worries, stress

_____ to handle feelings of depression

_____ to enhance a good meal

_____ to get drunk and lose control

_____ to conform to peer pressure

_____ to rebel against authority

_____ to relieve boredom

_____ to have an excuse to express anger

_____ other (specify)

Do your reasons for drinking promote abuse or responsible use? How do you respond physically to alcohol? What have you learned about drinking from your family, your friends, and cultural messages? What do your answers tell you about your own vulnerability to addiction?

cases, the reason for abusing the drug lies in the individual's motives, not in the chemical properties of the drug itself.

Debating the Causes of Addiction

The biological and learning models both contribute to our understanding of drug abuse and addiction. Yet among many researchers and public-health professionals these views are quite polarized (see Table 16.3 on the next page). What we have here is a case of either–or thinking on a national scale, with passions running high because of the implications for the treatment of alcoholics and other addicts.

The argument is most heated in the debate over whether former alcoholics can learn to drink moderately without becoming intoxicated and dependent again on alcohol. Those who advocate the disease model say there is no such thing as a "former" alcoholic; once an addict has even a single drink, he or she will not be able to stop. In this view, problem drinkers who learn to cut back to social-drinking levels were never true alcoholics in the first place. Those who champion the learning model, on the other hand, argue that once a person no longer *needs* to become drunk, he or she can learn to drink socially and in moderation (Marlatt, 1996). Longitudinal studies find that many people do shift from problem drinking to moderate drinking as they mature; if they change from a hard-drinking environment to one that supports moderation; if they no longer have a psychological need to drink heavily; and if they learn better ways of coping with problems than by getting smashed (Marlatt et al., 1993; Vaillant, 1983).

How can we assess these two positions critically? Can we locate a common ground between them? Because alcoholism and problem drinking occur for many reasons, neither model offers the only solution. Many alcoholics cannot learn to drink moderately,

AVOID EMOTIONAL REASONING
Many people feel passionately that controlled drinking for alcoholics is impossible. How can we move beyond emotional reasoning on this important issue?

TABLE 16.3   Biological and Learning Models of Addiction Contrasted

The biological and learning models of addiction differ in how they explain drug abuse and the solutions they propose:

The Biological Model	The Learning Model
Addiction is genetic, biological.	Addiction is a way of coping.
Once an addict, always an addict.	A person can grow beyond the need for alcohol or other drugs.
An addict must abstain from the drug forever.	Most problem drinkers can learn to drink in moderation.
A person is either addicted or not.	The degree of addiction will vary, depending on the situation.
The solution is medical treatment and membership in groups that reinforce one's permanent identity as a recovering addict.	The solution involves learning new coping skills and changing one's environment.
An addict needs the same treatment and group support forever.	Treatment lasts only until the person no longer abuses the drug.

Source: Adapted from Peele & Brodsky, 1991.

especially if they have had drinking problems for many years (Vaillant, 1995). On the other hand, although total-abstinence groups like Alcoholics Anonymous have saved lives, they do not work for everyone. According to its own surveys and those done independently, one-third to one-half of all people who join AA drop out. Many of these dropouts benefit from programs such as Rational Recovery, Moderation Management, and DrinkWise, which teach people how to drink moderately and keep their drinking under control (Marlatt, 1996; Peele & Brodsky, 1991; Rosenberg, 1993).

So instead of asking, "Can addicts and problem drinkers learn to drink moderately?" we should ask, "What are the factors that make it likely or unlikely that someone can learn to control problem drinking?" Alcoholics who are most likely to become controlled drinkers have a history of less severe dependence on the drug; they lead more stable lives (they don't have criminal records, they have jobs and families); and they believe that controlled drinking is possible (Rosenberg, 1993). Alcoholics who believe that one drink will set them off—those who accept the alcoholics' creed, "first drink, then drunk"—are in fact more likely to behave that way. Ironically, then, the course that alcoholism takes may reflect, in part, a person's belief in the disease model or the learning model.

As you can see, abuse and addiction reflect an interaction of physiology and psychology, person and culture. To summarize, problems with drugs are most likely to occur under these conditions:

■ When a person has a physiological vulnerability to a drug;

■ When a person believes he or she has no control over the drug;

■ When laws or customs encourage or teach people to take a drug in binges, and moderate use is neither encouraged nor taught;

■ When a person comes to rely on a drug as a way of coping with problems, suppressing anger or fear, or relieving pain;

■ When members of a person's peer group drink heavily or use other drugs excessively.

QUICK Q U I Z

If you are addicted to passing exams, try these questions:

1. What is the most reasonable conclusion about the role of genes in alcoholism? (a) Without a key gene, a person cannot become alcoholic; (b) the presence of a key gene will almost always cause a person to become alcoholic; (c) genes may work in combination to increase a person's vulnerability to some kinds of alcoholism.

2. Which cultural practice is associated with *low* rates of alcoholism? (a) gradual introduction to drinking in family settings, (b) infrequent but binge drinking, (c) drinking as a rite of passage into adulthood, (d) policies of prohibition

3. In a 1997 national survey, 52 percent of American college students said they drink to get drunk and 41.5 percent said they usually binge when drinking. To reduce this problem, some schools and fraternities are instituting "zero tolerance" programs—permitting no alcohol at all. According to the research described in this section, are such policies likely to work? Why or why not?

4. Heroin, cocaine, barbiturates, methadone, and tranquilizers were all, at first, thought to be nonaddictive. But in each case some people became addicted, and abuse of the drug became a problem. What are some reasons for the failure to find a completely nonaddictive mood-altering drug?

Answers:

1. c 2. a 3. Abstinence policies are not likely to work unless they address the *reasons* that students binge; change the student culture that fosters binge drinking; and teach students how to drink moderately. 4. Perhaps some people are biologically disposed to become addicted to any mind-altering drug. Perhaps the psychological need for addiction exists in the individual and not in the chemical properties of the drug. Perhaps the chemistry of the drug is less important than the cultural practices that encourage drug abuse among some groups. If that is so, we will never find a recreational drug that is nonaddictive for everyone.

WHAT'S AHEAD

● **What's the difference between schizophrenia and a "split personality"?**

● **Why do most researchers consider schizophrenia a brain disorder?**

● **Could schizophrenia begin in the womb?**

SCHIZOPHRENIA

To be schizophrenic is best summed up in a repeating dream that I have had since childhood. In this dream I am lying on a beautiful sunlit beach but my body is in pieces. . . . I realize that the tide is coming in and that I am unable to gather the parts of my dismembered body together to run away. The tide gets closer and just when I am on the point of drowning I wake up screaming in panic. This to me is what schizophrenia feels like; being fragmented in one's personality and constantly afraid that the tide of illness will completely cover me. (Quoted in Rollin, 1980)

In 1911, Swiss psychiatrist Eugen Bleuler coined the term **schizophrenia** to describe cases in which the personality loses its unity. People with schizophrenia do not have a "split" or "multiple personality," however. As the preceding quotation illustrates, schizophrenia is a fragmented condition in which words are split from meaning, actions from motives, perceptions from reality. It is an example of a **psychosis**, a mental condition that involves distorted perceptions of reality and an inability to function in most aspects of life.

schizophrenia A psychotic disorder or group of disorders marked by positive symptoms (e.g., delusions, hallucinations, disorganized and incoherent speech, and inappropriate behavior) and negative symptoms (e.g., emotional flatness and loss of motivation).

psychosis An extreme mental disturbance involving distorted perceptions and irrational behavior; it may have psychological or organic causes. (Plural: *psychoses*.)

Symptoms of Schizophrenia

If depression is the common cold of psychological disorder, said psychiatrist Donald Klein (1980), schizophrenia is its cancer: elusive, complicated, and varying in form. In general, schizophrenia produces two categories of symptoms. *Active* or *positive symptoms* involve an exaggeration or distortion of normal thinking processes and behavior. These symptoms are called "positive" because they are *additions* to normal behavior; healthy people do not have delusions that their brains are receiving Martian signals. In contrast, *negative symptoms* involve the *loss* or absence of normal traits and abilities, such as the ability to speak fluently and feel warm emotions.

The most common active symptoms include the following:

A common hallmark of schizophrenia is delusional thinking. Margaret Mary Ray suffered from the delusion that talk-show host David Letterman was in love with her.

1 *Bizarre delusions* (false beliefs), such as the belief that dogs are extraterrestrials disguised as pets. Some people with schizophrenia have paranoid delusions, taking innocent events—a stranger's cough, a helicopter overhead—as evidence that the world is plotting against them. Some have delusions of identity, believing that they are Moses, Jesus, Joan of Arc, or some other famous person. Some, like Margaret Mary Ray, whose story opened this chapter, have delusions that a celebrity loves them.

2 *Hallucinations and heightened sensory awareness.* Schizophrenic hallucinations, which feel intensely real to the sufferer, usually take the form of voices speaking odd, garbled words; a running conversation in the head; or two or more voices conversing with each other. But some hallucinations are tactile (e.g., feeling insects crawling over the body) or visual (e.g., seeing a famous actress in the mirror). People with schizophrenia also have difficulty in filtering out sensory stimulation and distracting sounds, making it difficult and sometimes impossible for them to concentrate.

3 *Disorganized, incoherent speech* consisting of an illogical jumble of ideas and symbols, linked by meaningless rhyming words or by remote associations called *word salads*. A patient of Bleuler's wrote, "Olive oil is an Arabian liquor-sauce which the Afghans, Moors and Moslems use in ostrich farming. The Indian plantain tree is the whiskey of the Parsees and Arabs. Barley, rice and sugar cane called artichoke, grow remarkably well in India. The Brahmins live as castes in Baluchistan. The Circassians occupy Manchuria and China. China is the Eldorado of the Pawnees" (Bleuler, 1911/1950).

4 *Grossly disorganized and inappropriate behavior* that may range from childlike silliness to unpredictable and violent agitation. The person may wear three overcoats and gloves on a hot day, start collecting garbage, or hoard scraps of food. Some people with schizophrenia completely withdraw into a private world, sitting for hours without moving, a condition called *catatonic stupor*. In *Diary of a Schizophrenic Girl*, Marguerite Sechehaye wrote, "A wall of brass separates me from everybody and everything. In the midst of desolation, in indescribable distress, in absolute solitude, I am terrifyingly alone."

In contrast to these positive symptoms, negative symptoms include loss of motivation; poverty of speech (making only brief, empty replies in conversation, because of diminished thought rather than an unwillingness to speak); and, most notably, emotional flatness—unresponsive facial expressions, poor eye contact, and diminished emotionality. These negative symptoms may appear months before active ones do, and they often persist when the active symptoms are in remission.

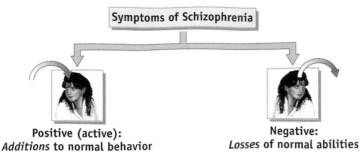

Symptoms of Schizophrenia

Positive (active):
Additions to normal behavior

Bizarre delusions
Hallucinations
Incoherent speech
(e.g., "word salads")
Inappropriate/
disorganized behavior

Negative:
Losses of normal abilities

Loss of motivation
Emotional flatness
Impoverished speech
(e.g., brief, empty replies)
Social withdrawal

Cases of schizophrenia vary enormously in severity, duration, and likelihood of recovery. In some individuals, the symptoms appear abruptly, often in response to a stressful situation; in such cases, the prognosis for recovery is relatively good. In other individuals, the onset is more gradual. Negative symptoms slowly emerge, and friends and family report a slow change in personality. The person may stop working or bathing, become isolated and withdrawn, and start behaving in peculiar ways. In these cases, the outlook is less predictable. The more breakdowns and relapses the individual has had, the poorer the chances for complete recovery (Eaton et al., 1992a, 1992b). Yet many people suffering from this illness learn to control the symptoms, while working and having good family relationships (Harding, Zubin, & Strauss, 1992).

The mystery of schizophrenia is that we could go on listing symptoms and variations all day and never finish. Some people with schizophrenia are almost completely impaired in all spheres; others do extremely well in certain areas. Still others have normal moments of lucidity in otherwise withdrawn lives. One adolescent crouched in a

When people with schizophrenia are asked to draw pictures, their drawings are often distorted, lack color, include words, and reveal flat emotion. One patient was asked to copy a picture of flowers from a magazine (above). The initial result is shown below on the left. The drawing in the center shows improvement, and the drawing on the right shows how much the patient progressed after several months of treatment.

rigid catatonic posture in front of a television for the month of October; later, he was able to report on all the highlights of the World Series he had seen. A middle-aged man, hospitalized for 20 years, believing he was a prophet of God and that monsters were coming out of the walls, was able to interrupt his ranting to play a good game of chess (Wender & Klein, 1981).

Unraveling the Mysteries of Schizophrenia

Any disorder that has so many variations and symptoms will pose many problems for diagnosis and explanation. One psychologist concluded that the concept of schizophrenia is "almost hopelessly in tatters" (Carson, 1989), and some would like to drop the label entirely (Sarbin, 1992). Others argue that the label is worth keeping because the same core signs of schizophrenia appear in cultures around the world: hallucinations, bizarre delusions, inappropriate behavior, and disorders of thought and sensation.

Biological Findings. Using brain-imaging techniques, longitudinal studies, and dissections of brains, many researchers are trying to pinpoint the biological factors that might be causes of schizophrenia. They are searching for genetic factors, abnormalities in the brain and neurotransmitters, and abnormalities in prenatal development:

1 *Genetic predispositions.* A person has a considerably greater risk of developing schizophrenia if an identical twin develops the disorder, and this is true even if the person is reared apart from the affected sibling (Gottesman, 1991, 1994). Moreover, children with one schizophrenic parent have a lifetime risk of 12 percent, and children with two schizophrenic parents have a lifetime risk of 35–46 percent, compared to a risk in the general population of only 1–2 percent (Goldstein, 1987). (See Figure 16.6.)

These and similar findings indicate the existence of a genetic contribution to the disorder, and researchers all over the world are trying to track down the genes that might be involved in specific symptoms such as hallucinations and sensitivity to sounds (Blouin et al., 1998; Leonard et al., 1998). However, no single gene has been found— or is likely to be found, many researchers believe, given all the different forms that schizophrenia takes (Levinson et al., 1998). In any case, genes alone cannot predict who will develop the disorder. Even among identical twins, when one develops it, the chances that the other will do so are slightly less than half (Torrey et al., 1994). And remember that even if 12 percent of all children with one schizophrenic parent develop the disorder, that means that 88 percent of them do not.

FIGURE 16.6
GENETIC VULNERABILITY TO SCHIZOPHRENIA

This graph, based on combined data from 40 European twin and adoption studies conducted over seven dacades, shows that the closer the genetic relationship to a person with schizophrenia, the higher the risk of developing the disorder. (Based on Gottesman, 1991).

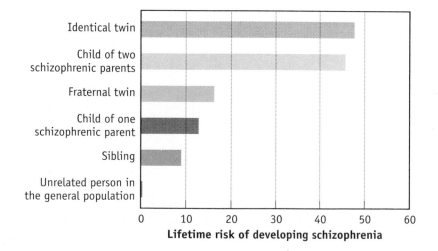

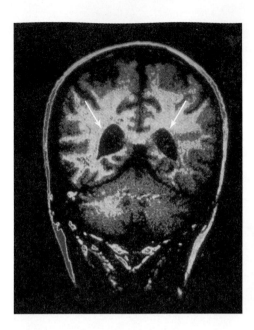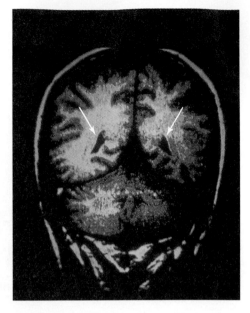

FIGURE 16.7

SCHIZOPHRENIA AND THE BRAIN

MRI scans show that a person with schizophrenia (left) is more likely than a healthy person (right) to have enlarged ventricles, or spaces, in the brain (see arrows) (Andreasen et al., 1994).

2 *Structural brain abnormalities.* Some individuals with schizophrenia show signs of cerebral damage: decreased brain weight, a decrease in the volume of the temporal lobe or limbic regions, reduced numbers of neurons in the prefrontal cortex, or enlargement of the *ventricles*, the spaces in the brain filled with cerebrospinal fluid (see Figure 16.7) (Akbarian et al., 1996; Heinrichs, 1993; Zorrilla et al., 1997). Schizophrenics are also more likely than healthy individuals to have abnormalities in the thalamus, the traffic-control center that filters sensations and focuses attention (Andreasen et al., 1994; Gur et al., 1998).

A recently discovered problem in brain research, however, is that the antipsychotic medications that many schizophrenics take *can affect the brain.* Thus a brain difference that appears to be a cause of schizophrenia might instead be a result of medication. In one study, patients who had never taken medication did not differ from healthy control subjects except in the size of the thalamus (Gur et al., 1998).

3 *Neurotransmitter abnormalities.* Abnormalities in several neurotransmitters, including serotonin, glutamate, and most notably dopamine, have been associated with schizophrenia. For example, many schizophrenics have high levels of activity in brain areas served by dopamine, and a particular kind of dopamine receptor is more common in their brains than in those of healthy people (Seeman et al., 1993; Wong et al., 1986). However, similar neurotransmitter abnormalities are also found in many other mental disorders, such as depression and alcoholism, making it difficult to know whether these abnormalities play a specific role in schizophrenia (Spoont, 1992).

4 *Prenatal abnormalities.* Damage to the fetal brain increases the likelihood of schizophrenia (and, again, of other mental disorders). In some cases, the damage may occur because of malnutrition: Babies conceived during times of famine have twice the schizophrenia rate as babies whose mothers ate normal diets during pregnancy (Susser et al., 1996). Another culprit may be an infectious virus during prenatal development (Hooper, 1999; Torrey et al., 1994). There is a significant association between a mother's exposure to the influenza virus during the second trimester of pregnancy, when the fetal brain is forming crucial connections, and the onset of schizophrenia in the child 20 to 30 years later (Bracha et al., 1991; Mednick, Huttunen, & Machón, 1994).

The Vulnerability-Stress Approach. Although the evidence for brain abnormalities in schizophrenia is compelling, many researchers believe that the onset and course of this disorder—like those of depression, antisocial personality disorder, and addiction—are best explained by an interactive theory (Gottesman, 1991). Proponents of the *vulnerability-stress model* observe that genes or brain damage alone will not inevitably produce schizophrenia, and a vulnerable person who lives in a good environment may never show full-fledged signs of the disorder.

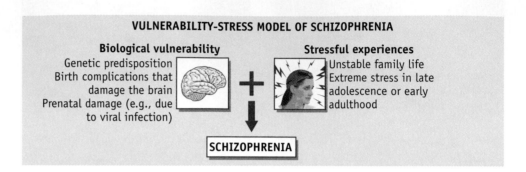

For many years, the Copenhagen High-Risk Project has followed 207 children at risk for schizophrenia (because they had a schizophrenic parent) and a control group of 104 low-risk children. The project has identified several factors that, *in combination*, increase the likelihood of schizophrenia: the existence of schizophrenia in the family; physical trauma during childbirth that might damage the brain; exposure to the flu virus or other prenatal trauma during the second trimester of gestation; and unstable, stressful environments (Mednick, Parnas, & Schulsinger, 1987; Olin & Mednick, 1996).

The combination of individual vulnerabilities and environmental stresses shows how several factors may combine to produce any given case of schizophrenia. To make matters even more complicated, different factors may predominate in different kinds of schizophrenia; this may explain why some schizophrenics recover and others do not. For example, schizophrenia caused primarily by prenatal exposure to the flu may be different from the kind caused primarily by genetic predispositions. The riddle of schizophrenia is likely to be several riddles, each remaining to be solved.

QUICK QUIZ

The following quiz is not a hallucination.

1. A patient with schizophrenia hears voices in her head when no one is around. Is this an example of a positive symptom or a negative one?

2. Many researchers suspect that high levels of the neurotransmitter _____ contribute to schizophrenia.

3. *True or false:* Most people with schizophrenia have a schizophrenic parent.

Answers:

1. positive 2. dopamine 3. false

MENTAL DISORDER AND PERSONAL RESPONSIBILITY

We have come to the end of a long walk along the spectrum of psychological problems—from those that are normal conditions of life, such as occasional anxiety or even "caffeine-induced sleep disorder," to mental disorders that can be severely disabling, such as schizophrenia.

One of the great debates generated by all diagnoses of mental disorder concerns the question of personal responsibility. In law and in everyday life, many people reach for a psychological diagnosis to exonerate themselves of responsibility for their actions. Romance writer Janet Dailey, found guilty of plagiarizing whole passages from another writer, said she was suffering from "a psychological problem that I never even suspected I had." Lyle and Erik Menendez, convicted of murdering their wealthy parents, claimed they suffered from a form of posttraumatic stress disorder resulting from years of abuse. Growing numbers of college students and graduate students are claiming to suffer from attention deficit/hyperactivity disorder so that they may be given more time for exams and papers (Ranseen, 1998).

Of course, many people *do* suffer from mental impairments that make it difficult or even impossible for them to focus their attention or control their behavior. Determining when a person has such an impairment and when he or she is claiming an unjustified excuse becomes especially important in cases of criminal behavior. In the United States and Canada, in order to prove that a defendant had diminished responsibility for a crime, the defense must show clear and convincing evidence that the defendant had a severe mental condition and not just a personality defect or a bad day at work. Few lawyers take advantage of the insanity defense; in fact, it is used in only 0.9 percent of all U.S. felony cases, and it succeeds in only about a quarter of those cases (Silver, Cirincione, & Steadman, 1994). Nonetheless, some defense attorneys, aided by the testimony of psychiatrists and psychologists, keep trying to expand the legal grounds for diminished responsibility, searching for mental disorders that might lessen the severity of the sentence a guilty person receives.

When thinking about the relationship of mental disorder to personal responsibility, we face a dilemma. The law recognizes, rightly, that people who are mentally incompetent, delusional, or disturbed should not be judged by the same standards as mentally healthy individuals. At the same time, society has an obligation to protect its citizens from harm and to reject easy excuses for violations of the law. To balance these two positions, we need to find ways to ensure that people who commit crimes or behave reprehensibly face the consequences of their behavior; and also to ensure that people who are suffering from psychological problems have the compassionate support of society in their search for help. After all, psychological problems of one kind or another are problems that all of us will have at some time in our lives.

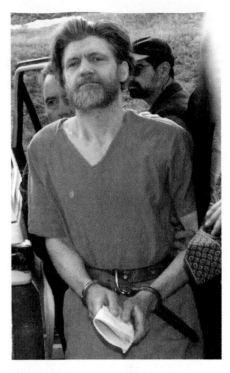

Ted Kaczynski (the "Unabomber") killed three people and injured at least 22 in his campaign against technology. He pleaded guilty in order to avoid a trial, because his lawyers were planning to argue that he was ill with schizophrenia. Kaczynski chose life in prison rather than the mitigating defense of insanity. Was he insane or no different from others who have committed crimes on behalf of unpopular political causes? Even if he does have a mental disorder, is he responsible for his actions?

TAKING PSYCHOLOGY WITH YOU

WHEN A FRIEND IS SUICIDAL

Suicide can be frightening to those who find themselves fantasizing about it, and it is devastating to the family and friends of those who go through with it. In North America, most people who commit suicide are over the age of 45, but suicide rates are rapidly increasing among young people. Suicide has become a leading cause of death for teenagers and college students (Garland & Zigler, 1994; *New York Times*, March 20, 1998).

Although many people believe that women are more likely than men to attempt suicide, whereas men are more likely to succeed, this gender difference is more apparent than real and depends on culture and circumstances. In Finland, for example, more males than females attempt suicide; and in Canada and the United States, men in prison have high rates of attempted suicide (Canetto & Sakinofsky, 1998). Moreover, men's efforts to commit suicide are not always as obvious as those of women: Some men provoke confrontations with the police, hoping to be shot; others try to destroy themselves with drugs.

Suicidal people believe that life is unendurable. This belief may be rational in the case of people who are terminally ill and in pain, but more often it reflects the distorted thinking of someone suffering from depression. Often, suicidal individuals do not really want to die; they just want to escape intolerable conditions or feelings of despair (Baumeister, 1990).

Friends and family members can help prevent a suicide by becoming informed and by recognizing the danger signs:

■ **Take all suicide threats seriously.** Some people assume they can't do anything about it when a friend talks about committing suicide. "He'll just do it at another place, another time," they think. In fact, most suicides occur during an acute crisis. Once the person gets through the crisis, the desire to die fades. One researcher tracked down 515 people who had attempted suicide by jumping off the Golden Gate Bridge many years earlier. Less than 5 percent had actually committed suicide in the subsequent decades (Seiden, 1978).

Some people believe that if a friend is talking about suicide, he or she won't really do it. This belief is also false. Few people commit suicide without signaling their intentions. Most are ambivalent: "I want to kill myself, but I don't want to be dead—at least not forever." Most suicidal people want relief from the terrible pain of feeling that nobody cares, that life is not worth living. Getting these thoughts and fears out in the open is an important first step.

■ **Know the danger signs.** A depressed person is at risk of trying to commit suicide if he or she has tried to do it before; has become withdrawn and listless; has a history of depression; reveals specific plans for carrying out the suicide or gives away cherished possessions; expresses no concern about religious prohibitions or the impact on family members; and has access to a lethal method, such as a gun (Garland & Zigler, 1994).

■ **Take constructive action.** If you believe a friend is in danger of suicide, do not be afraid to ask, "Are you thinking of suicide?" This question does not "put the idea" in anyone's mind. If your friend is contemplating the action, he or she will probably be relieved to talk about it, and you will know that it is time to get help. Let your friend talk without argument or disapproval. Don't try to talk your friend out of it by debating whether suicide is right or wrong, and don't put on phony cheerfulness. If your friend's words or actions scare you, say so. By listening nonjudgmentally, you are showing that you care. By allowing your friend to unburden his or her grief, you help the person get through the immediate crisis.

Most of all, do not leave your friend alone. If necessary, get the person to a counselor, health professional, or emergency room of a hospital; or call a local suicide hot line. Don't worry about doing the wrong thing. In an emergency, the worst thing you can do is nothing at all.

SUMMARY

DILEMMAS OF DIAGNOSIS

1. The prevalence of a behavior does not indicate whether it is disordered. When defining *mental disorder*, mental-health professionals emphasize the violation of cultural standards, whether the behavior is maladaptive for the individual or society, and the emotional suffering caused by the behavior.

2. *The Diagnostic and Statistical Manual of Mental Disorders (DSM)*, which is used throughout the world, is designed to provide objective criteria and categories for diagnosing mental disorders. Critics argue that the diagnosis of mental disorders is inherently a subjective process that can never be entirely objective. They believe the DSM fosters overdiagnosis, overlooks the influence of diagnostic labels on clients and therapists, confuses serious disorders with normal problems, and creates an illusion of objectivity. Supporters of the DSM believe that when the DSM criteria are used correctly, reliability in diagnosis improves; and that although some diagnoses are indeed subjective and culture-specific, not all diagnoses reflect society's biases.

ANXIETY DISORDERS

3. *Generalized anxiety disorder* involves continuous, chronic anxiety, with signs of nervousness, worry, and irritability. When anxiety results from exposure to uncontrollable or unpredictable danger, it can lead to *posttraumatic stress disorder*, which involves mentally reliving the trauma, "psychic numbing," and increased physiological arousal. *Panic disorder* involves sudden, intense attacks of profound fear, with feelings of impending doom. Panic attacks are common in the aftermath of stress or frightening experiences; those who go on to develop a disorder tend to interpret the attacks as a sign of impending disaster.

4. *Phobias* are unrealistic fears of specific situations, activities, or things. *Agoraphobia*, the fear of being away from a safe place or person, is the most disabling phobia. It often begins with a panic attack, which the person tries to avoid in the future by staying close to "safe" places, and hence becomes a "fear of fear."

5. *Obsessive-compulsive disorder* (OCD) involves recurrent, unwished-for thoughts or images (obsessions) and repetitive, ritualized behaviors (compulsions) that a person feels unable to control. Parts of the brain having to do with fear and response to threat are more active than normal in people with OCD.

MOOD DISORDERS

6. Symptoms of *major depression* include distorted thinking patterns, low self-esteem, physical ailments such as fatigue and loss of appetite, and prolonged grief and despair. In *bipolar disorder*, a person experiences episodes of both depression and *mania* (excessive euphoria). Women are more likely than men to be treated for major depression, but psychologists disagree on whether the difference is real or due to misdiagnosis of men's symptoms.

7. *Biological* explanations of depression emphasize low levels of the neurotransmitters serotonin and norepinephrine, and the role of genetic predispositions. *Social* explanations emphasize the circumstances of people's lives, such as work and family life, motherhood, and experiences with violence. *Attachment* theories argue that depression results from broken or conflicted relationships or a history of insecure attachment. *Cognitive* explanations attribute depression to particular attributions (the tendency to view the origin of one's unhappiness as internal, stable, and uncontrollable), a *pessimistic explanatory style*, and habits of brooding or rumination. *Vulnerability-stress models* look at interactions between individual vulnerabilities (genetic dispositions, cognitive habits, and personality traits) and environmental stress.

PERSONALITY DISORDERS

8. *Personality disorders* are characterized by rigid, self-destructive traits that cause distress or an inability to get along with others. They include *paranoid, narcissistic*, and *antisocial personality disorders*.

9. A person with antisocial personality disorder lacks empathy and remorse, is unafraid of punishment, is impulsive, and lacks self-control. The disorder may involve a neurological defect that is genetic or is caused by damage to the brain and central nervous system at birth or during childhood, parental rejection and abuse, or a combination of biological vulnerability and stressful, violent environments. Not all persons with APD are violent—some are charming but heartless con artists—and many people who are violent do not have APD.

DISSOCIATIVE DISORDERS

10. *Dissociative disorders* involve a split in consciousness or identity. They include *amnesia, fugue*, and *dissociative identity disorder (multiple personality disorder*, or MPD). In MPD, two or more distinct personalities and identities appear to exist within one person. Considerable controversy surrounds the validity and nature of MPD. Some clinicians think it is common, often goes undiagnosed, and originates in childhood trauma. Others hold a *sociocognitive* explanation, arguing that most cases are manufactured in unwitting collusion between therapists who believe in the disorder and suggestible patients who find it a plausible explanation for their problems.

DRUG ABUSE AND ADDICTION

11. The effects of drugs depend on whether they are used moderately or are abused. Signs of *substance abuse* include impaired ability to work or get along with others, use of the drug in hazardous situations, recurrent arrests for drug use, and conflicts with others caused by drug use.

12. According to the *biological* or *disease model* of addiction, some people have a biological vulnerability to alcoholism and other addictions, due to a genetic factor that affects their metabolism, biochemistry, or personality traits. Advocates of the *learning model* of addiction point out that addiction patterns vary according to culture, learning, and accepted practice; that many people

can stop taking drugs without experiencing withdrawal symptoms; that drug abuse depends on the reasons for taking a drug; and that abuse increases when people are not taught moderate use.

13. Although the biological and learning models are polarized on many issues, the evidence suggests that addiction and abuse result from an interaction between biological and psychological vulnerability and a person's culture, learning history, and situation.

SCHIZOPHRENIA

14. *Schizophrenia* is a psychotic disorder involving *positive* or *active symptoms* (including delusions, hallucinations, disorganized speech called *word salads*, and inappropriate behavior, including *catatonic stupor*) and *negative symptoms* (including loss of motivation, poverty of speech, and emotional flatness). Cases of schizophrenia vary in severity, duration, and prognosis.

15. Causes of schizophrenia may involve genetic predispositions; structural brain abnormalities; neurotransmitter abnormalities; abnormalities of prenatal development resulting from maternal malnutrition, viral infection, or other trauma during the second trimester; and, in the *vulnerability-stress model*, interactions between such factors and a person's environment during childhood or young adulthood.

MENTAL DISORDER AND PERSONAL RESPONSIBILITY

16. The diagnosis of mental disorder raises important questions of personal responsibility in the law and in everyday life. Psychologists and others struggle to decide when a mental disorder is merely an excuse for bad behavior, and when it truly does reduce people's responsibility for actions they cannot control.

KEY TERMS

insanity 576

mental disorder 577

Diagnostic and Statistical Manual of Mental Disorders (DSM) 577

generalized anxiety disorder 582

posttraumatic stress disorder (PTSD) 582

panic disorder (panic attack) 582

phobia 583

social phobia 584

agoraphobia 584

obsessive-compulsive disorder (OCD) 584

major depression 586

mania 586

bipolar disorder 587

learned helplessness 589

vulnerability-stress model of depression 589

personality disorders 591

paranoid personality disorder 591

narcissistic personality disorder 591

antisocial personality disorder (APD) 592

vulnerability-stress model of APD 593

dissociative disorders 595

amnesia (dissociative) 595

fugue 596

dissociative identity disorder (multiple personality disorder—MPD) 596

sociocognitive explanation of MPD 598

substance abuse 599

biological or disease model of addiction 600

learning model of addiction 601

schizophrenia 605

psychosis 605

positive and negative symptoms of schizophrenia 606

"word salads" 606

catatonic stupor 606

vulnerability-stress model of schizophrenia 610

LOOKING BACK

- Is insanity the same thing as having a mental disorder? (p. 576)

- What are three approaches to defining "mental disorder"? (pp. 576–577)

- Why were slaves who dreamed of freedom once considered to be mentally ill? (p. 576)

- Why is the standard guide to the diagnosis of mental disorders controversial? (pp. 579–580)

- What is the difference between ordinary anxiety and an anxiety disorder? (p. 582)

- Why is the most disabling of all phobias known as the "fear of fear"? (p. 584)

- When is checking the stove before leaving home a sign of caution—and when does it signal a disorder? (p. 585)

- How can you tell whether you have major depression or just the blues? (p. 586)

- What are the "poles" in bipolar disorder? (p. 587)

- How do some people think themselves into depression? (p. 589)

- When does being self-centered become a disorder? (p. 591)

- What do a charming but heartless tycoon and a remorseless killer have in common? (p. 592)

- Why are some people seemingly incapable of feeling guilt and shame? (p. 593)

- Can people actually forget who they are? (p. 596)

- Why are many clinicians and researchers skeptical about multiple personality disorder? (pp. 596–598)

- In what ways might genes contribute to alcoholism? (p. 600)

- Why is alcoholism more common in Ireland than in Italy? (p. 601)

- Why don't policies of abstinence from alcohol reduce problem drinking? (p. 602)

- If you take morphine to control chronic pain, does that mean you will become addicted to it? (p. 602)

- What's the difference between schizophrenia and a "split personality"? (p. 605)

- Why do most researchers consider schizophrenia a brain disorder? (pp. 608–609)

- Could schizophrenia begin in the womb? (p. 609)

17 APPROACHES TO TREATMENT AND THERAPY

Your vision will become clear only when you can look into your own heart. . . . Who looks outside, dreams; who looks inside, awakes.

PSYCHOANALYST CARL JUNG

Murray is a smart fellow with just one problem: He procrastinates. He can't seem to settle down and write his term papers. He keeps getting incompletes, swearing he will do those papers soon, but before long the incompletes turn to Fs. Why does Murray do this, manufacturing his own misery? What kind of therapy might help him?

Sally complains of anxieties, irritability, and continuing problems in her marriage. Although she is successful at work, she feels like a fraud, a useless member of society, and a burden to her family. She weeps often. Why is Sally so unhappy, and what can she do about it?

Jerry, a college student, is brought to the hospital by the campus police, who found him wandering around, dazed and confused. He is anxious and talkative, and he reports hearing angry voices that accuse him of being a spy. What treatment can help Jerry?

Margaret's parents were drug addicts who abandoned her when she was a baby. She lived in four foster homes before finding a family that truly cared for her. She eventually went to college and entered a satisfying career. Today, Margaret is married and loves her husband, but she finds that she still has many inhibitions and insecurities. What can Margaret do to get over them?

People seek professional help for many difficulties and disorders, ranging from common problems and stresses of life, such as family conflict or fear of public speaking, to the delusions of schizophrenia. In this chapter, we will evaluate two major approaches to treatment. (1) *Biological treatments* include drugs or direct intervention in brain function; they are prescribed by psychiatrists or other physicians in a hospital or on an outpatient basis. (2) *Psychotherapy* covers an array of psychological approaches, including psychodynamic therapies, cognitive and behavior therapies, family therapy, and humanist therapies. In addition, we will consider *self-help groups*, which provide support or advice, and *community programs*, which provide skills training, rehabilitation counseling, and community interventions.

Each of these approaches can successfully handle some problems but not others. Each can help some individuals but not others. Finding the right treatment depends not only on having a good practitioner but also on being an educated consumer. In this chapter we will review the research on the effectiveness and limitations of drugs, psychotherapy, self-help approaches, and community alternatives. We will assess which kinds of therapy work best for which problems and consider the risks of unvalidated "pop" therapies.

WHAT'S AHEAD

- **What kinds of drugs are used to treat psychological disorders?**
- **Are antidepressants always the best treatment for depression?**
- **Can mental disorders be cured by brain surgery?**
- **Why is "shock therapy" hailed by some clinicians but condemned by others?**

BIOLOGICAL TREATMENTS FOR MENTAL DISORDERS

Over the centuries, individuals trying to understand and treat psychological disorders have often taken a biological approach, viewing mental disorders as diseases that can be treated medically. Today, biological treatments are enjoying a resurgence, in part because of evidence that some disorders have a genetic component or involve a biochemical or neurological abnormality (see Chapter 16), and in part because of the failure of traditional psychotherapies to help chronic sufferers of some disorders.

The Question of Drugs

The most widespread biological treatment is medication. Because drugs are so widely prescribed these days, both for severe disorders such as schizophrenia and for more common problems such as anxiety and depression, consumers need to understand what these drugs are, how they can best be used, and what their limitations are.

Drugs Commonly Prescribed for Mental Disorders. The main classes of drugs used in the treatment of mental and emotional disorders are these:

1 **Antipsychotic drugs,** also called *neuroleptics*—such as chlorpromazine (Thorazine), haloperidol (Haldol), and clozapine (Clozaril)—are used in the treatment of schizophrenia and other psychoses. Many antipsychotic drugs block or reduce the sensitivity of brain receptors that respond to the neurotransmitter dopamine. Some also increase levels of serotonin, a neurotransmitter that inhibits dopamine activity. A new drug that lowers the neurotransmitter glutamate has successfully blocked schizophrenia-like symptoms in rats, without apparent side effects, and awaits human testing (Moghaddam & Adams, 1998).

Antipsychotic drugs can reduce a patient's agitation, delusions, and hallucinations, and they can shorten schizophrenic episodes. However, they offer little relief from other symptoms of schizophrenia, such as jumbled thoughts, difficulty concentrating,

These photos show the effects of antipsychotic drugs on the symptoms of a young man with schizophrenia. In the photo on the left, he was unmedicated; in the photo on the right, he had taken medication. However, these drugs do not help all people with psychotic disorders.

or inability to interact with others. And they are not effective for everyone with schizophrenia; one study found that drugs help only about 60 percent of all schizophrenics (Valenstein, 1998).

Even when medication works, many schizophrenics stop taking it because of unpleasant side effects, which can be dangerous if a drug is taken over many years. About one-fourth of all adults who take these drugs, and fully one-third of elderly patients who do so, develop a neurological disorder called *tardive* (late-appearing) *dyskinesia*, which is characterized by hand tremors and other involuntary muscle movements (Saltz et al., 1991). However, some of the newer antipsychotic drugs, like Clozaril, appear to reduce the risk of tardive dyskinesia (Weiden, 1999). Another disease, *neuroleptic malignant syndrome*, which occurs more rarely, produces fever, delirium, and sometimes death.

"Before Prozac, she loathed company."

2 **Antidepressant drugs** are used primarily in the treatment of depression, anxiety, phobias, and obsessive-compulsive disorder. *Monoamine oxidase (MAO) inhibitors*, such as Nardil, elevate the level of norepinephrine and serotonin in the brain by blocking or inhibiting an enzyme that deactivates these neurotransmitters. *Tricyclic antidepressants*, such as Elavil, boost norepinephrine and serotonin levels by preventing the normal reabsorption, or "reuptake," of these substances by the cells that have released them. *Selective serotonin reuptake inhibitors (SSRIs)*, such as Prozac, work on the same principle as the tricyclics but specifically target serotonin.

Antidepressants are nonaddictive, but they can produce some unpleasant physical reactions, including dry mouth, headaches, constipation, nausea, restlessness, gastrointestinal problems, weight gain, and, in as many as one-third of all patients, decreased sexual desire and blocked or delayed orgasm.

3 **Tranquilizers**, such as Valium and Xanax, increase the activity of the neurotransmitter gamma-aminobutyric acid (GABA). They are the drugs most often prescribed by general physicians for patients who complain of depressed mood, panic, or anxiety. However, they are not effective for depression or panic disorder. And, while they may help an anxious person temporarily feel calmer during an acute experience of anxiety, they are not considered the treatment of choice over a long period of time. One reason is that a significant percentage of people who take tranquilizers overuse the drugs and develop problems with withdrawal and tolerance (i.e., they need larger and larger doses) (Lader & Morton, 1991). Xanax can also result in rebound panic attacks if it is not taken exactly on schedule. That is why antidepressants are generally preferable to tranquilizers in treating mood and anxiety disorders.

4 A special category of drug, a salt called **lithium carbonate**, often helps people who suffer from bipolar disorder (depression alternating with manic euphoria). It may produce its effects by moderating levels of norepinephrine or by protecting brain cells

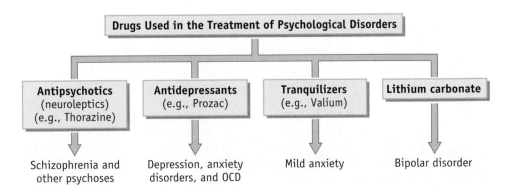

Drugs Used in the Treatment of Psychological Disorders

Antipsychotics (neuroleptics) (e.g., Thorazine)	**Antidepressants** (e.g., Prozac)	**Tranquilizers** (e.g., Valium)	**Lithium carbonate**
Schizophrenia and other psychoses	Depression, anxiety disorders, and OCD	Mild anxiety	Bipolar disorder

antipsychotic drugs Drugs used primarily in the treatment of schizophrenia and other psychotic disorders.

antidepressant drugs Drugs used primarily in the treatment of mood disorders, especially depression and anxiety.

tranquilizers Drugs commonly but often inappropriately prescribed for patients who complain of unhappiness, anxiety, or worry.

lithium carbonate A drug frequently given to people suffering from bipolar disorder.

from being overstimulated by glutamate (Nonaka, Hough, & Chuang, 1998). Lithium must be given in exactly the right dose, and levels of the drug in the bloodstream must be carefully monitored, because too little will not help and too much is toxic.

The increasing popularity of drugs as a method of treatment poses a problem for clinical psychologists, who, unlike psychiatrists, are not currently licensed to prescribe medication. Many psychologists are now lobbying for prescription rights, arguing that they should have access to the full range of treatment possibilities (DeLeon & Wiggins, 1996). But they have run into resistance from the medical profession, which argues that even with increased training, psychologists will not be qualified to prescribe medication, and also from psychologists who are concerned about the medicalizing of their field and who want psychology to remain a distinct alternative to psychiatry (DeNelsky, 1996).

Some Cautions About Drug Treatments. Drugs have helped many people who have gone from therapy to therapy without relief. Although medication cannot magically eliminate people's problems, it can be a useful first step in treatment. By improving sleep patterns, appetite, and energy, it can help people concentrate on solving their problems. But some words of caution are in order. Many psychiatrists and drug companies are trumpeting the benefits of medication without informing the public of its limitations. Here are some of those limitations:

1 *The placebo effect.* All new drugs, like new psychotherapies, promise quick and effective cures. But the **placebo effect** (see Chapter 2) ensures that some people will respond positively to a new drug just because of the enthusiasm surrounding it and their own expectations that the drug will make them feel better. After a while, when placebo effects decline, many drugs turn out to be neither as effective as promised nor as widely applicable. This has happened repeatedly with each new generation of tranquilizer and is happening again with antidepressants.

The belief that antidepressants are the treatment of choice for depression is widespread, so we were as surprised as anyone to discover the large amount of evidence questioning that belief (Valenstein, 1998). One meta-analysis found that although clinicians considered antidepressants helpful, the patients' ratings showed no advantage for the drugs beyond the placebo effect (Greenberg et al., 1992). Another meta-analysis, of 19 double-blind studies involving more than 2,000 depressed patients, found that 75 percent of the drugs' effectiveness was due to the placebo effect or other nonchemical factors, and only 25 percent to the chemical properties of the drug (Kirsch & Sapirstein, 1998). Even Prozac, which arrived with much fanfare and enthusiasm, is no more effective than the older generation of antidepressants (Greenberg et al., 1994).

2 *High relapse and dropout rates.* A person may have short-term success with antipsychotic or antidepressant drugs. However, in part because of their unpleasant side effects, half to two-thirds of people stop taking them (McGrath et al., 1990; Torrey, 1988). Individuals who take antidepressants without also learning how to cope with their problems are also more likely to relapse in the future (Antonuccio et al., 1999).

THINKING CRITICALLY

AVOID EMOTIONAL REASONING

A magazine announces that Prozac is "a breakthrough drug for depression." Other headlines announce that Clozaril is a miracle cure for people with schizophrenia. Announcements of "miracle cures" always generate emotional excitement. Why should the public be cautious before concluding that these drugs are really miracles?

3 *Dosage problems.* The challenge with drugs is to find the "therapeutic window," the amount that is enough but not too much. Many questions remain about which drug best suits which problem, what the proper dose should be, how long the drug should and can be taken, and so forth (Gutheil, 1993).

To complicate matters, the same dose of a drug may be metabolized differently in men and women, old people and young people, and different ethnic groups (Willie et al., 1995). When psychiatrist Keh-Ming Lin moved from Taiwan to the United States, he was amazed to learn that the dosage of antipsychotic drugs given to American patients with schizophrenia was often 10 times higher than the dose for Chinese patients. In subsequent studies, Lin and his colleagues confirmed that Asian patients require significantly lower doses of the medication for optimal treatment (Lin, Poland, & Chien, 1990). Similarly, African-Americans suffering from depression or bipolar disorder seem to need lower dosages of tricyclic antidepressants and lithium than other ethnic groups do (Strickland et al., 1991, 1995). Groups may differ in the dosages they can tolerate because of variations in metabolic rates, amount of body fat, the number or type of drug receptors in the brain, or cultural practices such as smoking and eating habits.

4 *Long-term risks.* We noted that antipsychotic drugs can have dangerous, even fatal consequences if taken for many years. Antidepressants, in contrast, are assumed to be quite safe, but the effects of taking them for many years are still unknown. The general public and even many physicians do not realize that new drugs are often tested on only a few hundred people for only a few weeks or months, even when the drug is one that patients might take for many years. For example, clozapine was tested in controlled trials that lasted only six weeks (*FDA Drug Bulletin*, 1990). Ritalin is given to many children diagnosed with attention deficit/hyperactivity disorder, but no studies have examined the drug's effect on children who take it for longer than 14 months (National Institutes of Health, 1998). Many physicians and the public, feeling reassured if a drug is effective in the short run, overlook the possibility of long-term risks.

Without question, drugs have rescued some people from emotional despair, suicide, or years in a mental hospital. They have enabled severely depressed or disturbed people to function and even respond to psychotherapy. But we need to think critically about drug treatments for mental disorders because many doctors prescribe drugs routinely, often without accompanying psychotherapy for the person's problems. The overprescription of drugs is partly a result of pressure from managed-care organizations, which prefer to pay for one patient visit for a prescription rather than ten visits for psychotherapy, and from drug companies, which are spending fortunes to market and promote these highly profitable products (Antonuccio et al., 1999; Critser, 1996).

The overprescription of drugs for mood disorders in North America also occurs because of a common but mistaken assumption: that if a disorder appears to have biological origins or involve biochemical abnormalities in the brain, then biological treatments must be most appropriate. But in fact, changing your behavior and thoughts—through psychotherapy or other new experiences—can also change the way your brain functions. This point was dramatically illustrated in a PET-scan study of people with obsessive-compulsive disorder (see Figure 17.1). Among those who were taking Prozac, the metabolism of glucose in the brain improved, suggesting that the drug was having a beneficial effect. But two studies found exactly the *same* brain changes in patients who were getting cognitive-behavior therapy and no medication (Baxter et al., 1992; Schwartz et al., 1996). Cognitive-behavior therapy with depressed patients also restores their brain-wave sleep profiles to normal, unlike antidepressants (Thase et al., 1998).

placebo effect The apparent success of a medication or treatment that is due to the patient's expectations or hopes rather than to the drug or treatment itself.

ANALYZE ASSUMPTIONS

Many people assume that if a disorder involves a biological abnormality, a biological treatment such as medication is the best solution. What is the logical error in this assumption?

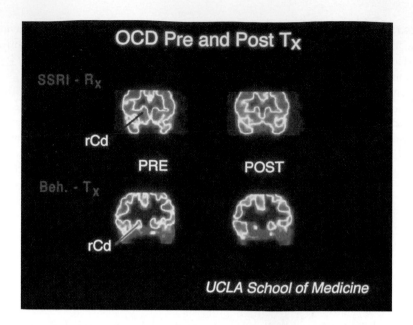

FIGURE 17.1
PSYCHOTHERAPY AND THE BRAIN

These PET scans show the brains of two persons with obsessive-compulsive disorder before and after behavior therapy (bottom row) or treatment with an SSRI (top row). Before either treatment, the glucose metabolic rates in the right caudate nucleus (rCd) were elevated. After either treatment, this area calmed down, becoming less active. Behavior therapy was thus as effective as medication (Schwartz et al., 1996).

In sum, drugs used for treating psychological problems are neither totally miraculous nor totally worthless. Their effectiveness depends on the individual, the problem, and whether medication is combined with psychotherapy.

Surgery and Electroshock

For centuries, physicians treated mental illness by trying to change brain function directly. In the seventeenth century, for example, physicians tried to release the "psychic pressures" they believed were causing a person's symptoms by drilling holes in the person's skull—a method called *trepanning*. **Psychosurgery**—surgery designed to destroy selected areas of the brain thought to be responsible for emotional disorders or disturbed behavior—continued well into the twentieth century.

The most famous form of modern psychosurgery was invented in 1935, when a Portuguese neurologist, Egas Moniz, drilled two holes into the skull of a mental patient and used a specially designed instrument to cut or crush nerve fibers running from the prefrontal lobes to other areas. This operation, called a *prefrontal lobotomy*, was supposed to reduce the patient's emotional symptoms without impairing intellectual ability. The procedure—which, incredibly, was never assessed or validated scientifically—was performed on tens of thousands of people. In America, the lobotomy was popularized by Walter Freeman, who personally performed more than 3,500 operations. Tragically, lobotomies left many patients apathetic, withdrawn, and unable to care for themselves (Valenstein, 1986). Yet Moniz won a Nobel Prize for his work.

With the advent of antipsychotic drugs in the 1950s, the number of lobotomies declined, but other forms of psychosurgery took their place. These surgeries, too, had unpredictable and often devastating consequences for the patient; today, they are rarely used. Some neurosurgeons, however, have not given up on the effort to cure mental illness by operating on the brain: They are burning holes in the frontal lobes of the brain (a procedure called a cingulotomy) of severely depressed or anxious patients whose symptoms have not responded to other treatments (Marino & Cosgrove, 1997). This procedure has no greater scientific justification than lobotomy did, and so far assessments of whether it "works" have come entirely from the patients' psychiatrists—not even the patients themselves (Vertosick, 1997).

psychosurgery Any surgical procedure that destroys selected areas of the brain believed to be involved in emotional disorders or violent, impulsive behavior.

electroconvulsive therapy (ECT) A procedure used in cases of prolonged and severe major depression, in which a brief brain seizure is induced.

Another controversial procedure is **electroconvulsive therapy (ECT)**, or "shock therapy," which is used for the treatment of severe depression. An electrode is placed on one or both sides of the head, and a brief current is turned on. The current triggers a seizure that typically lasts one minute, causing the body to convulse. A colleague told us about a man who was given ECT in the early 1950s: The convulsions sent the man flying off the table and shattered his legs. Cases such as this reinforced the impression of ECT as a barbaric and painful practice, and the method lost favor, especially when drugs seemed so promising. But in the 1980s, when drugs were proving to have limited effectiveness in some severely depressed patients, researchers began to reexamine ECT.

Today, the technique has been vastly modified and the voltage has been reduced. Patients are given muscle relaxants and anesthesia, so they can sleep through the procedure and their convulsions are minimized. Because ECT works faster than drugs, ECT is sometimes used on people who are at risk of committing suicide, when there is a risk of waiting until antidepressants or psychotherapy take effect (Holmes, 1997). ECT can be effective in such cases, although no one knows how or why it works. But it is *ineffective* with other disorders, such as schizophrenia or alcoholism, though it is occasionally misused for these conditions.

ECT's supporters argue that it is foolish to deny suffering, depressed patients a way out of their misery, especially if their misery is making them suicidal. They cite research showing that when ECT is used properly, it is safe and effective and causes no long-term cognitive impairment, memory loss, or detectable brain damage (Coffey, 1993; Devanand et al., 1994; Endler, 1991). Critics reply that ECT is too often used improperly, and that repeated use can damage the brain (Breggin, 1991). One psychiatrist has called its use "like hitting [someone] with a two-by-four" (Fisher, 1985). ECT continues to inspire passion, pro and con.

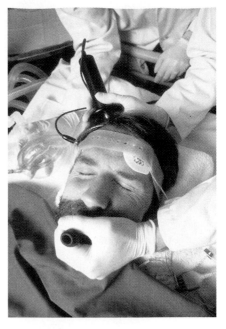

Electroconvulsive therapy has been used successfully to treat severe depression that has not responded to other treatments. But its supporters and critics continue to disagree vehemently about its use and potential for misuse.

QUICK QUIZ

ECT is not helpful in answering quizzes, but concentration is.

A. Match these treatments with the problems for which they are typically used.

1. antipsychotic drugs
2. antidepressant drugs
3. lithium carbonate
4. electroconvulsive therapy

a. suicidal depression
b. bipolar disorder
c. schizophrenia
d. depression and anxiety
e. obsessive-compulsive disorder

B. Give four reasons why the public should be cautious about concluding that drugs for psychological disorders are miracle cures.

C. Jezebel has had occasional episodes of depression that seem to be getting worse. Her physician prescribes an antidepressant. Before taking it, what questions should Jezebel ask herself—and the doctor?

Answers:

A. 1. c 2. d, e 3. b 4. a B. (1) Placebo effects are common; (2) dropout and relapse rates are high; (3) appropriate dosages can be difficult to determine and can vary by sex, age, and ethnicity; and (4) some drugs have unknown or long-term risks. C. Jezebel might want to ask these questions: Has the physician taken her full medical and psychological history, or prescribed the drug casually? Has the physician explored with her the possible reasons for her depression, or referred her to a mental-health professional who will do so? Would psychotherapy be appropriate, either with or without medication? Does the medication have any unpleasant physical effects or long-term risks? Will the doctor continue to monitor her reactions to the drug on a regular basis?

WHAT'S AHEAD

- Why are psychodynamic therapies called "depth" therapies?
- How can therapies based on learning principles change self-defeating habits?
- How do cognitive therapists help people get rid of self-defeating thoughts?
- Why do humanist therapists focus on the "here and now" instead of the "why and how"?
- Why do family therapists prefer to treat families rather than individuals?

KINDS OF PSYCHOTHERAPY

All good psychotherapists want to help clients think about their lives in new ways and find solutions to the problems that plague them. In this section we will consider the major schools of psychotherapy. To illustrate the philosophy and methods of each one, we will focus on a fictional fellow named Murray, whose problem with procrastination opened this chapter. Murray's difficulty in finishing his assignments is getting him into trouble academically, to say nothing of trouble with his parents, and he is understandably upset. What kind of therapy might help him?

Psychodynamic Therapy

Sigmund Freud was the father of the "talking cure," as one of his patients called it. He believed that intensive analysis of a patient's past and unconscious motives would produce *insight*, the patient's awareness of the reason for his or her symptoms and unhappiness. With insight and emotional release, the symptoms would disappear. Freud's method of *psychoanalysis* has evolved into many different forms of *psychodynamic therapy*, which share the goal of exploring the unconscious dynamics of personality, such as defenses and conflicts (see Chapter 13). Their proponents refer to them as "depth" therapies because the goal is to delve into unconscious processes rather than concentrate on "superficial" symptoms and conscious beliefs.

To bring unconscious conflicts into awareness, psychoanalytic and psychodynamic therapists often ask the client to talk about his or her dreams, fantasies, and memories. They encourage the person to *free associate*, saying whatever comes to mind. For example, by free associating to his dreams, his fantasies about work, and his early memories, our friend Murray might gain the insight that he procrastinates as a way of expressing anger toward his parents. He might realize that he is angry because they insist that he study for a career he dislikes. Ideally, Murray will come to this insight by himself. If the analyst suggests it, Murray might feel too defensive to accept it.

A major element of psychodynamic therapy is **transference**, the client's transfer (displacement) of emotional elements of his or her inner life—usually feelings about the parents—outward onto the analyst. Have you ever found yourself responding to a new acquaintance with unusually quick affection or dislike and later realized it was because the person reminded you of a relative that you loved or loathed? That experience is similar to transference. In therapy, a woman who failed to resolve her Oedipal love for her father might believe she has fallen in love with her analyst. A man who is unconsciously angry at his mother for rejecting him might become furious with his analyst for going on vacation. Through analysis of transference, psychodynamic therapists believe, clients can resolve their emotional conflicts.

In orthodox psychoanalysis, the client meets with the therapist as often as several times a week, for a period of years. The analyst listens to the client's free associations and dreams but rarely comments on them. There is no rush to solve the problem that brought the client into therapy. In fact, a person may come in complaining of a symptom such as anxiety or headaches, and the therapist may not get around to that

"HAVE A COUPLE OF DREAMS, AND CALL ME IN THE MORNING."

transference In psychodynamic therapies, a critical step in which the client transfers unconscious emotions or reactions, such as emotional feelings about his or her parents, onto the therapist.

symptom for months or even years. The analyst views the symptom as only the tip of the mental iceberg. Some traditional analysts do not attempt cures at all. The goal, they say, is understanding, not change.

Today, however, most psychodynamic therapists reject the orthodox psychoanalytic approach, while retaining the key ideas of transference, free association, and probing for unconscious motives (Westen, 1998). They sit facing the client; they participate more actively; and they are more goal-directed. Many practice time-limited or *brief psychodynamic therapy*, consisting of 15, 20, or 25 sessions. Without delving into the client's entire history, the therapist listens to the client's problems and formulates the main issue, or *dynamic focus* (Strupp & Binder, 1984). The rest of the therapy focuses on the person's self-defeating habits and recurring problems. The therapist looks for clues in the client's behavior in therapy to identify and change these patterns.

Behavior and Cognitive Therapy

Unlike psychodynamic therapists, psychologists who practice behavior or cognitive therapy (or, more commonly, a mixture of the two) would focus on helping Murray change his current behavior and attitudes rather than on striving for insight. "Mur," they would say, "you have lousy study habits. And you have a set of beliefs about studying, writing papers, and success that are woefully unrealistic." Such therapists would not worry much about Murray's past, his parents, or his unconscious anxieties.

The image of the psychoanalyst's couch is ingrained in popular culture, though most analysts now face their clients. In the movie *Antz,* an ant named Z-4195 complains to his analyst, "When you are the middle child in a family of five million you never get too much attention. What about my needs? What about me? I feel so insignificant." The analyst's interpretation: "You *are* insignificant."

Behavioral Techniques. Behavior therapists draw on techniques derived from the behavioral principles of classical and operant conditioning that we discussed in Chapter 7. (You may want to review those principles before going on.) Here are some of their methods:

1 **Systematic desensitization** *is a step-by-step process of desensitizing a client to a feared object or experience.* It is based on the classical-conditioning procedure of *counterconditioning*, in which a stimulus for an unwanted response (such as fear) is paired with some other stimulus or situation that elicits a response incompatible with the undesirable one (see Chapter 7). In this case, the incompatible response is usually relaxation. The client learns to relax deeply while imagining or looking at a

In this "virtual reality" version of systematic desensitization, people with spider phobias are gradually exposed to computerized but extremely lifelike images of spiders in a realistic, three-dimensional environment.

sequence of feared stimuli, arranged in a hierarchy ranging from the least frightening to the most frightening. The sequence for a person who is terrified of flying might be to read about airplane safety, look at pictures or models of airplanes, visit an airport and watch planes taking off, sit in a plane while it is on the ground, take a short flight, and then take a long flight. At each step the person must become relaxed and comfortable before going on. Eventually, the fear responses are extinguished.

2 **Aversive conditioning** *substitutes punishment for the reinforcement that has perpetuated a bad habit.* Suppose a woman who bites her nails is reinforced each time she does so by relief from her anxiety and a brief good feeling. A behavior therapist might have her wear a rubber band around her wrist and ask her to snap

GET ➜ INVOLVED

CURE YOUR FEARS

In Chapter 16, a Get Involved exercise asked you to identify your greatest fear. Now see whether systematic desensitization procedures will help you conquer it. Write down a list of situations that evoke your fear, starting with one that produces little anxiety (e.g., seeing a photo of a tiny brown spider) and ending with the most frightening one possible (e.g., touching a live tarantula at the pet store). Then find a quiet room where you will have no distractions or interruptions, sit in a comfortable reclining chair, and relax all the muscles of your body. Breathe slowly and deeply. Imagine the first, easiest scene, remaining as relaxed as possible. Do this until you can confront the image without becoming the least bit anxious. When that happens, go on to the next scene in your hierarchy. Do not try this all at once; space out your sessions over time. Does it work?

IN THE BLEACHERS   By Steve Moore

Batters overcoming *bonkinogginophobia*, a fear of the ball.

systematic desensitization A step-by-step process of desensitizing a client to a feared object or experience; it is based on the classical-conditioning procedure of counterconditioning.

aversive conditioning A method in which punishment is substituted for the reinforcement that is perpetuating a bad habit.

exposure treatment A method in which a person suffering from an anxiety disorder, such as a phobia or panic attacks, is taken directly into the feared situation until the anxiety subsides.

it (hard!) each time she bites her nails or feels the desire to do so. The goal is to make sure that she receives no continuing rewards for the undesirable behavior.

3 **Exposure treatments, *sometimes called "flooding," have clients who are suffering from specific anxieties confront the feared situation or memory directly.*** (Normally, people who are afraid of some situation or traumatic memory do everything they can to *avoid* confronting or thinking of it. This only makes the fear worse.) For example, a person who is trying to avoid thinking of a traumatic event might be asked to imagine the event over and over, until it no longer evokes the same degree of panic. Likewise, a person suffering from agoraphobia might be taken into the very situation that he or she fears most—a department store, say, or a subway—and would remain there, with the therapist, until the panic and anxiety declined. Notice how different this approach is from a psychodynamic one, in which the goal is to uncover the presumably unconscious reason that the agoraphobic feels afraid of going out.

4 **Behavioral records and contracts help clients identify the reinforcers (rewarding consequences) that are keeping their unwanted habits going.** For example, a man who wants to curb his overeating may not be aware of how much he eats throughout the day to relieve tension; a behavioral record might show that he eats more junk food than he realized in the late afternoon. Once the unwanted behavior is identified, along with the reinforcers that have been maintaining it, a treatment program can be designed to change it; the man might find other ways to reduce stress and make sure that he is nowhere near junk food in the late afternoon.

The therapist also helps people set *behavioral goals*, small step by small step. A husband and wife who fight over housework, for instance, might be asked to draw up a contract indicating who will do what, with specified rewards for carrying out their duties. With such a contract, they can't fall back on accusations such as "You never do anything around here."

5 **Skills training provides practice in behaviors that are necessary for achieving the person's goals.** It is not enough to tell someone "Don't be shy" if the person does not know how to make small talk with others; skills training would teach the shy person how to converse in social settings (for example, by focusing on other people rather than on his or her own insecurity). Countless skills-training programs are available—for parents who don't know how to discipline children, for people who don't know how to manage anger, for children and adults who don't know how to express their wishes clearly, and so on.

A behaviorist would treat Murray's procrastination in several ways. Murray might not be aware of how he actually spends his time when he is avoiding his studies. Afraid that he hasn't time to do everything, he does nothing. Keeping a behavioral diary would let Murray know exactly how he spends his time, and how much time he should realistically allot to a project. Instead of having a vague, impossibly huge goal, such as "I'm going to reorganize my life," Murray would establish specific small goals, such as reading the two books necessary for an English paper and writing one page of an assignment. The therapist might also offer skills training to make sure Murray knows how to reach these goals.

Cognitive Techniques. Of course, people's thoughts, feelings, and motivations can influence their behavior. *Cognitive therapy* helps clients identify the beliefs and expectations that might be unnecessarily prolonging their unhappiness, conflicts, and other problems. To a cognitive therapist, expressing emotions is not enough to get rid of them, if the thoughts behind the emotions remain (Greenberger & Padesky, 1995). So cognitive therapists require clients to examine the evidence for their beliefs. (You could say they teach critical thinking.)

For example, anger typically results from the perception that you have been insulted or treated unfairly (see Chapter 11), and depression often arises from pessimistic, self-defeating thoughts, such as the belief that the sources of your misery are permanent, have do to with your failings rather than temporary circumstances, and will never change (see Chapter 16). A cognitive therapist would help an angry person consider other interpretations for the irritating behavior of others and to become more empathic about other people's possible motives. That dope on the freeway who cut in front of you was probably not really trying to kill you; and maybe your father's strict discipline was intended not to control you but to protect you. Similarly, a cognitive therapist would help a depressed person substitute positive thoughts for pessimistic ones ("my love is doomed"; "I'm no good at anything") and would then encourage the person to seek out situations that confirm the new ways of thinking.

One of the oldest and best-known schools of cognitive therapy is Albert Ellis's rational emotive therapy, now called *rational emotive behavior therapy* (Ellis, 1993; Ellis & Blau, 1998). In this approach, the therapist uses rational arguments to directly challenge a client's unrealistic beliefs or expectations. For example, says Ellis, people

Cognitive therapists encourage clients to emphasize the positive—say, the early sunny signs of spring—rather than always focusing on the negative—the lingering icy clutch of winter. Poet Michael Casey described the first daffodil that bravely rises through the snow as "a gleam of laughter in a sullen face."

GET ➜ INVOLVED

MIND OVER MOOD

See whether cognitive-therapy techniques can help you control your moods. Think of a time recently when you felt a particularly strong emotion, such as depression, anger, or anxiety. On a piece of paper, record (1) the situation—who was there, what happened, and when; (2) your feeling at the time, from weak to strong; and (3) the thoughts that were going through your mind (e.g., "She never cares about what I want to do"; "I hate being angry"; "He's going to leave me"). Then examine your thoughts. What is the worst thing that could happen if those thoughts are true? *Are* your thoughts accurate, or are you "mind-reading" the other person's intentions and motives? Is there another way to think about this situation or the other person's behavior? If you practice this exercise repeatedly, you may learn how your thoughts affect your moods—and find out that you have more control over your feelings than you realized (from Greenberger & Padesky, 1995).

who are emotionally upset often overgeneralize: They decide that one annoying act by someone means that person is totally bad in every way. Or they may interpret their own normal human failings as evidence that their fundamental selves and souls are rotten to the core. The rational emotive behavior therapist directly challenges these thoughts and interpretations, showing the client why they are irrational and misguided.

Another popular cognitive approach, devised by Aaron Beck (1976, 1991), avoids direct challenges to the client's beliefs. Instead, the therapist encourages the person to test those beliefs against the evidence, to stop trying to read other people's minds ("I *know* he's out to get me"), and to avoid turning normal upsets and setbacks into catastrophes—a common mistake that cognitive therapists call "catastrophizing."

A cognitive therapist might treat Murray's procrastination by having Murray write down his thoughts about work, read the thoughts as if someone else had said them, and then write a rational response to each one. This technique would encourage Murray to examine the validity of his assumptions and beliefs. Many procrastinators are perfectionists; if they cannot do something perfectly, they will not do it at all. Unable to accept their limitations, they set impossible standards and catastrophize:

Negative thought	Rational response
This paper isn't good enough; I'd better rewrite it for the twentieth time.	Good enough for what? It won't win a Pulitzer Prize, but it is a pretty good paper.
If I don't get an A+ on this paper, my life will be ruined.	My life will be a lot worse if I keep getting incompletes. It's better to get a B or even a C than do nothing at all.
My professor is going to think I'm an idiot when he reads this. I'll feel humiliated by his criticism.	He's not accused me of being an idiot yet. If he makes some criticisms, I can learn from them and do better next time.

Strict behaviorists consider thoughts to be "behaviors" that are modifiable by learning principles; they do not regard thoughts as causes of behavior. But most psychologists believe that thoughts and behavior influence each other, which is why cognitive-behavior therapy is more common than either form alone.

Humanist and Existential Therapy

Humanist therapies, like their parent philosophy humanism, start from the assumption that people seek self-actualization and self-fulfillment. The therapist generally does not dig into past conflicts but aims instead to help clients feel better about themselves and free themselves from self-imposed limits. (It was the humanists who changed the term for a person in therapy from "patient," which implies that the person is ill, to "client," which implies that the person simply has a problem.) Humanist therapists want to know how clients subjectively perceive their own situations, so they can help them develop the will and confidence to bring about change. That is why they explore what is going on "here and now," not the issues of "why and how."

In *client-centered* (nondirective) *therapy*, developed by Carl Rogers, the therapist's role is to listen to the client's needs in an accepting, nonjudgmental way and offer what Rogers called *unconditional positive regard* (see Chapter 13). Whatever the client's specific complaint is, the goal is to build the client's self-esteem and help the person feel that he or she is accepted and respected. Thus, a Rogerian might assume that Murray's procrastination masks his low self-regard, and that Murray is out of touch with his real feelings and wishes. Perhaps he is not passing his courses because he is trying to please his parents by majoring in economics, when he would secretly rather become an artist.

Rogers (1961) believed that effective therapists must be warm, genuine, and honest in expressing their feelings, and they must show accurate, empathic understanding of the client's problems. The therapist's support for the client, according to Rogers, will eventually be adopted by the client, who will become more self-accepting. Once that is accomplished, the person can accept the limitations of others too.

Existential therapy helps clients explore the meaning of existence and face with courage the great questions of life, such as death, freedom, free will, alienation from oneself and others, loneliness, and meaninglessness. Existential therapists, like humanist therapists, believe that our lives are not inevitably determined by our pasts or our circumstances—that we have the power to choose our own destinies. As Irvin Yalom (1989) explained, "the crucial first step in therapy is the patient's assumption of responsibility for his or her life predicament. As long as one believes that one's problems are caused by some force or agency outside oneself, there is no leverage in therapy."

Yalom argues that the goal of therapy is to help clients cope with the inescapable realities of life and death and the struggle for meaning. However grim our experiences may be, he believes, "they contain the seeds of wisdom and redemption." Perhaps the most remarkable example of a man able to find seeds of wisdom in a barren landscape was Victor Frankl (1905–1997), who developed a form of existential therapy after surviving a Nazi concentration camp. In that pit of horror, Frankl (1955) observed, some people maintained their sanity because they were able to find meaning in the experience, shattering though it was.

Some observers believe that, ultimately, all therapies are existential. In different ways, therapy helps people determine what is important to them, what values guide them, and what changes they will have the courage to make. An existential therapist might help Murray think about the significance of his procrastination, what his ultimate goals in life are, and how he might find the strength to carry out his ambitions.

Humanist psychologist Carl Rogers emphasized the importance of the therapist's warmth and empathy, an idea that virtually all therapists now endorse.

Therapy in Social Context

Murray's situation is getting worse. His father has begun to call him Tomorrow Man, which upsets his mother, and his younger brother the math major has been calculating how much tuition money Murray's incompletes are costing. His older sister Isabel, the biochemist who never had an incomplete in her life, now proposes that all of them go to a family therapist. "Murray's not the only one in this family with complaints," she says.

Family Therapy. Family therapists would maintain that Murray's problem developed in a social context, that it is sustained by a social context, and that any change he makes will affect that context. One leading family therapist, Salvador Minuchin (1984), compared the family to a kaleidoscope, a changing pattern of mosaics in which the pattern is larger than any one piece. In this view, efforts to isolate and treat one member of the family without the others are doomed. Only if all family members reveal their differing perceptions of each other can mistakes and misperceptions be identified. A teenager, for instance, may see his mother as crabby

Family therapist Alan Entin uses photographs to help people identify themes and problems in their family histories. When one woman was asked to talk about a photo of her parents (left), she began to cry; she felt that it revealed her father's alienation from her and the rest of his family. Does the picture on the right convey a happy cohesive family to you, or a divided one? Shortly after it was taken, the couple divorced; the father took custody of the children . . . and the mother kept the dog (Entin, 1992).

and nagging when actually she is tired and worried. A parent may see a child as rebellious when in fact the child is lonely and desperate for attention.

Family members are usually unaware of how they influence one another. By observing the entire family (or, in the case of couples, both partners), the family therapist hopes to discover tensions and imbalances in power and communication. For example, in some families a child may have an illness or develop a psychological problem that affects the workings of the whole family. One parent may become overinvolved with the sick child while the other parent retreats, and each may start blaming the other. The child, in turn, may cling to the illness as a way of expressing anger, keeping the parents together, getting the parents' attention, or asserting control (Luepnitz, 1988).

Some family therapists look for patterns of behavior across generations (Carter & McGoldrick, 1988; Kerr & Bowen, 1988). The therapist and client may create a *genogram*, a family tree of psychologically significant events across as many generations as possible (McGoldrick & Gerson, 1985; Coupland, Serovich, & Glenn, 1995). This method often reveals the origins of current problems and conflicts, as you can see in Figure 17.2.

Even when it is not possible to treat the whole family, some therapists will treat individuals in a *family systems* perspective, which recognizes that people's behavior in a family is as interconnected as that of t.wo dancers (Bowen, 1978; Lerner, 1989). Clients learn that if they change in any way, even for the better, their families may protest noisily or may send subtle messages that read, "Change back!" Why? Because when one family member changes, each of the others must change too. As the saying goes, it takes two to tango, and if one dancer stops, so must the other. But most people do not like change. They are comfortable with old patterns and habits, even those that cause them trouble. They want to keep tangoing, even if their feet hurt.

In general, family therapists would observe how Murray's procrastination fits his family dynamics. Perhaps it allows Murray to get his father's attention and his

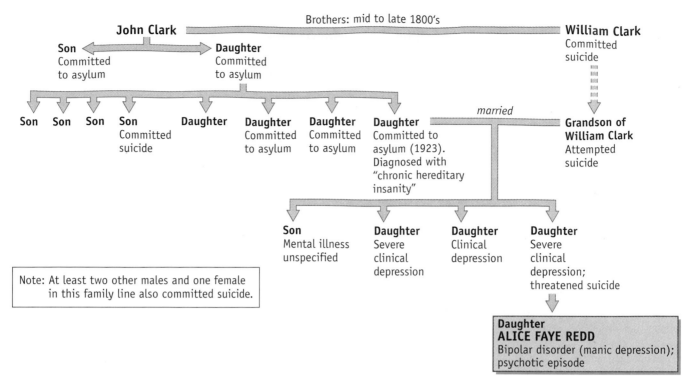

FIGURE 17.2
ONE FAMILY'S GENOGRAM OF MENTAL ILLNESS

Genograms can reveal patterns of behavior and mental disorders across generations in a family (McGoldrick & Gerson, 1985). Alice Faye Redd was convicted of defrauding elderly investors of $10 million, money she then lost in lavish spending and extravagant investment schemes. Prosecution and defense psychiatrists agreed that she suffers from a form of manic depression (bipolar disorder). Alice Redd's daughter, Rebecca Hagelin, constructed this multi-generation family record of depression and suicide in an effort to have her mother committed for treatment, but the court sentenced Redd to 15 years in prison.

mother's sympathy. Perhaps it keeps Murray from facing his greatest fear: that if he does finish his work, it will not measure up to his father's high standards. The therapist will not only help Murray change his work habits but also help his family deal with a changed Murray.

Group Therapy. Some therapists also take advantage of a lesson from social psychology—namely, that the influence of other people may accomplish what a single therapist cannot. In *group therapy*, people with the same or different problems are put together to find solutions. Members learn that their problems are not unique. They also learn that they cannot get away with their usual excuses because others in the group have tried them all (Yalom, 1995). Group therapies are commonly used in institutions, such as prisons and mental hospitals. They are also popular among people who have social difficulties, such as shyness and anxiety, or who share a common traumatic experience, such as sexual assault (Becker et al., 1984). Keep in mind that therapy groups are not the

GET ➡ INVOLVED

CLIMB YOUR FAMILY TREE

Using the example of a genogram in Figure 17.2, draw a diagram of a trait or behavior that has recurred in your family. It might be a problem, such as alcoholism, violence, or parental abandonment; an illness or disability that affected family dynamics, such as asthma or diabetes; or a positive quality, such as creativity or musical ability. What does this exercise show you about patterns across generations?

same as self-help groups, which we will discuss in the next section, or programs designed for personal growth rather than psychotherapy.

Psychotherapy in Practice

The four approaches to psychotherapy that we have discussed may seem quite different. In theory, they are, and so are the techniques resulting from them (see Review 17.1). Yet in practice, many psychotherapists draw on methods and ideas from various approaches, avoiding strong allegiances to any one theory or school of thought. This flexibility enables them to treat clients with whatever methods are most appropriate and effective.

Moreover, all successful therapies share some common elements. One is that they replace a client's self-defeating, pessimistic, or unrealistic life story—the "story" each of us develops over time to explain our lives—with one that is more hopeful or attainable (Freedman & Combs, 1996; Howard, 1991). Some therapists explicitly focus on helping clients change their life stories and hence to change their own role in them. For example, therapist David Epston worked with an immigrant woman named Marisa, who had been abused and rejected all her life. "To tell a story about your life turns it into a history," he told her, "one that can be left behind, and makes it easier for you to create a future of your own design" (quoted in O'Hanlon, 1994). Marisa came to see that she could tell a new story about her experiences. Instead of seeing the tragedies that had befallen her as evidence that she was a worthless victim, as she always had, she now saw the same events as evidence of her strength and endurance. "My life has a future now," she told him. "It will never be the same again."

REVIEW 17.1

THE MAJOR SCHOOLS OF THERAPY COMPARED

		Primary Goal	Methods
	Psychodynamic	Insight into unconscious motives and feelings	Probing the unconscious through dream analysis, free association, transference, other forms of "talk therapy"
	Cognitive-behavior	Modification of behavior and irrational beliefs	Behavioral techniques such as systematic desensitization and flooding; exercises to identify and change faulty beliefs
	Humanist	Insight; self-acceptance and self-fulfilment	Providing a safe, nonjudgmental setting in which to discuss life issues
	Family	Modification of individual habits and family patterns	Working with couples, families, and sometimes individuals to identify and change patterns that perpetuate problems

QUICK QUIZ

Match each method with the therapy most likely to use it.

1. free association
2. systematic desensitization
3. facing the fear of death
4. reappraisal of thoughts
5. unconditional positive regard
6. genogram
7. contract specifying duties

a. cognitive therapy
b. psychoanalysis
c. humanist therapy
d. behavior therapy
e. family therapy
f. existential therapy

Answers:

1.b 2.d 3.f 4.a 5.c 6.e 7.d

WHAT'S AHEAD

- **What is the "scientist-practitioner gap"—and why has it been widening?**
- **What does research tell us about the effectiveness of psychotherapy?**
- **What sorts of people make the best therapists—and the best clients?**
- **Which form of psychotherapy is most likely to help if you are anxious or depressed?**
- **Under what conditions can psychotherapy be harmful?**

EVALUATING PSYCHOTHERAPY

Poor Murray! He is getting a little baffled by all these therapies. He wants to make a choice soon—no sense in procrastinating about that, too! Is there any scientific evidence, he wonders, that might help him decide which therapy to seek, or are they all alike?

The Scientist-Practitioner Gap

Many psychotherapists believe that trying to evaluate psychotherapy using standard empirical methods is an exercise in futility. Psychotherapy is an art, they say, not a science. Laboratory and survey studies capture only a small and shadowy image of the complex exchange that takes place between a therapist and a client (Edelson, 1994; Elliott & Morrow-Bradley, 1994). Clinical experience, many therapists say, is therefore more valuable to them than research.

Scientific psychologists agree that research has little to say about the existential aims of therapy, such as helping people come to terms with illness and death or helping them choose which values to live by. But scientists, and many clinicians themselves, are concerned that when therapists fail to keep up with empirical findings in the field, their clients may pay the price (Dawes, 1994; Watters & Ofshe, 1999). Regardless of their particular philosophy or school of therapy, all therapists, scientists believe, should be aware of research on the most beneficial methods for particular psychological problems; on topics relevant to their practice, such as memory, hypnosis, and child development; and on ineffective or potentially harmful techniques.

Consider projective tests, which, as we discussed in Chapter 13, can help children who have been through traumatic experiences express their feelings through drawing or play. During the 1980s, some therapists began using projective methods for

Controlled experiments find that doll play does not reliably diagnose abuse because *nonabused* children are fascinated with the doll's genitals, too. In one study, children were examined by a doctor and later asked to use the doll to show what the doctor had done to them. The doctor, who was videotaped, had never touched the children's genitals, but half of the children alleged that he had, often in bizarre ways. For example, this little girl pounded a stick into the doll's vagina to describe what the doctor supposedly did to her (Bruck et al., 1995).

EXAMINE THE EVIDENCE

New therapies often claim remarkable, fast cures. Why should smart consumers examine the evidence for and against these therapies rather than be persuaded by enthusiastic testimonials?

another purpose: to determine *whether* a child had been sexually abused. They claimed they could identify a child who had been abused by observing how the child played with "anatomically detailed" dolls (dolls with prominent genitals)—and that is how many of them testified in hundreds of court cases (Ceci & Bruck, 1995). Unfortunately, these therapists did not test their beliefs by using a fundamental scientific procedure: a control group. They had not asked, "How do *nonabused* children play with these dolls?" When psychological scientists did ask this question and conducted controlled research to answer it, they found that most children, abused or not, are fascinated with the dolls' genitals. Abused children do not play any differently with the dolls than nonabused children do, and hence you cannot diagnose abuse on the basis of children's doll play (Koocher et al., 1995; Poole & Lamb, 1998).

Over the years, the disagreement between scientists and therapists on the importance of research has intensified, leading to what some psychologists call the *scientist-practitioner gap*. One reason for the growing split has been the rise of professional schools that are unconnected to academic psychology departments and that train students solely to do therapy (Dawes, 1994). Graduates of these schools sometimes know little about research methods or about research assessing therapy techniques.

The scientist-practitioner gap has also widened because of the proliferation of new therapies trying to get a foothold in a crowded market. As we noted way back in Chapter 1, the word *therapist* is unregulated; anyone can set up any kind of program and claim it is a new "therapy." New therapies are often started by a charismatic leader, who may or may not have professional training in psychology. They are then endorsed by enthusiastic practitioners who have been trained by the therapy's founder, usually in brief workshops that last a weekend or a week.

Some of these therapies are packaged and promoted with little or no scientific support at all (Beyerstein, 1999). For example, Thought Field Therapy (TFT), originated by Roger Callahan, assumes that emotional problems are caused by "perturbations" (disturbances) in "a subtle energy field" rather than by cognitions, environmental events, or chemical imbalances. Callahan claims he can successfully cure people on the phone, using his special patented Voice Technology™ method to assess their perturbations (Gallo, 1998). Another unvalidated therapy, Neurolinguistic Programming (NLP), claims to cure people by enhancing their communication skills through matching their learning styles with their "brain types." The U.S. National Research Council concluded that there is no credible evidence for NLP's claims (Druckman & Swets, 1988).

Other new therapies repackage established techniques, giving them new names. For example, Eye Movement Desensitization and Reprocessing (EMDR) is built on the tried-and-true desensitization and exposure techniques of behavior therapy for treating anxiety (Lohr, Tolin, & Lilienfeld, 1998). But EMDR's founder, Francine Shapiro (1995), added eye-movement exercises: Clients move their eyes from side to side, following the therapist's moving finger, while concentrating on the memory to be desensitized. Shapiro's (1994) explanation for why such eye movements work is that "the system may become unbalanced due to a trauma or through stress engendered during a developmental window, but once appropriately catalyzed and maintained in a dynamic state by EMDR, it transmutes information to a state of therapeutically appropriate resolution." (If you do not understand that, don't worry; we don't either.)

Shapiro has trained thousands of therapists in EMDR, and she claims it can cure everything from posttraumatic stress disorder and panic attacks to eating disorders and sexual dysfunction. Although her method has won endorsements from some prominent psychologists, there is no evidence from controlled studies that EMDR is any better than standard exposure treatments (Lohr et al., 1995; Rosen, 1999). One clinical researcher who reviewed the evidence concluded that the eye movements that are supposedly essential to this technique do not constitute "anything more than pseudoscientific window dressing" (Lilienfeld, 1996).

The fundamental questions for consumers who are thinking critically about any form of psychotherapy should be: Does it work any better than a placebo? Does its rationale make sense, or is it just a fancy form of psychobabble? Is it successful because of its promoters' ability to inspire and persuade, or because it uses techniques known to be effective? In "Taking Psychology with You," we consider other guidelines for becoming a smart consumer of psychotherapy. Now let's take a look at what research can tell us about mainstream therapies that have been around for a while.

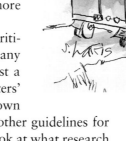

Assessing Therapy's Effectiveness

Despite the skepticism about research on the part of many therapists, many clinical psychologists have been conducting good research on clinical practice. Economic pressures and the rise of managed-care health programs now require psychotherapists to produce clear, research-based guidelines for which therapies are most effective, which therapies are best for which disorders, and which therapies are ineffective or potentially harmful (Barlow, 1996; Chambless et al., 1996, 1998). To develop these guidelines, clinical researchers conduct *controlled clinical trials*, in which people with a given problem or disorder are randomly assigned to one or more treatment groups or to a control group. Hundreds of studies have been designed to test the effectiveness of different kinds of therapy. Here are the overall results to date:

1 *For the common emotional problems of life, short-term treatment is usually sufficient.* Many psychodynamic therapists believe that the longer therapy goes on, the more successful it will be. Of course, people with severe mental disorders do often require and benefit from continued therapeutic care. But for most problems, a limited number of treatments is enough. About half of all people in therapy improve within 8 to 11 sessions, according to self-reports and objective measures of improvement (see Figure 17.3). And 76 percent improve within six months to a year; after a year, further change is minimal (Howard et al., 1986; Kopta et al., 1994).

2 *Psychotherapy is better than doing nothing at all.* People who receive almost any standard professional treatment improve more than people who do not get help (Lambert & Bergin, 1994; Lipsey & Wilson, 1993; Maling & Howard, 1994; Robinson, Berman, & Neimeyer, 1990; Smith, Glass, & Miller, 1980).

3 *People who have less serious problems and are motivated to improve do the best in psychotherapy.* Emotional disorders, self-defeating habits, and problems coping with crises are more successfully treated than are long-standing personality problems and psychotic disorders (Kopta et al., 1994). Clients who make the best use of therapy tend to have more adaptive levels of functioning to begin with, are prepared for treatment, and are ready to change (Orlinsky & Howard, 1994).

FIGURE 17.3
IS MORE THERAPY BETTER?

In one study, about half of all patients improved in only 8 sessions and about three-fourths improved by the 26th session (Howard et at., 1986). Subsequent research confirmed that the benefits of therapy occur within 8 to 11 sessions for half of all clients, and most of the rest need no more than a year of treatment (Kopta et al., 1994).

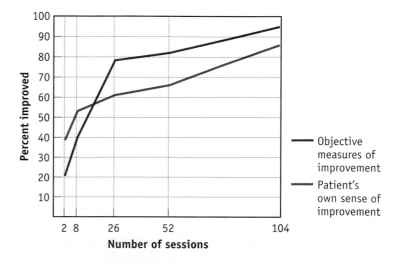

4 *In some cases, psychotherapy is harmful because of the therapist's incompetence, biases, unethical behavior, or lack of knowledge.* Individual therapists can do great harm by behaving unethically, incompetently, or prejudicially (Garnets et al., 1991; Lambert & Bergin, 1994; López, 1989; Peterson, 1992). Some psychologists are concerned that therapeutic malpractice may be increasing because of the recent surge in the number of therapists who use unvalidated methods (Dawes, 1994; Watters & Ofshe, 1999).

Because of these findings, most of the research on psychotherapy now focuses on three questions: What are the common ingredients in all successful therapies? Which kinds of therapy are best suited for which problems? And under what conditions can therapy be harmful?

When Therapy Helps

Psychotherapy is a social exchange, and like all such exchanges, its success depends on the qualities of the participants and the fit between them.

Successful Clients and Therapists. Clients who are likely to do well in therapy have a strong sense of self and are also unhappy and motivated enough to want to work on their problems. They tend to have support from their families and a personal style of dealing actively with problems instead of avoiding them (Gaston et al., 1989). Basic personality traits also influence whether a person will be able to change in therapy. As we saw in Chapter 13, some people are characteristically negative and bitter; others are more agreeable and positive, even in the midst of emotional crises. Hostile, negative individuals are more resistant to treatment and are less likely to benefit from it (Orlinsky & Howard, 1994).

The personality of the therapist is also critical to the success of any therapy, particularly the qualities that Carl Rogers praised: empathy, expressiveness, warmth, and genuineness. The most successful therapists make their clients feel respected, accepted, and understood. They are actively invested in the interaction with the client, instead of detached in the manner of Freud (Orlinsky & Howard, 1994).

Apart from the individual qualities of the client and the therapist, successful therapy depends on the bond they establish between them, called the **therapeutic alliance**. In a good therapeutic alliance, the two parties share an emotional connection, and they respect and understand one another. They agree on the goals of treatment and thus are more likely to meet them. For example, in one large-scale study of people being treated for alcohol abuse or dependence, those who had a strong therapeutic alliance with their therapists (as measured by a questionnaire filled out by both parties) were drinking much less alcohol a year after therapy ended. This was true regardless of which of three different treatment programs they had been in (Connors et al., 1997).

Cultural and Group Differences. Many therapists and clients establish successful therapeutic alliances and work well together, without having the same ethnic origins. But sometimes cultural differences cause misunderstandings that result from ignorance or prejudice (Comas-Díaz & Greene, 1994; Cross & Fhagen-Smith, 1996; Franklin, 1993; Sue, 1998). For example, a lifetime of experience with racism may keep some African-American clients from revealing feelings that they believe a white therapist would not understand or accept. And black therapists frequently have to deal with clients and co-workers who are bigoted or uncomfortable with them, or who fail to understand or accept them (Boyd-Franklin, 1989; Markowitz, 1993). Misunderstandings and prejudice may be a major reason that Asian-, Mexican-, and African-American psychotherapy clients are more likely to stay in therapy, and thus benefit from it, when their therapists match their own ethnicity

therapeutic alliance The bond of confidence and mutual understanding established between therapist and client, which allows them to work together to solve the client's problems.

(Sue, 1998). If such clients stay in therapy and do not drop out early, however, most are as likely to do as well with an "unmatched" therapist.

In establishing a bond with clients, therapists must distinguish normal cultural patterns from individual psychological problems (Pedersen et al., 1996). Two Irish-American clinicians, Monica McGoldrick and John Pearce (1996), described problems that are typical of Irish-American families. These problems arise from Irish history and religious beliefs, and they are deeply ingrained. "In general, the therapist cannot expect the family to turn into a physically affectionate, emotionally intimate group, or to enjoy being in therapy very much," they observed. "The notion of Original Sin—that you are guilty before you are born—leaves them with a heavy sense of burden. Someone not sensitized to these issues may see this as pathological. It is not. But it is also not likely to change and the therapist should help the family tolerate this inner guilt rather than try to get rid of it."

More and more psychotherapists are becoming "sensitized to the issues" caused by cultural differences (Sue, 1998). For example, Latino and Asian clients are likely to react to a formal interview with a therapist with relative passivity and deference, leading some therapists to diagnose a shyness problem that is only a cultural norm. Latinos may respond to catastrophic stress with an *ataque nervioso*, a nervous attack of screaming, swooning, and agitation. The attack is a culturally determined response, but an uninformed clinician might label it as a sign of pathology (Malgady, Rogler, & Costantino, 1987). Similarly, *susto*, or "loss of the soul," is a common response in Latin American cultures to extreme grief or fright; the person believes that his or her soul has departed along with that of the deceased relative. A psychiatrist unfamiliar with this culturally determined response might conclude that the sufferer was delusional or psychotic.

The American Psychiatric Association (1994) recommends that therapists consider a person's cultural background when making a diagnosis or suggesting treatment. For example, one New York psychiatrist, originally from Peru, treated a woman suffering from *susto* by prescribing a tradition important in her culture: a mourning ritual to help her accept the loss of her uncle. This ritual "was quite powerful for her," the psychiatrist told the *New York Times* (December 5, 1995). "She didn't need any antidepressants, and within a few meetings, including two with her family, her symptoms lifted and she was back participating fully in life once again."

Being aware of cultural differences, however, does not mean that the therapist should stereotype clients (Sue, 1998). Some Asians, after all, do have problems with excessive shyness, some Latinos do have emotional disorders, and some Irish do not feel any burden of guilt! It does mean that therapists must ensure that their clients find them to be trustworthy, understanding, and effective; and it means that clients must be aware of their prejudices, too.

Some psychotherapists fit their approach to the client's cultural background. For example, most Puerto Rican children know the tales of Juan Bobo (left), a foolish child ("bobo") who is always getting into trouble. The therapists on the right have adapted these stories for Puerto Rican children who are coping with new problems and temptations in America. The children and their mothers watch a videotape of the folktale, discuss it together, and later role-play its major themes, such as controlling aggression and understanding right from wrong. This method has been more successful than traditional therapies in reducing the children's transitional anxieties and improving their attention spans and imaginations (Costantino, Malgady, & Rogler, 1986).

Each school of therapy approaches problems differently. Empirical research helps determine which method is best suited for which problem.

Which Therapy for Which Problem? By now, Murray is really motivated to change. He just read a study showing that procrastinators not only get worse grades than other students, but also have more stress and illness during the semester (Tice & Baumeister, 1997). It is time to select a therapeutic approach.

The APA's Division of Clinical Psychology convened a task force to assess the research evaluating specific methods for specific problems (Chambless et al., 1996, 1998). To qualify as an *empirically validated treatment*, a method had to have been tested repeatedly against a placebo or another treatment, and it had to have its efficacy demonstrated by at least two different investigators. Although the task force could not assess every therapy in existence, one key finding emerged clearly: For many problems and most emotional disorders, cognitive and behavior therapies are the method of choice. These therapies are particularly effective for the following problems:

▪ *Depression.* Cognitive therapy's greatest success has been in the treatment of mood disorders, especially depression. It is often more effective than antidepressant drugs alone, and people in cognitive therapy are also less likely than those on drugs to relapse when the treatment is over. The reason may be that the lessons learned in cognitive therapy last a long time, according to follow-ups done from 15 months to many years after treatment (Antonuccio et al., 1999; McNally, 1994; Seligman et al., 1998; Whisman, 1993).

▪ *Anxiety disorders.* Exposure techniques are more effective than any other treatment for posttraumatic stress disorder, simple phobias, and agoraphobia. Systematic desensitization is usually all that is necessary in effectively treating phobias such as fear of dogs or of public speaking. And according to major controlled studies, cognitive-behavior therapy is far more effective than medication for panic disorder, generalized anxiety disorder, and obsessive-compulsive disorder (Kozak et al., 2000; Schwartz et al., 1996). Similarly, a meta-analysis of 80 studies found that although medication helps people with panic disorder in the short run, cognitive-behavior therapy has better results over time (Heisel, 1998).

▪ *Anger and impulsive violence.* Cognitive therapy is extremely successful, for males and females alike, in reducing hotheadedness, chronic anger, abusiveness, and hostility; it also teaches people how to express anger more calmly and constructively (Deffenbacher et al., 1998). For example, it has been used to help young male athletes learn to control angry outbursts that lead to physical and verbal abuse (Abrams & Feindler, 1998).

▪ *Health problems.* Cognitive and behavioral therapies are highly successful in helping people cope with chronic pain, chronic fatigue syndrome, headaches, and irritable bowel syndrome; quit smoking or overcome cocaine and alcohol dependence; recover from eating disorders such as bulimia and binge eating; and manage other health problems (Butler et al., 1991; J. Skinner et al., 1990; Wilson & Fairburn, 1993).

▪ *Childhood and adolescent behavior problems.* Behavior therapy is the most effective treatment for behavior problems that range from bed-wetting to defiant rebelliousness. A meta-analysis of more than 100 studies of children and adolescents found that behavioral treatments worked better than other treatments regardless of the child's age, the therapist's experience, or the specific problem (Weisz et al., 1987, 1995).

Cognitive therapy can even prevent mood disorders from developing in the first place. One such intervention program targeted 69 fifth- and sixth-grade children

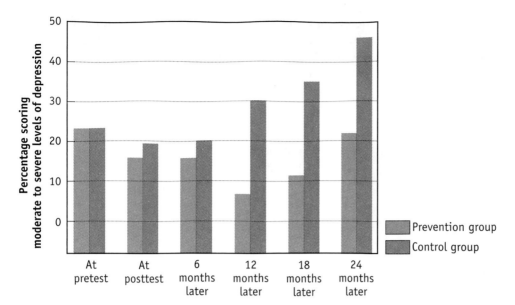

Prevention group
Control group

FIGURE 17.4
INOCULATING CHILDREN AGAINST DEPRESSION

This graph shows the percentage of children who were at moderate to high risk of depression (pretest), and their depression scores after a cognitive intervention (posttest) and during four follow-up assessments. Notice that the effects of the intervention were still strong two years later, as the children entered adolescence (Gillham et al., 1995).

who were considered at risk of depression because they scored high on a children's depression inventory, came from homes with high levels of parental conflict, or both. The children were taught to identify pessimistic beliefs, examine the evidence for and against those beliefs, and generate positive ways of coping. A control group of children who were also at risk of depression did not get this training. As you can see in Figure 17.4, after the training, children in the intervention group had lower depression scores than did those in the control group at all four follow-up sessions. The differences still held two years later, when the children were entering adolescence and when depression rates in the control group shot up steeply (Gillham et al., 1995). A later study of more than 200 college students at risk of depression produced similarly positive results (Seligman et al., 1998).

The APA task force also reported that young adults with schizophrenia are greatly helped by family intervention therapies that teach parents behavioral skills in dealing with their troubled children, and that educate the family in coping with the illness constructively (Chambless et al., 1998; Goldstein & Miklowitz, 1995). Nine studies found that in a two-year period, only 30 percent of the schizophrenic patients in such family-intervention treatments relapsed, compared to 65 percent of those whose families were not involved.

Of course, as the APA task force acknowledged, these important findings do not tell the whole story (nor have we listed every effective therapy the task force identified). Cognitive-behavior therapies are designed for specific, identifiable problems, but sometimes people seek therapy for less clearly defined reasons. They may wish to introspect about their feelings and lives, find solace and courage, or explore moral issues. "Depth" approaches may be well suited for such individuals. Moreover, in spite of their many successes, behavior and cognitive therapies have had their failures, especially with personality disorders and psychoses (Brody, 1990; Foa & Emmelkamp, 1983). These therapies are not highly effective with people who do not want to change and who are not motivated to carry out a behavioral or cognitive program.

Some problems, and some clients, are immune to any single kind of therapy but may respond to *combined* methods. For example, people who have severe and recurrent depressions sometimes respond better to a combination of antidepressants and psychotherapy than to either method alone (Thase et al., 1997). A promising treatment for sex offenders combines cognitive therapy, aversive conditioning, sex education, group therapy, reconditioning of sexual fantasies, and social-skills training (Abel et al., 1988; Kaplan, Morales, & Becker, 1993).

This illustration summarizes the factors contributing to successful therapy: qualities of the participants, the kind of therapy, and the affinity between therapist and client:

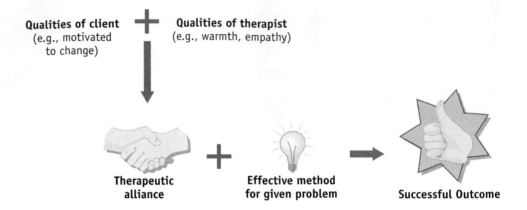

Qualities of client
(e.g., motivated to change)

Qualities of therapist
(e.g., warmth, empathy)

Therapeutic alliance

Effective method for given problem

Successful Outcome

When Therapy Harms

Every treatment and intervention carries risks, and so does psychotherapy. Some people are seriously harmed or unduly influenced by the treatment or by the therapist; their emotional state may deteriorate and their symptoms may worsen. Some clients become excessively dependent, relying on the therapist for all decisions; some therapists actively foster this dependency for financial or psychological motives (Johnson, 1988). Clients can also be harmed by the following:

1 *Coercion to accept the therapist's advice, sexual intimacies, or other unethical behavior.* Some therapists abuse their clients' trust, pressuring them, in subtle or overt ways, to behave in ways the clients would otherwise find reprehensible (Peterson, 1992). Some therapy groups even acquire cultlike attributes, persuading their members that their mental health depends on staying in the group and severing their connections to their "toxic" or "evil" families (Mithers, 1994; Watters & Ofshe, 1999). Such "psychotherapy cults" are created by the therapist's use of techniques that foster the client's dependency and isolation, prevent the client from terminating therapy, and reduce the client's ability to think critically (Temerlin & Temerlin, 1986). In Pennsylvania in 1997, 13 former patients of a group practice called Genesis Associates filed lawsuits claiming that they had been victims of these techniques.

2 *Bias on the part of a therapist who does not understand the client because of the client's gender, culture, religion, or sexual orientation.* A therapist may try to induce the client to conform to the therapist's standards and values, even if they are not appropriate to the client or in the client's best interest (Brodsky, 1982; López, 1989). For example, for many years, gay men and lesbians who entered therapy were told that homosexuality is a mental illness that could be "cured." Some of the so-called treatments were harsh, such as shock applied to the genitals for "inappropriate" arousal. Although the American Psychological Association and the American Psychiatric Association have gone on record opposing therapies that claim to turn gays into heterosexuals, these therapies still surface from time to time, most recently promoted in a campaign by Christian fundamentalists who believe homosexuality is a sin.

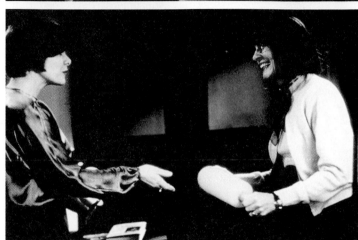

Movies often portray therapists as silly, evil, or unethical. In *Prince of Tides,* Barbra Streisand plays a psychiatrist who becomes sexually involved with her client's brother, who then becomes her client too. In *Good Will Hunting,* Robin Williams plays a therapist who reveals his own personal problems to his client and, at one point, physically threatens him. In *The First Wives Club,* Diane Keaton learns that her husband and her therapist, shown with her here encouraging Keaton to "ventilate" her anger with a bat, were having an affair. Such films imply that these offenses by therapists are common, accepted, harmless practices. But they can be harmful to clients and are all prohibited by the APA's ethical guidelines.

3 *Therapist-induced disorders resulting from inadvertent suggestions or influence.* In a healthy therapeutic alliance, therapists and clients come to agree on an explanation for the client's problems. Of course, the therapist will influence this explanation, according to his or her training and philosophy. This is why Freudian patients have dreams of erotic symbols, and patients in Jungian therapy have dreams of archetypes! However, some therapists so zealously believe in the prevalence of certain problems that they induce the client to produce the symptoms they are looking for (McHugh, 1993b; Merskey, 1995; Watters & Ofshe, 1999).

Therapist influence is a likely reason for the huge number of people diagnosed with multiple personality disorder in the 1980s and 1990s (see Chapter 16). It also helps account for *pseudomemories*, memories that clients construct about events that did not happen. For example, people in primal scream therapy "remember" being born, people in fetal therapy "remember" their lives in the womb, and people in past-lives therapy "remember" being Julius Caesar (or whomever) (Spanos, 1996). The risk to patients increases when a therapist uses hypnosis, sodium amytal (a barbiturate misleadingly called "truth serum"), guided imagery, and other techniques that enhance the client's suggestibility. As we noted in Chapter 10, a significant minority of therapists—between one-fourth and one-third—are using one or more of these techniques specifically to help clients "retrieve" memories of abuse (Poole et al., 1995).

To avoid these risks and take advantage of what good therapy has to offer, it is important to become an educated consumer of psychotherapeutic services.

QUICK QUIZ

Have you formed an alliance with these quizzes?

1. Which of the following is the most important predictor of successful therapy? (a) how long it lasts, (b) the insight it provides the client, (c) the bond between therapist and client, (d) whether the therapist and client are matched according to gender

2. The most important attribute of a good therapist is (a) years of training, (b) warmth and empathy, (c) objective detachment, (d) intellectual ability.

3. In general, which type of psychotherapy is most effective for anxiety and depression?

4. What are three possible sources of harm in psychotherapy?

5. Ferdie, who spends all his free time playing softball, joins a self-help group called "Sportaholics Anonymous" (SA). The group tells him he is suffering from sport addiction and that the only cure is SA. After a few months, Ferdie announces that the group doesn't seem to be helping him and he's going to quit. The other members reply with personal testimonials of how SA has helped them. They tell Ferdie that he is in denial and that his doubts about the group are actually a sign that it's working. What are some problems with their argument?

Answers:

1. c 2. b 3. cognitive-behavior 4. coercion, bias, and therapist-induced disorders 5. The group members have violated the principle of falsifiability (see Chapter 2): That is, they will accept no evidence that disproves their claims. If a person is helped by the group, they say it works; if a person is not helped by the group, they still say it works but the person doesn't know it yet or is "denying" its benefits. They are also arguing by anecdote: Ferdie is not hearing testimonials from people who have dropped out of the group and were not helped by it. Arguing by anecdote is not scientific reasoning, nor is it a way to determine a group's or therapy's effectiveness.

WHAT'S AHEAD

● **What community resources can help people who have serious mental disorders?**
● **What can a self-help group offer that relatives, friends, and psychotherapists cannot?**

ALTERNATIVES TO PSYCHOTHERAPY

Psychotherapy is used for all sorts of problems, but sometimes it is not enough and sometimes it is too much. *Community and rehabilitation programs* aim to help people who are seriously mentally ill or who have disabilities that require more than psychotherapy. *Self-help groups and programs* are designed for people who have problems that do not require professional help.

Community and Rehabilitation Psychology

Many people assume that most individuals who are seriously mentally ill live in hospitals and other institutions, but in the United States, this is not true. The Community Mental Health Centers Act of 1963 called for a nationwide network of mental health centers to replace mental hospitals, which often merely served as warehouses for the mentally ill. But the law was never funded, and thousands of patients were simply "dumped." Between 1955 and 1992 the number of people in mental institutions plummeted from 559,000 to 90,000 (Shogren, 1994). Today, the majority of those with severe mental disorders spend most of their lives in boarding houses, hotel rooms, hostels, jails, hallways, abandoned buildings, halfway houses, or the streets.

At halfway houses, people with mental disorders live "halfway" between hospitalization and independence. They learn to take care of themselves and others, they get job training, and they receive some therapy until they are able to live on their own.

The question of how best to treat them is crucial to these individuals, their families, and society. One answer has been provided by *community psychologists* and other mental-health workers who set up programs to help mentally ill people in their own communities rather than in hospitals (Dion & Anthony, 1987; Orford, 1992). These programs emphasize community support, including outpatient services at local clinics and close contact with family and friends (Harding, Zubin, & Strauss, 1987). The nature of the support depends on the nature of the disorder or disability.

For example, people with schizophrenia need a comprehensive program to help them function in the everyday world. Although drugs are helpful—even essential—they are not sufficient; a drug can reduce symptoms but cannot teach a person how to get (or hold) a job. One successful approach is the *clubhouse model*, a program for mentally ill people that provides rehabilitation counseling, job and skills training, and a support network. Members may live at the clubhouse until they are ready to be on their own, and they may visit the clubhouse at any time (Foderaro, 1994). Other community approaches include family therapy, foster care and family home alternatives, and family support groups (Hatfield & Lefley, 1987; Orford, 1992).

Sadly, community approaches are not available for all who need them. Many mentally ill patients live in nursing homes and board-and-care homes that are unregulated and poorly staffed. For the most part, patients are no better off in these facilities than they were in state institutions (Shadish, Lurigio, & Lewis, 1989). And general hospitals, which are burdened with people who have mental problems, often give patients medication and release them when there are no services and families to care for them. Back on the street, many patients stop taking their medication. Their psychotic symptoms return, they are rehospitalized, and the revolving-door cycle continues.

Increasingly, community psychologists are working with children as well as adults, to prevent or treat problems such as aggressive or disruptive behavior, drug abuse, and difficulty controlling emotions or getting along with others. Community psychologists have developed programs that target not only the child, but also the child's environment in school and at home. Thus, these programs are collaborative, involving the child's parents, teachers, and if necessary physician; the interventions usually occur in the child's community rather than the psychologist's office.

Rehabilitation psychologists are concerned with the assessment and treatment of people who are physically disabled, either temporarily or permanently. They work primarily with people who have chronic pain, severe physical injuries, epilepsy, arthritis, cancer, and addictions. They conduct research to find the best ways to teach disabled people to work and live independently, overcome motivational slumps, improve their sex lives, and follow healthy regimens. The rehabilitation approach to treatment is flexible, often including behavior therapy, group counseling, job training, and community intervention. Because more people are surviving traumatic injuries and living long enough to develop chronic medical conditions, rehabilitation is one of the fastest-growing areas of health care (Frank, Gluck, & Buckelew, 1990).

The Self-help Movement

Not all psychological problems require the aid of a professional. Sometimes the best approach to coping with a problem is to share it with others who are in the same boat you are, or to try to fix it yourself.

Self-help Groups. Self-help or social–support groups are devoted to particular problems or life crises. These groups are available for alcoholics, people who live with alcoholics, abusive parents or spouses, gay fathers, divorced people, women who have had mastectomies, parents of murdered children, rape victims, diabetics, widows and widowers, stepparents, cancer patients, relatives of patients, and people with just about any other concern you can think of. An estimated 7 to 15 million adults in North America belong to a self-help group (Christensen & Jacobson, 1994).

Formal and informal support groups provide a setting for sharing concerns and exchanging constructive advice, as these men with AIDS are doing.

A survey of 1,900 randomly selected Americans found that about 40 percent participate regularly in a small group that provides emotional support for its members. About two-thirds of these groups are organized around prayer or Bible study and the others around shared problems or interests. Regardless of the kind of group, members say that the primary benefits are the awareness that they are not alone, encouragement when they are feeling down, and help in feeling better about themselves (Wuthnow, 1995).

Self-help groups offer understanding, empathy, and solutions to shared problems. Such groups can be reassuring and supportive in ways that family, friends, and psychotherapists are not (Dunkel-Schetter, 1984; Wyatt & Mickey, 1987). For example, people with disabilities face unique challenges that involve coping not only with physical problems but also with the condescension, hostility, and prejudice of many nondisabled people (Linton, 1998; Robertson, 1995). Other disabled people, who share these challenges, can provide useful advice and resources.

Self-help groups, however, do not provide psychotherapy for specific problems, and they are not designed to help people with serious psychological difficulties. They are not subject to legal regulations or professional standards, and they vary widely in their philosophies and methods. Some are accepting and tolerant, offering support, cohesiveness, and spiritual guidance. Others are confrontational and coercive, and members who disagree with the premises of the group may be made to feel deviant or defensive. If you choose to become part of a support group, be sure it falls in the first category.

DON'T OVERSIMPLIFY

Many people buy self-help books uncritically and then blame themselves if the books don't help them. Others think just about all self-help books are pretty dumb. How can people find a middle ground between overestimating the value of these books and dismissing them all as useless?

Self-help Books. A major part of the self-help movement in the United States and Canada consists of advice books, many of them written by psychologists. These books, which address nearly every personal or relationship problem you can think of, are as popular as ice cream in August. But do they work?

The answer is—sometimes. Self-help books that propose a specific program for the reader to follow can be as effective as treatment administered by a therapist, as long as the reader follows the recommendations (Christensen & Jacobson, 1994). However, not all books are based on solid psychological principles, and the fact that a book has been written by a psychologist is no guarantee of its merit. An APA committee investigated the merits of self-help books and tapes, and concluded that "unfortunately, [psychologists] have

February 21, 1999

THE NEW YORK TIMES BOOK REVIEW

Best Sellers

Advice, How-to and Miscellaneous

1 HOW TO GET WHAT YOU WANT AND WANT WHAT YOU HAVE, by John Gray. (HarperCollins, $24.95.) A guide to personal success. (†) 2 2

2 LIFE STRATEGIES, by Phillip C. McGraw. (Hyperion, $21.95.) How to find what matters in your life and what to do about it. (†) 1 4

3 SUGAR BUSTERS! by H. Leighton Steward et al. (Ballantine, $22.) A diet designed for losing weight, increasing energy and combating disease. (†) 3 33

4 ONE DAY MY SOUL JUST OPENED UP, by Iyanla Vanzant. (Fireside/S&S, $13.) How to raise one's morale and realize one's ambitions. (†) 11

These best-selling "how to" books promise to help you "get what you want," "find what matters in your life," lose weight while "combating disease," and raise your morale and ambitions. The pep talks in such books, however, are generally too vague to be helpful.

published untested materials, advanced exaggerated claims, and accepted the use of misleading titles that encourage unrealistic expectations regarding outcome" (Rosen, 1981). This situation remains unchanged today.

Recognizing that self-help books and programs can be effective, however, the head of the APA committee offered some guidelines for evaluating a self-help book (Rosen, 1981):

■ *The authors should be qualified, which means that they have conducted good research or are thoroughly versed in the field.* Personal testimonials by people who have survived difficulties or tragedy can be inspirational, of course, but an author's own experience is not grounds for generalizing to everyone.

■ *The book should include evidence of the program's effectiveness* and not simply the author's claims that it works. Many self-help books offer untested advice, and some products, such as "subliminal" tapes, are based on claims that are flat-out wrong (see Chapter 6).

■ *The advice should be organized in a systematic, step-by-step program,* not as a vague pep talk to "take charge of your life" or "find love in your heart"; and the reader should be told how to evaluate his or her progress.

■ *The book should not promise the impossible.* This lets out books that promise you perfect sex, total love, or high self-esteem in 30 hours or 30 days.

Some books do meet all of these criteria. One is *Changing for Good* (Prochaska, Norcross, & DiClemente, 1994), which describes the common ingredients of effective change that apply to people in and out of therapy. But as long as people yearn for a magic bullet to cure their problems—a pill, a book, a subliminal tape—quick-fix solutions will find an audience.

QUICK QUIZ

Help yourself by taking this quiz.

1. What kind of psychologist is trained to help people cope with chronic illness or disability or recover from injury?

2. What are four guidelines for assessing the merits of a self-help book or program?

Answers:

1. a rehabilitation psychologist 2. The author should be qualified and knowledgeable; the program should have been tested for effectiveness; the program should be presented in clear steps rather than as a pep talk; the program should not promise the impossible.

ASK QUESTIONS

The benefits of psychotherapy are well documented, but we can ask questions about its implicit messages. Does psychotherapy foster unrealistic expectations of personal change? Does it promote individualism at the expense of community and relationships?

How much can therapy change a person?

THE SEVEN DWARFS AFTER THERAPY

THE VALUE AND VALUES OF PSYCHOTHERAPY

Modern psychotherapy has been of enormous value to many people. But psychotherapists have raised some important questions about the *values* inherent in what they do (Cushman, 1995; Hillman & Ventura, 1992; Wallach & Wallach, 1983). How much personal change is possible, and do some therapists promise their clients too much? Does psychotherapy, by encouraging people to look inward to their feelings and woes, foster a preoccupation with the self? Can self-fulfillment be achieved without also improving one's relationships and contributing to the larger world?

In his book *The Shrinking of America*, psychotherapist Bernie Zilbergeld (1983) argued that psychotherapy, while beneficial in most cases, promotes three myths that increase people's dissatisfaction with themselves: People should always be happy, and if they are not happy they need fixing; almost any change is possible; and change is relatively easy. In contrast, as discussed in Chapter 15, Eastern cultures have a less optimistic view of change, and they tend to be more tolerant of events they regard as being outside of human control. In the Japanese practice of Morita therapy, therefore, clients are taught to accept and live with their most troubling emotions, instead of trying to eradicate these psychological weeds from the lawn of life (Reynolds, 1987). Some Western psychotherapists now teach techniques of mindful meditation and greater self-acceptance instead of constant self-improvement (Kabat-Zinn, 1994).

Today, most therapists are realistic about what psychotherapy can and cannot do. In the hands of an empathic and knowledgeable practitioner, psychotherapy can help you make decisions and clarify your values and goals. It can teach you new skills and new ways of thinking. It can help you get along better with your family and break out of destructive family patterns. It can get you through bad times when no one seems to care or understand.

But psychotherapy cannot transform you into someone you're not. It cannot cure a disorder overnight. It cannot provide a life without problems. And it is not intended to substitute for experience—for work that is satisfying, relationships that are sustaining, activities that are enjoyable. As Socrates knew, the unexamined life is not worth living. But as an anonymous philosopher added, the unlived life is not worth examining.

TAKING PSYCHOLOGY WITH YOU

BECOMING A SMART CONSUMER OF THERAPY

In North America today, a vast array of therapies fills the marketplace. To protect themselves, as well as to get the best possible help, consumers need to be informed and know how to choose wisely. Some people spend more time looking for a good dentist than

for a good therapist. You would not be likely to keep going to a dentist, year after year, if your toothache got worse and the dentist merely kept promising to make it go away. Yet some people stay in therapy, year after year, with no resolution of their problems. The research

discussed in this chapter suggests the following guidelines for making the best use of therapy:

■ *Knowing when to start.* If you have a persistent problem that you do not know how to solve, one that causes you considerable unhappiness and that has lasted six months or more, it may be time to look for help.

- **Setting goals.** Try to identify exactly what you expect from therapy, and discuss your goals with the therapist. Do you want to solve a problem in your relationships or in your emotional life? Are your goals realistic? Some therapies, as we saw in this chapter, are designed not for solving problems but for exploring ideas and feelings. If you know what you want from therapy, you are less likely to feel disappointed later. You will also be better able to select a therapist who can meet your needs.

- **Choosing a therapist.** As we saw in Chapter 1, a person must have an advanced degree and a period of supervised training to become a licensed psychologist, psychiatrist, counselor, or social worker. Your school counseling center is a good place to start if you are looking for a therapist or a referral. You might also seek out a university psychology clinic, where you can get therapy with a graduate student in training; these students are closely supervised and the fees will be lower. If you know the kind of therapy you want, check your phone book; many therapists are listed according to the kind of therapy they do.

- **Choosing a therapy.** As we saw, not all therapies are equally effective for all problems. You should not spend four years in psychodynamic therapy for panic attacks, which can generally be helped in a few sessions of cognitive-behavior therapy. Likewise, as the APA task force recommends, if you have a specific emotional problem, such as depression, anger, or anxiety, or if you are coping with chronic health problems, look for a cognitive or cognitive–behavior therapist. However, if you just want to discuss your life with a wise and empathic person, the kind of therapy may not matter so much.

- **Negotiating the fee.** The amount of payment does not affect the success of the therapy (Orlinsky, 1994; Yoken & Berman, 1984). As a consumer, you can often negotiate a fee depending on what you can afford. If you have medical insurance that pays for psychotherapy, find out what kind of therapies your policy covers.

- **Deciding when to leave.** If you begin a time-limited treatment, such as 12 sessions of brief therapy or a seven-session airplane-phobia program, you ought to stick with it to the end. In unlimited therapy, however, you have the right to determine when enough is enough, especially if the therapist has been unable to help you with your problem after a considerable length of time.

If you have made a real effort to work with a therapist and there has been no result after ample time and effort, the reason could have as much to do with the treatment or therapist as with you. But as we have cautioned repeatedly, don't expect quick fixes or miracle cures. Successful therapy requires motivation, persistence, a willingness to face possibly unwelcome truths, and the courage to change.

SUMMARY

BIOLOGICAL TREATMENTS FOR MENTAL DISORDERS

1. Over the centuries, people trying to understand and treat psychological disorders have often taken a biological approach, and today, biological treatments are enjoying a resurgence.

2. Medications most commonly prescribed for mental disorders include *antipsychotic drugs*, used in treating schizophrenia and other psychotic disorders; *antidepressants*, used in treating depression, anxiety disorders, and obsessive-compulsive disorder; *tranquilizers*, often prescribed for emotional problems; and *lithium carbonate*, a salt used to treat bipolar disorder. Antidepressants are generally more effective for mood disorders than are tranquilizers, which can become addictive.

3. Drawbacks of drug treatment include the *placebo effect*; high dropout and relapse rates among people who take medications without also learning how to cope with their problems; the difficulty of finding the correct dose (the *therapeutic window*) for each individual, compounded by the fact that a person's ethnicity, sex, and age can influence a drug's effectiveness; and the long-term risks of medication, known and unknown. Medication can be helpful and can even save lives, but it should not be prescribed mindlessly and routinely, especially when nondrug therapies can work as well as drugs for many mood and behavioral problems.

4. When drugs or psychotherapy have failed to help seriously disturbed people, some psychiatrists have intervened directly in the brain. *Psychosurgery*, which destroys selected areas of the brain thought to be responsible for a psychological problem, is rarely done today. *Electroconvulsive therapy (ECT)*, in which a

brief current is sent through the brain, has been used successfully to treat suicidal depression. However, controversy exists about its effects on the brain and the appropriateness of its use.

KINDS OF PSYCHOTHERAPY

5. The hundreds of existing psychotherapies basically fall into four schools: (1) *Psychodynamic ("depth") therapies* include Freudian *psychoanalysis* and its modern variations, which explore unconscious dynamics. *Brief psychodynamic therapy* is a time-limited version that focuses on one major dynamic issue. (2) *Behavior and cognitive therapies* draw on principles of learning and cognition. Behavior therapists use such methods as systematic desensitization, aversive conditioning, flooding or exposure, behavioral contracts, and skills training. Cognitive therapists aim to change the irrational thoughts involved in negative emotions and self-defeating actions. (3) *Humanist and existential therapies* attempt to help people feel better about themselves by focusing on here-and-now issues and helping people cope with philosophical dilemmas, such as the meaning of life and the fear of death. (4) *Family therapies* share the view that individual problems develop in the context of the whole family network. Some family therapists use a *genogram* to identify patterns of behavior across generations. Finally, some therapists treat individuals in *group therapy*, hoping that the influence of other people with psychological problems will help the participants improve.

6. In practice, many therapists are flexible, drawing on many methods and ideas. And whatever their nature, successful therapies share some elements, such as efforts to help clients form more adaptive "life stories."

EVALUATING PSYCHOTHERAPY

7. A *scientist-practitioner gap* has developed because of the different assumptions held by researchers and many clinicians regarding the value of empirical research for doing psychotherapy and for assessing its effectiveness. The gap has led to a proliferation of scientifically unvalidated psychotherapies.

8. *Controlled clinical trials* show that, overall, psychotherapy is better than no treatment at all; that it is most effective with people who have the least serious disorders and who are motivated to improve; that for problems other than chronic mental disorders, short-term treatment is as effective as long-term therapy; and that sometimes therapy can be harmful.

9. The clients who benefit most from psychotherapy are motivated to solve their problems and willing to take responsibility for them. Good therapists are empathic, warm, and constructive. Successful therapy requires a *therapeutic alliance* between the therapist and the client, so that they understand each other and can work together. When therapist and client are of different ethnicities, both must try to avoid prejudice, misunderstanding, and stereotyping.

10. Some therapies are demonstrably better than others for specific problems. Behavior and cognitive-behavior therapies are the most effective for depression, anxiety disorders, anger, certain health problems and eating disorders, and childhood and adolescent behavior problems. Depth therapies may be most effective for people who want to introspect about their lives. And some individuals, such as sex offenders and chronic sufferers of schizophrenia, respond well to combined techniques.

11. In some cases, therapy is harmful. The therapist may foster the client's dependency; be coercive, biased, or unethical; or inadvertently create disorders through undue influence or suggestion, as in the case of therapist-induced *pseudomemories*.

ALTERNATIVES TO PSYCHOTHERAPY

12. People who have severe mental disorders, such as schizophrenia, or who have physical disabilities resulting from disease or injury, may benefit from alternatives to individual psychotherapy. *Community psychologists* set up programs in the community to treat mental-health problems, using many strategies, including the *clubhouse model*. *Rehabilitation psychologists* are concerned with the assessment and treatment of people who are physically disabled. *Self-help groups* are organized around a specific problem or common interest; they can be immensely helpful, but they vary widely in their methods and results. Self-help books can be helpful too, if they are based on empirically validated research and tested programs.

THE VALUE AND VALUES OF PSYCHOTHERAPY

13. Consumers need to choose a therapist carefully and be realistic about what they expect of psychotherapy. Therapy can help you in many ways, but it cannot transform you into something you are not, and it cannot substitute for the family, friends, and work that everyone needs.

KEY TERMS

LOOKING BACK

- What kinds of drugs are used to treat psychological disorders? (pp. 618–619)

- Are antidepressants always the best treatment for depression? (pp. 620–621)

- Can mental disorders be cured by brain surgery? (p. 622)

- Why is "shock therapy" hailed by some clinicians but condemned by others? (p. 623)

- Why are psychodynamic therapies called "depth" therapies? (p. 624)

- How can therapies based on learning principles change self-defeating habits? (pp. 625–626)

- How do cognitive therapists help people get rid of self-defeating thoughts? (pp. 627–628)

- Why do humanist therapists focus on the "here and now" instead of the "why and how"? (p. 628)

- Why do family therapists prefer to treat families rather than individuals? (pp. 629–630)

- What is the "scientist-practitioner gap"—and why has it been widening? (p. 634)

- What does research tell us about the effectiveness of psychotherapy? (pp. 635–636)

- What sorts of people make the best therapists—and the best clients? (p. 636)

- Which form of psychotherapy is most likely to help if you are anxious or depressed? (p. 638)

- Under what conditions can psychotherapy be harmful? (pp. 640–641)

- What community resources can help people who have serious mental disorders? (p. 643)

- What can a self-help group offer that relatives, friends, and psychotherapists cannot? (p. 644)

EPILOGUE
TAKING PSYCHOLOGY WITH YOU

We [human beings] never stop investigating. We are never satisfied that we know enough to get by. Every question we answer leads on to another question. This has become the greatest survival trick of our species.

ZOOLOGIST DESMOND MORRIS

You have come a long way since the beginning of this book. It is now time to stand back and ask yourself where you've been and what you've learned from the many studies, topics, and controversies that you have read about. What fundamental principles emerge, and how can you take them with you into your own life? By now, you probably won't be surprised that different psychologists would answer these questions differently. Still, we believe that a "big picture" exists in the study of psychology, and that it reveals five fundamental determinants of human behavior.

THE FIVE STRANDS OF HUMAN EXPERIENCE

In Chapter 1, we described five general perspectives on human behavior that guide the assumptions and methods of psychologists. Each of these perspectives on human experience offers questions to ask when trying to understand or change a particular aspect of your own life:

1 *Biological influences.* As physical creatures, we are influenced by our bodies and our brains. Physiology affects the rhythms of our lives, our perceptions of reality, our ability to learn, the intensity of our emotions, our temperaments, and in some cases our vulnerability to emotional disorder.

Thus, when you are distressed, you might want to start by asking yourself what might be going on in your body. Do you have a physical condition that might be affecting your behavior? Do you have a temperamental tendency to be easily aroused or to be calm? Are alcohol or other drugs altering your ability to make decisions or behave as you would like? Might an irregular schedule be disrupting your physical functions and impairing your efficiency? Are you under unusual pressures that increase your physical stress?

2 *Learning influences.* From the moment of birth, we begin learning and are exquisitely sensitive to our environments. What we do and how we do it are often a result of our learning histories and the specific situations we are in. We respond to the environment, and, in turn, our actions have consequences that influence future behavior. The right environment and rewards can help us cope better with disabilities, get along better with others, and even become more creative and happy. The wrong kind can foster boredom, hostility, and discontent.

So, as you analyze a situation, you will want to examine the contingencies and consequences governing your behavior and that of others. What rewards are maintaining your behavior? Of the many messages being aimed at you by television, books, parents, friends, and teachers, which have the greatest influence? Who are your role models, the people you most admire and wish to emulate?

3 *Social and cultural influences.* Although most Westerners think of themselves as independent creatures, everyone conforms to some extent to the expectations and demands of others. Spouses, lovers, friends, bosses, parents, and perfect strangers "pull our strings" in ways we may not recognize. We conform to group pressures, obey authorities, and blossom or wilt in close relationships. Throughout life, we need "contact comfort"—sometimes in the literal touch or embrace of others and sometimes in shared experience or conversation. Although many universals of behavior unite humanity, "human nature" also varies from one culture to another. Culture dictates a set of norms and roles for how employers and employees, strangers and friends, and men and women are supposed to act. Whenever you find yourself wondering irritably why "*those* people are behaving that way," chances are that a cultural difference or misunderstanding is at work.

So, in solving problems, you might think about the people in your life who are affecting you. Do your friends and relatives support you or hinder you in achieving your goals? How do your ethnicity and nationality affect you? What gender roles do they specify for you and your partners in close relationships, and what would happen if you ignored the norms of your role? Are your conflicts with others a result of cultural misunderstandings—due, for instance, to differing rules for expressing emotion?

4 *Cognitive influences.* Our species is, above all, the animal that explains things. These explanations may not always be realistic or sensible, but they continually influence our actions and choices. When you have a problem, ask yourself how you are framing the situation you are in. Are your explanations of what is causing the problem reasonable? Have you tested them? Are you wallowing in negative thoughts? Do you attribute your successes to luck but take all the blame for your failures—or do you take credit for your successes and blame everyone else for your failures? Do you assume the worst about others? Do you make external attributions or internal ones? Are you responding to other people's expectations in a mindless way?

5 *Psychodynamic influences.* People are often unaware of the reasons they are getting themselves in trouble, just as they are unaware of the defense mechanisms they use to rationalize mistakes and protect self-esteem. If you find that you are repeating self-defeating patterns, expectations, and emotional reactions, you might want to consider why. Do other people "push your buttons" for reasons you cannot explain? Are you displacing feelings about your parents onto your friends or intimates? Are you carrying around "unfinished business" from childhood losses and hurts?

Keep in mind that no single one of these factors operates in isolation from the others. The forces that govern our behavior are as intertwined as strands of ivy on a wall, and it can be hard to see where one strand begins and another ends. This message, if enough people believed it, would probably put an end to the pop-psych industry, which promotes single, simple answers to real-life complexities. Some simplifiers of psychology try to reduce human problems to biochemical imbalances or genetic defects. Others argue that anyone can "fulfill any potential," regardless of biology or environment, and that solving problems is merely a matter of having enough determination.

In this book, we have tried to show that the concerns and dilemmas of life do not divide up neatly according to the chapters of an introductory psychology text (even ours). For example, to understand shyness or loneliness, you might consider whether you have a temperamental disposition toward introversion and shyness; your personal learning history; childhood experiences and what you observed from adult role models; how stress, diet, drugs, and sleep patterns might be affecting your mood; and whether you come from a culture that encourages or prohibits assertiveness. It may seem daunting to keep so many factors in mind. But once you get into the habit of seeing a situation from many points of view, relying on single-answer approaches will feel like wearing blinders. And it's a habit that will inoculate you against appealing pop-psych ideas that are unsupported by evidence.

PSYCHOLOGY IN YOUR LIFE

If the theories and findings in this book are to be of long-lasting value to you, they must jump off the printed page and into your daily life. To give you some practice in applying them, we will look at an all-too-common problem—what to do when love is dwindling in a close relationship—and offer some ideas about where to look in this book for principles and findings that may shed light on it. Our list is far from exhaustive; feel free to come up with additional ideas.

Let's say you have been romantically involved with someone for a year. When the relationship began, you felt very much in love, and you thought your feelings were returned. But for a long time now, your partner's treatment of you has been anything but loving. In fact, your partner makes fun of your faults in front of others and yells at you about the slightest annoyance. Sometimes your partner ignores you for days on end, as if to punish you for some imagined wrong. Your friends advise you to leave the relationship, yet you can't shake the feeling that your partner really loves you. You still occasionally have a great time together, and your partner appears distressed whenever you threaten to leave. You wish you could either improve the relationship or get out, and your inability to act leaves you feeling angry and depressed.

How might each of the following topics help you resolve this problem? We suggest that you try to come up with your own answers, aided by these chapter references, before you look at ours:

- Approach-avoidance conflicts (Chapter 12)
- Intermittent reinforcement (Chapter 7)
- Observational learning (Chapter 7)
- Locus of control (Chapter 13)
- Cognitive-dissonance theory (Chapter 9)
- Gender differences in emotion and love (Chapters 11 and 12)
- Attribution theory (Chapter 8)

Here are a few reasons why these topics might apply, but, again, feel free to think of others:

- *Approach-avoidance conflicts* may characterize your relationship, which may help explain why you are both attracted to and repelled by it and why the closer you approach, the more you want to leave (and vice versa). When a goal is both attractive and painful, it is not unusual to feel uncertain and to vacillate about possible courses of action.

- *Intermittent reinforcement* may explain why you persist in apparently self-defeating behavior. If staying in the relationship brought only punishment or if your partner always ignored you, it would be easier to leave. But your partner intermittently gives you good times, and when behavior is occasionally rewarded, it becomes resistant to extinction.

- Past *observational learning* may help account for your present behavior. Perhaps your parents have a relationship like the one you are in, and their way of interacting is what you have learned to expect in your own relationships.

- If you have an *external locus of control,* you feel that you cannot control what is happening to you, that you are merely a victim of fate, chance, or the wishes of others. People with an internal locus of control feel more in charge of their lives and are less inclined to blame outside circumstances for their difficulties.

- *Cognitive-dissonance theory* suggests that you may be trying to keep your attitudes and behavior consistent. The cognition "I am in this relationship and choose to be with this person" is dissonant with "This person ignores and mistreats me." Because you are still unable to break up and alter the first cognition, you are working on the second cognition, hoping that your partner will change for the better.

- Research on *gender differences* finds that men and women often have different unstated rules about expressing emotion and different definitions of love. Perhaps traditional gender roles are preventing you and your partner from communicating your true preferences and feelings.

- *Attribution theory* addresses the consequences of holding dispositional explanations of another person's behavior (it's due to something about the person) or situational explanations (it's due to something about the circumstances). Unhappy couples tend to make dispositional attributions when the partner does something wrong or thoughtless ("My partner is mean"); happy couples look for situational attributions ("My partner is under a lot of pressure at work"). You might test different possible reasons that your partner is treating you badly. Is the behavior characteristic of your partner in many situations, or might it be a result of stress, particular problems with you, or other difficulties?

Understanding your situation, of course, does not lead automatically to a solution. Depending on the circumstances, you might choose to cope with the situation as it is (Chapter 15); change your attributions about your partner (Chapter 8); use learning principles to try to alter your own or your partner's behavior (Chapter 7); consider how your perceptions and beliefs are affecting your emotions (Chapter 11); seek psychotherapy, with or without your partner (Chapter 17); or leave the relationship.

Our example was an individual problem, but the applications of psychology extend beyond personal concerns to social ones, as we have seen throughout this book: disputes between neighbors and nations; prejudice and cross-cultural relations; the best ways to rear moral, considerate, and competent children; the formulation of social policies, such as ways of improving school performance or reducing drug abuse; and countless other issues.

Of course, research findings often change as new questions are asked, new methods become available, and new theories evolve. Indeed, some findings become dated in a year, thanks to the speed of the information explosion. That is why the one chapter that may ultimately be most useful to you is the one you may have assumed to be least useful: Chapter 2, "How Psychologists Do Research." The best way to take psychology with you is to understand its basic ways of approaching problems and questions—that is, its principles of critical and scientific thinking. Old theories give way to new ones, dated results yield to contemporary ones, dead-end investigations halt and new directions are taken. But the methods of psychology continue, and critical thinking is their hallmark.

Drawing by Lorenz; © 1989 The New Yorker Magazine, Inc.

*"I still don't have all the answers,
but I'm beginning to ask the right questions."*

APPENDIX

STATISTICAL METHODS

Nineteenth-century English statesman Benjamin Disraeli reportedly once named three forms of dishonesty: "lies, damned lies, and statistics." It is certainly true that people can lie with the help of statistics. It happens all the time: Advertisers, politicians, and others with some claim to make either use numbers inappropriately or ignore certain critical ones. (When hearing that "four out of five doctors surveyed" recommended some product, have you ever wondered just how many doctors were surveyed and whether they were representative of all doctors?) People also use numbers to convey a false impression of certainty and objectivity when the true state of affairs is uncertainty or ignorance. But it is people, not statistics, that lie. When statistics are used correctly, they neither confuse nor mislead. On the contrary, they expose unwarranted conclusions, promote clarity and precision, and protect us from our own biases and blind spots.

If statistics are useful anywhere, it is in the study of human behavior. If human beings were all alike, and psychologists could specify all the influences on behavior, there would be no need for statistics. But any time we measure human behavior, we are going to wind up with different observations or scores for different individuals. Statistics can help us spot trends amid the diversity.

This appendix will introduce you to some basic statistical calculations used in psychology. Reading the appendix will not make you into a statistician, but it will acquaint you with some ways of organizing and assessing research data. If you suffer from a "number phobia," relax: You do not need to know much math to understand this material. However, you should have read Chapter 2, which discussed the rationale for using statistics and described various research methods. You may want to review the basic terms and concepts covered in that chapter. Be sure that you can define *hypothesis, sample, correlation, independent variable, dependent variable, random assignment, experimental group, control group, descriptive statistics, inferential statistics* and *test of statistical significance*. (Correlation coefficients, which are described in some detail in Chapter 2, will not be covered here.)

To read the tables in this appendix, you will also need to know the following symbols:

N = the total number of observations or scores in a set

X = an observation or score

Σ = the Greek capital letter sigma, read as "the sum of"

$\sqrt{}$ = the square root of

(*Note:* Boldfaced terms in this appendix are defined in the glossary at the end of the book.)

ORGANIZING DATA

Before we can discuss statistics, we need some numbers. Imagine that you are a psychologist and that you are interested in that most pleasing of human qualities, a sense of humor. You suspect that a well-developed funny bone can protect people from the negative emotional effects of stress. You already know that in the months following a stressful event, people who score high on sense-of-humor tests tend to feel less tense and moody than more sobersided individuals do. You realize, though, that this correlational evidence does not prove cause and effect. Perhaps people with a healthy sense of humor have other traits, such as flexibility or creativity, that act as the true stress buffers. To find out whether humor itself really softens the impact of stress, you do an experiment.

First, you randomly assign subjects to two groups, an experimental group and a control group. To keep our calculations simple, let's assume there are only 15 people per group. Each person individually views a silent film that most North Americans find fairly stressful, one showing Australian aboriginal boys undergoing a puberty rite involving genital mutilation. Subjects in the experimental group are instructed to make up a humorous monologue while watching the film. Those in the control group are told to make up a straightforward narrative. After the film, each person answers a mood questionnaire that measures current feelings of tension, depression, aggressiveness, and anxiety. A person's overall score on the questionnaire can range from 1 (no mood disturbance) to 7 (strong mood disturbance). This procedure provides you with 15 "mood disturbance" scores for each group. Have people who tried to be humorous reported less disturbance than those who did not?

Constructing a Frequency Distribution

Your first step might be to organize and condense the "raw data" (the obtained scores) by constructing a **frequency distribution** for each group. A frequency distribution shows how often each possible score actually occurred. To construct one, you first order all the possible scores from highest to lowest. (Our mood disturbance scores will be ordered from 7 to 1.) Then you tally how often each score was actually obtained. Table A.1 gives some hypothetical raw data for the two groups, and Table A.2 shows the two frequency distributions

TABLE A.1   Some Hypothetical Raw Data

These scores are for the hypothetical humor-and-stress study described in the text.

Experimental group	4,5,4,4,3,6,5,2,4,3,5,4,4,3,4
Control group	6,4,7,6,6,4,6,7,7,5,5,5,7,6,6

based on these data. From these distributions you can see that the two groups differed. In the experimental group, the extreme scores of 7 and 1 did not occur at all, and the most common score was the middle one, 4. In the control group, a score of 7 occurred four times, the most common score was 6, and no one obtained a score lower than 4.

Because our mood scores have only seven possible values, our frequency distributions are quite manageable. Suppose, though, that your questionnaire had yielded scores that could range from 1 to 50. A frequency distribution with 50 entries would be cumbersome and might not reveal trends in the data clearly. A solution would be to construct a *grouped frequency distribution* by grouping adjacent scores into equal-sized *classes* or *intervals*. Each interval could cover, say, five scores (1–5, 6–10, 11–15, and so forth). Then you could tally the frequencies within each *interval*. This procedure would reduce the number of entries in each distribution from 50 to only 10, making the overall results much easier to grasp. However, information would be lost. For example, there would be no way of knowing how many people had a score of 43 versus 44.

Graphing the Data

As everyone knows, a picture is worth a thousand words. The most common statistical picture is a **graph,** a drawing that depicts numerical relationships. Graphs appear at several points in this book, and are routinely used by psychologists to convey their findings to others. From graphs, we can get a general impression of what the data are like, note the relative frequencies of different scores, and see which score was most frequent.

In a graph constructed from a frequency distribution, the possible score values are shown along a horizontal line (the *x-axis* of the graph) and frequencies along a vertical line (the *y-axis*), or vice versa. To construct a **histogram,** or **bar graph,** from our mood scores, we draw rectangles (bars) above each score, indicating the number of times it occurred by the rectangle's height (Figure A.1).

A slightly different kind of "picture" is provided by a **frequency polygon,** or **line graph.** In a frequency polygon, the frequency of each score is indicated by a dot placed directly over the score on the horizontal axis, at the appropriate height on the vertical axis. The dots for the various scores are then joined together by straight lines, as in Figure A.2. When necessary an "extra" score, with a frequency of zero, can be added at each end of the horizontal axis, so that the polygon will rest on this axis instead of floating above it.

TABLE A.2   Two Frequency Distributions

The scores are from Table A.1.

Experimental Group			Control Group		
Mood Disturbance Score	Tally	Frequency	Mood Disturbance Score	Tally	Frequency
7		0	7	////	4
6	/	1	6	//// /	6
5	///	3	5	///	3
4	//// //	7	4	//	2
3	///	3	3		0
2	/	1	2		0
1		0	1		0
		N = 15			*N* = 15

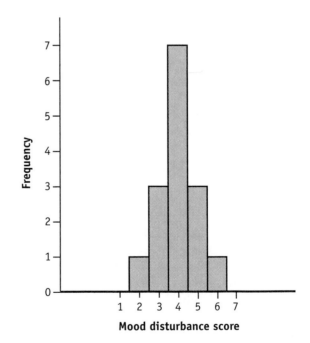

FIGURE A.1
A HISTOGRAM

This graph depicts the distribution of mood disturbance scores shown on the left side of Table A.2.

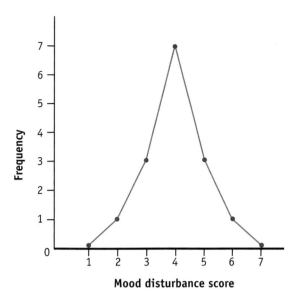

FIGURE A.2
A FREQUENCY POLYGON
This graph depicts the same data as Figure A.1.

A word of caution about graphs: They may either exaggerate or mask differences in the data, depending on which units are used on the vertical axis. The two graphs in Figure A.3, although they look quite different, actually depict the same data. Always read the units on the axes of a graph; otherwise, the shape of a histogram or frequency polygon may be misleading.

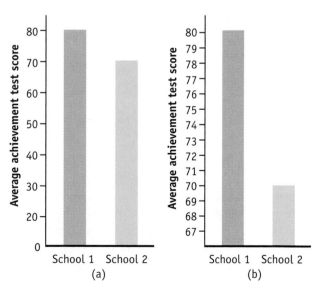

FIGURE A.3
SAME DATA, DIFFERENT IMPRESSIONS
These two graphs depict the same data, but have different units on the vertical axis.

DESCRIBING DATA

Having organized your data, you are now ready to summarize and describe them. As you will recall from Chapter 2, procedures for doing so are known as **descriptive statistics.** In the following discussion, the word *score* will stand for any numerical observation.

Measuring Central Tendency

Your first step in describing your data might be to compute a **measure of central tendency** for each group. Measures of central tendency characterize an entire set of data in terms of a single representative number.

The Mean. The most popular measure of central tendency is the arithmetic mean, usually called simply the **mean.** It is often expressed by the symbol *M.* Most people are thinking of the mean when they say "average." We run across means all the time: in grade point averages, temperature averages, and batting averages. The mean is valuable to the psychologist because it takes all the data into account and it can be used in further statistical analyses. To compute the mean, you simply add up a set of scores and divide the total by the number of scores in the set. Recall that in mathematical notation, Σ means "the sum of," X stands for the individual scores, and N represents the total number of scores in a set. Thus the formula for calculating the mean is:

$$M = \frac{\Sigma X}{N}$$

Table A.3 shows how to compute the mean for our experimental group. Test your ability to perform this calculation by computing the mean for the control group yourself. (You can find the answer, along with other control group statistics,

---

TABLE A.3   Calculating a Mean and a Median

The scores are from the left side of Table A.1.

Mean (*M*)

$$M = \frac{4 + 5 + 4 + 4 + 3 + 6 + 5 + 2 + 4 + 3 + 5 + 4 + 4 + 3 + 4}{15}$$

$$= \frac{60}{15}$$

$$= 4$$

Median

Scores, in order: 2, 3, 3, 3, 4, 4, 4, $\boxed{4,}$ 4, 4, 4, 5, 5, 5, 6

↑
Median

on page A-7.) Later, we will describe how a psychologist would compare the two means statistically to see if there is a significant difference between them.

The Median. Despite its usefulness, sometimes the mean can be misleading, as we noted in Chapter 2. Suppose you piled some children on a seesaw in such a way that it was perfectly balanced, and then a 200-pound adult came and sat on one end. The center of gravity would quickly shift toward the adult. In the same way, one extremely high score can dramatically raise the mean (and one extremely low score can dramatically lower it). In real life, this can be a serious problem. For example, in the calculation of a town's mean income, one millionaire would offset hundreds of poor people. The mean income would be a misleading indication of the town's actual wealth.

When extreme scores occur, a more representative measure of central tendency is the **median,** or midpoint in a set of scores or observations ordered from highest to lowest. In any set of scores, the same *number* of scores falls above the median as below it. The median is not affected by extreme scores. If you were calculating the *median* income of that same town, the one millionaire would offset only one poor person.

When the number of scores in the set is odd, calculating the median is a simple matter of counting in from the ends to the middle. However, if the number of scores is even, there will be two middle scores. The simplest solution is to find the mean of those two scores and use that number as the median. (When the data are from a grouped frequency distribution, a more complicated procedure is required, one beyond the scope of this appendix.) In our experimental group, the median score is 4 (see Table A.3 again). What is it for the control group?

The Mode. A third measure of central tendency is the **mode,** the score that occurs most often. In our experimental group, the modal score is 4. In our control group, it is 6. In some distributions, all scores occur with equal frequency, and there is no mode. In others, two or more scores "tie" for the distinction of being most frequent. Modes are used less often than other measures of central tendency. They do not tell us anything about the other scores in the distribution; they often are not very "central"; and they tend to fluctuate from one random sample of a population to another more than either the median or the mean.

Measuring Variability

A measure of central tendency may or may not be highly representative of other scores in a distribution. To understand our results, we also need a **measure of variability** that will tell us whether our scores are clustered closely around the mean or widely scattered.

The Range. The simplest measure of variability is the **range,** which is found by subtracting the lowest score from the highest one. For our hypothetical set of mood disturbance scores, the range in the experimental group is 4 and in the control group it is 3. Unfortunately, though, simplicity is not always a virtue. The range gives us some information about variability but ignores all scores other than the highest and lowest ones.

The Standard Deviation. A more sophisticated measure of variability is the **standard deviation (SD).** This statistic takes every score in the distribution into account. Loosely speaking, it gives us an idea of how much, on the average, scores in a distribution differ from the mean. If the scores were all the same, the standard deviation would be zero. The higher the standard deviation, the more variability there is among scores.

To compute the standard deviation, we must find out how much each individual score deviates from the mean. To do so we simply subtract the mean from each score. This gives us a set of *deviation scores.* Deviation scores for numbers above the mean will be positive, those for numbers below the mean will be negative, and the positive scores will exactly balance the negative ones. In other words, the sum of the deviation scores will be zero. That is a problem, since the next step in our calculation is to add. The solution is to *square* all the deviation scores (that is, to multiply each score by itself). This step gets rid of negative values. Then we can compute the average of the *squared* deviation scores by adding them up and dividing the sum by the number of scores (N). Finally, we take the square root of the result, which takes us from squared units of measurement back to the same units that were used originally (in this case, mood disturbance levels).

The calculations just described are expressed by the following formula:

$$SD = \sqrt{\frac{\Sigma(X - M)^2}{N}}$$

Table A.4 shows the calculations for computing the standard deviation for our experimental group. Try your hand at computing the standard deviation for the control group.

Remember, a large standard deviation signifies that scores are widely scattered, and that therefore the mean is not terribly typical of the entire population. A small standard deviation tells us that most scores are clustered near the mean, and that therefore the mean is representative. Suppose two classes took a psychology exam, and both classes had the same mean score, 75 out of a possible 100. From the means alone, you might conclude that the classes were similar in performance. But if Class A had a standard deviation of 3 and Class B had a standard deviation of 9, you would know

TABLE A.4   Calculating a Standard Deviation

Scores (X)	Deviation scores (X − M)	Squared deviation scores (X − M)²
6	2	4
5	1	1
5	1	1
5	1	1
4	0	0
4	0	0
4	0	0
4	0	0
4	0	0
4	0	0
4	0	0
3	−1	1
3	−1	1
3	−1	1
2	−2	4
	0	14

$$SD = \sqrt{\frac{\Sigma(X - M)^2}{N}} = \sqrt{\frac{14}{15}} = \sqrt{.93} = .97$$

Note: When data from a sample are used to estimate the standard deviation of the population from which the sample was drawn, division is by $N - 1$ instead of N, for reasons that will not concern us here.

that there was much more variability in performance in Class B. This information could be useful to an instructor in planning lectures and making assignments.

Transforming Scores

Sometimes researchers do not wish to work directly with raw scores. They may prefer numbers that are more manageable, such as when the raw scores are tiny fractions. Or they may want to work with scores that reveal where a person stands relative to others. In such cases, raw scores can be transformed to other kinds of scores.

Percentile Scores. One common transformation converts each raw score to a **percentile score** (also called a *centile rank*). A percentile score gives the percentage of people who scored at or below a given raw score. Suppose you learn that you have scored 37 on a psychology exam. In the absence of any other information, you may not know whether to celebrate or cry. But if you are told that 37 is equivalent to a percentile score of 90, you know that you can be pretty proud of yourself; you have scored as well as, or higher than, 90 percent of those who have taken the test. On the other hand,

if you are told that 37 is equivalent to a percentile score of 50, you have scored only at the median—only as well as, or higher than, half of the other students. The highest possible percentile rank is 99, or more precisely, 99.99, because you can never do better than 100 percent of a group when you are a member of the group. (Can you say what the lowest possible percentile score is? The answer is on page A-7.) Standardized tests such as those described in previous chapters often come with tables that allow for the easy conversion of any raw score to the appropriate percentile score, based on data from a larger number of people who have already taken the test.

Percentile scores are easy to understand and easy to calculate. However, they also have a drawback: They merely rank people and do *not* tell us how far apart people are in terms of raw scores. Suppose you scored in the 50th percentile on an exam, June scored in the 45th, Tricia scored in the 20th, and Sean scored in the 15th. The difference between you and June may seem identical to that between Tricia and Sean (five percentiles). But in terms of *raw* scores you and June are probably more alike than Tricia and Sean, because exam scores usually cluster closely together around the midpoint of the distribution and are farther apart at the extremes. Because percentile scores do not preserve the spatial relationships in the original distribution of scores, they are inappropriate for computing many kinds of statistics. For example, they cannot be used to calculate means.

Z-scores. Another common transformation of raw scores is to **z-scores,** or **standard scores.** A z-score tells you how far a given raw score is above or below the mean, using the standard deviation as the unit of measurement. To compute a z-score, you subtract the mean of the distribution from the raw score and divide by the standard deviation:

$$z = \frac{X - M}{SD}$$

Unlike percentile scores, z-scores preserve the relative spacing of the original raw scores. The mean itself always corresponds to a z-score of zero, since it cannot deviate from itself. All scores above the mean have positive z-scores and all scores below the mean have negative ones. When the raw scores form a certain pattern called a *normal distribution* (to be described shortly), a z-score tells you how high or low the corresponding raw score was, relative to the other scores. If your exam score of 37 is equivalent to a z-score of +1.0, you have scored 1 standard deviation above the mean. Assuming a roughly normal distribution, that's pretty good, because in a normal distribution only about 16 percent of all scores fall at or above 1 standard deviation above the mean. But if your 37 is equivalent to a z-score of −1.0, you have scored 1 standard deviation below the mean—a poor score.

Z-scores are sometimes used to compare people's performance on different tests or measures. Say that Elsa earns a score of 64 on her first psychology test and Manuel, who is taking psychology from a different instructor, earns a 62 on his first test. In Elsa's class, the mean score is 50 and the standard deviation is 7, so Elsa's z-score is (64 − 50)/7 = 2.0. In Manuel's class, the mean is also 50, but the standard deviation is 6. Therefore, his z-score is also 2.0 [(62 − 50)/6]. Compared to their respective classmates, Elsa and Manuel did equally well. *But be careful:* This does *not* imply that they are equally able students. Perhaps Elsa's instructor has a reputation for giving easy tests and Manuel's for giving hard ones, so Manuel's instructor has attracted a more industrious group of students. In that case, Manuel faces stiffer competition than Elsa does, and even though he and Elsa have the same z-score, Manuel's performance may be more impressive.

You can see that comparing z-scores from different people or different tests must be done with caution. Standardized tests, such as IQ tests and various personality tests, use z-scores derived from a large sample of people assumed to be representative of the general population taking the tests. When two tests are standardized for similar populations, it is safe to compare z-scores on them. But z-scores derived from special samples, such as students in different psychology classes, may not be comparable.

Curves

In addition to knowing how spread out our scores are, we need to know the *pattern* of their distribution. At this point we come to a rather curious phenomenon. When researchers make a very large number of observations, many of the physical and psychological variables they study have a distribution that approximates a pattern called a **normal distribution.** (We say "approximates" because a *perfect* normal distribution is a theoretical construct and is not actually found in nature.) Plotted in a frequency polygon, a normal distribution has a symmetrical, bell-shaped form known as a **normal curve** (see Figure A.4).

A normal curve has several interesting and convenient properties. The right side is the exact mirror image of the left. The mean, median, and mode all have the same value and are at the exact center of the curve, at the top of the "bell." Most observations or scores cluster around the center of the curve, with far fewer out at the ends, or "tails" of the curve. Most important, as Figure A.4 shows, when standard deviations (or z-scores) are used on the horizontal axis of the curve, the percentage of scores falling between the mean and any given point on the horizontal axis is always the same. For example, 68.26 percent of the scores will fall between plus and minus 1 standard deviation from the mean; 95.44 percent of the scores will fall between plus and minus 2 standard deviations from the mean; and 99.74 percent of the scores will fall between plus and minus 3 standard

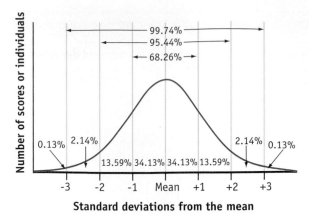

FIGURE A.4

A NORMAL CURVE

When standard deviations (or z-scores) are used along the horizontal axis of a normal curve, certain fixed percentages of scores fall between the mean and any given point. As you can see, most scores fall in the middle range (between +1 and −1 standard deviations from the mean).

deviations from the mean. These percentages hold for any normal curve, no matter what the size of the standard deviation. Tables are available showing the percentages of scores in a normal distribution that lie between the mean and various points (as expressed by z-scores).

The normal curve makes life easier for psychologists when they want to compare individuals on some trait or performance. For example, since IQ scores from a population form a roughly normal curve, the mean and standard deviation of a test are all the information you need in order to know how many people score above or below a particular score. On a test with a mean of 100 and a standard deviation of 15, about 68.26 percent of the population scores between 85 and 115—1 standard deviation below and 1 standard deviation above the mean (see Chapter 9).

Not all types of observations, however, are distributed normally. Some curves are lopsided, or *skewed*, with scores clustering at one end or the other of the horizontal axis (see Figure A.5). When the "tail" of the curve is longer on the right than on the left, the curve is said to be positively, or right, skewed. When the opposite is true, the curve is said to be negatively, or left, skewed. In experiments, reaction times typically form a right-skewed distribution. For example, if people must press a button whenever they hear some signal, most will react quite quickly; but a few will take an unusually long time, causing the right "tail" of the curve to be stretched out.

Knowing the shape of a distribution can be extremely valuable. Paleontologist Stephen Jay Gould (1985) has told how such information helped him cope with the news that he had a rare and serious form of cancer. Being a researcher, he immediately headed for the library to learn all he could about his disease. The first thing he found was that it was incurable,

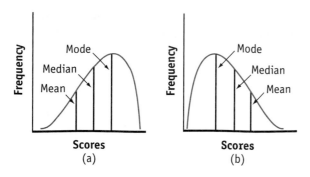

FIGURE A.5
SKEWED CURVES

Curve (a) is skewed negatively, to the left. Curve (b) is skewed positively, to the right. The direction of a curve's skewness is determined by the position of the long tail, not by the position of the bulge. In a skewed curve, the mean, median, and mode fall at different points.

with a median mortality of only eight months after discovery. Most people might have assumed that a "median mortality of eight months" means "I will probably be dead in eight months." But Gould realized that although half of all patients died within eight months, the other half survived longer than that. Since his disease had been diagnosed in its early stages, he was getting top-notch medical treatment, and he had a strong will to live, Gould figured he could reasonably expect to be in the half of the distribution that survived beyond eight months. Even more cheering, the distribution of deaths from the disease was right-skewed: The cases to the left of the median of eight months could only extend to zero months, but those to the right could stretch out for years. Gould saw no reason why he should not expect to be in the tip of that right-hand tail.

For Stephen Jay Gould, statistics, properly interpreted, were "profoundly nurturant and life-giving." They offered him hope and inspired him to fight his disease. Today, Gould is as active professionally as he ever was. The initial diagnosis was made in July of 1982.

ANSWERS:

Control group statistics:

$$\text{Mean} = \frac{\Sigma X}{N} = \frac{87}{15} = 5.8$$

$$\text{Median} = 6$$

$$\text{Standard Deviation} = \sqrt{\frac{\Sigma(X - M)^2}{N}} = \sqrt{\frac{14.4}{15}}$$

$$= \sqrt{.96} = .98$$

Lowest possible percentile score: 1 (or, more precisely, .01)

DRAWING INFERENCES

Once data are organized and summarized, the next step is to ask whether they differ from what might have been expected purely by chance (see Chapter 2). A researcher needs to know whether it is safe to infer that the results from a particular sample of people are valid for the entire population from which the sample was drawn. **Inferential statistics** provide this information. They are used in both experimental and correlational studies.

The Null Versus the Alternative Hypothesis

In an experiment, the scientist must assess the possibility that his or her experimental manipulations will have no effect on the subjects' behavior. The statement expressing this possibility is called the **null hypothesis.** In our stress-and-humor study, the null hypothesis states that making up a funny commentary will not relieve stress any more than making up a straightforward narrative will. In other words, it predicts that the difference between the means of the two groups will not deviate significantly from zero. Any obtained difference will be due solely to chance fluctuations. In contrast, the **alternative hypothesis** (also called the experimental or research hypothesis) states that on the average the experimental group will have lower mood disturbance scores than the control group.

The null hypothesis and the alternative hypothesis cannot both be true. Our goal is to reject the null hypothesis. If our results turn out to be consistent with the null hypothesis, we will not be able to do so. If the data are inconsistent with the null hypothesis, we will be able to reject it with some degree of confidence. Unless we study the entire population, though, we will never be able to say that the alternative hypothesis has been proven. No matter how impressive our results are, there will always be some degree of uncertainty about the inferences we draw from them. Since we cannot prove the alternative hypothesis, we must be satisfied with showing that the null hypothesis is unreasonable.

Students are often surprised to learn that in traditional hypothesis testing it is the null hypothesis, not the alternative hypothesis, that is tested. After all, it is the alternative hypothesis that is actually of interest. But this procedure does make sense. The null hypothesis can be stated precisely and tested directly. In the case of our fictitious study, the null hypothesis predicts that the difference between the two means will be zero. The alternative hypothesis does not permit a precise prediction because we don't know how much the two means might differ (if, in fact, they do differ). Therefore, it cannot be tested directly.

Testing Hypotheses

Many computations are available for testing the null hypothesis. The choice depends on the design of the study, the size of the sample, and other factors. We will not cover any specific tests here. Our purpose is simply to introduce you to the kind of *reasoning* that underlies hypothesis testing. With that in mind, let us return once again to our data. For each of our two groups we have calculated a mean and a standard deviation. Now we want to compare the two sets of data to see if they differ enough for us to reject the null hypothesis. We wish to be reasonably certain that our observed differences did not occur entirely by chance.

What does it mean to be "reasonably certain"? How different from zero must our result be to be taken seriously? Imagine, for a moment, that we had infinite resources and could somehow repeat our experiment, each time using a new pair of groups, until we had "run" the entire population through the study. It can be shown mathematically that if only chance were operating, our various experimental results would form a normal distribution. This theoretical distribution is called "the sampling distribution of the difference between means," but since that is quite a mouthful, we will simply call it the *sampling distribution* for short. If the null hypothesis were true, the mean of the sampling distribution would be zero. That is, on the average, we would find no difference between the two groups. Often, though, because of chance influences or *random error,* we would get a result that deviated to one degree or another from zero. On rare occasions, the result would deviate a great deal from zero.

We cannot test the entire population, though. All we have are data from a single sample. We would like to know whether the difference between means that we actually obtained would be close to the mean of the theoretical sampling distribution (if we *could* test the entire population) or far away from it, out in one of the "tails" of the curve. Was our result highly likely to occur on the basis of chance alone or highly unlikely?

Before we can answer that question, we must have some precise way to measure distance from the mean of the sampling distribution. We must know exactly how far from the mean our obtained result must be to be considered "far away." If only we knew the standard deviation of the sampling distribution, we could use it as our unit of measurement. We don't know it, but fortunately, we can use the standard deviation of our *sample* to estimate it. (We will not go into the reasons that this is so.)

Now we are in business. We can look at the mean difference between our two groups and figure out how far it is (in terms of standard deviations) from the mean of the sampling distribution. As mentioned earlier, one of the convenient things about a normal distribution is that a certain fixed percentage of all observations falls between the mean of the distribution and any given point above or below the mean. These percentages are available from tables. Therefore, if we know the "distance" of our obtained result from the mean of the theoretical sampling distribution, we automatically know how likely our result is to have occurred strictly by chance.

To give a specific example, if it turns out that our obtained result is 2 standard deviations above the mean of the theoretical sampling distribution, we know that the probability of its having occurred by chance is less than 2.3 percent. If our result is 3 standard deviations above the mean of the sampling distribution, the probability of its having occurred by chance is less than .13 percent—less than 1 in 800. In either case, we might well suspect that our result did not occur entirely by chance after all. We would call the result **statistically significant.** (Psychologists usually consider any highly unlikely result to be of interest, no matter which direction it takes. In other words, the result may be in either "tail" of the sampling distribution.)

To summarize: Statistical significance means that if only chance were operating, our result would be highly improbable, so we are fairly safe in concluding that more than chance was operating—namely, the influence of our independent variable. We can reject the null hypothesis, and open the champagne. As we noted in Chapter 2, psychologists usually accept a finding as statistically significant if the likelihood of its occurring by chance is 5 percent or less (see Figure A.6). This cutoff point gives the researcher a reasonable chance of confirming reliable results as well as reasonable protection against accepting unreliable ones.

Some cautions are in order, though. As noted in Chapter 2, conventional tests of statistical significance have drawn serious

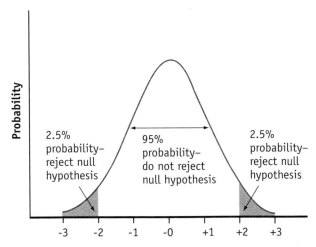

FIGURE A.6
STATISTICAL SIGNIFICANCE

This curve represents the theoretical sampling distribution discussed in the text. The curve is what we would expect by chance if we did our hypothetical stress-and-humor study many times, testing the entire population. If we used the conventional significance level of .05, we would regard our obtained result as significant only if the probability of getting a result that far from zero by chance (in either direction) totaled 5 percent or less. As shown, the result must fall far out in one of the tails of the sampling distribution. Otherwise, we cannot reject the null hypothesis.

criticisms in recent years. Statistically significant results are not always psychologically interesting or important. Further, statistical significance is related to the size of the sample. A large sample increases the likelihood of reliable results. But there is a trade-off: The larger the sample, the more probable it is that a small result having no practical importance will reach statistical significance. On the other hand, with the sample sizes typically used in psychological research, there is a good chance of falsely concluding that an experimental effect has *not* occurred when one actually has (Hunter, 1997). For these reasons, it is always useful to know how much of the total variability in scores was accounted for by the independent variable (the **effect size**). (The computations are not discussed here.) If only 3 percent of the variance was accounted for, then 97 percent was due either to chance factors or to systematic influences of which the researcher was unaware. Because human behavior is affected by so many factors, the amount of variability accounted for by a single psychological variable is often modest. But sometimes the effect size is considerable even when the results don't quite reach significance.

Oh, yes, about those humor findings: Our fictitious study is similar to two more-complicated ones done by Herbert M. Lefcourt and Rod A. Martin (1986). Women who tried to be funny reported less mood disturbance than women who merely produced a straightforward narrative. They also grimaced and fidgeted less during the film, suggesting that they really did feel less stress. The results were not statistically significant for men, for reasons that were not clear. Other findings, however, suggest that humor can shield both sexes from stress (see Chapter 15). *The moral:* When gravity gets you down, try a little levity.

SUMMARY

1. When used correctly, statistics expose unwarranted conclusions, promote precision, and help researchers spot trends amid diversity.

2. Often, the first step in data analysis is to organize and condense data in a *frequency distribution,* a tally showing how often each possible score (or interval of scores) occurred. Such information can also be depicted in a *histogram* (bar graph) or a *frequency polygon* (line graph).

3. *Descriptive statistics* summarize and describe the data. *Central tendency* is measured by the *mean, median,* or, less frequently, the *mode.* Since a measure of central tendency may or may not be highly representative of other scores in

a distribution, it is also important to analyze variability. A large *standard deviation* means that scores are widely scattered about the mean; a small one means that most scores are clustered near the mean.

4. Raw scores can be transformed into other kinds of scores. *Percentile scores* indicate the percentage of people who scored at or below a given raw score. *Z-scores* (*standard scores*) indicate how far a given raw score is above or below the mean of the distribution.

5. Many variables have a distribution approximating a *normal distribution,* depicted as a *normal curve.* The normal curve has a convenient property: When standard deviations are used as the units on the horizontal axis, the percentage of scores falling between any two points on the horizontal axis is always the same. Not all types of observations are distributed normally, however. Some distributions are *skewed* to the left or right.

6. *Inferential statistics* can be used to test the *null hypothesis* and to tell a researcher whether a result differed significantly from what might have been expected purely by chance. Basically, hypothesis testing involves estimating where the obtained result would have fallen in a theoretical *sampling distribution* based on studies of the entire population in question. If the result would have been far out in one of the "tails" of the distribution, it is considered statistically significant. A statistically significant result may or may not be psychologically interesting or important, so many researchers also compute the *effect size.*

KEY TERMS

frequency distribution A-1
graph A-2
histogram/bar graph A-2
frequency polygon/line graph A-2
descriptive statistics A-3
measure of central tendency A-3
mean A-3
median A-4
mode A-4
measure of variability A-4
range A-4
standard deviation A-4

deviation score A-4
percentile score A-5
z-score (standard score) A-5
normal distribution A-6
normal curve A-6
right- and left-skewed distributions A-6
inferential statistics A-7
null hypothesis A-7
alternative hypothesis A-7
sampling distribution A-8
statistically significant A-8
effect size A-9

GLOSSARY

absolute threshold   The smallest quantity of physical energy that can be reliably detected by an observer.

accommodation   In Piaget's theory, the process of modifying existing cognitive structures in response to experience and new information.

acculturation   The process by which members of minority groups come to identify with and feel part of the mainstream culture.

achievement tests   Tests designed to assess skills and knowledge that have been learned.

activation-synthesis theory   The theory that dreaming results from the cortical synthesis and interpretation of neural signals triggered by activity in the lower part of the brain.

adrenal hormones   Hormones that are produced by the adrenal glands and that are involved in emotion and stress; they include cortisol, epinephrine, and norepinephrine.

agoraphobia   A set of phobias, often set off by a panic attack, involving the basic fear of being away from a safe place or person.

algorithm   A problem-solving strategy guaranteed to produce a solution even if the user does not know how it works.

altered state of consciousness   A state of consciousness that differs from ordinary wakefulness or sleep.

alternative hypothesis   An assertion that the independent variable in a study will have a certain predictable effect on the dependent variable; also called an experimental or research hypothesis.

amnesia (dissociative)   When no organic causes are present, a dissociative disorder involving partial or complete loss of memory for threatening information or traumatic experiences.

amygdala [uh-MIG-dul-uh]   A brain structure involved in the arousal and regulation of emotion and the initial emotional response to sensory information.

anorexia nervosa   An eating disorder characterized by fear of being fat, a distorted body image, radically reduced consumption of food, and emaciation.

antidepressant drugs   Drugs used primarily in the treatment of mood disorders, especially depression and anxiety.

antipsychotic drugs   Drugs used primarily in the treatment of schizophrenia and other psychotic disorders.

antisocial personality disorder   A disorder (sometimes called psychopathy or sociopathy) characterized by antisocial behavior such as lying, stealing, manipulating others, and sometimes violence; a lack of guilt, shame, and empathy; and impulsivity.

applied psychology   The study of psychological issues that have direct practical significance and the application of psychological findings.

aptitude tests   Tests designed to assess the ability to acquire skills and knowledge in the future.

archetypes [AR-ki-tipes]   Universal, symbolic images that appear in myths, art, stories, and dreams; to Carl Jung, they reflect the collective unconscious.

arithmetic mean   An average that is calculated by adding up a set of quantities and dividing the sum by the total number of quantities in the set.

assimilation   In Piaget's theory, the process of absorbing new information into existing cognitive structures.

attribution theory   The theory that people are motivated to explain their own and other people's behavior by attributing causes of that behavior to a situation or a disposition.

autonomic nervous system   The subdivision of the peripheral nervous system that regulates the internal organs and glands.

availability heuristic   The tendency to judge the probability of a type of event by how easy it is to think of examples or instances.

aversive conditioning   In behavior therapy, a method in which punishment is substituted for the reinforcement that is perpetuating a bad habit.

axon   A neuron's extending fiber that conducts impulses away from the cell body and transmits them to other neurons.

basic concepts   Concepts that have a moderate number of instances and that are easier to acquire than those having few or many instances.

basic psychology   The study of psychological issues in order to seek knowledge for its own sake rather than for its practical application.

behavior modification   The application of conditioning techniques to teach new responses or to reduce or eliminate maladaptive or problematic behavior.

behavioral genetics   An interdisciplinary field of study concerned with the genetic bases of behavior and personality.

behaviorism   An approach to psychology that emphasizes the study of observable behavior and the role of the environment as a determinant of behavior.

binocular cues   Visual cues to depth or distance requiring two eyes.

biofeedback   A method for learning to control bodily functions, including ones usually thought to be involuntary, by attending to feedback from an instrument that monitors the function and signals changes in it.

biological perspective   A psychological approach that emphasizes bodily events and changes associated with actions, feelings, and thoughts.

biological rhythm   A periodic, more or less regular fluctuation in a biological system; may or may not have psychological implications.

bipolar disorder A mood disorder in which episodes of both depression and mania (excessive euphoria) occur.

brain stem The part of the brain at the top of the spinal cord, consisting of the medulla and the pons.

brightness Lightness or luminance; the dimension of visual experience related to the amount of light emitted from or reflected by an object.

bulimia An eating disorder characterized by episodes of excessive eating (bingeing) following by forced vomiting or use of laxatives (purging).

case study A detailed description of a particular individual being studied or treated.

cell body The part of the neuron that keeps it alive and determines whether it will fire.

central nervous system (CNS) The portion of the nervous system consisting of the brain and spinal cord.

cerebellum A brain structure that regulates movement and balance, and that is involved in the learning of certain kinds of simple responses.

cerebral cortex A collection of several thin layers of cells covering the cerebrum; it is largely responsible for higher mental functions. (*Cortex* is Latin for "bark" or "rind.")

cerebral hemispheres The two halves of the cerebrum.

cerebrum [suh-REE-brum] The largest brain structure, consisting of the upper part of the brain. Divided into two hemispheres, it is in charge of most sensory, motor, and cognitive processes. (From the Latin for "brain.")

childhood (infantile) amnesia The inability to remember events and experiences that occurred during the first two or three years of life.

chromosomes Within every body cell, rod-shaped structures that carry the genes.

chunk A meaningful unit of information; it may be composed of smaller units.

circadian [sur-CAY-dee-un] rhythm A biological rhythm with a period (from peak to peak or trough to trough) of about 24 hours; from the Latin *circa*, "about," and *dies*, "a day."

classical conditioning The process by which a previously neutral stimulus acquires the capacity to elicit a response through association with a stimulus that already elicits a similar or related response.

cochlea (KOCK-lee-uh) A snail-shaped, fluid-filled organ in the inner ear, containing the receptors for hearing.

coefficient of correlation A measure of correlation that ranges in value from -1.00 to +1.00.

cognitive dissonance A state of tension that occurs when a person simultaneously holds two cognitions that are psychologically inconsistent, or when a person's belief is incongruent with his or her behavior.

cognitive ethology The study of cognitive processes in nonhuman animals.

cognitive perspective A psychological approach that emphasizes mental processes in perception, memory, language, problem solving, and other areas of behavior.

cognitive schema An integrated mental network of knowledge, beliefs, and expectations concerning a particular topic or aspect of the world.

collective unconscious To Carl Jung, the universal memories and experiences of humankind, represented in the unconscious images and symbols of all people.

collectivist cultures Cultures in which the self is regarded as embedded in relationships, and harmony with one's group is prized above individual goals and wishes.

concept A mental category that groups objects, relations, activities, abstractions, or qualities having common properties.

conditioned response (CR) The classical-conditioning term for a response that is elicited by a conditioned stimulus; it occurs after the conditioned stimulus is associated with an unconditioned stimulus.

conditioned stimulus (CS) The classical-conditioning term for an initially neutral stimulus that comes to elicit a conditioned response after being associated with an unconditioned stimulus.

conditioning A basic kind of learning that involves associations between environmental stimuli and the organism's responses.

cones Visual receptors involved in color vision.

confirmation bias The tendency to look for or pay attention only to information that confirms one's own belief.

consciousness Awareness of the environment and of one's own existence, sensations, and thoughts.

conservation The understanding that the physical properties of objects—such as the number of items in a cluster or the amount of liquid in a glass—can remain the same even when their form or appearance changes.

consolidation The process by which a long-term memory becomes durable and stable.

contact comfort In primates (including humans), the innate pleasure derived from close physical contact; it is the basis of an infant's first attachment.

continuous reinforcement A reinforcement schedule in which a particular response is always reinforced.

control condition In an experiment, a comparison condition in which subjects are not exposed to the same treatment as in the experimental condition.

convergence The turning of the eyes inward, which occurs when they focus on a nearby object.

corpus callosum [CORE-puhs cah-LOW-suhm] The bundle of nerve fibers connecting the two cerebral hemispheres.

correlation A measure of how strongly two variables are related to one another.

correlational study A descriptive study that looks for a consistent relationship between two phenomena.

counterconditioning In classical conditioning, the process of pairing a conditioned stimulus with a stimulus that elicits a response that is incompatible with an unwanted conditioned response.

critical thinking   The ability and willingness to assess claims and to make judgments on the basis of well-supported reasons and evidence, rather than emotion or anecdote.

cross-sectional study   A study in which subjects of different ages are compared at a given time.

crystallized intelligence   Cognitive skills and specific knowledge of information acquired over a lifetime; it is heavily dependent on education and tends to remain stable over the lifetime.

cue-dependent forgetting   The inability to retrieve information stored in memory because of insufficient cues for recall.

culture   A program of shared rules that govern the behavior of members of a community or society, and a set of values, beliefs, and attitudes shared by most members of that community.

dark adaptation   A process by which visual receptors become maximally sensitive to dim light.

decay theory   The theory that information in memory eventually disappears if it is not accessed; it applies more to short-term than to long-term memory.

declarative memories   Memories of facts, rules, concepts, and events ("knowing that"); they include semantic and episodic memories.

deductive reasoning   A form of reasoning in which a conclusion follows necessarily from certain premises; if the premises are true, the conclusion must be true.

deep processing   In the encoding of information, the processing of meaning rather than simply the physical or sensory features of a stimulus.

defense mechanisms   Methods used by the ego to prevent unconscious anxiety or threatening thoughts from entering consciousness.

deindividuation   In groups or crowds, the loss of awareness of one's own individuality.

dendrites   A neuron's branches that receive information from other neurons and transmit it toward the cell body.

dependent variable   A variable that an experimenter predicts will be affected by manipulations of the independent variable.

depressants   Drugs that slow down activity in the central nervous system.

descriptive methods   Methods that yield descriptions of behavior but not necessarily causal explanations.

descriptive statistics   Statistical procedures that organize and summarize a body of data.

dialectical reasoning   A process in which opposing facts or ideas are weighed and compared, with a view to determining the best solution or to resolving differences.

difference threshold   The smallest difference in stimulation that can be reliably detected by an observer when two stimuli are compared; also called the *just noticeable difference (jnd)*.

diffusion of responsibility   In organized or anonymous groups, the tendency of members to avoid taking responsibility for actions or decisions because they assume that others will do so.

discriminative stimulus   A stimulus that signals when a particular response is likely to be followed by a certain type of consequence.

display rules   Social and cultural rules that regulate when, how, and where a person may express (or must suppress) emotions.

dissociation   A split in consciousness in which one part of the mind operates independently of others.

dissociative disorders   Conditions in which consciousness or identity is split or altered.

dissociative identity disorder   A controversial disorder marked by the appearance within one person of two or more distinct personalities, each with its own name and traits; formerly called *multiple personality disorder (MPD)*.

dizygotic twins   *See* fraternal twins.

DNA (deoxyribonucleic acid)   The chromosomal molecule that transfers genetic characteristics by way of coded instructions for the structure of proteins.

doctrine of specific nerve energies   The doctrine that different sensory modalities, such as vision and hearing, exist because signals received by the sense organs stimulate different nerve pathways leading to different areas of the brain.

double-blind study   An experiment in which neither the subjects nor the individuals running the study know which subjects are in the control group and which are in the experimental group until after the results are tallied.

effect size   In an experiment, the amount of variance in the data accounted for by the independent variable.

ego   In psychoanalysis, the part of personality that represents reason, good sense, and rational self-control.

egocentric thinking   Seeing the world from only your own point of view; the inability to take another person's perspective.

elaborative rehearsal   Association of new information with already stored knowledge and analysis of the new information to make it memorable.

electroconvulsive therapy (ECT)   A procedure used in cases of prolonged and severe major depression, in which a brief brain seizure is induced.

electroencephalogram (EEG)   A recording of neural activity detected by electrodes.

emotion   A state of arousal involving facial and bodily changes, brain activation, cognitive appraisals, subjective feelings, and tendencies toward action.

emotion work   Expression of an emotion, often because of a role requirement, that the person does not really feel.

emotional intelligence   The ability to identify your own and other people's emotions accurately, express your emotions clearly, and regulate emotions in yourself and others.

empirical   Relying on or derived from observation, experimentation, or measurement.

endocrine glands   Internal organs that produce hormones and release them into the bloodstream.

endorphins [en-DOR-fins]   Chemical substances in the nervous system that are similar in structure and action to opiates; they are involved in pain reduction, pleasure, and memory, and they are known technically as *endogenous opioid peptides*.

entrainment   The synchronization of biological rhythms with external cues, such as fluctuations in daylight.

entrapment   A gradual process in which individuals escalate their commitment to a course of action to justify their investment of time, money, or effort.

episodic memories   Memories of personally experienced events and the contexts in which they occurred.

equilibrium   The sense of balance.

ethnic identity   A person's identification with a racial, religious, or ethnic group.

ethnocentrism   The belief that one's own ethnic group, nation, or religion is superior to all others.

evolution   A change in gene frequencies within a population over many generations; a mechanism by which genetically influenced characteristics of a population may change.

evolutionary psychology   A field of psychology emphasizing evolutionary mechanisms that may help explain human commonalities in cognition, development, emotion, social practices, and other areas of behavior.

experiment   A controlled test of a hypothesis in which the researcher manipulates one variable to discover its effect on another.

experimenter effects   Unintended changes in subjects' behavior due to cues inadvertently given by the experimenter.

explicit memory   Conscious, intentional recollection of an event or of an item of information.

exposure treatment   In behavior therapy, a method in which a person suffering from an anxiety disorder, such as a phobia or panic attacks, is taken directly into the feared situation until the anxiety subsides.

extinction   The weakening and eventual disappearance of a learned response. In classical conditioning, it occurs when the conditioned stimulus is no longer paired with the unconditioned stimulus; in operant conditioning, it occurs when a response is no longer followed by a reinforcer.

extrinsic reinforcers   Reinforcers that are not inherently related to the activity being reinforced, such as money, prizes, and praise.

facial feedback   The process by which the facial muscles send messages to the brain about the basic emotion being expressed.

factor analysis   A statistical method for analyzing the intercorrelations among various measures or test scores; clusters of measures or scores that are highly correlated are assumed to measure the same underlying trait, ability, or aptitude (factor).

feature detectors   Cells in the visual cortex that are sensitive to specific features of the environment.

feminist psychology   A psychological approach that analyzes the influence of social inequities on gender relations and on the behavior of the two sexes.

field research   Descriptive or experimental research conducted in a natural setting outside the laboratory.

fixed-interval schedule   An intermittent schedule of reinforcement in which a reinforcer is delivered for the first response made after a fixed period of time has elapsed since the last reinforcer.

fixed-ratio schedule   An intermittent schedule of reinforcement in which reinforcement occurs only after a fixed number of responses.

fluid intelligence   The capacity for deductive reasoning and the ability to use new information to solve problems; it is relatively independent of education and tends to declines in old age.

fraternal (dizygotic) twins   Twins that develop from two separate eggs fertilized by different sperm; they are no more alike genetically than are any other pair of siblings.

frequency distribution   A summary of how frequently each score in a set occurred.

frequency polygon (line graph)   A graph showing a set of points obtained by plotting score values against score frequencies; adjacent points are joined by straight lines.

frontal lobes   Lobes at the front of the brain's cerebral cortex; they contain areas involved in short-term memory, higher-order thinking, initiative, social judgment, and (in the left lobe, typically) speech production.

fugue   [FEWG] A dissociative disorder in which a person flees home and forgets his or her identity.

functionalism   An early psychological approach that emphasized the function or purpose of behavior and consciousness.

fundamental attribution error   The tendency, in explaining other people's behavior, to overestimate personality factors and underestimate the influence of the situation.

g factor   A general intellectual ability assumed by some theorists to underlie specific mental abilities and talents.

ganglion cells   Neurons in the retina of the eye that gather information from receptor cells (by way of intermediate bipolar cells); their axons make up the optic nerve.

gate-control theory   The theory that the experience of pain depends in part on whether pain impulses get past a neurological "gate" in the spinal cord and thus reach the brain.

gender identity   The fundamental sense of being male or female; it is independent of whether the person conforms to the social and cultural rules of gender.

gender schema   A mental network of knowledge, beliefs, metaphors, and expectations about what it means to be male or female.

gender typing   The process by which children learn the abilities, interests, personality traits, and behaviors associated with being masculine or feminine in their culture.

generalized anxiety disorder   A continuous state of anxiety marked by feelings of worry and dread, apprehension, difficulties in concentration, and signs of motor tension.

genes   The functional units of heredity; they are composed of DNA and specify the structure of proteins.

genetic marker   A segment of DNA that varies among individuals, has a known location on a chromosome, and can function as a genetic landmark for a gene involved in a physical or mental condition.

genome   The full set of genes in each cell of an organism (with the exception of sperm and egg cells).

gestalt principles Principles that describe the brain's organization of sensory building blocks into meaningful units and patterns.

glial cells Nervous-system cells that aid the neurons by providing them with nutrients, insulating them, and removing cellular debris when "they die."

graph A drawing that depicts numerical relationships.

groupthink In close-knit groups, the tendency for all members to think alike for the sake of harmony and to suppress disagreement.

heritability A statistical estimate of the proportion of the total variance in some trait that is attributable to genetic differences among individuals within a group.

heuristic A rule of thumb that suggests a course of action or guides problem solving but does not guarantee an optimal solution.

higher-order conditioning In classical conditioning, a procedure in which a neutral stimulus becomes a conditioned stimulus through association with an already established conditioned stimulus.

hindsight bias The tendency to overestimate one's ability to have predicted an event once the outcome is known; the "I knew it all along" phenomenon.

hippocampus A brain structure involved in the storage of new information in memory.

histogram (bar graph) A graph in which the heights (or lengths) of bars are proportional to the frequencies of individual scores or classes of scores in a distribution.

hormones Chemical substances, secreted by organs called *glands*, that affect the functioning of other organs.

hue The dimension of visual experience specified by color names and related to the wavelength of light.

humanist psychology A psychological approach that emphasizes personal growth and the achievement of human potential rather than the scientific understanding and assessment of behavior.

hypnosis A procedure in which the practitioner suggests changes in the sensations, perceptions, thoughts, feelings, or behavior of the subject.

hypothalamus A brain structure involved in emotions and drives vital to survival, such as fear, hunger, thirst, and reproduction; it regulates the autonomic nervous system.

hypothesis A statement that attempts to predict or to account for a set of phenomena; scientific hypotheses specify relationships among events or variables and are empirically tested.

id In psychoanalysis, the part of personality containing inherited psychic energy, particularly sexual and aggressive instincts.

identical (monozygotic) twins Twins that develop when a fertilized egg divides into two parts that develop into separate embryos.

implicit memory Unconscious retention in memory, as evidenced by the effect of a previous experience or previously encountered information on current thoughts or actions.

independent variable A variable that an experimenter manipulates.

individualist cultures Cultures in which the self is regarded as autonomous, and individual goals and wishes are prized above duty and relations with others.

induction A method of child rearing in which the parent appeals to the child's own resources, abilities, sense of responsibility, and feelings for others in correcting the child's misbehavior.

inductive reasoning A form of reasoning in which the premises provide support for a conclusion, but it is still possible for the conclusion to be false.

infantile amnesia *See* childhood amnesia.

inferential statistics Statistical procedures that allow researchers to draw inferences about how statistically meaningful a study's results are.

infradian [in-FRAY-dee-un] rhythm A biological rhythm that occurs less frequently than once a day; from the Latin for "below a day."

intelligence An inferred characteristic of an individual, usually defined as the ability to profit from experience, acquire knowledge, think abstractly, act purposefully, or adapt to changes in the environment.

intelligence quotient (IQ) A measure of intelligence originally computed by dividing a person's mental age by his or her chronological age and multiplying the result by 100; it is now derived from norms provided for standardized intelligence tests.

intermittent (partial) schedule of reinforcement A reinforcement schedule in which a particular response is sometimes but not always reinforced.

internal desynchronization A state in which biological rhythms are not in phase (synchronized) with one another.

intrapsychic Within the mind (psyche) or self.

intrinsic reinforcers Reinforcers that are inherently related to the activity being reinforced, such as enjoyment of the task and the satisfaction of accomplishment.

inventories Standardized objective questionnaires requiring written responses; they typically include scales on which people are asked to rate themselves.

just-world hypothesis The notion that many people need to believe that the world is fair and that justice is served; that bad people are punished and good people rewarded.

justification of effort The tendency of individuals to increase their liking for something that they have worked hard or suffered to attain; a common form of dissonance reduction.

kinesthesis (KIN-es-THEE-sis) The sense of body position and movement of body parts; also called *kinesthesia*.

language A system that combines meaningless elements such as sounds or gestures to form structured utterances that convey meaning.

language acquisition device According to many psycholinguists, an innate mental module that allows young children to develop language if they are exposed to an adequate sampling of conversation.

latent learning   A form of learning that is not immediately expressed in an overt response; it occurs without obvious reinforcement.

lateralization   Specialization of the two cerebral hemispheres for particular operations.

learning   A relatively permanent change in behavior (or behavioral potential) due to experience.

learning perspective   A psychological approach that emphasizes how the environment and experience affect a person's or animal's actions; it includes *behaviorism* and *social-cognitive learning theories*.

libido [luh-BEE-do]   In psychoanalysis, the psychic energy that fuels the life or sexual instincts of the id.

limbic system   A group of brain areas involved in emotional reactions and motivated behavior.

linkage studies   Studies that look for patterns of inheritance of genetic markers in large families in which a particular condition is common.

lithium carbonate   A drug frequently given to people suffering from bipolar disorder.

localization of function   Specialization of particular brain areas for particular functions.

locus of control   A general expectation about whether the results of a person's actions are under her or his control (internal locus) or beyond the person's control (external locus).

long-term memory (LTM)   In the three-box model of memory, the memory system involved in the long-term storage of information.

long-term potentiation   A long-lasting increase in the strength of synaptic responsiveness, thought to be a biological mechanism of long-term memory.

longitudinal study   A study in which subjects are followed and periodically reassessed over time.

loudness   The dimension of auditory experience related to the intensity of a pressure wave.

lucid dream   A dream in which the dreamer is aware of dreaming.

magnetic resonance imaging   *See* MRI.

maintenance rehearsal   Rote repetition of material in order to maintain its availability in memory.

major depression   A mood disorder involving disturbances in emotion (excessive sadness), behavior (loss of interest in one's usual activities), cognition (thoughts of hopelessness), and body function (fatigue and loss of appetite).

mastery (learning) goals   Goals framed in terms of increasing one's competence and skills.

mean   *See* arithmetic mean.

measure of central tendency   A number intended to characterize an entire set of data.

measure of variability   A number that indicates how dispersed scores are around the mean of the distribution.

median   A measure of central tendency; the value at the midpoint of a distribution of scores when the scores are ordered from highest to lowest.

medulla [muh-DUL-uh]   A structure in the brain stem responsible for certain automatic functions, such as breathing and heart rate.

melatonin   A hormone, secreted by the pineal gland, that is involved in the regulation of daily biological rhythms.

menarche [menARRkee]   The onset of menstruation.

menopause   The cessation of menstruation and of the production of ova; usually a gradual process lasting up to several years.

mental age (MA)   A measure of mental development expressed in terms of the average mental ability at a given age; for instance, a child with a mental age of 8 performs on a test of mental ability at the level of the average 8-year-old.

mental disorder   Any behavior or emotional state that causes an individual great suffering or worry, is self-defeating or self-destructive, or is maladaptive and disrupts the person's relationships or the larger community.

mental image   A mental representation that mirrors or resembles the thing it represents; mental images can occur in many and perhaps all sensory modalities.

mental set   A tendency to solve problems using procedures that worked before on similar problems.

meta-analysis   A procedure for combining and analyzing data from many studies; it determines how much of the variance in scores across all studies can be explained by a particular variable.

metacognition   The knowledge or awareness of one's own cognitive processes.

Minnesota Multiphasic Personality Inventory (MMPI)   A widely used objective personality test.

mnemonics   Strategies and tricks for improving memory, such as the use of a verse or a formula.

mode   A measure of central tendency; the most frequently occurring score in a distribution.

monochronic cultures   Cultures in which time is organized sequentially; schedules and deadlines are valued over people.

monocular cues   Visual cues to depth or distance, which can be used by one eye alone.

monozygotic twins   *See* identical twins.

motivated forgetting   Forgetting that occurs because of a desire to eliminate awareness of painful, embarrassing, or otherwise unpleasant experiences.

motivation   A process within a person or animal that causes movement toward a goal or away from an unpleasant situation.

MRI (magnetic resonance imaging)   A method for studying body and brain tissue, using magnetic fields and special radio receivers.

multiple personality disorder   *See* dissociative identity disorder.

myelin sheath   A fatty insulation that may surround the axon of a neuron.

narcissistic personality disorder   A disorder characterized by an exaggerated sense of self-importance and self-absorption.

natural selection   The evolutionary process in which individuals with genetically influenced traits that are adaptive in a particular environment tend to survive and to reproduce in greater numbers than do other individuals; as a result, their traits become more common in the population.

need for achievement A learned motive to meet personal standards of success and excellence in a chosen area (abbreviated *nAch*).

need for affiliation The motive to associate with other people, as by seeking friends, moral support, companionship, or love.

need for power A learned motive to dominate or influence others.

negative correlation An association between increases in one variable and decreases in another.

negative reinforcement A reinforcement procedure in which a response is followed by the removal, delay, or decrease in intensity of an unpleasant stimulus; as a result, the response becomes stronger or more likely to occur.

nerves Bundles of neural fibers (axons and sometimes dendrites) in the peripheral nervous system.

network models Models of long-term memory that represent its contents as a vast network of interrelated concepts and propositions.

neuromatrix theory The theory that a matrix of neurons in the brain is capable of generating pain (and other sensations) in the absence of signals from sensory nerves.

neuron A cell that conducts electrochemical signals; the basic unit of the nervous system; also called a *nerve cell*.

neurotransmitter A chemical substance that is released by a transmitting neuron at the synapse and that alters the activity of a receiving neuron.

nonconscious processes Mental processes occurring outside of and not available to conscious awareness.

normal curve A symmetrical, bell-shaped frequency polygon representing a normal distribution.

normal distribution A theoretical frequency distribution having certain special characteristics. For example, the distribution is symmetrical; the mean, mode, and median all have the same value; and the farther a score is from the mean, the less the likelihood of obtaining it.

norms In test construction, established standards of performance.

norms (social) Rules that regulate human life, including social conventions, explicit laws, and implicit cultural standards.

null hypothesis An assertion that the independent variable in a study will have no effect on the dependent variable.

object permanence The understanding that an object continues to exist even when you cannot see it or touch it.

object-relations school A psychodynamic approach that emphasizes the importance of the infant's first two years of life and the baby's formative relationships, especially with the mother.

observational learning A process in which an individual learns new responses by observing the behavior of another (a model) rather than through direct experience; sometimes called *vicarious conditioning*.

observational study A study in which the researcher carefully and systematically observes and records behavior without interfering with the behavior; it may involve either naturalistic or laboratory observation.

obsessive-compulsive disorder (**OCD**) An anxiety disorder in which a person feels trapped in repetitive, persistent thoughts (obsessions) and repetitive, ritualized behaviors (compulsions) designed to reduce anxiety.

occipital [ahk-SIP-uh-tuhl] lobes Lobes at the lower back part of the brain's cerebral cortex; they contain areas that receive visual information.

Oedipus complex In psychoanalysis, a conflict in which a child desires the parent of the other sex and views the same-sex parent as a rival.

operant conditioning The process by which a response becomes more or less likely to occur, depending on its consequences.

operational definition A precise definition of a term in a hypothesis, which specifies the operations for observing and measuring the process or phenomenon being defined.

operations In Piaget's theory, mental actions that are cognitively reversible.

opiates Drugs, derived from the opium poppy, that relieve pain and commonly produce euphoria.

opponent-process theory A theory of color perception, which assumes that the visual system treats pairs of colors as opposing or antagonistic.

panic disorder An anxiety disorder in which a person experiences recurring *panic attacks*, periods of intense fear and feelings of impending doom or death, accompanied by physiological symptoms such as rapid breathing and pulse, and dizziness.

papillae [pa-PILL-ee] Knoblike elevations on the tongue, containing the taste buds. (Singular: *papilla.*)

parallel distributed processing (**PDP**) An alternative to the information-processing model of memory, in which knowledge is represented as connections among thousands of interacting processing units, distributed in a vast network, and all operating in parallel.

paranoid personality disorder A disorder characterized by habitually unreasonable and excessive suspiciousness, jealousy, or mistrust; paranoid symptoms may also occur in schizophrenia and other psychoses.

parapsychology The study of purported psychic phenomena such as ESP and mental telepathy.

parasympathetic nervous system The subdivision of the autonomic nervous system that operates during relaxed states and that conserves energy.

parietal [puh-RYE-uh-tuhl] lobes Lobes at the top of the brain's cerebral cortex; they contain areas that receive information on pressure, pain, touch, and temperature.

percentile score A score that indicates the percentage of people who scored at or below a given raw score; also called *centile rank*.

perception The process by which the brain organizes and interprets sensory information.

perceptual constancy The accurate perception of objects as stable or unchanged despite changes in the sensory patterns they produce.

perceptual illusion   An erroneous or misleading perception of reality.

perceptual set   A habitual way of perceiving, based on expectations.

performance goals   Goals framed in terms of performing well in front of others, being judged favorably, and avoiding criticism.

peripheral nervous system (PNS)   All portions of the nervous system outside the brain and spinal cord; it includes sensory and motor nerves.

personality   A distinctive and relatively stable pattern of behavior, thoughts, motives, and emotions that characterizes an individual throughout life.

personality disorders   Rigid, maladaptive personality patterns that cause personal distress or an inability to get along with others.

PET scan (positron-emission tomography)   A method for analyzing biochemical activity in the brain, using injections of a glucose-like substance containing a radioactive element.

phobia   An exaggerated, unrealistic fear of a specific situation, activity, or object.

pitch   The dimension of auditory experience related to the frequency of a pressure wave; height or depth of a tone.

pituitary gland   A small endocrine gland at the base of the brain, which releases many hormones and regulates other endocrine glands.

placebo   An inactive substance or fake treatment used as a control in an experiment or given by a medical practitioner to a patient.

placebo effect   The apparent success of a medication or treatment that is due to the patient's expectations or hopes rather than to the drug or treatment itself.

polychronic cultures   Cultures in which time is organized horizontally; people tend to do several things at once and value relationships over schedules.

pons   A structure in the brain stem involved in, among other things, sleeping, waking, and dreaming.

positive correlation   An association between increases in one variable and increases in another.

positive reinforcement   A reinforcement procedure in which a response is followed by the presentation of, or increase in intensity of, a reinforcing stimulus; as a result, the response becomes stronger or more likely to occur.

positron-emission tomography   *See* PET scan.

posttraumatic stress disorder (PTSD)   An anxiety disorder in which a person who has experienced a traumatic or life-threatening event has symptoms such as psychic numbing, reliving of the trauma, and increased physiological arousal.

power assertion   A method of child rearing in which the parent uses punishment and authority to correct the child's misbehavior.

primary control   An effort to modify reality by changing other people, the situation, or events; a "fighting back" philosophy.

primary emotions   Emotions considered to be universal and biologically based; they generally include fear, anger, sadness, joy, surprise, disgust, and contempt.

primary punisher   A stimulus that is inherently punishing; an example is electric shock.

primary reinforcer   A stimulus that is inherently reinforcing, typically satisfying a physiological need; an example is food.

priming   A method for measuring implicit memory in which a person reads or listens to information and is later tested to see whether the information affects performance on another type of task.

principle of falsifiability   The principle that a scientific theory must make predictions that are specific enough to expose the theory to the possibility of disconfirmation; that is, the theory must predict not only what will happen, but also what will not happen.

proactive interference   Forgetting that occurs when previously stored material interferes with the ability to remember similar, more recently learned material.

procedural memories   Memories for the performance of actions or skills ("knowing how").

projective tests   Psychological tests used to infer a person's motives, conflicts, and unconscious dynamics on the basis of the person's interpretations of ambiguous stimuli.

proposition   A unit of meaning that is made up of concepts and expresses a single idea.

prototype   An especially representative example of a concept.

psychedelic drugs   Consciousness-altering drugs that produce hallucinations, change thought processes, or disrupt the normal perception of time and space.

psychoactive drug   A drug capable of influencing perception, mood, cognition, or behavior.

psychoanalysis   A theory of personality and a method of psychotherapy developed by Sigmund Freud; it emphasizes unconscious motives and conflicts.

psychoanalysis   A theory of personality and a method of psychotherapy, originally formulated by Sigmund Freud, that emphasizes unconscious motives and conflicts.

psychodynamic perspective   A psychological approach that emphasizes unconscious dynamics within the individual, such as inner forces, conflicts, or the movement of instinctual energy.

psychodynamic theories   Theories that explain behavior and personality in terms of unconscious energy dynamics within the individual.

psychological tests   Procedures used to measure and evaluate personality traits, emotional states, aptitudes, interests, abilities, and values.

psychology   The scientific study of behavior and mental processes and how they are affected by an organism's physical state, mental state, and external environment; the term is often represented by Ψ, the Greek letter psi (usually pronounced "sy").

psychometrics   The measurement of mental abilities, traits, and processes.

psychoneuroimmunology (PNI)   The study of the relationships among psychology, the nervous and endocrine systems, and the immune system.

psychosis   An extreme mental disturbance involving distorted perceptions and irrational behavior; it may have psychological or organic causes. (Plural: *psychoses.*)

psychosurgery   Any surgical procedure that destroys selected areas of the brain believed to be involved in emotional disorders or violent, impulsive behavior.

puberty   The age at which a person becomes capable of sexual reproduction.

punishment   The process by which a stimulus or event weakens or reduces the probability of the response that it follows.

random assignment   A procedure for assigning people to experimental and control groups in which each individual has the same probability as any other of being assigned to a given group.

range   A measure of the spread of scores, calculated by subtracting the lowest score from the highest score.

rapid eye movement (REM) sleep   Sleep periods characterized by eye movement, loss of muscle tone, and dreaming.

reasoning   The drawing of conclusions or inferences from observations, facts, or assumptions.

recall   The ability to retrieve and reproduce from memory previously encountered material.

reciprocal determinism   In social-cognitive theories, the two-way interaction between the environment and the individual in determining and shaping personality factors.

recognition   The ability to identify previously encountered material.

reinforcement   The process by which a stimulus or event strengthens or increases the probability of the response that it follows.

relearning method   A method for measuring retention that compares the time required to relearn material with the time used in the initial learning of the material.

reliability   In test construction, the consistency of scores derived from a test, from one time and place to another.

REM sleep   *See* rapid eye movement sleep.

representative sample   A group of subjects, selected from a population for study, which matches the larger population on important characteristics such as age and sex.

reticular activating system (RAS)   A dense network of neurons found in the core of the brain stem; it arouses the cortex and screens incoming information.

retina   Neural tissue that lines the back of the eyeball's interior and contains the receptors for vision.

retinal disparity   The slight difference in lateral separation between two objects, as seen by the left eye and the right eye.

retroactive interference   Forgetting that occurs when recently learned material interferes with the ability to remember similar material stored previously.

rods   Visual receptors that respond to dim light but that are not involved in color vision.

role   A given social position that is governed by a set of norms for proper behavior.

Rorschach Inkblot Test   A projective personality test that asks respondents to interpret abstract, symmetrical inkblots.

saturation   Vividness or purity of color; the dimension of visual experience related to the complexity of light waves.

schizophrenia   A psychotic disorder or group of disorders marked by positive symptoms (e.g., delusions, hallucinations, disorganized and incoherent speech, and inappropriate behavior) and negative symptoms (e.g., emotional flatness and loss of motivation).

secondary control   An effort to accept reality by changing your own attitudes, goals, or emotions; a "learn to live with it" philosophy.

secondary emotions   Emotions that some cultures recognize or emphasize and others apparently do not, including blends of feeling or variations in intensity and nuance.

secondary punisher   A stimulus that has acquired punishing properties through association with other punishers.

secondary reinforcer   A stimulus that has acquired reinforcing properties through association with other reinforcers.

selective attention   The focusing of attention on selected aspects of the environment and the blocking out of others.

self-efficacy   A person's belief that he or she is capable of producing desired results, such as mastering new skills and reaching goals.

self-fulfilling prophecy   An expectation that comes true because of the tendency of the person holding it to act in ways to bring it about.

self-serving bias   The tendency, in explaining one's own behavior, to take credit for one's good actions and rationalize one's mistakes.

semantic memories   Memories of general knowledge, including facts, rules, concepts, and propositions.

semicircular canals   Sense organs in the inner ear, which contribute to equilibrium by responding to rotation of the head.

sensation   The detection of physical energy emitted or reflected by physical objects; it occurs when energy in the external environment or the body stimulates receptors in the sense organs.

sense receptors   Specialized cells that convert physical energy in the environment or the body to electrical energy that can be transmitted as nerve impulses to the brain.

sensory adaptation   The reduction or disappearance of sensory responsiveness that occurs when stimulation is unchanging or repetitious.

sensory deprivation   The absence of normal levels of sensory stimulation.

sensory memory   A memory system that momentarily preserves extremely accurate images of sensory information.

separation anxiety   The distress that most children develop, at about 7 to 9 months of age, when their primary caregivers temporarily leave them with strangers or in a new situation; it varies according to cultural practices.

serial-position effect   The tendency for recall of the first and last items on a list to surpass recall of items in the middle of the list.

set point   The genetically influenced weight range for an individual, thought to be maintained by a biological mechanism that regulates food intake, fat reserves, and metabolism.

sex hormones   Hormones that regulate the development and functioning of reproductive organs and that stimulate the development of male and female sexual characteristics; they include androgens, estrogens, and progesterone.

sex-typing *See* gender typing.

sexual script Scenarios that specify proper sexual behavior for a person in a given situation, varying with the person's age, culture, and gender.

shaping An operant-conditioning procedure in which successive approximations of a desired response are reinforced.

short-term memory (STM) In the three-box model of memory, a limited-capacity memory system involved in the retention of information for brief periods; it is also used to hold information retrieved from long-term memory for temporary use.

signal-detection theory A psychophysical theory that divides the detection of a sensory signal into a sensory process and a decision process.

significance tests Statistical tests that show how likely it is that a study's results occurred merely by chance.

single-blind study An experiment in which subjects do not know whether they are in an experimental or a control group.

social cognition An area in social psychology concerned with social influences on thought, memory, perception, and other cognitive processes.

social identity The part of a person's self-concept that is based on his or her identification with a nation, culture, or ethnic group or with gender or other roles in society.

social-cognitive theories Theories that emphasize how behavior is learned and maintained through observation and imitation of others, positive consequences, and cognitive processes such as plans, expectations, and beliefs.

social-cognitive theories (of personality) Theories that emphasize how personality traits are learned and maintained depending on the specific situation and the individual's cognitive processes, such as plans, expectations, and beliefs.

socialization The processes by which children learn the behaviors, attitudes, and expectations required of them by their society or culture.

sociobiology An interdisciplinary field that emphasizes evolutionary explanations of social behavior in animals, including human beings.

sociocultural perspective A psychological approach that emphasizes social and cultural influences on behavior.

somatic nervous system The subdivision of the peripheral nervous system that connects to sensory receptors and to skeletal muscles; sometimes called the *skeletal nervous system*.

source amnesia The inability to distinguish what you originally experienced from what you heard or were told about an event later.

spinal cord A collection of neurons and supportive tissue running from the base of the brain down the center of the back, protected by a column of bones (the spinal column).

spontaneous recovery The reappearance of a learned response after its apparent extinction.

standard deviation (SD) A commonly used measure of variability that indicates the average difference between scores in a distribution and their mean; more precisely, the square root of the average squared deviation from the mean.

standardize In test construction, to develop uniform procedures for giving and scoring a test.

state-dependent memory The tendency to remember something when the rememberer is in the same physical or mental state as during the original learning or experience.

states of consciousness Distinctive and discrete patterns in the functioning of consciousness, characterized by particular modes of perception, thought, memory, or feeling.

statistically significant A term used to refer to a result that is extremely unlikely to have occurred by chance.

stereotype A summary impression of a group, in which a person believes that all members of the group share a common trait or traits (positive, negative, or neutral).

stereotype threat A burden of doubt a person feels about his or her performance, due to negative stereotypes about his or her group's abilities.

stimulants Drugs that speed up activity in the central nervous system.

stimulus discrimination The tendency to respond differently to two or more similar stimuli. In classical conditioning, it occurs when a stimulus similar to the conditioned stimulus fails to evoke the conditioned response; in operant conditioning, it occurs when an organism learns to make a response in the presence of other, similar stimuli that differ from it on some dimension.

stimulus generalization After conditioning, the tendency to respond to a stimulus that resembles one involved in the original conditioning. In classical conditioning, it occurs when a stimulus that resembles the conditioned stimulus elicits the conditioned response; in operant conditioning, it occurs when a response that has been reinforced (or punished) in the presence of one stimulus occurs (or is suppressed) in the presence of other, similar stimuli.

structuralism An early psychological approach that emphasized the analysis of immediate experience into basic elements.

subconscious processes Mental processes occurring outside of conscious awareness but accessible to consciousness when necessary.

successive approximations In the operant-conditioning procedure of shaping, behaviors that are ordered in terms of increasing similarity or closeness to the desired response.

superego In psychoanalysis, the part of personality that represents conscience, morality, and social standards.

suprachiasmatic [soo-pruh-kie-az-MAT-ick] nucleus (SCN) An area of the brain containing a biological clock that governs circadian rhythms.

surveys Questionnaires and interviews that ask people directly about their experiences, attitudes, or opinions.

sympathetic nervous system The subdivision of the autonomic nervous system that mobilizes bodily resources and increases the output of energy during emotion and stress.

synapse The site where a nerve impulse is transmitted from one nerve cell to another; it includes the axon terminal, the synaptic cleft, and receptor sites in the membrane of the receiving cell.

systematic desensitization In behavior therapy, a step-by-step process of desensitizing a client to a feared object or experience; it is based on the classical-conditioning procedure of counterconditioning.

tacit knowledge Strategies for success that are not explicitly taught but that instead must be inferred.

taste buds Nests of taste-receptor cells.

telegraphic speech A child's first word combinations, which omit (as a telegram does) unnecessary words.

temperaments Physiological dispositions to respond to the environment in certain ways; they are present in infancy and are assumed to be innate.

temporal lobes Lobes at the sides of the brain's cerebral cortex, just above the ears; they contain areas involved in hearing, memory, perception, emotion, and (in the left lobe, typically) language comprehension.

thalamus A brain structure that relays sensory messages to the cerebral cortex.

Thematic Apperception Test (TAT) A personality test that asks respondents to interpret a series of drawings showing ambiguous scenes of people; usually scored for various motives such as the needs for affiliation, power, and achievement.

theory An organized system of assumptions and principles that purports to explain a specified set of phenomena and their interrelationships.

theory of mind A system of beliefs about the way your own mind and other people's minds work, and of how people are affected by their beliefs and feelings; emerges at age 4 or 5.

therapeutic alliance The bond of confidence and mutual understanding established between therapist and client, which allows them to work together to solve the client's problems.

timbre The distinguishing quality of a sound; the dimension of auditory experience related to the complexity of the pressure wave.

tolerance Increased resistance to a drug's effects accompanying continued use; as tolerance develops, larger doses are required to produce effects once brought about by smaller ones.

trait A characteristic of an individual, describing a habitual way of behaving, thinking, and feeling.

tranquilizers Drugs commonly but often inappropriately prescribed for patients who complain of unhappiness, anxiety, or worry.

transference In psychodynamic therapies, a critical step in which the client transfers unconscious emotions or reactions, such as emotional feelings about his or her parents, onto the therapist.

trichromatic theory A theory of color perception that proposes three mechanisms in the visual system, each sensitive to a certain range of wavelengths; their interaction is assumed to produce all the different experiences of hue.

two-factor theory of emotion The theory that emotions depend on both physiological arousal and a cognitive interpretation of that arousal.

ultradian [ul-TRAY-dee-un] rhythm A biological rhythm that occurs more frequently than once a day; from the Latin for "beyond a day."

unconditional positive regard To Carl Rogers, love or support given to another person with no conditions attached.

unconditioned response (UR) The classical-conditioning term for a reflexive response elicited by a stimulus in the absence of learning.

unconditioned stimulus (US) The classical-conditioning term for a stimulus that elicits a reflexive response in the absence of learning.

validity The ability of a test to measure what it was designed to measure.

validity effect The tendency of people to believe that a statement is true or valid simply because it has been repeated many times.

variable-interval schedule An intermittent schedule of reinforcement in which a reinforcer is delivered for a response made after a variable period of time has elapsed since the last reinforcer.

variable-ratio schedule An intermittent schedule of reinforcement in which reinforcement occurs after a variable number of responses.

variables Characteristics of behavior or experience that can be measured or described by a numeric scale; variables are manipulated and assessed in scientific studies.

volunteer bias A shortcoming of findings derived from a sample of volunteers instead of a representative sample; the volunteers may differ from those who did not volunteer.

withdrawal symptoms Physical and psychological symptoms that occur when someone addicted to a drug stops taking it.

z-score (standard score) A number that indicates how far a given raw score is above or below the mean, using the standard deviation of the distribution as the unit of measurement.

BIBLIOGRAPHY

Abel, Gene G.; Mittelman, Mary; Becker, Judith V.; et al. (1988). Predicting child molesters' response to treatment. *Annals of the New York Academy of Sciences, 528,* 223–234.

Abramovitch, Henry (1995). The nightmare of returning home: A case of acute onset nightmare disorder treated by lucid dreaming. *Israel Journal of Psychiatry and Related Sciences, 32,* 140–145.

Abrams, David B., & Wilson, G. Terence (1983). Alcohol, sexual arousal, and self-control. *Journal of Personality and Social Psychology, 45,* 188–198.

Abrams, Mitchell, & Feindler, Eva (1998). Violence reduction via anger management for male athletes. Paper presented at the annual meeting of the American Psychological Association, San Francisco.

Abramson, Lyn Y.; Metalsky, Gerald I.; & Alloy, Lauren B. (1989). Hopelessness depression: A theory-based subtype of depression. *Psychological Review, 96,* 358–372.

Adams, James L. (1986). *Conceptual blockbusting: A guide to better ideas* (3rd ed.). Boston: Addison-Wesley.

Ader, Robert (1997). The role of conditioning. In A. Harrington (ed.), *The placebo effect: An interdisciplinary exploration.* Cambridge, MA: Harvard University Press.

Adler, Nancy E.; Boyce, Thomas; Chesney, Margaret A.; et al. (1994). Socioeconomic status and health: The challenge of the gradient. *American Psychologist, 49,* 15–24.

Affleck, Glenn; Tennen, Howard; Croog, Sydney; & Levine, Sol (1987). Causal attribution, perceived control, and recovery from a heart attack. *Journal of Social and Clinical Psychology, 5,* 339–355.

Ainsworth, Mary D. S. (1973). The development of infant–mother attachment. In B. M. Caldwell & H. N. Ricciuti (eds.), *Review of child development research* (Vol. 3). Chicago: University of Chicago Press.

Ainsworth, Mary D. S. (1979). Infant–mother attachment. *American Psychologist, 34,* 932–937.

Akbarian, Schahram; Kim, J. J.; Potkin, Steven G.; et al. (1996). Maldistribution of interstitial neurons in prefrontal white matter of the brains of schizophrenic patients. *Archives of General Psychiatry, 53,* 425–436.

Alagna, Sheryle W., & Hamilton, Jean A. (1986). Science in the service of mythology: The psychopathologizing of menstruation. Paper presented at the annual meeting of the American Psychological Association, Washington, DC.

Albee, George W. (1985, February). The answer is prevention. *Psychology Today,* 60–64.

Aldag, Ramon J., & Fuller, Sally R. (1993). Beyond fiasco: A reappraisal of the groupthink phenomenon and a new model of group decision processes. *Psychological Bulletin, 113,* 533–552.

Alkon, Daniel L. (1989). Memory storage and neural systems. *Scientific American, 261,* 42–50.

Allen, Laura S., & Gorski, Robert A. (1992). Sexual orientation and the size of the anterior commissure in the human brain. *Proceedings of the National Academy of Sciences, 89,* 7199–7202.

Allison, David B., & Faith, Myles S. (1997). Issues in mapping genes for eating disorders. *Psychopharmacology Bulletin, 33,* 359–368.

Allison, David B., & Heshka, Stanley (1993). Emotion and eating in obesity? A critical analysis. *International Journal of Eating Disorders, 13,* 289–295.

Alloy, Lauren B., & Abramson, Lyn Y. (1998). The Temple–Wisconsin cognitive vulnerability to depression (CVD) project. Paper presented at the annual meeting of the American Psychological Association, San Francisco.

Alloy, Lauren B.; Fedderly, Sharon S.; Kennedy-Moore, Eileen; & Cohan, Catherine L. (1998). Dysphoria and social interaction: An integration of behavioral confirmation and interpersonal perspectives. *Journal of Personality and Social Psychology, 74,* 1566–1579.

Allport, Gordon W. (1937). *Personality: A psychological interpretation.* New York: Holt, Rinehart and Winston.

Allport, Gordon W. (1954/1979). *The nature of prejudice.* Reading, MA: Addison-Wesley.

Allport, Gordon W. (1961). *Pattern and growth in personality.* New York: Holt, Rinehart and Winston.

Alpert, Bené; Field, Tiffany; Goldstein, Sheri; & Perry, Susan (1990). Aerobics enhances cardiovascular fitness and agility in preschoolers. *Health Psychology, 9,* 48–56.

Amabile, Teresa M. (1983). *The social psychology of creativity.* New York: Springer-Verlag.

Amabile, Teresa M.; Phillips, Elise D.; & Collins, Mary Ann (1993). Creativity by contract: Social influences on the creativity of professional artists. Paper presented at the annual meeting of the American Psychological Association, Toronto, Canada.

Ambert, Anne-Marie (1997). *Parents, children, and adolescents: Interactive relationships and development in context.* New York: Haworth Press.

American Psychiatric Association (1994). *The diagnostic and statistical manual of mental disorders* (4th ed.). Washington, DC: American Psychiatric Association.

Amering, Michaela, & Katschnig, Heinz (1990). Panic attacks and panic disorder in cross-cultural perspective. *Psychiatric Annals, 20,* 511–516.

Anastasi, Anne (1988). *Psychological testing* (6th ed.). New York: Macmillan.

Anastasi, Anne, & Urbina, Susana (1997). *Psychological testing* (7th ed.). Upper Saddle River, NJ: Prentice-Hall.

Andersen, Barbara L.; Kiecolt-Glaser, Janice K.; & Glaser, Ronald (1994). A biobehavioral model of cancer stress and disease course. *American Psychologist, 49,* 389–404.

Anderson, Craig A.; Miller, Rowland S.; Riger, Alice L.; et al. (1994). Behavioral and characterological attributional styles as predictors of depression and loneliness: Review, refinement, and test. *Journal of Personality and Social Psychology, 66,* 549–558.

Anderson, John R. (1990). *The adaptive nature of thought.* Hillsdale, NJ: Erlbaum.

Andreasen, Nancy C.; Arndt, Stephan; Swayze, Victor, II; et al. (1994). Thalamic abnormalities in schizophrenia visualized through magnetic resonance image averaging. *Science, 266,* 294–298.

Angell, Marcia, & Kassirer, Jerome P. (1998, September 17). Alternative medicine: The risks of untested and unregulated remedies [Editorial]. *New England Journal of Medicine, 339,* 839–841.

Antonuccio, David O.; Danton, William G.; DeNelsky, Garland Y.; et al. (1999). Raising questions about antidepressants. *Psychotherapy and Psychosomatics, 68,* 3–14.

APA Commission on Violence and Youth (1993). *Violence and youth: Psychology's response.* Washington, DC: American Psychological Association.

APA Research Office (1998). *APA doctorate employment survey, 1996.* Washington, DC: American Psychological Association.

Arendt, Hannah (1963). *Eichmann in Jerusalem: A report on the banality of evil.* New York: Viking.

Arendt, Josephine; Skene, Debra J.; Middleton, B.; et al. (1997). Efficacy of melatonin treatment in jet lag, shift work, and blindness. *Journal of Biological Rhythms, 12,* 604–617.

Arkes, Hal R. (1993). Some practical judgment and decision-making research. In N. J. Castellan, Jr., et al. (eds.), *Individual and group decision making: Current issues.* Hillsdale, NJ: Erlbaum.

Arkes, Hal R.; Boehm, Lawrence E.; & Xu, Gang (1991). The determinants of judged validity. *Journal of Experimental Social Psychology, 27,* 576–605.

Arkes, Hal R.; Faust, David; Guilmette, Thomas J.; & Hart, Kathleen (1988). Eliminating the hindsight bias. *Journal of Applied Psychology, 73,* 305–307.

Arnett, Jeffrey J. (1999). Adolescent storm and stress, reconsidered. *American Psychologist, 54,* 317–326.

Aron, Arthur; Aron, Elaine N.; & Allen, Joselyn (1998). Motivations for unreciprocated love. *Personality and Social Psychology Bulletin, 24,* 787–796.

Aron, Arthur, & Westbay, Lori (1996). Dimensions of the prototype of love. *Journal of Personality and Social Psychology, 70,* 535–551.

Aronson, Elliot (1999a). Dissonance, hypocrisy, and the self concept. In J. E. Harmon-Jones & J. Mills (eds.), *Cognitive dissonance: Progress on a pivotal theory in social psychology.* Washington, DC: American Psychological Association.

Aronson, Elliot (1999b). *The social animal* (8th ed.). New York: Freeman.

Aronson, Elliot, & Mills, Judson (1959). The effect of severity of initiation on liking for a group. *Journal of Abnormal and Social Psychology, 59,* 177–181.

Aronson, Elliot, & Patnoe, Shelley (1997). *Cooperation in the classroom: The jigsaw method.* New York: Longman.

Aronson, Elliot; Stephan, Cookie; Sikes, Jev; Blaney, Nancy; & Snapp, Matthew (1978). *The jigsaw classroom.* Beverly Hills, CA: Sage.

Aronson, Elliot; Wilson, Timothy D.; & Akert, Robin A. (1999). *Social psychology: The heart and the mind* (3rd ed.). New York: Longman.

Arroyo, Carmen G., & Zigler, Edward (1995). Racial identity, academic achievement, and the psychological well-being of economically disadvantaged adolescents. *Journal of Personality and Social Psychology, 69,* 903–914.

Asch, Solomon E. (1952). *Social psychology.* Englewood Cliffs, NJ: Prentice-Hall.

Asch, Solomon E. (1965). Effects of group pressure upon the modification and distortion of judgments. In H. Proshansky & B. Seidenberg (eds.), *Basic studies in social psychology.* New York: Holt, Rinehart and Winston.

Aserinsky, Eugene, & Kleitman, Nathaniel (1955). Two types of ocular motility occurring in sleep. *Journal of Applied Physiology, 8,* 1–10.

Aspinwall, Lisa G., & Brunhart, Susanne M. (1996). Distinguishing optimism from denial: Optimistic beliefs predict attention to health threats. *Personality and Social Psychology Bulletin, 22,* 993–1003.

Aspinwall, Lisa G., & Taylor, Shelley E. (1997). A stitch in time: Self-regulation and proactive coping. *Psychological Bulletin, 121,* 417–436.

Atkinson, John W. (ed.) (1958). *Motives in fantasy, action, and society.* Princeton, NJ: Van Nostrand.

Atkinson, Richard C., & Shiffrin, Richard M. (1968). Human memory: A proposed system and its control processes. In K. W. Spence & J. T. Spence (eds.), *The psychology of learning and motivation: Vol. 2. Advances in research and theory.* New York: Academic Press.

Atkinson, Richard C., & Shiffrin, Richard M. (1971, August). The control of short-term memory. *Scientific American, 225*(2), 82–90.

AuBuchon, Peter G., & Calhoun, Karen S. (1985). Menstrual cycle symptomatology: The role of social expectancy and experimental demand characteristics. *Psychosomatic Medicine, 47,* 35–45.

Axel, Richard (1995, October). The molecular logic of smell. *Scientific American,* 154–159.

Azrin, Nathan H., & Foxx, Richard M. (1974). *Toilet training in less than a day.* New York: Simon & Schuster.

Azuma, Hiroshi (1984). Secondary control as a heterogeneous category. *American Psychologist, 39,* 970–971.

Bahill, A. Terry, & Karnavas, William J. (1993). The perceptual illusion of baseball's rising fastball and breaking curveball. *Journal of Experimental Psychology: Human Perception & Performance, 19,* 3–14.

Bahrick, Harry P. (1984). Semantic memory content in permastore: Fifty years of memory for Spanish learned in school. *Journal of Experimental Psychology: General, 113,* 1–29.

Bahrick, Harry P.; Bahrick, Phyllis O.; & Wittlinger, Roy P. (1975). Fifty years of memory for names and faces: A cross-sectional approach. *Journal of Experimental Psychology: General, 104,* 54–75.

Bailey, J. Michael; Bobrow, David; Wolfe, Marilyn; & Mikach, Sarah (1995). Sexual orientation of adult sons of gay fathers. *Developmental Psychology, 31,* 124–129.

Bailey, J. Michael; Gaulin, Steven; Agyei, Yvonne; & Gladue, Brian A. (1994). Effects of gender and sexual orientation on evolutionarily relevant aspects of human mating psychology. *Journal of Personality and Social Psychology, 66,* 1081–1093.

Bailey, J. Michael, & Pillard, Richard C. (1995). Genetics of human sexual orientation. *Annual Review of Sex Research, 6,* 126–150.

Bailey, J. Michael, & Zucker, Kenneth J. (1995). Childhood sex-typed behavior and sexual orientation: A conceptual analysis and quantitative review. *Developmental Psychology, 31,* 43–55.

Baillargeon, Renée (1994). How do infants learn about the physical world? *Current Directions in Psychological Science, 5,* 133–140.

Baker, Mark C. (1999). Innateness and the universality of universal grammar: Evidence from Mohawk. Paper presented at the annual meeting of the American Association for the Advancement of Science, Anaheim.

Baker, Robert A. (1992). *Hidden memories: Voices and visions from within.* Buffalo, NY: Prometheus.

Baker, Robin (1996). *The sperm wars: The science of sex.* New York: Basic Books.

Baltes, Paul B. (1983). Life-span developmental psychology: Observations on history and theory revisited. In R. M. Lerner (ed.), *Developmental psychology: Historical and philosophical perspectives.* Hillsdale, NJ: Erlbaum.

Baltes, Paul, & Graf, Peter (1996). Psychological aspects of aging: Facts and frontiers. In D. Magnusson (ed.), *The lifespan development of individuals.* Cambridge, England: Cambridge University Press.

Baltes, Paul B.; Sowarka, Doris; & Kliegl, Reinhold (1989). Cognitive training research on fluid intelligence in old age: What can older adults achieve by themselves? *Psychology and Aging, 4,* 217–221.

Bancroft, John; Sherwin, Barbara B.; Alexander, G. M.; et al. (1991). Oral contraceptives, androgens, and the sexuality of young women: II. The role of androgens. *Archives of Sexual Behavior, 20,* 121–135.

Bandura, Albert (1977). *Social learning theory.* Englewood Cliffs, NJ: Prentice-Hall.

Bandura, Albert (1986). *Social foundations of thought and action: A social cognitive theory.* Englewood Cliffs, NJ: Prentice-Hall.

Bandura, Albert (1990). Self-regulation of motivation through goal systems. In R. A. Dienstbier (ed.), *Nebraska Symposium on Motivation, 1989.* Lincoln: University of Nebraska Press.

Bandura, Albert (1992). Self-efficacy mechanism in psychobiologic functioning. In R. Schwarzer (ed.), *Self-efficacy: Thought control of action.* Washington, DC: Hemisphere.

Bandura, Albert (1994). Self-efficacy. In *Encyclopedia of human behavior* (Vol. 4). Orlando, FL: Academic Press.

Bandura, Albert (ed.) (1995). *Self-efficacy in changing societies*. New York: Cambridge University Press.

Bandura, Albert; Ross, Dorothea; & Ross, Sheila A. (1963). Vicarious reinforcement and imitative learning. *Journal of Abnormal and Social Psychology, 67,* 601–607.

Banks, Martin S. (in collaboration with Philip Salapatek) (1984). Infant visual perception. In P. Mussen (series ed.), M. M. Haith & J. J. Campos (vol. eds.), *Handbook of child psychology: Vol. 2. Infancy and developmental psychobiology* (4th ed.). New York: Wiley.

Barber, Theodore X. (1979). Suggested ("hypnotic") behavior: The trance paradigm versus an alternative paradigm. In E. Fromm & R. E. Shor (eds.), *Hypnosis: Developments in research and new perspectives* (2nd ed.). New York: Aldine.

Barbuto, J. E. (1997). A critique of the Myers-Briggs Type Indicator and its operationalization of Carl Jung's psychological types. *Psychological Reports, 80,* 611–625.

Bargh, John A. (1999, January 29). The most powerful manipulative messages are hiding in plain sight. *Chronicle of Higher Education,* B6.

Barinaga, Marcia (1992). Challenging the "no new neurons" dogma. *Science, 255,* 1646.

Barkley, Russell A. (1997). *ADHD and the nature of self control*. New York: Guilford.

Barkow, Jerome H.; Cosmides, Leda; & Tooby, John (eds.) (1992). *The adapted mind: Evolutionary psychology and the generation of culture*. New York: Oxford University Press.

Barlow, David H. (ed.) (1991). Special issue on diagnoses, dimensions, and DSM-IV: The science of classification. *Journal of Abnormal Psychology, 100,* 243–412.

Barlow, David H. (1996). Health care policy, psychotherapy research, and the future of psychotherapy. *American Psychologist, 51,* 1050–1058.

Barlow, David H.; Chorpita, Bruce F.; & Turovsky, J. (1996). Fear, panic, anxiety, and disorders of emotion. In D. A. Hope et al. (eds.), *Nebraska Symposium on Motivation, 1995: Perspectives on anxiety, panic, and fear.* Lincoln: University of Nebraska Press.

Baron, Miron (1993). The D2 dopamine receptor gene and alcoholism: A tempest in a wine cup? *Biological Psychiatry, 34,* 821–823.

Barondes, Samuel H. (1998). *Mood genes: Hunting for origins of mania and depression*. New York: W. H. Freeman.

Barone, David F.; Maddux, James E.; & Snyder, C. R. (1997). *Social cognitive psychology: History and current domains*. New York: Plenum Press.

Barrish, Barbara M. (1996). The relationship of remembered parental physical punishment to adolescent self-concept. *Dissertation Abstracts International, Section B, 57,* 2171.

Barsky, S. H.; Roth, M. D.; Kleerup, E. C.; et al. (1998). Histopathologic and molecular alterations in bronchial epithelium in habitual smokers of marijuana, cocaine, and/or tobacco. *Journal of the National Cancer Institute, 90,* 1198–1205.

Bartlett, Frederic C. (1932). *Remembering*. Cambridge, England: Cambridge University Press.

Bartoshuk, Linda M. (1993). Genetic and pathological taste variation: What can we learn from animal models and human disease? In D. J. Chadwick, J. Marsh, & J. Goode (eds.), *The molecular basis of smell and taste transduction* (CIBA Foundation Symposia Series, No. 179). New York: Wiley.

Bartoshuk, Linda M. (1998). Born to burn: Genetic variation in taste. Paper presented at the annual meeting of the American Psychological Association, San Francisco.

Bartoshuk, Linda M., & Beauchamp, Gary K. (1994). Chemical senses. *Annual Review of Psychology, 45,* 419–449.

Bartoshuk, Linda M.; Duffy, V. B.; Lucchina, L. A.; Prutkin, J.; & Fast, K. (1998). PROP (6-n-propylthiouracil) supertasters and the saltiness of NaCl. *Annals of the New York Academy of Sciences, 855,* 793–796.

Bashore, Theodore R., & Rapp, Paul E. (1993). Are there alternatives to traditional polygraph procedures? *Psychological Bulletin, 113,* 3–22.

Bashore, Theodore R.; Ridderinkhof, K. Richard; & van der Molen, Maurits W. (1997). The decline of cognitive processing speed in old age. *Current Directions in Psychological Science, 6,* 163–169.

Basic Behavioral Science Task Force of the National Advisory Mental Health Council (1996). Basic behavioral science research for mental health: Vulnerability and resilience. *American Psychologist, 51,* 22–28.

Bauer, Patricia J., & Dow, Gina A. (1994). Episodic memory in 16- and 20-month-old children: Specifics are generalized but not forgotten. *Developmental Psychology, 30,* 403–417.

Baum, William M. (1994). *Understanding behaviorism: Science, behavior, and culture*. New York: Addison Wesley Education.

Baumeister, Roy F. (1990). Suicide as escape from self. *Psychological Review, 97,* 90–113.

Baumeister, Roy, & Bratslavsky, Ellen (1999). Passion, intimacy, and time: Passionate love as a function of change in intimacy. *Personality and Social Psychology Review, 3,* 49–67.

Baumeister, Roy F.; Stillwell, Arlene M.; & Heatherton, Todd F. (1994). Guilt: An interpersonal approach. *Psychological Bulletin, 115,* 243–267.

Baumeister, Roy F.; Stillwell, Arlene M.; & Wotman, Sara R. (1990). Victim and perpetrator accounts of interpersonal conflict: Autobiographical narratives about anger. *Journal of Personality and Social Psychology, 59,* 994–1005.

Baumrind, Diana (1966). Effects of authoritative parental control on child behavior. *Child Development, 37,* 887–907.

Baumrind, Diana (1971). Current patterns of parental authority. *Developmental Psychology Monograph, 4* (1, Part 2).

Baumrind, Diana (1989). Rearing competent children. In W. Damon (ed.), *Child development today and tomorrow.* San Francisco: Jossey-Bass.

Baumrind, Diana (1991). Parenting styles and adolescent development. In R. Lerner, A. C. Petersen, & J. Brooks-Gunn (eds.), *The encyclopedia of adolescence.* New York: Garland.

Baumrind, Diana (1995). Commentary on sexual orientation: Research and social policy implications. *Developmental Psychology, 31,* 130–136.

Baxter, Lewis R.; Schwartz, Jeffrey M.; Bergman, Kenneth S.; et al. (1992). Caudate glucose metabolic rate changes with both drug and behavior therapy for obsessive–compulsive disorder. *Archives of General Psychiatry, 49,* 681–689.

Bechara, Antoine; Dermas, Hanna; Tranel, Daniel; & Damasio, Antonio R. (1997). Deciding advantageously before knowing the advantageous strategy. *Science, 275,* 1293–1294.

Beck, Aaron T. (1976). *Cognitive therapy and the emotional disorders*. New York: International Universities Press.

Beck, Aaron T. (1988). Cognitive approaches to panic disorder: Theory and therapy. In S. Rachman & J. D. Maser (eds.), *Panic: Psychological perspectives.* Hillsdale, NJ: Erlbaum.

Beck, Aaron T. (1991). Cognitive therapy: A 30-year retrospective. *American Psychologist, 46,* 368–375.

Becker, Judith V.; Skinner, Linda J.; Abel, Gene G.; & Cichon, Joan (1984). Time-limited therapy with sexually dysfunctional sexually assaulted women. *Journal of Social Work and Human Sexuality, 3,* 97–115.

Becker, Marshall H. (1993). A medical sociologist looks at health promotion. *Journal of Health and Social Behavior, 34,* 1–6.

Beckerman, Stephen; Lizarralde, Roberto; Ballew, Carol; et al. (1998). The Barí partible paternity project: Preliminary results. *Current Anthropology, 39,* 164–167.

Bee, Helen (1997). *The developing child* (8th ed.). New York: Longman.

Beer, Jeremy M.; Arnold, Richard D.; & Loehlin, John C. (1998). Genetic and environmental influences on MMPI factor scales: Joint model fitting to twin and adoption data. *Journal of Personality and Social Psychology, 74,* 818–827.

Bekenstein, Jonathan W., & Lothman, Eric W. (1993). Dormancy of inhibitory interneurons in a model of temporal lobe epilepsy. *Science, 259,* 97–100.

Bell, Alan P.; Weinberg, Martin S.; & Hammersmith, Sue K. (1981). *Sexual preference: Its development in men and women.* Bloomington: Indiana University Press.

Bell, Derrick (1992). *Faces at the bottom of the well: The permanence of racism.* New York: Basic Books.

Bellugi, Ursula; Bihrle, Amy; Neville, Helen; et al. (1992). Language, cognition, and brain organization in a neurodevelopmental disorder. In M. R. Gunnar et al. (eds.), *Developmental behavioral neuroscience: The Minnesota Symposia on Child Psychology.* Hillsdale, NJ: Erlbaum.

Belmont, Lillian, & Marolla, Francis A. (1973). Birth order, family size, and intelligence. *Science, 182,* 1096–1101.

Belsky, Jay; Campbell, Susan B.; Cohn, Jeffrey F.; & Moore, Ginger (1996). Instability of infant parent attachment security. *Developmental Psychology, 32,* 921–924.

Belsky, Jay; Hsieh, Kuang-Hua; & Crnic, Keith (1996). Infant positive and negative emotionality: One dimension or two? *Developmental Psychology, 32,* 289–298.

Bem, Daryl J., & Honorton, Charles (1994). Does psi exist? Replicable evidence for an anomalous process of information transfer. *Psychological Bulletin, 115,* 4–18.

Bem, Sandra L. (1993). *The lenses of gender.* New Haven, CT: Yale University Press.

Benet-Martínez, Verónica, & John, Oliver P. (1998). *Los Cinco Grandes* across cultures and ethnic groups: Multitrait multimethod analyses of the Big Five in Spanish and English. *Journal of Personality and Social Psychology, 75,* 729–750.

Benjamin, Ludy T., Jr. (1998). Why Gorgeous George, and not Wilhelm Wundt, was the founder of psychology: A history of popular psychology in America. Invited address presented at the National Institute on the Teaching of Psychology, St. Petersburg Beach.

Bennett, William, & Gurin, Joel (1982). *The dieter's dilemma: Eating less and weighing more.* New York: Basic Books.

Bentall, R. P. (1990). The illusion of reality: A review and integration of psychological research on hallucinations. *Psychological Bulletin, 107,* 82–95.

Bereiter, Carl, & Bird, Marlene (1985). Use of thinking aloud in identification and teaching of reading comprehension strategies. *Cognition and Instruction, 2,* 131–156.

Berenbaum, Sheri A., & Snyder, Elizabeth (1995). Early hormonal influences on childhood sex-typed activity and playmate preferences: Implications for the development of sexual orientation. *Developmental Psychology, 31,* 31–42.

Berger, F.; Gage, F. H.; & Vijayaraghavan, S. (1998). Nicotinic receptor-induced apoptotic cell death of hippocampal progenitor cells. *Journal of Neuroscience, 18,* 6871–6881.

Berkman, Lisa F.; Leo-Summers, L.; & Horwitz, R. I. (1992). Emotional support and survival after myocardial infarction: A prospective, population-based study of the elderly. *Annals of Internal Medicine, 117,* 1003–1009.

Berkman, Lisa, & Syme, S. Leonard (1979). Social networks, host resistance, and mortality: A nine-year follow-up study of Alameda County residents. *American Journal of Epidemiology, 109,* 186–204.

Berko, Jean (1958). The child's learning of English morphology. *Word, 14,* 150–177.

Bernhardt, Paul C; Dabbs, James M., Jr.; Fielden, Julie A.; & Lutter, Candice D. (1998). Testosterone changes during vicarious experiences of winning and losing among fans at sporting events. *Physiology and Behavior, 65,* 59–62.

Bernieri, Frank J.; Davis, Janet M.; Rosenthal, Robert; & Knee, C. Raymond (1991). Interactional synchrony and the social affordance of rapport: A validation study. Unpublished manuscript, Oregon State University, Corvallis.

Bernieri, Frank J.; Davis, Janet M.; Rosenthal, Robert; & Knee, C. Raymond (1994). Interactional synchrony and rapport: Measuring synchrony in displays devoid of sound and facial affect. *Personality and Social Psychology Bulletin, 20,* 303–311.

Bernieri, Frank J.; Gillis, John S.; Davis, Janet M.; & Grahe, Jon E. (1996). Dyad rapport and the accuracy of its judgment across situations: A lens model analysis. *Journal of Personality and Social Psychology, 71,* 110–129.

Berry, John W. (1994). Acculturative stress. In W. J. Lonner & R. S. Malpass (eds.), *Psychology and culture.* Needham Heights, MA: Allyn & Bacon.

Bettelheim, Bruno (1967). *The empty fortress.* New York: Free Press.

Beyerstein, Barry L. (1996). Graphology. In G. Stein (ed.), *The encyclopedia of the paranormal.* Amherst, NY: Prometheus Books.

Beyerstein, Barry L. (1999). Fringe psychotherapies: The public at risk. In W. Sampson (ed.), *A guide to alternative medicine.* London: Gordon and Breech.

Birdwhistell, Ray L. (1970). *Kinesics and context: Essays on body motion communication.* Philadelphia: University of Pennsylvania Press.

Bishop, Katherine M., & Wahlsten, Douglas (1997). Sex differences in the human corpus callosum: Myth or reality? *Neuroscience and Biobehavioral Reviews, 21,* 581–601.

Bjork, Daniel W. (1993). *B. F. Skinner: A life.* New York: Basic Books.

Blagrove, Mark (1996). Problems with the cognitive psychological modeling of dreaming. *Journal of Mind and Behavior, 17,* 99–134.

Blakemore, Colin, & Cooper, Grahame F. (1970). Development of the brain depends on the visual environment. *Nature, 228,* 477–478.

Blass, Thomas (1993). What we know about obedience: Distillations from 30 years of research on the Milgram paradigm. Paper presented at the annual meeting of the American Psychological Association, Toronto.

Blatt, Sidney J.; Auerbach, John S.; & Levy, Kenneth N. (1997). Mental representations in personality development, psychopathology, and the therapeutic process. *Review of General Psychology, 1,* 351–374.

Blazer, Dan G.; Kessler, Ronald C.; & Swartz, Marvin S. (1998). Epidemiology of recurrent major and minor depression with a seasonal pattern: The National Comorbidity Survey. *British Journal of Psychiatry, 172,* 164–167.

Bleuler, Eugen (1911/1950). *Dementia praecox or the group of schizophrenias.* New York: International Universities Press.

Bliss, T. V., & Collingridge, G. L. (1993). A synaptic model of memory: Long-term potentiation in the hippocampus. *Nature, 361*(6407), 31–39.

Blouin, J. L; Dombroski, B. A.; Nath, S. K.; et al. (1998). Schizophrenia susceptibility loci on chromosomes 13q32 and 8p21. *Nature Genetics, 20,* 70–73.

Blum, Deborah (1997). *Sex on the brain: The biological differences between men and women.* New York: Viking.

Blum, Deborah (1998, September/October). Face it! *Psychology Today,* 32–39, 66–67.

Boesch, Cristophe (1991). Teaching among wild chimpanzees. *Animal Behavior, 41,* 530–532.

Bohannon, John N., & Stanowicz, Laura (1988). The issue of negative evidence: Adult responses to children's language errors. *Developmental Psychology, 24,* 684–689.

Bohannon, John N., & Symons, Victoria (1988). Conversational conditions of children's imitation. Paper presented at the biennial Conference on Human Development, Charleston, South Carolina.

Bohman, Michael; Cloninger, R.; Sigvardsson, S.; & von Knorring, Anne-Liis (1987). The genetics of alcoholisms and related disorders. *Journal of Psychiatric Research, 21,* 447–452.

Bolger, Niall; Foster, Mark; Vinokur, Amiram D.; & Ng, Rosanna (1996). Close relationships and adjustment to a life crisis: The case of breast cancer. *Journal of Personality and Social Psychology, 70,* 283–294.

Bolshakov, Vadim Y., & Siegelbaum, Steven A. (1994). Postsynaptic induction and presynaptic expression of hippocampal long-term depression. *Science, 264,* 1148–1152.

Bond, Rod, & Smith, Peter B. (1996). Culture and conformity: A meta-analysis of studies using Asch's (1952b, 1956) line judgment task. *Psychological Bulletin, 119,* 111–137.

Bonnet, Michael H. (1990). The perception of sleep onset in insomniacs and normal sleepers. In R. R. Bootzin, J. F. Kihlstrom, & D. L. Schacter (eds.), *Sleep and cognition.* Washington, DC: American Psychological Association.

Boring, Edwin G. (1953). A history of introspection. *Psychological Bulletin, 50,* 169–187.

Bornstein, Robert F.; Leone, Dean R.; & Galley, Donna J. (1987). The generalizability of subliminal mere exposure effects: Influence of stimuli perceived without awareness on social behavior. *Journal of Personality and Social Psychology, 53,* 1070–1079.

Borys, Shelley, & Perlman, Daniel (1985). Gender differences in loneliness. *Personality and Social Psychology Bulletin, 11,* 63–74.

Bosworth, H. B., & Schaie, K. Warner (1999). Survival effects in cognitive function, cognitive style, and sociodemographic variables in the Seattle Longitudinal Study. *Experimental Aging Research, 25,* 121–139.

Bothwell, R. K., Deffenbacher, K. A., & Brigham, J. C. (1987). Correlation of eyewitness accuracy and confidence: Optimality hypothesis revised. *Journal of Applied Psychology, 72,* 691–698.

Bouchard, Claude; Tremblay, A.; Despres, J. P.; et al. (1990, May 24). The response to long-term overfeeding in identical twins. *New England Journal of Medicine, 322,* 1477–1482.

Bouchard, Thomas J., Jr. (1995). Nature's twice-told tale: Identical twins reared apart—what they tell us about human individuality. Paper presented at the annual meeting of the Western Psychological Association, Los Angeles.

Bouchard, Thomas J., Jr. (1997a). The genetics of personality. In K. Blum & E. P. Noble (eds.), *Handbook of psychiatric genetics.* Boca Raton, FL: CRC Press.

Bouchard, Thomas J., Jr. (1997b). IQ similarity in twins reared apart: Findings and responses to critics. In R. J. Sternberg & E. Grigorenko (eds.), *Intelligence: Heredity and environment.* New York: Cambridge University Press.

Bouchard, Thomas J., Jr., & McGue, Matthew (1981). Familial studies of intelligence: A review. *Science, 212,* 1055–1058.

Bousfield, W. A. (1953). The occurrence of clustering in the recall of randomly arranged associates. *Journal of General Psychology, 49,* 229–240.

Bowen, Murray (1978). *Family therapy in clinical practice.* New York: Jason Aronson.

Bower, Bruce (1998, February 21). All fired up: Perception may dance to the beat of collective neuronal rhythms. *Science News, 153,* 120–121.

Bower, Gordon H., & Clark, M. C. (1969). Narrative stories as mediators of serial learning. *Psychonomic Science, 14,* 181–182.

Bowers, Kenneth S.; Regehr, Glenn; Balthazard, Claude; & Parker, Kevin (1990). Intuition in the context of discovery. *Cognitive Psychology, 22,* 72–110.

Bowlby, John (1969). *Attachment and loss: Vol. 1. Attachment.* New York: Basic Books.

Bowlby, John (1973). *Attachment and loss: Vol. 2. Separation.* New York: Basic Books.

Boyd-Franklin, Nancy (1989). *Black families in therapy: A multisystems approach.* New York: Guilford Press.

Boysen, Sarah T., & Berntson, Gary G. (1989). Numerical competence in a chimpanzee *(Pan troglodytes). Journal of Comparative Psychology, 103,* 23–31.

Bracha, H. Stefan; Torrey, E. Fuller; Bigelow, Llewellyn B.; et al. (1991). Subtle signs of prenatal maldevelopment of the hand ectoderm in schizophrenia: A preliminary monozygotic twin study. *Biological Psychiatry, 30,* 719–725.

Bradford, John M., & Pawlak, Anne (1993). Effects of cyproterone acetate on sexual arousal patterns of pedophiles. *Archives of Sexual Behavior, 22,* 629–641.

Brainerd, C. J.; Reyna, V. F.; & Brandse, E. (1995). Are children's false memories more persistent than their true memories? *Psychological Science, 6,* 359–364.

Brannon, Elizabeth M., & Terrace, Herbert S. (1998). Ordering of the numerosities 1 to 9 by monkeys. *Science, 282,* 746–749.

Braungert, J. M.; Plomin, Robert; DeFries, J. C.; & Fulker, D. W. (1992). Genetic influence on tester-rated infant temperament as assessed by Bayley's Infant Behavior Record: Nonadoptive and adoptive siblings and twins. *Developmental Psychology, 28,* 40–47.

Breggin, Peter R. (1991). *Toxic psychiatry.* New York: St. Martin's Press.

Brehm, Jack W. (1999). The intensity of emotion. *Personality and Social Psychology Review, 3,* 2–22.

Breland, Keller, & Breland, Marian (1961). The misbehavior of organisms. *American Psychologist, 16,* 681–684.

Brennan, Patricia A., & Mednick, Sarnoff A. (1994). Learning theory approach to the deterrence of criminal recidivism. *Journal of Abnormal Psychology, 103,* 430–440.

Brewer, Marilynn B., & Gardner, Wendi (1996). Who is this "we"? Levels of collective identity and self representations. *Journal of Personality and Social Psychology, 71,* 83–93.

Briggs, John (1984, December). The genius mind. *Science Digest, 92*(12), 74–77, 102–103.

Brigham, John C., & Malpass, Roy S. (1985, Fall). The role of experience and contact in the recognition of faces of own- and other-race persons. *Journal of Social Issues, 41,* 139–155.

Brockner, Joel, & Rubin, Jeffrey Z. (1985). *Entrapment in escalating conflicts: A social psychological analysis.* New York: Springer-Verlag.

Brodsky, Annette M. (1982). Sex, race, and class issues in psychotherapy research. In J. H. Harvey & M. M. Parks (eds.), *Psychotherapy research and behavior change: Vol. 1. The APA Master Lecture Series.* Washington, DC: American Psychological Association.

Brody, D. J.; Pirkle, J. L.; Kramer, R. A.; et al. (1994). Blood lead levels in the US population: Phase 1 of the Third National Health and Nutrition Examination Survey (NHANES III, 1988 to 1991). *Journal of the American Medical Association, 272,* 277–283.

Brody, Nathan (1990). Behavior therapy versus placebo: Comment on Bowers and Clum's meta-analysis. *Psychological Bulletin, 107,* 106–109.

Bromberger, Joyce T., & Matthews, Karen A. (1996). A "feminine" model of vulnerability to depressive symptoms: A longitudinal investigation of middle-aged women. *Journal of Personality and Social Psychology, 70,* 591–598.

Brooks-Gunn, J. (1986). Differentiating premenstrual symptoms and syndromes. *Psychosomatic Medicine, 48,* 385–387.

Brown, Alan S. (1991). A review of the tip-of-the-tongue experience. *Psychological Bulletin, 109,* 204–223.

Brown, George W. (1993). Life events and affective disorder: Replications and limitations. *Psychosomatic Medicine, 55,* 248–259.

Brown, Jonathon D. (1991). Staying fit and staying well. *Journal of Personality and Social Psychology, 60, 555–561.*

Brown, Paul (1994). Toward a psychobiological study of dissociation. In S. J. Lynn & J. Rhue (eds.), *Dissociation: Clinical, theoretical and research perspectives.* New York: Guilford Press.

Brown, Robert, & Middlefell, Robert (1989). Fifty-five years of cocaine dependence [Letter to the editor]. *British Journal of Addiction, 84, 946.*

Brown, Roger (1986). *Social psychology* (2nd ed.). New York: Free Press.

Brown, Roger; Cazden, Courtney; & Bellugi, Ursula (1969). The child's grammar from I to III. In J. P. Hill (ed.), *Minnesota Symposium on Child Psychology* (Vol. 2). Minneapolis: University of Minnesota Press.

Brown, Roger, & Kulik, James (1977). Flashbulb memories. *Cognition, 5,* 73–99.

Brown, Roger, & McNeill, David (1966). The "tip of the tongue" phenomenon. *Journal of Verbal Learning and Verbal Behavior, 5, 325–337.*

Brown, Ryan P., & Josephs, Robert A. (1999). A burden of proof: Stereotype relevance and gender differences in math performance. *Journal of Personality and Social Psychology, 76, 246–257.*

Brown, Steven P. (1996). A meta-analysis and review of organizational research on job involvement. *Psychological Bulletin, 120, 235–255.*

Brownell, Kelly D., & Rodin, Judith (1994). The dieting maelstrom: Is it possible and advisable to lose weight? *American Psychologist, 49, 781–791.*

Bruck, Maggie; Ceci, Stephen J.; Francoeur, E.; & Renick, A. (1995). Anatomically detailed dolls do not facilitate preschoolers' reports of a pediatric examination involving genital touching. *Journal of Experimental Psychology: Applied, 1, 95–109.*

Buck, Linda, & Axel, Richard (1991). A novel multigene family may encode odorant receptors: A molecular basis for odor recognition. *Cell, 65, 175–187.*

Buck, Ross (1984). *The communication of emotion.* New York: Guilford Press.

Budiansky, Stephen (1998). *If a lion could talk: Animal intelligence and the evolution of consciousness.* New York: Free Press.

Burack, J. H.; Barrett, D. C.; Stall, R. D.; et al. (1993). Depressive symptoms and CD4 lymphocyte decline among HIV-infected men. *Journal of the American Medical Association, 270, 2568–2573.*

Burgess, Cheryl A.; Kirsch, Irving; Shane, Howard; et al. (1998). Facilitated communication as an ideomotor response. *Psychological Science, 9, 71–74.*

Burke, Deborah M.; Burnett, Gayle; & Levenstein, Peggy (1978). Menstrual symptoms: New data from a double-blind study. Paper presented at the annual meeting of the Western Psychological Association, San Francisco.

Burke, Deborah M.; MacKay, Donald G.; Worthley, Joanna S.; & Wade, Elizabeth (1991). On the tip of the tongue: What causes word finding failures in young and older adults? *Journal of Memory and Language, 30,* 237–246.

Burke, Phyllis (1996). *Gender shock.* New York: Basic Books.

Bursik, Krisanne (1998). Moving beyond gender differences: Gender role comparisons of manifest dream content. *Sex Roles, 38, 203–214.*

Bushman, Brad J.; Baumeister, Roy; & Stack, Angela D. (1999). Catharsis, aggression, and persuasive influence: Self-fulfilling or self-defeating prophecies? *Journal of Personality and Social Psychology, 76, 367–376.*

Buss, David M. (1993). Sexual strategies theory: An evolutionary perspective on human mating. *Psychological Review, 100, 204–232.*

Buss, David M. (1994). *The evolution of desire: Strategies of human mating.* New York: Basic Books.

Buss, David M. (1995). Evolutionary psychology: A new paradigm for psychological science. *Psychological Inquiry, 6, 1–30.*

Buss, David M. (1996). Sexual conflict: Can evolutionary and feminist perspectives converge? In D. M. Buss & N. Malamuth (eds.), *Sex, power, conflict: Evolutionary and feminist perspectives.* New York: Oxford University Press.

Bussey, Kay, & Bandura, Albert (1992). Self-regulatory mechanisms governing gender development. *Child Development, 63, 1236–1250.*

Butcher, James N.; Dahlstrom, W. Grant; Graham, John R.; Tellegen, Auke; & Kaemmer, Beverly (1989). *Minnesota Multiphasic Personality Inventory—II: Manual for administration and scoring.* Minneapolis: University of Minnesota Press.

Butcher, James N.; Lim, Jeeyoung; & Nezami, Elahe (1998). Objective study of abnormal personality in cross-cultural settings: The MMPI-2. *Journal of Cross-Cultural Psychology, 29, 189–211.*

Butler, S.; Chalder, T.; Ron, M.; et al. (1991). Cognitive behaviour therapy in chronic fatigue syndrome. *Journal of Neurology, Neurosurgery and Psychiatry, 54, 153–158.*

Butterfield, E. C., & Belmont, J. M. (1977). Assessing and improving the executive cognitive functions of mentally retarded people. In I. Bialer & M. Sternlict (eds.), *Psychological issues in mental retardation.* New York: Psychological Dimensions.

Buunk, Bram; Angleitner, Alois; Oubaid, Viktor; & Buss, David M. (1996). Sex differences in jealousy in evolutionary and cultural perspective: Tests from the Netherlands, Germany, and the United States. *Psychological Science, 7, 359–363.*

Byne, William (1993). Sexual orientation and brain structure: Adding up the evidence. Paper presented at the annual meeting of the International Academy of Sex Research, Pacific Grove, CA.

Byne, William (1995). Science and belief: Psychobiological research on sexual orientation. *Journal of Homosexuality, 28, 303–344.*

Cabezas, A.; Tam, T. M.; Lowe, B. M.; et al. (1989). Empirical study of barriers to upward mobility of Asian Americans in the San Francisco Bay area. In G. Nomura (ed.), *Frontiers of Asian American studies.* Pullman: Washington State University Press.

Cahill, Larry; Prins, Bruce; Weber, Michael; & McGaugh, James L. (1994). ß-Adrenergic activation and memory for emotional events. *Nature, 371,* 702–704.

Camera, Wayne J., & Schneider, Dianne L. (1994). Integrity tests: Facts and unresolved issues. *American Psychologist, 49, 112–119.*

Campbell, Frances A., & Ramey, Craig T. (1994). Effects of early intervention on intellectual and academic achievement: A follow-up study of children from low-income families. *Child Development, 65, 684–698.*

Campbell, Frances A., & Ramey, Craig T. (1995). Cognitive and school outcomes for high risk students at middle adolescence: Positive effects of early intervention. *American Educational Research Journal, 32,* 743–772.

Campbell, Jennifer; Trapnell, Paul D.; Heine, Steven J.; et al. (1996). Self-concept clarity: Measurement, personality correlates, and cultural boundaries. *Journal of Personality and Social Psychology, 70, 141–156.*

Campbell, Joseph (1949/1968). *The hero with 1,000 faces* (2nd ed.). Princeton, NJ: Princeton University Press.

Cancian, Francesca M. (1987). *Love in America: Gender and self-development.* Cambridge, England: Cambridge University Press.

Canetto, Silvia S. (1992). Suicide attempts and substance abuse: Similarities and differences. *Journal of Psychology, 125, 605–620.*

Canetto, Silvia S., & Sakinofsky, Isaac (1998). The gender paradox in suicide. *Suicide and Life-Threatening Behavior, 28, 1–23.*

Canino, Glorisa (1994). Alcohol use and misuse among Hispanic women: Selected factors, processes, and studies. *International Journal of the Addictions, 29, 1083–1100.*

Carani, C.; Bancroft, J.; Granata, A.; et al. (1992). Testosterone and erectile function, nocturnal penile tumescence and rigidity, and erectile response to visual erotic stimuli in hypogonadal and eugonadal men. *Psychoneuroendocrinology, 17, 647–654.*

Cardeña, Etzel; Lewis-Fernández, Roberto; Bear, David; et al. (1994). Dissociative disorders. In *DSM-IV Sourcebook*. Washington, DC: American Psychiatric Press.

Carroll, James M., & Russell, James A. (1996). Do facial expressions signal specific emotions? Judging emotion from the face in context. *Journal of Personality and Social Psychology, 70,* 203–218.

Carskadon, Mary A.; Mitler, Merrill M.; & Dement, William C. (1974). A comparison of insomniacs and normals: Total sleep time and sleep latency [Abstract]. *Sleep Research, 3,* 130.

Carson, Robert C. (1989). What happened to schizophrenia? Reflections on a taxonomic absurdity. Paper presented at the annual meeting of the American Psychological Association, New Orleans.

Carstensen, Laura L., & Charles, Susan T. (1998). Emotion in the second half of life. *Current Directions in Psychological Science, 7,* 144–149.

Carter, Betty, & McGoldrick, Monica (eds.) (1988). *The changing family life cycle: A framework for family therapy* (2nd ed.). New York: Gardner Press.

Cartwright, Rosalind D. (1990). A network model of dreams. In R. R. Bootzin, J. F. Kihlstrom, & D. L. Schacter (eds.), *Sleep and cognition.* Washington, DC: American Psychological Association.

Cartwright, Rosalind (1996). Dreams and adaptations to divorce. In D. Barrett (ed.), *Trauma and dreams.* Cambridge: Harvard University Press.

Cartwright, Rosalind; Young, Michael A.; Mercer, Patricia; & Bears, Michael (1998). Role of REM sleep and dream variables in the prediction of remission from depression. *Psychiatry Research, 80,* 249–255.

Carver, Charles S. (1998). Resilience and thriving: Issues, models, and linkages. *Journal of Social Issues, 54,* 245–266.

Carver, Charles S., & Baird, Eryn (1998). The American dream revisited: Is it *what* you want or *why* you want it that matters? *Psychological Science, 9,* 289–292.

Carver, Charles S.; Pozo, Christina; Harris, Suzanne D.; et al. (1993). How coping mediates the effect of optimism on distress: A study of women with early stage breast cancer. *Journal of Personality and Social Psychology, 65,* 375–390.

Carver, Charles S., & Scheier, Michael F. (1994). Situational coping and coping dispositions in a stressful transaction. *Journal of Personality and Social Psychology, 66,* 184–195.

Carver, Charles S., & Scheier, Michael F. (1999). Optimism. In C. R. Snyder (ed.), *Coping: The psychology of what works.* New York: Oxford University Press.

Caspi, Avshalom, & Moffitt, Terrie E. (1991). Individual differences are accentuated during periods of social change: The sample case of girls at puberty. *Journal of Personality and Social Psychology, 61,* 157–168.

Cattell, Raymond B. (1965). *The scientific analysis of personality.* Baltimore, MD: Penguin.

Cattell, Raymond B. (1973). *Personality and mood by questionnaire.* San Francisco: Jossey-Bass.

Ceci, Stephen J. (1996). *On intelligence: A bioecological treatise on intellectual development.* Cambridge, MA: Harvard University Press.

Ceci, Stephen J., & Bruck, Maggie (1993). Suggestibility of the child witness: A historical review and synthesis. *Psychological Bulletin, 113,* 403–439.

Ceci, Stephen J., & Bruck, Maggie (1995). *Jeopardy in the courtroom: A scientific analysis of children's testimony.* Washington, DC: American Psychological Association.

Cejka, Mary Ann, & Eagly, Alice H. (1999). Gender-stereotypic images of occupations correspond to the sex segregation of employment. *Personality and Social Psychology Bulletin, 25,* 413–423.

Cermak, Laird S., & Craik, Fergus I. M. (eds.) (1979). *Levels of processing in human memory.* Hillsdale, NJ: Erlbaum.

Cervone, Daniel (1997). Social-cognitive mechanisms and personality coherence. *Psychological Science, 8,* 43–50.

Chambless, Dianne L. (1988). Cognitive mechanisms in panic disorder. In S. Rachman & J. D. Maser (eds.), *Panic: Psychological perspectives.* Hillsdale, NJ: Erlbaum.

Chambless, Dianne L., & Members of the Division 12 Task Force (1996). An update on empirically validated therapies. *Clinical Psychologist, 49,* 5–18.

Chambless, Dianne L.; and the Task Force on Psychological Interventions (1998). Update on empirically validated therapies II. *Clinical Psychologist, 51,* 3–16.

Chance, June E., & Goldstein, Alvin G. (1995). The other-race effect in eyewitness identification. In S. L. Sporer, G. Koehnken, & R. S. Malpass (eds.), *Psychological issues in eyewitness identification.* Hillsdale, NJ: Erlbaum.

Chance, Paul (1989, November). The other 90%. *Psychology Today,* 20–21.

Chance, Paul (1999). *Learning and behavior* (4th ed.). Pacific Grove: Brooks/Cole.

Chang, Edward C. (1998). Dispositional optimism and primary and secondary appraisal of a stressor. *Journal of Personality and Social Psychology, 74,* 1109–1120.

Chaves, J. F. (1989). Hypnotic control of clinical pain. In N. P. Spanos & J. F. Chaves (eds.), *Hypnosis: The cognitive-behavioral perspective.* Buffalo, NY: Prometheus Books.

Checkley, Stuart A.; Murphy, D. G.; Abbas, M.; et al. (1993). Melatonin rhythms in seasonal affective disorder. *British Journal of Psychiatry, 163,* 332–337.

Chehab, Farid F.; Mounzih, K.; Lu, R.; & Lim, M. E. (1997, January 3). Early onset of reproductive function in normal female mice treated with leptin. *Science, 275,* 88–90.

Cheney, Dorothy L., & Seyfarth, Robert M. (1985). Vervet monkey alarm calls: Manipulation through shared information? *Behavior, 94,* 150–166.

Chipuer, Heather M.; Rovine, Michael J.; & Plomin, Robert (1990). LISREL modeling: Genetic and environmental influences on IQ revisited. *Intelligence, 14,* 11–29.

Chodorow, Nancy (1978). *The reproduction of mothering.* Berkeley: University of California Press.

Chodorow, Nancy (1992). *Feminism and psychoanalytic theory.* New Haven, CT: Yale University Press.

Choi, Incheol; Nisbett, Richard E.; & Norenzayan, Ara (1999). Causal attribution across cultures: Variation and universality. *Psychological Bulletin, 125,* 47–63.

Chomsky, Noam (1957). *Syntactic structures.* The Hague, Netherlands: Mouton.

Chomsky, Noam (1980). Initial states and steady states. In M. Piatelli-Palmerini (ed.), *Language and learning: The debate between Jean Piaget and Noam Chomsky.* Cambridge, MA: Harvard University Press.

Chorney, M. J.; Chorney, K.; Seese, N.; et al. (1998). A quantitative trait locus associated with cognitive ability in children. *Psychological Science, 9,* 159–166.

Chorpita, Bruce F., & Barlow, David H. (1998). The development of anxiety: The role of control in the early environment. *Psychological Bulletin, 124,* 3–21.

Chrisler, Joan C.; Johnston, Ingrid K; Champagne, Nicole M.; & Preston, Kathleen E. (1994). Menstrual joy: The construct and its consequences. *Psychology of Women Quarterly, 18,* 375–387.

Christensen, Andrew, & Jacobson, Neil S. (1994). Who (or what) can do psychotherapy: The status and challenge of nonprofessional therapies. *Psychological Science, 5,* 8–14.

Christensen, Larry, & Burrows, Ross (1990). Dietary treatment of depression. *Behavior Therapy, 21,* 183–194.

Chua, Streamson C., Jr.; Chung, Wendy K.; Wu-Peng, S. Sharon; et al. (1996). Phenotypes of mouse *diabetes* and rat *fatty* due to mutations in the OB (leptin) receptor. *Science, 271,* 994–996.

Church, A. Timothy, & Lonner, Walter J. (1998). The cross-cultural perspective in the study of personality: Rationale and current research. *Journal of Cross-Cultural Psychology, 29,* 32–62.

Cialdini, Robert B. (1993). *Influence: The psychology of persuasion.* New York: Quill/Morrow.

Cialdini, Robert B.; Trost, Melanie R.; & Newsom, Jason T. (1995). Preference for consistency: The development of a valid measure and the discovery of surprising behavioral implications. *Journal of Personality and Social Psychology, 69,* 318–328.

Cinque, Guglielmo (1999). *Adverbs and functional heads: A cross-linguistic approach.* New York: Oxford University Press.

Cioffi, Delia, & Holloway, James (1993). Delayed costs of suppressed pain. *Journal of Personality and Social Psychology, 64,* 274–282.

Cioffi, Frank (1998). *Freud and the question of pseudoscience.* Chicago, IL: Open Court.

Clark, David M., & Ehlers, A. (1993). An overview of the cognitive theory and treatment of panic disorder. *Applied and Preventive Psychology, 2,* 131–139.

Clark, Margaret S.; Milberg, Sandra; & Erber, Ralph (1987). Arousal state dependent memory: Evidence and some implications for understanding social judgments and social behavior. In K. Fiedler & J. P. Forgas (eds.), *Affect, cognition and social behavior.* Toronto, Canada: Hogrefe.

Clarke, Peter, & Evans, Susan H. (1998). *Surviving modern medicine.* Rutgers, NJ: Rutgers University Press.

Cloninger, C. Robert (1990). *The genetics and biology of alcoholism.* Cold Springs Harbor, ME: Cold Springs Harbor Press.

Clopton, Nancy A., & Sorell, Gwendolyn T. (1993). Gender differences in moral reasoning: Stable or situational? *Psychology of Women Quarterly, 17,* 85–101.

Coats, Erik J.; Janoff-Bulman, Ronnie; & Alpert, Nancy (1996). Approach versus avoidance goals: Differences in self-evaluation and well-being. *Personality and Social Psychology Bulletin, 22,* 1057–1067.

Coffey, C. E. (1993). Structural brain imaging and ECT. In C. E. Coffey (ed.), *The clinical science of electroconvulsive therapy.* Washington, DC: American Psychiatric Association.

Cohen, David B. (1999). *Stranger in the nest: Do parents really shape their child's personality, intelligence, or character?* New York: Wiley.

Cohen, Dov (1998). Culture, social organization, and patterns of violence. *Journal of Personality and Social Psychology, 75,* 408–419.

Cohen, Dov; Nisbett, Richard E.; Bowdle, Brian F.; & Schwarz, Norbert (1996). Insult, aggression, and the Southern culture of honor: An "experimental ethnography." *Journal of Personality and Social Psychology, 70,* 945–960.

Cohen, Sheldon; Doyle, W. J.; Skoner, D. P.; et al. (1997). Social ties and susceptibility to the common cold. *Journal of the American Medical Association, 277,* 1940–1944.

Cohen, Sheldon; Evans, Gary W.; Krantz, David S.; & Stokols, Daniel (1980). Physiological, motivational, and cognitive effects of aircraft noise on children. *American Psychologist, 35,* 231–243.

Cohen, Sheldon; Frank, Ellen; Doyle, William J.; et al. (1998). Types of stressors that increase susceptibility to the common cold in healthy adults. *Health Psychology, 17,* 214–223.

Cohen, Sheldon, & Herbert, Tracy B. (1996). Health psychology: Psychological factors and physical disease from the perspective of human psychoneuroimmunology. *Annual Review of Psychology, 47,* 113–142.

Cohen, Sheldon; Tyrrell, David A.; & Smith, Andrew P. (1993). Negative life events, perceived stress, negative affect, and susceptibility to the common cold. *Journal of Personality and Social Psychology, 64,* 131–140.

Cohn, Lawrence D. (1991). Sex differences in the course of personality development: A meta-analysis. *Psychological Bulletin, 109,* 252–266.

Cole, Michael, & Cole, Sheila R. (1993). *The development of children* (2nd ed.). New York: Freeman.

Collaer, Marcia L., & Hines, Melissa (1995). Human behavioral sex differences: A role for gonadal hormones during early development? *Psychological Bulletin, 118,* 55–107.

Collins, Allan M., & Loftus, Elizabeth F. (1975). A spreading-activation theory of semantic processing. *Psychological Review, 82,* 407–428.

Collins, Barry E., & Brief, Diana E. (1995). Using person-perception vignette methodologies to uncover the symbolic meanings of teacher behaviors in the Milgram paradigm. *Journal of Social Issues, 51,* 89–106.

Collins, Rebecca L. (1996). For better or worse: The impact of upward social comparison on self-evaluations. *Psychological Bulletin, 119,* 51–69.

Colman, Andrew (1991). Crowd psychology in South African murder trials. *American Psychologist, 46,* 1071–1079.

Comas-Díaz, Lillian, & Greene, Beverly (1994). *Women of color: Integrating ethnic and gender identities in psychotherapy.* New York: Guilford Press.

Comuzzie, Anthony G., & Allison, David B. (1998). The search for human obesity genes. *Science, 280,* 1374–1377.

Condon, William (1982). Cultural microrhythms. In M. Davis (ed.), *Interaction rhythms: Periodicity in communicative behavior.* New York: Human Sciences Press.

Connors, Gerard J.; Carroll, Kathleen M.; DiClemente, Carlo C.; et al. (1997). The therapeutic alliance and its relationship to alcoholism treatment participation and outcome. *Journal of Consulting and Clinical Psychology, 65,* 588–598.

Considine, R. V.; Sinha, M. K.; Heiman, M. L.; et al. (1996). Serum immunoreactive-leptin concentrations in normal-weight and obese humans. *New England Journal of Medicine, 334,* 292–295.

Cooper, M. Lynne; Frone, Michael R.; Russell, Marcia; & Mudar, Pamela (1995). Drinking to regulate positive and negative emotions: A motivational model of alcohol use. *Journal of Personality and Social Psychology, 69,* 990–1005.

Cooper, M. Lynne; Shapiro, Cheryl M.; & Powers, Anne M. (1998). Motivations for sex and risky sexual behavior among adolescents and young adults: A functional perspective. *Journal of Personality and Social Psychology, 75,* 1528–1558.

Copi, Irving M., & Burgess-Jackson, Keith (1992). *Informal logic* (2nd ed.). New York: Macmillan.

Coren, Stanley (1996). Daylight saving time and traffic accidents. *New England Journal of Medicine, 334,* 924.

Corkin, Suzanne (1984). Lasting consequences of bilateral medial temporal lobectomy: Clinical course and experimental findings in H. M. *Seminars in Neurology, 4,* 249–259.

Corkin, Suzanne; Amaral, David G.; Gonzalez, R. Gilberto; et al. (1997). H. M.'s medial temporal lobe lesion: Findings from magnetic resonance imaging. *Journal of Neuroscience, 17,* 3964–3979.

Cornelius, Randolph R. (1991). Gregorio Marañon's two-factor theory of emotion. *Personality and Social Psychology Bulletin, 17,* 65–69.

Cose, Ellis (1994). *The rage of a privileged class.* New York: HarperCollins.

Cosmides, Leda; Tooby, John; & Barkow, Jerome H. (1992) Introduction: Evolutionary psychology and conceptual integration. In J. H. Barkow, L. Cosmides, & J. Tooby (eds.), *The adapted mind: Evolutionary psychology and the generation of culture.* New York: Oxford University Press.

Costa, Paul T., Jr., & McCrae, Robert R. (1994). "Set like plaster"? Evidence for the stability of adult personality. In R. Heatherton & J. Weinberger (eds.), *Can personality change?* Washington, DC: American Psychological Association.

Costa, Paul T., Jr.; McCrae, Robert R.; Martin, Thomas A.; et al. (1999). Personality development from adolescence through adulthood: Further cross-cultural comparisons of age differences. In V. J. Molfese & D. Molfese (eds.), *Temperament and personality development across the life span*. Hillsdale, NJ: Erlbaum.

Costantino, Giuseppe; Malgady, Robert G.; & Rogler, Lloyd H. (1986). Cuento therapy: A culturally sensitive modality for Puerto Rican children. *Journal of Consulting and Clinical Psychology, 54,* 639–645.

Council, J. R.; Kirsch, Irving; & Grant, D. L. (1996). Imagination, expectancy and hypnotic responding. In R. G. Kunzendorf, N. K. Spanos, & B. J. Wallace (eds.), *Hypnosis and imagination*. Amityville, NY: Baywood.

Coupland, Scott K.; Serovich, Julianne; & Glenn, J. Edgar (1995). Reliability in constructing genograms: A study among marriage and family therapy doctoral students. *Journal of Marital and Family Therapy, 21,* 251–263.

Courtney, J. G.; Longnecker, M. P.; Theorell, T.; & Gerhardsson de Verdier, M. (1993). Stressful life events and the risk of colorectal cancer. *Epidemiology, 4,* 407–414.

Cowen, Emory L.; Wyman, Peter A.; Work, William C.; & Parker, Gayle R. (1990). The Rochester Child Resilience Project (RCRP): Overview and summary of first year findings. *Development and Psychopathology, 2,* 193–212.

Coyne, J. C. (1990). Interpersonal processes in depression. In G. I. Keitner (ed.), *Depression and families: Impact and treatment*. Washington, DC: American Psychiatric Press.

Craik, Fergus I. M., & Tulving, Endel (1975). Depth of processing and the retention of words in episodic memory. *Journal of Experimental Psychology: General, 104,* 268–294.

Crain, Stephen (1991). Language acquisition in the absence of experience. *Behavioral & Brain Sciences, 14,* 597–650.

Crair, Michael C.; Gillespie, Deda C.; & Stryker, Michael P. (1998). The role of visual experience in the development of columns in cat visual cortex. *Science, 279,* 566–570.

Crandall, Christian S., & Martinez, Rebecca (1996). Culture, ideology, and antifat attitudes. *Personality and Social Psychology Bulletin, 22,* 1165–1176.

Crandall, James E. (1984). Social interest as a moderator of life stress. *Journal of Personality and Social Psychology, 47,* 164–174.

Crawford, Mary, & Marecek, Jeanne (1989). Psychology constructs the female: 1968–1988. *Psychology of Women Quarterly, 13,* 147–165.

Crews, Frederick (ed.) (1998). *Unauthorized Freud: Doubters confront a legend*. New York: Viking.

Crick, Francis, & Mitchison, Graeme (1995). REM sleep and neural nets. *Behavioural Brain Research, 69,* 147–155.

Critchlow, Barbara (1983). Blaming the booze: The attribution of responsibility for drunken behavior. *Personality and Social Psychology Bulletin, 9,* 451–474.

Critchlow, Barbara (1986). The powers of John Barleycorn: Beliefs about the effects of alcohol on social behavior. *American Psychologist, 41,* 751–764.

Critser, Greg (1996, June). Oh, how happy we will be: Pills, paradise, and the profits of the drug companies. *Harper's,* 39–48.

Croizen, Jean-Claude, & Claire, Theresa (1998). Extending the concept of stereotype threat to social class: The intellectual underperformance of students from low socioeconomic backgrounds. *Personality and Social Psychology Bulletin, 24,* 588–594.

Cronbach, Lee J. (1990). *Essentials of psychological testing* (5th ed.). New York: Harper & Row.

Crook, John H. (1987). The nature of conscious awareness. In C. Blakemore & S. Greenfield (eds.), *Mindwaves: Thoughts on intelligence, identity, and consciousness*. Oxford, England: Basil Blackwell.

Cross, William E. (1971). The Negro-to-Black conversion experience: Toward a psychology of Black liberation. *Black World, 20,* 13–27.

Cross, William E. (1991). *Shades of black: Diversity in African-American identity*. Philadelphia, PA: Temple University Press.

Cross, William E., Jr., & Fhagen-Smith, Peony (1996). Nigrescence and ego identity development: Accounting for differential black identity patterns. In P. B. Pedersen, J. G. Draguns, W. J. Lonner, & J. E. Trimble (eds.), *Counseling across cultures* (4th ed.). Thousand Oaks, CA: Sage.

Crowley, Thomas J.; MacDonald, Marilyn J.; Whitmore, Elizabeth A.; & Mikulich, Susan K. (1998). Cannabis dependence, withdrawal and reinforcing effects among adolescents with conduct symptoms and substance use disorders. *Drug and Alcohol Dependence, 50,* 27–37.

Csikszentmihalyi, Mihaly, & Larson, Reed (1984). *Being adolescent: Conflict and growth in the teenage years*. New York: Basic Books.

Culbertson, Frances M. (1997). Depression and gender: An international review. *American Psychologist, 52,* 25–31.

Currie, Elliot (1998). *Crime and punishment in America*. New York: Henry Holt.

Curtiss, Susan (1977). *Genie: A psycholinguistic study of a modern-day "wild child."* New York: Academic Press.

Curtiss, Susan (1982). Developmental dissociations of language and cognition. In L. Obler & D. Fein (eds.), *Exceptional language and linguistics*. New York: Academic Press.

Cushman, Philip (1995). *Constructing the self, constructing America: A cultural history of psychotherapy*. New York: Addison-Wesley.

Cvetkovich, George T., & Earle, Timothy C. (1994). Risk and culture. In W. J. Lonner & R. Malpass (eds.), *Psychology and culture*. Boston: Allyn & Bacon.

Czeisler, Charles A.; Duffy, Jeanne F.; Shanahan, Theresa L.; et al. (1999). Stability, precision, and near-24-hour period of the human circadian pacemaker. *Science, 284,* 2177–2181.

Czeisler, Charles A.; Shanahan, T. L.; Klerman, E. B.; et al. (1995). Suppression of melatonin secretion in some blind patients by exposure to bright light. *New England Journal of Medicine, 332,* 6–11.

Dabbs, James M., Jr.; Alford, Elizabeth Carriere; & Fielden, Julie A. (1998). Trial lawyers and testosterone: Blue-collar talent in a white-collar world. *Journal of Applied Social Psychology, 28,* 84–94.

Dabbs, James M., Jr.; Carr, Timothy S.; Frady, Robert L.; & Riad, Jasmin K. (1995). Testosterone, crime, and misbehavior among 692 male prison inmates. *Personality and Individual Differences, 18,* 627–633.

Dabbs, James M., Jr.; Hargrove, Marian F.; & Heusel, Colleen (1996). Testosterone differences among college fraternities: Well-behaved vs. rambunctious. *Personality and Individual Differences, 20,* 157–161.

Dabbs, James M., Jr.; Strong, Rebecca; & Milun, Rhonda (1997). Exploring the mind of testosterone: A beeper study. *Journal of Research in Personality, 31,* 577–587.

Dadds, Mark R.; Bovbjerg, Dana H.; Redd, William H.; & Cutmore, Tim R. H. (1997). Imagery in human classical conditioning. *Psychological Bulletin, 122,* 89–103.

Daly, Martin, & Wilson, Margo (1983). *Sex, evolution, and behavior* (2nd ed.). Belmont, CA: Wadsworth.

Damasio, Antonio R. (1994). *Descartes' error: Emotion, reason, and the human brain*. New York: Grosset/Putnam.

Damasio, Hanna; Grabowski, Thomas J.; Frank, Randall; Galaburda, Albert M.; & Damasio, Antonio R. (1994). The return of Phineas Gage: Clues about the brain from the skull of a famous patient. *Science, 264,* 1102–1105.

Damasio, Hanna; Grabowski, Thomas J.; Tranel, Daniel; Hichwa, R. D.; & Damasio, Antonio R. (1996). A neural basis for lexical retrieval. *Nature, 380,* 499–505.

Damon, William (1995). *Greater expectations: Overcoming the culture of indulgence in America's homes and schools*. New York: Free Press.

Darley, John M. (1995). Constructive and destructive obedience: A taxonomy of principal agent relationships. In A. G. Miller, B. E. Collins, & D. E. Brief (eds.), Perspectives on obedience to authority: The legacy of the Milgram experiments. *Journal of Social Issues, 51*(3), 125–154.

Darley, John, & Latané, Bibb (1968). Bystander intervention in emergencies: Diffusion of responsibility. *Journal of Personality and Social Psychology, 8,* 377–383.

Darwin, Charles (1859). *On the origin of species* [A facsimile of the first edition, edited by Ernst Mayer, 1964]. Cambridge, MA: Harvard University Press.

Darwin, Charles (1872/1965). *The expression of the emotions in man and animals.* Chicago: University of Chicago Press.

Darwin, Charles (1874). *The descent of man and selection in relation to sex* (2nd ed.). New York: Hurst.

Dasen, Pierre R. (1994). Culture and cognitive development from a Piagetian perspective. In W. J. Lonner & R. S. Malpass (eds.), *Psychology and culture.* Needham Heights, MA: Allyn & Bacon.

Daum, Irene, & Schugens, Markus M. (1996). On the cerebellum and classical conditioning. *Psychological Science, 5,* 58–61.

Davey, Graham C. (1992). Classical conditioning and the acquisition of human fears and phobias: A review and synthesis of the literature. *Advances in Behaviour Research and Therapy, 14,* 29–66.

Davidson, Richard J. (1992). Anterior cerebral asymmetry and the nature of emotion. *Brain and Cognition, 20,* 125–151.

Davidson, Richard J. (1995). Cerebral asymmetry, emotion, and affective style. In R. J. Davidson & K. Hugdahl (eds.), *Brain asymmetry.* Cambridge, MA: Massachusetts Institute of Technology.

Davies, Michaela; Stankov, Lazar; & Roberts, Richard D. (1998). Emotional intelligence: In search of an elusive construct. *Journal of Personality and Social Psychology, 75,* 989–1015.

Davis, Christopher G.; Nolen-Hoeksema, Susan; & Larson, Judith (1998). Making sense of loss and benefiting from the experience: Two construals of meaning. *Journal of Personality and Social Psychology, 75,* 561–574.

Davis, Karen D.; Kiss, Z. H.; Luo, L.; et al. (1998). Phantom sensations generated by thalamic microstimulation. *Nature, 391,* 385–387.

Davis, Penelope J. (1999). Gender differences in autobiographical memory for childhood emotional experiences. *Journal of Personality and Social Psychology, 76,* 498–510.

Davis, T. L. (1995). Gender differences in masking negative emotions: Ability or motivation? *Developmental Psychology, 31,* 660–667.

Dawes, Robyn M. (1994). *House of cards: Psychology and psychotherapy built on myth.* New York: Free Press.

Dawson, Drew; Lack, Leon; & Morris, Mary (1993). Phase resetting of the human circadian pacemaker with use of a single pulse of bright light. *Chronobiology International, 10,* 94–102.

Dawson, Neal V.; Arkes, Hal R.; Siciliano, C.; et al. (1988). Hindsight bias: An impediment to accurate probability estimation in clinicopathologic conferences. *Medical Decision Making, 8*(4), 259–264.

Dean, Geoffrey (1987, Spring). Does astrology need to be true? Part II: The answer is no. *Skeptical Inquirer, 11,* 257–273.

Dean, Geoffrey (1992). The bottom line: Effect size. In B. Beyerstein & D. Beyerstein (eds.), *The write stuff: Evaluations of graphology—the study of handwriting analysis.* Buffalo, NY: Prometheus Books.

Deaux, Kay (1985). Sex and gender. *Annual Review of Psychology, 36,* 49–81.

Deaux, Kay, & Major, Brenda (1990). A social-psychological model of gender. In D. L. Rhode (ed.), *Theoretical perspectives on sexual difference.* New Haven, CT: Yale University Press.

de Bono, Edward (1985). *de Bono's thinking course.* New York: Facts on File.

deCharms, R. Christopher; Blake, David T.; & Merzenich, Michael M. (1998). Optimizing sound features for cortical neurons. *Science, 280,* 1439–1443.

Deci, Edward L., & Ryan, Richard M. (1987). The support of autonomy and the control of behavior. *Journal of Personality and Social Psychology, 53,* 1024–1037.

Deffenbacher, Jerry L.; Dahlen, Eric R.; Lynch, Rebekah S.; et al. (1998). Application of Beck's cognitive therapy to general anger reduction. Paper presented at the annual meeting of the American Psychological Association, San Francisco.

Deffenbacher, Jerry L.; Oetting, Eugene R.; Lynch, Rebekah S.; & Morris, Chad D. (1996). The expression of anger and its consequences. *Behaviour Research and Therapy, 34,* 575–590.

de Lacoste-Utamsing, Christine, & Holloway, Ralph L. (1982). Sexual dimorphism in the human corpus callosum. *Science, 216,* 1431–1432.

DeLeon, Patrick H., & Wiggins, Jack G., Jr. (1996). Prescription privileges for psychologists. *American Psychologist, 51,* 225–229.

DeLoache, Judy S. (1995). Early understanding and use of symbols: The model model. *Current Directions in Psychological Science, 4,* 109–113.

Dement, William (1978). *Some must watch while some must sleep.* New York: Norton.

Dement, William (1992). *The sleepwatchers.* Stanford, CA: Stanford Alumni Association.

DeNelsky, Garland Y. (1996). The case against prescription privileges for psychologists. *American Psychologist, 51,* 207–212.

Dennett, Daniel C. (1991). *Consciousness explained.* Boston: Little, Brown.

DePaulo, Bella M. (1992). Nonverbal behavior and self-presentation. *Psychological Bulletin, 111,* 203–243.

de Rivera, Joseph (1989). Comparing experiences across cultures: Shame and guilt in America and Japan. *Hiroshima Forum for Psychology, 14,* 13–20.

DeValois, Russell L., & DeValois, Karen K. (1975). Neural coding of color. In E. C. Carterette & M. P. Friedman (eds.), *Handbook of perception* (Vol. 5). New York: Academic Press.

Devanand, Devangere P.; Dwork, Andrew J.; Hutchinson, Edward R.; et al. (1994). Does ECT alter brain structure? *American Journal of Psychiatry, 151,* 957–970.

Devine, Patricia G. (1995). Breaking the prejudice habit: Progress and prospects. Award address paper presented at the annual meeting of the American Psychological Association, New York.

Devine, Patricia G.; Evett, Sophia R.; & Vasquez-Suson, Kristin A. (1996). Exploring the interpersonal dynamics of intergroup contact. In R. M. Sorrentino & E. T. Higgins (eds.), *Handbook of motivation and cognition: Vol. 3. The interpersonal context.* New York: Guilford Press.

Devlin, B.; Daniels, Michael; & Roeder, Kathryn (1997). The heritability of IQ. *Nature, 388,* 468–471.

Devolder, Patricia A., & Pressley, Michael (1989). Metamemory across the adult lifespan. *Canadian Psychology, 30,* 578–587.

de Waal, Frans (July, 1997). Are we in anthropodenial? *Discover,* 50–53.

De Wolff, Marianne, & van Ijzendoorn, Marinus H. (1997). Sensitivity and attachment: A meta-analysis on parental antecedents of infant attachment. *Child Development, 68,* 571–591.

Dewsbury, Donald A. (1996). Animal research: Getting in and getting out. *General Psychologist, 32,* 19–25.

Diamond, Marian C. (1993, Winter–Spring). An optimistic view of the aging brain. *Generations, 17,* 31–33.

Dickinson, Alyce M. (1989). The detrimental effects of extrinsic reinforcement on "intrinsic motivation." *Behavior Analyst, 12,* 1–15.

Dien, D. S. (1982). A Chinese perspective on Kohlberg's theory of moral development. *Developmental Review, 2,* 331–341.

Digman, John M. (1996). The curious history of the five-factor model. In J. S. Wiggins (ed.), *The five-factor model of personality: Theoretical perspectives.* New York: Guilford Press.

Digman, John M., & Shmelyov, Alexander G. (1996). The structure of temperament and personality in Russian children. *Journal of Personality and Social Psychology, 71,* 341–351.

DiLalla, David.; Carey, Gregory; Gottesman, Irving I.; & Bouchard, Thomas J., Jr. (1996). Heritability of MMPI personality indicators of psychopathology in twins reared apart. *Journal of Abnormal Psychology, 105,* 491–499.

di Leonardo, Micaela (1987). The female world of cards and holidays: Women, families, and the work of kinship. *Signs, 12,* 1–20.

Dinges, David F.; Whitehouse, Wayne G.; Orne, Emily C.; et al. (1992). Evaluating hypnotic memory enhancement (hypermnesia and reminiscence) using multitrial forced recall. *Journal of Experimental Psychology: Learning, Memory, and Cognition, 18,* 1139–1147.

Dion, George L., & Anthony, William A. (1987). Research in psychiatric rehabilitation: A review of experimental and quasi-experimental studies. *Rehabilitation Counseling Bulletin, 30,* 177–203.

Dion, Kenneth L., & Dion, Karen K. (1993). Gender and ethnocultural comparisons in styles of love. *Psychology of Women Quarterly, 17,* 463–474.

Dixon, N. F. (1980). Humor: A cognitive alternative to stress? In I. G. Sarason & C. D. Spielberger (eds.), *Stress and anxiety* (Vol. 7). Washington, DC: Hemisphere.

Doering, Charles H.; Brodie, H. K. H.; Kraemer, H. C.; et al. (1974). Plasma testosterone levels and psychologic measures in men over a 2-month period. In R. C. Friedman, R. M. Richard, & R. L. Vande Wiele (eds.), *Sex differences in behavior.* New York: Wiley.

Dollard, John, & Miller, Neal E. (1950). *Personality and psychotherapy: An analysis in terms of learning, thinking, and culture.* New York: McGraw-Hill.

Dolnick, Edward (1990, July). What dreams are (really) made of. *Atlantic Monthly, 226,* 41–45, 48–53, 56–58, 60–61.

Domhoff, G. William (1996). *Finding meaning in dreams: A quantitative approach.* New York: Plenum.

Doty, Richard M.; Peterson, Bill E.; & Winter, David G. (1991). Threat and authoritarianism in the United States, 1978–1987. *Journal of Personality and Social Psychology, 61,* 629–640.

Dovidio, John F.; Gaertner, Samuel L.; & Validzic, Ana (1998). Intergroup bias: Status, differentiation, and a common in-group identity. *Journal of Personality and Social Psychology, 75,* 109–120.

Downey, Geraldine; Freitas, Antonio L.; Michaelis, Benjamin; & Khouri, Hala (1998). The self-fulfilling prophecy in close relationships: Rejection sensitivity and rejection by romantic partners. *Journal of Personality and Social Psychology, 75,* 545–560.

Drieschner, K., & Lange, A. (1999). A review of cognitive factors in the etiology of rape: Theories, empirical studies, and implications. *Clinical Psychology Review, 19,* 57–77.

Druckman, Daniel, & Swets, John A. (eds.) (1988). *Enhancing human performance: Issues, theories, and techniques.* Washington, DC: National Academy Press.

Dubbert, Patricia M. (1992). Exercise in behavioral medicine. *Journal of Consulting and Clinical Psychology, 60,* 613–618.

Duncan, Paula D.; Ritter, Philip L.; Dornbusch, Sanford M.; et al. (1985). The effects of pubertal timing on body image, school behavior, and deviance. *Journal of Youth and Adolescence, 14,* 227–235.

Dunkel-Schetter, Christine (1984). Social support and cancer: Findings based on patient interviews and their implications. *Journal of Social Issues, 40*(4), 77–98.

du Verglas, Gabrielle; Banks, Steven R.; & Guyer, Kenneth E. (1988). Clinical effects of fenfluramine on children with autism: A review of the research. *Journal of Autism and Developmental Disorders, 18,* 297–308.

Dweck, Carol S. (1992). The study of goals in psychology. *Psychological Science, 3,* 165–167.

Dweck, Carol S., & Sorich, Lisa A. (1999). Mastery-oriented thinking. In C. R. Snyder (ed.), *Coping: The psychology of what works.* New York: Oxford University Press.

D'Zurilla, Thomas J., & Sheedy, Collete F. (1991). Relation between problem-solving ability and subsequent level of psychological stress in college students. *Journal of Personality and Social Psychology, 61,* 841–846.

Eastman, Charmane I.; Young, Michael A.; Fogg, Louis F.; et al. (1998). Bright light treatment of winter depression: A placebo-controlled trial. *Achives of General Psychiatry, 55,* 883–889.

Eaton, William W.; Bilker, Warren; Haro, Josep M.; et al. (1992a). Long-term course of hospitalization for schizophrenia: II. Change with passage of time. *Schizophrenia Bulletin, 18,* 229–241.

Eaton, William W.; Mortensen, Preben B.; Herrman, Helen; et al. (1992b). Long-term course of hospitalization for schizophrenia: I. Risk for rehospitalization. *Schizophrenia Bulletin, 18,* 217–228.

Ebbinghaus, Hermann M. (1885/1913). *Memory: A contribution to experimental psychology* (H. A. Ruger & C. E. Bussenius, trans.). New York: Teachers College Press, Columbia University.

Eberlin, Michael; McConnachie, Gene; Ibel, Stuart; & Volpe, Lisa (1993). Facilitated communication: A failure to replicate the phenomenon. *Journal of Autism and Developmental Disorders, 23,* 507–530.

Eccles, Jacquelynne S. (1993). Parents and gender-role socialization during the middle childhood and adolescent years. In S. Oskamp & M. Costanzo (eds.), *The Claremont Symposium on Applied Social Psychology: Gender issues in contemporary society.* Newbury Park, CA: Sage.

Eccles, Jacquelynne S.; Midgley, Carol; Wigfield, Allan; et al. (1993). Development during adolescence: The impact of stage–environment fit on young adolescents' experiences in schools and in families. *American Psychologist, 48,* 90–101.

Eckensberger, Lutz H. (1994). Moral development and its measurement across cultures. In W. J. Lonner & R. Malpass (eds.), *Psychology and culture.* Needham Heights, MA: Allyn & Bacon.

Edelson, Marshall (1994). Can psychotherapy research answer this psychotherapist's questions? In P. F. Talley, H. H. Strupp, & S. F. Butler (eds.), *Psychotherapy research and practice: Bridging the gap.* New York: Basic Books.

Edenberg, Howard J.; Foroud, Tatiana; Koller, D. L.; et al. (1998). A family-based analysis of the association of the dopamine D2 receptor (DRD2) with alcoholism. *Alcohol Clinical and Experimental Research, 22,* 505–512.

Edwards, Kari, & Smith, Edward E. (1996). A disconfirmation bias in the evaluation of arguments. *Journal of Personality and Social Psychology, 71,* 5–24.

Edwards, Lynne K., & Edwards, Allen L. (1991). A principal-components analysis of the Minnesota Multiphasic Personality Inventory Factor Scales. *Journal of Personality and Social Psychology, 60,* 766–772.

Efran, Jay S.; Greene, Mitchell A.; & Gordon, Don E. (1998, March/April). Lessons of the new genetics: Finding the right fit for our clients. *Family Therapy Networker, 22,* 26–41.

Ehrenreich, Barbara (1978). *For her own good: 150 years of the experts' advice to women.* New York: Doubleday.

Eich, E., & Hyman, R. (1992). Subliminal self-help. In D. Druckman & R. A. Bjork (eds.), *In the mind's eye: Enhancing human performance.* Washington, DC: National Academy Press.

Eisenberg, Nancy (1995). Prosocial development: A multifaceted model. In W. M. Kurtines & J. L. Gewirtz (eds.), *Moral development: An introduction.* Boston: Allyn & Bacon.

Eisenberg, Nancy; Fabes, Richard A.; Murphy, Bridget; et al. (1996). The relations of children's dispositional empathy-related responding to their emotionality, regulation, and social functioning. *Developmental Pschology, 32,* 195–209.

Eisenberger, Robert; Armeli, Stephen; & Pretz, Jean (1998). Can the promise of reward increase creativity? *Journal of Personality and Social Psychology, 74,* 704–714.

Eisenberger, Robert, & Cameron, Judy (1996). Detrimental effects of reward: Reality or myth? *American Psychologist, 51,* 1153–1166.

Eisenberger, Robert, & Cameron, Judy (1998). Reward, intrinsic interest, and creativity: New findings [Comment]. *American Psychologist, 53,* 676–679.

Ekman, Paul (1994). Strong evidence for universals in facial expressions: A reply to Russell's mistaken critique. *Psychological Bulletin, 115,* 268–287.

Ekman, Paul; Friesen, Wallace V.; & O'Sullivan, Maureen (1988). Smiles when lying. *Journal of Personality and Social Psychology, 54,* 414–420.

Ekman, Paul; Friesen, Wallace V.; O'Sullivan, Maureen; et al. (1987). Universals and cultural differences in the judgments of facial expression of emotion. *Journal of Personality and Social Psychology, 53,* 712–717.

Ekman, Paul, & Heider, Karl G. (1988). The universality of a contempt expression: A replication. *Motivation and Emotion, 12,* 303–308.

Elliot, Andrew J., & Harackiewicz, Judith M. (1994). Goal setting, achievement orientation, and intrinsic motivation: A mediational analysis. *Journal of Personality and Social Psychology, 66,* 968–980.

Elliot, Andrew J., & Sheldon, Kennon M. (1998). Avoidance personal goals and the personality–illness relationship. *Journal of Personality and Social Psychology, 75,* 1282–1299.

Elliott, Robert, & Morrow-Bradley, Cheryl (1994). Developing a working marriage between psychotherapists and psychotherapy researchers: Identifying shared purposes. In P. F. Talley, H. H. Strupp, & S. F. Butler (eds.), *Psychotherapy research and practice: Bridging the gap.* New York: Basic Books.

Ellis, Albert (1993). Changing rational-emotive therapy (RET) to rational emotive behavior therapy (REBT). *Behavior Therapist, 16,* 257–258.

Ellis, Albert, & Blau, S. (1998). Rational emotive behavior therapy. *Directions in Clinical and Counseling Psychology, 8,* 41–56.

Emery, C. Eugene, Jr. (1998, January–February). Psychic forecasts were a big flop (again). *Skeptical Inquirer, 22,* 6–8.

Emery, Robert E., & Laumann-Billings, Lisa (1998). An overview of the nature, causes, and consequences of abusive family relationships. *American Psychologist, 53,* 121–135.

Emmons, Robert A., & King, Laura A. (1988). Conflict among personal strivings: Immediate and long-term implications for psychological and physical well-being. *Journal of Personality and Social Psychology, 54,* 1040–1048.

Endler, Norman S. (1991). Electroconvulsive therapy: Myths and realities. Paper presented at the annual meeting of the American Psychological Association, San Francisco.

Englander-Golden, Paula; Whitmore, Mary R.; & Dienstbier, Richard A. (1978). Menstrual cycle as focus of study and self-reports of moods and behavior. *Motivation and Emotion, 2,* 75–86.

Ennis, Robert H. (1985). Critical thinking and the curriculum. *National Forum, 65*(1), 28–30.

Entin, Alan D. (1992). Family photographs: Visual icons and emotional history. Paper presented at the annual meeting of the American Psychological Association, Washington, DC.

Epstein, Seymour (1994). Integration of the cognitive and the psychodynamic unconscious. *American Psychologist, 49,* 709–724.

Erikson, Erik H. (1950/1963). *Childhood and society* (2nd ed.). New York: Norton.

Erikson, Erik H. (1982). *The life cycle completed.* New York: Norton.

Eriksson, P. S.; Perfilieva, E; Bjork-Eriksson, T.; et al. (1998). Neurogenesis in the adult human hippocampus. *Nature Medicine, 4,* 1313–1317.

Eron, Leonard D. (1982). Parent–child interaction, television violence, and aggression of children. *American Psychologist, 37,* 197–211.

Eron, Leonard D. (1995). Media violence: How it affects kids and what can be done about it. Invited address presented at the annual meeting of the American Psychological Association, New York.

Ervin-Tripp, Susan (1964). Imitation and structural change in children's language. In E. H. Lenneberg (ed.), *New directions in the study of language.* Cambridge, MA: MIT Press.

Escera, Carles; Cilveti, Robert; & Grau, Carles (1992). Ultradian rhythms in cognitive operations: Evidence from the P300 component of the event-related potentials. *Medical Science Research, 20,* 137–138.

Evans, Christopher (1984). *Landscapes of the night* (edited and completed by Peter Evans). New York: Viking.

Evans, Gary W.; Bullinger, Monika; & Hygge, Staffan (1998). Chronic noise exposure and physiological response: A prospective study of children living under environmental stress. *Psychological Science, 9,* 75–77.

Evans, Gary W.; Lepore, Stephen J.; & Schroeder, Alex (1996). The role of interior design elements in human responses to crowding. *Journal of Personality and Social Psychology, 70,* 41–46.

Ewart, Craig K. (1995). Self-efficacy and recovery from heart attack. In J. E. Maddux (ed.), *Self-efficacy, adaptation, and adjustment: Theory, research, and application.* New York: Plenum.

Ewart, Craig K., & Kolodner, Kenneth B. (1994). Negative affect, gender, and expressive style predict elevated ambulatory blood pressure in adolescents. *Journal of Personality and Social Psychology, 66,* 596–605.

Exner, John E. (1993). *The Rorschach: A comprehensive system: Vol. 1. Basic foundations* (3rd ed.). New York: Wiley.

Eyferth, Klaus (1961). [The performance of different groups of the children of occupation forces on the Hamburg–Wechsler Intelligence Test for Children.] *Archiv für die Gesamte Psychologie, 113,* 222–241.

Eysenck, Hans J. (1993). Prediction of cancer and coronary heart disease mortality by means of a personality inventory: Results of a 15-year follow-up study. *Psychological Reports, 72,* 499–516.

Fackelmann, Kathleen (1998, August 22). Stroke rescue: Can cells injected into the brain reverse paralysis? *Science News, 154,* 120–122.

Fagan, Joseph F., III (1992). Intelligence: A theoretical viewpoint. *Current Directions in Psychological Science, 1,* 82–86.

Fagot, Beverly I. (1985). Beyond the reinforcement principle: Another step toward understanding sex role development. *Developmental Psychology, 2,* 1097–1104.

Fagot, Beverly I. (1993, June). Gender role development in early childhood: Environmental input, internal construction. Invited address presented at the annual meeting of the International Academy of Sex Research, Monterey, CA.

Fagot, Beverly I.; Hagan, R.; Leinbach, Mary D.; & Kronsberg, S. (1985). Differential reactions to assertive and communicative acts of toddler boys and girls. *Child Development, 56,* 1499–1505.

Fagot, Beverly I., & Leinbach, Mary D. (1993). Gender-role development in young children: From discrimination to labeling. *Developmental Review, 13,* 205–224.

Fairchild, Halford H. (1985). Black, Negro, or Afro-American? The differences are crucial! *Journal of Black Studies, 16,* 47–55.

Falk, Ruma, & Greenbaum, Charles W. (1995). Significance tests die hard: The amazing persistence of a probabilistic misconception. *Theory & Psychology, 5*(1), 75–98.

Fausto-Sterling, Anne (1997). Beyond difference: A biologist's perspective. *Journal of Social Issues, 53,* 233–258.

Fazio, Russell H.; Jackson, Joni R.; Dunton, Bridget C.; & Williams, Carol J. (1995). Variability in automatic activation as an unobtrusive measure of racial attitudes: A bona fide pipeline? *Journal of Personality and Social Psychology, 69,* 1013–1027.

FDA Drug Bulletin (1990, April). Two new psychiatric drugs. *20*(1), 9.

Feather, N. T. (1966). Effects of prior success and failure on expectations of success and subsequent performance. *Journal of Personality and Social Psychology, 3,* 287–298.

Feather, N. T. (ed.) (1982). *Expectations and actions: Expectancy value models in psychology.* Hillsdale, NJ: Erlbaum.

Feeney, Dennis M. (1987). Human rights and animal welfare. *American Psychologist, 42,* 593–599.

Feeney, Judith A., & Noller, Patricia (1990). Attachment style as a predictor of adult romantic relationships. *Journal of Personality and Social Psychology, 58,* 281–291.

Fehr, Beverley (1993). How do I love thee . . . ? Let me consult my prototype. In S. Duck (ed.), *Individuals in relationships* (Vol. 1). Newbury Park, CA: Sage.

Fehr, Beverley; Baldwin, Mark; Collins, Lois; et al. (1999). Anger in close relationships: An interpersonal script analysis. *Personality and Social Psychology Bulletin, 25,* 299–312.

Fein, Steven, & Spencer, Steven J. (1997). Prejudice as self-image maintenance: Affirming the self through derogating others. *Journal of Personality and Social Psychology, 73,* 31–44.

Feingold, Alan (1988). Cognitive gender differences are disappearing. *American Psychologist, 43,* 95–103.

Feldman, Robert S. (1997). *Development across the life span.* Upper Saddle River, NJ: Prentice-Hall.

Fernald, Anne, & Mazzie, Claudia (1991). Prosody and focus in speech to infants and adults. *Developmental Psychology, 27,* 209–221.

Fernandez, Ephrem, & Turk, Dennis C. (1992). Sensory and affective components of pain: Separation and synthesis. *Psychological Bulletin, 112,* 205–217.

Fernández-Dols, José-Miguel, & Ruiz-Belda, María-Angeles (1995). Are smiles a sign of happiness? Gold medal winners at the Olympic games. *Journal of Personality and Social Psychology, 69,* 1113–1119.

Fernea, Elizabeth, & Fernea, Robert (1994). Cleanliness and culture. In W. J. Lonner & Malpass (eds.), *Psychology and culture.* Boston: Allyn & Bacon.

Festinger, Leon (1957). *A theory of cognitive dissonance.* Evanston, IL: Row, Peterson.

Festinger, Leon (1980). Looking backward. In L. Festinger (ed.), *Retrospections on social psychology.* New York: Oxford University Press.

Festinger, Leon, & Carlsmith, J. Merrill (1959). Cognitive consequences of forced compliance. *Journal of Abnormal and Social Psychology, 58,* 203–210.

Festinger, Leon; Pepitone, Albert; & Newcomb, Theodore (1952). Some consequences of deindividuation in a group. *Journal of Abnormal and Social Psychology, 47,* 382–389.

Festinger, Leon; Riecken, Henry W.; & Schachter, Stanley (1956). *When prophecy fails.* Minneapolis: University of Minnesota Press.

Feuerstein, Reuven (1980). *Instrumental enrichment: An intervention program for cognitive modifiability.* Baltimore, MD: University Park Press.

Field, Tiffany M. (1998). Massage therapy effects. *American Psychologist, 53,* 1270–1281.

Fields, Howard (1991). Depression and pain: A neurobiological model. *Neuropsychiatry, Neuropsychology, and Behavioral Neurology, 4,* 83–92.

Fiez, J. A. (1996). Cerebellar contributions to cognition. *Neuron, 16,* 13–15.

Fincham, Frank D.; Beach, Steven R. H.; Harold, Gordon T.; & Osborne, Lori N. (1997). Marital satisfaction and depression: Different causal relationships for men and women? *Psychological Science, 8,* 351–357.

Fincham, Frank D., & Bradbury, Thomas N. (1993). Marital satisfaction, depression, and attributions: A longitudinal analysis. *Journal of Personality and Social Psychology, 64,* 442–452.

Fingarette, Herbert (1988). *Heavy drinking: The myth of alcoholism as a disease.* Berkeley: University of California Press.

Fischer, Agneta H. (1993). Sex differences in emotionality: Fact or stereotype? *Feminism & Psychology, 3,* 303–318.

Fischer, Ann R.; Tokar, David M.; Good, Glenn E.; & Snell, Andrea F. (1998). More on the structure of male role norms. *Psychology of Women Quarterly, 22,* 135–155.

Fischer, Pamela C.; Smith, Randy J.; Leonard, Elizabeth; et al. (1993). Sex differences on affective dimensions: Continuing examination. *Journal of Counseling and Development, 71,* 440–443.

Fischhoff, Baruch (1975). Hindsight is not equal to foresight: The effect of outcome knowledge on judgment under uncertainty. *Journal of Experimental Psychology: Human Perception and Performance, 1,* 288–299.

Fishbein, Harold D. (1996). *Peer prejudice and discrimination.* Boulder, CO: Westview Press.

Fisher, Ann R., & Good, Glenn E. (1998). New directions for the study of gender role attitudes: A cluster analytic investigation of masculinity ideologies. *Psychology of Women Quarterly, 22,* 371–384.

Fisher, Kathleen (1985, March). ECT: New studies on how, why, who. *APA Monitor, 16,* 18–19.

Fisher, Ronald J. (1994). Generic principles for resolving intergroup conflict. *Journal of Social Issues, 50,* 47–66.

Fisher, S. E.; Vargha-Khadem, F.; Watkins, K. E.; et al. (1998). Localisation of a gene implicated in a severe speech and language disorder. *Nature Genetics, 18,* 168–170.

Fisher, Sarah; Guenin, Krista; Alter, R. J.; & Flannagan, Jeff (1999). Sweet and enduring: Quantity and consistency of long-term autobiographical memories. Paper presented at the annual meeting of the American Psychological Society, Denver.

Fisher, Seymour, & Greenberg, Roger P. (1996). *Freud scientifically appraised: Testing the theories and therapy.* New York: John Wiley.

Fiske, Alan P., & Haslam, Nick (1996). Social cognition is thinking about relationships. *Current Directions in Psychological Science, 5,* 143–148.

Fiske, Susan T. (1993). Controlling other people: The impact of power on stereotyping. *American Psychologist, 48,* 621–628.

Fivush, Robyn, & Hamond, Nina R. (1991). Autobiographical memory across the school years: Toward reconceptualizing childhood amnesia. In R. Fivush & J. A. Hudson (eds.), *Knowing and remembering in young children.* New York: Cambridge University Press.

Flacks, Richard, & Thomas, Scott L. (1998, November 27). Among affluent students, a culture of disengagement. *Chronicle of Higher Education,* A48.

Flavell, John H. (1992). Cognitive development: Past, present, and future. *Developmental Psychology, 28,* 998–1005.

Flavell, John H. (1993). Young children's understanding of thinking and consciousness. *Current Directions in Psychological Science, 2,* 40–43.

Flavell, John H. (1996). Piaget's legacy. *Psychological Science, 7,* 200–203.

Flavell, John H.; Green, F. L.; & Flavell, E. R. (1990). Developmental changes in young children's knowledge about the mind. *Cognitive Development, 5,* 1–27.

Flor, Herta; Kerns, Robert D.; & Turk, Dennis C. (1987). The role of spouse reinforcement, perceived pain, and activity levels of chronic pain patients. *Journal of Psychosomatic Research, 31,* 251–259.

Flynn, James R. (1987). Massive IQ gains in 14 nations: What IQ tests really measure. *Psychological Bulletin, 95,* 29–51.

Flynn, James R. (1999). Searching for justice: The discovery of IQ gains over time. *American Psychologist, 54,* 5–20.

Foa, Edna, & Emmelkamp, Paul (eds.) (1983). *Failures in behavior therapy.* New York: Wiley.

Foderaro, Lisa W. (1994, November 8). "Clubhouse" helps mentally ill find the way back. *New York Times,* B1, B3.

Fogelman, Eva (1994). *Conscience and courage: Rescuers of Jews during the Holocaust.* New York: Anchor Books.

Ford, D. E.; Mead, L. A.; Chang, P. P.; et al. (1998). Depression is a risk factor for coronary artery disease in men: The precursors study. *Archives of Internal Medicine, 158,* 1422–1426.

Fordham, Signithia (1991, Spring). Racelessness in private schools: Should we deconstruct the racial and cultural identity of African-American adolescents? *Teachers College Record, 92,* 470–484.

Foreyt, John P.; Goodrick, G. Ken; Reeves, Rebecca S.; et al. (1993). Response of free-living adults to behavioral treatment of obesity: Attrition and compliance to exercise. *Behavior Therapy, 24,* 659–669.

Forgas, Joseph P. (1998). On being happy and mistaken: Mood effects on the fundamental attribution error. *Journal of Personality and Social Psychology, 75,* 318–331.

Forgas, Joseph P., & Bond, Michael H. (1985). Cultural influences on the perception of interaction episodes. *Personality and Social Psychology Bulletin, 11,* 75–88.

Forrest, F.; Florey, C. du V.; Taylor, D.; et al. (1991, July 6). Reported social alcohol consumption during pregnancy and infants' development at 18 months. *British Medical Journal, 303,* 22–26.

Foulkes, D. (1962). Dream reports from different states of sleep. *Journal of Abnormal and Social Psychology, 65,* 14–25.

Fouts, Roger, with Mills, Stephen Tukel (1997). *Next of kin: What chimpanzees have taught me about who we are.* New York: William Morrow.

Fouts, Roger S., & Rigby, Randall L. (1977). Man–chimpanzee communication. In T. A. Seboek (ed.), *How animals communicate.* Bloomington: University of Indiana Press.

Fox, Nathan A. (1992). The role of individual differences in infant personality in the formation of attachment relationships. In E. J. Susman, L. V. Feagans, et al. (eds.), *Emotion, cognition, health, and development in children and adolescents.* Hillsdale, NJ: Erlbaum.

Fox, Nathan A., & Davidson, Richard J. (1988). Patterns of brain electrical activity during facial signs of emotion in 10-month-old infants. *Developmental Psychology, 24,* 230–236.

Fox, Ronald E. (1994). Training professional psychologists for the twenty-first century. *American Psychologist, 49,* 200–206.

Frank, Robert G.; Gluck, John P.; & Buckelew, Susan P. (1990). Rehabilitation: Psychology's greatest opportunity? *American Psychologist, 45,* 757–761.

Frankl, Victor E. (1955). *The doctor and the soul: An introduction to logotherapy.* New York: Knopf.

Franklin, Anderson J. (1993, July/August). The invisibility syndrome. *Family Therapy Networker,* 33–39.

Franklin, Karen (1998). Psychosocial motivations of hate crimes perpetrators: Implications for educational interventions. Paper presented at the annual meeting of the American Psychological Association, San Francisco, CA.

Franz, Carol E. (1997). Stability and change in the transition to midlife: A longitudinal study of midlife adults. In M. E. Lachman & J. B. James (eds.), *Multiple paths of midlife development.* Chicago: University of Chicago Press.

Frasure-Smith, Nancy; Lesperance, F.; Juneau, M.; Talajic, M.; & Bourassa, M. G. (1999). Gender, depression, and one-year prognosis after myocardial infarction. *Psychosomatic Medicine, 61,* 26–37.

Frederich, R. C.; Hamann, A.; Anderson, S.; et al. (1995). Leptin levels reflect body lipid content in mice: Evidence for diet-induced resistance to leptin action. *Nature Medicine, 1,* 1311–1314.

Freed, C. R.; Breeze, R. E.; Rosenberg, N. L.; & Schneck, S. A. (1993). Embryonic dopamine cell implants as a treatment for the second phase of Parkinson's disease: Replacing failed nerve terminals. *Advances in Neurology, 60,* 721–728.

Freedman, Hill, & Combs, Gene (1996). *Narrative therapy.* New York: Norton.

Freud, Anna (1967). *Ego and the mechanisms of defense (The writings of Anna Freud, Vol. 2)* (Rev. ed.). New York: International Universities Press.

Freud, Sigmund (1900/1953). The interpretation of dreams. In J. Strachey (ed.), *The standard edition of the complete psychological works of Sigmund Freud* (Vols. 4 and 5). London: Hogarth Press.

Freud, Sigmund (1905a). Fragment of an analysis of a case of hysteria. In J. Strachey (ed. and trans.), *Standard edition of the complete psychological works of Sigmund Freud* (Vol. 7). London: Hogarth Press.

Freud, Sigmund (1905b). Three essays on the theory of sexuality. In J. Strachey (ed.), *Standard edition of the complete psychological works of Sigmund Freud* (Vol. 7). London: Hogarth Press.

Freud, Sigmund (1920/1960). *A general introduction to psychoanalysis* (Joan Riviere, trans.). New York: Washington Square Press.

Freud, Sigmund (1923/1962). *The ego and the id* (Joan Riviere, trans.). New York: Norton.

Freud, Sigmund (1924a). The dissolution of the Oedipus complex. In J. Strachey (ed.), *Standard edition of the complete psychological works of Sigmund Freud* (Vol. 19). London: Hogarth Press.

Freud, Sigmund (1924b). Some psychical consequences of the anatomical distinction between the sexes. In J. Strachey (ed.), *Standard edition of the complete psychological works of Sigmund Freud* (Vol. 19). London: Hogarth Press.

Freud, Sigmund (1961). Ernst L. Freud (ed.), *Letters of Sigmund Freud, 1873–1939.* London: Hogarth Press.

Freyd, Jennifer J. (1996). *Betrayal trauma: The logic of forgetting childhood abuse.* Cambridge, MA: Harvard University Press.

Fridlund, Alan J. (1994). *Human facial expression: An evolutionary view.* San Diego: Academic Press.

Friedman, Meyer, & Rosenman, Ray (1974). *Type A behavior and your heart.* New York: Knopf.

Friedman, William; Robinson, Amy; & Friedman, Britt (1987). Sex differences in moral judgments? A test of Gilligan's theory. *Psychology of Women Quarterly, 11,* 37–46.

Friedrich, W. (1998). Normative sexual behavior in children: A contemporary sample. *Pediatrics, 101,* 4.

Frieze, Irene Hanson, & McHugh, Maureen C. (1998). Measuring feminism and gender role attitudes. *Psychology of Women Quarterly, 22,* 349–352.

Frijda, Nico H. (1988). The laws of emotion. *American Psychologist, 43,* 349–358.

Frome, Pamela M., & Eccles, Jacquelynne S. (1998). Parents' influence on children's achievement-related perceptions. *Journal of Personality and Social Psychology, 74,* 435–452.

Fry, P. S. (1995). Perfectionism, humor, and optimism as moderators of health outcomes and determinants of coping styles of women executives. *Genetic, Social, and General Psychology Monographs, 121,* 211–245.

Fry, William F. (1994). The biology of humor. *Humor: International Journal of Humor Research, 7,* 111–126.

Frye, Richard E.; Schwartz, B. S.; & Doty, Richard L. (1990). Dose-related effects of cigarette smoking on olfactory function. *Journal of the American Medical Association, 263,* 1233–1236.

Fuchs, C. S.; Stampfer, M. J.; Colditz, G. A.; et al. (1995, May 11). Alcohol consumption and mortality among women. *New England Journal of Medicine, 332,* 1245–1250.

Gaertner, Samuel L.; Mann, Jeffrey A.; Dovidio, John F.; et al. (1990). How does cooperation reduce intergroup bias? *Journal of Personality and Social Psychology, 59,* 692–704.

Gage, Fred H.; Kempermann, G.; Palmer, T. D.; et al. (1998). Multipotent progenitor cells in the adult dentate gyrus. *Journal of Neurobiology, 36,* 249–266.

Gagnon, John, & Simon, William (1973). *Sexual conduct: The social sources of human sexuality.* Chicago: Aldine.

Galanter, Eugene (1962). Contemporary psychophysics. In R. Brown, E. Galanter, H. Hess, & G. Mandler (eds.), *New directions in psychology.* New York: Holt, Rinehart and Winston.

Galanter, Marc (1989). *Cults: Faith, healing, and coercion.* New York: Oxford University Press.

Gallant, Jack L.; Braun, Jochen; & Van Essen, David C. (1993). Selectivity for polar, hyperbolic, and Cartesian gratings in macaque visual cortex. *Science, 259,* 100–103.

Gallant, Sheryle J.; Hamilton, Jean A.; Popiel, Debra A.; et al. (1991). Daily moods and symptoms: Effects of awareness of study focus, gender, menstrual-cycle phase, and day of the week. *Health Psychology, 10,* 180–189.

Gallo, Fred (1998). *Energy therapies.* Washington, DC: American Psychological Association.

Gallo, Linda C., & Eastman, Charmane I. (1993). Circadian rhythms during gradually delaying and advancing sleep and light schedules. *Physiology and Behavior, 53,* 119–126.

Galotti, Kathleen (1989). Approaches to studying formal and everyday reasoning. *Psychological Bulletin, 105,* 331–351.

Ganaway, George K. (1991). Alternative hypotheses regarding satanic ritual abuse memories. Paper presented at the annual meeting of the American Psychological Association, San Francisco.

Ganaway, George (1995). Hypnosis, childhood trauma, and dissociative identity disorder: Toward an integrative theory. *International Journal of Clinical and Experimental Hypnosis, 33,* 127–144.

Gao, Jia-Hong; Parsons, Lawrence M.; Bower, James M.; et al. (1996). Cerebellum implicated in sensory acquisition and discrimination rather than motor control. *Science, 272,* 545–547.

Garb, Howard N.; Florio, Colleen M.; & Grove, William M. (1998). The validity of the Rorschach and the Minnesota Multiphasic Personality Inventory: Results from meta-analyses. *Psychological Science, 9,* 402–404.

Garcia, Julio; Helms, Wes; & Garcia, Lisette (in preparation). White men can't jump. Tufts University.

Garcia, John, & Koelling, Robert A. (1966). Relation of cue to consequence in avoidance learning. *Psychonomic Science, 4,* 23–124.

Gardner, Howard (1983). *Frames of mind: The theory of multiple intelligences.* New York: Basic Books.

Gardner, Howard (1993). *Creating minds.* New York: Basic Books.

Gardner, Howard (1995). Perennial antinomies and perpetual redrawings: Is there progress in the study of mind? In R. L. Solso & D. W. Massar (eds.), *The science of the mind: 2001 and beyond.* New York: Oxford University Press.

Gardner, R. Allen, & Gardner, Beatrice T. (1969). Teaching sign language to a chimpanzee. *Science, 165,* 664–672.

Garland, Ann F., & Zigler, Edward (1994). Adolescent suicide prevention: Current research and social policy implications. *American Psychologist, 48,* 169–182.

Garmezy, Norman (1991). Resilience and vulnerability to adverse developmental outcomes associated with poverty. *American Behavioral Scientist, 34,* 416–430.

Garner, David M., & Wooley, Susan C. (1991). Confronting the failure of behavioral and dietary treatments for obesity. *Clinical Psychology Review, 11,* 729–780.

Garnets, Linda; Hancock, Kristin A.; Cochran, Susan D.; et al. (1991). Issues in psychotherapy with lesbians and gay men: A survey of psychologists. *American Psychologist, 46,* 964–972.

Garry, Maryanne; Manning, Charles G.; & Loftus, Elizabeth F. (1996). Imagination inflation: Imagining a childhood event inflates confidence that it occurred. *Psychonomic Bulletin & Review, 3,* 208–214.

Garven, Sena; Wood, James M.; Malpass, Roy S.; & Shaw, John S., III (1998). More than suggestion: The effect of interviewing techniques from the McMartin Preschool case. *Journal of Applied Psychology, 83,* 347–359.

Gaston, Louise; Marmar, Charles R.; Gallagher, Dolores; & Thompson, Larry W. (1989). Impact of confirming patient expectations of change processes in behavioral, cognitive, and brief dynamic psychotherapy. *Psychotherapy, 26,* 296–302.

Gawande, Atul (1998, September 21). The pain perplex. *New Yorker, 86,* 88, 90, 92–94.

Gay, Peter (1988). *Freud: A life for our time.* New York: Norton.

Gaziano, J. Michael, & Hennekens, Charles (1995, July 1). Royal colleges' advice on alcohol consumption [Editorial]. *British Medical Journal, 311,* 3–4.

Gazzaniga, Michael S. (1967). The split brain in man. *Scientific American, 217*(2), 24–29.

Gazzaniga, Michael S. (1983). Right hemisphere language following brain bisection: A 20-year perspective. *American Psychologist, 38,* 525–537.

Gazzaniga, Michael S. (1985). *The social brain: Discovering the networks of the mind.* New York: Basic Books.

Gazzaniga, Michael S. (1988). *Mind matters.* Boston: Houghton Mifflin.

Gazzaniga, Michael S. (1998). *The mind's past.* Berkeley, CA: University of California Press.

Geary, David C. (1995). Reflections of evolution and culture in children's cognition: Implications for mathematical development and instruction. *American Psychologist, 50,* 24–37.

Geller, E. Scott, & Lehman, Galen R. (1988). Drinking–driving intervention strategies: A person–situation–behavior framework. In M. D. Laurence, J. R. Snortum, & F. E. Zimring (eds.), *The social control of drinking and driving.* Chicago: University of Chicago Press.

Gelles, Richard J., & Straus, Murray A. (1988). *Intimate violence: The causes and consequences of abuse in the American family.* New York: Simon & Schuster/Touchstone.

Gerbner, George (1988). Telling stories in the information age. In B. D. Ruben (ed.), *Information and behavior* (Vol. 2). New Brunswick, NJ: Transaction Books.

Gibson, Eleanor, & Walk, Richard (1960). The "visual cliff." *Scientific American, 202,* 80–92.

Gillham, Jane E.; Reivich, Karen J.; Jaycox, Lisa H.; & Seligman, Martin E. P. (1995). Prevention of depressive symptoms in schoolchildren: A two-year follow-up. *Psychological Science, 6,* 343–351.

Gilligan, Carol (1982). *In a different voice.* Cambridge, MA: Harvard University Press.

Gilmore, David D. (1990). *Manhood in the making: Cultural concepts of masculinity.* New Haven, CT: Yale University Press.

Gladue, Brian A. (1994). The biopsychology of sexual orientation. *Current Directions in Psychological Science, 3,* 150–154.

Glanzer, Murray, & Cunitz, Anita R. (1966). Two storage mechanisms in free recall. *Journal of Verbal Learning and Verbal Behavior, 5,* 351–360.

Glazer, Myron P., & Glazer, Penina M. (1990). *The whistleblowers: Exposing corruption in government and industry.* New York: Basic Books.

Gleaves, David H. (1996). The sociocognitive model of dissociative identity disorder: A reexamination of the evidence. *Psychological Bulletin, 120,* 42–59.

Gobodo-Madikizela, Pumla (1994). The notion of the "collective" in South African "political" murder cases: The "deindividuation" argument revisited. Paper presented to the biennial conference of the American Psychology and Law Society, Santa Fe, NM.

Gold, Paul E. (1987). Sweet memories. *American Scientist, 75,* 151–155.

Goldin-Meadow, S., & Mylander, C. (1998). Spontaneous sign systems created by deaf children in two cultures. *Nature, 391,* 279–281.

Goldman-Rakic, Patricia S. (1996). Opening the mind through neurobiology. Invited address at the annual meeting of the American Psychological Association, Toronto, Canada.

Goldstein, Michael J. (1987). Psychosocial issues. *Schizophrenia Bulletin, 13*(1), 157–171.

Goldstein, Michael, & Miklowitz, David (1995). The effectiveness of psychoeducational family therapy in the treatment of schizophrenic disorders. *Journal of Marital and Family Therapy, 21,* 361–376.

Goleman, Daniel (1982, March). Staying up: The rebellion against sleep's gentle tyranny. *Psychology Today,* 24–25, 27–28, 31–32, 35.

Goleman, Daniel (1995). *Emotional intelligence.* New York: Bantam.

Golub, Sharon (1992). *Periods: From menarche to menopause.* Newbury Park, CA: Sage.

Goodman, Gail S.; Qin, Jianjian; Bottoms, Bette L.; & Shaver, Phillip R. (1995). *Characteristics and sources of allegations of ritualistic child abuse* (Final report to the National Center on Child Abuse and Neglect, Washington, DC). [Executive summary and complete report available from NCCAN, 1-800-394-3366.]

Goodman, Gail S.; Rudy, L.; Bottoms, B.; & Aman, C. (1990). Children's concerns and memory: Issues of ecological validity in the study of children's eyewitness testimony. In R. Fivush & J. Hudson (eds.), *Knowing and remembering in young children.* New York: Cambridge University Press.

Goodwin, Donald W.; Knop, Joachim; Jensen, Per; et al. (1994). Thirty-year follow-up of men at high risk for alcoholism. In Thomas F. Babor & Victor M. Hesselbrock (eds.), *Types of alcoholics: Evidence from clinical, experimental, and genetic research.* New York: New York Academy of Sciences.

Goodwyn, Susan, & Acredolo, Linda (1998). Encouraging symbolic gestures: A new perspective on the relationship between gesture and speech. In J. Iverson & S. Goldin-Meadow (eds.), *The nature and functions of gesture in children's communication.* San Francisco: Jossey-Bass.

Gopnik, Myrna (1991). Familial aggregation of a developmental language disorder. *Cognition, 39,* 1–50.

Gopnik, Myrna; Choi, Sooja; & Baumberger, Therese (1996). Cross-linguistic differences in early semantic and cognitive development. *Cognitive Development, 11,* 197–227.

Gopnik, Myrna, & Goad, Heather (1997). What underlies inflectional error patterns in genetic dysphasia? *Journal of Neurolinguistics, 10,* 109–137.

Gore, P. M., & Rotter, Julian B. (1963). A personality correlate of social action. *Journal of Personality, 31,* 58–64.

Goren, C. C.; Sarty, J.; & Wu, P. Y. (1975). Visual following and pattern discrimination of face-like stimuli by newborn infants. *Pediatrics, 56,* 544–549.

Gorn, Gerald J. (1982). The effects of music in advertising on choice behavior: A classical conditioning approach. *Journal of Marketing, 46,* 94–101.

Gottesman, Irving I. (1991). *Schizophrenia genesis: The origins of madness.* New York: Freeman.

Gottesman, Irving I. (1994). Perils and pleasures of genetic psychopathology. Distinguished Scientist Award address presented at the annual meeting of the American Psychological Association, Los Angeles.

Gottfried, Adele Eskeles; Fleming, James S.; & Gottfried, Allen W. (1994). Role of parental motivational practices in children's academic intrinsic motivation and achievement. *Journal of Educational Psychology, 86,* 104–113.

Gottman, John (1994, May/June). Why marriages fail. *Family Therapy Networker,* 40–48.

Gould, Elizabeth; Beylin, A.; Tanapat, Patima; et al. (1999). Learning enhances adult neurogenesis in the hippocampal formation. *Nature Neuroscience, 2,* 260–265.

Gould, Elizabeth; Tanapat, Patima; McEwen, Bruce S.; et al. (1998). Proliferation of granule cell precursors in the dentate gyrus of adult monkeys is diminished by stress. *Proceedings of the National Academy of Science, 95,* 3168–3171.

Gould, James L., & Gould, Carol G. (1995). *The animal mind.* San Francisco: Freeman.

Gould, Stephen Jay (1981/1996). *The mismeasure of man* (Rev. ed.). New York: W.W. Norton.

Gould, Stephen Jay (1985, June). The median isn't the message. *Discover, 6,* 40–42.

Gould, Stephen Jay (1987). *An urchin in the storm.* New York: Norton.

Gould, Stephen Jay (1994, November 28). Curveball [Review of *The Bell Curve,* by Richard J. Herrnstein and Charles Murray]. *New Yorker,* 139–149.

Graf, Peter, & Schacter, Daniel A. (1985). Implicit and explicit memory for new associations in normal and amnesic subjects. *Journal of Experimental Psychology: Learning, Memory, and Cognition, 11,* 501–518.

Graham, Jill W. (1986). Principled organizational dissent: A theoretical essay. *Research in Organizational Behavior, 8,* 1–52.

Graham, Sandra (1994). Motivation in African Americans. *Review of Educational Research, 64,* 55–117.

Grandin, Temple (1996). *Thinking in pictures and other reports from my life with autism.* New York: Doubleday.

Green, Donald P.; Glaser, Jack; & Rich, Andrew (1998). From lynching to gay bashing: The elusive connection between economic conditions and hate crime. *Journal of Personality and Social Psychology, 75,* 82–92.

Greenberg, Gary (1997). Right answers, wrong reasons: Revisiting the deletion of homosexuality from the *DSM. Review of General Psychology, 1,* 256–270.

Greenberg, Roger P.; Bornstein, Robert F.; Greenberg, Michael D.; & Fisher, Seymour (1992). A meta-analysis of antidepressant outcome under "blinder" conditions. *Journal of Consulting and Clinical Psychology, 60,* 664–669.

Greenberg, Roger P.; Bornstein, Robert F.; Zborowski, Michael J.; et al. (1994). A meta-analysis of fluoxetine outcome in the treatment of depression. *Journal of Nervous and Mental Disease, 182,* 547–551.

Greenberger, Dennis, & Padesky, Christine A. (1995). *Mind over mood: A cognitive therapy treatment manual for clients.* New York: Guilford Press.

Greene, Robert L. (1986). Sources of recency effects in free recall. *Psychological Bulletin, 99,* 221–228.

Greenfield, Patricia (1976). Cross-cultural research and Piagetian theory: Paradox and progress. In K. F. Riegel & J. A. Meacham (eds.), *The developing individual in a changing world: Vol. 1. Historical and cultural issues.* The Hague, Netherlands: Mouton.

Greenough, William T. (1984). Structural correlates of information storage in the mammalian brain: A review and hypothesis. *Trends in Neurosciences, 7,* 229–233.

Greenough, William T. (1991). The animal rights assertions: A researcher's perspective. *Psychological Science Agenda* (American Psychological Association), *4*(3), 10–12.

Greenough, William T., & Anderson, Brenda J. (1991). Cerebellar synaptic plasticity: Relation to learning vs. neural activity. *Annals of the New York Academy of Sciences, 627,* 231–247.

Greenough, William T., & Black, James E. (1992). Induction of brain structure by experience: Substrates for cognitive development. In M. Gunnar & C. A. Nelson (eds.), *Behavioral developmental neuroscience: Vol. 24. Minnesota Symposia on Child Psychology*. Hillsdale, NJ: Erlbaum.

Greenough, William T.; Cohen, N. J.; & Juraska, J. M. (1999). New neurons in old brains: Learning to survive? *Nature Neuroscience, 2,* 203–205.

Greenwald, Anthony G.; Draine, Sean C.; & Abrams, Richard L. (1996). Three cognitive markers of unconscious semantic activation. *Science, 273,* 1699–1702.

Greenwald, Anthony G.; Spangenberg, Eric R.; Pratkanis, Anthony R.; & Eskenazi, Jay (1991). Double-blind tests of subliminal self-help audiotapes. *Psychological Science, 2,* 119–122.

Gregory, Richard L. (1963). Distortion of visual space as inappropriate constancy scaling. *Nature, 199,* 678–679.

Griffin, Donald R. (1992). *Animal minds.* Chicago: University of Chicago Press.

Griggs, Richard A., & Cox, J. R. (1982). The elusive thematic-materials effect in Wason's selection task. *British Journal of Psychology, 73,* 407–420.

Grigorenko, Elena L., & Sternberg, Robert J. (1998). Dynamic testing. *Psychological Bulletin, 124,* 75–111.

Grinspoon, Lester, & Bakalar, James B. (1993). *Marihuana, the forbidden medicine.* New Haven, CT: Yale University Press.

Gronbaek, M.; Deis, A.; Sorensen, T. I.; et al. (1995, May 6). Mortality associated with moderate intakes of wine, beer, or spirits. *British Medical Journal, 310,* 1165–1169.

Gross, James J. (1998). Antecedent- and response-focused emotion regulation: Divergent consequences for experience, expression, and physiology. *Journal of Personality and Social Psychology, 74,* 224–237.

Grossman, Michele, & Wood, Wendy (1993). Sex differences in intensity of emotional experience: A social role interpretation. *Journal of Personality and Social Psychology, 65,* 1010–1022.

Gruber, Barry L.; Hersh, Stephen P.; Hall, Nicholas R.; et al. (1993). Immunological responses of breast cancer patients to behavioral interventions. *Biofeedback and Self-Regulation, 18,* 1–22.

Grusec, Joan E., & Goodnow, Jacqueline J. (1994). Impact of parental discipline methods on child's internalization of values: A reconceptualization of current points of view. *Developmental Psychology, 30,* 4–19.

Guilford, J. P. (1988). Some changes in the structure-of-intellect model. *Educational and Psychological Measurement, 48,* 1–4.

Gur, R. E.; Maany, V.; Mozley, P. D.; et al. (1998). Subcortical MRI volumes in neuroleptic-naive and treated patients with schizophrenia. *American Journal of Psychiatry, 155,* 1711–1717.

Guralnick, M. J. (ed.) (1997). *The effectiveness of early intervention.* Baltimore: Brookes.

Gutheil, Thomas G. (1993). The psychology of pharmacology. In M. Schacter (ed.), *Psychotherapy and medication.* Worthvale, NJ: Jason Aronson.

Gwiazda, Jane; Thorn, Frank; Bauer, Joseph; & Held, Richard (1993). Emmetropization and the progression of manifest refraction in children followed from infancy to puberty. *Clinical Vision Sciences, 8,* 337–344.

Haber, Ralph N. (1970, May). How we remember what we see. *Scientific American, 222,* 104–112.

Haimov, I., & Lavie, P. (1996). Melatonin—a soporific hormone. *Current Directions in Psychological Science, 5,* 106–111.

Halaas, Jeffrey L.; Gajiwala, Ketan S.; Maffei, Margherita; et al. (1995). Weight-reducing effects of the plasma protein encoded by the obese gene. *Science, 269,* 543–546.

Hall, C. S.; Domhoff, G. W.; Thick, K. A.; & Weesner, K. E. (1982). The dreams of college men and women in 1950 and 1980: A comparison of dream content and sex differences. *Sleep, 5,* 188–194.

Hall, Edward T. (1959). *The silent language.* Garden City, NY: Doubleday.

Hall, Edward T. (1976). *Beyond culture.* New York: Anchor.

Hall, Edward T. (1983). *The dance of life: The other dimension of time.* Garden City, NY: Anchor Press/Doubleday.

Hall, Edward T., & Hall, Mildred R. (1987). *Hidden differences: Doing business with the Japanese.* Garden City, NY: Anchor Press/Doubleday.

Hall, Edward T., & Hall, Mildred R. (1990). *Understanding cultural differences.* Yarmouth, ME: Intercultural Press.

Hall, G. Stanley (1899). A study of anger. *American Journal of Psychology, 10,* 516–591.

Hall, Judith A. (1987). On explaining gender differences: The case of nonverbal communication. In P. Shaver & C. Hendrick (eds.), *Sex and gender: Vol. 7. Review of personality and social psychology.* Beverly Hills, CA: Sage.

Halliday, G. (1993). Examination dreams. *Perceptual and Motor Skills, 77,* 489–490.

Halpern, Diane (1995). *Thought and knowledge: An introduction to critical thinking* (3rd ed.). Hillsdale, NJ: Erlbaum.

Halpern, Diane (1998). Teaching critical thinking for transfer across domains. *American Psychologist, 53,* 449–455.

Hamer, Dean H.; Hu, Stella; Magnuson, Victoria L.; et al. (1993). A linkage between DNA markers on the X chromosome and male sexual orientation. *Science, 261,* 321–327.

Haney, Craig; Banks, Curtis; & Zimbardo, Philip (1973). Interpersonal dynamics in a simulated prison. *International Journal of Criminology and Penology, 1,* 69–97.

Haney, Craig, & Zimbardo, Philip (1998). The past and future of U.S. prison policy: Twenty-five years after the Stanford Prison Experiment. *American Psychologist, 53,* 709–727.

Hardie, Elizabeth A. (1997). PMS in the workplace: Dispelling the myth of cyclic function. *Journal of Occupational and Organizational Psychology, 70,* 97–102.

Harding, Courtenay M.; Zubin, Joseph; & Strauss, John S. (1987). Chronicity in schizophrenia: Fact, partial fact, or artifact? *Hospital and Community Psychiatry, 38,* 477–486.

Harding, Courtenay M.; Zubin, Joseph; & Strauss, John S. (1992). Chronicity in schizophrenia: Revisited. *British Journal of Psychiatry, 161*(Suppl. 18), 27–37.

Hare, Robert D. (1965). Temporal gradient of fear arousal in psychopaths. *Journal of Abnormal Psychology, 70,* 442–445.

Hare, Robert D. (1993). *Without conscience: The disturbing world of the psychopaths among us.* New York: Pocket Books.

Hare-Mustin, Rachel T. (1991). Sex, lies, and headaches: The problem is power. In T. J. Goodrich (ed.), *Women and power: Perspectives for therapy.* New York: Norton.

Hare-Mustin, Rachel T., & Marecek, Jeanne (1990). Gender and the meaning of difference: Postmodernism and psychology. In R. Hare-Mustin & J. Maracek (eds.), *Psychology and the construction of gender.* New Haven, CT: Yale University Press.

Haritos-Fatouros, Mika (1988). The official torturer: A learning model for obedience to the authority of violence. *Journal of Applied Social Psychology, 18,* 1107–1120.

Harkins, Stephen G., & Szymanski, Kate (1989). Social loafing and group evaluation. *Journal of Personality and Social Psychology, 56,* 934–941.

Harlow, Harry F. (1958). The nature of love. *American Psychologist, 13,* 673–685.

Harlow, Harry F., & Harlow, Margaret K. (1966). Learning to love. *American Scientist, 54,* 244–272.

Harlow, Harry F.; Harlow, Margaret K.; & Meyer, D. R. (1950). Learning motivated by a manipulation drive. *Journal of Experimental Psychology, 40,* 228–234.

Harmon-Jones, Eddie, & Allen, John J. B. (1998). Anger and frontal brain activity: EEG asymmetry consistent with approach motivation despite negative affective valence. *Journal of Personality and Social Psychology, 74,* 1310–1316.

Harmon-Jones, Eddie; Brehm, Jack W.; Greenberg, Jeff; et al. (1996). Evidence that the production of aversive consequences is not necessary to create cognitive dissonance. *Journal of Personality and Social Psychology, 70,* 5–16.

Harris, Judith R. (1998). *The nurture assumption.* New York: Free Press.

Harris, Naomi G. Singer; Bellugi, Ursula; Bates, Elizabeth; et al. (1997). Contrasting profiles of language development in children with Williams and Down syndromes. *Developmental Neuropsychology, 13,* 345–370.

Hart, John, Jr.; Berndt, Rita S.; & Caramazza, Alfonso (1985, August 1). Category-specific naming deficit following cerebral infarction. *Nature, 316,* 339–340.

Hartung, Cynthia M., & Widiger, Thomas A. (1998). Gender differences in the diagnosis of mental disorders: Conclusions and controversies of the DSM-IV. *Psychological Bulletin, 123,* 260–278.

Hasher, Lynn, & Zacks, Rose T. (1984). Automatic processing of fundamental information: The case of frequency of occurrence. *American Psychologist, 39,* 1372–1388.

Hatfield, Agnes B., & Lefley, Harriet P. (eds.) (1987). *Families of the mentally ill: Coping and adaptation.* New York: Guilford Press.

Hatfield, Elaine; Cacioppo, John T.; & Rapson, Richard L. (1994). *Emotional contagion.* New York: Cambridge University Press.

Hatfield, Elaine, & Rapson, Richard L. (1996). *Love and sex: Cross-cultural perspectives.* Boston: Allyn & Bacon.

Hawkins, Scott A., & Hastie, Reid (1990). Hindsight: Biased judgments of past events after the outcomes are known. *Psychological Bulletin, 107,* 311–327.

Haynes, Suzanne, & Feinleib, Manning (1980). Women, work, and coronary heart disease: Prospective findings from the Framingham heart study. *American Journal of Public Health, 70,* 133–141.

Hazan, Cindy, & Shaver, Phillip R. (1994). Attachment as an organizational framework for research on close relationships. *Psychological Inquiry, 5,* 1–22.

Hebl, Michelle R., & Heatherton, Todd F. (1998). The stigma of obesity in women: The difference in black and white. *Personality and Social Psychology Bulletin, 24,* 417–426.

Hecht, Marvin A., & LaFrance, Marianne (1998). License or obligation to smile: The effect of power and sex on amount and type of smiling. *Personality and Social Psychology Bulletin, 24,* 1332–1342.

Heinrichs, R. Walter (1993). Schizophrenia and the brain: Conditions for a neuropsychology of madness. *American Psychologist, 48,* 221–233.

Heisel, Marnin J. (1998). A meta-analysis of psychotherapy and pharmacotherapy for panic disorder. Paper presented at the annual meeting of the American Psychological Association, San Francisco.

Heller, Wendy; Nitschke, Jack B.; & Miller, Gregory A. (1998). Lateralization in emotion and emotional disorders. *Current Directions in Psychological Science, 7,* 26–32.

Helmes, Edward, & Reddon, John R. (1993). A perspective on developments in assessing psychopathology: A critical review of the MMPI and MMPI-2. *Psychological Bulletin, 113,* 453–471.

Helson, Ravenna, & McCabe, Laurel (1993). The social clock project in middle age. In B. F. Turner & L. E. Troll (eds.), *Women growing older.* Newbury Park, CA: Sage.

Hendrick, Susan S., & Hendrick, Clyde (1992). *Romantic love.* Newbury Park, CA: Sage.

Hendrick, Susan S., & Hendrick, Clyde (1997). Love and satisfaction. In R. J. Sternberg & M. Hojjat (eds.), *Satisfaction in close relationships.* New York: Guilford Press.

Hendrix, William H.; Steel, Robert P.; Leap, Terry L.; & Summers, Timothy P. (1991). Development of a stress-related health promotion model: Antecedents and organizational effectiveness outcomes. *Journal of Social Behavior and Personality, 6,* 141–162.

Henley, Nancy (1995). Body politics revisited: What do we know today? In P. J. Kalbfleisch & M. J. Cody (eds.), *Gender, power, and communication in human relationships.* Hillsdale, NJ: Erlbaum.

Henry, Bill; Caspi, Avshalom; Moffitt, Terrie E.; & Silva, Phil A. (1996). Temperamental and familial predictors of violent and nonviolent criminal convictions: Age 3 to age 18. *Developmental Psychology, 32,* 614–623.

Herbert, Tracy B., & Cohen, Sheldon (1993). Depression and immunity: A meta-analytic review. *Psychological Bulletin, 113,* 472–486.

Herdt, Gilbert (1984). *Ritualized homosexuality in Melanesia.* Berkeley: University of California Press.

Herek, Gregory M. (1998). The social psychology of homophobias and heterosexisms. Invited address presented at the annual meeting of the American Psychological Association, San Francisco.

Herek, Gregory M., & Capitanio, J. P. (1996). "Some of my best friends": Intergroup contact, concealable stigma, and heterosexuals' attitudes toward gay men and lesbians. *Personality and Social Psychology Bulletin, 22,* 412–424.

Herman, John H. (1992). Transmutative and reproductive properties of dreams: Evidence for cortical modulation of brainstem generators. In J. Antrobus & M. Bertini (eds.), *The neuropsychology of dreaming.* Hillsdale, NJ: Erlbaum.

Herman, Louis M. (1987). Receptive competencies of language-trained animals. In J. S. Rosenblatt, C. Beer, M. C. Busnel, & P. J. B. Slater (eds.), *Advances in the study of behavior* (Vol. 17). Petaluma, CA: Academic Press.

Herman, Louis M.; Kuczaj, Stan A.; & Holder, Mark D. (1993). Responses to anomalous gestural sequences by a language-trained dolphin: Evidence for processing of semantic relations and syntactic information. *Journal of Experimental Psychology: General, 122,* 184–194.

Herman, Louis M., & Morrel-Samuels, Palmer (1996). Knowledge acquisition and asymmetry between language comprehension and production: Dolphins and apes as general models for animals. In M. Bekoff, D. Jamieson, et al. (eds.), *Readings in animal cognition.* Cambridge, MA: MIT Press.

Herman-Giddens, Marcia E.; Slora, E. J.; Wasserman, R. C.; et al. (1997). Secondary sexual characteristics and menses in young girls seen in office practice: A study from the Pediatric Research in Office Settings network. *Pediatrics, 99,* 505–512.

Heron, Woodburn (1957). The pathology of boredom. *Scientific American, 196*(1), 52–56.

Herrnstein, Richard J., & Murray, Charles (1994). *The bell curve: Intelligence and class structure in American life.* New York: Free Press.

Herz, Rachel S., & Cupchik, Gerald C. (1995). The emotional distinctiveness of odor-evoked memories. *Chemical Senses, 20,* 517–528.

Hicks, Robert D. (1991). The police model of satanism crime. In J. T. Richardson, J. Best, & D. G. Bromley (eds.), *The satanism scare.* New York: Aldine de Gruyter.

Higgins, E. Tory (1998). Promotion and prevention: Regulatory focus as a motivational principle. *Advances in Experimental Social Psychology, 30,* 1–46.

Higley, J. D.; Hasert, M. L.; Suomi, S. J.; & Linnoila, M. (1991). A nonhuman primate model of alcohol abuse: Effects of early experience, personality, and stress on alcohol consumption. *Proceedings of the National Academy of Science, 88,* 7261–7265.

Hilgard, Ernest R. (1977/1986). *Divided consciousness: Multiple controls in human thought and action* (2nd ed.). New York: Wiley.

Hilgard, Josephine R. (1979). *Personality and hypnosis: A study of imaginative involvement* (2nd ed.). Chicago: University of Chicago Press.

Hill, Harlan F.; Chapman, C. Richard; Kornell, Judy A.; et al. (1990). Self-administration of morphine in bone marrow transplant patients reduces drug requirement. *Pain, 40,* 121–129.

Hill, James O., & Peters, John C. (1998). Environmental contributions to the obesity epidemic. *Science, 280,* 1371–1374.

Hillman, James, & Ventura, Michael (1992). *We've had a hundred years of psychotherapy—and the world's getting worse.* San Francisco: Harper-Collins.

Hilsman, Ruth, & Garber, Judy (1995). A test of the cognitive diathesis–stress model of depression in children: Academic stressors, attributional style, perceived competence, and control. *Journal of Personality and Social Psychology, 69,* 370–380.

Hilts, Philip J. (1995). *Memory's ghost: The strange tale of Mr. M. and the nature of memory.* New York: Simon & Schuster.

Hines, Terence M. (1998). Comprehensive review of biorhythm theory. *Psychological Reports, 83,* 19–64.

Hirsch, Helmut V. B., & Spinelli, D. N. (1970). Visual experience modifies distribution of horizontally and vertically oriented receptive fields in cats. *Science, 168,* 869–871.

Hirst, William; Neisser, Ulric; & Spelke, Elizabeth (1978, January). Divided attention. *Human Nature, 1,* 54–61.

Hobson, J. Allan (1988). *The dreaming brain.* New York: Basic Books.

Hobson, J. Allan (1990). Activation, input source, and modulation: A neurocognitive model of the state of the brain mind. In R. R. Bootzin, J. F. Kihlstrom, & D. L. Schacter (eds.), *Sleep and cognition.* Washington, DC: American Psychological Association.

Hochschild, Arlie (1983). *The managed heart.* Berkeley: University of California Press.

Hockett, Charles F. (1960). The origins of speech. *Scientific American, 203,* 89–96.

Hodges, Ernest V. E., & Perry, David G. (1999). Personal and interpersonal antecedents and consequences of victimization by peers. *Journal of Personality and Social Psychology, 76,* 677–685.

Hoffman, Martin L. (1990). Empathy and justice motivation. *Motivation and Emotion, 14,* 151–172.

Hoffman, Martin L. (1994). Discipline and internalization. *Developmental Psychology, 30,* 26–28.

Hofstede, Geert, & Bond, Michael H. (1988). The Confucius connection: From cultural roots to economic growth. *Organizational Dynamics,* 5–21.

Hogg, Michael A., & Abrams, Dominic (1988). *Social identifications: A social psychology of intergroup relations and group processes.* New York: Routledge.

Holden, Constance (1997). Thumbs up for acupuncture [News report]. *Science, 278,* 1231.

Holden, George W., & Miller, Pamela C. (1999). Enduring and different: A meta-analysis of the similarity in parents' child rearing. *Psychological Bulletin, 125,* 223–254.

Holmes, David S. (1997). *Abnormal psychology* (3rd ed.). New York: HarperCollins.

Honts, Charles R. (1994). Psychophysiological detection of deception. *Current Directions in Psychological Science, 3,* 77–82.

Hooker, Evelyn (1957). The adjustment of the male overt homosexual. *Journal of Projective Techniques, 21,* 18–31.

Hoon, M. A.; Adler, E.; Lindemeier, J.; et al. (1999). Putative mammalian taste receptors: A class of taste-specific GPCRs with distinct topographic selectivity. *Cell, 96,* 541–551.

Hooper, Judith (1999, February). A new germ theory. *Atlantic,* 41–53.

Hoptman, Matthew J., & Davidson, Richard J. (1994). How and why do the two cerebral hemispheres interact? *Psychological Bulletin, 116,* 195–219.

Horgan, John (1995, November). Get smart, take a test: A long-term rise in IQ scores baffles intelligence experts. *Scientific American, 273,* 12,14.

Horm, J., & Anderson, K. (1993). Who in America is trying to lose weight? *Annals of Internal Medicine, 119,* 672–676.

Horn, G., & Hinde, R. A. (eds.) (1970). *Short-term changes in neural activity and behaviour.* New York: Cambridge University Press.

Horner, Althea J. (1991). *Psychoanalytic object relations therapy.* New York: Jason Aronson.

Horney, Karen (1926/1973). The flight from womanhood. *The International Journal of Psycho-Analysis, 7,* 324–339. [Reprinted in J. B. Miller (ed.), *Psychoanalysis and women.* New York: Brunner/Mazel, 1973.]

Hornstein, Gail (1992). The return of the repressed: Psychology's problematic relations with psychoanalysis, 1909–1960. *American Psychologist, 47,* 254–263.

House, James S.; Landis, Karl R.; & Umberson, Debra (1988, July 19). Social relationships and health. *Science, 241,* 540–545.

Howard, George S. (1991). Culture tales: A narrative approach to thinking, cross-cultural psychology, and psychotherapy. *American Psychologist, 46,* 187–197.

Howard, Kenneth; Kopta, S. Mark; Krause, Merton S.; & Orlinsky, David (1986). The dose–effect relationship in psychotherapy. *American Psychologist, 41,* 159–164.

Howe, Mark L., & Courage, Mary L. (1993). On resolving the enigma of infantile amnesia. *Psychological Bulletin, 113,* 305–326.

Howe, Mark L.; Courage, Mary L.; & Peterson, Carole (1994). How can I remember when "I" wasn't there? Long-term retention of traumatic experiences and emergence of the cognitive self [Special issue: The recovered memory/false memory debate]. *Consciousness and Cognition, 3,* 327–355.

Hrdy, Sarah B. (1988). Empathy, polyandry, and the myth of the coy female. In R. Bleier (ed.), *Feminist approaches to science.* New York: Pergamon.

Hu, S.; Pattatucci, A. M.; Patterson C.; et al. (1995). Linkage between sexual orientation and chromosome Xq28 in males but not in females. *Nature Genetics, 11,* 248–256.

Hubbard, Ruth (1990). *The politics of women's biology.* New Brunswick, NJ: Rutgers University Press.

Hubel, David H., & Wiesel, Torsten N. (1962). Receptive fields, binocular interaction and functional architecture in the cat's visual cortex. *Journal of Physiology* (London), *160,* 106–154.

Hubel, David H., & Wiesel, Torsten N. (1968). Receptive fields and functional architecture of monkey striate cortex. *Journal of Physiology* (London), *195,* 215–243.

Hughes, Judith M. (1989). *Reshaping the psychoanalytic domain: The work of Melanie Klein, W. R. D. Fairbairn, & D. W. Winnicott.* Berkeley, CA: University of California Press.

Hultsch, David F.; Hertzog, Christopher; Small, Brent J.; & Dixon, Roger A. (1999). Use it or lose it: Engaged lifestyle as a buffer of cognitive decline in aging? *Psychology and Aging, 14,* 245–263.

Hunt, Earl; Streissguth, Ann P.; Kerr, Beth; & Olson, Heather C. (1995). Mothers' alcohol consumption during pregnancy: Effects on spatial-visual reasoning in 14-year-old children. *Psychological Science, 6,* 339–342.

Hunt, Morton M. (1959/1967). *The natural history of love.* New York: Minerva Press.

Hunt, Morton M. (1993). *The story of psychology.* New York: Doubleday.

Hunter, John E. (1997). Needed: A ban on the significance test. *Psychological Science, 8,* 3–7.

Huntington's Disease Collaborative Research Group (1993). A novel gene containing a trinucleotide repeat that is expanded and unstable on Huntington's disease chromosomes. *Cell, 72,* 971–983.

Hupka, Ralph B. (1981). Cultural determinants of jealousy. *Alternative Lifestyles, 4,* 310–356.

Hupka, Ralph B. (1991). The motive for the arousal of romantic jealousy. In P. Salovey (ed.), *The psychology of jealousy and envy.* New York: Guilford Press.

Hur, Yoon-Mi; McGue, Matt; & Iacono, William G. (1998). The structure of self-concept in female preadolescent twins: A behavioral genetic approach. *Journal of Personality and Social Psychology, 74,* 1069–1077.

Hyde, Janet S.; Fennema, Elizabeth; & Lamon, Susan J. (1990). Gender differences in mathematics performance: A meta-analysis. *Psychological Bulletin, 107,* 139–155.

Hyde, Janet S., & Linn, Marcia C. (1988). Gender differences in verbal ability: A meta-analysis. *Psychological Bulletin, 104,* 53–69.

Hyman, Ira E., Jr., & Pentland, Joel (1996). The role of mental imagery in the creation of false childhood memories. *Journal of Memory and Language, 35,* 101–117.

Hyman, Ray (1994). Anomaly or artifact? Comments on Bem and Honorton. *Psychological Bulletin, 115,* 25–27.

Iacono, William G., & Lykken, David T. (1997). The scientific status of research on polygraph techniques: The case against polygraph tests. In D. L. Faigman, D. Kaye, M. J. Saks, & J. Sanders (eds.), *Modern scientific evidence: The law and science of expert testimony.* St. Paul, MN: West.

Inglehart, Ronald (1990). *Culture shift in advanced industrial society.* Princeton, NJ: Princeton University Press.

Inglis, James, & Lawson, J. S. (1981). Sex differences in the effects of unilateral brain damage on intelligence. *Science, 212,* 693–695.

Irons, Edward D., & Moore, Gilbert W. (1985). *Black managers: The case of the banking industry.* New York: Praeger/Greenwood.

Irvine, Janice M. (1990). *Disorders of desire: Sex and gender in modern American sexology.* Philadelphia: Temple University Press.

Islam, Mir Rabiul, & Hewstone, Miles (1993). Intergroup attributions and affective consequences in majority and minority groups. *Journal of Personality and Social Psychology, 64,* 936–950.

Iyengar, Sheena A., & Lepper, Mark R. (1999). Rethinking the value of choice: A cultural perspective on intrinsic motivation. *Journal of Personality and Social Psychology, 76,* 349–366.

Izard, Carroll E. (1990). Facial expressions and the regulation of emotions. *Journal of Personality and Social Psychology, 58,* 487–498.

Izard, Carroll E. (1994a). Four systems for emotion activation: Cognitive and noncognitive processes. *Psychological Review, 100,* 68–90.

Izard, Carroll E. (1994b). Innate and universal facial expressions: Evidence from developmental and cross-cultural research. *Psychological Bulletin, 115,* 288–299.

Jacobsen, Paul B; Bovbjerg, Dana H.; Schwartz, Marc D.; et al. (1995). Conditioned emotional distress in women receiving chemotherapy for breast cancer. *Journal of Consulting & Clinical Psychology, 63,* 108–114.

Jacobson, John W.; Mulick, James A.; & Schwartz, Allan A. (1995). The history of facilitated communication: Science, pseudoscience, and antiscience. *American Psychologist, 50,* 750–765.

James, Jacquelyn B., & Lewkowicz, Corinne J. (1997). Themes of power and affiliation across time. In M. E. Lachman & J. B. James (eds.), *Multiple paths of midlife development.* Chicago: University of Chicago Press.

James, William (1890/1950). *Principles of psychology* (Vol. 1). New York: Dover.

James, William (1902/1936). *The varieties of religious experience.* New York: Modern Library.

Jang, Kerry L.; McCrae, Robert R.; Angleitner, Alois; et al. (1998). Heritability of facet-level traits in a cross-cultural twin sample: Support for a hierarchical model of personality. *Journal of Personality and Social Psychology, 74,* 1556–1565.

Janis, Irving L. (1982). *Groupthink: Psychological studies of policy decisions and fiascoes* (2nd ed.). Boston: Houghton Mifflin.

Janis, Irving L. (1989). *Crucial decisions: Leadership in policymaking and crisis management.* New York: Free Press.

Janis, Irving L.; Kaye, Donald; & Kirschner, Paul (1965). Facilitating effects of "eating-while-reading" on responsiveness to persuasive communications. *Journal of Personality and Social Psychology, 1,* 181–186.

Janoff-Bulman, Ronnie (1999). Rebuilding shattered assumptions after traumatic life events: Coping processes and outcomes. In C. R. Snyder (ed.), *Coping: The psychology of what works.* New York: Oxford University Press.

Jellinek, E. M. (1960). *The disease concept of alcoholism.* New Haven, CT: Hillhouse Press.

Jenkins, Jennifer M., & Astington, Janet W. (1996). Cognitive factors and family structure associated with theory of mind development in young children. *Developmental Psychology, 32,* 70–78.

Jenkins, John G., & Dallenbach, Karl M. (1924). Obliviscence during sleep and waking. *American Journal of Psychology, 35,* 605–612.

Jenkins, Sharon Rae (1994). Need for power and women's careers over 14 years: Structural power, job satisfaction, and motive change. *Journal of Personality and Social Psychology, 66,* 155–165.

Jensen, Arthur R. (1969). How much can we boost IQ and scholastic achievement? *Harvard Educational Review, 39,* 1–123.

Jensen, Arthur R. (1981). *Straight talk about mental tests.* New York: Free Press.

Johnson, Catherine (1988). *When to say goodbye to your therapist.* New York: Simon & Schuster.

Johnson, Marcia K. (1995). The relation between memory and reality. Paper presented at the annual meeting of the American Psychological Association, New York.

Johnson, Mark H.; Dziurawiec, Suzanne; Ellis, Hadyn; & Morton, John (1991). Newborns' preferential tracking of face-like stimuli and its subsequent decline. *Cognition, 40,* 1–19.

Johnson, Robert, & Downing, Leslie (1979). Deindividuation and valence of cues: Effects of prosocial and antisocial behavior. *Journal of Personality and Social Psychology, 37,* 1532–1538.

Joiner, Thomas E. (1994). Contagious depression: Existence, specificity to depressed symptoms, and the role of reassurance seeking. *Journal of Personality and Social Psychology, 67,* 287–296.

Jones, James M. (1991). Psychological models of race: What have they been and what should they be? In J. D. Goodchilds (ed.), *Psychological perspectives on human diversity in America.* Washington, DC: American Psychological Association.

Jones, Mary Cover (1924). A laboratory study of fear: The case of Peter. *Pedagogical Seminary, 31,* 308–315.

Jones, Steve (1994). *The language of genes.* New York: Anchor/Doubleday.

Jorgensen, Randall S.; Johnson, Blair T.; Kolodziej, Monika E.; & Schreer, George E. (1996). Elevated blood pressure and personality: A meta-analytic review. *Psychological Bulletin, 120,* 293–320.

Judd, Charles M.; Park, Bernadette; Ryan, Carey S.; et al. (1995). Stereotypes and ethnocentrism: Diverging interethnic perceptions of African American and white American youth. *Journal of Personality and Social Psychology, 69,* 460–481.

Jung, Carl (1967). *Collected works.* Princeton, NJ: Princeton University Press.

Jusczyk, Peter W. (1997). Finding and remembering words: Some beginnings by English-learning infants. *Current Directions in Psychological Science, 6,* 170–174.

Kabani, Noor Jehan; MacDonald, David; Evans, Alan; & Gopnik, Myrna (1997). Neuroanatomical correlates of familial language impairment: A preliminary report. *Journal of Neurolinguistics, 10,* 203–214.

Kabani, Noor Jehan; MacDonald, David; Evans, Alan; & Gopnik, Myrna (1998). "Neuroanatomical correlates of familial language impairment: A preliminary report": Erratum. *Journal of Neurolinguistics, 11,* 329.

Kabat-Zinn, Jon (1994). *Wherever you go, there you are: Mindfulness meditation in everyday life.* New York: Hyperion.

Kaczynski, Richard (1997). The satanic ritual abuse controversy: A case of groupthink? Paper presented at the annual meeting of the American Psychological Association, Chicago.

Kagan, Jerome (1984). *The nature of the child.* New York: Basic Books.

Kagan, Jerome (1993). The meanings of morality. *Psychological Science, 4,* 353, 357–360.

Kagan, Jerome (1994). *Galen's prophecy: Temperament in human nature.* New York: Basic Books.

Kagan, Jerome (1998a). How we become what we are. Paper presented at the annual meeting of the Family Therapy Network Symposium, Washington, DC.

Kagan, Jerome (1998b). *Three seductive ideas.* Cambridge, MA: Harvard University Press.

Kagan, Jerome; Kearsley, Richard B.; & Zelazo, Philip R. (1978). *Infancy: Its place in human development.* Cambridge, MA: Harvard University Press.

Kahneman, Daniel, & Treisman, Anne (1984). Changing views of attention and automaticity. In R. Parasuraman, D. R. Davies, & J. Beatty (eds.), *Varieties of attention.* New York: Academic Press.

Kameda, Tatsuya, & Sugimori, Shinkichi (1993). Psychological entrapment in group decision making: An assigned decision rule and a groupthink phenomenon. *Journal of Personality and Social Psychology, 65,* 282–292.

Kandel, Eric R., & Schwartz, James H. (1982). Molecular biology of learning: Modulation of transmitter release. *Science, 218,* 433–443.

Kanin, Eugene J. (1985). Date rapists: Differential sexual socialization and relative deprivation. *Archives of Sexual Behavior, 14,* 219–231.

Kanter, Rosabeth Moss (1977/1993). *Men and women of the corporation.* New York: Basic Books.

Kanwisher, Nancy, & Downing, Paul (1998). Separating the wheat from the chaff. *Science, 282,* 57–58.

Kaplan, Abraham (1967). A philosophical discussion of normality. *Archives of General Psychiatry, 17,* 325–330.

Kaplan, Meg S.; Morales, Miguel; & Becker, Judith V. (1993). The impact of verbal satiation of adolescent sex offenders: A preliminary report. *Journal of Child Sexual Abuse, 2,* 81–88.

Karasek, Robert, & Theorell, Tores (1990). *Healthy work: Stress, productivity, and the reconstruction of working life.* New York: Basic Books.

Karau, Steven J., & Williams, Kipling D. (1993). Social loafing: A meta-analytic review and theoretical integration. *Journal of Personality and Social Psychology, 65,* 681–706.

Karney, Benjamin R.; Bradbury, Thomas N.; Fincham, Frank D.; & Sullivan, Kieran T. (1994). The role of negative affectivity in the association between attributions and marital satisfaction. *Journal of Personality and Social Psychology, 66,* 413–424.

Karni, Avi; Tanne, David; Rubenstein, Barton S.; Askenasy, Jean J. M.; & Sagi, Dov (1994). Dependence on REM sleep of overnight improvement of a perceptual skill. *Science, 265,* 679–682.

Karraker, Katherine H.; Vogel, D. A.; & Lake, M. A. (1995). Parents' gender-stereotyped perceptions of newborns: The eye of the beholder revisited. *Sex Roles, 33,* 687–701.

Kashima, Yoshihisa; Yamaguchi, Susumu; Kim, Uichol; et al. (1995). Culture, gender, and self: A perspective from individualism–collectivism research. *Journal of Personality and Social Psychology, 69,* 925–937.

Kasser, Tim, & Ryan, Richard M. (1996). Further examining the American dream: Correlates of financial success as a central life aspiration. *Personality and Social Psychology Bulletin, 22,* 280–287.

Katigbak, Marcia S.; Church, A. Timothy; & Akamine, Toshio X. (1996). Cross-cultural generalizability of personality dimensions: Relating indigenous and imported dimensions in two cultures. *Journal of Personality and Social Psychology, 70,* 99–114.

Katz, Jonathan Ned (1995). *The invention of heterosexuality.* New York: Dutton.

Katz, Lilian G. (1993, Summer). All about me. *American Educator, 17*(2), 18–23.

Katz, Lori, & Epstein, Seymour (1991). Constructive thinking and coping with laboratory-induced stress. *Journal of Personality and Social Psychology, 61,* 789–800.

Katz, Phyllis A., & Ksansnak, Keith R. (1994). Developmental aspects of gender role flexibility and traditionality in middle childhood and adolescence. *Developmental Psychology, 30,* 272–282.

Katz, Stuart, & Lautenschlager, Gary J. (1994). Answering reading comprehension items without passages on the SAT-I, the ACT, and the GRE. *Educational Assessment, 2,* 295–308.

Kaufman, Joan, & Zigler, Edward (1987). Do abused children become abusive parents? *American Journal of Orthopsychiatry, 57,* 186–192.

Keane, M. M.; Gabrieli, J. D. E.; & Corkin, S. (1987). Multiple relations between fact-learning and priming in global amnesia. *Society for Neuroscience Abstracts, 13,* 1454.

Keating, Caroline F. (1994). World without words: Messages from face and body. In W. J. Lonner & R. Malpass (eds.), *Psychology and culture.* Needham Heights, MA: Allyn & Bacon.

Kelly, Anita E., & McKillop, Kevin J. (1996). Consequences of revealing personal secrets. *Psychological Bulletin, 120,* 450–465.

Kelly, Dennis (1981). Disorders of sleep and consciousness. In E. Kandel & J. Schwartz (eds.), *Principles of neural science.* New York: Elsevier-North Holland.

Kelman, Herbert C., & Hamilton, V. Lee (1989). *Crimes of obedience: Toward a social psychology of authority and responsibility.* New Haven, CT: Yale University Press.

Keltner, Dacher, & Buswell, Brenda N. (1997). Embarrassment: Its distinct form and appeasement functions. *Psychological Bulletin, 122,* 250–270.

Kempermann, G.; Brandon, E. P.; & Gage, F. H. (1998). Environmental stimulation of 120/SvJ mice causes increased cell proliferation and neurogenesis in the adult dentate gyrus. *Current Biology, 8,* 939–942.

Kendall [no first name] (1999). Women in Lesotho and the (Western) construction of homophobia. In E. Blackwood & S. E. Wieringa (eds.), *Female desires: Same-sex relations and transgender practices across cultures.* New York: Columbia University Press.

Kenny, Michael G. (1986). *The passion of Ansel Bourne: Multiple personality in American culture.* Washington, DC: Smithsonian Press.

Kenrick, Douglas T., & Trost, Melanie R. (1993). The evolutionary perspective. In A. E. Beall & R. J. Sternberg (eds.), *The psychology of gender.* New York: Guilford Press.

Kephart, William M. (1967). Some correlates of romantic love. *Journal of Marriage and the Family, 29,* 470–474.

Kerr, Michael E., & Bowen, Murray (1988). *Family evaluation: An approach based on Bowen theory.* New York: Norton.

Kerr, Norbert L. (1995). Norms in social dilemmas. In D. Schroeder (ed.), *Social dilemmas: Perspectives on individuals and groups.* Westport, CT: Praeger.

Kessler, Ronald C.; McGonagle, Katherine A.; Zhao, Shanyang; et al. (1994). Lifetime and 12-month prevalence of DSM-III-R psychiatric disorders in the United States: Results from the National Comorbidity Study. *Archives of General Psychiatry, 51,* 8–19.

Kessler, Ronald C.; Sonnega, A.; Bromet, E.; et al. (1995). Posttraumatic stress disorder in the National Comorbidity Survey. *Archives of General Psychiatry, 52,* 1048–1060.

Kiecolt-Glaser, Janice; Garner, Warren; Speicher, Carl; et al. (1985a). Psychosocial modifiers of immunocompetence in medical students. *Psychosomatic Medicine, 46,* 7–14.

Kiecolt-Glaser, Janice; Glaser, Ronald; Williger, D.; et al. (1985b). Psychosocial enhancement of immunocompetence in a geriatric population. *Health Psychology, 4,* 25–41.

Kiecolt-Glaser, Janice; Malarkey, William B.; Chee, MaryAnn; et al. (1993). Negative behavior during marital conflict is associated with immunological down-regulation. *Psychosomatic Medicine, 55,* 395–409.

Kiecolt-Glaser, Janice K.; Page, Gayle G.; Marucha, Phillip T.; et al. (1998). Psychological influences on surgical recovery: Perspectives from psychoneuroimmunology. *American Psychologist, 53,* 1209–1218.

Kihlstrom, John F. (1994). Hypnosis, delayed recall, and the principles of memory. *International Journal of Clinical and Experimental Hypnosis, 40,* 337–345.

Kihlstrom, John F. (1995). From a subject's point of view: The experiment as conversation and collaboration between investigator and subject. Invited address presented at the annual meeting of the American Psychological Society, New York.

Kihlstrom, John F. (1998). Dissociations and dissociation theory in hypnosis: Comment on Kirsch and Lynn (1998). *Psychological Bulletin, 123,* 186–191.

Kihlstrom, John F.; Barnhardt, Terrence M.; & Tataryn, Douglas J. (1992). The psychological unconscious: Found, lost, and regained. *American Psychologist, 47,* 788–791.

Kihlstrom, John F., & Harackiewicz, Judith M. (1982). The earliest recollection: A new survey. *Journal of Personality, 50,* 134–148.

Kim, Karl H. S.; Relkin, Norman R.; Lee, Kyoung-Min; & Hirsch, Joy (1997). Distinct cortical areas associated with native and second languages. *Nature, 388,* 171–174.

King, M., & Woollett, E. (1997). Sexually assaulted males: 115 men consulting a counseling service. *Archives of Sexual Behavior, 26,* 579–588.

King, Pamela (1989, October). The chemistry of doubt. *Psychology Today, 58,* 60.

King, Patricia M., & Kitchener, Karen S. (1994). *Developing reflective judgment: Understanding and promoting intellectual growth and critical thinking in adolescents and adults.* San Francisco: Jossey-Bass.

Kinsbourne, Marcel (1982). Hemispheric specialization and the growth of human understanding. *American Psychologist, 37,* 411–420.

Kinsey, Alfred C.; Pomeroy, Wardell B.; & Martin, Clyde E. (1948). *Sexual behavior in the human male.* Philadelphia: Saunders.

Kinsey, Alfred C.; Pomeroy, Wardell B.; Martin, Clyde E.; & Gebhard, Paul H. (1953). *Sexual behavior in the human female.* Philadelphia: Saunders.

Kirkpatrick, Lee A., & Davis, Keith A. (1994). Attachment style, gender, and relationship stability: A longitudinal analysis. *Journal of Personality and Social Psychology, 66,* 502–512.

Kirsch, Irving (1997). Response expectancy theory and application: A decennial review. *Applied and Preventive Psychology, 6,* 69–70.

Kirsch, Irving, & Lynn, Steven Jay (1995). The altered state of hypnosis: Changes in the theoretical landscape. *American Psychologist, 50,* 846–858.

Kirsch, Irving, & Lynn, Steven J. (1998). Dissociation theories of hypnosis. *Psychological Bulletin, 123,* 100–113.

Kirsch, Irving; Montgomery, G.; & Sapirstein, G. (1995). Hypnosis as an adjunct to cognitive behavioral psychotherapy: A meta-analysis. *Journal of Consulting and Clinical Psychology, 63,* 214–220.

Kirsch, Irving, & Sapirstein, Guy (1998). Listening to Prozac but hearing placebo: A meta-analysis of antidepressant medication. *Prevention & Treatment, 1,* Article 0002a, posted electronically June 26, 1998 on the website of the American Psychological Association.

Kirsch, Irving; Silva, Christopher E.; Carone, James E.; et al. (1989). The surreptitious observation design: An experimental paradigm for distinguishing artifact from essence in hypnosis. *Journal of Abnormal Psychology, 98,* 132–136.

Kirschenbaum, B.; Nedergaard, M.; Preuss, A.; et al. (1994). In vitro neuronal production and differentiation by precursor cells derived from the adult human forebrain. *Cerebral Cortex, 4,* 576–589.

Kitayama, Shinobu, & Markus, Hazel R. (1994). Introduction to cultural psychology and emotion research. In S. Kitayama & H. R. Markus (eds.), *Emotion and culture: Empirical studies of mutual influence.* Washington, DC: American Psychological Association.

Kitchener, Karen S., & King, Patricia M. (1990). The Reflective Judgment Model: Ten years of research. In M. L. Commons (ed.), *Models and methods in the study of adolescent and adult thought: Vol. 2. Adult development.* Westport, CT: Greenwood Press.

Kitchener, Karen S.; Lynch, Cindy L.; Fischer, Kurt W.; & Wood, Phillip K. (1993). Developmental range of reflective judgment: The effect of contextual support and practice on developmental stage. *Developmental Psychology, 29,* 893–906.

Kitzinger, Celia, & Wilkinson, Sue (1995). Transitions from heterosexuality to lesbianism: The discursive production of lesbian identities. *Developmental Psychology, 31,* 95–104.

Kleim, J. A.; Swain, R. A.; Armstrong, K. A.; et al. (1998). Selective synaptic plasticity within the cerebellar cortex following complex motor skill learning. *Neurobiology of Learning and Memory, 69,* 274–289.

Klein, Donald F. (1980). Psychosocial treatment of schizophrenia, or psychosocial help for people with schizophrenia? *Schizophrenia Bulletin, 6,* 122–130.

Klein, Raymond, & Armitage, Roseanne (1979). Rhythms in human performance: 12-hour oscillations in cognitive style. *Science, 204,* 1326–1328.

Klein, Stanley B., & Kihlstrom, John F. (1998). On bridging the gap between social-personality psychology and neuropsychology. *Personality and Social Psychology Review, 2,* 228–242.

Kleinke, Chris L.; Peterson, Thomas R.; & Rutledge, Thomas R. (1998). Effects of self-generated facial expressions on mood. *Journal of Personality and Social Psychology, 74,* 272–279.

Kleinman, Arthur (1988). *Rethinking psychiatry: From cultural category to personal experience.* New York: Free Press.

Kleinmuntz, Benjamin, & Szucko, Julian J. (1984, March 29). A field study of the fallibility of polygraph lie detection. *Nature, 308,* 449–450.

Klerman, Gerald L.; Weissman, Myrna M.; Rounsaville, Bruce J.; & Chevron, Eve S. (1984). *Interpersonal psychotherapy of depression.* New York: Basic Books.

Klima, Edward S., & Bellugi, Ursula (1966). Syntactic regularities in the speech of children. In J. Lyons & R. J. Wales (eds.), *Psycholinguistics papers.* Edinburgh, Scotland: Edinburgh University Press.

Klimoski, R. (1992). Graphology and personnel selection. In B. Beyerstein & D. Beyerstein (eds.), *The write stuff: Evaluations of graphology—the study of handwriting analysis.* Buffalo, NY: Prometheus Books.

Klohnen, Eva C., & Bera, Stephan (1998). Behavioral and experiential patterns of avoidantly and securely attached women across adulthood: A 31-year longitudinal perspective. *Journal of Personality and Social Psychology, 74,* 211–223.

Kluft, Richard P. (1987). The simulation and dissimulation of multiple personality disorder. *American Journal of Clinical Hypnosis, 30,* 104–118.

Kluft, Richard P. (1993). Multiple personality disorders. In D. Spiegel (ed.), *Dissociative disorders: A clinical review.* Lutherville, MD: Sidran.

Kluger, Richard (1996). *Ashes to ashes: America's hundred-year cigarette war, the public health, and the unabashed triumph of Philip Morris.* New York: Knopf.

Knight, Raymond A.; Prentky, Robert A.; & Cerce, David D. (1994). The development, reliability, and validity of an inventory for the multidimensional assessment of sex and aggression. *Criminal Justice and Behavior, 21,* 72–94.

Kohlberg, Lawrence (1964). Development of moral character and moral ideology. In M. Hoffman & L. W. Hoffman (eds.), *Review of child development research.* New York: Russell Sage Foundation.

Kohlberg, Lawrence (1976). Moral stages and moralization: The cognitive-developmental approach. In T. Lickona (ed.), *Moral development and behavior.* New York: Holt, Rinehart and Winston.

Kohlberg, Lawrence (1984). *Essays on moral development: Vol. 2. The psychology of moral development: The nature and validity of moral stages.* San Francisco: Harper & Row.

Köhler, Wolfgang (1925). *The mentality of apes.* New York: Harcourt, Brace.

Köhler, Wolfgang (1959). Gestalt psychology today. Presidential address to the American Psychological Association, Cincinnati. [Reprinted in E. R. Hilgard (ed.), *American psychology in historical perspective: Addresses of the presidents of the American Psychological Association, 1892–1977.* Washington, DC: American Psychological Association, 1978.]

Kohn, Alfie (1992). *No contest: The case against competition* (Rev. ed.). Boston: Houghton Mifflin.

Kohn, Alfie (1993). *Punished by rewards.* Boston: Houghton Mifflin.

Kohn, Melvin, & Schooler, Carmi (1983). *Work and personality: An inquiry into the impact of social stratification.* Norwood, NJ: Ablex.

Kohn, Paul M.; Lafreniere, Kathryn; & Gurevich, Maria (1991). Hassles, health, and personality. *Journal of Personality and Social Psychology, 61,* 478–482.

Kolb, B., & Whishaw, I. Q. (1998). Brain plasticity and behavior. *Annual Review of Psychology, 49,* 43–64.

Kolbert, Elizabeth (1995, June 5). Public opinion polls swerve with the turns of a phrase. *New York Times, 144,* A1.

Konishi, Masakazu (1993). Listening with two ears. *Scientific American, 268,* 66ff.

Koocher, Gerald P.; Goodman, Gail S.; White, C. Sue; et al. (1995). Psychological science and the use of anatomically detailed dolls in child sexual-abuse assessments. *Psychological Bulletin, 118,* 199–222.

Kopta, Stephen M.; Howard, Kenneth I.; Lowry, Jenny L.; & Beutler, Larry E. (1994). Patterns of symptomatic recovery in psychotherapy. *Journal of Consulting and Clinical Psychology, 62,* 1009–1016.

Korn, James H. (1998). *Illusions of reality: A history of deception in social psychology.* New York: State University of New York Press.

Koski, Lilah R., & Shaver, Phillip R. (1997). Attachment and relationship satisfaction across the lifespan. In R. J. Sternberg & M. Hojjat (eds.), *Satisfaction in close relationships.* New York: Guilford Press.

Koss, Mary P. (1993). Rape: Scope, impact, interventions, and public policy responses. *American Psychologist, 48,* 1062–1069.

Kosslyn, Stephen M. (1980). *Image and mind.* Cambridge, MA: Harvard University Press.

Kozak, Michael J.; Liebowitz, Michael R.; & Foa, Edna B. (2000). Cognitive-behavior therapy and pharmacotherapy for OCD: The NIMH-sponsored collaborative study. In W. K. Goodman, M. Rudorfer, & J. Maser (eds.), *Treatment challenges in obsessive compulsive disorder.* Mahwah, NJ: Erlbaum.

Krantz, David S., & Manuck, Stephen B. (1984). Acute psychophysiologic reactivity and risk of cardiovascular disease: A review and methodological critique. *Psychological Bulletin, 96,* 435–464.

Krieger, Nancy, & Sidney, S. (1996). Racial discrimination and blood pressure: The CARDIA study of young black and white adults. *American Journal of Public Health, 86,* 1370–1378.

Kring, Ann M., & Gordon, Albert H. (1998). Sex differences in emotion: Expression, experience, and physiology. *Journal of Personality and Social Psychology, 74,* 686–703.

Kripke, Daniel F. (1974). Ultradian rhythms in sleep and wakefulness. In E. D. Weitzman (ed.), *Advances in sleep research* (Vol. 1). Flushing, NY: Spectrum.

Kroll, Barry M. (1992). *Teaching hearts and minds: College students reflect on the Vietnam War in literature.* Carbondale: Southern Illinois University Press.

Krupa, David J.; Thompson, Judith K.; & Thompson, Richard F. (1993). Localization of a memory trace in the mammalian brain. *Science, 260,* 989–991.

Kuhl, Patricia K.; Andruski, Jean E.; Chistovich, Inna A.; et al. (1997, August 1). Cross-language analysis of phonetic units in language addressed to infants. *Science, 277,* 684–686.

Kuhl, Patricia K.; Williams, Karen A.; Lacerda, Francisco; et al. (1992, January 31). Linguistic experience alters phonetic perception in infants by 6 months of age. *Science, 255,* 606–608.

Kuhn, Deanna; Weinstock, Michael; & Flaton, Robin (1994). How well do jurors reason? Competence dimensions of individual variation in a juror reasoning task. *Psychological Science, 5,* 289–296.

Kunda, Ziva (1990). The case for motivated reasoning. *Psychological Bulletin, 108,* 480–498.

Kutchins, Herb, & Kirk, Stuart A. (1997). *Making us crazy: DSM—The psychiatric bible and the creation of mental disorders.* New York: Free Press.

LaBerge, Stephen (1986). *Lucid dreaming.* New York: Ballantine Books.

LaBerge, Stephen, & Levitan, Lynne (1995). Validity established of Dream-Light cues for eliciting lucid dreaming. *Dreaming: Journal of the Association for the Study of Dreams, 5,* 159–168.

Lachman, Margie E., & Weaver, Suzanne L. (1998). The sense of control as a moderator of social class differences in health and well-being. *Journal of Personality and Social Psychology, 74,* 763–773.

Lachman, Sheldon J. (1996). Processes in perception: Psychological transformations of highly structured stimulus material. *Perceptual and Motor Skills, 83,* 411–418.

Lader, Malcolm, & Morton, Sally (1991). Benzodiazepine problems. *British Journal of Addiction, 86,* 823–828.

LaFromboise, Teresa; Coleman, Hardin L. K.; & Gerton, Jennifer (1993). Psychological impact of biculturalism: Evidence and theory. *Psychological Bulletin, 114,* 395–412.

Laird, James D. (1974). Self-attribution of emotion: The effects of expressive behavior on the quality of emotional experience. *Journal of Personality and Social Psychology, 29,* 475–486.

Lakoff, Robin T. (1990). *Talking power.* New York: Basic Books.

Lakoff, Robin T., & Coyne, James C. (1993). *Father knows best: The use and abuse of power in Freud's case of "Dora."* New York: Teachers College Press.

Lambert, Michael J., & Bergin, Allen E. (1994). The effectiveness of psychotherapy. In A. E. Bergin & S. L. Garfield (eds.), *Handbook of psychotherapy and behavior change* (4th ed.). New York: Wiley.

Land, Edwin H. (1959). Experiments in color vision. *Scientific American, 200*(5), 84–94, 96, 99.

Landine, Jeffrey, & Stewart, John (1998). Relationship between metacognition, motivation, locus of control, self-efficacy, and academic achievement. *Canadian Journal of Counseling, 32,* 200–212.

Landrine, Hope (1988). Revising the framework of abnormal psychology. In P. Bronstein & K. Quina (eds.), *Teaching a psychology of people.* Washington, DC: American Psychological Association.

Lang, Peter (1995). The emotion probe: Studies of motivation and attention. *American Psychologist, 50,* 372–385.

Langer, Ellen J. (1983). *The psychology of control.* Beverly Hills, CA: Sage.

Langer, Ellen J. (1989). *Mindfulness.* Reading, MA: Addison-Wesley.

Langer, Ellen J.; Blank, Arthur; & Chanowitz, Benzion (1978). The mindlessness of ostensibly thoughtful action: The role of placebic information in interpersonal interaction. *Journal of Personality and Social Psychology, 36,* 635–642.

Latané, Bibb; Williams, Kipling; & Harkins, Stephen (1979). Many hands make light the work: The causes and consequences of social loafing. *Journal of Personality and Social Psychology, 37,* 822–832.

Laudenslager, Mark L. (1988). The psychology of loss: Lessons from humans and nonhuman primates. *Journal of Social Issues, 44,* 19–36.

Laumann, Edward O., & Gagnon John H. (1995). A sociological perspective on sexual action. In R. G. Parker & J. H. Gagnon (eds.), *Conceiving sexuality: Approaches to sex research in a postmodern world.* New York: Routledge.

Laumann, Edward O.; Gagnon, John H.; Michael, Robert T.; & Michaels, Stuart (1994). *The social organization of sexuality.* Chicago: University of Chicago Press.

Laurence, J. R., & Perry, C. (1988). *Hypnosis, will, and memory: A psycho-legal history.* New York: Guilford Press.

Laursen, Brett, & Collins, W. Andrew (1994). Interpersonal conflict during adolescence. *Psychological Bulletin, 115,* 197–209.

Lavie, Peretz (1976). Ultradian rhythms in the perception of two apparent motions. *Chronobiologia, 3,* 21–218.

Lavie, Peretz (1996). *The enchanted world of sleep* (Anthony Berris, trans.). New Haven, CT: Yale University Press.

Lazarus, Richard S. (1991). Cognition and motivation in emotion. *American Psychologist, 46,* 352–367.

Lazarus, Richard S., & Folkman, Susan (1984). *Stress, appraisal, and coping.* New York: Springer.

LeDoux, Joseph E. (1994, June). Emotion, memory, and the brain. *Scientific American, 220,* 50–57.

LeDoux, Joseph E. (1996). *The emotional brain.* New York: Simon & Schuster.

Lee, John Alan (1973). *The colours of love.* Ontario, Canada: New Press.

Lee, John Alan (1988). Love-styles. In R. J. Sternberg & M. L. Barnes (eds.), *The psychology of love.* New Haven, CT: Yale University Press.

Lee, Tatia M. C.; Blashko, Carl A.; Janzen, Henry L.; et al. (1997). Pathophysiological mechanism of seasonal affective disorder. *Journal of Affective Disorders, 46,* 25–38.

Lefcourt, Herbert M., & Martin, Rod A. (1986). *Humor and life stress.* New York: Springer-Verlag.

Lehman, Adam K., & Rodin, Judith (1989). Styles of self-nurturance and disordered eating. *Journal of Consulting and Clinical Psychology, 57,* 117–122.

Leibel, Rudolph L.; Rosenbaum, Michael; & Hirsch, Jules (1995). Changes in energy expenditure resulting from altered body weight. *New England Journal of Medicine, 332,* 621–628.

Lenneberg, Eric H. (1967). *Biological foundations of language.* New York: Wiley.

Lent, James R. (1968, June). Mimosa cottage: Experiment in hope. *Psychology Today,* 51–58.

Leonard, S.; Gault, J.; Moore, T.; et al. (1998, July 10). Further investigation of a chromosome 15 locus in schizophrenia: Analysis of affected sibpairs from the NIMH Genetics Initiative. *American Journal of Medical Genetics, 81,* 308–312.

Lepore, Stephen J. (1997). Expressive writing moderates the relation between intrusive thoughts and depressive symptoms. *Journal of Personality and Social Psychology, 73,* 1030–1037.

Lepore, Stephen J.; Silver, Roxanne C.; Wortman, Camille B.; & Wayment, Heidi A. (1996). Social constraints, intrusive thoughts, and depressive symptoms among bereaved mothers. *Journal of Personality and Social Psychology, 70,* 271–282.

Lepper, Mark R.; Greene, David; & Nisbett, Richard E. (1973). Undermining children's intrinsic interest with extrinsic rewards. *Journal of Personality and Social Psychology, 28,* 129–137.

Leproult, Rachel; Copinschi, Georges; Buxton, Orfeu; & Van Cauter, Eve (1997). Sleep loss results in an elevation of cortisol levels the next evening. *Sleep, 20,* 865–870.

Leproult, Rachel; Van Reeth, Olivier; Byrne, Maria M.; et al. (1997). Sleepiness, performance, and neuroendocrine function during sleep deprivation: Effects of exposure to bright light or exercise. *Journal of Biological Rhythms, 12,* 245–258.

Lerner, Harriet G. (1989). *The dance of intimacy.* New York: Harper & Row.

Lerner, Jennifer S.; Goldberg, Julie H.; & Tetlock, Philip E. (1998). Sober second thought: The effects of accountability, anger, and authoritarianism on attributions of responsibility. *Personality and Social Psychology Bulletin, 24,* 563–574.

Lerner, Melvin J. (1980). *The belief in a just world: A fundamental delusion.* New York: Plenum.

Lesch, Klaus-Peter; Bengel, Dietmar; Heils, Armin; et al. (1996). Association of anxiety-related traits with a polymorphism in the serotonin transporter gene regulatory region. *Science, 274,* 1527–1531.

Lester, Barry M.; LaGasse, Linda L.; & Seifer, Ronald (1998, October 23). Cocaine exposure and children: The meaning of subtle effects. *Science, 282,* 633–634.

LeVay, Simon (1991). A difference in hypothalamic structure between heterosexual and homosexual men. *Science, 253,* 1034–1037.

Levenson, Robert W. (1992). Autonomic nervous system differences among emotions. *Psychological Science, 3,* 23–27.

Levenson, Robert W.; Carstensen, Laura L.; & Gottman, John M. (1994). Influence of age and gender on affect, physiology, and their interrelations: A study of long-term marriages. *Journal of Personality & Social Psychology, 67,* 56–68.

Levenson, Robert W.; Ekman, Paul; & Friesen, Wallace V. (1990). Voluntary facial action generates emotion-specific autonomic nervous system activity. *Psychophysiology, 27,* 363–384.

Levenstein, Susan; Ackerman, S.; Kiecolt-Glaser, Janice K.; & Dubois, A. (1999, January 6). Stress and peptic ulcer disease. *Journal of the American Medical Association, 281,* 10–11.

Leventhal, Howard, & Nerenz, D. R. (1982). A model for stress research and some implications for the control of stress disorders. In D. Meichenbaum & M. Jaremko (eds.), *Stress prevention and management: A cognitive behavioral approach*. New York: Plenum.

Levine, Joseph, & Suzuki, David (1993). *The secret of life: Redesigning the living world*. Boston: WGBH Educational Foundation.

Levine, Robert V.; Martinez, Todd S.; Brase, Gary; & Sorenson, Kerry (1994). Helping in 36 U.S. cities. *Journal of Personality and Social Psychology, 67,* 69–82.

Levinson, D. F.; Mahtani, M. M.; Nancarrow, D. J.; et al. (1998). Genome scan of schizophrenia. *American Journal of Psychiatry, 155,* 741–750.

Levitan, Alexander A., & Ronan, William J. (1988). Problems in the treatment of obesity and eating disorders. *Medical Hypnoanalysis Journal, 3,* 131–136.

Levy, Becca (1996). Improving memory in old age through implicit self-stereotyping. *Journal of Personality and Social Psychology, 71,* 1092–1107.

Levy, David A. (1997). *Tools of critical thinking: Metathoughts for psychology*. Boston: Allyn & Bacon.

Levy, Jerre (1985, May). Right brain, left brain: Fact and fiction. *Psychology Today,* 38–39, 42–44.

Levy, Jerre; Trevarthen, Colwyn; & Sperry, Roger W. (1972). Perception of bilateral chimeric figures following hemispheric deconnection. *Brain, 95,* 61–78.

Levy, Kenneth N.; Blatt, Sidney J.; & Shaver, Phillip R. (1998). Attachment styles are parental representations. *Journal of Personality and Social Psychology, 74,* 407–419.

Levy, Robert I. (1984). The emotions in comparative perspective. In K. R. Scherer & P. Ekman (eds.), *Approaches to emotion*. Hillsdale, NJ: Erlbaum.

Lewin, Kurt (1948). *Resolving social conflicts*. New York: Harper.

Lewis, Dorothy O. (ed.) (1981). *Vulnerabilities to delinquency*. New York: Spectrum Medical and Scientific Books.

Lewis, Dorothy O. (1992). From abuse to violence: Psychophysiological consequences of maltreatment. *Journal of the American Academy of Child and Adolescent Psychiatry, 31,* 383–391.

Lewis, Helen B. (1971). *Shame and guilt in neurosis*. New York: International Universities Press.

Lewis, Michael (1997). *Altering fate: Why the past does not predict the future*. New York: Guilford Press.

Lewontin, Richard C. (1970). Race and intelligence. *Bulletin of the Atomic Scientists, 26*(3), 2–8.

Lewontin, Richard C.; Rose, Steven; & Kamin, Leon J. (1984). *Not in our genes: Biology, ideology, and human nature*. New York: Pantheon.

Lewy, Alfred J.; Ahmed, Saeeduddin; Jackson, Jeanne L.; & Sack, Robert L. (1992). Melatonin shifts human circadian rhythms according to a phase response curve. *Chronobiology International, 9,* 380–392.

Lewy, Alfred J.; Ahmed, Saeeduddin; & Sack, Robert L. (1995). Phase shifting the human circadian clock using melatonin. *Behavior and Brain Research, 73,* 131–134.

Lewy, Alfred J.; Bauer, Vance K.; Cutler, Neil L.; et al. (1998). Morning vs. evening light treatment of patients with winter depression. *Archives of General Psychiatry, 55,* 890–896.

Lewy, Alfred J., & Sack, Robert L. (1997). Exogenous melatonin's phase-shifting effects on the endogenous melatonin profile in sighted humans: A brief review and critique of the literature. *Journal of Biological Rhythms, 12,* 588–594.

Lichtenstein, Sarah; Slovic, Paul; Fischhoff, Baruch; et al. (1978). Judged frequency of lethal events. *Journal of Experimental Psychology: Human Learning and Memory, 4,* 551–578.

Lickona, Thomas (1983). *Raising good children*. New York: Bantam.

Lightdale, Jenifer R., & Prentice, Deborah A. (1994). Rethinking sex differences in aggression: Aggressive behavior in the absence of social roles. *Personality and Social Psychology Bulletin, 20,* 34–44.

Lilienfeld, Scott O. (1993, Fall). Do "honesty" tests really measure honesty? *Skeptical Inquirer, 18,* 32–41.

Lilienfeld, Scott O. (1996, January/February). EMDR treatment: Less than meets the eye? *Skeptical Inquirer,* 25–31.

Lilienfeld, Scott O. (1999, September/October). Projective measures of personality and psychopathology: How well do they work? *Skeptical Inquirer,* 32–39.

Lillard, Angeline (1998). Ethnopsychologies: Cultural variations in theories of mind. *Psychological Bulletin, 123,* 3–32.

Lin, Keh-Ming; Poland, Russell E.; & Chien, C. P. (1990). Ethnicity and psychopharmacology: Recent findings and future research directions. In E. Sorel (ed.), *Family, culture, and psychobiology*. New York: Legas.

Linday, Linda A. (1994). Maternal reports of pregnancy, genital, and related fantasies in preschool and kindergarten children. *Journal of the American Academy of Child and Adolescent Psychiatry, 33,* 416–423.

Lindsay, D. S., & Read, J. D. (1994). Psychotherapy and memories of childhood sexual abuse: A cognitive perspective. *Applied Cognitive Psychology, 8,* 281–338.

Lindvall, O.; Sawle, G.; Widner, H.; et al. (1994). Evidence for long-term survival and function of dopaminergic grafts in progressive Parkinson's disease. *Annals of Neurology, 35,* 172–180.

Linton, Marigold (1978). Real-world memory after six years: An in vivo study of very long-term memory. In M. M. Gruneberg, P. E. Morris, & R. N. Sykes (eds.), *Practical aspects of memory*. London: Academic Press.

Linton, Simi (1998). *Claiming disability: Knowledge and identity*. New York: New York University Press.

Linville, P. W.; Fischer, G. W.; & Fischhoff, B. (1992). AIDS risk perceptions and decision biases. In J. B. Pryor & G. D. Reeder (eds.), *The social psychology of HIV infection*. Hillsdale, NJ: Erlbaum.

Lipsey, Mark W., & Wilson, David B. (1993). The efficacy of psychological, educational, and behavioral treatment: Confirmation from meta-analysis. *American Psychologist, 48,* 1181–1209.

Lissner, L.; Odell, P. M.; D'Agostino, R. B.; et al. (1991, June 27). Variability of body weight and health outcomes in the Framingham population. *New England Journal of Medicine, 324* (26), 1839–1844.

Locher, R.; Suter, P. M.; & Vetter, W. (1998). Ethanol suppresses smooth muscle cell proliferation in the postprandial state: A new antiatherosclerotic mechanism of ethanol? *American Journal of Clinical Nutrition, 67,* 338–341.

Locke, Edwin A., & Latham, Gary P. (1990). Work motivation and satisfaction: Light at the end of the tunnel. *Psychological Science, 1,* 240–246.

Locke, Edwin A.; Shaw, Karyll; Saari, Lise; & Latham, Gary (1981). Goal-setting and task performance: 1969–1980. *Psychological Bulletin, 90,* 125–152.

Loehlin, John C. (1992). *Genes and environment in personality development*. Newbury Park, CA: Sage.

Loehlin, John C.; Horn, J. M.; & Willerman, L. (1996). Heredity, environment, and IQ in the Texas adoption study. In R. J. Sternberg & E. Grigorenko (eds.), *Intelligence: Heredity and environment*. New York: Cambridge University Press.

Loewen, E. Ruth; Shaw, Raymond J.; & Craik, Fergus I. (1990). Age differences in components of metamemory. *Experimental Aging Research, 16*(1–2), 43–48.

Loftus, Elizabeth F. (1980). *Memory*. Reading, MA: Addison-Wesley.

Loftus, Elizabeth F. (1996). Memory distortion and false memory creation. *Bulletin of the American Academy of Psychiatry and the Law, 24,* 281–295.

Loftus, Elizabeth F., & Greene, Edith (1980). Warning: Even memory for faces may be contagious. *Law and Human Behavior, 4*, 323–334.

Loftus, Elizabeth F., & Ketcham, Katherine (1994). *The myth of repressed memory.* New York: St. Martin's Press.

Loftus, Elizabeth F.; Miller, David G.; & Burns, Helen J. (1978). Semantic integration of verbal information into a visual memory. *Journal of Experimental Psychology: Human Learning and Memory, 4*, 19–31.

Loftus, Elizabeth F., & Palmer, John C. (1974). Reconstruction of automobile destruction: An example of the interaction between language and memory. *Journal of Verbal Learning and Verbal Behavior, 13*, 585–589.

Loftus, Elizabeth F., & Pickrell, Jacqueline E. (1995). The formation of false memories [Special issue on false memories]. *Psychiatric Annals, 25*, 720–725.

Loftus, Elizabeth F., & Zanni, Guido (1975). Eyewitness testimony: The influence of the wording of a question. *Bulletin of the Psychonomic Society, 5*, 86–88.

Lohr, Jeffrey M.; Kleinknecht, R. A.; Tolin, D. F.; & Barrett, R. H. (1995). The empirical status of the clinical application of eye movement desensitization and reprocessing. *Journal of Behavior Therapy and Experimental Psychiatry, 26*, 285–302.

Lohr, Jeffrey M.; Tolin, D. F.; & Lilienfeld, Scott O. (1998). Efficacy of eye movement desensitization and reprocessing: Implications for behavior therapy. *Behavior Therapy, 29*, 123–156.

Lonner, Walter J. (1995). Culture and human diversity. In E. Trickett, R. Watts, & D. Birman (eds.), *Human diversity: Perspectives on people in context.* San Francisco: Jossey-Bass.

López, Steven R. (1989). Patient variable biases in clinical judgment: Conceptual overview and methodological considerations. *Psychological Bulletin, 106*, 184–203.

López, Steven R. (1995). Testing ethnic minority children. In B. B. Wolman (ed.), *The encyclopedia of psychology, psychiatry, and psychoanalysis.* New York: Henry Holt.

Lott, Bernice (1997). The personal and social consequences of a gender difference ideology. *Journal of Social Issues, 53*, 279–298.

Lott, Bernice, & Maluso, Diane (1993). The social learning of gender. In A. E. Beall & R. J. Sternberg (eds.), *The psychology of gender.* New York: Guilford Press.

Louie, Therese A. (1999). Decision makers' hindsight bias after making favorable and unfavorable feedback. *Journal of Applied Psychology, 84*, 29–41.

Lovaas, O. Ivar (1977). *The autistic child: Language development through behavior modification.* New York: Halsted Press.

Lovaas, O. Ivar; Schreibman, Laura; & Koegel, Robert L. (1974). A behavior modification approach to the treatment of autistic children. *Journal of Autism and Childhood Schizophrenia, 4*, 111–129.

Lucchina, L. A.; Curtis, O. F.; Putnam, P.; et al. (1998). Psychophysical measurement of 6-n-propylthiouracil (PROP) taste perception. *Annals of the New York Academy of Sciences, 855*, 816–819.

Lucio, Emilia; Ampudia, Amada; Durán, Consuelo; & Leon, Ivonne (1998). Norms of the MMPI-2 for Mexican population. Paper presented at the annual meeting of the International Association for Cross-Cultural Psychology, Bellingham, WA.

Luengo, M. A.; Carrillo-de-la-Peña, M. T.; Otero, J. M.; & Romero, E. (1994). A short-term longitudinal study of impulsivity and antisocial behavior. *Journal of Personality and Social Psychology, 66*, 542–548.

Luepnitz, Deborah A. (1988). *The family interpreted: Feminist theory in clinical practice.* New York: Basic Books.

Lugaresi, Elio; Medori, R.; Montagna, P.; et al. (1986, October 16). Fatal familial insomnia and dysautonomia with selective degeneration of thalamic nuclei. *New England Journal of Medicine, 315*, 997–1003.

Luria, Alexander (1968). *The mind of a mnemonist* (L. Soltaroff, trans.). New York: Basic Books.

Luria, Alexander R. (1980). *Higher cortical functions in man* (Rev. ed.). New York: Basic Books.

Lutz, Catherine (1988). *Unnatural emotions.* Chicago: University of Chicago Press.

Lyketsos, C. G.; Hoover, D. R.; Guccione, M.; et al. (1993). Depressive symptoms as predictors of medical outcomes in HIV infection: Multicenter AIDS Cohort Study. *Journal of the American Medical Association, 270*, 2563–2567.

Lykken, David T. (1981). *A tremor in the blood: Uses and abuses of the lie detector.* New York: McGraw-Hill.

Lykken, David, & Tellegen, Auke (1996). Happiness is a stochastic phenomenon. *Psychological Science, 7*, 186–189.

Lynch, James J. (1985). *Language of the heart: The body's response to human dialogue.* New York: Basic Books.

Lynn, Steven Jay; Rhue, Judith W.; & Weekes, John R. (1990). Hypnotic involuntariness: A social cognitive analysis. *Psychological Review, 97*, 69–184.

Lytton, Hugh, & Romney, David M. (1991). Parents' differential socialization of boys and girls: A meta-analysis. *Psychological Bulletin, 109*, 267–296.

Lyubomirsky, Sonja; Caldwell, Nicole D.; & Nolen-Hoeksema, Susan (1998). Effects of ruminative and distracting responses to depressed mood on retrieval of autobiographical memories. *Journal of Personality and Social Psychology, 75*, 166–177.

Maas, James B. (1998). *Power sleep.* New York: Villard.

MacArthur Foundation Research Network on Successful Midlife Development (1999). *Report of latest findings.* Orville G. Brim, Director. 2145 14th Avenue, Vero Beach, FL 32960. [Also reported 2/16/99 in the *New York Times*, "New study finds middle age is prime of life," by Erica Goode, Health & Fitness section.]

Maccoby, Eleanor E. (1990). Gender and relationships: A developmental account. *American Psychologist, 45*, 513–520.

Maccoby, Eleanor E. (1998). *The two sexes: Growing up apart, coming together.* Cambridge, MA: Belknap Press/Harvard University Press.

MacKavey, William R.; Malley, Janet E.; & Stewart, Abigail, J. (1991). Remembering autobiographically consequential experiences: Content analysis of psychologists' accounts of their lives. *Psychology and Aging, 6*, 50–59.

MacKinnon, Donald W. (1962). The nature and nurture of creative talent. *American Psychologist, 17*, 484–495.

MacKinnon, Donald W. (1968). Selecting students with creative potential. In P. Heist (ed.), *The creative college student: An unmet challenge.* San Francisco: Jossey-Bass.

MacLean, Paul (1993). Cerebral evolution of emotion. In M. Lewis & J. M. Haviland (eds.), *Handbook of emotions.* New York: Guilford Press.

Macrae, C. Neil; Milne, Alan B.; & Bodenhausen, Galen V. (1994). Stereotypes as energy-saving devices: A peek inside the cognitive toolbox. *Journal of Personality and Social Psychology, 66*, 37–47.

Maddux, James E. (1993, Summer). The mythology of psychopathology: A social cognitive view of deviance, difference, and disorder. *General Psychologist, 29*, 34–45.

Maddux, James E. (ed.) (1995). *Self-efficacy, adaptation, and adjustment: Theory, research, and application.* New York: Plenum.

Maddux, James E. (1996). The social-cognitive construction of difference and disorder. In D. F. Barone, J. E. Maddux, & C. R. Snyder (eds.), *Social cognitive psychology: History and current domains.* New York: Plenum.

Maddux, James E., & Mundell, Clare E. (1997). Disorders of personality. In V. Derlega, B. Winstead, & W. Jones (eds.), *Personality: Contemporary theory and research* (2nd ed.). Chicago: Nelson-Hall.

Maffei, M.; Halaas, J.; Ravussin, E.; et al. (1995). Leptin levels in human and rodent: Measurement of plasma leptin and ob RNA in obese and weight-reduced subjects. *Nature Medicine, 1,* 1155–1161.

Major, Brenda; Spencer, Steven; Schmader, Toni; et al. (1998). Coping with negative stereotypes about intellectual performance: The role of psychological disengagement. *Personality and Social Psychology Bulletin, 24,* 34–50.

Malamuth, Neil M., & Dean, Karol (1990). Attraction to sexual aggression. In A. Parrot & L. Bechhofer (eds.), *Acquaintance rape: The hidden crime.* Newark, NJ: Wiley.

Malamuth, Neil M.; Linz, Daniel; Heavey, Christopher L.; et al. (1995). Using the confluence model of sexual aggression to predict men's conflict with women: A 10-year follow-up study. *Journal of Personality and Social Psychology, 69,* 353–369.

Malarkey, William B.; Kiecolt-Glaser, Janice K.; Pearl, Dennis; & Glaser, Ronald (1994). Hostile behavior during marital conflict alters pituitary and adrenal hormones. *Psychosomatic Medicine, 56,* 41–51.

Malatesta, Carol Z. (1990). The role of emotions in the development and organization of personality. In R. A. Thompson et al. (eds.), *Nebraska Symposium on Motivation, 1988.* Lincoln: University of Nebraska Press.

Malgady, Robert G.; Rogler, Lloyd; & Costantino, Giuseppe (1987). Ethnocultural and linguistic bias in mental health evaluation of Hispanics. *American Psychologist, 42,* 228–234.

Maling, Michael S., & Howard, Kenneth I. (1994). From research to practice to research to . . . . In P. F. Talley, H. H. Strupp, & S. F. Butler (eds.), *Psychotherapy research and practice: Bridging the gap.* New York: Basic Books.

Malinosky-Rummell, Robin, & Hansen, David J. (1993). Long-term consequences of childhood physical abuse. *Psychological Bulletin, 114,* 68–79.

Malnic, B.; Hirono, J.; Sato, T.; & Buck, L. B. (1999). Combinatorial receptor codes for odors. *Cell, 96,* 713–723.

Manning, Carol A.; Hall, J. L.; & Gold, Paul E. (1990). Glucose effects on memory and other neuropsychological tests in elderly humans. *Psychological Science, 1,* 307–311.

Manning, Carol A.; Ragozzino, Michael E.; & Gold, Paul E. (1993). Glucose enhancement of memory in patients with probable senile dementia of the Alzheimer's type. *Neurobiology of Aging, 14,* 523–528.

Mansfield, Elizabeth D., & McAdams, Dan P. (1996). Generativity and themes of agency and community in adult autobiography. *Personality and Social Psychology Bulletin, 22,* 721–731.

Marcus, Gary F. (1999). *The algebraic mind.* Cambridge, MA: MIT Press.

Marcus, Gary F.; Pinker, Steven; Ullman, Michael; et al. (1992). Overregularization in language acquisition. *Monographs of the Society for Research in Child Development, 57* (Serial No. 228), 1–182.

Marcus, G. F.; Vijayan, S.; Rao, S. Bandi; & Vishton, P. M. (1999, January 1). Rule learning by seven-month-old infants. *Science, 283,* 77–79.

Margo, Geoffrey M.; Greenberg, Roger P.; Fisher, Seymour; & Dewan, Mantosh (1993). A direct comparison of the defense mechanisms of non-depressed people and depressed psychiatric inpatients. *Comprehensive Psychiatry, 34,* 65–69.

Marino, Raul, Jr., & Cosgrove, G. Rees (1997). Neurosurgical treatment of neuropsychiatric illness. *Psychiatric Clinics of North America, 20,* 933–943.

Markowitz, Laura M. (1993, July/August). Walking the walk. *Family Therapy Networker,* 19–31.

Markus, Hazel R., & Kitayama, Shinobu (1991). Culture and the self: Implications for cognition, emotion, and motivation. *Psychological Review, 98,* 224–253.

Marlatt, G. Alan (1996). Models of relapse and relapse prevention: A commentary. *Experimental and Clinical Psychopharmacology, 4,* 55–60.

Marlatt, G. Alan; Larimer, Mary E.; Baer, John S.; & Quigley, Lori A. (1993). Harm reduction for alcohol problems: Moving beyond the controlled drinking controversy. *Behavior Therapy, 24,* 461–503.

Marlatt, G. Alan, & Rohsenow, Damaris J. (1980). Cognitive processes in alcohol use: Expectancy and the balanced placebo design. In N. K. Mello (ed.), *Advances in substance abuse* (Vol. 1). Greenwich, CT: JAI Press.

Marriott, Bernadette M. (ed.) (1994). *Food components to enhance performance.* Washington, DC: National Academy Press.

Marshall, Grant N.; Wortman, Camille B.; Vickers, Ross R., Jr.; et al. (1994). The five-factor model of personality as a framework for personality health research. *Journal of Personality and Social Psychology, 67,* 278–286.

Martin, Rod A., & Dobbin, James P. (1988). Sense of humor, hassles, and immunoglobulin A: Evidence for a stress-moderating effect of humor. *International Journal of Psychiatry in Medicine, 18,* 93–105.

Martin, Stacia K., & Eastman, Charmane I. (1998). Medium-intensity light produces circadian rhythm adaption to simulated night-shift work. *Sleep, 21,* 154–165.

Maslow, Abraham H. (1970). *Motivation and personality* (2nd ed.). New York: Harper & Row.

Maslow, Abraham H. (1971). *The farther reaches of human nature.* New York: Viking.

Masten, Ann S., & Coatsworth, J. Douglas (1998). The development of competence in favorable and unfavorable environments. *American Psychologist, 53,* 205–220.

Masters, William H., & Johnson, Virginia E. (1966). *Human sexual response.* Boston: Little, Brown.

Matarazzo, Joseph (1984). Behavioral immunogens and pathogens in health and illness. In B. L. Hammonds & C. J. Scheirer (eds.), *Psychology and health: The master lecture series* (Vol. 3). Washington, DC: American Psychological Association.

Matsumoto, David (1996). *Culture and psychology.* Pacific Grove, CA: Brooks-Cole.

Matthews, John (ed.) (1994). *McGill working papers in linguistics* (Vol. 10 [1&2]) [Special issue: Linguistic aspects of familial language impairment]. Montreal, Quebec: McGill University.

Matthews, Karen A.; Wing, Rena R.; Kuller, Lewis H.; et al. (1990). Influences of natural menopause on psychological characteristics and symptoms of middle-aged healthy women. *Journal of Consulting and Clinical Psychology, 58,* 345–351.

Mawhinney, T. C. (1990). Decreasing intrinsic "motivation" with extrinsic rewards: Easier said than done. *Journal of Organizational Behavior Management, 11,* 175–191.

Maxfield, Michael, & Widom, Cathy S. (1996). The cycle of violence: Revisited 6 years later. *Archives of Pediatric and Adolescent Medicine, 150,* 390–395.

Mayer, John D.; McCormick, Laura J.; & Strong, Sara E. (1995). Mood-congruent memory and natural mood: New evidence. *Personality and Social Psychology Bulletin, 21,* 736–746.

Mayer, John D., & Salovey, Peter (1997). What is emotional intelligence? In P. Salovey & D. Sluyter (eds.), *Emotional development and emotional intelligence: Implications for educators.* New York: Basic Books.

Mazur, Allen, & Lamb, Theodore A. (1980). Testosterone, status, and mood in human males. *Hormones and Behavior, 14,* 236–246.

Mazza, James J.; Reynolds, William M.; & Grover, Jennifer H. (1995). Exposure to violence, suicidal ideation and depression in school-based adolescents. Paper presented at the annual meeting of the American Psychological Association, New York.

Mazzoni, Guiliana A. L.; Loftus, Elizabeth F.; Seitz, Aaron; & Lynn, Steven J. (1999). Changing beliefs and memories through dream interpretation. *Applied Cognitive Psychology, 13*, 125–144.

McAdams, Dan P. (1988). *Power, intimacy, and the life story: Personological inquiries into identity.* New York: Guilford Press.

McClearn, Gerald E.; Johanson, Boo; Berg, Stig; et al. (1997). Substantial genetic influence on cognitive abilities in twins 80 or more years old. *Science, 176*, 1560–1563.

McClelland, David C. (1961). *The achieving society.* New York: Free Press.

McClelland, David C. (1975). *Power: The inner experience.* New York: Irvington.

McClelland, David C. (1985). *Human motivation.* Glenview, IL: Scott, Foresman.

McClelland, David C. (1987). Characteristics of successful entrepreneurs. *Journal of Creative Behavior, 3*, 219–233.

McClelland, David C.; Atkinson, John W.; Clark, Russell A.; & Lowell, Edgar L. (1953). *The achievement motive.* New York: Appleton-Century-Crofts.

McClelland, James L. (1994). The organization of memory: A parallel distributed processing perspective. *Revue Neurologique, 150*, 570–579.

McClintock, Martha K., & Herdt, Gilbert (1996). Rethinking puberty: The development of sexual attraction. *Current Directions in Psychological Science, 6*, 178–183.

McConnell, James V. (1962). Memory transfer through cannibalism in planarians. *Journal of Neuropsychiatry, 3* (Monograph Supplement 1).

McCord, Joan (1989). Another time, another drug. Paper presented at the conference, Vulnerability to the Transition from Drug Use to Abuse and Dependence, Rockville, MD.

McCord, Joan (1992). The Cambridge–Somerville study: A pioneering longitudinal-experimental study of delinquency prevention. In J. McCord & R. E. Tremblay (eds.), *Preventing antisocial behavior: Interventions from birth through adolescence.* New York: Guilford Press.

McCrae, Robert R. (1987). Creativity, divergent thinking, and openness to experience. *Journal of Personality and Social Psychology, 52*, 1258–1265.

McCrae, Robert R., & Costa, Paul T., Jr. (1988). Do parental influences matter? A reply to Halverson. *Journal of Personality, 56*, 445–449.

McCrae, Robert R., & Costa, Paul T., Jr. (1996). Toward a new generation of personality theories: Theoretical contexts for the five-factor model. In J. S. Wiggins (ed.), *The five-factor model of personality: Theoretical perspectives.* New York: Guilford Press.

McCrae, Robert R., & Costa, Paul T., Jr. (1997). Personality trait structure as a human universal. *American Psychologist, 52*, 509–516.

McCrae, Robert R.; Costa, Paul T., Jr.; de Lima, Margarida Pedroso; et al. (1999). Age differences in personality across the adult life span: Parallels in five cultures. *Developmental Psychology, 35*, 466–477.

McDonald, Kim A. (1998, August 14). Scientists consider new explanations for the impact of exercise on mood. *Chronicle of Higher Education,* A15–A16.

McDonough, Laraine, & Mandler, Jean M. (1994). Very long-term recall in infancy. *Memory, 2*, 339–352.

McEwen, Bruce S. (1983). Gonadal steroid influences on brain development and sexual differentiation. *Reproductive Physiology IV (International Review of Physiology), 27*, 99–145.

McFarland, Cathy, & Buehler, Roger (1998). The impact of negative affect on autobiographical memory: The role of self-focused attention to moods. *Journal of Personality and Social Psychology, 75*, 1424–1440.

McFarlane, Jessica M.; Martin, Carol L.; & Williams, Tannis M. (1988). Mood fluctuations: Women versus men and menstrual versus other cycles. *Psychology of Women Quarterly, 12*, 201–223.

McFarlane, Jessica M., & Williams, Tannis M. (1994). Placing premenstrual syndrome in perspective. *Psychology of Women Quarterly, 18*, 339–373.

McGaugh, James L. (1990). Significance and remembrance: The role of neuromodulatory systems. *Psychological Science, 1*, 15–25.

McGaugh, James L. (1999). Making memories that linger: Emotional arousal, stress hormones and brain systems. Invited address at the annual meeting of the Western Psychological Association, Irvine.

McGinnis, Michael, & Foege, William (1993, November 10). Actual causes of death in the United States. *Journal of the American Medical Association, 270*, 2207–2212.

McGlone, Jeannette (1978). Sex differences in functional brain asymmetry. *Cortex, 14*, 122–128.

McGlynn, Susan M. (1990). Behavioral approaches to neuropsychological rehabilitation. *Psychological Bulletin, 108*, 420–441.

McGoldrick, Monica, & Gerson, Randy (1985). *Genograms in family assessment.* New York: Norton.

McGoldrick, Monica, & Pearce, John K. (1996). Family therapy with Irish Americans. In M. McGoldrick, J. Giordano, & J. K. Pearce (eds.), *Ethnicity and family therapy* (2nd ed.). New York: Guilford Press.

McGrath, Ellen; Keita, Gwendolyn P.; Strickland, Bonnie; & Russo, Nancy F. (eds.) (1990). *Women and depression: Risk factors and treatment issues.* Washington, DC: American Psychological Association.

McGregor, Ian, & Holmes, John G. (1999). How storytelling shapes memory and impressions of relationship events over time. *Journal of Personality and Social Psychology, 76*, 403–419.

McGregor, Ian, & Little, Brian R. (1998). Personal projects, happiness, and meaning: On doing well and being yourself. *Journal of Personality and Social Psychology, 74*, 494–512.

McGue, Matt; Bouchard, Thomas J., Jr.; Iacono, William G.; & Lykken, David T. (1993). Behavioral genetics of cognitive ability: A life-span perspective. In R. Plomin & G. E. McClearn (eds.), *Nature, nurture, and psychology.* Washington, DC: American Psychological Association.

McGue, Matt, & Lykken, David T. (1992). Genetic influence on risk of divorce. *Psychological Science, 3*, 368–373.

McGue, Matt; Pickens, Roy W.; & Svikis, Dace S. (1992). Sex and age effects on the inheritance of alcohol problems: A twin study. *Journal of Abnormal Psychology, 101*, 3–17.

McHugh, Paul R. (1993a). History and the pitfalls of practice. Unpublished manuscript, Johns Hopkins University.

McHugh, Paul R. (1993b, December). Psychotherapy awry. *American Scholar,* 17–30.

McKee, Richard D., & Squire, Larry R. (1992). Equivalent forgetting rates in long-term memory for diencephalic and medial temporal lobe amnesia. *Journal of Neuroscience, 12*, 3765–3772.

McKee, Richard D., & Squire, Larry R. (1993). On the development of declarative memory. *Journal of Experimental Psychology: Learning, Memory, and Cognition, 19*, 397–404.

McKim, Margaret K.; Cramer, Kenneth M.; Stuart, Barbara; & O'Connor, Deborah L. (1999). Infant care decisions and attachment security: The Canadian Transition to Child Care Study. *Canadian Journal of Behavioural Science, 31*, 92–106.

McKinlay, John B.; McKinlay, Sonja M.; & Brambilla, Donald (1987). The relative contributions of endocrine changes and social circumstances to depression in mid-aged women. *Journal of Health and Social Behavior, 28*, 345–363.

McLeod, Beverly (1985, March). Real work for real pay. *Psychology Today,* 42–44, 46, 48–50.

McNally, Richard J. (1994). *Panic disorder: A critical analysis.* New York: Guilford Press.

McNally, Richard J. (1996). Cognitive bias in the anxiety disorders. In D. A. Hope et al. (eds.), *Nebraska Symposium on Motivation, 1995: Perspectives on anxiety, panic, and fear.* Lincoln: University of Nebraska Press.

McNally, Richard J. (1998). Panic attacks. In *Encyclopedia of mental health* (Vol. 3). New York: Academic Press.

McNaughton, B. L., & Morris, R. G. M. (1987). Hippocampal synaptic enhancement and information storage within a distributed memory system. *Trends in Neuroscience, 10*, 408–415.

McNeill, David (1966). Developmental psycholinguistics. In F. L. Smith & G. A. Miller (eds.), *The genesis of language: A psycholinguistic approach.* Cambridge, MA: MIT Press.

Mealey, Linda (1996). Evolutionary psychology: The search for evolved mental mechanisms underlying complex human behavior. In J. P. Hurd (ed.), *Investigating the biological foundations of human morality* (Vol. 37). Lewiston, NY: Edwin Mellen Press.

Medawar, Peter B. (1979). *Advice to a young scientist.* New York: Harper & Row.

Medawar, Peter B. (1982). *Pluto's republic.* Oxford, England: Oxford University Press.

Mednick, Martha T. (1989). On the politics of psychological constructs: Stop the bandwagon, I want to get off. *American Psychologist, 44*, 1118–1123.

Mednick, Sarnoff A. (1962). The associative basis of the creative process. *Psychological Review, 69*, 220–232.

Mednick, Sarnoff A.; Huttunen, Matti O.; & Machón, Ricardo (1994). Prenatal influenza infections and adult schizophrenia. *Schizophrenia Bulletin, 20*, 263–267.

Mednick, Sarnoff A.; Parnas, Josef; & Schulsinger, Fini (1987). The Copenhagen High-Risk Project, 1962–86. *Schizophrenia Bulletin, 13*, 485–495.

Medvec, Victoria H.; Madey, Scott F.; & Gilovich, Thomas (1995). When less is more: Counterfactual thinking and satisfaction among Olympic medalists. *Journal of Personality and Social Psychology, 69*, 603–610.

Meeus, Wim H. J., & Raaijmakers, Quinten A. W. (1995). Obedience in modern society: The Utrecht studies. In A. G. Miller, B. E. Collins, & D. E. Brief (eds.), *Perspectives on obedience to authority: The legacy of the Milgram experiments. Journal of Social Issues, 51*(3), 155–175.

Meindl, J. R., & Lerner, M. J. (1985). Exacerbation of extreme responses to an out-group. *Journal of Personality and Social Psychology, 47*, 71–84.

Meltzoff, Andrew N., & Gopnik, Alison (1993). The role of imitation in understanding persons and developing a theory of mind. In S. Baron-Cohen, H. Tager-Flusberg, & D. Cohen (eds.), *Understanding other minds.* New York: Oxford University Press.

Melzack, Ronald (1973). *The puzzle of pain.* New York: Basic Books.

Melzack, Ronald (1992, April). Phantom limbs. *Scientific American, 266*, 120–126. [Reprinted, Special issue, "Mysteries of the Mind," 1997.]

Melzack, Ronald (1993). Pain: Past, present and future. *Canadian Journal of Experimental Psychology, 47*, 615–629.

Melzack, Ronald; Israel, R.; Lacroix, R.; & Schultz, G. (1997). Phantom limbs in people with congenital limb deficiency or amputation in early childhood. *Brain, 120*, 1603–1620.

Melzack, Ronald, & Wall, Patrick D. (1965). Pain mechanisms: A new theory. *Science, 13*, 971–979.

Mendes de Leon, C. F.; Krumholz, H. M.; Seeman, T. S.; et al. (1998). Depression and risk of coronary heart disease in elderly men and women: New Haven EPESE, 1982–1991. Established populations for the epidemiologic studies of the elderly. *Archives of Internal Medicine, 158*, 2341–2348.

Mercer, Jane (1988, May 18). Racial differences in intelligence: Fact or artifact? Talk presented at San Bernardino Valley College, San Bernardino, CA.

Merikle, Philip M., & Skanes, Heather E. (1992). Subliminal self-help audiotapes: A search for placebo effects. *Journal of Applied Psychology, 77*, 772–776.

Merrill, L. L.; Newell, C. E.; Milner, J. S.; Koss, M. P.; et al. (1998). Prevalence of premilitary adult sexual victimization and aggression in a Navy recruit sample. *Military Medicine, 163*, 209–212.

Merskey, Harold (1992). The manufacture of personalities: The production of MPD. *British Journal of Psychiatry, 160*, 327–340.

Merskey, Harold (1995). The manufacture of personalities: The production of multiple personality disorder. In L. M. Cohen, J. N. Berzoff, & M. R. Elin (eds.), *Dissociative identity disorder: Theoretical and treatment controversies.* Northvale, NJ: Jason Aronson.

Merton, Robert K. (1948). The self-fulfilling prophecy. *Antioch Review, 8*, 193–210.

Mesquita, Batja, & Frijda, Nico H. (1992). Cultural variations in emotions: A review. *Psychological Bulletin, 112*, 179–204.

Metalsky, Gerald I.; Joiner, Thomas E., Jr.; Hardin, Tammy S.; & Abramson, Lyn Y. (1993). Depressive reactions to failure in a naturalistic setting: A test of the hopelessness and self-esteem theories of depression. *Journal of Abnormal Psychology, 102*, 101–109.

Meyer-Bahlburg, Heino F. L.; Ehrhardt, Anke A.; Rosen, Laura R.; et al. (1995). Prenatal estrogens and the development of homosexual orientation. *Developmental Psychology, 31*, 12–21.

Mickelson, Kristin D.; Kessler, Ronald C.; & Shaver, Phillip R. (1997). Adult attachment in a nationally representative sample. *Journal of Personality and Social Psychology, 73*, 1092–1106.

Milgram, Stanley (1963). Behavioral study of obedience. *Journal of Abnormal and Social Psychology, 67*, 371–378.

Milgram, Stanley (1974). *Obedience to authority: An experimental view.* New York: Harper & Row.

Miller, George A. (1956). The magical number seven, plus or minus two: Some limits on our capacity for processing information. *Psychological Review, 63*, 81–97.

Miller, George A. (1969, December). On turning psychology over to the unwashed. *Psychology Today*, 53–55, 66–68, 70, 72, 74.

Miller, Inglis J., & Reedy, Frank E. (1990). Variations in human taste bud density and taste intensity perception. *Physiology and Behavior, 47*, 1213–1219.

Miller, J. G.; Bersoff, D. M.; & Harwood, R. L. (1990). Perceptions of social responsibilities in India and in the United States: Moral imperatives or personal decisions? *Journal of Personality and Social Psychology, 58*, 33–47.

Miller, Neal E. (1978). Biofeedback and visceral learning. *Annual Review of Psychology, 29*, 421–452.

Miller, Neal E. (1985). The value of behavioral research on animals. *American Psychologist, 40*, 423–440.

Miller, Paul A., & Eisenberg, Nancy (1988). The relation of empathy to aggressive and externalizing/antisocial behavior. *Psychological Bulletin, 103*, 324–344.

Miller, Scott D., & Triggiano, Patrick J. (1992). The psychophysiological investigation of multiple personality disorder: Review and update. *American Journal of Clinical Hypnosis, 35*, 47–61.

Miller, Todd Q.; Smith, Timothy W.; Turner, Charles W.; et al. (1996). A meta-analytic review of research on hostility and physical health. *Psychological Bulletin, 119*, 322–348.

Miller-Jones, Dalton (1989). Culture and testing. *American Psychologist, 44*, 360–366.

Milner, Brenda (1970). Memory and the temporal regions of the brain. In K. H. Pribram & D. E. Broadbent (eds.), *Biology of memory.* New York: Academic Press.

Milner, J. S., & McCanne, T. R. (1991). Neuropsychological correlates of physical child abuse. In J. S. Milner (ed.), *Neuropsychology of aggression*. Norwell, MA: Kluwer Academic.

Milton, Julie, & Wiseman, Richard (1999). Does psi exist? Lack of replication of an anomalous process of information transfer. *Psychological Bulletin, 125*, 387–391.

Minuchin, Salvador (1984). *Family kaleidoscope*. Cambridge, MA: Harvard University Press.

Mischel, Walter (1973). Toward a cognitive social learning reconceptualization of personality. *Psychological Review, 80*, 252–253.

Mischel, Walter, & Shoda, Yuichi (1995). A cognitive affective system theory of personality: Reconceptualizing situations, dispositions, dynamics, and invariance in personality structures. *Psychological Review, 102*, 246–268.

Mishkin, Mortimer, & Appenzeller, Tim (1987). The anatomy of memory. *Scientific American, 256*, 80–89.

Mishkin, M.; Suzuki, W. A.; Gadian, D. G.; & Vargha-Khadem, F. (1997). Hierarchical organization of cognitive memory. *Philosophical Transactions of the Royal Society of London, B: Biological Science, 352*, 1461–1467.

Mistry, Jayanthi, & Rogoff, Barbara (1994). Remembering in cultural context. In W. J. Lonner & R. Malpass (eds.), *Psychology and culture*. Needham Heights, MA: Allyn & Bacon.

Mitchell, Valory, & Helson, Ravenna (1990). Women's prime of life: Is it the 50s? *Psychology of Women Quarterly, 14*, 451–470.

Mithers, Carol L. (1994). *Reasonable insanity: A true story of the seventies*. Reading, MA: Addison-Wesley.

Modigliani, Andre, & Rochat, François (1995). The role of interaction sequences and the timing of resistance in shaping obedience and defiance to authority. In A. G. Miller, B. E. Collins, & D. E. Brief (eds.), *Perspectives on obedience to authority: The legacy of the Milgram experiments. Journal of Social Issues, 51*(3), 107–125.

Moffitt, Terrie E. (1993). Adolescence-limited and life-course-persistent antisocial behavior: A developmental taxonomy. *Psychological Review, 100*, 674–701.

Moghaddam, Bita, & Adams, Barbara W. (1998, August 28). Reversal of phencyclidine effects by a group II metabotropic glutamate receptor agonist in rats. *Science, 281*, 1349–1352.

Montagner, Hubert (1985). Approche ethologique des systems à interaction du nouveau né et du jeune enfant. [An ethological approach of the interaction systems of the infant and the young child.] *Neuropsychiatrie de l'Enfance et de l'Adolescence, 33*, 59–71.

Monteith, Margo J. (1996). Contemporary forms of prejudice-related conflict: In search of a nutshell. *Personality and Social Psychology Bulletin, 22*, 461–473.

Moore, Robert Y. (1997). Circadian rhythms: Basic neurobiology and clinical applications. *Annual Review of Medicine, 48*, 253–266.

Moore, Timothy E. (1992, Spring). Subliminal perception: Facts and fallacies. *Skeptical Inquirer, 16*, 273–281.

Moore, Timothy E. (1995). Subliminal self-help auditory tapes: An empirical test of perceptual consequences. *Canadian Journal of Behavioural Science, 27*, 9–20.

Moore, Timothy E., & Pepler, Debra J. (1998). Correlates of adjustment in children at risk. In G. W. Holden, R. Geffner, et al. (eds.), *Children exposed to marital violence: Theory, research, and applied issues*. Washington, DC: American Psychological Association.

Moorhead, Gregory; Ference, Richard; & Neck, Chris P. (1991). Group decision fiascoes continue: Space shuttle *Challenger* and a revised groupthink framework. *Human Relations, 44*, 539–550.

Morelli, Gilda A.; Rogoff, Barbara; Oppenheim, David; & Goldsmith, Denise (1992). Cultural variation in infants' sleeping arrangements: Questions of independence. *Developmental Psychology, 28*, 604–613.

Morris, Michael W., & Peng, Kaiping (1994). Culture and cause: American and Chinese attributions for social and physical events. *Journal of Personality and Social Psychology, 67*, 949–971.

Morrison, John H., & Hof, Patrick R. (1997, October 17). Life and death of neurons in the aging brain. *Science, 278*, 412–419.

Moscovici, Serge (1985). Social influence and conformity. In G. Lindzey & E. Aronson (eds.), *Handbook of social psychology* (Vol. 2, 3rd ed.). New York: Random House.

Moscovitch, Morris; Winocur, Gordon; & Behrmann, Marlene (1997). What is special about face recognition? Nineteen experiments on a person with visual object agnosia and dyslexia but normal face recognition. *Journal of Cognitive Neuroscience, 9*, 555–604.

Mozell, Maxwell M.; Smith, Bruce P.; Smith, Paul E.; et al. (1969). Nasal chemoreception in flavor identification. *Archives of Otolaryngology, 90*, 367–373.

Mroczek, Daniel K., & Kolarz, Christian M. (1998). The effect of age on positive and negative affect: A developmental perspective on happiness. *Journal of Personality and Social Psychology, 75*, 1333–1349.

Muehlenhard, Charlene L. (1988). "Nice women" don't say yes and "real men" don't say no: How miscommunication and the double standard can cause sexual problems. *Women & Therapy, 7*, 95–108.

Muehlenhard, Charlene L., & Cook, Stephen (1988). Men's self-reports of unwanted sexual activity. *Journal of Sex Research, 24*, 58–72.

Mueller, Claudia M., & Dweck, Carol S. (1998). Praise for intelligence can undermine children's motivation and performance. *Journal of Personality and Social Psychology, 75*, 33–52.

Mulick, James (1994, November/December). The non-science of facilitated communication. *Science Agenda* (APA newsletter), 8–9.

Müller, Ralph-Axel; Courchesne, Eric; & Allen, Greg (1998). The cerebellum: So much more [Letter to the editor]. *Science, 282*, 879–880.

Murphy, Sheila T.; Monahan, Jennifer L.; & Zajonc, R. B. (1995). Additivity of nonconscious affect: Combined effects of priming and exposure. *Journal of Personality and Social Psychology, 69*, 589–602.

Myers, Ronald E., & Sperry, R. W. (1953). Interocular transfer of a visual form discrimination habit in cats after section of the optic chiasm and corpus callosum. *Anatomical Record, 115*, 351–352.

Nadel, Lynn, & Zola-Morgan, Stuart (1984). Infantile amnesia: A neurobiological perspective. In M. Moscovitch (ed.), *Infantile memory: Its relation to normal and pathological memory in humans and other animals*. New York: Plenum.

Nadon, Robert; Hoyt, Irene, P.; Register, Patricia A.; & Kihlstrom, John (1991). Absorption and hypnotizability: Context effects reexamined. *Journal of Personality and Social Psychology, 60*, 144–153.

Nash, Michael R. (1987). What, if anything, is regressed about hypnotic age regression? A review of the empirical literature. *Psychological Bulletin, 102*, 42–52.

Nash, Michael R., & Nadon, Robert (1997). Hypnosis. In D. L. Faigman, D. Kaye, M. J. Saks, & J. Sanders (eds.), *Modern scientific evidence: The law and science of expert testimony*. St. Paul, MN: West.

Nathan, Debbie (1994, Fall). Dividing to conquer? Women, men, and the making of multiple personality disorder. *Social Text, 40*, 77–114.

National Institutes of Health (1998, November 19). *Consensus report on Ritalin*. Washington, DC: Author.

National Victim Center & Crime Victims Research and Treatment Center (1992). *Rape in America: A report to the nation*. Fort Worth, TX: National Victim Center.

Needleman, Herbert L.; Riess, Julie A.; Tobin, Michael J.; et al. (1996). Bone lead levels and delinquent behavior. *Journal of the American Medical Association, 275*, 363–369.

Neher, Andrew (1996). Jung's theory of archetypes: A critique. *Journal of Humanistic Psychology, 36,* 61–91.

Neisser, Ulric (ed.) (1998). *The rising curve: Long-term gains in IQ and related measures.* Washington, DC: American Psychological Association.

Neisser, Ulric, & Harsch, Nicole (1992). Phantom flashbulbs: False recollections of hearing the news about *Challenger.* In E. Winograd & U. Neisser (eds.), *Affect and accuracy in recall: Studies of "flashbulb memories."* New York: Cambridge University Press.

Neitz, Maureen, & Neitz, Jay (1995). Numbers and ratios of visual pigment genes for normal red–green color vision. *Science, 267,* 1013–1016.

Nelson, Thomas O., & Dunlosky, John (1991). When people's judgments of learning (JOLs) are extremely accurate at predicting subsequent recall: The "delayed JOL effect." *Psychological Science, 2,* 267–270.

Nelson, Thomas O., & Leonesio, R. Jacob (1988). Allocation of self-paced study time and the "labor in vain effect." *Journal of Experimental Psychology: Learning, Memory, and Cognition, 14,* 676–686.

Neugarten, Bernice (1979). Time, age, and the life cycle. *American Journal of Psychiatry, 136,* 887–894.

Newman, Leonard S., & Baumeister, Roy F. (1994). "Who would wish for the trauma?" Explaining UFO abductions. Paper presented at the annual meeting of the American Psychological Association, Los Angeles.

Newman, Lucille F., & Buka, Stephen (1991, Spring). Clipped wings. *American Educator,* 27–33, 42.

Nezu, Arthur M.; Nezu, Christine M.; & Blissett, Sonia E. (1988). Sense of humor as a moderator of the relation between stressful events and psychological distress: A prospective analysis. *Journal of Personality and Social Psychology, 54,* 520–525.

NICHD Early Child Care Research Network (1997). The effects of infant–child care on infant–mother attachment security. (Results of the NICHD study of early child care.) *Child Development, 68,* 860–879.

Nickerson, Raymond (1998). Confirmation bias: A ubiquitous phenomenon in many guises. *Review of General Psychology, 2,* 175–220.

Nickerson, Raymond, & Adams, Marilyn Jager (1979). Long-term memory for a common object. *Cognitive Psychology, 11,* 287–307.

Nigg, Joel T., & Goldsmith, H. Hill (1994). Genetics of personality disorders: Perspectives from personality and psychopathology research. *Psychological Bulletin, 115,* 346–380.

NIH Technology Assessment Panel on Integration of Behavioral and Relaxation Approaches into the Treatment of Chronic Pain and Insomnia (1996). *Journal of the American Medical Association, 276,* 313–318.

Nisbett, Richard E. (1993). Violence and U.S. regional culture. *American Psychologist, 48,* 441–449.

Nisbett, Richard E., & Ross, Lee (1980). *Human inference: Strategies and shortcomings of social judgment.* Englewood Cliffs, NJ: Prentice-Hall.

Noble, Ernest P. (1998, August 28). DRD2 gene and alcoholism. *Science, 281,* 1287–1288.

Noble, Ernest P.; Blum, Kenneth; Ritchie, T.; Montgomery, A.; & Sheridan, P. J. (1991). Allelic association of the D2 dopamine receptor gene with receptor-binding characteristics in alcoholism. *Archives of General Psychiatry, 48,* 648–654.

Nolen-Hoeksema, Susan (1991). Responses to depression and their effects on the duration of depressive episodes. *Journal of Abnormal Psychology, 100,* 569–582.

Nolen-Hoeksema, Susan, & Girgus, Joan S. (1994). The emergence of gender differences in depression during adolescence. *Psychological Bulletin, 115,* 424–443.

Nonaka, S.; Hough, C. J.; & Chuang, De-Maw (1998, March 3). Chronic lithium treatment robustly protects neurons in the central nervous system against excitotoxicity by inhibiting N-methyl-D-aspartate receptor-mediated calcium influx. *Proceedings of the National Academy of Sciences, 95,* 2642–2647.

Norman, Donald A. (1988). *The psychology of everyday things.* New York: Basic Books.

Nowicki, Stephen, & Strickland, Bonnie R. (1973). A locus of control scale for children. *Journal of Consulting Psychology, 40,* 148–154.

Nurnberger, John I., & Gershon, Elliot S. (1992). In E. S. Paykel (ed.), *Handbook of affective disorders* (2nd ed.). New York: Guilford Press.

Nyberg, L.; Backman, L.; Erngrund, K.; et al. (1996). Age differences in episodic memory, semantic memory, and priming: Relationships to demographic, intellectual, and biological factors. *Journal of Gerontology: Psychological Sciences, 51,* 234–240.

Oatley, Keith (1990). Do emotional states produce irrational thinking? In K. J. Gilhooly, M. T. G. Keane, R. H. Logie, & G. Erdos (eds.), *Lines of thinking* (Vol. 2). New York: Wiley.

Oatley, Keith, & Duncan, Elaine (1994). The experience of emotions in everyday life. *Cognition and Emotion, 8,* 369–381.

Oatley, Keith, & Jenkins, Jennifer M. (1996). *Understanding emotions.* Cambridge, MA: Blackwell.

Ofshe, Richard J., & Watters, Ethan (1994). *Making monsters: False memory, psychotherapy, and sexual hysteria.* New York: Scribners.

Ogden, Jenni A., & Corkin, Suzanne (1991). Memories of H. M. In W. C. Abraham, M. C. Corballis, & K. G. White (eds.), *Memory mechanisms: A tribute to G. V. Goddard.* Hillsdale, NJ: Erlbaum.

O'Hanlon, Bill (1994, November/December). The third wave. *Family Therapy Networker,* 18–29.

Olds, James (1975). Mapping the mind onto the brain. In F. G. Worden, J. P. Swazy, & G. Adelman (eds.), *The neurosciences: Paths of discovery.* Cambridge, MA: Colonial Press.

Olds, James, & Milner, Peter (1954). Positive reinforcement produced by electrical stimulation of septal area and other regions of the rat brain. *Journal of Comparative and Physiological Psychology, 47,* 419–429.

O'Leary, Virginia E., & Ickovics, J. R. (1994). Resilience and thriving in response to challenge: An opportunity for a paradigm shift in women's health. *Women's Health: Research on Gender, Behavior, and Policy, 1,* 127.

Olin, Su-Chin S., & Mednick, Sarnoff A. (1996). Risk factors of psychosis: Identifying vulnerable populations premorbidly. *Schizophrenia Bulletin, 22,* 223–240.

Oliver, Mary Beth, & Hyde, Janet S. (1993). Gender differences in sexuality: A meta-analysis. *Psychological Bulletin, 114,* 29–51.

Olujic, M. B. (1998). Embodiment of terror: Gendered violence in peacetime and wartime in Croatia and Bosnia-Herzegovina. *Medical Anthropology Quarterly, 12,* 31–50.

Orford, Jim (1992). *Community psychology: Theory and practice.* New York: Wiley.

Orlinsky, David E. (1994). Research-based knowledge as the emergent foundation for clinical practice in psychotherapy. In P. F. Talley, H. H. Strupp, & S. F. Butler (eds.), *Psychotherapy research and practice: Bridging the gap.* New York: Basic Books.

Orlinsky, David E., & Howard, Kenneth I. (1994). Unity and diversity among psychotherapies: A comparative perspective. In B. Bongar & L. E. Beutler (eds.), *Foundations of psychotherapy: Theory, research, and practice.* New York: Oxford University Press.

Ortony, Andrew, & Turner, Terence J. (1990). What's basic about basic emotions. *Psychological Review, 97,* 315–331.

Ó Scalaidhe, Séamas P.; Wilson, Fraser A. W.; & Goldman-Rakic, Patricia S. (1997). Areal segregation of face-processing neurons in prefrontal cortex. *Science, 278,* 1135–1138.

O'Sullivan, Lucia F.; Byers, E. Sandra; & Finkelman, Larry (1998). A comparison of male and female college students' experiences of sexual coercion. *Psychology of Women Quarterly, 22,* 177–195.

Oyserman, Daphna, & Saltz, Eli (1993). Competence, delinquency, and attempts to attain possible selves. *Journal of Personality and Social Psychology, 65,* 360–374.

Page, Gayle G.; Ben-Eliyahu, Shamgar; Yirmiya, Raz; & Liebeskind, John C. (1993). Morphine attenuates surgery-induced enhancement of metastatic colonization in rats. *Pain, 54,* 21–28.

Panksepp, Jaak (1998). Attention deficit hyperactivity disorders, psychostimulants, and intolerance of childhood playfulness: A tragedy in the making? *Current Directions in Psychological Science, 7,* 91–98.

Panksepp, Jaak; Herman, B. H.; Vilberg, T.; et al. (1980). Endogenous opioids and social behavior. *Neuroscience and Biobehavioral Reviews, 4,* 473–487.

Park, Denise C.; Smith, Anderson D.; & Cavanaugh, John C. (1990). Metamemories of memory researchers. *Memory and Cognition, 18,* 321–327.

Parker, Elizabeth S.; Birnbaum, Isabel M.; & Noble, Ernest P. (1976). Alcohol and memory: Storage and state dependency. *Journal of Verbal Learning and Verbal Behavior, 15,* 691–702.

Parker, Gwendolyn M. (1997). *Trespassing: My sojourn in the halls of privilege.* Boston: Houghton Mifflin.

Parker, Kevin C. H.; Hanson, R. Karl; & Hunsley, John (1988). MMPI, Rorschach, and WAIS: A meta-analytic comparison of reliability, stability, and validity. *Psychological Bulletin, 103,* 367–373.

Parlee, Mary B. (1982). Changes in moods and activation levels during the menstrual cycle in experimentally naive subjects. *Psychology of Women Quarterly, 7,* 119–131.

Parlee, Mary B. (1994). The social construction of premenstrual syndrome: A case study of scientific discourse as cultural contestation. In M. G. Winkler & L. B. Cole (eds.), *The good body: Asceticism in contemporary culture.* New Haven, CT: Yale University Press.

Parsons, Michael W., & Gold, Paul E. (1992). Glucose enhancement of memory in elderly humans: An inverted-**U** dose response curve. *Neurobiology of Aging, 13,* 401–404.

Patterson, Charlotte J. (1992). Children of lesbian and gay parents. *Child Development, 63,* 1025–1042.

Patterson, Charlotte J. (1995). Sexual orientation and human development: An overview. *Developmental Psychology, 31,* 3–11.

Patterson, Francine, & Linden, Eugene (1981). *The education of Koko.* New York: Holt, Rinehart and Winston.

Patterson, Gerald R.; Forgatch, Marion S.; Yoerger, Karen L.; & Stoolmiller, Mike (1998). Variables that initiate and maintain an early-onset trajectory for juvenile offending. *Development and Psychopathology, 10,* 531–547.

Patterson, Gerald R.; Reid, John; & Dishion, Thomas (1992). *Antisocial boys.* Eugene, OR: Castalia.

Paul, Richard W. (1984, September). Critical thinking: Fundamental to education for a free society. *Educational Leadership,* 4–14.

Paunonen, Sampo V. (1998). Hierarchical organization of personality and prediction of behavior. *Journal of Personality and Social Psychology, 74,* 538–556.

Pearlin, Leonard (1982). Discontinuities in the study of aging. In T. K. Hareven & K. J. Adams (eds.), *Aging and life course transitions: An interdisciplinary perspective.* New York: Guilford Press.

Pedersen, Paul B.; Draguns, Juris G.; Lonner, Walter J.; & Trimble, Joseph E. (eds.) (1996). *Counseling across cultures* (4th ed.). Thousand Oaks, CA: Sage.

Peele, Stanton, & Brodsky, Archie, with Arnold, Mary (1991). *The truth about addiction and recovery.* New York: Simon & Schuster.

Pellegrini, Anthony D., & Galda, Lee (1993). Ten years after: A reexamination of symbolic play and literacy research. *Reading Research Quarterly, 28,* 163–175.

Pendergrast, Mark (1995). *Victims of memory* (2nd ed.). Hinesburg, VT: Upper Access Press.

Penfield, Wilder, & Perot, Phanor (1963). The brain's record of auditory and visual experience: A final summary and discussion. *Brain, 86,* 595–696.

Pennebaker, James W. (1995). Emotion, disclosure, and health: An overview. In J. W. Pennebaker (ed.), *Emotion, disclosure, and health.* Washington, DC: American Psychological Association.

Pennebaker, James W.; Colder, Michelle; & Sharp, Lisa K. (1990). Accelerating the coping process. *Journal of Personality and Social Psychology, 58,* 528–527.

Pennebaker, James W.; Kiecolt-Glaser, Janice; & Glaser, Ronald (1988). Disclosure of traumas and immune function: Health implications for psychotherapy. *Journal of Consulting and Clinical Psychology, 56,* 239–245.

Penninx, B. W.; Guralnik, J. M.; Pahor, M.; et al. (1998). Chronically depressed mood and cancer risk in older persons. *Journal of the National Cancer Institute, 90,* 1888–1893.

Peplau, Letitia A.; Conley, Terri; Spalding, Leah; & Veniegas, Rosemary (2000). The development of sexual orientation in women. *Annual Review of Sex Research,* in press.

Peplau, Letitia A., & Conrad, Eva (1989). Beyond nonsexist research: The perils of feminist methods in psychology. *Psychology of Women Quarterly, 13,* 379–400.

Peplau, Letitia A., & Gordon, Steven L. (1985). Women and men in love: Gender differences in close heterosexual relationships. In V. O'Leary, R. Unger, & B. Wallston (eds.), *Women, gender, and social psychology.* Hillsdale, NJ: Erlbaum.

Peplau, Letitia A., & Spalding, Leah (2000). The close relationships of lesbians, gay men and bisexuals. In C. Hendrick & S. Hendrick (eds.), *Close relationships: A sourcebook.* Thousand Oaks, CA: Sage.

Pepperberg, Irene M. (1990). Cognition in an African gray parrot (*Psittacus erithacus*): Further evidence for comprehension of categories and labels. *Journal of Comparative Psychology, 104,* 41–52.

Pepperberg, Irene M. (1994). Numerical competence in an African gray parrot (*Psittacus erithacus*). *Journal of Comparative Psychology, 108,* 36–44.

Perloff, Robert (1992, Summer). "Where ignorance is bliss, 'tis folly to be wise." *The General Psychologist Newsletter, 28,* 34.

Perry, Samuel W., & Heidrich, George (1982). Management of pain during debridement: A survey of U.S. burn units. *Pain, 13,* 267–280.

Pert, Candace B., & Snyder, Solomon H. (1973). Opiate receptor: Demonstration in nervous tissue. *Science, 179,* 1011–1014.

Pesetsky, David (1999). Introduction to symposium: Grammar: What's innate? Paper presented at the annual meeting of the American Association for the Advancement of Science, Anaheim.

Peterson, Bill E., & Stewart, Abigail J. (1993). Generativity and social motives in young adults. *Journal of Personality and Social Psychology, 65,* 186–198.

Peterson, Christopher; Seligman, Martin E. P.; Yurko, Karen H.; et al. (1998). Catastrophizing and untimely death. *Psychological Science, 9,* 127–130.

Peterson, Lloyd R., & Peterson, Margaret J. (1959). Short-term retention of individual verbal items. *Journal of Experimental Psychology, 58,* 193–198.

Peterson, Marilyn R. (1992). *At personal risk: Boundary violations in professional–client relationships.* New York: Norton.

Petrie, Keith J.; Booth, Roger J.; & Pennebaker, James W. (1998). The immunological effects of thought suppression. *Journal of Personality and Social Psychology, 75,* 1264–1272.

Pettigrew, Thomas F. (1997). Generalized intergroup contact effects on prejudice. *Personality and Social Psychology Bulletin, 23,* 173–185.

Pfungst, Oskar (1911/1965). *Clever Hans (the horse of Mr. von Osten): A contribution to experimental animal and human psychology.* New York: Holt, Rinehart and Winston.

Phillips, D. P.; Ruth, T. E.; & Wagner, L. M. (1993, November 6). Psychology and survival. *Lancet, 342*(8880), 1142–1145.

Phinney, Jean S. (1990). Ethnic identity in adolescents and adults: Review of research. *Psychological Bulletin, 108,* 499–514.

Phinney, Jean S. (1996). When we talk about American ethnic groups, what do we mean? *American Psychologist, 51,* 918–927.

Piaget, Jean (1929/1960). *The child's conception of the world.* Paterson, NJ: Littlefield, Adams.

Piaget, Jean (1932). *The moral judgment of the child.* New York: Macmillan.

Piaget, Jean (1952a). *The origins of intelligence in children.* New York: International Universities Press.

Piaget, Jean (1952b). *Play, dreams, and imitation in childhood.* New York: Norton.

Piaget, Jean (1984). Piaget's theory. In P. Mussen (series ed.) & W. Kessen (vol. ed.), *Handbook of child psychology: Vol. 1. History, theory, and methods* (4th ed.). New York: Wiley.

Pinker, Steven (1994). *The language instinct: How the mind creates language.* New York: Morrow.

Pinker, Steven (1997). *How the mind works.* New York: Norton.

Piper, August, Jr. (1997). *Hoax and reality: The bizarre world of multiple personality disorder.* Northvale, NJ: Jason Aronson.

Pittenger, David J. (1993). The utility of the Myers–Briggs Type Indicator. *Review of Educational Research, 63,* 467–488.

Plant, E. Ashby, & Devine, Patricia G. (1998). Internal and external motivation to respond without prejudice. *Journal of Personality and Social Psychology, 75,* 811–832.

Plomin, Robert (1989). Environment and genes: Determinants of behavior. *American Psychologist, 44,* 105–111.

Plomin, Robert; Corley, Robin; Caspi, Avshalom; et al. (1998). Adoption results for self-reported personality: Evidence for nonadditive genetic effects? *Journal of Personality and Social Psychology, 75,* 211–218.

Plomin, Robert; Corley, Robin; DeFries, J. C.; & Fulker, D. W. (1990). Individual differences in television viewing in early childhood: Nature as well as nurture. *Psychological Science, 1,* 371–377.

Plomin, Robert, & DeFries, John C. (1985). *Origins of individual differences in infancy: The Colorado Adoption Project.* New York: Academic Press.

Plous, Scott L. (1991). An attitude survey of animal rights activists. *Psychological Science, 2,* 194–196.

Plous, Scott L. (1996). Attitudes toward the use of animals in psychological research and education: Results from a national survey of psychologists. *American Psychologist, 51,* 1167–1180.

Plutchik, Robert; Conte, Hope R.; Karasu, Toksoz; & Buckley, Peter (1988, Fall/Winter). The measurement of psychodynamic variables. *Hillside Journal of Clinical Psychology, 10,* 132–147.

Polefrone, Joanna M., & Manuck, Stephen B. (1987). Gender differences in cardiovascular and neuroendocrine response to stressors. In R. C. Barnett, L. Biener, & G. K. Baruch (eds.), *Gender and stress.* New York: Free Press.

Poole, Debra A. (1995). Strolling fuzzy-trace theory through eyewitness testimony (or vice versa). *Learning and Individual Differences, 7,* 87–93.

Poole, Debra A., & Lamb, Michael E. (1998). *Investigative interviews of children.* Washington, DC: American Psychological Association.

Poole, Debra A.; Lindsay, D. Stephen; Memon, Amina; & Bull, Ray (1995). Psychotherapy and the recovery of memories of childhood sexual abuse: U.S. and British practitioners' opinions, practices, and experiences. *Journal of Consulting and Clinical Psychology, 63,* 426–437.

Pope, Harrison G., & Katz, David L. (1992). Psychiatric effects of anabolic steroids. *Psychiatric Annals, 22,* 24–29.

Pope, Kenneth S. (1996). Memory, abuse, and science: Questioning claims about the false memory syndrome epidemic. *American Psychologist, 51,* 957–974.

Portenoy, Russell K. (1994). Opioid therapy for chronic nonmalignant pain: Current status. In H. L. Fields & J. C. Liebeskind (eds.), *Progress in pain research and management: Vol. 1. Pharmacological approaches to the treatment of chronic pain.* Seattle: International Association for the Study of Pain.

Postmes, Tom, & Spears, Russell (1998). Deindividuation and antinormative behavior: A meta-analysis. *Psychological Bulletin, 123,* 238–259.

Potter, W. James (1987). Does television viewing hinder academic achievement among adolescents? *Human Communication Research, 14,* 27–46.

Poulin-Dubois, Diane; Serbin, Lisa A.; Kenyon, Brenda; & Derbyshire, Alison (1994). Infants' intermodal knowledge about gender. *Developmental Psychology, 30,* 436–442.

Powell, Russell A., & Boer, Douglas P. (1994). Did Freud mislead patients to confabulate memories of abuse? *Psychological Reports, 74,* 1283–1298.

Powell, Russell A., & Boer, Douglas P. (1995). Did Freud misinterpret reported memories of sexual abuse as fantasies? *Psychological Reports, 77,* 563–570.

Pratkanis, Anthony, & Aronson, Elliot (1992). *Age of propaganda: The everyday use and abuse of persuasion.* New York: Freeman.

Pratt, L. A.; Ford, D. E.; Crum, R. M.; et al. (1996, December 15). Depression, psychotropic medication, and risk of myocardial infarction: Prospective data from the Baltimore ECA follow-up. *Circulation, 94,* 3123–3129.

Premack, David, & Premack, Ann James (1983). *The mind of an ape.* New York: Norton.

Press, Gary A.; Amaral, David G.; & Squire, Larry R. (1989, September 7). Hippocampal abnormalities in amnesic patients revealed by high-resolution magnetic resonance imaging. *Nature, 341,* 54–57.

Prochaska, James O.; Norcross, John C.; & DiClemente, Carlo C. (1994). *Changing for good.* New York: Morrow.

Punamaeki, Raija-Leena, & Joustie, Marja (1998). The role of culture, violence, and personal factors affecting dream content. *Journal of Cross-Cultural Psychology, 29,* 320–342.

Radetsky, Peter (1991, April). The brainiest cells alive. *Discover, 12,* 82–85, 88, 90.

Radke-Yarrow, Marian; Zahn-Waxler, Carolyn; & Chapman, M. (1983). Prosocial dispositions and behavior. In P. Mussen (series ed.), *Handbook of child psychology: Vol. 4. Socialization, personality, and social development.* New York: Wiley.

Raglin, John S. (1990). Exercise and mental health. Beneficial and detrimental effects. *Sports Medicine, 9,* 323–329.

Raglin, John S., & Morgan, William P. (1987). Influence of exercise and quiet rest on state anxiety and blood pressure. *Medicine and Science in Sports and Exercise, 19,* 456–463.

Räikkönen, Katri; Matthews, Karen A.; Flory, Janine D.; et al. (1999). Effects of optimism, pessimism, and trait anxiety on ambulatory blood pressure and mood during everyday life. *Journal of Personality and Social Psychology, 76,* 104–113.

Raine, Adrian (1996). Autonomic nervous system factors underlying disinhibited, antisocial, and violent behavior. Biosocial perspectives and treatment implications. *Annals of the New York Academy of Sciences, 794,* 46–59.

Raine, Adrian; Brennan, Patricia; & Mednick, Sarnoff A. (1994). Birth complications combined with early maternal rejection at age one year predispose to violent crime at age 18 years. *Archives of General Psychiatry, 51,* 984–988.

Raine, Adrian; Meloy, J. R.; Bihrle, S.; et al. (1998). Reduced prefrontal and increased subcortical brain functioning assessed using positron emission tomography in predatory and affective murderers. *Behavioral Science and Law, 16,* 319–332.

Ramey, Craig T., & Ramey, Sharon Landesman (1998). Early intervention and early experience. *American Psychologist, 53,* 109–120.

Ranseen, John D. (1998). Lawyers with ADHD: The special test accommodation controversy. *Professional Psychology: Research and Practice, 29,* 450–459.

Rapkin, Andrea J.; Chang, Li C.; & Reading, Anthony E. (1988). Comparison of retrospective and prospective assessment of premenstrual symptoms. *Psychological Reports, 62,* 55–60.

Raskin, David C.; Honts, Charles R.; & Kircher, John C. (1997). The scientific status of research on polygraph techniques: The case for polygraph tests. In D. L. Faigman, D. Kaye, M. J. Saks, & J. Sanders (eds.), *Modern scientific evidence: The law and science of expert testimony.* St. Paul, MN: West.

Raso, Jack (1996, July/August). Alternative health education and pseudo-credentialing. *Skeptical Inquirer,* 39–45.

Rathbun, Constance; DiVirgilio, Letitia; & Waldfogel, Samuel (1958). A restitutive process in children following radical separation from family and culture. *American Journal of Orthopsychiatry, 28,* 408–415.

Ravussin, Eric; Lillioja, Stephen; Knowler, William; et al. (1988). Reduced rate of energy expenditure as a risk factor for body-weight gain. *New England Journal of Medicine, 318,* 467–472.

Ravussin, Eric; Pratley, R. E.; Maffei, M.; et al. (1997). Relatively low plasma leptin concentrations precede weight gain in Pima Indians. *Nature Medicine, 3,* 238–240.

Reber, Paul J.; Stark, Craig E. L.; & Squire, Larry R. (1998). Contrasting cortical activity associated with category memory and recognition memory. *Learning & Memory, 5,* 420–428.

Rechtschaffen, Allan; Gilliland, Marcia A.; Bergmann, Bernard M.; & Winter, Jacqueline B. (1983). Physiological correlates of prolonged sleep deprivation in rats. *Science, 221,* 182–184.

Redd, W. H.; Dadds, M. R.; Futterman, A. D.; et al. (1993). Nausea induced by mental images of chemotherapy. *Cancer, 72,* 629–636.

Redelmeier, Donald A., & Tversky, Amos (1996). On the belief that arthritis pain is related to the weather. *Proceedings of the National Academy of Sciences, 93,* 2895–2896.

Redmond, D. E., Jr.; Roth, R. H.; Spencer, D. C.; et al. (1993). Neural transplantation for neurodegenerative diseases: Past, present, and future. *Annals of the New York Academy of Sciences, 695,* 258–266.

Reed, Geoffrey M. (1990). Stress, coping, and psychological adaptation in a sample of gay and bisexual men with AIDS. Unpublished doctoral dissertation, University of California, Los Angeles.

Reed, Geoffrey M.; Kemeny, Margaret E.; Taylor, Shelley E.; et al. (1994). Realistic acceptance as a predictor of decreased survival time in gay men with AIDS. *Health Psychology, 13,* 299–307.

Reedy, F. E.; Bartoshuk, L. M.; Miller, I. J.; et al. (1993). Relationships among papillae, taste pores, and 6-n-propylthiouracil (PROP) suprathreshold taste sensitivity. *Chemical Senses, 18,* 618–619.

Regier, Darrel A.; Narrow, William E.; Rae, Donald S.; et al. (1993). The de facto US mental and addictive disorders service system: Epidemiologic Catchment Area prospective 1-year prevalence rates of disorders and services. *Archives of General Psychiatry, 50,* 85–94.

Reich, Theodore; Edenberg, Howard J.; Goate, Alison; et al. (1998, May 8). Genome-wide search for genes affecting the risk for alcohol dependence. *American Journal of Medical Genetics, 81,* 207–15.

Reid, R. L. (1991). Premenstrual syndrome. *New England Journal of Medicine, 324,* 1208–1210.

Rescorla, Robert A. (1988). Pavlovian conditioning: It's not what you think it is. *American Psychologist, 43,* 151–160.

Restak, Richard M. (1983, October). Is free will a fraud? *Science Digest, 91*(10), 52–55.

Restak, Richard M. (1994). *The modular brain.* New York: Macmillan.

Reuter-Lorenz, Patricia A.; Jonides, John; Smith, Edward E.; et al. (1999). Age differences in the frontal lateralization of verbal and spatial working memory revealed by PET. Paper presented at the annual meeting of the Cognitive Neuroscience Society, Washington, DC.

Reuter-Lorenz, Patricia A.; Stanczak, Louise; & Miller, Andrea C. (2000). Neural recruitment and cognitive aging: Two hemispheres are better than one, especially as you age. *Psychological Science,* in press.

Reynolds, Brent A., & Weiss, Samuel (1992). Generation of neurons and astrocytes from isolated cells of the adult mammalian central nervous system. *Science, 255,* 1707–1710.

Reynolds, David K. (1987). *Water bears no scars: Japanese lifeways for personal growth.* New York: Morrow.

Ricaurte, George A.; Forno, Lysia; Wilson, Mary; et al. (1988). (+ or –) 3, 4-Methylenedioxy-methamphetamine selectively damages central serotonergic neurons in nonhuman primates. *Journal of the American Medical Association, 260,* 51–55.

Rice, George; Anderson, Carol; Risch, Neil; & Ebers, George (1999, April 23). Male homosexuality: Absence of linkage to microsatellite markers at Xq28. *Science, 284,* 665–667.

Rice, Mabel L. (1989). Children's language acquisition. *American Psychologist, 44,* 149–156.

Richards, Ruth L. (1991). Everyday creativity and the arts. Paper presented at the annual meeting of the American Psychological Association, San Francisco.

Richardson, John T. E. (ed.) (1992). *Cognition and the menstrual cycle.* New York: Springer-Verlag.

Richardson-Klavehn, Alan, & Bjork, Robert A. (1988). Measures of memory. *Annual Review of Psychology, 39,* 475–543.

Ridley-Johnson, Robyn; Cooper, Harris; & Chance, June (1983). The relation of children's television viewing to school achievement and I.Q. *Journal of Educational Research, 76,* 294–297.

Riessman, Catherine K. (1990). *Divorce talk: Women and men make sense of personal relationships.* New Brunswick, NJ: Rutgers University Press.

Riley, Vernon; Spackman, Darrel; & Santisteban, George (1975). The role of physiological stress on breast tumor incidence in mice. *Proceedings of the American Association of Cancer Research, 16,* 152.

Rind, Bruce, & Tromovitch, Philip (1997). A meta-analytic review of findings from national samples on psychological correlates of child sexual abuse. *Journal of Sex Research, 34,* 237–255.

Rind, Bruce; Tromovitch, Philip; & Bauserman, Robert (1998). A meta-analytic examination of assumed properties of child sexual abuse using college samples. *Psychological Bulletin, 124,* 22–53.

Ristau, Carolyn A. (ed.) (1991). *Cognitive ethology: The minds of other animals.* Hillsdale, NJ: Erlbaum.

Roberts, John E.; Gotlib, Ian H.; & Kassel, Jon D. (1996). Adult attachment security and symptoms of depression: The mediating roles of dysfunctional attitudes and low self-esteem. *Journal of Personality and Social Psychology, 70,* 310–320.

Roberts, Susan B.; Savage, J.; Coward, W. A.; et al. (1988). Energy expenditure and intake in infants born to lean and overweight mothers. *New England Journal of Medicine, 318,* 461–466.

Robertson, Barbara A. (1995). Creating a disability community. Paper presented at the annual meeting of the American Psychological Association, New York.

Robins, Lee N.; Davis, Darlene H.; & Goodwin, Donald W. (1974). Drug use by U.S. Army enlisted men in Vietnam: A follow-up on their return home. *American Journal of Epidemiology, 99*, 235–249.

Robins, Lee N.; Tipp, Jayson; & Przybeck, Thomas R. (1991). Antisocial personality. In L. N. Robins & D. A. Regier (eds.), *Psychiatric disorders in America.* New York: Free Press.

Robinson, Leslie A.; Berman, Jeffrey S.; & Neimeyer, Robert A. (1990). Psychotherapy for the treatment of depression: A comprehensive review of controlled outcome research. *Psychological Bulletin, 108*, 30–49.

Rocha, Beatriz A.; Scearce-Levie, Kimberly; Lucas, Jose J.; et al. (1998). Increased vulnerability to cocaine in mice lacking the serotonin-1–receptor. *Nature, 393*, 175–178.

Roe, R. A.; Zinovieva, I. L.; Dienes, E.; & Ten Horn, L. A. (1998). Test of a model of work motivation in the Netherlands, Hungary and Bulgaria. Paper presented at the annual meeting of the International Association for Cross-Cultural Psychology, Bellingham, WA.

Roediger, Henry L., III (1990). Implicit memory: Retention without remembering. *American Psychologist, 45*, 1043–1056.

Roediger, Henry L., & McDermott, Kathleen B. (1995). Creating false memories: Remembering words not presented in lists. *Journal of Experimental Psychology: Learning, Memory, & Cognition, 21*, 803–814.

Rogers, Carl (1951). *Client-centered therapy: Its current practice, implications, and theory.* Boston: Houghton Mifflin.

Rogers, Carl (1961). *On becoming a person.* Boston: Houghton Mifflin.

Rogers, Ronald W., & Prentice-Dunn, Steven (1981). Deindividuation and anger-mediated interracial aggression: Unmasking regressive racism. *Journal of Personality and Social Psychology, 41*, 63–73.

Rokeach, Milton, & Ball-Rokeach, Sandra (1989). Stability and change in American value priorities, 1968–1981. *American Psychologist, 44*, 775–784.

Rollin, Henry (ed.) (1980). *Coping with schizophrenia.* London: Burnett.

Rosch, Eleanor H. (1973). Natural categories. *Cognitive Psychology, 4*, 328–350.

Rose, Suzanna; Zand, Debra; & Cini, Marie A. (1993). Lesbian courtship scripts. In E. D. Rothblum & K. A. Brehony (eds.), *Boston marriages.* Amherst: University of Massachusetts Press.

Roseman, Ira J.; Wiest, Cynthia; & Swartz, Tamara S. (1994). Phenomenology, behaviors, and goals differentiate discrete emotions. *Journal of Personality and Social Psychology, 67*, 206–221.

Rosen, Gerald M. (1981). Guidelines for the review of do-it-yourself treatment books. *Contemporary Psychology, 26*, 189–191.

Rosen, Gerald M. (1999). Treatment fidelity and research on eye movement desensitization and reprocessing (EMDR). *Journal of Anxiety Disorders, 13*, 173–184.

Rosen, R. D. (1977). *Psychobabble.* New York: Atheneum.

Rosenberg, Harold (1993). Prediction of controlled drinking by alcoholics and problem drinkers. *Psychological Bulletin, 113*, 129–139.

Rosenhan, David L. (1973). On being sane in insane places. *Science, 179*, 250–258.

Rosenthal, Norman E. (1998). *Winter blues: Seasonal affective disorder. What it is and how to overcome it.* New York: Guilford Press.

Rosenthal, Robert (1966). *Experimenter effects in behavioral research.* New York: Appleton-Century-Crofts.

Rosenthal, Robert (1994). Interpersonal expectancy effects: A 30-year perspective. *Current Directions in Psychological Science, 3*, 176–179.

Rosenzweig, Mark R. (1984). Experience, memory, and the brain. *American Psychologist, 39*, 365–376.

Ross, Colin (1995). The validity and reliability of dissociative identity disorder. In L. M. Cohen, J. N. Berzoff, & M. R. Elin (eds.), *Dissociative identity disorder: Theoretical and treatment controversies.* Northvale, NJ: Jason Aronson.

Ross, Lee (1977). The intuitive psychologist and his shortcomings: Distortions in the attribution process. In L. Berkowitz (ed.), *Advances in experimental social psychology* (Vol. 10). New York: Academic Press.

Roth, David L., & Holmes, David S. (1985). Influence of physical fitness in determining the impact of stressful life events on physical and psychologic health. *Psychosomatic Medicine, 47*, 164–173.

Rothbaum, Fred M.; Weisz, John R.; & Snyder, Samuel S. (1982). Changing the world and changing the self: A two-process model of perceived control. *Journal of Personality and Social Psychology, 42*, 5–37.

Rotter, Julian B. (1982). *The development and applications of social learning theory: Selected papers.* New York: Praeger.

Rotter, Julian B. (1990). Internal versus external control of reinforcement: A case history of a variable. *American Psychologist, 45*, 489–493.

Rovee-Collier, Carolyn (1993). The capacity for long-term memory in infancy. *Current Directions in Psychological Science, 2*, 130–135.

Rowe, John W., & Kahn, Robert L. (1998). *Successful aging.* New York: Pantheon.

Rowe, Walter F. (1993, Winter). Psychic detectives: A critical examination. *Skeptical Inquirer, 17*, 159–165.

Roy, Mark P.; Steptoe, Andrew; & Kirschbaum, Clemens (1998). Life events and social support as moderators of individual differences in cardiovascular and cortisol reactivity. *Journal of Personality and Social Psychology, 75*, 1273–1281.

Rozin, Paul; Lowery, Laura; & Ebert, Rhonda (1994). Varieties of disgust faces and the structure of disgust. *Journal of Personality and Social Psychology, 66*, 870–881.

Rubin, Jeffrey Z. (1994). Models of conflict management. *Journal of Social Issues, 50*, 33–45.

Ruggiero, Vincent R. (1988). *Teaching thinking across the curriculum.* New York: Harper & Row.

Ruggiero, Vincent R. (1997). *The art of thinking: A guide to critical and creative thought* (5th ed.). New York: HarperCollins.

Rumbaugh, Duane M. (1977). *Language learning by a chimpanzee: The Lana project.* New York: Academic Press.

Rumbaugh, Duane M.; Savage-Rumbaugh, E. Sue; & Pate, James L. (1988). Addendum to "Summation in the chimpanzee (*Pantroglodytes*)." *Journal of Experimental Psychology: Animal Behavior Processes, 14*, 118–120.

Rumelhart, David E., & McClelland, James L. (1987). Learning the past tenses of English verbs: Implicit rules or parallel distributed processing. In B. MacWhinney (ed.), *Mechanisms of language acquisition.* Hillsdale, NJ: Erlbaum.

Rumelhart, David E.; McClelland, James L.; & the PDP Research Group (1986). *Parallel distributed processing: Explorations in the microstructure of cognition* (Vols. 1 and 2). Cambridge, MA: MIT Press.

Rushton, J. Philippe (1988). Race differences in behavior: A review and evolutionary analysis. *Personality and Individual Differences, 9*, 1009–1024.

Russell, Diana E. H. (1990). *Rape in marriage* (Rev. ed.). Bloomington: Indiana University Press.

Russell, James A. (1991). In defense of a prototype approach to emotion concepts. *Journal of Personality and Social Psychology, 60*, 37–47.

Russell, James A., & Fehr, Beverley (1994). Fuzzy concepts in a fuzzy hierarchy: Varieties of anger. *Journal of Personality and Social Psychology, 67*, 186–205.

Rusting, Cheryl L., & Nolen-Hoeksema, Susan (1998). Regulating responses of anger: Effects of rumination and distraction on angry mood. *Journal of Personality and Social Psychology, 74*, 790–803.

Ryan, Richard M.; Chirkov, Valery I.; Little, Todd D.; et al. (1999). The American dream in Russia: Extrinsic aspirations and well-being in two cultures. *Personality and Social Psychology Bulletin, 25*, in press.

Ryff, Carol D., & Keyes, Corey L. M. (1995). The structure of psychological well-being revisited. *Journal of Personality and Social Psychology, 69*, 719–727.

Rymer, Russ (1993). *Genie: An abused child's flight from silence.* New York: HarperCollins.

Saarni, Carolyn (1989). Children's understanding of strategic control of emotional expression in social transactions. In C. Saarni & P. L. Harris (eds.), *Children's understanding of emotion.* Cambridge, England: Cambridge University Press.

Sack, Robert L., & Lewy, Alfred J. (1997). Melatonin as a chronobiotic: Treatment of circadian desynchrony in night workers and the blind. *Journal of Biological Rhythms, 12*, 595–603.

Sackett, Paul R. (1994). Integrity testing for personnel selection. *Current Directions in Psychological Science, 3*, 73–76.

Sacks, Oliver (1985). *The man who mistook his wife for a hat and other clinical tales.* New York: Simon & Schuster.

Saffran, J. R.; Aslin, R. N.; & Newport, E. L. (1996). Statistical learning by 8-month-old infants. *Science, 274*, 1926–1928.

Sagan, Eli (1988). *Freud, women, and morality: The psychology of good and evil.* New York: Basic Books.

Sagarin, Brad; Cialdini, Robert B.; & Rice, William E. (1998). Creating critical consumers: Instilling resistance to unethical persuasion. Paper presented at the annual meeting of the American Psychological Association, San Francisco.

Sahley, Christie L.; Rudy, Jerry W.; & Gelperin, Alan (1981). An analysis of associative learning in a terrestrial mollusk: I. Higher-order conditioning, blocking, and a transient US preexposure effect. *Journal of Comparative Physiology, 144*, 1–8.

Salthouse, Timothy A. (1998). The what and where of cognitive aging. Address presented at the annual meeting of the American Psychological Association, San Francisco.

Saltz, Bruce L.; Woerner, M. G.; Kane, J. M.; Lieberman, J. A.; et al. (1991, November 6). Prospective study of tardive dyskinesia incidence in the elderly. *Journal of the American Medical Association, 266*(17), 2402–2406.

Samelson, Franz (1979). Putting psychology on the map: Ideology and intelligence testing. In A. R. Buss (ed.), *Psychology in social context.* New York: Irvington.

Sameroff, Arnold J.; Seifer, Ronald; Barocas, Ralph; et al. (1987). Intelligence quotient scores of 4-year-old children: Social-environmental risk factors. *Pediatrics, 79*, 343–350.

Sapolsky, Robert M. (1997). *The trouble with testosterone: And other essays on the biology of the human predicament.* New York: Touchstone.

Sapolsky, Robert M. (1998, March/April). Is biology destiny? *Family Therapy Networker, 22*, 33–35.

Sarbin, Theodore R. (1991). Hypnosis: A fifty year perspective. *Contemporary Hypnosis, 8*, 1–15.

Sarbin, Theodore R. (1992). The social construction of schizophrenia. In W. Flack, D. R. Miller, & M. Wiener (eds.), *What is schizophrenia?* New York: Springer-Verlag.

Savage-Rumbaugh, Sue, & Lewin, Roger (1994). *Kanzi: The ape at the brink of the human mind.* New York: Wiley.

Savage-Rumbaugh, Sue; Shanker, Stuart; & Taylor, Talbot (1998). *Apes, language and the human mind.* New York: Oxford University Press.

Saxe, Leonard (1994). Detection of deception: Polygraph and integrity tests. *Current Directions in Psychological Science, 3*, 69–73.

Saywitz, Karen; Goodman, Gail S.; Nicholas, Elissa; & Moan, Susan (1991). Children's memory for genital exam: Implications for child sexual abuse. *Journal of Consulting and Clinical Psychology, 59*, 682–691.

Scarborough, Elizabeth, & Furumoto, Laurel (1987). *Untold lives: The first generation of American women psychologists.* New York: Columbia University Press.

Scarr, Sandra (1984). Intelligence: What an introductory psychology student might want to know. In A. M. Rogers & C. J. Scheirer (eds.), *The G. Stanley Hall Lecture Series* (Vol. 4). Washington, DC: American Psychological Association.

Scarr, Sandra (1993). Biological and cultural diversity: The legacy of Darwin for development. *Child Development, 64*, 1333–1353.

Scarr, Sandra (1997). Why child care has little impact on most children's development. *Current Directions in Psychological Science, 6*, 143–148.

Scarr, Sandra; Pakstis, Andrew J.; Katz, Soloman H.; & Barker, William B. (1977). Absence of a relationship between degree of white ancestry and intellectual skill in a black population. *Human Genetics, 39*, 69–86.

Scarr, Sandra, & Weinberg, Robert A. (1994). Educational and occupational achievement of brothers and sisters in adoptive and biologically related families. *Behavioral Genetics, 24*, 301–325.

Schachter, Stanley, & Singer, Jerome E. (1962). Cognitive, social, and physiological determinants of emotional state. *Psychological Review, 69*, 379–399.

Schacter, Daniel L. (1996). *Searching for memory: The brain, the mind, and the past.* New York: Basic Books.

Schacter, Daniel L. (1999). The seven sins of memory: Insights from psychology and cognitive neuroscience. *American Psychologist, 54*, 182–203.

Schacter, Daniel L.; Chiu, C.-Y. Peter; & Ochsner, Kevin N. (1993). Implicit memory: A selective review. *Annual Review of Neuroscience, 16*, 159–182.

Schacter, Daniel L.; Reiman, E.; Curran, T.; et al. (1996). Neuroanatomical correlates of veridical and illusory recognition memory: Evidence from positron emission tomography. *Neuron, 17*, 267–274.

Schaie, K. Warner (1993). The Seattle longitudinal studies of adult intelligence. *Current Directions in Psychological Science, 2*, 171–175.

Schaie, K. Warner (1994). The course of adult intellectual development. *American Psychologist, 49*, 304–313.

Schank, Roger C., & Abelson, Robert P. (1995). Knowledge and memory: The real story. In R. S. Wyer, Jr., et al. (eds.), *Advances in social cognition* (Vol. 8). Hillsdale, NJ: Erlbaum.

Schank, Roger C., with Childers, Peter (1988). *The creative attitude.* New York: Macmillan.

Schein, Edgar; Schneier, Inge; & Barker, Curtis H. (1961). *Coercive persuasion.* New York: Norton.

Scherer, Klaus R. (1997). The role of culture in emotion-antecedent appraisal. *Journal of Personality and Social Psychology, 73*, 902–922.

Schlossberg, Nancy K. (1984). Exploring the adult years. In A. M. Rogers & C. J. Scheirer (eds.), *The G. Stanley Hall Lecture Series* (Vol. 4). Washington, DC: American Psychological Association.

Schlossberg, Nancy K., & Robinson, Susan P. (1996). *Going to plan B.* New York: Simon & Schuster/Fireside.

Schmelz, M.; Schmidt, R.; Bickel, A.; et al. (1997). Specific C-receptors for itch in human skin. *Journal of Neuroscience, 17*, 8003–8008.

Schneider, Allen M., & Tarshis, Barry (1986). *An introduction to physiological psychology* (3rd ed.). New York: Random House.

Schneider, Edward L. (1999, February 5). Aging in the third millennium. *Science, 283*, 796–797.

Schnell, Lisa, & Schwab, Martin E. (1990, January 18). Axonal regeneration in the rat spinal cord produced by an antibody against myelin-associated neurite growth inhibitors. *Nature, 343,* 269–272.

Schuckit, Marc A. (1998). Relationship among genetic, environmental, and psychological variables in predicting alcoholism. Invited address presented at the annual meeting of the American Psychological Association, San Francisco.

Schuckit, Marc A., & Smith, T. L. (1996). An 8-year follow-up of 450 "sons of alcoholic and control subjects. *Archives of General Psychiatry, 53,* 202–210.

Schulkin, Jay (1994). Melancholic depression and the hormones of adversity: A role for the amygdala. *Current Directions in Psychological Science, 3,* 41–44.

Schulman, Michael, & Mekler, Eva (1994). *Bringing up a caring child* (Rev. ed.). New York: Doubleday.

Schulz, Richard, & Decker, Susan (1985). Long-term adjustment to physical disability: The role of social support, perceived control, and self-blame. *Journal of Personality and Social Psychology, 48,* 1162–1172.

Schuman, Howard, & Scott, Jacqueline (1989). Generations and collective memories. *American Journal of Sociology, 54,* 359–381.

Schwartz, Jeffrey; Stoessel, Paula W.; Baxter, Lewis R.; et al. (1996). Systematic changes in cerebral glucose metabolic rate after successful behavior modification treatment of obsessive–compulsive disorder. *Archives of General Psychiatry, 53,* 109–113.

Scofield, Michael (1993, June 6). About men: Off the ladder. *New York Times Magazine,* p. 22.

Sears, Pauline, & Barbee, Ann H. (1977). Career and life satisfactions among Terman's gifted women. In J. C. Stanley, W. C. George, & C. H. Solano (eds.), *The gifted and the creative: A fifty-year perspective.* Baltimore, MD: Johns Hopkins University Press.

Seeman, Philip.; Guan, Hong-chang; & Van Tol, Hubert H. (1993). Dopamine D4 receptors elevated in schizophrenia. *Nature, 365,* 441–445.

Segal, Julius (1986). *Winning life's toughest battles.* New York: McGraw-Hill.

Segall, Marshall H. (1994). A cross-cultural research contribution to unraveling the nativist/empiricist controversy. In W. J. Lonner & R. Malpass (eds.), *Psychology and culture.* Needham Heights, MA: Allyn & Bacon.

Segall, Marshall H.; Campbell, Donald T.; & Herskovits, Melville J. (1966). *The influence of culture on visual perception.* Indianapolis: Bobbs-Merrill.

Segall, Marshall H.; Dasan, Pierre R.; Berry, John W.; & Poortinga, Ype H. (1999). *Human behavior in global perspective: An introduction to cross-cultural psychology* (2nd ed.). Boston, MA: Allyn & Bacon.

Segall, Marshall H.; Lonner, Walter J.; & Berry, John W. (1998). Cross-cultural psychology as a scholarly discipline: On the flowering of culture in behavioral research. *American Psychologist, 53,* 1101–1110.

Segerstrom, Suzanne C.; Taylor, Shelley E.; Kemeny, Margaret E.; & Fahey, John L. (1998). Optimism is associated with mood, coping, and immune change in response to stress. *Journal of Personality and Social Psychology, 74,* 1646–1655.

Seiden, Richard (1978). Where are they now? A follow-up study of suicide attempters from the Golden Gate Bridge. *Suicide and Life-Threatening Behavior, 8,* 203–216.

Seidenberg, Mark S. (1997). Language acquisition and use: Learning and applying probabilistic constraints. *Science, 275,* 1599–1603.

Seidenberg, Mark S., & Petitto, Laura A. (1979). Signing behavior in apes: A critical review. *Cognition, 7,* 177–215.

Seidlitz, Larry, & Diener, Ed (1998). Sex differences in the recall of affective experiences. *Journal of Personality and Social Psychology, 74,* 262–271.

Seifer, Ronald; Schiller, Masha; Sameroff, Arnold; et al. (1996). Attachment, maternal sensitivity, and infant temperament during the first year of life. *Developmental Psychology, 32,* 12–25.

Sekuler, Robert, & Blake, Randolph (1994). *Perception* (3rd ed.). New York: Knopf.

Seligman, Martin E. P. (1975). *Helplessness: On depression, development, and death.* San Francisco: Freeman.

Seligman, Martin E. P. (1991). *Learned optimism.* New York: Knopf.

Seligman, Martin E. P., & Hager, Joanne L. (1972, August). Biological boundaries of learning: The sauce-béarnaise syndrome. *Psychology Today,* 59–61, 84–87.

Seligman, Martin E.P.; Schulman, Peter; DeRubeis, Robert J.; & Hollon, Steven D. (1998). The prevention of depression and anxiety. Paper presented at the annual meeting of the American Psychological Association, San Francisco.

Selye, Hans (1956). *The stress of life.* New York: McGraw-Hill.

Serbin, Lisa A.; Powlishta, Kimberly K.; & Gulko, Judith (1993). The development of sex typing in middle childhood. *Monographs of the Society for Research in Child Development, 58*(2, Serial No. 232), v–74.

Serdula, Mary K.; Collins, M. E.; Williamson, David F.; et al. (1993). Weight control practices of U.S. adolescents and adults. *Annals of Internal Medicine, 119,* 667–671.

Serpell, Robert (1994). The cultural construction of intelligence. In W. J. Lonner & R. S. Malpass (eds.), *Psychology and culture.* Needham Heights, MA: Allyn & Bacon.

Shadish, William R., Jr.; Lurigio, Arthur J.; & Lewis, Dan A. (1989). After deinstitutionalization: The present and future of mental health long-term care policy. *Journal of Social Issues, 45*(3), 1–16.

Shapiro, A. Eugene, & Wiggins, Jack G. (1994). A PsyD degree for every practitioner. *American Psychologist, 49,* 207–210.

Shapiro, Deane H.; Schwartz, Carolyn E.; & Astin, John A. (1996). Controlling ourselves, controlling our world. *American Psychologist, 51,* 1213–1230.

Shapiro, Francine (1994). EMDR: In the eye of a paradigm shift. *Behavior Therapist, 17,* 153–156.

Shapiro, Francine (1995). *Eye movement desensitization and reprocessing.* New York: Guilford Press.

Shatz, Marilyn, & Gelman, Rochel (1973). The development of communication skills: Modifications in the speech of young children as a function of the listener. *Monographs of the Society for Research in Child Development, 38.*

Shaver, Phillip R., & Hazan, Cindy (1993). Adult romantic attachment: Theory and evidence. In D. Perlman & W. H. Jones (eds.), *Advances in personal relationships* (Vol. 4). London: Kingsley.

Shaver, Phillip R.; Schwartz, Judith; Krison, Donald; & O'Connor, Cary (1987). Emotion knowledge: Further exploration of a prototype approach. *Journal of Personality and Social Psychology, 52,* 1061–1086.

Shaver, Phillip R.; Wu, Shelley; & Schwartz, Judith C. (1992). Cross-cultural similarities and differences in emotion and its representation: A prototype approach. In M. S. Clark (ed.), *Review of Personality and Social Psychology* (Vol. 13). Newbury Park, CA: Sage.

Shaw, Daniel S.; Keenan, Kate; & Vondra, Joan I. (1994). Developmental precursors of externalizing behavior: Ages 1 to 3. *Developmental Psychology, 30,* 355–364.

Shaywitz, Bennett A.; Shaywitz, Sally E.; Pugh, Kenneth R.; et al. (1995). Sex differences in the functional organization of the brain for language. *Nature, 373,* 607–609.

Shedler, Jonathan; Mayman, Martin; & Manis, Melvin (1993). The illusion of mental health. *American Psychologist, 48,* 1117–1131.

Sheldon, Kennon M., & Elliot, Andrew J. (1999). Goal striving, need satisfaction, and longitudinal well-being: The self-concordance model. *Journal of Personality and Social Psychology, 76,* 482–497.

Shepard, Roger N., & Metzler, Jacqueline (1971). Mental rotation of three-dimensional objects. *Science, 171,* 701–703.

Shepperd, James A. (1995). Remedying motivation and productivity loss in collective settings. *Current Directions in Psychological Science, 4,* 131–140.

Sherif, Muzafer (1958). Superordinate goals in the reduction of intergroup conflicts. *American Journal of Sociology, 63,* 349–356.

Sherif, Muzafer; Harvey, O. J.; White, B. J.; Hood, William; & Sherif, Carolyn (1961). *Intergroup conflict and cooperation: The Robbers Cave experiment.* Norman, OK: University of Oklahoma Institute of Intergroup Relations.

Sherman, Bonnie R., & Kunda, Ziva (1989). Motivated evaluation of scientific evidence. Paper presented at the annual meeting of the American Psychological Society, Arlington, VA.

Sherman, Jeffrey W., & Bessenoff, Gayle R. (1999). Stereotypes as source-monitoring cues: On the interaction between episodic and semantic memory. *Psychological Science, 10,* 106–110.

Shermer, Michael (1997). *Why people believe weird things: Pseudoscience, superstition, and other confusions of our time.* New York: Freeman.

Sherwin, Barbara B. (1988). A comparative analysis of the role of androgen in human male and female sexual behavior: Behavioral specificity, critical thresholds, and sensitivity. *Psychobiology, 16,* 416–425.

Sherwin, Barbara B. (1998a). Estrogen and cognitive functioning in women. *Proceedings of the Society for Experimental Biological Medicine, 217,* 17–22.

Sherwin, Barbara B. (1998b). Use of combined estrogen–androgen preparations in the postmenopause: Evidence from clinical studies. *International Journal of Fertility and Women's Medicine, 43,* 98–103.

Shields, Stephanie A. (1975). Functionalism, Darwinism, and the psychology of women: A study in social myth. *American Psychologist, 30,* 739–754.

Shields, Stephanie A. (1991). Gender in the psychology of emotion: A selective research review. In K. T. Strongman (ed.), *International review of studies on emotion* (Vol. 1). New York: Wiley.

Shih, Margaret; Pittinsky, Todd L.; & Ambady, Nalini (1999). Stereotype susceptibility: Identity salience and shifts in quantitative performance. *Psychological Science, 10,* 80–83.

Shin, Lisa M.; Kosslyn, Stephen M.; McNally, Richard K.; et al. (1997). Visual imagery and perception in posttraumatic stress disorder. *Archives of General Psychiatry, 54,* 233–241.

Shogren, Elizabeth (1994, August 18). Treatment against their will. *Los Angeles Times,* A1, A14–16.

Shotland, R. Lance, & Straw, Margaret (1976). Bystander response to an assault: When a man attacks a woman. *Journal of Personality and Social Psychology, 34,* 990–999.

Shweder, Richard A.; Mahapatra, Manamohan; & Miller, Joan G. (1990). Culture and moral development. In J. W. Stigler, R. A. Shweder, & G. Herdt (eds.), *Cultural psychology: Essays on comparative human development.* Cambridge, England: Cambridge University Press.

Sidanius, Jim; Pratto, Felicia; & Bobo, Lawrence (1996). Racism, conservatism, affirmative action, and intellectual sophistication: A matter of principled conservatism or group dominance? *Journal of Personality and Social Psychology, 70,* 476–490.

Siegel, Alan B. (1991). *Dreams that can change your life.* Los Angeles: Jeremy Tarcher.

Siegel, Judith M. (1990). Stressful life events and use of physician services among the elderly: The moderating role of pet ownership. *Journal of Personality and Social Psychology, 58,* 1081–1086.

Siegel, Ronald K. (1989). *Intoxication: Life in pursuit of artificial paradise.* New York: Dutton.

Siegler, Robert (1996). *Emerging minds: The process of change in children's thinking.* New York: Oxford University Press.

Silver, Eric; Cirincione, Carmen; & Steadman, Henry J. (1994). Demythologizing inaccurate perceptions of the insanity defense. *Law and Human Behavior, 18,* 63–70.

Silverstein, Brett, & Perlick, Deborah (1995). *The cost of competence: Why inequality causes depression, eating disorders, and illness in women.* New York: Oxford University Press.

Silverstein, Brett; Peterson, Barbara; & Perdue, Lauren (1986). Some correlates of the thin standard of bodily attractiveness in women. *International Journal of Eating Disorders, 5,* 145–155.

Sims, Ethan A. (1974). Studies in human hyperphagia. In G. Bray & J. Bethune (eds.), *Treatment and management of obesity.* New York: Harper & Row.

Singer, Jerome L. (1984). The private personality. *Personality and Social Psychology Bulletin, 10,* 7–30.

Singer, Margaret T.; Temerlin, Maurice K.; & Langone, Michael D. (1990). Psychotherapy cults. *Cultic Studies Journal, 7,* 101–125.

Skinner, B. F. (1938). *The behavior of organisms: An experimental analysis.* New York: Appleton-Century-Crofts.

Skinner, B. F. (1948). Superstition in the pigeon. *Journal of Experimental Psychology, 38,* 168–172.

Skinner, B. F. (1948/1976). *Walden Two.* New York: Macmillan.

Skinner, B. F. (1956). A case history in the scientific method. *American Psychologist, 11,* 221–233.

Skinner, B. F. (1961, November). Teaching machines. *Scientific American,* 91–102.

Skinner, B. F. (1972). The operational analysis of psychological terms. In B. F. Skinner, *Cumulative record* (3rd ed.). New York: Appleton-Century-Crofts.

Skinner, B. F. (1990). Can psychology be a science of mind? *American Psychologist, 45,* 1206–1210.

Skinner, Ellen A. (1996). A guide to constructs of control. *Journal of Personality and Social Psychology, 71,* 549–570.

Skinner, J. B.; Erskine, A.; Pearce, S. A.; et al. (1990). The evaluation of a cognitive behavioural treatment programme in outpatients with chronic pain. *Journal of Psychosomatic Research, 34,* 13–19.

Skreslet, Paula (1987, November 30). The prizes of first grade. *Newsweek,* 8.

Slade, Pauline (1984). Premenstrual emotional changes in normal women: Fact or fiction? *Journal of Psychosomatic Research, 28,* 1–7.

Slobin, Daniel I. (ed.) (1985). *The cross-linguistic study of language acquisition* (Vols. 1 and 2). Hillsdale, NJ: Erlbaum.

Slobin, Daniel I. (ed.) (1991). *The cross-linguistic study of language acquisition* (Vol. 3). Hillsdale, NJ: Erlbaum.

Slotkin, Theodore A. (1998). Fetal nicotine or cocaine exposure: Which one is worse? *Journal of Pharmacology and Experimental Therapeutics, 285,* 931–945.

Smith, Carlyle (1995). Sleep states and memory processes. *Behavioural Brain Research, 69,* 137–145.

Smith, Carolyn A.; Lizotte, Alan J.; Thornberry, Terence P.; et al. (1997). Resilient youth: Identifying factors that prevent high-risk youth from engaging in delinquency and drug use. In J. Hagan (ed.), *Delinquency and disrepute in the life course.* Greenwich, CT: JAI Press.

Smith, Craig A.; Haynes, Kelly N.; Lazarus, Richard S.; & Pope, Lois K. (1993). In search of the "hot" cognitions: Attributions, appraisals, and their relation to emotion. *Journal of Personality and Social Psychology, 65,* 916–929.

Smith, David N. (1998). The psychocultural roots of genocide: Legitimacy and crisis in Rwanda. *American Psychologist, 53,* 743–753.

Smith, James F., & Kida, Thomas (1991). Heuristics and biases: Expertise and task realism in auditing. *Psychological Bulletin, 109,* 472–489.

Smith, Larissa L., & Reise, Steven P. (1998). Gender differences on negative affectivity: An IRT study of differential item functioning on the Multidimensional Personality Questionnaire Stress Reaction Scale. *Journal of Personality and Social Psychology, 75,* 1350–1362.

Smith, Mary Lee; Glass, Gene; & Miller, Thomas I. (1980). *The benefits of psychotherapy.* Baltimore, MD: Johns Hopkins University Press.

Smith, Michael D.; Keltner, Dacher; & Gonzaga, Gian C. (1998). Love and desire: New evidence for distinct displays of emotion. Paper presented at the annual meeting of the American Psychological Association, San Francisco.

Smith, N.; Tsimpli, I.-M., & Ouhalla, J. (1993). Learning the impossible: The acquisition of possible and impossible languages by a polyglot savant. *Lingua, 91,* 279–347.

Smith, Peter B., & Bond, Michael H. (1993/1994). *Social psychology across cultures: Analysis and perspectives.* Boston: Allyn & Bacon.

Smith, Timothy W.; Limon, Jeffery P.; Gallo, Linda C.; & Ngu, Le Q. (1996). Interpersonal control and cardiovascular reactivity: Goals, behavioral expression, and the moderating effects of sex. *Journal of Personality and Social Psychology, 70,* 1012–1024.

Smither, Robert D. (1998). *The psychology of work and human performance* (3rd ed.). New York: Longman.

Smyth, Joshua M., & Pennebaker, James W. (1999). Sharing one's story: Translating emotional experiences into words as a coping tool. In C. R. Snyder (ed.), *Coping: The psychology of what works.* New York: Oxford University Press.

Snodgrass, Sara E. (1985). Women's intuition: The effect of subordinate role on interpersonal sensitivity. *Journal of Personality and Social Psychology, 49,* 146–155.

Snodgrass, Sara E. (1992). Further effects of role versus gender on interpersonal sensitivity. *Journal of Personality and Social Psychology, 62,* 154–158.

Snodgrass, Sara E.; Hecht, Marvin A.; & Ploutz-Snyder, Robert (1998). Interpersonal sensitivity: Expressivity or perceptivity? *Journal of Personality and Social Psychology, 74,* 238–249.

Snow, Barry R; Pinter, Isaac; Gusmorino, Paul; et al. (1986). Sex differences in chronic pain: Incidence and causal mechanisms. Paper presented at the annual meeting of the American Psychological Association, Washington, DC.

Snowdon, Charles T. (1997). The "nature" of sex differences: Myths of male and female. In P. A. Gowaty (ed.), *Feminism and evolutionary biology.* New York: Chapman and Hall.

Snyder, C. R., & Shenkel, Randee J. (1975, March). The P. T. Barnum effect. *Psychology Today,* 52–54.

Snyder, James J., & Patterson, Gerald R. (1995). Individual differences in social aggression: A test of a reinforcer model of socialization in the natural environment. *Behavior Therapy, 26,* 371–391.

Snyder, Robert A. (1993, Spring). The glass ceiling for women: Things that don't cause it and things that won't break it. *Human Resource Development Quarterly,* 97–106.

Solomon, Jennifer C. (1996). Humor and aging well: A laughing matter or a matter of laughing? *American Behavioral Scientist, 39,* 249–271.

Solomon, Paul R. (1979). Science and television commercials: Adding relevance to the research methodology course. *Teaching of Psychology, 6,* 26–30.

Solomon, Robert C. (1994). *About love.* Lanham, MD: Littlefield Adams.

Sommer, Robert (1969). *Personal space: The behavioral basis of design.* Englewood Cliffs, NJ: Prentice-Hall.

Sommer, Robert (1977, January). Toward a psychology of natural behavior. *APA Monitor.* (Reprinted in *Readings in psychology 78/79.* Guilford, CT: Dushkin, 1978.)

Sorce, James F.; Emde, Robert N.; Campos, Joseph; & Klinnert, Mary D. (1985). Maternal emotional signaling: Its effect on the visual cliff behavior of 1-year-olds. *Developmental Psychology, 21,* 195–200.

Spanos, Nicholas P. (1991). A sociocognitive approach to hypnosis. In S. J. Lynn & J. W. Rhue (eds.), *Theories of hypnosis: Current models and perspectives.* New York: Guilford Press.

Spanos, Nicholas P. (1996). *Multiple identities and false memories: A sociocognitive perspective.* Washington, DC: American Psychological Association.

Spanos, Nicholas P.; Burgess, Cheryl A.; Roncon, Vera; et al. (1993). Surreptitiously observed hypnotic responding in simulators and in skill-trained and untrained high hypnotizables. *Journal of Personality and Social Psychology, 65,* 391–398.

Spanos, Nicholas P.; Menary, Evelyn; Gabora, Natalie J.; et al. (1991). Secondary identity enactments during hypnotic past-life regression: A sociocognitive perspective. *Journal of Personality and Social Psychology, 61,* 308–320.

Spanos, Nicholas P.; Stenstrom, Robert J.; & Johnson, Joseph C. (1988). Hypnosis, placebo, and suggestion in the treatment of warts. *Psychosomatic Medicine, 50,* 245–260.

Spearman, Charles (1927). *The abilities of man.* London: Macmillan.

Speltz, Matthew L.; Greenberg, Mark T.; & Deklyen, Michelle (1990). Attachment in preschoolers with disruptive behavior: A comparison of clinic-referred and nonproblem children. *Development and Psychopathology, 2,* 31–46.

Spence, Janet T. (1985). Gender identity and its implications for concepts of masculinity and femininity. In T. Sonderegger (ed.), *Nebraska Symposium on Motivation, 1984.* Lincoln: University of Nebraska Press.

Spence, Janet T., & Hahn, Eugene D. (1997). The Attitudes Toward Women Scale and attitude change in college students. *Psychology of Women Quarterly, 22,* 17–36.

Spencer, M. B., & Dornbusch, Sanford M. (1990). Ethnicity. In S. S. Feldman & G. R. Elliott (eds.), *At the threshold: The developing adolescent.* Cambridge, MA: Harvard University Press.

Sperling, George (1960). The information available in brief visual presentations. *Psychological Monographs, 74*(498).

Sperry, Roger W. (1964). The great cerebral commissure. *Scientific American, 210*(1), 42–52.

Sperry, Roger W. (1982). Some effects of disconnecting the cerebral hemispheres. *Science, 217,* 1223–1226.

Spiegel, D.; Bloom, J. R.; Kraemer, H. C.; Gottheil, E. (1989, October 14). Effect of psychosocial treatment on survival of patients with metastatic breast cancer. *Lancet, 2*(8668), 888–891.

Spilich, George J.; June, Lorraine; & Renner, Judith (1992). Cigarette smoking and cognitive performance. *British Journal of Addiction, 87,* 113–126.

Spitz, Herman H. (1997). *Nonconscious movements: From mystical messages to facilitated communication.* Mahwah, NJ: Erlbaum.

Spitzer, Robert L., & Williams, Janet B. (1988). Having a dream: A research strategy for *DSM-IV. Archives of General Psychiatry, 45,* 871–874.

Spoont, Michele R. (1992). Modulatory role of serotonin in neural information processing: Implications for human psychopathology. *Psychological Bulletin, 112,* 330–350.

Sporer, Siegfried L.; Penrod, Steven; Read, Don; & Cutler, Brian (1995). Choosing, confidence, and accuracy: A meta-analysis of the confidence-accuracy relation in eyewitness identification studies. *Psychological Bulletin, 118,* 315–327.

Sprecher, Susan; Sullivan, Quintin; & Hatfield, Elaine (1994). Mate selection preferences: Gender differences examined in a national sample. *Journal of Personality and Social Psychology, 66,* 1074–1080.

Spring, Bonnie; Chiodo, June; & Bowen, Deborah J. (1987). Carbohydrates, tryptophan, and behavior: A methodological review. *Psychological Bulletin, 102,* 234–256.

Springer, S. P., & Deutsch, G. (1998). *Left brain, right brain*. New York: Freeman.

Squier, Leslie H., & Domhoff, G. William (1998). The presentation of dreaming and dreams in introductory psychology textbooks: A critical examination with suggestions for textbook authors and course instructors. *Dreaming, 8,* 149–168.

Squire, Larry R. (1987). *Memory and the brain*. New York: Oxford University Press.

Squire, Larry R.; Ojemann, Jeffrey G.; Miezin, Francis M.; et al. (1992). Activation of the hippocampus in normal humans: A functional anatomical study of memory. *Proceedings of the National Academy of Science, 89,* 1837–1841.

Squire, Larry R., & Zola-Morgan, Stuart (1991). The medial temporal lobe memory system. *Science, 253,* 1380–1386.

Staats, Carolyn K., & Staats, Arthur W. (1957). Meaning established by classical conditioning. *Journal of Experimental Psychology, 54,* 74–80.

Stajkovic, Alexander D., & Luthans, Fred (1998). Self-efficacy and work-related performance: A meta-analysis. *Psychological Bulletin, 124,* 240–261.

Stam, Henderikus J. (1989). From symptom relief to cure: Hypnotic interventions in cancer. In N. P. Spanos & J. F. Chaves (eds.), *Hypnosis: The cognitive-behavioral perspective*. Buffalo, NY: Prometheus Books.

Stanovich, Keith (1996). *How to think straight about psychology* (4th ed.). New York: HarperCollins.

Stanton, Annette L., & Franz, Robert (1999). Focusing on emotion: An adaptive coping strategy? In C. R. Snyder (ed.), *Coping: The psychology of what works*. New York: Oxford University Press.

Staples, Brent (1994). *Parallel time*. New York: Pantheon.

Staples, Susan L. (1996). Human response to environmental noise: Psychological research and public policy. *American Psychologist, 51,* 143–150.

Stapley, Janice C., & Haviland, Jeannette M. (1989). Beyond depression: Gender differences in normal adolescents' emotional experiences. *Sex Roles, 20,* 295–308.

Stattin, Haken, & Magnusson, David (1990). *Pubertal maturation in female development*. Hillsdale, NJ: Erlbaum.

Staub, Ervin (1996). Cultural–social roots of violence. *American Psychologist, 51,* 117–132.

Staudinger, Ursula M.; Fleeson, William; & Baltes, Paul B. (1999). Predictors of subjective physical health and global well-being: Similarities and differences between the United States and Germany. *Journal of Personality and Social Psychology, 76,* 305–319.

Steele, Claude M. (1992, April). Race and the schooling of Black Americans. *Atlantic Monthly,* 68–78.

Steele, Claude M. (1997). A threat in the air: How stereotypes shape intellectual identity and performance. *American Psychologist, 52,* 613–629.

Steele, Claude M., & Aronson, Joshua (1995). Stereotype threat and the intellectual test performance of African-Americans. *Journal of Personality and Social Psychology, 69,* 797–811.

Steinberg, Laurence D. (1990). Interdependence in the family: Autonomy, conflict and harmony in the parent–adolescent relationship. In S. S. Feldman & G. R. Elliott (eds.), *At the threshold: The developing adolescent*. Cambridge, MA: Harvard University Press.

Steinberg, Laurence D.; Dornbusch, Sanford M.; & Brown, B. Bradford (1992). Ethnic differences in adolescent achievement: An ecological perspective. *American Psychologist, 47,* 723–729.

Steiner, Robert A. (1989). *Don't get taken!* El Cerrito, CA: Wide-Awake Books.

Stempel, Jennifer J.; Beckwith, Bill E.; & Petros, Thomas V. (1986). The effects of alcohol on the speed of memory retrieval. Paper presented at the annual meeting of the American Psychological Association, Washington, DC.

Stenberg, Craig R., & Campos, Joseph (1990). The development of anger expressions in infancy. In N. Stein, B. Leventhal, & T. Trabasso (eds.), *Psychological and biological approaches to emotion*. Hillsdale, NJ: Erlbaum.

Stephan, K. M.; Fink, G. R.; Passingham, R. E.; et al. (1995). Functional anatomy of the mental representation of upper movements in healthy subjects. *Journal of Neurophysiology, 73,* 373–386.

Stephan, Walter G.; Ageyev, Vladimir; Coates-Shrider, Lisa; et al. (1994). On the relationship between stereotypes and prejudice: An international study. *Personality and Social Psychology Bulletin, 20,* 277–284.

Stephens, Mitchell (1991, September 20). The death of reading. *Los Angeles Times Magazine,* 10, 12, 16, 42, 44.

Stern, Kathleen, & McClintock, Martha K. (1998). Regulation of ovulation by human pheromones. *Nature, 392,* 177–179.

Stern, Marilyn, & Karraker, Katherine H. (1989). Sex stereotyping of infants: A review of gender labeling studies. *Sex Roles, 20,* 501–522.

Sternberg, Esther M., & Gold, Philip W. (1997). The mind–body interaction in disease [Special issue: Mysteries of the mind]. *Scientific American,* 8–15.

Sternberg, Robert J. (1986). *Intelligence applied: Understanding and increasing your intellectual skills*. San Diego: Harcourt Brace Jovanovich.

Sternberg, Robert J. (1988). *The triarchic mind: A new theory of human intelligence*. New York: Viking.

Sternberg, Robert J. (1997). Construct validation of a triangular love scale. *European Journal of Social Psychology, 27,* 313–335.

Sternberg, Robert J., & Wagner, Richard K. (1989). Individual differences in practical knowledge and its acquisition. In P. Ackerman, R. J. Sternberg, & R. Glaser (eds.), *Individual differences*. New York: Freeman.

Sternberg, Robert J.; Wagner, Richard K.; & Okagaki, Lynn (1993). Practical intelligence: The nature and role of tacit knowledge in work and at school. In H. Reese & J. Puckett (eds.), *Advances in lifespan development*. Hillsdale, NJ: Erlbaum.

Sternberg, Robert J.; Wagner, Richard K.; Williams, Wendy M.; & Horvath, Joseph A. (1995). Testing common sense. *American Psychologist, 50,* 912–927.

Sternberg, Robert J., & Williams, Wendy M. (1997). Does the GRE predict meaningful success in the graduate training of psychologists? A case study. *American Psychologist, 52,* 630–641.

Stevenson, Harold W.; Chen, Chuansheng; & Lee, Shin-ying (1993, January 1). Mathematics achievement of Chinese, Japanese, and American children: Ten years later. *Science, 259,* 53–58.

Stevenson, Harold W., & Stigler, James W. (1992). *The learning gap*. New York: Summit.

Stewart, Abigail J., & Ostrove, Joan M. (1998). Women's personality in middle age: Gender, history, and midcourse corrections. *American Psychologist, 53,* 1185–1194.

Stewart, Abigail J., & Vandewater, Elizabeth A. (1999). "If I had it to do over again . . . ": Midlife review, midcourse corrections, and women's well-being in midlife. *Journal of Personality and Social Psychology, 76,* 270–283.

Stimpson, Catherine (1996, Winter). Women's studies and its discontents. *Dissent, 43,* 67–75.

Stoch, M. B., & Smythe, P. M. (1963). Does undernutrition during infancy inhibit brain growth and subsequent intellectual development? *Archives of Diseases in Childhood, 38,* 546–552.

Strack, Fritz; Martin, Leonard L.; & Stepper, Sabine (1988). Inhibiting and facilitating conditions of the human smile: A nonobtrusive test of the facial-feedback hypothesis. *Journal of Social and Personality Psychology, 54,* 768–777.

Straus, Murray A., & Kantor, Glenda Kaufman (1994). Corporal punishment of adolescents by parents: A risk factor in the epidemiology of depression, suicide, alcohol abuse, child abuse, and wife beating. *Adolescence, 29,* 543–561.

Streissguth, Ann P.; Barr, Helen M.; Bookstein, Fred L.; et al. (1999). The long-term neurocognitive consequences of prenatal alcohol exposure: A 14-year study. *Psychological Science, 10*, 186–190.

Strickland, Bonnie R. (1989). Internal–external control expectancies: From contingency to creativity. *American Psychologist, 44*, 1–12.

Strickland, Bonnie R. (1995). Research on sexual orientation and human development: A commentary. *Developmental Psychology, 31*, 137–140.

Strickland, Tony L.; Lin, Keh-Ming; Fu, Paul; et al. (1995). Comparison of lithium ratio between African-American and Caucasian bipolar patients. *Biological Psychiatry, 37*, 325–330.

Strickland, Tony L.; Ranganath, Vijay; Lin, Keh-Ming; et al. (1991). Psychopharmacological considerations in the treatment of black American populations. *Psychopharmacology Bulletin, 27*, 441–448.

Stroebe, Wolfgang; Stroebe, Margaret; Abakoumkin, Georgios; & Schut, Henk (1996). The role of loneliness and social support in adjustment to loss: A test of attachment versus stress theory. *Journal of Personality and Social Psychology, 70*, 1241–1249.

Strupp, Hans H., & Binder, Jeffrey (1984). *Psychotherapy in a new key.* New York: Basic Books.

Stunkard, Albert J. (ed.) (1980). *Obesity.* Philadelphia: Saunders.

Stunkard, Albert J.; Harris, J. R.; Pedersen, N. L.; & McClearn, G. E. (1990, May 24). The body-mass index of twins who have been reared apart. *New England Journal of Medicine, 322*, 1483–1487.

Sue, Stanley (1998). In search of cultural competence in psychotherapy and counseling. *American Psychologist, 53*, 440–448.

Suedfeld, Peter (1975). The benefits of boredom: Sensory deprivation reconsidered. *American Scientist, 63*(1), 60–69.

Sullivan, Michael J. L.; Tripp, Dean A.; & Santor, Darcy (1998). Gender differences in pain and pain behavior: The role of catastrophizing. Paper presented at the annual meeting of the American Psychological Association, San Francisco.

Sulloway, Frank J. (1992). *Freud, biologist of the mind: Beyond the psychoanalytic legend* (Rev. ed.). Cambridge, MA: Harvard University Press.

Suomi, Stephen J. (1987). Genetic and maternal contributions to individual differences in rhesus monkey biobehavioral development. In N. Krasnegor, E. Blass, M. Hofer, & W. Smotherman (eds.), *Perinatal development: A psychobiological perspective.* New York: Academic Press.

Suomi, Stephen J. (1989). Primate separation models of affective disorders. In J. Madden (ed.), *Adaptation, learning, and affect.* New York: Raven Press.

Suomi, Stephen J. (1991). Uptight and laid-back monkeys: Individual differences in the response to social challenges. In S. Branch, W. Hall, & J. E. Dooling (eds.), *Plasticity of development.* Cambridge, MA: MIT Press.

Super, Charles A., & Harkness, Sara (1994). The developmental niche. In W. J. Lonner & R. Malpass (eds.), *Psychology and culture.* Needham Heights, MA: Allyn & Bacon.

Susman, Elizabeth J.; Inoff-Germain, Gale; Nottelmann, Editha D.; et al. (1987). Hormones, emotional dispositions, and aggressive attributes in young adolescents. *Child Development, 58*, 1114–1134.

Susser, Ezra; Neugebauer, Richard; Hoek, Hans W.; et al. (1996). Schizophrenia after prenatal famine: Further evidence. *Archives of General Psychiatry, 53*, 25–31.

Symons, Donald (1979). *The evolution of human sexuality.* New York: Oxford University Press.

Tabandeh, H.; Lockley, S. W.; Buttery, R.; et al. (1998). Disturbance of sleep in blindness. *American Journal of Ophthalmology, 126*, 707–712.

Taffel, Ronald (1990, September/October). The politics of mood. *Family Therapy Networker, 49–53, 72.

Tajfel, Henri; Billig, M. G.; Bundy, R. P.; & Flament, C. (1971). Social categorization and intergroup behavior. *European Journal of Social Psychology, 1*, 149–178.

Tajfel, Henri, & Turner, John C. (1986). The social identity theory of intergroup behavior. In S. Worchel & W. G. Austin (eds.), *Psychology of intergroup relations.* Chicago: Nelson-Hall.

Tangney, June P.; Wagner, Patricia E.; Hill-Barlow, Deborah; et al. (1996). Relation of shame and guilt to constructive versus destructive responses to anger across the lifespan. *Journal of Personality and Social Psychology, 70*, 797–809.

Tartter, Vivien C. (1986). *Language processes.* New York: Holt, Rinehart and Winston.

Taub, David M. (1984). *Primate paternalism.* New York: Van Nostrand Reinhold.

Taubes, Gary (1998). As obesity rates rise, experts struggle to explain why. *Science, 280*, 1367–1368.

Tavris, Carol (1989). *Anger: The misunderstood emotion* (Rev. ed.). New York: Simon & Schuster/Touchstone.

Taylor, Donald M., & Porter, Lana E. (1994). A multicultural view of stereotyping. In W. J. Lonner & R. Malpass (eds.), *Psychology and culture.* Needham Heights, MA: Allyn & Bacon.

Taylor, Shelley E. (1995). *Health psychology* (3rd ed.). New York: McGraw Hill.

Taylor, Shelley E., & Brown, Jonathon D. (1994). Positive illusions and well-being revisited: Separating fact from fiction. *Psychological Bulletin, 116*, 21–27.

Taylor, Shelley E.; Lichtman, Rosemary R.; & Wood, Joanne V. (1984). Attributions, beliefs about control, and adjustment to breast cancer. *Journal of Personality and Social Psychology, 46*, 489–502.

Taylor, Shelley E., & Lobel, Marci (1989). Social comparison activity under threat: Downward evaluation and upward contacts. *Psychological Review, 96*, 569–575.

Taylor, Shelley E.; Repetti, Rena; & Seeman, Teresa (1997). Health psychology: What is an unhealthy environment and how does it get under the skin? *Annual Review of Psychology* (Vol. 48). Palo Alto, CA: Annual Reviews.

Temerlin, Jane W., & Temerlin, Maurice K. (1986). Some hazards of the therapeutic relationship. *Cultic Studies Journal, 3*, 234–242.

Tennen, Howard, & Affleck, Glenn (1999). Finding benefits in adversity. In C. R. Snyder (ed.), *Coping: The psychology of what works.* New York: Oxford University Press.

Terman, Lewis M., & Oden, Melita H. (1959). *Genetic studies of genius: Vol. 5. The gifted group at mid-life.* Stanford, CA: Stanford University Press.

Terman, Michael; Terman, Jiuan Su; & Ross, Donald C. (1998). A controlled trial of timed bright light and negative air ionization for treatment of winter depression. *Archives of General Psychiatry, 55*, 875–882.

Terrace, H. S. (1985). In the beginning was the "name." *American Psychologist, 40*, 1011–1028.

Terry, Deborah J. (1994). Determinants of coping: The role of stable and situational factors. *Journal of Personality and Social Psychology, 66*, 895–910.

Terry, Deborah J., & Hynes, Gloria J. (1998). Adjustment to a low-control situation: Reexamining the role of coping responses. *Journal of Personality and Social Psychology, 74*, 1078–1092.

Thase, Michael E.; Fasiczka, A. L.; Berman, S. R.; et al. (1998). Electroencephalographic sleep profiles before and after cognitive behavior therapy of depression. *Archives of General Psychiatry, 55*, 138–144.

Thase, Michael E.; Greenhouse, J. B.; Frank, E.; et al. (1997). Treatment of major depression with psychotherapy or psychotherapy–pharmacotherapy combinations. *Archives of General Psychiatry, 54*, 1009–1015.

Thibodeau, Ruth, & Aronson, Elliot (1992). Taking a closer look: Reasserting the role of the self-concept in dissonance theory. *Personality and Social Psychology Bulletin, 18,* 591–602.

Thigpen, Corbett H., & Cleckley, Hervey M. (1984). On the incidence of multiple personality disorder: A brief communication. *International Journal of Clinical and Experimental Hypnosis, 32,* 63–66.

Thoma, Stephen J. (1986). Estimating gender differences in the comprehension and preference of moral issues. *Developmental Review, 6,* 165–180.

Thomassen, R.; van Schaick, H. W.; & Blansjaar, B. A. (1998). Prevalence of dementia over age 100. *Neurology, 50,* 283–286.

Thompson, Clara (1943/1973). Penis envy in women. *Psychiatry, 6,* 123–125. (Reprinted in J. B. Miller (ed.), *Psychoanalysis and women.* New York: Brunner/Mazel, 1973.)

Thompson, Richard F. (1983). Neuronal substrates of simple associative learning: Classical conditioning. *Trends in Neurosciences, 6,* 270–275.

Thompson, Richard F. (1986). The neurobiology of learning and memory. *Science, 233,* 941–947.

Thompson, Suzanne C.; Nanni, Christopher; & Levine, Alexandra (1994). Primary versus secondary and central versus consequence-related control in HIV-positive men. *Journal of Personality and Social Psychology, 67,* 540–547.

Thorndike, Edward L. (1898). Animal intelligence: An experimental study of the associative processes in animals. *Psychological Review Monograph Supplement, 2* (Whole No. 8).

Thorndike, Edward L. (1903). *Educational psychology.* New York: Columbia University Teachers College.

Thornhill, Randy (1980). Rape in *Panorpa* scorpion-flies and a general rape hypothesis. *Animal Behavior, 28,* 52–59.

Thun, M. J.; Peto, R.; Lopez, A. D.; et al. (1997). Alcohol consumption and mortality among middle-aged and elderly U.S. adults. *New England Journal of Medicine, 337,* 1705–1714.

Tice, Dianne M., & Baumeister, Roy F. (1997). Longitudinal study of procrastination, performance, stress, and health: The costs and benefits of dawdling. *Pschological Science, 8,* 454–458.

Tiefer, Leonore (1995). *Sex is not a natural act and other essays.* Boulder, CO: Westview Press.

Timmers, Monique; Fischer, Agneta H.; & Manstead, Antony S. R. (1998). Gender differences in motives for regulating emotions. *Personality and Social Psychology Bulletin, 24,* 974–985.

Todes, Daniel P. (1997). From the machine to the ghost within: Pavlov's transition from digestive physiology to conditional reflexes. *American Psychologist, 52,* 947–955.

Tolman, Edward C. (1938). The determiners of behavior at a choice point. *Psychological Review, 45,* 1–35.

Tolman, Edward C., & Honzik, Chase H. (1930). Introduction and removal of reward and maze performance in rats. *University of California Publications in Psychology, 4,* 257–275.

Torrey, E. Fuller (1988). *Surviving schizophrenia* (Rev. ed.). New York: Harper & Row.

Torrey, E. Fuller; Bowler, Ann E.; Taylor, Edward H.; & Gottesman, Irving I. (1994). *Schizophrenia and manic–depressive disorder.* New York: Basic Books.

Totterdell, Peter; Kellett, Steve; Teuchmann, Katja; & Briner, Rob B. (1998). Evidence of mood linkage in work groups. *Journal of Personality and Social Psychology, 74,* 1504–1515.

Tougas, Francine; Brown, Rupert; Beaton, Ann M.; & Joly, Stéphane (1995). Neosexism: Plus ça change, plus c'est pareil. *Personality and Social Psychology Bulletin, 21,* 842–849.

Triandis, Harry C. (1994). *Culture and social behavior.* New York: McGraw-Hill.

Triandis, Harry C. (1995). *Individualism and collectivism.* Boulder, CO: Westview Press.

Triandis, Harry C. (1996). The psychological measurement of cultural syndromes. *American Psychologist, 51,* 407–415.

Trichopoulos, Dimitrios; Li, F. P.; & Hunter, D. J. (1996, September). What causes cancer? *Scientific American, 275,* 80–87.

Trivers, Robert (1972). Parental investment and sexual selection. In B. Campbell (ed.), *Sexual selection and the descent of man.* New York: Aldine de Gruyter.

Tronick, Edward Z.; Morelli, Gilda A.; & Ivey, Paula K. (1992). The Efe forager infant and toddler's pattern of social relationships: Multiple and simultaneous. *Developmental Psychology, 28,* 568–577.

Tulving, Endel (1985). How many memory systems are there? *American Psychologist, 40,* 385–398.

Tversky, Amos, & Kahneman, Daniel (1973). Availability: A heuristic for judging frequency and probability. *Cognitive Psychology, 5,* 207–232.

Tversky, Amos, & Kahneman, Daniel (1981). The framing of decisions and the psychology of choice. *Science, 211,* 453–458.

Twenge, Jean M. (1997). Attitudes toward women, 1970–1995: A meta-analysis. *Psychology of Women Quarterly, 21,* 35–51.

Tyler, Tom R. (1997). The psychology of legitimacy: A relational perspective on voluntary deference to authorities. *Personality and Social Psychology Review, 1,* 323–345.

Uchida, K., & Toya, S. (1996). Grafting of genetically manipulated cells into adult brain: Toward graft-gene therapy. *Keio Journal of Medicine* (Japan), *45,* 81–89.

Uchino, Bert N.; Cacioppo, John T.; & Kiecolt-Glaser, Janice K. (1996). The relationship between social support and physiological processes: A review with emphasis on underlying mechanisms and implications for health. *Psychological Bulletin, 119,* 488–531.

Uchino, Bert N.; Cacioppo, John T.; Malarkey, William; & Glaser, Ronald (1995). Individual differences in cardiac sympathetic control predict endocrine and immune responses to acute psychological stress. *Journal of Personality and Social Psychology, 69,* 736–743.

Usher, JoNell A., & Neisser, Ulric (1993). Childhood amnesia and the beginnings of memory for four early life events. *Journal of Experimental Psychology: General, 122,* 155–165.

Utman, Christopher H. (1997). Performance effects of motivational state: A meta-analysis. *Personality and Social Psychology Review, 1,* 170–182.

Vaillant, George E. (1983). *The natural history of alcoholism: Causes, patterns, and paths to recovery.* Cambridge, MA: Harvard University Press.

Vaillant, George E. (ed.) (1992). *Ego mechanisms of defense.* Washington, DC: American Psychiatric Press.

Vaillant, George E. (1995). *The natural history of alcoholism revisited.* Cambridge, MA: Harvard University Press.

Valenstein, Elliot (1986). *Great and desperate cures.* New York: Basic Books.

Valenstein, Elliot (1998). *Blaming the brain: The truth about drugs and mental health.* New York: Free Press.

Valian, Virginia (1998). *Why so slow? The advancement of women.* Cambridge, MA: MIT Press.

Van Cantfort, Thomas E., & Rimpau, James B. (1982). Sign language studies with children and chimpanzees. *Sign Language Studies, 34,* 15–72.

Van de Castle, R. (1994). *Our dreaming mind.* New York: Ballantine Books.

Vandenberg, Brian (1985). Beyond the ethology of play. In A. Gottfried & C. C. Brown (eds.), *Play interactions.* Lexington, MA: Lexington Books.

Vanman, Eric J.; Paul, Brenda Y.; Ito, Tiffany A.; & Miller, Norman (1997). The modern face of prejudice and structural features that moderate the effect of cooperation on affect. *Journal of Personality and Social Psychology, 73,* 941–959.

van Praag, H.; Kempermann, G.; & Gage, F. H. (1999). Running increases cell proliferation and neurogenesis in the adult mouse dentate gyrus. *Nature Neuroscience, 2,* 266–270.

Verhaeghen, Paul, & Salthouse, Timothy A. (1997). Meta-analyses of age-cognition relations in adulthood: Estimates of linear and nonlinear age effects and structural models. *Psychological Bulletin, 122,* 231–249.

Vertosick, Frank T. (1997, October). Lobotomy's back. *Discover,* 66–72.

Viken, Richard J.; Rose, Richard J.; Kaprio, Jaakko; & Koskenvuo, Markku (1994). A developmental genetic analysis of adult personality: Extraversion and neuroticism from 18 to 59 years of age. *Journal of Personality and Social Psychology, 66,* 722–730.

Vila, J., & Beech, H. R. (1980). Premenstrual symptomatology: An interaction hypothesis. *British Journal of Social and Clinical Psychology, 19,* 73–80.

Vita, A. J.; Terry, R. B.; Hubert, H. B.; & Fries, J. F. (1998). Aging, health risks, and cumulative disability. *New England Journal of Medicine, 338,* 1035–1041.

Von Lang, Jochen, & Sibyll, Claus (eds.) (1984). *Eichmann interrogated: Transcripts from the archives of the Israeli police.* New York: Random House.

Voyer, Daniel; Voyer, Susan; & Bryden, M. P. (1995). Magnitude of sex differences in spatial abilities: A meta-analysis and consideration of critical variables. *Psychological Bulletin, 117,* 250–270.

Vroon, Piet (1997). *Smell: The secret seducer* (Paul Vincent, trans.). New York: Farrar, Straus, & Giroux.

Wadden, Thomas A.; Foster, G. D.; Letizia, K. A.; & Mullen, J. L. (1990, August 8). Long-term effects of dieting on resting meta-bolic rate in obese outpatients. *Journal of the American Medical Association, 264,* 707–711.

Wagenaar, Willem A. (1986). My memory: A study of autobiographical memory over six years. *Cognitive Psychology, 18,* 225–252.

Wakefield, Jerome C. (1992). The concept of mental disorder: On the boundary between biological facts and social values. *American Psychologist, 47,* 373–388.

Walker, Anne (1994). Mood and well-being in consecutive menstrual cycles: Methodological and theoretical implications. *Psychology of Women Quarterly, 18,* 271–290.

Walker, Edward L. (1970). Relevant psychology is a snark. *American Psychologist, 25,* 1081–1086.

Walker, Lawrence J.; de Vries, Brian; & Trevethan, Shelley D. (1987). Moral stages and moral orientations in real-life and hypothetical dilemmas. *Child Development, 58,* 842–858.

Walker-Andrews, Arlene S. (1997). Infants' perception of expressive behaviors: Differentiation of multimodal information. *Psychological Bulletin, 121,* 437–456.

Wallach, Michael A., & Wallach, Lise (1983). *Psychology's sanction for selfishness: The error of egoism in theory and therapy.* New York: Freeman.

Wallbott, Harald G.; Ricci-Bitti, Pio; & Bänninger-Huber, Eva (1986). Non-verbal reactions to emotional experiences. In K. R. Scherer, H. G. Wallbott, & A. B. Summerfield (eds.), *Experiencing emotion: A cross-cultural study.* Cambridge, England: Cambridge University Press.

Waller, Niels G.; Kojetin, Brian A.; Bouchard, Thomas J., Jr.; et al. (1990). Genetic and environmental influences on religious interests, attitudes, and values: A study of twins reared apart and together. *Psychological Science, 1,* 138–142.

Walsh, B. Timothy, & Devlin, Michael J. (1998). Eating disorders: Progress and problems. *Science, 280,* 1387–1390.

Wandersman, Abraham, & Nation, Maury (1998). Urban neighborhoods and mental health: Psychological contributions to understanding toxicity, resilience, and interventions. *American Psychologist, 53,* 647–656.

Wang, Alvin Y.; Thomas, Margaret H.; & Ouellette, Judith A. (1992). The keyword mnemonic and retention of second-language vocabulary words. *Journal of Educational Psychology, 84,* 520–528.

Wark, Gillian R., & Krebs, Dennis (1996). Gender and dilemma differences in real-life moral judgment. *Developmental Psychology, 32,* 220–230.

Warren, Gayle H., & Raynes, Anthony E. (1972). Mood changes during three conditions of alcohol in-take. *Quarterly Journal of Studies on Alcohol, 33,* 979–989.

Washburn, David A., & Rumbaugh, Duane M. (1991). Ordinal judgments of numerical symbols by macaques *(Macaca mulatta). Psychological Science, 2,* 190–193.

Watson, John B. (1925). *Behaviorism.* New York: Norton.

Watson, John B., & Rayner, Rosalie (1920). Conditioned emotional reactions. *Journal of Experimental Psychology, 3,* 1–14.

Watters, Ethan, & Ofshe, Richard (1999). *Therapy's delusions.* New York: Scribner.

Webb, Wilse B., & Cartwright, Rosalind D. (1978). Sleep and dreams. In M. Rosenzweig & L. Porter (eds.), *Annual Review of Psychology, 29,* 223–252.

Webster, Richard (1995). *Why Freud was wrong.* New York: Basic Books.

Wechsler, David (1955). *Manual for the Wechsler Adult Intelligence Scale.* New York: Psychological Corporation.

Weder, Alan B., & Schork, Nicholas J. (1994). Adaptation, allometry, and hypertension. *Hypertension, 24,* 145–156.

Wegner, Daniel M., & Gold, Daniel B. (1995). Fanning old flames: Emotional and cognitive effects of suppressing thoughts of a past relationship. *Journal of Personality and Social Psychology, 68,* 782–792.

Wegner, Daniel M.; Schneider, David J.; Carter, Samuel R., III; & White, Teri L. (1987). Paradoxical effects of thought suppression. *Journal of Personality and Social Psychology, 53,* 5–13.

Weiden, Peter (1999). *Breakthroughs in anti-psychotic medications.* New York: W. W. Norton.

Weil, Andrew T. (1972/1986). *The natural mind: A new way of looking at drugs and the higher consciousness.* Boston: Houghton Mifflin.

Weil, Andrew T. (1974a, June). Parapsychology: Andrew Weil's search for the true Geller. *Psychology Today,* 45–50.

Weil, Andrew T. (1974b, July). Parapsychology: Andrew Weil's search for the true Geller—Part II. The letdown. *Psychology Today,* 74–78, 82.

Weiner, Bernard (1986). *An attributional theory of motivation and emotion.* New York: Springer-Verlag.

Weiss, Bahr; Dodge, Kenneth A.; Bates, John E.; & Petitt, Gregory S. (1992). Some consequences of early harsh discipline: Child aggression and a maladaptive social information processing style. *Child Development, 63,* 1321–1335.

Weisz, John R.; Weiss, Bahr; Alicke, Mark D.; & Klotz, M. L. (1987). Effectiveness of psychotherapy with children and adolescents: A meta-analysis for clinicians. *Journal of Consulting and Clinical Psychology, 55,* 542–549.

Weisz, John R.; Weiss, Bahr; Han, Susan S.; et al. (1995). Effects of psychotherapy with children and adolescents revisited: A meta-analysis of treatment outcome studies. *Psychological Bulletin, 117,* 450–468.

Weitzenhoffer, André M. (1996). Catalepsy tests: What do they tell us? *International Journal of Clinical and Experimental Hypnosis, 44,* 307–323.

Wellenkamp, Jane (1995). Cultural similarities and differences regarding emotional disclosure: Some examples from Indonesia and the Pacific. In J. W. Pennebaker (ed.), *Emotion, disclosure, and health.* Washington, DC: American Psychological Association.

Wells, Gary L.; Small, Mark; Penrod, Steven; et al. (1998). Eyewitness identification procedures: Recommendations for lineups and photospreads. *Law and Human Behavior, 22,* 602–647.

Wender, Paul H., & Klein, Donald F. (1981). *Mind, mood, and medicine: A guide to the new biopsychiatry.* New York: Farrar, Straus & Giroux.

Werner, Emmy E. (1989). High-risk children in young adulthood: A longitudinal study from birth to 32 years. *American Journal of Orthopsychiatry, 59,* 72–81.

West, Candace, & Zimmerman, Don H. (1991). Doing gender. In J. Lorber & S. A. Farrell (eds.), *The social construction of gender.* Newbury Park, CA: Sage.

West, Melissa O., & Prinz, Ronald J. (1987). Parental alcoholism and childhood psychopathology. *Psychological Bulletin, 102,* 204–218.

Westen, Drew (1998). The scientific legacy of Sigmund Freud: Toward a psychodynamically informed psychological science. *Psychological Bulletin, 124,* 333–371.

Westermeyer, Joseph (1995). Cultural aspects of substance abuse and alcoholism: Assessment and management. *Psychiatric Clinics of North America, 18,* 589–605.

Wheeler, David L. (1998, September 11). Neuroscientists take stock of brain-imaging studies. *Chronicle of Higher Education,* A20–A21.

Whisman, Mark A. (1993). Mediators and moderators of change in cognitive therapy of depression. *Psychological Bulletin, 114,* 248–265.

Whitam, Frederick L.; Diamond, Milton; & Martin, James (1993). Homosexual orientation in twins: A report on 61 pairs and 3 triplet sets. *Archives of Sexual Behavior, 22,* 187–206.

White, Sheldon H., & Pillemer, David B. (1979). Childhood amnesia and the development of a socially accessible memory system. In J. F. Kihlstrom & F. J. Evans (eds.), *Functional disorders of memory.* Hillsdale, NJ: Erlbaum.

Whiting, Beatrice B., & Edwards, Carolyn P. (1988). *Children of different worlds: The formation of social behavior.* Cambridge, MA: Harvard University Press.

Whiting, Beatrice, & Whiting, John (1975). *Children of six cultures.* Cambridge, MA: Harvard University Press.

Wickelgren, Ingrid (1997). Estrogen stakes claim to cognition [Research news]. *Science, 276,* 675–678.

Widner, H.; Tetrud, J.; Rehncrona, S.; et al. (1993). Fifteen months' follow-up on bilateral embryonic mesencephalic grafts in two cases of severe MPTP-induced Parkinsonism. *Advances in Neurology, 60,* 729–733.

Widom, Cathy S. (1989). Does violence beget violence? A critical examination of the literature. *Psychological Bulletin, 106,* 3–28.

Wiggins, Jerry S. (ed.) (1996). *The five-factor model of personality: Theoretical perspectives.* New York: Guilford Press.

Williams, Kipling D., & Karau, Steven J. (1991). Social loafing and social compensation: The effects of expectations of co-worker performance. *Journal of Personality and Social Psychology, 61,* 570–581.

Williams, Redford B., Jr.; Barefoot, John C.; & Shekelle, Richard B. (1985). The health consequences of hostility. In M. A. Chesney & R. H. Rosenman (eds.), *Anger and hostility in cardiovascular and behavioral disorders.* New York: Hemisphere.

Willie, Charles V.; Rieker, Patricia P.; Kramer, Bernard M.; & Brown, Bertram S. (eds.) (1995). *Mental health, racism, and sexism* (Rev. ed.). Pittsburgh: University of Pittsburgh Press.

Willis, Sherry L. (1987). Cognitive training and everyday competence. In K. W. Schaie (ed.), *Annual review of gerontology and geriatrics* (Vol. 7). New York: Springer.

Wilner, Daniel; Walkley, Rosabelle; & Cook, Stuart (1955). *Human relations in interracial housing.* Minneapolis: University of Minnesota Press.

Wilson, Edward O. (1975). *Sociobiology: The new synthesis.* Cambridge, MA: Belknap/Harvard University Press.

Wilson, Edward O. (1978). *On human nature.* Cambridge, MA: Harvard University Press.

Wilson, G. Terence, & Fairburn, Christopher G. (1993). Cognitive treatments for eating disorders. *Journal of Consulting and Clinical Psychology, 61,* 261–269.

Winick, Myron; Meyer, Knarig Katchadurian; & Harris, Ruth C. (1975). Malnutrition and environmental enrichment by early adoption. *Science, 190,* 1173–1175.

Winnicott, D. W. (1957/1990). *Home is where we start from.* New York: Norton.

Winter, David G. (1993). Power, affiliation, and war: Three tests of a motivational model. *Journal of Personality and Social Psychology, 65,* 532–545.

Wispé, Lauren G., & Drambarean, Nicholas C. (1953). Physiological need, word frequency, and visual duration thresholds. *Journal of Experimental Psychology, 46,* 25–31.

Witelson, Sandra F.; Glazer, I. I.; & Kigar, D. L. (1994). Sex differences in numerical density of neurons in human auditory association cortex. *Society for Neuroscience Abstracts, 30* (Abstract No. 582.12).

Wittchen, Hans-Ulrich; Kessler, Ronald C.; Zhao, Shanyang; & Abelson, Jamie (1995). Reliability and clinical validity of UM-CIDI *DSM-III-R* generalized anxiety disorder. *Journal of Psychiatric Research, 29,* 95–110.

Wolfe, C., & Spencer, S. (1996). Stereotypes and prejudice: Their overt and subtle influence in the classroom. *American Behavioral Scientist, 40,* 176–185.

Wong, Dean F.; Wagner, Henry N.; Tune, Larry E.; et al. (1986). Positron emission tomography reveals elevated D-sub-2 dopamine receptors in drug-naïve schizophrenics. *Science, 234,* 1558–1563.

Wood, James M.; Nezworski, Teresa; & Stejskal, William J. (1996). The comprehensive system for the Rorschach: A critical examination. *Psychological Science, 7,* 3–10.

Wood, Wendy; Lundgren, Sharon; Ouellette, Judith A.; et al. (1994). Minority influence: A meta-analytic review of social influence processes. *Psychological Bulletin, 115,* 323–345.

Woody, Erik Z., & Bowers, Kenneth S. (1994). A frontal assault on dissociated control. In S. J. Lynn & J. W. Rhue (eds.), *Dissociation: Clinical, theoretical and research perspectives.* New York: Guilford.

Woody, Erik, & Sadler, Pamela (1998). On reintegrating dissociated theories: Comment on Kirsch and Lynn (1998). *Psychological Bulletin, 123,* 192–197.

Wooley, Susan; Wooley, O. Wayne; & Dyrenforth, Susan (1979). Theoretical, practical, and social issues in behavioral treatments of obesity. *Journal of Applied Behavior Analysis, 12,* 3–25.

Wright, Daniel B. (1993). Recall of the Hillsborough disaster over time: Systematic biases of "flashbulb" memories. *Applied Cognitive Psychology, 7,* 129–138.

Wright, R. L. D. (1976). *Understanding statistics: An informal introduction for the behavioral sciences.* New York: Harcourt Brace Jovanovich.

Wurtman, Richard J. (1982). Nutrients that modify brain function. *Scientific American, 264*(4), 50–59.

Wurtman, Richard J., & Lieberman, Harris R. (eds.) (1982–1983). Research strategies for assessing the behavioral effects of foods and nutrients. *Journal of Psychiatric Research, 17*(2).

Wuthnow, Robert (1995). *Sharing the journey: Support groups and America's new quest for community.* New York: Free Press.

Wyatt, Gail E., & Mickey, M. Ray (1987). Ameliorating the effects of child sexual abuse: An exploratory study of support by parents and others. *Journal of Interpersonal Violence, 2,* 403–414.

Wygant, Steven A. (1997). Moral reasoning about real-life dilemmas: Paradox in research using the Defining Issues Test. *Personality and Social Psychology Bulletin, 23,* 1022–1033.

Yalom, Irvin D. (1989). *Love's executioner and other tales of psychotherapy.* New York: Basic Books.

Yalom, Irvin D. (1995). *The theory and practice of group psychotherapy* (4th ed.). New York: Basic Books.

Yang, Kuo-shu, & Bond, Michael H. (1990). Exploring implicit personality theories with indigenous or imported constructs: The Chinese case. *Journal of Personality and Social Psychology, 58,* 1087–1095.

Yapko, Michael (1994). *Suggestions of abuse: True and false memories of childhood sexual trauma.* New York: Simon & Schuster.

Yazigi, R. A.; Odem, R. R.; & Polakoski, K. L. (1991, October 9). Demonstration of specific binding of cocaine to human spermatozoa. *Journal of the American Medical Association, 266*(14), 1956–1959.

Yoder, Janice D. (1999). *Women and gender: Transforming psychology.* Upper Saddle River, NJ: Prentice Hall.

Yoder, Janice D., & Kahn, Arnold S. (1993). Working toward an inclusive psychology of women. *American Psychologist, 48,* 846–850.

Yoken, Carol, & Berman, Jeffrey S. (1984). Does paying a fee for psychotherapy alter the effectiveness of treatment? *Journal of Consulting and Clinical Psychology, 52,* 254–260.

Young, Malcolm P., & Yamane, Shigeru (1992). Sparse population coding of faces in the inferotemporal cortex. *Science, 256,* 1327–1331.

Young-Eisendrath, Polly (1993). *You're not what I expected: Learning to love the opposite sex.* New York: Morrow.

Zahn-Waxler, Carolyn (1996). Environment, biology, and culture: Implications for adolescent development. *Developmental Psychology, 32,* 571–573.

Zajonc, Robert B. (1968). Attitudinal effects of mere exposure. *Journal of Personality and Social Psychology, 9* (Monograph Suppl. 2), 1–27.

Zajonc, Robert B., & Markus, Gregory B. (1975). Birth order and intellectual development. *Psychological Review, 82,* 74–88.

Zellman, Gail, & Goodchilds, Jacqueline (1983). Becoming sexual in adolescence. In E. R. Allgeier & N. B. McCormick (eds.), *Changing boundaries: Gender roles and sexual behavior.* Palo Alto, CA: Mayfield.

Zhang, Yiying; Proenca, Ricardo; Maffei, Margherita; et al. (1994). Positional cloning of the mouse obese gene and its human homologue. *Nature, 372*(6505), 425–432.

Zilbergeld, Bernie (1983). *The shrinking of America: Myths of psychological change.* Boston: Little, Brown.

Zimbardo, Philip G. (1970). The human choice: Individuation, reason, and order versus deindividuation, impulse, and chaos. In W. J. Arnold & D. Levine (eds.), *Nebraska Symposium on Motivation, 1969.* Lincoln: University of Nebraska Press.

Zimbardo, Philip G., & Leippe, M. R. (1991). *The psychology of attitude change and social influence.* New York: McGraw-Hill.

Zimmer, Lynn, & Morgan, John P. (1997). *Marijuana myths, marijuana fact: A review of the scientific evidence.* New York: Lindesmith Center.

Zinberg, Norman (1974). The search for rational approaches to heroin use. In P. G. Bourne (ed.), *Addiction.* New York: Academic Press.

Zorrilla, L.T.; Cannon, T.D.; Kronenberg, S.; Mednick, S.A.; et al. (1997, December 15). Structural brain abnormalities in schizophrenia: A family study. *Biological Psychiatry, 42,* 1080–1086.

CREDITS

Text, Table, and Figure Credits

CHAPTER 2 *Page 46:* Figure 2.2, from R. L. Wright, "Correlations in understanding statistics," *Understanding Statistics: An Informal Introduction for the Behavioral Sciences.* © 1976 by Harcourt Brace & Company. Reprinted by permission of the publisher.
CHAPTER 3 *Page 78:* Figure 3.1, (a) Adapted from "Evolutionary psychology: A new paradigm for psychological science" by David M. Buss, in *Psychological Inquiry*, 6, 1–30, (1995). Copyright © 1995 by The American Psychological Association. Reprinted by permission, (b) Reuters/Fred Prouser/Archive Photos; *p. 79:* Figure 3.2, adapted from Evolutionary psychology: A new paradigm for psychological science by David M. Buss, in *Psychological Inquiry*, 6, 1–30, (1995). Copyright © 1995 by The American Psychological Association. Reprinted by permission; *p. 93:* Figure 3.5, from J. Horgan "Get smart, take a test: A long term rise in IQ scores baffles intelligence experts" from *Scientific American* 11-1995, p. 14. Reproduced by permission of Dimitry Schildlovsky.
CHAPTER 4 *Page 114:* Figure 4.7, Hank Morgan/ Science Source/ Photo Researchers, Inc., *(left)*, Michael E. Phelps/Mazziotta UCLA School of Medicine *(right)*; *p. 115:* Figure 4.8, Howard Sochurek, Inc; *p. 121:* Figure 4.12, from Kim, Relkin, Lee & Hirsch, "Nature" 388, 171–174 (1997). Courtesy of Dr. Joy Hirsch, Head, FMRI Laboratory Memorial Sloan-Kettering Cancer Center; *p. 132:* Figure 4.16, Copyright © 1992 The Time Inc. Magazine Company. Reprinted by permission.
CHAPTER 5 *Page 152:* Figure 5.3, from "Physiology of sleep and dreaming" by Dennis Kelly from Principles of Neural Science. Copyright © 1981 by Elsevier Science Publishing Company. Reprinted by permission of the publisher; *p. 172:* Excerpt from Encounters: A Psychologist Reveals Case Studies of Abduction by Extraterrestrials by Edith Fiore. Copyright © 1989. Reprinted by permission of Bantam Doubleday Dell Publishing Group, Inc.
CHAPTER 6 *Page 194:* Figure 6.5, © Josef Albers Foundation/Yale University Press, Figure 6.6, M. C. Escher's "Circle Limit IV" © 1999 Cordon Art B.V.–Baarn–Holland. All rights reserved; *p. 201:* Table 6.1, from "Sound intensity levels in the environment." Reprinted by permission of the American Academy of Otolaryngology-Head and Neck Surgery, Washington D. C.; *p. 206:* Figure 6.11, from "Taste Test" from *Archives of Otolarynology*, 90, pp. 367–373, 1969. Copyright © 1969 American Medical Association. Reprinted by permission; *p. 213:* Monkmeyer Press.
CHAPTER 7 *Page 226:* Figure 7.1, The Granger Collection; *p. 229:* Figure 7.3, from "Acquisition and extinction of a salivary response" by Ivan P. Pavlov from *Conditioned Reflexes*, trans. G. V. Anrep. Copyright © 1927. Reprinted by permission of Oxford University Press, Oxford, England; *p. 242:* Figure 7.6, from "Teaching Machines" by B.F. Skinner in *Scientific American*, November 1961, p. 96. Reprinted by permission of Margaret C. Gladbach, Estate of Mary E. and Dan Todd; *p. 251:* Figure 7.7, from "Turning Play into Work" by David Green and Mark R. Lepper, *Psychology Today*, September 1974. Reprinted with permission from Psychology Today Magazine, Copyright © 1974 (Sussex Publishers, Inc.); *p. 256:* Figure 7.8, from "Introduction and removal of reward and maze performance in rats" by E. C. Tolman and C. H. Honzik from *Psychology*, 4 (1930). Reprinted by permission of University of California Publications.
CHAPTER 8 *Page 267:* Figure 8.1, Copyright 1965 by Stanley Milgram. From the film OBEDIENCE, distributed by Penn Media Sales; *p. 282:* Figure 8.2, from p. 440 Aronson, Wilson & Akert. "When will bystanders help?" in *Social Psychology*, 2nd Edition (Addison-Wesley Longman); *p. 292:* Figure 8.5, from S. Keen, Faces of the Enemy: Reflections of the Hostile Imagination. Copyright © 1986 by Sam Keen. All rights reserved. Reprinted by permission of HarperCollins Publishers, Inc. *(top left & right; bottom left)*, Francois de Mulder/Corbis *(top right)*; *p. 294:* Figure 8.6, from R. Rogers and S. Prentice-Dunn, 1981, *Journal of Personality and Social Psychology*, 41, p. 68. Copyright © 1981 by the American Psychological Association. Reprinted with permission.
CHAPTER 9 *Page 312:* Table 9.1, from "Two Kinds of Reasoning" by Kathleen Galotti in *Psychological Bulletin*, 105, 1989, 331–351. Copyright © 1989 by the American Psychological Association. Adapted with permission of the publisher and the author; *p. 314:* Excerpt from King, Patricia M., and Kitchener, Karen Strohm. *Developing Reflective Judgment: Understanding and Promoting Intellectual Growth and Critical Thinking in Adolescents and Adults.* Copyright © 1994 Jossey-Bass Inc., Publishers. Reprinted by permission; *p. 326:* Table 9.2, from "Sample items from the Stanford-Binet Intelligence Scale" by Lewis M. Terman and Maud A. Merrill. Copyright © 1973 by Houghton Mifflin Co. Reprinted by permission of Riverside Publishing Co.; *p. 327:* Figure 9.3, from "Performance tasks on the Weschler tests" by Lee J. Cronbach from *Essentials of Psychological Testing, 4th edition*, p. 208. Copyright © 1984 by HarperCollins Publishers. Reprinted by permission; *p. 337:* Figure 9.6, From "Knowledge of Number: Its Evolution and Ontogeny" by Susan Carey in *Science*, Vol. 282, 23 October 1998, p. 641. Reprinted by permission of Elizabeth Brannon.
CHAPTER 10 *Page 356:* © 1985, 1976 Golden Books Publishing Company, Inc. All rights reserved; *p. 365:* Figure 10.4, from "Serial Position Effect" in *Memory* by Elizabeth Loftus, 1980, p. 25. © 1980 by Addison Wesley Publishing Co. Reprinted by permission; *p. 368:* Figure 10.5, from Michael G. Wessell, "Retention in short term memory," *Cognitive Psychology*, p. 98. © 1982 by Harper & Row, Publishers, Inc. Reprinted by permission; *p. 372:* Figure 10.7 Fig. 3, from Reber, PJ, Stark, CEL & Squire, LR (1998). Contrasting cortical activity associated with category memory and recognition memory. Learning & Memory, 5, p. 420–428; *p. 375:* Figure 10.9b, from "A Forgetting Curve for Personal Events" by Marigold Linton in *Psychology Today*, Vol. 13:2, July 1979. Reprinted by permission from Psychology Today Magazine. Copyright © 1970. (Sussex Publishers, Inc.).
CHAPTER 11 *Page 393: (top row, left to right)* Matrix International, Inc., Erika Stone, Laura Dwight, Eric Gay/AP/Wide World Photos, *(bottom row, left to right)* Reuters/Fred Prouser/Archive Photos, Henry Fuseli, "Mad Kate," 1806-07. Oil on canvas. 91 × 71 cm. Goethe Museum, Frankfurt, Germany. The Bridgeman Art Library International Ltd., The New York Public Library, Astor, Lenox, and Tilden Foundations; *Page 397:* Illustration

11.01, from Chimeric Faces, Figure 5.5, p. 146 in Keith Oatley and Jennifer J. Jenkins, *Understanding Emotions*, 1996. Reproduced by permission of Blackwell Publishers; *p. 411:* Adapted from Bernieri, Davis, Rosenthal, and Knee;

CHAPTER 12 *Page 448:* Figure 12.03, (a) from Mueller, Claudia M., & Dweck, Carol S. (1998). Praise for intelligence can undermine children's motivation and performance. *Journal of Personality and Social Psychology*, 75, 33–52. Copyright © 1998 by the American Psychological Association. Reprinted with permission, (b) Dan Bosler/Tony Stone Images; *p. 449:* Figure 12.4, from Iyengar, Sheena A., Lepper, Mark R. (1999), Rethinking the value of choice: A cultural perspective on intrinsic motivation. *Journal of Personality and Social Psychology*, 76, 349–366. Copyright © 1999 by American Psychological Association. Reprinted with permission.

CHAPTER 13 *Page 463:* Dr. Stephen J. Suomi; *p. 477:* Review Chart 13.1, excerpt from "The Ego and the Id" by Sigmund Freud, trans. by James Strachey. Copyright © by James Strachey. Reprinted by permission of W. W. Norton and Co., Inc.; *p. 491:* Excerpt from "The P. T. Barnum Effect" by Snyder, C. R. and Randee J. Shenkel in *Psychology Today*, March 1975. Reprinted with permission from Psychology Today Magazine, Copyright © 1975 (Sussex Publishers, Inc.).

CHAPTER 14 *Page 507:* Mimi Forsyth/Monkmeyer Press Photo Service *(left)*, Marcia Weinstein *(right)*; *p. 515:* Figure 14.3, from Kay Bussey and Albert Bandura, "Gender-linked activities" in *Child Development*, 63. © The Society for Research in Child Development, Inc. Reprinted by permission.

CHAPTER 15 *Page 548:* Figure 15.1, "Stress and the Cold", *The New York Times* HEALTH May 12, 1998. Adapted with permission; *p. 553:* Figure 15.2, Tom Sobolik/Black Star *(top); p. 561:* Figure 15.3, from "Resilience and Thriving in Response to Challenge: An Opportunity for a Paradigm Shift in Women's Health" by V.E. O'Leary and J.R. Ickovics, 1994, *Women's Health: Research on Gender, Behavior, and Policy*, V1 , p. 127. Reprinted by permission; *p 562:* Figure 15.04, "Fitness and health" in *Abnormal Psychology* by David Holmes 1991. © 1991 by Addison Wesley Longman Publishers. Reprinted by permission of Addison Wesley Longman Publishers.

CHAPTER 16 *Page 587:* Figure 16.1A, from "Depression's double standard," by Kristin Leutwyler in "Mysteries of the Mind," special issue published by Scientific American, June 1995, p. 54. Reprinted by permission of Bryan Christie; *p. 588:* Figure 16.2, Courtesy of Dr. Michael E. Phelps and Dr. John C. Mazziotta, UCLA School of Medicine; *p. 590:* Figure 16.3, from p. 102, by Gerald I. Metalsky, Thomas E. Joiner Jr., Tammy S. Hardin & Lyn Y. Abramson (1993). Depressive reactions to failure in a naturalistic setting: A test of the hopelessness and self-esteem theories of depression. *Journal of Abnormal Psychology*, 101–109. Copyright © 1993 by The American Psychological Association. Reprinted by permission; *p. 593:* Figure 16.4 from "Antisocial Personality Disorder" in *Journal of Psychology*, F.1A, 1985. Reprinted with permission of the Helen Dwight Reid Educational Foundation. Published by Heldref Publications, 1319 Eighteenth St., NW, Washington, DC 20036-1802. Copyright © 1985; *p. 602:* Figure 16.5, from "Drug Use by U.S. Army Enlisted Men in Vietman: A Follow up on the Return Home" by Robins, Davis & Goodwin in *American Journal of Epidemiology*, Vol 99, pp. 239–249, 1974. Reprinted by permission; *p. 604:* Table 16.3, Reprinted with the permission of Simon & Schuster, Inc., from *The Truth About Addiction and Recovery* by Stanton Peele and Archie Brodsky with Mary Arnold. Copyright © 1991 by Stanton Peele and Archie Brodsky with Mary Arnold; *p. 609:* © Howard Sochurek, Inc. All rights reserved.

CHAPTER 17 *Page 622:* Figure 17.1, System One/Jeffrey M. Schwartz; © 1996, American Medical Association, from "Archives of General Psychiatry," February 1996, Vol. 53, pp. 109–113; *p. 635:* Figure 17.3, From "The dose-effect relationship in psychotherapy" by Kenneth I. Howard from *American Psychologist*, 41, February 1986, p. 160. Copyright © 1986 by the American Psychological Association. Reprinted by permission of the publisher and the author.

Photographs and Cartoons

Page abbreviations are as follows: (T) top; (C) center; (B) bottom, (L) left, (R) right.

CHAPTER 1 *Page xxxiv:* Amana America, Inc.; *p. 2:* (L) Mark E. Gibson/The Stock Market, (TC) PhotoEdit, (BC) William Thompson/Picture Cube, (R) William Thompson/Index Stock Imagery, Inc.; *p. 3:* (L) Thomas A. Kelly/Gail Mooney/Corbis, (R) Stock Boston; *p. 4:* Punch/Rothco; *p. 8:* (L) Magnum Photos, Inc., (R) International Stock Photography Ltd.; *p. 9:* (L) Andre Kole, (R) Tanenbuam/Sygma Photo News; *p. 10:* (L) AP/Wide World Photos, (R) Courtesy of Natural Nectar Corp.; *p. 11:* (L) Matrix International, Inc., (R) Frank Trapper/Sygma Photo News; *p. 14:* Archives of the History of American Psychology–The University of Akron; *p. 16:* (T) New York Public Library, (B) The Image Works; *p. 19:* Les Jorgensen/Amana America, Inc.; *p. 24:* (L) George Rule Photography, (R) PhotoEdit; *p. 26:* (L) Sean McCann/United States Olympic Committee, (R) Ed Kashi; *p. 27: Bent Offerings* by Don Addis. By permission of Don Addis and Creators Syndicate.

CHAPTER 2 *Page 32:* Amana America, Inc.; *p. 34:* Courtesy of FRONTLINE/WGBH Educational Foundation; *p. 36:* (T) Jose L. Pelaez/The Stock Market, (B) Unicorn Stock Photos; *p. 38:* From Susan Curtiss, *Genie: A Modern Day Wild Child*, Academic Press, used by permission; *p. 40:* (T) Copyright © 1990 Los Angeles Times, (B) Jonathan Nourok/PhotoEdit; *p. 42:* © The New Yorker Collection 1998 Roz Chast from cartoonbank.com. All rights reserved; *p. 43:* Copyright 1994, Los Angeles Times Syndicate. Reprinted with permission; *p. 54: Miss Peach* by Mell Lazarus. By permission of Mell Lazarus and Creators Syndicate; *p. 59:* Rainbow.

CHAPTER 3 *Page 64:* Amana America, Inc.; *p. 66:* Photo Researchers, Inc.; *p. 67:* Photo Researchers, Inc.; *p. 69:* (T) Copyright British Museum, (B) Breck P. Kent, *p. 70:* (BL) Laura Dwight, (BC) Woodfin Camp & Associates, (BR) Harlow Primate Laboratory; *p. 72:* Stock Boston; *p. 74:* Richter/Cartoonists & Writers Syndicate; *p. 76:* Dan Bosler/Tony Stone Images; *p. 77:* Magnum Photos, Inc.; *p. 78:* Reuters/Fred Prouser/Archive Photos; *p. 79:* Art Wolfe/Tony Stone Images; *p. 83:* © The New Yorker Collection, 1981. Charles Addams from cartoonbank.com. All rights reserved; *p. 84:* Index Stock Imagery, Inc.; *p. 85:* (T) Dennis Stock/Magnum Photos, Inc., (B) Photo Researchers, Inc.; *p. 86:* REAL LIFE ADVENTURES © 1999 GarLanCo. Reprinted with permission of UNIVERSAL PRESS SYNDICATE. All rights reserved; *p. 87:* Liaison Agency, Inc.; *p. 88:* William Thompson/The Picture Cube; *p. 93:* (L) Shelly Katz, (R) Photo Researchers, Inc.

CHAPTER 4 *Page 98:* Vince Michaels/Tony Stone Images; *p. 100:* Howard Sochurek, Inc; *p. 102:* Roe Di Bona; *p. 106:* (T) Marc

NAME INDEX

Abel, G. G., 640
Abelson, R. P., 382
Abramovitch, H., 153
Abrams, D. B., 166
Abrams, M., 288, 638
Abrams, R. L., 216
Abramson, L. Y., 589
Acredolo, L., 504
Adams, B. W., 618
Adams, M. J., 385
Ader, R., 235
Adler, N. E., 549
Affleck, G., 558, 564
Ahmed, S., 143
Ainsworth, M. D. S., 40, 423–424
Akamine, T. X., 460
Akbarian, S., 609
Akert, R. A., 282, 283, 285, 322
Alagna, S., 146
Albee, G. W., 577
Aldag, R. J., 282
Alford, E. C., 147
Alkon, D. L., 370
Allen, G., 117
Allen, J., 428
Allen, J. J. B., 397
Allen, L. S., 439
Allison, D. B., 84, 85, 88
Alloy, L. B., 588, 589
Allport, G. W., 290, 294–295, 459
Alpert, B., 561
Alpert, N., 447
Amabile, T. M., 341
Amaral, D. G., 371
Ambady, N., 329
Ambert, A.-M., 526
Amering, M., 583
Ames, A., 399
Anastasi, A., 328, 329, 458, 483
Andersen, B. L., 550, 570
Anderson, B. J., 107
Anderson, C. A., 589
Anderson, J. R., 363
Anderson, K., 86
Andreasen, N. C., 609
Angell, M., 134, 570
Antonuccio, D. O., 620, 621, 638
Anthony, W. A., 643
Appelwhite, M., 278
Appenzeller, T., 372
Arendt, H., 179, 299
Arendt, J., 143
Aristotle, 392
Arkes, H. R., 276, 323

Armeli, S., 341
Armitage, R., 140
Arnett, J. J., 525, 527
Arnold, R. D., 465
Aron, A., 427, 428
Aron, E. N., 428
Aronson, E., 276, 282, 283, 285, 291, 292,
    297, 298, 322, 323, 328
Arroyo, C. G., 521
Asch, S. E., 280
Aserinsky, E., 150
Ashton-Warner, S., 324
Asimov, I., 442
Aslin, R. N., 76
Aspinwall, L. G., 556, 560
Astin, J. A., 558
Astington, J. W., 509
Atkinson, J. W., 443
Atkinson, R. C., 358
AuBuchon, P. G., 146
Auerbach, J. S., 486
Axel, R., 207
Aziz, T., 409
Azrin, N. H., 247
Azuma, H., 559

Bahill, A. T., 199
Bahrick, H. P., 356, 376
Bahrick, P. O., 356
Bailey, J. M., 78, 438, 439
Baillargeon, R., 508
Baird, E., 442
Bakalar, J. B., 167
Baker, J., 409
Baker, M. C., 74
Baker, R., 79
Baker, R. A., 172
Baldwin, F., 497
Ball-Rokeach, S., 441
Baltes, P. B., 532, 535, 536, 537, 558
Bancroft, J., 432
Bandura, A., 254, 256, 466, 467, 515, 571
Banks, C., 268
Banks, M. S., 212
Banks, S. R., 109
Bänninger-Huber, E., 415
Barbee, A. H., 334
Barber, T. X., 171
Barbuto, J. E., 459
Barefoot, J. C., 553
Bargh, J. A., 216
Barinaga, M., 106
Barker, C. H., 278
Barkley, R. A., 579

Barkow, J. H., 68, 70
Barlow, D. H., 581, 582, 583, 589, 635
Barnhardt, T. M., 486
Baron, M., 601
Barondes, S. H., 587, 588
Barone, D. F., 254
Barrish, B. M., 249
Barsky, S. H., 167
Bartlett, F. C., 348–349
Bartoshuk, L. M., 205, 206
Bashore, T. R., 400, 534
Bauer, P. J., 380
Baum, W. M., 257
Baumberger, T., 76
Baumeister, R. F., 172, 404, 412, 417, 427,
    429, 437, 612, 638
Baumrind, D., 439, 519, 520
Bauserman, B., 538
Baxter, L. R., 621
Beauchamp, G. K., 205
Bechara, A., 308
Beck, A. T., 583, 628
Becker, J. V., 631, 640
Becker, M. H., 562, 570
Beckerman, S., 79
Beckwith, B. E., 164
Bee, H., 499
Beech, H. R., 146
Beer, J. M., 465
Behrmann, M., 192
Bekenstein, J. W., 109
Bell, A. G., 200
Bell, A. P., 438
Bell, D., 293
Bellugi, U., 74
Belmont, J. M., 329
Belmont, L., 92
Belsky, J., 425, 462
Bem, D. J., 218
Bem, S. L., 21, 514
Benedict, R., 65
Benet-Martínez, V., 460
Benjamin, L. T., Jr., 14
Bennett, W., 86, 87
Bentall, R. P., 576
Bera, S., 428
Bereiter, C., 330
Berenbaum, S. A., 514
Berger, F., 106
Bergin, A. E., 635, 636
Berkman, L. F., 565
Berko, J., 75
Berman, J. S., 635, 647
Berndt, R. S., 363

SUBJECT INDEX

Introduction to Psychology
Suzy Scherf

Lecture 11: How Do We Interact?

Human Mating Strategies

Don't Men and Women have the Same Mate Preferences?

What if someone of the opposite sex approached you and began a conversation. You find this person attractive and pleasant to talk to. After a few moments of conversation they ask you either:

1. "Would you go out with me tonight?"

2. "Would you come over to my apartment tonight?"

3. "Would you go to bed with me tonight?"

How would you respond?

Don't Men and Women have the Same Mate Preferences?

1. "Would you go out with me tonight?"
   Men: 50% Yes, 50% No
   Women: 50% Yes, 50% No

2. "Would you come to my apartment tonight?"
   Men: 69% Yes, 31% No
   Women: 6% Yes, 94% No

3. "Would you go to bed with me tonight?"
   Men: 75% Yes, 25% No
   Women: 0% Yes, 100% No

Sexual Selection

- Traits spread b/c they lead to more offspring than they cost.

- Sexual Selection favors traits that provide benefits <u>only</u> in the mating context.

- Often acts unevenly in the two sexes because of differences in reproductive rate.

Sexual Selection: The Peacock

Come on Mamma. I got what you need!

A long-tailed male is more likely to die than a short-tail male, but he's also more likely to reproduce!

Sexual Selection

- When males > females reproductive rate (most mammals):

  1. Fertile females have lots of possible mates

  2. Fertile males have to compete for a few available fertile females

- Sexual selection favors traits that help increase the <u># of matings</u> in the **fast** sex:

- Sexual selection favors traits that help increase the <u>quality of matings</u> in the **slow** sex:

The Case of Humans

Women can produce about 1 child/year
- limited by gestation
- in EEA probably limited to about 1 child/5-6 years
- breast milk only food for infants then - prevents ovulation

Would increasing the number of partners increase her reproductive rate?

No - her reproductive rate is limited by her physiology not by the shortage of males!

The Case of Humans

Men can produce an unlimited number of children/year
- if they do not invest in their offspring
- limited by the number of available partners

Would increasing the number of partners increase his reproductive rate?

YES- his reproductive rate is limited by his access to available fertile women!

The Case of Humans

Men do tend to invest in their offspring
- paternal investment slows down a man's reproductive rate
- human mating practices impose limits on a man's reproductive rate

In a perfectly monogamous system, the men's and women's reproductive rates would be equal.

Human mating systems approach monogamy - but the degree to which they don't influences differences in reproductive rates

Evidence for a Mostly Monogamous Mating System

- In 85% of human cultures allow polygyny!

- Prohibitions on polygyny are very recent ($\approx$ 500 years)

- Marital infidelity

- Marriage, divorce, re-marriage

The extent of polygyny = the extend of sex differences in mating strategies.

Sexual Selection in Humans

- Members of the fast sex compete

- Members of the slow sex choose

- Because of a tendency toward weak polygyny:

  - Women expected to be more choosy

  - Men expected to be more competitive - but also a bit choosy since they do invest in offspring

- Sexual Selection can shape desires that influence competition and choosiness behaviors

Are Men More Competitive and are Women more Choosy?

1. "Would you go out with me tonight?"
   Men: 50%
   Women: 50%

2. "Would you come to my apartment tonight?"
   Men: 69% Yes
   Women: 6% Yes

3. "Would you go to bed with me tonight?"
   Men: 75% Yes
   Women: 0% Yes

Are Men More Competitive and are Women more Choosy?

1. Women are more chossy than men.

2. Men aren't indiscriminate

Men

Women

Likelihood of consenting to intercourse

5 yrs   Time Known   1 hr.

How does Parental Investment Influence Mating Strategies?

Parental investment - anything that a parent does for a particular offspring that helps the offspring and reduces the parent's ability to invest in other offspring.

- limited resources
- gestation and lactation
- food, shelter, protection
- biparental investment in humans - rare in mammals
- most likely to evolve in species with very helpless young

How does Parental Investment Influence Mating Strategies?

- Parental investment is different for men and women

- Women have obvious physical investment

- Men do not make the physiological investment, but do invest with resources - it is an economic investment

- Women make physiological and economic investments in their offspring, while men only invest economically

How does Parental Investment Influence Mating Strategies?

Any trait that indicates good physiological health in women should be selectively preferred in men.

Any trait that helps a woman get parental investment from a man will spread!

Any trait that indicates good economic investment from males should be selectively preferred in women.

Mating Preferences in Men and Women

Physical Attractiveness:

Perceptions of attractiveness have been shaped by evolution as indicators of fitness (fertility and health)

Correlates of Fitness that shape our attractiveness judgments many are indicators that the person is not too stressed by parasites
1. Youth
2. Clear Skin
3. Bright eyes
4. Shiny Hair
5. Symmetrical facial and non-facial features

Mating Preferences in Men and Women

Physical Attractiveness:

Symmetry

Face Symmetry

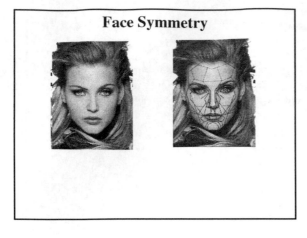

Face Symmetry

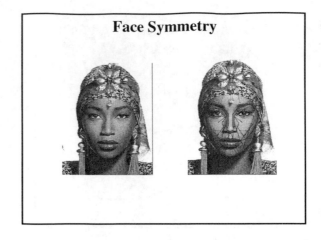

Face Symmetry

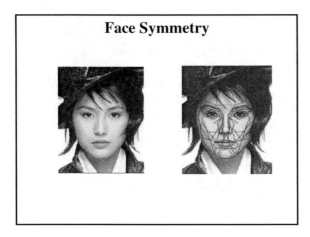

Face Symmetry

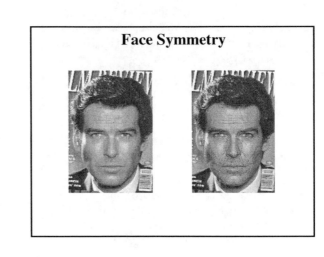

Face Symmetry

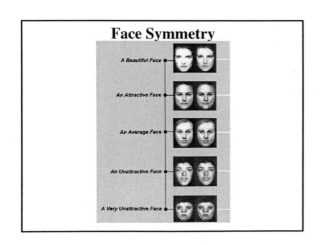

A Beautiful Face

An Attractive Face

An Average Face

An Unattractive Face

A Very Unattractive Face

Face Symmetry

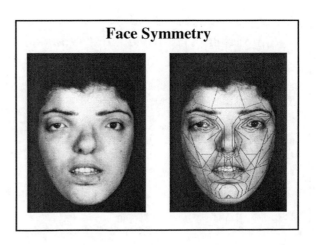

Mating Preferences in Men and Women

Physical Attractiveness:

Men and women have equal criteria for attractiveness

What's Different between the Sexes?

- The emphasis placed on attractiveness in mate selection!

- Across cultures, men overwhelmingly place physical attractiveness as a higher priority for mate selection than do women.

Mating Preferences in Men and Women

Why do men place a higher emphasis on physical attractiveness?

- Physical attractiveness is an indicator of physiological health - a major investment needed by women for their offspring.

- Attractiveness is an indicator of potential physiological investment capabilities on the part of women.

Mating Preferences in Men and Women

What other indicators of potential fecundity do <u>men</u> attend to in mate selection?

How attractive is this woman?

How attractive is this woman?

How attractive is this woman?

Waist-Hip Ratio

WHR = 0.5   WHR = 0.7   WHR = 0.9

5

Waist-Hip Ratio is Related to Fecundity

- Higher WHR is correlated with <u>low fertility</u> and higher susceptibility to a range of degenerative diseases

- High WHR reflects a low level of estrogen - as in pregnancy women, prepubescent girls, and post-menopausal women

- Really low WHR probably does not exist in nature

Waist-Hip Ratio is Related to Fecundity

- An increase from .7 to .8 in WHR results in a 30% decrease in likelihood of pregnancy

- A woman's WHR does reflect her reproductively relevant hormone profile!

Mating Preferences in Men and Women

When might women place a high emphasis on the physical attractiveness of their mate?

- During one-night stands!

- <u>Sneaker-strategy</u> for having access to resources from one man - and getting good genes from another.

Mating Preferences in Men and Women

What kind of traits to <u>women</u> place as a higher priority for mate selection than do men?

- Good economic potential!

- WHY? Because that's how men invest in their offspring!

Sex Differences in Reproductive Strategies

1. Reflect differences in reproductive rate – time off the market due to physiological and/or economic investment in offspring

2. Reflect mate preferences based on differences in reproductive rate

3. Women looking for good genes and economic resources in men

4. Men looking for good genes

Sex Differences in Reproductive Strategies

5. Women's genes and investment automatically linked

6. Men's genes and investment not automatically linked

As a result, there is an asymmetry between men's and women's **parental confidence**

Sex Differences in Parental Confidence

How confident are you in your ability to identify your own offspring?

- Women (and her relatives) are **100%** confident in her ability to identify her offspring

- Men (and his relatives) are **never 100%** confident in his ability to identify his offspring

Sex Differences in Parental Confidence: Women

- Since a man's investment and his genes are not automatically linked, women can recruit them separately

- This opportunity to recruit these resources separately results in a **mixed reproductive strategy**

Sex Differences in Parental Confidence: Women

- Women trying to get the best of both worlds

- A strategy focused only on getting the best genes or only on getting the most resources from men is <u>not</u> as successful as a mixed strategy

Women's Mixed Reproductive Strategy

A woman playing a mixed reproductive strategy will accept genes and resources from different men!

Sex Differences in Parental Confidence: Men

- Since men never have complete parental confidence they risk being cuckolded

- **<u>Cuckoldry</u>** is investing in offspring that aren't yours' or your biological relatives'

- There is some selection pressure on men to desert their partners and children and seek additional mates

Men's Mixed Reproductive Strategy

A man playing a mixed reproductive strategy will invest heavily in one partner and her offspring but still attempt to attract additional mates.

Mixed Reproductive Strategies

If you ask about men's and women's selectivity across several characteristics and many levels of involvement:

1. Women set higher standards than men - related to choosiness

2. Setting high standards eliminates potential mates, while relaxing standards increases access to potential mates

Mixed Reproductive Strategies

3. Women set higher standards on attractiveness for one-night-stand partners than they do for marriage partners

4. Overall, both men and women set the highest standards for potential marriage partners

5. Men relax their standards on all characteristics for their one-night-stand partners

Counter-Strategies

Men's and women's mixed reproductive strategies are often in <u>competition</u> with one another.

How do men and women's mating strategies deal with this competition?

Both men and women have developed <u>counter-strategies</u> in their mating strategies such that men are sensitive to cuckoldry and women are sensitive to men's reallocation of their parental investment

Counter-Strategies: Men

Men have to avoid investing in offspring that aren't genetically related to them.

Men have evolved a counter-strategy to giving investment where there are no genes.

1. Men can attempt to secure a sexually faithful mate

2. If his mate is unfaithful, he can leave his partner and minimize his investment in her offspring

Counter-Strategies: Men

Men rate <u>sexual fidelity as the most important</u> characteristic in a long-term mate and sexual infidelity as the most negative trait in a long-term mate!

On the other hand, men don't show a preference for fidelity in a short-term mate.

Counter-Strategies: Men

- In fact, men are 10x more likely to divorce a woman if he has low paternity certainty in their children and they are much less likely to invest in these children after the divorce!

- Women intuitively know this about men and seem to use this sensitivity to the risk of cuckoldry in competing for mates. (She's a ho!)

Counter-Strategies: Women

- When a man invests in another woman and her offspring, the amount of time and resources he can invest in his own offspring are reduced.

- Women have also developed counter-strategies to defend against having her partner invest in other women and their offspring.

Counter-Strategies: Women

- Women are much more threatened by emotional infidelity than by sexual infidelity.

- Emotional infidelity is a stronger signal to women that their men are investing in another woman and potentially her offspring.

Facultative Influences on Reproductive Strategy

Why are some individuals so jealous?

Why do some women seem to lower their reproductive fitness by having many sexual partners?

Why don't some men invest at all in their offspring?

Facultative Influences on Reproductive Strategy

One essential factor may be expectations about the local availability of parental investment.

In particular, the abundance of investing men predicts the payoffs of alternative reproductive strategies.

Facultative Influences on Reproductive Strategy

	Lots of Investing Males	Few Investing Males
Women	Sexual Fidelity that fosters male investment	Sexual access facilitates short-term investment so increase the number of sexual partners
Men	Parental Investment - lots of courtship that pays off	Maximize the number of sexual partners since most of the offspring are only receiving maternal investment anyway

Facultative Influences on Reproductive Strategy

In fact, children show lasting responses to the presence or absence of a father as an indication that investing males are scarce.

- Girls reared in father-absent homes engages in sexual activity at earlier ages and are less choosy about their partners.

- Boys reared in father-absent homes engage in more interpersonal manipulation and dominance striving

Facultative Influences on Reproductive Strategy

Adult's expectations about the necessity of male paternal investment influence their mate-attracting strategy.

- Women who believe that investing males are scarce are more likely to use overtly sexual mate-attracting tactics.

- Women who believe that there are an abundance of investing males downplay their sexuality – offering higher sexual fidelity

Facultative Influences on Reproductive Strategy

Adult's expectations about the necessity of male paternal investment influence their mate-attracting strategy.

- Men who believe in the scarcity of investing males also use sexually overt mate-attracting strategies.

- Men who believe that there are an abundance of high investing males are more likely to attract mates by displaying their ability and willingness to invest.

Facultative Influences on Reproductive Strategy

- When men and women assume male investment to be rare in the population, they both show mate-attracting behaviors that reduce the likelihood of long-term bonding.

- When men and women assume male investment to be frequent in the population, they behave in ways that maximize their chances of securing a long-term relationship.

Facultative Influences on Reproductive Strategy: Human Mate Poaching

- One big mating problem: Many desirable mates already mated and thus not available

- One potential strategy to deal with this problem is to attract someone who is already in a romantic relationship

Human Mate Poaching

- Some mate poaching strategies designed to elicit a short-term fling and others to elicit a long-term partnership

- Schmitt and Buss (2001) - poaching assumed to involved <u>premeditated actions</u> by a poacher that are <u>intended to lure someone away</u> from an established relationship

Human Mate Poaching
Schmitt and Buss (2001)

- How often does mate poaching occur?

  - 70% of undergrad sample reported some experience with being a poacher

  - 30% of undergrad men reported that women often try to poach them

  - 25% of undergrad women reported that men often try to poach them

Human Mate Poaching
Schmitt and Buss (2001)

- How often does mate poaching occur?

  - Mature women (over 30) more likely to poach than were undergrad women for long-term relationship

  - Mature men more likely to have experienced short-term attempts to have their mate attracted away from them

---

Human Mate Poaching: S & B (2001)

- What kind of personality traits do poachers and poachees possess?

Traits	Poachers	Successful Poachers	Poachees	Successful Poachees
Extraversion			√	
Meanness	√			√
Unconscientious	√			√
Neuroticism				√
Openness to Experience			√	

Human Mate Poaching: S & B (2001)

- What kind of sexuality attributes do poachers and poachees possess?

Traits	Poachers	Successful Poachers	Poachees	Successful Poachees
Sexual Attractiveness		√	√	
Relationship Exclusivity	-√	-√	-√	-√
Erotophillic Disposition	√			√
Emotional Investment			√	-√

Human Mate Poaching: S & B (2001)

- What motivates people to poach?

Benefits	Men: fling	Men: relationship	Women: fling	Women: relationship
Gain more attractive mate	√	√		
Gain more resources			√	
Gain partner with resources to give			√	√
Enjoy sexual variety	√			

Human Mate Poaching: S & B (2001)

- What motivates people to avoid poaching?

Costs	Men: fling	Men: relationship	Women: fling	Women: relationship
Loose Resources		√		
Future concerns of infidelity		√		√
Available competition		√		√
Uncertain future		√		√

Human Mate Poaching: S & B (2001)

- What strategies to people use to poach?

Strategy	Men: fling	Men: relationship	Women: fling	Women: relationship
Enhance physical beauty			√	√
Derogate rivals looks			√	
Demonstrate resources	√	√		
Be generous	√	√		

Human Mate Poaching: S & B (2001)

- What strategies to people use to poach?

Strategy	Men: fling	Men: relationship	Women: fling	Women: relationship
Provide easy sexual access			√	
Suggest easy sexual access			√	√
Arrange easy sexual access			√	
Develop emotional connection	√	√		
Display dominance	√			

Human Mate Poaching: S & B (2001)

- Mate poaching strategies less effective the more committed the existing relationship is

- Mate poaching strategies less effective than general romantic attraction strategies

- Mate poaching strategies different for men and women in a predictable way based on knowledge of human mating strategies

Human Mate Poaching: Counter Strategies

- Men: tend to guard mates by displaying resources and physically threatening intrasexual rivals

- Women: tend to guard mates by enhancing their own appearance and verbally showing signs of partner possession

Human Mate Poaching: Counter Strategies

- Men: who desire to poach tend to increase resources and emotional commitment with current partner

- Women: who desire to poach tend to increase sexual frequency and discount their physical appearance with their current partner